B L A C K S E A
P9-CKU-459
N
Ephesus
Antioch
Damascu
A N
S E A
Jerusalem
Alexandria
E LOWENSTEIN

THE INTERPRETER'S BIBLE

THE INTERPRETER'S BIBLE

IN TWELVE VOLUMES

VOLUME

I. General Articles on the Bible; General Articles on the Old Testament; Genesis; Exodus

II. Leviticus; Numbers; Deuteronomy; Joshua; Judges; Ruth; Samuel

III. Kings; Chronicles; Ezra; Nehemiah; Esther; Job

IV. Psalms; Proverbs

V. Ecclesiastes; Song of Songs; Isaiah; Jeremiah

VI. Lamentations; Ezekiel; Daniel; Hosea; Joel; Amos; Obadiah; Jonah; Micah; Nahum; Habakkuk; Zephaniah; Haggai; Zechariah; Malachi

VII. General Articles on the New Testament; Matthew; Mark

VIII. Luke; John

IX. Acts; Romans

X. Corinthians; Galatians; Ephesians

XI. Philippians; Colossians; Thessalonians; Timothy; Titus; Philemon; Hebrews

XII. James; Peter; John; Jude; Revelation; General Articles; Indexes

VOLUME VIII

THE GOSPEL ACCORDING TO

ST. LUKE

THE GOSPEL ACCORDING TO

ST. JOHN

EDITORIAL BOARD

THE
INTERPRETER'S BIBLE

The Holy Scriptures

IN THE KING JAMES AND REVISED STANDARD VERSIONS

WITH GENERAL ARTICLES AND

INTRODUCTION, EXEGESIS, EXPOSITION

FOR EACH BOOK OF THE BIBLE

IN TWELVE VOLUMES

VOLUME

VIII

Ἐν ἀρχῇ ἦν ὁ λόγος

Abingdon

NASHVILLE

For information address Abingdon,
Nashville, Tennessee 37203.

ISBN 0-687-19214-5

Library of Congress Catalog Card Number: 51-12276

Twenty-fourth Printing 1982

MANUFACTURED BY THE PARTHENON
PRESS AT NASHVILLE, TENNESSEE,
UNITED STATES OF AMERICA

ABBREVIATIONS AND EXPLANATIONS

Abbreviations

Canonical books and bibliographical terms are abbreviated according to common usage

Amer. Trans. — *The Bible, An American Translation,* Old Testament, ed. J. M. P. Smith
Apoc.—Apocrypha
Aq.—Aquila
ASV—American Standard Version (1901)
Barn.—Epistle of Barnabas
Clem.—Clement
C.T.—Consonantal Text
Did.—Didache
Ecclus.—Ecclesiasticus
ERV—English Revised Version (1881-85)
Exeg.—Exegesis
Expos.—Exposition
Goodspeed—*The Bible, An American Translation,* New Testament and Apocrypha, tr. Edgar J. Goodspeed
Herm. Vis., etc.—The Shepherd of Hermas: Visions, Mandates, Similitudes
Ign. Eph., etc.—Epistles of Ignatius to the Ephesians, Magnesians, Trallians, Romans, Philadelphians, Smyrnaeans, and Polycarp
KJV—King James Version (1611)
LXX—Septuagint
Macc.—Maccabees
Moffatt—*The Bible, A New Translation,* by James Moffatt
M.T.—Masoretic Text
N.T.—New Testament
O.T.—Old Testament
Polyc. Phil.—Epistle of Polycarp to the Philippians
Pseudep.—Pseudepigrapha
Pss. Sol.—Psalms of Solomon
RSV—Revised Standard Version (1946-52)
Samar.—Samaritan recension
Symm.—Symmachus
Targ.—Targum
Test. Reuben, etc.—Testament of Reuben, and others of the Twelve Patriarchs
Theod.—Theodotion
Tob.—Tobit
Vulg.—Vulgate
Weymouth—*The New Testament in Modern Speech,* by Richard Francis Weymouth
Wisd. Sol.—Wisdom of Solomon

Quotations and References

Boldface type in Exegesis and Exposition indicates a quotation from either the King James or the Revised Standard Version of the passage under discussion. The two versions are distinguished only when attention is called to a difference between them. Readings of other versions are not in boldface type and are regularly identified.

In scripture references a letter (*a, b,* etc.) appended to a verse number indicates a clause within the verse; an additional Greek letter indicates a subdivision within the clause. When no book is named, the book under discussion is understood.

Arabic numbers connected by colons, as in scripture references, indicate chapters and verses in deuterocanonical and noncanonical works. For other ancient writings roman numbers indicate major divisions, arabic numbers subdivisions, these being connected by periods. For modern works a roman number and an arabic number connected by a comma indicate volume and page. Bibliographical data on a contemporary work cited by a writer may be found by consulting the first reference to the work by that writer (or the bibliography, if the writer has included one).

Greek Transliterations

α = a	ε = e	ι = i	ν = n	ρ = r	φ = ph
β = b	ζ = z	κ = k	ξ = x	σ(ς) = s	χ = ch
γ = g	η = ē	λ = l	ο = o	τ = t	ψ = ps
δ = d	θ = th	μ = m	π = p	υ = u, y	ω = ō

Hebrew and Aramaic Transliterations

I. HEBREW ALPHABET

א = ʾ	ה = h	ט = ṭ	מ(ם) = m	פ(ף) = p, ph	שׁ = s, sh
ב = b, bh	ו = w	י = y	נ(ן) = n	צ(ץ) = ç	ת = t, th
ג = g, gh	ז = z	כ(ך) = k, kh	ס = ṣ	ק = q	
ד = d, dh	ח = ḥ	ל = l	ע = ʿ	ר = r	

II. MASORETIC POINTING

Pure-long	Tone-long	Short	Composite *shᵉwa*
◌ָ = â	◌ָ = ā	◌ַ = a	◌ֲ = ᵃ
◌ֵ = ê	◌ֵ = ē	◌ֶ = e	◌ֱ = ᵉ
◌ִ *or* ◌ִי = î		◌ִ = i	
וֹ *or* ◌ֹ = ô	◌ֹ = ō	◌ָ = o	◌ֳ = ᵒ
וּ = û		◌ֻ = u	

Note: (*a*) The *páthaḥ* furtive is transliterated as a *ḥaṭeph-páthaḥ.* (*b*) The simple *shᵉwa,* when vocal, is transliterated ᵉ. (*c*) The tonic accent, which is indicated only when it occurs on a syllable other than the last, is transliterated by an acute accent over the vowel.

TABLE OF CONTENTS

VOLUME VIII

THE GOSPEL ACCORDING TO ST. LUKE

THE GOSPEL ACCORDING TO ST. JOHN

MAPS

The Gospel According to

ST. LUKE

Introduction and Exegesis by S. MacLean Gilmour

Exposition Chs. 1-6 by Walter Russell Bowie

Exposition Chs. 7-12 by John Knox

Exposition Chs. 13-18 by George Arthur Buttrick

Exposition Chs. 19-24 by Paul Scherer

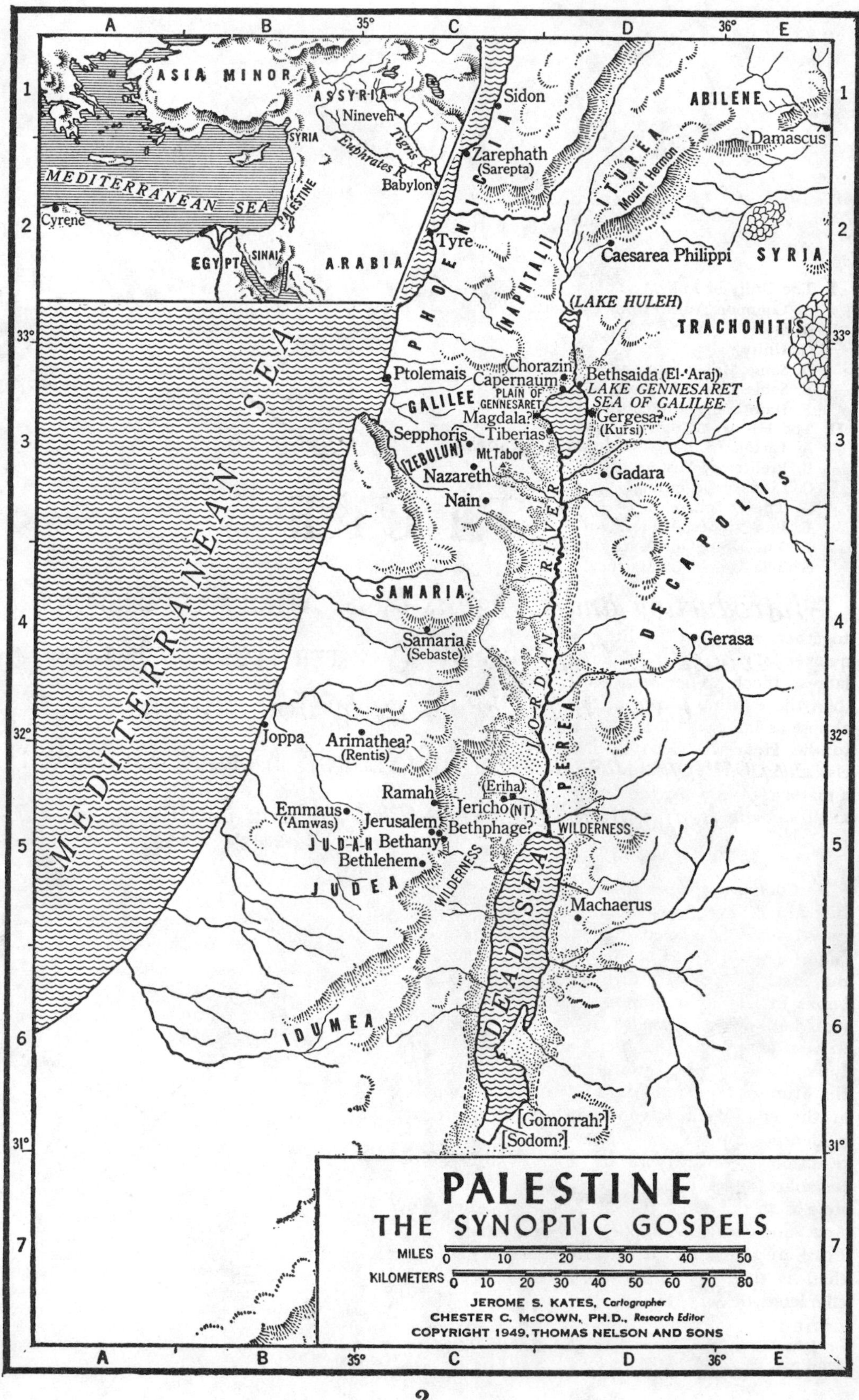

ASIA MINOR
ASSYRIA
Nineveh
Tigris R.
Euphrates R.
Babylon
SYRIA
PALESTINE
MEDITERRANEAN SEA
Cyrene
EGYPT
SINAI
ARABIA
Sidon
Zarephath
(Sarepta)
PHOENICIA
Tyre
(NAPHTALI)
ITUREA
Mount Hermon
ABILENE
Damascus
Caesarea Philippi
SYRIA
(LAKE HULEH)
TRACHONITIS
Ptolemais
Chorazin
Capernaum
Bethsaida (El-'Araj)
LAKE GENNESARET
SEA OF GALILEE
PLAIN OF GENNESARET
GALILEE
Magdala?
Gergesa?
(Kursi)
Sepphoris
Tiberias
(ZEBULUN)
Mt.Tabor
Nazareth
Gadara
Nain
DECAPOLIS
JORDAN RIVER
SAMARIA
Samaria
(Sebaste)
Gerasa
PEREA
Joppa
Arimathea?
(Rentis)
(Eriha)
Ramah
Jericho (NT)
Emmaus
('Amwas)
Jerusalem
Bethphage?
WILDERNESS
JUDAH
Bethany
Bethlehem
JUDEA
WILDERNESS
DEAD SEA
Machaerus
IDUMEA
[Gomorrah?]
[Sodom?]
PALESTINE
THE SYNOPTIC GOSPELS
MILES 0 10 20 30 40 50
KILOMETERS 0 10 20 30 40 50 60 70 80
JEROME S. KATES, Cartographer
CHESTER C. McCOWN, PH.D., Research Editor
COPYRIGHT 1949, THOMAS NELSON AND SONS

LUKE

INTRODUCTION

The Gospel of Luke and the book of Acts together represent a little more than one quarter of the New Testament and form its largest block. They constitute a unit larger than the Pauline corpus of thirteen letters and almost as large as those letters plus the Epistle to the Hebrews. Even if there were nothing else, their sheer bulk would give Luke and Acts a major claim on the interest of the New Testament student.

I. The Unity of Luke-Acts

A. Common Authorship.—The common authorship of Luke and Acts is obvious and is universally recognized. The second volume claims (Acts 1:1) to be by the same author as the first. The earliest direct references to the books in Christian literature assert their common authorship. Irenaeus in *Against Heresies,* written about A.D. 185, ascribed both books to Luke; [1] and so also, according to the witness of the Muratorian canon, did the church of Rome at the end of the second century. Linguistic evidence supports the claims of preface and tradition. Nearly twice as many words are peculiar in the New Testament to Luke and Acts as to the other two Synoptic Gospels and Acts, and words and phrases characteristic of Luke are found in Acts at a ratio much higher than is true of words and phrases that are characteristic of Matthew or of Mark.[2] The case for identifying the author of Luke with the author of Acts is therefore a strong one.[3]

B. Style.—Like the rest of the New Testament, Luke and Acts were written in the popular, nonliterary Greek that served as the international language of the day. In no sense was the author of Luke-Acts a classicist. Yet he had a sense of Greek style and of rhetorical sentence structure which gives him rank next in the New Testament to the author of the Epistle to the Hebrews as a writer. (See article, "The Language of the N.T.," Vol. VII, pp. 43-59.) Luke knew the rules of good Greek grammar and syntax and was accustomed to observe them. This is most evident in the balanced periodic sentence with which the Gospel begins, but is also to be observed in sufficient measure elsewhere to justify Jerome's comment that Luke "of all the evangelists was the most polished in his use of the Greek language." [4]

Some of the distinctive features of Luke's style can be noted in connection with the omissions, changes, and improvements he made in the material he took over from Mark. In such instances we can be certain, as rarely we can be elsewhere, that the phrasing is Luke's rather than that of his source. In accordance with good

[1] III. 1. 1.

[2] John C. Hawkins, *Horae Synopticae* (Oxford: Clarendon Press, 1899), pp. 140-43.

[3] It has been challenged by A. C. Clark (*The Acts of the Apostles* [Oxford: Clarendon Press, 1933]) on the ground of numerous differences in small parts of speech, but W. L. Knox (*The Acts of the Apostles* [Cambridge: University Press, 1948], pp. 2-14, 100-9) demonstrates that Clark's linguistic researches actually tend to confirm the assumption that "the same hand is responsible for the final compilation both of the Acts and the Gospel."

[4] *Epistles* XX. 4.

Hellenistic literary practice he omits Semitic and Latin "barbarisms" wherever possible. "Boanerges," "Iscariot," "abba," "hosanna," "Gethsemane," and "Golgotha" are not used, and the phrases "Talitha cumi" and "Eloi, Eloi, lama sabachthani" are missing. The Greek *hekatontarchēs* is substituted for the Latin "centurion," and the Latin *quadrans* (Mark 12:42) is not reproduced. The Marcan "amen" is frequently omitted and occasionally changed to "truly." "Rabbi" is replaced with "master" or "Lord." "Satan" is retained in Luke 11:18 (Mark 3:26) but is dropped in favor of "devil" in Luke 4:2 (Mark 1:13) and Luke 8:12 (Mark 4:15). "Simon the Cananaean" is translated "Simon . . . the Zealot." Even those words of foreign origin that are retained are frequently qualified by a participle or other expression meaning "named" or "called"—for example, "a city called Bethsaida" and "the feast of Unleavened Bread . . . which is called the Passover." "Straightway," "again," and "much," among Mark's favorite adverbs, are used infrequently or not at all. Of the 151 instances in Mark of the use of the historical present only one survives (Luke 8:49=Mark 5:35). Mark's faulty use of the Greek imperfect to introduce a single and definite saying is often corrected to the aorist. Compound verbs are consistently preferred to Mark's simple forms. Mark's monotonous use of co-ordinate clauses connected by "and" is varied by the employment of another conjunction or of a participial or similar complex construction. Periphrastic introductions ("and it came to pass that"—omitted by the RSV as redundant) are frequently prefixed to Marcan passages. Again and again Luke purges Mark's repetitious style as in the following instances:

Mark 1:32: "And at even, when the sun did set. . . ."

Luke 4:40: "Now when the sun was setting. . . ."

Mark 12:44: "All that she had, even all her living."

Luke 21:4: "All the living that she had."

He regularly smooths Mark's involved constructions, as in the following passage:

Mark 3:7-8: "And a great multitude from Galilee followed him, and from Judea, and from Jerusalem, and from Idumaea, and from beyond Jordan; and they about Tyre and Sidon, a great multitude, when they had heard what great things he did, came unto him."

Luke 6:17: "And a great multitude of people out of all Judea and Jerusalem, and from the seacoast of Tyre and Sidon, which came to hear him. . . ."

With all his excellent command of Greek, Luke has incorporated material, chiefly in the birth and infancy narratives and in the first half of the book of Acts, that is replete with Hebraisms. This may be the result of a deliberate attempt on Luke's part to give his narrative an archaic flavor at these points by modeling it on the Septuagint. But the possibility cannot be ruled out that in the initial chapters of the Gospel such passages as the Magnificat and the Benedictus are translations or adaptations of early Christian hymns (see Exeg., *ad loc.*) or that some of the speeches in Acts, especially in the earlier chapters, are based on primitive Christian sermons (see Intro. to Acts, Vol. IX).

The extent to which Luke used sources for the material peculiar to his Gospel is discussed elsewhere (see below, pp. 14-15). That such passages as the story of the penitent sinner, the parable of the good Samaritan, the story of Martha and Mary, the parable of the prodigal son, and the story of the walk to Emmaus, are not entirely Luke's own free composition may be taken for granted. But their exquisite style is Luke's. Much the same might be said of such speeches as the inaugural sermon of Jesus' ministry in the synagogue at Nazareth, and of Paul's addresses at Athens and before Agrippa. Whatever basic material Luke may have used owes its present rhetorical grandeur to a master in the art of Greek composition. And such narratives as that of Jesus and the repentant thief, of Paul's arrest and protective custody at Jerusalem, and of the shipwreck of the apostle and of his company off the island of Malta, are vivid and memorable word pictures that help us to understand why Luke in the sixth century was declared to have been a painter.[5] He was a superb artist with the pen if not with the brush.[6]

C. Unity.—Luke and Acts are not just two books by the same early Christian author that happen to have been preserved because of the canonical status accorded them in the second century. They are two volumes of one and the same work, conceived and composed as a unit.[7] The preface to the gospel volume should be regarded as a preface to the whole. The "narrative of the things which have been accomplished among us" refers to the story of the rise and expansion of Christianity that is the subject matter of both books. In good Hellenistic fashion the secondary preface at the beginning of the Acts volume refers to "the first book" and briefly recapitulates its content.

[5] Theodorus Lector, *Collectaneorum* 1. 7.

[6] For a discussion of Luke's language and style see H. J. Cadbury, *The Making of Luke-Acts* (New York: The Macmillan Co., 1927), pp. 213-38.

[7] *Ibid.*, pp. 1-11.

The first volume begins at Jerusalem with the prediction to Zechariah of the birth of a son who would "turn many of the sons of Israel to the Lord their God" and "make ready for the Lord a people prepared." It goes on to tell of the miraculous birth of the Messiah and, when its historical section really begins, of the Messiah's baptism at the hands of his forerunner. It gives an account of Jesus' Galilean ministry, of his rich teaching interlude on his last journey to Jerusalem, of his condemnation by the Jewish Sanhedrin in Jewry's capital city, and of his crucifixion by the Romans at the instigation of his Jewish enemies. The risen Christ appears to his disciples and shows them that Scripture had foretold what was to happen: "Thus it is written, that the Christ should suffer and on the third day rise from the dead, and that repentance and forgiveness of sins should be preached in his name to all nations, beginning from Jerusalem" (Luke 24:46-47). Finally, the risen Christ assures his faithful and believing followers that he will send the promise of his Father upon them and bids them stay in the city until they should be clothed with power from on high.

The second volume resumes the narrative at Jerusalem. It goes on to give a vivid account of the gift of the Holy Spirit at Pentecost that fulfilled the promise with which the first volume had ended. In succeeding chapters we are told that the Christianity that was first preached in Jerusalem was carried by Greek-speaking evangelists to Samaria, the seacoast Palestinian towns, and as far as Phoenicia, Cyprus, and Antioch. At Antioch something new happened —the Lord Jesus was preached "to the Greeks also." Under the leadership of Paul and Barnabas the new religion was then taken to the Roman province of Galatia. Here opposition of Jews made the apostles declare: "It was necessary that the word of God should be spoken first to you. Since you thrust it from you, and judge yourselves unworthy of eternal life, behold we turn to the Gentiles" (Acts 13:46). Paul and Barnabas succeeded in convincing the Jerusalem leadership that Gentiles should be admitted to the fellowship of the church without requiring their circumcision, that is, without demanding that they first become full-fledged Jews, and henceforth the story is largely that of the spread of Greek Christianity. The new world-embracing religion was taken, chiefly by the great Apostle to the Gentiles, to the provinces of the Levant and of eastern Europe, and the narrative ends with Paul "preaching the kingdom of God and teaching about the Lord Jesus Christ quite openly and unhindered" in Rome. The faith that had arisen in an obscure and remote city on the periphery of the empire was now firmly established at its very center.

D. Some Major Interests.—In the preface to his first volume Luke declares that his intention is to relate the story of the rise and expansion of Christianity—"the things which have been accomplished among us"—according to good canons of literary form. His purpose was to write history and to create literature. But his historical and literary interests were often subordinated in the body of his work to his concerns as a practical churchman. A number of these can still be distinguished.

1. Luke wished to show that Christianity was not a subversive sect.

From the beginning Christianity had to govern its community activities and develop its institutional life in the light of the Roman attitude toward religious cults. In general this was a policy of legal or tacit recognition of all foreign religions that did not threaten imperial unity and whose deities promised to add further assurances of divine protection to the state. In the case of Judaism it involved a somewhat unwilling toleration of this religion as the historic faith of a well-defined racial group, together with discouragement of proselytizing activities. The Christian church, therefore, took its rise within a situation in which it had ultimately to seek legal status or suffer the consequences of being treated as a subversive element in society.

During the first few decades of its history Christianity was regarded as a Jewish sect by Roman officials, who failed to distinguish the church from the synagogue. Christians profited by this situation and enjoyed a freedom from interference that greatly facilitated the spread of their faith. Paul had no illusions about the ultimate overthrow of Roman hegemony at the end of this age, but in the meantime he regarded Caesar as the embodiment of justice on earth and Roman authority as ordained of God and entitled to obedience and respect (Rom. 13:1-7).

With the rapid growth of the Christian community, adherents of the new religion were gradually deprived of their original immunity from state interference. Judaism made every effort to repudiate Christianity and to disown any responsibility for it, and Roman officials gradually became cognizant of a distinction between the two groups. The result was sporadic and local persecution, such as that under Nero at Rome in A.D. 64.

Even the tradition in the Gospel of Mark reveals an effort on the part of early Christians to prove that Christianity was not fundamentally anti-Roman. The paragraph about the payment of the poll tax would serve to allay any fears concerning the attitude of Jesus to the state, and would govern the responsibilities of members of the Christian community. Mark's passion narrative made it clear that the Jews, and the Jews only, had been responsible for Jesus' crucifixion. The Roman procurator Pilate had consented to it most unwillingly.

This apologetic element is still more pointed in Matthew's Gospel. When Pilate was seated on the tribunal, his wife warned him not to do anything to "that just man." When his proposal to release Jesus rather than the notorious prisoner Barabbas was rejected by "the crowd," the procurator dramatically washed his hands as a symbol of his own innocency, and declared that the execution of the judgment was entirely a Jewish affair. "All the people" accepted the odium with alacrity. "His blood be on us and on our children!" Finally, when the "chief priests and the Pharisees" asked for a Roman guard to throw around the sepulcher to prevent the theft of Jesus' body by his erstwhile followers, Pilate refused his co-operation. The Roman authorities had not been implicated in the judicial murder of the founder of the Christian church.

This interest is carried still further by the author of Luke-Acts. The incident of the denarius becomes a deliberate demonstration of Jesus' political loyalty. Pilate asserted on no less than three different occasions that he had not been able to find any basis for a criminal charge against Jesus. Herod Antipas had also examined him but had found no grounds for legal action. It was the Jewish retinue of Herod, not the Roman soldiers, that mocked Jesus. Pilate proposed only to scourge and then release him, but he was intimidated into giving sentence by the clamorous insistence of the Jews. The Roman centurion at the Cross confessed, not that Jesus was the Son of God (as in Mark), but that "certainly this man was innocent!"

Having demonstrated in his gospel volume that the crucifixion of Jesus had been due to the virulent animosity of the Jews and not to the intervention of the Roman authorities, Luke proceeds in his Acts volume to show that the church, in its relationships with the state, could be absolved from any suspicion of anti-Roman bias. A Roman centurion at Caesarea was Peter's first non-Jewish convert. The Roman governor of Cyprus became a believer. Paul, the greatest of Christian missionaries, had been born a Roman citizen. The Roman magistrates in Philippi formally apologized to him and to Silas for their illegal imprisonment, and the very jailer and his household were baptized. Gallio, the governor of Achaia, abruptly dismissed the charges brought against Paul in Corinth. State officials in Ephesus who were charged with the oversight of the imperial cult in the province of Asia were friends of Paul, and the city clerk cleared him and his Macedonian companions of all responsibility in the matter of the Ephesian riot. The Roman officer and garrison in Jerusalem twice rescued Paul from a Jewish mob. Though Claudius Lysias sent him under arrest to the procurator in Caesarea, he also wrote a letter professing his confidence in Paul's innocence. Felix kept Paul in prison only because he wanted him to bribe his freedom. Festus agreed with Herod Agrippa II and Bernice that Paul had done nothing worthy of death or imprisonment, and Agrippa asserted that he might have been set free had he not appealed to Caesar. The Roman centurion Julius treated him with the utmost consideration on the voyage to Rome, and in the capital city he was permitted to carry on his work with a minimum of interference.

It is even possible that Luke expresses his apologetic purpose in his preface. According to the usual interpretation, the evangelist declares a desire to instruct and establish Theophilus in the faith. But perhaps it was the Roman official's misinformation about Christianity with which he was concerned. He may have wished him to "know the truth" about certain incriminating reports he had received.[8]

2. Luke wished to support the claim that the church had superseded the synagogue as the true Israel and was entitled to the recognition and protection that the state had heretofore afforded Judaism.

Jesus was indeed the supernaturally accredited Messiah of Jewish expectation. Early Christians had visited the temple regularly and had been regarded with favor by "all the people." Jesus had been raised to life "to give repentance to Israel and forgiveness of sins." Only the willful perversity of the mass of the Jews had driven Paul and Barnabas to embark upon a mission to the heathen. Paul himself had been "a Pharisee, a son of Pharisees." It had been his custom to preach the gospel in Jewish synagogues, and he had gone elsewhere only when compelled to do so by the enmity of the Jews. He had tried to placate Jewish sensibilities by such acts as the circumcision of Timothy and the observance of the rites of ceremonial purification. The charge that he had desecrated the temple on his last visit to Jerusalem was due to an egregious error and had been refuted to the

[8] See H. J. Cadbury, "The Purpose Expressed in Luke's Preface," *The Expositor*, Ser. 8, XXI (1921), 431-41.

satisfaction of the procurator Felix. He told the Jews in Rome that his presence in chains among them was for the sake of "the hope of Israel." The quotation from Isaiah that is given almost at the end of the Acts volume points the moral of the whole work: Christians are not apostates from Judaism! The Jews had stubbornly refused to heed God's message, and the church has now entered into possession of all the privileges that had formerly been theirs as the people of God.

3. Luke was eager to stress the fact that Christianity was a world religion that recognized no racial limitations.

Luke's version of Jesus' genealogy traced Jesus' ancestry to Adam, the primal man, rather than to Abraham, the father of the Jewish people. The prophet Simeon took the infant Jesus into his arms and declared that he was to be "a light for revelation to the Gentiles" as well as "glory" to the people Israel. In the inaugural sermon of his ministry Jesus asserted that Elijah had not been sent to the widows of Israel but to Zarephath in the land of Sidon, and that Elisha had not cleansed the many lepers in Israel but only Naaman the Syrian. A Samaritan rather than a Jew was the hero of one of Jesus' most memorable parables. When Jesus healed ten lepers, only one, a grateful Samaritan, returned to praise God and give thanks. At least one incident in the ministry of Jesus was located in Samaria. There is no counterpart in Luke to Jesus' command in Matthew, "Go nowhere among the Gentiles, and enter no town of the Samaritans" (Matt. 10:5). There is nothing in Luke comparable to the saying of Jesus in Matthew, "I was sent only to the lost sheep of the house of Israel" (Matt. 15:24). The story in Mark of the Syrophoenician woman whose request Jesus granted only grudgingly is not reproduced. The risen Lord declares that "repentance and remission of sins" should be preached in his name to "all nations."

The Gospel of Luke therefore prepares the way for the story in the Acts volume of the spread of Christianity to Samaria, to the coastal districts of Palestine, to Syria, to the Levant, to eastern Europe, and finally to the capital of the Roman Empire. We are prepared for Peter's comment after his visit to the centurion Cornelius, "Truly I perceive that God shows no partiality, but in every nation any one who fears him and does what is right is acceptable to him" (Acts 10:34-35). We are prepared for the words spoken by Paul and Barnabas to the Jews at Pisidian Antioch:

"It was necessary that the word of God should be spoken first to you. Since you thrust it from you, and judge yourselves unworthy of eternal life, behold, we turn to the Gentiles. For so the Lord has commanded us, saying,

'I have set you to be a light for the Gentiles,
that you may bring salvation to the uttermost
parts of the earth'" (Acts 13:46-47).

We are prepared for Paul's great statement of universal religion in his speech before the Areopagus in Athens (Acts 17:26-28). The Gospel of Luke anticipates the declaration of the apostle Paul with which the book of Acts comes to an end, "Let it be known to you then that this salvation of God has been sent to the Gentiles; they will listen" (Acts 28:28).

E. Some Lesser Interests.—A variety of secondary interests characterize the narrative of Luke-Acts.[9]

1. Luke gives prominence to the work of the Spirit. As against six references to the Spirit in Mark and twelve in Matthew, there are seventeen in the Gospel of Luke and fifty-seven in the book of Acts. "The Holy Spirit" is by far the most common phrase, but "the Spirit" is frequently employed, "the Spirit of the Lord" occurs on several occasions, and "the Spirit of Jesus" is used in Acts 16:7.

In the gospel volume the Spirit is mentioned particularly frequently in the two introductory chapters. Zechariah was informed by an angel that his son John would be "filled with the Holy Spirit" from the moment of his birth. Gabriel told Mary that she would conceive by the supernatural agency of the Holy Spirit. Elizabeth was "filled with the Holy Spirit" when she greeted Mary, and Zechariah when he uttered the Benedictus. It was the Holy Spirit that directed, informed, and inspired the prophet Simeon at the time he greeted the infant Jesus in the temple.

As in the Gospel of Mark, John the Baptist predicts that Jesus would baptize "with the Holy Spirit" in contrast to his own baptism with water, but Luke adds the note that Jesus' baptism would also be "with fire." When Jesus was baptized by John, Luke asserts that the Holy Spirit descended upon him "in bodily form, as a dove." Both the Marcan temptation narrative and that used by Matthew and Luke had mentioned Jesus' guidance in the wilderness by the Spirit, but Luke prefixes a note that Jesus had been "full of the Holy Spirit" from the time of his Jordan experience. In the inaugural sermon of his ministry at Nazareth, Jesus quotes the passage from Isa. 61:1-2 that begins, "The Spirit of the Lord God is upon me." The thanksgiving of Jesus that Matthew also records (Matt. 11:25-27) is prefaced by Luke

[9] See Cadbury, *Making of Luke-Acts*, pp. 239-96.

with the words "he rejoiced in the Holy Spirit" (Luke 10:21). The risen Christ assures his disciples that he will send his Father's "promise" upon them and bids them stay in Jerusalem until they receive this "power from on high."

The book of Acts describes the fulfillment of Christ's promise at Pentecost. The Holy Spirit came from heaven with a sound like that of a mighty wind, and in appearance like tongues of fire, and rested on the apostles, who were then enabled to speak in various languages. This outpouring was interpreted by Peter as the fulfillment of the prophecy in Joel 2:25-32. Peter and John conferred the gift of the Spirit by the laying on of hands on those Samaritans whom Philip the evangelist had converted. The Spirit was "poured out" on Cornelius and other Gentiles at Caesarea and was granted to certain disciples at Ephesus (after Paul had laid his hands upon them) who had hitherto known only the baptism of John. Peter, Stephen, Barnabas, Paul, and the Christian converts at Pisidian Antioch are variously described as "full of" or "filled with" the Holy Spirit. Luke declares that the Holy Spirit had been the inspiration of David and of Isaiah when they had uttered prophecies, of Philip the evangelist when he had spoken to the Ethiopian eunuch, and of Agabus when he had foretold a famine in the days of Claudius and when he had predicted Paul's fate at Jerusalem. The Spirit gave directions to Peter; "caught up" Philip on the road from Jerusalem to Gaza and deposited him at Azotus; directed the church at Antioch to commission Barnabas and Saul for missionary work; sanctioned the decision of the apostolic conference at Jerusalem; forbade Paul and Timothy "to speak the word" in Asia and to enter the province of Bithynia; and had appointed the Ephesian elders to be "guardians of the flock."

2. Luke emphasizes the prayer life of Jesus and the place of prayer in the life of the early church.

Jesus engaged in prayer after his baptism. He retired to the wilderness for prayer after the healing of a leper. He spent the night in prayer before he chose the company of the twelve. He had prayed before he asked the disciples, "Who do the people say that I am?" He was praying at the time of his transfiguration. His own practice of prayer inspired his disciples to ask for a model prayer. He had been engaged in prayer just before his arrest. His last words on the Cross were a prayer: "Father, into thy hands I commit my spirit!" His parables of the importunate friend, of the unjust judge, and of the Pharisee and the tax collector illustrate his teaching on prayer.

The practice of prayer was also characteristic of the early church. The apostles prayed before they cast lots to choose a successor to Judas. The seven Hellenists were set apart with prayer and "the laying on of hands." Barnabas and Saul were commissioned for their missionary work by the church at Antioch after a period of "fasting and praying." Peter and John attended the temple "at the hour of prayer." After the apostles were released from arrest by the chief priests and the elders, their friends prayed that they might be empowered to speak the word with boldness. Stephen was martyred with a prayer on his lips. The Holy Spirit was granted to the converted Samaritans in answer to the prayer of Peter and John. Cornelius, Peter's first Gentile convert, was a man who "prayed constantly to God." Peter's vision at Joppa followed a period of prayer. The apostle prayed before he restored Tabitha to life. He was released from prison during the persecution of Herod Agrippa when the church that had gathered in the home of Mary, the mother of John Mark, made earnest prayer to God on his behalf. Paul and Silas were miraculously released from prison at Philippi after "praying and singing hymns to God." And Paul and his companions prayed with the disciples at Tyre before taking leave of them to go to Jerusalem.

3. Luke shows a marked interest in the role of women in the gospel tradition and in the history of the early church.

Stories about Mary, the mother of Jesus, Elizabeth, the mother of John the Baptist, and the prophetess Anna form a large part of the introductory birth narratives. Reference is made elsewhere to the attention that is given to Jesus' relationships with women in the special tradition that is in the body of the Gospel (see Intro., p. 14). Jesus' words to the "daughters of Jerusalem" who bewailed and lamented him as he was taken out to be crucified, as well as the enumeration of the women who told the apostles of the empty tomb, show that this interest was extended into the passion narrative.

Women often enter into the story in the book of Acts: Sapphira, the wife of Ananias; Priscilla, the wife of Aquila; Drusilla, the wife of Felix; Bernice, the sister of Herod Agrippa II; Tabitha; Mary, the mother of John Mark; the maid Rhoda; Lydia of Thyatira; the slave girl whom Paul freed of "a spirit of divination"; Damaris of Athens; and the four daughters of Philip the evangelist. Incidental reference is made in Acts 23:16 to the fact that Paul had a sister in Jerusalem.

4. The birth and infancy narratives in the gospel volume testify to an interest in Jesus' origins that had not existed at the time the

Gospel of Mark had been written. Luke extends this interest to the supernatural events associated with the birth of John the Baptist.

5. Mark's Gospel had given no account of any resurrection appearances of Christ, and Luke undertakes to supply this deficiency. He tells of appearances to two disciples on a journey to a village in the environs of Jerusalem and to the company of the eleven assembled at Jerusalem, and hints at an earlier appearance to Simon. This interest in the Resurrection is carried over into the opening chapter of the book of Acts, which speaks of appearances to the apostles over a period of forty days. The risen Christ appears and disappears at will, asserts that he is not a disembodied spirit, eats a piece of broiled fish, gives a variety of instructions to his followers, and finally ascends by physical levitation into a cloud and is taken up into heaven.

6. There is a marked sympathy for the poor in Luke's account of the gospel tradition. The Magnificat declares that God has

> filled the hungry with good things,
> and the rich he has sent empty away.

The birth narratives stress Jesus' humble origin. John the Baptist teaches that men should share their possessions with the needy. In his sermon at Nazareth, Jesus declares in the words of Isaiah's prophecy that the Spirit of the Lord has anointed him "to preach good news to the poor." "Blessed are you poor, for yours is the kingdom of God" is a beatitude pronounced over the disciples, and a corresponding woe is directed against the absent rich.

7. The proper stewardship of wealth is stressed in both Luke and Acts. The parables of the rich fool, of the dishonest steward, and of the rich man and Lazarus serve this end. Sayings of Jesus that encourage almsgiving are quoted. After his first contact with Jesus, Zacchaeus promises to give half his goods to feed the poor. Paul supports his advice to the Ephesian elders to "help the weak" with a saying of Jesus, "It is more blessed to give than to receive." Many early Christians are said to have pooled their resources for distribution "to each as any had need." Barnabas is cited as one who contributed all the proceeds of the sale of a piece of property to this common fund, and the story of Ananias and Sapphira illustrates the gruesome fate of those who had lied "to the Holy Spirit" when they claimed to have given their all.

F. Date and Authorship.—Any judgment regarding the date and authorship of Luke-Acts must be based in the main on data derived from the Acts volume. The reader is therefore referred for a full discussion of these questions to the Introduction to the book of Acts in Vol. IX. Here it will suffice to state the assumptions on these matters that underlie the present studies in the Gospel.

Luke's use of Mark as a major source (see below, pp. 16 ff.) and various passages in the Gospel that appear to reflect the destruction of Jerusalem by Titus (see Exeg. of Luke 19:41-44; 21:20-24) make it certain that Luke-Acts could not have been written earlier than A.D. 70. Some interpreters have held that on a number of occasions, both in the Gospel and in the Acts, Luke betrays a familiarity with Josephus' *Antiquities*. If this were the case, Luke-Acts would have to be dated after A.D. 93, but it is now generally admitted that the "proof" that Luke had read Josephus falls short of demonstration.[10]

There appear to be good grounds for accepting the patristic tradition that Marcion used Luke's Gospel (see below, pp. 22-23). Since Luke-Acts was conceived and executed as a unit, both volumes must have been in use at least in parts of the church before A.D. 140. But a date much earlier than this can be accepted as a reasonable *terminus ad quem*. The collected corpus of Paul's letters was known to most Christians who wrote after A.D. 100.[11] It is hard to believe that it could have been ignored by the author of Luke-Acts if it had already been in circulation.

A date for Luke-Acts in the eighties or nineties of the first century could also account for the evident concern of the author to emphasize the favorable attitude that the state had adopted toward the church in the persons of its founder and its greatest missionary (see above, pp. 5-6). Both the Gospel and the book of Acts were written at a time when Christians were suspected of covert disloyalty and were being regarded with a measure of hostility by imperial officials. Both volumes make a plea for state toleration of the new religion on the ground that the history of the church had been devoid of political offense. The little we know of the relationships between church and state during the reign of Domitian (A.D. 81-96) suggests that the stresses of this period could have occasioned the writing of Luke-Acts.[12]

The Introduction to the book of Acts (Vol. IX) points out that "general considerations of

[10] *Beginnings of Christianity*, ed. F. J. Foakes Jackson and Kirsopp Lake (London: Macmillan & Co., 1922), II, 355-58.

[11] A. E. Barnett, *Paul Becomes a Literary Influence* (Chicago: University of Chicago Press, 1941).

[12] See Donald W. Riddle, "The Occasion of Luke-Acts," *Journal of Religion*, X (1930), 545-62.

external evidence, and even linguistic and literary considerations, cannot solve the problem" of authorship. The only plausible alternative to the traditional ascription of Luke and Acts to Luke the physician, the companion of Paul, is the view that Luke was the author of only one of the sources employed by the final editor in the Acts volume, the so-called "we" sections—probably excerpts from Luke's travel diary. On this latter hypothesis we know nothing about the *auctor ad Theophilum* beyond what emerges from his writings as characteristic of his interests and concerns. The Introduction to Acts rather hesitantly favors "the case for the tradition." The present writer is impressed with the case against it.[13] A strong argument can be advanced for the hypothesis that the two-volume work was written for the Roman church.

II. The History of the Tradition in Luke's Gospel

The study of gospel sources and origins has proceeded largely by a process of analysis, and an account of 150 years of fruitful research is given elsewhere (see Vol. VII, pp. 60-74). Perhaps it is now possible to reconstruct the history of the tradition in Luke's Gospel. Free use is made in these paragraphs of the positive results of literary, historical, and form criticism, but their tools and techniques are not intruded.

A. Factors in the Preservation of the Tradition.—No doubt the language that Jesus normally used was Aramaic. For several centuries it had been the lingua franca of Palestinian Jews and in Jesus' day was still their primary oral and literary medium. From the beginning of the Hellenistic era, however, and particularly after Pompey's capture of Jerusalem in 63 B.C., Aramaic had been in competition with a Greek dialect, now known as "koine" or "popular" Greek. This had become the international language of the Greco-Roman world. It had become the language of commerce, of politics, and of unpretentious literature; and every Jew who wished to trade, to do business with the Roman governing power, or to reach any non-Semitic reading public, had to be bilingual.

Even apart from such activities the Palestinian Jew must often have found that a working knowledge of Greek was indispensable. A league of independent cities called the Decapolis or "ten-city" district had been established as early as the time of Pompey and was Greek in culture and organization. While most of its member cities were situated on the eastern frontier of Palestine, its most important constituent, Scythopolis, lay to the west of the Jordan. Caesarea, the capital city of the Roman procurator; Tiberias, the capital of the tetrarchy of Herod Antipas; Samaria; Jericho; in fact every important urban center in Palestine with the exception of Jerusalem was predominantly non-Jewish in population and had become an outpost of Hellenistic influence. Even Jerusalem housed many Jewish repatriates whose native language was Greek.

Jesus was reared in the village of Nazareth in Galilee. No doubt Nazareth itself was wholly Jewish, but it was little more than a suburb of Sepphoris. Sepphoris was the largest city outside Jerusalem and, like the other cities, Greek in culture and in language. It is improbable that Jesus avoided all contacts with its bustling life. Perhaps our ideas of Jesus' activities as a carpenter are unnecessarily pastoral. He may have helped build houses and towers for Greeks as well as plows and ox yokes for Jews. Two of Jesus' inner circle of followers bore the pure Greek names of Philip and Andrew, and such men would almost certainly be Greek-speaking. Jesus himself is said to have conversed with a Roman centurion, with a woman from Syrophoenicia, and with Pontius Pilate, and in each instance Greek was probably the language he employed. Though he appears to have avoided non-Jewish areas in Palestine and to have restricted his ministry in the main to his own race, we may suspect that Jesus also had some fluency in Greek. Like most Jews of his time he would be forced to acquire it.

Nevertheless most of his teaching, even in translation, still bears the marks of its Semitic origin. Some of it has the characteristic features of Semitic poetry: parallelism, antithesis, and rhythm. Much of it makes use of such typically Jewish methods of illustration as the parable and the example story. Most of it employs familiar imagery of everyday life in the Palestine of Jesus' day. Jesus spoke to Jewish hearers as a Jewish teacher, legislator, and prophet, and employed categories of thought and vehicles of teaching similar to his fellow Jews.

It would be incorrect to think of Jesus as a professional teacher of religion, but the courtesy title of rabbi was frequently given him during his lifetime, and his inner circle of followers may well have regarded the preservation of his sayings as an obligation and a privilege of their association with him. Jewish rabbis were accustomed to communicate a body of oral tradition to their pupils, and the latter made a point of remembering it. The amazing plasticity of the human memory has no better illustration than in those students of Shammai and Hillel and Gamaliel who could recollect and repeat thousands of individual interpretations and applica-

[13] See Hans Windisch, "The Case Against the Tradition," *Beginnings of Christianity*, II, 298-348.

tions of the Jewish law. One teacher described his best student as "a plastered cistern that loses not a drop." [14] Jesus' disciples and auditors were not professional theologians, but neither were they completely unlettered. They were men who had been impressed with his teaching. They were conscious of the importance of remembering it, and were aided in the task of recollection by the fact that it was vivid and concrete.

B. Preliterary History of the Tradition.—The primitive church was a missionary community. It consisted of "eyewitnesses and ministers of the word." It was composed of men and women who believed that Jesus the crucified and the risen was the Messiah of Jewish expectation. Its adherents were convinced that Jesus' message and mission had been divinely vindicated and demonstrated by the Resurrection. Jesus the Christ was the clue to history, the key to the meaning of life, and the word of God to man. He had revealed God's purposes by what he had done, by what he had said, and by what he had been. This was the gospel that those who believed were privileged and compelled to proclaim.

The first message of the good news of Jesus the Christ was therefore the proclamation of enthusiastic evangelists. The motive for the preservation and communication of the tradition at the beginning was a missionary one. Stories of God's visitation and redemption of his people in Christ were told and retold, not primarily to inform or to instruct, but to convert. Theology rather than history shaped the content of the earliest message about Jesus. The good news was transmitted at the start by preachers, not by historians or biographers.[15]

Since the early church believed that God had spoken above all in the suffering, the death, and the rising again of the Messiah, it was the passion and resurrection narratives that formed the core of the earliest Christian message. If the speech that Luke has credited to the apostle Peter in Acts 2:14-40 is a reproduction of primitive Jerusalem preaching and not what someone has called "a triumph of archaeology," we can trace the outline of a typical sermon. First came a reference to the ministry of Jesus (vs. 22). Then his crucifixion was declared to be part of "the definite plan and foreknowledge of God" (vs. 23). The climax was reached in the proclamation of Jesus' resurrection and exaltation as Messiah and Lord (vss. 24, 32, 36), and the sermon concluded with the message of forgiveness of sins dependent on repentance and baptism, and a promise of the gift of the Holy Spirit (vs. 38).[16]

In I Cor. 15:3-11 Paul recalls the message he had delivered to his Corinthian hearers "as of first importance," and that he on his part had received from the church before him. Again it was the death, the burial, and the resurrection of Christ, and the consequences for believers of these events that made up its content. That was the primitive *kerygma* or evangel, the message that was "a stumbling-block to Jews and folly to Gentiles, but to those who are called, . . . the power of God and the wisdom of God" (I Cor. 1:23-24).

Stories of Jesus' last days in Jerusalem, of the Last Supper with his disciples, of his arrest, of his trials before the Sanhedrin and Pilate, of his crucifixion, burial, and resurrection, were early woven into a more or less fixed and continuous narrative. It was shaped in part by such passages in the Old Testament as Pss. 22 and 69, and Isa. 53, scripture that the early church believed had foretold and illuminated the Cross; but in the main it was determined by the actual course of events. Early missionaries often searched the Scriptures to try to understand what had happened. They rarely invented a story to fulfill a text. In their formative stages the narratives of the Passion and the Resurrection were subject to the control of "eyewitnesses" as well as of "ministers" of the word.

Nevertheless it is clear that variant accounts of at least some events circulated in different parts of the early church. Paul supports the belief in the Resurrection by reference to a number of appearances of the risen Lord to individuals and to groups. Mark bases the belief on the discovery by certain women of the empty tomb. Matthew combines both lines of argument by appending to Mark's account a story of a resurrection appearance to eleven disciples in Galilee. Luke's narrative contains further independent material, and the same is true to some extent of the closing chapters of the Gospel of John and perhaps also of the noncanonical Gospel of Peter. The differences in the versions involve matters of content as well as of emphasis and of order, and it cannot be maintained that any one is historically preferable at every point to the others.

While the passion and resurrection narratives furnished the main vehicle of the early Christian message, stories from the life and ministry of Jesus also proved useful for preaching pur-

[14] Pirke Aboth 2:10.

[15] See Martin Dibelius, *From Tradition to Gospel*, tr. Bertram Lee Woolf (New York: Charles Scribner's Sons, 1935).

[16] See C. H. Dodd, *The Apostolic Preaching and Its Developments* (London: Hodder & Stoughton, 1936), pp. 3-73.

poses. In the form the early preachers cast them they were simple, terse, and concrete. They introduced other people only to the extent that witnesses or auditors set the stage for Jesus or responded appropriately to his act or utterance. Each narrative centered about some striking saying or action. Examples of such "pronouncement stories"[17] are the healing of the paralytic (Mark 2:1-12=Luke 5:17-26), Jesus and his disciples in the grainfield (Mark 2:23-28=Luke 6:1-5), and Jesus and the question of paying taxes to Caesar (Mark 12:13-17= Luke 20:20-26).

Early Christian preachers soon discovered that stories about Jesus as a miracle worker appealed to the interest of their hearers and helped to demonstrate the claim that he had been supernaturally accredited as God's Messiah. The narratives of the calming of the storm (Mark 4:35-41=Luke 8:22-25), the healing of the Gerasene demoniac (Mark 5:1-20= Luke 8:26-39), and the feeding of the five thousand (Mark 6:35-44=Luke 9:12-17) are illustrative of different types. They are more descriptive and detailed than pronouncement stories, and often interest in the miraculous for its own sake has displaced devotional, didactic, and hortatory motives. Like similar stories elsewhere miracle narratives in the gospel tradition assume a more or less stereotyped form: the seriousness of the situation (or of the illness) is described; the methods and means of effecting the miracle are reported; and its success is stressed by recording the impression it made on observers or the subsequent behavior of the patient.[18]

Still other types of narrative belonged to the repertory of the early preacher. An interest in men and women who had formed part of Jesus' environment or entourage preserved, and sometimes created, legends about John the Baptist, Peter, Zacchaeus, Judas, Martha and Mary, the penitent sinner, Pilate's wife, and others. In the course of time this interest was extended to Jesus' infancy, and later still to his birth and to those who were first aware of its significance. The accounts of the Baptism, the Temptation, and the Transfiguration, as well as occasional mythological traits in such miracle stories as that of Jesus' walking on the water, show that the early church came to regard certain events in the life of Jesus as epiphanies of a divine being. On the whole, however, there is a singular lack of mythological interest at the earliest levels of the tradition.[19]

[17] Vincent Taylor, *The Formation of the Gospel Tradition* (London: Macmillan & Co., 1933), pp. 63-87.

[18] Dibelius, *From Tradition to Gospel*, pp. 70-103.

[19] *Ibid.*, pp. 266-86.

At the beginning the stories about Jesus and those who had been associated with him and his ministry were told as isolated units, as individual short sermons, but in the course of time sequences were developed. One such sequence is now incorporated in Mark 2:1–3:6 (cf. Luke 5:17–6:11). It relates six conflicts between Jesus and Jewish religious leaders in and about Capernaum. Another is now preserved in two parallel forms in Mark 6:35–7:30 and Mark 8:1-26. Each commences with a miracle story, according to which Jesus fed a crowd of people, followed in each case by accounts of a crossing of the Sea of Galilee, a conflict with Pharisees, and a miracle of healing.

Some sayings of Jesus were preserved within the narrative framework of pronouncement stories, miracle stories, and other types of narrative, but most of them were transmitted without context. If the preservation of the tradition about Jesus' deeds was the work in the main of the early missionary, the preservation of his words was due in large part to the teacher. Narratives of Jesus' mighty works were employed to convert the unbeliever and to confirm the faithful. His utterances were used to inform, inspire, and discipline individual and corporate Christian behavior.[20]

Several types of such hortatory sayings may be distinguished. One useful classification has grouped them as follows: [21] (*a*) "wisdom" sayings, analogous to those found in such Jewish collections as the books of Proverbs and Ecclesiasticus; (*b*) prophetic and apocalyptic sayings that announce the kingdom of God, issue a call to repentance, promise salvation to those who are prepared, and threaten with disaster such as refuse to heed; (*c*) legislative enactments that correct or supplement the law of Moses; (*d*) first person singular ("I") sayings that reveal a consciousness of messianic authority; and (*e*) parables and related forms of teaching, many of them illustrating the message of the kingdom of God but others with a wider range of reference.

The formation at an early stage of narrative sequences has already been noted. There was a similar development in the history of the didactic tradition. Originally unrelated sayings were connected in patterns. Three parables on the general theme of sowing are grouped in Mark 4. Mark 9:42-50 is a sequence suggested by the recurring phrase "causes to sin" and the words "fire" and "salt." Several sayings

[20] *Ibid.*, pp. 233-65.

[21] Rudolf Bultmann, *Die Geschichte der synoptischen Tradition* (2d ed.; Göttingen: Vandenhoeck & Ruprecht, 1931), pp. 73-222; cf. "The Study of the Synoptic Gospels," tr. F. C. Grant, *Form Criticism* (Chicago: Willett, Clark & Co., 1934), pp. 52-60.

about wealth and admittance to the kingdom of God are assembled in Mark 10:23-31. What may originally have been a little Jewish apocalypse has been elaborated by the addition of eschatological sayings of Christian origin in Mark 13.

C. Literary Beginnings.—All this wealth of narrative and teaching matter was first transmitted in Aramaic and by word of mouth. If any of it was ever committed to writing in the language of its origin, it must have had only a brief and limited circulation. The new faith soon broke through its Palestinian chrysalis and began to make converts among Greek-speaking Jews in Syria, the Levant, Egypt, and still farther afield, and with the passage of time also among non-Jews. The church's Aramaic-speaking membership was rapidly overshadowed and outnumbered by its Greek-speaking constituency. By the time Paul wrote his Epistle to the Romans, not more than twenty-five years after the Crucifixion, it is clear that Christianity had become very largely a non-Jewish religion and it is a fair inference that this had been the case for many years. In all probability the gospel tradition was transferred from oral to written form after Greek had displaced Aramaic as the normal language of the Christian preacher and catechist.

The sheer bulk of the Jewish oral tradition compelled the rabbis in the second century to commit it to writing as the Mishnah. The need for a written tradition became evident to Christians at an earlier date. Christian preachers and teachers were not scholars who had been meticulously trained, as rabbinical students were, but simple men who held that God had set them apart for their duties. The need of such "lay preachers" for a normative version of the tradition in writing was soon apparent. Furthermore the small company of "eyewitnesses" was rapidly outnumbered by "ministers of the word" who, like Paul, had not known Christ "after the flesh." Some sort of control over their proclamation of the gospel was desirable. Finally, the growth of the church had brought with it an increase in the complexity and gravity of the moral and ecclesiastical problems with which the Christian catechist had to cope. A greater systematization of the hortatory tradition was required than had been possible while it remained in fluid oral form. In all probability the process of committing the material to writing began within fifteen or twenty years after the Resurrection. In all probability, also, the process was a gradual one. For many decades oral and written tradition vied with each other for authority within the church, and as late as the middle of the second century Bishop Papias of Hierapolis declared: "I was never accustomed to consider material from books of as much benefit to me as from a living and abiding voice." [22]

D. The Q Source.—Written collections of Jesus' sayings may have preceded any formal written Gospel. The existence of one such collection is to be inferred from the occurrence in Luke of a large amount of teaching matter that is almost identical in form and wording with parallel material in Matthew. While some students of the literary phenomena involved still prefer to speak of Q as a stratum rather than as a document, the assumption that it circulated as a collection in written form provides an answer to many questions that arise in the course of Synoptic analysis. Since the agreement between Luke and Matthew in this area of overlapping is an agreement of one Greek text with another, it follows that Q was a Greek rather than an Aramaic document. Speculation as to an earlier literary history in Aramaic is hypothetical and remote. Attempts to date Q are based on little more than conjecture, but the collection can scarcely have been much earlier than A.D. 50 or much later than A.D. 65. Its provenance appears to have been Palestinian.

Since the very existence of Q is only a deduction from the data of literary analysis, any reconstruction of it must be hypothetical. The author of Luke, as we can see from his use of Mark, ordinarily incorporated his sources in blocks, employed them without extensive systematization or conflation, and followed the order of his material as he found it. It is therefore reasonable to assume that both the order and the wording of Q are best preserved in Luke's Gospel. The abstraction from Luke of non-Marcan matter that Luke has in common with Matthew will give us Q in its approximate outline and content. According to a recent reconstruction,[23] Q contained 252 Lukan verses or parts of verses. Included in that count, however, are a few passages occurring only in Luke but whose relationship to adjacent "double tradition" is such as to suggest that they were drawn from the same source.

A glance over this material shows that Q consisted of four parables, a wealth of apologetic and ethical teaching, and a few narratives introducing discourses. Apparently this early document contained no miracle stories, unless the story of the centurion's faith is so interpreted. Attention given to the office and teaching of John the Baptist may have been in-

[22] Eusebius *Church History* III. 39. 3.

[23] F. C. Grant, *The Growth of the Gospels* (New York: Abingdon Press, 1933), pp. 74-81.

tended to correct claims by John's followers that the founder of their sect was superior to Jesus as a religious teacher. The narrative of Jesus' temptation in Q served as a commentary on his entire life and mission. Jesus' instructions to the twelve read like a program for church missionaries. His controversies with Pharisees and lawyers illuminated the growing rift between church and synagogue. His warnings, encouragement, and advice to men on trial for their faith had relevance to times of conflict and persecution. The exhortations to watchfulness and faithfulness, the message of the kingdom of God and of the conditions of admittance to it, the emphasis on the urgency, the duties, the cost, and the rewards of discipleship, the legislation of individual and group behavior, and the assurance of the imminent and catastrophic but triumphant day of the Son of man, met the disciplinary and hortatory needs of the struggling and growing church, beset with difficulties but buoyed up by hopes of eschatological deliverance. It is probable, therefore, that Q was compiled as a manual for Christian catechists in their instruction of converts.

E. Luke's Special Tradition.—Undoubtedly many collections of Jesus' sayings and discourses were made in one part or other of the primitive church. Sources that stressed the Jewishness of Jesus and the continuity of the new faith with Judaism supplied at least some of the special matter that Matthew incorporated in his Gospel. The rich tradition of narratives, parables, and sayings that is peculiar to Luke must have been drawn from some special source or sources at the disposal of the Third Evangelist.

It is possible, of course, that Luke obtained his special tradition entirely from oral sources, or that it had formed part of Q and for some reason was not incorporated by Matthew. But both of these hypotheses are open to objection. Except for the fact that no parallel version of it is extant, a good part of Luke's special tradition has just as much claim as the so-called Q material to documentary origin. Since Matthew's use of almost all of Mark suggests that he may have exploited his other sources in similar fashion, his omission of such a rich body of teaching as that in the special Lukan matter would be difficult to understand had it stood in his version of Q. It is probable, therefore, that Luke employed other collections of Jesus' teaching in addition to Q, and reckoned them among the compilations that he declares "many" had undertaken.

It would be hazardous to assume that all Luke's special tradition ever circulated as a single document, or that all of it had had some previous documentary history. The birth and infancy narratives differ in style and content from the rest of the Lukan matter and appear to have been originally independent of it. Whether they all come from one source or not, and whether Luke found them in oral or written form, still remain matters of dispute (see Exeg., *ad loc.*). The greater part of the special matter in the passion and resurrection narratives was probably derived from sources Luke knew only in oral form. Even in the main body of the Gospel the special tradition, which amounts to 279 verses,[24] must be described as cognate rather than homogeneous, and such narratives as the call of Simon and the sons of Zebedee and the raising from the dead of the widow's son at Nain need not have had a documentary base. Nevertheless it is convenient to refer to the special tradition in the main body of Luke's Gospel by the symbol L and to discuss it as a block.

One feature of this special tradition is the place it made for Jesus' relationships with women: the widow of Nain; the penitent sinner; the women who provided for Jesus and his disciples out of their means; Martha and Mary; the woman whose blessing Jesus corrected with a striking saying; and the crippled woman whom he healed by exorcism. In contrast to Q there is a highly developed interest in the miraculous. Jesus' escape from the mob at Nazareth and Simon's extraordinary catch of fish are traits incidental to more inclusive narratives. In addition there are at least four full-fledged miracle stories: the resurrection of the young man of Nain; the healing of a crippled woman; the healing of a man suffering from dropsy; and the healing of ten lepers, one of whom was a grateful Samaritan. Luke's special material is unique among major gospel sources in that it makes little or no place for eschatology in Jesus' message. Its tradition has affinities with Jewish prophecy and Jewish wisdom but not with Jewish apocalyptic. It portrays Jesus as a prophet and teacher and healer but not as one destined to be the supernatural "Son of man."

The L sources were particularly rich in parables. Four of these teach by examples that are to be imitated or avoided rather than by direct analogy and therefore constitute a class by themselves in the parabolic tradition of the Gospels: the good Samaritan; the rich fool; the rich man and Lazarus; and the Pharisee and the tax collector. Three of the other thirteen that were in Luke's special sources are variants of parables also occurring in the tradition peculiar to Matthew: the great banquet; the lost sheep; and the pounds. The lost sheep, the

[24] *Ibid.*, pp. 92-93.

lost coin, and the lost son (ch. 15) form a sequence that may have been earlier than Luke's use of it.

The two passages on dividing an inheritance and on faithfulness in the administration of wealth, as well as the parables of the rich fool, the dishonest steward, and the rich man and Lazarus, are concerned with the stewardship of material resources. The parables of the importunate friend, of the widow and the judge, and of the Pharisee and the tax collector deal with the proper practice of prayer. The rules of etiquette for guests and the rules of hospitality for the host are examples of what has been termed Jesus' "table talk." The story of the penitent sinner, the story of Jesus and Zacchaeus, and the parables of the lost sheep, the lost coin, and the lost son are illustrations of Jesus' love and compassion for repentant sinners.

The provenance of most of the L material, like that of the Q source, appears to have been Palestinian. It is not so clear that the miracle stories would have been at home in a purely Semitic environment, particularly that of the resurrection of the widow's son. Luke's version of Jesus' rejection at Nazareth, whether it had a documentary base or not, presupposes the church's Gentile mission. A Hellenistic community on the fringe of Palestine, such as the seacoast town of Caesarea, could have provided the setting in which Luke's tradition was preserved, collected, and in some instances created. For the most part L material has as good a claim as Q matter to early origin, but the miracle narratives imply a highly developed interest in this aspect of Jesus' ministry and may require a later date.

F. The Gospel of Mark.—The first reduction of parts of the oral tradition to writing was a response to the catechetical needs of the primitive church, but its more strictly evangelistic concerns also required some literary fixation of the narratives. The passion story appears to have been the earliest to achieve formulation as a continuous account. Pronouncement stories, miracle stories, legends, and myths circulated separately during the oral period of their transmission and perhaps also in the earlier stages of their literary history. In time cognate matter was grouped into sequences, and the Gospel of Mark represents a further development of this literary process.

In the main Mark's work was that of an editor rather than that of an author. He selected and arranged the Christian tradition with which he was familiar and superimposed a vague chronological and geographical framework. But his Gospel is by no means planless. By prefixing selected narratives, discourses, miracle stories, myths, parables, and sayings to the passion story, the evangelist shows forth Jesus as the Messiah: foretold by John the Baptizer; accredited by his authority over demons; opposed by Pharisees and scribes and the political flunkies of Herod Antipas; recognized in his true character first by unclean spirits; confessed by Peter; revealed to the eye of faith by his transfiguration; betrayed by a member of his immediate group of followers; crucified by Pontius Pilate at the instigation of the Sanhedrin; made manifest to believers through his suffering on the Cross; and known to have triumphed over death by the discovery of the empty tomb. Though Mark is only one stage in the process of fixing the tradition, it is a most dramatic and definitive one.

G. The Gospel of Matthew.—The Gospel of Matthew is best described as a revised and enlarged edition of Mark. The author used Mark as it stands and almost in its entirety. His method of composition was to follow Mark's text until some phrase or incident suggested the desirability of illustration or elaboration. He then worked Q or other appropriate material into the Marcan context, returning after this excursus to the Marcan text at the point at which he had temporarily abandoned it. Only at the beginning and the end is his Gospel completely independent of Mark. When Mark was written, the church had not yet developed any concern for the origins of its martyred Messiah. Mark was satisfied to begin his account with the ministry of John the Baptizer and with John's baptism of Jesus. But during the interval between the appearance of Mark and the publication of Matthew the motives that tend to create and transmit religious legends had come into play. In order to satisfy a growing interest among churchmen Matthew prefixed a genealogy which reflected one stage in christological reflection and a cycle of birth and infancy narratives that articulated a later and more supernatural doctrine of the Messiah's generation. Mark ended rather abruptly with the discovery of the empty tomb. Matthew appended an account of the appearance of the risen Christ to his eleven disciples in Galilee and concluded with the famous missionary commission.

H. The Gospel of Luke.—While Mark and Matthew are complete in themselves, Luke is the first volume of a two-volume work. The fundamental unity of Luke-Acts has already been discussed (see above, pp. 3-5). It has been obscured in part by an accident of manuscript transmission whereby Luke has been included in the "Gospel" section of the canon and Acts in the "Apostle" section. This canonical separation by the Gospel of John is an unfortunate divorce. The gospel volume tells of the rise of Christianity in its Palestinian environment. The Acts volume relates the expansion of the new world religion into Syria, the Levant, and eastern Europe, and ends with its firm establishment at the heart of the Roman Empire.

Luke, like Matthew, made Mark the basis of his Gospel, but his method of composition differed. In the body of his Gospel he incorporated his material in great blocks—five blocks of Mark alternating with four of Q and the special tradition that has been designated by the symbol L. At the end he redrafted Mark's passion narrative with material of his own composition and with two accounts of appearances of the risen Christ to disciples in or about Jerusalem. To the beginning he prefixed a cycle of birth and infancy stories completely different from Matthew's, instinct with poetic beauty and couched in the sonorous phraseology of the Septuagint. Renan called the resulting work "the most beautiful book ever written."

J. Recapitulation.—It has required a section of this Introduction to reconstruct the history of the tradition in Luke's Gospel. In his own preface Luke summarized the whole process in a single sentence. He distinguished four levels, and to recall them is to recapitulate the study just made. First there were the events themselves: "The things which have been accomplished among us." Then came the oral tradition: "They were delivered to us by those who from the beginning were eyewitnesses and ministers of the word." Then the oral tradition was committed to writing and various attempts were made to assemble it: "Many have undertaken to compile a narrative." Finally came the evangelist's own contribution: "It seemed good to me also, having followed all things closely for some time past, to write an orderly account. . . ."

III. Some Special Problems in the Source Analysis of Luke

A. Proto-Luke Hypothesis.—B. H. Streeter[25] advanced the hypothesis that Q and L—the latter comprising almost all the special tradition in Luke except that in 1:1–2:52—were already combined in what amounted to a gospel before Luke became acquainted with Mark, and perhaps by Luke himself. The Gospel of Luke is therefore a new edition of this "Proto-Luke," revised and enlarged by the addition of Marcan matter. As a corollary Streeter maintained that the non-Marcan sections of Luke (that is, Proto-Luke) formed the framework of the final edition, into which copious extracts from Mark were inserted at convenient places. The argument of this original article (with modifications and elaborations) was presented again in Streeter's *Four Gospels*[26] and was worked out in detail by Vincent Taylor in *Behind the Third Gospel*.[27] Taylor even published the "text" of Proto-Luke under the title *The First Draft of St. Luke's Gospel*.[28] Since the Streeter-Taylor hypothesis has had considerable vogue both in British and American circles, it will be in order to subject it to critical examination.[29]

We may ask, first: Would QL constitute a complete gospel?

There are four blocks of non-Marcan matter in the body of Luke's Gospel: (*a*) 5:1-11; (*b*) 6:20–8:3; (*c*) 9:51–18:14; and (*d*) 19:1-27. The first consists of Luke's account of the call of Simon and the sons of Zebedee. This appears to be a variant of Mark 1:16-20 (see Exeg., *ad loc.*), just as is the other variant in John 21:1-14, and apart from Proto-Luke assumptions there is no need to postulate a documentary base for it. In the second block most of the material is derived from Q and provided by the evangelist with editorial links. Some of the so-called "L" matter that is appended probably had an oral rather than a documentary base, for example, the miracle story of the raising from the dead of the widow's son at Nain. The third and by far the largest of the blocks begins with an incident that may have been drawn from a special source, the story of the inhospitable Samaritans. But from 9:57 to 13:30 the bulk of the matter again is Q, with a few inserts of special tradition and with some obviously editorial links. From 13:31 to 18:14 most of the content is derived from some special source or sources, with a few Q inserts and many editorial introductions, conclusions, and generalizations. In the fourth and final block the story of Jesus and Zacchaeus is special tradition, and the parable of the pounds is an independent version of Matt. 25:14-30.

If this non-Marcan matter is abstracted from Luke, it will be seen to have even less homogeneity than its Q content by itself and even less claim to have constituted the main body of a gospel. Did it have a beginning that would have suited a gospel? Streeter and Taylor held that Luke 3:1–4:30 was that beginning, a block of narratives and sayings untouched (or almost untouched) by Mark. There is certainly a pre-

[25] "Fresh Light on the Synoptic Problem," *Hibbert Journal*, XX (1921), 103-12.

[26] New York: The Macmillan Co., 1925, pp. 201-22.

[27] Oxford: Clarendon Press, 1926.

[28] "Theology Reprints No. 1"; London: Society for Promoting Christian Knowledge, 1927.

[29] For more detailed argument see S. MacLean Gilmour, "A Critical Re-Examination of Proto-Luke," *Journal of Biblical Literature*, LXVII (1948), 143-52.

ponderance of non-Marcan matter here, but most of it appears either to be editorial in origin or tradition that had previously circulated only in oral form. The genealogy (Luke 3:23-38) is a variant of the one that now forms the preface to Matthew's Gospel and may have circulated independently of any connected source. The story of Jesus' rejection at Nazareth (Luke 4:16-30) is Luke's own expansion of Mark 6:1-6, representing Jesus at the very outset of his ministry as conscious of his world mission, and forecasting his ultimate rejection by the Jews. Streeter declared that the chronological data in Luke 3:1-2*a* look like the opening words of a gospel and then drew the conclusion that they constituted the preamble to Luke's preliminary draft. But their present setting is more reasonably explained as their original one. The evangelist was fond of associating events in the gospel story with the wider history of the times. Zechariah had been priest "in the days of Herod, king of Judea" (Luke 1:5), and Jesus had been born at the time of Quirinius' first enrollment (Luke 2:1-2). The sixfold synchronization of John's appearance as a prophet with the activities of distinguished contemporaries is simply a more elaborate application of the same technique. Luke is careful to note the termination of John's work: "But Herod the tetrarch, who had been reproved by him . . . shut up John in prison" (Luke 3:19-20).

If it is difficult to consider the special tradition in Luke 3:1–4:30 as the beginning of a gospel, it is even more difficult to regard the non-Marcan matter in Luke 22:14–24:50 as a suitable "conclusion." In his reconstruction of Luke's special passion and resurrection narrative Taylor unduly minimized the Marcan content of Luke's account and regarded much that was editorial, or editorial inference from Mark, as extracts from an independent source. Probably only the following passages can claim to form a special literary tradition (see Exeg.):

22:15-17, 21, 23. The Last Supper.

22:25-27. Discourse on true greatness (L here overlaps with Mark 10:42-45).

22:28-30. Discourse on the disciples as future judges of the twelve tribes (L here overlaps with Matt. 19:28).

22:31-32. A prediction of the disciples' desertion, and a commission to Simon.

22:36-38. The saying about buying a sword.

23:28*b*-31. Words of Jesus on the road to Calvary.

24:13-21, 25-35. The risen Christ on the road to Emmaus.

24:36-43. An appearance of the risen Christ in Jerusalem.

It is difficult to discover any evidence in these passages that Luke had access to a continuous account of the Passion and the Resurrection other than Mark's.

On examination, then, Proto-Luke scarcely maintains itself as a complete gospel. In the course of composing his gospel volume, Luke used in addition to Mark and Q a number of cognate literary sources that can loosely be called L. In the body of his Gospel Luke used L mainly to supplement Q. In the introductory chapters he used a fund of oral tradition, some matter from Mark and Q, and some special tradition about John the Baptist's preaching that may have existed quite apart from a documentary L. In the passion and resurrection narratives he used a few L passages to supplement Mark but depended in the main on oral tradition and on his own dramatic and literary genius to achieve the recasting of the narrative that he desired.

A second question: Did QL provide Luke with the framework for the final draft of his Gospel?

There is general agreement that the problem does not arise until we come to the third chapter of the Gospel. Luke prefixed the birth and infancy narratives to his final draft in order to satisfy the emerging interest of the church in the nativity and childhood of its Lord, an interest that had probably not existed when Mark was composed or, for that matter, when "Proto-Luke" is supposed to have been compiled. Furthermore it is probable that Luke took these narratives in large part from an oral rather than a documentary cycle of tradition.

In the body of his Gospel Luke alternates five blocks of Mark (4:31-44; 5:12–6:16; 8:4–9:50; 18:15-43; and 19:28–22:13) with the four blocks of L or Q plus L that have already been noted (see p. 16). At the beginning, on the other hand, a relatively small amount of Marcan matter is conflated with a relatively large amount of non-Marcan, or is recast and expanded with considerable editorial freedom.

Doubts have already been expressed that any continuous block of non-Marcan material has been incorporated by Luke in 3:1–4:30. On the contrary, matter drawn from Q has been supplemented with special tradition, partly oral and partly documentary, and with Luke's own editorial introductions, connections, generalizations, and free composition. To this conclusion must now be added the other, that at crucial points in 3:1–4:30 Luke betrays unmistakable dependence on Mark (see Exeg.). Unlike his practice in later sections he uses Mark with freedom, making selections from Mark's material, conflating it with non-Marcan tradition, and supplementing it with matter drawn from a variety of more or less cognate sources. But throughout it is Mark that is basic rather than a hypothetical (and probably imaginary) "Proto-Luke."

Luke's use of Mark and his other sources in 22:14–24:50 is comparable. Freedom is used in selecting from and rearranging Mark, but the skeleton of the passion story remains our earliest Gospel, not the heterogeneous selection of tradition used to expand and redraft it.

It is clear, then, that Luke was able to draw on a variety of tradition with which to amplify and recast Mark's account, but his basic dependence on Mark is equally clear, and the hypothesis that a "Proto-Luke" constituted the framework of his gospel volume may be dismissed.

B. Omission of Marcan Matter from Luke's Gospel.—The fact that the Gospel of Mark survived the centuries has made it possible to demonstrate that Luke used it as a major source (see Vol. VII, pp. 62-63). He employed over 60 per cent of its 661 verses, and these Marcan passages constitute approximately one third of the 1,148 verses of his Gospel. As we have seen immediately above it was Mark, not Q or L or a hypothetical combination of Q and L in a "Proto-Luke," that provided him with the framework of his gospel volume.

Nevertheless there are numerous passages in Mark that are omitted by Luke. Matthew reproduced no less than 93 per cent of his major source, but Luke chose to use it more sparingly. Can we determine his motives in this?

Minor editorial revision in the interests of clarity, brevity, or style requires no comment. Mark's account of Herod's execution of John the Baptist (Mark 6:17-29) may have been excluded as an irrelevant excursus. Its omission certainly improves the connection of Marcan material at that point, and Luke's editorial matter in 3:19-20 reflects familiarity with it. The request of the sons of Zebedee in Mark 10:35-41 may have been interpreted as derogatory, and an inclination to idealize the original disciples could account for its omission. Mark's story of the cursing of the fig tree and its consequent withering (Mark 11:12-14, 20-25) may have seemed as incongruous and incomprehensible to Luke as it does to many a modern reader. A considerable number of Marcan passages were omitted because Luke wished to employ, or had already employed, variants from other sources:

Mark 1:16-20. The call of Simon, Andrew, James, and John; cf. Luke 5:1-11 (L).

Mark 3:19*b*-30. The Beelzebub controversy; cf. Luke 11:14-26 (Q).

Mark 4:26-33. The parables of the seed growing secretly and of the mustard seed; cf. Luke 13:18-21 (Q).

Mark 6:1-6. Jesus' rejection at Nazareth; cf. Luke 4:16-30 (L).

Mark 10:42-45. Sayings about true greatness; cf. Luke 22:25-27 (L).

Mark 12:28*c*-34. The scribe's question about the great commandment; cf. Luke 10:25-28 (L).

Mark 14:3-9. The anointing of Jesus by a woman at Bethany; cf. Luke 7:36-39, 44-50 (L).

The catena of sayings in Mark 9:41-50 was unused, but two of them appear in variant forms in other contexts (Luke 17:2 [Q] and 14:34 [Q]). Luke may have believed that the single verse in 16:18 (Q) reproduced the gist of the controversy with the Pharisees about divorce (Mark 10:2-12).

Mark 6:45–8:26, often called Luke's "great omission," has no parallels whatever in the Third Gospel. It relates the following incidents: Jesus' walk on the sea; healing activity at Gennesaret; controversy with Pharisees about the tradition of the elders; Jesus and the Syrophoenician woman; healing of the deaf stammerer by means of spittle; feeding of the four thousand; controversy with Pharisees about a sign from heaven; discourse in a boat as Jesus and his disciples cross the lake; and the healing of a blind man by means of spittle.

It is a plausible conjecture that Mark 8:1-26 originally belonged to a source independent of Mark 6:30–7:37 and parallel at this point to it. The two groups of material contain an interesting series of doublets. Both begin with a miraculous feeding of a crowd of people, followed by a crossing of the lake and a discussion between Jesus and his disciples, in which the latter reveal a failure to understand the meaning of the miracle of the loaves and the fish. Both groups contain an account of a controversy with Pharisees and end with a miracle of healing effected by the use of spittle. It is no solution of our problem, however, to postulate an earlier form of Mark that Luke used and from which Mark 8:1-26 was missing. Luke's disuse of Mark 6:45–7:37 would still remain unexplained. The hypothesis that Luke used a mutilated copy of Mark is also too desperate for serious consideration.

The controversy with the Pharisees about scribal tradition in Mark 7:1-23 may have seemed remote from the interests of the public for which Luke was writing. The story of Jesus' reluctant healing of the daughter of the Syrophoenician woman may have run counter to the evangelist's desire to represent Jesus as ministering readily to non-Jews. Luke may have recognized that the story of the feeding of the four thousand was a doublet of the earlier narrative he had already employed. The two miracles of healing by means of spittle are the only two instances in the gospel tradition in which Jesus is said to have employed physical methods in exorcism, and Luke (as well as Matthew, for that matter) may have hesitated to associate Jesus in this way with popular healers familiar to his Gentile readers. Finally—and this may have been the decisive factor in the omission—Luke clearly had more material than he could easily compress into the space he had at his disposal. The gospel volume of Luke-Acts must have filled a papyrus roll of thirty feet or more, and this was as long as a reader could conveniently manipulate. As an editor Luke may have felt that some omission as well as abbreviation of available material was mandatory.

IV. The Text of Luke

A. History of the Greek Text of Luke.—We have just seen that the Gospel would fill one papyrus roll; Acts would fill another. Since the author was consciously creating "literature," he may have employed the literary or "uncial" script, that is, capital letters. At first the two rolls containing Luke and Acts would have been copied by the same scribe or group of scribes, but early in the second century "Luke" was attached to the "Gospel" section of the nascent canon, and subsequently its textual history differs from that of its original companion.

Early in the second century, also, sheets of papyrus began to be bound into books or "codices," and these came into general use for the reproduction of Christian literature. No copy of Luke in roll form has so far been discovered, but in 1931, Chester Beatty, an American collector living in England, announced the purchase from Egyptian dealers of (among others) a fragmentary third-century papyrus codex (p^{45}) that contains parts of the four Gospels and the book of Acts. Passages from Luke 6 and 9–14 are preserved, and this is the earliest manuscript of the Third Gospel known to scholars.

Papyrus was an exceedingly fragile writing material and could be preserved for any length of time only in a very dry climate. It was therefore natural that Christians should soon turn to the use of the more durable parchment. The earliest Christian parchment codices known to exist are early fourth-century uncials, probably of a scriptorium at Alexandria. Codex Vaticanus (B) is now in the Vatican Library at Rome, where it was first listed in a catalogue of the year 1481. Originally it contained both the Old Testament and the New Testament in Greek, but the latter part of the New Testament is now missing. Codex Sinaiticus (א) was first discovered in 1844 in the monastery of St. Catherine on Mount Sinai. Forty-three leaves are now in the Leipzig University Library and the rest in the British Museum. This codex has the text of the Epistle of Barnabas and of the Shepherd of Hermas as well as of the entire Greek Bible. Both Codex Vaticanus and Codex Sinaiticus include the complete text of Luke.

Other famous uncials that contain Luke's Gospel are documents that date from the fifth century: Alexandrinus (A), part of the British Museum collection since its inception in 1757; Ephraemi Rescriptus (C), a manuscript now in Paris that was erased and rewritten with nonbiblical material in the twelfth century, but whose original text is still decipherable (parts of Luke's Gospel are missing); the Washington manuscript of the Gospels (W) in the Freer Gallery of Art; and Codex Bezae (D) in the Cambridge University Library (the earliest New Testament manuscript to contain a Latin translation parallel to the Greek text).

Manuscript transmission of literature, in fact even printed transmission, tends to be faulty. Minor changes are introduced into the text, either unintentionally, through accidental omission, addition, or through misinterpretation, or deliberately, in order to increase the clarity, and occasionally to improve on the meaning of the original. Variations even in the earliest types of the New Testament text that scholarship can recover continue to plague the interpreter. No "pure" form of Luke, or of any other part of the New Testament, can yet be distinguished. Even the Chester Beatty Gospel Papyrus and the earliest parchment uncials have been edited. But the process of change and embellishment accelerated in the early medieval period, until a text of the New Testament came into general use in the church—in so far as the church in the Middle Ages used a Greek text at all—that contained a combination of earlier readings and many more or less distinctive variants of its own. This so-called "ecclesiastical" text is found in most uncials (apart from those mentioned above), in almost all quotations from the New Testament by church fathers since the fourth century, in all translations after A.D. 400 (that is, all translations other than Old Latin, Old Syriac, and Coptic), and in most manuscripts written in the running hand ("cursive" script) that began to be used for literature in the ninth century and became almost universal by the twelfth. Such manuscripts are called "minuscules."

Paper as a writing material was first used in China. Arabs became acquainted with its method of manufacture and began to employ it as early as the eighth century. It was introduced into western Europe as one by-product of the Crusades. A few paper manuscripts of the New Testament date from as early as the twelfth and thirteenth centuries and share the characteristics of late parchment minuscules. But parchment also continued in use until after the invention of printing.

B. Printed Greek Text.—Printed books appearing before A.D. 1500 are often called *incunabula* (books in "swaddling clothes"). Among them are over a hundred printings of the Vulgate, almost a dozen pre-Luther German Bibles, and the first printing of the Hebrew Old Testament, but no edition of the Greek New Testament. An ambitious project of a Bible polyglot that would print the New Testament in Greek and Latin and the Old Testament in Hebrew, Greek, and Latin was begun as early as 1502 by the Spanish Cardinal Jiménez, but was not actually published until 1520. The honor of preparing the first Greek New Testament to be printed goes to the Renaissance humanist Erasmus. It was published by the Swiss printer Froben in 1516.

Erasmus prepared his Greek text after little more than ten months labor, employing half a dozen minuscule manuscripts that were in the library at Basel. One of these, now designated by the numeral 1, contains a most valuable and interesting text, but Erasmus made little use of it. The result is that Erasmus' printed text represents the more or less standardized ecclesiastical text that was to be found in the bulk of late medieval manuscripts.

Erasmus' text continued to be basic to later printings of the Greek New Testament. In 1550 the Parisian printer Robert Estienne brought out an edition dedicated to Henry II of France, called the "Regia." This included a number of variants found in fifteen manuscripts that Estienne was able to consult in Paris. The Regia in turn was the basis of a Greek text published by Théodore de Bèze in 1598. This latter appears to have been the main text employed by the translators of the King James Version of 1611.

The Erasmus-Estienne-Bèze type of Greek text came to be known in the early seventeenth century as the "textus receptus," and no serious modifications were introduced for almost 250 years. The first attempt to edit a Greek New Testament independently of the received text, and by employing the most ancient manuscripts available, was by a German philologist, Karl Lachmann, whose first edition appeared in 1831. Between 1841 and 1872 another German scholar, Konstantin von Tischendorf, brought out eight still more famous editions. The eighth, the culmination of his labors, is based on Codex Sinaiticus and has an immense and still invaluable critical apparatus of variant readings.

The greatest of the nineteeth-century critical editions of the Greek New Testament was published in 1881 after almost thirty years of work by two Cambridge scholars, B. F. Westcott and F. J. A. Hort. Westcott and Hort made use of critical principles enunciated in the eighteenth century by two German scholars, Bengel and Griesbach, but they elaborated and grounded them much more thoroughly in the history of the New Testament text. They recognized that a type of text represented by Codex Bezae, by the Old Latin and Old Syriac versions, and by quotations in the writings of the earliest fathers was widely used in the post-apostolic age. Nevertheless they did not regard this so-called "Western" text as primitive. They believed it was characterized by a love of paraphrase, a tendency to harmonize one section of the New Testament with another, and a readiness to adopt alterations and additions from sources that ultimately did not receive canonical status. Instead of the "Western" text they preferred what they called "Neutral" readings, found chiefly in codices Vaticanus and Sinaiticus (the latter less pure than the former), the Coptic versions, most quotations from the New Testament in the writings of Clement of Alexandria and of Origen, and to some extent in codices Alexandrinus and Ephraemi Rescriptus.

In preparing their text, then, Westcott and Hort followed the Neutral text, especially the readings of Codex Vaticanus. They made only one important exception to this rule. When a shorter reading occurs in the Western text, they preferred it on grounds of "intrinsic probability." Since the tendency of Codex Bezae and its allies was, they believed, to add and to expand and to paraphrase, any shorter reading they give has claims to originality.

The King James Version was based on the "textus receptus," mainly the embellished Greek text that had widespread currency in the medieval church. The English Revised Version of 1881 and the American Standard Version of 1901 were profoundly influenced by the principles of text reconstruction as they had been stated by Westcott and Hort. The Revised Standard Version of 1946 reflects in turn some of the modifications of the theories of Westcott and Hort that have been made during the past fifty years. Codices Vaticanus and Sinaiticus are no longer regarded as primitive and unrevised. The readings of Codex Bezae and its allies are given more consideration than Westcott and Hort were prepared to accord them. The readings of the Chester Beatty Gospel Papyrus are given weight because of their early attestation and because of the apparent excellence of the text as a whole. The possibility is seriously entertained that other text types worthy of ranking with Westcott and Hort's Neutral and Western may yet be isolated or are already in process of isolation (for example, the "Caesarean" as represented in the uncials W and Θ, the minuscules 13 and 1 and their allies, and to some extent in the Chester Beatty papyri). As a result the English text of the Revised Standard Version is based on a more or less "eclectic" Greek text—each separate reading having been weighed by the translators on its merits. Nevertheless even these most recent revisers are heavily indebted to the Westcott and Hort edition. While modern textual research may have modified some of Westcott and Hort's theories, it has not yet established a text that can admittedly supersede it. (See also article "The Text and Ancient Versions of the New Testament," Vol. I.)

C. Attempt to Recover the Original Greek Text of Luke.—The difficulties involved in establishing one New Testament Greek text as a whole as preferable to another have no better illustration than in the case of Luke and Acts. Variations between Codex Bezae and its allies on the one hand and Codex Vaticanus and its supporters on the other are more interesting and widespread in the text of these books than elsewhere, but at the same time of such a nature as to suggest that they arose after Luke and Acts ceased to be copied as a single work. The more important variants in the Western text of Luke are shorter readings, and the judgment of many modern scholars is in agreement with that of Westcott and Hort, that in these instances Codex Bezae is to be preferred to Codex Vaticanus. In Acts, on the other hand, most of the Western variations—more numerous and substantial than in Luke—appear to be additions to or expansions of an original form that is more closely approximated in Codex Vaticanus. Nevertheless there are not lacking those who would maintain that the Neutral text here is the result of a deliberate revision and abbreviation.

It would therefore be hazardous to defend the superiority of one text family over another throughout both volumes of Luke-Acts. The texts are clearly "mixed" in content and in quality. One may be preferable to another at one point and inferior at another. One bold attempt to provide a solution to the textual difficulties that arise in Luke and Acts was made in the late seventeenth century by Jean Le Clerc and renewed in 1895 by Friedrich Blass. According to their hypothesis, Luke and Acts went through two editions under the direction of their original author. Codex Bezae is based on the later edition of the Gospel and the earlier edition of the Acts. Despite its attractive features the hypothesis leaves many questions unanswered and has not generally commended itself. The exact relationship of the Western and the Neutral texts of Luke and Acts to each other and to the autographs is a problem that still awaits solution.

The text of Acts is given further consideration elsewhere (see Intro. to Acts in Vol. IX). Here it will be useful to mention only a few of the more important variations between codices Vaticanus and Bezae (and their allies) in the gospel volume, leaving a more detailed discussion of them, as well as all reference to minor but not necessarily unimportant differences, to the exegesis of the passages in question.

The following inclusions in Codex Bezae are absent from Codex Vaticanus:

1. Following 6:4: "On the same day he saw a man breaking the Sabbath by working and said to him: 'If you are doing this deliberately, you are blessed; but if you are acting out of ignorance, you are transgressing the law and are accursed.' "
2. Added to 9:55: "And he said, 'You do not know what manner of spirit you are of.' "
3. In 11:2-4 clauses are added that expand the shorter form of the Lord's Prayer as found in Codex Vaticanus to its more familiar longer version. Also the words of Matt. 6:7 are added to vs. 2.
4. Following 22:42, vss. 43-44—the angelic visitation and Jesus' agony in the garden —are inserted.
5. Added to 23:38: "in letters of Greek and Latin and Hebrew."
6. Added to 23:53: "and when he had laid him there, he had a stone placed before the tomb that twenty men could scarcely roll."

The following are the chief omissions by Codex Bezae of matter that is included in Codex Vaticanus:

1. The latter part of 22:19 and all of 22:20.
2. Jesus' words from the Cross in 23:34 were omitted in the original but were later added by some early corrector ("And Jesus said, '. . . what they do' ").
3. The first sentence of 24:6: "He is not here, but has risen."
4. All of 24:12: "But Peter rose . . . what had happened."

5. The concluding phrase of 24:36: "And he said to them, 'Peace to you!' "
6. The entire verse, 24:40: "And when he had said this, he showed them his hands and his feet."
7. The concluding phrase of 24:51: "and was carried up into heaven."

Westcott and Hort held that the additional matter attested by Codex Bezae and itemized above was secondary and they gave it no place in their text. The readings contained in Codex Vaticanus but absent from Codex Bezae were called "Western non-interpolations" by the Cambridge scholars, who disliked to use the obvious term "Neutral interpolations" because of the high respect they had for Codex Vaticanus. While few today would hesitate to regard Codex Vaticanus as an edited text, and less weight would be given today to Westcott and Hort's "genealogical evidence" of manuscripts, modern scholarship nevertheless agrees substantially with the judgment of the great nineteenth-century editors. The longer "Western" readings are generally suspicious, while the shorter readings of Codex Bezae and its allies give the impression of originality.

D. Marcion's "Gospel."—Marcion was born about A.D. 85 at the Black Sea port of Sinope in the Roman province of Pontus. He was reared a Christian. According to one account, his father was bishop of Sinope, but Marcion's own early connection with the shipping trade implies that his father had been a wealthy shipowner. Possibly the two activities were not mutually exclusive. At some point in his career Marcion was excommunicated by the church at Sinope, presumably because of views that were regarded locally as heretical. He then made his way to Ephesus and perhaps also to Smyrna. After an unfriendly reception from Christians in Asia Minor, he went to Rome about A.D. 139.

In Rome, Marcion joined himself to the long-established Christian community and made it a gift that would approximate $30,000. At first his relations with the Roman church appear to have been amicable. After a few years, however, they were disturbed by his reforming zeal, and particularly by the publication of a book which set forth his peculiar doctrines and which he entitled *The Antitheses.* Other literary activities included the editing and publication of a "Gospel" and an "Apostle," which he hoped would displace the Jewish scriptures as the Christian Bible. The final break came in A.D. 144. It is interesting to note that Marcion's original cash contribution was then refunded!

For fifteen years or so after his Roman excommunication Marcion carried on an active program of propaganda and organization. Marcionite churches were established throughout the empire. Although bitterly attacked by orthodox church leaders, Marcionism continued to flourish for some centuries.

Marcion's interpretation of Christianity does not directly concern us here. It will suffice to say that he wished to purge Christianity of its Jewish elements and to establish it as a completely new religion. He believed that the Jewish Bible contained the revelation of an inferior, anthropomorphic, creator-god; a god of justice untempered with mercy; the god of the Jews who was jealous, exacting, and resentful. The supreme God on the other hand, the Highest Principle, was the God of love whom Jesus had first made known to men. In accordance with these ideas Marcion rejected the Jewish Bible in its entirety and undertook to substitute for it a "closed" canon of Christian scripture. As far as we know, Marcion's "Gospel" and "Apostle" were the first Christian "New Testament," although the term itself did not come into use until later in the century. Certainly the process of defining the much more inclusive orthodox New Testament, and of giving it equal weight with the Old Testament, was in part a reaction against Marcion's radical views —another instance of the church's debt to heretics!

Marcion's *Antitheses* and his text of the Christian scriptures are known to us only through the medium of quotations from them by orthodox apologists who had undertaken to refute his ideas, particularly Tertullian, Epiphanius, and Adamantius (Pseudo-Origen). Such sources, in addition to a prejudice that often led to a distortion of Marcion's positions, are necessarily fragmentary. Nevertheless much of the *Antitheses* and of Marcion's Christian Bible can be reconstructed from them.

In the "Apostle" section Marcion placed what now form ten letters of Paul, that is, all the letters of the Catholic corpus except the three "Pastorals" and the Epistle to the Hebrews. The letter now known as Ephesians was known to Marcion as "Laodiceans." He arranged his Pauline letters apparently in order of their anti-Jewishness, beginning the collection with Galatians and ending it with Philippians. He also edited the letters, particularly the Epistle to the Romans, making many omissions in the interest of his peculiar theological beliefs.

Marcion's "Gospel" apparently contained no non-Lukan matter. On the other hand much that is in our text of Luke was missing. Marcion's text began with the words that are now in Luke 3:1*a* and then proceeded to relate Jesus' "descent" (presumably from heaven) to Capernaum and his healing of a demoniac there (Luke 4:31-37). Marcion therefore made no use of Luke's preface or of his birth and infancy narratives. In what follows, also, omissions of Luke's text as we know it are numerous. A recent study has estimated that of the 1,148 verses in Luke, 682 were certainly in Marcion's "Gospel," 283 were certainly absent, and 183 must be classified as doubtful.[30]

From very early times it has been assumed that Marcion issued an abbreviated and tendentious edition of Luke. Epiphanius expressly declared that Marcion had only Luke's Gospel at his disposal.[31] The one dissenting voice among the ancients was Hippolytus, who asserted that Mark rather than Luke had been employed.[32] Adolf von Harnack, in an exhaustive study of Marcion published in 1921,[33] supported the traditional opinion and held that any attempt to challenge it would be futile.

In an essay on the early history of the New Testament canon John Knox[34] questioned this ancient assumption and demonstrated that it is far from proved. Nevertheless he hesitated to accept the alternative, seriously raised in Germany in the nineteenth century, that Luke expanded Marcion. His own tentative hypothesis is that both Marcion's "Gospel" and our canonical Luke made use of a common source, and that this primitive "Proto-Luke" is more closely approximated in the former than in the latter.

Knox himself points out two weighty objections to his hypothesis: (*a*) the late date it requires for the preparation and publication of Luke-Acts; and (*b*) the plausibility of the abridgment theory. The question of the date of Luke-Acts is discussed elsewhere in this Introduction (see pp. 9-10 and cf. also Intro. to Acts, Vol. IX). While none of the evidence necessitates composition earlier than the middle of the second century, there is certainly no compelling reason—unless one shares Knox's conclusion that the publication of Paul's letters as a *corpus* preceded the publication of Luke-Acts—to regard it as a post-Marcion product. The hypothesis that Marcion abridged Luke's Gospel falls short of demonstration but is by no means untenable. And there is a third objection, namely, that Knox's "Proto-Luke" is as superfluous in the source reconstruction of the Gospel of Luke as the Streeter-Taylor "halfway house."

If Marcion's "Gospel" was based on Luke—or even on a major Lukan source—the reconstruction that has been made of it from patristic quotations becomes a further and important witness to the early Lukan text. Harnack showed that the text that Marcion had employed was characterized by Western readings, and he believed that already occasional passages had been harmonized with the text of Mark and Matthew. In a critical apparatus Marcion's readings lend themselves readily to grouping with the Lukan readings of Codex Bezae and its allies.

V. Outline of Contents

I. Preface (1:1-4)
II. Jesus' birth and boyhood (1:5–2:52)
- A. Annunciations to Zechariah and to Mary (1:5-56)
  1. The promise to Zechariah of the birth of John (1:5-25)
  2. The promise to Mary of the birth of Jesus (1:26-38)
  3. Mary's visit to Elizabeth (1:39-56)
- B. Births of John and Jesus (1:57–2:20)
  1. The birth of John (1:57-80)
  2. The birth of Jesus (2:1-20)
- C. Jesus' infancy and childhood (2:21-52)
  1. Jesus' circumcision and presentation (2:21-40)
  2. An incident from Jesus' boyhood (2:41-52)

III. Introduction to Jesus' public ministry (3:1–4:13)
- A. John the Baptist (3:1-20)
  1. John's message (i). (3:1-6)
  2. John's message (ii). (3:7-9)
  3. John's message (iii). (3:10-14)
  4. John's message (iv). (3:15-17)
  5. Summary of John's message and an account of Herod and John (3:18-20)
- B. Prelude to Jesus' public ministry (3:21–4:13)
  1. Jesus' baptism (3:21-22)
  2. Jesus' genealogy (3:23-38)
  3. Jesus' temptations (4:1-13)

IV. Jesus' Galilean ministry (4:14–9:50)
- A. Beginning of Jesus' public ministry (4:14-30)
  1. Return to Galilee (4:14-15)
  2. Rejection at Nazareth (4:16-30)
- B. Jesus' ministry in and about Capernaum (4:31–5:16)
  1. Healing of a demoniac (4:31-37)
  2. Healing of Simon's wife's mother (4:38-39)
  3. Healings on the evening after the sabbath (4:40-41)

[30] John Knox, *Marcion and the New Testament* (Chicago: University of Chicago Press, 1942), pp. 107-8.

[31] *Heresies* XLII. 9.

[32] *Refutation* VII. 18. In an earlier work, *Against All Heresies,* Hippolytus had conformed to the general opinion. See Pseudo-Tertullian *Against All Heresies* 6, and Philastrius *Heresies* 45.

[33] *Marcion: Das Evangelium vom fremden Gott* (Leipzig: J. C. Hinrichs, 1921).

[34] *Marcion and the New Testament.*

4. Epilogue to a day at Capernaum (4:42-44)
5. Call of the first disciples (5:1-11)
6. Healing of a leper (5:12-16)

C. Controversies with Pharisees (5:17–6:11)
1. Healing of a paralytic (5:17-26)
2. Levi's call (5:27-28)
3. Jesus as a guest in Levi's house (5:29-32)
4. Parable of the wedding guests (5:33-35)
5. Parables of the patch and of the wine-skins (5:36-39)
6. Concerning plucking and eating grain on the sabbath (6:1-5)
7. Concerning a healing on the sabbath (6:6-11)

D. The great sermon (6:12-49)
1. Choosing of the twelve (6:12-16)
2. Introduction to Jesus' sermon (6:17-19)
3. The Beatitudes (6:20-23)
4. The woes (6:24-26)
5. The law of love (6:27-35)
6. The law of mercy (6:36-45)
7. Parable of the two houses (6:46-49)

E. Jesus' healing ministry (7:1-17)
1. Healing of the centurion's slave (7:1-10)
2. Raising from the dead of the young man of Nain (7:11-17)

F. Jesus and John the Baptist (7:18-35)
1. Jesus and the emissaries of John (7:18-23)
2. Jesus' estimate of John (7:24-30)
3. Parable of the peevish children (7:31-35)

G. Jesus and a penitent sinner (7:36-50)

H. Jesus as an itinerant teacher and wonder-worker (8:1-56)
1. Jesus begins an itinerant ministry (8:1-3)
2. Parable of the seed and the soils (8:4-8)
3. Purpose of parables (8:9-10)
4. Explanation of the parable (8:11-15)
5. Parable of the lamp and other sayings (8:16-18)
6. Jesus' spiritual kindred (8:19-21)
7. Stilling of the storm (8:22-25)
8. The Gerasene demoniac (8:26-39)
9. Jairus' daughter; a woman with a hem-orrhage (8:40-56)

J. Jesus and his disciples (9:1-50)
1. Mission of the twelve (9:1-6)
2. Herod hears rumors about Jesus (9:7-9)
3. Return of the apostles and Jesus' de-parture from Galilee (9:10-11)
4. Feeding of five thousand (9:12-17)
5. Peter's confession; Jesus' first prediction of his passion (9:18-22)
6. Motif of martyrdom (9:23-27)
7. The Transfiguration (9:28-36)
8. Exorcism of a demon from a boy (9:37-43*a*)
9. Jesus' second prediction of his passion (9:43*b*-45)
10. Dispute about rank (9:46-48)
11. An exorcist who was not a follower (9:49-50)

V. Jesus on the journey to Jerusalem (9:51–19:27)

A. Jesus sets his face toward Jerusalem (9:51-62)
1. Hostile Samaritans (9:51-56)
2. Conditions of discipleship (9:57-62)

B. Mission of the seventy (10:1-24)
1. Instructions to the missioners (10:1-16)
2. Jesus' words to the seventy on their return (10:17-20)
3. Jesus' prayer of thanksgiving (10:21-22)
4. Jesus' blessing on his disciples (10:23-24)

C. Jesus answers questions (10:25-42)
1. Jesus and a lawyer's question (10:25-28)
2. Parable of the good Samaritan (10:29-37)
3. Martha and Mary (10:38-42)

D. Teaching on prayer (11:1-13)
1. The Lord's Prayer (11:1-4)
2. Parable of the importunate friend (11:5-8)
3. Assurance that prayer will be answered (11:9-13)

E. Concerning the exorcism of demons (11:14-28)
1. Beelzebub controversy (11:14-23)
2. Parable of a demoniac and his relapse (11:24-26)
3. Jesus corrects a woman's blessing (11:27-28)

F. Concerning signs (11:29-36)
1. Sign of Jonah and related sayings (11:29-32)
2. Parables about the lamp and the eye (11:33-36)

G. Denunciations of Pharisees and lawyers (11:37-54)
1. Denunciations of Pharisees (11:37-44)
2. Denunciations of lawyers (11:45-52)
3. Opposition of scribes and Pharisees to Jesus (11:53-54)

H. On the responsibilities and privileges of discipleship (12:1–13:9)
1. Warning, encouragement, and advice to disciples (12:1-12)
2. On dividing an inheritance (12:13-15)
3. Parable of the rich fool (12:16-21)
4. The providence of God (12:22-31)
5. Heavenly treasure (12:32-34)
6. Allegory of the waiting servants (12:35-38)
7. Parable of the Householder and the thief (12:39-40)
8. Parable of the faithful and unfaithful servants (12:41-46)
9. Supplementary sayings emphasizing re-sponsibility (12:47-48)
10. Reflections on the purpose and issue of Christ's ministry (12:49-50)
11. Messianic divisions (12:51-53)
12. Interpreting the present time (12:54-56)
13. Wisdom of reconciliation (12:57-59)
14. Call to repentance (13:1-5)
15. Parable of the fig tree (13:6-9)

LUKE

J. Sabbath teaching in a synagogue (13:10-21)
   1. On the sabbath healing of a crippled woman (13:10-17)
   2. Parable of the mustard seed (13:18-19)
   3. Parable of the leaven (13:20-21)
K. Teaching in the course of the journey (13:22-35)
   1. On admission to the kingdom of God (13:22-30)
   2. Warning from Pharisees (13:31-33)
   3. Lament over Jerusalem (13:34-35)
Table talk in the house of a Pharisee (14:1-24)
   1. Healing of a man with dropsy (14:1-6)
   2. Rules of etiquette for guests at a feast (14:7-11)
   3. Rules of hospitality for a host (14:12-14)
   4. Parable of the great banquet (14:15-24)
M. On the conditions of discipleship (14:25-35)
   1. Renunciation as a condition of discipleship (14:25-27)
   2. Parables of the tower builder and of the king preparing for war (14:28-33)
   3. Worthlessness of tasteless salt (14:34-35)
N. On God's love for the lost (15:1-32)
   1. Parable of the lost sheep (15:1-7)
   2. Parable of the lost coin (15:8-10)
   3. Parable of the lost son (15:11-32)
O. On the use and abuse of wealth (16:1-31)
   1. Parable of the dishonest steward (16:1-9)
   2. Faithfulness in the administration of wealth (16:10-12)
   3. Exclusive demands of God's service (16:13)
   4. God knows the hearts of men (16:14-15)
   5. The law and the gospel (16:16-18)
   6. Parable of the rich man and Lazarus (16:19-31)
P. On forgiveness, faith, God's grace, and man's ingratitude (17:1-19)
   1. On those who cause others to sin; forgiveness; faith (17:1-6)
   2. Parable of the farmer and his slave (17:7-10)
   3. The grateful Samaritan (17:11-19)
Q. On the kingdom and the Son of man (17:20-37)
   1. Advent of the kingdom of God (17:20-21)
   2. Sudden coming of the Son of man (17:22-37)
R. Parables on the proper practice of prayer (18:1-14)
   1. Parable of the widow and the judge (18:1-8)
   2. Parable of the Pharisee and the tax collector (18:9-14)
S. Conditions of entrance to the kingdom (18:15-34)
   1. Jesus and little children (18:15-17)
   2. A rich man rejects discipleship (18:18-27)
   3. Reward of renunciation (18:28-30)
   4. Jesus again predicts his passion (18:31-34)
T. Jesus in Jericho (18:35–19:27)
   1. Healing of a blind beggar (18:35-43)
   2. Jesus and Zacchaeus (19:1-10)
   3. Parable of the pounds (19:11-27)

VI. Jesus' ministry in Jerusalem (19:28–24:12)
A. Jesus enters Jerusalem (19:28-46)
   1. Approach to Jerusalem (19:28-38)
   2. Jesus justifies the jubilation of his disciples (19:39-40)
   3. Prediction of the siege and destruction of Jerusalem (19:41-44)
   4. Cleansing of the temple (19:45-46)
B. Various attempts to incriminate Jesus (19:47–21:4)
   1. Antipathy of the Sanhedrin to Jesus (19:47-48)
   2. The Sanhedrin's challenge to Jesus' authority (20:1-8)
   3. Allegory of the vineyard and its wicked tenants (20:9-18)
   4. Question about paying the head tax to Caesar (20:19-26)
   5. Question about the resurrection (20:27-40)
   6. Question about the Davidic descent of the Christ (20:41-44)
   7. Jesus warns against the scribes (20:45-47)
   8. The widow's gift to the temple treasury (21:1-4)
C. Events that will mark the end of the age (21:5-38)
   1. Prediction that the temple would be destroyed (21:5-6)
   2. Preliminary signs of the approaching end (21:7-19)
   3. Fate of Jerusalem (21:20-24)
   4. Coming of the Son of man (21:25-28)
   5. Parable of the fig tree in leaf (21:29-31)
   6. A prediction and a certification (21:32-33)
   7. Injunction to watchfulness and prayer (21:34-36)
   8. Summary of Jesus' life and work in Jerusalem (21:37-38)
D. Jesus' last supper (22:1-23)
   1. Conspiracy of the chief priests and the scribes (22:1-2)
   2. Judas' plot to betray Jesus (22:3-6)
   3. Preparation for the Passover (22:7-13)
   4. The Last Supper (22:14-23)
E. The farewell discourse (22:24-38)
   1. True greatness (22:24-27)
   2. The disciples as the future rulers of the twelve tribes (22:28-30)
   3. Prediction of the disciples' desertion and a commission to Simon (22:31-32)
   4. Prediction of Peter's denial (22:33-34)
   5. Saying about buying a sword (22:35-38)
F. The arrest (22:39-65)
   1. Jesus' prayer on the Mount of Olives (22:39-46)
   2. Betrayal and arrest (22:47-54*a*)

3. Peter's denial (22:54*b*-62)
4. Mockery and mistreatment of Jesus (22:63-65)

G. The condemnation (22:66–23:25)
1. Hearing before the Sanhedrin (22:66-71)
2. Jesus brought before Pilate (23:1-5)
3. Jesus' examination by Herod Antipas (23:6-16)
4. Jesus surrendered to the Jews by Pilate (23:17-25)

H. Calvary (23:26-56)
1. Simon of Cyrene compelled to carry the Cross (23:26)
2. The road to Calvary (23:27-32)
3. The Crucifixion (23:33-38)
4. The penitent criminal (23:39-43)
5. Miracles that marked the last hours on the Cross (23:44-45)
6. Jesus' death (23:46-49)
7. Jesus' burial (23:50-56)

J. Discovery of the empty tomb (24:1-12)

VII. The risen Christ (24:13-53)
A. The risen Christ on the road to Emmaus (24:13-35)
B. Appearance of the risen Christ in Jerusalem (24:36-43)
C. Christ's final message to his disciples (24:44-49)
D. Christ's final parting from his disciples (24:50-53)

VI. Selected Bibliography

BULTMANN, RUDOLF. *Die Geschichte der synoptischen Tradition.* 2d ed. revised. Göttingen: Vandenhoeck & Ruprecht, 1931.

CADBURY, HENRY J. *The Making of Luke-Acts.* New York: The Macmillan Co., 1927.

CREED, JOHN MARTIN. *The Gospel According to St. Luke.* London: Macmillan & Co., 1930.

EASTON, BURTON SCOTT. *The Gospel According to St. Luke.* New York: Charles Scribner's Sons, 1926.

KLOSTERMANN, ERICH. *Das Lukas-Evangelium.* "Handbuch zum Neuen Testament," Vol V. 2d ed. revised. Tübingen: J. C. B. Mohr, 1929.

LOISY, ALFRED. *Les Évangiles Synoptiques.* 2 vols. Ceffonds: pub. by the author, 1907-8.

MAJOR, H. D. A., MANSON, T. W., and WRIGHT, C. J. *The Mission and Message of Jesus.* New York: E. P. Dutton & Co., 1938.

MANSON, WILLIAM. *The Gospel of Luke* ("The Moffatt New Testament Commentary"). London: Hodder & Stoughton, 1930.

MONTEFIORE, C. G. "The Gospel According to Luke," *The Synoptic Gospels,* II, 360-646. 2d ed. revised. London: Macmillan & Co., 1927.

WEISS, JOHANNES. *Die Schriften des Neuen Testaments,* II, 406-525. 2d ed. revised. Göttingen: Vandenhoeck & Ruprecht, 1907.

WELLHAUSEN, JULIUS. *Das Evangelium Lucae.* Berlin: Georg Reimer, 1904.

LUKE

TEXT, EXEGESIS, EXPOSITION

1 Forasmuch as many have taken in hand to set forth in order a declaration of those things which are most surely believed among us,

1 Inasmuch as many have undertaken to compile a narrative of the things which have been accomplished among us,

---

I. PREFACE (1:1-4)

When an ancient work exceeded the physical limits of a single volume, it was customary to put the preface to the whole at the beginning of the first roll or codex and to recapitulate it at the beginning of each subsequent one. Luke adopts this practice here and in Acts 1:1. The prologue, then, must be read as an introduction to the Acts as well

---

1:1. *The Supreme Event.*—**The things which have been accomplished among us.** There is an important suggestion in the RSV translation here, as compared with the words in the KJV. Luke was thinking not only of **those things which are most surely believed;** he was thinking of the things which had been brought to positive fulfillment. His stress is upon the life of Jesus as a unique and incomparable event. God had revealed himself. The message of salvation had not been partially or tentatively set forth; it had been **accomplished.**

Not only the Gospels but the whole of the N.T. proclaims this conviction that in Jesus

2 Even as they delivered them unto us, which from the beginning were eyewitnesses, and ministers of the word;

2 just as they were delivered to us by those who from the beginning were eyewitnesses

---

as to the gospel volume. An author's dedication of his work to an individual—sometimes a patron who underwrote the cost of its publication—was also a literary convention and does not imply in this instance that Luke's account of the rise and expansion of Christianity was intended only for private circulation. The preface is a fine example of rhetorical balance and periodic structure. Its style conforms to the best Greek model, while that of the matter which follows in the first chapter is characteristically Semitic.

1:1. A reference to **many** authorities was a convention in ancient prefaces. Nevertheless it is clear that the author of Luke-Acts has incorporated a variety of sources and that the adjective is more than rhetorical. The verse does not imply any criticism of earlier narratives. They were precedents that justified Luke's own venture. **The things which have been accomplished among us** (RSV) is preferable to the alternative translation in the KJV. The events that are narrated in the second volume are included with those that form the subject matter of the first.

2. Earlier compilers had received the gospel tradition—largely, no doubt, in oral form—from **eyewitnesses and ministers.** According to Acts 1:21-22; 10:37; and Luke 3:1-2 (cf. Mark 1:1), Luke considered John the Baptist's ministry the **beginning** of the gospel story. **To us,** i.e., to the Christian community.

God has entered into history in a way that was unprecedented and could never be surpassed. It was this, according to Paul, that was "the mystery hidden for ages and generations but now made manifest" (Col. 1:26). Jesus was more than an exemplar of heroic human virtues; more than a teacher of luminous truth. He was the channel of a power by which a new age was ushered in. In him God "has delivered us from the dominion of darkness and transferred us to the kingdom of his beloved Son, in whom we have redemption, the forgiveness of sins" (Col. 1:13). "If any one is in Christ, he is a new creation; the old has passed away, behold, the new has come" (II Cor. 5:17). Jesus in his life and death and resurrection represented not merely one more and better reflection of the meaning of God. Instead, the faith of the N.T. dared to say, "In him dwells the whole fullness of deity bodily" (Col. 2:9). For human understanding of the nature of God, Jesus Christ is final.

That is a supreme truth—the truth of the finality of Jesus. Yet as with other great truths, it is possible to interpret it in a narrow way that distorts its meaning. Orthodoxy has sometimes borne itself as though its duty was to define what has been, rather than to proclaim what can be. It has been so closely concerned to recognize nothing except what Jesus in his career on earth seemed to authorize that it has been blind to the wider implications of the living spirit of Christ. It has refused to see, for example, that the Christian gospel ought to have a message for the economic and the social complexities of modern civilization, even though Jesus himself said no direct word concerning these—since obviously they did not exist in the century when he lived. It has preached a false finality for the message of Jesus, confining this to the literal limits of his recorded word, or even reducing it to a shrunken preoccupation by the individual with his own soul, and calling this the "pure gospel." Jesus is final in that the grace of God which came in him can never be transcended. But the real *finality* of that which the Gospel of Luke thinks of as having been once and for all **accomplished** is the gift in him of a life which has an infinite *fertility*. The implications of what he was and what he brought to life go on expanding and ripening beyond all reckoning. To be concerned thus that the revelation of God in Jesus shall energize every creative purpose of the centuries is to make it "final" in the supreme sense that it will be expressed in every one of life's triumphant ends.

2. ***The Many Witnesses.***—**Those who from the beginning were eyewitnesses and ministers of the word.** Certainly there was a larger number of these than can now be known. Many of them were humble folk, and their names have long since been forgotten. But they had all contributed to the remembered truth about Jesus which Luke wanted to record.

Two thoughts emerge. The first is the recognition of the importance not only of those who are counted as the great figures, but of those who were the humble ones. The importance of the original twelve disciples is obvious; also of

3 It seemed good to me also, having had perfect understanding of all things from the very first, to write unto thee in order, most excellent Theophilus,

and ministers of the word, 3 it seemed good to me also, having followed all things closely[a] for some time past, to write an orderly account for you, most excellent

[a] Or *accurately*.

3. Luke believed himself peculiarly fitted to improve on the work of his predecessors. **Having followed all things closely** (RSV) is preferable to the KJV translation. Similar constructions were used by Greek authors to assert familiarity with the course of events. For the gospel volume, at any rate, Luke must have achieved this by some measure of research. There is no compelling reason to abandon **from the very first** (KJV) as a translation of the Greek. On the other hand the rendering **an orderly account** (RSV) avoids a possible misconstruction of the older English version. Luke claims a better arrangement of the source material rather than greater chronological exactitude. **Theophilus** means "one who loves God," but the fact that the word often occurs in ancient literature as a proper name makes it improbable that it is symbolic or pseudonymous in Luke's use of it. **Most excellent** is a title that is given in Acts 23:26; 24:2; and 26:25 to the Roman procurator of Judea, and frequently in Greco-Roman literature to high government officials. The conclusion that Luke is addressing some such individual is therefore not unwarranted (cf. Goodspeed's "Your Excellency").

the others who are mentioned by name in the Gospels and the book of Acts. But these were only part of the number of those who had seen Jesus and had heard him and had begun to follow him. What the recollections of some of these contributed may have had as great significance and value as what could be told by the more prominent men. Here is a reminder of the role which may be played in every generation by any man or woman who has caught at firsthand some of the meaning of Christ. They were and are ministers of the word.

The second thought is this: When Luke refers to eyewitnesses, there is foundation here for confidence in the knowledge which has come down to us of the historic Jesus. That confidence has been befogged by some tendencies in modern N.T. criticism. Form criticism in the hands of its more extreme exponents has tended to produce the idea that the Gospels are made up of vague communal traditions, fragments of sermons about Jesus, secondhand impressions. But the word **eyewitnesses** which Luke here uses recalls the fact that for many years after Jesus' crucifixion, and during the time when the fundamental materials for the Gospels were being gathered, there may have been those who could testify—in the words of I John 1:1, "That . . . which we have heard, which we have seen with our eyes, which we have looked upon and touched with our hands, concerning the word of life."

Always a great personality can stamp itself so deeply upon the memory of friends and companions that the vivid picture of him can be retained and transmitted through many years. William Lawrence, bishop of Massachusetts, knew and loved that supreme preacher of the late nineteenth century, Phillips Brooks. Thirty-seven years after Brooks's death, Lawrence wrote his *Life of Phillips Brooks*,[1] as to which he said in his preface, "I have depended entirely upon my own memories." The interval between the death of Brooks and the writing of that book, which is a graphic portrayal of the nature and genius of Brooks, was thirty-seven years, approximately the period between the crucifixion and the writing of the Gospel of Mark. But Lawrence, who was then eighty years of age, lived to be over ninety, and up to the very end, more than forty-seven years after Brooks's death, with a mind still fresh and eager, he could tell of Brooks as he had known him. How much more must the incomparable fact of Jesus have stamped itself upon the memories of those who had known him and who, for as long as they lived, could keep the story of what he was and what he did from drifting into fantasy or vagueness.

> From all that we can learn of it the primitive church was not made up exclusively of simple-minded people, who were prepared to accept anything. . . . In such a community doubtful statements would not easily pass muster, and evidence would be scrutinized. It must never be forgotten, too, that for many years personal disciples of Jesus were still alive and were held in peculiar honor. Their testimony was always available on matters of historical fact, and we know that it was given.[2]

[1] New York: Harper & Bros., 1930.

[2] Ernest Findlay Scott, *The Validity of the Gospel Record* (New York: Charles Scribner's Sons, 1938), pp. 19-20.

4 That thou mightest know the certainty of those things, wherein thou hast been instructed.

Theoph'i-lus, 4 that you may know the truth concerning the things of which you have been informed.

4. The usual interpretation of this verse is that Theophilus had already received instruction in the faith and that Luke was writing to confirm him in it. H. J. Cadbury has shown that it is open to quite another construction. If the reports that had reached Theophilus of the new religion were unfriendly, Luke may have been seeking in Luke-Acts to come to its defense. "If so, Theophilus was not a catechumen but an influential non-Christian . . . , to whom this work is nominally dedicated or addressed with the intention of meeting incriminating reports or impressions by the presentation of exonerating facts" (*The Beginnings of Christianity,* ed. F. J. Foakes Jackson and Kirsopp Lake [London: Macmillan & Co., 1922], II, 510) . Certainly one of the leading interests of Luke-Acts was to show that Christianity was not a politically subversive sect (see Intro., pp. 5-6) .

4. ***The Truth in Its Fullness.***—What was **the truth concerning the things of which you have been informed?** It was twofold. A person's understanding suffers a great loss when either one of the two aspects is forgotten.

In the first place, the truth of the evangel had to do with the facts of the life of the historical Jesus. Sometimes the "quest of the historical Jesus" has amounted to little more than a bare, cold analysis of details which seemed in themselves to be ordinary, or has bogged down in a confusion of conflicting opinions as to what actually can be known about the man of Nazareth. Many Christian theologians reacted from that and turned to seek a mystical Christ—an ideal and an inspiration which they regard as somehow having come to us and as remaining with us whether facts of history can be attested or not. But that would remove Christian faith from one of the very foundation stones which unquestionably Luke regarded as essential. He wanted Theophilus and anyone else by whom his Gospel might be read to know the vivid reality of the Master whom men in Galilee and in Jerusalem knew. The importance of that must never be forgotten. C. H. Dodd wrote:

> Some religions can be indifferent to historical fact, and move entirely upon the plane of timeless truth. Christianity cannot. It rests upon the affirmation that a series of events happened, in which God revealed Himself in action, for the salvation of men.[3]

And Donald M. Baillie has written:

> Indispensable, surely, is the actual portrait of the historical Jesus, connecting these claims [as to his divine significance] firmly with historical reality. Apart from that, we do not know why we should say these things *about a particular historical figure,* Jesus the carpenter of Nazareth. In short, we do not know who it is about whom we say these marvellous things, and therefore cannot know why we say them.[4]

If thus awareness of the historical Jesus is the beginning of faith, it is not the end of it. Luke was never interested in the narrative of what went on from Bethlehem to Calvary as a mere chronicle. The history he wrote was also theology—history with a meaning and an immense significance. It was the history of him who came to be the Christ, revealer of God, redeemer. It is possible to write a life of Jesus which would be just one more interesting human drama. But that is not what Luke was writing. He meant to tell of a career that transcended all ordinary categories and brought not merely information to men's minds but transformation to their souls.

This double aspect of the truth has been summed up by Gerhard Kittel in one cogent paragraph:

> The Jesus of History is valueless and unintelligible unless He be experienced and confessed by faith as the living Christ. But, if we would be true to the New Testament, we must at once reverse this judgment. The Christ of faith has no existence, is mere noise and smoke, apart from the reality of the Jesus of History. These two are utterly inseparable in the New Testament. They cannot even be thought of apart. There is no word about Christ which is not referred to Him who suffered under Pontius Pilate, and which is not at the same time intended as the Gospel applicable to all men of every time and in every place. Anyone who attempts first to separate the two and then to describe only one of them has nothing in common with the New Testament.[5]

[3] *History and the Gospel* (New York: Charles Scribner's Sons, 1938), p. 15.

[4] *God Was in Christ* (New York: Charles Scribner's Sons, 1948), p. 52.

[5] "The Jesus of History," in G. K. A. Bell and D. A. Deissmann, eds., *Mysterium Christi* (London: Longmans, Green & Co., 1930), p. 49. Used by permission.

5 ¶ There was in the days of Herod, the king of Judea, a certain priest named Zacharias, of the course of Abia: and his wife *was* of the daughters of Aaron, and her name *was* Elisabeth.

5 In the days of Herod, king of Judea, there was a priest named Zech-a-ri'ah,[b] of the division of A-bi'jah; and he had a wife of the daughters of Aaron, and her name

[b] Greek *Zacharias.*

II. Jesus' Birth and Boyhood (1:5–2:52)

A. Annunciations to Zechariah and to Mary (1:5-56)

1. The Promise to Zechariah of the Birth of John (1:5-25)

Originally this story may have belonged to a collection of legends about John the Baptist that circulated independently of the Christian tradition. It must be admitted that there is little in it or in its companion account of John's birth that demands an assumption of Christian authorship. The hypothesis has even been advanced that the story of the promise of Jesus' birth and the story of his nativity have been deliberately modeled on the more primitive Johannine narratives and then interwoven with them. However this may be, it is probable that Luke found most of the material that is now in his first two chapters already integrated in a source. Their Semitic style has been regarded by some interpreters as evidence that the narratives have been translated from a Hebrew or Aramaic document. This hypothesis would not require us to assume that Luke himself was the translator, for there is little evidence that the evangelist had any competence as a Semitic scholar. Others have attributed the language and structure of the stories to Luke's own artistic genius. He has deliberately phrased a body of oral tradition in the vocabulary of the Greek Bible and adapted it to the narrative style of the O.T. The evidence of familiarity with Jewish custom as well as idiom throughout Luke's first two chapters is in favor of the former hypothesis, but the idea in 1:26-38 that Jesus' conception was supernatural is difficult to reconcile with a theory that this paragraph originated in strictly Jewish circles. No doubt Luke has edited whatever material he had at his disposal in the interests of the larger story he has to tell. He was an author in his own right, and his work is never simply that of collation.

5. Judea is used here (and in 4:44; 6:17; 7:17; 23:5; Acts 10:37) for the whole of Palestine. **Herod** the Great died in 4 B.C. This cycle of stories therefore assumes that John the Baptist and Jesus were born before that date. Priests among the Jews had long been divided into twenty-four "divisions," each responsible for the conduct of temple worship for one week at semiannual intervals (Josephus *Antiquities* VII. 14. 7). **Zechariah**

5-6. *The Lowly Saints.*—Three names are mentioned here: Herod, Zechariah, and Elizabeth, and the second and third of these are very different from the first. Herod was one of the most evil figures of his age, cruel, sensual, with no standard of judgment higher than his own relentless will for power. It may well be that many in Israel estimated their time by this man who seemed to be its dominant representative. What could it be but an evil time when a man so evil overshadowed it? In every generation men may pass that same estimate—in modern times, for instance, may think that the age must be mean, cynical, and decadent because of what they read in the headlines of newspapers about the cheap or corrupt lives of many who are prominent in politics, in the getting of wealth, in the world of entertainment. But meanwhile, in Herod's time there was another sort of person, quiet, inconspicuous, and yet more important than Herod, men and women who were the sound core of society and gave it such real wholesomeness as it did possess. Then and always there were and are the lowly and humble men in whom the strength of the present and the promise of the future lie.

From another point of view also there is a suggestion in those words concerning Zechariah and Elizabeth, that **they were both righteous before God, walking in all the commandments and ordinances of the Lord blameless.** The division which arose in the first century between the new Christian fellowship and the Jewish church from which it was gradually separated sometimes led to what was in danger of being a disparagement of the old religion. The fact that the Pharisees were condemned created the impression that Judaism in general stood condemned. But it needs to be remembered that it was out of the heritage of Israel that

6 And they were both righteous before God, walking in all the commandments and ordinances of the Lord blameless.

7 And they had no child, because that Elisabeth was barren; and they both were *now* well stricken in years.

8 And it came to pass, that, while he executed the priest's office before God in the order of his course,

9 According to the custom of the priest's office, his lot was to burn incense when he went into the temple of the Lord.

was Elizabeth. 6 And they were both right-
eous before God, walking in all the com-
mandments and ordinances of the Lord
blameless. 7 But they had no child, be-
cause Elizabeth was barren, and both were
advanced in years.
8 Now while he was serving as priest
before God when his division was on duty,
9 according to the custom of the priesthood,
it fell to him by lot to enter the temple

belonged to **the division of Abijah.** According to I Chr. 24:10, this was the eighth. **Elizabeth** is also said to have been of priestly descent.

6-7. The piety of the priest and his wife is articulated in negative terms of Jewish legalism; cf. Paul's boast in Phil. 3:6*b*: "as to righteousness under the law blameless." Like Abraham and Sarah, they were childless and **advanced in years.** The story makes it clear that their childlessness was not a consequence of divine displeasure.

8-10. And it came to pass, that (KJV) is a Semitic formula of introduction that occurs occasionally in Mark and Matthew and frequently in Luke-Acts. It is consistently omitted by the RSV as superfluous in English. Even within each division priests were so numerous that the privilege of performing any significant sacerdotal act was awarded

Jesus himself came, and that there was in Judaism a spiritual force which would produce souls that were accounted **righteous before God.**

8-11. ***Elements of Worship.***—Three times in these verses there is the word **incense.** The use of incense is familiar in Roman Catholic churches, but very few churches in Protestant Christendom would think of using it. Certainly it is not needful that they should. Yet the description here of the priest Zechariah burning incense in the temple, as it had been burned by an unending succession of the priests of the Lord, leads out to a wider suggestion which is worth following in thought—not in regard to incense specifically, but in regard to symbolic acts in general as an aid to worship.

The use of incense is very ancient and very widespread. Often it was connected with crude pagan ideas of an anthropomorphic god pleased by the actual scent of the sweet-smelling smoke. In the early centuries of Judaism incense was regarded as one of the marks of heathenism, but by the time of the Priestly Code a new thought regarding it had been developed. It was incorporated into Jewish worship as a symbol of the ascending prayers of souls that reach up to God. In the last book of the O.T. it is prophesied that "in every place incense shall be offered unto my name, and a pure offering" (Mal. 1:11). When Zechariah went into the temple on this day which Luke describes, he was carrying out the custom of worship which was many centuries old.

Forms of worship change. They vary and they ought to vary according to their use or lack of use in helping men to worship in the truest and fullest way. There is always a danger that any particular form may come through long use to seem to have some sort of semimagical validity. Acts which have lost their understood meaning may become a mechanical substitute for the freshly conscious lifting up of the mind and soul to God. Thus, as Evelyn Underhill recognizes in her notable book, form may "smother spirit, ritual action take the place of spontaneous prayer, the outward and visible sign obscure the inward grace." [6]

But there is a larger truth which Evelyn Underhill's book richly brings out and which all churches would do well to ponder. Unless leaders of worship do recognize the instinctive need of the human personality for methods of devotion which wake the whole human organism, worship may become "thin, abstract and notional." Man is

> not "pure" spirit, and is not capable of "pure" spiritual acts. Even though in his worship he moves out toward absolutes, and in and through that worship absolutes are revealed to his soul, it is at his own peril that he leaves the world of sense behind, in his approach to the God Who created and informs it. This humbling truth must govern all his responses to Reality. . . . It is true that in its highest reaches worship becomes an act of pure

[6] *Worship* (New York: Harper & Bros., 1937), p. 14. Used by permission.

10 And the whole multitude of the people were praying without at the time of incense.

11 And there appeared unto him an angel of the Lord standing on the right side of the altar of incense.

12 And when Zacharias saw *him,* he was troubled, and fear fell upon him.

of the Lord and burn incense. **10** And the
whole multitude of the people were pray-
ing outside at the hour of incense. **11** And
there appeared to him an angel of the
Lord standing on the right side of the altar
of incense. **12** And Zech-a-ri'ah was trou-
bled when he saw him, and fear fell upon

---

by lot. To **burn incense** was therefore an honor that might not often be bestowed on any member of the priestly order, and the occasion would be one of particular solemnity for Zechariah. We are not told whether this particular **hour of incense** was after the morning or after the evening sacrifice. "May the God of mercy enter the sanctuary and be pleased to accept the sacrifice of his people!" was the traditional formula of public prayer at such times.

11-13. On a similar occasion the high priest John Hyrcanus (135-104 B.C.) is said to have heard a divine voice announce that his sons had conquered Antiochus (Josephus *Antiquities* XIII. 10. 3). **An angel of the Lord** had also appeared to Manoah's barren

---

love; but never for man an act stripped of all contingency. Because of the unity of our being, sensible stimulation of eye and ear, or even of taste, touch, and smell, can give supra-sensible suggestions to us and awaken, nourish, and deepen the worshipping sense; and the exclusive spirituality which rejects these homely aids merely defeats its own ends.[7]

No church would be wise to accept in hasty imitation a ritual or cultus from some other church or to crowd upon a particular congregation ways of worship which are not actually an expression of its own felt needs. At the same time, there can rightly be, and indeed there is, an awakening realization in Protestantism that an extreme reaction from practices which had once grown superstitious has led to a too drastic abandonment of much that might give to worship color and richness and depth. In a booklet put forth by the Commission on Worship of the Federal Council of the Churches of Christ in America there is a section entitled "The Arts Have a Distinct Function in Aiding Worship." The paragraphs which follow rightly underscore the word "aiding," i.e., the outward elements in worship must always be subsidiary, and must never be allowed to bulk so large in importance that they overshadow the supreme matter, which is the direct awareness of God himself. But when that is remembered, it is rightly said also:

We are so constituted that the soul is often reached through the senses, and the arts of architecture, decoration, and music have always had a place in conjunction with worship, and in the service of the Church have reached the highest phases of their own development. . . . Art speaks to the spiritual imagination by its use, symbol and color and light and harmony make abstract conceptions comprehensible, even when these cannot be clothed in formal words and sentences.[8]

[7] *Ibid.*, pp. 14-15, 26.

12-13. ***The Overcoming of Fear.***—Out of these verses a double truth emerges. In the first place, there is the recognition that a sudden consciousness of the reality of God can overwhelm a soul with awe. When the angel appeared to Zechariah, **fear fell upon him.** His human nature shrank before the divine glory, as a man might cover his eyes against some intolerable light. This same instinctive shrinking occurred with others also. When Gabriel appeared to Mary in Nazareth, she was "greatly troubled." When the shepherds on the plains of Bethlehem saw their vision of the heavenly hosts "they were filled with fear." That sort of fear has its rightful place in any deep religious experience. It is not a craven fear. Instead, it is the startled awareness of those tremendous heights and depths by which the soul finds itself confronted, of an infinity upon which its littleness looks out to recognize the awful contrast between itself and the unfathomable wonder with which it is surrounded.

But in the Gospel of Luke the description of experience does not end with fear. **Do not be afraid,** the angel said to Zechariah. "Do not be afraid," said Gabriel to Mary. "Be not afraid," said the angel to the shepherds. First there is, as there ought to be, the deep hush of the soul before God, an abasement of our human pride, a waiting for the heavenly word. Then that word, when it comes, is the message of encour-

[8] S. Arthur Devan, *Seven Principles of Worship*, p. 14.

13 But the angel said unto him, Fear not, Zacharias: for thy prayer is heard; and thy wife Elisabeth shall bear thee a son, and thou shalt call his name John.

14 And thou shalt have joy and gladness; and many shall rejoice at his birth.

him. 13 But the angel said to him, "Do
not be afraid, Zech-a-ri'ah, for your prayer
is heard, and your wife Elizabeth will bear
you a son, and you shall call his name
John.

14 And you will have joy and gladness,
and many will rejoice at his birth;

---

wife (according to Judg. 13:3) and had promised that she would conceive and bear a son (Samson). It was the duty of the officiating priest to offer a prayer on behalf of the people after the incense had been kindled by the live coals on the altar. No mention has heretofore been made of Zechariah's personal petition. **John** is a Semitic name meaning "God is gracious," but there is no indication that Luke has reflected on its etymology.

14-15. The **many** who are to share the father's **joy** are John's future adherents, although Luke and his readers would also have included the Christian church. They will **rejoice** that such a man has been born into the world. **In the sight of the Lord** means "in God's estimate" (cf. Gen. 10:9). According to Num. 6:3, Nazarites were forbidden the

---

agement and of power. Because a soul has had the pure humility to bow down before the glory of God, it is ready for the free gift of his grace by which its faith can be exalted.

13-17. ***Greatness in the Eyes of God.***—Here is the magnificent prophecy of the significance which the greatness of John the Baptist should have for history. He was to be a man **great before the Lord, . . . filled with the Holy Spirit,** coming **in the spirit and power of Elijah;** and his high destiny should be to **turn many . . . to the Lord their God.** Greatness in the eyes of the world is measured in terms other than those: measured in terms not of service but of self-aggrandizement; in terms material rather than spiritual; in terms immediate and visible, rather than invisible and only at long length to be revealed. But greatness as God sees it is the greatness promised for the son of Zechariah —the greatness of the man linked with eternal purposes of redemption, who will make himself an obedient instrument for these.

Many will rejoice at his birth, said the angel. That prophecy could seem true, and yet not true. There was rejoicing for his parents at the coming of a long-desired child. There would be rejoicing for them and for all others who had any spiritual discernment as this child began to grow up into a man of spiritual devotion and incalculable courage. But there would be some quarters in which there would be no rejoicing. Pharisees coming down to the Jordan river and hearing John denounce them as a brood of snakes would not look like men rejoicing. Herod and his wife and that sinuous daughter of hers, Salome, would have an emotion a long way from joy about this man who denounced royal sins. Instead of being glad that he had been born, the one thing they wanted was to bring him to his end and bury him. That is the kind of emotion which the man dedicated to the service of God may excite in his own generation, and the greater he is, the more implacable may be the hostility he arouses.

But the longer, truer judgment of mankind does rejoice in the birth of the man who brings to his own age and to subsequent ages a sense of the immediacy of God. Such men have been, as Thomas Carlyle has said "modellers, patterns, and in a wide sense creators, of whatsoever the general mass of men contrived to do or to attain; . . . the soul of the whole world's history, it may justly be considered, were the history of these."[9] John the Baptist was of that mighty line. Elijah and Elisha, Hosea and Amos, Isaiah and Jeremiah, had walked the stage of the world before him, dwarfing kings and conquerors by their presence; and after him were to come others of that prophetic fellowship. The apostles of Christian missions, battlers for those convictions which they believed they had received from God, Athanasius and Augustine, Bernard of Cluny and Savonarola, John Huss and Martin Luther, with their differences of thought and against their changing backgrounds, all were alike in this: from the direct contact of mind and heart with the experienced reality of God, they drew the messages which burned in them like fire and would not let them rest until they were delivered. In every age we need the pulse and passion of that prophetic fervor. In every century the dry fagots of our dulled possibilities need that rekindling by the divine fire which only the prophetic souls can bring. Deep in the heart of the world, in spite of surface evidences that seem to deny the

[9] *On Heroes, Hero-Worship, and the Heroic in History,* "The Hero as Divinity."

15 For he shall be great in the sight of the Lord, and shall drink neither wine nor strong drink; and he shall be filled with the Holy Ghost, even from his mother's womb.

16 And many of the children of Israel shall he turn to the Lord their God.

17 And he shall go before him in the spirit and power of Elias, to turn the hearts of the fathers to the children, and the disobedient to the wisdom of the just; to make ready a people prepared for the Lord.

18 And Zacharias said unto the angel, Whereby shall I know this? for I am an old man, and my wife well stricken in years.

19 And the angel answering said unto him, I am Gabriel, that stand in the presence of God; and am sent to speak unto thee, and to show thee these glad tidings.

20 And, behold, thou shalt be dumb, and not able to speak, until the day that these things shall be performed, because thou believest not my words, which shall be fulfilled in their season.

15 for he will be great before the Lord,
and he shall drink no wine nor strong
drink,
and he will be filled with the Holy
Spirit,
even from his mother's womb.
16 And he will turn many of the sons of
Israel to the Lord their God,
17 and he will go before him in the spirit
and power of Elijah,
to turn the hearts of the fathers to the
children,
and the disobedient to the wisdom of
the just,
to make ready for the Lord a people
prepared."
18 And Zech-a-ri'ah said to the angel, "How
shall I know this? For I am an old man,
and my wife is advanced in years." 19 And
the angel answered him, "I am Gabriel,
who stand in the presence of God; and I
was sent to speak to you, and to bring you
this good news. 20 And behold, you will
be silent and unable to speak until the day
that these things come to pass, because you
did not believe my words, which will be

---

use of **wine** or **strong drink**—the latter an inclusive term for intoxicating liquor other than that from grapes. But if the prediction means that John was to be a Nazarite, one must note that it is not said that he would allow his hair to grow uncut. Perhaps only some such contrast as in Eph. 5:18 is intended: "Do not get drunk with wine . . . but be filled with the Spirit." In the O.T. **the Holy Spirit** was only a temporary gift of God, even to the most exceptional individual. John is to **be filled with it. From his mother's womb** probably means "while he is still unborn" (cf. 1:41).

16-17. John will not only perform the ancient function of a prophet, but will also make the people ready for God's rule, as predicted of God's forerunner in Mal. 4:5-6. It is not directly stated that he will be **Elijah** redivivus (as in Matt. 11:14 and Mark 9:13), but one who will exhibit Elijah's **spirit and power. The Lord** means God. Luke has not reworked his material in the interests of Christian messianism.

18-20. Like Abraham on a similar occasion (Gen. 15:8) **Zechariah** is incredulous and demands some proof that the promise will be fulfilled. He had prayed without any conviction that his prayer would be answered. The **angel** identifies himself as **Gabriel,** one of the seven archangels who **stand in the presence of God** (Rev. 1:4; Tob. 12:15). His words

---

fact, there is always a hunger for the prophet. There is a yearning for the voice which speaks with no stumbling accents of self-consciousness but with the flaming conviction of a self which has been caught up into communion with the purposes of the most high God.

15-17. ***The Consecration of John.*—He shall drink no wine nor strong drink, and he will be filled with the Holy Spirit.** Mark the two influences which thus unite. From the human side this child should be dedicated by such means as the most reverent and earnest custom had devised. He should be a Nazarite, vowed to self-discipline and to abstinence, i.e., as far as human devotion could make it possible, John should be a ready instrument, self-controlled and clean. Into such a vessel God's Holy Spirit might come completely. So John might be adequate for the supreme service which a man may render, to **turn many . . . to the Lord their God** and **to make ready for the Lord a people prepared** (see also Expos. on vss. 67-79).

21 And the people waited for Zacharias, and marveled that he tarried so long in the temple.

22 And when he came out, he could not speak unto them: and they perceived that he had seen a vision in the temple; for he beckoned unto them, and remained speechless.

23 And it came to pass, that, as soon as the days of his ministration were accomplished, he departed to his own house.

24 And after those days his wife Elisabeth conceived, and hid herself five months, saying,

25 Thus hath the Lord dealt with me in the days wherein he looked on *me,* to take away my reproach among men.

26 And in the sixth month the angel Gabriel was sent from God unto a city of Galilee, named Nazareth,

fulfilled in their time." 21 And the people
were waiting for Zech-a-ri'ah, and they
wondered at his delay in the temple.
22 And when he came out, he could not
speak to them, and they perceived that he
had seen a vision in the temple; and he
made signs to them and remained dumb.
23 And when his time of service was ended,
he went to his home.

24 After these days his wife Elizabeth
conceived, and for five months she hid
herself, saying, 25 "Thus the Lord has done
to me in the days when he looked on me,
to take away my reproach among men."

26 In the sixth month the angel Gabriel
was sent from God to a city of Galilee

had deserved credence and would **be fulfilled,** but the sign that **Zechariah** had requested would also be a punishment for unbelief. Luke had a special interest in punitive miracles (Acts 1:18; 5:5, 10; 12:23; 13:11).

21-23. When he had burned the incense, the officiating priest was expected to issue from the sanctuary and bless the assembled worshipers. Zechariah's inability to perform this function upon his tardy reappearance was correctly interpreted by the impatient congregation as evidence **that he had seen a vision in the temple.** After a similar supernatural vision and audition, the prophet Daniel had **remained dumb** until the heavenly man had touched his lips and freed his speech (Dan. 10:15-16). Zechariah's **time of service** would end with the next sabbath. Priests were at liberty to live anywhere in Judea when not on duty. Zechariah's place of residence is vaguely described in 1:39 as a Judean city in "the hill country."

24-25. Nothing is known of any ancient custom that required an expectant mother to seclude herself. Explanations of Elizabeth's retirement based on the presumed psychology of an elderly woman have no warrant in the text. Probably the **five months** of secrecy are mentioned only to prepare the way for the next story. They account for the fact that the angel's announcement to Mary of her kinswoman's pregnancy could be delayed until "the sixth month" (vs. 36) and still come as news and serve as a sign. Childlessness was considered a **reproach** among Semitic peoples (cf. Gen. 30:23). Sterility was always blamed in the O.T. on the woman.

2. The Promise to Mary of the Birth of Jesus (1:26-38)

The doctrine of the Virgin Birth is not articulated as part of the primitive Christian *kerygma* in the epistles of Paul or in the early chapters of the book of Acts. There is no hint of it in Mark's Gospel or in the common tradition of Matthew and Luke. It has no place in the birth and infancy narratives in Luke 2:1-52 which assume throughout that Joseph was one of Jesus' parents (2:27, 33, 41, 43, 48). It is implied in the editorial parenthesis ("as was supposed") in Luke's version of Jesus' genealogy (3:23) but no-

26-29. ***The Favor of the Lord.*—The angel came in unto her, and said, Hail, thou that art highly favored, the Lord is with thee: blessed art thou among women.** Those words now chime in with every instinctive recognition. What other thought could there be than that the one who was to be the mother of Jesus was blessed above all other women?

27 To a virgin espoused to a man whose name was Joseph, of the house of David; and the virgin's name *was* Mary.

28 And the angel came in unto her, and said, Hail, *thou that art* highly favored, the Lord *is* with thee: blessed *art* thou among women.

named Nazareth, 27 to a virgin betrothed to a man whose name was Joseph, of the house of David; and the virgin's name was Mary. 28 And he came to her and said, "Hail, O favored one, the Lord is with

where else in the body of the Third Gospel. For that matter, apart from the first chapter of Matthew, the only reference to the doctrine in the N.T. is in this paragraph.

Even in this account the doctrine is explicit only in the words "since I have no husband" (vs. 34). If this clause were missing the angel's promises could apply to a son whom Mary was to conceive in natural wedlock. The late Canon B. H. Streeter believed that the reading of the O.L. MS b, which omits vs. 34, may represent the original Lukan text (*The Four Gospels* [New York: The Macmillan Co., 1925], pp. 267-68). Frederick C. Grant is a more recent interpreter to hold that the clauses in 1:34 and 3:23 are early interpolations (*An Introduction to New Testament Thought* [New York and Nashville: Abingdon-Cokesbury Press, 1950], pp. 230-32). But the textual evidence for this conclusion is not impressive. It seems more probable that the doctrine of Christ's supernatural generation was already familiar to the author of the Third Gospel and that he edited his source material to convey it.

The real significance of the Virgin Birth in early Christian thought was theological. It declared what had been the faith of the church from the beginning, that God had come into human life for our salvation in Jesus Christ. Luke was writing for a church that was already disturbed by schismatic and heretical teachers (Acts 20:28-30). One of the earliest heresies was the denial of Christ's humanity. The Docetists held that Christ had been a divine being who only seemed to be human. He had not actually taken our flesh upon him, or suffered, or died. From the time of Ignatius and the framers of the Apostles' Creed, and possibly as early as Luke's day, the doctrine of the Virgin Birth asserted that Christ was truly man as well as truly God. The Son of God had been conceived by a human mother—a virgin in accordance with O.T. prophecy as the church read it in the LXX text of Isa. 7:14—when "the power of the Most High had overshadowed her." He was "made like his brethren in every respect, so that he might become a merciful and faithful high priest in the service of God" (Heb. 2:17).

26-27. Gabriel ("the hero of God") is again the messenger. He had also been the vehicle of revelation to Daniel (Dan. 8:16; 9:21). **Nazareth** is identified as **a city of Galilee** for the benefit of Gentile readers unfamiliar with Palestinian geography. **Of the house of David** is a phrase that modifies **Joseph,** not **Mary.** The tradition of Jesus' Davidic descent was manifestly based on Joseph's lineage (2:4; 3:23, cf. Matt. 1:20). **Joseph** plays a much more important role in the Matthaean than in the Lukan cycle of birth stories.

28-29. Blessed art thou among women is missing from codices Sinaiticus and Vaticanus. The words were borrowed from vs. 42 and interpolated at this point in most later MSS. In

Yet by the ordinary reckonings of the world, what sort of favor was it that Mary received? Such favor certainly as many would have been reluctant to claim. She would go presently on a long and wearying journey to a small town, not because she wanted to go, but as the Gospel states, because the commands of the foreign masters of her country made her go. There in Bethlehem, on a winter's night, the pains of childbirth would come upon her. No seeming glory would be round about her then. No, not even seeming mercy. There was to be no room for her or her baby in the inn. He must be born in a stable and cradled nowhere but in the straw of the oxen's crib. At the moment she may have seemed to herself only one more figure in the eternal agony of motherhood amid conditions as hard and harsh as any woman ever faced before.

And after Bethlehem, what followed? The return to Nazareth and the long years of obscurity and poverty there in the village hidden among its hills. Her baby of Nazareth would grow up into the man who must go out into a life which she soon perceived would be one of increasing danger. Humble people loved him;

29 And when she saw *him,* she was troubled at his saying, and cast in her mind what manner of salutation this should be.

30 And the angel said unto her, Fear not, Mary: for thou hast found favor with God.

31 And, behold, thou shalt conceive in thy womb, and bring forth a son, and shalt call his name JESUS.

you!"[c] 29 But she was greatly troubled at
the saying, and considered in her mind
what sort of greeting this might be. 30 And
the angel said to her, "Do not be afraid,
Mary, for you have found favor with God.
31 And behold, you will conceive in your
womb and bear a son, and you shall call
his name Jesus.

[c] Other ancient authorities add *"Blessed are you among women!"*

---

time the angelic salutation became the Ave Maria of the Latin translations. There is sporadic support in early Christian literature for the view—incompatible with the future tenses in vs. 35—that the angel's utterance marked the moment of Mary's conception. Zechariah had been **troubled** at the sight of the angel (vs. 12), but it was by the angel's **saying** that Mary was disturbed.

30-31. You have found favor with God (cf. Gen. 6:8; etc.) reiterates the content of the title that the angel had already conferred. Luke does not cite the Immanuel prophecy of Isa. 7:14 (cf. Matt. 1:23), although he may well have had it in mind. But compare also the angel's words to Hagar in Gen. 16:11. **Jesus** is the Greek equivalent of the Semitic "Joshua," which means "the Lord is salvation." Luke does not interpret the name etymologically (contrast Matt. 1:21*b*).

---

while many other people, and they the more powerful ones, regarded him with increasing hatred. At last one day he would be taken by the priests and rulers of his own nation, accused before the Roman governor, led to a hilltop amidst a jeering crowd, and there hung upon a cross. That was the career which actually would follow the salutation of the angel. That was the **favor with God.**

If Mary had wanted unbroken happiness, she plainly did not get it. If she had measured God's favor by the presence of this, then she would have had to say, when all was added up, that the promise of favor which she had heard from the lips of the angel was only an illusion. But the truth lay deeper, and lies deeper now. The world thinks that God's favor is in ease and pleasure and prosperity. Some of these may come from God's bestowing hand, but they are not identical with blessings. A man or woman may know at last that God's supreme favor may have been revealed in the things that were desperately hard but by confronting which the soul has become heroic. No mother would regret at last the pangs of motherhood nor the vicarious sufferings which she has had to experience as her child faced the difficulties or dangers of his growing life. God's favor for a man may be in some frustration of expected success which throws him back upon himself and makes him summon up reserves of courage and endurance which he otherwise might never have known. It may come through a collision into which he is driven for conscience' sake with evil forces of this world which will batter him and bruise him and almost break his hopes in pieces. God's favor for a nation or for the world may be more richly bestowed not in easy and piping times, but in a great challenge when a people's real faith is winnowed and put to a costly test. Lives that might think themselves fortunate because they have never been called upon to face great difficulties may end with nothing to show but feebleness. It is the lives which have been given something great to do and to bear, even though they may have been bruised in the process, which have truly known the favor of God.

29, 34, 37, 38. *Revelation and Response.*—Here in these four verses one notes the stages of a spiritual experience. It was the supreme experience of Mary of Nazareth, but the significance of it did not stop with her. It suggests, in principle at least, what may happen in different circumstances for other souls.

Note first that the divine revelation came to Mary as something that disturbed her to the point of fear. Often it does so come. In some moment when the divine reality with its divine purpose suddenly breaks in upon the human consciousness, the effect of it is overwhelming. The soul trembles and shrinks before the awful magnitude of the new life to which its own possibilities, which previously have seemed so little, now are called.

If the first stage is awe, the second is perplexity. **How can this be?** When the trembling passes away, there is still the uncertainty that

32 He shall be great, and shall be called the Son of the Highest; and the Lord God shall give unto him the throne of his father David:

33 And he shall reign over the house of Jacob for ever; and of his kingdom there shall be no end.

32 He will be great, and will be called
the Son of the Most High;
and the Lord God will give to him the
throne of his father David,
33 and he will reign over the house of
Jacob forever;
and of his kingdom there will be no
end."

32-33. Jesus is to be the Davidic Messiah of popular Jewish hope. The angel's words recall the predictions of II Sam. 7:13-16 (cf. Pss. 2:7; 89:26-27) and Isa. 9:6-7.

leaves one timid. One gropes as in an unknown land, blinded by the very light of the new consciousness of God. One must try to walk in the way of the heavenly purpose, but what is the way? How can any clear path be found through the difficulties and confusions that seem so much more certain than one's own strength?

Then comes a third fact: The voice as of an angel that speaks to one's own insufficiency, and brings a message of the heavenly grace that must be trusted before its ways are known. **With God nothing will be impossible.** That is the conviction which can come, one knows not how, to still one's own perplexities and to make one sure that the revelation of God's purpose will fulfill itself.

Then the crowning fact is obedience. Purely and humbly Mary put herself into the hands of God. **Let it be to me according to your word** was her answer to the angel. That is the one way always by which God's revelation to a human soul is validated. The assurance of its truth does not lie in analysis or speculation. When in its depths a soul has felt that God has called it to some new commitment, then the one supreme requirement is to answer to that feeling. To be ready to obey: that is the one open door to knowledge and growth, and to a glad discovery of the fulfillment of life to which God's grace leads on.

32-33. *The Sovereign Lord.*—Of his kingdom there will be no end. Such the Gospel tells us were the angel's words. But times and occasions were to come when those words would seem fantastic. Over the cross of Jesus there would be written, "This is the King of the Jews"; but that writing was in mockery. Not only Pilate but most other men in Judea would listen with only a cool contempt to the suggestion that Jesus of Nazareth was a king.

Yet the long wonder is that the angel's words have been coming true. He who was born of Mary was never the kind of king that human pride and lust for power were looking for. But he who said his kingdom was not of this world has nevertheless been building a kingdom in this world. He has represented a sovereignty of mind and spirit which even those who oppose him have not been able to deny. Read Charles Rann Kennedy's *The Terrible Meek* and Ibsen's *Emperor and Galilean.* As the years go on, that sovereignty of his increases wherever men's consciences are sensitive. That is true in individual lives. E. Stanley Jones tells of the answer of an earnest Hindu when he was asked one day what he thought of Christ. He said: "There is no one else who is seriously bidding for the heart of the world except Jesus Christ. There is no one else on the field."[1] It is true of the influence which is resident in and expressed through the Christian church. Ecclesiastical history has often been discreditable with its dissensions and divisions, but there is a power of attraction in Christ which is increasingly drawing people from all nations together. As it is said in the general introduction to *Man's Disorder and God's Design,* the report of the First Assembly of the World Council of Churches in Amsterdam, "In Him, a reign of love and forgiveness has been inaugurated, moulding the hearts and lives of men, calling them to find their common centre and desire in Him, and so to discover that real community for which mankind is longing."[2] Moreover, those words which have to do particularly with the church suggest the still wider field of human life into which the sovereignty of Jesus must be extended. In the chancel of Westminster Abbey, above the spot where generation after generation of the kings of England have been crowned, there are inscribed these words from the book of Revelation, "The kingdoms of this world are become the kingdoms of our Lord, and of his Christ" (Rev. 11:15). Certainly it is tragically evident that the "real community for which mankind is longing" can never be built by threats and national self-assertions. It can be built only when the imagination and will of the

[1] *The Christ of the Indian Road* (New York: Abingdon Press, 1925), p. 51.

[2] New York: Harper & Bros., 1948.

34 Then said Mary unto the angel, How shall this be, seeing I know not a man?
35 And the angel answered and said unto her, The Holy Ghost shall come upon thee, and the power of the Highest shall overshadow thee: therefore also that holy thing which shall be born of thee shall be called the Son of God.

34 And Mary said to the angel, "How can
this be, since I have no husband?" 35 And
the angel said to her,

"The Holy Spirit will come upon you,
and the power of the Most High will
overshadow you;
therefore the child to be born[d] will be
called holy,
the son of God.

[d] Other ancient authorities add *of you.*

---

34. In some earlier form of the story the angel's words in vs. 31 may not have implied an immediate conception and Mary's astonishment may have been due to the intimation that she was to become the mother of the Davidic Messiah. As Luke records it, however, the question hinges on the words **since I have no husband** (see above). **Mary** is astonished that she is to have a son before her marriage. Roman Catholic interpreters have discovered support in this verse for their dogma that **Mary** had taken a vow of perpetual virginity: **seeing I know not a man** (KJV) declares her intention of remaining a virgin as much as it describes her present status. This is not only difficult exegesis; it also raises the further question: Why, then, had she become betrothed to Joseph?

35. The **angel** explains the theory of supernatural conception. Since his words are cast in the parallelism of Hebrew poetry, the second statement is a repetition of the first. **The Holy Spirit** is therefore the equivalent of **the power of the Most High.** It is impersonal, as in the O.T., and later trinitarian doctrine must not be read into the verse. The last part of it involves translation difficulties. The RSV is preferable to the KJV. Another possible rendering: "Therefore the child to be born will be holy; he will be called Son of God." **Son of God** involves the idea of physical (or metaphysical) relationship to deity, whereas **Son of the Most High** (RSV) in vs. 32 was only a title that God would confer on Jesus as Messiah.

---

peoples of the world are captured by the spirit of him whose greatness was that he came not to be ministered unto but to minister.

34-35. ***The Virgin Birth.***—In this question of Mary there is one of the few passages in the Gospels which refer specifically to the birth of Jesus as being a physical miracle (cf. Exeg., and see Elwood Worcester, *Studies in the Birth of the Lord*[3]). In 1922 there was issued a notable report of a Commission on Christian Doctrine appointed by the archbishops of Canterbury and York, and in this there is a summary of two positions held by devoted and Christian men concerning the Virgin Birth. "Many of us hold," says the report, "that belief in the Word made flesh is integrally bound up with belief in the Virgin Birth, and that this will increasingly be recognized." But it is noted that others hold "that a full belief in the historical Incarnation is more consistent with the supposition that our Lord's birth took place under the normal conditions of human generation." The concluding sentence runs thus: "We . . . recognize that both the views outlined above are held by members of the Church, as of the Commission, who fully accept the reality of our Lord's Incarnation, which is the central truth of the Christian faith."[4]

Such a statement, which could be paralleled in other quarters, can lift the whole question out of perplexity and fear. It may be, as the first chapters in this Gospel indicate, that Jesus was born miraculously of Mary and not of Mary and Joseph. But it may be also that this was a wondering tradition which had grown up in Christian circles with which Luke was acquainted—a tradition which, as the Exeg. points out, has no echo in the earliest Gospel of Mark, nor in any of the letters of Paul, nor in the Gospel of John. Certainly, therefore, the saving evangel of the reality of God come to earth in Christ could be proclaimed, and was proclaimed, without it. If the birth of Jesus was not by physical miracle, Jesus himself is not thereby made one whit the less miraculous. All birth is a miracle, and the supreme miracle, in any case, was the actual entrance into the world of one who in his mind and spirit completely expressed and embodied the reality of God.

[3] New York: Charles Scribner's Sons, 1932.

[4] New York: The Macmillan Co., 1938, pp. 82, 83.

36 And, behold, thy cousin Elisabeth, she hath also conceived a son in her old age; and this is the sixth month with her, who was called barren.

37 For with God nothing shall be impossible.

38 And Mary said, Behold the handmaid of the Lord; be it unto me according to thy word. And the angel departed from her.

39 And Mary arose in those days, and went into the hill country with haste, into a city of Juda;

36 And behold, your kinswoman Elizabeth
in her old age has also conceived a son;
and this is the sixth month with her who
was called barren. 37 For with God nothing
will be impossible." 38 And Mary said, "Be-
hold I am the handmaid of the Lord; let it
be to me according to your word." And
the angel departed from her.

39 In those days Mary arose and went with haste into the hill country, to a city

36-37. Mary had not asked the angel to authenticate his message as Zechariah had done (vs. 18). Nevertheless a sign is given. Elizabeth's pregnancy **in her old age** demonstrates that **with God nothing will be impossible**—a statement modeled on Gen. 18:14. Two conflicting tendencies can be observed in the gospel tradition about John and Jesus: (*a*) to subordinate John to Jesus to a greater extent than history seems to warrant (cf. John 1:19-34); and (*b*) to link John and Jesus more closely than the facts seem to permit —as in this opening chapter of Luke's Gospel. There is nothing elsewhere in the N.T. to suggest that John and Jesus were related by blood. Luke 7:18-20 (Matt. 11:2-3) implies that John had never heard of Jesus—or at least had never suspected that he might be Messiah—until reports of his ministry reached him in prison. Luke appears to assume that Mary was of priestly (non-Davidic) descent. The **sixth month** of this verse later influenced the Christian calendar. In the fourth century the birth of Jesus was fixed at the time of the winter solstice, and John's birth was then dated six months earlier. (June 24 was the date of the summer solstice according to the reckoning of the Julian calendar.)

38. Mary's words are those of humble acquiescence in God's will. There is no account of the fulfillment of the angel's prophecy as in vss. 24-25. The story is not cast in the framework of a vision. **And the angel departed from her** was meant to be understood literally.

3. Mary's Visit to Elizabeth (1:39-56)

The third scene in the series connects Gabriel's annunciations to Zechariah and to Mary with the birth narratives of John and Jesus.

Is the description which Luke gives in his first chapters therefore less true? To answer that question, consider how truth may be conveyed. Burnett H. Streeter in one of his books gives a striking illustration of two avenues of truth. He is speaking of Venice, one of the most romantic cities of the earth. If we have not been to Venice, how, he asks, shall we best know its beauty and its wonder? One way would be to read Baedeker's guidebook, which lists every fact and place in Venice with complete objectivity and in meticulous detail. Another way would be to look at one of the paintings in which J. M. W. Turner made Venice visible. We might not be able to identify in that radiant canvas of his some exact spot in Venice portrayed with photographic accuracy. But there in the glory of his coloring is the true Venice—its mood, its mystery, its incomparable charm. Similarly, not every detail in Luke may be objectively exact, e.g., a host of angels visible in the shining Judean sky, a song of angels floating audibly down. In the whole picture of the annunciation and the birth, we may be moving in the realm, not of prose, but of poetry, into which the adoring worship of men who had experienced the incomparable greatness of Jesus lifted their imagination as to the way in which he came. Whether he was born by miraculous generation or whether, as the later chapters of Luke's own Gospel suggest, he was the son of Joseph, in either case the spiritual truth that Luke conveys remains exalted. His conception was of the Holy Spirit. The purpose of God did descend to earth as radiantly as by a proclamation of the Angel Gabriel, and for the mother of Jesus, God did choose the maid of Nazareth in her meek obedience and in the lovely purity of her virgin soul.

37, 38. See Expos., vss. 29, 34, 37, 38.

40 And entered into the house of Zacharias, and saluted Elisabeth.

41 And it came to pass, that, when Elisabeth heard the salutation of Mary, the babe leaped in her womb; and Elisabeth was filled with the Holy Ghost:

42 And she spake out with a loud voice, and said, Blessed *art* thou among women, and blessed *is* the fruit of thy womb.

43 And whence *is* this to me, that the mother of my Lord should come to me?

44 For, lo, as soon as the voice of thy salutation sounded in mine ears, the babe leaped in my womb for joy.

45 And blessed *is* she that believed: for there shall be a performance of those things which were told her from the Lord.

46 And Mary said, My soul doth magnify the Lord,

of Judah, 40 and she entered the house of
Zech-a-ri'ah and greeted Elizabeth. 41 And
when Elizabeth heard the greeting of Mary,
the babe leaped in her womb; and Elizabeth was filled with the Holy Spirit 42 and
she exclaimed with a loud cry, "Blessed
are you among women, and blessed is the
fruit of your womb! 43 And why is this
granted me, that the mother of my Lord
should come to me? 44 For behold, when
the voice of your greeting came to my ears,
the babe in my womb leaped for joy.
45 And blessed is she who believed that
there would be[e] a fulfillment of what was
spoken to her from the Lord." 46 And
Mary said,

"My soul magnifies the Lord,

[e] Or *believed, for there will be.*

39-40. The vague references to Mary's destination are of no help to the reader. Luke intends us to understand that the journey was undertaken **with haste** because of the angel's report (vs. 36).

41-42. Elizabeth's unborn babe is prophetically aware of the unborn Messiah, and his inspiration (cf. vs. 15) is transferred to his mother. The future mother of the forerunner recognizes the future mother of the Christ.

43. For a similar expression of unworthiness, see II Sam. 24:21. **My Lord** had been a messianic title (Ps. 110:1), but Luke and his readers would fill it with Christian content.

44-45. Elizabeth explains to Mary how it was that she had recognized her as the mother of the Messiah, and congratulates her on her faith in the angel's words. If the KJV (cf. RSV mg.) of vs. 45 is preferred, Elizabeth explains to Mary why she calls her **blessed.**

46*a*. Mary is the speaker according to all Greek MSS and almost all translations. "Elizabeth" appears in the oldest O.L. MSS, and in quotations from this passage in Luke by Irenaeus (late second century A.D.) and a few other church fathers. MS support for "Elizabeth" is therefore not impressive. Nevertheless many interpreters prefer it for reasons of intrinsic probability. The Magnificat (so-called from the first word in the Latin versions of the psalm) has been closely modeled on the Song of Hannah in I Sam.

40-45. *The Power of Faith.*—What Elizabeth says here is echoed in a larger way all through the N.T. Blessed is belief. If one will only trust, there are no limits to what God may bring to pass. One remembers words of Jesus: "Have faith in God" (Mark 11:22); "According to your faith be it done to you" (Matt. 9:29); "Your faith has made you well" (Matt. 9:22).

But how can one have faith? How shall one believe? Often the drag of difficulty or discouragement, or the sheer dead weight of the material world, pulls too heavily the other way. There is a great sentence of C. H. Dodd's that may well be remembered and meditated upon. Faith, he wrote, "is an act which is the negation of all activity, a moment of passivity out of which the strength for action comes, because in it God acts."[5] Faith is our act in that it begins with the turning of a heart desirously toward God. But then it depends no longer upon any action of our own. It is the quiet surrender of the self to the spirit of God, which then takes hold and brings to fulfillment in us the faith which is his gift and which opens the way for all his continued giving.

46-55. *The Magnificat.*—This song of praise has to do with Mary, but in a deeper and longer way it has to do with Mary's Son. Here is the song of her rejoicing. Yet the reason for her rejoicing was not in that which she herself

[5] *The Epistle of Paul to the Romans* (London: Hodder & Stoughton, 1932; "The Moffatt New Testament Commentary"), p. 16.

47 And my spirit hath rejoiced in God my Saviour.

48 For he hath regarded the low estate of his handmaiden: for, behold, from henceforth all generations shall call me blessed.

49 For he that is mighty hath done to me great things; and holy *is* his name.

50 And his mercy *is* on them that fear him from generation to generation.

47 and my spirit rejoices in God my
Savior,
48 for he has regarded the low estate of
his handmaiden.
For behold, henceforth all generations
will call me blessed;
49 for he who is mighty has done great
things for me,
and holy is his name.
50 And his mercy is on those who fear
him
from generation to generation.

2:1-10; Hannah's song was the joyous praise to God of a woman whose long period of childlessness had been ended by God's response to her prayer (I Sam. 1:11); and it is therefore Elizabeth's situation that resembles Hannah's. It is Elizabeth who has just been filled with prophetic inspiration (vs. 41). Zechariah's rejoicing (vss. 67-79) would parallel Elizabeth's better than Mary's. Vs. 48*a* is said to have more meaning on Elizabeth's lips than on Mary's. And it is urged that vs. 56 reads as if "Elizabeth" were the subject of the verb in vs. 46. On the other hand it has been pointed out that for Elizabeth to sing a song of praise for God's goodness to her would be belated in this context; the song should have appeared after vs. 25. For this reason, and in view of the MS attestation, it is difficult to reject **and Mary said** as the original Lukan reading. But the dispute is academic, for neither Mary nor Elizabeth can seriously be considered as the author of the psalm. Almost every phrase in the Magnificat has its parallel in I Sam. 1:11; I Sam. 2:1-10, or elsewhere in the O.T. Luke or his source took a Jewish (or Jewish-Christian) hymn of praise and fitted it to this situation, possibly by the interpolation of vs. 48.

Vss. 46*b*-50 express a sense of personal thankfulness to God for his mighty acts, while vss. 51-55 praise him for Israel's deliverance from oppressors; cf. the similar structure of Hannah's song (I Sam. 2:1-10).

46*b*-47. In the parallelism of Hebrew poetry the second clause repeats the first, and there is therefore no distinction between **my soul** and **my spirit. Magnifies**="declares the greatness of."

48. This is the only verse in the psalm that relates it specifically to its present context. Luke intends us to understand vs. 48*a* as a reference to the annunciation. **The low estate** translates a Greek word that is used in the LXX text of I Sam. 1:11 for Hannah's "affliction"—i.e., her childlessness (cf. Gen. 29:32). But it can also be given a more general application (II Sam. 16:12; Ps. 25:18; etc.). Goodspeed: "For he has noticed his slave in her humble station." Vs. 48*b* is more appropriate as Mary's prophetic utterance than as Elizabeth's (but cf. Leah's boast in Gen. 30:13). **Henceforth** presumably means that Elizabeth's benediction (vs. 45) is to be the first of a long series.

49-50. Compare Deut. 10:21; Pss. 103:17; 111:9.

---

might do, but in that which might be done by him who was to be born of her. The earliest church saw the Magnificat as an expression of the kind of salvation God wrought through Jesus. It was a salvation that the great ones of the earth would not welcome. There was dynamite within it. It was to challenge the selfish powers of this earth and exalt **those of low degree.**

The Christian gospel, when it is true to itself, must always have in it the explosive power from which some will shrink in fear. In the period between World Wars I and II, that devoted Christian of Japan, Kagawa, who had been giving his life in service in the slums of Tokyo, came on a brief visit to the United States. A sensitive woman who heard him speak wrote to her minister thus, "Kagawa said what we need is fire." Then she repeated, "What is fire?" and went on to give her answer: "Fire is the leaven of discontent that somebody puts in to make life better than it was the day before. You must foster within the church your own revolutionists, not for doings primarily, but

51 He hath showed strength with his arm; he hath scattered the proud in the imagination of their hearts.

52 He hath put down the mighty from *their* seats, and exalted them of low degree.

53 He hath filled the hungry with good things; and the rich he hath sent empty away.

54 He hath holpen his servant Israel, in remembrance of *his* mercy;

55 As he spake to our fathers, to Abraham, and to his seed for ever.

56 And Mary abode with her about three months, and returned to her own house.

57 Now Elisabeth's full time came that she should be delivered; and she brought forth a son.

58 And her neighbors and her cousins heard how the Lord had showed great mercy upon her; and they rejoiced with her.

51 He has shown strength with his arm,
he has scattered the proud in the imagination of their hearts,
52 he has put down the mighty from their thrones,
and exalted those of low degree;
53 he has filled the hungry with good things,
and the rich he has sent empty away.
54 He has helped his servant Israel,
in remembrance of his mercy,
55 as he spoke to our fathers,
to Abraham and to his posterity for-ever."
56 And Mary remained with her about three months, and returned to her home.

57 Now the time came for Elizabeth to be delivered, and she gave birth to a son.
58 And her neighbors and kinsfolk heard that the Lord had shown great mercy to

---

51-55. God is the subject. The verses have been interpreted as anticipations of a redemption that is yet to be accomplished—viewed from the vantage point of the messianic age. But this interpretation is forced. It is easier to understand them as extolling God's mighty deeds in days of old. The language is that of the Greek O.T. (LXX), where parallels to almost every phrase can be discovered. "He has routed the proud-minded" (Goodspeed) is a more intelligible rendering of the Hebrew idiom in vs. 51*b*. The canticle ends with a rehearsal of God's ancient promise. **As he spoke to our fathers** can be read as a parenthesis, but this would be an awkward construction in Greek as well as in English.

56. Mary's visit ended shortly before the birth of the Baptist. Did she return to her parental **home?** She was married to Joseph when Jesus was born (see Exeg., 2:1-7), but when did her marriage take place? Luke was not concerned with such questions.

B. Births of John and Jesus (1:57–2:20)

1. The Birth of John (1:57-80)

57-58. The angel's prediction that many would rejoice at John's birth (vs. 14) had John's later followers in mind rather than Elizabeth's **neighbors and kinsfolk.** Therefore there is no reason why we should not translate vs. 58*b* with Goodspeed (cf. the Vulg.): "And they came and congratulated her."

---

for doing this: to make the leaven of discontent which is light or fire. Once it is kindled, nothing else matters, no organization, nothing; and unless it is kindled, nothing matters."

The self-satisfied and complacent would shrink in resentment from such words as those. To talk of the church needing revolutionists within it would seem an outrage. What warrant is there in the creeds and traditions of the church for any such statement? What right does anyone have to suggest that the church must be invaded by the propaganda of any particular kind of social change, and more particularly by a sort of social change which conflicts with vested interests and rooted preconceptions, and therefore to many is abhorrent?

So the literalist would say; but in saying that, he would miss the whole swift flash of truth which can light the facts up into significance. The name is not important. It is the reality that matters, and it is true that the church does need the leaven of discontent. It cannot be true to Christ unless it is making people restless before the facts of an unchristian world, restless and rebellious against unemployment and needless poverty, against the drab wretchedness of

59 And it came to pass, that on the eighth day they came to circumcise the child; and they called him Zacharias, after the name of his father.

60 And his mother answered and said, Not *so;* but he shall be called John.

61 And they said unto her, There is none of thy kindred that is called by this name.

62 And they made signs to his father, how he would have him called.

63 And he asked for a writing table, and wrote, saying, His name is John. And they marveled all.

her, and they rejoiced with her.
59 And on the eighth day they came to circumcise the
child; and they would have named him
Zech-a-ri'ah after his father,
60 but his mother said, "Not so; he shall be called
John."
61 And they said to her, "None of your kindred is called by this name."
62 And they made signs to his father, inquiring what he would have him called.
63 And he asked for a writing tablet, and
wrote, "His name is John." And they all

59. There is O.T. precedent for allowing neighbors to take part in naming a child (Ruth 4:17) but none for postponing the ceremony until the **eighth day** (cf. also 2:21). The earliest Jewish parallel only substantiates the practice in the medieval period, but it may go back to Roman times. The alternative would be to assume that Luke has adapted his narrative to Greco-Roman custom. Circumcision was performed according to rabbinical rules by an expert. Jewish children were more frequently **named** after their grandfather than their **father.**

60-63. Probably Luke thinks of Elizabeth as inspired to insist on **John** as a name. The implication of the narrative is that Zechariah was deaf as well as dumb—an exaggeration of the punishment that had been meted out to him by the angel (vs. 20). **A writing tablet** was ordinarily a block of wood covered with wax. **Saying** is a Semitism that often serves only to introduce a direct quotation and that is omitted (but not consistently) by the RSV. The deaf-mute's confirmation of his wife's unusual choice of a name for their child is accepted by the company as an astonishing evidence of the supernatural.

city tenements, against the starved misery of exploited sharecroppers, white or black, against the kind of insecurity of livelihood that creeps like a shadow toward every wage earner the instant he is past his prime. That great apostle of God, G. A. Studdert-Kennedy, said something once that in a single phrase laid bare his heart. He said that he had "a passion of pity for the poor." There ought to be in all the Christian church "a passion of pity for the poor" and for all who are oppressed; and those who do not have it will be among those for whom the impact of Christ means downfall and in whose place must rise then a different sort of man.

59-66. ***The Past and the Future.***—Note the innate conservatism of the family group. Here at the circumcision of the child they would have named him Zechariah after his father. The name of John had no precedent. Therefore to give this name to the baby would not seem right or proper.

In all Jewish thought and immemorial practice, the giving of a name meant much more than attaching a casual label. In a very intimate and vital way the name must be appropriate to the person. Name and facts should correspond.[6] Note the special meaning of O.T. names such as those of Isaac (Gen. 21:3, 6), of Jacob (Gen. 27:36), of Moses (Exod. 2:10), and the extraordinary symbolical names given to their children by Isaiah and Hosea. Consider, too, the names that were changed to indicate some new phase of an individual's destiny: the name of Abram changed to Abraham; Jacob changed to Israel; Cephas changed to Peter; Saul changed to Paul. So now a family name was to be altered. Zechariah had received from the angel of his vision the new and commanding thought that his child should not be named after himself. He should be named John, and the giving of that new name was associated with a promise of the manner of man he should grow up to be and of the great new work that he should do.

Zechariah, and Elizabeth with him, were right in insisting on that name. They were

[6] See G. B. Gray, articles on "name" and "names" in James Hastings, ed., *Dictionary of the Bible* (Edinburgh: T. & T. Clark, 1904), III, 478-85.

64 And his mouth was opened immediately, and his tongue *loosed,* and he spake, and praised God.

65 And fear came on all that dwelt round about them: and all these sayings were noised abroad throughout all the hill country of Judea.

66 And all they that heard *them* laid *them* up in their hearts, saying, What manner of child shall this be? And the hand of the Lord was with him.

67 And his father Zacharias was filled with the Holy Ghost, and prophesied, saying,

marveled. 64 And immediately his mouth
was opened and his tongue loosed, and
he spoke, blessing God. 65 And fear came
on all their neighbors. And all these things
were talked about through all the hill
country of Judea; 66 and all who heard
them laid them up in their hearts, saying,
"What then will this child be?" For the
hand of the Lord was with him.

67 And his father Zech-a-ri'ah was filled
with the Holy Spirit, and prophesied,
saying,

---

64. Zechariah has served his sentence (vss. 13, 20) and his physical handicap is lifted. **Loosed** is supplied in the Greek only by Codex Bezae and its allies, but its insertion can be justified in the English translation as necessary to the sense.

65-66*a*. Luke often notes that fear is a response to the manifestation of the supernatural (1:12, 30; Acts 5:5). **Things** (or "events") is the better translation (cf. 2:19, 51). **The hill country of Judea** (cf. vs. 39) centered about Hebron. Greatness could be expected of a **child** who had been born under such remarkable circumstances. But legends arise after events, not before them.

66*b*. This reflection reads as though it originally belonged with the conclusion in vs. 80.

67-79. These verses look like an insertion into the narrative at some stage in its history, perhaps suggested by vs. 64.

67. The Holy Spirit is usually the vehicle of prophecy and of revelation in Luke-Acts (cf. Ezek. 11:24-25).

The Benedictus is named from the translation of the first word of the song in the Vulg. Like the Magnificat it was an early Christian hymn. Vss. 68-75 may even have been of Jewish origin. They are largely a chain of O.T. phrases, among them Pss. 41:13 and 111:9 (vs. 68); Ps. 132:17 (vs. 69); Ps. 106:10 (vs. 71); and Mic. 7:20; Ps. 106:45; and Ps. 105:8-9 (vss. 72-73). Specifically Christian content is introduced in vss. 76-79.

---

aware of something that had come from on high to change their accustomed pattern. They represented a perception more keen than that which parents sometimes have. Too often the impulse that runs all through a family is that which the kinsfolk in this case expressed—the impulse to think that what has been must continue to be. A family has had its own customs and its own habits of thought; why change them? A father may want his son to follow his own profession, to grow up with his same interests and his same ideas. A mother may want her child to develop in the conventional manner to which she has been accustomed. It is not only that the family name shall be inherited; along with the name it is thought that there ought to go the set of opinions and particular purposes which have been associated with it. That is a natural feeling, but it may nevertheless be disastrously mistaken. A heavenly voice may be trying to break through the closed circle of the human notions to indicate that the new generation is to be different from the former one, to have a new message and to embody a new meaning for its world. That would be true for John, the son of Zechariah. It is often true for others of the sons of men. And the great need is that parents should realize this as Zechariah did, and not be caught instead in the dull conservatism which the kinsfolk expressed when they assumed that the present must be governed by the past.

67-75. ***Heavenly Light on History.***—In the words of these nine verses the personal joy of Zechariah is lifted up into relationship with a larger patriotism. He is thinking of the gift of his child as part of a far larger and greater gift. What God had given him would be the channel of God's mercy for a whole people, in which every individual would have a share.

Zechariah is looking a long way back. The essential worth of life for him and for his child

68 Blessed *be* the Lord God of Israel; for he hath visited and redeemed his people,

69 And hath raised up a horn of salvation for us in the house of his servant David;

70 As he spake by the mouth of his holy prophets, which have been since the world began:

71 That we should be saved from our enemies, and from the hand of all that hate us;

72 To perform the mercy *promised* to our fathers, and to remember his holy covenant;

73 The oath which he sware to our father Abraham,

74 That he would grant unto us, that we, being delivered out of the hand of our enemies, might serve him without fear,

75 In holiness and righteousness before him, all the days of our life.

68 "Blessed be the Lord God of Israel,
for he has visited and redeemed his people,
69 and has raised up a horn of salvation for us
in the house of his servant David,
70 as he spoke by the mouth of his holy prophets from of old,
71 that we should be saved from our enemies,
and from the hand of all who hate us;
72 to perform the mercy promised to our fathers,
and to remember his holy covenant,
73 the oath which he swore to our father
Abraham, 74 to grant us
that we, being delivered from the hand of our enemies,
might serve him without fear,
75 in holiness and righteousness before him all the days of our life.

68-69. God is praised for the fulfillment of Jewish messianic hopes. He has raised up a leader from among the descendants of **David. Horn** is a common metaphor in the O.T. for "power" or "strength." The Greek gives a literal translation of a typically Semitic idiom, and both of our English versions follow it. Goodspeed paraphrases: "a mighty Savior."

70. The language suggests that this verse was Luke's own composition (cf. Acts 3:21; 4:25; etc.). **From of old** does more justice to the meaning of the phrase than **since the world began.** The earliest messianic passage in the O.T. appears to be Nathan's speech to David (II Sam. 7:12-16).

71. Salvation from sins is not mentioned until vs. 77. The deliverance of the nation from its political **enemies** is all that is implied in this verse and in vs. 74. This deliverance was to be the work of the Messiah according to popular phrasings of the Jewish hope, and the articulation of that hope in vss. 68-75 does not betray any evidence of Christian reinterpretation.

72-73. Freedom from foreign tyranny will be the fulfillment of God's promised **mercy** and **his holy covenant** with **Abraham.**

74-75. Political independence will make it possible for men **to serve God without fear** and **in holiness and righteousness.**

---

is linked with what had been true ever since the days of Abraham. God had made a covenant with Israel, and it was because of that covenant that this nation had indestructible significance. It was a covenant which the great soul of the nation's progenitor had accepted, and the meaning of which the prophets had illuminated and proclaimed. Observe how thus the whole interpretation of history is lifted up above the common plane. Ordinarily a people would estimate the favor of God in immediate and material terms. If they were to believe in a divine redemption, they would want to see it evidenced in the here and now. But to Zechariah's perception God had already **visited and redeemed his people.** He had done so because he had planted in their life a spiritual quality and had given to them a spiritual commission which no outward happenings could destroy. Whoever and whatever might be their enemies, they could escape from them into the citadel of a deep inner security of faith. Whatever might be the events of the moment, this nation could still have the heroic confidence of those to whom it was granted that they could serve God **without fear.**

76 And thou, child, shalt be called the prophet of the Highest: for thou shalt go before the face of the Lord to prepare his ways;

77 To give knowledge of salvation unto his people by the remission of their sins,

78 Through the tender mercy of our God; whereby the dayspring from on high hath visited us,

79 To give light to them that sit in darkness and *in* the shadow of death, to guide our feet into the way of peace.

76 And you, child, will be called the
prophet of the Most High;
for you will go before the Lord to
prepare his ways,
77 to give knowledge of salvation to his
people
in the forgiveness of their sins,
78 through the tender mercy of our God,
when the day shall dawn upon[f] us
from on high
79 to give light to those who sit in dark-
ness and in the shadow of death,
to guide our feet into the way of
peace."

[f] Or *whereby the dayspring will visit.* Other ancient authorities read *since the dayspring has visited.*

---

76. The psalm passes from praise to prediction, and the attention of the reader is deflected from God's Messiah to the Messiah's forerunner. The title that had been predicted for Jesus was "the Son of the Most High" (vs. 32). The Baptist is to be called **the prophet of the Most High.** The second half of the verse is based on a combination of Mal. 3:1*a* and Isa. 40:3 (see Exeg., Luke 7:27 and 3:4). **Before the Lord** in vs. 15 had meant "before God," but Luke understands it to mean "before the Messiah" in this instance (cf. 3:4).

77-78*a*. The Baptist's historical role as a preacher of repentance (3:3) is anticipated. He would inform the **people** whom the Messiah was to redeem of the **salvation** that consists **in the forgiveness of their sins** and that is made available to them **through the tender mercy of our God.**

78*b*-79. The RSV makes the best of a Greek text that bristles with difficulties (for an alternative translation see the RSV mg.). John will fulfill his mission when the messianic age—**the dayspring from on high**—breaks in upon history. The future tense is better attested in the MSS than the aorist—the English perfect of the KJV. Therefore the redemption that was announced as accomplished in vs. 68 is regarded here as still in prospect. Vs. 79*a* is a reminiscence of Isa. 9:2 (cf. Ps. 107:10). Men who have lived heretofore **in darkness and in the shadow of death**—the speaker includes himself among them—will learn **the way of peace**—i.e., the way of "salvation" (Heb. *shālôm*).

76-79. *The Herald of God.*—In these last verses of the prophecy attributed to Zechariah, which has become the chant used in churches as the Benedictus, the thought of God's purpose for a people converges into the declaration of what one man, as a representative of that people's soul, would do. Here is set forth the meaning that the ministry of John the Baptist would fulfill. Follow the description as it not only applies to John but as it might apply in essential spirit to any life. No other person, of course, will duplicate John's special role. No one will live or act in circumstances identical with his. But the ideals here set forth are those which again and again can be lifted up like a relighted torch. What is the highest destiny to which any person can aspire? Is it to be measured in obvious personal profit, in the applause of the world, in the shallow estimates of the unthinking crowd? Our deeper recognition knows that it is not to be so measured. Very different are the considerations which can throw a heavenly light upon our human opportunity. The supreme achievement in any career would be to do essentially for its own generation what it was prophesied that John should do for his: so to walk in the light of God's countenance as to open the way for his increasing presence in our world; to teach people to find their only ultimate salvation, not in the manipulations of their power or pride, but through the humble and contrite heart that can reach out for the forgiveness of their sins; to bring in the dawn of a new day that only God can give, so that **those who sit in darkness and in the shadow of death** may be guided **into the way of peace.** How pointedly those words out of the past must stab us wide awake to realize our twentieth-

80 And the child grew, and waxed strong in spirit, and was in the deserts till the day of his showing unto Israel.

2 And it came to pass in those days, that there went out a decree from Caesar Augustus, that all the world should be taxed.

80 And the child grew and became strong in spirit, and he was in the wilderness till the day of his manifestation to Israel.

2 In those days a decree went out from Caesar Augustus that all the world

80. Compare 2:40, 52. No doubt this summary report of John's early years followed originally upon vs. 66. That John's youth was spent **in the wilderness**—i.e., in sparsely settled districts rather than **in the deserts**—may be Luke's deduction from the traditional scene of the Baptist's ministry. **The day of his manifestation to Israel:** Luke has in mind the story that he tells in 3:1-6.

2. The Birth of Jesus (2:1-20)

Luke's beautiful pastoral narrative is folk poetry—saga that love and reverence wove about God's good, glad gift of Christ to men. Attempts to find pagan antecedents to it in the Roman tale of Romulus and Remus and the shepherds who nurtured them, in the Iranian account of the shepherds who watched over the birth of Mithra, or in some hypothetical messianic legend borrowed by Hellenistic Judaism from Egyptian Osiris mythology, have not led to any conclusive results. Nor is it clear that David's shepherd origins (I Sam. 16:11) or the tradition that Bethlehem had a "tower of flocks" (Gen. 35:21 [Targ.]; Mic. 4:8) have contributed anything to it. If pre-Christian motifs helped to shape the Lukan story, they have not been documented.

According to Luke, Joseph and Mary had been residents of Nazareth in Galilee (cf. 1:26). Jesus was born in the stable of an inn in Bethlehem because the exigencies of an imperial census had brought his parents to the city of David. In contrast the birth stories in Matthew assume that Jesus was born in Bethlehem because that was where Joseph

century needs. **In darkness and in the shadow of death:** how many people have learned the literal meaning of that in a century of world wars and of growing fear! Where will there be, and when will there come, the spirit-filled men with enlightened minds and consecrated souls who can lead humanity upward into the way of peace?

80. ***The Value of Solitude.***—There is a striking suggestion here as to the way in which one who was to do a public work made his preparation. For a long time before he appeared at the fords of the Jordan river and began to preach, John was in the wilderness, i.e., he deliberately went out into the empty land, away from the towns and from the crowded roads. He separated himself from men in order that he might be alone with God. In this he was not singular. Elijah, likewise, when he appeared to Ahab, came from no one knew where. Amos, when he confronted the crowds in Bethel, came unheralded from the gaunt wilderness of Tekoa. In the hearts of these men burned the consciousness that they must be spokesmen of God. How were they to determine, then, what it was that they must say? By joining in the miscellaneous strife of tongues, by listening to the general voice, by echoing the average opinion? No. Rather they went apart where their minds and souls might dwell in a great quiet of contemplation and become like still waters which alone can mirror the stars. The modern world is more confused and clamorous than the world of John. Therefore there is not less but the more need that those who are to speak a message for God should learn the meaning of deliberate withdrawal. They may not have to go for long periods into a physical wilderness as John did; they may not have to retire into some monastic cloister; but they do need to create in the midst of crowded life a space for independent thinking. Resolutely they must take time to get far enough away from the distractions of the common world to hear those heavenly voices which can be heard only by those who have made themselves receptively ready for a divine communion.

2:1. ***The Transient and the Eternal Power.***—**A decree went out from Caesar Augustus.** In the year to which those words refer the most powerful person on earth was Caesar Augustus, emperor of Rome. Born in 63 B.C. and named

2 (*And* this taxing was first made when Cyrenius was governor of Syria.)

should be enrolled. 2 This was the first enrollment, when Qui-rin′i-us was governor

and Mary had their residence. The family left Bethlehem and settled in Nazareth only after an interlude in Egypt, in response to oracles that warned against threats to the life of the Christ child. All this raises the question: Was Jesus born in Bethlehem? Or did both Luke and Matthew discount the tradition that Jesus had come out of Nazareth and tell their variant stories of his birth at Bethlehem in order that he might better fulfill Jewish messianic expectations? The matter is one of considerable historical interest but no longer of any religious importance.

2:1-3. The implication of 1:26 is that Jesus was born six months after the birth of John the Baptist. Therefore **in those days** cannot have any reference to the time of John's "manifestation to Israel" (1:80*b*). Luke seeks to set his story against the background of secular history (cf. 3:1-2). **Caesar Augustus** ruled from 27 B.C. to A.D. 14. No other source makes any mention of a census of **all the world**—a hyperbole for the Roman Empire—during his reign. An enrollment in the province of Syria for purposes of taxation was undertaken in A.D. 6 (or 7) when **Quirinius was governor.** The references to it by Josephus (*Jewish War* II. 8. 1; VII. 8. 1) imply that this census was **the first enrollment,** for it raised a storm of protest among the Jews and led to an insurrection in Galilee that was suppressed only with some difficulty (cf. Acts. 5:37). Since **Quirinius** was never

Gaius Octavius, he was the great nephew of Julius Caesar, who had led the Roman legions across the Rubicon and carried them to conquests wider than had been won before. Adopted by Julius Caesar as his son and heir, he stood in obvious danger after Caesar's assassination. But steadily he won his way to power against Mark Antony and other rivals, and at last he was seated on the imperial throne and given by the Roman senate the title of Augustus.

The Roman dominion extended all over the Mediterranean world and reached across to the island of Britain, and went eastward into Asia. Wherever the Roman legions marched, men made way before them. Augustus himself was responsible for notable achievements. Concerning Rome itself, it was said of him that he found it brick and left it marble.

> His legions policed the provinces up to the extreme barbarian confines. He made the Italian roads a marvel of efficiency, and established or completed a similar network overseas. Mile-stones and pillars at the crossroads gave the traveller his bearings. . . . He did much, too, in the way of building new cities and amplifying old ones at strategic points in the interior, cities which should dominate the new roads and be centres of Roman influence.[7]

So it was that under the rule of Augustus the very name of Rome meant wealth, power, and authority.

Then, in a corner of a conquered province which was part of the Roman Empire, one night a baby was born. It was in a little town to which the mother and her husband had come because the decree of Caesar Augustus had compelled them to make the journey there. Both of them were poor, and when they came to the town, no one took any notice of their coming and no one helped them to find a place in which to stay. Since the only shelter they could get was a stable, it was in a stable that the baby was born, a baby whose name was Jesus.

The rest of the town was not concerned. And certainly no flicker of awareness or interest stirred in the general world outside. In far-off Rome, Caesar Augustus could not have known about it, or listened if by any chance he had been told. Who cared what had happened in insignificant Palestine? And particularly who cared for any event so common as that a woman had borne a child? Birth was as common as the day. What did it matter that one life more or less should be added to the shifting panorama of the earth?

As between Caesar Augustus and the child born in Palestine, who would have had any question as to which was the significant figure? Surely Caesar Augustus would tower above the horizons of history, while a child born in one of his provinces would be lost among the multitudes that existed beneath his shadow. But it has not been so. Great as he was, Caesar Augustus is now only an echo of ancient times, while the name of the child he had never heard of is spoken by millions with reverence and love in prayers that go up from single hearts and in

[7] John Buchan, *Augustus* (Boston: Houghton Mifflin Co., 1937), pp. 290-91, 309.

3 And all went to be taxed, every one
into his own city.
4 And Joseph also went up from Galilee, out of the city of Nazareth, into Judea, unto the city of David, which is called Bethlehem, (because he was of the house and lineage of David,)

of Syria. 3 And all went to be enrolled, each
to his own city. 4 And Joseph also went up
from Galilee, from the city of Nazareth, to Judea, to the city of David, which is called Bethlehem, because he was of the house

---

Roman legate in Syria during the lifetime of Herod the Great, and Luke's earlier narratives assume that John the Baptist—and therefore Jesus also—was born while Herod was still king of Judea (1:5), it would appear that the evangelist has been guilty of an anachronism. Many ingenious attempts have been made to escape this conclusion, but all fall short of demonstration. Furthermore it is improbable that any Roman census would have required a man to report to the home of his ancestors. Such a procedure would have been almost as impracticable in Roman times as it would be in our own, and the Roman state was interested in a man's property, not in his pedigree.

4-5. The suggestion that **Joseph** had to journey to **Bethlehem** because he owned property in that city has no warrant in Luke's story. In any case **Mary** would not have been obliged to accompany him. **His betrothed** has the support of the best Greek MSS, but

---

the worship of numberless churches and great cathedrals. As John Buchan wrote in a chapter that described Augustus' funeral, men "comforted themselves, reflecting that Augustus was a god, and that gods do not die." But though Augustus represented the imperial power that men tried to deify in his person, that power did go down to death. Meanwhile, the one born in Palestine "was to proclaim a kingdom mightier than the Roman, and to tell of a world saved not by Man who became God, but by God who became Man." [8]

Something mightier than a proclamation by an emperor had happened. A decree went out from Caesar Augustus: that was one fact. But here was the more tremendous fact: "God sent forth his Son" (Gal. 4:4). The whole meaning of Christian history is summed up in that contrast. Life and the spirit's inner life are more powerful than things. It appeared that Caesar Augustus had all the resources of power in his hands; but his power has gone and the ancient Rome over which he ruled was doomed to fall to catastrophe and to ruin. Meanwhile the power of Jesus has lived and gone on increasing, because it is the power of light and love which can reach into men's hearts and make them different and new.

4. ***Which Is Called Bethlehem.***—The meaning of the name "Bethlehem" is "the house of bread," and thought and imagination will linger upon the significance of that word.

Doubtless the origin of the name was due to the simple fact that Bethlehem is in the midst of a relatively fertile region. That is a rare thing in Palestine, which in large part is a barren land. Around it are great regions which are still more barren. Below it is the long, grim wilderness of Sinai; to the east, beyond the region of the Jordan Valley, rise the harsh ramparts of Moab; and beyond these the empty spaces of deserts, inhabited only by the Arab Bedouins, stretch away toward the deep heart of Asia. Even to the west of the Jordan Valley there is the gaunt and lonely Tekoa, from which came the prophet Amos. But around Bethlehem the land was of a gentler kind. There wheat ripened in the fields and the figs and olives grew. In Bethlehem and its neighborhood people might live with a reasonable security of subsistence.

Surely it is not irrelevant that the birth of Jesus was thus associated with the town whose name is "the house of bread." The love of God, of which his birth was the supreme expression, is not indifferent to simple and basic human needs. Jesus himself was no aloof ascetic. One of the first petitions in the prayer he taught his disciples is "Give us this day our daily bread." He liked those familiar and friendly contacts with people which are most instinctively made when men sit down to eat their food together. Read the Gospels and see how often in their brief story there is mention of Jesus going to this or that house to dine—to Simon Peter's house in Capernaum, to the wedding feast in Cana, to Matthew the publican's, to the house of Zacchaeus, to Mary and Martha's house at Bethany, to the house of Simon the Pharisee, to the upper room where Jesus ate with the disciples at the very end; and even after his resur-

[8] *Ibid.*, p. 346.

5 To be taxed with Mary his espoused wife, being great with child.

6 And so it was, that, while they were there, the days were accomplished that she should be delivered.

7 And she brought forth her firstborn

and lineage of David, 5 to be enrolled with
Mary, his betrothed, who was with child.
6 And while they were there, the time
came for her to be delivered. 7 And she
gave birth to her first-born son and

"his wife," a reading found in the O.L. MSS and in the Sinaitic Syriac, is intrinsically preferable. Its displacement may have been due to the harmonization of vs. 5 with 1:27. **His espoused wife** is a meaningless combination of both readings that occurs in later MSS.

6-7. With the simplicity that is often the mark of his literary genius, Luke tells the story of Jesus' humble birth in a single sentence (in the Greek text). **Her first-born son:** Luke refers in 8:19 to Jesus' brothers. Mark gives the names of four, and mentions at least

---

rection, to the house of the two disciples at Emmaus, where he was known in the breaking of bread. He was never indifferent either to human need or to human happiness. His life had a balance and roundedness such as few of the world's great creators of religions have even approached. He moved in two worlds at once, and yet without ever seeming to be less but rather more a participant in this one. He had about him the power of an endless life, and yet he gave himself so intimately and so completely to the homely human contacts that the simplest matters of everyday existence were made beautiful. When he wanted to illustrate the meaning of the kingdom of God, he spoke of the sower scattering the grain that would ripen into the harvest, or of the woman kneading leaven into the meal, of a man at the end of a journey knocking at his friend's house for bread. As he looked at men's efforts to gain their livelihood, he said, "Your heavenly father knoweth that ye have need of all these things" (Matt. 6:32). He did not want them to be anxious or to struggle as those who think that everything depends on their own fret and tension. But he himself had lived and worked in Nazareth, and he knew the practical necessities on which life rests. The love of God understands these things, he said, and God cares. And if his children are obedient to his purpose, he will provide.

But Bethlehem, which has represented the birth to men of the love of God in Jesus, is a house of bread not only in the physical sense. It suggests the house of that living bread which feeds all that is fullest in men's souls.

Jesus saw always that double aspect of life: "Man shall not live by bread alone," he said, "but by every word that proceedeth out of the mouth of God" (Matt. 4:4). He knew then, and he would know now, that no satisfaction of their economic wants, vital, urgent, and primary though these are, can ultimately feed the best in our human life. If we are able to create, as we must try to do, a social order in which every family can have a decent home and in which every child can grow up in security and contentment and with some sufficient taste of the physical beauty of this earth, even then we should not have reached fulfillment. The proof of that is in the multitude of houses—one may not fully call them homes—where there is everything that money can command, and yet no joy. People may have the wealth of Croesus to live on, but if they do not know how to live, life will grow bitter, disillusioned, and despairing. Something inside men and women will starve unless it is fed by him who said he had come to be the bread of life.

4-7. *When the Christ Child Could Not Come In.*—There was no place for them in the inn. There are no words in the whole Gospel of Luke upon which the minds of Christians have dwelt more meditatively and more tenderly than upon these. Out of what is stated here the scene shapes itself again as vividly to the imagination as though it were beheld by actual eyes: a little town in darkness, a jostling crowd of people arriving here and pressing ahead of one another for harborage, Joseph and Mary of Nazareth coming wearily to the end of their long road; no room for them in the rude village inn, and nothing to do then but to find a corner in a stable where Mary could come to rest. Christian poets have caught the strange and wistful wonder of it all, as in Phillips Brooks's "O Little Town of Bethlehem," G. K. Chesterton's "There Fared a Mother Driven Forth," and Joyce Kilmer's "There Was a Gentle Hostler."

Of course the picture as Luke gives it cannot be pressed too far, as though we could identify persons and their motives in a Bethlehem that was. But one reason why it lays such a hold upon the mind and heart is that the crowded inn of the story becomes also an eternal parable

son, and wrapped him in swaddling clothes, and laid him in a manger; because there was no room for them in the inn.

wrapped him in swaddling cloths, and laid him in a manger, because there was no place for them in the inn.

---

two sisters (Mark 6:3). An alternative translation to **manger** would be "stall" (Moffatt), and to **inn** would be "guest room" (cf. 22:11). The ox and the ass were introduced into apocryphal versions of the story from Isa. 1:3. The later tradition that Jesus was born in a cave is first mentioned by Justin (*ca.* A.D. 150). In the early fourth century the Basilica of Constantine was built behind its traditional site.

---

of the human soul. Therefore in that everlastingly present sense, why was there—why is there—no room in the inn for the Christ child who is at its doors?

In the first place, simply because of other guests who would have got there first. In the imagined scene at Bethlehem, if Mary and Joseph had come earlier to the inn, they doubtless would have been received. If they were turned away, it was not that there was any ill will against them, but simply because the innkeeper was so harried with other people that he had no patience to look at any more. His house was a caravansary and those who had happened to arrive first had filled it up. These travelers from Nazareth had come late, the inn was crowded, they could not get in; and that was all there was to that. Just so casually, through the near drift of circumstances, and not through any particularly hostile will, may Jesus be excluded from the inn of our hearts. We have merely filled all the space we have with other guests. We do not mean to be irreligious, but our thoughts and feelings are so occupied with other matters that religion cannot find a place. We too are like a caravansary where the first come are the first served. In this world with its noisy and demanding clamor the crowd of common thoughts and common interests has poured in upon us and taken possession of our time and our attention, and when Christ comes with his infinite gift for the enrichment of our souls, there is no room for him in the inn.

In the second place, it might be said that the reason why there was no room in the inn for Mary and Joseph and for the Christ child who was to be born was because nobody knew that they were coming, and did not recognize their importance when they came. If the one who had charge of the inn had dreamed who Mary's child would be, he would have found means to welcome him. Like most of the rest of us, he would have been flattered at the idea of welcoming greatness. If someone could only have told him that here was the world's Savior, that here was the One by whose name every little town and place he touched should be made significant forever, then he would have rearranged his guests and sent some of them to find lodgings elsewhere, that Mary the mother of Jesus might come in. But he did not know. That is the way it always is. We never do know when the great possibilities of God are at our doors unless we have taken the pains to keep our spirits sensitive. The mystery waiting to bring to us the birth of a redeeming Savior may be at our doors, and all that we shall see will be some ordinary stranger whom we shall wave away, saying, "There is no room in my inn."

There is another course of thought along which we might be led concerning the theme which has been suggested. When the reality of Christ is at our doors, what may be the signs of his presence?

In the first place, the note of his coming will be joy. When anything happens in life that is or might be joyous, then we need to understand that the reality of Jesus may be coming near. Love has come to a man and a woman, or some great friendship has begun, or new opportunities open into a work which gives happier self-expression than has been known before. If a man chooses, he may take these things self-confidently, as if he himself had deserved them and created them. Or he may realize with a sense of wonder how widely life seems to be expanding beyond anything which he himself could have brought to pass. A child is born into a human home, and a man and woman may treat that great gift with a natural but shallow pride, and with no more than that. On the other hand, they may let the birth of that little child unlock for them the larger sense of the mystery and wonder of life. They may know that it is God who is giving himself to them, and then they will want to widen all the ways of their recognition so that most fully the heavenly blessing may come in.

In the second place, the sign that Jesus may be near us is when we stand in the presence of innocence. The curse of our world is not so apt to be its evil as its disillusionment. We can fight evil and gain strength in the battling with it, as long as we know unmistakably that evil is evil, and as long as we believe in the beauty and worthwhileness of good. But our danger is that

19 But Mary kept all these things, and pondered *them* in her heart.

herds told them. 19 But Mary kept all these things, pondering them in her heart.

happened (1:26-38), and therefore did not share in the general surprise. Instead she treasured a memory of the events and reflected on them. Those who believe that the shepherds' watch and the angels' chorus are to be taken literally can claim that the story is based on this firsthand report. But it is unwise to impose the prose of history on the

poetry. It will depend upon the suggestions which we do or do not welcome. Some potentially great event can be a mere common thing which happens in a stable, or it can, instead, be illumined by the halo of a divine significance.

To all human souls there comes as truly as to those who listened to the shepherds some report of a glory which might belong to them. There are things of which at least they know enough to make it possible for them to ponder further. They know that there is such a thing as a Christian consciousness, such a thing as life lived with reference to religious values. They know that their own growing experience ought to be sensitive to the best they have heard and learned from every influence which speaks of life as something large and high. Sayings have come to them to which they can never quite be deaf, whether those sayings are from literature, from poetry, from their fathers and mothers, or from their happiest friends. They can, of course, dismiss these with the mistaken hardness of a supposed sincerity. With the poor, raw crudity which calls itself realism, they can shrug their shoulders at these reports of something divine which invests our humanness. But if they do so, then life is apt to begin and to end on a level that is not much higher than a stable. Only if they hide the great suggestions in their hearts, ponder them and try to live in the growing light which these will kindle, can they go forward into the high worth which life has for them to inherit.

This is why we need worship as perhaps the world has never needed it before. We have plenty of ideas, but a dearth of deep assurance. We have plenty of bright ideas and gaily painted ambitions upon which we ride as children ride upon the prancing horses of a merry-go-round. We like the motion and the music; but when we climb down from all our riding, we discover that we have gone through many revolutions only to arrive nowhere. We like to hear people talk, provided they will give us, like a motion picture, a series of new impressions so rapid that we do not concentrate on any one. What we must learn is to be quiet before the voices which speak to us of the unseen reality of life. Those voices may come in forms no more impressive than those of the shepherds; but they come. Someone we know has been aware of God. Someone has given us an incentive to believe that there is something more to life than its everyday appearances, and that it is never understood until it is interpreted in that light which has broken upon the most sensitive spirits in the hour of their communion with the infinite. Before such messengers there can at least be wonder, and it is wonder that opens the mind and heart to truth.

19. *The Heavenly Meditation.*—Let thought dwell on that one word **pondered.** According to the beautiful suggestion of the Gospel here, the mother of Jesus held in her heart all the intimations of a divine significance for her child which had come to her in the moments of highest inspiration. She had felt then with great certainty what God wanted her to know. She had not let the vision fade.

There is a message here for all parents. It is always possible for a man and woman to forget their accountability to God. The child is theirs, and they rear it as though only the poor, shallow impulses of their own uninspired minds had to be consulted; or they hold themselves subject to the foolish ideals which in ignominious forgetfulness of the soul's true greatness they worship. They pay their deference to social convention, to the demands of fashion, to the supposed advantages of a frivolous popularity. This and that the child must do because the child wants to, because other children are doing it, because it is the road of least resistance. So the whole conduct of the child's life is a thing of shreds and patches, a poor, cheap product of chance and caprice, with no pattern of noble purpose weaving it into dignity, vagrant in its development because the high thought of its accountability to God is lost in the glitter of lesser things. The pity of the failure is so much the more great because there is so much to disguise it. There are children in every community who because of the politeness and refinement of their surroundings will always reflect a certain measure of charm, who, well-dressed and well-mannered, may seem on the surface all that a child should be, yet in the center of their souls, where the high consciousness of religion and duty should have dwelt, have only emptiness.

20 And the shepherds returned, glorifying and praising God for all the things that they had heard and seen, as it was told unto them.

20 And the shepherds returned, glorifying and praising God for all they had heard and seen, as it had been told them.

---

poetry of faith. Had Jesus' mission as "Christ the Lord" been attested by such a portent at his birth, it would be difficult to understand the later attitude of his parents (2:50) and fellow townsmen (4:22).

On the other hand, is there any such supreme honor as belongs to those who do rightly discharge their responsibilities to train young souls in the strength of their accountability to God? It is a great thing if a man takes brick and stone, and bowing his imagination down before the infinite ideals of beauty, learns patiently to be the servant of these until he has wrought from his materials the architectural glory which centuries will wonder at. It is a great thing when a Michelangelo takes the marble and beneath its rough uncouthness sees the loveliness of the vision which his skillfulness will carve into the statue. But how much mightier a thing is it when men and women in the realized wonder of their parenthood fashion from the imperishable stuff of the human soul the life that measures up to the stature of its full manhood in the sight of God.

20. *When the Great Moment Has Gone.*— And the shepherds returned. It was the road back. The shepherds had had their great experience, and now it was over. They had been to the stable in Bethlehem, but they could not linger there. They returned to their familiar pastures and the commonplace tending of their sheep. Back from a shining happiness, they must go to humdrum things.

The road back is always the hard road. It is easy to go with hurrying feet when expectation leads ahead. But it is not so easy to know what to do when the expectation has culminated in an experience which was fleeting, and when eagerness cools into the wistful realization that a great emotion has begun to ebb. The trouble with many people, and the reason which keeps them from being happy, is that so often they seem to be walking upon the road back.

Certainly to all children, and often to adults, there is a sense of letdown when the Christmas season and its festivities have come and gone. But much more serious is the fact that the high beliefs which the Christmas gospel and the Christmas hymns symbolize may also fade. The poetry of the spirit turns into dull prose. Men and women may lose the sense that life has above it the mystery of infinite skies. They may disparage whatever they begin to think is visionary, and emphasize what they call realism. That realism presents a drab and harshly lighted world which no longer includes things so beautiful and spacious that they must bow down before them as divine. Much modern literature is keyed to this stark note, and the result is that multitudes of people, being affected by what they read and by what the general mood of the time makes familiar, are ashamed to trust their desire to find in life some high religious meaning. They are walking on a road back, busy not with preserving but with abandoning their youthful ideals, bent upon adjusting themselves to the ordinary world instead of believing that the ordinary world can be made over in the light of what they once saw in some earlier hour of spiritual illumination.

So it might have been with the shepherds. But note that the first four words of the sentence are not the end. **And the shepherds returned, glorifying and praising God for all the things that they had heard and seen.** That is to say that on the road back they took with them undimmed and undiminished the expansion of soul which had been theirs in their most exalted moments.

What was it that they carried with them which would last? In the first place, recognition that their highest happiness had its source in God. That is a recognition which all men need to preserve. Have there not been in every life moments when there was some sudden experience so beautiful and so full of loveliness that the life knew it had been touched by an inspiration which came from God? "Ah, yes, that is very well," men may say, "there have been rare occasions when I have felt what might be called inspiration, but on the ordinary days I do not feel it." So it may be. But do we remember the days when we did? That is the important point: to remember them and let the music of their great fact keep echoing in our recollection. The shepherds were thanking God not for what they saw and heard at that moment. As they returned from Bethlehem, the skies were blank above them, and under their feet was only the common earth; but they were **glorifying and praising God for all the things that they had heard and seen.**

In the second place, the shepherds not only

21 And when eight days were accomplished for the circumcising of the child, his name was called JESUS, which was so named of the angel before he was conceived in the womb.

21 And at the end of eight days, when he was circumcised, he was called Jesus, the name given by the angel before he was conceived in the womb.

C. Jesus' Infancy and Childhood (2:21-52)

1. Jesus' Circumcision and Presentation (2:21-40)

Luke's infancy narratives refer to Joseph and Mary as Jesus' parents without any accommodation to the doctrine of the Virgin Birth. Jesus' father and mother conformed to the practice of pious Jewish families by circumcising their son, presenting him in the temple, and offering a sacrifice for their own purification as the law prescribed. The temple scene is the main center of interest. It provides Luke with an opportunity to tell of Simeon and Anna and their prophetic insight concerning the child and his mission.

21. Jesus' circumcision is implied. His infancy followed the pattern of orthodox Jewish piety, and Luke's readers are provided with further evidence that Christianity had its roots in Judaism. But the emphasis of the verse rests on the naming of the child (cf. 1:59). Luke is careful to point out that the name was given in accordance with the angel's proclamation (1:31).

saw that their happiness had its source in God; they saw that this had focused in something very simple and human.

Once men supposed that God must be very distant. He must reveal himself in terror and awe. He moved among the clouds of Sinai or dwelt in dreadful silence behind the curtain in the holy of holies in the temple shrine. But the shepherds learned a more wondrous truth. When God wanted to come near to human life, he chose a human family and a little human child. He drew near in that crude and accidental shelter in Bethlehem. Because life was there and love was there, even the stable gave room enough for God to enter in.

God will not be found in some strange and distant day if he cannot be found now. But he can be found now in the things which are most close—in the familiar blessings of friendship and affection, in the daily beauty of patience and devotion and faith and love which may be given altogether beyond one's deserving. When men recognize this, though the road may lead back to the places of routine work, they can go, as the shepherds went, **glorifying and praising God** for all that they have seen and heard.

Finally, the shepherds knew that what they had beheld in Bethlehem should reach out and on to illimitable consequence. They did not yet know how. But they had learned that it would be so. This little child in Mary's arms should be a king. They could not have understood then that the throne of his exaltation would be a cross and his crown would be a crown of thorns. They could not know how he would rule the hearts of men wherein the old hardness of sin must first be broken by his own sacrifice. But dimly at least they did know that somehow he was royal, that the new power which had come so silently there in Bethlehem should increase in spiritual majesty and go marching at length to its conquest along the highways of the world.

Similarly, in later times we cannot foresee God's when or how. We do not yet know how business can be Christianized; how the economic order can be made over to express the values of Jesus; how the relationship between nations can be lifted above the law of the jungle into some redeeming expression of the law of love. But there is one thing that the high moments of knowledge have made sure. It is the truth that only in Christ does life find its real interpretation. When in our homes and in our nearest contacts with any human personality we touch that which we instinctively recognize as Christlike, we are sure that we have come into contact with that which alone holds in its hands the keys of human destiny. When we have known that once, we can go back to the routine duties still **glorifying and praising God** for that which in a moment of vision had been seen and heard.

21. ***The Value of Tradition.***—In much of the N.T. the word "circumcision" is associated with disparagement. In the thought of Paul as expressed again and again in his epistles, the party of the circumcision meant the stubborn reactionaries who blocked the new gospel of Christ's saving spirit. Yet here is the fact that Jesus himself was circumcised. In facing what seems thus

22 And when the days of her purification according to the law of Moses were accomplished, they brought him to Jerusalem, to present *him* to the Lord;

23 (As it is written in the law of the Lord, Every male that openeth the womb shall be called holy to the Lord;)

24 And to offer a sacrifice according to that which is said in the law of the Lord, A pair of turtledoves, or two young pigeons.

25 And, behold, there was a man in Jerusalem, whose name *was* Simeon; and the same man *was* just and devout, waiting for the consolation of Israel: and the Holy Ghost was upon him.

22 And when the time came for their
purification according to the law of Moses,
they brought him up to Jerusalem to pre-
sent him to the Lord 23 (as it is written in
the law of the Lord, "Every male that
opens the womb shall be called holy to
the Lord") 24 and to offer a sacrifice ac-
cording to what is said in the law of the
Lord, "a pair of turtledoves, or two young
pigeons." 25 Now there was a man in Jeru-
salem, whose name was Simeon, and this
man was righteous and devout, looking for
the consolation of Israel, and the Holy

22*a*. Their purification became **her purification** in later MSS in order to make the text conform to the regulation in Lev. 12:6. As a Jewish mother, Mary was considered "unclean" for seven days after the birth of her child (Lev. 12:2) and was expected to remain in ceremonial isolation for another thirty-three days (Lev. 12:4)—a total of forty days in Bethlehem. Luke believes Joseph also was required to observe this legal provision.

22*b*-23. An interruption of the main narrative. The rite of presentation was distinct from that of purification, but Luke has evidently confused the two. The quotation is a free one from Exod. 13:2. The law provided for the "redemption" of the first-born **male** by the offering of a substitute (Exod. 13:13). Luke omits any notice of this. He interprets Jesus' presentation as an act of dedication to the service of God in the light of the O.T. story about Samuel (I Sam. 1:24-28).

24. The quotation is from Lev. 12:8. It details the **sacrifice** that was to be offered for purification by a mother who could not afford a lamb.

25-26. Some interpreters have identified **Simeon** with a rabbi of the early first century A.D. who was the son of Hillel and the father of Gamaliel (Acts 5:34; 22:3); but the name was too common among Jews to warrant such an inference. Vss. 26 and 29 imply that the prophet was an aged man. **The consolation of Israel** means "the fulfillment of Jewish messianic hopes" (as often in rabbinical literature). The author of II Peter does justice to O.T. and early Christian ideas when he says, "No prophecy ever came by the

---

to be a contradiction, one notes first the value that there may be in old traditions and observances. In those to whom by the grace of God the nurture of the child Jesus had been given, there was the right desire that his life should be linked with all the rich inheritance of Israel. Jesus himself kept that same spirit. He came as a new creator for the values of life, but he was never an iconoclast. He said, "Think not that I have come to abolish the law and the prophets; I have come not to abolish them but to fulfill them" (Matt. 5:17). Yet Paul was right when he learned from the whole example of his master's life that however worthy of regard old forms and ways had been, they must be broken through if and when they became so hardened that they shut life up instead of letting it expand. The natural thing is that the old customs shall be reverently carried on. So it was with the child Jesus, as the opening words of the collect for the feast of the Circumcision in the Book of Common Prayer are a reminder, "Almighty God, who madest thy blessed Son to be circumcised, and obedient to the law for man." But then the prayer goes on beyond its reference to the formal law to the petition, "Grant us the true circumcision of the Spirit." Every rite and ceremony originally was an effort to express a spiritual purpose. As long as it does that, it is to be reverenced. When it fails to do that, then the spirit must seek expression in some new and living way.

22-32. ***The Glory of Israel.***—What does a man most want to see before he dies? There might be many answers to that question: his own reputation secure, his name honored, his family prosperous. But Simeon, **this man . . . righteous and devout,** had a different desire. His desire had no narrow reference to himself. The one thing he wanted was to see the unfold-

26 And it was revealed unto him by the Holy Ghost, that he should not see death, before he had seen the Lord's Christ.

27 And he came by the Spirit into the temple: and when the parents brought in the child Jesus, to do for him after the custom of the law,

28 Then took he him up in his arms, and blessed God, and said,

29 Lord, now lettest thou thy servant depart in peace, according to thy word:

30 For mine eyes have seen thy salvation,

31 Which thou hast prepared before the face of all people;

32 A light to lighten the Gentiles, and the glory of thy people Israel.

Spirit was upon him. 26 And it had been
revealed to him by the Holy Spirit that he
should not see death before he had seen
the Lord's Christ. 27 And inspired by the
Spirit[h] he came into the temple; and when
the parents brought in the child Jesus,
to do for him according to the custom of
the law, 28 he took him up in his arms
and blessed God and said,

29 "Lord, now lettest thou thy servant
depart in peace,
according to thy word;
30 for mine eyes have seen thy salvation
31 which thou hast prepared in the presence of all peoples,
32 a light for revelation to the Gentiles,
and for glory to thy people Israel."

[h] Or *in the Spirit.*

---

impulse of man, but men moved by the Holy Spirit spoke from God" (II Pet. 1:21). Paul had laid down a rule of thumb by which men might distinguish true revelations by **the Holy Spirit** from false (I Cor. 12:1-3; cf. Did. 11:7-12). **The Lord's Christ** is a pre-Christian Jewish title that means "God's Messiah"—"God's anointed one."

27-28. Simeon was inspired to come **into the temple** at the right moment. When Jesus' **parents brought in the child Jesus,** the prophecy that he should live to see the Messiah was fulfilled. **To do for him according to the custom of the law** must refer to the rite of presentation, for the rite of purification did not concern the child.

The use of the Nunc Dimittis in Christian liturgy has been traced to as early as the fifth century (*Apostolic Constitutions* VII. 48). Whether it ever circulated in the primitive church as a hymn after the fashion of the Magnificat and the Benedictus is difficult to determine. It lends itself to Luke's interest in stressing the universalism of the gospel. While the Christ was still a babe in arms, a Jewish prophet foresaw that his messianic salvation was intended for all mankind. The theme of an old man who anticipates the greatness of a divine child can also be documented in stories about Asita and the infant Buddha. Given a similar phenomenon in religion, men of different races, places, and times tend to give it a similar explanation.

29. The introductory words of the psalm are a statement of fact ("thou lettest . . . depart") not a prayer. The oracle—**according to thy word** refers to vs. 26—has been fulfilled, and Simeon is content to die. The figure in the Greek text is that of a master freeing his slave.

30-32. The **salvation** that Simeon had **seen**—"the Lord's Christ" of vs. 26—was intended for all peoples. The KJV construes **glory** as well as **light** in apposition to **salvation,** and this does justice to the rhythm of the Greek text. Phrases from the LXX version of Isa. 40:5; 52:10; 42:6; 49:6; and 46:13 have been built into these verses.

---

ing of God's promise for his people, and for that a new personality was needed. If just once he could look upon the face that had the light of God on it, he would die content. So when the child Jesus was put in his arms, his intuition made him know that his desire was satisfied. Here was the beginning of salvation.

Very noteworthy also are the last words of Simeon's thanksgiving. They express the flowering of that highest understanding which began to emerge among the prophets and to which the Gospel of Luke is attuned. It is the recognition that the spiritual treasures which God had given to Israel were meant as a gift for all mankind. The glory of Israel should not be in keeping that treasure to itself; its glory should be in making all its life **a light to lighten the Gentiles.** The corollaries of that truth go far. Any Christian church is false to the gospel if it is concerned only with its own prestige and

33 And Joseph and his mother marveled at those things which were spoken of him.

34 And Simeon blessed them, and said unto Mary his mother, Behold, this *child*

33 And his father and his mother marveled at what was said about him; **34** and Simeon blessed them and said to Mary his mother,

---

33. Joseph is substituted for **his father** in inferior MSS. The amazement of Jesus' parents would be in order if the story of Simeon's prescience belonged originally to a source that knew nothing of the angel's annunciation and the nativity narrative. Joseph and Mary learn for the first time that their child is to be God's Messiah. Another explanation: Jesus' **father** and **mother** were astonished at the declaration that he was to be "a light for revelation to the Gentiles," as well as the Savior of Israel.

34-35. Simeon pronounced his blessing on both parents but addressed this further prediction only to the **mother.** This involves a certain awkwardness in style that is also apparent in the parenthesis in vs. 35*a*. Perhaps Luke substituted **Mary his mother** for

---

has no burning missionary desire to make the gospel of Jesus Christ reach out with redemption to all life everywhere.

33-34. ***The Formidableness of the Gospel.***—The words of this verse are solemn words:

> **Behold, this child is set for the fall and rising of many in Israel,**
> **and for a sign that is spoken against.**

They strike a different note from the story of Bethlehem which has preceded them. That story has in it an unexampled loveliness. It touches the most beautiful chords of instinctive sentiment in men's hearts. Yet the danger is that the sentiment may be only aesthetic and shallow, and may not reflect the deeper consequences which the Incarnation has involved.

The part of the Gospel of Luke which is always associated with Christmas is the festival of the child Jesus. We may thank God that it is thus the festival of the Holy Child and that thereby all childhood has been made more significant and precious. But we err if we fail to carry our thoughts forward to the man into whom the child of Bethlehem should grow. We may detach the picture of the infancy and revel in it with a kind of pleasant satisfaction which can be an escape from the adult realities of religion. The second collect for Christmas Day in the Book of Common Prayer includes a longer and graver thought: "O God, who makest us glad with the yearly remembrance of the birth of thine only Son Jesus Christ; Grant that as we joyfully receive him for our Redeemer, so we may with sure confidence behold him when he shall come to be our Judge." The Incarnation does not speak of small things or sweet things only. It points forward to something which is noble because of the sternness in it. The child who was born in Bethlehem would grow up into the man whose spiritual mission was not to send peace but a sword. To Israel and to all people he would bring a judgment, according to which men would fall or rise.

Anybody who had happened along the streets of Bethlehem might have looked good-naturedly at the baby lying in Mary's arms, but by no means everybody would have looked good-naturedly at the Son of man who afterward went out from Nazareth. He came, as he himself said, to set men at variance one with another. He came with that great cleavage which a shining moral and spiritual force must always make in human life. Some men loved him with the utmost of their devotion and followed him to their death; but other men hated him. They were persuaded that there was nothing which their world needed so much as to have him die. To some of the people in his nation who were ordinarily accounted the best men the nation had—to eminent citizens, to leading men of affairs, to the authoritative men of the church and state—the man Jesus came to seem intolerable. He offended their prejudices; he challenged their conventions; he set up standards of right and wrong which blasted their respectability. He outraged them because they felt that he was always ignoring the best people and championing the common crowd. Doubtless there were not many people in Palestine who, like Herod, would have killed the child. Caiaphas and Annas and Pilate very probably would not have done so. If we could conceive that in their day somebody had invented a kind of Christmas, a pleasant, cheerful Christmas unrelated to any drastic issues of their life, they might have entered into it good-humoredly enough. But the man Jesus was another matter. They had no compunctions about killing him. He antagonized the interests which they were determined to defend. He set up principles for life which every stubborn instinct in them re-is set for the fall and rising again of many in Israel; and for a sign which shall be spoken against;

35 (Yea, a sword shall pierce through thy own soul also;) that the thoughts of many hearts may be revealed.

"Behold, this child is set for the fall
and rising of many in Israel,
and for a sign that is spoken against
35 (and a sword will pierce through your
own soul also),
that thoughts out of many hearts may
be revealed."

"them" in an earlier form of Simeon's prophecy and then introduced the prediction of Mary's grief at the tragic fate of her son. Mark fails to mention Joseph when he enumerates members of Jesus' family (Mark 6:3), and Matthew and Luke make no reference to him in the body of their Gospels. If it is legitimate to infer from this that Joseph died before the beginning of Jesus' public ministry, one can account for the hypothetical changes in vss. 34-35. Only Mary was to witness the fulfillment of Simeon's words, and she herself was to suffer bitterly in the course of it. But this is to support one hypothesis by another, and it must be admitted that even the rest of the prophecy suggests reflection after the event. God has ordained **this child** to separate the righteous from the unrighteous

---

jected. So in all succeeding times, if men honestly mean to be Christians, they cannot stop with the sentiment of Christmas. The question which must be answered is whether in actual fact we are glad or sorry that there came once into our world, and that there comes into the midst of our conscience, the influence which was and is the full grown Jesus. He comes not only with the child's appeal, but with the everlasting man's authority: to force us to decisions which must be very difficult, to compel us to review and reshape the values of our living, to renounce some of the things that pride or greed or lust of power clings to, and to accept instead the royal imperatives of his law of service. It is never easy to face the real implications of Christ. "But who may abide the day of his coming? and who shall stand when he appeareth?" (Mal. 3:2.) And as Jesus himself said, "When the Son of man comes, will he find faith on earth?" (18:8.)

If the answer to that question is to be "yes," then it will involve certain definite realizations for our here and now.

The judgments of Jesus by which men will fall or rise are not the judgments of the world. The world judges by numbers and mass and money. It wants to know of any life or of any situation whether the majority is on its side, whether the weight of opinion of the so-called "best people" is already with it, whether it commands financial support. The mind of the world often acts according to a kind of crowd contagion and may be very much afraid of individual differences, even for conscience' sake. But Christ everywhere and always would put the spiritual values above the material ones. He would maintain always and everywhere the sacred worth of human personality; and therefore any policy in business or economics or social relationships, or anything else which has become so obsessed with ideas and prejudices that it is relatively indifferent to the consequences of these on human lives, is a repudiation of the spirit of Christ. He came to bring redemption through love, and he lived and died in that supremely heroic faith—and as it seemed on Calvary, a forlorn faith. The Christian must try to hold that faith whatever happens, and the worst indictment against the church is that the world may not believe that it does. There are men who are officers in Christian churches, who yet in word and in act will be as violent and as ruthless as any non-Christian when they are dealing as employers with employees, or arguing as members of the privileged social class against some movement of the unprivileged that they fear and hate. The personal and social issues of our modern times are terribly complicated, and right and wrong are never altogether on one side. But in one respect every man who does not want to fall before the judgment of Jesus must be on one side. He must be on the one side of those who are trying as best they can to purify and discipline their own hearts, to keep themselves from being controlled by blinded selfishness, to follow as far and as fast as they can Christ's great belief that only in the effort to understand, to sympathize, and to treat all men as brothers in God's sight can human relationships at length be redeemed.

35. *The Profundities of Life.*—The Spanish writer, Miguel de Unamuno, in his book, *The Tragic Sense of Life in Man and in Peoples,*[1] has written, "May God deny you peace but give you glory." Here is a recognition that all real life will have its element of tragedy and that only through tragedy will fulfillment come.

[1] Tr. J. E. Crawford Flitch (New York: The Macmillan Co., 1921).

36 And there was one Anna, a prophetess, the daughter of Phanuel, of the tribe of Aser: she was of a great age, and had lived with a husband seven years from her virginity;

37 And she *was* a widow of about fourscore and four years, which departed not from the temple, but served *God* with fastings and prayers night and day.

36 And there was a prophetess, Anna, the daughter of Phan'u-el, of the tribe of Asher; she was of a great age, having lived with her husband seven years from her virginity,
37 and as a widow till she was eighty-four. She did not depart from the temple, worshiping with fasting and prayer

---

among **many in Israel.** Some are to reject him and fall (Isa. 8:14-15); others are to accept him and rise. He is to be **a sign** (cf. 11:30) that many will dispute. This is part of the purpose of God, for by their attitude to the Christ, men will reveal their true nature.

36-38. An aged **prophetess** also hailed the advent of God's Messiah. It is not certain from the Greek text whether we are to understand that she was **eighty-four** years of age or had been a **widow** for that length of time. A famous widow of Jewish apocryphal legend

---

In our English Bibles, in connection with the words which here (vs. 35) Luke ascribes to Simeon, there is a striking detail of punctuation. The KJV and the RSV—though curiously not the ASV—put into parenthesis the words **and a sword will pierce through your own soul also.** With this parenthesis the final words, **that thoughts out of many hearts may be revealed,** go back to what Simeon has said of Jesus, rather than being linked with what he is saying to Mary herself.

Yet both references express the truth. There was tragedy in the life of Jesus; and it is supremely through him who "came unto his own, and his own received him not," who was wounded for the world's transgressions, and who at last was crucified, that the deepest thoughts of men concerning the meaning and the ultimate glory of life have been revealed. But the life of Mary also had its tragic element, as the life of a mother so often does. Motherhood begins in pain, and for her it began also in poverty and loneliness. But the greater pain was that which was yet to come to her spirit as she saw her son go out at length into a life full of risk and danger that was moving on to a catastrophe which she could not prevent and could not wholly understand. Religious reverence looking at her has seen in Mary the symbol of vicarious suffering, and innumerable Christian souls passing through darkness of their own have been comforted by the thought that their experience was not strange but has been endured by the mother of the Lord himself. Often it is as "Our Lady of Sorrows" that she has been venerated most.

However that may be, the great truth is that it is only those who have suffered who can reveal the full meaning of life for other souls. The sword of affliction to a human heart may sometimes seem to be only disaster; but by strange paradox, the wound it makes may so enlarge that heart with sympathy and understanding that others in their need will turn to it for interpretation and inspiration. George Matheson, who was blind and had suffered other griefs, wrote this: "I cannot keep the song of the lark when I get the seal of sonship; I must enter into the pain of my Lord. Yet that pain is better than the world's joy. . . . Put the scar of sympathy in my heart! Let me feel my brother's thorn!" [2]

Cardinal Mercier, the hero of Belgium in World War I, dying of an agonizing illness, said:

> I leave my fate in God's hands, and only ask one thing of Him: to draw such glory as is possible from my humble person, at whatever price it may cost. . . . I thank the good Lord for having permitted me to follow Him, at least part of the way towards Calvary and to have suffered on the Cross. Suffering—that is the complete apostleship.[3]

So, in any place and in any century sorrow may be the redeeming sword of revelation. In the words of William R. Inge: "A generation which wishes for a religion without tears must find it difficult to adjust its beliefs to the teaching of the New Testament and to the facts of life." [4]

36-38. ***Receptive Spirits.***—Those **who were looking for the redemption of Jerusalem** were doubtless a minority. The majority of people, then as now, had their eyes on something very

[2] *The Representative Men of the Bible* (New York: A. C. Armstrong & Son, 1902), p. 172.

[3] John R. Gade, *The Life of Cardinal Mercier* (New York: Charles Scribner's Sons, 1934), pp. 279, 285.

[4] *Personal Religion and the Life of Devotion* (New York: Longmans, Green & Co., 1924), p. 88.

38 And she coming in that instant gave thanks likewise unto the Lord, and spake of him to all them that looked for redemption in Jerusalem.

39 And when they had performed all things according to the law of the Lord, they returned into Galilee, to their own city Nazareth.

night and day. 38 And coming up at that
very hour she gave thanks to God, and
spoke of him to all who were looking for
the redemption of Jerusalem.
39 And when they had performed every-
thing according to the law of the Lord,
they returned into Galilee, to their own

---

is said to have lived to the ripe age of 105 (Judith 16:23). Anna's piety is described in terms of popular hyperbole. **At that very hour** presumably means at the time that Simeon uttered his prediction. **Of him** obviously refers to the child Jesus. **The redemption of Jerusalem** is equivalent to "the consolation of Israel" (vs. 25)—i.e., the messianic age.

39-40. Having recorded the Jewish piety of Jesus' parents, Jesus' own unimpeachable origins within the folds of orthodox Judaism, and the prophetic anticipations of Jesus' role as Messiah, Luke's infancy cycle ends with the simple notice that Joseph and Mary returned to **Nazareth, to their own city.** There is nothing that indicates any familiarity with the events that are narrated in Matt. 2. A comment on Jesus' growth as a child is appended after the model of the note about John in 1:80. The Baptist was "in the wilderness." It is implied that Jesus lived as a normal child in the family circle. The Baptist grew "strong in spirit." Jesus was **filled with wisdom** and **the favor of God was upon him.**

---

different: on getting ahead with the day's business; on maintaining things as they were, so far as these were profitable; perhaps on getting rich; but anyhow, not consciously on redemption. Yet there were those whose great desire was on the plane of the spirit, humble and simple and quiet folk, men and women of prayer and of devotion. There always are such as these. Even in the worst times and in the worst circumstances, there are the seven thousand in Israel who have not bowed the knee to Baal. These are the ones and the only ones through whom God can proclaim a message about redemption (see Expos. on 3:15). It is only when people are in expectation that the seers and saints can convey their saving word.

39. ***The Obscure Environment.***—What was Nazareth? A humble town in the hills of Galilee, a little place of which it was asked contemptuously "Can anything good come out of Nazareth?" (John 1:46); a village made up of ordinary houses where dwelt a little handful of seemingly ordinary folk. Yet in Nazareth Jesus lived nearly all his life. In Nazareth he grew to that fullness of body, mind, and spirit which made him what he was. So God's spiritual miracles may happen in very quiet ways. The life of Jesus in Nazareth was to show that God's revelation can blossom in the midst of common life and his message be conveyed in experience fulfilling itself in the everyday relationships of the familiar place.

In short, Jesus revealed that no circumstances need be humdrum and that a heavenly light can always be found in the here and now. What are some of the manifest ways in which this was true for him?

First, he had a readiness to see and to mark all the innumerable facts of simple beauty which surrounded him. The objects which Jesus looked at were the same objects that any man could see, but in his regard they became different. He looked at lilies growing in the Galilean fields, at nesting birds, at flocks of sheep and the shepherds with them coming back at evening. He watched men sowing grain in the field, or the men working in the vineyards, or toiling in the fishing fleets on the lake. He stopped to listen to little children playing in the market place and to let them gather around him while he took some of them into his arms. Here was the common stuff out of which life and the world can be made anywhere and everywhere. But to Jesus it was never common. It was full of the suggestions of God—of the goodness of God in the miracle of the growing grain, of the wonder of God in the child's imagination, of the grace of God in the patience and courage of men about their daily work.

In the second place, he always found the best in people. He had a marvelous way of seeing the most undreamed of possibilities in ordinary human beings. He could see powers lying latent which no one else had ever surmised. He could see that a little group of untutored fishermen had in them energies which could turn a world upside down. Presently he would per-

40 And the child grew, and waxed strong in spirit, filled with wisdom; and the grace of God was upon him.

41 Now his parents went to Jerusalem every year at the feast of the passover.

city, Nazareth. 40 And the child grew and became strong, filled with wisdom; and the favor of God was upon him.

41 Now his parents went to Jerusalem every year at the feast of the Passover.

---

2. An Incident from Jesus' Boyhood (2:41-52)

The early church appears to have had no interest in the life of Jesus before his emergence as a teacher, and it preserved no tradition of his boyhood apart from this one incident. At a later date unfettered imagination undertook to make up the deficiency. Compilations of legends such as the Gospel of Thomas (see M. R. James, *The Apocryphal New Testament* [Oxford: Clarendon Press, 1924], pp. 49-70) gave marvelous and often grotesque and repulsive accounts of Jesus as an exhibitionist and as a boy wonder. The simplicity and restraint of Luke's story stand out in contrast. No doubt the story was originally independent of the nativity cycle. It refers without affectation to Jesus' parents (vss. 41, 43) and to his father (vs. 48). It betrays no knowledge of any supernatural portents that could account for Jesus' concern for "his Father's house." Luke uses it to illustrate Jesus' growth in wisdom and in the favor of God (vss. 40, 52) and to connect the birth and infancy cycle with the narratives of the baptism and the public ministry.

Josephus' egotistic description of his cleverness as a youth has been cited as a remote analogy in Jewish literature to Luke's story: "While still a mere boy, about fourteen years old, I won universal applause for my love of letters; insomuch that the chief priests and the leading men of the city used constantly to come to me for precise information on some particular in our ordinances" (*Life* 9). Erich Klostermann quotes a passage from an Egyptian source about a twelve year old grandson of Ramses II: "The boy grew and became strong. . . . He surpassed the scribe who had to instruct him. The boy . . . began to talk to the scribes in the school in [the temple of Ptah; all who heard him] were

---

ceive that in Mary Magdalene were the makings of a saint. When he looked at anyone, he was not looking at the surface which was all that other people saw. His intuition looked straight into that person's soul; and as his understanding shone there like sunlight shining on a garden, the roots of hidden desires and the secret seeds of half-ashamed goodness began to quiver, and presently out of the soil of that man's or woman's heart new graces began to grow. The woman of Samaria would say, "Come, see a man who told me all that I ever did" (John 4:29). That was the way he made her feel; but that was not all. It was not only that he made people think that he understood them so deeply as to be aware of everything they had done. He made them feel also that he understood what they ought to be, and more important, what they could be. When he stood by them, they felt that anything was possible.

In the third place, he showed that God can be found in every plain act of faithfulness which waits to be performed. Much of his life in Nazareth must have been made up of work in the carpenter shop and of the routine relationships of the little town. He would find God in the synagogue worship, as we definitely know that he did, and in his own communion with his Father. But these were not the only moments in which life was filled for him with a complete religious worth. When he put into his work the thoroughness which made it not only honest but complete; when in the midst of the neighbors of Nazareth he spoke, as every man may be called upon to speak, truth in the face of falsehood; when he championed some cause that was unpopular; when he defended someone who was weak against the cruelty of the strong —in those acts as surely as when he knelt in prayer he could be a shining witness of the spirit of God.

Some people never find God or know that they might find him because they suppose that God must be identified with some far-off and surprising thing. They do not walk the road that would lead to him through the simple process of taking the next clear step in spiritual obedience. It is not in imaginary flights that men will most surely find God. They will find him in the growing confidence that life is good which comes to those who are going steadily ahead in the direction of the next goodness that they know.

40-46. *Jesus and the Teachers.*—They found him in the temple, sitting among the teachers, listening to them and asking them questions.

42 And when he was twelve years old, they went up to Jerusalem after the custom of the feast.

43 And when they had fulfilled the days, as they returned, the child Jesus tarried behind in Jerusalem; and Joseph and his mother knew not *of it.*

44 But they, supposing him to have been in the company, went a day's journey; and they sought him among *their* kinsfolk and acquaintance.

45 And when they found him not, they turned back again to Jerusalem, seeking him.

46 And it came to pass, that after three days they found him in the temple, sitting in the midst of the doctors, both hearing them, and asking them questions.

47 And all that heard him were astonished at his understanding and answers.

42 And when he was twelve years old, they
went up according to custom; 43 and when
the feast was ended, as they were returning,
the boy Jesus stayed behind in Jerusalem.
His parents did not know it, 44 but sup-
posing him to be in the company they
went a day's journey, and they sought him
among their kinsfolk and acquaintances;
45 and when they did not find him, they
returned to Jerusalem, seeking him.
46 After three days they found him in the
temple, sitting among the teachers, listen-
ing to them and asking them questions;
47 and all who heard him were amazed at

much amazed" (*Das Lukas-Evangelium* [2d ed.; Tübingen, J. C. B. Mohr, 1929; "Handbuch zum Neuen Testament"], p. 45). It is true that the note of youthful precocity is frequently sounded in ancient biographical literature and was introduced in time into the Christian story. The apocryphal Gospel of Thomas represents Jesus as instructing the rabbis (ch. 19). Christian art has often portrayed the scene under the caption "The Boy Jesus Teaching in the Temple." But the stress in Luke's story is on Jesus' early interest in matters of religion. "Jesus Learning in the Temple" would be a better title. In the course of their instruction Jesus asks questions of the teachers, and answers those they propound.

41. Attendance at three annual festivals was prescribed for male Israelites by the regulations in Exod. 23:14-17; Deut. 16:16; etc. Women were not obliged to make the pilgrimage but frequently did so (I Sam. 1:7; 2:19).

42-45. Talmudic tradition asserts that even boys of tender years were required to make their appearance in the temple at festivals. **When he was twelve years old** indicates only that the incident took place after Jesus had attained his adolescence. It is not stated that it was the occasion of his first visit. **The feast** of the Passover and of Unleavened Bread occupied a period of seven days (see Exeg., 22:1). **The boy Jesus** had been allowed a measure of independence. As his parents began their return to Galilee, they "supposed he was in the caravan" (Moffatt) and looked for him only at the end of **a day's journey.**

46-47. After three days of search? Or does this number include the two days of travel referred to in the preceding verses? **In the temple:** in one of the halls of its outer courts. Rabbis taught by question, answer, and discussion. We are to understand that several were engaging on this occasion in debate.

The picture which these words present has sometimes been distorted. In Hofmann's well-known painting of the twelve-year-old Jesus in the temple the artist has portrayed the boy standing erect in the midst of the listening elders, as though he were authoritatively expounding the truth to them. What Luke suggests is simpler. He was **listening to them and asking them questions.**

In some of the apocryphal gospels the attempt was made to glorify Jesus, as it was supposed, by elaborate stories of precocious wisdom and of exhibitions, even as a child, of supernatural power. It was a right Christian judgment that never let those apocryphal writings get into the N.T. canon. The full picture of Jesus does not depend upon exaggerations. The boy of twelve did not go to Jerusalem with overbearing confidence to lay down the law. He went with the eagerness of an open mind

48 And when they saw him, they were
amazed: and his mother said unto him,
Son, why hast thou thus dealt with us?
behold, thy father and I have sought thee
sorrowing.
49 And he said unto them, How is it
that ye sought me? wist ye not that I must
be about my Father's business?
50 And they understood not the saying
which he spake unto them.
51 And he went down with them, and
came to Nazareth, and was subject unto
them: but his mother kept all these say-
ings in her heart.
52 And Jesus increased in wisdom and
stature, and in favor with God and man.

his understanding and his answers. 48 And
when they saw him they were astonished;
and his mother said to him, "Son, why
have you treated us so? Behold, your father
and I have been looking for you anxious-
ly." 49 And he said to them, "How is it
that you sought me? Did you not know that
I must be in my Father's house?" 50 And
they did not understand the saying which
he spoke to them. 51 And he went down
with them and came to Nazareth, and was
obedient to them; and his mother kept
all these things in her heart.
52 And Jesus increased in wisdom and
in stature,[i] and in favor with God and
man.

[i] Or *years.*

48-50. Jesus' parents **were astonished. His mother** expressed their anxiety by words of inquiry and rebuke that were greeted with surprise by the Christ child. Why should they not have known where to find him? **About my Father's business** cannot be dismissed as an impossible translation, but the RSV alternative **in my Father's house** is more appropriate after an implied interrogative of place. The early church believed that Jesus stood in a unique relationship to God, and that occasionally he made use of an address to the deity in which this was implied (see Exeg., 10:21-22). In an unobtrusive way this christological reflection has left its impress on Luke's story. In his first recorded utterance Jesus spoke of God as "my Father" in a sense that distinguished this relationship from one that was open to all, and his parents **did not understand the saying.**

51. Jesus' consciousness that he was the Son of God did not interfere in any way with his filial duties on the human level. **All these things** as in 1:65; 2:19.

52. Another concluding sentence after the fashion of 1:80 and 2:40, possibly modeled in this instance on I Sam. 2:26, "And the child Samuel grew on, and was in favour both with the LORD, and also with men."

---

and with simplicity of spirit. He realized later that there was much which these teachers of the law did not understand, but his first instinctive attitude was that of winsome respect for those who were believed to be interpreters of the truth of God. It was part of the very fact of the Incarnation that he should increase in wisdom, and this meant that in his boyhood years he had tuned himself to those influences from which he could learn. Undoubtedly he had gone to the synagogue school in Nazareth. He had brought from there the best gift which can be acquired: the desire to learn more. It was this desire that he was expressing in Jerusalem, as there among the teachers he was **listening to them and asking them questions.** It was a mark of his divine sonship that he could be so free from small complacency, so outreaching toward any truth by which his own conception of the purpose of his Father for him could grow.

40-52. ***The Attractiveness of Jesus.***—In vs. 40 it was said of Jesus that "the favor of God was upon him." That was the great and primary fact. The power and beauty of his life were due to the shining in him and through him of a light whose source was higher than this earth. But this vs. 52 adds another suggestion. Not only was the life of Jesus related radiantly to the Unseen; it was related also with a happy naturalness to human circumstances. He was not only **in favor with God;** he had a friendliness which won the responsive friendliness of people.

It is important to remember this when we attempt to shape our whole picture of what Jesus was. As his life moved on with its strong, sure purposes, he encountered in some quarters a bitter and, in the end, a deadly opposition. A little group of those who became implacably his enemies brought him finally to the Cross. But it would be a mistake to think that Jesus was separated from people generally by an antagonistic gulf. Exactly the contrary was true. He grew up in Nazareth in favor with

3 Now in the fifteenth year of the reign of Tiberius Caesar, Pontius Pilate being governor of Judea, and Herod being tetrarch of Galilee, and his brother Philip tetrarch of Iturea and of the region of Trachonitis, and Lysanias the tetrarch of Abilene,

3 In the fifteenth year of the reign of Ti-be′ri-us Caesar, Pontius Pilate being governor of Judea, and Herod being tetrarch of Galilee, and his brother Philip tetrarch of the region of It-u-rae′a and Trach-o-ni′tis, and Ly-sa′ni-as tetrarch of

III. Introduction to Jesus' Public Ministry (3:1–4:13)

A. John the Baptist (3:1-20)

1. John's Message (i). (3:1-6=Mark 1:2-5)

3:1-2*a*. Editorial. The beginning of John's ministry. Mark had regarded the mission and message of John the Baptizer as the "beginning of the gospel of Jesus Christ," and so also (it would appear) had the Q document. Luke shares the viewpoint of his sources. In accordance with Greek literary custom (Thucydides, Polybius, Josephus, etc.) and also with good O.T. precedent (Amos 1:1; Jer. 1:2; etc.), he synchronizes his story with the political and ecclesiastical history of its times. The death of Augustus Caesar had occurred on August 19, A.D. 14. **The fifteenth year of the reign of Tiberius Caesar** would therefore correspond to A.D. 28-29. As the only fixed date in gospel chronology, this is an

men. It was said of him later that "the common people heard him gladly" (Mark 12:37). He could fascinate men—rough men originally—and make them lay aside everything else and follow him. It was not a somber personality which thus won men's loyalty and affection, but one who had about him the quality of friendliness and cheer. There are deep aspects of Jesus' life at the end which have made him be called the "Man of Sorrows." But it is equally true that in an instinctive sense he was a man of joy. The Fourth Gospel depicts him at a wedding feast in Cana; he goes to another great feast to which Matthew the publican had invited all his friends; he sits at another banquet in the house of Simon the Pharisee. When his enemies wanted to slander him, they did it by exaggerating his zest for life, which all men knew. They said that he was "a man gluttonous, and a winebibber, a friend of publicans and sinners" (Matt. 11:19). From the point of view of their drab, conventional religion, they could not understand how one could be so debonair as Jesus seemed to be.

Many people since that time, both without and within the church, have made the mistake of the Pharisees. They have supposed that somehow there must be an incompatibility between religion and the bright enjoyment of this world. They have divorced it from poetry and turned it into dogmatic prose. They have divorced it even from beauty and made religion a thing of drab clothes and drab demeanor. They have turned it into a hard, inward discipline of spirit and have forgotten that all life ought to be baptized into a larger meaning if religion is to be true to the beauty of Christ. Worst of all, they have treated religion as though it had nothing necessarily to do with the everyday matter of keeping human contacts warm and lovely. Some persons of official standing in the church, both clerical and lay, have a kind of formal piety but are poison to live with, like Mr. Murdstone in *David Copperfield.* It has been rightly said that not much credit can be given to any man's religion whose very dog and cat are not the better for it. How much more, then, ought human beings, and especially all the near and dear circle of a home, to be the better for it? In the "intentions" drawn up by a group from the Society of Friends, who were shaping a rule of life which they would follow together, one commitment was "to share myself with my household (an hour daily in relaxed converse, such hours cumulative if I miss a day)." Such mindfulness of one's relationship with other persons and with the need to keep those relationships deep and true is fundamentally Christian. In Nazareth and elsewhere Jesus gave himself greatly to those he loved. Except for the minority who, because of their own perverted reasons, rejected him, he must have made all life seem brighter to those among whom he came. That is what it means to say that he was **in favor with . . . man.** Those who are to be his disciples must humbly but eagerly be trying to let his spirit be reflected in themselves.

3:1-2. ***The Shadow and the Substance of Power.***—Here is another dramatic juxtaposition of names (see Expos. on 2:1). Tiberius Caesar and John the son of Zechariah; Tiberius in the palace of the emperor at Rome, John the son of Zechariah in the wilderness. One man had imperial rank and power; beside him

2 Annas and Caiaphas being the high priests, the word of God came unto John the son of Zacharias in the wilderness.

Ab-i-le'ne, 2 in the high-priesthood of Annas and Ca'ia-phas, the word of God came to John the son of Zech-a-ri'ah in

important calculation of the beginning of John's ministry, even if it is Luke's rather than traditional in the church. **Judea**—together with Samaria and Idumaea—was administered as a subdivision of the province of Syria from the deposition and exile of Archelaus in A.D. 6 to the transfer of the territory to Agrippa I in A.D. 41. For this period it was ruled by a succession of Roman "procurators" of equestrian rank. **Governor** is a loose rendering of the title in the Gospels. **Pontius Pilate,** fifth in the series, held office from A.D. 26 to A.D. 36. **Galilee** (and Perea) had been entrusted after the death of Herod the Great in 4 B.C. to **Herod Antipas,** a younger full brother of Archelaus. Antipas had the title of **tetrarch** and remained in power until he was exiled to Gaul by Caligula in A.D. 39. **Philip,** a half brother, and according to Josephus the best of the Herods, ruled as **tetrarch,** until his death in A.D. 34, over various territories that comprised northeastern Palestine—among them **Ituraea and Trachonitis. Abilene** was the district centering about Abila, a town in the Lebanon, northeast of Mount Hermon. At one time it had formed part of the Roman puppet kingdom of Chalcis, and from 40 B.C. to 36 B.C. was ruled by a king named **Lysanias.** Later it was organized by itself as a tetrarchy. Various extrabiblical references (Josephus *Antiquities* XVIII. 6. 10; XIX. 5. 1; XX. 7. 1; *Jewish War* II. 11. 5; 12. 8; *Corpus Inscr. Graec.* No. 4521) lend plausibility to the hypothesis that another Lysanias with the title of **tetrarch** governed **Abilene** at some period in the first century of the Christian era before A.D. 37. If this is the case, Luke should not be charged with a historical anachronism, or accused of having misread Josephus (see Vol. IX, Intro. to Acts). **Annas** (Ananos) had been high priest from A.D. 6 to A.D. 15, and **Caiaphas,** his son-in-law, held office from A.D. 18 to A.D. 36. Jewish practice had been to appoint the high priest for life, but in Roman times his tenure of office was limited, perhaps because the Romans disliked to see so much power concentrated in the hands of one man. Does Luke mean only to suggest that **Annas** was the "power behind the throne" (cf. John 18:13)? As a matter of fact the office of high priest was held by members of Annas' immediate family for fifty years after his official retirement. On the other hand it is possible that the words **and Caiaphas** are a gloss by some early scribe who wished to bring Luke into harmony with Matthew. Neither Mark nor Luke mentions the name of the high priest in his passion account. Did Luke make the mistaken assumption that it was **Annas?** In Acts 4:6 he names **Annas** as holder of the office.

2*b*-4. Like the O.T. prophet Amos (3:8), John was compelled to prophesy because God had spoken. In the true sense of the Greek word "prophet," he was one who "spoke

the other one seemed obscure and unimportant. But the centuries have set the two men in a different perspective from the short and obvious estimate of their time. Tiberius is remembered only with the abstract interest of historians. John is linked with associations that will live as long as religion lives. The man whose greatness was that of conditions and circumstance fades, the man whose greatness was in character endures. The second man was a channel for something mightier than himself. **The word of God came to John . . . in the wilderness.**

Here was the essential secret of this man's power. Like the prophets of old and like the men of unique spiritual force in every generation, he believed that he had been called—called to be a spokesman not for his own small ideas but for the truth that is given from on high. John's mind and soul were no mere mirrors—which is all that many men's ever are—to reflect the moods and opinions of the time. He had lived for years in the solitudes of the desert, a lonely man, and yet not lonely, for he had companionship with eternal things. There in the open spaces he watched great stars blaze in the untroubled sky. There apart from the clamor of men he kept the vigil of his own meditation and his prayer. There, with no chatter of the crowd to listen to, he listened to the voice of God; and when he came to the Jordan Valley and began to preach at the verge of the river, where the stream of traffic went back and forth, it is no wonder that those who heard him were arrested. In this man's speech there was a

3 And he came into all the country about Jordan, preaching the baptism of repentance for the remission of sins;

the wilderness; 3 and he went into all the region about the Jordan, preaching a baptism of repentance for the forgiveness of

on behalf of" God. Presumably **in the wilderness** is a reference to the barren and sparsely settled lower Jordan Valley rather than to the rocky wasteland west of the Dead Sea. Mark (1:4-5) locates John's ministry as well as his call "in the wilderness." Luke alters his source to make the Baptist a peripatetic prophet in **all the region about the Jordan.** Luke 7:24 (Q) supports Mark. See Exeg., Mark 1:4, Vol. VII, for a discussion of **a baptism of repentance for the forgiveness of sins.** Luke also corrects Mark by omitting the quotation from Mal. 3:1. The LXX text of Isa. 40:3 is followed by both Mark and Luke—with minor variants. In the original prophecy "in the wilderness" is to be construed with "prepare." The prophet expected that the return of the Babylonian exiles to Palestine would be supernaturally facilitated. By connecting **in the wilderness** with **the voice,** and by changing "the paths of our God" of the LXX to **his paths,** the Synoptic Gospels make **Lord** mean "Messiah," and find biblical support for their interpretation of John as the herald and forerunner of the Christ.

note which they had never heard before. There were none of the quibbles and equivocations, none of the vagueness and uncertainty, which most men betray when they talk upon crucial themes. In what John said, there was no "If it so please you" or "If you will kindly listen"; no "I think so" or "It may be thus and thus." Instead, his message was as swift and straight as lightning. It had the blazing and shadowless intensity of the desert noonday sun. It was plain that here was a man whose whole soul was on fire with a flame that came from a source that is higher than this earth. He had gained his convictions not by piecing together little scraps of human shrewdness and probabilities; he gained those convictions from the direct communion of his soul with the reality of the living God. His was the inspiration which comes at rare intervals through the years to the great souls who have lived and meditated in a vast communion as though they belonged not to this world but to an unseen one. Before the eyes of John the show of things dissolved. He foresaw the awful destinies which God should judge; and to his sight the judgment was impending. Therefore when he spoke it seemed as though something more than one impassioned man was speaking. He did not say, "Thus saith John." He said, "Thus saith the Lord."

3. ***The Power of the Word.***—Consider the significance of that one word **preaching.** John the Baptist was a preacher, and that is all that he was. The baptism which he performed for those who were moved by what he said was the consequence of his preaching, and thus can be considered as bound up with it in one unity. Besides his preaching there is no record of anything that he did. His whole ministry was in the power of the spoken word.

Now and then someone arises with the shallow and weak suggestion that we need a moratorium on preaching. For the wrong kind of preaching—the preaching which is careless or halfhearted or conventional—we need not only a moratorium but a morgue. But to say that for preaching in its great full meaning there should be a moratorium is to express only the dull defeatism produced in those who have never discovered what preaching at its best can be. The power of the spoken word when the Spirit of God breathes in it is limitless. Remember John Wesley and George Whitefield bringing their vast awakening to multitudes of souls in eighteenth-century England. Remember what Dwight L. Moody did a century later to light new fires of consecration in many men and women, among whom was Sir Wilfred Grenfell. Remember what Phillips Brooks brought to Boston, and what other preachers later than he have given to their own communities. Consider also how, in the twentieth century, newspapers and books and particularly the radio have immeasurably extended the possible influence of the man who has something vital to say. Whether for good or for evil, the spoken word heard by the ears of listeners immediately present or transmitted in the press or over the radio has proved in the twentieth century to be a gigantic force in shaping the history of our earth. Remember, on the one hand, Hitler, on the other hand, Winston Churchill. If in the light of these facts any Christian preacher disparages his opportunity, it is only a sorry disparagement of himself. Never has there been a time when the pulpit and the word which goes out from it could represent a more thrilling opportunity for the man who may be a spokesman of the truth of God.

4 As it is written in the book of the words of Esaias the prophet, saying, The voice of one crying in the wilderness, Prepare ye the way of the Lord, make his paths straight.

5 Every valley shall be filled, and every mountain and hill shall be brought low; and the crooked shall be made straight, and the rough ways *shall be* made smooth;

6 And all flesh shall see the salvation of God.

sins. 4 As it is written in the book of the words of Isaiah the prophet,

"The voice of one crying in the wilderness:
Prepare the way of the Lord,
make his paths straight.
5 Every valley shall be filled,
and every mountain and hill shall be brought low,
and the crooked shall be made straight,
and the rough ways shall be made smooth;
6 and all flesh shall see the salvation of God."

5-6. Editorial. Luke's universalism prompts him to expand Mark's quotation to include the promise of Isa. 40:5 that **all flesh shall see the salvation of God.** The literal removal of physical obstacles had been anticipated by the original text. This is interpreted as a prediction of John's work of moral and spiritual preparation.

4-6. *The Maker of the Road for God.*—Here is a description of the servant of God which spans the ages. Isaiah expressed it long ago. It was caught up and applied to John the Baptist. It may well be lifted up as an ideal to be prayed for in every generation. The imagery is of the physical world; the meaning, of course, has to do with the spiritual world. In the course of history men have built all sorts of roads: roads of commerce, roads of conquest. But the one road supremely needing to be built is the way of the Lord, a highway along which his holiness and truth shall find their access to all areas of human life. The man who is concerned with that may often seem like the voice of John the Baptist **crying in the wilderness;** nevertheless, the voice of the great true man can always help to do what Isaiah prophesied. It can help to fill up the valleys of ignorance, to bring down the mountains and hills of stubborn prejudice and pride, to straighten men's crooked thinking, to smooth the rough ground of instinctive resistance which human nature interposes before the feet of God.

4. *The Great Inheritance.*—**As it is written.** Brief words, but in them there is a long suggestion. Into the present there comes the authority of the past.

John the Baptist seems, on the one hand, utterly independent. He would speak no shibboleths nor stereotyped traditions; he interpreted in living accents the living reality of an immediately communicated God. But on the other hand, and at the same time, there was in his preaching the authority of all that the great souls had proclaimed in earlier years. The hope and expectation of the past throbbed through what he had to say to his own present. His message, fresh and original as it was, was yet no mere overflowing of something that had its boundaries in himself. It was like the flooding of a spring fed by inexhaustible waters whose secret channels led from the deepest ground of the devotion of the far-off years.

There are two errors which men may make in relation to the heritage from the past. The first of these is that they may ignore it. In too many modern circles there is a debonair assumption that nothing matters except what is supposed to be new. The morality and religion which have come down through the centuries are waved aside as though they had no claim upon the up-to-date attention. Among some representatives of a restless generation acceptance of the newest notion may be a substitute for thinking. Said an observant professor with a gift for caustic phrase, "The trouble with our time is that we have the movie-mind and the jazz-emotion." With that mind the impulse is to turn impatiently away from the contemplation of anything which has the steadiness of history. The only thing that seems interesting is the latest suggestion that flickers on the screen.

The second error is that of those who do not ignore the past altogether but when they do turn back to the past, get bogged down in it instead of being inspired to go beyond it. This is what the human race used to be, says the man whose newly acquired smattering of biology and anthropology has begun to ferment in his mind; therefore, he concludes, with an unsteady flourish of supposed logic, that is what the human race *is.* It is controlled by animal in-

7 Then said he to the multitude that came forth to be baptized of him, O gen-

7 He said therefore to the multitudes

2. John's Message (ii). (3:7-9=Matt. 3:7-10)

7-9. Luke omits the Marcan description of the desert prophet's dress and fare, and elaborates his preaching of repentance and judgment. The **multitudes** that present themselves for baptism are a **brood of vipers.** Like snakes that flee before a fire, the penitents have become apprehensive of the judgment that is to close their age. But their merely formal **repentance** must issue in a new way of life that goes beyond perfunctory alms-

stincts. Man was a lustful, pugnacious, marauding savage at the beginning; and fundamentally that is what he is now. There is no use wasting time in sentimental ideals for human behavior. The best thing, say some who pretend to have the Freudian psychology for their sure warrant, is to recognize that human beings are going to express the same instincts with which the human race started out; and in order not to be restrained by inconvenient complexes, people should be taught that whenever there is something which they very much want to do, they may feel conveniently assured that the biological conscience is thereby indicating it as the very thing they ought to do. Remembrance of the evolutionary past becomes thus a warrant for never having to trouble to rise above it. If a man can say of some selfish and passionate instinct, "This was written into the constitution of human beings at the beginning," then he can take that **it is written** as the excuse why his life is habitually marked with it still. But it is evident that the message which comes to us from the figure of John the Baptist has no agreement with either of these two conceptions. He did not ignore the past; neither did he diligently search it for its most indulgent precedents. He took from it the power of its growing meaning. When it was said of his preaching that he fulfilled what had been written long before, the thing which had been written that he fulfilled was the long record of those noblest desires which are the expanding glory of the human soul.

As it is written. Yes, **it is written** in the long story of humanity that goodness has always been there—dim oftentimes and flickering like a feeble spark which the wind almost extinguishes, red sometimes with the smoke of mingled evil, yet undying and indomitable, passing at last with white flame into the torches of brighter souls. **It is written** that from the beginning there has been something in the heart of man that could respond to **Prepare ye the way of the Lord.** In all his long struggle has been written the instinct to fill up the valleys and bring low the mountains, that something better might find a plain path by which to enter in. Man's real life is not the thing he started from; it is the possibility he is moving toward. It is not the print of heavy feet down in the primeval clay; it is the lift of eyes toward the stars and the sun. **It is written** that man is made for the coming of Christ. **It is written** that all existence finds its meaning only as it becomes the road for the advent of the divine. That is the way John the Baptist read the past. That is the way the only true prophets of life for us must read the meaning of the past which culminates in our own day.

7-14. ***The Fearlessness of John.***—Because John had unqualified convictions, he was a man of uncalculating courage. He was no respecter of persons. He would preach to the average people and tell them the truth as he saw it, and he would not soften or change that truth when more formidable elements appeared in his congregation. He dealt with the Roman soldiers as directly as he dealt with anyone else. He asked no favors from and gave no odds to the taxgatherers and other rich and influential folk. When the scribes and Pharisees came out from Jerusalem, the ordinary crowd made room for these exalted persons; but they got no deference from John. On the contrary, he met them with a rebuke which must have amazed and halted them as completely as though he had struck them in the face. **O generation of vipers,** he said, **who hath warned you to flee from the wrath to come?** The Pharisees were outraged; but the multitude, when they had caught their breath, were undoubtedly delighted. From that time on, John became a hero in their eyes. He had this one supreme quality which all idols of the people must possess. Because he had no fear, all ordinary men felt themselves sheltered by him, and their own uncertain natures seemed to catch a new quality of courage from his contagion. They loved John for the enemies he dared to make. They began to think there was nothing he might not do because they saw that there was nothing of which he was afraid.

7-9. ***False Reliance.***—Luke here attributes to John the same devastating condemnation of racial and religious pride which is recorded by Matthew, and it may be that he recorded these

eration of vipers, who hath warned you to flee from the wrath to come?

8 Bring forth therefore fruits worthy of repentance, and begin not to say within yourselves, We have Abraham to *our* father: for I say unto you, That God is able of these stones to raise up children unto Abraham.

9 And now also the axe is laid unto the root of the trees: every tree therefore which bringeth not forth good fruit is hewn down, and cast into the fire.

10 And the people asked him, saying, What shall we do then?

that came out to be baptized by him, "You brood of vipers! Who warned you to flee
from the wrath to come? 8 Bear fruits that
befit repentance, and do not begin to say to yourselves, 'We have Abraham as our father'; for I tell you, God is able from these stones to raise up children to Abra-
ham. 9 Even now the ax is laid to the root
of the trees; every tree therefore that does not bear good fruit is cut down and thrown into the fire."

10 And the multitudes asked him, "What

giving, prayer, and fasting. They are not to be lulled by pride of race (cf. Rom. 2:17-29) into any false sense of security. In true prophetic fashion (cf. Amos, Jeremiah), John asserts that God would still be God even if those who claim **Abraham** as **father** should perish. In vigorous hyperbole he declares that God could **raise up children to Abraham** from the lifeless **stones** of the desert. Furthermore **the wrath to come** is not some distant threat. **Even now the ax is laid to the root of the trees.** Those whose conduct does not **befit** their pretensions face imminent judgment.

3. John's Message (iii). (3:10-14)

10-14. Moral precepts are now introduced, presumably from a source other than Q. **Coats** were tunics or undershirts. **Let him impart,** viz., "one." The Romans farmed out the right to collect various taxes in Palestine to petty Jewish contractors. The **tax collectors** of the Gospels were their deputies. They were heartily disliked and despised by their

words with even greater satisfaction than was true of the other evangelist. For the message of Luke's Gospel conspicuously breaks out beyond the bounds of old inherited complacency. Salvation does not belong of right to the Jew; it will belong to all those who shall be included in the outreaching mercy of God in Christ. That emphasis of Luke leads straight on to the emphasis of Paul. Nevertheless, the spirit of smug assurance which drew upon itself the shattering condemnation of John the Baptist has been by no means exorcised. In the ranks of every religion, and among the members of every Christian denomination, there are those who seem to think that their acceptance in the eyes of God is based upon ancestral title deeds. Has not the family always belonged to this particular church? Did not their father own a pew there? Does not their ecclesiastical status have its roots going back into richly respectable soil? And who are these strangers and nobodies that seem to be coming in nowadays to the church that once belonged to "the best people"? So the proud may ask. But time does not dull the edge of John the Baptist's words when he assailed men who fortified themselves by claiming Abraham as their father. In effect, he was saying, "Never mind telling me about your roots. What about your fruits?" "Even now the ax is laid to the root of the trees; every tree therefore that does not bear good fruit is cut down and thrown into the fire" (Matt. 3:10).

10-14. ***The Message of John.***—It is true that John's "ethical teaching . . . was by no means radical" (see Exeg.), i.e., his injunctions would not seem violent or unreasonable. They moved within the limits of what might be expected of not too extraordinary people. Nevertheless, they were important, and they were radical too in the sense of having to do with the plain and practical foundations of sound behavior on which all the higher spiritual superstructure must be built. There is often a danger that even people who think they are religious may forget this fact—forget that first of all they must be honest and considerate and kind. When these fundamentals are neglected, all efforts at spiritual development may be very unsubstantial and insecure. C. E. Montague, the British essayist, in a book written after World War I, spoke of the little French villages which had been so beaten and ground to powder by bombardment that the very bricks of them were dust that had to be mingled with

11 He answereth and saith unto them, He that hath two coats, let him impart to him that hath none; and he that hath meat, let him do likewise.

12 Then came also publicans to be baptized, and said unto him, Master, what shall we do?

13 And he said unto them, Exact no more than that which is appointed you.

14 And the soldiers likewise demanded of him, saying, And what shall we do? And he said unto them, Do violence to no man, neither accuse *any* falsely; and be content with your wages.

15 And as the people were in expectation, and all men mused in their hearts of John, whether he were the Christ, or not;

then shall we do?" 11 And he answered
them, "He who has two coats, let him
share with him who has none; and he who
has food, let him do likewise." 12 Tax col-
lectors also came to be baptized, and said
to him, "Teacher, what shall we do?"
13 And he said to them, "Collect no more
than is appointed you." 14 Soldiers also
asked him, "And we, what shall we do?"
And he said to them, "Rob no one by
violence or by false accusation, and be
content with your wages."
15 As the people were in expectation,
and all men questioned in their hearts
concerning John, whether perhaps he were

---

countrymen, partly because Roman taxes were regarded as an unwarranted imposition by a foreign overlord, and partly because the method of collecting the levies lent itself to extortion all down the line. Jews were not enrolled in Roman legions, but presumably native **soldiers** could be recruited by Herod Antipas for his own personal service. No doubt they were often able to supplement their **wages** by intimidating civilians.

If these are typical samples of John's ethical teaching, it was by no means radical. The well to do were urged to **share** their surplus of clothing and **food** and those whose profession offered temptations of unjust or dishonest enrichment were warned against the vice of avarice.

4. John's Message (iv). (3:15-17=Matt. 3:11-12)

The interesting interrelationships of Matthew, Mark (1:7-8), and Luke at this point are not easily explained. Did Mark draw his account of John's preaching from Q or has there been some harmonization of our texts by early copyists?

15. Editorial introduction to John's prophecy of the coming Messiah.

---

the clay and baked again. "To some such remaking of bricks, some shaping and hardening anew of the most elementary, plainest units of rightness in action, we have to get back." The elaborate plans for social and economic and international welfare depend upon the "humdrum decencies, patiently practised through millions of undistinguished lives. . . . And now, just when there seems to be such a babble as never before about those grandiose structures, bricks have run short."[5]

15. ***Conditions of Spiritual Awakening.***—**As the people were in expectation.** Those words are the prelude to great facts which are to follow. John the Baptist had been preaching to the crowds who came to hear him. He had given his message not only of repentance but of hope. A power mightier than any of his own was presently coming. His business was to "prepare the way of the Lord." He himself had done his best, but he could not achieve his purpose unless the people responded. Their hearts had to be stirred. They needed to be expectant if God's salvation was actually to appear.

Always that kind of expectancy is essential if God's spirit is to be poured out and received. Here is something for all Christians, and especially for all the Christian laity, to remember: the greatest preaching cannot prevail unless the minds and hearts of people reach out with welcome toward whatever it brings of truth. Carlyle in *Heroes and Hero-Worship* laid his powerful emphasis upon the fact that revelation may depend first upon the great individual. His flaming personality is like the lightning that brings down the fire from heaven. But that is not the whole truth. Such fire will be a single flash, and will kindle nothing unless those to whom it comes have brought on their part the fuel of some great desire that waits to

[5] *Disenchantment* (New York: Brentano's, 1922), p. 259.

16 John answered, saying unto *them* all,
I indeed baptize you with water; but one
mightier than I cometh, the latchet of
whose shoes I am not worthy to unloose: he
shall baptize you with the Holy Ghost and
with fire:
17 Whose fan *is* in his hand, and he will
thoroughly purge his floor, and will gather
the wheat into his garner; but the chaff
he will burn with fire unquenchable.

the Christ, 16 John answered them all, "I
baptize you with water; but he who is
mightier than I is coming, the thong of
whose sandals I am not worthy to untie;
he will baptize you with the Holy Spirit
and with fire. 17 His winnowing fork is in
his hand, to clear his threshing floor, and
to gather the wheat into his granary, but
the chaff he will burn with unquenchable
fire."

16-17. John vitalized the Jewish messianic hope by announcing the **coming** of one **who is mightier,** one for whom he himself was **not worthy** to perform even the menial service of a slave. He thought of the Messiah's mission in terms of conventional Jewish imagery. As a farmer takes a **winnowing fork,** separates **the wheat** from **the chaff** by throwing the trodden grain against the wind, stores **the wheat in his granary,** and burns **the chaff,** so the Messiah would separate the evil from the good. John contrasts his own baptism **with water** and the Messiah's baptism **with fire,** i.e., the **unquenchable fire** of the Day of Judgment that would purge the body of God's people and consume the sinners. Was the phrase **with the Holy Spirit and** added to John's original message at some early date to do justice to Christian experience?

---

be set ablaze in their own minds and hearts. How much do we want God? What great expectancy are we cherishing? On the answer to those questions will depend whether or not even such a great voice as that of John the Baptist can lead people to be ready for Christ.

16. ***The One Greater than John.*—He who is mightier than I is coming.** We cannot surely know the meaning of John in such words as these. He may have been thinking in terms of the eruption of some dramatic power, expecting the coming of an apocalyptic figure clothed with the terrible might of God. When he said that one mightier than he was coming, he proclaimed what did come true, but in a way very different from what he probably expected. The kingdom which Jesus established would be a mightier fact than any influence John himself had set in motion.

In what way was this true? In the first place, the way and work of Jesus were greater than John's in that he gave men a motive and a power to achieve the obligations to which he called them. John had thought he could frighten men into salvation. Jesus fascinated them into following him, and as they followed him they saw revealed the meaning of life as God would have it be. He showed them the pattern of God's larger purpose for each man's soul. He made it plain that God's most direct relationship to them was not so much with reference to their sins, but with reference to their better selves. What therefore was good in them God had put there, and the love of God was reaching out to awake that goodness to such a passion of high desire that it could overcome all that was mean and evil in their souls. That was the new emotion, a heart-warming and heart-changing emotion, by which men were to be led toward goodness.

Secondly, Jesus offered to men a fellowship. John had treated men as individuals only, but Jesus knew that goodness and salvation were not merely individual but social. He said, "Fear not, little flock, for it is your Father's good pleasure to give you the kingdom" (12:32). He did not say, "Fear not, you unrelated individuals, for to you shall be given the kingdom." He taught men how to live together so that out of their experience the spirit of the kingdom might emerge. The world has been a long time learning the necessity of those redeeming relationships without which, as Jesus so well knew, the kingdom of God's grace will never be realized upon this earth. We have caught a glimpse of the reality in that most beautiful of human achievements, the genuinely Christian home. We have heard that same reality preached and to some degree have experienced it in the fellowship of the church. But often the relationships which are truly Christian have stopped at the door which leads from the home and the church into the street. Our money-making and our business and the prevailing character of our economic life have been largely pagan and not Christian. We have attempted the impossible task of pretending that we were continuing to be Christians while we adapted ourselves every day to conditions and to motives which are the antithesis

18 And many other things in his exhortation preached he unto the people.
19 But Herod the tetrarch, being reproved by him for Herodias his brother Philip's wife, and for all the evils which Herod had done,
20 Added yet this above all, that he shut up John in prison.

18 So, with many other exhortations, he
preached good news to the people. 19 But
Herod the tetrarch, who had been reproved
by him for He-ro′di-as, his brother's wife,
and for all the evil things that Herod
had done, 20 added this to them all, that
he shut up John in prison.

---

5. Summary of John's Message and an Account of Herod and John (3:18-20)

18-20. Editorial. God's gift of Christ to mankind was the content of the early Christian gospel. Because John had proclaimed the Messiah's coming, Luke can say **he preached good news to the people** (the KJV does not do justice to the verb εὐηγγελίζετο). There is no version here or later of Mark's narrative of John's execution (Mark 6:19-29), although Luke 9:9 (Mark 6:16) assumes that the readers of the Gospel are familiar with it. **Herod** Antipas had married **Herodias** after divorcing a daughter of the Nabataean king Aretas (Josephus *Antiquities* XVIII. 5. 1). Mark had erroneously identified Herodias' first husband with Philip, who was her son-in-law. Her former marriage had been with an older half brother of Herod, also known as Herod. If Luke knew the complicated Herodian family tree, his reading **his brother's wife** (the KJV is based on late MSS that have harmonized Luke with Matthew and Mark at this point) is a deliberate correction. Mark appears to assume that **Herod . . . shut up John in prison** at Tiberias. Josephus declares that the site of the Baptist's imprisonment as well as of his execution was Machaerus, a fortress in Perea to the east of the Dead Sea.

---

of the spirit of Christ. But existence cannot be divided; and if our souls are to be saved in unity and peace, the spirit of those who are "in Christ" must reach out to leaven all human relationships everywhere.

Again, the vision of Jesus was more profound than that of John because he saw that great results will not come suddenly. John thought that the kingdom might be achieved by some catastrophic act of God. Jesus knew that it must be built by the grace of God through those who are willing to live, to work, to suffer, and if need be, to die for the Father's purposes. We are always being tempted to the hasty hopes of John. Men have supposed in their religious life that some great revival will make all things new and that the church will be permanently better afterward; but often the hoped for result does not come. Men think also that some whirlwind of reform in political conditions will accomplish the desired results. Throw out the rascals, defeat the corruptionists, send a few notorious evildoers to prison, and all will be well. But all is not well. The evil spirit, if he is merely driven out by some spasmodic effort, will be back again in a few years with seven other spirits worse than himself. The process of redemption always must be patient and gradual. It must be wrought out through men and women who do not suppose that a single stroke will decide the battles which are waged on the arena of this world's right and wrong. The way of the coming of the kingdom of God may involve many disappointments, many victories which may be only partial, and temporary defeats which must be endured; and it will require a kind of consecration which is willing, as Jesus was, to face crosses and go past these into life.

18-20. ***The Recalcitrant Conscience.***—Herod could put John in prison, but in the ultimate he could not keep him there. The moral truth which John spoke broke through all prison walls to deal decisively with Herod and men like him, then and now. The trouble with the Herod type of man is that he cannot bring himself to face an unwelcome fact. He may fight against it with a kind of frustrated fury, as Pharaoh fought against the demands of Moses. He may shrink before it with hostility that nevertheless has fear at its heart, as Ahab shrank before Elijah. He may respond with loud contempt, as Amaziah the priest of Bethel tried to make answer to the prophet Amos. He may listen cynically yet uneasily, as Festus listened to the apostle Paul. But in every case this type of man tries to silence and shut out of his conscious world the truth he does not want to hear. Only the rare spirit is big enough to accept rebuke and to profit by it. The ability to do so was one of the saving aspects of the

21 Now when all the people were baptized, it came to pass, that Jesus also

21 Now when all the people were bap-

B. Prelude to Jesus' Public Ministry (3:21–4:13)

1. Jesus' Baptism (3:21-22=Mark 1:9-11)

21-22. In his rephrasing of Mark, Luke fails to note specifically that Jesus was **baptized** by John, but there is little reason to conclude from this that he was troubled by the tradition. Matthew felt he had to explain it (Matt. 3:14-15), and John omitted it altogether. Luke's interest in Jesus' prayer life (see Intro., p. 8) may have been responsible for the introduction of the words **and was praying,** but they also served to accommodate Jesus' example to the rite as it was practiced in the later church. The gift of **the Holy** (the adjective is Luke's addition) **Spirit** does not automatically follow upon baptism, but is associated with the act of prayer—in Acts 8:15-17 with prayer and "the

character of David (see II Sam. 12:1-14). That perhaps was one of the decisive reasons why David could be thought of as a man after God's own heart (I Sam. 13:14).

21-22. ***The Baptism of Jesus.***—Luke has heightened here the description of the baptism as compared with the way the scene is described by Mark and by Matthew (see Exeg.). In the picture as Luke draws it the Holy Spirit would seem to have come in a hovering symbol which the whole multitude could see. In Mark and Matthew there is not this effort to dramatize the spiritual fact with a miraculous sign. The profound meaning of the baptism lies in a realm deeper than that. It was Jesus himself, and not the crowd, who was conscious of the descent of the Spirit. It was in Jesus' consciousness that the baptism had its supreme significance.

Why was he baptized? Middleton Murry[6] makes the blunt answer that Jesus, like every other human being, had been conscious of sin, and therefore as a sinner he came to John for baptism. But this runs counter to the whole N.T. tradition. The sole conception of Jesus which emerges in the early church is of one who, although tempted in all points like other human beings, was altogether without sin. If that is so, then why the baptism? There are various strands that weave together to make a full answer. Jesus had heard of the work of John and of the moral awakening which it was producing. In the selflessness which was always his, he may have wanted first of all just to bring his own comradeship to the side of John. It may be also that the expectation which John's message had aroused among the people was to him like a signal that the time had come for him to enter upon the mission which through long years in Nazareth he had been meditating. Even if all his life up to that hour was sinless, there was still a possibility of a subtle sin: the sin of shrinking from what might lie ahead, the conceivable sin of the lower rather than the higher choice. He would be baptized, therefore, not for repentance, but for the utter consecration of being completely ready. And in the third place, one remembers that Jesus never thought of himself in isolation. He identified himself in utter sympathy with his nation's needs. He was a son of Israel, and all that belonged to his people in heritage as well as in hope he took upon himself. Vicariously, therefore, he would be baptized into their need for repentance, and with them and for them express the urgency of commitment to the kingdom of God.

21. ***Jesus Praying.***—We remember that Jesus taught others to pray. We remember that he gave to the disciples the immortal words of the Lord's Prayer. We are sure that he would wish us to pray. But all this may represent a rather remote relationship. If he is simply the teacher to us of a spiritual duty, we should not feel in that a very intimate relationship with him. But the fact is far more near and living than that. Jesus himself prayed. Here is not a solitary reference, but the first of many references in this Gospel to Jesus' **praying.** He felt the same need and he sought the same strength which we experience. He is not a mentor standing at a distance and telling us what to do. He is the great pioneer of souls that would draw close to the infinite riches of God. That is the everlasting kinship which his humanness has with us.

It is not to be suggested, of course, that this is all there is of the personality of Jesus. In the mystery of his soul and of that soul's origin there are relationships with God the Father too vast and wonderful for us to fathom. Paul said in his matchless phrase, "God was in Christ reconciling the world unto himself" (II Cor. 5:19). The Nicene Creed proclaims that Jesus was "God of God, Light of Light, Very God

[6] *Jesus, Man of Genius* (New York: Harper & Bros., 1926).

being baptized, and praying, the heaven was opened,

tized, and when Jesus also had been baptized and was praying, the heaven was

laying on of hands" (cf. Hippolytus *Church Order* 46; Tertullian *On Baptism* 7-8). In Mark it is possible to interpret the baptismal experience as one personal to Jesus himself ("he saw the heavens opened"), but in Luke it is externalized (**the heaven was opened**). Furthermore the descent of **the Holy Spirit** becomes a miracle—**in bodily form.** In early rabbinical literature the sound of **a voice . . . from heaven** (*bath qôl,* an "echo" of the voice of God) is likened to the cooing of **a dove,** and Luke may have been employing familiar symbolism in his simile. The evangelist accepts the view that Jesus was Messiah from the moment of his miraculous conception, but the earlier christological

of very God, Begotten, not made, Being of one substance with the Father." All this is not to be forgotten. But the very meaning of the Incarnation is that, whatever else we say about the divine mystery of God in Christ, we must also say in those other great words of the N.T. that he humbled himself, "being born in the likeness of men" (Phil. 2:7), and was "in every respect . . . tempted as we are" (Heb. 4:15); i.e., Jesus reveals to us the divine possibilities in human life, not under conditions different from ours, but by walking exactly on our pathway and holding out his hand always for us to come with him. When he says to us, "Pray," he says it only because he can say to us at the same time, "I prayed. I knew the need of it and I know what it can do."

What was it that Jesus sought in prayer? Certainly, first of all, companionship with his Father. Above and beyond all human companionship he knew that only God could know and meet the utmost reaches of his soul. If out of our conjecture we may know anything about his praying, then certainly we may know this: that when he prayed, he was not asking, first of all, for any specific thing. He was not trying to use God—as so much of our poor blundering prayer may try to use him—as a source of favors. He did not supremely want God's gifts, even the greatest gifts. He wanted God. He wanted to feel again and again the immense expansion of his own soul which came in those moments when he knew that he was utterly in communion with his Father. In the Gospel of John there is one tremendous verse in which the truth comes as from Jesus' lips, "I and the father are one" (John 10:30). No others have ever reached high enough to dare say that. But Jesus said it and in those words is the mystic center of his praying. He was conscious then that he was not alone and could never be alone; no matter how much his human companions might fail him, there was a Companion that would never fail. There was a knowledge that understood him to the utmost, a purpose that undergirded him and overarched him, a love that went with him all the way. So for all his followers this must be the first meaning of prayer—to seek not for some emergency favor which God might grant, but rather for God himself, and to be still until we learn that at the heart of things there is One upon whom we may unfailingly rely.

The second thing which we may believe that Jesus sought in prayer was illumination. He prayed not only that he might feel God, but that he might see more clearly where the ways of God would lead. In prayer his soul climbed up above the dust and confusion of the world into that serene atmosphere of a heavenly purity in which all things were seen in God's perspective. Among those who learn from him there are always men and women whose purity of heart gives them in some degree at least this same luminousness of understanding. They may not be among the persons best educated; they may not be among those who can describe in learned words what they believe about the ways of God. But because of their prayers they know with a kind of blessed instinct where those ways lead. They have a sense of right and wrong which does not play them false.

Finally, the third thing which we may believe that Jesus sought through prayer was power. Certainly he gained it. Wherever he went, he radiated power. Men knew instinctively that he was equal to any occasion. They knew that no obstruction, either of human will or fateful circumstance, could ever be strong enough to dismay him. It is true that in this tragic earth, shot through with the consequences of human sin, not even he, God's greatest son, could achieve everything he aimed at. He had taken our humanity upon him, and human life does not always end in victory. In overwhelming outer aspects his life seemed to be defeated. Gethsemane looked like defeat. The Cross looked like defeat. Yet anyone who considers the ultimate miracle of Jesus' life knows that he himself was victorious. Even in the most apparent disaster his soul moved on, high, poised, unshaken, toward the fulfillment and triumph

22 And the Holy Ghost descended in a bodily shape like a dove upon him, and a voice came from heaven, which said, Thou art my beloved Son; in thee I am well pleased.

23 And Jesus himself began to be about thirty years of age, being (as was supposed) the son of Joseph, which was *the son* of Heli,

opened, 22 and the Holy Spirit descended upon him in bodily form, as a dove, and a voice came from heaven, "Thou art my beloved Son;[j] with thee I am well pleased."[k]

23 Jesus, when he began his ministry, was about thirty years of age, being the son (as was supposed) of Joseph, the son

[j] Or *my Son, my* (or *the*) *Beloved.*
[k] Other ancient authorities read *today I have begotten thee.*

---

interpretation of the baptism as the time when he became God's Son is still apparent in the words of the heavenly voice that are quoted from Mark. A strong case can be made for Goodspeed's translation: "You are my Son, my Beloved! You are my Chosen!" i.e., Jesus is addressed as Messiah under three synonyms. Codex Bezae and some of its allies make this "adoptionist" Christology more explicit by substituting the words of Ps. 2:7: "Thou art my Son; today have I begotten thee" (cf. RSV mg.).

2. Jesus' Genealogy (3:23-38)

23-38. When he began his ministry renders a Greek participle (ἀρχόμενος) that troubled even the earliest interpreters, and the exact meaning of which in this context still remains obscure. By his use of the qualifying **about,** Luke emphasizes that his estimate

---

of his life. Richard C. Trench in his sonnet that begins

> Lord, what a change within us one short hour
> Spent in Thy presence will prevail to make,

has expressed the truth that power can come to all Christians who learn their Lord's meaning of prayer. And a brave Englishman of the nineteenth century, Henry M. Stanley, wrote in his journal, "You may know when prayer is answered, by that glow of content which fills one who has flung his cause before God, as he rises to his feet." [7]

23. *The Man Sometimes Forgotten.*—**Jesus, . . . being the son (as was supposed) of Joseph.** The question of the Virgin Birth implied here in the parenthetical words has already been considered (see Expos. on 1:34). Whatever may be one's conclusion about that, there is the fact that Joseph stood in the relationship of a father to Jesus as he grew up in Nazareth, and in the providence of God that relationship may have had profound significance.

After the story of the journey to Jerusalem when Jesus was twelve years old, Joseph does not again appear. The assumption is that he had died before Jesus was grown, and that on the shoulders of Jesus thus there fell the chief responsibility for the family. He who had previously been thought of as the carpenter's son was now the carpenter. In the house and in the shop the headship had to be his.

But what of the earlier years when the older man was there? Certainly the likelihood is that the foundations for much of Jesus' later life were being laid then, and that Joseph had a deep share in what was happening. In Jewish family life the relationship between a father and a son was traditionally very close. There was not only the natural affection of the flesh; there was also the bond of a shared religion. It was the duty of the father to make sure that his son should understand his spiritual inheritance in Israel. Of course it was possible for this to become a perfunctory matter. It might be the passing on of words and forms, and little more. But on the other hand, it could be vastly more than that. It could be the building of the bridge by which a boy passed over from a sensitive and unsure childhood to a manhood that should walk on a sure way. And this was what the influence of Joseph apparently did mean to Jesus. Here was a boy of infinite capacity for joy or for sufferng, and here was a man who loved him. A boy is not much helped toward faith in God by words his father may repeat, but his whole faith may be begun and undergirded by what his father is. Great convictions are not built out of abstract ideas; they grow out of the deep experiences of the heart. When Jesus went out at length from Nazareth to

[7] *The Autobiography of Henry M. Stanley*, ed. Dorothy Stanley (Boston: Houghton Mifflin Company, 1909), p. 519.

24 Which was *the son* of Matthat, which
was *the son* of Levi, which was *the son*
of Melchi, which was *the son* of Janna,
which was *the son* of Joseph,
25 Which was *the son* of Mattathias,
which was *the son* of Amos, which was *the*
son of Naum, which was *the son* of Esli,
which was *the son* of Nagge,
26 Which was *the son* of Maath, which
was *the son* of Mattathias, which was *the*
son of Semei, which was *the son* of Joseph,
which was *the son* of Juda,
27 Which was *the son* of Joanna, which
was *the son* of Rhesa, which was *the son*
of Zorobabel, which was *the son* of Sala-
thiel, which was *the son* of Neri,
28 Which was *the son* of Melchi, which
was *the son* of Addi, which was *the son*
of Cosam, which was *the son* of Elmodam,
which was *the son* of Er,
29 Which was *the son* of Jose, which
was *the son* of Eliezer, which was *the son*
of Jorim, which was *the son* of Matthat,
which was *the son* of Levi,

of He′li, 24 the son of Matthat, the son of
Levi, the son of Mel′chi, the son of Jan′-
na-i, the son of Joseph, 25 the son of Mat-
ta-thi′as, the son of Amos, the son of
Na′hum, the son of Es′li, the son of Nag′-
ga-i, 26 the son of Ma′ath, the son of Mat-
ta-thi′as, the son of Sem′e-in, the son of
Jo′sech, the son of Joda, 27 the son of Jo-
an′an, the son of Rhesa, the son of Ze-rub′-
ba-bel, the son of She-al′ti-el,[l] the son of
Ne′ri, 28 the son of Mel′chi, the son of
Addi, the son of Cosam, the son of El-ma′-
dam, the son of Er, 29 the son of Jesus, the
son of E-li-e′zer, the son of Jorim, the son

[l] Greek *Salathiel.*

of **thirty years of age** is not to be taken too strictly. The sixth-century Roman monk Dionysius Exiguus apparently used this passage (in conjunction with 3:1) as a point of departure when, in preparing a calendar for the Roman church based on *anno Domini* rather than on *anno urbis conditae,* he calculated that Jesus had been born in the year 753 of the founding of the city of Rome. Other equations could have been reached had he started from the data in the first chapter—where it is assumed that both John the Baptist and Jesus were born before the death of Herod the Great, i.e., before 4 B.C. (cf. Matt. 2:1)—from 2:1-7, or from John 8:57—where it is implied that Jesus was nearer fifty than thirty at the height of his public ministry. That the genealogy cannot be harmonized with Matthew's was apparent to the scribe responsible for the text of Codex Bezae, who simply incorporated Matthew's list of names (in Luke's order) at this point. Early in the third century (see the letter of Julius Africanus to Aristides as quoted by Eusebius *Church History* I. 7) the theory was current that Matthew's genealogy symbolized Christ's royalty, and Luke's his priesthood. Some of the more notable variations are: fifty-six names to **Abraham** instead of forty-two; **Heli** (vs. 23) instead of "Jacob" as

preach and teach and heal, he had one great word for God. That word was Father. Every reference that he made to fatherhood was as though to something so beautiful that it needed no argument or elaboration. "Your Father knoweth"; "How much more shall your Father give." He would not instinctively have spoken so unless a human father's understanding had first interpreted for him the fatherhood of God. Joseph perhaps died early, but in a larger sense he did not die. That quiet, unassuming man may have gone on to the end in the heart of the incomparable son. Because of a faith in the unseen love that Joseph had helped to make him sure of, Jesus could teach his disciples to pray "Our Father" and in the last hour on the Cross could say, "Father, into thy hands I commend my spirit."

23-38. ***The Lineage of Jesus.***—Probably it would be safe to say that Jesus never spent time contemplating his family tree. But there are definite reasons (see Exeg.) why Matthew and Luke worked out and framed the genealogies which they related to him. The details of these cannot be taken too seriously, which is obvious since they do not wholly agree. Nevertheless,

30 Which was *the son* of Simeon, which
was *the son* of Juda, which was *the son*
of Joseph, which was *the son* of Jonan,
which was *the son* of Eliakim,

31 Which was *the son* of Melea, which
was *the son* of Menan, which was *the son*
of Mattatha, which was *the son* of Nathan,
which was *the son* of David,

32 Which was *the son* of Jesse, which
was *the son* of Obed, which was *the son* of
Booz, which was *the son* of Salmon, which
was *the son* of Naasson,

33 Which was *the son* of Aminadab,
which was *the son* of Aram, which was *the
son* of Esrom, which was *the son* of Phares,
which was *the son* of Juda,

34 Which was *the son* of Jacob, which
was *the son* of Isaac, which was *the son* of
Abraham, which was *the son* of Thara,
which was *the son* of Nachor,

of Matthat, the son of Levi, **30** the son of
Symeon, the son of Judas, the son of
Joseph, the son of Jonam, the son of E-li'a-
kim, **31** the son of Me'le-a, the son of
Men'na, the son of Mat'ta-tha, the son of
Nathan, the son of David, **32** the son of
Jesse, the son of O'bed, the son of Bo'az,
the son of Sala, the son of Nah'shon, **33** the
son of Am-min'a-dab, the son of Admin,
the son of Ar'ni, the son of Hez'ron, the
son of Pe'rez, the son of Judah, **34** the son of
Jacob, the son of Isaac, the son of Abra-
ham, the son of Te'rah, the son of Na'hor,

Jesus' grandfather; seven different immediate ancestors of **Zerubbabel** (vss. 26-27); **Neri** instead of "Jechoniah" as the father of **Shealtiel** (vs. 27); and Jesus' descent traced through **Nathan** (vs. 31) instead of "Solomon." It is also noteworthy that Luke carries Jesus' lineage back from **Abraham**, the father of the Jewish nation, to **Adam**, the father of the human race. Was this extension made by Luke himself to stress the universalism of Jesus as Christ? (See Intro., p. 7.) **Cainan** (vs. 36) is derived from the LXX rather than the M.T. of Gen. 10:24. Both Luke's genealogy and Matthew's date from a time when it was important for the church to demonstrate that Jesus was the Messiah of Jewish expectation by proving that he was descended from **David.** When the new religion began to attract non-Jews in numbers, this christological argument was subordinated to others more likely to appeal to Gentiles. Nevertheless Luke incorporates this version of Jesus' family tree, perhaps out of loyalty to his sources, even though—since he accepts the account of Jesus' supernatural generation—he no longer believes it proves anything. The parenthesis (**as was supposed**) is his editorial apology for doing so, and at the same time evidence that the list as a whole was not Luke's own compilation. Two methods of

---

there emerge from them two suggestions of the relationship of the life of Jesus to other lives which are of true importance. Matthew's concern is that the lineage of Jesus shall be led unmistakably through David, the great king, back to Abraham himself, the father of the Jewish race. Luke's purpose is a still wider one. He wants to identify the life of Jesus not only with one nation but with all mankind. He was **the son of Adam, the son of God.** To the query in the Exeg.: "Was this extension made by Luke himself to stress the universalism of Jesus as Christ?" the answer would seem surely to be "Yes."

The two great values indicated would thus belong to Jesus, and it is well to remember that they always should be preserved side by side. No life ought to be dissociated from its national and racial inheritance. There can be a noble worth in patriotism. But in the words of Edith Cavell, the British nurse who, for the aid she gave to escaping soldiers, died without bitterness as a martyr before a German firing squad in Belgium in World War I, "Patriotism is not enough." A soul rooted in all that is best in the life of its own people must go out even to enemies and aliens. That is the way it was with Jesus. In deep devotion he was the son of Israel. Yet not the less, but all the more because of this, he was to be that which the Gospel of Luke consistently represents him, the lover and redeemer both of the Jews and the Gentiles, the supreme Son of the Father who made himself the brother of all mankind.

35 Which was *the son* of Saruch, which was *the son* of Ragau, which was *the son* of Phalec, which was *the son* of Heber, which was *the son* of Sala,

36 Which was *the son* of Cainan, which was *the son* of Arphaxad, which was *the son* of Sem, which was *the son* of Noe, which was *the son* of Lamech,

37 Which was *the son* of Mathusala, which was *the son* of Enoch, which was *the son* of Jared, which was *the son* of Maleleel, which was *the son* of Cainan,

38 Which was *the son* of Enos, which was *the son* of Seth, which was *the son* of Adam, which was *the son* of God.

4 And Jesus being full of the Holy Ghost returned from Jordan, and was led by the Spirit into the wilderness,

35 the son of Se'rug, the son of Re'u, the
son of Pe'leg, the son of Eber, the son of
She'lah, 36 the son of Ca-i'nan, the son of
Ar-pha'xad, the son of Shem, the son of
Noah, the son of Lamech, 37 the son of
Methuselah, the son of Enoch, the son of
Ja'red, the son of Ma-ha'la-le-el, the son of
Ca-i'nan, 38 the son of Enos, the son of
Seth, the son of Adam, the son of God.

4 And Jesus, full of the Holy Spirit, returned from the Jordan, and was led

---

glossing over the conflict between the genealogy and the birth narratives are still employed: (*a*) Luke gives the genealogy of Mary rather than of **Joseph**—so Annius of Viterbo (*ca.* A.D. 1490); Roman Catholic exegetes; Luther—and (*b*) Jesus was legally Joseph's son—so Alfred Plummer, *The Gospel According to St. Luke* (New York: Charles Scribner's Sons, 1896; "International Critical Commentary"), p. 103; *et al.*

3. Jesus' Temptations (4:1-13=Matt. 4:1-10)

In its present form the temptation narrative is a commentary on the entire course of Jesus' ministry. Time and again Jesus must have been tempted to authenticate his mission by a display of miraculous power (Mark 8:11-12) or to undertake the role of political Messiah (John 6:15), and the church knew that he had consistently refused to do so, recognizing in such proposals the promptings of Satan (Mark 8:33). No doubt the O.T. account of Israel's forty years of testing in the wilderness also helped to shape the narrative. All Jesus' answers are quotations from Deut. 6–8 (cf. especially Deut. 8:2-3). Nevertheless, although the details of the Q story may be the work of Christian reflection, Mark also records this initial period of testing. Perhaps Jesus retired to think through the implications of his baptismal experience, and he may very conceivably have spoken later of the decisions he made and the alternatives he rejected.

4:1*a*. Editorial introduction. In the O.T. the **Spirit** is a sporadic and temporary influx of divine energy that enabled certain individuals to see visions, prophesy, or perform remarkable feats of strength. Paul insists that the **Spirit** is an abiding possession of the true believer, and responsible for the characteristic virtues of a Christ-filled life. Luke still shares the O.T. (and early Christian) concept, but speaks of Peter (Acts 4:8), Stephen (Acts 6:5), Barnabas (Acts 11:24), Paul (Acts 13:9), and (here) pre-eminently

---

4:1. *Jesus Tempted.*—**Jesus, full of the Holy Spirit, returned from the Jordan, and was led by the Spirit for forty days in the wilderness, tempted by the devil.** As a narrative of fact, the knowledge of this could have come to the evangelists from only one source. Jesus was alone in the wilderness. Consequently, if others were to understand what happened there, it must have been because Jesus himself in some moment of intimate communion with his disciples told them of it. There would seem to be abundant reason to believe that this was so. As James Moffatt has written:

> The wonderful account of the three temptations of Jesus is a record of inward struggle which forms

2 Being forty days tempted of the devil. And in those days he did eat nothing: and when they were ended, he afterward hungered.

by the Spirit 2 for forty days in the wilderness, tempted by the devil. And he ate nothing in those days; and when they

---

Jesus as **full of the Holy Spirit,** i.e., possessed by the Spirit in uncommon measure. Luke's topography is vague. Does he mean that Jesus **returned** to Galilee?

1*b*-2. Read with the RSV: **Led by the Spirit for forty days.** Vs. 2 combines intimations of both Mark and Q: the **forty days in the wilderness** were marked by recurrent temptation (Mark 1:13*a*) and continuous fast (Matt. 4:2; contrast Mark 1:13*c*). The specific temptations (unknown to Mark) were a sequel (cf. Matt. 4:2). Matthew has altered the order of the second and the third temptations, perhaps in the interests of a better climax, but other variations between the two accounts are minor. In the **O.T. the devil** (the Semitic "Satan" occurs in Mark) had played only a minor role. Even in the late book of Job he had not been more than one of the angels whose special duty it was to call God's attention to the shortcomings of the children of men. But in the intertestamental literature, probably under the influence of Persian dualism (Ahriman over against Ormazd), he had taken on the character of an evil deity opposed to God, and so was regarded by the early church. For Paul he was "the god of this world" who had "blinded the minds of the unbelievers" (II Cor. 4:4). No doubt Jesus also thought of Satan and "his kingdom" (11:18), as did his Jewish contemporaries and later Christians, as the great obstacle in the way of the rule of God.

---

a masterpiece of description. Look for the artist, however, not in some community-group or in an unknown disciple who depicted the conflict out of his own psychological intuitions, but in Jesus himself; he was the artist to whom we owe the delineation of the profound experience.[8]

The narrative is cast in dramatic form: the arena of the temptation, of course, was in Jesus' own mind and soul, and the force that assailed him was invisible. But it had an objective reality as vivid and urgent as though the devil's figure had physically confronted Jesus and spoken to him in words audible to the physical ear.

The whole fact of the temptation is linked immediately with the critical experience of the baptism. There Jesus knew with an instant and overwhelming certainty that now his God-ordained ministry had begun. He must go out into the silence and solitude to face in his own thought and for his own decision the alternatives which lay before him. He must determine exactly what God's will for him involved. When any human personality tries in its own measure to answer a question such as that, the plausible voices of shrewdness or self-seeking or sinuous argument of some half-good-half-evil appearing as the wholly-good will speak within it. The reality of the Incarnation meant that Jesus in his far vaster way would know that same experience. He was "one who in every respect has been tempted as we are" (Heb. 4:15). The strange truth is that this sort of temptation comes not accidentally but as part of the very necessity of the life which God is fashioning. There is a vivid conjunction of words in the Gospel of Mark: "'Thou art my beloved Son; with thee I am well pleased.' The Spirit immediately drove him out into the wilderness" (Mark 1:11-12). At the first sound of the words, that seems a strange way to treat a beloved son. Yet it is ever the way that leads to growth and greatness. All wise parents know that they cannot shield a little boy completely, or keep him protected from the contacts of this world. He has got to be sent out more and more to learn his own way, to make his own choices, to grapple with actual life and overcome it even though he may be bruised. So it was in the supreme degree with the divine Son. The love of God must confront him with decisions difficult to make, and let him hear the plausible voice of false alternatives in order that clearly and greatly he could commit himself to what is truth.

2-4. ***The First Temptation.***—In both Matthew and Luke the temptation which is described in these verses stands first. Here, as in the narrative to follow, the spiritual significance must be discerned within the dramatic form and symbol into which it has been cast. This first temptation does not mean that Jesus liter-

[8] *Jesus Christ the Same* (New York and Nashville: Abingdon-Cokesbury Press, 1940), p. 28.

3 And the devil said unto him, If thou be the Son of God, command this stone that it be made bread.
4 And Jesus answered him, saying, It is written, That man shall not live by bread alone, but by every word of God.
5 And the devil, taking him up into a high mountain, showed unto him all the kingdoms of the world in a moment of time.

were ended, he was hungry. 3 The devil
said to him, "If you are the Son of God,
command this stone to become bread."
4 And Jesus answered him, "It is written,
'Man shall not live by bread alone.'"
5 And the devil took him up, and showed
him all the kingdoms of the world in a

3-4. In a state of hunger induced by his **long fast** Jesus is tempted to turn **this stone** (plural in Matthew) into **bread.** In a country of which not more than one fifth of the land was arable under the best of conditions, and which was frequently plagued by extremes of drought and flood, **bread** was a precious commodity. In late Jewish literature visionaries loved to dwell on the marvelous fertility of nature that would mark the new age. So the editor of the book of Amos pictures the time

> When the plowman shall overtake the reaper,
> And the treader of grapes him who sows the seed
> (Amos 9:13 Amer. Trans.);

and the author of the pre-Christian book of Enoch speaks of the vines that would yield wine in abundance, the seed that would reproduce itself a thousandfold, and the olives from which men would press vast quantities of oil (Enoch 10:19). Jesus was invited to assume a role that would have satisfied his own immediate needs and have fulfilled popular messianic hopes, but he repudiated the temptation. The quotation is from Deut. 8:3—given more fully in Matthew. Man's most urgent needs are not physical and the meeting of such needs was not Jesus' mission. "My food is to do the will of him who sent me, and to accomplish his work" (John 4:34).

5-8. In late Judaism as well as in the early church (John 12:31; etc.) **the devil** was the real power behind **all the kingdoms of the world** (τῆς οἰκουμένης, "the inhabited world," in the Hellenistic era the countries bordering on the Mediterranean, and in Jesus' day practically the Roman Empire). Luke apparently thinks of Jesus as lifted up

ally considered a kind of magical act by which the round stones of the hillside should be changed into a loaf of bread which he would then take up and eat. **He was hungry,** as the Gospel says, but his consciousness never stopped with himself. His experience of hunger was making him think of hungry people everywhere. He had grown up among the poor, and he knew their lot. He knew how many there were who had little to eat, who might be anxious often for bare subsistence. He never forgot man's nature and needs. He would teach his disciples to pray, "Give us this day our daily bread." He knew that nothing could gain him so quick a following as to give people first of all what they most instinctively wanted: better conditions of life, some relative abundance instead of poverty. Suppose he should dedicate his power of leadership to producing that? Certainly that would not be an evil thing. It might seem altogether good. Exactly there was the subtlety of the temptation. It was good, but for Jesus it could not be the highest good. People would follow him "for the loaves and fishes" and meanwhile might be unconcerned for the supreme gift which they needed to receive—bread for their souls rather than bread for their bodies only. It was a matter of emphasis, and Jesus knew where his emphasis had to fall. He could not take the short road to popularity. In the too-brief time that was to be his he must help men most of all to hunger for God.

5-8. ***The Second Temptation.***—Matthew puts this second temptation as the third and final one. It will appear presently why the Lukan order is accepted here.

Jesus had rejected what in modern terms we might call the temptation to be a Messiah for the people's economic life—to set himself to

6 And the devil said unto him, All this power will I give thee, and the glory of them: for that is delivered unto me; and to whomsoever I will, I give it.
7 If thou therefore wilt worship me, all shall be thine.
8 And Jesus answered and said unto him, Get thee behind me, Satan: for it is written, Thou shalt worship the Lord thy God, and him only shalt thou serve.

moment of time,
6 and said to him, "To you I will give all this authority and their glory; for it has been delivered to me, and I give it to whom I will.
7 If you, then, will worship me, it shall all be yours."
8 And Jesus answered him, "It is written,
'You shall worship the Lord your God,
and him only shall you serve.' "

---

into air, for **into a high mountain** is an interpolation from Matthew found only in inferior MSS. Vs. 5*c* is peculiar to Luke's version. The devil's temporal power had **been delivered** to him by God. For centuries the Jews had been ground under the heel of foreign conquerors—Babylonian, Persian, Greek, and then Roman. In much popular eschatology the Messiah was expected to reverse the situation. The oppressed would rise under his leadership, overthrow pagan rule, and establish Jewish hegemony over the world. Jesus is tempted to construe his mission in this light. But according to the logic of a pessimistic world view, such power could be assumed only as a grant from **the devil,** and its acceptance would be tantamount to devil **worship.** The invitation is rejected, once again with a Deuteronomic quotation, this time from Deut. 6:13.

---

better their material conditions. This second temptation was to be the Messiah who would satisfy the patriotic passion of his people.

There were many in Israel who hoped that the Messiah would come manifestly as a conqueror, the man on horseback with sword of deliverance in his hand. The oppression of Rome rested heavily upon their bodies and their souls. They wanted to be free. They wanted to win a glory for Israel which apocalyptic books had pictured. What if Jesus, with his unparalleled personal power, should arouse the fighting blood of Israel and all the other oppressed peoples within the Roman Empire and in the end dethrone Tiberius? Does that seem too fantastic to have been suggested to Jesus—an impossible meaning for the words of the tempter, **To you I will give all this authority and their glory. . . . If you, then, will worship me?** But it is not fantastic. Milton's poetical genius expressed the realities of that temptation in *Paradise Lost.* But it can be seen not in poetry only, but in unmistakable present fact in this twentieth century. We have actually seen what gives substance to the sort of temptation that was brought to Jesus. Was it unthinkable that he could have taken seriously the tempter's words that there was a way by which he himself might become physically the master of his world? Look at what has happened before our eyes. For a quarter of a century after World War I there was a man who seemed insignificant and inconsequential. He lived in a nation which had been conquered, humiliated, and discouraged. He had no obvious resources of power whatsoever, and the forces ranged against him were gigantic. But the enormous force of that man's purpose and passion burned through opposition as an acetylene torch will burn through steel. Presently that man whose name was Adolf Hitler, had so incredibly followed his vision of imperial conquest that he came within a hairbreadth of being the ruler of all Europe and arbiter of the destinies of the world. Between him and Jesus there was a great gulf, a gulf as between night and day. But underneath both is this fact which gives its meaning to the second temptation: That as there was almost no limit to what this man of the twentieth century by himself did accomplish, so there was complete plausibility in the tempter's words to Jesus that there was no limit to what he could accomplish if he would follow the way the prince of this world could show him. The heroic quality of Jesus' renunciation must be seen against the reality of what the devil said. Jesus could have had limitless power, at a price. It was a price he would not pay—though in many generations men have been willing to pay it, the price of holding that the end justifies the means, and that God does not intend us to be too scrupulous about how we get what we want so long as we can claim that we have a good purpose in the getting. That is the suggestion which often seems so sensible but actually may be satanic. Against it stand the words of Jesus:

> **You shall worship the Lord your God,**
> **and him only shall you serve.**

9 And he brought him to Jerusalem, and set him on a pinnacle of the temple, and said unto him, If thou be the Son of God, cast thyself down from hence:
10 For it is written, He shall give his angels charge over thee, to keep thee:
11 And in *their* hands they shall bear thee up, lest at any time thou dash thy foot against a stone.
12 And Jesus answering said unto him, It is said, Thou shalt not tempt the Lord thy God.

9 And he took him to Jerusalem, and set him on the pinnacle of the temple, and said to him, "If you are the Son of God, throw yourself down from here; 10 for it is written,

'He will give his angels charge of you,
to guard you,'

11 and

'On their hands they will bear you up,
lest you strike your foot against a stone.' "

12 And Jesus answered him, "It is said, 'You shall not tempt the Lord your God.' "

9-12. The Greek word translated **temple** (ἱερόν) usually refers to the whole complex of buildings rather than to the central shrine, and **pinnacle** could mean "battlement," or even the outer temple wall, as well as "summit." Josephus pictures the giddy heights of the royal cloister on the south side of the temple hill, towering there above a deep ravine (Josephus *Antiquities* XV. 11. 5). The devil tempted Jesus to prove that he was the Messiah by thrusting himself into peril and compelling God to intervene for his safety by miracle. He quotes the LXX text of Ps. 91:11-12, interpreting it as a messianic prediction, and challenges Jesus to put its promises to the test. It was this passage that Shakespeare had in mind when he made Antonio say: "The devil can cite Scripture for his purpose" (*The Merchant of Venice,* Act 1, scene 3). Again Jesus refuses to comply, enforcing his refusal from Deut. 6:16. Scripture forbids any such challenge to God's good faith.

9-12. *The Supreme Temptation.*—Thus in Luke's Gospel the narrative comes to its real climax, even though at first the immensity of it does not appear. Here is the temptation that was most subtle and in which the untruth that the tempting voice tried to urge was most plausibly disguised as truth.

Consider what had happened. Jesus had made two absolute choices involving two great renunciations. He had determined that he would not seek an easy following by ministering only to people's temporal wants. Neither would he buy devotion by appealing to men's combative passions. He would take a longer and more difficult road toward the world's redemption. Now it was as though the tempter said to him: "I am beaten. I admit that in your consecration you are completely God's son. Therefore you can expect no more perplexity or hardship. Since you are God's son, certainly from this time on he will protect you on all your way. Nothing henceforth can hurt you. Into whatever seeming danger you may go, you can be sure that God's angels will be there to bear you up in their protecting hands."

Dramatically, as always, the temptation narrative puts the thought into particular expression. **He took him to Jerusalem, and set him on the pinnacle of the temple, and said to him, "If you are the Son of God, throw yourself down."** That does not mean that Jesus entertained the actual idea of any such piece of exhibitionism as that. Rather it objectifies in an extreme illustration the whole area of physical risk which his life might face. Why might it not be, as the tempter said: "You cannot be hurt. You can depend upon angelic deliverance always. That will be the sign that you are the chosen son of God"?

Conceivably Jesus might have believed that, just as innumerable men and women who have thought that they trusted God have believed it. How often is it said of such and such a person, "He obviously deserves God's favor and surely he will have it." How often, on the other hand, have men cried out in bitterness against what seemed to them some inexplicable failure of God to protect a saintly life from suffering. It *must* be true, they have thought, that if a person is good enough, he will have a protecting angel at his side. That is what the tempter wanted Jesus to assume: that it was right to expect from God the Father what seemed so reasonable. He would go forward to his ministry, *provided* . . . . He would believe that no opposition could successfully stand in his way, and that there could be no serious disaster. If so, then he could go confidently ahead. But there in that extreme moment Jesus determined that there should be no "if." It might be that

13 And when the devil had ended all
the temptation, he departed from him
for a season.
14 ¶ And Jesus returned in the power
of the Spirit into Galilee: and there went
out a fame of him through all the region
round about.
15 And he taught in their synagogues,
being glorified of all.

13 And when the devil had ended every
temptation, he departed from him until
an opportune time.
14 And Jesus returned in the power of
the Spirit into Galilee, and a report con-
cerning him went out through all the sur-
rounding country. 15 And he taught in
their synagogues, being glorified by all.

---

13. Editorial conclusion. **Until an opportune time:** Satan is introduced again as the instigator of Jesus' betrayal (22:3).

IV. Jesus' Galilean Ministry (4:14–9:50)

A. Beginning of Jesus' Public Ministry (4:14-30)

1. Return to Galilee (4:14-15, based on Mark 1:14-15)

14-15. As in Mark and Matthew, Jesus' public ministry begins in **Galilee** after the temptation prelude. He **returned in the power of the Spirit:** cf. 3:22; 4:1. Luke makes no mention of John's imprisonment in the interim (Matt. 4:12; Mark 1:14). According to Luke, the only interruption of the Galilean ministry before Jesus' final departure for Jerusalem (9:51) was a brief interlude in "the country of the Gerasenes, which is opposite Galilee" (8:26)—unless Luke's alteration of Mark's "Galilee" (Mark 1:39) to "Judea" in 4:44 was intended to imply a preaching tour at this point that extended into other parts of Palestine. **Glorified**="honored" (Goodspeed).

---

in his Father's high purpose, as yet unrevealed, the road for him might be not a quickly triumphant road, but a tragic one. **Thou shalt not tempt** [make trial of] **the Lord thy God,** he said. He did not lay down conditions. He would face whatever awaited him, even if at the end of the vista there might be the shadow of a cross.

13. ***After the Temptations—What?***—Would the experience in the wilderness mark the conclusion of the temptations which came to Jesus? In principle, yes; in repetition of the fact, no. There in those long days of his self-searching and his communion with God, he had settled once for all the principles to which his life would be committed. Yet those principles would be assailed again and again by the subtle suggestions that might have diverted him from them. He would have to reaffirm his determination not to let his concern for people's physical needs, their poverty and their sicknesses, and their desire for some immediate material advantage, swerve him from a greater ministry to their empty souls. He must keep on saying, "Do not labor for the food which perishes, but for the food which endures to eternal life" (John 6:27). He would have to resist more than once the fierce pressure of nationalistic desire by those like the Zealots who would have liked "to come and take him by force to make him king" (John 6:15). Often too he must have heard the voice of the last and most plausible temptation, the temptation to make his faith in his Father depend upon his being shielded from disaster. On the very last night of his life, in Gethsemane, that temptation had to be wrestled with again in agony. So the struggle was not ended in the wilderness. But the essential victory had been won. Jesus' decisions had been so deep and sure that they could not afterward be taken by surprise or shaken.

A double truth is there for all our contemplation: on the one hand, the fact that great moral and spiritual commitments will be assailed in subsequent times and therefore no soul must carelessly or forgetfully drop its guard; on the other hand, the happier fact that it is possible for decisions to be made so deeply and so surely and with such clear prevision of their consequences that the strength of them can never afterward be overcome.

15. ***Significance of the Synagogue.***—Here is the first mention in this Gospel of something which has had immense significance in all religious history. The institution of the **synagogue** was one of the supreme contributions of Israel. In the early times recorded in the O.T., worship centered around the various "high places" until later when it was concentrated at the temple in Jerusalem. Both at the local shrines and at the temple, worship was largely a matter

16 ¶ And he came to Nazareth, where he had been brought up: and, as his custom was, he went into the synagogue on the sabbath day, and stood up for to read.

16 And he came to Nazareth, where he had been brought up; and he went to the synagogue, as his custom was, on the sab-

2. Rejection at Nazareth (4:16-30)

Luke omits the summary of Jesus' message in Mark 1:15 and puts a representative illustration of it in its place. The narrative is based on Mark 6:1-6—omitted at the corresponding point (following 8:56) in the Third Gospel—but it is uncertain whether Luke expanded Mark on his own initiative, or discovered the material in some special source and adapted it to Mark. At any rate he altered Mark's order to make the incident a dramatic frontispiece to Jesus' public ministry. Matthew also implies a preliminary visit to Nazareth (Matt. 4:13) before the commencement of the work at Capernaum (in contrast to Mark), and the notice may have stood in Q.

16. Worship in a Palestinian synagogue consisted of the recitation of the Shema, a prayer, a fixed lection from the Law (*pārāshāh*), a free lection from the Prophets (*haphṭārāh*), an explanation and application of one or both of the scriptural passages, and a blessing by a priest or a prayer by a layman. The scripture was read in Hebrew, but a translator turned it, verse by verse, into Aramaic. There was no official "minister." An invitation to read and to preach could be extended by the ruling elders to any competent member of the congregation or visitor (cf. Acts 13:15). It was the practice to stand up **to read,** and to sit down to preach (vss. 20-21).

of sacrifice and ritual. When the temple was destroyed and most of the Jews were led away into captivity, it seemed a shattering and ultimate disaster. How could they sing the Lord's song in a strange land? How could they worship, now that the familiar altars were destroyed? The answer was the rise of the synagogue, the meeting place of Jewish worshipers, not now for the ritual of material sacrifice, but for the offering up of prayer and praise and for listening to instruction in the law. Religion moved more and more from the realm of cultus and of outward acts toward the cultivation of mind and heart and moral conscience. Christian worship would be built upon that foundation of the synagogue and would be patterned after it. Its contribution, therefore, to the conception and expression of all high religion has been inestimable. As Ernest F. Scott has written:

> The rise of the Synagogue may be compared, in its historical significance, with the invention of printing, though in some ways it marked an even greater revolution. [By the synagogue God's] worship was made independent of everything that was sensuous and external. He was the righteous God, and desired that men should serve Him by moral obedience. They were to meet before Him to meditate on His will, as it was revealed in His holy law.[9]

16. *Churchgoing: The Divine Example.*— And he went to the synagogue, as his custom was, on the sabbath day. Those four words, **as his custom was,** are a striking phrase, the more so because they occur only twice in the Gospel. The first instance is here; the other one comes near the end of Jesus' life, when he "went, as was his custom, to the Mount of Olives" (22:39). Both times the custom had to do with prayer. Instinctively and habitually Jesus prayed, not only in the solitary hours of his own communion, but in the public worship of God's people. To put it in modern terms, he made a practice of going to church.

Why did he do this? Nazareth was a little place, inhabited by ordinary people. The service in the synagogue could hardly have seemed in itself to be particularly inspiring. Nevertheless, Jesus was there. What made him choose to go?

In the first place, perhaps he recognized that there were associations of time and place which make the approach to God more sure. Shallow talk may often be heard from people who say that they do not need to go to church because God can be worshiped anywhere. Why cannot he be found equally well out under the open sky, on the hills, in the fields? Why cannot he be found when people are playing, as well as when they are going to church—as a matter of fact, on a golf club veranda, on the first tee, or the eighteenth green? Theoretically, he might be. And of course, in honest fact, he generally is not. Jesus knew in shining reality that which some lightly prate about: that God is everywhere. Jesus did find him in the beauty of the

[9] *The Nature of the Early Church* (New York: Charles Scribner's Sons, 1941), pp. 71-72.

17 And there was delivered unto him the book of the prophet Esaias. And when he had opened the book, he found the place where it was written,

18 The Spirit of the Lord *is* upon me, because he hath anointed me to preach

bath day. And he stood up to read; 17 and there was given to him the book of the prophet Isaiah. He opened the book, and found the place where it was written,

18 "The Spirit of the Lord is upon me,
because he has anointed me to preach
good news to the poor.

---

17. Since it is improbable that the book or "codex" form of papyrus was yet in use, we might better translate with Goodspeed: "And the roll of the prophet Isaiah was handed to him, and he unrolled it." The Law was read through over a period of three years—one year in Babylonia—but the reader chose his own selection from the Prophets.

18-19. The greater part of this short lection is from the LXX text of Isa. 61:1-2. **To heal the broken-hearted** is a clause in the source that is omitted by the best Lukan MSS.

Galilean lilies or under the silences of the stars; but he knew God there because he knew him also in the place where since he was a little boy he had gone to think of him, in the house of worship consecrated to his presence, where the revelation of himself was both intensely and particularly set forth.

Also, the synagogue linked the present with the past. Here the worship of today had its continuity with all the rich meaning of Israel's long yesterdays. The hopes, the desires, the needs of the immediate life could no longer seem occasional and accidental. They became a part of the yearning and the promise of all the generations.

Furthermore, the synagogue meant fellowship. And it is in fellowship that the fire of the spirit may kindle best. For a soul in isolation the fire may die, as the fire dies out in a coal set off by itself; but as coals, each one of which was only partially glowing, when brought together turn into flame, so do the souls of men when they are brought together in corporate worship attain the glowing heat which one by one they might have lost.

Such were some of the values to which Jesus gave his silent and steady testimony when he went, **as his custom was,** to the synagogue. Those who in their complacency imagine that public worship has no importance for them may well look at him and consider whether he represents for them agreement or rebuke.

17-18. ***The Gospel that Sets Life Free.***—It was characteristic of Jesus that he should have selected this passage from Isaiah which glows with the message of God's pity and compassion. Here was the perfect description of the ministry which he himself should fulfill—

> **To preach good news to the poor.**
> **. . . . .**
> **to set at liberty those who are oppressed,**
> **to proclaim the acceptable year of the Lord.**

The power God sent to earth in Jesus was the power of his love. The only weapon Jesus ever used to win his way was love. So he lived and so he taught, and in the end he imparted that same spirit to his disciples. He made them know that as their lives reached out to touch and help the lives of others, their own personalities would be touched by the greatness of God.

When those who have the name of Christians and ought to be followers of their Lord fail to show that they are in any real sense bringing **good news to the poor** and setting **at liberty those who are oppressed,** the deepest reason may be that the springs of their emotions have been stifled by too much dust of indifferent things. They have their technical interests, but as they move in the presence of the voiceless pathos that is in so much of human life, they do not feel it and they do not greatly care. It may be claimed that there are some creative influences which have nothing to do with the emotions. Perhaps there may be. There are certain kinds of poetry and certain kinds of music that seem to move in a realm which has very little to do with the heart; but their light is a cold glitter, like the shining of the aurora above the polar ice. The greatest splendors of imagination in every realm have their roots in the emotions. Shakespeare is the loftiest genius of our English poetry, and no one can read Shakespeare without perceiving that here was a man whose warm understanding went deep down into all the ground of human life. And certainly the kind of imagination which carries the world forward into more generous and hopeful adventures for social betterment comes from those men and women who have emotions that make them care. Nobody can strive passionately for justice who has not first himself suffered in his sympathy. No one can have a flame of indignation against the cruel callousness of piled up wealth or devote himself with

the gospel to the poor; he hath sent me to heal the broken-hearted, to preach deliverance to the captives, and recovering

He has sent me to proclaim release
to the captives
and recovering of sight to the blind,

To set at liberty those who are oppressed is from the LXX text of Isa. 58:6. Both the LXX original and Luke's version should be punctuated as follows:

> The Spirit of the Lord is upon me,
> Because he has anointed me;
> He has sent me to preach good news to the poor;
> To proclaim release to the captives . . .

The original expressed some postexilic prophet's consciousness of mission. The same passage underlies Jesus' words to the emissaries of John the Baptist in 7:22 (Matt. 11:5). Therefore Jesus as well as the evangelist may have interpreted it as illuminating his commission. In its Lukan context **he has anointed me** refers to Jesus' baptism. It is

his whole-souled power to the bringing in of a social order of more equal opportunity unless he first has that compassion for the poor which Jesus expressed in what he said in Nazareth. None of us can take our everyday business or profession and lift it up out of the arid dust of mean detail into something greatly inspired and inspiring unless the fire of human emotion is burning in our hearts, i.e., unless all that we do is warmed and made to glow by a sense of its reference to the things that really count for the sweetness and strength of life.

To remember Jesus is to find it harder to be cruel or selfish or pitiless; to remember him is to have something in us so drawn to him that we are more eager to be generous, understanding, compassionate, and kind. To remember him is to know that out of the heart are the issues of life. And someday, looking into our own heart and remembering him, we may be moved to cry: "O God, let the healing waters which may come from the fountain of cleansing tears, as well as from the fountain of a great rejoicing, begin to flow in me!"

18. *The Redemption of Suffering.*—**He hath sent me to heal the broken-hearted.** It will be seen that these words are omitted in the RSV although they are included in the KJV (see Exeg.). But they have a deep relevance to the actual spirit of Jesus' ministry. He was in truth one who healed **the broken-hearted.** He touched life not only at its points of joy and power, as pagan ideas of gods come down to earth had sometimes assumed that the godlike ones must do. He brought the consciousness of the presence of God not only on the heights but in the valleys also, not only in the lights but in the shadows, not only in those moments when life soars up on wings but in those other moments when it walks with lame and weary feet upon a heavy road. Jesus in his life and teaching did not set himself to give a verbal explanation of this world's inescapable paradox of sorrow and of seeming evil; but for himself and for others he made sorrow redeeming through his revelation of a spirit which could transfigure it with courage and steady it with trust, and that has been the effect of his spirit from that time until this. Whenever sad people think of him, something happens to their sadness. They may not understand it any better; but there is newness in the way they feel. Their iciness is melted; all that was hard and frozen turns into a stream of gentle emotion which waters in their souls a garden where the flowers of a fragrant peace begin to grow. They are not afraid of sadness now, for the love of God is walking by their side.

18. *Making the Blind to See.*—When Jesus said that one result of the spirit of the Lord in him was **recovering of sight to the blind,** we may believe that the first and direct reference was to physical healing. There are numerous accounts in the Gospels of blind men who came to Jesus begging for his help whom Jesus made to see. The healing power of Jesus is something that we can never fully define or explain. But we may hold as indubitable the words which were written not by a Christian, but by a learned orthodox Jew, Joseph Klausner: "This force which Jesus had, comprises some secret, some mystical element, still not properly studied by the ordinary psychologists and physicians and scientists, who are conversant only with the laws of nature so far determined by science." [1]

But we may be equally sure that physical healing was not the only and probably not the chief result of the spirit which Jesus had in mind. Repeatedly the Gospels make it evident

[1] *Jesus of Nazareth* (New York: The Macmillan Co., 1925), p. 270.

of sight to the blind, to set at liberty them that are bruised,

19 To preach the acceptable year of the Lord.

to set at liberty those who are oppressed,

19 to proclaim the acceptable year of the Lord."

---

characteristic of Luke's conception of Jesus that he was sent **to preach good news to the poor** (cf. 6:20). The Hebrew original of **the acceptable year of the Lord** is best translated "the year of the LORD's favor" (Amer. Trans.). In our context the phrase has reference to the messianic age.

---

that he did not wish people to be drawn to him primarily for some benefit to their body. He wanted most of all to reach their minds and souls and to set these free. The people whom he regarded as most blind were not those whose physical eyes were sightless. According to the Fourth Gospel some of the Pharisees took offense at the suggestion which they caught from him and they demanded, "Are we also blind?" Jesus said to them, "If you were blind, you would have no guilt; but now that you say, 'We see,' your guilt remains" (John 9:40-41). Their fault was in a moral and spiritual obtuseness which did not recognize the reality of God.

The great gift of Jesus was that he did open men's eyes not only to the wonder and majesty but to the nearness of God. He helped them to see some of the light of God's presence in the ordinary place and in ordinary people. There is an arresting suggestion in the description in Mark 8:22-26 of the healing of a blind man. After Jesus had touched him first, he asked him, "Do you see anything?" He looked up and said, "I see men; but they look like trees, walking." Spiritually speaking, a great many people have no more sight than that. It is possible for us to go among men and women and perceive their faces and watch their figures move this way and that, but all the while see them only as trees walking. We do not see their souls. We do not stop to contemplate what they are within. We treat them as instruments of our convenience and part of the outward mechanism of our living. And too seldom do we stop to consider with sympathy and imagination what in themselves they really are. This may be true even in our nearest associations. It is entirely possible for a man to sink into such a rut of stupid self-absorption that all his wife really means to him is a convenient automaton whose business it is to see that he gets his breakfast when he wants it, to keep the children quiet when he wants to be still, to have the house pleasant when he comes home in the evening, and to be sure that he is not bothered by difficulties with servants or with too many bills. It is possible for a woman to regard her husband as an economic machine whose function is to give her the money she needs for her conveniences and her luxuries, to be her escort when she wants amusement, and not to have any inconvenient larger interests which interfere with what she wants to do. It is possible for us all to treat people in our business and our office not as individuals but merely implements. But then ultimately the healing touch of Jesus may come to us so that we are restored and, like the blind man in Mark's Gospel, we see "everything clearly." We wake to the fact that there is a whole world which to our stolidity and selfishness had been invisible. These men and women whom we have treated so impassively that perhaps we have made them impassive too are human souls filled with needs and with nobilities, with hunger after sympathy and understanding, and the power to give sympathy and understanding back, with temptations and with moral triumphs, with all their drama of obscure and yet heroic faithfulness, and it may be with powers greater than they are aware of waiting some touch of confidence in order to be released.

18. *The Captive Who Is Free.*—He has sent me to proclaim release to the captives. The captivity referred to here is evidently moral and spiritual. Thought is not moving now on the plane of opening the doors of physical jails, but rather of setting men free from the invisible but terribly real imprisonment into which their souls may fall.

There are various forms of captivity. There is a captivity into which men are slowly and gradually drawn and the existence of which they will try to deny. It is the captivity which comes through seductions of the flesh, because of which a man may yield more and more to his appetites and passions until at length he is a slave to dissipation and degradation. From that kind of captivity the challenging purity of Jesus called men to emerge, and the fire of his inspiration could cut through the chains that held them.

There is another captivity into which men go willingly. It is seen most clearly in discouraged and disorganized times. Individuals feel a sense of inadequacy and frustration; they

20 And he closed the book, and he gave
it again to the minister, and sat down.
And the eyes of all them that were in the
synagogue were fastened on him.
21 And he began to say unto them, This
day is this Scripture fulfilled in your ears.
22 And all bare him witness, and won-
dered at the gracious words which pro-
ceeded out of his mouth. And they said,
Is not this Joseph's son?
23 And he said unto them, Ye will
surely say unto me this proverb, Physician,

20 And he closed the book, and gave it
back to the attendant, and sat down; and
the eyes of all in the synagogue were fixed
on him. 21 And he began to say to them,
"Today this scripture has been fulfilled in
your hearing." 22 And all spoke well of
him, and wondered at the gracious words
which proceeded out of his mouth; and
they said, "Is not this Joseph's son?" 23 And
he said to them, "Doubtless you will quote

---

20. The synagogue **attendant** (*ḥazzān*) was a general factotum, whose duties ranged from teaching children to scourging criminals, and included that of taking the scripture roll from the ark and returning it. As in Acts 6:15 and 10:4, the verb that here is translated **were fixed** suggests an atmosphere of suspense.

21. "Today this scripture that you have just heard has been fulfilled" is a more attractive rendering than either the KJV or the RSV. According to Luke, Jesus' first public announcement claims that he is the fulfillment of the O.T. prediction. The Messiah has come and with him the new era of "the Lord's favor"—the kingdom of God.

22. Read with the RSV: **And all spoke well of him.** Some Marcan matter is now worked into the account and the transition is not easy. The comment **"Is not this Joseph's son?"**—like its counterpart in Mark 6:3—suggests hostility rather than surprise.

23. **Physician, heal yourself:** "Charity begins at home"; a proverb with equivalents in every age and language. The Oxyrhynchus Papyrus fragment (early third century A.D.) has a variant that has obviously been adapted to fit the Lukan application: "Jesus

---

grow hopeless as to working out any successful destiny of their own. There is, as Erich Fromm has put it in the title of his book, an *Escape from Freedom.* People deliberately seek to yield up their individualities with all the burden of their unsure choices to some masterful spirit who claims the right to rule. Thus millions of people in Nazi Germany submitted themselves with a kind of fanatical relief to Adolf Hitler. Thus Communists find a fierce sense of power by surrendering their own independence and becoming unquestioning devotees of the "party line."

That kind of captivity, like the first kind, degrades the dignity of the human soul. Yet the strange fact is that the supreme fulfillment of a life is not apart from captivity, but through it—if only the meaning of captivity is greatly understood. There is a shining truth in the first two lines of George Matheson's hymn:

> Make me a captive, Lord,
> And then I shall be free.[2]

Here, in what seems a paradox, is yet the plain, sure truth. On that word "Lord" the emphasis must fall. When a soul is taken possession of by the purifying and inspiring purpose of God himself, then for the first time that soul finds for itself an immense and joyous freedom. It is lifted up above the plane of mean entanglements, like a bird launched from the earth into the sky. That was what Jesus came to make men understand. Only when they give their imaginations and wills in glad surrender to the service of God's kingdom will all the glorious possibilities within them be released.

20-28. ***Jesus Among His Own People.***—It seems that in this passage Luke is combining material which had come to him from two different sources, so that the whole picture as he presents it is not quite consistent (see Exeg.). The two strands of thought which he has interwoven need to be followed separately.

The words which give the clue to the first thought are those in vs. 24. They take us back to the description in Mark 6:1-6, which of course was earlier than the Gospel of Luke. In the scene in the synagogue at Nazareth as Mark describes it, there is from the first moment a mood of suspicion and of half hostility among the townsfolk. They are astonished at Jesus, but it is a grudging and sour astonishment. He appears to be saying extraordinary things, but they are skeptical of their truth.

[2] Used by permission of McClure, Naismith, Brodie & Co.

heal thyself: whatsoever we have heard
done in Capernaum, do also here in thy
country.

24 And he said, Verily I say unto you,
No prophet is accepted in his own country.

25 But I tell you of a truth, many widows
were in Israel in the days of Elias, when
the heaven was shut up three years and six
months, when great famine was throughout
all the land;

26 But unto none of them was Elias
sent, save unto Sarepta, *a city* of Sidon,
unto a woman *that was* a widow.

to me this proverb, 'Physician, heal yourself;
what we have heard you did at Ca-per'na-um,
do here also in your own country.' "
24 And he said, "Truly, I say to you,
no prophet is acceptable in his own country.
25 But in truth, I tell you, there were
many widows in Israel in the days of
Elijah, when the heaven was shut up three
years and six months, when there came a
great famine over all the land;
26 and
Elijah was sent to none of them but only
to Zar'e-phath, in the land of Sidon, to a

---

said: No prophet is acceptable in his own country, and no physician performs cures on those who know him" (Oxyrhynchus Papyrus I. 11). The proverb's application suggests that the whole narrative originally was located later in Jesus' ministry, for Luke has not yet reported any activity at **Capernaum.**

24. Also Marcan matter (Mark 6:4). Were vss. 22*c* and 24 missing from the source Luke was employing at this point? The narrative would flow more freely without them.

25-27. The example of two O.T. prophets might serve to silence a complaint that Jesus' "mighty works" ought to have been performed in his native village (vs. 23), though the parallelism is not complete since Capernaum was presumably a Jewish town. However, it has little bearing on the observation that "no prophet is acceptable in his own country" (vs. 24). The **Elijah** incident is narrated in I Kings 17:8-24. The statement that **the heaven was shut up three years and six months** is also made in Jas. 5:17-18. According to I Kings 18:1, the duration of the drought was less than three years. In apocalyptic literature "three and a half years" (the half of seven—"a time, and times, and half a time" [Dan. 7:25; Rev. 12:14; etc.]) had become the stereotyped period of evil and distress, and this may explain the change in chronology. **Zarephath, in the land of**

How did he get all this supposed wisdom? Did he not grow up in their midst, the son and brother of people just like themselves? How could he be so distinguished as to be worth listening to? Jesus could not help but understand what they were whispering together, so he said: "A prophet is not without honor, except in his own country, and among his own kin, and in his own house" (Mark 6:4). Or as Luke puts it, **Truly, I say to you, no prophet is acceptable in his own country.** Then the account in Mark goes on to say, "He could do no mighty work there."

Here was a sad fact manifest in supreme degree with reference to Jesus, but observable again and again in human relationships. God's truth may come in ways which we do not choose to recognize. In our lesser circumstances and occasions we may make the same sort of blunder which the townsfolk in Nazareth made. We will not pay heed to someone who might bring us closer to God, just because we do not have humility enough to listen. Familiarity may make us deaf to some divine message which might come to us every day from someone close to our side. How many men and women there are in this world who, when it is too late, may realize with an infinitely bitter regret that they never took the trouble to accept what was said to them by some voice that now is heard no more. A man's mother follows him with the gentle but inexorable expectation of her love. From the time when he was a little boy she has been saying to him in a thousand ways all the great things which she wants him to live up to. But he may not ever have stopped to listen deeply. "Oh, that is just her imagination," he says to himself. "Of course she says all this, but I cannot take it seriously; mothers are like that, anyway." So he goes on with a good-humored but empty inattention, never rebuffing the love which is held out to him, but never quite accepting it either. The same may be true when the voice which speaks to us is the voice of a husband or wife or friend. Or sometimes the mood may be harsher and more like the mood of the people of Nazareth. Pride is in it, and the beginning of resentment. A man's son may

27 And many lepers were in Israel in the time of Eliseus the prophet; and none of them was cleansed, saving Naaman the Syrian.

28 And all they in the synagogue, when they heard these things, were filled with wrath,

29 And rose up, and thrust him out of the city, and led him unto the brow of the hill whereon their city was built, that they might cast him down headlong.

30 But he, passing through the midst of them, went his way,

woman who was a widow. 27 And there
were many lepers in Israel in the time of
the prophet Elisha; and none of them
was cleansed, but only Na'a-man the Syr-
ian." 28 When they heard this, all in the
synagogue were filled with wrath. 29 And
they rose up and put him out of the city,
and led him to the brow of the hill on
which their city was built, that they might
throw him down headlong. 30 But passing
through the midst of them he went away.

Sidon, is the modern Ṣarafand, a town on the coast road, midway between Sidon and Tyre. It would be clear to the readers of the Gospel that **a woman** living there would be Syrophoenician by race. The **Elisha** story is found in II Kings 5:1-14. Again the point is that a prophet of God ministered to a non-Jew.

28-30. In Mark 6:5-6 there is no reference to any overt act of hostility to Jesus. **All in the synagogue were filled with wrath** because the benefits of Jesus' mission were to accrue to others. Modern Nazareth is situated on a steep slope, but changes in topography since the first century A.D. have been such that it is impossible to locate **the brow of the hill** that Luke had in mind, if indeed it was not entirely a literary detail. **Passing through the midst of them** implies that Jesus was miraculously invulnerable to mob violence (cf. John 7:30).

Placed as it is, at the beginning of Jesus' public ministry, the Nazareth story serves as a prelude to the whole of Luke-Acts—to the entire account of the emergence of Christianity as a non-Jewish religion. Many of the main motifs are introduced: the *praeparatio evangelica* in the O.T.; the endowment with the Spirit; the good news to the poor; the proclamation of the messianic age; the hostility of the Jews; and the mission to the Gentiles. The rejection of Jesus by his fellow townsmen prepares the reader for the

---

have in some decision that affects himself and his father and his family a more sensitive appreciation of the things that really count than his father has, but the father may be angered at the very suggestion that this could be so. The clear eyes of a girl may see some truth more fully than her mother, but the mother will not have it so. Here are human relationships, but nevertheless, as in supreme degree through the Incarnation, the reality of heaven may be pressing in upon our human lives. It is a perilous thing to refuse it just because we think its source is too simple and too near to be impressive.

The second strand of thought in Luke's narrative has to do with the section beginning with vss. 25-28. Here is the particular message which made the people of Nazareth angry. Jesus was saying to them that often in the history of Israel it had been shown that God's goodness could not be appropriated by those who thought they had a special claim on God, but that it went out to all those who were eager and receptive—and those who were thus eager might be not those of orthodox privilege, but the stranger and the alien. Always there is a tendency to resent that. A church wants to keep its religious privileges to itself; it does not want to be annoyed with unduly difficult claims for Christian missions. The congregation's business, it thinks, is to nurture its own life, and moreover, it is God's business that this precious life of its own should be thus nurtured. Men who decide the policies of nations in their legislative assemblies often have the same idea; whatever happens, the nation's special interests must stand first. Anyone who suggests that other peoples of the earth might be equally important in God's sight is to be pushed aside as an intolerable nuisance. Still there are many places where a message such as that which Jesus spoke on that sabbath in the synagogue would be as unwelcome as it was in Nazareth.

29-30. ***Passing Through the Midst.***—In their anger the townsfolk of Nazareth would have done violence to Jesus if they had quite dared. But here with one swift phrase the evangelist suggests the moral majesty in Jesus' bearing by which men were awed. He did not have to

31 And came down to Capernaum, a city of Galilee, and taught them on the sabbath days.

32 And they were astonished at his doctrine: for his word was with power.

33 ¶ And in the synagogue there was a man, which had a spirit of an unclean devil, and cried out with a loud voice,

34 Saying, Let *us* alone; what have we to do with thee, *thou* Jesus of Nazareth? art thou come to destroy us? I know thee who thou art; the Holy One of God.

31 And he went down to Ca-per'na-um, a city of Galilee. And he was teaching
them on the sabbath; 32 and they were as-
tonished at his teaching, for his word was
with authority. 33 And in the synagogue
there was a man who had the spirit of an unclean demon; and he cried out with a
loud voice, 34 "Ah![p] What have you to do
with us, Jesus of Nazareth? Have you come to destroy us? I know who you are, the

[p] Or *Let us alone.*

rejection of Christ by the Sanhedrin, and the rejection of the gospel by the Jewish nation. We are prepared at the beginning of the work for Paul's statement with which it ends: "Let it be known to you then that this salvation of God has been sent to the Gentiles; they will listen" (Acts 28:28; cf. Intro., p. 7).

B. Jesus' Ministry in and About Capernaum (4:31–5:16)

There are unmistakable traces of the use of Mark in 3:1–4:30, but the first great block of Marcan matter is incorporated in 4:31-44. Only minor changes in the interests of clarity, brevity, and style have been imposed on the source.

1. Healing of a Demoniac (4:31-37=Mark 1:21-28)

31-32. Went down: from the Galilean highlands to a town situated 686 feet below sea level. Capernaum has been identified with Tell Ḥûm, the site of extensive ruins on the northwestern shore of the Sea of Galilee. In Jesus' day it was an important toll station on the trade route from Ptolemais to Damascus and a port for maritime trade with Philip's tetrarchy and the Decapolis. It was therefore strategically located as a center for Jesus' Galilean ministry. For the benefit of non-Jewish readers Luke describes it as **a city of Galilee.**

33-34. The synagogue at Capernaum is said in 7:5 (Q) to have been built by an officer in the Roman army. The ruins of the most ancient synagogue yet found in Galilee are at Tell Ḥûm. Although it dates from about A.D. 200, Jack Finegan believes that "the Capernaum synagogue stands on the site and follows the plan of an earlier synagogue or of earlier synagogues, and therefore may be safely regarded as a reconstruction of the one in which Jesus himself taught" (*Light from the Ancient Past* [Princeton: University Press, 1946], p. 228). **The spirit of an unclean demon:** the widespread Oriental belief in demonic possession as the cause of disease is scarcely to be found in the O.T. but it flourished in late Judaism under Babylonian and Persian influence. It pervades the gospel tradition. It is likely that many of the miracle stories in the Gospels have been borrowed from popular Jewish and Hellenistic cycles and attached to Jesus. There is also an observable tendency on the part of the evangelists to heighten and embellish the reputation that Jesus had in their sources as a healer and exorcist. Nevertheless even in his own lifetime it is clear that Jesus was widely known as a healer, particularly of what we should now describe as mental and nervous diseases. **Ah!** is an interjection of dismay. **Have you**

meet the threat of violence by any sign of counterviolence. He simply passed **through the midst of them** and **went his way.**

31-37. ***The Authority of Jesus.***—Noticeable first of all are the words in vs. 31, which is linked to vs. 16. The evangelist has already made clear in one brief phrase, "as his custom was," that when Jesus went to the synagogue in Nazareth on the sabbath he was doing that which had long been his habit. Now in Capernaum, likewise, he is in the synagogue on the sabbath day. The form of the narrative which follows reflects the fact more than once suggested in the Gospels that Jesus did not wish his messiahship to be bruited about in public conversation and excitement, but the spirits of evil

35 And Jesus rebuked him, saying, Hold thy peace, and come out of him. And when the devil had thrown him in the midst, he came out of him, and hurt him not.

36 And they were all amazed, and spake among themselves, saying, What a word *is* this! for with authority and power he commandeth the unclean spirits, and they come out.

37 And the fame of him went out into every place of the country round about.

38 ¶ And he arose out of the synagogue, and entered into Simon's house. And Simon's wife's mother was taken with a great fever; and they besought him for her.

39 And he stood over her, and rebuked the fever; and it left her: and immediately she arose and ministered unto them.

Holy One of God." 35 But Jesus rebuked
him, saying, "Be silent, and come out of
him!" And when the demon had thrown
him down in the midst, he came out of
him, having done him no harm. 36 And
they were all amazed and said to one an-
other, "What is this word? For with au-
thority and power he commands the un-
clean spirits, and they come out." 37 And
reports of him went out into every place in
the surrounding region.

38 And he arose and left the synagogue,
and entered Simon's house. Now Simon's
mother-in-law was ill with a high fever,
and they besought him for her. 39 And
he stood over her and rebuked the fever.
and it left her; and immediately she rose
and served them.

come to destroy us? i.e., into the world. The demon speaks for the whole regiment of Satan. In late Judaism the freeing of men from enslavement to Belial and the destruction of all evil spirits were acknowledged functions of the Messiah (cf. Test. Simeon 6:6 and Test. Zebulun 9:8). **The Holy One of God** is a messianic title (cf. John 6:69).

35. Be silent. Mark had imposed a theory of "the messianic secret" on his source material. By virtue of their supernatural knowledge the demons had recognized Jesus as Messiah, but he had ordered them not to betray the fact. Luke takes over Mark's phrase but not his doctrine (cf. also vs. 41*b*). **Having done him no harm** is a Lukan addition to heighten the miraculous.

36-37. Read **What is this word?** with the RSV. It is to be understood in the light of its Marcan source: "What is this? A new teaching!" (Mark 1:27.)

This story of miraculous healing exhibits the more or less stereotyped form of such narratives in the Gospels: (*a*) the demon recognizes the exorcist and attempts to evade his authority; (*b*) the exorcist reproves the demon and employs a formula of exorcism; (*c*) the demon takes a violent departure from the individual he had possessed; and (*d*) the bystanders are astonished at the event.

2. Healing of Simon's Wife's Mother (4:38-39=Mark 1:29-31)

38-39. The reader is unprepared for Simon and his intimacy with Jesus. Luke had omitted Mark's account of the disciple's call (Mark 1:16-20) and has not yet given his own (5:1-11). Paul confirms the fact that Simon (Cephas) was a married man (I Cor. 9:5). In Mark, Andrew and James and John are mentioned as well as Simon, and an

recognized him and cried out the truth. (For the general belief in demons and their entrance into human beings, see Exeg.) The significance of the narrative, for the evangelist as he wrote it and for the first Christians as they read it, is in its testimony to a power in Jesus that went beyond all ordinary bounds. In every company and in the face of every circumstance he carried authority and power. When he commanded the unclean spirits, they came out. Names and labels for men's difficulties may change, but the great fact abides. It is still **with authority and power** that the spirit of the living Christ comes to those who are in the grip of evil.

38-39. ***Whose Memory Is Here?***—In the nature of the healing thus described there is no striking significance as compared with numerous other acts of healing which Jesus wrought. Many instances of his power were greater than this. But there is an aspect of the scene which the Gospel here describes that does have exceeding interest. For this is the most intimate reference in any of the Gospels to the family life and relationships of one of the disciples.

40 ¶ Now when the sun was setting, all they that had any sick with divers diseases brought them unto him; and he laid his hands on every one of them, and healed them.

41 And devils also came out of many, crying out, and saying, Thou art Christ the Son of God. And he rebuking *them* suffered them not to speak: for they knew that he was Christ.

40 Now when the sun was setting, all those who had any that were sick with various diseases brought them to him; and he laid his hands on every one of them
and healed them. 41 And demons also came out of many, crying, "You are the Son of God!" But he rebuked them, and would not allow them to speak, because they knew that he was the Christ.

---

editorial slip on Luke's part allows the plural to remain in **they besought him** (and in the **them** of vs. 39). **And he stood over her,** i.e., at the head of her bed. Luke gilds the lily. The **fever** was **high,** and after the exorcism the woman rose **immediately.** Vs. 39*b* emphasizes the success of the miracle. The detail may be unhistorical, for the Talmud expressly prohibits the table service of men by women (Kiddushin 70*a*). In the early days of the church "the twelve" were accustomed "to serve tables" as well as to preach (Acts 6:2).

3. Healings on the Evening After the Sabbath (4:40-41=Mark 1:32-34)

40-41. When the sun was setting: i.e., when sabbath regulations were no longer binding. By adding **he laid his hands on . . . them,** Luke specifies the technique of healing that Jesus used on this occasion. In Mark, Jesus healed "many" (Mark 1:34); in Luke, **every one.** "Natural" diseases are apparently distinguished from illnesses due to demon possession. The best MSS support the RSV reading: **You are the Son of God!** This messianic appellation, and the following phrase **but he rebuked them,** were inserted by Luke at this point from Mark 3:11-12, which has no parallel otherwise in the Third Gospel. Luke's narrative—as well as Mark's—is an enthusiastic generalization of Jesus' healing powers.

Most of them are presented to us as individuals whose background we do not see. In the case of James and John their father is mentioned; and so at another place is their mother. But of none of the others of the twelve is even that much said. It is of Simon Peter and of him only that we learn that he had a wife and a house where his wife's mother also lived.

How did this fact, which appears first in the Gospel of Mark, get into the record? The healing itself, as we have noted, was not sensational. The person healed was hardly one who for her own sake would have been chosen to appear in the tradition. We know nothing else of her, and mothers-in-law are not customarily selected as figures upon whom the light of happy attention falls. But there is one possibility which would furnish a clear and sure explanation of why this particular healing finds its place in the gospel record. It is the possibility, strongly declared as a fact in the early church, that Mark's Gospel—in which this incident first is told—embodies direct reminiscences of Simon Peter. Certainly there would have been nothing that Peter himself would have remembered more vividly than what happened in the days directly after his call by Jesus and what happened in his own house. So the brief sentences are more than a cool statement. They may be the open door leading straight back into the warm personal recollection of the first of the followers of Jesus.

40-41. ***The Compassionate Christ.***—In these verses there is one conception which to us will seem remote, but there is also another which is timeless. In that first century there was the familiar and almost universal belief in demons and in demon possession. We do not often use that diagnosis for a disease, although modern psychological studies of the profound and shadowy depths of human personality may make us less inclined than we used to be to rule out strange influences for evil which can be called demonic. However that may be, the picture presented in vs. 40 abides with its promise and its benediction. One reads the words, and before the mind's eye the scene is re-enacted: the pathetic multitude of sick folk brought together by the gates of the town at the end of the day, and in the midst of them the figure of Jesus with his infinite compassion and his unearthly power to help and heal. Modern conclusions about psychosomatic medicine have given increasing substance to belief in the part which

42 And when it was day, he departed and
went into a desert place: and the people
sought him, and came unto him, and stayed
him, that he should not depart from them.
43 And he said unto them, I must preach
the kingdom of God to other cities also:
for therefore am I sent.
44 And he preached in the synagogues
of Galilee.
5 And it came to pass, that, as the peo-
ple pressed upon him to hear the word
of God, he stood by the lake of Gennesaret,

42 And when it was day he departed
and went into a lonely place. And the
people sought him and came to him, and
would have kept him from leaving them;
43 but he said to them, "I must preach the
good news of the kingdom of God to the
other cities also; for I was sent for this
purpose." 44 And he was preaching in the
synagogues of Judea.[q]
5 While the people pressed upon him
to hear the word of God, he was stand-

[q] Other ancient authorities read *Galilee*.

---

4. Epilogue to a Day at Capernaum (4:42-44=Mark 1:35-39)

42-44. The Marcan version of this narrative leaves the impression that Jesus' departure from Capernaum was a flight. He sought to escape the insistent demands of the residents. By omitting Mark's "and there he prayed" (Mark 1:35)—the Third Evangelist more often adds some such statement (3:21; 5:16; 6:12)—Luke implies that Jesus **departed** in order to extend his mission. It is **the people** who seek Jesus, rather than the disciples as in Mark 1:36, for the latter—according to Luke—had not yet been chosen. For the same reason Luke omits Mark's "Let us go" (Mark 1:38). **I must preach the good news of the kingdom of God to the other cities also** is a clarification of Mark's "that I may preach there also" (Mark 1:38) and the first occurrence in Luke of Jesus' characteristic message. **I was sent for this purpose** is a christological interpretation of Mark's "for this is why I came out" (Mark 1:38). For a similar phrasing of Jesus' sense of commission see John 8:42. The weight of MS evidence supports **Judea** (RSV) rather than **Galilee** (KJV), though the latter stands in Mark 1:39. Luke often uses **Judea** for Palestine (1:5; 6:17; 7:17; 23:5; Acts 10:37) and would seem to do so here. Did he wish to correct Mark's picture of a ministry strictly limited at the outset to Galilee?

5. Call of the First Disciples (5:1-11)

Luke had omitted Mark's account of the call of Simon and his associates to discipleship (Mark 1:16-20) but now, at a later point in the sequence of events, he inserts this variant. The story makes no mention of Andrew.

---

religious faith can play in healing. And over and beyond that is the fact of the spiritual peace and power that come to needy souls when they are brought to Jesus. Read Henry Twells's hymn, "At even, when the sun was set," and ponder its verses as they lead on to the final one that is a prayer addressed to Christ:

Thy touch has still its ancient power,
No word from thee can fruitless fall;
Hear, in this solemn evening hour,
And in thy mercy heal us all.

42-44. *Trying to Restrain Christ.*—The suggestion of these verses is already largely covered by the Exeg. Here, as so often, one finds the emphasis of Luke upon the outreach of Jesus' message. It cannot be confined within the expected limits. It is an evangel which belongs not to one town or province or particular people, but to God's children everywhere. Yet in vs. 42 there is a curious foretokening of a spirit which is too often met with among those who have come into contact with Christ. The people among whom Jesus moved in Capernaum **would have kept him from leaving them;** exactly thus would some companies of those who call themselves Christians like to do. Note the churches which are entirely willing to be little self-satisfied conventicles where people meet for their own complacent practices of worship, but feel no responsibility to be a point of departure from which the influence of Christ shall go out far and wide. They think of Christianity as a sort of privilege and prerogative of their own. In effect, they believe that the presence of Christ ought to be content to confine itself to such respectable surroundings and to stay there.

5:1-7. *The Larger Venture.*—The Exeg. is right in warning against the temptation to

2 And saw two ships standing by the lake: but the fishermen were gone out of them, and were washing *their* nets.

3 And he entered into one of the ships, which was Simon's, and prayed him that he would thrust out a little from the land. And he sat down, and taught the people out of the ship.

4 Now when he had left speaking, he said unto Simon, Launch out into the deep, and let down your nets for a draught.

5 And Simon answering said unto him, Master, we have toiled all the night, and have taken nothing: nevertheless at thy word I will let down the net.

ing by the lake of Gen-nes'a-ret. 2 And he
saw two boats by the lake; but the fisher-
men had gone out of them and were wash-
ing their nets. 3 Getting into one of the
boats, which was Simon's, he asked him
to put out a little from the land. And he
sat down and taught the people from the
boat. 4 And when he had ceased speaking,
he said to Simon, "Put out into the deep
and let down your nets for a catch." 5 And
Simon answered, "Master, we toiled all
night and took nothing! But at your word

5:1-3. In Luke **the word of God** is Jesus' own preaching (8:11, 21; 11:28); in Acts it is the apostolic message (Acts 4:31; 6:2; etc.). **The lake of Gennesaret** is a name derived from the plain that lies to the south of Capernaum (Matt. 14:34; Mark 6:53), a designation peculiar in the N.T. to Luke, and more accurate than Mark's "sea" (cf. Josephus *Antiquities* XVIII. 2. 1). According to Luke, Simon had been associated with Jesus for some time before his formal call.

4-9. The story of the miraculous draught of fish has a parallel in John 21:3-14, where it appears to foreshadow the success of the later Christian mission and is associated with the senior disciple's rehabilitation after disgrace. In Luke's source, or in the oral form in

---

allegorize this narrative of the disciples' extraordinary catch. Many sermons have been preached which made fantastic play with the nature and number of fish, and more especially when the preacher reached over to the similar story in John 21 and essayed to explain why the number of fish was 153. Yet when all this area of exaggeration is remembered, it remains true that there are suggestions in the story which go beyond the physical facts. As with so many of the miracles, vistas of spiritual truths which are timeless open out through the events of the particular place and time. The men by the Sea of Galilee had toiled all night and taken nothing. They were tired and a bit discouraged; but when Jesus spoke to them, his words gave them a lift to make another effort. Exactly such is his effect in greater things. His word can make those who have grown discouraged in their spiritual endeavors try again. Secondly, in the plain matter of the place where they were to go to work, Jesus told these fishermen to **put out into the deep.** They responded, and they got the results that they would not have won if they had stayed in the shallows by the shore. Whether it was meant so or not, this has become a symbol of what would happen for their souls. When Peter and the others were called to leave their fishing boats and to follow Jesus on an unpredictable way and into what would prove to be a costly allegiance, they were putting out into deep waters. Paul was putting out into the deep when he launched the mission to the Gentiles. All the great pioneers and evangelists have done the same. They have gone out in the strength of the spirit represented by William Carey, forerunner of modern missions, who, before he set out in lonely courage for his work in India, preached to a little group of ministers on the theme "Attempt Great Things for God, Expect Great Things from God."

1-11. *Simon Peter and James and John.*—In the scene which is here described we see for the first time together the three men who were to be closest to Jesus in his ministry. These were the three whom he took with him at especially critical times. These were the three who alone were permitted to enter with him when he went into the house of Jairus, where Jairus' little daughter was lying dead (8:51). It was the same three who were his companions on the Mount of Transfiguration (9:28). One or the other of these is frequently conspicuous in the narrative of the Gospel, and the names of two of them at least stand at the top of the roll which Christendom remembers.

First there was **Simon.** In the Fourth Gospel there is a striking sentence which reveals as with a flash of light what Jesus did for him. According to John 1:42, Jesus, when he first saw him, said to him: "So you are Simon the

6 And when they had this done, they inclosed a great multitude of fishes: and their net brake.

7 And they beckoned unto *their* partners, which were in the other ship, that they should come and help them. And they came, and filled both the ships, so that they began to sink.

I will let down the nets." 6 And when they
had done this, they enclosed a great shoal
of fish; and as their nets were breaking,
7 they beckoned to their partners in the
other boat to come and help them. And
they came and filled both the boats, so

---

which the story reached the evangelist, it may also have been a postresurrection narrative with some similar symbolical purpose. But Luke has obscured this by making the miracle the occasion of Simon's call. The temptation to allegorize Luke's version must be resisted. Whatever the original symbolism in Luke's source—and in John's version—Luke's fish are fish, not Christian converts. **Master** appears six times in Luke as a title for Jesus. Nondisciples employ "teacher." The **great shoal of fish** numbers "a hundred and fifty-three" in John 21:11. **Their partners in the other boat** are the sons of Zebedee (vs. 10), but need not have been specified in the original story. **Simon Peter** occurs nowhere else in Luke as a double name. Codex Bezae omits the nickname and its reading may be original. In that case "Peter" is first used in 6:14. **Depart from me, for I am a sinful man, O Lord** may originally have presupposed the story of Peter's denial. In its present setting it is an expression of dismay evoked by the supernatural. **Lord** as a title for Jesus appears twenty-one times in Luke. Twelve of the instances are in material peculiar to the Third Gospel.

---

son of John? You shall be called Cephas (which means Rock)." "You are . . . you shall be." Note the significance of those words. The swift understanding of Jesus recognized the manner of man this Simon was, eager and outgoing, but unsure, with great possibilities in him undeveloped. He saw also what he would make this man become, and he began to call him already by the name that henceforth should continually remind him of what by the grace of God he should some day be.

If in after years someone had asked Simon Peter what his ministry had meant to him, he might have replied in some such way as this: "I was a rough man, knowing nothing much except the rough life of the fishing fleet. I wanted something better; but I never had much confidence in myself. I had hot impulses; but I never seemed to carry them fully through. I had as much courage as most men; but even so, I could not always count on it to last. Nobody would have ever expected of me that I would do anything that mattered much; but Jesus came one day and called me. He made me his friend. The one thing I began to want then was not to disappoint him. I said I would stick to him through thick and thin, and instead of that, I left him and denied him. But even at the worst I knew he loved me. I felt his love so much that it seemed as though the hands of God himself had hold of me and would not let me go. And in the end that saved me and made me know that I could be the sort of man that from the beginning I knew he was expecting me to be."

The other best known one of the three who were called from the fishing boats was **John.** He and his brother **James** in temperament appear to have been much alike. It was these two brothers who wanted to call down fire from heaven on the Samaritan village which would not receive their Master (9:54). It was these two who wanted places of honor at his right hand in his kingdom (Mark 10:35-45). Together they were called the "sons of thunder" (Mark 3:17). Perhaps both of them were transformed by the spirit of Jesus. Certainly according to the tradition of the early church, John was. On down the years he has been remembered not only as the Beloved Disciple but as one whose supreme message was that God is love.

If later he had told his own story, it might have been something like this that he would have said: "I was a very different sort of person once, hot-tempered, proud, quick to pick up a grudge. Then came Jesus. I saw him deal with people in a different way. I saw what love could do. One day I wanted to get God to curse a village which rebuffed us and to burn it up with a lightning bolt. But I learned from Jesus that that is not the way God works. He does not come as lightning but as love, love that gets inside a man's heart and melts his stubbornness, shames his pride, and awakens his own love in answer."

8 When Simon Peter saw *it,* he fell down at Jesus' knees, saying, Depart from me; for I am a sinful man, O Lord.

9 For he was astonished, and all that were with him, at the draught of the fishes which they had taken:

10 And so *was* also James, and John, the sons of Zebedee, which were partners with Simon. And Jesus said unto Simon, Fear not; from henceforth thou shalt catch men.

that they began to sink. 8 But when Simon
Peter saw it, he fell down at Jesus' knees,
saying, "Depart from me, for I am a sinful
man, O Lord." 9 For he was astonished,
and all that were with him, at the catch
of fish which they had taken; 10 and so also
were James and John, sons of Zeb'e-dee,
who were partners with Simon. And Jesus
said to Simon, "Do not be afraid; hence-

10-11. Although the **sons of Zebedee** are also mentioned in John 21:2, they appear to have been introduced into this narrative—rather inadroitly—in order to adapt it to Mark 1:19. **Do not be afraid; henceforth you will be catching men** is Luke's substitute for the invitation in Mark 1:17. Simon alone is addressed (cf. the singular **thou** of the KJV),

---

8. *Condemnation, but Encouragement.*— Simon Peter . . . fell down at Jesus' knees, saying, "Depart from me, for I am a sinful man, O Lord." So Peter cried out in that moment when he was overwhelmed by a sudden sense of a divine power and goodness that made his own self seem small and unworthy. He felt that he could not bear to be in Jesus' presence. That scene of a man facing the visible Jesus as he once walked in Galilee cannot be duplicated. Yet out of actual experience some part at least of the emotions in it can be understood. Who is there that cannot remember the effect upon him of some personality immensely better than himself? We may have thought that we were as good as we needed to be, since we had not seen any better revelation which shocked us by contrast. Then suddenly we became aware of that other life and its difference from ours. We saw the man at our side quietly rise in an emergency to reveal a moral courage which we had not begun to think of. We saw him take upon his shoulders unselfish burdens, and help those who stumbled in this pathetic human pilgrimage up the hard hills. We saw his figure outlined upon the spiritual mountaintops against the sky while we were down in the valleys cultivating the easy fields of our own interests. Then for the first time we began to see ourselves as we really were. Then the idea of sinfulness became no longer a somnolent phrase to be repeated in a prayer of general confession. It became acute and personal disquiet. We knew that we ourselves had sinned not against an abstract code, but against the real meaning of life which, now that we had seen it, we could no longer deny.

But does this mean, then, that one is bogged down in an ultimate sense of failure? Not if we press through to the real truth. Our humiliation is our hope. Although Simon Peter cried out, **Depart from me, for I am a sinful man, O Lord,** Jesus did not depart. Through thick and thin, through failure and through half success, he stood close, determined that however much Peter might falter, in the end he should not fail. So it always is with the spirit of Jesus. Through some human personality that partially reflects him, or in some other more silent and hidden way, he comes now as he came to the disciples long ago, not only to reveal our present selves, but to reveal the possible self which we can see in him. We know what we mean when we say that some particular quality of life is Christlike. We feel its shining goodness, and yet a goodness which is not remote or dazzling, but quick to stoop to our need and to light us on our own better way.

10-11. *Jesus' Call.*—This is Luke's abbreviated record of what is more circumstantially and vividly described in Mark 1:16-20. The climax is, of course, the same. Jesus calls four men to come with him, and they do come. They commit themselves from that moment to be not ordinary fishermen, but followers of him who said that he would teach them to fish for men.

Certain thoughts emerge. In the first place, it is well to try to feel the human warmth and the essential simplicity of that scene. Sometimes there is an impression that there was a sort of miraculous suddenness about the response of these men. Because the narrative does not tell of what may have gone before, it is often assumed that Jesus came that day as a complete stranger and the fishermen answered to this stranger's compulsion. But it would seem much more probable that Jesus had met these men before. Capernaum was not far from Nazareth, and Jesus may well have gone often to the lakeside town. Already a friend, he was one toward whom these fishermen's hearts were warm. So when he bade them come with him, they knew without any supernatural persuasion that was what they deeply wanted to do.

11 And when they had brought their ships to land, they forsook all, and followed him.

12 ¶ And it came to pass, when he was in a certain city, behold a man full of leprosy; who seeing Jesus fell on *his* face, and besought him, saying, Lord, if thou wilt, thou canst make me clean.

13 And he put forth *his* hand, and touched him, saying, I will: be thou clean. And immediately the leprosy departed from him.

14 And he charged him to tell no man: but go, and show thyself to the priest, and offer for thy cleansing, according as Moses commanded, for a testimony unto them.

forth you will be catching men." 11 And
when they had brought their boats to land,
they left everything and followed him.
12 While he was in one of the cities,
there came a man full of leprosy; and
when he saw Jesus, he fell on his face
and besought him, "Lord, if you will, you
can make me clean." 13 And he stretched
out his hand, and touched him, saying,
"I will; be clean." And immediately the
leprosy left him. 14 And he charged him
to tell no one; but "go and show yourself
to the priest, and make an offering for
your cleansing, as Moses commanded, for

---

but as in Mark 1:20, his **partners** also **left everything and followed** Jesus. Codex Bezae smooths out such roughnesses by rewriting both verses: "James and John, sons of Zebedee, were his partners. He said to them: 'Do not remain ordinary fishermen. Come and let me make you fishers of men!' And when they heard the invitation, they left everything on the land and followed him."

6. Healing of a Leper (5:12-16=Mark 1:40-45)

Luke resumes his use of Mark at the point at which he had interrupted it to introduce the preceding narrative.

12-14. As it is described in Lev. 13, **leprosy** was a term that covered a variety of ulcerous diseases, some of them curable. The leper was expected to separate himself and to cry "Unclean, unclean" as a warning to others of his condition (Lev. 13:45-46). Not until a priest had pronounced him "clean" and he had made the prescribed offerings, could he be readmitted to society (Lev. 14:1-32). Jesus **touched** the leper as part of the

---

Consider further how little they knew that day and how little Jesus required that they know. They could have had no conception of the infinite significance of this one who spoke to them. They could not have passed the most elementary catechism on Christology. They could not know either what were the tremendous ends toward which the life of Jesus would be moving. All they knew was that when they looked at him, they wanted to be with him more than they would want any other imaginable thing. So they responded when he called them and went to be with him from that day on. They would learn amazing lessons. They would be led on to a kind of devotion which then they could hardly have conceived. But at first the essential matter was simply that they should say "Yes" when Jesus said "Come with me." That is the heart of discipleship always. To become a disciple does not depend upon knowledge and learning and original orthodoxy. It depends upon the impulse of the spirit that wants to follow Jesus; and when that impulse is obeyed, all the rest will come.

12-14. ***The Healing of the Leper.***—Not only was leprosy, or what people believed to be leprosy (see Exeg.), a disease dreadful in itself, but it had the ghastly consequence of making its victim a human outcast. To feel that tragedy read *Ben Hur* (Bk. VI, chs. i-ii; Bk. VIII, ch. iv). To realize the degree of unreckoning compassion which it took to minister to a leper, remember Francis of Assisi and read Robert Louis Stevenson's letter concerning Father Damien. In the scene as presented here in Luke we have a picture both of Jesus' instant pity and of his healing power. One notes also his readiness to fit in when he could do so with the established pattern of the Jewish church. The time would come when the fellowship of Jesus' disciples would become a church that would break with Judaism, but that was because it appeared at last that the old forms were too hard and fixed to accommodate the new spirit. Here Jesus himself, and the disciples at first, kept those practices which were the inheritance of many faithful generations. When Jesus had healed this leper, he did not ignore the estab-

15 But so much the more went there a fame abroad of him: and great multitudes came together to hear, and to be healed by him of their infirmities.

16 ¶ And he withdrew himself into the wilderness, and prayed.

a proof to the people."[r] 15 But so much the more the report went abroad concerning him; and great multitudes gathered to hear and to be healed of their infirmities. 16 But he withdrew to the wilderness and prayed.

[r] Greek *to them*.

---

healer's technique. **Go and show yourself to the priest** is a command that is repeated in 17:14, the only other story in the Gospels about the healing of lepers. **An offering for . . . cleansing** would have to be made by the officiating **priest** in the temple at Jerusalem. The story assumes that Jesus contemplated no break with Jewish sacerdotalism. Like most other miracle stories, it served originally to satisfy the widespread interest of early Christians in Jesus' activities as a wonderworker.

15-16. According to Luke, Jesus **withdrew to the wilderness** to escape the throng of suppliants. Mark appears to assume that he was already "in the country" where people flocked to him "from every quarter." Luke again emphasizes that Jesus **prayed** at a crisis in his ministry.

---

lished method by which the community safeguarded itself in a matter of this kind. He sent the leper to the priest in order that the healing might be certified and the man might be permitted to go freely among the people. Thus from Jesus himself may be learned the lesson that new workers in God's name do not have to be contemptuous of what a community has established through its ordinary common sense.

15-16. ***The Ultimate Need.***—As one looks at these two verses, they seem to present a strange contradiction of what one would expect. Great multitudes are gathering around Jesus to listen to him **and to be healed of their infirmities.** What, supposedly, would follow then? Why, naturally, a statement that he stayed and healed them. But that is exactly what does not follow. Instead it is recorded that **he withdrew to the wilderness and prayed.** And why was that? No one can give the answer categorically, but spiritual meditation may well linger here and try at least to surmise the directions in which the answer may be sought.

It may be that Jesus realized that there was too much mass excitement and that the motives for it were too shallow. Here perhaps were many people whose only thought was that they could get something specific out of him. They had bodily ailments, and their entire consciousness was taken up with these. If they could be rid of them, they would be completely satisfied. But the thought of Jesus went deeper than that. Was he thinking now, as he would be thinking in the circumstances described later in vss. 20-24, not only of the infirmities of men's bodies but of the more decisive infirmities of the soul? So it may be that he did not want to see the swift mounting of a crowd emotion that fed upon a desire for miracles, and in its immediate excitement had no readiness to listen to a message of men's need for the more profound gifts of God.

May it have been, on the other hand, that Jesus felt his own need to gain again at its source the power which he was called upon to give out? One reflects upon that other incident when a woman touched him in the crowd and Jesus, turning, said, "I perceive that power has gone forth from me" (8:46). Often he would go apart alone to pray, sometimes rising early in the morning, sometimes in the evening to spend the whole night in prayer. The demands upon his sympathy and compassion and upon the energies of his own human body were endless. In order that he might respond to the pitiful thirst for help of those who flocked to him, he had to separate himself from time to time that through communion with his Father the reservoirs of his own soul might be filled again from the fountains that were on high.

Or finally, there may be a still greater truth. It is possible that Jesus went apart to pray not only in order that from that prayer he might come back to do the particular thing which people wanted then, but rather because in that praying itself the supreme blessing might be given. We do not easily grasp that possibility. Life may become so much a matter of direct activity, so largely measured by results which are visible and which, therefore, alone we think to be practical, that we have little consciousness of what may be accomplished by one who at the moment is not in obvious contact with his neighbor, but off somewhere in silent communion, interceding for him. Yet that inter-

17 And it came to pass on a certain day, as he was teaching, that there were Pharisees and doctors of the law sitting by, which were come out of every town of Galilee, and Judea, and Jerusalem: and the power of the Lord was *present* to heal them.

17 On one of those days, as he was teaching, there were Pharisees and teachers of the law sitting by, who had come from every village of Galilee and Judea and from Jerusalem; and the power of the Lord

---

C. Controversies with Pharisees (5:17–6:11)

Luke 5:17–6:11 (Mark 2:1–3:6) is a collection of stories about Jesus in controversy with Pharisaic opponents, together with some auxiliary matter. By recalling the words and example of Jesus they support the church's right to preach forgiveness of sins, to associate with those whom the synagogue had excommunicated, to disregard Jewish fasts, and to break Jewish sabbath laws. No doubt Mark found them already assembled, and Luke took them over almost as they stood in Mark.

1. Healing of a Paralytic (5:17-26=Mark 2:1-12)

The first narrative in the series combines a vivid account of Jesus as a healer (vss. 17-20*a*, 24*b*-26) and a pronouncement story about Jesus' authority to forgive sins (vss. 20*b*-24*a*).

17. Pharisees were members of a Jewish sect distinguished by its strict adherence to the written law and the supplementary interpretation. The name (or nickname) was derived from a Hebrew word (פרושים) meaning "the separated," i.e., those who avoided ceremonial defilement. They themselves preferred to be called "companions" (חברים). **Teachers of the law** is a Lukan paraphrase (for Gentile readers) of Mark's "scribes"—

---

cession may be the channel through which alone the prevailing help of God comes down.

17-22. *The Stereotyped Mind.*—There were Pharisees and teachers of the law sitting by. Here were men who ought to have been coming with eagerness to see the power of God that was being newly released through Jesus. But instead they sat on the side lines and watched him with cold criticism. Presently they would see an act of healing which left simplehearted people wondering and grateful. But to them it was only an occasion for offense. They considered that Jesus had no right to invoke the grace of God in such terms as he dared to use. **Who is this,** they said, **that speaks blasphemies?**

These Pharisees and teachers of the law were not essentially bad men. In their original and essential purpose they were good men. They were bent on preserving what they believed to be the authorized commandments and codes for religious speech and conduct. The trouble was that they had lost imagination, and so had become insensitive to the new ideas which are necessary to creative hope and faith. A. Edward Newton said with gentle wit, "But for the unimpeachable integrity of Charles Lamb we might well doubt his observation that 'lawyers were children once.' "[2] Those Pharisees and teachers of the law whom Luke introduces here were the type who grow so old and crusty in their minds that one might well have doubted whether they ever had been children. Yet they too were children once, with the blessedness of a child's possession of a mind not fixed in stubborn patterns and a spirit still expectant. Now they had no alertness to new realities; they were only lawyers, jealous for what they thought had been established in the long ago. Similarly, many men and women who are not lawyers by profession may yet in their individual attitudes to life, in their civic loyalties, in their religious and ecclesiastical prejudices, lose all signs that they once were children instead of their legalistic and dusty present selves. "Whosoever shall not receive the kingdom of God as a little child, he shall not enter therein," said Jesus (Mark 10:15). It is a calamitous thing when any person fails to carry into maturity some of the everlasting meaning of the child's expectancy and the child's desire.

17-26. *The Son of Man.*—At this point Luke begins to recount five incidents which in substantially the same form and in precisely the same order have been described in Mark 2:1–3:6. This practical identity of material indicates the importance of these incidents in the thought of the early church. One emphasis is in them all: the repeated emphasis upon the

[2] "Newton on Blackstone," *The Atlantic Monthly*, CLIX (1937), 3.

18 ¶ And, behold, men brought in a
bed a man which was taken with a palsy:
and they sought *means* to bring him in, and
to lay *him* before him.
19 And when they could not find by
what *way* they might bring him in because
of the multitude, they went upon the house-
top, and let him down through the tiling
with *his* couch into the midst before Jesus.
20 And when he saw their faith, he said
unto him, Man, thy sins are forgiven thee.
21 And the scribes and the Pharisees
began to reason, saying, Who is this which
speaketh blasphemies? Who can forgive
sins, but God alone?

was with him to heal.[s] 18 And behold,
men were bringing on a bed a man who
was paralyzed, and they sought to bring
him in and lay him before Jesus;[t] 19 but
finding no way to bring him in, because of
the crowd, they went up on the roof and
let him down with his bed through the tiles
into the midst before Jesus. 20 And when
he saw their faith he said, "Man, your
sins are forgiven you." 21 And the scribes
and the Pharisees began to question, say-
ing, "Who is this that speaks blasphemies?
Who can forgive sins but God only?"

[s] Other ancient authorities read *was present to heal them.*
[t] Greek *him.*

---

professional experts in Jewish legalism. **The Lord** is a reference in this instance to God. Luke appears to think of **the power . . . to heal** as a sporadic gift (cf. 6:19).

18-20*a*. The **bed** would resemble a stretcher. The narrative has in mind a one-story (and probably one-room) house. The **crowd,** spilling out into the courtyard, prevented access to Jesus through the door. **The roof** would be a flat thatch of straw or branches, coated with clay, and reached by an outside staircase. Luke presupposes non-Palestinian architecture when he speaks of **tiles** that could be lifted.

20*b*-24*a*. If these verses were originally part of a separate narrative, they do not necessarily imply a correlation of sickness and sin, although that was common enough in Judaism. Jesus' exercise of the right of absolution—referred to elsewhere only in 7:47—would serve to support the church's proclamation of forgiveness, a divine prerogative according to the O.T. and rabbinical tradition. Vs. 23 (Mark 2:9) links this bit of early Christian apologetic with the miracle story in which it is embedded, and which

---

authority of Jesus. Here in the account of the healing of the paralytic it is the authority to forgive sins; in the succeeding incidents it is his authority to associate with sinners, to set aside the strict conventions of the Jewish code, to be free from the letter even of the sabbath law.

In this particular scene in the synagogue three aspects are conspicuous. In the first place, there is the faith that moved the friends of the paralyzed man and which, it is to be supposed, was burning in him too. It turned out to be a not easy or simple matter for him to get into the presence of Jesus. Crowds that pressed around Jesus filled the house and overflowed beyond. But these friends of the sick man, once they had made up their minds to bring him where Jesus was, were not to be deterred. If they could not get in the door, then they would get him through the roof, and that was what they did. It was no wonder that Jesus' heart leaped up to welcome a faith and resolution such as that. What great answers to human faith might there not be in every generation if men were as undiscouraged and determined to bring their needs to God as those friends of the paralytic were to bring this man to the feet of Jesus!

The second matter to note is what Jesus said. To him body and soul were bound up together in a living unity. There could be no wholeness of life unless the soul was at peace with God. Therefore he spoke directly to this man's first and most important need: **Your sins are forgiven you,** he said. When that was true, then strength and healing of the body could follow. This could be a sign of the inward healing, but it was secondary to it. Even if the man's body had remained crippled, the greater blessing could have been wrought. To release a soul from its inner fear and darkness, to give the spiritual power of an inner peace, was more than to give the body the physical strength to walk.

In the third place, note the name by which Jesus called himself. Here is the first instance in the Gospel of Luke of the title **Son of man.** It is a striking fact that this title is never used in the Gospel as on the lips of others, and yet is recorded scores of times as having been used by Jesus himself. It was thus no preferred or invented phrase of the early church. Rather

22 But when Jesus perceived their thoughts, he answering said unto them, What reason ye in your hearts?

23 Whether is easier, to say, Thy sins be forgiven thee; or to say, Rise up and walk?

24 But that ye may know that the Son of man hath power upon earth to forgive sins, (he said unto the sick of the palsy,) I say unto thee, Arise, and take up thy couch, and go into thine house.

25 And immediately he rose up before them, and took up that whereon he lay, and departed to his own house, glorifying God.

26 And they were all amazed, and they glorified God, and were filled with fear, saying, We have seen strange things to-day.

22 When Jesus perceived their questionings,
he answered them, "Why do you question
in your hearts? 23 Which is easier, to say,
'Your sins are forgiven you,' or to say,
'Rise and walk'? 24 But that you may know
that the Son of man has authority on
earth to forgive sins" — he said to the man
who was paralyzed — "I say to you, rise,
take up your bed and go home." 25 And
immediately he rose before them, and took
up that on which he lay, and went home,
glorifying God. 26 And amazement seized
them all, and they glorified God and were
filled with awe, saying, "We have seen
strange things today."

---

demonstrated Jesus' right to say: **Your sins are forgiven you. The Son of man** occurs in the Gospels only on the lips of Jesus. In the Similitudes of Enoch (46:2-4; 69:26-27, 29) the title is applied to the supernatural being who is to be God's vicegerent at the end of the present age and in the Day of Judgment. In the Gospels, also, it is ordinarily an apocalyptic synonym for "Messiah." Whether Jesus himself employed the term, remains a debated question. The hypothesis that it is to be explained as an overliteral translation into Greek of an Aramaic phrase meaning nothing more than "man" does not commend itself in this instance. It is clear that both Mark and Luke have Jesus' messianic **authority** in mind.

24*b*-26. He said to the man who was paralyzed is stylistically as awkward in Greek as in English, and this observation supports the hypothesis that two originally disparate narratives have been fused. According to an almost stereotyped formula, the cure by fiat is verified by the subsequent behavior of the patient and the impression it made on the onlookers. **Amazement** and **awe** were emotions evoked by the successful healer rather than the successful controversialist.

---

it was a recollection of the actual word of Jesus so certainly fixed in the tradition that it could not be forgotten. What did it mean? In part it may have meant what it represented in the book of Ezekiel, where it is used more than ninety times to indicate the prophet whom God had raised up to carry his message to his people. In part it may have been charged for Jesus with the immense overtones of Dan. 7:13, in which "one like the Son of man" appears in the clouds of heaven before the "Ancient of days," and is given "Dominion, and glory, and a kingdom," as representative of the saints who shall possess the kingdom forever. And it may be that its meaning went on to embrace the still more majestic prophecies of the Similitudes of Enoch, in which the Son of man is to sit upon a throne of glory, as God's vicegerent, to whom "the sum of judgment" is assigned.

It is true, of course, that we cannot fathom the consciousness of Jesus himself. But it was a meaning not less than all this that the conception of Jesus as the **Son of man** held for the early church. In an unparalleled way he represented and transmitted the majesty as well as the mercy of God. And when their faith reached up to what Jesus had revealed, they felt in the love which came to them through him nothing less than God's forgiveness. That has been proved in Christian experience ever since. Browning was right when he wrote in "An Epistle":

> So, the All-Great, were the All-Loving too—
> So, through the thunder comes a human voice
> Saying, "O heart I made, a heart beats here!"

Through the love that was incarnate, man can trust the infinite love that was in the beginning and will be to the end.

27 ¶ And after these things he went forth, and saw a publican, named Levi, sitting at the receipt of custom: and he said unto him, Follow me.

28 And he left all, rose up, and followed him.

29 And Levi made him a great feast in his own house: and there was a great company of publicans and of others that sat down with them.

30 But their scribes and Pharisees murmured against his disciples, saying, Why do ye eat and drink with publicans and sinners?

27 After this he went out, and saw a tax collector, named Levi, sitting at the tax office; and he said to him, "Follow me." **28** And he left everything, and rose and followed him.

29 And Levi made him a great feast in his house; and there was a large company of tax collectors and others sitting at table[u] with them. **30** And the Pharisees and their scribes murmured against his disciples, saying, "Why do you eat and drink with

[u] Greek *reclining*.

---

2. Levi's Call (5:27-28=Mark 2:13-14)

27. A publican (KJV; *publicanus* in the Vulg.) was a lessee of the right to collect a Roman tax, and **tax collector** (RSV) is a better translation into English of the Greek name for a mere henchman. **Levi** is identified in Mark as a "son of Alphaeus." A certain James "the son of Alphaeus" is included in all Synoptic Gospel lists of the twelve disciples (Mark 3:18; etc.), but there is no suggestion in either Mark or Luke that **Levi** became a member of that inner circle. The author of the Gospel of Matthew has apparently confused **Levi** with Matthew, substituting the latter name in Matt. 9:9 and describing him in Matt. 10:3 as a "tax collector." **The tax office** need not have been more than a roadside table.

3. Jesus as a Guest in Levi's House (5:29-32=Mark 2:15-17)

29-32. It is an open question whether Mark thought of Jesus as the host or the guest at the **great feast,** but Luke leaves no room for difference of opinion (cf. 19:5). **Sitting at table** is a modernization of the Greek word for "reclining" (RSV mg.). The presence of **the Pharisees and their scribes** at such a meal appears to be an incongruous element in the narrative, and many interpreters believe that the statement that they **murmured against his disciples** probably reflects a situation in which Judaism was charging the church with admitting riffraff to its membership. Nevertheless Jesus' association with men

---

27-32. ***Friend of the Common Crowd.***—Here in Luke the name of the tax collector is Levi, and it is Levi also in the earlier account in Mark 2:13-17. But in the First Gospel the tax collector's name is Matthew (Matt. 9:9). Whichever name is right, or whether the two names were interchangeable, the picture is the same. This man, like Peter, Andrew, and James and John before him, felt the immense attraction of Jesus. Thenceforth collecting taxes would seem to him a cheap thing as compared with the magnetism of this strong influence that drew him on. He left the whole business behind, and went to follow Jesus.

Then the first thing he did was to beg Jesus to come to his house for a feast to which he invited a number of his associates and friends. No wonder the Pharisees were outraged! They themselves would have lost caste by sitting down in such a low-class crowd. They would have been too uncomfortable in that company to endure it. But Jesus, what of him? Remembering him and what he was, one knows that when he sat in Levi's house with that unrefined collection, he did not come down to what had been their level. (It is a shallow and pitiful mistake when anyone imagines that in order to be pleasant and popular and hail fellow well met, one must make oneself a cheap imitation of men's least worthy words and habits.) Jesus, by being himself, lifted Levi's friends instinctively toward his level, because when they looked at him, that was where all that was secretly aspiring in them desired to be. He had no embarrassment or constraint in the midst of those whom the community called its sinners. He loved them even as they were, and he loved them with the warmth of God's own expectation of what they might become. There in the midst of them he felt the deep joy of

31 And Jesus answering said unto them, They that are whole need not a physician; but they that are sick.

32 I came not to call the righteous, but sinners to repentance.

33 ¶ And they said unto him, Why do the disciples of John fast often, and make prayers, and likewise *the disciples* of the Pharisees; but thine eat and drink?

34 And he said unto them, Can ye make the children of the bridechamber fast, while the bridegroom is with them?

35 But the days will come, when the bridegroom shall be taken away from them, and then shall they fast in those days.

tax collectors and sinners?" 31 And Jesus
answered them, "Those who are well have
no need of a physician, but those who are
sick; 32 I have not come to call the right-
eous, but sinners to repentance."
33 And they said to him, "The disciples
of John fast often and offer prayers, and
so do the disciples of the Pharisees, but
yours eat and drink." 34 And Jesus said to
them, "Can you make wedding guests fast
while the bridegroom is with them? 35 The
days will come, when the bridegroom is
taken away from them, and then they will

---

and women outside the pale of Jewish legalism is well fixed in the gospel tradition, and it would be hazardous to assume that the whole story has been derived from the saying in vs. 32. Sharing a meal with those who did not observe the law was included by the rabbis among the "things that shame a pupil of the scribes" (Berakoth 43*b*). Luke's addition of **to repentance** narrows the reference in vs. 32, which may originally have implied "to the kingdom."

4. Parable of the Wedding Guests (5:33-35=Mark 2:18-20)

33-35. The better MSS support the RSV punctuation of vs. 33 as a statement rather than a question (contrast Mark). **The disciples of the Pharisees** is a peculiar phrase, for a Pharisee as a *rabbi* could have disciples, but not as a *Pharisee.* It is a plausible conjecture that **the Pharisees** were introduced into the story—at some pre-Marcan stage—to make it another "conflict." In that case the earlier contrast was between the practice of **the disciples of John** and that of Jesus' followers. "Groomsmen" is the specific meaning of the Semitism translated **wedding guests.** The gospel tradition makes it clear that neither Jesus nor his disciples practiced fasting, but the Didache, an early second-century Christian catechism, indicates that the early church did so: "Let not your fasts be with the hypocrites [Jews], for they fast on Mondays and Thursdays, but do you fast on Wednesdays and Fridays" (Did. 8:1). Therefore vs. 35 may be an early allegorical addition to a parable that originally compared the kingdom of God to a wedding festival. It makes Jesus declare that his disciples were justified in fasting after his death, although it was known both that they had not done so during his lifetime and that this omission had been approved by Jesus. It is improbable that Jesus predicted his death and justified a later ecclesiastical practice after this fashion.

---

his life's mission, which was, as he said to his critics, **not to call the righteous, but sinners to repentance.** Whenever the fellowship of Jesus as expressed in the Christian church lets that supreme motive slip away, it is no longer Christian. Always its spirit must be evangelistic. Its only leaders who are true to the motive of their Master are those who in their different ways and in their different places do what Bishop Joseph B. Lightfoot of Durham declared that William Booth had done: he had "recalled us to this lost ideal of the work of the Church—*the universal compulsion of the souls of men.*" [3]

33-39. ***Christian Gaiety.***—This may be a composite passage, made up, as the Exeg. suggests, of earlier and later traditions. Vs. 39 is absent from a number of important MSS. The general meaning of the whole passage, however, can be readily discerned. Jesus was under constant criticism because he did not make his disciples observe the strict and sometimes long-

[3] Harold Begbie, *Life of General William Booth* (New York: The Macmillan Co., 1920), II, 4.

36 ¶ And he spake also a parable unto them; No man putteth a piece of a new garment upon an old; if otherwise, then both the new maketh a rent, and the piece that was *taken* out of the new agreeth not with the old.

37 And no man putteth new wine into old bottles; else the new wine will burst the bottles, and be spilled, and the bottles shall perish.

38 But new wine must be put into new bottles; and both are preserved.

39 No man also having drunk old *wine* straightway desireth new; for he saith, The old is better.

6 And it came to pass on the second sabbath after the first, that he went through the corn fields; and his disciples plucked the ears of corn, and did eat, rubbing *them* in *their* hands.

fast in those days." 36 He told them a para-
ble also: "No one tears a piece from a new
garment and puts it upon an old garment;
if he does, he will tear the new, and the
piece from the new will not match the
old. 37 And no one puts new wine into
old wineskins; if he does, the new wine
will burst the skins and it will be spilled,
and the skins will be destroyed. 38 But new
wine must be put into fresh wineskins.
39 And no one after drinking old wine de-
sires new; for he says, 'The old is good.' "[v]

6 On a sabbath,[w] while he was going
through the grainfields, his disciples
plucked and ate some ears of grain, rub-

[v] Other ancient authorities read *better*.
[w] Other ancient authorities read *On the second first sabbath* (on the second sabbath after the first).

5. Parables of the Patch and of the Wineskins
(5:36-39=Mark 2:21-22)

36-38. According to Mark, the first of these two parables declared that a patch of unbleached cloth will shrink after it has been sewed on a coat, and leave a tear that is worse than ever. Its parallelism with its twin is not as direct in Luke's version, which deplores ruining **a new garment** in order to patch **an old,** since **the piece from the new will not match the old. New wine** is unfermented wine (therefore "must"). **Old wineskins** are hard and dry, and **will burst** when the fermentation occurs. The parables teach that one must not mix the new with the old, but pass no judgment on the relative merits of the one and the other. In their Marcan and Lukan application they point the moral that the new Christian message and the old ceremonial forms of Judaism are incompatible; more specifically, that the new gospel has nothing to do with the old rite of fasting. Since their original context cannot be recovered, it is idle to speculate on the truth Jesus meant them to illustrate.

39. Omitted by Codex Bezae and its allies, and probably to be regarded as an interpolated apology for the relative failure of Christian missions among Jews.

6. Concerning Plucking and Eating Grain on the Sabbath
(6:1-5=Mark 2:23-28)

6:1-2. On the second sabbath after the first (KJV) is a difficult reading with strong support in the MSS, and its very difficulty is an argument in its favor. A reckoning in terms of post-Passover sabbaths is given in Lev. 23:15-16, and perhaps Luke had in mind the second sabbath in such a series. Barley is harvested in Palestine shortly before the

faced customs of the Jewish code. John the Baptist made his disciples follow those restrictions; the Pharisees said John the Baptist knew enough to recognize the importance of correct behavior if people were to be accounted respectably religious. Why did not Jesus make his own disciples more punctilious? The answer was that in him and through him something new and thrilling had come into the midst of life. The expansive power of his message of the life and love in God could not be expressed in conventional form. There was in Christ, and there always must be in Christianity, something of the pure gaiety of a spirit so free in God that it can be debonair.

6:1-5. ***The Old and the New.***—In this incident one must see not only what is in the foreground, but what is in the background also.

2 And certain of the Pharisees said unto them, Why do ye that which is not lawful to do on the sabbath days?

3 And Jesus answering them said, Have ye not read so much as this, what David did, when himself was ahungered, and they which were with him;

4 How he went into the house of God, and did take and eat the showbread, and gave also to them that were with him; which it is not lawful to eat but for the priests alone?

5 And he said unto them, That the Son of man is Lord also of the sabbath.

6 And it came to pass also on another sabbath, that he entered into the synagogue and taught: and there was a man whose right hand was withered.

bing them in their hands. 2 But some of the
Pharisees said, "Why are you doing what is
not lawful to do on the sabbath?" 3 And
Jesus answered, "Have you not read what
David did when he was hungry, he and
those who were with him: 4 how he entered
the house of God, and took and ate the
bread of the Presence, which it is not law-
ful for any but the priests to eat, and also
gave it to those with him?" 5 And he said to
them, "The Son of man is lord of the sab-
bath."

6 On another sabbath, when he entered
the synagogue and taught, a man was there

Passover, and wheat shortly after. Therefore the story, if it is primitive, affords the incidental information that Jesus' ministry extended over a period that included at least two Passovers. The O.T. prohibition of sabbath labor had been supplemented in rabbinical tradition by a list of thirty-nine "major occupations" that were proscribed, among them harvesting and threshing (Shabbath 7:2). To pluck heads of grain in a neighbor's field was not considered an act of theft (Deut. 23:25), but to do so on the sabbath was a form of "harvesting," and was declared to be a breach of the law.

3-4. Jesus defends the legality of his disciples' act by an appeal to David's action **when he was hungry** (I Sam. 21:1-6). Human need can override the letter of the law. Luke omits Mark's mistaken reference to Abiathar (instead of Ahimelech) as high priest. **The bread of the Presence:** Twelve cakes that were placed each sabbath on a "table of pure gold" in the sanctuary, and eaten only by priests (Lev. 24:5-9). For an interesting insertion by Codex Bezae at this point see Intro., p. 21.

5. Another line of defense: The authority of the Messiah to set aside sabbath legislation. No doubt the church found this a useful argument in its controversy with Jews over the celebration of the Christian Sunday, but it is difficult to think of it as primitive. If the hypothesis that **Son of man** is an overliteral translation of an Aramaic phrase (בר אנשא) meaning "man" is accepted in this instance, Mark (followed by Luke and Matthew) has misinterpreted a far-reaching principle. Mark 2:27*b* is its natural premise, although its omission—if it was original—by Luke and Matthew (and by Codex Bezae and its allies in their text of Mark) is difficult to explain.

7. Concerning a Healing on the Sabbath (6:6-11=Mark 3:1-6)

The fifth and last in this conflict series. Luke later incorporates two similar stories (13:10-17; 14:1-6). In each instance the motif of miracle is subordinated to that of controversy.

That background has to do with what Jesus' disciples at the moment knew and took for granted, but which we may forget. Here in the foreground is Jesus—decisively setting aside the accepted sabbath code. But in the background is the fact of the Jesus who was no scorner of the sabbath, but who, on the contrary, held it dear. He had grown up in its atmosphere of worship in Nazareth. When he went back to Nazareth, he went to the synagogue on the sabbath, "as his custom was." All the great and holy traditions of Israel were rooted in Jesus' affection. But he had what many of the Pharisees, with their minds grown stiff and formal, lacked. He had the vivid consciousness of the life and love of God coming directly into touch

7 And the scribes and Pharisees watched
him, whether he would heal on the sab-
bath day; that they might find an accusa-
tion against him.
8 But he knew their thoughts, and said
to the man which had the withered hand,
Rise up, and stand forth in the midst.
And he arose and stood forth.

whose right hand was withered. 7 And the
scribes and the Pharisees watched him, to
see whether he would heal on the sabbath,
so that they might find an accusation
against him. 8 But he knew their thoughts,
and he said to the man who had the with-
ered hand, "Come and stand here." And

6-7. The Gospel According to the Hebrews, a lost variant of our Matthew, represented the cripple as addressing Jesus: "I was a stonemason, seeking a living with my hands; I implore you, Jesus, to restore me to health that I may not need to beg in shame" (Jerome *On Matthew* XII. 2). To **heal on the sabbath,** except in cases of extremity, was contrary to rabbinical interpretation of the law (Shabbath 22:6).

8-10. It is possible to interpret the first half of Jesus' double question as an ironical comparison of his own motives with those of his opponents—their malice makes them the real sabbathbreakers. Others see in it an idea similar to the one expressed in Jas. 4:17:

---

with the needs of his human children, concerned with these, compassionate for these, using old ordinances in so far as they ministered to these, and altering them whenever they became not benefits but barriers to his grace. The immediate fact must be more controlling than the rigid formula. As that was the mind of Christ, so it ought to be the controlling spirit in Christianity everywhere. There must be reverence for the old, but over and beyond that there must be the recognition that God's redeeming mercy will be forever making for itself new ways of approach to the needs of men.

7-11. ***Limitations of the Scribes.*—Scribes and Pharisees.** That is a familiar phrase in the Gospel, and usually it has an unpleasant overtone. Scribes and Pharisees were nearly always antagonistic to Jesus, impatient and supercilious. Yet the Pharisees, and the scribes who were the most learned of the Pharisaic party, ought to have been admirable men. They had knowledge; they revered the religious inheritance which had come to them from the past; they were studious. What was the matter with them, then? The matter was that they paid the penalty of their own excessive and lopsided virtue. They were so intent upon what used to be that they were blind to what might be henceforward. They had grown spiritually nearsighted and astigmatic. They peered so narrowly into old books that they never lifted their eyes to look out of the window upon the new and exciting facts which were going by. They knew all about what God had said once, and in their preoccupation with that it did not even occur to them that they had better be listening for what God was saying then. That is always the danger of the scribe. He is like a mole who burrows underground and cannot find his way on the surface. He is like a deep-sea fish that has become accustomed to the glimmering half-light and the half-immobility of old drowned years.

So the scribes of the first century could not or would not recognize the new and thrilling message from God which was coming through Jesus. They had no elasticity of spiritual comprehension which could make them respond to a power that had not already been included in the precedents they knew. Common people in the presence of Jesus could be filled with amazement and could glorify God (5:26). Ideally, the people ought to have been able to learn God's glory from what the scribes taught, but the scribes failed them; and those who are scribes and no more always do thus fail. They have no fresh word for a new generation. They can only tell how people ought to live if the world were the same as it used to be a few hundred years ago. But the world never is. It is always different, and if men are to hear God's message for their immediate problems and their immediate needs, they must hear it through some immediate sense of the truth as it comes from Jesus, and not from the scribe who listens with straining ear only to catch some echo of a word of God faintly resounding from the distant wall of dead centuries.

8. ***The Divine Discernment.*—He knew their thoughts.** These are arresting and formidable words. Jesus did not have to wait to hear what the Pharisees would say or to watch what they would do. As he looked at their faces, his swift perception saw what was going on secretly in their minds and hearts. The light of the truth of God that was in him had a penetrating certainty which could be terrible. The evil in men

9 Then said Jesus unto them, I will ask you one thing; Is it lawful on the sabbath days to do good, or to do evil? to save life, or to destroy *it?*

10 And looking round about upon them all, he said unto the man, Stretch forth thy hand. And he did so: and his hand was restored whole as the other.

11 And they were filled with madness; and communed one with another what they might do to Jesus.

12 And it came to pass in those days, that he went out into a mountain to pray, and continued all night in prayer to God.

he rose and stood there. **9** And Jesus said
to them, "I ask you, is it lawful on the
sabbath to do good or to do harm, to save
life or to destroy it?" **10** And he looked
around on them all, and said to him,
"Stretch out your hand." And he did so,
and his hand was restored. **11** But they
were filled with fury and discussed with
one another what they might do to Jesus.
12 In these days he went out into the
hills to pray; and all night he continued

"Whoever knows what is right to do and fails to do it, for him it is sin." Not **to do good** in this instance is **to do evil.** It is difficult to force the second half of the parallelism into either explanation, for it would be violent exegesis to conclude from it that the sabbath healing of **the man who had the withered hand** was a matter of life or death. Many interpreters believe the double question was once independent of its present setting.

11. No doubt the Pharisees, as guardians of the law, were suspicious of Jesus from the beginning. Luke and Matthew omit Mark's mysterious reference to a conspiracy "with the Herodians." According to Exod. 31:14 and 35:2, death was the penalty for violating the sabbath law; but there is no evidence that it was enforced in Roman times, and no formal charge of sabbath defilement was ever laid against Jesus.

D. The Great Sermon (6:12-49)

1. Choosing of the Twelve (6:12-16=Mark 3:13-19*a*)

12. Into the hills (RSV) rather than **into a mountain** (KJV).

---

could not mask itself or hide from his recognition. Thus in him there was represented a divine fact of which life must always take account. In many homes of an earlier generation there used to be on the wall the woven and framed words "Thou God Seest Me." That reminder belonged, it is true, to the austere mood of Puritanism, and it gave sometimes a note to religion that was undoubtedly grim. But nevertheless it represented a recognition of that which must never be lost if religion is to retain a serious and disciplined responsibility. In a generation which tends to let the individual grow soft through the excuse that his life is as good as the crowd expects, there is need to remember the searching and eternal truth of God, by which, and not by the world's chatter and compromise, a man's morality and religion will be judged.

But there is another side to the truth which the words in the Gospel suggest. As Jesus knew the thoughts of men when they were evil, so also he knew those thoughts when they were good. He recognized and by his encouragement he warmed into growth even the little seeds of goodness which people might be wistfully aware of in themselves but hardly dared to trust. He knew the aspirations which might be stirred in their souls, the divine upreaching, and the quivering of spiritual wings that had not yet learned to fly. Because he saw these possibilities, he helped men and women to see them too. That is the way he dealt with Simon Peter and with Mary Magdalene. That is how he could see in Matthew the taxgatherer the man who should be a disciple. So he expressed not only the judgment but also the mercy of the all-seeing eyes of God. That fact can come as encouragement to unsure souls in every time. It is not only what we already are—or are not—that God perceives, but what by his grace we may be. Browning has expressed that truth in "Rabbi Ben Ezra," the truth that it is not the acts that we have yet achieved, but the direction of our thoughts; not the goodness we have won, but the goodness that we do deeply crave; not the selves of today, but the selves that may be unfolding for tomorrow—these are what we are "worth to God."

12. ***The All-Night Vigil.***—Imagination may linger reverently upon this scene. At the end of the day Jesus goes up into the hills. He felt,

13 ¶ And when it was day, he called
unto him his disciples: and of them he
chose twelve, whom also he named apostles;
14 Simon, (whom he also named Peter,)
and Andrew his brother, James and John,
Philip and Bartholomew,

in prayer to God. 13 And when it was day,
he called his disciples, and chose from
them twelve, whom he named apostles;
14 Simon, whom he named Peter, and An-
drew his brother, and James and John,

---

13. Jesus chose **twelve** from among a much larger group (cf. vs. 17). Apart from Peter, the sons of Zebedee, and Judas Iscariot, the members of this inner circle remain little more than names. Apocryphal "Acts" of Andrew, Matthew, Thomas, and others proliferated in the third and later centuries. Paul's use of "the twelve" (I Cor. 15:5) as a title for the disciples makes improbable any hypothesis that the number was arbitrarily fixed by the early church. It is possible that Jesus himself intended "the twelve" to symbolize the true Israel that would enter God's kingdom. In early church usage **apostles** included Paul and Barnabas and other missionaries (Rom. 16:7). The limitation of the title to the original group (Matt. 10:2; Mark 6:30; Rev. 21:14; and six times in Luke) would therefore appear to be late. It is an anachronism on Luke's part to assert that Jesus conferred it.

14-16. Peter ("rock") is almost certainly a translation of the Aramaic "Cephas" (John 1:42 and often in Galatians and I Corinthians). The nickname may represent an estimate of the disciple's character, despite his behavior at Gethsemane and after Jesus' arrest. More probably it recalls the fact that, as the first disciple to be called, or as the first of Jesus' followers to be convinced of his Lord's resurrection (24:33-34; I Cor. 15:5), he was "the rock" on which the church was built (Matt. 16:18). The gospel tradition differs as to when the name was conferred: according to the Fourth Gospel, at Jesus' first

---

as many a man in his lesser way has felt, the lift of the spirit which comes when one goes from the lower levels of the earth to the heights from which the far perspectives of the landscape open, around which there is the great silence of the clean upper air, above which is the profundity of the sky. There, alone and apart from all the distractions of the world below, Jesus let his mind and soul commune with God: while the sun went down and the shadows lengthened; while the stars came out and the constellations moved across the great arc of heaven; hour after hour until at length the dawn flushed above the Trans-Jordan mountains and the morning came. Certainly he was not uttering petitions all that time, or speaking any words. He was revealing what prayer at its most intense can be: an undistracted listening to God.

What was it that in this instance he sought and what was it he heard? No doubt it was illumination for the choice he was presently to make. That next day he would select the men who were to be most intimately with him as his disciples. He wished to make that choice in the light of a heavenly purpose, and to invoke God's grace for these men who should be with him. As to the essential answer to that prayer, history bears witness. Men who by all outward signs seemed very ordinary—fishermen, tax collectors, and others from backgrounds too undistinguished to have been recorded—were made into such representatives of their Lord that ultimately they turned the world upside down. Nothing that was in those men themselves could have accomplished that. The power of the mightier world that overarches this world of ours came down to them through Jesus' intercession—came at least to all of them but one. Among those chosen was Judas Iscariot, doubtless because Jesus trusted him as he trusted the others of the twelve. Yet Judas would betray him. Here, then, appears what seems the tragic contradiction of a prayer answered and yet unanswered. How can it be supposed that the Father did answer the prayer of Jesus that his disciples should be faithful if Judas was to fall away? To this question the reply is that though God's grace is fully given, there is in every man the awful freedom to refuse it. There was available to Judas the same inspiration that made the other disciples great. That was the answer to his Master's prayer. But the inspiration which God offers is never compulsory. It is the privilege and the peril of every man that he can determine whether he will let the flame of the spirit burn in him or whether he will blow it out.

13-16. ***The Twelve Apostles.***—Here is the full list of those whom Jesus chose to be most intimately with him. Among these names the most memorable are those of **Peter** and **John** (see

15 Matthew and Thomas, James the *son* of Alpheus, and Simon called Zelotes,

and Philip, and Bartholomew, **15** and Matthew, and Thomas, and James the son of Alphaeus, and Simon who was called the

---

encounter with him (John 1:42); according to Mark and Luke, when the twelve were chosen (although most Lukan MSS read "Simon Peter" in 5:8); and according to Matthew, after he had confessed Jesus' messiahship at Caesarea Philippi (Matt. 16:18). **Andrew** is a pure Greek name. Since Luke had not reproduced Mark's earlier reference to him (Mark 1:16), he now identifies him for the readers of the Gospel as Peter's **brother. James and John** have already been introduced as "sons of Zebedee" (5:10), and that title is not used in this instance. Mark's enigmatical "sons of thunder" is also omitted. **Philip**—another pure Greek name—is described in John 1:44 and 12:21 as a native of Bethsaida. The disciple is not to be confused with the evangelist of Acts 6:5; 8:4-13, 26-40. **Bartholomew** is patronymic (perhaps "son of Ptolemy"). **Matthew** has sometimes been identified with the "Nathanael" of the Fourth Gospel, since both names mean "gift of

---

Expos. on 5:1-11), but in their different ways the others are significant too.

First among those others there is **James.** He, as we have already seen, was one of the three whom Jesus drew out from the twelve in general to be with him at certain great moments of his own experience. James, like his brother John, was originally a man of hot and sudden temper. But in that temper was a fire which could forge an unbreakable devotion. He would lay down his life later for the sake of his Lord (Acts 12:2). Moreover, there was an incident in the life of James—as of his brother John also—which is often thought of in a way that obscures the element of nobility that was in it. In Mark 10:35-45 it is told that James and John came to Jesus, asking that they might sit at his right hand and at his left hand in his glory. The other disciples were greatly annoyed when they heard that. They considered it an evidence of a pushing ambition which wanted to get ahead of the others in ultimate honor and reward. It is true that James and his brother did ask for posts of honor. The element of self-seeking which was there needed to be rebuked, and Jesus did rebuke it. But consider a deeper fact. How did they happen to make any such request of Jesus as that they might have seats of honor next to him in his kingdom? What made them think there would be any kingdom? Certainly there was no outward evidence of it as Jesus led his little band of peasant followers along the dusty roads to Jerusalem. Jesus had no army, no powerful following, no worldly pomp or obvious power whatever. But James and John had an instinctive consciousness of Jesus' greatness. They had got above the level, which some men never transcend, of judging reality in material terms. They saw in Jesus the spiritual power which they believed would be ultimately more decisive than any forces of this earth. It is that perception more than anything else which makes a man choose Christ and cleave to him.

Among the twelve was **Andrew.** There is something pathetic about Andrew, and for our present knowledge, puzzling too. He was Simon Peter's brother, as James was the brother of John, yet he was not included among the three who were of the innermost circle. One wonders whether Andrew was sometimes wistful that he was left out and whether he wondered why. Whatever may be the fact concerning that, here was a man who without resentment played his full part in loyalty and service. According to the Fourth Gospel, it was Andrew who was drawn to Jesus before Simon Peter was, and who went and called his brother to come with him. It was Andrew, according to that same Gospel, who first looked about and saw "a lad here who has five barley loaves and two fish" (John 6:9), and who, even when he questioned their sufficiency, nevertheless had the practical sense to tell Jesus of this food with which the feeding of the multitude might begin. It was to Andrew that Philip went when he knew that there were certain Greeks who wanted to see Jesus, because he evidently thought that Andrew could arrange it (John 12:22). Here was a man whose mind was not on his own honors or lack of them, but a man, on the contrary, quick to see each chance for helpfulness and to go out to meet it. Such men must stand high in the ultimate reckoning of the kingdom of their Lord.

There was **Matthew,** who was called from the receipt of custom. Not much is known of him, although his name is associated with the Gospel that comes first in the N.T. But this one fact stands clear: He was a man who as a tax collector was making money. He could have stayed in that position and kept on making money. But when he saw Jesus, he left all that behind. Relatively, his possessions did not

16 And Judas *the brother* of James, and Judas Iscariot, which also was the traitor.

Zealot, 16 and Judas the son[x] of James, and Judas Iscariot, who became a traitor.

[x] Or *brother.*

God." **Thomas** is a Hellenized form of the Hebrew word for "twin" (cf. John 11:16; etc.). It is arbitrary exegesis to identify **James the son of Alphaeus** with either "Levi the son of Alphaeus" (Mark 2:14) or "James the younger" (Mark 15:40). The second Simon in the list is called "the Cananaean" in Mark, a title that is probably the transliteration into Greek of an Aramaic word (קנאנא) that Luke translates **the Zealot.** The title may have been nothing more than a nickname, for there is no evidence that members of the revolutionary party in Palestine were known as "Zealots" before A.D. 66. No doubt **Judas the son of James** is the "Judas (not Iscariot)" of John 14:22, although it is clear that there has been some primitive confusion about the name of this particular disciple. He is called "Thaddaeus" in most MSS of Mark and Matthew, and the Codex Bezae text of those Gospels has "Lebbaeus." The second **Judas** in the list is called "the son of Simon Iscariot" in John 6:71, etc. **Iscariot** is probably a Hebraism meaning "man of Kerioth"—a village on the southern fringes of Judea. Another list of the same names, in slightly different order, and omitting Judas Iscariot, appears in Acts 1:13.

---

seem important to him any more. To be in the fellowship of Jesus was worth all that it was going to cost.

After Matthew on the list comes **Thomas.** According to the narrative of the Fourth Gospel, and in the thought of Christendom ever since, he is the man who doubted. If so, then there is encouragement for many would-be Christians that this sort of man was included in Jesus' fellowship. There are two kinds of doubt. There is the doubt which grows out of an essential cynicism, the doubt that is the sour fruit of mean and careless living which is incapable of producing any sure convictions. But there is also the doubt of utterly sincere and honest minds who will not say what they do not think, and who in their intellectual integrity will not pretend to build belief until they have for it a foundation of certain fact. Tennyson wrote:

> There lives more faith in honest doubt,
> Believe me, than in half the creeds.[4]

He was not disparaging creeds. It is a great thing to have a creed which a man says as though the trumpet of his glad assurance were sounding in every word. But there are some creeds which are merely parrotlike and perfunctory. There are men who will not say a creed in such a spirit, but they stand wistful and silent wishing they could say it with their minds and hearts. Jesus welcomed a man like that, and he will welcome those who are like that now. The essential thing is for a man to keep close to him in loyalty, as Thomas was ready to do, come what might (John 11:16). Out of that sort of loyalty the light of conviction will come. It will be true, as Jesus said, "If any man's will is to do his will, he shall know whether the teaching is from God" (John 7:17).

Of most of the others among the twelve we do not know much. According to the record, they seem to have been less important figures. Yet it is their relative insignificance that makes them enduringly significant. The work of God is not done only by the outstanding men whose names will be celebrated later. Much of it is done by those who are anonymous. Who registered and passed on those memories of the life and teaching of Jesus which are embodied in the Gospels? We cannot fully know. Who spread the Christian gospel when it began to reach out beyond Jerusalem? The records tell us the names of some, but there are other men and women whose names are nowhere written —little people, not great or eloquent, who nevertheless were witnesses for their Lord. "Those who were scattered went about preaching the word" (Acts 8:4). "Those who were scattered . . . traveled as far as Phoenicia and Cyprus and Antioch" (Acts 11:19). Who "those" were no history records. Similarly in other great advances of the church, the humble believers sometimes preceded and always undergirded the work of those whose names endure, e.g., in the island of Britain Christianity was planted early in the Christian era; certainly by the second and more probably by the first century the church was there. Who made it possible? Apparently not any men with shining names, but men obscure and now forgotten; perhaps some Christian soldier among the Roman legions, perhaps a merchant or some other traveler from Gaul. As in the beginning

[4] *In Memoriam,* Part XCVI, st. iii.

17 ¶ And he came down with them, and stood in the plain, and the company of his disciples, and a great multitude of people out of all Judea and Jerusalem, and from the seacoast of Tyre and Sidon, which came to hear him, and to be healed of their diseases;

18 And they that were vexed with unclean spirits: and they were healed.

19 And the whole multitude sought to touch him: for there went virtue out of him, and healed *them* all.

17 And he came down with them and
stood on a level place, with a great crowd
of his disciples and a great multitude of
people from all Judea and Jerusalem and
the seacoast of Tyre and Sidon, who came
to hear him and to be healed of their dis-
eases; 18 and those who were troubled
with unclean spirits were cured. 19 And all
the crowd sought to touch him, for power
came forth from him and healed them all.

---

2. Introduction to Jesus' Sermon (6:17-19, based on Mark 3:7-10)

17-19. After a night of prayer in the hills, Jesus had summoned his disciples and chosen an inner circle. Then **he came down with them and stood on a level place.** "The sea" is the setting in Mark, and "the mountain" in Matt. 5:1. Surrounded by the twelve, the larger company of his followers, and a **multitude of people** representative of the entire nation, he healed the sick and then "lifted up his eyes on his disciples" and spoke to them.

It is clear that some common source underlies Luke's "Sermon on the Plain" (6:20*b*-49) and Matthew's "Sermon on the Mount" (Matt. 5:3–7:27). Both discourses begin with beatitudes. Both have sections, in the same relative order, on love for one's enemies and on passing judgment. Both have the parable of the healthy and the diseased trees. And both end with the parable of the two houses. Only three of the thirty verses in Luke's sermon (6:39, 40, 45*a*, 45*b*) appear in other contexts in Matthew, and only six and one half are missing altogether (6:24-26, 27*b*, 28*a*, 34, 35*a*, 37*b*, 38*a*). On the other hand, of the much longer sermon in Matthew (107 verses), one quarter (27 verses) is paralleled in Luke's version, slightly more than one third (37 verses) can be found in various other Lukan contexts, and the larger part (43 verses) is peculiar to the First Gospel. The most probable solution of the literary problem involved is that Luke took over the sermon much as it stood in Q, and that Matthew expanded it. Luke's sermon consists of (*a*) introductory blessings and woes (vss. 20-26); (*b*) ethical legislation (vss. 27-45); and (*c*) concluding parable (vss. 46-49). In the central section of the Sermon on the Mount Matthew stresses the superiority of the new righteousness to the teaching of the scribes (Matt. 5:17-48) and to the practice of the Pharisees (Matt. 6:1-18), but no Jewish foils are used for the legislation in Luke. Although Luke presupposes a crowd of auditors in the background (7:1), Jesus' words were directed in the first instance to his disciples—the larger company referred to in 6:13, 17. (See also Vol. VII, pp. 155-64, 278-79.)

Jesus had among his disciples those who by comparison seemed the lesser men—**Philip . . . Bartholomew . . . James the son of Alphaeus, Simon . . . the Zealot, Judas the son of James**—so always there are those who seem the lesser ones but who nevertheless have their indispensable part to play in his service.

Last in the list comes that shadowed name **Judas Iscariot, who became a traitor.** The question of why he was a traitor belongs later in the Expos. of this Gospel. Here there is one thought to be remembered. It is the somber fact that human personality can come directly into touch with Jesus and then repudiate him. Yet even in that tragic possibility there is revealed the dignity which God has given to every human soul. It is not to be coerced. It has the awful choice of freedom.

17-19. ***The Timeless Touch of Christ.***—These verses are a swift summary of the great works of Jesus, presented here without detail. But out of the few words vivid suggestions emerge. Multitudes flocked around him. Why? The evangelist mentions first that they **came to hear him.** This was Jesus who had said of himself in Nazareth that he was anointed to preach good news to the poor, release to the captive, liberty for those who were oppressed. The deep hunger in the hearts of ordinary folk reached out to him—the hunger for a word from God which would give them hope and confidence and something to live for and to live by. That

20 ¶ And he lifted up his eyes on his disciples, and said, Blessed *be ye* poor: for yours is the kingdom of God.
21 Blessed *are ye* that hunger now: for ye shall be filled. Blessed *are ye* that weep now: for ye shall laugh.

20 And he lifted up his eyes on his disciples, and said:
"Blessed are you poor, for yours is the kingdom of God.
21 "Blessed are you that hunger now, for you shall be satisfied.
"Blessed are you that weep now, for you shall laugh.

3. The Beatitudes (6:20-23=Matt. 5:3-6, 11-12)

The beatitudes in Luke are four in number, are addressed in the second person to the disciples, and emphasize the reversal of values that will take place in the age to come, whereas Matthew's are nine, refer—except in the last instance—to the faithful in general, and stress the spiritual and moral qualities that characterize those who will enter the kingdom of heaven. Luke's version looks the more primitive.

20. There may be a reminiscence of this beatitude in Jas. 2:5. It has often been pointed out that the Hebrew word for "poor" (עניים) had come in late Judaism (Pss. 9:12; 35:10; etc.) to mean "saintly" or "pious," and that Jesus may have used an Aramaic original of our Greek in some such sense. This interpretation has the doubtful merit of harmonizing Luke's first beatitude with Matthew's but the antithesis in vs. 24 shows that Luke had in mind those who were **poor** in money and possessions. Jesus elsewhere asserts that riches constitute an almost insuperable barrier to **the kingdom of God** (18:24-25; Mark 10:23, 25).

21. Luke's second and third beatitudes have also been "spiritualized" in Matthew's version. For **hunger now** there is "hunger and thirst for righteousness," and for **weep now** and **laugh,** "mourn" and "be comforted."

hunger is in the hearts of people always. And they had come **to be healed of their diseases** and freed from the **unclean spirits which** were their deepest trouble. Our diagnoses now would not be the same as those of the first century, but there are diseases into the cure of which the spirit of Christ will enter, and there are unclean spirits which his grace alone can cast out. **Power came forth from him** in first-century Galilee, and from the living Christ that power still can come.

20-22. ***God's Poor.***—In these verses is Luke's parallel to Matt. 5:3-6. But there is a striking and significant difference. There is reason to think that Matthew's form represents a later and less sharp reflection of the original words of Jesus (cf. Exeg.). According to Matthew, the blessing is promised to those who spiritually are the lowly and the humble; according to Luke, the blessing is upon those who are poor in the plain and obvious aspect of economic poverty and upon those who in actual circumstances of community life are the disadvantaged. For them there shall come a reversal of their human lot. The poor, the hungry, the sad, the oppressed and scorned, whom the world pushes aside with contempt or cruelty, are within the sure compassion of the eternal love. **God himself will right their lot.**

If, then, these words of Luke do express the mind of Jesus, here are some of the realizations that come into light. The first is the remembrance of Jesus' own association with the poor. He grew up in the little town where most people had no more than enough to live on, if indeed they always had that. He knew how difficult the winning of a livelihood could be, and what everyday heroism had often to be displayed by humble people to earn a family's support. He had for men and women such as these a quick and understanding pity that was a reflection of the pity that must be in the heart of God. But he had more than pity. As he looked at the poor and compared them with others in the community, who seemed materially to be so much better off, he saw that poverty could create qualities which deserved the ultimate recompense of God. He never condemned wealth as such, but he saw how wealth might encase men in a hard shell of their seeming sufficiency so that they were no longer sensitive to the spiritual values of life. Christian experience in subsequent times has shown that poverty might be the price at which the highest blessings can be won. In the long history of Catholic Christianity, those who were called the "religious," as against those who were still part of the secular world, have taken as their

22 Blessed are ye, when men shall hate you, and when they shall separate you *from their company,* and shall reproach *you,* and cast out your name as evil, for the Son of man's sake.

23 Rejoice ye in that day, and leap for joy: for, behold, your reward *is* great in heaven: for in the like manner did their fathers unto the prophets.

24 But woe unto you that are rich! for ye have received your consolation.

25 Woe unto you that are full! for ye shall hunger. Woe unto you that laugh now! for ye shall mourn and weep.

26 Woe unto you, when all men shall speak well of you! for so did their fathers to the false prophets.

22 "Blessed are you when men hate you, and when they exclude you and revile you, and cast out your name as evil,
on account of the Son of man! 23 Rejoice
in that day, and leap for joy, for behold, your reward is great in heaven; for so their fathers did to the prophets.

24 "But woe to you that are rich, for you have received your consolation.

25 "Woe to you that are full now, for you shall hunger.

"Woe to you that laugh now, for you shall mourn and weep.

26 "Woe to you, when all men speak well of you, for so their fathers did to the false prophets.

22-23. **Exclude you,** i.e., from the synagogue. **Cast out your name as evil** is probably a Semitism meaning "issue an evil report about you" (cf. Jas. 2:7; I Pet. 4:14). This beatitude may not have been original with Jesus. Its references to hatred, excommunication, reproach, and slander appear to imply forms of persecution experienced by the early church, and **their fathers** is a phrase that reflects a sense of alienation from the Jewish community.

4. The Woes (6:24-26)

24-26. The woes have no parallel in Matthew and are exact antitheses to the preceding beatitudes. Men who find complete satisfaction in this world's goods will be excluded from God's kingdom. People who are content to satisfy only their physical needs in the present age will experience a time when God will send "a famine in the land, not a famine of bread, nor a thirst for water, but of hearing the words of the Lord"

---

first vow the vow of poverty. Francis of Assisi became the witness of a life made radiant when he utterly abjured all the world's riches. William James, a philosopher sensitive to spiritual realities in a materialistic age, wrote:

> Poverty indeed *is* the strenuous life,—without brass bands or uniforms or hysteric popular applause or lies or circumlocutions; and . . . one wonders whether a revival of the belief that poverty is a worthy religious vocation may not be . . . the spiritual reform which our time stands most in need of.[5]

There are ideologies which speak directly to depressed and exploited people, and promise them by way of revolution the rewards they never yet have had. The spirit of Jesus cannot be linked with the kind of revolution that is the product of fanaticism and of ruthless force; but it does make men know that the fundamental injustices of the economic order are an affront to God, and that the power of his righteousness is on the side of their correction. But above all and through all, Jesus would lay his emphasis upon those qualties among the poor which can make their life deserve enrichment: simplicity of heart, the capacity to find happiness in oneself and in the love of people rather than in the luxury of things, experience that is not surfeited and so can reach up in expanding desire toward God.

24-26. ***The Perils of Prosperity.***—Here is the reversal of the picture which Luke has drawn in the words preceding. There he was describing the rewards which the goodness of God would give at last to the poor. Here he is setting forth the warning to the rich.

As we seek to understand the emphasis of Jesus, we must not rashly generalize from what he said in some special circumstance. When the rich young ruler came with his question about how he might inherit eternal life, Jesus confronted him with a drastic demand. He saw that for that particular person nothing less than a heroic renunciation could set him spiritually free. But this was not a demand that Jesus al-

[5] *The Varieties of Religious Experience* (New York: Longmans, Green & Co., 1903), pp. 367-68.

27 ¶ But I say unto you which hear, Love your enemies, do good to them which hate you,

28 Bless them that curse you, and pray for them which despitefully use you.

29 And unto him that smiteth thee on the *one* cheek offer also the other; and him that taketh away thy cloak forbid not *to take thy* coat also.

30 Give to every man that asketh of thee; and of him that taketh away thy goods ask *them* not again.

27 "But I say to you that hear, Love
your enemies, do good to those who hate
you, 28 bless those who curse you, pray for
those who abuse you. 29 To him who strikes
you on the cheek, offer the other also; and
from him who takes away your cloak do
not withhold your coat as well. 30 Give to
every one who begs from you; and of him
who takes away your goods, do not ask

(Amos 8:11). Concentration on the pleasures of this life will lead to deep distress when the new age dawns: "My servants shall sing for joy of heart, but ye shall cry for sorrow of heart, and shall howl for vexation of spirit" (Isa. 65:14). Flattery in ancient times was the reward of **false prophets,** and universal acclaim should therefore lull no man into a sense of complacency.

5. The Law of Love (6:27-35=Matt. 5:39-47)

27-28. Does vs. 27*a* imply a return to the source after a rhetorical apostrophe? **Love your enemies** is not a sentiment. It is a strategy to combat attitude, utterance, and act. **Abuse** (RSV) in the sense of "mistreat" (cf. KJV).

29-30. A separate section in Matthew, where it illustrates the principle of non-resistance to evil. The second singular imperative—in contrast to the second plural of the preceding and following verses—also points to some editorial rearrangement on Luke's part. **Cloak** was the outer garment and **coat** the undergarment or "tunic." Vs. 29*b* appears to postulate an act of robbery, while Matthew's version—where the garments are mentioned in reverse order—implies a dispute before a magistrate. Matthew's parallel to vs. 30 enjoins a readiness to give and to lend. This may be primitive, for 30*b* appears to reproduce the thought of 29*b*.

---

ways made. Zacchaeus apparently was a man of substance, and so perhaps was Matthew; but there is no record that Jesus commanded them to give everything away. Nevertheless, it is true that he saw plainly, and may have spoken unsparingly, as indicated in these verses of Luke, about the spiritual perils of wealth. The danger that comes to the souls of those who are rich in this world's goods is exactly that which is indicated here. The rich may already have received their **consolation,** may be **full now,** may **laugh now,** may be satisfied because **all men speak well** of them, i.e., they may no longer be eager for the gifts of God, because they think they have already got everything worth desiring; they have no hunger for the invisible, because their visible possessions seem to be enough; they take life lightly and laugh off its deeper wants; they may be satisfied with the fawning and flattery of those who want their favors and so say nothing to them but what is smooth and pleasant.

Luther put the fact in his blunt way: "Rich folks' children," he once remarked, "seldom turn out well. They are complacent, arrogant, and conceited, and think they need to learn nothing because they have enough to live on, anyway." [6] William James wrote:

> The desire to gain wealth and the fear to lose it are our chief breeders of cowardice and propagators of corruption. There are thousands of conjunctures in which a wealth-bound man must be a slave, whilst a man for whom poverty has no terrors becomes a freeman.[7]

But still more devastating are the words in the book of Revelation, words that represent the eternal warning of Christ to those whom the satisfactions of this world may have wrapped in soft complacency. "You say, I am rich, I have prospered, and I need nothing; not knowing that you are wretched, pitiable, poor, blind and naked" (Rev. 3:17).

27-36. ***The Supreme Ideal.***—One would need to meditate upon this passage not for a moment

[6] Arthur C. McGiffert, *Martin Luther, The Man and His Work* (New York: The Century Co., 1911), p. 4.

[7] *Varieties of Religious Experience,* p. 368.

31 And as ye would that men should do to you, do ye also to them likewise.

32 For if ye love them which love you, what thank have ye? for sinners also love those that love them.

33 And if ye do good to them which do good to you, what thank have ye? for sinners also do even the same.

34 And if ye lend *to them* of whom ye hope to receive, what thank have ye? for sinners also lend to sinners, to receive as much again.

35 But love ye your enemies, and do good, and lend, hoping for nothing again; and your reward shall be great, and ye shall be the children of the Highest: for he is kind unto the unthankful and *to* the evil.

them again. 31 And as you wish that men
would do to you, do so to them.
32 "If you love those who love you,
what credit is that to you? For even sin-
ners love those who love them. 33 And if
you do good to those who do good to you,
what credit is that to you? For even sinners
do the same. 34 And if you lend to those
from whom you hope to receive, what
credit is that to you? Even sinners lend
to sinners, to receive as much again. 35 But
love your enemies, and do good, and lend,
expecting nothing in return;[y] and your
reward will be great, and you will be sons
of the Most High; for he is kind to the

[y] Other ancient authorities read *despairing of no man.*

---

31. In a different context and relative order in Matthew's sermon (Matt. 7:12). Luke omits the statement that "the Golden Rule" is the quintessence of Scripture. A non-Jew once offered to become a proselyte if Hillel (*ca.* 20 B.C.) could teach him the law while he stood on one leg. The rabbi said to him: "What you do not like, do not to your neighbor. That is the entire law, and all the rest is commentary" (Shabbath 31*a*). A negative version of the maxim is also credited to Confucius in the *Analects* (V. 11; XII. 2; XV. 23), the *Great Learning* (X. 2), the *Li Ki* (XXVIII. 1), and the *Doctrine of the Steadfast Mean* (XIII. 3).

32-34. Three examples show that mere reciprocity is not an adequate ethic for Jesus' followers. **Credit,** i.e., "in the sight of God." **Sinners** (vs. 32) is a generalization of Matthew's "tax collectors." Vs. 34 intrudes the motif of lending that had been omitted in the parallel to Matt. 5:42 (vs. 30)—another indication that Luke has reworked his material. **From whom you hope to receive,** i.e., "who will repay."

35. Expecting nothing in return (RSV) is a translation that is based on the rendering in the Vulg. This is the only occurrence in the N.T. of the verb that is involved. Elsewhere

---

only, but through all his days. The loftiness of the challenge which Jesus here presents exalts us with the sense of the glory of God, and in the same moment humbles us to the dust with the consciousness of our utter inability to measure up to the ideal he set before his disciples.

Yet we may begin with a thought which puts the law of love on a plane where at least we can admit its relevance to our daily choice and effort. Jesus is not asking for feelings and emotions which we cannot control. Love does not mean some artificially created sentiment. It does not mean that we must first force ourselves to find all other persons congenial. To love is not necessarily to like. (Surely God himself in his love, which is measureless and unconditioned, cannot like everything he sees in his imperfect children to whom he gives himself.) In Jesus' summary of the great commandments of the law, he said that each one is to love his neighbor as himself. How, actually, do we love ourselves? We do not look at ourselves in the mirror and think how amiable we are. To love ourselves is a much more practical and positive matter than that. It means to want for ourselves the best that life can give and to reach out and try to get it. That kind of self-love can be mean and cramping unless it is enlarged by a pure and humble recognition of what the real values of life are which God would have us gain. Then love of self can be lifted up to mean the soul's desire for that ultimate enrichment which God can give. That, then, is what the love of one's neighbor should mean. It is regarding him as worthy of all the best in life that God can help us make available for him.

But how to do that? How can we ever sufficiently surmount the inertia of our self-concern? How can we sufficiently overcome our quick impulse to resent injury, our anger and pride,

36 Be ye therefore merciful, as your Father also is merciful.
37 Judge not, and ye shall not be judged: condemn not, and ye shall not be condemned: forgive, and ye shall be forgiven:

ungrateful and the selfish. 36 Be merciful, even as your Father is merciful.
37 "Judge not, and you will not be judged; condemn not, and you will not be condemned; forgive, and you will be

it always means "despairing." Hence Goodspeed: "never despairing." The RSV mg. translates a variant that is found in some MSS: "despairing of no man." The medieval church interpreted the phrase as prohibiting the collection of interest on loans. Vs. 35*b* looks like a prosaic abbreviation of the saying in Matt. 5:45 (the sun and the rain). Jesus' ethic is not based on any calculation that it will convert **enemies** into friends or overcome evil with good (contrast Paul's teaching in Rom. 12:20-21). It is an imitation of God's generosity.

6. The Law of Mercy (6:36-45; cf. Matt. 5:48; 7:1-5; 15:14; 10:24-25; 7:16-20; 12:33-35)

36. A new theme, to which a variety of somewhat refractory didactic matter has been subordinated. Matthew reads "perfect" instead of **merciful;** there the verse concludes the preceding section on the law of love.

37. Connected with the foregoing in most Greek MSS by the conjunction "and." The passive construction in late Jewish literature is sometimes a device for avoiding the use of the divine name, and so most interpreters understand it in this sequence. **Judge not** "that God may not judge you," etc. More probably the sayings are bits of practical Jewish wisdom, comparable to much in the books of Proverbs and Ecclesiasticus (cf. Goodspeed: "Do not judge others, and they will not judge you").

our self-assertion, and the slowness of our sympathy? How can we ever in these ways translate into actual conduct the kind of spirit which Jesus has set forth in the illustrations which these verses contain? We know that we cannot. The great stars shine in the sky, but they are too high for us to touch them. Nevertheless, we know this: Now and then some figure rises on the human scene who does approximate the incredible ideals of Jesus—a Francis of Assisi, going with radiant joy upon God's way when he had left all the cluttering things of this earth behind; a Mahatma Gandhi attaining a peace and power of soul beyond all common measurement, because he had cleansed his heart from hate and from every thought of violence and had committed himself completely to the persuasive power of love. Even the least of us have glimpses of what that means. Meanwhile, we can trust that Jesus, who set the goal so high and far, will have compassionate understanding for the slow steps of those who are at such a distance from it, provided the eyes of their desire are turned in its direction.

What is written here in Luke parallels the longer passage in Matt. 5, and for a richer interpretation of the message in both Gospels one should turn to the Expos. there.

37. ***The Danger in Judgment.***—There is a judgment of God which is inescapable, and of that solemn judgment Jesus often spoke. All men's lives stand in the light of that; but men are not to make the arrogant assumption that they can take the place of God and do his judging for him. Wheat and tares must grow together until God determines the harvest. Meanwhile, each man must be patient, hopeful, and forgiving. In the Lord's Prayer Jesus taught his disciples that only as they did forgive could they be forgiven. His unerring insight is made only the more authoritative by what modern psychology has begun to understand. When a man judges, the likelihood is that he himself self-consciously at that moment is judging and condemning himself. We do not wish explicitly to acknowledge our own faults, but when we note in others that which we are actually most ashamed of in ourselves, we get a kind of vicarious relief by projecting there the condemnation which we ourselves deserve. Only the man who does not evade the facts by a harsh criticism of others can have the humility and truthfulness which will confess his own faults, and so escape the just judgment of others, and receive not the judgment but the redeeming mercy of God.

38 Give, and it shall be given unto you; good measure, pressed down, and shaken together, and running over, shall men give

forgiven; [38] give, and it will be given to you; good measure, pressed down, shaken

---

38. The metaphor is borrowed from the grain trade. Read with Goodspeed "they will pour" (cf. KJV) rather than with the RSV. Lap is perhaps the best that can be done with a word that means a large pocket or fold that overlaps a girdle on a garment. Also used metaphorically in Isa. 65:6-7; Ps. 79:12; etc. The proverb in 38*b* has a different application in Mark 4:24*b*.

---

38. ***The World's Idea.***—Many of the men of influence in the time of Jesus, if they had heard these words of his, would have listened to them with a scornful incredulity. The Herods would have had no interest in a principle of life that put the emphasis on giving instead of getting. Neither would Pilate, nor Caiaphas, nor the rest of the high priests. They took what they could of the world's advantages, and held on to what they had.

That has often been the world's idea of wisdom, not only in ancient times, but now. R. H. Tawney has expressed a present fact in the title of his book, *Our Acquisitive Society*. Much of our modern life is characterized by the struggle to gain and multiply possessions. It is true that material achievements can be made the basis of a more abundant life, but the danger is that preoccupation with them may become an obsession which warps all sense of values. Success may be estimated in terms of money and of what money will buy. Boys and young men who must choose between possible alternatives for their lifework may have caught from older men the impulse to ask only how much profit they can make. The determining question may not be "What can I contribute in some particular field by way of service?" but rather it may be "What can be got out of it for me?"

There is a second way in which people seek to gain by getting. It is not now by gaining material things but by getting what feeds their inner craving for importance. As in the Greek myth of Narcissus, they have fallen in love with themselves. This means that a man or woman has ceased to look at life objectively. Everything is judged in relation to his or her own subjective feeling, for the person who is narcissistic is interested in other people in exactly the proportion to which they contribute to his self-esteem. If they praise him, flatter him, serve him, he will be expansive toward them. If they criticize him or oppose him, he will dislike them no matter what the objective right on their side may be. He is jealous of all interests that do not somehow fit into and magnify his own importance. The result is that his contacts are increasingly grudging. He cannot go out freely and gladly into life because he can never be self-forgetful.

Meanwhile, the world is full of pitiful rich people who are wretched in the midst of their possessions, and yet are driven by their pride to maintain an outward shell of apparent sufficiency, when all their life within is emptiness; and full also of those who, after having for many years tried to make all the worthwhileness of life flow inward instead of outward, have discovered at last that all the world around them and the people who live in it have been sucked dry of interest, so that life in its normal relationships seems a thing no longer to be endured. Whether the things we seek to get are material things or immaterial emotions, the penalty of our insatiate getting is always the same. The Dead Sea is an old example, but it lies there as much a contemporary reality as it ever was. Drawing everything into itself and giving nothing out, it has produced only a motionless stagnation.

38. ***The Way of Jesus.***—Looking at those whose principle was to grab and get, and seeing the mechanical glitter of their apparent success, Jesus nevertheless knew that that success was false. That kind of life is the road to death, he said. If you want to gain, you must give. If you want to win abundant life, you must be ready to fling away that which most lives covet. He did not merely utter sayings such as those; he himself was as good as his word. What he had he would give, and all he was he would give. He did not grudge his time. The Gospels give us glimpses of what his days were like. The sick thronged upon him at the gates of Capernaum in the evening. He went away into the wilderness to pray, and before the dawn his disciples were hunting for him because the people were clamoring to have him in their midst again. He did not grudge his strength. "I perceive that power has gone forth from me," he said once (8:46), when a woman worn with long illness reached out her eager hands of faith to touch him in the crowd. Power was always going out of him, but he renewed his strength at the fountains of the life of God and came back to pour out his help

into your bosom. For with the same measure that ye mete withal it shall be measured to you again.

39 And he spake a parable unto them; Can the blind lead the blind? shall they not both fall into the ditch?

together, running over, will be put into your lap. For the measure you give will be the measure you get back."

39 He also told them a parable: "Can a blind man lead a blind man? Will they

---

39. The disastrous consequences of judgment for both the judge and the object of his criticism. Matthew used the proverb to criticize the leadership of the Pharisees (Matt. 15:14; cf. also Matt. 23:16).

---

again. He did not grudge even his life. "The Son of man came to seek and to save that which was lost," he said (19:10), "and to give his life as a ransom for many" (Matt. 20:28). From the beginning to the end he was ready to spend and to be spent. His spirit was never like a lake that gathers its sequestered waters into itself. It was like a river born in the mountain but flowing toward the plains, drawing from a thousand sources of the rains and snows of God, but pouring these out in fertility and power through all the wide valley of the world through which it flows.

Too many human personalities give us the impression of something fenced in and guarded. They are cautious lest they go too far, do too much, commit themselves to a loyalty too unreservedly. But Jesus gave to those who knew him a magnificent and unparalleled sense of unimpeded life. Men felt when they were with him that no matter how deeply their needs drew upon him, they could not empty what his immense responsive spirit had to give. And the extraordinary part of it was that it always seemed as though he were not giving so much as receiving. The more he poured out, the more there poured into him resources of sufficiency and joy. He received from God, but also he received from men. His own words were true of himself, **Give and it will be given to you; good measure, pressed down, shaken together, running over, will be put into your lap.** No man ever loved as he loved, but neither was ever any man loved as he was loved. Think of the human marvel of it, the marvel which so often we forget because we treat it like a thing of course. This man of Nazareth who gave no material gifts to anybody, who never answered the wrongheaded hopes for worldly advantage which some even of his closest followers cherished, who may seem to have left at his death only the power of a personality, nevertheless in his lifetime and through all the centuries since, has commanded and still commands the kind of adoration which can lift men completely out of themselves to a new level of living and of dying.

The words in some of the great Christian hymns are typical:

> Jesus, the very thought of thee
> With sweetness fills the breast.[8]
>
> . . . .
>
> Jesus, my Lord, I thee adore;
> O make me love thee more and more![9]

To the measure in which he meted, it has been measured to him again. He who gave most has gained most. He, the lover of mankind, has been supremely beloved.

39. ***The Blind Guide.***—Thus, as so often, Jesus expressed a truth by means of one single, swift illustration so unmistakable that even the dullest could see and understand. He had reference here to the kind of presumption which makes a man who is fundamentally ignorant of the real directions of life take it upon himself to tell others the way to go. Perhaps he was thinking of the Pharisees, as when in Matt. 23:16 he called them "blind guides." Perhaps he included in his reference a wider group than they. At any rate, the significance of what he said reaches out to include many others than first-century Pharisees.

The blind guides of more modern times may be men who consider themselves religious, as the Pharisees did, but whose religion is intolerant and harsh and lacking human sympathy. On the other hand, the contemporary blind guides may more probably be those who are not religious at all, but instead are the arrogant and aggressive secularists. They come to their generation with a loud proclamation of their own wisdom. They will direct the choices of their times to where they ought to go. But as a matter of fact, their vision is so twisted that they are no better than the blind. Sometimes there comes a surprising confession of what the fact has been. In *Ends and Means* Aldous Huxley is asking whether the world as a whole, and particularly the human beings in it, and their works, have value and meaning. "This," he says, "is a question which, a few

[8] Medieval Latin hymn, tr. Edward Caswall.

[9] Henry Collins, "Jesus, my Lord, my God, my All."

40 The disciple is not above his master: but every one that is perfect shall be as his master.

41 And why beholdest thou the mote that is in thy brother's eye, but perceivest not the beam that is in thine own eye?

not both fall into a pit?
40 A disciple is not above his teacher, but every one when he is fully taught will be like his teacher.
41 Why do you see the speck that is in your brother's eye, but do not notice the

40. An obscure saying in its Lukan context. Are blind guides compared to teachers who cannot impart more to their pupils than they themselves know? Matthew adds his version to the account of the mission of the twelve (Matt. 10:24-25), where it means that no disciple can expect a better fate than his master's.

41-42. These verses follow immediately upon the prohibition of judgment in Matthew's Gospel. Any useful criticism must begin with self-examination and reform. The

years ago, I should not even have posed. For, like some of my contemporaries, I took it for granted that there was no meaning." [1] Why did he think there was no meaning? Was it because there really is none; because a thorough search of the whole ground of life's realities, fully explored and appraised with a far-reaching and reverent truthfulness, shows that no meaning is there? Listen to Huxley's answer:

> I had motives for not wanting the world to have a meaning; consequently assumed that it had none, and was able without any difficulty to find satisfying reasons for this assumption.
>
> Most ignorance is vincible ignorance. We don't know because we don't want to know. It is our will that decides how and upon what subjects we shall use our intelligence. Those who detect no meaning . . . generally do so because, for one reason or another, it suits their books that the world should be meaningless.[2]

Of course, if we have reasons for wanting the world to be meaningless, it can seem so; and with every one of us there is always the possibility that these reasons will subtly creep in. We may be living on the level of this world, and therefore we do not want to believe too vividly in another one. We are governed by motives which are selfish and short, and therefore we do not want to be disturbed by long-range possibilities. We have wanted to think that the mean little measuring rod of our small estimate of life is large enough, but that is simply the evidence of our blindness. Unless the eyes of our ordinary perception have been lighted by that revelation of the meaning of life which comes from God, then we and our blind contemporaries alike will fall into the ditch.

40. ***Teacher and Disciple.***—There is no categorical way of interpreting this verse. Perhaps it is a single saying that has floated into this context from some origin that we do not know. It might have either of two meanings. In one there might be an element of irony. The pupil of a blind, opinionated teacher, when he was fully taught, would be like his teacher. And the ironic twist in that conclusion would be the fact that the measure of the pupil's success would be the measure of his failure, for the more he learned, the less he would know. On the other hand, this sentence about a disciple may have a different origin and a quite different meaning. It may be linked with such a word of Jesus as Mark 8:34-35, or with such an answer as Jesus gave to James and John in Mark 10:35-45. Here the likeness of the disciples to the teacher comes with the learning of a heroic lesson: the laying down of selfish ambition, that one may catch the secret of triumphant life from him who went on his way to the Cross.

41-42. ***The Sin of Self-Assurance.***—Jesus' most unsparing condemnation was launched not against sins of the flesh, but against the sins of the hard mind and the arrogant spirit. Those whom he recognized as most alien to himself were Pharisees who insisted vehemently upon the mint, anise, and cummin of the law, but had scant concern for those qualities of life which matter most. He could thrust through their pretense of spiritual wisdom with a satire that was devastating.[3] The type of man whom he indicted belongs not to the past only, but equally to the present. Very familiar are individuals who have gained eminence and power in some particular area of achievement and assume that they are entitled to give instruction and be listened to on broad decisions which affect everybody. A man may have made a conspicuous success as an inventor, a manufacturer, a business executive; and he assumes therefore that he can advise on all human relationships—on politics and government, on public conduct, and on the sphere proper for

[1] New York: Harper & Bros., 1937, p. 312. Used by permission.

[2] *Ibid.*

[3] See Matt. 23; also T. R. Glover, *The Jesus of History* (London: Student Christian Movement Press, 1917), ch. iii.

42 Either how canst thou say to thy brother, Brother, let me pull out the mote that is in thine eye, when thou thyself beholdest not the beam that is in thine own eye? Thou hypocrite, cast out first the beam out of thine own eye, and then shalt thou see clearly to pull out the mote that is in thy brother's eye.

43 For a good tree bringeth not forth corrupt fruit; neither doth a corrupt tree bring forth good fruit.

44 For every tree is known by his own fruit. For of thorns men do not gather figs, nor of a bramble bush gather they grapes.

45 A good man out of the good treasure of his heart bringeth forth that which is good; and an evil man out of the evil treasure of his heart bringeth forth that which is evil: for of the abundance of the heart his mouth speaketh.

log that is in your own eye?
42 Or how can you say to your brother, 'Brother, let me take out the speck that is in your eye,' when you yourself do not see the log that is in your own eye? You hypocrite, first take the log out of your own eye, and then you will see clearly to take out the speck that is in your brother's eye.

43 "For no good tree bears bad fruit, nor again does a bad tree bear good fruit;
44 for each tree is known by its own fruit. For figs are not gathered from thorns, nor are grapes picked from a bramble bush.
45 The good man out of the good treasure of his heart produces good, and the evil man out of his evil treasure produces evil; for out of the abundance of the heart his mouth speaks.

---

speck (RSV) and the **beam** (KJV), the gnat and the camel (Matt. 23:24), and the camel and the needle's eye (18:25; Mark 10:25) are hyperboles in Jesus' teaching that reveal a gentle touch of humor.

43-45. The conjunction **for** links the parable with vss. 41-42. A transposition of the clauses in vs. 43 would have made for a better connection. A bad man cannot utter a good precept. In Matthew's Sermon on the Mount, the sayings (Matt. 7:16-18) enforce the warning against false prophets. Vs. 45 has a parallel only in another Matthaean version (Matt. 12:33-35). **Heart** in Semitic anatomy was the seat of the intellect. In view of the final clause of the generalization, **produces good** must mean "utters good words," but Luke's context justifies a wider reference: Character makes the man!

---

religion. "Let me show you how to look at things," he says to men in general. "Let me teach you to see straight." Meanwhile, he is not conscious that his own vision is twisted by ignorance and full of blind spots of his own particular prejudices. He thinks he will take the speck out of his **brother's eye,** and does not notice **the log** that is in his **own eye.** Such men may belong to the church and may call themselves Christians, but if in genuine humility they should come into the presence of Christ, they would know that it is their own eyes rather than the eyes of those whom they presume to benefit that are in need of drastic treatment.

43-45. ***Out of the Good Treasure.***—At first sight the meaning of this chapter would seem to be the general truth that what a man is will certainly be revealed. In other words, there is no ultimate concealment of a man's real character, good or bad. But the Exeg. suggests what may be a more specific connection with the passage immediately preceding. In Semitic thought the **heart** symbolized the active intellect rather than, as to us, the seat of feeling and emotion. To bring good treasure out of the heart, therefore, in the passage here means to bring that kind of helpful thought and counsel which, as has been suggested above, a man can give only when he can cleanse his own mind from its spots of ignorance and error. To change the figure, he cannot give to someone else the good food of helpful counsel unless there is in himself a deep-rooted honesty and truth which can produce that kind of fruit. A further suggestion comes in the word **abundance.** If one is to speak to others the word that will enrich their lives, there must be something substantial in one's own thinking. The content of the mind must not be left to chance. It needs to be stored with lovely recollections which, as Wordsworth wrote when he had seen the daffodils, will

> . . . flash upon that inward eye
> Which is the bliss of solitude.

46 ¶ And why call ye me, Lord, Lord, and do not the things which I say?

47 Whosoever cometh to me, and heareth my sayings, and doeth them, I will show you to whom he is like:

48 He is like a man which built a house, and digged deep, and laid the foundation on a rock: and when the flood arose, the stream beat vehemently upon that house, and could not shake it; for it was founded upon a rock.

49 But he that heareth, and doeth not, is like a man that without a foundation built a house upon the earth; against which the stream did beat vehemently, and immediately it fell; and the ruin of that house was great.

46 "Why do you call me 'Lord, Lord,'
and not do what I tell you? 47 Every one
who comes to me and hears my words and
does them, I will show you what he is like:
48 he is like a man building a house, who
dug deep, and laid the foundation upon
rock; and when a flood arose, the stream
broke against that house, and could not
shake it, because it had been well built.[z]
49 But he who hears and does not do them
is like a man who built a house on the
ground without a foundation; against
which the stream broke, and immediately it
fell, and the ruin of that house was great."

[z] Other ancient authorities read *founded upon the rock*.

---

7. Parable of the Two Houses (6:46-49=Matt. 7:21, 24-27)

46. A saying that is pregnant with pathos in Luke's version, but impersonal in Matthew's. **Lord** originally meant no more than "sir" or "master," but would be filled with much richer content by readers of the Gospel. All MSS support the double form of address.

47-49. The one **house** had a **foundation upon rock,** the other was **built . . . on the ground,** and the disaster was due to a flooded river. More typically Palestinian topography and climate are reflected in Matthew's version, where one house was built on rock and the other on sand, and the disaster was caused by the impact of winter storms. Luke may have edited the original to stress the importance of good construction rather than the selection of a good site. **Because it had been well built** is the better attested reading. A similar parable has been preserved in rabbinical tradition: "To whom can we compare a man who has studied diligently in the Law and has many good works? To a man who has laid a foundation of stones and built upon them with unbaked bricks. Even if great floods come and wash against them, the stones will not be dislodged. And to whom can we compare a man who has studied the Law but has no good works? To a man who has built first with bricks and then with stones. Even a little water will cause the stones to tumble at once" (Aboth R. Nathan 24).

William Lyon Phelps once said that the happiest man is the man who has the most interesting thoughts; and the man who can be most happy in what he gives to others is the man who has meditated much on that which is both interesting and inspiring.

46-49. *The Eternal Foundation.*—This unforgettable saying of Jesus which concludes this chapter of Luke, and which is in Matthew's Gospel too (7:24-27), might well be the last word in much preaching and teaching of the Gospels. Yet it is not only the last word but also the first, the commencement as well as the climax of the truth. If any life is to have the stability which Christ can give, it must be built unmistakably in thought and act upon Christ at the beginning.

That is true for the individual. Someone may have a shallow and reckless notion that he is sufficient to himself. He can build his own life on any basis that happens to be easy and agreeable. As long as the weather is fair, his foolishness may not be evident. But one day there come the floods, the muddy waters of some sudden passion, the rushing current of unforeseen temptation. Because his character has no sure foundation in those principles which loyalty to Christ would have given, his whole moral structure may collapse. Equally that is true for the relationships between individuals which ought to be most precious. Friendships cannot endure if they are based only on the sands of selfishness. Marriages do not endure when they have no ground except in physical attraction, and have never been undergirded by the deeper loyalties and love which only a

7 Now when he had ended all his sayings in the audience of the people, he entered into Capernaum.

7 After he had ended all his sayings in the hearing of the people he en-

E. Jesus' Healing Ministry (7:1-17)

1. Healing of the Centurion's Slave (7:1-10=Matt. 8:5-10)

The dialogue is almost identical in Luke and in Matthew, but not the narrative framework. The latter in both instances may be secondary, for the saying of Jesus, not his miracle of healing, is still the real climax of the story. John 4:46-53 preserves another variant.

7:1. Editorial. **Capernaum** had already been associated in Q (Matt. 8:5) with the story of the centurion—the only specific geographical note that is known to have stood in that source.

---

consecrated purpose can assure. And the same truth holds for all larger associations, including the church itself. Traditions are not enough, dogmatic orthodoxies are not enough, the deposit of formal creeds is not enough. The one decisive question is whether the real life of the church reaches down for its anchorage beneath all partial authorities to rest upon the never forgotten will of the Lord of the church himself.

A parish of distinguished history, St. Paul's, in Richmond, Virginia, was celebrating its centennial in the nineteen-forties. The anniversary preacher wanted to know the facts about the building of the church and the laying of the cornerstone. But there was no inscription to indicate which the cornerstone was, and when a search was made for the original records as to the identity of the cornerstone and what had been placed inside it, it was found that those records had been burned in the great fire which destroyed much of the city at the end of the War Between the States. With all the greater vividness, then, the preacher built his sermon upon Paul's strong words, "For no other foundation can any one lay than that which is laid, which is Jesus Christ" (I Cor. 3:11). It did not matter that the material cornerstone could not be identified. It did not matter that no one knew what might be in it. The one thing that did matter for that church and for every other church would be that its everlasting foundation should be the living Christ.

7:1-17. ***The Continuing Miracle.***—Just as in Mark (1:22 ff.) a reference to Jesus' impressive teaching is followed by an account of several miracles, so here and in the corresponding section of Matthew the great sermon of Jesus is followed by striking acts of power. Jesus' words, we are told elsewhere by Luke, were "words of grace" (4:22); they were also words of power. Not only did he teach "as one that had authority," but he also demonstrated the reality of this authority by his deeds. Luke describes here only two of these; but one of them involves a healing at a distance (with an explicit reference to Jesus' **authority**), and the other, the raising of a man from the dead. Such stories as these circulated and were prized in the early church, not simply because they seemed to prove something about the person and career of the historical Jesus, but because they illustrated the meaning of the continuing presence of Christ. Christ as known in the church was still speaking words, not only of "grace and truth," but also of power and life. Though no longer present in the flesh (he was not present in the incident of the centurion's slave), Christ was still healing men sick in body and soul and was still raising men from the death of sin.

It is this continuing fact which explains the survival and early circulation of these stories and makes them still true and important. Only as God gives us to experience this present power of Christ is understanding of the miracle stories of the Gospels possible or belief in them significant. The important question is not "Did Jesus work miracles in Galilee?" but "Is he miraculously present and miraculously potent now?" Unless we find ourselves answering this second question with a confident and adoring "Yes," it really does not matter how we answer the first.

1-10. ***The Compassionate Christ.***—As there are many opportunities to observe, Luke preeminently among the gospel writers emphasizes the human compassion of Jesus. He does so not only with striking consistency but with an accent all his own. The breadth and extensiveness of this compassion, as well as its depth and quality, come frequently into view. In this section (i.e., vss. 1-17), the compassion of Jesus is illustrated in two stories, one about a woman and the other about the slave of a foreigner.

2 And a certain centurion's servant, who was dear unto him, was sick, and ready to die.

3 And when he heard of Jesus, he sent unto him the elders of the Jews, beseeching him that he would come and heal his servant.

4 And when they came to Jesus, they besought him instantly, saying, That he was worthy for whom he should do this:

5 For he loveth our nation, and he hath built us a synagogue.

6 Then Jesus went with them. And when he was now not far from the house, the centurion sent friends to him, saying unto him, Lord, trouble not thyself; for I am not worthy that thou shouldest enter under my roof:

tered Ca-per′na-um. 2 Now a centurion had
a slave who was dear[a] to him, who was
sick and at the point of death. 3 When he
heard of Jesus, he sent to him elders of
the Jews, asking him to come and heal his
slave. 4 And when they came to Jesus, they
besought him earnestly, saying, "He is
worthy to have you do this for him, 5 for
he loves our nation, and he built us our
synagogue." 6 And Jesus went with them.
When he was not far from the house, the
centurion sent friends to him, saying to
him, "Lord, do not trouble yourself, for
I am not worthy to have you come under

[a] Or *valuable.*

2. Vs. 9 presupposes—and vs. 5 implies—that the **centurion** was a non-Jew. Presumably he was an officer in the Jewish army of Herod Antipas. Read **slave** (RSV) instead of **servant** (KJV) throughout, except in vs. 7.

3-5. The centurion does not appear in person, as he does in Matthew, but sends a delegation of Jewish **elders**—representatives of the local synagogue. They support his plea with a glowing testimonial that has no counterpart in Matthew's version. An Egyptian inscription from the second century B.C. tells of a pagan official who had assisted Jews in the erection of a **synagogue** at Athribis.

6-8. A second delegation—this time of **friends**—intercepts **Jesus** on his way to the centurion's **house** and quotes the words that come more naturally in Matthew's version

The slave is described as **dear** to his owner. On that account the latter asks his Jewish friends to intercede with the Jewish teacher, of whose wonderful powers he has heard. One hopes that **dear** means "highly honored," valued as a person—sometimes slaves *were* thus valued—but the word (ἔντιμος) was also used of things, and slaves were often thought of and dealt with as things. Moffatt translates here "whom he valued very highly," and Goodspeed, "whom he thought a good deal of." Was the slave a valued thing, or was he an honored person? Whichever he seemed to the centurion, we can be sure that *Jesus* left Capernaum to save a person. One hopes that in the centurion also was that same interest and that same feeling. Luke probably understands it so, possibly seeing an indication of the soldier's humane character in the testimonial offered by **the elders of the Jews.** Is this Gentile officer, when he speaks of not being **worthy** and not "presuming," thinking only of the fact that he is not a Jew? And does he send a delegation of Jewish **elders** because he supposes that Jesus will receive them more willingly than he would have received the soldier himself? If so, he does not understand the attitude of the humane Jesus as Luke is seeking here and everywhere to present it.

There is an interesting contrast between the testimonial of the **elders** and the centurion's estimate of himself. The elders say, **He is worthy;** he says, **I am not worthy.** (The adjectives in Greek are different, but the meaning is the same; and in any case, the term used in vs. 4 appears in vs. 7.) He feels his own unworthiness, whether to go to Jesus or to receive him in his own house; but others see him differently. Perhaps there is a connection. The realization in our own hearts that we "do not deserve" helps make us deserving in the eyes of others—and in one sense of the word "deserving," even in the eyes of God. It is a principal emphasis of Luke's Gospel that one is never worthy of the goodness of God. It is never true to say of anyone: **He is worthy to have you do this for him.** No amount of benevolence can put one in position to claim God's help as a right; it is always a gift to be received humbly and gratefully. We remember the words of the penitent son in ch. 15: "I am no longer worthy to be called

7 Wherefore neither thought I myself worthy to come unto thee: but say in a word, and my servant shall be healed.

8 For I also am a man set under authority, having under me soldiers, and I say unto one, Go, and he goeth; and to another, Come, and he cometh; and to my servant, Do this, and he doeth *it.*

my roof; 7 therefore I did not presume to come to you. But say the word, and let my servant be healed. 8 For I am a man set under authority, with soldiers under me: and I say to one, 'Go,' and he goes; and to another, 'Come,' and he comes; and to my

---

from the lips of the speaker himself. The centurion's reluctance in Luke's account to intrude himself personally on Jesus' attention serves to emphasize his humility, but the idea of intermediaries may have been borrowed from the story of the healing of Jairus' daughter (8:49), as well as the words **do not trouble yourself. Set under authority** is a difficult phrase. C. C. Torrey's "exercising authority" (*The Four Gospels* [New York: Harper & Bros., 1933], *ad loc.*) would help the interpreter, but that translation has an uneasy basis in a mistranslation hypothesis. Perhaps "familiar with authority" can be justified as a paraphrase, with the implication that God has delegated his authority to Jesus, just as Herod Antipas has conferred his upon the centurion.

---

your son," and the cry of the penitent publican in the temple (18:13), "God, be merciful to me a sinner!" The Jewish **elders,** for all their courtesy toward this foreigner, were in the last analysis wrong; the centurion, for all his good deeds, was right: he was **not worthy** to have Christ do this for him. But he was mistaken if he supposed that he needed to be **worthy** in order to seek or secure Christ's help. "The sacrifices of God are a broken spirit: a broken and a contrite heart, O God, thou wilt not despise" (Ps. 51:17).

7. *The Healing Word.*—The Exeg. properly warns us against allegorizing, but it can scarcely be doubted that in the preaching of the early church Jesus' act of healing the officer's slave from a distance served to illustrate not only the miraculous powers of Jesus during his earthly career but also his present power to save. Jesus is absent in the flesh, but his **word** is enough: **But say the word, and let my servant be healed.** This is a divine prerogative. "The worlds were framed by the word of God," writes the author of the Epistle to the Hebrews (11:3), who is remembering the first chapter of Genesis, "God said, Let there be light: and there was light." Instrumentalities in the ordinary sense were not needed; God had only to speak and it was done. Indeed, the **word** came to be thought of as being itself an agent of God. God "sends forth" his word; and we find such statements as "My word . . . shall not return unto me void, but it shall accomplish that which I please" (Isa. 55:11). In the same way Christ's word has power—healing power and, as we shall soon be reminded, life-giving power too. "Only speak, and my servant will be well." So Christ still has only to speak and our broken, thwarted lives are made whole. It would be foolish to suppose that the official had any such idea in his mind; on the other hand, it is not mere allegorizing for us to find such a meaning in this story. For the historical study of the Gospels involves not only finding out as best we can what happened, but also seeing the meaning which made the happening important and memorable to the first believers. They too had been **healed** by Christ's **word**—that fact made this sentence both true and religiously significant (see also Expos. on vss. 11-17).

8. *The Authority of Jesus.*—As we are reminded by the Exeg., **set under authority** is somewhat perplexing. The sequel seems to presuppose some such wording as "possessing authority." But we may not illegitimately suppose that the centurion's meaning is "I know what authority is—I am both subject to it and an exerciser of it. I know the implicit obedience which authority demands and secures—I both give it and receive it." In other words (as the Exeg. suggests), he is "familiar with authority." He has sensed the presence of authority in Jesus —authority far transcending any he either is subject to or exercises as a centurion. Perhaps the phrase **set under authority** is intended to remind one that he did not exercise the authority given him irresponsibly or arbitrarily; he too was under orders. If so, although the phrase says something very true and important about *human* authority (only the disciplined person is free; only he is qualified to command who has learned to obey), it is not necessarily to be supposed that the same condition was thought of as applying to *Jesus'* authority. Indeed, per-

9 When Jesus heard these things, he
marveled at him, and turned him about,
and said unto the people that followed
him, I say unto you, I have not found so
great faith, no, not in Israel.
10 And they that were sent, returning
to the house, found the servant whole that
had been sick.

slave, 'Do this,' and he does it." 9 When
Jesus heard this he marveled at him, and
turned and said to the multitude that fol-
lowed him, "I tell you, not even in Israel
have I found such faith." 10 And when
those who had been sent returned to the
house, they found the slave well.

---

9. One of the few sayings in the tradition—and no doubt a primitive one—that postulates an interest on Jesus' part in non-Jews. It is reasonable to assume that the centurion symbolized Gentile Christianity for Luke and his readers, but to press the point that he never met Jesus in the flesh and received his benefits only through intermediaries (so J. M. Creed) is allegory rather than sober exegesis. **Faith** in this instance is belief in Jesus' wonder-working power.

10. No word of command is given in Luke's version, but to explain the miracle on any theory of "coincidence" is an unwarranted rationalization. The cure in this case is effected at a distance—a feature of the miracle that appears elsewhere in the Synoptic tradition only in the story of the healing of the Syrophoenician woman's daughter (Matt. 15:21-28; Mark 7:24-30). In the latter instance, also, the petitioner is a Gentile, whose apt remark induces Jesus to perform a miracle of healing.

---

haps the phrase **set under authority** is meant to remind us of the superiority of Jesus' position; he possessed an ultimate authority. Yet on the other hand, it may well be that the gospel writer has in mind the fact that Jesus' authority is itself derived. The Fourth Gospel, for all the exalted view it takes of Jesus' person, does not hesitate to subordinate him to the Father ("I can do nothing on my own authority; . . . I seek not my own will but the will of him who sent me" [John 5:30]); and the Epistle to the Hebrews, with an equally high Christology, can say, "He learned obedience through what he suffered" (Heb. 5:8). But the basic fact underlying this story's preservation was that the church had actually been confronted in Christ with the authority of God himself, whose word was power.

9. ***The Unexpected Faith.***—We are told more than once in the Gospels that Jesus "marveled" at the "unbelief" of persons who, because of long training in the tradition of Israel, might have been expected to recognize the presence and activity of God; but here he "marvels" at the **faith** of one concerning whom he could have entertained no such expectation. The Exeg. calls attention to the fact that for Luke the centurion represents Gentile Christianity. Luke sees in the incident a prophecy of what was later to occur: Israel rejects Christ and the Gentile world accepts him. But we shall err if we find a merely partisan or polemical meaning in this story. It symbolizes the universal appeal of Christ—to men of every race and kind. One does not need to have a certain sort of cultural background to feel the attraction of Christ and to recognize the truth in him. It is true that he is the fulfillment of the old covenant and that his full meaning cannot be known except in the context which the whole history of Israel provides; he is "the glory of [his] people Israel." But he is also a "light to lighten the Gentiles"; and that light is not a reflected one—the Gentiles can see the light itself and can rejoice in it. Christ is able to make his appeal—to reveal the divine—directly to every human heart. Jesus, for Luke, is not the Jew only, but the man; his ancestry is traced (3:23-38) not to Abraham (as in Matthew), but to Adam. One who fails to see Christ as the "glory" of Israel (i.e., in the context of the covenants) fails to understand him; but one also fails to understand who does not see him as the "light" of the Gentiles. The meaning of Christ is on one side inextricably tied in with the history of ancient Israel; on the other it is as universal as mankind. Neither of these meanings must be ignored. It was the heresy of the Judaizers of Paul's period that they denied the second of them; later Gnostics and Marcionites denied the first. In every age one or the other has to some extent been obscured: we try to understand Christianity without reference to ancient Judaism, or we interpret it too exclusively and narrowly in Jewish terms. It is with this latter fallacy that this story is concerned. A Gentile officer could recognize God in Christ. So may other "outsiders" of

11 ¶ And it came to pass the day after, that he went into a city called Nain; and many of his disciples went with him, and much people.

12 Now when he came nigh to the gate of the city, behold, there was a dead man carried out, the only son of his mother, and she was a widow: and much people of the city was with her.

11 Soon afterward[b] he went to a city called Na'in, and his disciples and a great crowd went with him.
12 As he drew near to the gate of the city, behold, a man who had died was being carried out, the only son of his mother, and she was a widow; and a large crowd from the city was with

[b] Other ancient authorities read *Next day*.

2. Raising from the Dead of the Young Man of Nain (7:11-17)

The story of the centurion from Capernaum was followed in the Q source—if we are to judge from the order of its matter in Luke—by a collection of material about Jesus and John the Baptist. Jesus' answer to John's messengers in the first section of this sequence included the words "the dead are raised up" (vs. 22; Matt. 11:5). To illustrate them Luke prefixed a miracle story from his special source—or one that was known to him in oral form. An account that exhibits many of the same features has been preserved of Apollonius, a Hellenistic philosopher, healer, and exorcist of the first century A.D., who later became an object of cult worship. A young woman died at the hour of her marriage. Her bridegroom and the populace of Rome mourned her as she was carried on her bier by pallbearers. The healer stopped the funeral procession, touched the maiden, whispered a secret spell over her, and woke her from apparent death. The maiden then cried out, and returned to her father's house (Philostratus, *The Life of Apollonius of Tyana*, tr. F. C. Conybeare [New York: The Macmillan Co., 1912] I, 456-59). The O.T. doublets of Elijah and the son of the widow of Zarephath (I Kings 17:17-24) and of Elisha and the son of the Shunammite woman (II Kings 4:17-22, 32-37) are evidence that similar miracle stories were also at home within Jewish circles. Many interpreters believe that the miracle under discussion, as in the case of John's story of the raising of Lazarus (John 11:1-44), has also become the vehicle of symbolism—Jesus' life-giving power.

11-12. **Nain** is not mentioned elsewhere in the Bible. It has been identified with the modern Nein, a village six miles southeast of Nazareth and three miles northeast of Sôlem, the Shunammite setting of Elisha's miracle of resurrection. The fact that an ancient cemetery still lies outside its east **gate** is often, but precariously, cited as an instance of local color. **Only** is twice added elsewhere by Luke to miracle stories taken from his Marcan source (8:42; 9:38).

various types. The possibility of **faith** is as wide as the race.

11-17. ***The Dead Are Raised.***—The Exeg. points to parallels to this story in the O.T. and other ancient sources. There can be no doubt that stories of this kind circulated widely and were associated from time to time with various historical or legendary individuals. The Gospels present many instances of this type of transfer. Sometimes we allow ourselves to become anxious when scholars call our attention to this fact, feeling that something important for faith is involved in the suggestion that some narratives may rest upon stereotypes as much as upon actual incidents in Jesus' life. But in the last resort the important question is not whether an incident occurred exactly as it is described, but rather what the incident as described meant to the primitive church and whether that meaning was true. Here, as the Exeg. leads us to see, Luke tells the story partly to illustrate the statement to be made in the following paragraph, "The dead are raised up" (vs. 22). And that statement in turn is certainly not a mere reminiscence of a feature of Jesus' historical career; it is a testimony to the present power of the living Christ. Having risen from the dead, he gives the "power of an endless life" to those who belong to him. This meaning is not made explicit in Luke (as it is in the Fourth Gospel's account of the raising of Lazarus [John 11:23-26]), but we have to look only a little way beneath the surface to find it. And to find such a meaning, it is important to note, is far indeed from allegorizing; it is the soberest kind of exegesis. One observes in this particular story some of Luke's characteristic notes: the dead man was **the only son of his mother, and**

13 And when the Lord saw her, he had compassion on her, and said unto her, Weep not.

14 And he came and touched the bier: and they that bare *him* stood still. And he said, Young man, I say unto thee, Arise.

15 And he that was dead sat up, and began to speak. And he delivered him to his mother.

16 And there came a fear on all: and they glorified God, saying, That a great prophet is risen up among us; and, That God hath visited his people.

17 And this rumor of him went forth throughout all Judea, and throughout all the region round about.

her. 13 And when the Lord saw her, he
had compassion on her and said to her,
"Do not weep." 14 And he came and
touched the bier, and the bearers stood
still. And he said, "Young man, I say to
you, arise." 15 And the dead man sat up,
and began to speak. And he gave him to
his mother. 16 Fear seized them all; and
they glorified God, saying, "A great
prophet has arisen among us!" and "God
has visited his people!" 17 And this report
concerning him spread through the whole
of Judea and all the surrounding country.

13-14. The Lord was part of the confession of early Christians, and the church's favorite name for the exalted Christ. The title is never found in the narrative of Mark and Matthew, but occurs often in special Lukan matter, and is frequently employed by Luke himself in editorial introductions. It is characteristic of the late and apocryphal Gospel of Peter. Jesus' motive is one of **compassion.** No mention is made of faith on the woman's part. Jesus **touched the bier** to halt the cortege.

15-16. The story concludes, according to form, with proof of the success of the miracle. The bystanders are convinced that **a great prophet has arisen** with the miracle-working powers of Elijah and Elisha, and that his presence among them is evidence that "God has not forgotten his people!" (Goodspeed.)

17. Editorial conclusion. **Judea,** as in 1:5; 4:44; and 6:17, is the whole of Palestine.

---

she was a widow; Jesus **had compassion on her and said to her, "Do not weep";** after reviving the **young man,** Jesus **gave him to his mother.** Many writers on Luke discern his special and very tender concern for women (see Intro., pp. 8, 14); he is quick to seize on and to note in his Gospel the evidences that Jesus was especially considerate of women, as of the weak and underprivileged of every kind. But in this story are many reminders not only of Jesus' compassion, but of his authority as well: Jesus touches the bier and the bearers stop; he speaks a brief word of command and the young man obeys; **fear seized them all; . . . a great prophet has arisen.** Reading vs. 15, one cannot but wonder what the man said when he **began to speak.** Eugene O'Neill touches on this fascinating question in his *Lazarus Laughed* (see below, p. 417).

16. ***Fear and Glory.*—Fear** is frequently spoken of in the N.T. and often as an evil, or at best an inappropriate and unfortunate, thing. Jesus rebukes his disciples in the storm because they are "afraid" (Matt. 8:26); and when on another occasion they think they have seen a ghost, he says, "Have no fear" (Mark 6:50). The slothful servant in Jesus' parable of the talents "was afraid" and hid his lord's money (Matt. 25:25); Paul writes that we have not received "the spirit of slavery to fall back into fear" (Rom. 8:15); the writer to the Hebrews (2:15) speaks of Christ as freeing us from the "fear of death"; and I John 4:18 affirms that "perfect love casts out fear." On the other hand, the N.T. recognizes the appropriateness of fear under certain conditions. To this distinction between fear that is uncalled for and destructive and fear that is proper and creative we shall find ourselves recurring again and again in this Expos. (e.g., see on 8:25, 37; 12:4-7, 32). This verse is enough to tell us that Luke regards fear as often of this latter kind. **Fear seized them all** because they were manifestly standing in the very presence of the glory of God. One is reminded of the same combination of terms in 2:9: "The glory of the Lord shone around them and they were filled with fear"; but just as the shepherds end by going to Bethlehem to worship the newly born King, so here the fear leads to the "glorifying" of God. In both cases the fear is appropriate because it is a recognition of weakness and unworthiness in the presence of the ultimate goodness and power; in both cases the fear is creative because it issues in appropriate action; in both cases,

18 And the disciples of John showed him of all these things.
19 ¶ And John calling *unto him* two of his disciples sent *them* to Jesus, saying,

18 The disciples of John told him of all these things. 19 And John, calling to

F. Jesus and John the Baptist (7:18-35)

1. Jesus and the Emissaries of John (7:18-23=Matt. 11:2-6)

The passage answers a question that must have been of interest to the early Christian community. What did John think of Jesus?

18. Editorial introduction. Various references in the Gospels to the **disciples of John** (5:33; 11:1; etc.), the account in Acts 19:1-5 of disciples in Ephesus who had known only "the baptism of John," the polemic of the Fourth Gospel against John the Baptist and, as some scholars have argued, the sacred literature of the small sect in Iran that still claims John the Baptist as its founder, are evidence that followers of the Baptist remained independent of the Christian church for a hundred years or more, and were often in competition with it. The last direct reference to **John** in Luke's Gospel had told of his imprisonment (3:19-20). **All these things** would include Jesus' activities as a teacher as well as a healer.

19. **He who is to come** is the Messiah, not Elijah (as in Matt. 11:14; John 6:14). In his birth narratives Luke had related Jesus by blood to John. In his version of the

since it is the glory of God which has been revealed, the appropriate and creative response is an act of praise.

A great prophet . . . God. The Greek does not make absolutely clear whether the two sentences **a great prophet has arisen** and **God has visited his people** were parts of one remark, or whether some of the crowd expressed themselves in one way and some in the other. Moffatt sees one continuous statement: "'A great prophet has appeared among us,' they said; 'God has visited his people.'" The presence of a second ὅτι—**that** (KJV)—which often serves the purpose of quotation marks in the Greek of this period, rather indicates two separate remarks; so the RSV, KJV, Goodspeed, and most others understand the passage. Not that the point has any great importance: Luke undoubtedly regarded the two statements as thoroughly compatible and as belonging harmoniously together (as indeed they do), whether spoken by one group or by two different groups. Still, they represent two distinct, even if complementary, interpretations of the miracle which has elicited the awe and praise of the crowd. Some say, **A great prophet . . .**; others say, **God. . . .** One remark emphasizes the human person; the other, the divine event. One answers the question, "Who is this person?"; the other, "What has God done?" Whenever we reflect upon the meaning of Christ, both questions need to be asked; and neither has been truly asked or answered unless the other too is asked and answered. Luke likes this conception of God's "visiting" his people; cf. 1:68, 78, where again it occurs in close connection with the appearance of the "prophet." Eventually the meaning of what God had done in the event was realized as being much too great for any such phrase as **a great prophet** to be adequate as a description of the person. He became "Lord" (cf. vs. 13) and "Christ."

God has visited his people! As we have just seen, Luke likes this way of referring to God's act in Christ; and we can understand its appeal. The phrasing suggests the general transcendence of God, and yet his intimate nearness in this particular event. God is *God,* and therefore by definition remote from us (an object of awe and **fear**); but here he has drawn nigh, and nigh to help and save—for such is the connotation of the Greek term (it was used often of a doctor's visits). Note Goodspeed's translation to which the Exeg. calls attention. It hardly needs to be said that Luke, when he writes thus, is thinking not of this particular incident merely as such, but of the total event of which he regards the incident as typical. In the whole great happening—Jesus' life, death, and resurrection—God himself has come to our help; and because the happening culminated and issued in the church, his "visit" is more than a visit: "The dwelling of God is with men" (Rev. 21:3).

18-20. ***Christ or Another?***—Few matters about N.T. history are more tantalizingly obscure than the relationship between Jesus and John the Baptist, with whom in one way or another the next series of paragraphs in this chapter (vss. 18-35) are concerned. The Exeg.

Art thou he that should come? or look we for another?

20 When the men were come unto him, they said, John Baptist hath sent us unto thee, saying, Art thou he that should come? or look we for another?

21 And in that same hour he cured many of *their* infirmities and plagues, and of evil spirits; and unto many *that were* blind he gave sight.

22 Then Jesus answering said unto them, Go your way, and tell John what things ye have seen and heard; how that the blind see, the lame walk, the lepers are cleansed, the deaf hear, the dead are raised, to the poor the gospel is preached.

him two of his disciples, sent them to the
Lord, saying, "Are you he who is to come,
or shall we look for another?" **20** And
when the men had come to him, they said,
"John the Baptist has sent us to you, say-
ing, 'Are you he who is to come, or shall
we look for another?' " **21** In that hour he
cured many of diseases and plagues
and evil spirits, and on many that were
blind he bestowed sight. **22** And he an-
swered them, "Go and tell John what
you have seen and heard: the blind re-
ceive their sight, the lame walk, lepers
are cleansed, and the deaf hear, the dead
are raised up, the poor have good news

---

baptism story he had assumed that John had been made aware of Jesus' messianic mission. But now he incorporates material that is at cross-purposes with his own theory. It is possible that this passage gives the true picture. John may have heard of Jesus for the first time in prison, and only then have suspected that he might be the Messiah. In this case the question was the faint dawn of a new faith, not the dark night of a soul.

20-21. Vs. 20 is a repetition that is not necessary in Matthew's form of the narrative. Vs. 21 is also peculiar to Luke. A demonstration of mighty acts prepares John's disciples for Jesus' answer to their query.

22. This verse is a catena of phrases from Isa. 35:5-6 and 61:1 (cf. Luke 4:18), with the addition of **lepers are cleansed** and **the dead are raised up.** Jesus' answer is therefore

---

calls attention to the fact that seemingly contradictory views on this point belonged to the primitive tradition. Although vss. 18-23 suggest that John had no previous knowledge of Jesus, the following passage (vss. 24-30) seems to indicate much more than hearsay acquaintance with John on Jesus' part. Whether the Baptist had previously believed and was now doubting that Jesus was the Messiah, or whether (as is more probable) he was only now beginning to wonder if it might not be so—in either case one can understand his anxiety. He is in prison, with much time for reflection and no opportunity for action or verification. He hears about Jesus and the impression he is making on "the whole of Judea and all the surrounding country," but he misses much that he had expected in connection with the coming event of judgment and redemption (cf. vs. 23). "Can this be the Messiah?" he asks. There is a certain pathos in the way he puts his question, **Are you he who is to come, or shall we look for another?** i.e., "May we rest in the assurance that God has at last 'visited his people,' or must we continue only to wait in hope?" John, knowing that he probably faces death, wonders if he is entitled to the satisfaction of Simeon: "Lord, now lettest thou thy servant depart in peace, . . . for mine eyes have seen thy salvation" (2:29-30). Either Jesus is the Messiah, or the Messiah has not yet come; there is no alternative—Jesus has no competitor. Nor has he now: either Christ has redeemed us, or we are unredeemed; either we can rest in the knowledge that in Christ forgiveness and victory over sin and death have been decisively gained for us, or else we are condemned, probably to despair and at best to a merely wistful dream—more wish than hope—that this may still occur. For John it could be "Christ or another"; for us it is Christ or no one at all. Our question would need to be, "Are you he who should come, or has God forsaken us?"

21-22. ***The Proof of the Messiah.***—According to this well-attested story (cf. Matt. 11:2-6), which belongs to the most ancient stratum of the tradition, Jesus did not directly answer John's question. He did not speak concerning his own person, but rather pointed to the event, i.e., to what God was doing, to the signs that God's rule had begun. The Exeg. raises the question of what precisely these signs were. Were they the miracles merely as such? This is extremely unlikely. Certainly, as the Exeg. points out, this is not the meaning of the passages from the prophet which are cited in vs.

23 And blessed is *he,* whosoever shall not be offended in me.

preached to them. 23 And blessed is he who takes no offense at me."

---

indirect: The signs of the new age which the O.T. prophet had foretold are in evidence; draw your own conclusions from them! Doubtless Luke understood Jesus' words as a literal appeal to the evidence of the miraculous in his ministry. But they are metaphorical in the O.T. passage from which they were taken, and Jesus may also have used them figuratively.

23. "Who is repelled by nothing in me" is Moffatt's attempt to render a difficult idiom into modern English speech. The beatitude also presents difficulties of interpretation. Is it a veiled warning that Jesus and his work are not to be ignored? Or a guarded appeal for faith in his person? In either case Jesus avoids any direct assertion of messianic dignity, a feature that this passage shares with all the Synoptic tradition outside the passion narrative.

---

22. There the promises that "the eyes of the blind shall be opened"; that "the ears of the deaf shall be unstopped"; that the "lame man" will "leap as a hart" and "the tongue of the dumb" will "sing"—all these are obviously poetic ways of alluding to the joy of the new age when God's goodness will overflow for the blessing of men in manifold ways. We may assume that these phrases are cited by Jesus in the same spirit and with the same intention. There are many indications that in Jesus' thought although the actual dawn of the new age was still in the future, evidences of its approach were already appearing; in what he found occurring in his own ministry he saw unmistakable signs of the imminence of the kingdom of God. Certainly that was what the early church perceived. The beneficent miracles of Jesus were anticipations, proleptic manifestations, of the great salvation which would be consummated only in the age to come. The important thing is not that wonders merely as such have occurred, but that these express the wonderful goodness of God—as powerfully redemptive as that same goodness had in the beginning been powerfully creative. **The blind see, the lame walk, the lepers** are cured, . . . **the dead are raised**—it is as though a new world were coming into being, as indeed it was! And Luke characteristically places in the most emphatic position in this series of signs that "God has visited his people"—that the kingdom of God is already coming—the fact that the joyous **news** of its arrival is being brought to **the poor.** To what extent are these marks of the Messiah characteristic of the church as the continuing manifestation within history of the kingdom of God, the very body of Christ? Does the church embody the spirit of the new age? Do mighty creative and redemptive currents flow through it? Is the wonderful goodness of God being powerfully experienced and expressed in its life? Unless this is so, what can we say when the question is asked (as it is asked afresh in every generation), "Are you he who is to come, or shall we look for another?" and Christ must depend upon us to give the answer?

23. ***The Repellent Christ.***—Whether we take the position that John is only beginning to believe, or suppose that he is being troubled by doubts as to the truth of an earlier belief, this verse fits well enough into its context. In either case we are being told that there are facts which have the appearance of contradicting the clear implication of the preceding verse. What are these facts? What can Jesus have in mind here? The Exeg. quotes Moffatt's translation; Goodspeed's is similar: "Blessed is the man who finds nothing that repels him in me." Must not the meaning be that whereas the signs of the *kingdom* are manifest (vs. 22), Jesus himself does not suit any popular or traditional conception of the *Messiah?* He appears to be neither the kingly Son of David nor the heavenly Son of man. He has none of the trappings of messianic office, however conceived; indeed, he appears as a more than ordinarily humble man. As a matter of fact (as became clear later), he is on his way to be crucified. This proved to be the supremely repellent fact: even those who were willing to believe that this man who lived with no place to lay his head and preferred to associate with the despised was, or might be, the Christ—even these were not able to tolerate the idea of his being spat upon, ridiculed, scourged, and lifted up on a cross, the weak and helpless victim of Roman cruelty. We remember, "They all forsook him, and fled" (Mark 14:50); "We had hoped that he was the one to redeem Israel" (24:21); Peter's denial; and his earlier "God forbid, Lord! This shall never happen to you" (Matt. 16:22), after Jesus had predicted his coming suffering. And this **offense** at Christ's humiliation is the more likely because of his requirement that we also

24 ¶ And when the messengers of John were departed, he began to speak unto the people concerning John, What went ye out into the wilderness for to see? A reed shaken with the wind?

25 But what went ye out for to see? A man clothed in soft raiment? Behold, they which are gorgeously appareled, and live delicately, are in kings' courts.

26 But what went ye out for to see? A prophet? Yea, I say unto you, and much more than a prophet.

24 When the messengers of John had
gone, he began to speak to the crowds
concerning John: "What did you go out
into the wilderness to behold? A reed
shaken by the wind? 25 What then did you
go out to see? A man clothed in soft rai-
ment? Behold, those who are gorgeously
appareled and live in luxury are in kings'
courts. 26 What then did you go out to see?
A prophet? Yes, I tell you, and more than

---

2. Jesus' Estimate of John (7:24-30=Matt. 11:7-11)

The belief was current in late Judaism that Elijah was to reappear "in the last days" as a forerunner of the Messiah. According to one Christian tradition (Matt. 11:13-14), Jesus had identified John the Baptist as this Elijah redivivus. According to another (John 1:21), the Baptist himself had rejected the identification. In the form in which we have it our passage supports the affirmative in this debate.

24-25. No doubt many of Jesus' hearers had first been stirred by the preaching of **John.** Jesus' questions are ironical and metaphorical. "Did you expect to find some cringing timeserver in the desert, some self-indulgent man of ease?"

26-27. The obvious answer is "No!" They had gone out to see a **prophet**—a man who would preach austerity to others and practice it himself. But John was **more than a prophet.** The formula **it is written** introduces a quotation from scripture in early Christian literature, but what follows it in this instance has no exact counterpart in the O.T. It appears to be an adaptation to messianic doctrine of the LXX text of Mal. 3:1: "Behold, I send my messenger, and he shall prepare a way before my face." The change in personal pronouns makes the "quotation" refer to a herald of the Messiah rather than to a

---

take up a cross. He asks—he must ask—so much of us, so much more than we can give; and we often prefer to turn from him rather than to acknowledge our moral impotence and failure. He repels us, as the truth about ourselves and our duty often repels us. "Depart from me, for I am a sinful man, O Lord" (5:8).

24-28*a*. *More than a Prophet.*—Attention has been called to the obscurity that surrounds the relationship in which Jesus stood to John the Baptist (see on vss. 18-20). There can be no doubt that the two movements—Johannine and Christian—were closely related for a generation or more after both historical careers had ended; note what is implied on this point by Acts 18:25; 19:1-6. Many scholars would hold that this closeness stems from an original close connection between Jesus and John themselves. The association of the two individuals and the two movements and the importance of the Baptist in Christian beginnings are no doubt reflected in the fact that only the names of Jesus, Peter, and Paul occur more often in the N.T. than does the name of John the Baptist. Whatever the exact character of Jesus' relationship to John, it is clear that Jesus thought of him with the greatest respect and admiration. One can scarcely imagine terms of higher praise than are used in vss. 26-28*a*: "A prophet, do you say? Why this is the man about whom the prophets wrote, to whose coming they looked forward. Among those born of women none is greater than John." Although one may question points in this statement (see Exeg. on vss. 26-27), as a whole it must almost certainly go back to Jesus himself, since the tendency in the primitive church was to discount and disparage John (note that in the Fourth Gospel there is no word of praise for him whatever from any source). Words such as these on Jesus' lips mean that John was a man of altogether extraordinary moral stature. His character is nowhere delineated for us. The traits that stand out in this passage are integrity and strength--he was not weak or soft. People are often curious to see kings or nobles or rich men and will stand for hours to get a glimpse of royalty; but they found no such person in **the wilderness,** nor had they expected to. They found something better than a king; they found a **prophet.** There had been all the while many kings or half kings in Israel, but for many gen-

27 This is *he,* of whom it is written, Behold, I send my messenger before thy face, which shall prepare thy way before thee.

28 For I say unto you, Among those that are born of women there is not a greater prophet than John the Baptist: but he that is least in the kingdom of God is greater than he.

a prophet. 27 This is he of whom it is
written,

'Behold, I send my messenger before thy face,
who shall prepare thy way before thee.'

28 I tell you, among those born of women
none is greater than John; yet he who is
least in the kingdom of God is greater

---

precursor of God—identified as Elijah in Mal. 4:5-6. The same "quotation" also appears in Mark 1:2, where it is erroneously credited to Isaiah. Such a free paraphrase may have been pre-Christian, and it would be arbitrary exegesis to deny that Jesus could have used it. But the connection between vss. 26 and 28 is improved by its omission, and it is probably a christological proof text that was given its present setting by an early controversialist in order that the passage as a whole might support one Christian definition of John the Baptist's relationship to Jesus. But the addition, if it is such, must have been made very early, for the verse already stood in the Q source (cf. Matt. 11:10).

28. John marked a watershed in history. He was the last among the great of the old dispensation. But a new order has begun, and **he who is least in the kingdom of God is greater than he.** This is one of several kingdom references in the gospel tradition that show that Jesus thought of the new age of God's rule as a fact of present experience as well as the climactic event of the historical process.

---

erations there had been no prophets. Jesus affirms that one has now appeared—another Elijah or Amos. No wonder the people had gone out to see him! And when Jesus calls him a prophet, he does more than authenticate the man; he also authenticates his message; for what makes a man a prophet is "the word of God" which has come to him. But John was **more than a prophet.** He was more than a prophet because of his time; he had appeared at history's climactic moment; he had spoken to men "upon whom the end of the ages [had] come" (I Cor. 10:11). It is always true that these three elements combine to make the really great prophet: a great man, a great message, and a great time. John is **more than a prophet** because his "time" is "more than a time"; it is the moment when God's eternity is about to enter into time with a new, cleansing, and redemptive meaning. It is the moment of imminent judgment and salvation. John himself is part of the event he speaks of and shares its greatness.

28b. Less than a Christian.—Many students of the Gospels argue that this half verse was not originally a part of Jesus' own statement; that it is a remark of some early recorder of Jesus' words which came to be included among the words themselves. When it is remembered that no quotation marks or other punctuation was used in the earliest MSS, the possibility of such confusions cannot be denied, and indeed many actual instances are indubitable (e.g., John 3; who can say with certainty where the words being attributed to Jesus break off and the evangelist's begin? Vs. 13? Vs. 16?). The reason for the view that Jesus could not have spoken vs. 28*b* is that it seems to contradict so completely and sharply the immediately preceding statement, and at the same time can so easily be understood as the comment of some early Christian who was somewhat embarrassed by the high praise Jesus had conferred on John. After all, could even a member of John the Baptist's movement in the writer's time have expressed his admiration for John in more glowing terms? But if vs. 28*b* is such an interpolation, the insertion took place very early indeed because it belonged to the common source upon which Matthew also drew (cf. Matt. 11:11). Whatever the origin of this half verse, however, the important thing is its truth —and it *is* true. This man who was "more than a prophet" is in very truth less than the **least in the kingdom of God.** The Exeg. reminds us that in the N.T. the new age could be thought of as a fact of present experience; in the church and the Spirit the new age had already begun to be. Indeed, the phrase "the kingdom of God" seems occasionally to mean the church—which is the advance installment of our inheritance (Eph. 1:13-14), a "colony of heaven" (Phil. 3:20 Moffatt), to which we already belong. But this new order of the Spirit came into being only as a consequence of the total event—the life, death, and resurrection of Christ—and

29 And all the people that heard *him*, and the publicans, justified God, being baptized with the baptism of John.

30 But the Pharisees and lawyers rejected the counsel of God against themselves, being not baptized of him.

than he." 29 (When they heard this all the people and the tax collectors justified God, having been baptized with the baptism of John; 30 but the Pharisees and the lawyers rejected the purpose of God for themselves, not having been baptized by him.)

29-30. The RSV parentheses emphasize the probability that these verses are to be interpreted, not as part of Jesus' discourse, but as Luke's own comment on the reaction of Jesus' audience to it. **Justified God,** i.e., "acknowledged that God's plan was just." Luke often speaks of **lawyers** instead of "scribes" for the benefit of his Gentile readers.

could not have been possessed earlier. We have already observed the importance of the "time"; it was the nearness—indeed the actual beginning—of the event which made John "more than a prophet." But once the event had fully transpired, the Spirit given, and the church brought into being, something so supremely important had happened that those who stood within the new situation had privileges which even the most distinguished gifts or the most exalted character and calling could not earlier have bestowed. "Blessed are your eyes, for they see, and your ears, for they hear. Truly, I say to you, many prophets and righteous men longed to see what you see, and did not see it, and to hear what you hear, and did not hear it" (Matt. 13:16-17). The primary affirmation of Christian faith is that the life, death, and resurrection of Christ made a difference—a difference so tremendous as to require that we divide history by his coming. To be "in Christ" is to stand in a relationship to God which was not a possibility before him and is still not a possibility apart from him. The new order of relationships between men and God and among men was created through Christ—this is the "new creation" of which Paul speaks—and even **he who is least** in that new order is blessed beyond the greatest and most deserving of an earlier time. The Epistle to the Hebrews was written in order that a church which had forgotten its privileges might be awakened to the splendor of the meaning of Christ. God had previously spoken "by the prophets," but now "he has spoken to us by a Son" (Heb. 1:1-2), and the benefits falling to us are incalculably greater—as much greater as this Son is greater than Moses and Aaron or even the angels. But there is warning, too, in this reminder: "For if the message declared by angels was valid and every transgression or disobedience received a just retribution, how shall we escape if we neglect such a great salvation?" (Heb. 2:2-3.) This vivid awareness of the new situation, with greatly increased opportunities and obligations, was characteristic of the early church and is frequently expressed in the N.T. (e.g., the Sermon on the Mount in Matthew begins with setting forth the new blessedness [Matt. 5:1-11] and continues immediately with the new and more demanding law which Christ has brought). When the consciousness of the new situation is lost, the church grows cold (cf. Heb. 6:11-12; 10:32-39; Rev. 2:4). The important question is not how "great" we are, but whether we stand within **the kingdom of God,** where even **the least** has an incomparable greatness—greatness dependent not upon what we are but upon what God has done.

30. ***Rejecting God's Purpose.***—The statement that some of Jesus' hearers **rejected the purpose of God for themselves** is bound upon reflection to appear somewhat startling. For one thing, it says in effect that God *has* a purpose for us; and to say that is to make no easy or obvious statement. To affirm that in a world as incalculably vast as ours, a world which appears so heartless and impersonal in most of its operations—to affirm that in such a world God has a purpose for each of us (and this is surely implied) is to say a surprising and a profoundly significant thing. But the statement is surprising for another reason: it tells us that men have it in their power to reject God's purpose. In other words, God's will is not always done. In Matt. 18:14 Jesus says, "It is not the will of my Father . . . that one of these little ones should perish." Yet nothing is more certain and obvious than that the "little ones" do perish; every day's news tells us of the suffering or death of thousands of God's little ones. God's will can be defeated by human self-will. What a terrific responsibility it is given us to bear! We can reject **the purpose of God;** i.e., we can reject it for ourselves. Our action does not mean the failure of God's purpose except as it relates to ourselves. God's will is still sovereign: where he does not rule, he overrules; he makes the wrath of men to praise him. Although many things happen which are not in accordance with God's will, nothing happens outside of his will, i.e., outside of the area where he works and

31 ¶ And the Lord said, Whereunto then shall I liken the men of this generation? and to what are they like?

32 They are like unto children sitting in the market place, and calling one to another, and saying, We have piped unto you, and ye have not danced; we have mourned to you, and ye have not wept.

33 For John the Baptist came neither eating bread nor drinking wine; and ye say, He hath a devil.

31 "To what then shall I compare the men of this generation, and what are they
like? 32 They are like children sitting in the market place and calling to one another,

'We piped to you, and you did not dance;
we wailed, and you did not weep.'

33 For John the Baptist has come eating no bread and drinking no wine; and you

---

3. Parable of the Peevish Children (7:31-35=Matt. 11:16-19)

Interpreters are prone to allegorize. A parable is a story intended to make only one point clear and memorable. It is not a code in which each detail in one system has a counterpart in another. We must not look for any correspondence between the details of this parable and those of its application. In fact the two may originally have been independent in the tradition of Jesus.

31-32. Jesus' parables, as well as those in the rabbinical tradition, were often introduced by a double question. **The men of this generation** are compared with **children** who cannot agree on a game. The quotation should be punctuated as two separate statements. One group wishes to play "weddings," the other "funerals," and neither proposal is mutually acceptable. The parable reflects the discouragement that Jesus often experienced in his ministry, but he lightens it with a touch of humor.

33-35. John the Baptist was criticized for practicing asceticism, and Jesus for his failure to do so. Luke found **Son of man** in the Q source (cf. Matt. 11:19), but this

---

reigns, whether with healing and creative power or in judgment. So in the ultimate sense it is not God who fails when we reject his purpose, but rather ourselves. Luke is apparently identifying this **purpose of God** with accepting the "baptism of repentance for the forgiveness of sins" (3:3), to which men were called by John the Baptist; but the conception is capable of unlimited extension.

31-35. *Resisting the Truth.*—In a sense, as the Exeg. points out in the comment on vss. 33-35, this interesting and obviously very primitive little section further emphasizes and develops the idea of the Pharisees' rejection of God's purpose which was involved in their rejection of John. In an incidental way this vivid illustration throws a welcome light on the personality of Jesus. His humor shines through as it is seldom elsewhere in the tradition allowed to shine; and the statements that he came **eating and drinking** (a fact which laid him open to the scurrilous charges of his enemies), and that he was **a friend of tax collectors and sinners** remind us of Jesus' love of companionship, as well as of his compassion for all sorts and conditions of men. He was not an ascetic like John. (It is interesting to observe how often the accusations of Jesus' opponents reflect credit on him, e.g., this accusation of friendship with sinners, or "He saved others; he cannot save himself" [Mark 15:31].) The real purpose of these verses, however, is not to tell us something about the human personality of Jesus, but to affirm that those who have "rejected the purpose of God for themselves" will find reasons for rejecting every bearer of God's message and every representation of it, no matter how varied these may be and however inconsistent with one another the "reasons." There is a certain looseness in the words **what are they like?**—as is frequently true in the Gospels (cf. Matt. 13:44). Strictly speaking, **the men of this generation . . . are . . . like,** not the children who "call," but those who answer. (Note that the Exeg. takes a different view here, holding that two groups of children are making incompatible proposals to each other.) It is God (**wisdom** in vs. 35; cf. Prov. 1:20) who has called—called men to repentance and promised forgiveness—but **this generation** has rejected the call; and it has rejected the call just as decisively when it came through Jesus as when it came through John. The excuses are different in the two cases, but the real reason is the same: they have "rejected the purpose of God for themselves." Modern psychology uses the term "rationalization," and here is an admirable example of it. When we once set ourselves to resist the truth,

34 The Son of man is come eating and drinking; and ye say, Behold a gluttonous man, and a winebibber, a friend of publicans and sinners!
35 But wisdom is justified of all her children.
36 ¶ And one of the Pharisees desired him that he would eat with him. And he went into the Pharisee's house, and sat down to meat.

say, 'He has a demon.'
34 The Son of man has come eating and drinking; and you say, 'Behold, a glutton and a drunkard, a friend of tax collectors and sinners!'
35 Yet wisdom is justified by all her children."
36 One of the Pharisees asked him to eat with him, and he went into the Phari-

---

apocalyptic title may be a Christian substitution for an original "I." The **children of wisdom** must be the "people and the tax collectors" of vs. 29. By their attitude toward John and Jesus they have shown that God's wisdom, which spoke through these messengers, is right and true. Matthew reads "deeds" instead of **children**, and no satisfactory explanation of this divergence in the tradition has been advanced.

G. Jesus and a Penitent Sinner (7:36-50)

Luke made a place for this story because it illuminated the grounds for the charge in vs. 34 that Jesus was "a glutton and a drunkard, a friend of tax collectors and sinners." Jesus' concern for social and religious outcasts is a leading interest in Luke's special tradition (see Intro., pp. 14-15). Where there are no parallel documents for comparison, source analysis is admittedly hypothetical. Nevertheless there is good reason for assuming that Luke has woven together two distinct traditions: a story in vss. 36-40, 44-47*a*, and a parable in vss. 41-43. Vss. 48-50 introduce a new motif, and are possibly Luke's own composition. The point of the story is that one who loves much is forgiven much; the point of the parable is that one who is forgiven much, loves much. It is possible the story is a doublet of the one in Mark 14:3-9. Luke omitted the latter when he came to it in the course of composition. But the differences are more striking than the similarities, and it may have been Luke himself who borrowed "Simon" from the Marcan narrative as a name for Jesus' host, and took from it the details of the "alabaster flask," the ointment, and the anointing in vss. 37, 38, 46. These details introduce an element of premeditation into an act that is more naturally interpreted as spontaneous and impulsive.

36. No doubt Jesus numbered friendly Pharisees among his acquaintances (cf. 13:31), and twice elsewhere Luke speaks of Jesus at dinner in a **Pharisee's house** (11:37;

---

we can always find excellent "reasons" for objecting to all possible representations of it or arguments for it. The recalcitrant children would not play at either "weddings" or "funerals" because they were unwilling to play at all; so those who argued that John had **a demon** and that Jesus was **a glutton and a drunkard** did so because they had first rejected the truth to which each bore witness. This story also reminds us that witness can be borne to truth in many varied ways. There is no suggestion here that because John's way of life was so different from that of Jesus it had no value or place in God's purpose. The same appreciation of John is implied as is explicitly avowed in the preceding paragraph (vss. 24-28). God can speak many languages and use persons of many different gifts. Perhaps this suggests the meaning of the very obscure vs. 35. Those who belong to God, who possess the true **wisdom,** will recognize his truth under various forms and will respond to it gladly, just as others will reject it no matter what the form may be.

36-47. *Penitence or Love?*—This story is one of the most beautiful and appealing in the Gospels, and one of the most characteristically Lukan. Many of the important and distinctive interests of this writer are expressed in it—Jesus' sociability and enjoyment of hospitality; his sympathy with the lowly, and in particular with women; his love toward sinners; the forgiveness of sins, etc. The Exeg. calls attention to the signs of confusion in the mind of the writer as to just what the point of the story is, and indicates the very substantial grounds for the position taken by many commentators that Luke has here combined material from two sources. It is possible to take the story as a

37 And, behold, a woman in the city,
which was a sinner, when she knew that
Jesus sat at meat in the Pharisee's house,
brought an alabaster box of ointment,
38 And stood at his feet behind *him*
weeping, and began to wash his feet with
tears, and did wipe *them* with the hairs
of her head, and kissed his feet, and
anointed *them* with the ointment.

see's house, and sat at table. 37 And behold,
a woman of the city, who was a sinner,
when she learned that he was sitting at
table in the Pharisee's house, brought an
alabaster flask of ointment, 38 and stand-
ing behind him at his feet, weeping, she
began to wet his feet with her tears, and
wiped them with the hair of her head, and
kissed his feet, and anointed them with

14:1). But these instances of Pharisaic hospitality may be a literary device rather than a historical reminiscence, for on each occasion the host or his colleagues come in for criticism.

37-38. The city is nameless. Luke probably had Capernaum in mind. **A sinner** probably means "a prostitute." A private dinner in Palestine could take on the appearance of a public entertainment, and uninvited guests around the banquet table excited no comment (cf. 14:2; Mark 2:16). Jesus would have removed his sandals before entering the house, and when he reclined on a couch, his **feet** would be stretched out away from the table. Luke does not describe the woman as penitent but no doubt we are expected to deduce remorse from her **weeping.**

unit, however—Luke at least expects us to take it so—and the present comments are based on such an understanding. Taken thus, the story as a whole is apparently intended to explain not why the woman is forgiven, but why she loves. Her acts of devotion and her tears express not so much penitence before forgiveness as love and gratitude afterward. This is plainly the meaning of the parable in vss. 41-44 and in 47*b*; vs. 47*a*, although obviously difficult, can be understood as not altogether incongruous with that meaning: Luke may be thinking of the woman's love as an indication of a forgiveness, given or being given, not as a prior condition of it. For the distinction we are accustomed to make between the penitence that precedes forgiveness and the love and gratitude that follow it must not be pressed too hard. Indeed, the two are inseparable within the meaning of being forgiven, and to some degree identical, i.e., penitence always has love in it and love always contains a continuing penitence. It is simply not true to our experience to say that we do not know the love of God toward us or even begin to respond to it with love on our own part until after we have repented and been forgiven. Our penitence is itself an expression of love. It is the love within penitence which keeps it from being despair. One cannot really repent unless one is in process of being forgiven. In the same way, the love which we think of as following upon forgiveness always involves penitence, a continuing awareness of unworthiness. No one who loves ever finds himself worthy of love, whether man's or God's. We continue to rely upon the grace of those who love us; it is the nature of love to do this. The fact that our response to love, that of others and God's love, is thus complex may help explain the apparent confusion of point of view in this story. The woman is both penitent and loving; and she is both because she has been and is being forgiven, even though the word of forgiveness has not yet been pronounced.

37-38. ***Devotion to Christ.***—The principal meaning and value of this story as it was told and heard in the meetings of the first believers lay in the emphasis it places upon the appropriateness and worth of devotion to Christ. The most important element in the attitude of the N.T. Christians to Jesus is not their faith in him, but their love for him. To be a Christian it is more profoundly important to love Christ than to believe in him, although in actual fact the two go together: to love Christ is to believe in him and one cannot be said to believe in him in the N.T. sense of the word "faith" without loving him. But love comes first; so here Luke does not mention faith until in the appendix to the story (vs. 50). It must be so, for God is love and one can know him only in loving. This love of God was revealed, in the sense of being actively present, in Christ; and to him the church has always given herself in gratitude and devotion. The extravagance of this woman's actions—the washing of Jesus' feet with her tears, the drying of them with her hair, the kissing of his feet, the anointing of them from the **alabaster flask of ointment**—all of this seems appropriately to suggest the really inexpressible gratitude and love, transcending any

39 Now when the Pharisee which had bidden him saw *it,* he spake within himself, saying, This man, if he were a prophet, would have known who and what manner of woman *this is* that toucheth him; for she is a sinner.

40 And Jesus answering said unto him, Simon, I have somewhat to say unto thee. And he saith, Master, say on.

the ointment. 39 Now when the Pharisee who had invited him saw it, he said to himself, "If this man were a prophet, he would have known who and what sort of woman this is who is touching him, for she
is a sinner." 40 And Jesus answering said to him, "Simon, I have something to say to you." And he answered, "What is it,

---

39. **The Pharisee** had invited Jesus in the belief that he was a **prophet.** He now interprets an apparent failure to discern the character of the **woman** who was a **sinner** as evidence to the contrary.

40. The host is addressed as **Simon** for the first time. Presumably Luke means us to assume that Jesus' knowledge of the Pharisee's thoughts was supernatural.

---

human loyalty, which the earliest believers felt for Christ, who had died for them and now freely gave them all things. The acts of the woman were remembered and treasured because they were in a vicarious way their own acts. She did in the story just what they would have desired to do. In the corresponding Marcan story (14:3-9) this meaning is more explicitly brought out: "She has done a beautiful thing to me. For you always have the poor with you . . . but you will not always have me. She has done what she could; she has anointed my body beforehand for burying." She had done "what she could" and what very soon no one would be able to do. (Note that Mark ends his Gospel [16:1-8] with the story of how other women came to anoint Jesus' body and could not.) We have only the "memory" (Mark 14:9) of such expressions of devotion. But such a remembered act of gratitude and devotion can become a symbol of the continuing love of the risen Christ, which is the very life of the church; and it can be treasured the more because in the literal sense it cannot be repeated.

39. ***Not Less Knowledge but More.***—The Pharisee explains the behavior of Jesus toward the woman—behavior so different from what his own would have been—by assuming that Jesus knows less about her than he does; whereas the truth is that Jesus has acted as he has because he knows more. From the Pharisee's point of view the only alternative to lack of knowledge on Jesus' part, as an explanation of his unconventional conduct, would have been lack of virtue; and a less charitable person might have said, "If this man were a prophet, he would have refused to let this woman touch him, for it is obvious that she is a sinner." It is in the nature of any merely conventional morality to see in a deviation from its norms a sign either of ignorance or of immorality—"This person either is not good enough or does not know enough to act in the approved way." Such, we may grant, is usually the case; but by no means always. Sometimes one violates the approved way not because one knows less than others, but more; not because one is not good enough to meet the approved standards, but because one is too good to be bound by them. The charitable Pharisee is pitying Jesus for being stupid, for not knowing what he is doing, never realizing that Jesus is expressing a wisdom and a virtue so far beyond his own that the wisdom can appear to be folly and the virtue an offense. (So the Cross, Paul tells us, is foolishness to the Greeks and a scandal to the Jews [I Cor. 1:20 ff.].) It is the Pharisee who does not know! It is he who does not know that every human being is God's creature and the object of his care; that even the most shameless sinner can be forgiven; that no one is righteous in God's sight, but all stand equally in need of God's mercy; that love is the fulfillment of the law. It is he who is really ignorant! Later in this Gospel Jesus is to express his own sense of the tragedy of this deeper ignorance, and his pity: "And when he drew near and saw the city he wept over it, saying, 'Would that even today you knew the things that make for peace! . . . You did not know the time of your visitation'" (19:42-44). And out of the agony of the Cross he cried, "Father, forgive them; for they know not what they do" (23:34).

39, 44. ***Who or What Sort?***—Jesus knew **who** the woman was; the Pharisee knew—or thought he did—of **what sort** she was. The Pharisee had people arranged in classes; this woman was **a sinner.** He had rules governing his behavior toward the various classes or sorts. Having identified the class to which the woman belonged, he knew how she should be treated. But Jesus did not classify people; he did not concern himself much with what sort they were; he was always interested in who they were, i.e.,

41 There was a certain creditor which had two debtors: the one owed five hundred pence, and the other fifty.

42 And when they had nothing to pay, he frankly forgave them both. Tell me therefore, which of them will love him most?

43 Simon answered and said, I suppose that *he,* to whom he forgave most. And he said unto him, Thou hast rightly judged.

44 And he turned to the woman, and said unto Simon, Seest thou this woman? I entered into thine house, thou gavest me no water for my feet: but she hath washed my feet with tears, and wiped *them* with the hairs of her head.

45 Thou gavest me no kiss: but this woman, since the time I came in, hath not ceased to kiss my feet.

46 My head with oil thou didst not anoint: but this woman hath anointed my feet with ointment.

47 Wherefore I say unto thee, Her sins, which are many, are forgiven; for she loved

**Teacher?" 41 "A certain creditor had two
debtors; one owed five hundred denarii,
and the other fifty. 42 When they could not
pay, he forgave them both. Now which
of them will love him more?" 43 Simon
answered, "The one, I suppose, to whom
he forgave more." And he said to him,
"You have judged rightly." 44 Then turning toward the woman he said to Simon,
"Do you see this woman? I entered your
house, you gave me no water for my feet,
but she has wet my feet with her tears and
wiped them with her hair. 45 You gave me
no kiss, but from the time I came in she
has not ceased to kiss my feet. 46 You did
not anoint my head with oil, but she has
anointed my feet with ointment. 47 There-**

41-43. The original context of many of Jesus' parables has been lost, and this may be true of the parable of the two debtors. It teaches that a debtor's gratitude will be in proportion to the debt that the **creditor** has canceled. There is nothing in the story that precedes and follows it to suggest that the woman's emotions as she anointed Jesus were those of gratitude for an earlier assurance of forgiveness. God's forgiveness was the consequence of the woman's love, not its occasion. **Five hundred denarii** would approximate $100 in United States currency, but much more than that in terms of purchasing power.

44-47*a*. These verses continue the narrative of vss. 36-40. The host had failed to extend any special courtesies: **water** for a foot bath; a **kiss** of welcome; anointment of the **head** before a meal. He had treated Jesus as a casual guest—possibly as a social inferior. In contrast the woman had lavished evidences of her love upon him. The story reaches its climax in vs. 47*a*: **Therefore I tell you, her sins, which are many, are forgiven, for she loved much** (cf. I Pet. 4:8: "Love covers a multitude of sins"). Love is the qualification for divine forgiveness.

---

in persons themselves. In general it may be observed that Jesus was interested in concrete things, not in abstractions; and categories and classes are abstractions. Jesus said to Simon, **Do you see this woman?** That is no casual question, but an exceedingly searching one. And the answer would need to have been "No." The woman was exactly what Simon did not see and was not able to see. He could not see the woman herself because of his preoccupation with her sort. But Jesus saw the woman. It was of the very essence of Christ's ministry that he dealt directly, concretely, individually with persons, as the Gospels testify with scores of examples. It was on this account that conventional arrangements were never permitted to set up a barrier between himself and another, to limit his contacts with others, or to determine the character of his attitudes and relationships. How do we see people and act toward them: as persons or as sorts of persons?

47. *Degrees of Forgiveness.*—We are reminded again by this verse of the apparent confusion to which reference was made at the beginning of the discussion of this incident (see p. 141). Is the forgiveness the consequence of the love (as vs. 47*a* seems to indicate), or is the love the result of the forgiveness (as vs. 47*b* suggests)? It

much: but to whom little is forgiven, *the same* loveth little.

48 And he said unto her, Thy sins are forgiven.

49 And they that sat at meat with him began to say within themselves, Who is this that forgiveth sins also?

fore I tell you, her sins, which are many, are forgiven, for she loved much; but he who is forgiven little, loves little."
48 And he said to her, "Your sins are forgiven."
49 Then those who were at table with him began to say among themselves, "Who is

47*b*. But he who is forgiven little, loves little is in harmony with the point of the parable, but at variance with that of the story, and Luke may have added it when he integrated these two apparently incongruous traditions. It is just possible that the clause is a later scribal gloss for it is missing from the text of Codex Bezae, together with "for she loved much" of vs. 47*a*.

48-49. A new subject that is unrelated to anything that has gone before in the story or the parable but that has interesting similarities to the question under discussion in 5:20-21. Jesus pronounces absolution on the woman, and his table companions take offense at such an arrogation to himself of God's prerogative.

is possible that Luke did not feel the kind of logical difficulty here which we modern Westerners feel; note that a not dissimilar shift in point of view occurs in the story of the good Samaritan. (See on 10:29-37; the Fourth Gospel contains many instances of this kind of logical inconsistency.) The Exeg., it will be remembered, accounts for this feature of the story by supposing that Luke put together material from two sources. But however we ought to regard and explain the seeming contradiction, it is clear that Luke finds a correlation between degrees of forgiveness and degrees of love: the woman has been forgiven much and loves much; Simon loves little and has been forgiven little. We are thus reminded that the forgiveness of God is not a simple state, which is either received or not received, but that it may be received in many degrees. At first sight one might suppose the teaching of the story to be that the measure of our capacity to receive the forgiveness of God is the measure of our sin: the woman has been a notorious sinner, and Simon has been a respectable member of society, indeed, a Pharisee; it is possible, therefore, for the woman to know the meaning of God's forgiveness in a way Simon cannot know it. But to interpret the story in such a way would be to interpret it superficially—and falsely—for it is inconceivable that Jesus should have taught that one needed to be any particular kind of sinner in order to know, however fully, the meaning of God's mercy and love. No; the significant difference between the woman and Simon is not that she had been a worse sinner than he—it is possible that she had not been—but that she has realized more truly and deeply the reality of her sin. It is this deeper and truer understanding of her situation apart from Christ which has made possible for her the more intimate relationship with Christ. So in the parable of the prodigal son (15:11-32) it is not the fact that the younger son was a worse offender than his elder brother which explains his being able eventually to enter more deeply into the meaning of sonship, but rather the fact that "he came to himself," whereas the elder brother never did. So this woman had come to herself, i.e., had faced up to the moral situation in a way Simon had not done. Sometimes it seems harder for the respectable person to do this than for the notorious sinner; pride stands in the way of full realization and confession. That point is implicit in the present story, as well as in the parables of the prodigal son and of the publican and Pharisee (18:9-14), and is more explicit in such passages as Matt. 21:31, where Jesus, talking to "the chief priests and the elders," warns, "The tax collectors and the harlots go into the kingdom of God before you."

48-50. ***Forgiveness in Christ.***—According to any reading of this story, these verses, as the Exeg. points out, represent a kind of appendix. Here the point is the power of Jesus to forgive sins, as in 5:17-26 (cf. Mark 2:1-12). Just as has been urged in connection with previous stories of healing or the story of the raising of the widow's son from the dead (vss. 11-17), a paragraph like this became a part of the tradition, not primarily because of what it says about the career of Jesus, but because of the witness it bears to a continuing fact within the life of the church. "In Christ"—i.e., in the new order of life of which he is the head and center—the forgiveness of sins is to be found. This was not a matter of doctrinal belief, but of actual experience. Men and women, burdened with a

50 And he said to the woman, Thy faith
hath saved thee; go in peace.

8 And it came to pass afterward, that
he went throughout every city and vil-
lage, preaching and showing the glad tid-
ings of the kingdom of God: and the twelve
were with him,
2 And certain women, which had been
healed of evil spirits and infirmities, Mary
called Magdalene, out of whom went seven
devils,
3 And Joanna the wife of Chuza Herod's
steward, and Susanna, and many others,
which ministered unto him of their sub-
stance.

this, who even forgives sins?" 50 And he
said to the woman, "Your faith has saved
you; go in peace."
8 Soon afterward he went on through
cities and villages, preaching and bring-
ing the good news of the kingdom of God.
And the twelve were with him, 2 and also
some women who had been healed of
evil spirits and infirmities: Mary, called
Mag'da-lene, from whom seven demons
had gone out, 3 and Jo-an'na, the wife of
Chu'za, Herod's steward, and Susanna, and
many others, who provided for them[c] out
of their means.

[c] Other ancient authorities read *him*.

---

50. Your faith has saved you; go in peace is the same as the statement addressed in 8:48 (Mark 5:34) to the woman with a flow of blood, but the meaning of the first verb in the latter instance is necessarily "made you well." Forgiveness in this appendix to the story is the consequence of **faith** instead of "love."

H. Jesus as an Itinerant Teacher and Wonder-Worker (8:1-56)

1. Jesus Begins an Itinerant Ministry (8:1-3)

8:1*a*. Editorial.

1*b*-3. In addition to **the twelve** Jesus was accompanied by **certain women** whom he had restored to health of mind and body. For Luke's interest in the women who had been associated with Jesus' ministry and the life of the early church, see Intro., pp. 8, 14. Mark 15:40-41 also refers to women—not mentioned by name in Luke 23:49, 55—who had followed Jesus in Galilee and had "ministered" to him. **Mary, called Magdalene** is common to both lists. There is no good reason to identify her with the "sinner" of 7:37-50. Magdala, also known as Tarichaea, was a fishing village on the western bulge of the Galilean lake. **From whom seven demons had gone out,** i.e., the woman had been cured of a particularly serious mental disorder. **Joanna** is also mentioned with Mary Magdalene in 24:10. As the **wife** of one of **Herod's** officials she was presumably a woman of affluence and social standing; but there is no reference elsewhere in Jewish or Christian literature to **Chuza** or to his office as **steward.** Nothing is known of **Susanna** ("Lily"). **For them** (RSV) has much better attestation in the MSS than **unto him** (KJV). Jesus and his disciples did not depend on chance hospitality but were supported by women of **means.**

---

sense of guilt and separated from God and therefore from one another and their own true selves, have now been reached by God's love in Christ and brought within the new community of grace, and find themselves forgiven, i.e., pardoned and restored to that fellowship with God which means inner wholeness, or peace. This forgiveness was God's; but it had come to them through the event of which the life and death of Jesus had been the center, and within the life of the community in which the event had issued and in which Jesus was still known as Lord, and it had come as an utterly free, undeserved, and unexpected gift. Here is the empirical fact upon which all the doctrines of the person and work of Jesus were based. These doctrines are important; and some are truer than others. But more important and more true than any of them is the fact on which they are founded—the actual availability of the forgiveness of God within the new community. The early Christians believed that Jesus during his earthly life had forgiven sins, but this belief was important to them because of the fact that in Christ their own sins had been forgiven.

4 ¶ And when much people were gathered together, and were come to him out of every city, he spake by a parable:
5 A sower went out to sow his seed: and as he sowed, some fell by the wayside; and it was trodden down, and the fowls of the air devoured it.

4 And when a great crowd came together and people from town after town came
to him, he said in a parable: 5 "A sower
went out to sow his seed; and as he sowed, some fell along the path, and was trodden under foot, and the birds of the air de-

2. Parable of the Seed and the Soils (8:4-8=Mark 4:1-9)

The Marcan source, which Luke abandoned at 6:17, is resumed, and is followed with minor transpositions and abbreviations until 9:51. One great omission of Marcan matter (Mark 6:45–8:26) between 9:17 and 18 and two lesser omissions (Mark 6:1-6; 6:17-29) are discussed in the Intro. (pp. 18-19).

The parable is clear. Seed sown carelessly, or in poor soil, or on land infested with thorns, is unfruitful; but fertile soil produces abundantly and assures a good harvest. The only problem, as so often in the study of Jesus' teaching, is to recover the parable's application. Mark's interpretation (Mark 4:13-20; cf. Luke 8:9-15) is a Christian allegory, but its equation of the "seed" and "the word" probably does justice to the point of the original. Jesus meant the parable to encourage his disciples in the faith that his proclamation of "the good news of the kingdom of God" would prove fruitful. "Sowing" in rabbinical literature is a frequent metaphor for "teaching." A similar parable in II Esdras 8:41 illustrates the doctrine that not all mankind will be saved.

4. In Mark's version Jesus had been teaching "beside the sea" and was forced by the size of the crowd to put out in a boat and teach offshore. Luke had already used this stereotyped setting in 5:3, and substitutes an even vaguer one at this point. **A parable** for Mark's "parables," which had referred to a whole collection (Mark 4:1-34).

5. Despite the definite article in the Greek (cf. the ASV), **a sower** is the correct translation. In accordance with Semitic usage the definite article marks him as a representative of a class. **And was trodden under foot** is an amplification of the Marcan source.

8:4-8, 11-15. ***The Task of the Sower.***—In Mark (4:1-9) this parable of the sower stands as the first of the more formal (cf. Mark 2:17, 19-22; 3:23-27) parables of Jesus and is the occasion for an explanation on Jesus' part of why he uses the parable form in his teaching. Matthew and Luke closely follow Mark in both the parable itself and the explanation, and the student of the present passage should consult both the Exeg. and Expos. on Mark 4:1-20 and Matt. 13:1-23. The parables of Jesus almost certainly often circulated in the earliest period without context, so that it must frequently have been (and therefore must continue to be) uncertain just what Jesus was intending to illustrate by a particular parable. As the Exeg. indicates, however, the general intention of the parable of the sower is fairly clear. The conceiving of the teaching of truth under the analogy of the sowing of seed was common in the period. The Exeg. refers to the rabbinical literature and to II Esdras 8:41-43 (see also II Esdras 9:31-33). William Manson[4] quotes the following from Aristotle's *Nicomachean Ethics* X. 9. 6: "Reason has not (the same) operative force in all men. The soul of the hearer must be wrought first into a state of preparedness by the training of habit, like land that is to foster seeds." Jesus is apparently reflecting upon the results of his mission. Opposition has developed, and it is clear that only a limited number in Israel are going to hear and respond to the gospel of the kingdom. He finds comfort in the observation that only a part of the seed broadcast by any sower eventually bears fruit. Much of it falls on hard, barren, or preoccupied soil and yields nothing. This is to be expected; and the preacher, no more than the sower, must be discouraged; let him remember that some seed does fall **into good soil,** where it yields **a hundredfold.** Such is the probable intention of the parable; and nothing more definite or elaborate can properly be regarded as belonging to its original meaning. It was inevitable, however, that an allegorical meaning should be found in the various types of unpropitious soil (see Exeg. on vss. 11-15); and the truth of the statement that some hearers resemble the hard ground, others the shallow ground, and still

[4] *The Gospel of Luke* (London: Hodder & Stoughton, 1930; "The Moffatt New Testament Commentary"), *ad loc.*

6 And some fell upon a rock; and as
soon as it was sprung up, it withered away,
because it lacked moisture.
7 And some fell among thorns; and the
thorns sprang up with it, and choked it.
8 And other fell on good ground, and
sprang up, and bare fruit a hundredfold.
And when he had said these things, he
cried, He that hath ears to hear, let him
hear.
9 And his disciples asked him, saying,
What might this parable be?

voured it. 6 And some fell on the rock;
and as it grew up, it withered away, be-
cause it had no moisture. 7 And some fell
among thorns; and the thorns grew with
it and choked it. 8 And some fell into good
soil and grew, and yielded a hundredfold."
As he said this, he called out, "He who
has ears to hear, let him hear."
9 And when his disciples asked him

6-7. Rock for the word in Mark that means "a shallow crust of soil covering bedrock." According to Mark, the shoot was scorched because it had no root; according to this version, it **withered . . . because it had no moisture.**

8. An abbreviation that reproduces only the highest estimate that is given in Mark of the yield. For the fertility of the soil in Palestine under good conditions cf. Gen. 26:12. The hortatory conclusion occurs in Mark 4:9, 23, and Luke also uses it again in 14:35.

3. Purpose of Parables (8:9-10=Mark 4:10-12)

9-10. In Luke the **disciples** ask Jesus the meaning of **this parable;** in Mark, the purpose of "parables" in general. Despite this change Luke also presents the answer in two parts. These verses tell us that Jesus employed **parables** to veil the truth, to hide it from all but his most intimate followers, to confirm the mass of the people in ignorance and unbelief. This is an incredible theory, for the obvious purpose of parables was to make truth plain. In Mark's Gospel the verses break a good connection between Mark 4:10 and 13 and are presumably the composition of the evangelist. As he reflected on Jesus' ministry, Mark tried to account for the fact that most of his contemporaries had

---

others the crowded ground does not depend upon the original intention of the parable. Still, the major point is that it is the preacher's or teacher's task to sow **the word of God:** let him do this faithfully and generously, not allowing himself to be discouraged because much of his seed seems to be wasted. The preacher or teacher in every age, if he is serious and sensitive, is susceptible to the kind of disillusionment against which the parable is aimed. Such a one is likely to take to himself a measure of responsibility for the final outcome of his sowing which it is not appropriate that he should bear, and to feel an anxiety for results, which is not only futile but also baseless. Let him sow his seed, making sure that the seed is **the word of God.** The rest must be left to God.

It may not be inappropriate to point out in this connection—although it lies outside of the conscious purpose of the parable—that Jesus characteristically thinks of goodness as a living, growing thing, and therefore as being the work not of men, but of God. His parables often celebrate in one way or another the wonder of growth (note the parables of the mustard seed, of the seed growing secretly, etc.). The true good is not something man can construct, whether in himself or in others; it is the creation of God. We may assist in God's creative work by setting up favorable conditions for it, but only he can create the living plant or bring forth the living fruit. We may plant (and, it might be added, prepare the soil beforehand and cultivate it afterward), but only God can give the increase (I Cor. 3:6). Because God's kingdom is such a living creation, we cannot "build" it; we can only pray for it, prepare as best we can the way for its coming, and then wait for it **with patience.**

9-10. ***The Secret of the Kingdom.***—On Mark's view, taken over also by Matthew and Luke, that Jesus told parables in order to conceal the truth, see the Exeg. on these verses as well as the discussion in Vol. VII of Mark 4:10-12; Matt. 13:10-15. The view can be accounted for partly as a corollary of Mark's doctrine of the "messianic secret" and partly by the fact that many parables in circulation in the early church were actually enigmatic. This obscurity we would understand quite simply—the orig-

10 And he said, Unto you it is given to know the mysteries of the kingdom of God: but to others in parables; that seeing they might not see, and hearing they might not understand.

what this parable meant, 10 he said, "To you it has been given to know the secrets of the kingdom of God; but for others they are in parables, so that seeing they may not see, and hearing they may not under-

---

remained unresponsive. He felt that the failure of the Jews to understand must have been divinely ordained—cf. Paul's doctrine of God's "hardening" of Israel (Rom. 9–11). Jesus must have intended the very simplicity of the parables to hide their message from all but the inner circle. In reaching this conclusion Mark may have been influenced by the Hellenistic notion that the essence of religion is a "mystery" (**mysteries** in Luke), hidden from outsiders but revealed to the initiate. The word occurs nowhere else in the gospel tradition.

---

inal contexts which would have given the clues to the purposes of the several parables have been lost. (Imagine a collection of illustrations culled from the sermons of a modern preacher, published without any information as to the setting of each in a particular sermon or as to the point it was designed to illustrate—how uncertain and confused the reader would often be!) That Jesus deliberately hid the truth about himself (or about anything else) from those whom he was presumably teaching is incredible in view of what we know of Jesus' character and purpose, as well as of historical probabilities generally.

Still, when all of this is said, one cannot deny that the phrase **secrets of the kingdom of God** answers to reality. A mystery shrouds the inmost meaning of creation and of our own being, as well as of redemption and the ultimate fulfillment of God's purpose, which ordinary flesh-and-blood eyes cannot penetrate. Either the mystery is not expressed at all, or it must be expressed **in parables**; either the meaning is not grasped at all, or it is grasped imaginatively. Reality is a deep, deep thing which no science can begin to sound and no positivism can begin to compass. A modern writer has said, "Some people read God in prose translation." What is meant obviously is "try to read God"; for God cannot be read that way, nor can any true interpreter of the ways of God be thus read. And yet some people can read in no other way. They not only try to read poetry so, but also nature, the human heart, and the long story of the race—all of them in prose translation. Sometimes such a person deludes himself into believing that his deficiency is a virtue, that lack of imagination means the presence of superior intelligence. But if one reads Shakespeare in prose translation, one does not find Shakespeare; and if one reads the universe in prose translation, one misses most of it—no wonder one does not find the **secrets of the kingdom of God.** The woman who according to the Fourth Gospel once said to Jesus, "Thou hast nothing to draw with, and the well is deep" (John 4:11), spoke more wisely than she knew. The well *is* deep and many have nothing to draw with. It happened that he who was talking with her did have something to draw with, but how could she know that till after he had given her the water which was "a well of water springing up into everlasting life"? To anyone who fancies that he can reduce the concrete reality of God's world to a neat formula, or who fondly thinks he can dispose of all the hopes, faiths, and devotions of the race with a few "hard facts," we might say, "Thou hast nothing to draw with, and the well is deep."

The tragedy of those who, seeing, do not see is a familiar one. Thornton Wilder in his play *Our Town* reminds us poignantly of how insensitive we are to the color and flavor and beauty of our everyday life. The poets are constantly making us aware of how little we see. When Carl Sandburg in an old brickyard sees the moonlight making "a wide dreaming pansy of an old pond in the night";[5] when Joyce Kilmer sees a tree with "a nest of robins in her hair";[6] when Chester Firkins has in a subway express a "wild ride—with God,"[7] or Langston Hughes sees a polished spittoon as a "bright bowl of brass" on the "altar of the Lord";[8] when Shakespeare sees the daffodils taking "the winds of March with beauty,"[9] or Wordsworth finds in the meanest flower thoughts "that do often lie too deep for tears,"[1] or Madison Cawein watches the winds as "God's workmen," who "with large laughter and loud song" bear "on backs of might" up the "steep stair of sky, . . . huge tempest bulks"[2]—the poets are telling us what they see, and without intending

[5] "Nocturne in a Deserted Brickyard."

[6] "Trees."

[7] "On a Subway Express."

[8] "Brass Spittoons."

[9] *The Winter's Tale,* Act IV, scene 4.

[1] "Ode on the Intimations of Immortality."

[2] "The Winds."

11 Now the parable is this: The seed is the word of God.

12 Those by the wayside are they that hear; then cometh the devil, and taketh away the word out of their hearts, lest they should believe and be saved.

13 They on the rock *are they,* which, when they hear, receive the word with joy; and these have no root, which for a while believe, and in time of temptation fall away.

14 And that which fell among thorns are they, which, when they have heard, go forth, and are choked with cares and riches and pleasures of *this* life, and bring no fruit to perfection.

15 But that on the good ground are they, which in an honest and good heart, having

stand. 11 Now the parable is this: The seed
is the word of God. 12 The ones along the
path are those who have heard; then the
devil comes and takes away the word from
their hearts, that they may not believe
and be saved. 13 And the ones on the rock
are those who, when they hear the word,
receive it with joy; but these have no root,
they believe for a while and in time of
temptation fall away. 14 And as for what
fell among the thorns, they are those who
hear, but as they go on their way they are
choked by the cares and riches and pleas-
ures of life, and their fruit does not ma-
ture. 15 And as for that in the good soil,
they are those who, hearing the word, hold

4. Explanation of the Parable (8:11-15=Mark 4:13-20)

The "explanation" reflects missionary problems of the early church. Some who hear the gospel never have faith because of the machinations of the devil; others give up their faith under trial; and still others have their faith submerged by "the cares and pleasures" of this life. The emphasis in the parable is on the abundant harvest from fertile soil; in the "explanation," on the reasons why so much seed is wasted. Allegory, a Hellenistic device for imparting truth, was rarely employed by the rabbis and probably never used by Jesus.

11. The sower is not allegorized. **The word of God** in the N.T. is a technical name for "the gospel."

12. To make sense the four classes of hearers ought to be identified with the four kinds of soil in which the same seed is sown, but they appear to be identified with the seed. The narrator may be thinking in terms of the final crop, which is a product of both seed and soil, or the confusion may be a matter of careless diction. **That they may not believe and be saved** is a Lukan addition which relates the situation more explicitly to the difficulties of the early Christian mission.

13. Luke's use of **root** shows his dependence on Mark, for he had used "moisture" in his own version of the parable (vs. 6). **Fall away** is a proper synonym for Mark's "are offended."

14. Pleasures of life, for Mark's "desire for other things," **and their fruit does not mature,** for Mark's "and it proves unfruitful."

15. As in vs. 8 Luke does not distinguish between the various yields of the fertile soil. Those who hear **the word** do so with **an honest and good heart** and bear fruit **with patience.**

it are rebuking us for our blindness. The inmost meaning of our experience can be expressed only **in parables** and can be discerned only by those who know how to read and understand them.

The Bible expresses its conception of the nature and meaning of human life not in a metaphysic or a science, but in a story—the story of the Creation, the Fall, the Incarnation, the Atonement. It uses these terms because the meaning of our life, as it understands that meaning, is too deep for more "positive" or prosaic terms to express it. In a sense the whole of Christian theology is a parable. It must be so. With parables the truth is hidden from many; but without parables it would be hidden from all. Those who are able to understand the truth will be able to read the parables; where we do not understand, the situation is not that the parables have hidden the truth from us, but that we have been too blind to see it even with their help.

11-15. See Expos., vss. 4-8.

heard the word, keep *it,* and bring forth
fruit with patience.

16 ¶ No man, when he hath lighted a
candle, covereth it with a vessel, or putteth
it under a bed; but setteth *it* on a candle-
stick, that they which enter in may see
the light.

17 For nothing is secret, that shall not
be made manifest; neither *any thing* hid,
that shall not be known and come abroad.

it fast in an honest and good heart, and
bring forth fruit with patience.

16 "No one after lighting a lamp covers
it with a vessel, or puts it under a bed, but
puts it on a stand, that those who enter
may see the light. 17 For nothing is hid that
shall not be made manifest, nor anything
secret that shall not be known and come

---

5. Parable of the Lamp and Other Sayings (8:16-18=Mark 4:21-25)

16. A detached parable that stood in Q as well as in Mark, and whose original application cannot be recovered. Matthew's version is in the Sermon on the Mount (Matt. 5:15), where it exhorts the disciples not to hide their light. Luke uses the parable a second time in 11:33. There it seems to assert that Jesus himself is an answer to the demand for a "sign." In both instances Luke's form is based on Q, but in this verse **or puts it under a bed** has been added from Mark, and the **lamp,** as in Mark, appears to be a metaphor for the teaching of Jesus. **Vessel** is used instead of Mark's "bushel"—a grain and flour measure holding about a peck. Matthew's form of the parable presupposes a lamp that illuminated a one-room Palestinian house. Luke thinks of a **lamp** that had been placed on a **stand** in the vestibule of a Greco-Roman dwelling so **that those who enter may see the light.** Is this final clause in Luke an oblique reference to Gentile converts?

17. Another floating saying. Matthew used a slightly different Q version in Matt. 10:26*b,* where the proverb is appended to the counsel not to be afraid of persecutors, and gets its meaning from the verse that follows: "What I tell you in the dark, utter in the light." **Be known and** is from Q. The saying, as in Mark, seems to be related to the explanation of the purpose of parables in vs. 10. The meaning of Jesus' teaching is **hid** only temporarily; ultimately it will be **made manifest.** Luke uses the proverb again (in its Q form) in 12:2, where it refers to the hypocrisy of the Pharisees. Still another version is preserved in fragmentary form in the Oxyrhynchus Papyrus 654. iv.

16-17. *The Secret Shall Be Known.*—These verses, which follow upon the parable of the sower in Mark as well as here, effectively contradict the theory about Jesus' purpose in speaking in parables which is expressed in Mark 4:11-12 and repeated in Luke 8:9-10. Vs. 16 would seem to say in effect, as Luke understands it: "The parable in my teaching is intended to be not **a vessel** or other object for hiding the light, but **a stand** to enable the light to shine more clearly and widely." To be sure, to some hearers Jesus' teaching is sometimes obscure or even mystifying; but it is not the parables that make it so, but their own lack of experience, insight, and imagination. Vs. 17 in this context must mean that even if the truth is for a time hidden from our sight (this is true to some degree for all, and for some altogether), it will ultimately **be made manifest** and unmistakable in the actual stuff of our experience. Truth *will* prevail. Truth will eventually be embodied in events, and while we may be able now to close our eyes to its light, we shall not then be able to resist its power. The distinction between truth and reality is perhaps relevant and useful here. Truth might be defined as the description of reality. Reality is by definition normative, irresistible, invincible; to it all behavior must conform or else cease. To understand and obey the truth is to live; to misjudge it or to disregard it is to be destroyed. We may deny the truth about God, but we cannot escape the reality of God. God's kingdom will come, even if we have not learned in advance the secret of its coming and conformed our lives to its demand. The hidden will **be made manifest** and the **secret . . . shall . . . be known**—if no longer as truth about reality (to which one can adjust one's life and be saved), then as reality itself, from which there is no escape. One who defies or denies the truth—yes, who so much as neglects, hides, plays fast and loose with it—takes the way of death. The Fourth Gospel is not mistaken in seeing "light" and "life" as inseparably related. "In him was life, and the life was the light of men" (John 1:4);

18 Take heed therefore how ye hear: for whosoever hath, to him shall be given; and whosoever hath not, from him shall be taken even that which he seemeth to have.

19 ¶ Then came to him *his* mother and his brethren, and could not come at him for the press.

to light. 18 Take heed then how you hear; for to him who has will more be given, and from him who has not, even what he thinks that he has will be taken away."

19 Then his mother and his brothers came to him, but they could not reach

---

18. How you hear instead of Mark's "what you hear." **Even what he thinks that he has** for Mark's paradoxical "even what he has." In both Mark and Luke the proverb means: God will impart more truth to him who appropriates what he has already heard. The saying is also appended to the parable of the pounds (Matt. 25:29 and Luke 19:26), where it follows the command that money that had been entrusted to the third servant should be taken from him and given to the first.

6. Jesus' Spiritual Kindred (8:19-21=Mark 3:31-35)

19-21. See 11:27-28 and Mark 10:29-30 for similar sayings elsewhere in the gospel tradition (cf. Heb. 2:11). Bonds of the spirit bind the family of God, not those of blood.

"I am the way, and the truth, and the life" (John 14:6); "I am the light of the world; he who follows me will not walk in darkness, but will have the light of life" (John 8:12).

18. *Take Heed then How You Hear.*—The meaning of this verse in its present context is clear (the context is the same in Mark). In vs. 17 Jesus has given the sober reminder that God's kingdom will come, whether we see it coming and prepare for it or not. The fact that we may be too blind to see the light of truth will not keep us from knowing eventually the full power of truth—and this power, for those who have neglected the light, will be the power of judgment and destruction. It is important, therefore, that we *see* the light, that we *learn* the truth, that we *understand* what Jesus is saying about the nature and the nearness of God's rule; in other words, we must **take heed . . . how** [we] **hear.** We are accustomed to the distinction in the Gospels between "hearing" and "doing"—to the contrast between that hearing which is only hearing and that hearing which issues in action (cf., e.g., vs. 21; 6:48-49; Matt. 21:28-31; see also Jas. 1:22-25). In all these passages the emphasis is upon doing; hearing is taken for granted, as though it were a natural, or inevitable, or easy, or morally neutral thing. In the present passage, however, the importance and critical significance of hearing itself is stressed. It is necessary, of course, that we *will* the right, but we must also *understand* the right; and there is a *duty* to hear as well as to do. We are responsible not only for the faithfulness of our action, but also for the accuracy of our hearing and the truth of our understanding. We shall not be able to escape the final judgment by saying simply, "I did not know," if we shall have slighted our opportunities for learning. It is a fact of experience that we may suffer—and others may suffer through us—as often from our lack of knowledge as from our lack of virtue; and when the opportunity for knowledge is given us and we neglect it, lack of knowledge means lack of virtue. Our ignorance under such conditions, besides being practically costly to ourselves and others, is also sinful in God's sight. **Take heed then how you hear.**

Jesus not only warns of the importance of true understanding; he also gives us its principle or law: **to him who has will more be given, and from him who has not, even what he thinks that he has will be taken away.** Understanding is a faculty which grows more effective as it is used. As we learn, we acquire greater capacity to learn. As we use our opportunities for knowledge, more opportunities come to us. On the other hand, neglect and disuse of what we have means not only the impossibility of receiving more truth, but also the loss of the truth we "thought" was really and permanently ours. It is not surprising that this saying is found also in the parable of the pounds; it is a general principle applicable to life at many points.

19-21. *Jesus' Family.*—This story is more vividly told in Mark (3:31-35), who is followed almost word for word by Matthew (12:46-50); and the student of the present passage should consult the comment on these parallels. Luke's abridgment of the narrative is not merely in the interest of economy; he is seeking to mitigate somewhat the apparent harshness of the Marcan story. In Mark the effect of the story is to suggest repudiation by Jesus of his kinsmen, even his mother; to Luke this would seem

20 And it was told him *by certain* which
said, Thy mother and thy brethren stand
without, desiring to see thee.
21 And he answered and said unto them,
My mother and my brethren are these
which hear the word of God, and do it.

him for the crowd. 20 And he was told,
"Your mother and your brothers are standing outside, desiring to see you." 21 But
he said to them, "My mother and my
brothers are those who hear the word of
God and do it."

According to Mark's account, Jesus' family had been disturbed by the rumor that he was a lunatic—possessed by Beelzebub—and had come to interrupt his ministry. All this has disappeared from Luke's version, which is abbreviated and transposed to a new setting. By reading **those who hear the word of God and do it** instead of "whoever does the will of God" the evangelist has related the saying to that in vs. 15 and has made it an effective conclusion to the discourse. There is no reason to suppose that the **brothers** here are not brothers in the usual sense of the word.

---

not only unnatural but also intolerably harsh. He therefore makes changes, with the result that as the story stands in his Gospel, Jesus without rejecting his own family makes their coming the occasion for a remark about his larger, more inclusive family. (It is noteworthy that while in vs. 20 the words **mother** and **brothers** are used with the definite article, the same words in vs. 21 are without the article. Alfred Plummer[3] suggests the translations "mother to me" and "brothers to me," i.e., "equally dear.") The transposition, to which the Exeg. calls attention, may be explained in the same way: in Mark the context suggests that Jesus' mother and brothers were attempting to interfere with his work and had virtually aligned themselves with his enemies; Luke gives the story a new setting in which no such suggestion appears. We can understand Luke's difficulty with the passage in Mark; looked at simply as a story about a human being, it is harsh and incredible. But of course Mark and the early Christians generally did not look upon it so; this was a story about the Son of God, the Lord of the church. It is this risen and ascended Master whose only family is **those who hear the word of God and do it.** The story bears witness to the reality, the depth, and the divine quality of the κοινωνία ("community" or "fellowship") of the church. Those who belonged to that community belonged to Christ so completely and so intimately that they could speak of themselves as being "in Christ"; and ties stronger than any earthly bond of blood bound them together in this new family. Reflected in the story—at any rate as Mark understands it—is the fact that many of the first believers had been repudiated by their families: these had been rejected by their natural kinsmen, but they had found another home, a more adequate and congenial home, toward which they felt a far deeper loyalty and in which they found far deeper satisfactions. They belonged to the new brotherhood in Christ, God's new creation. But in the same way Christ belonged to them. He had died not only to sin (Rom. 6:10), but also to all contingent relationships, to all merely earthly bonds, nation and race as well as family. Something like this was undoubtedly the meaning of this story for those who first heard it told or read.

As to the incident as it originally happened, we may be sure that although Jesus did not speak harshly of his mother and brothers or repudiate them, he did relegate family loyalty to a definitely secondary place. This would be in line with his teaching at other points (cf., e.g., 9:59-61 and passages noted in the Exeg.). The kingdom of God and his righteousness must be sought first (Matt. 6:33)—taking precedence not only over individual interests, but over family interests as well. Jesus goes so far as to say (14:26): "If any one comes to me and does not hate his own father and mother and wife and children and brothers and sisters, . . . he cannot be my disciple." It is usual in reading such passages, and proper, to make allowance for Oriental hyperbole—of course Jesus is not teaching hatred of anyone—but the passionate feeling and force of this statement cannot be missed. The intensity of the emotion reflected in it, however, far from indicating callousness on Jesus' part to family privileges and obligations, probably means just the opposite: he knows in his own experience how subtly and powerfully love of family can sometimes compete with loyalty to the kingdom of God. Most of us are too self-centered or too insulated by habit or social convention to feel this conflict acutely—we do not love our families enough, or we do not love God enough, or both. But

[3] *A Critical and Exegetical Commentary on the Gospel According to St. Luke* (New York: Charles Scribner's Sons, 1896; "International Critical Commentary"), *ad loc.*

22 ¶ Now it came to pass on a certain day, that he went into a ship with his disciples: and he said unto them, Let us go over unto the other side of the lake. And they launched forth.

23 But as they sailed, he fell asleep: and there came down a storm of wind on the lake; and they were filled *with water,* and were in jeopardy.

22 One day he got into a boat with his disciples, and he said to them, "Let us go across to the other side of the lake." So they set out, 23 and as they sailed he fell asleep. And a storm of wind came down on the lake, and they were filling

7. Stilling of the Storm (8:22-25=Mark 4:35-41)

Nature miracles form a small group in the gospel tradition. It is frequently debated in these cases whether some popular tale has become attached to the person of Jesus, or whether a natural event has been transformed on reflection into a miracle. According to the latter hypothesis, in this instance Jesus' confident trust in God at a time of crisis calmed his disciples' fears, and their escape from the perils of the tempest was later ascribed to his miraculous powers. But Mark and Luke understood the incident as an exhibition of the supernatural, and this fact must not be obscured by any process of rationalization.

22. A vaguer introduction than in Mark, where Jesus had been teaching from a boat that was anchored offshore and then, in the evening of the same day, had begun the voyage with his disciples to **the other side of the lake.**

23-25. A sudden squall on the Sea of Galilee is said to be a common occurrence. Natural phenomena such as **the wind and the raging waves** are the work of spirits or

Jesus is passionately committed (in a way of which we rarely even dream) to God's will; and it is just because he also knows so well the appeal of other loyalties and feels so keenly the force of more limited, and limiting, responsibilities that he must make an act of such decisive rejection. To understand Jesus' words here one must love one's family not less, but more; but one must also love God with a devotion that goes beyond not only the attainment, but even the capacity of ordinary men. We shall therefore probably never be able to understand Jesus at this point—as at so many others. He is "too great for our small hearts." Few passages show so clearly and forcefully the "suprahistorical" character of the kingdom of God. It is the fact that Jesus' life had the quality which an incident like this suggests which made psychologically possible his being later held to be the very Son, or Logos, of God, incarnate among us. He asked of men what only God could ask; he gave to God what no mere man could give.

22-25. ***Peace in Storm.***—Although, as the Exeg. points out, the miracle of Jesus' power over natural phenomena is of the very essence of this story, it would be a mistake to suppose that it owes its place in the gospel tradition to what it seems to demonstrate about Jesus and his career on earth; it was remembered and was told and retold because of the comfort it gave Christians of later years who were involved **in danger,** especially from persecution by the state; they too were being tossed about on **raging waves.** The important martyrological interest of the Gospel of Mark, where this story first appears (see on Mark 4:35-41), makes this interpretation of the story more plausible there; but Luke-Acts also reflects the growing danger confronting the church from the state, and as we have seen (Intro., pp. 5-6), one of the primary purposes of that work was to mitigate this danger by presenting Christianity in a favorable light to the Roman authorities. In this story it is the Christians themselves who are being appealed to—just as in the Epistle to the Hebrews, which much more explicitly refers to the contemporary storm and describes our faith and hope in Christ as "a sure and steadfast anchor of the soul" (Heb. 6:19). The church is **in danger;** Jesus, it might appear, is **asleep. We are perishing!** the Christians cry. Then comes the assurance **(faith)** that Christ is not asleep, that he has power over **the wind and the raging waves.** We may assume that the statement that Jesus **rebuked the wind and the waves, . . . and there was a great calm** had two meanings: on the one hand, it symbolized the calm in the hearts of believers even in the midst of storm, calm born of faith in Christ; and on the other, the more objective calm which could be expected *after* the storm, the

24 And they came to him, and awoke him, saying, Master, Master, we perish. Then he arose, and rebuked the wind and the raging of the water: and they ceased, and there was a calm.

25 And he said unto them, Where is your faith? And they being afraid wondered, saying one to another, What manner of man is this! for he commandeth even the winds and water, and they obey him.

with water, and were in danger.
24 And
they went and woke him, saying, "Master,
Master, we are perishing!" And he awoke
and rebuked the wind and the raging
waves; and they ceased, and there was a
calm.
25 He said to them, "Where is your
faith?" And they were afraid, and they
marveled, saying to one another, "Who
then is this, that he commands even wind
and water, and they obey him?"

---

demons in all ancient folklore—a survival of animism. **Faith** in this instance means trust in the providence of God. The amazement of those who have witnessed a miracle is often stressed by the narrator of the story as confirmatory evidence.

8. The Gerasene Demoniac (8:26-39=Mark 5:1-20)

Mental disease was often explained in ancient times as the consequence of demon possession, and Jesus' healing ministry is frequently described in the Gospels as an act of exorcism. In this instance Jesus restores a raving lunatic to health of mind by ridding him of a host of evil spirits. Because they could exist only in human or animal bodies, they begged permission to enter a herd of swine, which then plunged over a precipice and perished in the lake. The unusual detail of this particular story convinces many interpreters that it is primitive. Others regard its elaborate form as an indication that the storyteller's art has had free play in its composition. The incident has frequently been rationalized on the precarious hypothesis of coincidence: Jesus healed a demented man; a herd of swine stampeded down a steep slope into the lake; and the two events were associated by those who described them. Whatever its origin, the story of the Gerasene demoniac articulates the faith of the church that Jesus came to free men from the power of Satan and points the truth that evil is self-destructive.

---

calm which Christ's victory over the powers of evil would bring. Christ himself has suffered the ravages of men's hostility—he was put to death on the cross—but he has risen from the dead. He demonstrated the power of God over the evil forces of sin and death; and this power is available to those who belong to him. The inner calm in the midst of storm rested upon the faith in the objective fact and significance of Christ's victory: "The kingdom of the world has become the kingdom of our Lord and of his Christ, and he shall reign for ever and ever" (Rev. 11:15).

> Fierce was the wild billow,
>   Dark was the night;
>
> . . . . . .
>
> Trembled the mariners,
>   Peril was nigh;[4]

but Christ was there and he was not asleep; he would bring the little ship of the church to safety and peace. "Take heart," he says on another similar occasion, "it is I; have no fear" (Mark 6:50).

The Exeg. points out that this story belongs, with a few others, to a separate category—the "nature miracles" of Jesus. In the early church, and still, they have the value of affirming the *cosmic* significance of Christ. Not only is history to be fulfilled in God's kingdom, but all of nature also will in some way beyond our understanding share in the redemption (see Rom. 8:19-22). Meantime it is subject to God's power; and to be "in Christ" is to be freed from all fear of what wind or sea may do to us. The fact that we are actually still subject to these fears and anxieties means that we are not yet fully "in Christ." The real situation is that "all things" are ours, whether the world or life or death or the present or the future—all are ours —because we are Christ's and "Christ is God's" (I Cor. 3:22); but we are not yet able to enter into full possession of our heritage. Still, in Christ it has been awarded to us, in the Spirit a token of it has been conferred, and sometime by God's mercy the fullness of it will be given.

25. ***Christian Fear.***—As by 7:16, so here we are reminded (and will be again in this Gospel) that there are various ways of being **afraid**—some appropriate and worthy, others ignoble and without justification. This distinction is

[4] Hymn ascribed to Anatolius, tr. John Mason Neale.

26 ¶ And they arrived at the country of the Gadarenes, which is over against Galilee.

27 And when he went forth to land, there met him out of the city a certain man, which had devils long time, and ware no clothes, neither abode in *any* house, but in the tombs.

26 Then they arrived at the country of the Ger'a-senes,[d] which is opposite Gali-
lee. 27 And as he stepped out on land, there met him a man from the city who had demons; for a long time he had worn no clothes, and he lived not in a house but

[d] Other ancient authorities read *Gadarenes,* others *Gergesenes.*

26. There has been some early confusion in the place named. **Gerasenes** is the best attested reading in Mark and Luke, but Gerasa, the modern Jerash, was forty miles southeast of the lake and therefore geographically impossible. "Gadarenes" has the best attestation in Matthew, but Gadara was also not a site that was **opposite Galilee.** It was seven miles to the south of the lake. Gergesa, halfway down the eastern shore, would fit the narrative, and "Gergesenes" has strong manuscript support in Luke, but the name was apparently introduced into Alexandrian texts of the N.T. in the early third century as a deliberate geographical correction.

27. **For a long time he had worn no clothes** is an editorial inference from vs. 35 (Mark 5:15). In popular thought **tombs** were the dwelling place of **demons,** and one whom they had possessed would naturally live there. Furthermore, in Palestine they were often caves or caverns hewn out of rock and could provide a place of refuge for one who was ostracized by society.

the more striking in this story because fears of both kinds appear in it: the disciples are obviously terrified at the storm, but it is only after the storm has been quieted and Jesus has said to them, **Where is your faith?** that we are told, **And they were afraid.** It is somewhat startling to find this assertion only after the ostensible occasion of fear is past. Mark makes the same distinction by the use of different Greek words. We read there (Mark 4:40): "He said to them, 'Why are you afraid [δειλοί]? Have you no faith?'" and then literally, "And they feared a great fear" (ἐφοβήθησαν φόβον μέγαν)—as though Mark would say, "They were afraid before Jesus quieted the storm, but now they were really afraid." Luke, who has not used the word δειλός, conveys the same impression: the disciples, who began by being afraid of the storm, ended by being more profoundly afraid in the presence of him who had mastered it. The first fear is to be rebuked—it means lack of faith—but the second is itself the consequence of faith. Various aspects of this true and creative fear appear in connection with various passages in this Gospel which have been or will be discussed (see on vss. 34, 37; 7:16; 12:4-7; etc.). In the present passage (as at 7:16) the fear is awe (**they marveled**) in the presence of the mysterious being and power of God. P. Vallery-Radot, the biographer of Pasteur, quotes Pasteur as rejecting positivism with these words: "Positivism . . . does not take into account the most important of positive notions, that of the Infinite. . . . When this notion seizes upon our understanding, we can but kneel."[5] This fear of God is a cleansing fear, driving out lesser and lower fears.

27. *A Man Who Had Demons.*—The Synoptic Gospels contain many stories of demon possession and of exorcism (see, e.g., 4:33-36). At first hearing and on first thought we are likely to regard such stories merely as evidences of ancient superstition which we have long since outgrown—as indeed they are—as being among the many reminders that the truth of God, because it has come to us through history, comes not unmixed with error. As we reflect further, however, we recognize that when the biblical writers speak of demon possession, they are not only speaking of an actual human condition which we too know, but are also describing that condition in a strikingly apt way. Modern psychology has only given new names to ancient demons. With such terms as paranoia, schizophrenia, etc., we diagnose scientifically certain human ills which the Gospels describe mythologically. The ancient terms are certainly less accurate; and we are greatly indebted to the new science for a clearer understanding of the conflicts in ourselves and in others and for the discovery of new techniques in resolving many of them. Still, much can be said also for the old terms. Besides being more graphic and vivid, they correspond more closely with the felt realities. The deeply disturbed or divided person is likely to *feel* himself possessed

[5] *The Life of Pasteur,* tr. Mrs. R. L. Devonshire (London: Constable & Co., 1914), pp. 342-43.

28 When he saw Jesus, he cried out, and fell down before him, and with a loud voice said, What have I to do with thee, Jesus, *thou* Son of God most high? I beseech thee, torment me not.

29 (For he had commanded the unclean spirit to come out of the man. For oftentimes it had caught him: and he was kept bound with chains and in fetters; and he brake the bands, and was driven of the devil into the wilderness.)

among the tombs. 28 When he saw Jesus, he
cried out and fell down before him, and
said with a loud voice, "What have you
to do with me, Jesus, Son of the Most
High God? I beseech you, do not torment
me." 29 For he had commanded the un-
clean spirit to come out of the man. (For
many a time it had seized him; he was
kept under guard, and bound with chains
and fetters, but he broke the bonds and
was driven by the demon into the desert.)

---

28. The victim is the mouthpiece of the demons. As in 4:33-37 the unclean spirits recognize the supernatural powers of **Jesus** before they are evident to men and take steps to counteract them. **I beseech you,** instead of Mark's "I adjure you by God," which Luke probably thought an incongruous formula for a demon.

29. We are told belatedly that Jesus had already begun the exorcism. This popular case history of a violent maniac is based on the description at the beginning of Mark's narrative.

—possessed by a power or by powers, more or other than human, who have somehow got into him and gained control over him. The true self is helpless to assert itself. Even the most sophisticated modern person in the midst of such conflict may easily resort to the terms of demon possession in speaking of his situation—for that is how it actually *feels* to him. But more than this, there is a certain more objective *truth* in these ancient terms. Our modern terms, we have said, are undoubtedly more accurate; but like all abstract and scientific terms, they may be in some ways less adequate, less profoundly realistic. The word **demons** calls attention not only to the alien and malign character of the disturbing influence, but also to the basically religious character of our "inner conflicts." We are involved in them because for one reason or another (which psychology can often help in identifying and in thus removing) we have been separated from the God who made us for himself and in whom alone we can find rest.

It is a commonplace in modern psychology that no absolute line can be drawn between the "normal" and the neurotic or psychotic individual. We are all involved in some measure of inner division and hostility. The term "possessed by demons" is in the N.T. applied only to abnormal cases; but Paul describes the normal or typical man in terms not too dissimilar: "I do not do the good I want, but the evil I do not want is what I do. . . . I delight in the law of God, in my inmost self, but I see in my members another law at war with the law of my mind and making me captive. . . . Wretched man that I am! Who will deliver me from this body of death?" (Rom. 7:19, 22-24.)

28. *The Tormenting Christ.*—In considering the preceding incident (vss. 22-25) we noted as remarkable that the word "fear" or "afraid" was not used till after the ostensible occasion of fear was past. So here it is startling to hear this man who is so manifestly wretched (ostracized from society, living unclothed "among the tombs," or else in "chains and fetters") speaking of Jesus as about to **torment** him. How can Jesus add to his torment? Actually, however, Jesus can and will; for Jesus purposes to cure and save him, and this curing and saving will involve suffering. To be saved we must recognize our need in all of its dimensions, and this acknowledgment is difficult and costly; it is easier to keep our illusions about ourselves. The first step toward wholeness and inner security is to face the facts; and the facts are disagreeable. It is pleasanter to "escape" from our wretchedness than fully and honestly to recognize and seek to understand it. Henry Nelson Wieman has written illuminatingly about a sentence of Alfred N. Whitehead, "Religion . . . is the transition from God the void to God the enemy, and from God the enemy to God the companion." [6] When we find ourselves confused and distraught, torn apart by many conflicting reactions to many diverse situations, lacking that knowledge of God which would unify our experience and give peace and wholeness to the soul, God is "the void." But when God first confronts us, he does so as "the enemy." He demands something of us which we

[6] *Religion in the Making* (New York: The Macmillan Co., 1926), pp. 16-17. Wieman's discussion is in *The Wrestle of Religion with Truth* (New York: The Macmillan Co., 1927), pp. 3-7.

30 And Jesus asked him, saying, What is thy name? And he said, Legion: because many devils were entered into him.

31 And they besought him that he would not command them to go out into the deep.

32 And there was there a herd of many swine feeding on the mountain: and they besought him that he would suffer them to enter into them. And he suffered them.

33 Then went the devils out of the man, and entered into the swine: and the herd ran violently down a steep place into the lake, and were choked.

34 When they that fed *them* saw what was done, they fled, and went and told *it* in the city and in the country.

30 Jesus then asked him, "What is your name?" And he said, "Legion"; for many demons had entered him. 31 And they begged him not to command them to depart into the abyss. 32 Now a large herd of swine was feeding there on the hillside; and they begged him to let them enter these. So he gave them leave. 33 Then the demons came out of the man and entered the swine, and the herd rushed down the steep bank into the lake and were drowned.

34 When the herdsmen saw what had happened, they fled, and told it in the

---

30. To control a demon an exorcist had to know his name. **"Legion"** was Latin for an army division of about six thousand, but the word had also been naturalized in Aramaic. According to popular diagnosis, the severity of an affliction was proportionate to the number of demons who had caused it (cf. vs. 2: "Mary, called Magdalene, from whom seven demons had gone out").

31-33. The demons admit defeat but parley for terms. **Into the abyss**—hell, the place of punishment (cf. Rev. 20:1-3)—is a substitute for Mark's vague "out of the country." The predominantly non-Jewish population of the east Jordan country would have had no scruples about raising **swine.** The **demons** are duped. The consequences of their request are catastrophic. Luke omits Mark's estimate that the **herd** numbered "about two thousand."

34-36. What had happened, from the point of view of **the herdsmen,** would be the loss of the swine. They **fled** and aroused the curiosity and superstitious concern of the neighborhood. The Gerasenes investigated, and found the demoniac **clothed and in his right mind**—dressed like a sane man and restored to mental health. That he was sitting

---

find it painful to give—a radical readjustment and reorientation, a new discipline. At this stage God is the "tormentor"—more tormenting than the many demons which possess us. But as we make the required acknowledgment and inner adjustment (this is repentance), God becomes "the companion," sustaining and strengthening, the source of life and peace. Facts, especially permanent and important facts, often have this double character—hostile if we challenge and thwart them; friendly and supporting if we accept and respond appropriately to them. God is the ultimate fact, the really permanent and important fact; and we must often know the pain of his judgment before we can know the joy of his salvation.

30. ***His Name Was Legion.***—In the present case, the man, when asked his name, replies, **Legion.** Luke explains: **for many demons had entered him.** Mark (5:9) makes the division in personality more graphic when he quotes the man himself as saying, "My name is Legion; for we are many"—the first personal pronoun being used in one sentence in both singular and plural number. The personality is so "shot" or torn to pieces by conflicting interests and drives that the "I" seems not one person, but a whole mob of people with conflicting purposes. The madman's malady is in a degree the sickness of us all. Our need of God under one of its most important aspects—perhaps the most important—is the need of that which will *unify* the world of our experience and therefore our own souls. Our existence is filled with a multitude of separate and often conflicting experiences. Impressions follow one another with bewildering rapidity and in bewildering variety. Crowding interests of all kinds demand our attention and effort, and we are confused and distracted. In perplexity, almost despair, we ask, "Must there not be under all of these a fundamental unity, some meaning in which I can find peace and resource? Beneath 'the many' must there not be 'the One'? Oh, that I

35 Then they went out to see what was done; and came to Jesus, and found the man, out of whom the devils were departed, sitting at the feet of Jesus, clothed, and in his right mind: and they were afraid.

36 They also which saw *it* told them by what means he that was possessed of the devils was healed.

37 ¶ Then the whole multitude of the country of the Gadarenes round about besought him to depart from them; for they were taken with great fear: and he went up into the ship, and returned back again.

38 Now the man, out of whom the devils were departed, besought him that he might be with him: but Jesus sent him away, saying,

39 Return to thine own house, and show how great things God hath done unto thee.

city and in the country. **35** Then people
went out to see what had happened, and
they came to Jesus, and found the man
from whom the demons had gone, sitting
at the feet of Jesus, clothed and in his
right mind; and they were afraid. **36** And
those who had seen it told them how he
who had been possessed with demons was
healed. **37** Then all the people of the sur-
rounding country of the Ger'a-senes[e] asked
him to depart from them; for they were
seized with great fear; so he got into the
boat and returned. **38** The man from whom
the demons had gone begged that he might
be with him; but he sent him away, saying,
39 "Return to your home, and declare how

[e] Other ancient authorities read *Gadarenes,* others *Gergesenes.*

at the feet of Jesus is a Lukan detail. Eyewitnesses of the exorcism supplement the swineherds' story, and their evidence helps to substantiate the miracle. All this is true to the form of miracle stories, whether sacred or profane, but is given here in greater detail than is usual in the gospel tradition.

37. All the people of the district is characteristic Lukan hyperbole. **For they were seized with great fear** explains the request that had stood unsupported in Mark. The affair was uncanny and its author inspired a sense of dread.

38-39. The man from whom the demons had gone wished to become a disciple but Jesus rejected his petition. **God** for Mark's equivocal "the Lord," and **throughout the whole city** for "in the Decapolis"—an independent league of Hellenistic cities that is never mentioned by name in Luke. Jesus' instructions are an apparent exception to the

knew where I might find him in whom the world superficially so chaotic is made significant and whole!" There is a sense in which **Legion** is the name of every man.

35. ***Religion and Sanity.***—Those who came out to see what had happened to the demon-possessed man found him **sitting at the feet of Jesus, clothed and in his right mind.** The fact that religion has so often appeared as a kind of frenzy—as irrational and irresponsible fanaticism, or sheer unrestrained emotionalism, or perverse idiosyncrasy ("he had worn no clothes, and he lived not in a house," etc.)—makes appropriate some emphasis upon this picture of the cured man. Frenzy is not the work of the Spirit of God, but of demons; it is the explosion of inner conflict, not the fruit of the Spirit of peace. To sit **at the feet of Jesus** (cf. 10:39-42) and to learn of him is to recover our sanity, for he is the Word of God by whom all things were made and are held together (cf. Col. 1:17), and we can live secure, coherent, and creative lives only through that same Word. Sanity must, of course, be sharply distinguished from a mere conventionality or a careful discretion; being sane does not always mean being "sensible." But though the truly religious man may act contrary to the opinions of his friends or contrary to the standards of the majority, he does so not in disregard of wisdom or truth, but in its service. The Christian way may seem nonsense to the Greeks; but it is never a mad frenzy or a distorting fanaticism. Nor is it ever a gratuitous or bumptious nonconformity, mere crankiness. The Christian sits **at the feet of Jesus, clothed and in his right mind.** This right mindedness involves an inner consistency and sanity and also an adequate and appropriate responsiveness to the full range of reality—the glad and obedient acknowledgment of truth wherever it may be found and whatever it may be.

35-39. ***Fear of the Good.***—Here is another instance, among the many in this Gospel, of the fear which Jesus sometimes inspired. When the people saw the madman **clothed and in his right mind,** we are told that **they were afraid,** and again, **they were seized with great fear.** So far

And he went his way, and published
throughout the whole city how great things
Jesus had done unto him.
40 And it came to pass, that, when Jesus
was returned, the people *gladly* received
him: for they were all waiting for him.
41 ¶ And, behold, there came a man
named Jairus, and he was a ruler of the
synagogue; and he fell down at Jesus' feet,
and besought him that he would come
into his house:
42 For he had one only daughter, about
twelve years of age, and she lay a dying.
But as he went the people thronged him.

much God has done for you." And he went
away, proclaiming throughout the whole
city how much Jesus had done for him.
40 Now when Jesus returned, the crowd
welcomed him, for they were all waiting
for him. 41 And there came a man named
Ja'i-rus, who was a ruler of the synagogue;
and falling at Jesus' feet he besought him
to come to his house, 42 for he had an only
daughter, about twelve years of age, and
she was dying.
As he went, the people pressed round

---

custom of enjoining sick persons who had been healed, or their friends, to keep the matter a strict secret—taken over from Mark by Luke in 5:14; 8:56. It is difficult to follow those interpreters who detect a contrast in vs. 39 between the command and its performance—the patient's **home** instead of **the whole city** and **God** as the agent instead of **Jesus.** Perhaps the theory of the messianic secret was not imposed on this story because it was localized outside the strictly Jewish parts of Palestine.

9. Jairus' Daughter; a Woman with a Hemorrhage (8:40-56=Mark 5:21-43)

Mark had a fondness for intercalating one story into the context of another, and Luke had used the same device on his own initiative in 7:36-50. It heightens the dramatic effect of the framework narrative, and in this instance the second episode occupies Jesus' attention during the necessary interval between his interview with Jairus and the arrival of the messenger from the ruler's house. The fact that the girl was twelve years of age and that the woman had been ailing for twelve years seemed significant to Luke, who rearranged his source to draw attention to it—vs. 42 is at the beginning of his story and at the end of Mark's. Luke has drastically abbreviated Mark's narrative.

40-42. Jesus **returned** to his point of departure as of vs. 22 (cf. vs. 37*c*)—presumably to the vicinity of Capernaum. Mark is less explicit, though characteristically prolix.

---

the story parallels previous ones: "fear seized them all" (7:16) when Jesus raised the son of the widow of Nain; "they were afraid" (8:25) when Jesus quieted the storm. But the correspondence does not continue: those at Nain "glorified God, saying, 'A great prophet has arisen among us!' and 'God has visited his people' "; and the disciples on the lake not only feared but also "marveled . . . , 'Who then is this . . . ?' " but the Gerasenes **asked him to depart from them.** In 7:16 and 8:25 the fear calls forth wonder and praise; here, only dismay and aversion. In the other cases, a worshipful awe; here, only a superstitious dread. In all the cases there is a recognition of supernatural and overwhelming *power;* the difference in the response depends upon whether the beauty and love of God are also recognized. In some ways the response of the Gerasenes is like that of those Pharisees in 11:14-15, who did not deny that Jesus cast out demons but asserted that he did so by the power of Beelzebub. So the Gerasenes **asked him to depart**—him of whom others had said, "God has visited his people!" They were incapable of seeing and seizing their one glorious opportunity; they saw only a manifestation of strange power and were blind to the glory of God. We live in the midst of mighty powers; we can know, in a way the ancients could not, that the universe is the balance and play of gigantic, incalculable forces. Are these *sheer* forces, as Bertrand Russell says in his familiar *A Free Man's Worship*[7] ("Blind to good and evil, reckless of destruction, omnipotent matter rolls on its relentless way")? If so, the only attitude men can take is either abject dread or proud defiance. The defiance uttered by Bertrand Russell is better than the dread expressed by the

[7] Portland, Maine: P. B. Mosher, 1927, p. 27.

43 ¶ And a woman having an issue of blood twelve years, which had spent all her living upon physicians, neither could be healed of any,

44 Came behind *him*, and touched the border of his garment: and immediately her issue of blood stanched.

him. 43 And a woman who had had
a flow of blood for twelve years[f] and
could not be healed by any one, 44 came
up behind him, and touched the fringe of
his garment; and immediately her flow of

[f] Other ancient authorities add *and had spent all her living upon physicians.*

Jairus as a name does not recur in Luke's narrative, is lacking in Matthew's version, and is absent from the Codex Bezae text of Mark. Originally anonymous individuals tend to get names with the passage of time, and this one may have been Luke's contribution to the tradition. **A ruler of the synagogue** was an official appointed by the elders to supervise the conduct of worship, and there could be several in larger synagogues (cf. Acts 13:15). **Only** is Luke's inference from Mark's "little daughter"—an affectionate diminutive in Greek.

43-44. The affliction was a continuous uterine discharge. The woman is named "Bernice" in ch. 7 of the Greek MSS of The Acts of Pilate, and "Veronica" in the Latin versions. "And who had suffered much under many physicians, . . . and was no better but rather grew worse" are comments in the Marcan source (5:26) which Luke has suppressed. This has often been cited as evidence that the author of Luke-Acts was "the beloved physician" (Col. 4:14)—his professional pride had been touched—but it may be nothing more than a simple abbreviation. **Which had spent all her living upon physicians** (KJV) is relegated by the RSV to the margin. It does not occur in codices Vaticanus and Bezae or in the Sinaitic Syriac. According to Mark, the sick woman touched Jesus' "garment." Matthew and Luke are more explicit. It was **the fringe** that she **touched.** A *çîçîth* or "sacred tassel" was tied by a blue thread to each of the four corners of the outer **garment** (Num. 15:38-39; Deut. 22:12)—a cloak that served as clothing by day and as a blanket at night. Such tassels were intended to remind Israelites of their obligations to the law, and are still affixed to the prayer shawl (the tallith) worn by orthodox Jews. The loose end of the cloak would have hung over Jesus' left shoulder, and the *çîçîth* attached to it could have been touched by one who **came up behind him**—perhaps because she was ceremonially unclean. For other references by Luke to cure by contact see Acts 19:12.

Gerasenes—but both attitudes are false and inappropriate if God is *good.* The major point of all these miracle stories is that he *is* good (the power would be taken for granted)—in Christ are embodied and expressed the power *and the love* of God. The healed demoniac goes home to tell not merely **how much God has done,** but how much he **had done for him.**

43-46. *Jesus' Sensitiveness to Human Need.*—This story of Jesus' healing of the ill woman serves the same general purpose as do many other stories in this section of the Gospel (cf. vss. 26-39; 7:11-23; etc.), viz., to emphasize and illuminate the will and power of Christ to heal and save. The particular value of this story, however, lies in its demonstration of the sensitiveness of Christ to every case of need—the fact that no needy person can be hidden from him. The woman is one of a great crowd. The disciples see only the crowd (**Master, the multitudes surround you and press upon you!**); but Jesus senses the presence of a particular individual, a very humble, retiring individual, who **came up behind him** lest she be seen, and ventured only to touch **the fringe** [or tassel] **of his garment.** The impression which the story makes of this sensitiveness on Jesus' part is enhanced by its position in the narrative. Both in Mark (5:21-43) and here the incident is presented as an interruption. Jesus has been appealed to in a very urgent case: the only daughter of an important and highly respected man, a ruler of the synagogue, is so ill that her death is momentarily feared. Jesus has accepted the appeal and is on his way to Jairus' house. Not only is he being jostled by the crowd; he is also engaged upon a very urgent mission. But he is not so preoccupied as not to know the need of this poor woman who was too modest to ask anything and who, now that she has been discovered, stands trembling before him. This passage belongs with such teachings of Jesus as **"It is not the will of my father . . . that one of these little ones should perish"** (Matt. 18:14),

45 And Jesus said, Who touched me?
When all denied, Peter and they that were
with him said, Master, the multitude
throng thee and press *thee,* and sayest
thou, Who touched me?

46 And Jesus said, Somebody hath
touched me: for I perceive that virtue is
gone out of me.

47 And when the woman saw that she
was not hid, she came trembling, and fall-
ing down before him, she declared unto
him before all the people for what cause
she had touched him, and how she was
healed immediately.

48 And he said unto her, Daughter, be
of good comfort: thy faith hath made thee
whole; go in peace.

49 ¶ While he yet spake, there cometh
one from the ruler of the synagogue's *house,*

blood ceased.
45 And Jesus said, "Who
was it that touched me?" When all denied
it, Peter[g] said, "Master, the multitudes sur-
round you and press upon you!"
46 But
Jesus said, "Some one touched me; for I
perceive that power has gone forth from
me."
47 And when the woman saw that she
was not hidden, she came trembling, and
falling down before him declared in the
presence of all the people why she had
touched him, and how she had been im-
mediately healed.
48 And he said to her,
"Daughter, your faith has made you well;
go in peace."

49 While he was still speaking, a man

[g] Other ancient authorities add *and those who were with him.*

45-46. According to Mark, the "disciples" answered Jesus' question with a brusque protest, but Luke makes **Peter** their respectful spokesman. **And those who were with him** is omitted by Codex Vaticanus and the Old Syriac versions, and the authenticity of the phrase is therefore open to question. **I perceive that power has gone forth from me** is a direct statement in Luke but only an inference of the evangelist's in Mark. Perhaps the original narrative explained the cure by "faith" rather than by magic (vs. 48).

47-48. When the woman saw that she was not hidden, for Mark's "knowing what had been done to her." The confession attests the miracle. Its public nature, and the fact that the woman had been healed **immediately,** are stressed in the Third Gospel. **Go in peace** is a Semitic benediction (e.g., I Sam. 1:17; 29:7).

49-50. The framework narrative is resumed. According to one translation of the verb that occurs in Mark, Jesus "ignored" the report that the girl had died (cf. RSV).

---

or "Not one [sparrow] is forgotten before God. Why, even the hairs of your head are all numbered. Fear not . . ." (12:6-7). There is always the temptation to doubt God's care for the individual: How can he know and care for me in view of the complexity and fullness of the world (**the multitudes**) and the incalculable importance of God's concerns? But Jesus says that he does—and so do our own hearts (though perhaps timidly and doubtfully, as did this woman's). And this story dramatically sets forth that same truth.

47. ***Not Hidden by the Crowd.***—The word **hidden** ordinarily suggests aloneness and separateness, but we know that one can be hidden in a crowd. This woman hoped to be hidden and in general succeeded. Often we try to hide ourselves from others in a crowd—we do not want to be noticed. We participate in the crowd's activities; we share—or at least are careful to express—only the crowd's attitudes and opinions; we are afraid to assume our full responsibilities or to use fully our privileges as individuals. We may thus be hidden from the very multitudes to which we so entirely belong. But we are not hidden from God. He has searched us and known us; he knows our downsitting and our uprising and has beset us behind and before (Ps. 139:1-2, 5). When the crowd cruelly or callously ignores or forgets us, in his mercy he sees and remembers us; when in cowardice we seek association with others in order to escape from ourselves, he judges us and calls us back to truth and life; when in the midst of the crowd, with all its busy activity and its strident noise, we sense our need of him, he is suddenly with us as intimately as though we were with him alone—as indeed we are.

> We touch him in life's throng and press,
> And we are whole again.[8]

50-53. ***Fear and Faith.***—The story of Jairus' daughter corresponds interestingly with the

[8] John Greenleaf Whittier, "We may not climb the heavenly steeps."

saying to him, Thy daughter is dead; trouble not the Master.

50 But when Jesus heard *it,* he answered him, saying, Fear not: believe only, and she shall be made whole.

51 And when he came into the house, he suffered no man to go in, save Peter, and James, and John, and the father and the mother of the maiden.

52 And all wept, and bewailed her: but he said, Weep not; she is not dead, but sleepeth.

53 And they laughed him to scorn, knowing that she was dead.

54 And he put them all out, and took her by the hand, and called, saying, Maid, arise.

55 And her spirit came again, and she arose straightway: and he commanded to give her meat.

from the ruler's house came and said,
"Your daughter is dead; do not trouble
the Teacher any more." 50 But Jesus on
hearing this answered him, "Do not fear;
only believe, and she shall be well." 51 And
when he came to the house, he permitted
no one to enter with him, except Peter
and John and James, and the father and
mother of the child. 52 And all were
weeping and bewailing her; but he said,
"Do not weep; for she is not dead but
sleeping." 53 And they laughed at him,
knowing that she was dead. 54 But taking
her by the hand he called, saying, "Child,
arise." 55 And her spirit returned, and she
got up at once; and he directed that some-

Luke understood it to mean "overheard." **Him** is ambiguous but must refer to Jairus. **And she shall be well** adds nothing to the terse assurance in Mark.

51. In Mark, Jesus dismisses the crowd before the house is reached; in Luke, at the house door. **Peter and John and James** are mentioned in this order in the better MSS. The same group of intimates witnesses the Transfiguration (9:28); according to Mark, also the agony in Gethsemane (Mark 14:33).

52-55. Mark presupposes a public wake, with professional mourners in attendance. This is probably Luke's assumption also, although he has abbreviated his source to the point of obscurity. Interpreters often rationalize this miracle. The bystanders thought the child was dead but Jesus knew better. He diagnosed her apparent death as coma. What seemed to others to be a miracle was merely a natural recovery. But Mark and Luke entertained no such notion. They understood the story to describe an act of resurrection. When Jesus said **she is not dead but sleeping,** he was not disputing appearances. According to Mark, he had not yet entered the death chamber. He meant that the child's death was not irrevocable. But his hearers took him literally (cf. John 11:11-13) and **laughed at him.** Jesus confounded their incredulity by a miracle. The child's immediate response to his command was its demonstration, and his direction **that something should be given her to eat** was convincing evidence that the dead had come back to life (cf. 24:41-43).

---

account of the son of the widow of Nain in 7:11-17. There it was a mother and her "only son"; here it is a father and "an only daughter." Each died only a little while before Jesus' arrival on the scene, and his words in raising them are very much alike. What was said as to the original significance of 7:11-17 in the life of the church is true of this story also: Christ, who rose from the dead, has tasted death for every man (Heb. 2:9), has abolished death (II Tim. 1:10); therefore, we are not to **fear** when death or any calamity assails us. Fear and faith are related to each other as they are in the earlier part of the story of the stilling of the storm in this same chapter. There the disciples are actually terrified and Jesus asks them, "Where is your faith?"; here Jairus is on the verge of fear and Jesus cautions him not to let the faith which had brought him to Jesus (vss. 41-42) weaken under this new test. Here is the logic of faith: if we trust at all we must trust to the uttermost. Faith in man may properly be partial; faith in God, however shaky it may be on occasions, is by definition all-inclusive. Either we do not trust God and have nothing; or we do trust him and possess all things. Nothing "can separate us from the love of Christ, . . . neither death, nor life" (Rom. 8:35-38).

The close allocation of the words **all were**

56 And her parents were astonished:
but he charged them that they should tell
no man what was done.

9 Then he called his twelve disciples
together, and gave them power and authority over all devils, and to cure diseases.
2 And he sent them to preach the kingdom of God, and to heal the sick.

thing should be given her to eat. 56 And
her parents were amazed; but he charged
them to tell no one what had happened.

9 And he called the twelve together and
gave them power and authority over
all demons and to cure diseases, 2 and he
sent them out to preach the kingdom of

---

56. The amazement of the **parents** is the miracle's final attestation. The injunction **to tell no one what had happened** is taken over from Mark, where it is related to the editorial view that Jesus wished to keep his messianic dignity a secret.

Luke may have had this gospel narrative in mind when he told the story about Peter's raising of Tabitha (Acts 9:36-42).

J. Jesus and His Disciples (9:1-50)

1. Mission of the Twelve (9:1-6=Mark 6:7-13)

Both Mark and Q had accounts of Jesus' missionary instructions to the twelve. Matthew was content to combine his two sources (Matt. 9:37–10:1, 5-15). Luke used a few details from the Q narrative to modify Mark's story at this point but reserved the bulk of it for another context (10:1-11).

Although we are not told that the twelve were ever employed on any other mission, there is little reason to doubt that Jesus had the extension of his ministry in mind when he chose them (Mark 3:14). He may well have intended to use his disciples as aides much more extensively than time and opportunity permitted. But this passage speaks of the disciples' work only in the vaguest terms (vs. 6); and no doubt Mark and Luke recorded it, not out of any objective interest in a historical event, but because it authorized the methods of early Christian evangelism.

9:1. In 10:17 the "seventy" report to Jesus that "even the demons are subject to us in your name." Nevertheless the idea that Jesus formally transferred personal **power** (Luke only) and divine **authority** to his followers looks like ecclesiastical theory. Luke 9:40 (Mark 9:18) reports the inability of the disciples on one occasion to practice exorcism.

2. Luke appears to have inserted this into Mark's account under the influence of the Q version (cf. Matt. 10:7-8).

---

weeping and bewailing her and **they laughed at him** is interesting (vss. 52-53). Those who were able to wail so freely were also ready to laugh. Were they professional wailers whose weeping was only a show? Or were both weeping and laughing expressions of the same bitterness? The **father and mother,** although certainly more acutely conscious of the fact of the death than anyone else and more deeply moved by it, neither wailed nor laughed; they trusted the goodness and the power of Christ. So will the Christian do in every vicissitude.

9:1-6. ***Preaching the Kingdom of God.***—What did it mean to preach the **kingdom of God?** It surely meant reminding the Jewish hearers of the fact of God's eternal and absolute sovereignty and of men's responsibility for unqualified loyalty and obedience. It also meant reminding them of the fact that God's righteous sovereignty would at the end of time vindicate itself among men, destroying the evil and establishing the good. But it meant too the good news—**gospel**—that this end of time had now arrived, or was on the point of arriving, and that in Christ, God had visited his people. The power **to cure diseases** and the **authority over all demons** were signs that the new age, the kingdom of God, was already beginning to make its presence known. What are we in our own generation to make of this assurance that the kingdom of God is at hand? It may seem remote from the realities of our world. But no denial of God's sovereignty can be the last word, whether it is accompanied by the blast of trumpets or the thunder of bombs. The final word, which will resolve forever the conflicts and frustrations of our human life, will not be spoken till the end of time when God's own

3 And he said unto them, Take nothing for *your* journey, neither staves, nor scrip, neither bread, neither money; neither have two coats apiece.

4 And whatsoever house ye enter into, there abide, and thence depart.

5 And whosoever will not receive you, when ye go out of that city, shake off the very dust from your feet for a testimony against them.

6 And they departed, and went through the towns, preaching the gospel, and healing every where.

7 ¶ Now Herod the tetrarch heard of all that was done by him: and he was perplexed, because that it was said of some, that John was risen from the dead;

8 And of some, that Elias had appeared; and of others, that one of the old prophets was risen again.

9 And Herod said, John have I beheaded; but who is this, of whom I hear such things? And he desired to see him.

God and to heal. 3 And he said to them,
"Take nothing for your journey, no staff,
nor bag, nor bread, nor money; and do not
have two tunics. 4 And whatever house you
enter, stay there, and from there depart.
5 And wherever they do not receive you,
when you leave that town shake off the dust
from your feet as a testimony against
them." 6 And they departed and went
through the villages, preaching the gospel
and healing everywhere.

7 Now Herod the tetrarch heard of all
that was done, and he was perplexed, because it was said by some that John had
been raised from the dead, 8 by some that
Elijah had appeared, and by others that
one of the old prophets had risen. 9 Herod
said, "John I beheaded; but who is this
about whom I hear such things?" And he
sought to see him.

3-6. Mark's version of the instructions had permitted a **staff** and "sandals," but these concessions to the necessities of the Hellenistic mission were not made in the Q account, which often reflects a strictly Palestinian milieu. The **bag** that was forbidden was one used by travelers to carry provisions. The Q version forbade the possession—Mark's the wearing—of **two tunics,** which were shirts or undergarments (cf. 3:11). The missioners were not to accept hospitality from more than one host in any one center and were not to waste precious time on any who would not **receive** their message. The rabbis held that even pagan dust was "unclean" and should be removed by a traveler returning to Palestine. To **shake off the dust from your feet as a testimony against them** may therefore have been a gesture by which a Christian declared that a **city** had no part in the true Israel (cf. Acts 13:51). The instructions reflect the apocalyptic atmosphere of early Christianity—the imminence of the kingdom and the need for haste in **preaching the gospel**—but are also true, so far as we can see, to the framework of Jesus' own thought.

2. Herod Hears Rumors About Jesus (9:7-9=Mark 6:14-16)

A passage that bridges a literary gap between the departure and the return of the twelve. The various popular estimates of Jesus' person agree with those reported by the disciples in a later story (9:19; Mark 8:27-28), and Mark may have taken them from that narrative to expand a reference in his source material to Herod's uneasy reflections.

7-8. Herod the tetrarch is a correction of Mark's "king Herod"—also made by Matthew. **All that was done** has a wider reference than to the missionary activity of the twelve. **John** the Baptist had stirred the interest and excited the imagination of large numbers of people, and Jesus doubtless seemed to many to be continuing his work. The idea that **Elijah** was to reappear "in the last days" occurs in Mal. 4:5; Ecclus. 48:10, and frequently in rabbinical literature. **That one of the old prophets had risen** is Luke's interpretation of Mark's "a prophet, like one of the prophets of old." None of the surmises identifies Jesus with the Messiah.

9. Luke omits the long parenthesis in Mark that tells of Herod's execution of John (see Intro., p. 18) and leaves his readers to make the easy inference. Only Luke says

10 ¶ And the apostles, when they were returned, told him all that they had done. And he took them, and went aside privately into a desert place belonging to the city called Bethsaida.

11 And the people, when they knew *it*, followed him: and he received them, and spake unto them of the kingdom of God, and healed them that had need of healing.

12 And when the day began to wear away, then came the twelve, and said unto him, Send the multitude away, that they may go into the towns and country round about, and lodge, and get victuals: for we are here in a desert place.

10 On their return the apostles told him what they had done. And he took them and withdrew apart to a city called Beth-sa'i-da. **11** When the crowds learned it, they followed him; and he welcomed them and spoke to them of the kingdom of God, and cured those who had need of healing. **12** Now the day began to wear away; and the twelve came and said to him, "Send the crowd away, to go into the villages and country round about, to lodge and get provisions; for we are here in a lonely place."

---

that **Herod** was perplexed. According to Mark, the tetrarch thought that Jesus was the Baptist redivivus. **And he sought to see him** is a statement in accord with 23:8 but in apparent contradiction to 13:31.

3. Return of the Apostles and Jesus' Departure from Galilee (9:10-11=Mark 6:30-34)

10-11. Bethsaida was a **city** on the north end of the lake, to the east of the Jordan. It had been rebuilt by Philip as the capital of his tetrarchy. By telescoping Mark's account Luke takes Jesus and his disciples out of Galilee before, instead of after, the feeding of the multitude. Such editorial redaction facilitates the omission of Mark 6:45–8:26 between 9:17 and 18 (see Intro., pp. 18-19) but involves **the crowds** that **followed** Jesus in a journey of ten miles or more, and overlooks the fact that the succeeding narrative was originally localized "in a lonely place" (vs. 12).

4. Feeding of Five Thousand (9:12-17=Mark 6:35-44)

This is the only miracle story in the tradition that is recorded in all four Gospels. Mark (8:1-9) and Matthew (15:32-38) also relate another variant. John (ch. 6) understood the incident to symbolize the Eucharist, and therefore omitted any reference to the institution of the latter in his account of the Last Supper (John 13). Christ himself was "the bread of life" that was given "for the life of the world" (John 6:48-51).

Frequent and ingenious attempts have been made to discover a "historical core" to the narrative. Jesus and his disciples, it is said, distributed their own small store of provisions, and their example stimulated a contagious generosity among others. But such rationalizations do not carry conviction. In all likelihood the story of the multiplication of the loaves and the fish is a miracle story that came in the course of narration to be

---

trumpets sound. But even so—even now—**the kingdom of God** is at hand, at hand as judgment upon what is, as promise of what shall ultimately be, and as challenge to what can be here and now. For though the perfect world must wait, the better world can come; and we are called to accept God's rule where we stand and to let him work through us.

10-17. *We Can Do More than We Think.*—When we let God thus work through us, more can be accomplished than we could hope or dream. The disciples, who have been given "authority over all demons and to cure diseases," are challenged to feed the **multitudes** who have been listening to Jesus' words until the evening: **You give them something to eat.** But this they thought they could not do: **We have no more than five loaves and two fish;** and **there were about five thousand men.** But Jesus holds them to their responsibility, directing them first to organize the crowd in orderly and manageable groups. (Does Luke think of one of these groups for each of the twelve?) Then Jesus took the food, and having given thanks, began to give it to the disciples, who distributed it to the **people**. And lo, all were

13 But he said unto them, Give ye them to eat. And they said, We have no more but five loaves and two fishes; except we should go and buy meat for all this people.

14 For they were about five thousand men. And he said to his disciples, Make them sit down by fifties in a company.

15 And they did so, and made them all sit down.

16 Then he took the five loaves and the two fishes, and looking up to heaven, he blessed them, and brake, and gave to the disciples to set before the multitude.

17 And they did eat, and were all filled: and there was taken up of fragments that remained to them twelve baskets.

13 But he said to them, "You give them
something to eat." They said, "We have
no more than five loaves and two fish—
unless we are to go and buy food for all
these people." 14 For there were about five
thousand men. And he said to his disciples,
"Make them sit down in companies, about
fifty each." 15 And they did so, and made
them all sit down. 16 And taking the five
loaves and the two fish he looked up to
heaven, and blessed and broke them, and
gave them to the disciples to set before
the crowd. 17 And all ate and were satis-
fied. And they took up what was left over,
twelve baskets of broken pieces.

---

regarded as a prototype of the Eucharist. Bread and fish on frescoes in the catacombs are symbols of the Lord's Supper. A similar story about a miraculous feeding of a hundred men had been told of Elisha (II Kings 4:42-44).

12-15. Barley **loaves** and smoked or pickled **fish** were the food of the poor in Palestine. Mark puts this numerical estimate of the crowd at the end of his narrative. **By fifties** instead of Mark's "by hundreds and by fifties."

16. The actions that are ascribed to Jesus were those employed by the celebrant of the Lord's Supper in the ritual of the early church. The presiding elder or bishop **blessed** the bread, **broke** it into fragments, and **gave** them to deacons to be distributed to the faithful. The priest in the western church still looks **up to heaven** when he consecrates the elements. But rabbinical notices show that a Jewish host observed much the same ritual at any common meal (cf. also 24:30; Acts 27:35).

17. The careful collection of larger fragments was accepted procedure after a Jewish meal, but the mention of **baskets of broken pieces** also served to emphasize the miraculous —the disciples had far more **left over** than they had when they started. **Twelve** in this version of the story ("seven" in Mark 8:8) corresponds to the number of the disciples.

---

fed—and a basketful of **broken pieces** was **left** over when each group had eaten. The **twelve baskets** suggest the uncalculating abundance of God's goodness (cf. 6:38). Whatever is available in the way of human resources, whatever is possible in the way of efficient organization, and the incalculable power of God, here are the factors which produced the amazing result: **All ate and were satisfied.** The disciples had forgotten the third—and most important—of these factors. "All things are possible to him who believes" (Mark 9:23). They could do more than they thought because Christ was there and was acting through them. "I can do all things in him who strengthens me" (Phil. 4:13).

10-17. ***The Bread of Life.***—The Exeg. properly disparages the attempts frequently made to reduce or deny the miraculous elements in this narrative. The exercise of the divine power of Christ is of the very essence of this story, as we have just been noting. Still, the greatest emphasis in the narrative is laid not upon the miracle as such, but upon the symbolic significance of this act of Jesus. Manson[9] points out "a remarkable feature" characteristic of the tradition of this feeding of the multitudes in all of the six forms in which it appears in the Gospels (Manson is including the two accounts of the feeding of four thousand as variants of this same tradition): "Not one of the six narratives states in so many words that Jesus multiplied the food. . . . The main interest of the original narrative lay not in the realm of physical miracle but in another quarter." This other interest is suggested by the "ritual actions with which Jesus accompanied the giving of the food" (see Exeg.). Here is an anticipation of the Last Supper and a symbol of the reality of the church and of Christ as the Lord of life. The Exeg. suggests that John 6:25-71 should be read in connection with the present passage, for there this symbolic meaning is made more explicit. On Jesus as the source of life see the

[9] *The Gospel of Luke*, pp. 104-5.

18 ¶ And it came to pass, as he was alone praying, his disciples were with him; and he asked them, saying, Whom say the people that I am?

19 They answering said, John the Baptist; but some *say*, Elias; and others *say*, that one of the old prophets is risen again.

20 He said unto them, But whom say ye that I am? Peter answering said, The Christ of God.

18 Now it happened that as he was praying alone the disciples were with him; and he asked them, "Who do the people
say that I am?" 19 And they answered,
"John the Baptist; but others say, Elijah; and others, that one of the old prophets
has risen." 20 And he said to them, "But
who do you say that I am?" And Peter an-

5. Peter's Confession; Jesus' First Prediction of His Passion (9:18-22=Mark 8:27-31)

The story of Peter's confession introduces a new section in Mark's Gospel (Mark 8:27–10:52) and forms a great divide. Jesus is the center of interest, no longer as a public figure, but as the suffering Messiah who seeks to prepare his disciples for the events of his passion. Luke's method of composition robs the incident of this place of pivotal importance. His "great insertion" (9:51–18:14), with its wealth of teaching matter, separates the first two Marcan prophecies of the Passion (9:22, 44) from the third (18:31), and the attention of the reader continues to be focused on Jesus' public ministry.

18-19. Jesus was **praying** on this occasion, as at other crises in his ministry in Luke's Gospel. The statement that Jesus was **alone** and that **the disciples were with him** is interpreted by B. H. Streeter (*The Four Gospels,* pp. 176-77) as evidence that Luke used a mutilated copy of Mark. The former assertion was dependent on Mark 6:45-47 and the latter on Mark 8:27*b*—the matter that in Luke's text was the immediate introduction to Peter's confession. But Luke may simply mean that Jesus was no longer accompanied by "the crowd." Cf. Mark 4:10 for similar phraseology. According to Mark, Jesus asked the question while he and his disciples were in the vicinity of Caesarea Philippi. Luke assumes that his readers have no interest in the place name. The popular surmises that are reported in this passage are the same as had already come to the ears of Herod (9:7-8). Luke again changes Mark's "one of the prophets" to read: **one of the old prophets has risen.**

20-21. Peter is the spokesman for the disciples. This is perhaps the crucial passage that bears on the question: Did Jesus think of his mission in terms of the messianic concept? If this incident rests on a historical reminiscence, it demonstrates that Jesus' dis-

Expos. on 7:11-17. But here "the bread" is thought of less as the source or means of life than as a symbol of fellowship—the new fellowship which men had with Christ and with one another in Christ, the new fellowship of the church. (On the possible significance of this incident in the career of Jesus see Vincent Taylor, "Life and Ministry of Jesus," Vol. VII, pp. 127-28, of this Commentary.)

18-22. *The Meaning of Christ.*—As the Exeg. indicates, the two questions **Who do the people say that I am?** and **Who do you say that I am?** have a particular significance (made especially clear in the Marcan context of the incident) as calling attention to the growing importance of the difference between the way Jesus was thought of by people generally and the way in which sooner or later he was thought of by his own disciples. Jesus was a public figure; the Gospels (Luke included) have emphasized the fact that he was widely known. Multitudes have been astounded by his acts and words: some have been moved to worshipful appreciation (e.g., 7:16-17); others, to fearful aversion (e.g., 8:37). But all were aware of him—not excluding those in high places (vss. 7-9)—and there has been no little speculation on who and what he was. The distinction is made in this passage between what men in general think about Jesus and what his own disciples think. Only those who belong to Christ are in position to say what he is. Note that others can interpret him only in terms of the old: **John the Baptist, or Elijah, or one of the old prophets.** Jesus' disciples alone perceive that he is something new and unprecedented, **the Christ of God.**

21 And he straitly charged them, and commanded *them* to tell no man that thing;

22 Saying, The Son of man must suffer many things, and be rejected of the elders and chief priests and scribes, and be slain, and be raised the third day.

swered, "The Christ of God." 21 But he
charged and commanded them to tell this
to no one, 22 saying, "The Son of man must
suffer many things, and be rejected by the elders and chief priests and scribes, and be killed, and on the third day be raised."

---

ciples came to interpret his mission in the light of messianic expectations and that he himself at least tacitly accepted the designation "Messiah." Those who regard the messianic interpretation of Jesus' life and work as early Christology that has been read back into the records consider the story a later articulation of Christian faith. The question of Jesus' messianic consciousness is one of historical rather than of religious importance. It was only in the early days of the church that it was a matter of any consequence to demonstrate that Jesus had fulfilled Jewish messianic hopes. Later Christology employed more adequate categories to explain the central fact of Christian experience—that God has come into human life in Jesus Christ for man's salvation. Nevertheless the conclusion that Jesus was driven to accept the messianic category as the only one that could do justice to his sense of mission commends itself to most interpreters as a historical datum. According to this understanding, Jesus accepted Peter's confession but declined to have it made public until he had reinterpreted the popular messianic concept in terms of service, suffering, and sacrifice.

22. **The Son of man** is a synonym for Messiah in this passage, but its employment does not settle the vexed question whether Jesus ever used the phrase, since the details of this prediction appear to have been filled in after the events. Seventy-one representatives of **the elders and chief priests and scribes** constituted the Sanhedrin, the final court of appeal for Jews in Palestine in all matters that were not specifically reserved by the Roman procurator for his own jurisdiction. **On the third day** instead of Mark's "after three days."

This does not mean that others cannot appreciate him, perhaps very highly: "the greatest of the prophets," or "a great poet," or "a spiritual genius," etc. But only the church can know that he is not simply superior, but unique. He is the Christ. Since, when Peter made his confession, the church was only in process of being created and had not fully come into being, even Jesus' disciples at this time did not really know this. To be sure, they gave the true answer in words, as Luke understands it; but they did not comprehend the true meaning of that answer. So Jesus tells them not to use the words until after the redemptive event is complete and the church is fully in existence. Only those who have witnessed the suffering and resurrection of Jesus can be in position to know who he is and what he has done. Only those who have been reconciled to God in Christ can know that "God was in Christ reconciling the world to himself" (II Cor. 5:19). He was **the Christ of God**—God's Christ, not ours. Most of the "messiahs"—as conceived and as occasionally appearing—were soldiers or kings dedicated to the fulfillment of the national purpose; Christ, in the sense in which Jesus was the Christ, was the gift of God for our redemption, not from human foes, but from sin and death. This redemption can be fully known only in the kingdom of God, which lies beyond history, but a foretaste of it is already available in the church, the "colony of heaven," and in the Spirit, the "earnest of our inheritance." But only those who are led by God's grace into the meaning of Christ's death and resurrection can know what it means to say, "Thou art the Christ." This experience the disciples (or some of them) were eventually to have, but they had not had it yet; therefore Jesus **charged . . . them to tell this to no one.** As the Exeg. indicates, there was no place in "the popular messianic concept" for "suffering and sacrifice." That concept must be "reinterpreted" if it is to apply to Jesus. Manson[1] writes: "Rejected and despised, and *yet* the Messiah! Nay, rejected and despised, and *therefore* the Messiah! This is the Christian 'mystery' into which Jesus' mind has been now initiated, and into which he must initiate his followers."

[1] *The Gospel of Luke, ad loc.*

23 ¶ And he said to *them* all, If any *man* will come after me, let him deny himself, and take up his cross daily, and follow me.

24 For whosoever will save his life shall lose it: but whosoever will lose his life for my sake, the same shall save it.

23 And he said to all, "If any man would come after me, let him deny himself and take up his cross daily and follow
me. 24 For whoever would save his life will lose it; and whoever loses his life for

6. Motif of Martyrdom (9:23-27=Mark 8:34–9:1)

23. The same saying has another setting in 14:27 (Matt. 10:38). Both in Mark and in Q it was a Christian summons to martyrdom that presupposes reflection on the death of Christ and an experience of persecution. **Let him deny himself,** i.e., "let him disregard all thought of himself." By adding **daily** to **take up his cross** Luke has toned down the demand to mean little more than "face the dangers of his Christian calling" (cf. I Cor. 15:31).

24. Also in Q (17:33; Matt. 10:39). Saving one's life by evading martyrdom and losing it at the final judgment are contrasted with losing one's life as a Christian martyr and saving it in the world to come.

23. *The Cost of Discipleship.*—Both in Mark and here Jesus' first prediction of his own death is followed immediately by the assertion that his disciples must also be ready to suffer. "There are three conditions of discipleship" (**come after me**), writes Plummer:[2] "Self-denial, bearing one's cross, and obedience" (**follow me**). **Let him deny himself,** as the Exeg. reminds us, means much more than "let him make sacrifices" or "let him give up particular interests or possessions." It is a demand for a radical reorientation of life—with self no longer the center. The will of God, as known through Christ, must take the place of our own wills. As Jesus says in John 4:34, "My food is to do the will of him that sent me, and to accomplish his work," so the disciple must learn to say. Even the devoutest Christian who observes his life, inner and outer, with this demand in mind will be appalled by the measure of his failure to meet it. It is "natural" to think habitually of ourselves, remembering others only when their needs inescapably confront us; Jesus is demanding that we think habitually of others, only occasionally remembering ourselves. On **take up his cross** see also what is said in the Exeg. and Expos. of the parallel passages in Matthew and Mark (Vol. VII, pp. 454-55, 769-71). Luke adds the word **daily.** There is a sense in which this represents a "toning down," as the Exeg. indicates: Mark undoubtedly means actual martyrdom. But in another sense the additional word adds to the rigor of the demand. Perhaps it is harder to "die daily" (I Cor. 15:31) than simply to die. Perhaps it is *continuing* self-denial which is so utterly impossible. Noble as is the martyr's heroic sacrifice in a great crisis, does it require as much of him as the necessity of steady and often lonely sacrifice of self over long years requires of another? But self-denial and bearing one's cross are futile unless we *follow* Jesus, i.e., take his yoke upon us and learn of him. Self-denial and martyrdom are useless and morbid unless they are done for Christ's sake, i.e., unless they are required by fidelity to our Lord.

[2] *Commentary on Luke, ad loc.*

24. *Saving and Losing Life.*—The **will save** of the KJV is not a simple future; the meaning is "wills to save," as the RSV manages to convey. The Exeg. indicates the original intention of this verse. As in the first form of vs. 23 (i.e., before the addition of **daily**), the primary reference is to the persecution and death which Jesus has now accepted as his destiny. He calls upon his disciples to share it with him, and promises them the eschatological reward which was soon to come. But the passage is true and relevant far beyond the limits of this particular situation and these particular eschatological terms. It is universally true that one who seeks first the security of his own **life,** i.e., his life in this world, ends by losing that which makes living ultimately significant, i.e., membership in the kingdom of God. It is more than the romantic pretention of a few poetic souls—it is a simple fact about most men—that they would rather die with a sense of the meaning of existence than to live without it. There are two ways to kill men: one is to rob them of life; the other is to rob life of its meaning. There are two ways to enslave men: one is to give them masters; the other is to take away their God. The second way, whether of killing or enslaving, is the more cruel and terrible, and is much the more frequent. Man does not live by bread

25 For what is a man advantaged, if he gain the whole world, and lose himself, or be cast away?

26 For whosoever shall be ashamed of me and of my words, of him shall the Son

my sake, he will save it. **25** For what does it profit a man if he gains the whole world and loses or forfeits himself? **26** For whoever

---

25. A restatement of vs. 24*a*. Wealth and power in this life count for nothing at the last assize.

26. The first reference in Luke's Gospel to the Second Coming. The saying articulates the "Son of man" Christology and the eschatological expectations of the early church.

---

alone. Man lives by the "word" of God. This word sets us free by ruling us. For what we most need—and want—is not things we can own, but the One to whom we can feel justified in belonging. The meaning of life is never found within life itself. It may find *us* there—indeed it must, since that is where we are—but it is never found there. Our life has meaning only as it is caught up into a larger meaning altogether beyond it: **Whoever loses his life for my sake, he will save it.** Often we think we have found the meaning of life in devotion to some art, to some intellectual quest, or to some cause. More frequently we think we have found it in our love for another person. We may not be altogether mistaken: art, quest, cause, and person may well be carriers of life's meaning. Any one of them may be the point where the transcendent meaning of life meets us and finds us. But they are carriers of the meaning; not the meaning itself. And if devotion to any of them is worthy and creative, and not a senseless, distorting, and destructive idolatry, it will be devotion not to art, quest, cause, or person, merely as such, but to God who fills infinity beyond them, makes himself known to us in them, and calls us through them to himself. Only as we lose our life *to him* do we **save it.**

25. ***Gaining the Whole World.***—As the Exeg. says, the essential idea here is the same as in vs. 24*a*, but it is freshly expressed. Here the stress falls not upon how we may lose our true life (although this conception is implied in **if he gains the whole world**), but upon the uncompensable nature of such a loss. This meaning is clearer in Mark (8:37), who adds at this point, "For what can a man give in return for his life?" Again (as in vs. 24*a*) it must be said that the reference in this verse is primarily eschatological; but again also the verse is capable of a far wider interpretation. Luke uses the word "life" in vs. 24, and **himself** here; the meaning is the same, not because **himself** means less than we might suppose, but because "life" means more, i.e., not because **himself** means only one's physical life, but because the term "life" means one's existence in a more ultimate sense than the merely physical. Mark 8:36 (RSV) has "life" here as well as in the preceding verse; but the KJV in translating "soul" was not altogether mistaken. Not that Jesus made a distinction between two elements in personality (as we do); life was one. But it could be lost at one level to be found at another; or as we might say it, one may need to lose one's life in order to find one's soul. We do not distort the meaning of this text, therefore, when we see in **himself** a reference to one's ultimate inner integrity—one's true being in God's sight, "What shall it profit a man, if he shall gain the whole world, and lose his own soul?" (Mark 8:36.) This question may seem rather remote from ordinary men: there is little chance of our gaining **the whole world** or even any significant part of it (although it is appalling to discover how tiny a fragment of it can tempt us and can turn us from God and our true life). But the corollary is also true and is perhaps more pertinent to the situation of modern men who must often see their world breaking up or in danger of doing so. That corollary is "What shall it matter to a man if he lose the whole world and keep his own soul?" There is no need to be afraid of what either men or circumstances can take from us or prevent our obtaining. There is only one thing to fear even in a fearful time: that is the moment or—far more dangerous—the deceptive series of moments of moral weakness when we shall ourselves surrender what no man otherwise can take from us, the integrity, the freedom, the *reality* of our souls.

26. ***Ashamed of Jesus.***—The primary martyrological reference of these verses appears here unmistakably. One must not be **ashamed** of confessing Christ when one is called on to bear witness to one's faith before the magistrate. If one is afraid, or for any reason refuses to make this confession, Christ will refuse to acknowledge that person as his own when he returns at the end of the age. If we are unwilling to suffer with him, we shall not be glorified with him (Rom. 8:17). The use of the word **ashamed** helps give the passage a wider relevance, for in

of man be ashamed, when he shall come in his own glory, and *in his* Father's, and of the holy angels.

27 But I tell you of a truth, there be some standing here, which shall not taste of death, till they see the kingdom of God.

is ashamed of me and of my words, of him will the Son of man be ashamed when he comes in his glory and the glory of the Father and of the holy angels. 27 But I tell you truly, there are some standing here who will not taste of death before they see the kingdom of God."

There is a tendency in the tradition to substitute **Son of man** for an original "I," and it has been noted that the title is missing in this instance from the Q version (Luke 12:9; Matt. 10:33).

27. At times in his teaching Jesus declared that **the kingdom of God** is already a fact of human experience. At other times, as in this saying, he speaks of it as an *eschaton*—an event of the last days. Both Jesus and the early church believed that God would inaugurate his rule within the lifetime of some of Jesus' auditors. Mark's "come with power" is omitted.

every generation (not merely in periods of persecution) the Christian may be tempted to a certain shame, i.e., where there is no occasion for actual fear. Paul as he addresses the Romans affirms that he is not "ashamed" of the gospel of Christ (Rom. 1:16), thus revealing that he has felt this temptation. In I Cor. 1:20-25 he indicates some part of the basis of this shame which he is too strong actually to feel: the "folly" and the "weakness" of "Christ crucified." It is still possible to be ashamed of Christ in the presence of the "power" and the "wisdom" of the world. When the church finds itself in the position, as it sometimes does, of seeming to set store by the prestige of the great ones of the world, or when it is ready to make the gospel dependent for its truth upon the nod of philosophers and scientists, it is being ashamed of Christ. It is striking that the passage speaks of being **ashamed** of Christ **and** [his] **words,** as though it would call attention particularly to the *teaching* of Jesus as a possible occasion of false shame. We are given no clue here as to what words of Christ were especially "scandalous" to the Jews or "foolish" to the Greeks, but they may well have been such words as are found in the present paragraph (i.e., vss. 23-27); certainly such words, if taken seriously, are bound to seem so to the secular world, and (must we not confess?) somewhat to us all, for the Christian is by no means altogether free from the spirit of this age. The teaching of Jesus is teaching about the kingdom of God; the ethical demands of his teaching are the demands laid upon us as members of the new age, when **the Son of man . . . comes in his glory and the glory of the Father and of the holy angels.** If we do not believe in the kingdom of God, if we do not deeply feel the reality and nearness of the new age, the **words** of Jesus will seem irrelevant and foolish, and we shall be **ashamed** of Christ. By the same token we cannot share in the glories of the kingdom. In denying Christ we deny our part in his victory. To be ashamed of Christ is to be ashamed to recognize our true self, for our true self is what we are as members of God's kingdom. He will be ashamed of the false self we shall have decided to be.

27. ***The Nearness of the Kingdom.***—This is one of several passages which place virtually beyond doubt the fact that Jesus, although he denied knowing the exact time (Mark 13:32), expected the end of the age within a relatively short period. **There are some standing here** must be a reference to the current generation; **the kingdom of God** was very near, "at hand" (cf. on vss. 1-6). Only in the least important sense, the literal and chronological, did this understanding prove not to be correct; and even here it is appropriate to remember, with II Pet. 3:8, "that with the Lord one day is as a thousand years, and a thousand years as one day." But beneath the vivid *hope* of the early coming of the kingdom lay the fervent *faith* in the reality of the kingdom and the recognition that in Christ the kingdom had already been manifested. Rudolf Otto and C. H. Dodd, in different ways, urge that Jesus himself saw in his own words and acts this present manifestation of the kingdom's power and righteousness; and whether or not one agrees with either of these in his exact formulation, one can scarcely deny the evidence that for Jesus the eschatological kingdom of God was more than an expectation, however confident. But whatever is concluded as to Jesus' own conscious intention, there can be no question that the early church saw in the life and death and resurrection of Jesus a strange and divine event after which nothing could be the same again. **The kingdom of God** was near, as it had not

28 ¶ And it came to pass about an eight days after these sayings, he took Peter and

28 Now about eight days after these

7. The Transfiguration (9:28-36=Mark 9:2-10)

Both Mark and Luke understood the incident of the Transfiguration as a divine confirmation of Jesus' messiahship. Jesus had tacitly accepted Peter's messianic designation, but had warned his disciples that he must suffer. To his most intimate followers it was shown that despite the "fate that awaited him," he was nevertheless God's "Son" and "Chosen."

As we have it, then, the story belongs to the field of Christian doctrine. After the Resurrection all Christians knew their Lord as the glorified Messiah. The gospel narrative declares that even during Jesus' lifetime a few intimate followers were permitted a glimpse of what he was to become.

If Mark 9:9 (cf. Luke 9:36*b*) is not just another editorial articulation of "the messianic secret," it may be an admission that the story gained currency only after the Resurrection. Many interpreters hold that the narrative was originally an account of an

been before. "God [had] visited his people" (see on 7:16). A new era of human history had begun. Of the distinctiveness and divine significance of this new era the church was the symbol. It was the kingdom of God already present within history—"a colony of heaven" (Phil. 3:20 Moffatt). In it the mighty works of Christ were to be repeated—only "greater works" would be done (John 14:12). In it the Spirit of Christ would be mightily operative; and in its fellowship and in its healing, saving work, men would be made aware of the reality and nearness of Christ. Has the church thus represented God's kingdom? Has the church been the actual continuation of Christ's presence and ministry? Has the church confronted men with the judgment of God and mediated to them his forgiveness in Christ? Such questions as these are really asking whether and to what extent the church *is* the church. The prophecy of vs. 27 may be thought of as having been fulfilled for **some standing here** at Pentecost; when will it be fulfilled for our generation?

28-36. ***The Truth of the Transfiguration.***—Whatever may have been the original form of this narrative, and whatever the character of the actual experience which produced it, we have here one of the most significant passages in the Gospels. It is either not true at all, or it is in one sense truer than anything else in the story of Jesus' earthly life; for it attempts to tell us what the real meaning of that life was. Jesus' life appeared to be and in a sense was an extraordinarily humble human life; so it was seen by his contemporaries, even for the most part by his disciples. But it was in reality part—in some ways the most important part—of the divine event toward which all creation had been moving and in which God was acting for the salvation of the world. Jesus was indeed "the Christ of God" (vs. 20) and would be "designated" such "by his resurrection from the dead" (Rom. 1:4). In the present passage this fact is set forth by anticipation. The Exeg. mentions the view held by many that the transfiguration scene is a resurrection appearance inserted at an earlier point in the narrative. Whether this is true or not, literally and actually, the suggestion undoubtedly contains a symbolic truth: the earthly life of Jesus could not be seen truly except when it was looked at from the standpoint of the Resurrection. Only after Jesus had risen from the dead could the historical life be seen in its true quality and with its true significance. This meant a transfiguration—i.e., Jesus' life appeared no longer as it had normally appeared to his disciples, but as invested with heavenly light and power. But such it really was. The Transfiguration is not illusion or distortion, but the truth. In it the true meaning of Jesus the Christ was for a moment at least glimpsed by his associates. The transfiguration of Jesus is incomparable and stands in a class by itself; but it may be appropriate to point out that this experience of seeing ordinary things transfigured is by no means rare. We often have the unexpected privilege of seeing some familiar, ordinary object assume, even if only for a moment, an altogether new and glorious aspect as we see it in a fresh perspective, and a realization of its true significance breaks in upon us. In such moments we know that the "transfiguration," far from hiding the reality, is revealing it. We may have looked on the object thousands of times before; now for the first time we see it.

29. ***As He Was Praying.***—Only Luke tells us that the Transfiguration took place while Jesus **was praying.** It is like Luke to lay stress upon the importance of prayer to Jesus—he often

John and James, and went up into a mountain to pray.

29 And as he prayed, the fashion of his countenance was altered, and his raiment *was* white *and* glistering.

30 And, behold, there talked with him two men, which were Moses and Elias:

31 Who appeared in glory, and spake of his decease which he should accomplish at Jerusalem.

sayings he took with him Peter and John
and James, and went up on the mountain
to pray. 29 And as he was praying, the ap-
pearance of his countenance was altered,
and his raiment became dazzling white.
30 And behold, two men talked with him,
Moses and Elijah, 31 who appeared in glory
and spoke of his departure, which he was

---

appearance of the risen Christ (cf. I Cor. 15:5-8) to Peter, James, and John that has been moved forward and made an incident in the life of Jesus. Others believe it is based on a historical reminiscence. "The remark of S. Peter [Mark 9:5] is precisely the kind of remark—half-related to the supposed situation, semi-reasonable, and yet fundamentally foolish—which might be made by a man in a dream, or in the strange, half-hypnotic condition in which men see visions (and hear voices)" (A. E. J. Rawlinson, *St. Mark* [London: Methuen & Co., 1925], p. 118).

28-29. About eight days after these sayings for Mark's "after six days." The **mountain** ("the holy mount" in II Pet. 1:18) is unnamed. **To pray** is a characteristic Lukan addition. Luke paraphrases Mark's "and he was transfigured before them."

30-31. Moses was the prototype (Deut. 18:15) and **Elijah** the forerunner (Mal. 4:5) of the Messiah in some Jewish speculation, and both—according to an interpretation of Deut. 34:6 in the Assumption of Moses and to the story in II Kings 2:11—had been directly translated to the heavens. They appear to be the "two witnesses" of the Messiah in Rev. 11:3-12. Allegorists have equated them with the Law and the Prophets. Only Luke refers to the subject of their discussion with Jesus. **His departure, which he was to accomplish** is a painfully literal translation of a Greek clause that could be rendered "the fate that awaited him."

---

speaks of him as praying (cf., e.g., vs. 18)—and it would have seemed appropriate to him that the experience of exaltation and revelation should come while Jesus was thus engaged. Although no analogy is being hinted at between Christ's unique experience and our own, nevertheless one cannot but reflect that it is in periods of prayer that we are most likely to witness, in whatever measure may be possible for us, the glory of God. We remember Isaiah's experience in the temple. To have "mountaintop experiences" it is not enough to go up on a mountain; one must go up on a "mountain to pray" (vs. 28). Luke is also the only evangelist to inform us what was the subject of Jesus' prayer: he was praying about "his departure which he was to accomplish at Jerusalem" (vs. 31), the same subject as of his teaching in vss. 21-26. Likewise, the final prayer of Jesus in Gethsemane, also in the presence of Peter, James, and John, dealt with this same theme. We can well understand that the approach of the Crucifixion would preoccupy Jesus' thoughts in prayer: Was it necessary that he die? Was it the Father's will? If so, he would faithfully accept his vocation of suffering, depending upon God to supply the needed strength. Is it possible that Peter's proposal that Jesus stay on the mountain had in Luke's mind a connection with this same departure—another way of saying, "God forbid, Lord! This shall never happen to you" (Matt. 16:22)? Jesus seeks on the mountain resources for his great ordeal; Peter supposes that he uses the mountain as a place of escape from the necessity of the ordeal. "Listen to him" (vs. 35; cf. Deut. 18:15) places the stamp of divine truth upon the teachings Jesus has just given, teachings about the necessity of his own death and about the gaining of life through the renunciation of life.

30-31. *Moses and Elijah.*—The Exeg. refers to the several considerations which may explain the inclusion of Moses and Elijah in the transfiguration vision: both are associated with the messiahship in Jewish belief, and according to certain traditions (cf. II Esdras 6:26), both were taken up into heaven, just as Jesus was soon to be taken up. Furthermore, in a passage so steeped in symbolism it is not far-fetched to suppose that Luke thinks of the association of Moses with the Law and of Elijah with the

32 But Peter and they that were with him were heavy with sleep: and when they were awake, they saw his glory, and the two men that stood with him.

33 And it came to pass, as they departed from him, Peter said unto Jesus, Master, it is good for us to be here: and let us make three tabernacles; one for thee, and one for Moses, and one for Elias: not knowing what he said.

34 While he thus spake, there came a cloud, and overshadowed them: and they feared as they entered into the cloud.

35 And there came a voice out of the cloud, saying, This is my beloved Son: hear him.

to accomplish at Jerusalem. 32 Now Peter
and those who were with him were heavy
with sleep but kept awake, and they saw
his glory and the two men who stood with
him. 33 And as the men were parting from
him, Peter said to Jesus, "Master, it is well
that we are here; let us make three booths,
one for you and one for Moses and one
for Elijah" — not knowing what he said.
34 As he said this, a cloud came and over-
shadowed them; and they were afraid as
they entered the cloud. 35 And a voice came
out of the cloud, saying, "This is my Son,

---

32. Peculiar to Luke, and probably editorial. Luke thinks of the incident as nocturnal. The RSV implies that **Peter** and his companions were fighting off drowsiness, but the KJV—on just as good authority—makes better sense: **and when they were awake.**

33. Peter's remark, as the KJV understands it, means that the three disciples wished to prolong a rewarding experience. The RSV offers another, and attractive, alternative: **It is well that we are here** to be of some service. Both Mark and Luke make the comment that Peter's proposal was inept, perhaps because they thought heavenly beings did not require earthly habitations.

34-35. The climax of the story. In Exod. 24:15-18; I Kings 8:10, and elsewhere in the O.T., a **cloud** (the Shekina) symbolized the presence of God. It was expected to reappear in the messianic period (II Macc. 2:8). The text is ambiguous; but presumably the **cloud** enveloped only Jesus and his heavenly associates. **This is my Son, my Chosen** (RSV) has better support in the MSS than the KJV reading, which agrees with the text of Mark. **Listen to him!** may have been added to an earlier form of the utterance from Deut. 18:15: the Messiah is the "Prophet" foretold by Moses.

Prophets. Thus Luke would be representing both Law and Prophets as confirming Christ's suffering messiahship and as being validated by him. Luke is very acutely aware of the essential identity of Christianity with the true Israel. Burton S. Easton[3] discovers the primary purpose of this author's work to be establishing the fact of this identity. The Marcionites a little later, and possibly their predecessors in Luke's own time, were denying it, asserting that the revelation in Christ stood absolutely alone. The church was right not only in regarding this denial as historically false, but also in recognizing it as dangerous. The revelation in Christ would not be complete, or itself, without the O.T. The O.T. anticipates and supports the N.T. The N.T. does not merely correct or supersede the O.T.; it also confirms and validates it. What is best and central in the O.T. leads directly into the N.T. Much in the N.T. could not be understood without the O.T. It is significant that Moses and Elijah **talked with him;** they did not merely listen. The O.T. conception of God—One, the Creator, the Lord of history, the righteous King, the final Judge, the divine Companion, self-revealing through the historical life of his people—is presupposed in the N.T. Jesus was a Jew and is utterly unintelligible except as such. When he wished to appeal to the highest possible sanction for his ethical teachings, he said, "This is the law and the prophets." But, for the Christian, the true meaning of the O.T. can be seen only by one who also sees Christ and "listens" to him. When Jesus says, "This is the Law and the Prophets," he is not only validating the O.T., but is also interpreting it. Moses and Elijah were also "transfigured"; i.e., in Christ's presence they too **appeared in glory.** In other words, just as the true meaning of Jesus himself can be discerned only in the light of the Resurrection, so the true meaning of the Law and the Prophets can be seen only there. The record of the revelation of God in Christ must include the O.T.,

[3] *The Purpose of Acts* (London: Society for Promoting Christian Knowledge, 1936).

36 And when the voice was past, Jesus was found alone. And they kept *it* close, and told no man in those days any of those things which they had seen.

37 ¶ And it came to pass, that on the next day, when they were come down from the hill, much people met him.

38 And, behold, a man of the company cried out, saying, Master, I beseech thee, look upon my son; for he is mine only child.

39 And, lo, a spirit taketh him, and he suddenly crieth out; and it teareth him that he foameth again, and bruising him, hardly departeth from him.

40 And I besought thy disciples to cast him out; and they could not.

my Chosen;[h] listen to him!" 36 And when
the voice had spoken, Jesus was found
alone. And they kept silence and told no
one in those days anything of what they
had seen.

37 On the next day, when they had
come down from the mountain, a great
crowd met him. 38 And behold, a man from
the crowd cried, "Teacher, I beg you to look
upon my son, for he is my only child;
39 and behold, a spirit seizes him, and he
suddenly cries out; it convulses him till he
foams, and shatters him, and will hardly
leave him. 40 And I begged your disciples

[h] Other ancient authorities read *my Beloved.*

---

36. They . . . told no one in those days is substituted for Jesus' charge to the disciples in Mark to tell no one "until the Son of man should have risen from the dead."

8. Exorcism of a Demon from a Boy (9:37-43*a*=Mark 9:14-27)

The compassionate healer in the valley of suffering succeeds the transfigured Christ on the holy mount. Raphael's masterpiece has immortalized the contrast.

37. On the next day, because Luke thought of the Transfiguration as a vision in the night.

38-39. For he is my only child is a sentimental addition to Mark's story. The symptoms suggest that epilepsy was the disease that is described. **Shatters him** is an overliteral translation. Read "exhausts him."

40. The failure of the **disciples** throws their Master's powers into greater relief.

---

but the record of the revelation of God in Israel is incomplete without the N.T.

36. ***They Kept Silence.***—As the Exeg. indicates, this verse stands in Luke for the more explicit statement in Mark that the disciples were admonished to say nothing about their experience on the mountain till after the Resurrection. In Mark the injunction belongs with other indications that it was only after the Resurrection that the full messianic status of Jesus was realized by his followers; at the very least the passage is, as Manson says, "A plain admission that the new Messianic ideas to which they had been introduced did not become operative until after Jesus' death."[4] To both evangelists, however, it would have seemed perfectly appropriate that these disciples should have **kept silence** after having had so wonderful an experience. In the course of Luke's narrative we have often been told of the "fear," "wonder," or "amazement" which Jesus' mighty acts called forth in those who witnessed them. This mood was often expressed in ecstatic cries; it could also be expressed in **silence.** Thus we are told in 2:19, "But Mary kept all these things, pondering them in her heart," in contrast to the shepherds who "returned, glorifying and praising God for all they had heard and seen." Silence may mean the mere absence of words; it may mean the presence of meanings too deep for words. "The Lord is in his holy temple; let all the earth keep silence before him." Such silence is pregnant and fruitful. Every great word and deed, of whatever kind, comes out of silence, i.e., it comes from depths of experience far beneath the surface. And however great the word or deed, it never succeeds in expressing fully or perfectly this deeper meaning. Thus, it is said, Vergil asked that the manuscript of *The Aeneid* be destroyed. The inner silence is always much greater than the spoken word—and gives that word any degree of greatness it may have.

37-43. ***From Mountain to Plain.***—The contrast between the scene of the Transfiguration and the present one can scarcely be exaggerated. No wonder Raphael saw its dramatic possibilities. Instead of the solitude of the **mountain,** we have a **great crowd;** instead of Elijah and

[4] *Gospel of Luke, ad loc.*

41 And Jesus answering said, O faithless and perverse generation, how long shall I be with you, and suffer you? Bring thy son hither.

42 And as he was yet a coming, the devil threw him down, and tare *him*. And Jesus rebuked the unclean spirit, and healed the child, and delivered him again to his father.

43 ¶ And they were all amazed at the mighty power of God. But while they wondered every one at all things which Jesus did, he said unto his disciples,

44 Let these sayings sink down into your ears: for the Son of man shall be delivered into the hands of men.

to cast it out, but they could not." 41 Jesus
answered, "O faithless and perverse generation, how long am I to be with you and
bear with you? Bring your son here."
42 While he was coming, the demon tore
him and convulsed him. But Jesus rebuked
the unclean spirit, and healed the boy,
and gave him back to his father. 43 And
all were astonished at the majesty of God.

But while they were all marveling at
everything he did, he said to his disciples,
44 "Let these words sink into your ears;
for the Son of man is to be delivered into

---

41. The reproach recalls God's own complaints in Num. 14:27 and Isa. 65:2. It voices a mood of weariness that is not easy to understand in its present setting. A **faithless and perverse generation** surely includes more than the disciples. Martin Dibelius sees a mythical trait in the words. Jesus speaks as a divine being who has appeared only temporarily in human form (*From Tradition to Gospel,* tr. Bertram Lee Woolf [New York: Charles Scribner's Sons, 1935], p. 278).

42-43*a*. Luke has effected a drastic compression of his Marcan source. **And gave him back to his father** is an added detail (cf. 7:15).

9. Jesus' Second Prediction of His Passion (9:43*b*-45=Mark 9:31-32)

Luke omits Mark's note about Jesus' clandestine return with his disciples to Galilee, and supplies his own introduction to the second prediction.

43*b*-44. The crowds might marvel at "all he was doing" (Goodspeed) but the **disciples** were again to be forewarned of the impending tragedy. The contrast is stronger

---

Moses "in glory," we have a distracted father and his epileptic child; instead of a reassuring voice from heaven, we have a complaint about the weakness or failure of Jesus' disciples, whom he had appointed and empowered to cast out "all demons and to cure diseases" (vs. 1). Implied also is a contrast even in Jesus himself: in the earlier passage, "as he was praying, . . . his countenance was altered, and his raiment became dazzling white"; he conversed with heavenly beings "in glory." Now he is not only disturbed by a case of particularly poignant human need, but is also bitterly disappointed by his disciples' impotence. He has just been communing with God; now he must deal with a demon. But the two pictures are intended to stand together. In both are Jesus' true messianic status and power set forth: the one whom God approved on the mountaintop is he through whom God now acts on the plain; he whom God has chosen has power over the demons. Jesus' messiahship is not a detached glory, but is relevant to even the most sordid human situation. Also the disciples' behavior in the two stories ties them together: the three who were "heavy with sleep" and confused in speech on the mountain show up no better and no worse than the rest who **could not** exorcise the demon. Perhaps Jesus has both sorts in mind —the confused and the impotent—when he cries out in a kind of desperation, **O faithless and perverse generation.** Finally, the responses to the two incidents on the part of the witnesses have the effect of giving a common frame to the pictures: in the one case "silence"; in the other, astonishment **at the majesty of God** (on the last clauses of vss. 38, 42, cf. 7:12, 15; 8:42).

43*b*-44. ***Delivered into Men's Hands.***—Here is Jesus' second prediction of his death; and again it appears in close connection with a reference to the enthusiastic response to him on the part of both the multitudes and his own disciples. In vss. 18-22, where the first prediction is found, it follows upon an account of the laudatory titles the people were giving Jesus, climaxed by the disciples' own ascription, "The Christ of God." Here we are told only that it was **while they were all marveling at everything he did** that he said, **The Son of man is to be delivered into the hands of men.** The contrast

45 But they understood not this saying, and it was hid from them, that they perceived it not: and they feared to ask him of that saying.

the hands of men." 45 But they did not understand this saying, and it was concealed from them, that they should not perceive it; and they were afraid to ask him about this saying.

---

in the Greek text than in either the KJV or the RSV ("You must let . . ."). **These words** apparently refer to the saying that follows, and **for,** which serves in the Greek only to introduce it, might better be omitted in the translation. Luke had reproduced all the details of the first prediction (vs. 22) from his Marcan source but abbreviates this one.

45. Mark's verse is expanded to suggest that God had never intended the disciples to understand the prophecy. This meaning disappears if the Greek subordinating conjunction implies only consequence—"so that they did not perceive it." But Luke's sentence then becomes painfully prolix.

---

is striking, especially if vs. 43*a* is taken into account—**the majesty of God** being **delivered** into men's hands—and is made more solemnly significant by **Let these words sink into your ears.** Thus again we are reminded of the wide gulf between Jesus' own conception of his vocation and the popular messianic idea (cf. on vss. 18-22). Jesus' throne was to be a cross, and his crown would be made of thorns. Not only did the Son of man humble himself to be made man, but as man he let other men do to him what they would. Having emptied himself to take the form of a slave, he "became obedient unto death, even the death of the cross" (Phil. 2:5-8). The carrier of God's purpose for mankind is delivered weak and helpless into our hands; and we scoff at him, spit upon him, and crucify him. What power God has given us! We can reject his purpose; we can crucify his love! This is the solemn truth; and the statement in vs. 44 does not misrepresent or exaggerate the awful meaning of human freedom. But it is not the whole story. In Mark the statement is followed by "after three days he will rise again"; Matthew agrees with Mark, but Luke, possibly for reasons of dramatic effect, omits the second clause (or perhaps, as Manson suggests, Luke is following a different tradition here). But we can be sure that the fact of the Resurrection is clearly present in Luke's mind also: It is true that **the Son of man is to be delivered into the hands of men;** but God will not leave him there. God's purpose may be thwarted in history, but it will not be permanently or ultimately defeated. God is able to overrule men's rebellion against his will and often makes the wrath of men to praise him. This is supremely true in this case: Jesus is put to death by blind and brutal men, but his death becomes the center of God's redeeming act: "with his stripes we are healed." So also in our own personal lives, "in everything God works for good with those who love him," and we can be in all times of trial "more than conquerors through him who loved us" (Rom. 8:28, 37).

45. *They Did Not Understand.*—As Luke sees it, the prediction of Jesus' death in vs. 44 was made to Jesus' disciples only—it was hopelessly beyond the comprehension of the crowd—but even they **did not understand.** It was part of the tragedy of the life of Jesus that those nearest him only meagerly understood him. From Luke's postresurrection point of view it seems almost inconceivable that they should not have understood his meaning in this case, and he can account for their blindness only by assuming that God **concealed** the truth **from them.** The fact is, however, that the real and inner meaning of Christ could not under any conditions have been understood till after the Resurrection, when the event was complete and the Spirit had come. We can believe that Jesus' disciples in this later period were constantly finding a new significance in sayings and incidents recalled, but, until then, not understood. Words of Jesus which foreshadowed his death would have been of this kind. We are reminded in our own lives how often it is true that we really sense the meaning of an experience only long after it has occurred. Only from the point of view of a later time can we see the earlier event in true perspective and therefore with its true significance. This reflection should make us more patient in the presence of some of the mysteries of God's providence.

Reference has been made to the tragic overtones in the words **They did not understand.** They bring to our minds the fact, illustrated constantly in history and on the smaller stage of our own lives, that absence of comprehension can sometimes have consequences as disastrous as the actual presence of evil purpose. Indeed, Jesus himself accounts even for the action of his enemies in putting him to death by this lack:

46 ¶ Then there arose a reasoning among them, which of them should be greatest.

47 And Jesus, perceiving the thought of their heart, took a child, and set him by him,

48 And said unto them, Whosoever shall receive this child in my name receiveth me; and whosoever shall receive me, receiveth him that sent me: for he that is least among you all, the same shall be great.

46 And an argument arose among them
as to which of them was the greatest. 47 But
when Jesus perceived the thought of their
hearts, he took a child and put him by his
side, 48 and said to them, "Whoever receives this child in my name receives me, and whoever receives me receives him who sent me; for he who is least among you all is the one who is great."

10. Dispute About Rank (9:46-48=Mark 9:33-37)

46. The KJV is probably correct when it implies that the dispute among the disciples had to do with precedence in the future kingdom of God (cf. Mark 10:37).

47-48. Luke interprets Mark to mean that Jesus' perception was supernatural. **Receives** must mean "cares for," and **in my name,** "because it is his duty as one of my followers." Probably the saying was originally independent of its present context. Jesus speaks much as does the Christ of the Gospel of John (John 12:44-45). Christian ethics are grounded in Christian theology. Christian service to the lowliest is done to the Lord of the church, and thereby to God. Mark's formulation of the saying about true greatness precedes the acted parable of the **child.** The early church regarded the reversal of popular values in vs. 48*b* as a characteristic element in Jesus' teaching. See 22:26 (Mark 10:43-44) for another version. We are reminded of the Matthaean beatitude: "Blessed are the meek, for they shall inherit the earth" (Matt. 5:5).

"They know not what they do" (23:34). It is as important to pray for growth in understanding as for growth in goodness.

46-48. ***Humility and Service.***—It is clear not only that Jesus loved children but also that they figured largely in his teaching. The best-known example of this is in Mark 10:13-16 (and parallels), where Jesus rebukes those who would prevent mothers from bringing their children to him, adding that it is to the children that the kingdom of God belongs. The conception is that one must become like a child—in his sincerity, simplicity, and humility—if one would enter the kingdom (for a discussion of this conception, so important in Jesus' teaching, see on 18:17). This same idea appears in connection with the present passage in its Matthaean form (Matt. 18:1-14). In Mark, however, as well as in Luke, the meaning is somewhat different. The exhortation is not that we must be like the child, but that we should "receive," "care for," or minister to the child. The child is here taken not as an example of character, but as the symbol of lowly human need. Instead of disputing about their own greatness, Jesus' disciples should be seeking out opportunities of service to God's little ones, i.e., to his humble and needy ones. In serving them we serve Christ, who identified himself during his earthly career with the most needy, and identifies himself with them still (cf. James Russell Lowell, "The Vision of Sir Launfal"). This idea is expressed in matchless form in the great parable in Matt. 25:31-46, in which those who have served their fellows have to be informed that they have served Christ; they seem surprised at learning that they are among the "blessed." The one who is **least among you all is the one who is great.** The word **least** suggests "humblest," but the reference is primarily not to the one who is *humbler* than the rest, but to the one who is the *servant* of the rest. As a matter of fact, humility can become a sterile and morbid thing if it is not geared to service. This meaning of vs. 48*b* is stated more fully in Mark 9:35, "He must be last of all and servant of all" (see also 22:26; Mark 10:43-44; Matt. 23:11). Montefiore says: "The Rabbis were never weary of preaching humility and its greatness. . . . But the combination of humility with *service* . . . was a special characteristic of the religion of Jesus, and a new thing when he preached it." [5] But it is this "combination" which gives reality and beauty to each. Without the other, each is artificial and theatrical.

[5] *Synoptic Gospels,* I, 218.

49 ¶ And John answered and said, Master, we saw one casting out devils in thy name; and we forbade him, because he followeth not with us.
50 And Jesus said unto him, Forbid *him* not: for he that is not against us is for us.
51 ¶ And it came to pass, when the time

49 John answered, "Master, we saw a
man casting out demons in your name, and
we forbade him, because he does not fol-
low with us." 50 But Jesus said to him,
"Do not forbid him; for he that is not
against you is for you."
51 When the days drew near for him to

11. An Exorcist Who Was Not a Follower (9:49-50=Mark 9:38-40)

49-50. Counsel to Christians not to proscribe the practice by outsiders of exorcism in the **name** of Jesus (cf. Moses' advice concerning Eldad and Medad in Num. 11:27-29). Luke reports instances of the successful use of the formula by Peter (Acts 3:6-8) and Paul (Acts 16:16-18) in the early days of the church as well as one unsuccessful attempt by Jews (Acts 19:13-17). The Paris Magical Papyrus 574, written in Egypt about A.D. 300, quotes a later version used by an exorcist who was probably neither Jew nor Christian: "I exorcise you by Jesus, the god of the Hebrews" (lines 3018-20). The better MSS support **against you** (RSV) and **for you** (RSV). Possibly Luke substituted these readings for Mark's "against us" and "for us" in order to gloss over an apparent conflict with the saying in 11:23 (Matt. 12:30).

V. Jesus on the Journey to Jerusalem (9:51–19:27)

Luke has substituted this extensive travel section for Mark's brief account (Mark 10:1–11:10) of Jesus' journey to Jerusalem. The greater part of it (9:51–18:14) is a "great insertion" into the framework of Mark's narrative. By this literary device the Third Evangelist found a place for a wealth of teaching tradition that was probably undated

49-50. *Pride and Intolerance.*—This incident follows in the same order in Mark, where 9:41 seems to bind Jesus' teaching about tolerance with his immediately preceding words about the real meaning of greatness. Luke omits this verse, but **in your name** remains to mark the connection in thought between the two paragraphs (cf. "in my name" in 9:48). And indeed there *is* a connection: concern for one's own status goes along with intolerance of others. Preoccupation with one's own importance and jealousy to maintain it inevitably prevent one's appreciating the good in others; one is not able to rejoice in the truth (I Cor. 13:6). Because one does not humbly and gratefully acknowledge God's grace in one's own life, one is not able to see God's grace working in others. One might also note, by way of connection, that in vss. 46-48 Jesus is rebuking selfishness in an individual, and in vss. 49-50 the same selfishness in a group. John in this story is identifying the kingdom of God with his own little company. In Mark the presumption of the disciples is stated even more boldly than in Luke, "We forbade him, because he was not following us." Luke softens this to **he does not follow with us;** but the point is the same: "We are the people! No one can act in Christ's name except us." But actually someone else *was* acting in Christ's name, and acting effectively—demons were being cast out; and Mark tells of "a mighty work." This was not the last time that a group, whether large or small, has set itself up as the sole medium of God's action in Christ; and groups and institutions as well as individuals can make proud claims to greatness, forgetting that "whoever would be great among you must be the servant of all." We have seen nations and classes of men becoming thus conceited about themselves and therefore intolerant of others; but this spirit is evilest and ugliest and most anomalous in a church. Walter Rauschenbush has written a prayer for the church which closes: "Baptize her afresh in the life-giving spirit of Jesus! . . . Put upon her lips the ancient gospel of her Lord. . . . Fill her with the prophets' scorn of tyranny, and with a Christ-like tenderness for the heavy-laden and down-trodden. . . . Bid her cease from seeking her own life, lest she lose it. Make her valiant to give up her life to humanity, that like her crucified Lord she may mount by the path of the cross to a higher glory." [6] (On vs. 50*b* see on 11:23.)

51-55. *He Set His Face.*—It is striking that this phrase, which "emphasizes the deliberate resolution" of Jesus (see Exeg.), appears in the same sentence with an equally clear refer-

[6] *Prayers of the Social Awakening* (Boston: Pilgrim Press, 1925), pp. 134-35.

was come that he should be received up, he
steadfastly set his face to go to Jerusalem,
52 And sent messengers before his face:
and they went, and entered into a village
of the Samaritans, to make ready for him.
53 And they did not receive him, because his face was as though he would go
to Jerusalem.

be received up, he set his face to go to
Jerusalem. And he sent messengers ahead
of him, 52 who went and entered a village
of the Samaritans, to make ready for him;
53 but the people would not receive him,
because his face was set toward Jerusalem.

---

and without context in his sources. According to Mark 10:1, Jesus crossed the Jordan and traveled through Perea. The initial story in Luke's section (9:51-56) is located in Samaria, but the only other reference to that half-alien province (17:11) does not imply direct passage through it, and, despite the opinion of many commentators, there is no real reason to believe that Luke was trying to correct the Marcan tradition. The fact that Jesus and his disciples arrived in the end at Jericho in Luke's account (18:35) as well as in Mark's (10:46) suggests that Luke was dependent on Mark for all his information about the journey. Most of the teaching in the travel section presumes the public that Jesus had in Galilee: the crowds (11:29; 12:1, 54; 14:25); a sabbath congregation in a synagogue (13:10); tax collectors and sinners (15:1); friendly Pharisees (11:37; 13:31; 14:1); hostile lawyers and Pharisees (10:25; 11:45, 53; 15:2; 16:14); and the ever-present company of the disciples. Luke's frequent references to travel (9:57; 10:38; 13:22; 14:25; 17:11; 18:35) are modeled on Mark's (10:17, 32, 46) and are probably editorial.

A. Jesus Sets His Face Toward Jerusalem (9:51-62)

1. Hostile Samaritans (9:51-56)

51*a*. Editorial. **To be received up,** i.e., "into heaven." A reference to the Ascension (24:50-53; Acts 1:9-11). Luke assumes that the events of the gospel story have been foreordained. **Steadfastly** (KJV) has no corresponding adverb in the Greek text but emphasizes the deliberate resolution that is implicit in the Semitism **he set his face** (cf. Jer. 21:10).

51*b*-53. A similar reference to Jesus' use of advance agents is found in 22:7-13. There is little reason to doubt that this incident was already located near **a village of the Samaritans** in Luke's source. John 4:1-42 also records a tradition that Jesus taught in Samaria. Josephus reports a collision about A.D. 50 between Galilean pilgrims and hostile Samaritans, which may explain why many preferred to take the circuitous route to Jerusalem through Perea. But that author also tells us in the same passage that the Samaritan route was the usual one (*Antiquities* XX. 6. 1).

---

ence to the fact that "the events of the gospel story have been foreordained." According to Luke, Jesus' passion (and this is involved in **received up**) has been determined upon by the purpose of God and is his inescapable destiny; and this fact Jesus himself knows (twice he has predicted it already). Nevertheless, he must summon his own resolution to go to his death; he must **set his face to go to Jerusalem.** Divine foreordination does not shut out the need for human determination and fortitude. These words also suggest that Jesus had *accepted* his fate; it would almost be true to say that he had *chosen* it. Evil was not forced upon him; he saw it coming and went to meet it. There is an approach here to the understanding of the Passion which is explicitly stated only in John (10:17-18): "For this reason the Father loves me, because I lay down my life. . . . No one takes it from me, but I lay it down of my own accord. I have power to lay it down." A clear vision of the Father's will; an understanding of the suffering of heart and body he must bear, and bear alone; a willing acceptance of his fate; a firm resolution to meet it without failure or flinching; a first deliberate step in the direction of it—all of this is involved in **he set his face to go to Jerusalem.** There was no one with whom he might share the awful burden of grief and joy he carried. He had tried twice to initiate his companions into his secret, but they could not understand. There is a striking sentence in

54 And when his disciples James and
John saw *this,* they said, Lord, wilt thou
that we command fire to come down from
heaven, and consume them, even as Elias
did?
55 But he turned, and rebuked them,
and said, Ye know not what manner of
spirit ye are of.
56 For the Son of man is not come to
destroy men's lives, but to save *them.* And
they went to another village.
57 ¶ And it came to pass, that, as they
went in the way, a certain *man* said unto
him, Lord, I will follow thee whithersoever
thou goest.

54 And when his disciples James and John
saw it, they said, "Lord, do you want us to
bid fire come down from heaven and con-
sume them?"[i] 55 But he turned and re-
buked them.[j] 56 And they went on to an-
other village.
57 As they were going along the road,
a man said to him, "I will follow you wher-

[i] Other ancient authorities add *as Elijah did.*
[j] Other ancient authorities add *and he said, "You do not know what manner of spirit you are of; for the Son of man came not to destroy men's lives but to save them."*

54. James and John wished to invoke a punitive miracle upon the villagers in accordance with O.T. precedent (II Kings 1:9-16). Marcion, codices Bezae and Alexandrinus, and many later authorities make this explicit by adding "as Elijah did" (RSV mg. [cf. KJV]). Some interpreters have advanced the suggestion that the nickname "sons of thunder" (in Mark 3:17 only) derives from this occasion; but this is mere conjecture.

55-56. Such stories as this usually reach their climax in a saying of Jesus, and various MSS undertook to supply the deficiency in this instance. Marcion, Codex Bezae, and many later authorities added "and he said 'You do not know what manner of spirit you are of' " (RSV mg. [cf. KJV]). The disciples were not to be governed by Elijah's hot-tempered example but by Jesus' teaching about nonresistance to evil (6:29). Marcion and many later authorities also expanded the same saying with the words: "For the Son of man came not to destroy men's lives but to save them" (RSV mg. [cf. KJV]). **Another village** could mean a more hospitable Samaritan one. However, since Jesus and his disciples were repulsed in Samaria, Luke may wish us to understand that they returned to the Galilean side of the border. The verse 17:11 is not decisive.

2. Conditions of Discipleship (9:57-62=Matt. 8:19-22)

57-58. Jesus warns an aspirant to discipleship to count its cost. If the saying is autobiographical, it must come from a period when Jesus as a teacher had been repudi-

Mark 10:32 which suggests that they were not unaware of the existence of the secret, although they were incapable of sharing it: "And they were on the road, going up to Jerusalem, and Jesus was walking ahead of them; and they were amazed, and those who followed were afraid." But this is in Mark; here we have only an incident reflecting upon how far the thoughts of Jesus' disciples were from being his —they want to **bid fire come down from heaven** to destroy an inhospitable Samaritan village. One who is soon to suffer death at men's hands without protest or resistance is expected to resent and punish a mere act of discourtesy! According to a disputed text, Jesus said to them: "You do not know what manner of spirit you are of." Implied may be: "You do not know what is going on in my mind and heart and how utterly out of tune with my mood such words as those are." "You do not understand," "they did not understand," "they know not"—how frequent this kind of comment as the end of Jesus' career approaches!

This passage also reminds us of the wonderful patience of God. It is we who in our sin want **to bid fire come down from heaven** to destroy the wrongdoer; God—not despite his holiness but because of it—is more patient.

57-62. ***The Demands of God's Kingdom.***—Earlier in this same chapter we find Jesus' description of the strenuous conditions of the disciple's life: "If any man would come after me, let him deny himself and take up his cross daily. . . . Whoever would save his life will lose it" (vss. 23-24). That description follows immediately upon Jesus' first prediction of his coming passion. In the present passage we have three concrete instances of the meaning of this

58 And Jesus said unto him, Foxes have holes, and birds of the air *have* nests; but the Son of man hath not where to lay *his* head.

59 And he said unto another, Follow me. But he said, Lord, suffer me first to go and bury my father.

60 Jesus said unto him, Let the dead bury their dead: but go thou and preach the kingdom of God.

61 And another also said, Lord, I will follow thee; but let me first go bid them farewell, which are at home at my house.

62 And Jesus said unto him, No man, having put his hand to the plow, and looking back, is fit for the kingdom of God.

ever you go." 58 And Jesus said to him,
"Foxes have holes, and birds of the air
have nests; but the Son of man has no-
where to lay his head." 59 To another he
said, "Follow me." But he said, "Lord, let
me first go and bury my father." 60 But he
said to him, "Leave the dead to bury their
own dead; but as for you, go and proclaim
the kingdom of God." 61 Another said, "I
will follow you, Lord; but let me first say
farewell to those at my home." 62 Jesus said
to him, "No one who puts his hand to the
plow and looks back is fit for the kingdom
of God."

---

ated by most of his countrymen. **Son of man** in this instance has none of the eschatological content usually associated with the title. To understand it as a mistranslation of the Aramaic phrase meaning "man" is to reduce the utterance to a pessimistic and inaccurate generalization. Perhaps vs. 58*c* was originally cast in the first person singular.

59-60. There is a higher loyalty than even filial duty. The proclamation of **the kingdom of God** brooks no delay. **The dead** are the "spiritually dead" who have not heeded the call of the kingdom. The resemblance of this story to that of Elijah and Elisha in I Kings 19:19-21 is too remote to support any theory of literary dependence.

61-62. Matthew has no parallel to these verses. It is difficult to believe that he would have suppressed them. Probably Luke provided the striking saying in vs. 62 with its present introduction and gave it this appropriate setting. No one who has ever tried to plow a straight furrow can miss the point: the task requires a man's uninterrupted attention. **Is fit for** probably means "is fitted to work for."

---

demand for self-denial; and it is not accidental that they fall immediately after the account of Jesus' setting "his face to go to Jerusalem" and his death. The passage records brief conversations with three men who are considering discipleship—there is probably no significance in the fact that Jesus takes the initiative in one case and the men in the other two. The point lies in the fact that they are all rejected, or at least discouraged. None of them apparently is capable of the passionate loyalty to the kingdom of God which is required; none of them is ready apparently to take up the cross which Jesus has now definitely and irrevocably accepted. This lack shows itself as unwillingness to give, in the first case, self-denying devotion to the kingdom of God; in the second, absolute priority; and in the third, exclusive attention. Only one who is able to forget his own physical needs and wants, who gives God's kingdom precedence over every other loyalty, and who is able to concentrate his attention on it alone —only such a one **is fit for the kingdom of God.** Can we consider such a passage without asking, "Who then can be saved?"

It is interesting that the obstacles to discipleship in these three cases are (*a*) concern with self, especially one's own comfort, and (*b*) a too-narrow group loyalty. The three men loved either themselves or their families too much, i.e., as compared with the kingdom of God. These are still the two major obstacles to the coming of the kingdom; and it is principally because both of them seem to belong ineradicably to our human nature and to the nature of human history that many despair of the kingdom of God within history. Only in a miraculously new order where men do not live on bread, and where they neither marry nor are given in marriage, can the kingdom of God fully come. Whether we agree with such a view or not, a passage like this is bound to disclose the grounds for it. Who is or can be sufficient for these things? Obviously we, like these men, are not **fit for the kingdom of God;** and if God were not compassionate toward the unfit, and willing and able to redeem them if they understand and confess their unfitness and seek his grace, none of us could have any hope.

Sometimes readers of this section are repelled

10 After these things the Lord appointed other seventy also, and sent them two and two before his face into every city and place, whither he himself would come.

10 After this the Lord appointed seventy[k] others, and sent them on ahead of him, two by two, into every town and place where he himself was about to come.

[k] Other ancient authorities read *seventy-two.*

B. Mission of the Seventy (10:1-24)

1. Instructions to the Missioners (10:1-16; cf. Matt. 9:37-38; 10:7-16; 11:21-23*a*; 10:40)

10:1. Luke's introduction is not altogether consistent with the material subordinated to it. Jesus sent his **seventy** emissaries **two by two** into localities **where he himself was about to come,** after the fashion of the messengers of 9:51-52. But the instructions that follow do not contemplate a merely preparatory mission, and in vs. 17 the **seventy** report back to him. At a later point Luke appears to forget all about the **seventy,** for in 22:35 the injunction in 10:4 is considered to have been delivered to the twelve (cf. 22:14). It is apparent that the Q source had contained an account of the instructions Jesus had given to the twelve before they embarked on their preaching mission. Matthew used it to supplement Mark's version (Matt. 10:1-16), but Luke reserved the greater part of it for use at this point. He had made Mark's account basic to his story in 9:1-6, and now, on the assumption that his sources referred to distinct missions, provides the bulk of the Q matter with a new context. Codex Vaticanus and some representatives of the Western text (including Codex Bezae) read "seventy-two." Similar variations in the use of the same number have been noted elsewhere. The traditional translators of the Hebrew Pentateuch into Greek are variously reckoned as seventy and as seventy-two. The Hebrew text of Gen. 10 gives the number of the Gentile nations as seventy, while the LXX gives it as seventy-two. It is often asserted that Luke intended the **seventy** to symbolize the later Gentile mission, just as the sending out of the twelve is said to have anticipated the mission to the Jews. It is true that seventy is often regarded in Jewish literature as the number of the Gentile nations. However, if this symbolism determined Luke's choice of the number, it is strange that he should imply that these missionaries were dispatched only to Jewish, or Samaritan, centers. It should also be noted that the Gentile mission is entrusted in 24:46-49 to the faithful eleven and their associates. Luke may have mentioned **seventy** as the number of the missionaries on this occasion only because it was a round number for a large company (cf. the seventy elders of Israel in Exod. 24:1; Num. 11:16).

by what appears to be Jesus' harshness. Is it natural or right that a prospective disciple should not have been permitted to bury his father; and another, to say good-by to his family? But the story is not told in such a way as to answer such questions (see also on 8:19-21). No attempt is made to describe fully the concrete situation in which Jesus' words were spoken; if we knew all the circumstances, doubtless his words would seem altogether appropriate. But this series of incidents is recorded with but one purpose—to set forth the supreme importance of the kingdom of God and the supreme loyalty which it demands of us. Everything is stripped away but what is relevant to that purpose. The same economy is characteristic of many biblical narratives and parables and must be taken into account when we interpret them.

10:1-12. ***The Preaching of the Kingdom.***—(See also on 9:1-6.) This passage, placed elsewhere in Matthew, here follows the story of the three halfhearted disciples; and we can readily understand Luke's so locating it. For the major point here too is the supreme importance of the kingdom of God, with special emphasis upon the terrible urgency of preaching it. The disciples are to pray for **laborers** and are to become laborers themselves. All the directions given them as they begin their mission (see Exeg.) are underscorings of the urgent importance of their task. Men are to be presented with the issue of ultimate significance—the kingdom of God. To accept the gospel is to accept salvation and life; to reject it is to choose judgment and death. Men have it in their power to accept or reject; but the preachers must not leave them in ignorance of the awful

2 Therefore said he unto them, The harvest truly *is* great, but the laborers *are* few: pray ye therefore the Lord of the harvest, that he would send forth laborers into his harvest.

3 Go your ways: behold, I send you forth as lambs among wolves.

4 Carry neither purse, nor scrip, nor shoes: and salute no man by the way.

5 And into whatsoever house ye enter, first say, Peace *be* to this house.

6 And if the son of peace be there, your peace shall rest upon it: if not, it shall turn to you again.

7 And in the same house remain, eating and drinking such things as they give: for the laborer is worthy of his hire. Go not from house to house.

2 And he said to them, "The harvest is
plentiful, but the laborers are few; pray
therefore the Lord of the harvest to send
out laborers into his harvest. 3 Go your
way; behold, I send you out as lambs in
the midst of wolves. 4 Carry no purse, no
bag, no sandals; and salute no one on the
road. 5 Whatever house you enter, first
say, 'Peace be to this house!' 6 And if a
son of peace is there, your peace shall rest
upon him; but if not, it shall return to
you. 7 And remain in the same house, eat-
ing and drinking what they provide, for
the laborer deserves his wages; do not go

---

2. A saying more appropriately located by Matthew before Jesus' choice of the twelve. People were ready for the message if only they could be reached. John 4:35-38 appears to be based on the same utterance.

3. A warning. Matthew places it near the end of the charge to the twelve and adds: "So be wise as serpents and innocent as doves" (RSV). Missionaries who were undergoing experiences of persecution in later decades would take comfort from the thought that Jesus had anticipated the dangers of their calling and had prepared his first followers for them.

4. Travel rules. **Purse** occurs elsewhere in the N.T. only in Luke 12:33 and 22:35-36. Mark (6:8) and Matthew (10:9) thought that the prohibition applied to money that would be carried in girdles, or "belts." **No bag** was to be taken for carrying victuals (cf. 9:3). **Sandals** translates a different Greek noun from the "sandals" of Mark 6:9, but both refer to the same sort of footwear. The wearing of them was enjoined in Mark's account of the instructions and apparently forbidden in the Q version. "Carry no [extra] sandals" would be a forced interpretation. Oriental salutations were ceremonious and time-consuming, and the need for haste would justify the neglect of them **on the road.**

5-7. Procedure by which missioners are to find lodging and entertainment. Courtesies that were to be omitted on the road are to be observed on entering a **house.** The blessing is regarded as something objective that will **return to** the giver if it is not accepted. **Son of peace** is a phrase that reflects the dislike of Semitic languages for attributive adjectives. In its present connection it probably means "one who is ready for the message of **peace** [salvation] that you bring." Hospitality is to be accepted on the principle that **the laborer deserves his wages.** This is one of the few sayings of Jesus to which Paul seems to allude (I Cor. 9:14; cf. I Cor. 9:7). It is also quoted in I Tim. 5:18. To change quarters would be to waste precious time (cf. 9:4).

---

meaning of their choice: to both groups they must say, **The kingdom of God has come near.** The relevance of this passage lies in the challenge it offers to the church, and especially its ministry in every generation. Are we taking our mission with anything like the seriousness indicated here? It may be argued that because the primitive preachers expected the immediate end of history and the coming of the kingdom of God, they inevitably felt a need for haste which we do not feel. The fact that we do not share this expectation may be regarded as part of the psychological explanation of our unfaithfulness and lassitude, but not in any degree as a moral justification of it. **The kingdom of God has come near**—this is true regardless of how long history is yet to last. The final eschatological salvation in Christ is present and available

8 And into whatsoever city ye enter,
and they receive you, eat such things as
are set before you:
9 And heal the sick that are therein, and
say unto them, The kingdom of God is
come nigh unto you.
10 But into whatsoever city ye enter, and
they receive you not, go your ways out
into the streets of the same, and say,
11 Even the very dust of your city,
which cleaveth on us, we do wipe off against
you: notwithstanding, be ye sure of this,
that the kingdom of God is come nigh unto
you.
12 But I say unto you, that it shall be
more tolerable in that day for Sodom, than
for that city.
13 Woe unto thee, Chorazin! woe unto
thee, Bethsaida! for if the mighty works
had been done in Tyre and Sidon, which

from house to house. [8] Whenever you en-
ter a town and they receive you, eat what
is set before you; [9] heal the sick in it and
say to them, 'The kingdom of God has
come near to you.' [10] But whenever you
enter a town and they do not receive you,
go into its streets and say, [11] 'Even the
dust of your town that clings to our feet,
we wipe off against you; nevertheless know
this, that the kingdom of God has come
near.' [12] I tell you, it shall be more toler-
able on that day for Sodom than for that
town.
13 "Woe to you, Cho-ra'zin! woe to you,

8-9. Missionary procedure in a hospitable **town. Eat what is set before you** is a repetition of the injunction in vs. 7*a*, and could be omitted in this sentence without loss. The same words in I Cor. 10:27 are applied by Paul to an entirely different situation, and it is unlikely that the apostle had Jesus' saying in mind. In Matt. 10:7-8 the proclamation of the new age is to precede the ministry to the sick. **To you** is not in Matthew's version and may be Luke's addition. As Luke records the announcement **the kingdom of God** is a new order that men may accept or reject without waiting for some future manifestation of it.

10-12. Missionary procedure in an inhospitable **town.** For vs. 11*a* see on 9:5. There is no early MS support for **unto you** (KJV) in vs. 11. The imminence of **the kingdom of God** is to be proclaimed even to those who have forfeited their right to share in it. What is a promise to others becomes a threat to them.

The following "woes" on cities in Galilee and Gaulanitis were also included by Matthew in his Gospel, but in a separate section and with their own introduction and conclusion (Matt. 11:20-24). Perhaps Luke, rather than the editor of Q, was responsible for inserting them into this context. They consist of observations in retrospect that appear to have no good connection with a charge to disciples. If they go back in substance to Jesus, they reflect a bitterness that is unusual in his teaching, and a disappointment that contrasts in tone with that expressed in 19:41. They are more easily understood as the verdict of the later church on the failure of these towns to respond to the ministry of Jesus, or the missionary efforts of early Palestinian Christians.

13-14. Chorazin is not mentioned in the Gospels except in this passage and its parallel in Matthew. It has been tentatively identified with some ruins now known as

wherever the gospel is preached. Men always stand in a crisis of judgment, and are faced now as certainly as men were then with the necessity of choosing either life or death, either heaven or hell. The church's principal task as preacher is to confront men with these alternatives. Are we doing this?

13-14. ***The Greater Judgment.***—These verses (as well as vs. 12) present an instance of a striking and pervasive emphasis of Jesus' teaching—what H. J. Cadbury calls "the principle of . . . proportionate duty." [7] There will be occasion to note this general principle again at 12:48. In the present passage the idea is applied to the duties of large societies. Chorazin and Bethsaida have had opportunities which other cities

[7] *Jesus: What Manner of Man* (New York: The Macmillan Co., 1947), p. 23.

have been done in you, they had a great while ago repented, sitting in sackcloth and ashes.

14 But it shall be more tolerable for Tyre and Sidon at the judgment, than for you.

15 And thou, Capernaum, which art exalted to heaven, shalt be thrust down to hell.

Beth-sa'i-da! for if the mighty works done in you had been done in Tyre and Sidon, they would have repented long ago, sitting in sackcloth and ashes. 14 But it shall be more tolerable in the judgment for Tyre and Sidon than for you. 15 And you, Caper'na-um, will you be exalted to heaven? You shall be brought down to Hades.

Kerâzeh, two or three miles to the northeast of Tel Ḥûm (Capernaum). The Gospels often tell us that Jesus worked in the vicinity of **Bethsaida,** but they never actually locate him in that center (see on 9:10). Therefore this Q narrative hints at a ministry, or a mission of the early church—**the mighty works done in you**—of which our other sources take no account. **Tyre** and **Sidon** had been bitterly cursed in postexilic times by the authors of Ezek. 26–28 and Isa. 23. From the point of view of a Jew they typified paganism at its worst. But **Chorazin** and **Bethsaida** were even more stubbornly impenitent and would fare far worse **in the** day of **judgment.**

15. A separate saying is devoted to **Capernaum,** closely associated in the gospel tradition with the ministry of Jesus. The language is modeled on a postexilic oracle against Nebuchadrezzar: "You said to yourself, 'I will ascend into heaven,' . . . but now you shall be brought down to Hades" (Isa. 14:13-15 [LXX]). The interrogative phrasing of 15*a* (cf. RSV) has very strong MS support, including the third-century Chester Beatty Gospel Papyrus (p[45]) and codices Sinaiticus, Vaticanus, and Bezae. This reading declares that the city is to be punished for its unwarranted pride, perhaps in the fact that it had been the scene of so great a part of Jesus' ministry. The reading in the KJV—with much

---

and regions have not had; therefore they rest under a greater responsibility and are incurring a greater judgment. After a very illuminating discussion of the general principle as Jesus understood and used it, Cadbury, without quoting this passage, comes near indeed to the meaning of it when he writes:

> In proportion to their advantages the rich [as Jesus often sees them] have so acted as to deserve no blessing, while the poor have often deserved better than might have been expected of them. So the Jew as contrasted with Samaritan or Gentile. Jesus' principle here merely echoes the stern words of the Lord in the book of Amos to the whole family that he had brought up out of the land of Egypt and led forty years in the wilderness to possess the land of the Amorite.
>
> You only have I known of all the families of the earth,
> Therefore I will visit upon you all your iniquities.
>
> What this would mean when applied to modern nations like our own is rarely recognized. Our moral condemnation of other peoples too often assumes that they are to be judged by identical standards and if we are more decent than they, all is well with us. But if we should begin with Jesus' principle of proportionate responsibility, we would recognize that it requires of a more highly favored people not slight moral superiority, but a really great difference. Our geographical remoteness from the friction centers of Europe and Asia, our great natural resources, our abundant Lebensraum, our educational standards, our long political experience with democratic institutions and our knowledge, if not our practice, of Christian ethical standards, put on us the duty of corresponding generosity, chivalry, understanding.[8]

Is it possible that Christ is saying to our own privileged nation, **It shall be more tolerable in the judgment** for the nations of Europe and Asia **than for you?**

15. ***Exaltation and Abasement.***—Here we are reminded of yet another pervasive characteristic of Jesus' thought—an alertness to the paradoxical nature of reality. The teaching here is a concrete application of the principle more generally stated at 18:14, "For every one who exalts himself will be humbled, but he who humbles himself will be exalted" (see also on 9:46-48). The present passage seems to take a further step and to say in effect, "The higher the position we give ourselves, the lower the position God will give us." (Cadbury, in the chapter just quoted, sees in such teachings as this and the foregoing an indication that Jesus liked to think in mathematical and quantitative terms of size, distance, proportion, etc. One recognizes at once that this is true; scores of

[8] *Ibid.*, pp. 26-27. By permission of The Macmillan Co.

16 He that heareth you heareth me; and he that despiseth you despiseth me; and he that despiseth me despiseth him that sent me.

16 "He who hears you hears me, and he who rejects you rejects me, and he who rejects me rejects him who sent me."

---

inferior MS attestation—is open to another interpretation somewhat more in accordance with that of the preceding "woes": "You were **exalted to heaven** by the very presence of Jesus, but will be **thrust down to hell** because you have failed to respond to his message."

16. Matthew's version, with two further verses on the same theme, also concludes the parallel section in his Gospel: "He who receives you receives me" (Matt. 10:40). Presumably the original stood at the end of the Q account of the charge. Other variants are in 9:48 (Mark 9:37; Matt. 18:5) and John 13:20. Has Luke added 16*a* to the saying in order to relate it more directly to the reception of the message, and changed "receives" to **rejects** in 16*b* and *c* because he has included vss. 13-15 in the charge?

---

sayings and parables confirm it.) If we exalt ourselves to heaven, we shall be cast into hell, just as the man who takes for himself the highest seat is forced to take the lowest (see on 14:8-9). So also we meet with the mythological belief that Lucifer and his angels were once in heaven, and that it was their ambitious attempt to take the highest place there—the place of God himself—which led to their being thrown into the pit. It is this story which is applied to Nebuchadrezzar in Isa. 14:12 ff. (see Exeg.). It could have been applied to some modern rulers. Indeed, it applies whenever any of us, in however humble a position, sets up his own will as a kind of ultimate for his life. Paul in Rom. 1:18 ff. gives a dark picture of the debasement which overtakes those who "exchanged the truth about God for a lie" about themselves. Note that **Capernaum** does not *reach* heaven—it only wishes or tries to do so—but it **shall** in fact **be brought down to Hades.** There is no way to take the kingdom of God by storm. We cannot possess heaven except as God gives it to us. Indeed, to try to seize it is to lose it.

16. ***Authority and Responsibility of the Preacher.***—Jesus often makes the "equals mark" and calls attention to equivalences, another example of the "mathematical" turn of mind of which Cadbury speaks (see on vs. 15). In 9:48, e.g., Jesus says that to serve a little child is to serve him, and that to serve him is to serve God. That same saying is apparently found in Matthew at the end of his version of the present passage, i.e., at the end of Jesus' instructions to the evangelists he is sending out, "He who receives you receives me, and he who receives me receives him who sent me"; and the text in Luke states the same truth in negative terms. The meaning of the equivalence between Jesus and God can be discussed more appropriately in connection with vs. 22; here the emphasis falls upon the equivalence Jesus affirms between himself and his evangelists: **he who rejects you rejects me.** We may view this statement in either of two ways. Most obviously and immediately the intention is to affirm the *authority* of the preacher. He goes out in Christ's name; he stands in Christ's place; he speaks for Christ. His message is not his own; it has been given to him. If men reject him and his message, he must not take the hurt of their rejection too much to himself; they have rejected him only because they have also, and first, rejected Christ and the truth. But the same text calls attention to the terrible *responsibility* under which the preacher stands. Let us suppose that the rejected preacher does not truly represent Christ, that he speaks his own words, not Christ's; and that he is rejected for his own sake, not for Christ's sake. Even so, it is likely that the text will still be true: **he who rejects you rejects me,** i.e., many who hear the preacher will not be able to distinguish between him and the Christ he claims to represent, and in rejecting him, will reject Christ also. Often the preacher himself is unable to make this distinction, and being rejected, comforts himself that he is suffering because of Christ, when really the church of Christ is being made to suffer because of him. In this connection one may recall an illuminating and salutary passage, I Pet. 4:13 ff., addressed to Christians undergoing persecution: "Rejoice in so far as you share Christ's sufferings. . . . If you are reproached for the name of Christ, you are blessed. . . . But let none of you suffer as a murderer, or a thief, or a wrongdoer, or a mischief-maker; yet if one suffers as a Christian, let him not be ashamed." He who rejects the disciple rejects the Master; but let us be sure that the disciple is rejected for Christ's sake,

17 ¶ And the seventy returned again with joy, saying, Lord, even the devils are subject unto us through thy name.

18 And he said unto them, I beheld Satan as lightning fall from heaven.

19 Behold, I give unto you power to tread on serpents and scorpions, and over all the power of the enemy; and nothing shall by any means hurt you.

20 Notwithstanding, in this rejoice not, that the spirits are subject unto you; but rather rejoice, because your names are written in heaven.

17 The seventy[l] returned with joy, saying, "Lord, even the demons are subject to us in your name!"
18 And he said to them, "I saw Satan fall like lightning from heaven.
19 Behold, I have given you authority to tread upon serpents and scorpions, and over all the power of the enemy; and nothing shall hurt you.
20 Nevertheless do not rejoice in this, that the spirits are subject to you; but rejoice that your names are written in heaven."

[l] Other ancient authorities read *seventy-two.*

---

2. Jesus' Words to the Seventy on Their Return (10:17-20)

The editor's hand can probably be noted at least in vs. 17*a.* By this introduction Luke has related an originally independent group of sayings to his own tradition of the mission of the seventy.

17. The **seventy** report back to Jesus as the twelve had done (9:10) and express joyful astonishment at their power to exorcise **demons** by the use of Jesus' **name** (see on 9:49). **Seventy-two** (RSV mg.) has the same MS support as in vs. 1, with the addition of the Chester Beatty Gospel Papyrus (p^{45}).

18. In a moment of ecstatic vision (during the absence of the missioners?) Jesus had seen **Satan** defeated and cast **from heaven** (cf. the imagery of Isa. 14:12; Rev. 12:7-9). Here, and in the saying in 11:20, Jesus interprets successful exorcism as evidence that the forces of evil are dethroned and the new age has begun.

19. There is an echo in this verse of Ps. 91:13. The **authority** that Jesus had delegated: a reference to vs. 9, or possibly to 9:1. **Serpents and scorpions** were apparently considered half-demonic (cf. Mark 16:18—a late addition to that Gospel). The final clause seems to imply a promise of preservation from death.

20. The real grounds for rejoicing (cf. Exod. 32:32-33; Ps. 69:28; Dan. 12:1; Enoch 104:1; Rev. 3:5; etc.).

---

and that Christ is not rejected for the disciple's sake.

17-20. ***Not What We Have but Whose We Are.***—**The seventy returned with joy** (cf. Ps. 126:6)—their mission had been successful—and Jesus sees in their triumph a sign of the reality and the imminence of God's kingdom. In an ecstasy he cries, **I saw Satan fall like lightning from heaven**—another reference to the myth of Lucifer (cf. vs. 15; Rev. 12:9-10). And yet there is peril in this kind of rejoicing; it can so easily pass into self-congratulation. Note that **the demons are subject to us in your name** in vs. 17 becomes simply **the spirits are subject to you** in vs. 20. The real source of the disciples' satisfaction must be not the consciousness of having great powers or authority, but the awareness of belonging to God in Christ. The disciple's joy is to be not in possessing, but in being possessed. And the greater an individual's authority in the church, and the more notable and conspicuous his gifts, the more profound and clear and constant must be his consciousness of belonging to Christ if he is to be saved from intolerable pride and selfishness. What good we are able to do must be seen to be—as it really is—not what *we* are able to do at all, but what God is able to do in us and through us. A reference to the several passages mentioned in the Exeg. of vs. 20 will remind us that the phrase **names . . . written in heaven** is an allusion to those who have been made the recipients of God's forgiveness and mercy. It is as though Jesus is cautioning his disciples that however much authority they may have, they still stand constantly in need of God's mercy, which he freely offers; and that when they cease being humbly, gratefully, and joyously aware of this mercy, their authority will have become a false and empty thing.

21 ¶ In that hour Jesus rejoiced in spirit, and said, I thank thee, O Father, Lord of heaven and earth, that thou hast hid these things from the wise and prudent, and hast revealed them unto babes: even so, Father; for so it seemed good in thy sight.

21 In that same hour he rejoiced in the Holy Spirit and said, "I thank thee, Father, Lord of heaven and earth, that thou hast hidden these things from the wise and understanding and revealed them to babes; yea, Father, for such was thy

3. Jesus' Prayer of Thanksgiving (10:21-22=Matt. 11:25-27)

Luke is fond of adding references to **the Holy Spirit** to his sources. Otherwise this passage is in almost verbal agreement with its Matthaean parallel. But Luke omits the verses that follow in Matthew's Gospel (Matt. 11:28-30), an omission that is difficult to understand if they stood in Luke's version of Q.

21. Paul's words to his Corinthian converts exhibit striking similarities: "For since, in the wisdom of God, the world did not know God through wisdom, it pleased God through the folly of what we preach to save those who believe" (I Cor. 1:21). **The wise and understanding:** Presumably the "scribes and Pharisees"—the professional students of

21. *Revealed to Babes.*—This passage (vss. 21-22) is found also in Matthew, but in a different connection. It is not difficult to see why Luke places it here, just after his account of the rejoicing of Jesus and his disciples over the results of the mission of the seventy. Those who take no pride in themselves, their possessions, or their accomplishments, but rather "rejoice that [their] names are written in heaven"—these are the **babes** for whom Christ now gives thanks. Distinguished from them are **the wise and understanding.** As the Exeg. says, immediately in mind are probably the scribes and Pharisees, but the words point to proud and confident "masters" of truth, whoever they may be. We are not to suppose that Jesus is denying to the more intelligent or the better informed, simply as such, any real insight into the truth of God—soon (vss. 25-28) he is going to say to one of the rabbis, "You have answered right; do this, and you will live." But there are at least three perils to which the learned are particularly subject: one is pride in oneself and one's powers; another is confidence in the ability of the mind to master all truth and to control all things; and the third is the habit of analyzing and classifying to the exclusion of any vision of things in their concreteness, wholeness, and simplicity. *Wisdom* is always humble and in a certain sense naïve; *learning* tends not to be the one and seeks not to be the other. Jesus is here talking about the *learned,* and remarks that humble folk who make no pretensions to scholarship or sophistication, but have not lost the ability to look freshly at reality and to hear what it says, are wiser than many of the scholars and know more of truth, i.e., the really important truth. The basic reason for this fact is that the really important truth is **revealed** truth; it is not discovered by us, but disclosed to us. Such truth is not *less* than our minds, so that we can seize, organize, secure, and be served by it; it is *more* than our minds so that we can only pray for it, wait for it, place ourselves in the way of receiving it, seek to serve it. If we are to know it, God must make it known. A much wider range of truth is of this **revealed** sort than is often recognized: poets know this, and children; the rest of us often do not (cf. on 8:9-10; 18:17).

The truth of God in Christ is revealed truth, and only those who are willing and able humbly to receive a revelation can know it. It is this fact that Paul has in mind when he says, in the passage cited by the Exeg., that the gospel of Christ is "foolishness" to the Greeks, i.e., it cannot be proved; it is not the conclusion of a rational argument. Nevertheless this foolishness is not the foolishness of ignorance. Indeed, it is not foolishness at all; it is the "wisdom of God." For **the wise and understanding** are likely to discover eventually that

> wisdom, without the so-called folly of faith, fails even to be wisdom. The task of wisdom is to give an adequate and rational account of the world and the meaning of human life. It is likely to begin by seeing that faith is not *rational* and that therefore it must be excluded from such an account; but it will end by discovering that reason is not *adequate.* Wisdom thus finds itself rejecting what wisdom itself cannot dispense with. The lower wisdom aims at logic and sacrifices adequacy; the true wisdom aims at adequacy, and discovers a deeper logic. The world by wisdom only cannot be truly wise. The world by wisdom knew not God; and yet without the knowledge of God there can be no wisdom.[9]

[9] *The Gospel, the Church and the World,* ed. Kenneth Scott Latourette (New York: Harper & Bros., 1946), p. 7. Used by permission.

22 All things are delivered to me of my Father: and no man knoweth who the Son is, but the Father; and who the Father is, but the Son, and *he* to whom the Son will reveal *him*.

gracious will.[m] 22 All things have been delivered to me by my Father; and no one knows who the Son is except the Father, or who the Father is except the Son and any one to whom the Son chooses to reveal him."

[m] Or *so it was well-pleasing before thee.*

---

the law and those who had dedicated themselves to the strict observance of all its regulations. **Babes:** The disciples—common folk who did not belong to the learned or pious elite.

22. The thought and language of this verse set it apart from the rest of the Synoptic tradition. Nowhere else does Jesus speak of God as a transcendent being who is hid from human knowledge, or of his own relationship to God as revealed truth that he mediates only to the chosen few. It is therefore difficult to regard this verse as primitive. It is easier to understand it as an early interpretation of Christianity: a "mystery" that a divine mediator has made known to the church. This would be a Christian version of an idea that had been popularized in the Hellenistic world by various Gnostic cults. The thought that only **the Father** and **the Son** know each other is characteristic of the Gospel of John (cf. John 10:15*a*: "As the Father knoweth me, even so know I the Father"). On the other hand, many believe that derivation of the logion from Q attests its authenticity.

---

22. ***The Unique Revelation in the Son.***—In this important verse the Christian position about the revelation of God in Christ, shadowed forth in vs. 21, is more explicitly stated. The gospel is not a philosophy; it is not the affirmation of a universal or abstract truth. It is the proclamation of an event, concrete and unique—an event which sets the whole meaning of human life in a new light. What this text is saying is that the God of Christian faith is known in no other way than through this event: **No one knows . . . who the Father is except the Son and any one to whom the Son chooses to reveal him.** This does not mean that there is no knowledge of God whatever except in Christ. The God who made us has not left himself anywhere without a witness. The heavens declare his glory, and his law is written in our hearts. To deny this would be to deny the very existence of God. He is the Father Almighty, the ground and the breath of all being, and we exist at all only because we are in him. But when we speak of God, we mean in particular God as he has made himself known to us; and God has made himself thus known only through Christ. Sometimes the revelation in Christ is interpreted and emphasized in such a way as virtually to deny the validity of experiences of God's reality and nearness which come to us without immediate or conscious connection with either Christ or the church; the doctrine thus interpreted seems arbitrary and harsh. But although to recognize our dependence upon an historical event for our knowledge of God does not mean a repudiation of the experiences of his reality and glory which have been vouchsafed to us in our common life, it does mean our perception of the fact that the God who is disclosed in these experiences is for us the God and Father of our Lord Jesus Christ, and that *this* God can make himself known to us in these experiences only because he has first made himself known in Christ. The clue to the interpretation of whatever intimations of the divine are given us in our common life is provided by the first-century event to which we find ourselves inevitably looking back, and by the historical community through which the concrete meaning of that event has been conveyed to us, and in which therefore the event itself is in a sense perpetuated.[1]

But not only does this text tell us that we cannot know **who the Father is** except through the Son, it implies also that no one can know **who the Son is** except through the Father. The historian's researches into the life and teachings of the "Jesus of history," however valuable, cannot by themselves yield knowledge of **who the Son is.** Paul writes, "No one can say 'Jesus is Lord' except by the Holy Spirit" (I Cor. 12:3). It is only as the God and Father of our Lord Jesus Christ becomes known to us that we enter into any true understanding of the meaning of Christ himself.

[1] The substance and to some extent the wording of this paragraph depend upon a longer discussion of the theme in John Knox, *On the Meaning of Christ* (New York: Charles Scribner's Sons, 1947), pp. 2-7.

23 ¶ And he turned him unto *his* disciples, and said privately, Blessed *are* the eyes which see the things that ye see:

24 For I tell you, that many prophets and kings have desired to see those things which ye see, and have not seen *them;* and to hear those things which ye hear, and have not heard *them.*

25 ¶ And, behold, a certain lawyer stood up, and tempted him, saying, Master, what shall I do to inherit eternal life?

23 Then turning to the disciples he said privately, "Blessed are the eyes which see what you see! 24 For I tell you that many prophets and kings desired to see what you see, and did not see it, and to hear what you hear, and did not hear it."

25 And behold, a lawyer stood up to put him to the test, saying, "Teacher, what

---

4. Jesus' Blessing on His Disciples (10:23-24=Matt. 13:16-17)

23-24. Jesus' mighty acts and gracious words are evidence that the ancient messianic hope has been realized. The disciples are living in the new age of God's rule. Luke draws attention to the fact that this interpretation of Jesus' ministry was not common knowledge. Jesus had communicated it **privately** to his most intimate followers.

C. Jesus Answers Questions (10:25-42)

1. Jesus and a Lawyer's Question (10:25-28)

A story that appears to be an independent version of the account in Mark of a scribe's question about the greatest commandment (Mark 12:28-34; cf. Matt. 22:37-40). At any rate Luke regarded it as a parallel, for he omitted the Marcan narrative at the point in his Gospel where otherwise he would have used it (following 20:39).

25. Lawyer translates a Greek title that would be more intelligible to Gentile readers than Mark's "scribe." Luke often makes the same substitution. In Mark the

---

23. ***Our Privileges.***—Again we have material which is placed elsewhere in Matthew, and again there is no difficulty in understanding Luke's (or his source's) placing it here. It concludes the section which began with the return of the seventy. Still the emphasis is upon the blessedness of the disciples. The presence of these verses in the Gospel reflects the joyous sense of privilege the early Christians had. Their religion was not a burden or a task; it was an inestimable treasure, a pearl of great price. Note in this section (i.e., vss. 17-24) the recurrence of such phrases and words as "returned with joy" (vs. 17), "rejoice" (vs. 20), "he rejoiced in the Holy Spirit" (vs. 21), "I thank thee, Father" (vs. 21), and now **Blessed are the eyes which see what you see!** This is the characteristic note of the N.T.; consider how many beatitudes it contains and how often the words "joy" and "hope" occur. The very word "gospel" (good news) expresses this essential character of N.T. religion and faith. Do we not often find ourselves looking back to this with a kind of wistfulness—to what L. P. Jacks called "the lost radiance of the Christian religion"? But in so far as it is really lost, the Christian religion has been lost because this radiance belongs to it essentially and inseparably.

Luke tells us that Jesus addressed this beatitude **privately** to his disciples. Does he mean that there is something esoteric and exclusive about the privileges of the believer? Occasionally in the N.T. one finds hints of such a teaching. Of course the blessedness is the blessedness of *the believer* and is in that sense by definition limited; but whatever may be in Luke's mind here, any idea of a closed circle of believers, a limited elite, was foreign to Jesus' mind, as many teachings show. The blessedness of the Christian is not of the sort one takes a selfish pride in and hugs to oneself; rather it carries within itself the impulse to share it with others—with all others. The motive back of all creative evangelistic and missionary activity in the church, from the beginning till now, has been the desire of Christians that others shall see what they see. The privileges of the Christian are in one sense special privileges—they belong to life within a particular community—but they are not restricted to any group or class; they are freely offered to all who will accept them.

24. See Expos., 7:28*b*.

25-28. ***Love the Fulfillment of the Law.***—Here begins one of the best-known and best-loved sections of this Gospel (vss. 25-37). The vss. 25-28 are paralleled in Mark (and in Matthew), but their use in the present passage to provide the setting for the parable of the good

26 He said unto him, What is written in
the law? how readest thou?
27 And he answering said, Thou shalt
love the Lord thy God with all thy heart,

shall I do to inherit eternal life?" 26 He
said to him, "What is written in the law?
How do you read?" 27 And he answered,
"You shall love the Lord your God with

---

question is: "Which commandment is the first of all?" Here it is the one that was asked by the "ruler" of the story in 18:18-30 (Mark 10:17-31): **What shall I do to inherit eternal life?** Did Luke, or his source, delete a question that had interest only for Jews and substitute one that would appeal more directly to Gentiles?

26-27. The lawyer combines Deut. 6:4 (the Shema) and Lev. 19:18 to summarize the law. In Mark (and Matthew) it is Jesus himself who associates these two O.T. texts. The same combination is also found in the Testaments of the Twelve Patriarchs (Issachar 5:2; 7:5; Dan 5:3).

Samaritan imparts a special significance. The heart of the passage is the summation of the law in love for God and neighbor, the bringing together of the Shema (which every good Jew repeated daily) and Lev. 19:18: "Thou shalt love thy neighbor as thyself." Sometimes Christians have been jealous to insist that Jesus was the first thus to sum up God's requirements of us, but the point cannot be justly made. Not only is the summary to be found in earlier Jewish sources (see Exeg.), but also, even here, it is the **lawyer,** or scribe, who actually proposes it; Jesus only accepts and concurs. But why does it matter who said it first? Jesus' originality is too great to need defending at points like this. The Exeg. calls attention to the similarities between this story in Luke and the story of the rich ruler in 18:18-30. In both a leader of repute asks how he may **inherit eternal life;** in both Jesus appeals to what the law says. But the other story ends with "One thing thou lackest" (though the law has been kept), and this one with **this do, and thou shalt live.** The explanation of the difference lies in the two ways of summarizing the law: in ch. 18 the summary is merely an aggregation of the several commandments, "Thou shalt not kill," "Thou shalt not commit adultery," etc.; here it is an appeal to that requirement of God which undergirds, unifies, and transcends all the separate rules and codes. One can and should go beyond the rules (that was the "lack" of the rich ruler; he had not done so); but one cannot go beyond love. This is made clear by the words **with all your heart, . . . soul, . . . strength, . . . mind.** "Love is the fulfilling of the law" (Rom. 13:10; note also Rom. 13:9; cf. on Matt. 5:17; Luke 6:27-31). The requirement of love "fulfills" the law in at least three respects: it goes not only beyond the rules, but also between the rules and under the rules. It goes *under* the rules in the sense of being concerned not primarily with acts as such (as rules must be), but with motives (see Matt. 5:21-48). It goes *between* the rules in the sense of covering our behavior in the whole wide range of our relationships; rules are perforce specific and leave gaps. The law was computed by the rabbis to contain 613 commandments (365 "thou shalt nots" and 248 "thou shalts"), but even so many rules were not enough to define duty in all the contingencies of existence; and if that was true then, how much more true would it be now in our vastly more complex society. Rules are rough-and-ready, approximate answers; love alone can prescribe precisely for each need and occasion. But the requirement of love also goes *beyond* the rules. To be sure, it asks less that is irrelevant and pointless; but it asks more that is significant. It is less restraining, but more demanding; less irritating and burdensome, but more costly. One who merely obeys rules is trying to save himself; one who loves is trying to serve God. The one obedience is slavery; the other "perfect freedom." And this is true because what we call "freedom" is really our experience of belonging with **heart, soul, strength,** and **mind** to what we know is worthy to possess us; and what can that be but the God who made us and made us for himself?

25-28. *Love Moves in Three Directions.*—But how can love be a requirement or a duty? It would appear that love, of all things, must be spontaneous and voluntary. This difficulty is partly met by emphasis upon the particular Greek word which is used here and is always used when love is enjoined as an obligation, ἀγαπᾶν. Montefiore, speaking of love for enemies as Jesus commanded it, writes: "What does 'love' mean? It means 'desire their well-being'; 'do good to them'; 'pray for their salvation.' It does not mean: 'Feel for them an emotion such as you feel for your wife, your sister, or your father.' 'Αγαπᾶν is not φιλεῖν." [2] And yet ἀγαπᾶν is not to be equated with ἀγαθοποιεῖν ("to do good")—as though it were a matter of deeds only. The very passage in Matthew on which

[2] *Synoptic Gospels,* II, 80.

and with all thy soul, and with all thy strength, and with all thy mind; and thy neighbor as thyself.

28 And he said unto him, Thou hast answered right: this do, and thou shalt live.

all your heart, and with all your soul, and with all your strength, and with all your mind; and your neighbor as yourself."
28 And he said to him, "You have answered right; do this, and you will live."

---

28. Jesus' words to the scribe in Mark's account: "You are not far from the kingdom of God." **Do this, and you will live:** an apparent reminiscence of Lev. 18:5. Paul also quotes the same passage (Gal. 3:12).

Montefiore is commenting (i.e., Matt. 5:21 ff.) clearly distinguishes between outer behavior and inner attitude, and insists that it is precisely a certain inner attitude that God requires. Perhaps there does not need to be a tender emotion toward our neighbors, but it *is* demanded that we "desire their well-being," that we have good will toward them; and the problem remains of how such an attitude can be either appropriately commanded or obediently given. Whatever answer would have been given to this question within the context of Judaism, there can be no doubt that the Christian finds a clue to it in God's love of us. Love moves in three directions: from God to us, from us to God, and toward one another. We can love God only because he has first loved us; and we are able to love our neighbors in the Christian sense only because we have been first loved of God. Both my neighbor and I are men for whom Christ died.

27b-37. Thy Neighbor as Thyself.—This is a quotation from the O.T., and although it is approved and appropriated by Jesus, probably does not represent the way in which he would have described the love of neighbor for which God asks if he had been discussing it without reference to the traditional **law**. Jesus has put his understanding of God's will into more congenial and characteristic terms in such passages as 9:23, "If any man would come after me, let him deny himself." "Deny thyself" says something more and other than "Love thy neighbor as thyself." **As thyself** seems to imply the duty, as well as the fact, of self-love—and this Jesus certainly did not intend. And yet there is a profound wisdom in this traditional ethical principle. Paul Ramsey writes:

> The words "as yourself" do not indicate how much love, or for that matter that any amount of love, may be withheld; instead, they describe the sort of love Christians should give to others. How exactly do you love yourself? Answer this question and you will know how a Christian should love his neighbor. You naturally love yourself for your own sake. You wish your own good. . . . You love yourself more than you love any good qualities or worth you may possess. . . . Self-love does not wait on worth. In fact it is the other way around: self-love makes you desire worth for yourself. Regardless of fluctuations in feeling, you love yourself on one day about as much as on any other. And regardless of differences in temperament or capacity for deep emotion, one person probably wishes his own good about as much as another person wishes for his.[8]

When, then, we are asked to love our neighbors, we are required to love them not vaguely or emotionally, but in very definite, practical, and realistic ways. It is so that we love ourselves.

The saying is wise in another sense. Looked at in one way this **law** resembles a law of nature, which defines not merely how things ought to act but how they *do* act. There is a sense in which we do inevitably love our neighbors as we love ourselves; it is how we regard ourselves which determines how we regard others. It is interesting that the "lawyer" after citing the commandment proceeds at once to the question, **And who is my neighbor?** For it is how I regard myself which determines whom I am going to regard as my neighbor. If what I most esteem in myself is something I share with only a small group of other men, my human interest will be largely limited to that group. If, on the other hand, the thing in myself by which I set largest store is something which every man at least potentially possesses, there will be no limit to my social concern. The **priest** and the **Levite** thought of themselves, esteemed themselves, primarily as priest and Levite; and the wounded man was neither. The Samaritan, however, thought of himself not primarily as a Samaritan of a certain class, or even as a Samaritan at all, but as a human being, and therefore to him the important thing was not that a Jew was in need of help, but that a man was.

For those who belong to the Christian tradition the significance of this common humanity is immeasurably deepened. For them the supremely important thing about themselves is that they stand in a certain relationship to God. The Christian makes the supremely significant affirmation about himself when he says: "God made me, judges me, in Christ has suffered to

[8] *Basic Christian Ethics* (New York: Charles Scribner's Sons, 1950), pp. 99-100. Used by permission.

29 But ne, willing to justify himself, said unto Jesus, And who is my neighbor?

29 But he, desiring to justify himself, said to Jesus, "And who is my neighbor?"

2. Parable of the Good Samaritan (10:29-37)

The Greek word for "parable" was used by the translators of the **LXX** to render the Hebrew noun *māshāl,* a derivative of a verb meaning "to be like." In Hebrew literature a *māshāl* could mean almost any kind of verbal image: riddle, proverb, taunt, simile, metaphor, prophetic oracle, detailed simile (similitude), illustrative narrative, example story, or even allegory. While "parable" in the Synoptic Gospels describes a similar range of figurative utterances, the word is restricted in common usage to three types: "similitude," "narrative parable," and "example story." The first and second teach by analogy, and the third by direct example that is to be imitated or avoided. "Example stories" were preserved only in Luke's special tradition and include, in addition to the one under discussion, those of the rich fool, the rich man and Lazarus, and the Pharisee and the tax collector.

Luke has a special interest in Samaritans, and he represents Jesus' attitude to them in a much more favorable light than does the tradition in Matthew (cf. Matt. 10:5). Some interpreters have therefore maintained that Luke, or his source, has revised the parable by the substitution of a Samaritan for an Israelite as the third character. Originally the conduct of a Jewish layman was contrasted with that of the professionally religious priest and Levite. It has been argued that Jesus, because of the antipathy of Jews for Samaritans, could hardly have spoken of a Samaritan who made regular trips from Jerusalem to Jericho and who was on good terms with the landlord of an inn. The words of a learned Jewish scholar are an apt commentary on this hypothesis: "Whether the Samaritan was original to the parable or not, at all events he is there now, and the conception of the good Samaritan is one which the world will not easily let go. For the parable is one of the simplest and noblest among the noble gallery of parables in the Synoptic Gospels. Love, it tells us, must know no limits of race and ask no enquiry. Who needs me is my neighbour. Whom at the given time and place I can help with my active love, he is my neighbour and I am his" (C. G. Montefiore, *The Synoptic Gospels* [2nd ed.; London: Macmillan & Co., 1927], II, 468).

29. To justify himself, i.e., to justify his question. The Scriptures say, "You shall love your neighbor as yourself," but what is meant by **neighbor?**

The lawyer's question seeks information on **neighbor** as object of one's love. We should expect some such answer as: "Your neighbor is anyone who needs your help." But

redeem me. Whatever else may be true about me, nothing matters as compared with this." But just that statement can be made also of every other man. In precisely the same sense God has made, judges, and offers to redeem all mankind. But it is only with man as man that God is concerned. And once I recognize this fact, I can no longer ascribe any great importance to racial, national, or cultural distinctions. God's love for me is no whit greater or less than his love for all my fellows.

One of the most terrible things about the world we live in is that it all but forces men to think of themselves in inadequate terms, to love themselves for the wrong reasons. The pride of one racial group forces another racial group to develop an equally false and divisive pride of its own. The selfishness of one industrial group forces another to develop a selfishness of its own. The nationalism of one country leads to the creation of an antagonistic nationalism in another. But such developments, understandable and perhaps, as things are, inevitable though they may be, do not belong to the essential order of the world. Humanity is really one; and the person who finds himself at his deepest level has found something which makes him kin with all sincere men.

29-37. *The Extravagance of Love.*—Students of this passage often find significance in the rather curious way in which the parable is related to the question it was told to answer. It seems to answer not the lawyer's question, **Who is my neighbor?** i.e., "Who is an appropriate object of neighborly love?" but some such question as "Who is a true bestower of neighborly love?" The same kind of shift in point of view was observed in the story of the penitent

30 And Jesus answering said, A certain
man went down from Jerusalem to Jericho,
and fell among thieves, which stripped him
of his raiment, and wounded *him,* and de-
parted, leaving *him* half dead.

31 And by chance there came down a
certain priest that way; and when he saw
him, he passed by on the other side.

32 And likewise a Levite, when he was
at the place, came and looked *on him,* and
passed by on the other side.

30 Jesus replied, "A man was going down
from Jerusalem to Jericho, and he fell
among robbers, who stripped him and beat
him, and departed, leaving him half-dead.
31 Now by chance a priest was going down
that road; and when he saw him he passed
by on the other side. 32 So likewise a Levite,
when he came to the place and saw him,

---

the emphasis in the story that follows is not on the man who fell among robbers, but on the Samaritan who had compassion on him. It illustrates **neighbor** as subject rather than as object. It is in answer to some such question as: "How can I act as neighbor?" "Whose neighbor am I?" "Neighbor" in vs. 36 bears a different meaning than the same word in vs. 29. "If it is given the meaning that it bears in the earlier verse, then the answer to the question is the strange one that those whom we should regard as our neighbours are those only who show loving-kindness towards us" (B. T. D. Smith, *The Parables of the Synoptic Gospels* [Cambridge: University Press, 1937], p. 182).

It is therefore possible that the story of the good Samaritan was originally independent of the narrative that precedes it and that the connection is due to the editorial artistry of the evangelist—or his source.

30. A man, presumably a Jew. The road **from Jerusalem to Jericho** is a little short of seventeen miles and falls more than thirty-four hundred feet. Josephus spoke of the road in the first century as "desolate and rocky" (*Jewish War* IV. 8. 3). Jerome declared in the late fourth century that it was still infested with Bedouin **robbers** (*On Jeremiah* I. 50).

31-32. Priests and Levites were not compelled to live in Jerusalem when off duty. The narrative may imply that one traveler was on his way to Jericho and the other to Jerusalem. Men whose interest in religion was professional might have been expected to exceed others in their concern for human need.

---

woman in 7:36-50. In each place the Exeg. suggests a combination of materials from two sources; it is also possible that a characteristic of Luke's mind is in evidence (see on 7:47). But whatever the explanation, it is doubtful that this change in point of view has any important meaning, as though, e.g., Jesus were saying to the lawyer, "You have not asked the right question. I shall answer not the question you have put to me, but the really appropriate question." The query in vs. 36 may indeed mean simply, "Which of these three showed that he truly loved his neighbor as himself?" Jesus' story directly exemplifies the meaning of the commandment in vs. 27*b*, but also indirectly answers the lawyer's question. Anyone in need is the neighbor to whom our good will must go out.

The story wonderfully illustrates the quality of this good will. Love of neighbor will not be calculating and restrained, as though one were merely doing one's duty; but will be, one might almost say, foolishly extravagant and lavish. Here is a constant note in Jesus' ethical teaching and probably the most characteristic. One hears it again and again in the Sermon on the Mount, where we are told to love our enemies, to go the second mile, to give our cloak, too. Many of the parables sound it—as when the employer pays all his laborers the full wage though some have worked only for an hour, and a father rewards with gifts and a great feast an utterly unworthy son. So here again we find the hallmark of Jesus: the fact that the **neighbor** was so completely a stranger, being of all things a Samaritan; the extravagance of his compassion, **pouring on oil and wine,** binding up the man's **wounds,** setting him **on his own beast,** bringing him **to an inn** and taking **care of him.** He could have stopped so much sooner than this and still have more than fulfilled any possible rule about one's duty to a wounded stranger. But he did not stop even then—leaving money to pay for the man's further care, and insisting that if more were needed, he should be allowed to pay the account on his

33 But a certain Samaritan, as he journeyed, came where he was; and when he saw him, he had compassion *on him,*

34 And went to *him,* and bound up his wounds, pouring in oil and wine, and set him on his own beast, and brought him to an inn, and took care of him.

35 And on the morrow when he departed, he took out two pence, and gave *them* to the host, and said unto him, Take care of him: and whatsoever thou spendest more, when I come again, I will repay thee.

36 Which now of these three, thinkest thou, was neighbor unto him that fell among the thieves?

37 And he said, He that showed mercy on him. Then said Jesus unto him, Go, and do thou likewise.

38 ¶ Now it came to pass, as they went, that he entered into a certain village: and a certain woman named Martha received him into her house.

passed by on the other side. 33 But a Sa-
maritan, as he journeyed, came to where he
was; and when he saw him, he had com-
passion, 34 and went to him and bound
up his wounds, pouring on oil and wine;
then he set him on his own beast and
brought him to an inn, and took care of
him. 35 And the next day he took out two
denarii[n] and gave them to the innkeeper,
saying, 'Take care of him; and whatever
more you spend, I will repay you when I
come back.' 36 Which of these three, do you
think, proved neighbor to the man who
fell among the robbers?" 37 He said, "The
one who showed mercy on him." And Jesus
said to him, "Go and do likewise."

38 Now as they went on their way, he
entered a village; and a woman named

[n] The denarius was worth about twenty cents.

33-34. **A Samaritan,** a layman in religion and one who was outside the pale of orthodox Judaism, is the only passer-by to exhibit **compassion. Oil and wine** are known from rabbinical sources to have been used as curative agents. The ass was the ordinary **beast** of burden in Palestine.

35. According to Matt. 20:2, a denarius—worth about twenty cents in silver content —could be regarded as a fair day's wage. Therefore **two denarii** might have represented several days' compensation to the innkeeper. **When I come back,** i.e., "on my return journey" rather than "after my return." The implication of the story is that the Samaritan was a merchant with business in Jerusalem.

36-37. Relates the story to its present context and points the moral. The lawyer's reply to Jesus' question reiterates the teaching of the parable.

3. Martha and Mary (10:38-42)

38-40. Another travel reference introduces the incident. The **village** is unnamed. The author of the Gospel of John declares that **Martha** and **Mary** were residents of

---

return. The good Samaritan is not trying to do his duty. The point is that he is not aware of *duty* at all—any more than we are aware of duty when we act generously toward ourselves. We act so toward ourselves because we want to; so the Samaritan acts toward the stranger. He loves his neighbor as he loves himself.

38-42. *Distracted with Much Serving.*—This story of Martha and Mary, one of the most exquisite in the Gospels, is found only in Luke. One can no more than guess as to why it is given its particular location in the narrative. Is it because the writer or his source wished to caution against a conception of the Christian life which would make it consist alone in deeds of benevolence, like that of the good Samaritan? This has been suggested, but is at best doubtful. Still, a major point of the story is undoubtedly that service of others is not enough; indeed, that it is possible to be **distracted with much serving.** It is possible to lose one's soul in a program of highly useful activity. Our service to others must be in a relation of constant alternation or rhythm with our sitting at the Lord's feet and listening to **his word.** This must be true not only if we are to save our souls, but also if our service itself is to be really helpful. Martha in the story is **distracted;** but it is also true that she is not giving really effective service. She is **anxious and troubled about many things** —many things that really do not matter to her guests. She is busy preparing an elaborate meal

39 And she had a sister called Mary, which also sat at Jesus' feet, and heard his word.

40 But Martha was cumbered about much serving, and came to him, and said, Lord, dost thou not care that my sister hath left me to serve alone? bid her therefore that she help me.

Martha received him into her house. **39** And
she had a sister called Mary, who sat at the Lord's feet and listened to his teaching.
40 But Martha was distracted with much serving; and she went to him and said, "Lord, do you not care that my sister has left me to serve alone? Tell her then to

---

Bethany (John 11:1; 12:1-3), and identifies the woman of Bethany who anointed Jesus shortly before his arrest (Mark 14:3) with the **Mary** of our story (John 12:3). Luke knew nothing of all this. While **Mary** gave her "undivided attention to the Lord" (I Cor. 7:35), Martha, the mistress of the **house,** was **distracted with much serving** (cf. Paul's complaint that a "married woman is anxious about worldly affairs" [I Cor. 7:34]).

—many dishes—when only a few are needed; really one would be ample (see Exeg. for variations in the MS reading here). She is thus wasting much of her time. And she is thus wasteful because she has lost the perspective in which all her activities must be viewed. Having at least for the moment lost the **word** of Christ, she has lost the true reason for her work; and the work itself, in ceasing thus to be significant and satisfying to her, ceases also to be either efficient or creative. For only **one thing** is ultimately needful, and other things are valuable only because that one thing is so important. That **one thing** is the **word** of the Lord. For man is really much more in need of finding meaning in life than he is of life itself (see also on 9:24). Indeed, men's frantic, nervous search for **many things** and their attempts to enjoy various novelties and luxuries are efforts to make up for or to hide the lack of the **one thing** which they really need and want.

38-42. ***Words of Life.***—The point just made is susceptible of a wide social application. Building an economic order in which every man shall have a fair share is one of the most important aims we can have, but it is not the only important thing in the world, or even ultimately the most important. Perhaps we can say that there are two most important things: one is seeing to it that every man has the fullest possible chance at life; the other is seeing, and enabling others to see, that life is supremely worth having a chance at. One is bare existence itself, the other, knowing the meaning or the meanings which alone make existence worth either having or giving up—and sometimes the only way to have life is to give it up. "Man shall not live by bread alone, but by every word that proceeds from the mouth of God" (Matt. 4:4). That has always been true—ever since the moment in our planet's history when, under God's creative hand, man took his first decisive step away from the beast. At that moment he began to live not by bread alone, as he had done theretofore, but by "words" also. That was what made him a man. And ever since there have been some benefactors who have given him bread and others who have given him words; and can there be any doubt as to which sort of beneficence is ultimately the more important? Without bread one cannot live; but without the words which give meaning to life, why should one desire to live? It is one who understood this very well, the author of the Fourth Gospel, who tells us that on one occasion when Jesus, after watching the multitude depart disappointed and angry because they had asked for bread and he had none to give, turned to his disciples with the question, "Will you also go away?" Their answer was, "Lord, to whom shall we go? You have the words of eternal life" (John 6:66 ff.).

38-42. ***The Good Portion.***—The quotation from John in the preceding paragraph will have reminded us that it is not only values beyond bread that are needed to give meaning to our life, but values beyond life itself. It is not for lack of *men's* words that we die—men's words are often confusing and darkening, not *words* at all in the true, high sense of the term—but for lack of God's imperious **word** which alone can really rule our hearts and set us free. We are what we belong to. What we need, what we cry for, is something worthy and able to possess us—really possess us, i.e., possess our hearts. Unless there is God, overarching and undergirding man's life, creating good, destroying evil, working out his purpose, our human life is an unspeakably pathetic thing, and the so-called achievements of art, science, and thought, as well as of social and economic planning, merely serve to accentuate its futility. Humanists sometimes talk as though faith in God functions as a substitute for concern for man, and has the effect of turning men's attention away from the social tasks confronting their generation. They

41 And Jesus answered and said unto
her, Martha, Martha, thou art careful and
troubled about many things:

42 But one thing is needful; and Mary
hath chosen that good part, which shall not
be taken away from her.

11 And it came to pass, that, as he was
praying in a certain place, when he
ceased, one of his disciples said unto him,
Lord, teach us to pray, as John also taught
his disciples.

help me." 41 But the Lord answered her,
"Martha, Martha, you are anxious and
troubled about many things; 42 one thing
is needful.[o] Mary has chosen the good por-
tion, which shall not be taken away from
her."

11 He was praying in a certain place,
and when he ceased, one of his dis-
ciples said to him, "Lord, teach us to pray,

[o] Other ancient authorities read *few things are needful, or only one.*

41-42. A saying that has been variously transmitted and that is open to a number of interpretations. (*a*) Representatives of the Western text omit all that is in the KJV and RSV between **Martha, Martha** and **Mary.** Moffatt adopts this reading. Martha's request is denied. It is more important to attend to Jesus' teaching than to be concerned for matters of food and drink (cf. 12:29-31). (*b*) The KJV translates a text that is supported by the bulk of the MSS and that tempers Jesus' rebuke. **But one thing is needful,** i.e., concern for the spiritual life. (*c*) The RSV translates the same text as the KJV, apparently because it is now known to have the support of the Chester Beatty Gospel Papyrus (p^{45}), but gives it a different interpretation: Martha had planned too lavish an entertainment. Simple hospitality would have sufficed—**one thing** only **is needful.** (*d*) The Syriac Peshitta and a few allies read: "Few things are needful." (*e*) Codices Sinaiticus and Vaticanus read: "Few things are needful, or only one" (RSV mg.; cf. Goodspeed)—apparently a combination of the readings discussed under (*c*) and (*d*).

D. Teaching on Prayer (11:1-13)

1. The Lord's Prayer (11:1-4=Matt. 6:9*b*-13)

The RSV translates the short text of Codex Vaticanus and its allies. The additional phrases that appear in the KJV have decidedly inferior MS support and are almost certainly to be taken as interpolations from Matthew by a scribe bent on harmonizing both versions. Matthew's longer form appears to be a liturgical expansion of Luke's, and is the one that came into common use in the church.

11:1-2*a*. Editorial introduction. Rabbinical teachers often formulated short prayers for the use of their followers. Luke tells us that the Lord's Prayer was the pattern Jesus

---

are at this point poor readers of the human heart or of human history. From the savage kneeling to wood and stone to Gamaliel Bradford, who tells us that

> . . . my one unchanged obsession, wheresoe'er my feet have trod
> Is a keen, enormous, haunting, never-sated thirst for God—[4]

in both cases and in all the cases between, the search for God is really a search for that which alone will justify either living oneself or helping others to live—the ultimate and transcendent meaning of human existence. It was Mary who chose **the good portion.**

This divine meaning of our existence is not far to seek, transcendent and ultimate though it is. It was present and accessible in Martha's humble home. Finding God is not finding a Reality strange and new; it is recognizing and responding to Someone whom we have always known, although perhaps we knew it not. It is answering "Yes" to a Voice one has often heard, but to which heretofore one may not have been willing or prepared to listen. But that Voice, though it speaks in our hearts, is not our voice. It comes from heights and depths we cannot scale or fathom. And the words the Voice speaks are not ours. They are the words of the One who is as far as he is near, in whom alone our partial, thwarted lives have meaning and wholeness, and for whose sake alone even the least of these little ones has infinite worth.

11:1. *Discipline in Prayer.*—No attempt will be made to discuss adequately the Lord's Prayer. The prayer in fuller form is found in Matt.

[4] "God." From *Shadow Verses* (New Haven: Yale University Press, 1920). Used by permission.

2 And he said unto them, When ye pray, say, Our Father which art in heaven, Hallowed be thy name. Thy kingdom come. Thy will be done, as in heaven, so in earth.

as John taught his disciples." 2 And he said to them, "When you pray, say:
"Father, hallowed be thy name. Thy

---

gave when **one of his disciples** asked him to imitate John the Baptist's example. Matthew locates his version in the Sermon on the Mount, where it follows a warning against ostentatious practice and verbose forms of prayer.

2*b*. Father as an address to deity was not original with Jesus. The O.T. and later Jewish literature refer to God as **Father** of the people Israel, and occasionally also as **Father** of the individual Israelite (Ecclus. 23:1, 4; 51:10; Wisd. Sol. 2:16; 14:3). But

---

6:9-13, and the reader is referred there for a more complete exposition. But there are a few features of the Lukan account which call for consideration here. For one thing, Luke tells us what was the original occasion for the giving of the prayer (Matthew simply records its text along with some teachings about prayer). We are told that Jesus gave the prayer in response to a specific request of one of his disciples, **Teach us to pray.** This request was prompted apparently, first, by the example of Jesus—the disciples recognized how much prayer meant to Jesus and wanted to know this meaning too (**He was praying in a certain place, and when he ceased, one of his disciples said to him . . .**); and second, by the example of John the Baptist in giving, as rabbis often did, a prayer to be said by his own disciples. They say, **Teach us to pray,** meaning apparently, "Teach us a prayer"; and Jesus gives them a very great and beautiful one. But of course learning to pray is much more than learning a prayer; and Luke may be intending to indicate his awareness of this fact by placing certain teachings of Jesus *about* prayer just after the text of the prayer itself. We are given very few glimpses of what the content of Jesus' own prayers may have been—in the nature of the case this would be true—but we are not left in doubt about the reality and importance of prayer to him. The few glimpses we have are enough to show that what prayer *may* mean to us it meant to him, only much more: the bringing to God of our deepest needs and most perplexing problems, and a waiting there for light and strength from him; the effective recognition that adequate living depends not so much upon what we do as upon what we permit God to do in us and through us; the conscious, purposeful act of letting God have his way with us, of yielding ourselves to him and his will for us. To be sure, Jesus brought his wants to God, but not as demands on God; rather he brought them to God in order that God might bring *them* into harmony with his own purpose: "Nevertheless not my will, but thine, be done." The consequence was a strength and peace which the world could not give. It was because prayer did not have this character and effect for Jesus' disciples that they asked, **Teach us to pray;** and many of Jesus' teachings bear directly on this theme. Paul tells us that the Spirit of Christ continues to teach us "how to pray" (Rom. 8:26).

We cannot learn to pray simply by learning the words of a prayer, but the repetition of such words may be part of this discipline. Certainly it is true that effective prayer is in a real sense an art—and to learn an art always requires careful method and persistent practice. Definite forms of prayer may be a very useful part of that method and practice; surely this prayer of Jesus will be such. The prayer is manifestly adapted to be said by a group (the first personal pronoun is always plural), and it is possible that the request of the disciples was for help in group prayer. In such prayer the use of some common form is almost indispensable. Whether we belong to "liturgical" or "nonliturgical" churches, all will acknowledge the contribution the Lord's Prayer has made to the common worship of Christendom, and incidentally to the discovery and maintenance of its unity.

2. *Father.*—With this one word the prayer begins in Luke; in Matthew we have the familiar longer form, "Our Father who art in heaven." There can be little doubt, as the Exeg. says, that Luke's form is the more primitive. Although Matthew's phrase is liturgically more appropriate and effective, and although it does no violence whatever to Jesus' meaning, still there is value in remembering that the original address was simply **Father.** We know from many passages in Matthew and Mark, as well as in Luke, that it was thus that Jesus himself addressed God (e.g., 23:34; Matt. 11:25-26; Mark 14:36).

The use of the same address here, therefore, has the effect of making the prayer more personal: Jesus is inviting his followers to share in his own prayer life; he is assuming that they

3 Give us day by day our daily bread.
4 And forgive us our sins; for we also forgive every one that is indebted to us.

kingdom come. 3 Give us each day our
daily bread;[p] 4 and forgive us our sins, for
we ourselves forgive every one who is in-

[p] Or *our bread for the morrow.*

Jesus' use of the name was characteristic of his thought of God, as it had not been of any of his predecessors. "What is significant is that he selected just this aspect of Jewish faith for his major emphasis" (Millar Burrows, *An Outline of Biblical Theology* [Philadelphia: Westminster Press, 1946], p. 73). In Semitic usage **name** was closely associated with "person" or "being." The **name** of God meant practically God himself. **Hallowed be thy name:** "May the time come when the holiness of God's being will be universally acknowledged." The first petition is therefore almost the equivalent of the second, **Thy kingdom come;** and both are eschatological—i.e., concerned with God and his activities in the "last days." There is some support in minuscule MSS and in the fathers for an alternative to the second petition: "Thy holy spirit come upon us and cleanse us." Some have maintained that this is the original Lukan reading. More probably it is an early paraphrase that transformed an eschatological petition into one that was related to the immediate needs of the believing community (cf. the three petitions that follow).

3. **Each day** instead of Matthew's "this day," demanded by Luke's choice of an imperative form that literally means "continually give us." The meaning of the adjective translated **daily** remains an exegetical puzzle, and any rendering is little more than a guess. The word ἐπιούσιον occurs in Christian literature only here, in Matt. 6:11, and Did. 8:2. It has been found once in extant pagan literature, but in a context that casts no light on its meaning. The early translations reflect the uncertainty. Old Syriac: "lasting"; the Peshitta: "for our needs"; Vulg. (of Matthew): "supersubstantial." Origen urged the translation "necessary for existence," and many modern scholars prefer that represented by the RSV mg.: **for the morrow.**

4. Luke's use of **every one who is indebted to us** makes it probable that **sins** is an interpretation—but a correct one—of "debts" (Matthew). Luke has probably generalized

will approach God just as he himself does. Christians have always been unable to think of Christ's relationship to God as being of the same kind as their own—which may be part of the explanation of the substitution of "Our Father who art in heaven" for **Father.** So in the Fourth Gospel Jesus makes a distinction, speaking of "ascending to my Father and your Father, to my God and your God" (John 20:17). We can understand this feeling and undoubtedly share it; would we not find it intolerable that John should have written in the verse just cited "our Father"? But even so, it is good to know that Jesus himself, whatever thoughts he may have had about his nature and mission, thinks of his disciples as saying **Father** as appropriately, as inevitably, as he says it himself. The Epistle to the Hebrews makes very moving use of the idea that Jesus shared not only our flesh but also our human approach to God (see Heb. 2:10-13; 5:7-8). His *religious* life was a *human* religious life. Only so could God through him bring "many sons to glory" (cf. Rom. 8:29, "first-born among many brethren"). When we see things so, we are able to recognize this prayer as being the "Lord's Prayer" in a new and more intimately personal sense: it is not only the prayer which Jesus gave his disciples, it is also his own prayer. This is the way *he* prayed. Paul lets us know (Rom. 8:15; Gal. 4:6) that much later it was the spontaneous cry of **Father** in the heart of the believer which bore witness to the presence of the Spirit of Christ. The one who in the days of his flesh taught his followers to say **Father,** now in the Spirit prompts that cry in their hearts and in the hearts of thousands who never heard his voice (see also I Pet. 1:17).

2-3. See on Matt. 6:9-11.

4a. Forgiveness.—This is one of many recorded teachings of Jesus in which God's forgiveness of us is described as contingent upon our forgiveness of others (cf. 6:37; Matt. 6:12, 14-15; 18:32-35). The teaching, at first sight at least, raises difficulties: it seems to make God's forgiveness not a free act of grace (as forgiveness must always be), but a reward for a virtue on our own part. Various efforts are made to mitigate the difficulty. Montefiore writes: "The γάρ ('for') is rather awkward. The meaning is not: 'Forgive us *because* we have forgiven.' But rather: we may ask you to forgive us, for we

And lead us not into temptation; but de-
liver us from evil.
5 And he said unto them, Which of you
shall have a friend, and shall go unto him

debted to us; and lead us not into tempta-
tion."
5 And he said to them, "Which of you

Matthew's "as we also have forgiven our debtors." The thought that we can expect God's forgiveness only as we ourselves show a forgiving spirit is a familiar emphasis in Jesus' teaching. The most interesting parallel that has been cited in Jewish literature is in Ecclus. 28:2 (Goodspeed):

> Forgive your neighbor his wrongdoing;
> Then your sins will be forgiven when you pray.

Temptation is an ambiguous term. It might mean "trial," i.e., suffering or persecution. More probably, "a situation in which one is exposed to the seductions of sin." Some of the early fathers felt that this fifth petition reflected on God's providence, and interpreted it to mean: "Do not allow us to fall into temptation"—a gloss that found its way into a few O.L. MSS.

2. Parable of the Importunate Friend (11:5-8)

An illustration with a quaint touch of humor (cf. the parable of the widow and the judge [18:1-8]). In both instances it must be remembered that a parable is a story intended to teach only one truth. The details are incidental. God is not compared to an unwilling neighbor or an unjust judge, nor is his answer to prayer attributed to selfish motives. The importance of persistence in prayer is the only moral, and the argument is indirect: If perseverance achieves its end in everyday human relationships, how much more in our relationships with God!

5-6. Journeys were often made at night to avoid travel in the heat.

have forgiven others. We have fulfilled the needful condition."[5] Manson explains: "The clause 'for we forgive, etc.,' states not the ground on which God bestows forgiveness but the ground on which men can receive it."[6] The heart of the matter, however, is the recognition of the close and intimate relationship of forgiveness with *repentance*. We are accustomed to the idea that forgiveness depends upon repentance (i.e., forgiveness can be *received* only by the penitent), but one is in no danger of thinking of repentance as the *price* of forgiveness, or of forgiveness as the *reward* of repentance. We recognize that repentance is the necessary condition because there can be no forgiveness except on the basis of truth; and repentance is essentially the realization of truth. It is facing up to the moral facts. It is, then, indispensable to forgiveness, not for any arbitrary reason, but in the nature of the case. We recognize also that repentance and forgiveness are the two sides of a single shield. If forgiveness depends upon repentance, it is true also that repentance depends upon forgiveness, i.e., it is the knowledge that Another is willing to forgive us that makes repentance (as distinguished from mere regret or remorse) possible. But the experience of repenting, besides involving, almost as a part of itself, the experience of being forgiven, involves also the forgiving of others, for one cannot repent of one's own sins against God without being at the same time forgiving toward one's neighbor. If we do not forgive others, it is clear that we have not been brought to that realization of our own sinfulness which in the nature of the case must precede and accompany God's forgiving act. It was pointed out in connection with 10:25-28 that love has three dimensions; the same insight of Jesus is being expressed here. Forgiveness works in three directions: God toward us (a willingness to forgive); we toward God (realization and acceptance); we toward others, or rather God toward others through us (forgiveness). It is one organic process—not to be reduced to terms of mathematical relationships or equivalences or of causal sequences. To forgive and to be forgiven belong inseparably together.

4b. See on Matt. 6:13.

5-8. ***Struggle in Prayer.***—Here is one of a number of stories told by Jesus which came to the gospel writer apparently without any con-

[5] *Synoptic Gospels,* II, 473.
[6] *Gospel of Luke,* p. 135.

at midnight, and say unto him, Friend,
lend me three loaves;
6 For a friend of mine in his journey is
come to me, and I have nothing to set be-
fore him?
7 And he from within shall answer and
say, Trouble me not: the door is now shut,
and my children are with me in bed; I
cannot rise and give thee.
8 I say unto you, Though he will not
rise and give him, because he is his friend,
yet because of his importunity he will rise
and give him as many as he needeth.
9 And I say unto you, Ask, and it shall
be given you; seek, and ye shall find; knock,
and it shall be opened unto you.

who has a friend will go to him at mid-
night and say to him, 'Friend, lend me
three loaves; 6 for a friend of mine has
arrived on a journey, and I have nothing
to set before him'; 7 and he will answer
from within, 'Do not bother me; the door
is now shut, and my children are with me
in bed; I cannot get up and give you any-
thing'? 8 I tell you, though he will not
get up and give him anything because he is
his friend, yet because of his importunity
he will rise and give him whatever he needs.
9 And I tell you, Ask, and it will be given
you; seek, and you will find; knock, and

7-8. Importunity implies repeated requests. The Vulg. prefixes to vs. 8: "But if he keeps on knocking."

3. Assurance That Prayer Will Be Answered (11:9-13=Matt. 7:7-11)

9-10. Ask, seek, and **knock** are three metaphors for petitionary prayer. The passive form in late Jewish literature is often used to avoid direct reference to God (cf. 6:37-38, and contrast Jas. 1:5). Jesus' assertion that prayer will be answered is absolute and

---

text to indicate Jesus' purpose in telling it. The immediate point of the story in and of itself would seem to be that even an unneighborly neighbor (contrast the good Samaritan) will do a neighborly act if he is made sufficiently uncomfortable otherwise. Under the same condition also the unrighteous judge (18:1-8), who neither fears God nor regards man, will give justice to the poor widow. In the case of the unrighteous judge it is said that Jesus told the parable "to the effect that they ought always to pray and not to lose heart," and it is possible that Jesus told both of these stories to encourage prayer. Luke shows that he thinks of the present parable as having that intention by placing it just before the exhortation, "Ask, and it will be given you . . . ," which has a quite different context in Matthew and probably did in Luke's source also. But although these parables may well have been told to encourage our forming the habit of prayer, it is by no means clear that they were told to enforce **importunity** in prayer, if by that word is meant a kind of urgent, almost strident, demand on God, a beating on the doors of heaven. It may just as well be true, or better, that the stories were told to discourage that kind of persistence—as though Jesus would say of it: "Such importunity is needed when a neighbor is inconsiderate or a judge is unjust; surely you do not need to approach God in that way. To be sure, the Gentiles think that they will be heard for their many words; but you are not to be like them, for your Father knows what you need before you ask him" (Matt. 6:7-8). If that was the original intention of the parable, then vss. 9-10, if interpreted accordingly, mean not "ask importunately," but "ask trustfully."

Not that there is no occasion and need for agony in prayer. The experience of praying can often be an experience of desperate struggle—like Jacob's wrestling with the angel. When Jesus prayed all night, as apparently he often did, we can be sure he was not simply and quietly waiting before God. One has only to remember Gethsemane to know this (cf. also Heb. 5:7). Yet the struggle is not with God, but with ourselves. We speak many words, or the same words over and over again, not because they are needed to persuade God (God does not hear our words as such), but because we are seeking to overcome our own pride, selfishness, or indifference. We agonize to get free of the bondage to our own wills which keeps us from really praying. The struggle in prayer, then, is not our struggle with God, but God's struggle with us. It is his hand that will not let us go (cf. Rom. 8:26).

9-13. ***Petitionary Prayer.***—This passage, which has a different context in Matthew, is here used to point up the teaching of the parable of the importunate friend (vss. 5-8). Plummer[7] sees in Luke's preface to the teaching,

[7] *Commentary on Luke, ad loc.*

10 For every one that asketh receiveth; and he that seeketh findeth; and to him that knocketh it shall be opened.

11 If a son shall ask bread of any of you that is a father, will he give him a stone? or if *he ask* a fish, will he for a fish give him a serpent?

12 Or if he shall ask an egg, will he offer him a scorpion?

13 If ye then, being evil, know how to give good gifts unto your children; how much more shall *your* heavenly Father give the Holy Spirit to them that ask him?

it will be opened to you.
10 For every one
who asks receives, and he who seeks finds,
and to him who knocks it will be opened.
11 What father among you, if his son asks
for[q] a fish, will instead of a fish give him a
serpent;
12 or if he asks for an egg, will
give him a scorpion?
13 If you then, who
are evil, know how to give good gifts to
your children, how much more will the
heavenly Father give the Holy Spirit to
those who ask him?"

[q] Other ancient authorities insert *a loaf, will give him a stone; or if he asks for.*

---

unqualified. "Ifs" and "buts" are left to the commentators! In this instance the interpreter can justify a theological reservation by reference to Jesus' own example: "Father, if thou art willing, remove this cup from me; nevertheless not my will, but thine, be done" (22:42). True petitionary prayer is an act of exploration. It seeks to discover God's will and to submit to it. But there is no suggestion of any such qualification in these verses.

11-13. The grounds for Jesus' confidence in the efficacy of prayer: If we can trust our human fathers, how much more our **heavenly Father!** The correlatives in Matthew are bread and stone, fish and serpent. In the best text of Luke (Codex Vaticanus and its allies) they are **fish** and **serpent, egg** and **scorpion.** Vs. 13 has sometimes been used as a proof text in support of the doctrine of original sin. But Jesus' argument is from the goodness in men to the perfect goodness of God. **The Holy Spirit** has probably been substituted for "good things" (Matt. 7:11).

And I tell you (the emphasis falls upon the personal pronoun [κἀγώ]), the evangelist's way of indicating this connection with what precedes, the meaning being: "The parable has said this to you and *I* also say to you. . . ." **Ask, seek, knock** are all *present* imperatives, the tense of continuing action, so that the meaning is "Continually ask," or "Keep on seeking and knocking"; this suits the sense usually found in the parable, "Ask importunately," but the meaning may just as easily be "Ask habitually and faithfully; do not be afraid to ask and do not be discouraged from asking." The main point in this passage is not that we will get whatever we ask for (although that seems to be said and must be commented on), but that we are not in the position of having to plead with God, as with a hostile judge or an indifferent neighbor, when we ask for what we need, whether it is bread or justice. God does not do for us, because we "importune" him, what he is not ready and eager to do for us in response to a simple request. In other words, God is *not* like the unneighborly neighbor or the unjust judge; he *is* like the loving father, only infinitely more loving. We can trust his goodness and do not need to "bother" or "tease" him into hearing or granting our requests.

To see that this is the major point of the teaching helps to place the real problem presented by these verses in true perspective. The problem can be stated in some such way as this: Jesus seems to be asserting without qualification that every request we make of God will be granted. But can he mean this? If so, we should have to say that he was mistaken. But allowing that he could have been mistaken at all, is it likely that he would have been mistaken on so obvious a point? Do we not know indeed that he himself made a request that was not granted? (Mark 14:36.) So the argument goes. But this approach is wrong: we do not have the right to press Jesus' teachings in this way. Jesus' mind was in more than one respect the mind of a poet. Now poets rarely qualify their statements. The poet sees a truth about life and affirms it simply and boldly. But few if any truths stand alone; no truth is the whole truth. And when we move from the realm of insight into the realm of action, we must confront truth with truth and hope to attain to wisdom. A little later we shall have occasion to observe the fact that Jesus was not interested in questions of moral casuistry (see on 12:13-21); he is just as little interested in what have been called the "scruples of theology." Montefiore writes:[8] "In the full magnificence and simplicity of his faith,

[8] *Synoptic Gospels,* II, 119.

14 ¶ And he was casting out a devil, and it was dumb. And it came to pass, when the devil was gone out, the dumb spake; and the people wondered.

15 But some of them said, He casteth out devils through Beelzebub the chief of the devils.

14 Now he was casting out a demon that was dumb; when the demon had gone out, the dumb man spoke, and the people
marveled. 15 But some of them said, "He
casts out demons by Be-el'ze-bul, the

E. Concerning the Exorcism of Demons (11:14-28)

1. Beelzebub Controversy (11:14-23=Matt. 9:32-34; 12:22-30)

Mark also contains the charge that Jesus' power of exorcism was due to collusion with Beelzebub (Mark 3:22-30). Matthew makes Mark's story basic to his account, amplifying it with Q materials. Luke omits the Marcan narrative at the point at which he would normally have included it (after 6:16), and now makes a place for the Q version.

14. The occasion of the calumny: an exorcism performed by Jesus.

15. The charge that a man was in league with the forces of evil was an exceedingly dangerous one in a superstitious age. In Mark it was made by "scribes" and in Matthew by "the Pharisees." Luke's indefinite **some of them** probably represents the reading in Q. The name that was given to **the prince of demons**—i.e., to Satan (vs. 18)—has been variously preserved. Codices Vaticanus and Sinaiticus: "Beezebul"; the Chester Beatty Gospel Papyrus (p^{45}), codices Ephraemi Rescriptus, Bezae, and others: **Beelzebul** (RSV); and the Latin and Syraic versions: **Beelzebub. Beelzebub** is derived from the Hebrew text of II Kings 1:2-3, where Baalzebub ("lord of flies") is a contemptuous perversion of Baalzebul ("lord of the temple"), the name of the god of Ekron. But **Beelzebul** in Aramaic was open to the derogatory interpretation "lord of dung." None of the forms has been found in Jewish literature as a name for Satan.

Jesus declares that every prayer will be answered. The case of a man asking for follies or absurdities or evils is not considered or thought of"—exactly! In the same way every magnificent generalization leaves something out of account. That does not mean the generalization is not true; but it is true as a great poem is true. It says one true thing; other things are true too, but they will be said in other poems or by other poets. The one true thing this "poem" would say is that God cares for us, that he listens to our prayers, that he rejoices to give us what we need.

If someone had challenged Jesus and, subjecting his "poem" to analysis, had asked him to discuss the "ifs" and "buts" to which the Exeg. refers, we cannot know what Jesus' reply would have been. Perhaps he would have responded with the same impatience he shows in 12:14. But surely it is clear that Jesus would never have said, "What father among you, if his son asks for a serpent, will he not give it to him?"

If you then, who are evil: Cf. "No one is good but God alone" (18:19).

Luke's substitution of **the Holy Spirit** (see Exeg.) is almost certainly aimed at mitigating the difficulty discussed above. God may not give us all "the good things" we happen to ask for, but he is always ready to give us his best gift—the gift of himself, the Holy Spirit. And incidentally this is the one gift he cannot give without our asking. A father can give his children the *things* they need, even though they never ask or even know; but he cannot give himself, i.e., his love, except to those who are ready and eager to receive it.

14-19. ***The Sign from Heaven.***—The Exeg. on vs. 16 points out the significance which Luke sees in this Beelzebub controversy. Jesus has just healed a dumb man—an act of power and goodness at which **the people marveled.** Note that in 7:18-23 (see comment there), when John the Baptist sends to Jesus to inquire whether he is "he who is to come," Jesus points to just such happenings as this healing as proof that the new age is on the point of arriving: "Go and tell John," he says to the messengers, "what you have seen and heard: the blind receive their sight, the lame walk, etc." As though he knew, however, that such facts would fail to convince everybody, he added, "And blessed is he who takes no offense at me." And now in the present passage we have a concrete instance of this failure. **The demon** has **gone out**—but not all who witness the healing know that "the kingdom of God has come upon [them]."

16 And others, tempting *him,* sought of him a sign from heaven.

17 But he, knowing their thoughts, said unto them, Every kingdom divided against itself is brought to desolation; and a house *divided* against a house falleth.

18 If Satan also be divided against himself, how shall his kingdom stand? because ye say that I cast out devils through Beelzebub.

prince of demons"; 16 while others, to test
him, sought from him a sign from heaven.
17 But he, knowing their thoughts, said
to them, "Every kingdom divided against
itself is laid waste, and house falls upon
house. 18 And if Satan also is divided
against himself, how will his kingdom
stand? For you say that I cast out demons

16. The Matthaean equivalent (Matt. 12:38) is more appropriately located as an introduction to the material parallel to vss. 29-32. If Luke's order is secondary, the transposition was deliberate. The evangelist believes that Jesus' healing miracles, properly understood (vs. 20), are in themselves an answer to the demand for **a sign from heaven.**

17. In the Marcan and Matthaean versions "house" means "household," and Jesus makes two parallel statements. The KJV interprets Luke's text similarly but the RSV translates the Greek text as it stands: **house falls upon house.** Luke understands **house** literally and the clause illustrates the content of the verb **laid waste.**

18. The charge is absurd. **Satan** would not undermine his own **kingdom** by giving Jesus authority over demonic powers.

Those who do not recognize "the finger of God" are apparently of two sorts (vss. 15-16): the prejudiced or cynical, and the insensitive or blind. The latter, having just looked at **a sign,** now ask for one. They are blind to the significance of what has happened. They want **a sign from heaven**—presumably something more spectacular than an act of healing. Casting out demons is nothing extraordinary—do not our **sons cast them out?** They may not be "offended" in Jesus (7:23); but they are unimpressed. **Heaven** has drawn near as healing and emancipating love; but they are incapable of seeing **heaven** near at hand. They can recognize it only in some manifestation of overwhelming power.

But not all who rejected Jesus did so because of failure to see **the sign;** some did so because they misinterpreted it: **He casts out demons by Beelzebul, the prince of demons.** They are aware of the extraordinary character of what is happening, but put the worst possible construction on it. Those in the one group are blind to the divine significance of healing and emancipating love; those in the other group deny its existence. Indeed, they go so far as to ascribe Jesus' actions to the promptings and the power of evil. It is to this group particularly that the teachings of vss. 17-22 are addressed. Jesus is pointing to the absurdity of supposing that evil casts out evil, to the essential and irreconcilable opposition between good and evil, and to the significance of his acts as betokening the final defeat of evil and the coming of God's reign (vss. 20-22).

Both groups are still with us, although we no longer talk about demoniacs and Beelzebub and signs from heaven. We too have our cynics who *will* not recognize manifestations of divine goodness in human life because they know in advance that there is no real goodness, i.e., except in themselves. For it is probably true that when we call "evil" everything outside ourselves, we show that whatever our theory on the point, we really regard ourselves as being good. How otherwise could we identify the evil? For this reason a certain moral pride or snobbishness, whether recognized or not, always goes along with cynicism. Jesus clearly has no doubt in his mind—nor do we—as to how his opponents would answer the question in vs. 19*a*: "By whom do your sons cast them out?" They will certainly not make in regard to themselves or their sons the judgment they have made concerning him. One ought to be exceedingly ready and quick to see the evil in oneself, and exceedingly ready and quick to see the goodness in others. As a matter of fact, it might be argued that we can really see goodness only in others (it turns into evil when we observe it in ourselves) and that we can really see evil (in all its range and depth) only in ourselves. These cynical critics of Jesus, perhaps because they are incapable of seeing the evil in themselves, are not able to recognize the divine goodness which so powerfully manifests itself in Jesus.

But the dull of heart are also still with us—those who seek **a sign from heaven** because they have not seen the signs of heaven within

19 And if I by Beelzebub cast out devils, by whom do your sons cast *them* out? therefore shall they be your judges.
20 But if I with the finger of God cast out devils, no doubt the kingdom of God is come upon you.

by Be-el′ze-bul. 19 And if I cast out demons by Be-el′ze-bul, by whom do your sons cast them out? Therefore they shall be your judges. 20 But if it is by the finger of God that I cast out demons, then the king-

---

19. The charge could as easily be brought against **your sons**—i.e., Jewish exorcists (cf. Acts 19:13; Josephus *Antiquities* VIII. 2. 5)—and they should be asked to answer it. Because this verse has no counterpart in Mark, and because it partially invalidates the interpretation of his healing ministry that Jesus gives in vs. 20—he would hardly have adduced Jewish exorcisms as evidence that "the kingdom of God has come"!—some scholars believe it did not belong to the earliest form of the tradition.

20. The finger of God is an O.T. expression (Exod. 8:19; Deut. 9:10; etc.), and perhaps preferable to Matthew's "the Spirit of God." Jesus declares that his power over **demons** comes from **God** and that it is evidence that the new age of God's rule has already begun (cf. 10:18). According to Jesus' teaching, the full manifestation of the **kingdom of God** belongs to the future. It will be introduced suddenly and catastrophically as the climax of the "last days." But in some measure it is already in being. Jesus himself is the vehicle of divine power already at work among men: **the kingdom of God has come upon you.**

---

our earthly life. One of the most dangerous heresies and one of the widest spread has always been that which puts God far off and makes religion a queer, abnormal thing. Religion at its best is but a natural response to the deepest implications of our common life. Worship is not a strange variety of excitement which takes one momentarily out of the world; it is sensitiveness to the profounder, subtler meanings *of* the world. It is appreciation raised to its highest power; it is man's answer to the mystery and beauty which overwhelms, but overbroods, the whole scene of his life. It is the inevitable result of going deeply into the significance of any experience. Edna St. Vincent Millay wrote:

> God, I can push the grass apart
> And lay my finger on Thy heart.[9]

One does not need to live abnormally to find God or see strange signs to know that he is near; one has only to live deeply and sensitively and in Christ's presence. God is near us in every manifestation of light and love and beauty. He has made himself known in his supremely authentic character in Jesus Christ, and in that character, within the Christian community, he confronts us in our sin and consoles us in our contrition. He is by our side whenever we do battle for justice and truth. We do not need **a sign;** we need to be able to recognize the many signs we have.

[9] From *Renascence*. Copyright, 1912, 1940, by Edna St. Vincent Millay. Used by permission.

20-22. *The Kingdom of God Has Come.*—Moffatt renders the closing clause in vs. 20, "The Reign of God has reached you already," and Goodspeed, "The kingdom of God has overtaken you." Those who insist that Jesus thought of the kingdom not as a future order, but as a present reality, lay a great deal of stress upon this passage.[1] The truth of the matter almost certainly is, however (as the Exeg. points out), that while the kingdom for Jesus is already in a real sense manifesting its nearness and its power, it nevertheless lies essentially in the future. The kingdom of God is a hope—but a hope that is not a hope only, because even now in Jesus' life and work it is beginning to be fulfilled. The kingdom is future in the sense in which the day is future when one sees the first red streaks of dawn; but in that moment the day can just as easily and truly be regarded as already present. Jesus can speak of the kingdom in both tenses; the same ambiguity can even more often be observed in Paul. In the present passage the contrast—and the likeness—is between **the finger of God** and **the kingdom of God.** In the new event of which Jesus' life is the center, only the **finger of God** is manifest; but it is the finger of *God* and is a sure promise of the early disclosure of his full power and reign, i.e., his **kingdom.** Matthew's parallel (12:28) has "Spirit [instead of **finger**] of God"; and it is worth noting that in Paul and elsewhere in the N.T. the Spirit is in the same way a token of the coming age, the "ear-

[1] C. H. Dodd, *The Parables of the Kingdom* (New York: Charles Scribner's Sons, 1936), pp. 43-46.

21 When a strong man armed keepeth his palace, his goods are in peace:

22 But when a stronger than he shall come upon him, and overcome him, he taketh from him all his armor wherein he trusted, and divideth his spoils.

23 He that is not with me is against me; and he that gathereth not with me scattereth.

dom of God has come upon you. 21 When a
strong man, fully armed, guards his own
palace, his goods are in peace; 22 but when
one stronger than he assails him and overcomes him, he takes away his armor in
which he trusted, and divides his spoil.
23 He who is not with me is against me,
and he who does not gather with me scatters.

21-22. In Mark and in Matthew the "strong man" of this parable is a householder, and the situation contemplated is one of violent robbery. In Luke the **strong man** is a prince whose **palace** is captured by armed assault. In both forms the one point is that Satan is now impotent. Allegory not only identifies Jesus with the **one stronger than he,** but also Satan's human victims with **his goods** and **his spoils** and the demons with **his armor.**

23. The first clause is in apparent conflict with 9:50*b*, but not for that reason alone is it to be regarded as secondary. Jesus declares that the kingdom of God is set over against the kingdom of Satan, and that there is no place for neutrals in the conflict. The metaphors of 23*b* refer to the work of a herdsman rather than a harvester.

---

nest" or "advance installment" of our inheritance. Heaven has not yet come, and until it does, victory and peace cannot be secure nor joy complete; but the Spirit has been given, and this is a sure guarantee, an actual foretaste, of the final fulfillment. The church is the community of this Spirit, and therefore Paul can speak of it as "a colony of heaven" (Phil. 3:20 Moffatt). Paul expected the intervening period to be very short—Christ would quickly return, bringing the present age to an end, and those to whom in the midst of this alien world the Spirit had been given would be finally at home in the kingdom of the Spirit. We have no expectation of an early end of this world; but like them we have the lively hope that the kingdom of this world either must become, or must give place to, the kingdom of God. We too know that in Christ the triumph of God's kingdom was decisively won, however long in our short human perspective its actual coming may be delayed; and that in the Spirit and the church a foretaste of this victory is offered us. **The kingdom of God has come upon us.**

Vss. 21-22 simply reinforce with a parable the idea that in Christ the power of Satan has been broken. In the midst of an evil time, especially so long afterward, it may seem absurd to believe such a statement. From the point of view of ordinary wisdom it *is* absurd. But from *that* point of view it was just as absurd nineteen centuries ago. Yet the primitive Christians went forth with joy and were led forth with peace, the mountains and the hills breaking forth before them into singing (Isa. 55:12); they "subdued kingdoms, wrought righteousness, obtained promises, . . . out of weakness were made strong" (Heb. 11:33-34). The secret of their faith and hope (as it must be of ours also) was the present possession of the Spirit. The love of God already poured out in their hearts by the Holy Spirit already given (Rom. 5:5) made them sure and invincible. Their hope was not mere hope; it was hope that had already begun to be fulfilled. The **finger of God** was already at work; he would soon make "bare his holy arm in the eyes of all the nations; and all the ends of the earth [should] see the salvation of our God" (Isa. 52:10).

23. ***No Neutrality Toward Christ.***—The Exeg. calls attention to the "apparent conflict" between this verse and 9:50*b*, "He that is not against you is for you," at the same time pointing out that both passages are one in affirming that "there is no place for neutrals" in the struggle between God and Satan. As is there indicated, both statements may well be authentic (the same person, however responsible, often makes apparently contradictory statements at different times); and, it may also be said, both statements may well be quite true (so rich and complex is reality that two logically incompatible affirmations are often both true and indispensable). The most plausible explanation of the present "contradiction" is suggested by Montefiore:

> They are not necessarily inconsistent, nor is it quite impossible that, on different occasions, Jesus might have said both one and the other. Here [i.e., in 11:23], a test is given by which a man is to test himself. If he is not for Jesus, he is against him. Before [i.e., in 9:50*b*], a test was given by which

24 When the unclean spirit is gone out of a man, he walketh through dry places, seeking rest; and finding none, he saith, I will return unto my house whence I came out.

25 And when he cometh, he findeth *it* swept and garnished.

26 Then goeth he, and taketh *to him* seven other spirits more wicked than himself; and they enter in, and dwell there: and the last *state* of that man is worse than the first.

24 "When the unclean spirit has gone
out of a man, he passes through waterless
places seeking rest; and finding none he
says, 'I will return to my house from which
I came.' 25 And when he comes he finds it
swept and put in order. 26 Then he goes
and brings seven other spirits more evil
than himself, and they enter and dwell
there; and the last state of that man becomes worse than the first."

2. Parable of a Demoniac and His Relapse
(11:24-26=Matt. 12:43-45*a*)

Jesus describes the ways of evil spirits as they were understood in his day. It is possible that the passage is nothing more than a warning to demoniacs who have been cured to guard against the danger of relapse. More probably it is a parable. If such is the case, its original context is no longer recoverable. In Matthew it asserts that any response of the Jewish people to Jesus' message is only temporary. They are a "wicked generation" whose last state will be worse than their first. In Luke it declares that it is not enough for a man to be freed from the power of Satan; a new dynamic must replace the old tyranny. To express it in Paul's phraseology, the faithful must be the temple of God and the dwelling place of God's Spirit (I Cor. 3:16).

24-25. Waterless places: In popular belief wasteland was the dwelling place of a disembodied demon (cf. Tob. 8:3; Mark 5:10; Rev. 18:2). But the demon finds no **rest** except in a human body.

26. Seven other spirits will give him support, and make a second exorcism difficult or impossible.

the disciples are to try others: if they are not against Jesus, they are to be considered as for him. Some think that only the "tolerant" saying is authentic; others that only the exclusive one is so.[2]

But there is no reason whatever why both may not be. And certainly the two together provide us with an admirable principle of judgment: "Am I on Christ's side actively and positively? No? Then I am against him. . . . But my brother? Is he working *against* Christ? No? Then he is to be welcomed as for him." Tolerance toward others; strictness toward oneself.

Notice, too, the way in which **he who is not with me** is further described as one **who does not gather with me.** In 9:50*b* Jesus is rebuking one of his disciples for an attitude of rejection toward one not of his immediate company. Jesus would "gather" the sheep; this disciple would "scatter" them. To be *with* Christ is to be a gatherer, a reconciler of men to God and to one another, a builder of mutuality, unity, and peace, a creator of human good. To be *against* him is to be a scatterer, a breeder or carrier of hatred and division, a destroyer. One cannot avoid being the one or the other (but see also on 12:49-56).

24-26. *The Danger of Emptiness.*—The Exeg. properly sums up the teaching of this striking parable, at least as Luke here understands it: "It is not enough for a man to be freed from the power of Satan; a new dynamic must replace the old tyranny." Would it not be correct to change the word "dynamic" to "rule" or "sovereignty" and to say, "It is not enough to escape from the rule of Satan; one must come under the rule of God"? Thus interpreted, the passage is seen to be clearly connected in thought with the preceding section (vss. 14-23). Either we serve God or we are in bondage to some evil spirit. There is no middle ground. Gertrude Stein in her autobiography[3] says of some intellectuals whom she met in Paris that it seemed to her they "suffered from a nothingness." She might have said "emptiness." She meant presumably that these men and women belonged to nothing, were mastered by no great loyalty, had, to use Vachel Lindsay's phrase, "no gods to serve." Their house was perhaps well furnished with

[2] *Synoptic Gospels*, II, 194.

[3] *The Autobiography of Alice B. Toklas* (New York: Harcourt, Brace & Co., 1933).

27 ¶ And it came to pass, as he spake these things, a certain woman of the company lifted up her voice, and said unto him, Blessed *is* the womb that bare thee, and the paps which thou hast sucked.

28 But he said, Yea, rather, blessed *are* they that hear the word of God, and keep it.

29 ¶ And when the people were gathered thick together, he began to say, This is an evil generation: they seek a sign; and there shall no sign be given it, but the sign of Jonas the prophet.

27 As he said this, a woman in the crowd raised her voice and said to him, "Blessed is the womb that bore you, and the breasts that you sucked!" 28 But he said, "Blessed rather are those who hear the word of God and keep it!"

29 When the crowds were increasing, he began to say, "This generation is an evil generation; it seeks a sign, but no sign shall be given to it except the sign of Jonah.

3. Jesus Corrects a Woman's Blessing (11:27-28)

In Mark's Gospel Jesus' saying about his true relatives (Mark 3:32-35) follows the account of the Beelzebub controversy. Luke has already used that Marcan passage in 8:19-21. In this context he incorporates another with much the same point from one of his special sources.

27. How happy is the mother of such a son! (cf. Pesiqta 149*a*: "Blessed is the hour in which the Messiah was created. Blessed is the womb from which he came").

28. Note 8:21; also Jas. 1:22: "Be doers of the word, and not hearers only."

F. Concerning Signs (11:29-36)

1. Sign of Jonah and Related Sayings (11:29-32=Matt. 12:38-42)

29a. Editorial introduction replacing one in Q which Luke has transferred to vs. 16 (see Exeg., *ad loc.*).

29b. According to a variant in Mark 8:12*b*, Jesus refused to give his countrymen any display of supernatural power. Paul declared that such a demand was characteristic

things, also perhaps **swept and put in order,** but it had no owner or occupant. For man was not created to be self-sufficient and independent, the master of his soul. He was designed to belong to Someone. As Augustine said, we are restless till we find rest in him. The human quest is a search for a Master, i.e., for someone to whom we shall be able to feel morally justified in belonging. If we do not find this Master, we either resort to some anesthetic—and no anesthetic can be more than temporarily effective—or we fall the victim of some destructive idolatry. The world is in a fearful state when its masses suffer from "a nothingness"; and such is frequently the case. It is this fact which explains totalitarianism, the twentieth-century idolatry. It is not the fact that the dictators have given the people bread which accounts for what success they have had, but the fact that they have given many people a sense of belonging to something greater than themselves, usually the state, and thus have given them relief—poor, shoddy relief, we would say, but still relief—from the nothingness or emptiness of life. This emptiness is what we sometimes call "secularism," and the sequel to it is demonism. Nature, we are told, abhors a vacuum; the same is true in the moral sphere.

27-28. *The Important Thing.*—As the Exeg. points out, Luke substitutes this brief story for the Marcan narrative about Jesus' mother and brothers, which he has already used in a different connection. For comment on the principal theme of both stories, viz., the fact that loyalty to God takes precedence even over family loyalty, see on 8:19-21. An additional theme is peculiar to the present story—the same theme as more clearly appears in Matt. 7:21; "Not every one who says to me, 'Lord, Lord,' shall enter the kingdom of heaven, but he who does the will of my Father who is in heaven." The woman is not so much complimenting Jesus' mother as complimenting *him,* and doing so (may we not say?) somewhat sentimentally. There are many indications that Jesus did not seek or want such personal tributes. The important thing was **the word of God, to hear . . . and keep it.**

29-32. *Preaching as a Sign.*—Luke's narrative now returns to those who seek **a sign** (see on 11:14-19). The Marcan parallel (8:11-12) reads: "The Pharisees came and began to argue with him, seeking from him a sign from heaven, to

30 For as Jonas was a sign unto the Ninevites, so shall also the Son of man be to this generation.

31 The queen of the south shall rise up in the judgment with the men of this generation, and condemn them: for she came from the utmost parts of the earth to hear the wisdom of Solomon; and, behold, a greater than Solomon *is* here.

32 The men of Nineveh shall rise up in the judgment with this generation, and shall condemn it: for they repented at the preaching of Jonas; and, behold, a greater than Jonas *is* here.

30 For as Jonah became a sign to the men
of Nin'e-veh, so will the Son of man be
to this generation. 31 The queen of the
South will arise at the judgment with the
men of this generation and condemn them;
for she came from the ends of the earth to
hear the wisdom of Solomon, and behold,
something greater than Solomon is here.
32 The men of Nin'e-veh will arise at the
judgment with this generation and condemn it; for they repented at the preaching of Jonah, and behold, something greater than Jonah is here.

---

of the Judaism of his day (I Cor. 1:22*a*). **Except the sign of Jonah** may have been omitted from the original form of the saying by Mark because he did not understand it. Did Jesus mean "except the message of repentance"?

30. Luke's explanation of **the sign of Jonah.** As **Jonah** proclaimed the judgment of God **to the men of Nineveh** in ancient times, so **the Son of man** will proclaim it **to this generation** in the last days. Matthew gives a different interpretation. He compares Jonah's "three days and three nights in the belly of the whale" with the Son of man's "three days and three nights in the heart of the earth."

31-32. Parallel sayings that occur in Matthew in reverse order. Possibly once independent of the preceding. Jesus contrasts the unresponsiveness of **the men of this generation** to the revelation he had brought, with the response of pagans in antiquity to the lesser revelations of **Solomon** and **Jonah. The queen of the South,** i.e., the queen of

---

test him [cf. Luke 11:16]. And he sighed deeply in his spirit, and said, 'Why does this generation seek a sign? Truly, I say to you, no sign shall be given to this generation.'" But Matthew and Luke add **except the sign of Jonah.** If this additional phrase goes back to Jesus, it is impossible to say what he meant by it. It is certain that Matthew saw in it a reference to the burial and resurrection of Jesus (Matt. 12:40), and Luke also probably so understood it. Moreover, there can be no doubt that it was in fact the Resurrection which later became the **sign** of the miraculous character of the whole event. So Paul writes: "The gospel concerning his Son, who was descended from David according to the flesh and designated Son of God in power . . . by his resurrection from the dead" (Rom. 1:3-4). But it is much more likely that Jesus himself was thinking of the message of repentance, as the Exeg. suggests. This preaching of the coming kingdom would not have been regarded as **a sign** at all by **an evil** (i.e., an unrepentant) **generation;** and it is possibly on that account that Mark omits any reference to it. In their sense of the word Jesus gave them "no sign." But preaching *can* be a sign, i.e., a medium of the Spirit, powerfully convincing men of God's reality, his righteousness, his judgment, and his mercy. In 16:31 we read, "If they do not hear Moses and the prophets, neither will they be convinced if some one should rise from the dead." Thus preaching is expressly compared with a resurrection and is declared to be as potent a sign. But in 16:31 it is the preaching of "Moses and the prophets" (cf. Solomon and Jonah in the present story) which has convincing power; how much more persuasive would be the preaching of Christ! Paul speaks of the Greeks' wanting wisdom (cf. **wisdom of Solomon**) and the Jews' a sign, but "we preach Christ crucified, a stumbling-block to Jews and folly to Gentiles, but to those who are called, both Jews and Greeks, Christ the power of God and the wisdom of God" (I Cor. 1:22-24). Paul clearly regards the preaching itself (κήρυγμα) or the gospel (εὐαγγέλιον) as being an act of God, a miracle (δύναμις); cf. Rom. 1:16; note also I Cor. 2:1-5. When in the last cited passage Paul speaks of preaching "in demonstration of the Spirit and power," he comes near to calling it a sign. In so far as Christian preaching fails to be such a "demonstration," it fails to be itself. Preaching in its true character is not merely *about* the miracle of Christ; it is itself a part of the continuing miracle. (On vss. 31-32 see also on 10:13-15.)

33 No man, when he hath lighted a candle, putteth *it* in a secret place, neither under a bushel, but on a candlestick, that they which come in may see the light.

33 "No one after lighting a lamp puts it in a cellar or under a bushel, but on a stand, that those who enter may see the

---

Sheba (I Kings 10:1-13), traditionally southwestern Arabia (the modern Yemen). **Something greater than:** The adjective is neuter in both verses (cf. Matt. 12:6). Probably a reference to the kingdom of God—manifest in the teaching and healing ministry of Jesus—rather than to Jesus' own person, as the KJV interprets it. Vs. 32 is omitted by Codex Bezae.

2. Parables About the Lamp and the Eye (11:33-36=Matt. 5:15; 6:22-23)

33. Luke has already made use of this parable (see on 8:16) in its Marcan context, where lamp appears to be a metaphor for Jesus' teaching. In its present setting the parable seems to assert that Jesus himself is the answer to the demand for a "sign." He is a **lamp** that has been lit and placed where all **who enter may see the light.** Possibly Luke has converts to Christianity in mind. Matthew: "It gives light to all in the house." **Or under a bushel:** From Mark 4:21; paraphrased by Luke in 8:16; omitted at this point by the Sinaitic Syriac, the Chester Beatty Gospel Papyrus (p^{45}), and some other Greek MSS; and possibly an interpolation from Matt. 5:16.

33-34. ***The Light and the Eye.***—Here are a parable and a metaphor of Jesus involving the terms **lamp** and **light,** which Luke places together. The first little parable occurs in a different setting in 8:16, and in still another context in Matt. 5:15. In Matt. 5:15 it is used to illustrate the truth that the disciples must let their light so shine that men, seeing their good works, may glorify God; in Luke 8:16 it serves to set forth Jesus' purpose in using parables (see comment there); and here the parable is used with yet another purpose. No passage could serve better to exemplify the fact, already noted several times, that often a parable of Jesus was remembered for its own sake and apart from any particular context, just as frequently today a story told by a preacher to illustrate a point in his sermon is remembered by hearers who have completely forgotten the point itself. And often such a story does not bear in itself any clear indication of what the point was: it might have been used to illustrate any number of truths, and only the original context could have told which. (In addition to the points mentioned above, e.g., this story might conceivably have been told to illustrate the truth that it is futile to take the first step toward a desirable goal if one is not going to take the remaining necessary or appropriate step or steps.)

This being true, the interpreter can be concerned only with what the parable means to the gospel writer and his readers. In the present case, as the Exeg. points out, Luke understands the parable to teach that Jesus himself is the "sign" some are seeking. So Paul says, "We preach Christ crucified" (see on vss. 29-32). He is the "sign" the Jews are seeking, as well as being the "wisdom" the Greeks desire. He is the "light of the world" (John 8:12). **The light,** i.e., the revelation of God, is *there,* like a **lamp . . . on a stand,** for all to see. It is not **in a cellar or under a bushel.** That men fail to see it, still ask for a sign, means not that the lamp is not lighted or visible, but that their **eye** is **not sound.**

What does Jesus mean by a sound eye? Presumably he means the possession of simple, undistorted, unclouded vision; the ability to look at things freshly and truly, to see things as they really are. Jesus' opponents had lost this ability. The kingdom of God was with men; and some saw it not at all, while others saw it as the kingdom of evil (cf. on vss. 14-18). It is solemn to remember that **the light**—even God's light—can shine only where there are eyes to see it; that not even God can reveal what men cannot receive or apprehend. Revelation by definition is a double process—it involves God's lighting **a lamp,** but it also involves men's having **sound** eyes. This double character can be illustrated at every level of experience: to take one example, nature for many is drab and dark. They have seen it again and again, but always with the same unseeing eyes. Sun and rain and stars and moon and grass and wind have become commonplace things. Such men therefore need various forms of artificial excitement to interrupt the dead monotony of what is all around them. In old times they sought and usually got a miracle of some kind; but now that interrup-

34 The light of the body is the eye: therefore when thine eye is single, thy whole body also is full of light; but when *thine eye* is evil, thy body also *is* full of darkness.

35 Take heed therefore, that the light which is in thee be not darkness.

36 If thy whole body therefore *be* full of light, having no part dark, the whole shall be full of light, as when the bright shining of a candle doth give thee light.

light. 34 Your eye is the lamp of your body;
when your eye is sound, your whole body is full of light; but when it is not sound, your body is full of darkness. 35 Therefore
be careful lest the light in you be darkness.
36 If then your whole body is full of light, having no part dark, it will be wholly bright, as when a lamp with its rays gives you light."

34-35. A parable and its moral, associated with the preceding (probably already in Q) only because of the recurring words **lamp** and **light.** Read **sound** and **not sound** with the RSV. The health of the **eye** determines whether a man can see or not. Beware of spiritual blindness! **The light in you:** Understanding in ancient times was believed to be the function of the heart. "Conscience" appears to have been first introduced into Christian vocabulary (from Stoic usage) by the apostle Paul.

36. An observation that has no parallel in Matthew. Omitted from the text of Luke by Codex Bezae and by some O.L. and Old Syriac MSS, probably because the editors could see no point in the verse. Variant readings in many Greek MSS are best understood as emendations in the interest of a deeper meaning. Torrey suspects that **it will be wholly bright** is a mistranslation of an Aramaic original which he would render "then all about you will be light." The verse would then assert: "The man who is full of light lights the world about him" (Torrey, *Four Gospels, ad loc.*); cf. Matt. 5:14*a*: "You are the light of the world."

---

tion is no longer available. The same nature, however, is to others a thrillingly new, a fresh, and radiant thing, constantly fascinating with some new side of itself, declaring the glory of God. Thus Wordsworth can sing:

> To me the meanest flower that blows can give
> Thoughts that do often lie too deep for tears.[4]

The same thing is true of the human world about us and of the story of our race. In both history and the associations of our common life God's light is shining if only we are capable of seeing it. And this is true in a supreme sense of Jesus Christ, in whom God laid bare his very heart (see on 10:22).

The thing which more than anything else makes the **eye . . . not sound** is the habit of looking at things with a view only to the use we can put them to for ourselves, rather than with a view to really seeing them for their own sake. This fact lies back of such sayings as that one must be like a little child to see the kingdom of God, or that one must be born again to see it. Only the humble and disinterested can behold the glory of God. It is self-interest or preoccupation with ourselves and with what things are worth *to us* which chiefly accounts for the distortions of our vision. Thus there is an accidental truth in the fact that of our two English versions, one speaks of the **eye** as being **evil,** the other, as **not sound. Not sound** is undoubtedly the better translation of πονηρός in this passage; but the word **evil** has its points, too. "This generation is an evil [πονηρά] generation," Jesus has said in vs. 29. Because it is filled with pride and greed and jealousy, it cannot see the light. Thus John (3:19) can say: "This is the judgment, that the light has come into the world, and men loved darkness rather than light, because their deeds were evil."

35-36. ***When Light Is Darkness.*—Be careful lest the light in you be darkness.** What is meant by this saying? Is it simply a striking way of saying, "Beware lest there be no light in you at all; only darkness"? In that case vs. 36 is to be understood as setting the contrast: With Christ there is only **light, no part dark;** without Christ there is only **darkness.** This may well have been Luke's meaning. One suspects, however, a subtler sense; and Matthew's form of the saying points more clearly in that direction, "If then the light in you is darkness, how great is the darkness!" (Matt. 6:23.) The reference seems to be to darkness not merely as the absence of light, but as a positive force; not so much to those who have not eyes and therefore do not see at all, as to those whose eyes are diseased (the adjective πονηρός may have that sense) so that they see falsely—so falsely that it

[4] "Ode on Intimations of Immortality," st. xi. See also on 8:9-10.

37 ¶ And as he spake, a certain Pharisee besought him to dine with him: and he went in, and sat down to meat.

37 While he was speaking, a Pharisee asked him to dine with him; so he went in

G. Denunciations of Pharisees and Lawyers (11:37-54)

There are seven "woes" against "scribes and Pharisees" in Matt. 23. Luke records three as directed against "Pharisees" and three as against "lawyers" (scribes).

In using this material the interpreter should keep the fact in mind that the gospel tradition was given its final form by Christian evangelists, teachers, and apologists during a period of acute conflict with Jewish opponents. It is probable that these sayings tell us more about the attitude of the early church to Judaism than they do about the attitude of the Jesus of history toward his Pharisaic contemporaries. Their bitterness may reflect the controversy of church and synagogue as much as that of Jesus and the Pharisees of his own time. There is no reason to doubt that many Pharisees in Jesus' day exhibited evidence of externalism in religion, of legalistic pedantry, of religious ostentation, and even of pious hypocrisy. It was Jesus' criticism of these features of their religion that aroused their bitter antagonism. But these are unfortunately concomitants of religion at more than one time and in more than one group, and the Pharisees hold no monopoly of them. It is increasingly recognized by Christian scholars that to interpret Pharisaism solely in the light of these polemical passages in the Gospels is to do it a grave injustice. The picture needs to be corrected by the study of such ethical and religious teachings of Pharisees as have been preserved in parts of II Esdras, Pirke Aboth, and the Mishnah. The best in Christianity ought to be compared with the best rather than the worst in Pharisaic Judaism if both are to be seen in the proper perspective (cf. D. W. Riddle, *Jesus and the Pharisees* [Chicago: University of Chicago Press, 1928]; R. T. Herford, *The Pharisees* [London: George Allen & Unwin, 1924]; G. F. Moore, *Judaism,* Vols. I-III [Cambridge: Harvard University Press, 1927]).

1. Denunciation of Pharisees (11:37-44=Matt. 23:25-26, 23, 6-7, 27)

37. In all probability Luke himself is responsible for this setting. It is not entirely a happy one, for Jesus' sayings on the occasion are scarcely appropriate as the table talk of a guest in a Pharisee's home. The denunciations may have stood in Q without any specific context. Together with some additional matter they are incorporated by Matthew in a discourse delivered by Jesus to "the crowds" and "his disciples" in the temple during his last week in Jerusalem. Matthew's setting was suggested by the brief warning against scribes reported by Mark (12:38), part of which Matthew has worked into his account. The Marcan passage is reproduced without amplification by Luke in 20:46. **While he was speaking:** "After he had spoken" gives the sense of the Greek.

would be better if they did not see at all. The very **light** in them is **darkness.** In addition to the darkness of ignorance they are plunged in the deeper darkness of perverted understanding. (Here we have again something like the distinction noted in comment on vss. 14-19.) "How great is the darkness!" "How great" meaning "how deep and complete"; but also "how terribly destructive." It is not ignorance, but false knowledge, which has chiefly blighted our world. Ignorance may make men victims or dupes of great evil; but it is false knowledge which makes them perpetrators of it. It is not those simply without light who pose the greater danger to mankind, but those in whom the **light is darkness.** In such men darkness has become an active and destructive force. The world is full of this active darkness. The Bible has it in mind when it speaks of the "power of darkness" (22:53; Col. 1:13), the "rulers of the darkness" (Eph. 6:12).

37-44. ***The Sins of the Pharisees.***—As the Exeg. reminds us, such passages as this (and through vs. 54) must be understood against the background of the hostility between church and synagogue which prevailed in many quarters in the period when the gospel tradition was taking final form. No doubt Jesus denounced certain common Pharisaic practices and characteristics; but that he did not do so in the violent and undiscriminating way in which he is alleged to have spoken in such passages as this, the record,

38 And when the Pharisee saw *it,* he marveled that he had not first washed before dinner.

39 And the Lord said unto him, Now do ye Pharisees make clean the outside of the cup and the platter; but your inward part is full of ravening and wickedness.

40 *Ye* fools, did not he, that made that which is without, make that which is within also?

41 But rather give alms of such things as ye have; and, behold, all things are clean unto you.

and sat at table. 38 The Pharisee was aston-
ished to see that he did not first wash before
dinner. 39 And the Lord said to him, "Now
you Pharisees cleanse the outside of the
cup and of the dish, but inside you are full
of extortion and wickedness. 40 You fools!
Did not he who made the outside make the
inside also? 41 But give for alms those things
which are within; and behold, everything
is clean for you.

38-39*a*. Ritual ablutions before meals were not prescribed by any regulation of the law, but were elaborately observed by Pharisees in obedience to the oral legislation of the scribes (cf. Mark 7:3-4). According to Mark 7:5—part of a long Marcan section omitted by Luke—Pharisees had complained on one occasion to Jesus that his disciples omitted the practice.

39*b*. The scrupulous care taken by **Pharisees** to assure the ceremonial purity of dishes is contrasted with their failure to purge their own hearts of **extortion** and **wickedness.** Probably an interpretation of the "woe" in Matthew, where the contrast is between the outer purity and inner impurity of the **cup** and the **dish.**

40. No parallel in Matthew. The reference is apparently to God. Another possible translation: "You fools! He who has set the outside aright has not thereby set the inside aright."

41. Hopelessly obscure in the Greek. "Purify those things which are within" would make sense, but depends on the precarious assumption that a Greek translator has confused the Aramaic verb "to purify" with that "to give alms."

---

critically examined, makes equally clear. This is one of many places where criticism as applied to the Scriptures has had results positive and constructive for religious faith. Can it be denied that some of the harsh language ascribed to Jesus in the anti-Pharisaic (sometimes anti-Semitic) passages creates a difficulty for faith? Montefiore was not a Christian, and Christian readers may well regard his words here as unfair; but we can hardly feel altogether secure and comfortable when he writes:

> He [Jesus] urged his disciples to love their enemies, but so far as we can judge he showed little love to those who opposed him. He urged that the lost sheep be actively sought out; but except in the way of sheer abuse and bitter vituperation, he did nothing to win over to his own conception of religion the Pharisees and Rabbis who ventured to criticise and dislike him.[5]

Historical criticism removes this difficulty: Jesus' attitude toward the Pharisees is not adequately set forth in such passages as this. We do not know what, if any, tradition lies back of vs. 37; but there are many other references to Jesus' friendly association with Pharisees—a fact hardly compatible with the wholesale denunciations which are sometimes attributed to him.

The only wholesome way for us to take Jesus' words in such passages as this is as denunciations not of men of another nation, age, and religion than ours, but rather of sins of omission and commission to which religious piety in every age and nation is especially subject. Jesus is denouncing not the sins of others merely, but our own sins. Such words as these are helpful only if we take them to ourselves; they apply only too well.

39-42. ***Externalism and Legalism.***—Jesus brings four charges against us, which the Exeg. describes as externalism, legalistic pedantry, religious ostentation, and hypocrisy. But these are at bottom all one, viz., concern with externals to the neglect of inner, i.e., real righteousness. The charge is made quite explicitly in vss. 39-41 (whatever the exact meaning of vss. 40-41), and is repeated in another form in vs. 42, for legalism is an aspect of externalism. We **cleanse the outside of the cup,** i.e., we are care-

[5] *Some Elements of the Religious Teaching of Jesus* (London: Macmillan & Co., 1910), p. 53.

42 But woe unto you, Pharisees! for ye tithe mint and rue and all manner of herbs, and pass over judgment and the love of God: these ought ye to have done, and not to leave the other undone.
43 Woe unto you, Pharisees! for ye love the uppermost seats in the synagogues, and greetings in the markets.

42 "But woe to you Pharisees! for you tithe mint and rue and every herb, and neglect justice and the love of God; these you ought to have done, without neglecting the others.
43 Woe to you Pharisees! for you love the best seat in the synagogues and

---

42. The first of the attacks found in Luke in the form of a "woe." According to the Mishnah, the tithe was demanded even of kitchen herbs. One tractate declares that **rue** was exempted. **Justice and the love of God** is practically a paraphrase of the summary of the law in 10:27. Matthew's version: "Justice and mercy and faith." **These you ought . . . the others** is omitted by Codex Bezae and by Marcion, and may be a scribe's interpolation in the other MSS from Matthew.

43. In 20:46 (Mark 12:38-39) it is the scribes who are charged with these ostentatious practices. **The best seat:** A semicircular bench in front of the ark and facing the congregation.

---

ful to keep the "form of godliness," but are loath to acknowledge and deal with the fact that **inside** we are **full of extortion and wickedness.** The principal reason for the emphasis on the external is that we *can* keep the **outside** clean, while the cleansing of the **inside** is altogether beyond our powers. We tend to define our duty in terms of external legalistic observances such as tithing **mint and rue and every herb** because we find it possible to do our duty only when it is so defined, and at the same time find it intolerable to acknowledge that we are not able to do our duty. The Pharisee in Jesus' parable in 18:9-14 is a legalist, certainly partly because he wants to be a "righteous" man; and unless righteousness is defined in terms of legalistic obedience, it is clear that he cannot be. Because he does not want to say, "God, be merciful to me a sinner!" he must think of God's requirements in external ways. We cannot recognize that we are subject to the demands of God's **justice** and **love** without recognizing the unattainability of any righteousness of our own; therefore we are inclined to set up a lower, more external, more attainable standard. Who of us can look into himself, honestly and in the light of God's truth, and not see "dead men's bones and all uncleanness" (Matt. 23:27)?

Modern psychology has given us new insights into the complicated relationships between the outside and the inside. We know, e.g., that an exterior of a certain kind often means an interior of exactly the opposite sort; that quite without a person's knowing it, he may **cleanse the outside of the cup** in order to hide from himself the fact that the **inside** is unclean. Just as an aggressive exterior may conceal terrible anxiety and insecurity, so an overhumble aspect may hide insufferable pride; instances of this type could be multiplied indefinitely.

43. *Legalism and Pride.*—The concern with externals, which expresses itself in legalism, stands in a double relation to religious pride. As we have seen (vss. 39-42), legalism is rooted in pride; but it also issues in it. One becomes a legalist because one is too proud to acknowledge that one is a sinner; but one's success in keeping the law that is substituted for God's profounder and more inclusive requirement of love makes one more proud still. The pride that *leads* to legalism is pride before *oneself;* the pride that *follows* from it is pride also before *others.* We **love the best seat in the synagogues and salutations in the market places.** "I thank thee that I fast twice a week and give tithes of all that I possess" (in other words, "I do all I ought to do") leads inevitably to "I thank thee that I am not as other men are."

The term **love** in vss. 42 and 43 is the same whether in Greek or English. How starkly the contrast is stated: instead of loving God we love **the best seat** and the **salutations,** deferential and preferential treatment both in church and in public (cf. Matt. 6:5). E. C. Colwell brings home to us the meaning of Matt. 23:8 when he translates ῥαββί as "doctor" and goes on to say, out of his own experience as an educator:

> Anyone who has been dean of a divinity school will testify that at all alumni meetings the first question is, "Why don't you give us a doctor's degree?" The alumni point with groans to the seven-year curriculum and with disdain to the lowly bachelor's degree they were given. They want to be called "doctor" even though the Scriptures they reverence forbid it. Their congregations support

44 Woe unto you, scribes and Pharisees, hypocrites! for ye are as graves which appear not, and the men that walk over *them* are not aware *of them*.

45 ¶ Then answered one of the lawyers, and said unto him, Master, thus saying thou reproachest us also.

46 And he said, Woe unto you also, *ye* lawyers! for ye lade men with burdens grievous to be borne, and ye yourselves touch not the burdens with one of your fingers.

salutations in the market places. 44 Woe
to you! for you are like graves which are not seen, and men walk over them without knowing it."
45 One of the lawyers answered him, "Teacher, in saying this you reproach us
also." 46 And he said, "Woe to you lawyers
also! for you load men with burdens hard to bear, and you yourselves do not touch

44. Contact with a dead body or with a tomb made one ceremonially "unclean" (Num. 19:16). Pharisees are compared to unmarked **graves.** They give no warning of their true nature, and **men** who associate with them are unwittingly corrupted. Matthew's version: "Scribes and Pharisees" are like whitewashed tombs, outwardly beautiful but inwardly unclean.

2. Denunciation of Lawyers (11:45-52=Matt. 23:4, 29-31, 34-36, 13)

45. An editorial introduction divides the denunciations into two separate series.

46. Burdens: Interpretations and applications of individual precepts of the law that had accumulated from the time of Ezra and that ultimately were committed to writing in the Mishnah (second century A.D.). The accusation appears to be that the **lawyers** do nothing to help those who cannot keep the regulations. Another interpretation: they themselves evade the responsibilities they impose on others.

and sometimes create the desire, for the local church feels ashamed of its status if it alone in the community has a minister who is not a doctor.[6]

How vulgar and petty our pride!

44. ***Unsuspected Carriers of Infection.***—The Matthaean parallel to vs. 44 (Matt. 23:27) repeats the idea of vs. 39 (Matt. 23:25); but the verse in Luke introduces an additional idea. The argument against the Pharisees, which began at vs. 39, now reaches its final stage: their concern for externals (vs. 39), which manifests itself in legalism (vs. 42) and spiritual pride (vs. 43), also makes them a source of peril to others. Men are deceived by their correct exteriors, put trust in them, and are defiled and corrupted by them. The most dangerous purveyor of racial prejudice, e.g., is the person who though filled with prejudice appears to have none—and if he himself thinks he has none, he is most dangerous of all! And how often it has happened that sanctimonious institutions and conventions have been responsible for subtly infecting masses of men with inhuman and destructive ideas!

45-52. ***Sins of the Clergy.***—In Matt. 23, to much of which this whole passage in Luke (vss. 37-54) is parallel, all of the "woes" are addressed indiscriminately to "scribes and Pharisees." In Luke the "woes" are divided: a series is addressed to the Pharisees (vss. 39-44) and another series to the scribes or **lawyers.** Virtually all scribes were Pharisees, but not all Pharisees were scribes. The scribes were the professional experts whose teachings and counsels the Pharisees followed. Moffatt translates vs. 45: "Teacher, when you say this you are insulting us as well," and Plummer, "Thou insultest even us."[7] As the passage stands, "insult" is not too strong a word—which confirms the question of authenticity discussed in both the Exeg. and Expos. on vss. 37-44. Three charges are brought against the professional teachers, and all of them are related in some way to the legalistic pedantry emphasized in the denunciation of the Pharisees. They may well be taken to heart by the professional custodians of any and every religious tradition.

Such custodians are always in danger of elaborating the requirements of the tradition until it becomes an intolerable burden (vs. 46). We run into a kind of paradox here. In the Expos. on 10:25-28 it was pointed out that Christ in a real sense asks more than any legal code asks. He asks for love, and love goes beyond any law.

[6] *An Approach to the Teaching of Jesus* (New York and Nashville: Abingdon-Cokesbury Press, 1947), p. 97.

[7] *Gospel According to Luke,* p. 312.

47 Woe unto you! for ye build the sepulchres of the prophets, and your fathers killed them.

48 Truly ye bear witness that ye allow the deeds of your fathers: for they indeed killed them, and ye build their sepulchres.

49 Therefore also said the wisdom of God, I will send them prophets and apos-

the burdens with one of your fingers. 47 Woe
to you! for you build the tombs of the
prophets whom your fathers killed. 48 So
you are witnesses and consent to the deeds
of your fathers; for they killed them, and
you build their tombs. 49 Therefore also

47-48. The lawyers share in the guilt of their ancestors, who murdered **the prophets.** But the argument is obscure. Matthew's version: Scribes and Pharisees pride themselves on their superiority to their fathers, but inadvertently bear witness in so doing that they are their sons.

49. The Wisdom of God: Possibly some lost Jewish apocryphal book from which the quotation is taken. Cf. Jer. 7:25-26. Others prefer to translate, "God, in his wisdom, said, . . ." Jesus himself is the speaker in Matthew, and the statement becomes a prediction.

It was emphasized that love is more demanding and costly; but that at the same time it is less irritating and burdensome. This last is true because love, as Jesus taught it, *is* God making himself known *in our hearts;* when we feel the demands of love, we feel them *from within.* That is why the service of God, which is the service of love, can be called "perfect freedom." It may be noted, too, that this love which makes demands also helps us meet them. Love both asks and gives. But laws, on the contrary, ask *from outside,* and they only *ask;* there is no *help* in laws. Thus we are told that the representatives of a legal tradition **load men with burdens hard to bear . . .** but **do not touch the burdens with one of** [their] **fingers.** Contrast Jesus' words in Matt. 11:28-30. To hear God's own word of command is to hear also the word of grace; this is not true of the commandments of men.

The scribes, like all guardians of a tradition, are also in danger of honoring the letter of the tradition but forgetting or losing its spirit (vss. 47-48). Religious teachers are quite properly, and almost by definition, conservative. But the conservative must be progressive or he fails to be conservative, i.e., he cannot really save the past except by making it a part of the living present.[8] The person who insists that the institutions of the past shall not be altered is not their friend—he is their enemy—for he is helping to make their eventual overthrow inevitable. False and ineffectual conservatives imagine that the way to preserve the unfinished building begun by the fathers is to put a fence around it and a tablet on it and to designate it holy ground that shall not be touched forever; the true and effective conservative knows that the only way to preserve it is to continue the building. The only things which will stand the test of time are the things which time itself is permitted to modify and adapt to new and larger uses. Furthermore, the true conservative must always remember that the most important heritage from the past is the spirit of progress itself. This is the particular point of Jesus' criticism of the scribes here (allowing for the obscurities in the text of which the Exeg. speaks). They stone the present prophets and build monuments to the ancient ones. They want to preserve the names of the prophets, but not the fact of prophecy. They want to keep the things of value the past has achieved but not the spirit and method by which those things were accomplished in their time. Often the sons and daughters of a revolution conserve everything about the revolutionists—their names, their houses, their portraits—everything except their spirit. In the same way the creative spirit of a religious tradition can die in the hands of those who are faithfully seeking to preserve the tradition itself.

Finally (vs. 52; vss. 49-51 receive special comment below) the scribes are accused of being positive obstacles to the salvation of men. The very persons who have been given **the key of knowledge,** who are appointed to open the door of the kingdom of God to men, are actually by teaching and example closing the door and keeping men out—men who, left alone, might have entered. (On the terrible responsibility of the religious leader see also Expos. on 10:16.)

49-51. ***The Solidarity of Life.***—These verses call for special comment because they are concerned, not (as the others in this section) with sins, but with punishment; and with punishment not of the Pharisees and scribes alone, but of the nation. In such a passage, not anti-Pharisaism particularly, but anti-Semitism, seems to manifest itself. To say this is to say that

[8] For an excellent brief discussion of this point see Wieman, *The Wrestle of Religion with Truth,* pp. 47-49.

tles, and *some* of them they shall slay and persecute:
50 That the blood of all the prophets, which was shed from the foundation of the world, may be required of this generation;
51 From the blood of Abel unto the blood of Zacharias, which perished between the altar and the temple: verily I say unto you, It shall be required of this generation.

the Wisdom of God said, 'I will send them prophets and apostles, some of whom they will kill and persecute,'
50 that the blood of all the prophets, shed from the foundation of the world, may be required of this generation,
51 from the blood of Abel to the blood of Zech-a-ri'ah, who perished between the altar and the sanctuary. Yes, I tell you, it shall be required of this genera-

---

Prophets and apostles: Possibly a Christianized version of "prophets, and wise men, and scribes" (Matthew), or perhaps **apostles** should be translated "messengers."

50-51. The implication is that **this generation** will be the last. It will be charged with all the misdeeds of its predecessors. Matthew's "righteous blood" is more appropriate than **the blood of all the prophets,** for neither of the individuals cited is properly described as a prophet. **Abel** (Gen. 4:8) is the first victim of murder referred to in the historical books of the O.T. and **Zechariah** (II Chr. 24:20-22) is the last. Luke's text lends no support to an ancient hypothesis, recently revived, that the **Zechariah** of this passage is to be identified with a Jew by that name who was murdered in the temple courts in A.D. 68 during Titus' siege of Jerusalem (Josephus *Jewish War* IV. 5. 4).

---

these words, in the midst of a passage of questionable authenticity as an utterance of Jesus (see on vss. 37-44), are especially questionable. One is bound to suspect that they reflect the experiences of a later period when Christians (note the apparently Christian word **apostles**) were in fact being often persecuted by Jews and when also the terrible suffering and slaughter of the Jewish War (A.D. 66-70) were vividly in mind, either in memory or in prospect. This passage sounds like some Christian's interpretation of the significance of that tragic event (like Matt. 27:25). It should be noted that even Luke does not ascribe the saying primarily or simply to Jesus; it is from **the Wisdom of God.** (There is nothing to require the quotation mark after vs. 49 in RSV.)

But whatever its source, and without regard to the particular way it is applied in this passage, this teaching calls attention to a basic fact in the moral order. There *is* such a thing as accumulating guilt; it does happen that a generation suffers for the sins and errors of previous generations. This is said in Exod. 20:5; and though later teachers in Israel sought to emphasize the fact of individual responsibility (cf. Jer. 31:29-30; Ezek. 18:1-24), the fact of human solidarity, of the intimate and inextricable interrelatedness of men within each generation, and of the generations themselves with one another is undeniable. One generation has over and over again suffered for others; e.g., wars always represent accumulations from the blindness and iniquity of earlier generations.

A given generation must be ready to accept its "punishment," not complaining about the "injustice" of its being forced to suffer for the fathers' sins, but in humility remembering that it is through these same fathers that most of the treasures of its life have been conveyed. To be an individual entirely cut off from humanity, to be a man not a part of mankind—if such were conceivable—would be an utterly intolerable agony. We belong together—that is our joy; and perhaps we can recognize the reality and worth of this kinship and realize the joy of it more fully because it is our grief as well.

But there is another reason why we should accept punishment for our fathers' sins humbly and without resentment: the sins are not exclusively our fathers'. Note the force of vs. 49, **I will send them prophets and apostles, some of whom they will kill and persecute, that the blood. . . .** The implication is that if the present generation had not itself shared in the sins of the fathers, it would not have suffered the punishment. Is it possible that one righteous generation could atone for all the sins of the past (as in a somewhat different sense one Man did) and give the race a new start? (Cf. 13:34; 19:41-42.) Such seems to be implied and such may be true; but certainly no such generation has appeared. The guilt for which a generation suffers may have been building up for centuries, but its own guilt is a part, not improbably the culminating and precipitating part, of the accumulation.

We must be humble also in remembering that just as we may have to suffer for our fathers, so we are contributing by our sins and errors to the suffering of our children. Moral responsibility is an awful, an incalculable, a ter-

52 Woe unto you, lawyers! for ye have taken away the key of knowledge: ye entered not in yourselves, and them that were entering in ye hindered.

53 And as he said these things unto them, the scribes and the Pharisees began to urge *him* vehemently, and to provoke him to speak of many things:

54 Laying wait for him, and seeking to catch something out of his mouth, that they might accuse him.

12 In the mean time, when there were gathered together an innumerable multitude of people, insomuch that they trode one upon another, he began to say unto his disciples first of all, Beware ye of the leaven of the Pharisees, which is hypocrisy.

tion. 52 Woe to you lawyers! for you have taken away the key of knowledge; you did not enter yourselves, and you hindered those who were entering."

53 As he went away from there, the scribes and the Pharisees began to press him hard, and to provoke him to speak of many things, 54 lying in wait for him, to catch at something he might say.

12 In the meantime, when so many thousands of the multitude had gathered together that they trod upon one another, he began to say to his disciples first, "Beware of the leaven of the Pharisees,

---

52. The legalistic pedantry of the **lawyers** had prevented them from knowing God and had **hindered** others. But Matthew's "you shut the kingdom of heaven against men" may be an earlier form of the saying than **you have taken away the key of knowledge.**

3. Opposition of Scribes and Pharisees to Jesus (11:53-54)

53-54. Editorial generalization.

H. On the Responsibilities and Privileges of Discipleship (12:1–13:9)

Teaching from Q and L sources has been arranged in the form of a loose discourse, addressed by Jesus in the first instance to "his disciples," but also with occasional reference to "the multitude" in the background (cf. 6:17–7:1).

1. Warning, Encouragement, and Advice to Disciples (12:1-12; cf. Matt. 10:26*b*-33; 12:32; 10:19-20)

12:1. Editorial introduction. **So many thousands:** For a similar hyperbole see Acts 21:20. **Beware,** etc., is a saying that serves to connect the subsequent material with the denunciations of ch. 11. In Mark 8:15, part of a long section that Luke omits, there is a similar warning: "Beware of the leaven of the Pharisees and the leaven of Herod." **Leaven** in Jewish literature and in the N.T. is usually a metaphor for evil. In Matt. 16:6 it refers to the teaching of the Pharisees and the Sadducees.

---

rifying thing; it must be so, or man would not be man and there could be no glory in his life. But without the God who suffers with us and "through suffering" is "bringing many sons to glory" (Heb. 2:10), in whom all the generations live and move and find their rest at last—without God, who could bear to live? It is only God who can assure us that our own suffering, besides being suffering for our fathers and ourselves, is in another sense for our children also.

12:1-12. ***The Supreme Worth of Truth.***—The Exeg. speaks of ch. 12 as being "in the form of a loose discourse," and commentators generally are unable to find any very coherent scheme. Except that most of the teachings or teaching sections are related in some way to the coming judgment and the kingdom of God, there seems to be little connection among them, nor is it possible to trace Luke's purpose in arranging them as he has. They must have been originally independent of one another, and many of them appear in Matthew in quite different contexts.

The present section is itself made up of originally disparate brief sayings, but it is surely not fanciful to see that Luke associates them because they all have something to do with the truth, particularly the truth in Christ—its supreme worth, its ultimate inviolability, its au-

2 For there is nothing covered, that shall not be revealed; neither hid, that shall not be known.

which is hypocrisy. 2 Nothing is covered up that will not be revealed, or hidden that

2. A saying that declares in 8:17 and in Mark 4:22 that the meaning of parables is hid only temporarily; in Matt. 10:26*b*—part of the missionary instructions to the twelve

thenticity, its sustaining power. Most of these teachings appear in substance—often in almost the same form—in other connections in this same Gospel, where they have been or will be severally discussed (on vs. 1 see on 11:37-52; on vss. 2-3 see on 8:16-17; on vss. 4-5 see on 7:16; 8:25, 35-39, 50-53; on vss. 6-7 see on 7:30; 8:43-46; 9:25; 12:22-34; on vss. 8-9 see on 9:26). On the assumption that the reader is consulting the cited passages, it is possible at this place to deal with the several teachings more summarily and briefly, and with reference to the particular aspect of their meaning which is pertinent in the present context.

The transition from the old theme to the new one is made by the caution against **the leaven of the Pharisees, which is hypocrisy** (vs. 1). The emphasis in 11:37-54 was on externalism and legalism, but hypocrisy is implied at several points, especially in vs. 44. Notice that in the Matthaean parallels (see Exeg.) the emphasis upon hypocrisy is clear and constant. It is certain that Jesus hated nothing so much as hypocrisy—and for the reason that it made impossible the kind of fellowship with others which he sought. Truth is the one indispensable prerequisite to any genuine community. For this reason the Gospels show that Jesus often found it easier to associate with "publicans and sinners" than with more respectable people. Not that "sinners" too might not be hypocritical; but apparently he found them less frequently so than those with a reputation to sustain and appearances to keep up. But truth is essential not only to human intercourse but also to any real life with God. (Indeed, as Jesus saw it, genuine human community and genuine life with God are one and the same thing—one community under two aspects [see on 10:25-28; 11:4*a*].) That is why repentance is indispensable; for repentance is simply an acknowledgment of the truth; repentance is moral honesty. Jesus could tolerate any sin more easily than the denial that one had sin, for such a denial is by definition unpardonable (see below on vs. 10). There can be no forgiveness—which is in its end meaning the restoration of fellowship—except on the basis of an honest facing of the moral facts. "Grace and truth" go together in the nature of things (cf. John 1:14). The Pharisee who did not live repentantly was not living truly; the same is true of any of us. Such a one may not be a hypocrite in the sense of consciously trying to deceive others; but he is not living *as himself*. He is playing a part—and that is what hypocrisy basically means.

Jesus knew how difficult this kind of truth is. We live in a world of appearances, where **hypocrisy** is a treacherous **leaven.** It is not merely a matter of the distinction between the "outer" and the "inner," but of differences of moral level within ourselves; for it usually happens that we deceive ourselves before we try to deceive others. It is not easy to get down to the bedrock of reality in ourselves through all the layers of self-deception which social tradition and convention and our own pride have imposed. Shakespeare's Polonius says to his son,

> This above all: to thine own self be true,
> And it must follow, as the night the day,
> Thou canst not then be false to any man.[9]

But the whole context of these lines leaves one gravely doubting that Polonius knows how radical and difficult a thing he has asked. Matthew Arnold shows greater understanding in his poem "Self-Dependence," which closes,

> Resolve to be thyself; and know that he,
> Who finds himself loses his misery!

But as the title suggests, the poem is more Stoic than Christian in feeling, and therefore to a degree false. For actually we are not self-dependent; despite Henley's "Invictus," we are not captains of our souls or masters of our fate. We are in fact like little children—that is why it is so important to *"become* like little children." That is why poverty of spirit and humility and mercifulness are virtues; they correspond to the realities of our moral situation. To be in all truth what we are involves a self-searching, a self-discipline, a constancy in prayer, and a dedication to the will of God which are costly indeed. But the reward is great beyond all describing; and the alternative is nothing less than being "cast into hell," as the next verses will say.

2-5. ***The Final Failure.***—For Jesus goes on to affirm that ultimately truth will have its way. The "play actor" must eventually face reality. He must stand alone—himself, his own self, his naked self—before the judgment seat of God.

[9] *Hamlet,* Act I, scene 3.

3 Therefore, whatsoever ye have spoken in darkness shall be heard in the light; and that which ye have spoken in the ear in closets shall be proclaimed upon the housetops.

4 And I say unto you my friends, Be not afraid of them that kill the body, and after that have no more that they can do.

5 But I will forewarn you whom ye shall fear: Fear him, which after he hath killed hath power to cast into hell; yea, I say unto you, Fear him.

6 Are not five sparrows sold for two farthings, and not one of them is forgotten before God?

will not be known.
3 Whatever you have said in the dark shall be heard in the light, and what you have whispered in private rooms shall be proclaimed upon the housetops.

4 "I tell you, my friends, do not fear those who kill the body, and after that have no more that they can do.
5 But I will warn you whom to fear: fear him who, after he has killed, has power to cast into hell;[s] yes, I tell you, fear him!
6 Are not five sparrows sold for two pennies? And not one

[s] Greek *Gehenna.*

—that the disciples are to proclaim in public the teaching of Jesus they had heard in private; and in this setting, that hypocrisy will be exposed.

3. A warning that it is useless for disciples to conceal their faith. Matthew's version is a direct exhortation to disciples to proclaim the message Jesus had given them. **Therefore** (KJV) is omitted without apparent justification by the editors of the RSV.

4-5. My friends: Used by Jesus of his disciples in John 15:14-15, but only here in the Synoptic tradition. Martyrdom holds no terrors; only God's judgment is to be feared. **Hell:** Gehenna (גי הנם) means "valley of Hinnom," a ravine to the west and south of Jerusalem. It is occasionally referred to in the O.T. as the site at which certain Israelites during the monarchy worshiped Molech by making their children "pass through the fire." Josiah polluted the valley ("with the bones of men") to put a stop to this pagan cult (II Kings 23:10-14), but it was revived under Jehoiachin; and Jeremiah prophesied that one day the valley would be known as the "valley of slaughter" (Jer. 7:30-32). A medieval Jewish commentator on the Psalms (Kimchi, *ca.* A.D. 1200) says that Gehenna was used as a garbage dump for Jerusalem and that a fire burned there constantly. Many modern scholars accept this statement without question, but there is no early evidence for fires in the valley except those connected with the Molech cult. In late Jewish literature (e.g., Enoch 27:2) Gehenna became the popular name for the place of future punishment. In the N.T. it is carefully distinguished from Hades (the O.T. Sheol). The souls of the wicked go to Hades after death, but both souls and bodies (cf. Matt. 10:28) are cast into Gehenna after the resurrection and final judgment. Gehenna occurs frequently in Matthew and Mark, but only here in Luke-Acts.

6-7. Among the great sayings in the gospel tradition on the infinite worth of the individual in the sight of God. The disciples can entrust themselves confidently to God's

---

Nothing is covered up that will not be revealed (see on 8:16-17). In that moment all illusion is stripped away and only the truth abides. In so far as we have relied on illusion and have not known ourselves in truth, the moment is one of unrelieved and terrible judgment. God appears as an enemy (see on 8:28), the awful and ultimate enemy. Because we have not known ourselves in truth, God has had no opportunity to make himself known to us as love. It is this last—this deepest—failure we are to fear (vss. 4-5). The worst men or circumstances can do to us is to **kill the body**—which sooner or later must be killed in any case—but one who has denied his own integrity, or hidden from himself, or let slip his hold upon the moral reality within himself, has lost his soul. He is ultimately lost. In violating one's own moral integrity one has made a treacherous attack from within upon the inmost citadel of the soul, where the spirit makes its final stand against the chaos of the world—a negation of all stability and value in one's life. What is this but being **cast into hell?** And who is not aware of how near he often is to the edge of this pit?

6-7. *God's Care for the Individual.*—This passage appears at first to be in striking contrast to the immediately preceding verses. "Yes, I tell

7 But even the very hairs of your head
are all numbered. Fear not therefore: ye
are of more value than many sparrows.
8 Also I say unto you, Whosoever shall
confess me before men, him shall the Son
of man also confess before the angels of
God:
9 But he that denieth me before men
shall be denied before the angels of God.
10 And whosoever shall speak a word
against the Son of man, it shall be forgiven
him: but unto him that blasphemeth

of them is forgotten before God. **7** Why,
even the hairs of your head are all num-
bered. Fear not; you are of more value
than many sparrows.
8 "And I tell you, every one who ac-
knowledges me before men, the Son of man
also will acknowledge before the angels of
God; **9** but he who denies me before men
will be denied before the angels of God.
10 And every one who speaks a word against

---

loving care, for it embraces even **sparrows,** among the cheapest articles sold for food on the market. **Two pennies:** The maximum price for ten sparrows was set at the equivalent of seven cents by an edict of the emperor Diocletian (late third century A.D.).

8-9. A promise and a threat. A variant of the latter is preserved separately in Mark 8:38 (Luke 9:26). **Son of man:** Matthew reads "I." Some scholars hold that the title throughout the Gospels is a christological designation read into the tradition by the early church. In this passage **Son of man** appears in the role of advocate for the faithful, not as judge. If the term is primitive, Jesus may mean by it someone other than himself. More probably he uses it to distinguish between himself as he is and as he will be. Matthew interprets **before the angels of God** as "before my Father who is in heaven."

10. In this context blasphemy **against the Holy Spirit** is probably to be understood in the light of vs. 12. The unbeliever who speaks **against** Christ **will be forgiven,** but not

---

you, fear him!" says Christ in vs. 5; and now, **Fear not,** in vs. 7. But of course what we are to fear is God; and what we are *not* to fear is poverty or want or any earthly circumstance. We are to be free from fear of such eventualities not only because they do not matter as compared with the thing of really first importance (this is the point of vs. 4), but also because we are the objects of God's care. The Exeg. describes these verses as containing one of "the great sayings" of the Gospels "on the infinite worth of the individual in the sight of God." There are many indications that Jesus thus regarded the human person (we shall be examining another passage with this same theme in vss. 22-24); and indeed, even without explicit assertions on this specific point we would have been in position to know this because it is integrally involved in Jesus' religious faith. This evaluation of the person is, after all, a matter of faith; one could hardly justify it rationally. Life is plentiful, and nature seems to care little for the individual; how do we know that God does? Note that Jesus says only that not a sparrow **is forgotten before God;** he does not say that every sparrow is protected or kept alive. Matthew's form of the utterance explicitly assumes the opposite: "One of them shall not fall on the ground without your Father" (Matt. 10:29). We are to be comforted and without fear not because God will keep us from suffering, but because he will know and in some way share our suffering and thus give meaning to it. Note that the value of the individual in God's sight is ultimate and absolute; nothing is said here about his being valuable because of the contribution he may make to the social whole. He is valuable simply as the object of God's love. On whatever grounds others may do so, here is the Christian's ground for resisting all the cruel tyrannies, whether of church or state.

8-9, 11-12. ***Bearing Witness to the Truth.***—These verses relate more closely to the major theme of the section. One must **acknowledge . . . before men** the truth one knows; there must be no holding back through fear or shame. (Virtually the same point is discussed at 9:26.) Nor does one who is on truth's side need to be anxious about what he shall answer when he is challenged (vss. 11-12). To lie or evade is complicated and intricate; to say the truth we know is simple and involves no careful stratagems. **The Holy Spirit will teach you in that very hour what you ought to say.**

10. ***The Unpardonable Sin.***—This verse in a slightly different form appears in the Beelzebub controversy in Mark and Matthew; and it seems to belong there more naturally than in the Lukan context. Indeed, it is not easy to see why Luke places it where he does or what meaning he thinks of it as having here. Manson

against the Holy Ghost it shall not be forgiven.
11 And when they bring you unto the synagogues, and *unto* magistrates, and powers, take ye no thought how or what thing ye shall answer, or what ye shall say:
12 For the Holy Ghost shall teach you in the same hour what ye ought to say.

the Son of man will be forgiven; but he who blasphemes against the Holy Spirit will not be forgiven.
11 And when they bring you before the synagogues and the rulers and the authorities, do not be anxious how or what you are to answer or what you are to say;
12 for the Holy Spirit will teach you in that very hour what you ought to say."

---

the believer who refuses to confess his faith when supernaturally prompted to do so. A variant of the saying in Mark 3:28-29, which is perhaps more primitive. Matt. 12:31-32 is a conflation of both. If **Son of man** in Luke's version originally meant "a man" (see on 5:24*a*; 6:5), the main difference between Mark and Q disappears. The contrast, then, is between blasphemy against man and blasphemy **against the Holy Spirit.**

11-12. A variant in Mark 13:11 (Luke 21:14-15). Matt. 10:19-20 is a conflation of Mark and Q. Christians on trial for their faith before Jewish courts and Gentile tribunals are to trust to divine inspiration for their defense. No such legal persecution was experienced by Jesus' followers during his lifetime. The saying clearly reflects the experience of the early church.

---

understands it to mean that "Jesus will accept patiently and forgivingly men's misrepresentations of himself, but the calumnies of men against the Spirit, which speaks in his faithful disciples, he will not condone."[10] Thus understood (in close connection with vs. 12), the statement was intended to encourage the disciples to bear their witness to Christ. A much more probable understanding is expressed in the Exeg.: **He who blasphemes against the Holy Spirit** is he who is disloyal to the divine truth which he has received and to which he has given inner acceptance.

As to just what Jesus said originally about "the unpardonable sin" and what he meant by it, the record does not make clear. It seems unlike Jesus to think of any sin as unforgivable; certainly it could be only sin for which repentance is for some reason impossible (cf. Heb. 12:17). But in that case the intention of the teaching would have been to point not to some one unpardonable sin, but to the condition under which any sin is unpardonable. Such a perverted sense of truth and value as would permit of one's regarding Jesus' divinely good deeds, or deeds wrought later by the Holy Spirit, as the work of Satan would constitute such a condition; and for that reason the Marcan and Matthaean setting of the story seems more fitting (see also the reference to the "unpardonable" sin in Expos., vss. 1-12).

In other generations, and perhaps to some extent still, this saying of Jesus has been the occasion of serious emotional distress among devout people. Probably the most famous instance is that of the English poet, William Cowper, whose fear that he had been guilty of this sin contributed to his recurrent insanity. Although his contemporary, John Wesley, was perhaps surer than he was entitled to be as to just what Jesus said or meant, there is truth and good health in his counsel:

> How immense is the number in every nation . . . of those who have been more or less distressed on account of this scripture! . . . Nay, there are few that are truly convinced of sin, who have not felt some uneasiness for fear they had committed, or should commit, this unpardonable sin. . . . But . . . how is it possible that anyone who reads his Bible can one hour remain in doubt concerning it, when our Lord himself . . . has so clearly told us. . . . This then, and this alone . . . is the blasphemy against the Holy Ghost: the saying that he had an unclean spirit; the affirming that Christ wrought his miracles by the power of an evil spirit. . . . Now, have *you* been guilty of this? . . . No more than you have cut your neighbor's throat, and set his house on fire. How marvelously then have you been afraid, where no fear is! Dismiss that vain terror; let your fear be more rational for the time to come. Be afraid of giving way to pride; be afraid of yielding to anger; be afraid of loving the world; be afraid of foolish and hurtful desires; but never more be afraid of committing the blasphemy against the Holy Ghost.[1]

But if blasphemy **against the Holy Ghost** is the deliberate turning of one's back to God's truth as it is known to us, the deliberate closing of one's eyes upon the "inward vision," then we

[10] *Gospel of Luke*, p. 151.

[1] From the works of John Wesley, quoted by Maurice J. Quinlan, "William Cowper and the Unpardonable Sin," *Journal of Religion*, XXIII (1943), 112.

13 ¶ And one of the company said unto him, Master, speak to my brother, that he divide the inheritance with me.

14 And he said unto him, Man, who made me a judge or a divider over you?

15 And he said unto them, Take heed, and beware of covetousness: for a man's

13 One of the multitude said to him,
"Teacher, bid my brother divide the in-
heritance with me." 14 But he said to him,
"Man, who made me a judge or divider
over you?" 15 And he said to them, "Take

---

2. On Dividing an Inheritance (12:13-15)

13-14. One of the multitude . . . : A formula by which this special tradition is fitted into discourse material taken largely from Q. Rabbis were experts on the civil regulations of the law as well as on its religious, ethical, cultic, and criminal ordinances. Jesus' refusal to arbitrate in the dispute is phrased in words that are reminiscent of the Israelite's question to Moses: "Who made you a prince and a judge over us?" (Exod. 2:14.)

15. Prepares the way for the parable that follows and anticipates its moral. Goodspeed's paraphrase: "A man's life does not belong to him, no matter how rich he is."

---

ought to be afraid of that, too—most of all afraid because through such deliberate blindness repentance may become impossible to us and even God's mercy be unable to reach us. The one thing sure is that there is no sin of which we can repent, which God is not able and willing to forgive.

13-15*a*. *Beware of Covetousness.*—No incident in the Gospels brings into such vivid relief what is really the most characteristic feature of Jesus' ethical teaching—viz., its intense preoccupation with the absolute will of God, with an implied indifference to more immediate questions of casuistry. The distinction of this particular passage is that in it the indifference is not merely implied, but is forcefully expressed: **Who made me a judge or divider over you?** The man had come to Jesus with what would seem to be a reasonable complaint against his brother. That some arrangement for the adjudication and settlement of such disputes as this about **inheritance** must exist so long as we have the disputes themselves, Jesus would almost certainly not have denied. His question, just noted (vs. 14), cannot be pressed to mean that Jesus did not recognize the need, as things were, of judges and dividers. He knows, however, not only that he is not such a judge and does not want to be, but also that the ethical questions with which such judges deal are not the ultimately important ones. In this case he brushes aside the immediate occasion (which lawyers and judges can handle) and focuses attention on the basic cause (with which God is concerned), viz., **covetousness.** Why is this man so concerned about his **inheritance?** Is it because of disinterested concern for justice? As Jesus sees it, he is concerned because he is covetous. Let him take the attitude which Jesus enjoins upon his disciples in the immediately following passage (vss. 22-34) or asks of the rich ruler in 18:18-30—then he will not be concerned about what his brother does with the inheritance, or rather, he will be glad to have his brother keep it. What other answer than this could a teacher give who has said, "If any one would sue you and take your coat, let him have your cloak as well"? (Matt. 5:40=Luke 6:29.) In other words, Jesus is saying in effect that we have ethical problems at the more superficial levels often only because we have not truly solved a deeper problem. Because this man is covetous, he is in trouble with his brother.

It is worth noting, however, that he has come to Jesus not with an ethical problem of his own at any level, but with a complaint against his brother. The basic trouble of the rich ruler in 18:18-30 was also, as Jesus saw it, this same covetousness; but one senses more sympathy for him than for this man. The difference is that the rich ruler came with a confession of his own need ("What shall I do . . . ?), while in the present passage the man comes with a charge against someone else. It is interesting that there are two stories in Luke (and in Luke only) in which someone asks Jesus to say something or other by way of rebuke or correction to a third person, and that in each case Jesus addresses his rebuke or correction to the complainant himself. (The other passage is, of course, 10:38-42.) We may complain about one another *to* one another, if we want to, and with more or less justification; but there is no possibility of getting through to God with our complaints against others. Before *God* we are confessors, not complainants. Before God we are not judges; we are being judged. The awesome thing about Jesus' teaching is that it represents so unerringly this ultimate divine point of view.

life consisteth not in the abundance of the things which he possesseth.

16 And he spake a parable unto them, saying, The ground of a certain rich man brought forth plentifully:

17 And he thought within himself, saying, What shall I do, because I have no room where to bestow my fruits?

18 And he said, This will I do: I will pull down my barns, and build greater; and there will I bestow all my fruits and my goods.

19 And I will say to my soul, Soul, thou hast much goods laid up for many years; take thine ease, eat, drink, *and* be merry.

20 But God said unto him, *Thou* fool, this night thy soul shall be required of thee: then whose shall those things be, which thou hast provided?

21 So *is* he that layeth up treasure for himself, and is not rich toward God.

heed, and beware of all covetousness; for
a man's life does not consist in the abun-
dance of his possessions." **16** And he told
them a parable, saying, "The land of a
rich man brought forth plentifully; **17** and
he thought to himself, 'What shall I do,
for I have nowhere to store my crops?'
18 And he said, 'I will do this: I will pull
down my barns, and build larger ones; and
there I will store all my grain and my
goods. **19** And I will say to my soul, Soul,
you have ample goods laid up for many
years; take your ease, eat, drink, be merry.'
20 But God said to him, 'Fool! This night
your soul is required of you; and the things
you have prepared, whose will they be?'
21 So is he who lays up treasure for himself,
and is not rich toward God."

---

3. Parable of the Rich Fool (12:16-21)

An "example story." The folly of a life devoted to the accumulation of material riches. A passage in Ecclus. 11:18-19 (Goodspeed) teaches a similar lesson:

> One man grows rich by carefulness and greed,
> And this will be his reward:
> When he says, "Now I can rest,
> And enjoy my goods,"
> He does not know when the time will come
> When he will die and leave them to others.

16-19. The monologue of a wealthy farmer who thinks only in terms of larger granaries and a life of **ease. Eat, drink, be merry,** cf. Eccl. 8:15; Tob. 7:10.

20. Material riches offer a man no protection against the uncertainty of life, and pass into the possession of others when he dies.

21. This points the obvious moral of the story. Possibly an addition by Luke to prepare the way for the section that follows. **Rich toward God:** No doubt Luke understands this in the light of vs. 33.

This is one of the elements in what we mean when we speak of the divinity of Christ.

15*b*-21. ***The True Security.***—Vs. 15*b* is awkward in the Greek and its exact meaning is uncertain. Our two versions present the same, and a quite possible, understanding of the text; the Exeg. calls attention to Goodspeed's. Another possible reading is, "It does not follow, because a man has abundance, that his life consists in wealth"; and still another, "A man's wealth is no guarantee for the continuance of life." Whatever interpretation we accept, it is clear that Jesus is challenging an accepted standard of values. He is denying that it is possible to achieve security by amassing property; one becomes secure only by being **rich toward God.**

L. P. Jacks writes:

> There is a coward and a hero in the breast of every man. Each of the pair has a "logic" of his own adapted to his particular purpose and aim—which is safety for the coward and victory for the hero. The two are perpetually at variance, the reason of the one being the unreason of the other, the truth of the one being the falsehood of the other.[2]

Now, the **rich man** of Jesus' story represents the coward in us trying to make his life secure. He

[2] *Religious Perplexities* (New York: George H. Doran, 1923), p. 17.

22 ¶ And he said unto his disciples, Therefore I say unto you, Take no thought for your life, what ye shall eat; neither for the body, what ye shall put on.

23 The life is more than meat, and the body *is more* than raiment.

24 Consider the ravens: for they neither sow nor reap; which neither have storehouse nor barn; and God feedeth them: how much more are ye better than the fowls?

22 And he said to his disciples, "There-
fore I tell you, do not be anxious about
your life, what you shall eat, nor about
your body, what you shall put on. 23 For
life is more than food, and the body more
than clothing. 24 Consider the ravens:
they neither sow nor reap, they have neither
storehouse nor barn, yet God feeds them.
Of how much more value are you than the

---

4. The Providence of God (12:22-31=Matt. 6:25-33)

Sayings that have no eschatological motivation and that in this respect are comparable to such Jewish wisdom teaching as is to be found in Proverbs, Ecclesiasticus, Pirke Aboth, and parts of the Testaments of the Twelve Patriarchs. Matthew incorporated this material in the Sermon on the Mount.

Jesus does not qualify his admonitions to complete and utter trust in God's providence. The interpreter must seek elsewhere in the biblical record for supplementary counsel to industry and forethought, if he deems such is wise and necessary. He may find justification for so doing in the fact that it is the attitude of anxiety that Jesus deprecates, not the attempt to provide for future needs.

22*a*. Editorial introduction.

22*b*-23. **Therefore:** The example of the rich fool illustrates the absurdity of anxiety about food and clothing. In Matthew, because worry is evidence of servitude to mammon. **Take no thought for your life** (KJV) was more correctly rendered by Tyndale "be not careful," i.e., "full of care." The revised versions follow the lead of this earlier English translation: **do not be anxious about your life.**

24. Worry shows lack of trust in God. **The ravens,** "the birds of the heaven" in Matthew. "The birds are an example not of idleness but of freedom from anxiety" (A. H. McNeile, *The Gospel According to Matthew* [London: Macmillan & Co., 1915], p. 87).

---

filled his barns, built new barns and filled them, too; he then said to his soul, **Soul, you have ample goods laid up for many years.** The coward, in other words, had found the "safety" he was out for. But Jesus saw in him not a coward only, but a **fool** as well—not only had he purchased his safety by surrendering every chance at victory, but also, as soon appears, the safety itself was chimerical: **This night your soul is required of you.** There is no security except the security of victory. One's life is made secure not by things, but by triumph over things. And this triumph does not consist, as the Stoics thought, in a hard-won independence of one's environment, a solitary self-sufficiency. It is not an achievement of self-discipline, although self-discipline is certainly involved in it. It is the consequence of joyous participation in a new order of the Spirit; it is the gift of God—"Thanks be to God, who gives us the victory" (I Cor. 15:57). One's life *does* consist in an **abundance,** but it is an abundance of another sort than that on which the "rich fool" relied. It is "through him who loved us" that we can be "in all things . . . more than conquerors. For," Paul continues, "I am sure [and of this only can we be sure] that neither death, nor life, . . . nor things present, nor things to come, . . . nor anything else in all creation, will be able to separate us from the love of God in Christ Jesus our Lord" (Rom. 8:37-39). To know this love is to be **rich toward God** (cf. on vss. 33-34).

The warning which this parable contains applies aptly to nations, especially strong and prosperous nations which are under a terrible temptation to try to build security by accumulating ever greater wealth and power (cf. Deut. 8).

22-31. *Trusting God.*—Here is another illustration of that poetic character of Jesus' teaching which was discussed in the Expos. on 11:9-13. If one wants to deal with this passage as one might deal with a page from a scientific or philosophical textbook, it is not difficult to show the absurdity of its statements. Indeed, how utterly romantic and extravagant! Most birds, it has been said, die of starvation; certainly millions of them do each year. And how

25 And which of you with taking thought can add to his stature one cubit?

26 If ye then be not able to do that thing which is least, why take ye thought for the rest?

27 Consider the lilies how they grow: they toil not, they spin not; and yet I say unto you, that Solomon in all his glory was not arrayed like one of these.

28 If then God so clothe the grass, which is to-day in the field, and to-morrow is cast into the oven; how much more *will he clothe* you, O ye of little faith?

birds! 25 And which of you by being anxious
can add a cubit to his span of life?[t] 26 If
then you are not able to do as small a thing
as that, why are you anxious about the rest?
27 Consider the lilies, how they grow; they
neither toil nor spin;[u] yet I tell you, even
Solomon in all his glory was not arrayed
like one of these. 28 But if God so clothes
the grass which is alive in the field today
and tomorrow is thrown into the oven, how
much more will he clothe you, O men of

[t] Or *to his stature.*

[u] Other ancient authorities read *Consider the lilies; they neither spin nor weave.*

25-26. Worry serves no useful purpose. The Greek noun translated **stature** (KJV) can also mean **span of life** (RSV) ; and the latter translation is preferred. To add a **cubit** —approximately twenty inches—to one's height would scarcely be described as a trifling thing (vs. 26) . Goodspeed: "Which of you with all his worry can add a single hour to his life?"

27-28. God lavishes his care on even the lowest forms of life. His children need have no fear that he will overlook their needs. **Lilies:** Still used by Arabs as a general term for wild flowers. The reading in the RSV mg., **they neither spin nor weave,** has the support of Codex Bezae, the early Syriac translations, and some other allies, and is preferred by several modern editors on the ground that the more common reading is a scribal harmonization of Luke's text with Matthew's. But **they toil not, they spin not** (KJV) —i.e., they perform neither man's nor woman's labor—has much more impressive MS attestation, and is also the reading of the Chester Beatty Gospel Papyrus (p^{45}) . Dried **grass**—which would include the "lilies" referred to in vs. 27—could be used as fuel.

---

about people? Is it not clear that God neither feeds us nor clothes us: that we feed and clothe ourselves and one another? And that if we do not, we starve or freeze? So we might argue, with complete plausibility, indeed with obvious truth. But the distinction of Jesus' teaching is not the soberness of its wisdom, but the magnificence of its truth; like the heavens it declares the glory of God. Such an utterance as this cannot, it is true, be called wise; but only because it is too great to be wise. The word "wise" does not apply to it at all, any more than to a lyric of Shelley or a statue of Michelangelo. This does not mean that the utterance is not true. Jesus is affirming here the appropriateness of an attitude of absolute trust in God. Who will deny that birds are fed and flowers clothed without anxiety or conscious strain on their part, and also that when we are most ourselves, we realize the essential anomalousness, in spite of the apparent necessity, of all our cares about ourselves? Do we not know in our hearts that these anxieties do not belong to our true life, that God did not intend things so?

The Exeg. expresses the opinion that the sayings "have no eschatological motivation." This may well be true if the emphasis is falling upon the word "motivation"; but that this teaching is related to, and in a sense conditioned by, Jesus' vivid expectation of **the kingdom of God** is a conclusion difficult to avoid. Martin Dibelius happens to use this passage in illustrating his understanding of how Jesus' most characteristic teachings are to be taken. He specifies five separate ways in which Jesus' intention in this teaching has been interpreted. Some have understood him to be making literally an absolute prohibition of any forethought or providence on our part, and have claimed to regard it as a practicable rule. Others have emphasized the tendency to exaggeration implicit in Oriental, and in particular Jesus', teaching, and have held that he means only that we should not be overburdened with anxiety. Again the prohibition has been understood as applying only to a special class—then the disciples; now the clergy. The fourth way of understanding is that of Schweitzer and others: an "interim ethic" applying only for the brief period believed to separate Jesus and his hearers from the end of history and the beginning of the eschatological kingdom of God. Martin

29 And seek not ye what ye shall eat,
or what ye shall drink, neither be ye of
doubtful mind.
30 For all these things do the nations
of the world seek after: and your Father
knoweth that ye have need of these things.
31 ¶ But rather seek ye the kingdom
of God; and all these things shall be added
unto you.
32 Fear not, little flock; for it is your
Father's good pleasure to give you the
kingdom.

little faith? 29 And do not seek what you
are to eat and what you are to drink, nor
be of anxious mind. 30 For all the nations
of the world seek these things; and your
Father knows that you need them. 31 In-
stead, seek his[v] kingdom, and these things
shall be yours as well.
32 "Fear not, little flock, for it is your
Father's good pleasure to give you the

[v] Other ancient authorities read *God's*.

29-30. Worry about material things is characteristic of pagans. "The knowledge that these things come from the Father as His gifts to His children, that they come not capriciously but out of His perfect knowledge of man's needs and His perfect love for His children, this is the true antidote to anxiety and fear" (Major, Manson, and Wright, *The Mission and Message of Jesus* [New York: E. P. Dutton & Co., 1938], p. 405).

31. His kingdom (RSV) has the support of all early MSS except the Chester Beatty Gospel Papyrus (p^{45}). Matthew's version adds "and his righteousness." Origen (*On Prayer* 2) quotes a similar saying: "Ask ye for the greater things, and the small shall be added unto you: and ask for the heavenly things, and the earthly shall be added unto you" (James, *Apocryphal N.T.*, p. 35).

5. Heavenly Treasure (12:32-34=Matt. 6:19-21)

Johannes Weiss, Albert Schweitzer, and their followers undertook to explain all Jesus' ethical teaching in the light of his belief in the imminence of the kingdom of God. Jesus meant his precepts to be taken literally and fulfilled literally, but they were a

---

Dibelius favors a fifth way, according to which the word is to be taken eschatologically, but in another sense:

> Jesus proclaims in an absolute way the pure will of God. This will is not confined to an interim and is thus not valid only for the period till the end of the world; it is God's actual demand upon men at all times and for all time. But it will attain its full validity only in the Kingdom of God. It is the sign of this passing age that the fulfillment of God's will is hampered and embarrassed by the conditions of our worldly existence. In the face of the coming end Jesus proclaims God's demand without regard to any such considerations. God's will does not depend upon the eschatological hope and expectation; it is eternal, like God. The eschatological expectation, however, gives the occasion for the proclamation of the divine will, without regard to the circumstances of everyday existence. The eschatological expectation makes men free from all conditions of this world, free to understand what is the pure, unconditional will of God.[3]

Thus a teaching like this stands in constant judgment upon our anxiety and selfish, feverish striving, and beckons us constantly toward the distant heights where something within us tells us we belong. Another great German scholar, Johannes Weiss, writes about this passage:

> In our modern world with its hurry and its striving, this song of banished care sounds like a strain from the lost paradise. Indeed none of us will accept it so completely from the heart as not to feel afterward some silent objections, and many a person, in the midst of his need and struggle, will bitterly reject it as not meant for him. . . . But has Jesus' word then no meaning for us? Once again we remind ourselves that "to be anxious" is not the same as "to pray and work." . . . "Do not be anxious: that is, "Have a free heart; be courageous and active; accept life each day new from God's hand and trust in him." . . . And how do we obtain such freedom from care? Jesus says to us, "Fill your soul with a really great care: strive after the kingdom of God; fight for the victory of the good in the world; seek for personal fulfillment; then what has hitherto oppressed you will seem petty and negligible.[4]

32. ***The Church and the Kingdom.***—This verse is of great importance in discussions of the relationship of Jesus to the church, which

[3] *The Sermon on the Mount* (New York: Charles Scribner's Sons, 1940), pp. 51-52. Used by permission.

[4] *Die Schriften des Neuen Testaments* (Göttingen: Vandenhoeck & Ruprecht, 1906), I, 273.

33 Sell that ye have, and give alms; provide yourselves bags which wax not old, a treasure in the heavens that faileth not, where no thief approacheth, neither moth corrupteth.

kingdom. 33 Sell your possessions, and give alms; provide yourselves with purses that do not grow old, with a treasure in the heavens that does not fail, where no thief

---

practicable ethic only on the assumption that the coming age would supersede the present in a matter of days or months. When the church abandoned the apocalyptic doctrine of the two ages, it was forced to qualify and to reinterpret Jesus' ethical teaching in terms of a philosophy of history that Jesus himself had not shared.

There are difficulties with this theory of "consistent eschatology." For one thing, much of Jesus' teaching shows no trace of eschatological presuppositions. Jesus often teaches in the Jewish "wisdom" tradition. For another, we have seen evidence that Jesus did not always think of the kingdom of God as wholly in the future. In some measure God's rule was already a fact. The kingdom was already breaking in upon history, although its full manifestation will be an event of the last days.

In the passage under consideration, Jesus' counsel to his followers to dispose of material possessions and to provide themselves with "a treasure in the heavens" is subordinated to the expectation of the kingdom but is not necessarily dependent on it. The imminence of death was the motive for unworldliness in vss. 16-21 and may also have been the underlying thought of these sayings in their original context. Jesus frequently drew attention to the corrupting influence of wealth but it must also be remembered that he had people of means among his followers and accepted their support (8:3).

32. An assurance peculiar to Luke. Whether or not it stood in Q must remain an open question. The sayings that follow are subordinated to it. Early Christians would interpret **little flock** as a reference to the church. **The kingdom** is here an *eschaton*—a future gift of God to the faithful.

33. The fact that the form of the saying in Matt. 6:19-20 preserves the parallelism of Semitic poetry supports the impression that it is more original. **Sell your possessions,**

---

manifestly came fully into being only after his death and resurrection.[5] At the very least the passage indicates that Jesus thought of his disciples whom he is addressing as being in some special sense the recipients of the benefits of the new age. **Fear not:** the exhortation involves confidence both that the kingdom is coming and that they will belong to it. The term **little flock** is reminiscent of Isa. 40:11 and of Ezek. 34:12, and must mean that Jesus thought of his disciples as a body, not only with affectionate devotion, but also as having important religious significance. He would hardly have so addressed them if he had not thought of them as being God's **little flock** as well as his own. And indeed, the latter part of the verse makes this quite explicit. But as the Exeg. reminds us, whatever was Jesus' intention in this teaching, there can be no question about the meaning the church of Luke's time found in it. That church conceived of itself as the nucleus or core of the coming new order. It was not long after the Resurrection that Christians were all but identifying the church with the kingdom of God.

[5] See R. Newton Flew, *Jesus and His Church* (New York: Abingdon Press, 1938), pp. 53-54.

In this they went too far; the kingdom of God transcends any human community, and no human institution can hope to embody it. In so far as we ever claim to do so, we are guilty of an act of almost blasphemous presumption. At the same time, it is not enough to say that the church is simply the herald of a completely future kingdom, or is in the position of merely waiting for it. In the church the kingdom is already in some measure present. The church *is* the church only in so far as it belongs not to this age only, but to the age which is to come and in Christ has already begun. There is a sense in which God has already given us **the kingdom.** How able and ready have we been to receive it? How adequately are we representing it? (See also on 9:27.)

33-34. ***Riches in Heaven.***—This passage, which ends a definite sequence of teachings within this chapter (vss. 13-34), invites comparison with the parable of the rich fool, which begins it. It makes essentially the same point—that material possessions do not give life security. In vss. 13-21 the uncertainty of *life* was emphasized; here, the uncertainty of *possessions* (to **moth** and **thief** we would need to add such

34 For where your treasure is, there will
your heart be also.
35 Let your loins be girded about, and
your lights burning;
36 And ye yourselves like unto men that
wait for their lord, when he will return

approaches and no moth destroys. 34 For
where your treasure is, there will your heart
be also.
35 "Let your loins be girded and your
lamps burning, 36 and be like men who are

---

and give alms: A command for Matthew's prohibition—"Do not lay up for yourselves treasures on earth." Distributing to the poor was one recognized way of obtaining **treasure in the heavens** (cf. 18:22=Mark 10:21). **No moth destroys:** Rugs and tapestries would be among the valuable **possessions** of Orientals.

34. This verse differs from Matthew's version only by slight variations in word order and by reading **your** instead of "thy" (ASV; KJV does not follow the Greek text here).

6. Allegory of the Waiting Servants (12:35-38)

A passage peculiar to Luke but having certain features in common with the parables of the doorkeeper (Mark 13:33-37) and of the wise and the foolish virgins (Matt. 25:1-13). The waiting servants appear to represent the early church; the absent master, the risen Christ; and the master's return, the Parousia or Second Coming. The allegory warns Christians to be on the watch for Christ's return, even though it may be long delayed (vs. 38). Certain genuine fragments of Jesus' teaching no doubt went into its construction (e.g., vs. 35). Allegory was a teaching device rarely employed by the rabbis and probably never used by Jesus, but one that soon became popular in Christian circles.

35. A metaphorical summons to preparedness. **Let your loins be girded:** The long Oriental robe would interfere with freedom of movement if it were not caught up about the waist (cf. Exod. 12:11).

36. Perhaps once a true similitude, but the allegorical interpretation now lies close at hand. No doubt Luke and his readers equated **the marriage feast** with Christ's sojourn

---

things as inflation, or the failure of stock market or bank). But whether we are remembering the fact that we must leave our possessions, or the fact that they may be lost or stolen or destroyed, the point is the same: our security, if it is really secure, cannot rest upon so precarious a foundation. As in the other passage also, however, it is clear that this real security is not a matter of individual self-sufficiency and the mere elimination of desire. It consists not primarily in the acceptance of poverty, but in the possession of another kind of riches—riches which make earthly possessions unimportant. We must be "rich toward God"; or as it is said here, our **treasure** must be **in the heavens.** (Note that this passage follows directly upon two references to the kingdom of God: "Seek his kingdom," and "It is your Father's good pleasure to give you the kingdom.") It is because God "has delivered us from the dominion of darkness and transferred us to the kingdom of his beloved Son" (Col. 1:13) that we are able—in the measure of our appropriation of this victory—to become independent of the "change and decay" to which all things are subject. Paul says to a small and socially despised group of Christians in Corinth, "All things are yours." Alexander the Great had claimed to have conquered the world; Paul is much bolder. We own the world, he says. "All things are yours, whether . . . the world or life or death or the present or the future, all are yours" (I Cor. 3:21-22). Paul means more here than that Christians have renounced the world—although renunciation in a certain sense is surely involved. He means that they have entered into a relationship with God in which all their other relationships are seen in their true character and have no more than their true importance. "All things are yours" because "you are Christ's; and Christ is God's" (I Cor. 3:23). Perhaps the deepest fallacy in the seeking of security through possessing things lies in the belief that possessing things is simply a matter of having them in our hands. Actually, things possess *us,* unless we are possessed by God. If God possesses us, we are possessed by nothing else, and therefore possess all things in the only way we can truly possess anything (see also on vss. 13-21; 18:18-30; Matt. 6:19-21).

35-46. ***Watchfulness and Faithfulness.***—Whatever the original text and context of these three parables, they stand in Luke as a reiterated warning, in view of Jesus' expected return,

from the wedding; that, when he cometh and knocketh, they may open unto him immediately.

37 Blessed *are* those servants, whom the lord when he cometh shall find watching: verily I say unto you, that he shall gird himself, and make them to sit down to meat, and will come forth and serve them.

38 And if he shall come in the second watch, or come in the third watch, and find *them* so, blessed are those servants.

39 And this know, that if the goodman of the house had known what hour the thief would come, he would have watched, and not have suffered his house to be broken through.

40 Be ye therefore ready also: for the Son of man cometh at an hour when ye think not.

waiting for their master to come home from
the marriage feast, so that they may open
to him at once when he comes and knocks.
37 Blessed are those servants whom the mas-
ter finds awake when he comes; truly, I say
to you, he will gird himself and have them
sit at table, and he will come and serve
them. 38 If he comes in the second watch, or
in the third, and finds them so, blessed are
those servants! 39 But know this, that if the
householder had known at what hour the
thief was coming, he would have been
awake and[w] would not have left his house
to be broken into. 40 You also must be
ready; for the Son of man is coming at an
hour you do not expect."

[w] Other ancient authorities omit *would have been awake and.*

---

in heaven after the Resurrection, and **when he comes and knocks** with his anticipated return as Son of man. For the picture of Christ knocking at the door cf. Rev. 3:20. In Matt. 25:11 it is the foolish virgins who knock.

37. A beatitude on watchfulness is followed by a saying that is indubitably allegorical. In ordinary life it is the servants who wait on their master (17:7-8). The **master** of this allegory is he who said: "I am among you as one who serves" (22:27). For other references to the new age under the imagery of a feast see 13:29; 22:30; Rev. 19:9.

38. A warning that the Parousia may be delayed. In Mark 13:35 the night is divided after the Roman custom into four watches. According to Jewish reckoning, **the second watch** was from 10 P.M. to 2 A.M., and **the third** from 2 A.M. to 6 A.M.

7. Parable of the Householder and the Thief (12:39-40=Matt. 24:43-44)

39-40. These verses continue to stress the importance of watchfulness, but without the employment of allegory. Unlike the unwary **householder,** whom the thief caught by surprise, the faithful must be prepared for the coming of **the Son of man,** even though they do not know the **hour** (cf. I Thess. 5:2; II Pet. 3:10; Rev. 3:3).

---

against laxness on the part of Christians and (especially in vss. 41-46) of their official leaders. There can be no question about the "eschatological motivation": Christians must be faithful to their duty because they "know neither the day nor the hour" (Matt. 25:13) when Christ will come. In the middle parable (vss. 39-40) it is simply the suddenness and unexpectedness of this return which are emphasized; in the other two there are also unmistakable allusions to the Christians as *servants* of Christ, left for a while with certain duties, and not knowing when the Master will return and demand an accounting. This theme of the absentee landlord or master is recurrent in the gospel accounts of Jesus' teaching (cf. 19:12-27; Matt. 24:45-51; 25:14-30; Mark 12:1-9; 13:32-37) and always is subject to this same eschatological interpretation. We must be faithful because the Day of Judgment is imminent. And so we must—for it would be a great mistake to suppose that the difference in spatial and temporal world view which lies between us and these ancient Christians makes any significant difference at the essential point with which eschatology is concerned. We live on the edge of eternity—either heaven or hell—quite as much as they. All apocalyptic pictures are in essence attempts at dramatizing or making vivid a continuing and awful fact about man's life: our actions, whether good or evil, have an ultimate significance and effects of infinite range and scope. We stand under incalculable responsibility. We must be faithful in little things be-

41 ¶ Then Peter said unto him, Lord, speakest thou this parable unto us, or even to all?

42 And the Lord said, Who then is that faithful and wise steward, whom *his* lord shall make ruler over his household, to give *them their* portion of meat in due season?

43 Blessed *is* that servant, whom his lord when he cometh shall find so doing.

44 Of a truth I say unto you, that he will make him ruler over all that he hath.

45 But and if that servant say in his heart, My lord delayeth his coming; and shall begin to beat the menservants and maidens, and to eat and drink, and to be drunken;

41 Peter said, "Lord, are you telling
this parable for us or for all?" 42 And the
Lord said, "Who then is the faithful and
wise steward, whom his master will set over
his household, to give them their portion
of food at the proper time? 43 Blessed is
that servant whom his master when he
comes will find so doing. 44 Truly I tell you,
he will set him over all his possessions.
45 But if that servant says to himself, 'My
master is delayed in coming,' and begins to
beat the menservants and the maidservants,

---

8. Parable of the Faithful and Unfaithful Servants (12:41-46=Matt. 24:45-51*a*)

Originally a parable that warned of the sudden advent of the kingdom. Some interpreters believe it was directed against the priestly aristocracy. Luke understands it as an allegorical caution to those in his day who constituted the ministry of the church. The servants, the master, and the return are cryptic terms for ecclesiastical officials, the risen Christ, and the Second Advent.

41-42*a*. Editorial insertion by Luke into Q matter (Matt. 24:43-51) to suggest that the following parable bears particularly on the responsibility of church officials. **Peter** is often made the spokesman of the disciples in the gospel tradition. **This parable:** probably Luke has vss. 35-38 in mind as well as vss. 39-40.

42*b*. Luke has substituted **steward** for "servant" (cf. Matthew's version and also vss. 43, 45, 46) in order to emphasize the great responsibility held in trust. Parables frequently begin with a question.

43-44. The faithful and wise **servant** will be rewarded by promotion from the office of overslave to that of estate manager.

45-46. The tyrannical and drunken **servant**, who takes advantage of his temporary authority, will be surprised by his master's unexpected return and will be **cut . . . in sunder** (KJV). **Punish** (RSV) attenuates the Greek verb but makes it possible to avoid under-

---

cause there are no little things; we must be faithful in God's absence because God is never absent. Eschatology, which seems to treat entirely of the awesome end of life, is really primarily concerned with its awesome nature. It is this awesome nature which leads us to expect the awesome end; not the expectation of the end which leads us to infer the nature. It is the vertical dimension in our experience, the depth and height of meaning we find in it, which is expressed in all our conceptions of a future heaven or hell if these conceptions are anything more than the most naïve fancies. Those conceptions have persisted, under however many forms, because they are not fancies, but answer, and answer indispensably, to the realized character of human life. Man stands each day and hour on the verge of either hell or heaven, i.e., of either utter and final defeat or utter and final victory. We must live in readiness for judgment because we are constantly under judgment; we must live in readiness for victory because victory is a constant possibility. This is the glory and the peculiar torment of human living.

The eschatological significance of these parables has been emphasized in what has been said because there can be no doubt that for Luke—and probably for Jesus also—such was their primary significance. H. J. Cadbury, although giving due weight to this fact, points out an additional meaning. The parables presuppose that much of our life will be lived without conscious experience of God's nearness.

46 The lord of that servant will come in
a day when he looketh not for *him,* and at
an hour when he is not aware, and will
cut him in sunder, and will appoint him
his portion with the unbelievers.
47 And that servant, which knew his
lord's will, and prepared not *himself,*
neither did according to his will, shall be
beaten with many *stripes.*
48 But he that knew not, and did commit things worthy of stripes, shall be beaten
with few *stripes.* For unto whomsoever
much is given, of him shall be much required; and to whom men have committed
much, of him they will ask the more.

and to eat and drink and get drunk, **46** the
master of that servant will come on a day
when he does not expect him and at an
hour he does not know, and will punish[x]
him, and put him with the unfaithful.
47 And that servant who knew his master's
will, but did not make ready or act according to his will, shall receive a severe beating.
48 But he who did not know, and did what
deserved a beating, shall receive a light
beating. Every one to whom much is given,
of him will much be required; and of him
to whom men commit much they will demand the more.

[x] Or *cut him in pieces.*

standing **unfaithful** (RSV) allegorically. The reference could be to "unfaithful servants." **Unbelievers** (KJV) would rather mean those who are punished by being committed to hell.

9. Supplementary Sayings Emphasizing Responsibility (12:47-48)

Appended by Luke to the parable to underline his interpretation of its message: a warning to leaders of the church that they in particular are to be ready for the advent of the Son of man.

47-48*a*. Note Amos 3:2. **Make ready or** adapts an independent saying to its present context. Probably Luke thought of the instructed and uninstructed servants as allegorical references respectively to the clergy and to the rank and file of the church. The responsibilities of Christian laymen were less onerous than those of their leaders, and their failure to be on the alert would be less severely penalized.

48*b*. Both statements express the same idea—synonymous parallelism. The force of the comparative is not to be pressed, for **the more** is probably only a variation in the interests of style for **much.** The saying now serves to generalize the principle of vs. 47, but no doubt once circulated independently.

Rather one must live *as though* seeing him that is invisible, remembering his strict demands and our responsibility, and waiting through the present interim until the *parousia.* Much has been said about the ethics of Jesus as interim ethics, but much clearer from these parables comes the notion of an absentee God. Like the apocalyptic term *parousia,* they remind us that normally we are on our own and alone. For long intervals we have no contact with the one to whom we are responsible. He is in a distant country and there is no certainty that he will return soon. Our business is to live as we should live, but without him. Normal rectitude, fidelity, diligence, are expected of us and not emergency behavior. Blessed is the servant whom his master, when he cometh, shall find so doing.[6]

47-48. *Proportionate Duty.*—The point which this little paragraph makes has been discussed in the Expos. on 10:13-14. Cadbury points to our familiarity with the distinction between graded and equal requirements, e.g., the income tax and the poll tax, and to the fact that it is characteristic of law in general to "require a flat minimum." Cadbury finds abundant indication that one of the decisive and pervasive characteristics of Jesus' mind was his habit of thinking about human responsibility in the other way. In the present passage Jesus formulates explicitly a principle which he is everywhere applying, especially in his dealings with more privileged groups. Commenting on the last clause of vs. 48, Cadbury says: "Were we to press the wording, 'To whom *much* is committed of him will *more* be required,' we might find something even more exacting than proportionate responsibility for the highly privileged. We might assume a kind of surtax in the moral realm." The reader will find illuminating Cadbury's whole discussion of this feature of Jesus' teaching and of its meaning for us.[7]

[6] *Jesus: What Manner of Man* (New York: The Macmillan Co., 1947), p. 45. Used by permission.

[7] *Ibid.,* pp. 23-31.

49 ¶ I am come to send fire on the earth; and what will I, if it be already kindled?

49 "I came to cast fire upon the earth; and would that it were already kindled!

10. Reflections on the Purpose and Issue of Christ's Ministry (12:49-50)

49. Fire: Sometimes interpreted as the fire of the Day of Judgment (3:16-17), as the fire of the Holy Spirit (Acts 2:3), or as the purifying fire of repentance that will prepare the way for the kingdom of God. In the light of vss. 51-53 it is evident that Luke thinks of it as the fire of conflict that will compel men to align themselves for or against the Messiah. Vs. 49*b* (like 50*b*) is without doubt an exclamation and is correctly punctuated in RSV.

49-53. ***Fire upon the Earth.***—This brief paragraph contains what seem to be three originally independent pieces of tradition: a saying about **fire;** a reference to Jesus' approaching passion as a **baptism** (see separate comment below); and a prediction of divisions, even within families, of which Jesus is to be the occasion. The Exeg. deals with the questions of their authenticity. Luke places them together as all referring to the coming crisis, the great day: it will be preceded by the **fire** of bitter divisions (in Luke's time, of course, prevalent and increasing) and by Jesus' own crucifixion. What vs. 49 meant in its original context we have no way of knowing. We can interpret it only as Luke understands it, and that apparently was as a symbol of the disturbance and division which Jesus introduced into the world. There can be no doubt about the fact of the divisions, that in this sense Jesus did **cast fire upon the earth.** Not only is there plenty of evidence of bitter divisions within families, but almost every part of the N.T. bears witness to the opposition of organized society as a whole to the Christian. The ancient church from the moment it was recognized was under an unremitting threat of persecution—and **fire** was not too strong a term for Luke to use in speaking of it. The author of I Pet. 4:12 also can speak of "the fiery ordeal which comes upon you to prove you." He tells his readers that they are not to be "surprised" at this ordeal: did not Christ also suffer? (Here again we see the fire of persecution and Jesus' own death brought together, as they are in vss. 49-50.)

We are reminded by this passage of the paradox that the peacemaker may, despite all his efforts, be the occasion of conflict. Jesus is the Prince of Peace—indeed, he is above all the peacemaker, the reconciler—and yet he can say that the effect of his coming is not to give peace on earth, but rather, as the Matthaean parallel has it, "a sword" (Matt. 10:34). One cannot have the kind of fidelity to truth discussed in vss. 1-12 and not find oneself often at odds, and sometimes at war, with the world. To be sure, the Christian will still seek to be the peacemaker. "If possible," Paul writes, "so far as it depends upon you, live peaceably with all" (Rom. 12:18; see also Col. 4:5). The author of I Peter is eager that Christians shall not be the cause of unnecessary friction or conflict. "Always be prepared," he says, "to make a defense to any one who calls you to account for the hope that is in you, yet do it with gentleness and reverence" (I Pet. 3:15; cf. also I Pet. 2:12-17). This same writer also recognizes that sometimes Christians may be persecuted not because they are Christians, but because they are wrongdoers or mischief-makers (I Pet. 4:15-16). In other words, there is no virtue in suffering that might have been avoided by a measure of kindness and respect toward one's opponents, nor is there any value in suffering for the wrong cause. In a famous letter to Trajan, the Roman emperor, Pliny, then governor of Pontus-Bithynia, says that although he is uncertain just what the beliefs of the Christians are and whether they are as such punishable, he has nevertheless put some Christians to death because he is "persuaded that whatever the nature of their creed a contumaceous and inflexible obstinacy certainly deserved punishment."[8] This may well be the prejudiced remark of a pagan official; but it may refer to a lack of "gentleness and reverence" on the part of the accused. Certainly it often happened that later Christians, seeking martyrdom, made no effort to be conciliatory. But the Christian who faithfully bears witness to Christ will be the victim of an inescapable amount of misunderstanding and hostility, no matter how gentle and tactful he may be, and in some periods and crises he will face actual persecution.

[8] *Letters* X. 96.

50 But I have a baptism to be baptized with; and how am I straitened till it be accomplished!

51 Suppose ye that I am come to give peace on earth? I tell you, Nay; but rather division:

52 For from henceforth there shall be five in one house divided, three against two, and two against three.

53 The father shall be divided against the son, and the son against the father; the mother against the daughter, and the daughter against the mother; the mother-in-law against her daughter-in-law, and the daughter-in-law against her mother-in-law.

50 I have a baptism to be baptized with;
and how I am constrained until it is ac-
complished! 51 Do you think that I have
come to give peace on earth? No, I tell
you, but rather division; 52 for henceforth
in one house there will be five divided,
three against two and two against three;
53 they will be divided, father against son
and son against father, mother against
daughter and daughter against her mother,
mother-in-law against her daughter-in-law
and daughter-in-law against her mother-in-
law."

---

50. This verse asserts that Jesus' mission cannot be accomplished except by his death—**baptism** is also used in this sense in Mark 10:38-39. Most of the passages that represent Jesus as anticipating his death are clearly "predictions after the event." This saying may also belong in that category, but there is nothing in it that compels the interpreter to deny its authenticity. If Jesus meditated on the fate of John the Baptist; if he foresaw the consequences of the growing opposition to his own ministry; if he discovered any clue to his own mission in the suffering servant passages in the book of Isaiah—if his thoughts moved along any or all of these lines, he may have been driven to anticipate his death and to reflect on its significance. But purely historical exegesis can give us no final answer to such questions.

11. Messianic Divisions (12:51-53=Matt. 10:34-36)

51-53. Probably an expansion of sayings that stood in Q. Matthew's version is modeled more closely on Mic. 7:6 and represents the conflict more explicitly as a revolt of the younger against the older generation. The passage ascribes a well-defined messianic consciousness to Jesus, and declares that he anticipated the divisions that would arise within families over the issue of adherence to Christ. On both counts its authenticity is open to dispute. **Three against two and two against three:** The father and the mother on one side, and the daughter, the son, and the son's wife on the other.

---

50. ***Jesus' Baptism of Suffering.***—Here is one of the most deeply moving sayings in the Gospels, and the commentator is bound to hesitate as he approaches it. There can be no doubt whatever that by **baptism** is meant the death of Jesus. Mark 10:38-39 clearly indicates such a use, and the verse itself can bear no other sense. Back of the figure may stand such passages as Pss. 69:2-3, 14-15; 42:7; 124:4-5; Isa. 43:2*a*. There is good ground for trusting the saying as an authentic word of Jesus himself (see Exeg.). As Montefiore[9] says, it is hard to believe that such an utterance would have been invented. It belongs with Jesus' prayer in Gethsemane, and his "cry of dereliction" from the Cross, in attributing to Jesus human feelings of weakness and fear which hardly suited the developing portrait of Jesus the Christ. Whatever may have been the route of transmission of such traditions as these, they make a very strong claim to authenticity at least in substance. But if they are authentic, they bring us near to the inmost heart of Jesus. And this is not least true of this poignant cry, "Would that it were over!" That Jesus may have foreseen his death the Exeg. makes clear; that he would have thought of it as a religiously significant event (a **baptism**) is also clear. There is no hint in the Gospels that Jesus was put to death because his enemies finally overtook him. On the contrary, he set his face to go to Jerusalem knowing that death might well be the result of his act (see on 9:51-55). He went to Jerusalem because he knew it was the will of God that he should do so. If, then, death awaited him there, that he suffer it was also God's will. The Fourth Gospel sees Jesus as the complete master of his fate, as dying

[9] *Synoptic Gospels*, II, 496.

54 ¶ And he said also to the people, When ye see a cloud rise out of the west, straightway ye say, There cometh a shower; and so it is.

55 And when *ye see* the south wind blow, ye say, There will be heat; and it cometh to pass.

56 *Ye* hypocrites, ye can discern the face of the sky and of the earth; but how is it that ye do not discern this time?

54 He also said to the multitudes, "When
you see a cloud rising in the west, you say
at once, 'A shower is coming'; and so it
happens. 55 And when you see the south
wind blowing, you say, 'There will be
scorching heat'; and it happens. 56 You
hypocrites! You know how to interpret the
appearance of earth and sky; but why do
you not know how to interpret the present
time?

12. Interpreting the Present Time (12:54-56)

54-56. A variant of this passage has been interpolated in many MSS to constitute Matt. 16:2*b*-3 but is not in the text of that Gospel in codices Vaticanus and Sinaiticus or in the Old Syriac versions. In it the signs by which "Pharisees and Sadducees" are said to prognosticate the weather are a red sky in the evening and a red sky in the morning. **A cloud rising in the west:** Winds from the Mediterranean were laden with moisture (cf. I Kings 18:44). **The south wind** blew in over arid and scorching plains. **You hypocrites!** was perhaps introduced into the saying because it was a frequent word of abuse. Some believe it was used because those who were addressed only pretended that they had no ability to draw obvious conclusions, but this interpretation is remote. Luke and his readers would understand that Jesus and his message were the signs by which **the multitudes** ought to have interpreted **the present time.** Men ought to have known that the age of God's rule was at hand—or had already begun—and to have governed themselves accordingly. It is conceivable that that was also what Jesus had in mind. The kingdom of God was breaking in upon history, but men who were weatherwise remained spiritually insensitive.

only because he chose to die (cf., e.g., John 10:17-18); that goes too far—and the proof that it goes too far is the fact that such sayings as the present one and the others mentioned just above are not to be found in John. Jesus did not choose to die—indeed, he shrank from death. But on the other hand, he was not the mere victim of external circumstances. He chose, in obedience to the Father's will, a course which led to death; and such passages as this indicate that he knew both that it would lead thither and that the purpose of God which decreed the course would give meaning to the death also.

Such shrinking from death as this passage reveals does not reflect upon the heroism of Jesus, as some have thought. Just the contrary is true. His sensitiveness to the bitterness of his fate only accentuates his courage and truth in facing and bearing it. To be sure, Jesus did not die like a Stoic; but neither had he lived like one. He had loved men and he had loved life; the Stoics aimed at loving neither. To suffer death through the hatred of men was to drink a bitter cup and to enter the deep waters. Nor does a recognition of Jesus' human attitude toward his passion reduce the religious and theological significance of his act. Note how the writer to the Hebrews emphasizes this very element in Jesus' life—this human weakness and finitude—as one of its most significant and religiously precious features: "For we have not a high priest who is unable to sympathize with our weaknesses, but one who in every respect has been tempted as we are, yet without sinning. . . . In the days of his flesh, Jesus offered up prayers and supplications, with loud cries and tears, to him who was able to save him from death. . . . Although he was a Son, he learned obedience through what he suffered; and being made perfect he became the source of eternal salvation to all who obey him" (Heb. 4:15; 5:7-9).

54-59. ***The Crucial Time.***—Except for the phrase **You hypocrites,** which does not appear in Matthew's version of this text and does not fit the context in Luke, there is no reason to distrust the authenticity of vss. 54-56 as an utterance of Jesus. The opprobrious term is excepted not only because it is improbable that Jesus would have addressed **the multitudes** in this way, but also because the remark seems to express disappointment at men's blindness rather than condemnation of their sin. In whatever terms precisely Jesus conceived of his mission and role, it is beyond question that he believed the kingdom of God—the final judg-

57 Yea, and why even of yourselves judge ye not what is right?

58 ¶ When thou goest with thine adversary to the magistrate, *as thou art* in the way, give diligence that thou mayest be delivered from him; lest he hale thee to the judge, and the judge deliver thee to the officer, and the officer cast thee into prison.

59 I tell thee, thou shalt not depart thence, till thou hast paid the very last mite.

57 "And why do you not judge for your-
selves what is right? 58 As you go with your
accuser before the magistrate, make an effort to settle with him on the way, lest he drag you to the judge, and the judge hand you over to the officer, and the officer put
you in prison. 59 I tell you, you will never
get out till you have paid the very last copper."

---

13. Wisdom of Reconciliation (12:57-59=Matt. 5:25-26)

Usually interpreted as a parable. As the defendant in a lawsuit for the recovery of a debt is well advised to reach an agreement with his "accuser" before the case is brought to court, so a man ought to **make an effort to settle with** anyone with whom he has differences before the Day of Judgment. No doubt Luke understood it after this fashion. It is an illustration of how men ought to act in "the present time." Originally it may have been a bit of wisdom teaching without eschatological reference: Settle your disputes out of court! Matthew employs it in the Sermon on the Mount to illustrate the application in a concrete instance of Jesus' teaching forbidding anger.

57. Transition to new material. "You should know what to do without any instruction from me."

58. The singular number (cf. KJV) is evidence that the matter in this verse had no original connection with what precedes it. **Officer:** translates a Greek word that is found in the papyri for a collector of revenue.

59. Copper (λεπτόν for the Hebrew פרוטה): The smallest coin in circulation. Luke avoids the Latinism (κοδράντης from the Latin *quadrans*) that Matthew uses ("penny" [RSV], worth about two "coppers").

---

ment and salvation—to be on the point of arriving, and that he felt the mighty, the incalculable significance of **the present time.** We can come nearest to understanding how he felt, perhaps, if we try to imagine how we should have felt had we been there but had known what we now know of the meaning of Christ. We now know that in these happenings in Palestine a strange and divine event was occurring, after which life would never be the same again; that what was taking place was nothing less than the disclosure to men of the ultimate nature and purpose of God; that God was reconciling the world to himself; that a new kind of human community was coming into existence; that a new epoch in the life of mankind was beginning. All of this we now know. Imagine that we had known it then! But Jesus, we may believe, did think of that **present time** in some such way. That was his message, "The kingdom of God is at hand!" This was the "weight of glory" he carried in his heart. No wonder he could find no one to carry it with him! No wonder the kingdom of God remained a "secret" which he tried constantly to share but could not! Who could have believed such a report?

It is usual that men do not sense the meaning of their own time, and it is perhaps inevitable that this should be true. Only in the perspective of the years, perhaps the centuries, can the true meaning of an epoch be seen—it will not be fully seen until history itself is ended and transcended and we know as also we are known. Not only was the significance of the event of which Jesus and his message were the center and the "sign" not recognized by his contemporaries during the earthly life; it was not recognized even by his own disciples till after the Resurrection, which placed it in a new light; and even then, decades of reflection were needed for the realization, even to the limits of the church's power of understanding, of its manifold richness.

Vss. 57-59 bring into a new context, and invest with a new significance, a saying more familiar to us in Matt. 5:25-26. Vs. 57 is a reference to the same blindness and dullness of heart implied in vss. 54-56. The Exeg. gives one interpretation of Luke's intention; Montefiore

13 There were present at that season some that told him of the Galileans, whose blood Pilate had mingled with their sacrifices.

2 And Jesus answering said unto them, Suppose ye that these Galileans were sinners above all the Galileans, because they suffered such things?

3 I tell you, Nay: but, except ye repent, ye shall all likewise perish.

13 There were some present at that very time who told him of the Galileans
whose blood Pilate had mingled with their
sacrifices. 2 And he answered them, "Do you
think that these Galileans were worse sinners than all the other Galileans, because
they suffered thus? 3 I tell you, No; but unless you repent you will all likewise perish.

---

14. Call to Repentance (13:1-5)

Disasters that overwhelm individuals do not prove that such people are worse sinners than others. But they ought to serve as a warning both to Galileans and Judeans that only timely repentance can avert destruction at the Day of Judgment.

13:1. Goodspeed translates (in accordance with Lukan [Acts 10:21; 12:20; etc.] and classical usage) : "some people came up." **At that very time:** An editorial note that makes the following paragraph part of the more inclusive discourse. The incident must have taken place in the environs of the temple in Jerusalem. Pilate had ordered some **Galileans** slain while they were in the act of slaughtering **their sacrifices,** perhaps because he suspected them of being insurrectionaries. Josephus makes no mention of this atrocity, although he does refer to comparable acts of violence against Jews in Jerusalem (*Antiquities* XVIII. 3. 2) and Samaritans on Mount Gerizim (*ibid.,* XVIII. 4. 1). The latter incident was responsible for the procurator's recall in A.D. 36. Were Jesus' informants enemies who were hoping he might make some seditious utterance? Or Jewish patriots who wished to rouse him to lead a revolt against Rome? Or simply purveyors of news? The story itself provides no answer to such questions.

2-3. All the other Galileans: A translation according to the sense of the Greek. Jesus repudiated the popular theory that suffering was the consequence of sin, but did not concern himself in this instance with any other answer to the problem. He interpreted the fate that had befallen the **Galileans** only as a warning to his hearers to heed the call to repentance before it would be too late.

---

suggests a slightly different one: "As in an earthly quarrel it is well to be reconciled with your adversary (you being in the wrong) before you enter the court, so, as between you and God, repent before the Judgment comes." [10]

13:1-5. ***Calamities and Repentance.***—We can only guess why the question was asked. Jesus' interrogators may have been trying to arouse his indignation so that he would lead a nationalistic movement; or they may have had a hostile desire to provoke him into a seditious word that could be reported to Rome; but perhaps, and more likely, they were curious to know his answer to their baffled minds. The Jew believed by and large that calamity is the wages of sin. But how could men be sinners in the act of preparing animals for sacrifice? Yet the tyrant slew them then and there, and thus mixed human and animal blood. Jesus replied to their instance with another instance: Were the eighteen people killed by a falling tower more wicked than other men? If the eighteen were building a tower of Pilate's aqueduct, as some exegetes propose, they were being paid from the temple funds which Pilate had confiscated; and therefore calamity, so the Jew might argue, was clearly their penalty.

Jesus cut across the current belief: **I tell you, Nay.** That was a radical stroke. But Jesus was a realist: He confronted the truth that calamity is no respecter of persons, even though that truth might double the mind's questionings.

> Streams will not curb their pride
> The just man not to entomb,
> Nor lightnings go aside
> To give his virtues room.[1]

Jesus did not tell us why tyrants are given free rein or towers fall. The answer is found only through another question, "Why am I given life?"; and in such a reply as Keats suggested,

[10] *Synoptic Gospels,* II, 498.

[1] Matthew Arnold, *Empedocles on Etna,* Act I, scene 2.

4 Or those eighteen, upon whom the
tower in Siloam fell, and slew them, think
ye that they were sinners above all men
that dwelt in Jerusalem?
5 I tell you, Nay: but, except ye repent,
ye shall all likewise perish.
6 ¶ He spake also this parable; A cer-
tain *man* had a fig tree planted in his vine-
yard; and he came and sought fruit there-
on, and found none.

4 Or those eighteen upon whom the tower
in Si-lo'am fell and killed them, do you
think that they were worse offenders than
all the others who dwelt in Jerusalem? 5 I
tell you, No; but unless you repent you will
all likewise perish."
6 And he told this parable: "A man had
a fig tree planted in his vineyard; and he
came seeking fruit on it and found none.

4-5. A fatal accident that had involved Judeans ought to serve a similar purpose. **The tower in Siloam** was a part of the fortifications of Jerusalem near an important spring and reservoir.

15. Parable of the Fig Tree (13:6-9)

Employed by Luke as a conclusion to the discourse that had begun with 12:2. Reiterates the theme of impending judgment. Israel has only a short period left for repentance.

The parable may be the ultimate source of Mark's story about the cursing of the fig tree (Mark 11:12-14). There has possibly been a confusion in the Marcan stream of tradition between what Jesus said and what Jesus did. Luke may have suspected some such connection between the parable and the story, for he omits the latter at the point where he might otherwise have used it (19:44).

A parable in the Story of Ahikar (Syriac Version 8:35) exhibits some resemblances to the one under discussion: "My son, thou hast been to me like that palm-tree that stood by a river, and cast all its fruit into the river, and when its lord came to cut it down, it said to him, 'Let me alone this year, and I will bring thee forth carobs.' And its lord said unto it, 'Thou hast not been industrious in what is thine own, and how wilt thou be industrious in what is not thine own?'" (Tr. J. Rendell Harris, in R. H. Charles, *The Apocrypha and Pseudepigrapha of the Old Testament* [Oxford: Clarendon Press, 1913], II, 775.)

6. A vineyard in Palestine contained fruit trees as well as vines. Goodspeed: "a garden."

"Call the world if you please, 'The vale of Soul-making.' Then you will find out the use of the world."[2] But such was the urgency of the gospel for Jesus that he himself gave no answer: he waved aside even so vast an issue as the meaning of pain.

He saw his nation headed for disaster. He would have no part with the insurrectionists. He opposed direct action not only because it would obviously be a blood bath of futility, but because there was no guarantee that insurrectionist leaders or Caiaphas would lead Israel more nobly than Rome. The nation had a mission: to make God known to the world. That mission was now laid again on Israel: the kingdom had come in new grace and vocation in him, the Son of man. Should Israel again prove recreant, the day of opportunity for the chosen would darken into a long midnight. All the towers would fall, for Rome would destroy the rebels and lay waste the land. Rome, though herself guilty of the pride of brute power, would be a scourge in the hand of God. We live in the midst of slaughters and calamities. What would Jesus say to our land and time?

6-10. ***Fruitlessness and Penitence: The Parable of the Fig Tree.***—These verses are on the same theme: "Except ye repent" . . . (vs. 3). Jesus' hearers could scarcely mistake his reference: he was speaking about them and their nation. Jesus often spoke in judgment tones about his own land, but the undertone was poignant love. Always the dominant system of government pleads with the preacher, "Speak unto us smooth things," and too many preachers acquiesce. But they part company with their Lord. If Jesus spoke to our land as to his own, his patriotism would be called in question.

[2] In a letter to George and Georgiana Keats dated April 28, 1819. See *The Complete Poetical Works and Letters of John Keats* (Boston: Houghton Mifflin Co., 1899), p. 369.

7 Then said he unto the dresser of his vineyard, Behold, these three years I come seeking fruit on this fig tree, and find none: cut it down; why cumbereth it the ground?

8 And he answering said unto him, Lord, let it alone this year also, till I shall dig about it, and dung *it:*

9 And if it bear fruit, *well:* and if not, *then* after that thou shalt cut it down.

10 And he was teaching in one of the synagogues on the sabbath.

7 And he said to the vinedresser, 'Lo, these
three years I have come seeking fruit on this
fig tree, and I find none. Cut it down; why
should it use up the ground?' 8 And he
answered him, 'Let it alone, sir, this year
also, till I dig about it and put on manure.
9 And if it bears fruit next year, well and
good; but if not, you can cut it down.' "

10 Now he was teaching in one of the

---

7. The details of the parable are not to be allegorized. "Three" is a recurring number in folk tales, and **three years** has no reference to the length of Jesus' ministry. The owner of the orchard had given the **fig tree** ample opportunity to demonstrate its fruitfulness. It had failed to do so, and must now be felled (cf. 3:9). **Use up the ground,** or "exhaust the soil."

8-9. The gardener urges the owner to give the tree another year of grace. **Well and good:** An apodosis that is unexpressed in the Greek text (a regular feature of the Semitic idiom, but also not uncommon in Greek).

J. Sabbath Teaching in a Synagogue (13:10-21)

1. On the Sabbath Healing of a Crippled Woman (13:10-17)

Closely related in structure and content to 6:6-11 (Mark 3:1-6) and 14:1-6. The nucleus in each instance is a saying that no doubt had proved useful to the church in its controversy with the synagogue over the matter of sabbath observance, and in each instance the miracle story appears to have been woven around the saying to provide it with a narrative setting. The argument in this variant is repeated in 14:2-6 (cf. Matt. 12:11-12*a*): If it is right to care for domestic animals on the sabbath, it is right to relieve human distress.

10. A synagogue scene as in 6:6.

When we give due weight to the rigor of truth in Jesus, it will not surprise us that he was crucified.

He said that Israel was privileged, like a fig tree in a vineyard. It had a sunny slope, and rose high above the vines: the sky was all its own. To the outward eye Israel's history was a succession of disasters, but real blessings are not in material prosperity: Israel had the covenant of God, the lineage of the prophets, and the commission to make God's way known on earth. This was privilege, a sunny vineyard.

The privilege spelled responsibility, as always. *Noblesse oblige.* The purpose of a fig tree is to bear figs. Leaves and shade are no substitute for fruit. But Israel had run to leaf—to an itch for wealth, and a hankering for power by which to confound her foes. It is the perennial failure of men and nations. Still God was patient: **Three years** means a long time. There is no occasion to allegorize the **three.** We should neither construe it as the law, the prophets, and the time of Jesus, nor take it as a reference to the length of Jesus' ministry. Three was a favorite number in such parables. In this instance it tells of the patience of God. **I have come** means in the tense of the verb "I keep coming." The startling matter in our life is not that disaster overtakes our transgression, but that the disaster is so long delayed.

Despite man's always postponed obedience, God is still patient. **This year** also is the index of grace. Jesus is surely **the dresser:** he "maketh intercession for us" (Rom. 8:34). Always he said that men can make a new start. To an age caught in the fetter of habit, as every age is caught, he told of a mercy that can break every fetter. "Repent, and believe in the gospel" (Mark 1:15) is his word. He meant it: a man or nation can turn again, and by act of faith receive power for creative life. The parable does not tell if the year of grace brought penitence. The open ending gives the story a more moving power. Yet the clear warning should not be sidestepped: "He will not always chide: neither will he keep his anger for ever" (Ps. 103:9).

11 ¶ And, behold, there was a woman which had a spirit of infirmity eighteen years, and was bowed together, and could in no wise lift up *herself*.

12 And when Jesus saw her, he called *her to him*, and said unto her, Woman, thou art loosed from thine infirmity.

13 And he laid *his* hands on her: and immediately she was made straight, and glorified God.

14 And the ruler of the synagogue answered with indignation, because that Jesus had healed on the sabbath day, and said unto the people, There are six days in which men ought to work: in them therefore come and be healed, and not on the sabbath day.

synagogues on the sabbath. 11 And there
was a woman who had had a spirit of in-
firmity for eighteen years; she was bent
over and could not fully straighten herself.
12 And when Jesus saw her, he called
her and said to her, "Woman, you are freed
from your infirmity." 13 And he laid his
hands upon her, and immediately she was
made straight, and she praised God. 14 But
the ruler of the synagogue, indignant be-
cause Jesus had healed on the sabbath, said
to the people, "There are six days on which
work ought to be done; come on those days
and be healed, and not on the sabbath

11-13. A spirit of infirmity, a spirit that caused weakness. Possibly substituted by Luke for an original "infirmity," for the rest of the story assumes a healing rather than an exorcism (cf. 6:10; 14:4).

14. The ruler of the synagogue is represented as avoiding a direct criticism of Jesus. He addresses himself to the congregation by recalling the words of Deut. 5:13.

11-13. *Crippleness Healed.*—Form criticism has taught that this story is a memory frame for a focal word of Jesus, in this instance the word in vss. 15-16. But the story is still rich in suggestion in its own right. Why did Jesus heal so few people in a land rife with suffering? Why did the few who were healed afterward die? The compassions of Jesus were instantly touched by crippleness: therefore his healings. Yet the compassion sought more than physical cure. In his eyes bodily sickness, even though not necessarily the result of transgression, was always the sign of a deeper ill: the sickness of the soul. Thus the healings wrought by Jesus are sign and promise of a deeper health. Actually we seek that better gift when we go to a doctor: recovery from bodily ills gives us chance to renew our quest for—what? Sickness regarded as a sign has points of contact with the view held in Jesus' day, that maladies are brought by invading demons—**a spirit of infirmity.**

This story is eloquent of our deeper need. **Eighteen years:** how long and strong is the bondage of sin! **Bent over:** her eyes on the ground, so that she could not see Jesus, as our eyes in recent decades have been intent to study and exploit the planet, like the man with the muck rake who could not see the angel above his head.[3] **Could not fully straighten herself:** human helplessness in a phrase! The ungodly man is even less able to straighten his crippleness into faith and reverence.

The description of the healing likewise has words that are stabs of truth. **He called:** to him there are no masses, for each man or woman is precious, and the need of any is claim upon his care. **He . . . said to her:** the word of assurance was spoken even before she reached him. **You are freed:** his power was stronger than any demonic fetter. **He laid his hands upon her:** even in the cure he did not stand aloof. "Daughter of Abraham" (vs. 16) is a tribute any Jew might covet: it is as if he had said "Child of heaven," for he told her thus that she belonged to God, not to any demonic spirit of infirmity.

The cure was complete: **She . . . glorified God.** Suppose she had used her liberation for license: she might almost better have stayed bound. But **she was made straight** in soul as well as in body, thus giving evidence that Jesus was intent on the deeper cure, of which the bodily cure was but a visible sign. Do we wish to be made whole to glorify God, or to be cured just enough to rid us of discomfort?

14-17. *The Question of the Sabbath.*—The opposition between the mind of Jesus and that of the religious leaders of Israel came to sharp and open clash on the question of the sabbath. The conflict continued beyond the first century; sabbath observance was a bone of contention between the synagogue and the early church. Therefore this story: it is told to teach converts

[3] John Bunyan, *The Pilgrim's Progress*, Part II.

15 The Lord then answered him, and said, *Thou* hypocrite, doth not each one of you on the sabbath loose his ox or *his* ass from the stall, and lead *him* away to watering?

16 And ought not this woman, being a daughter of Abraham, whom Satan hath bound, lo, these eighteen years, be loosed from this bond on the sabbath day?

17 And when he had said these things, all his adversaries were ashamed: and all the people rejoiced for all the glorious things that were done by him.

day." 15 Then the Lord answered him,
"You hypocrites! Does not each of you on
the sabbath untie his ox or his ass from
the manger, and lead it away to water it?
16 And ought not this woman, a daughter
of Abraham whom Satan bound for eight-
een years, be loosed from this bond on the
sabbath day?" 17 As he said this, all his
adversaries were put to shame; and all the
people rejoiced at all the glorious things
that were done by him.

---

15. Hypocrites: The plural may be an indication that the saying was originally independent of its present context. Another explanation: Jesus assumes that the people agree with the ruler and includes them in his rebuke. **Hypocrite** is probably a scribal correction, but one that must have been made as early as the Chester Beatty Gospel Papyrus (p^{45}).

16. The "loosing" of the **woman** from her infirmity—ascribed in accordance with the thought of the day to the activities of Satan—is compared to the "loosing" of an ox or an ass from its manger. Jews would not have admitted that the healing of **a woman** who had been ill for **eighteen years** was an emergency great enough to justify the infringement of sabbath legislation, but the early church saw a logic in the analogy, and the gospel evidence makes it clear that Jesus put human need above ritual requirements (see on 6:1-5).

17. Luke's concluding observation: Jesus had discomfited **all his adversaries** in sabbath controversy, and **all the people rejoiced** at his miracles of healing, **the glorious things that were done by him.**

---

the Christian law of the sabbath; or rather, of the new Sunday. We must give scribes and Pharisees their due: they knew that only through observance of the religious law could the purity of Israel be preserved and her mission fulfilled in the world. The law was "the yoke of the kingdom." The ruler of the synagogue here attacks the people for laxness in sabbath observance, but by implication his real condemnation was on Jesus for healing a woman on the sabbath.

Luke's Gospel deals three times with this issue (see Expos. on 6:6-11; 14:1-6; also Mark 3:1-6, and corresponding passages in Matthew). Jesus here offers three reasons for what seemed his radical breach of the law: (*a*) Jewish tradition itself supported him: some work was allowed on the sabbath, for a man was allowed to lead his ox to water, even though he was not permitted, in the scrupulous hairsplitting of the Talmud, to lift the water in a vessel to the animal's mouth. (*b*) The worth of human life justified him: a woman is more important than an ox, her bondage by demonic power more important than an ox's bondage by a rope, her eighteen years of infirmity more pitiable than an animal's tether for a few hours. (*c*) Conscience spoke an instant demand, and through conscience the voice of God: **Ought not this woman . . . be loosed?** These three tests are still radiant guidance: What does the best practice of the past teach us? What does the preciousness of human life require? What does God's spirit demand?

We should carefully note that Jesus never broke the sabbath; he broke only the scrupulosity of Jewish law concerning the sabbath. We affront his truth if we try to twist this story into an excuse for sabbath laxities. Jesus went regularly to the synagogue on the sabbath. He took reverent joy also in the temple worship. Sunday is given for rest, for kindliness, for the acknowledgment of God in praise and prayer. Nothing in this story impairs the centrality of worship in man's life. Christ is still "Lord also of the sabbath" (Mark 2:28). Vs. 17 may be a Lukan addition, but that fact does not make it untrue; the churches to which Luke wrote had found in Christ **glorious things,** and therefore rejoiced.

18 ¶ Then said he, Unto what is the kingdom of God like? and whereunto shall I resemble it?

19 It is like a grain of mustard seed, which a man took, and cast into his garden; and it grew, and waxed a great tree; and the fowls of the air lodged in the branches of it.

18 He said therefore, "What is the kingdom of God like? And to what shall I compare it? 19 It is like a grain of mustard seed which a man took and sowed in his garden; and it grew and became a tree, and the birds of the air made nests in its branches."

2. Parable of the Mustard Seed (13:18-19=Matt. 13:31-32)

A variant occurs in Mark 4:30-32. It had apparently been incorporated into a collection that Mark had used as a source. Luke omits the Marcan version at the point where he might have used it (following 8:18) and now employs the Q form. Matthew conflated Mark and Q and preserved the Marcan order.

The mustard plant was characterized by its rapid growth, and the whole process of growth was a mystery to the ancients. Therefore there are those who insist that the point of the parable is that the new age of God's rule will come suddenly and mysteriously. But this is to do violence to the passage in the interests of a hypothesis. The parable turns on the contrast between small beginnings and great results. Although the full realization of God's rule on earth as it is in heaven awaits the future, in some measure it is already manifest within the historical order.

18. He said therefore is obviously editorial. Both Mark and Luke (Q) introduce the parable with a double question although they differ in the wording of it. Matthew substitutes a statement.

19. The smallness of a **mustard seed** was proverbial (cf. 17:6; Matt. 17:20) but it is the Marcan version (followed by Matthew in this detail) that draws specific attention to the fact. The mustard was not a **garden** plant in Galilee and therefore Matthew substitutes "field." It is said to grow to heights of ten or twelve feet. On several occasions in the O.T. (Ezek. 17:22-23; 31:1-6; Dan. 4:10-12, 20-22) a kingdom is depicted as a **tree,** and the extension of its power as the nesting of **birds** in its **branches.** It is possible that the last clause is actually a quotation from one or other of these passages, and that it was added to the parable to give it a touch of allegory: the church will gather in even Gentile peoples!

18-19. ***Parable of the Mustard Seed.***—The ancients could not explain growth. It provoked their wonder: seeds "spring and grow up, he knoweth not how" (Mark 4:27). But that mystery and wonder are not central truth in this parable. The emphasis clearly is on a contrast: small beginnings lead to great results. A mustard seed was proverbially, although not actually, the smallest seed; yet it grew to the size of a bush so large that birds could "lodge" in it.

It is a vivid parable, filled with hope. In Jewish thinking the kingdom of God was not evolution, still less the accomplishment of man's hand and brain; it was God's act, an event so surprising, with such reversals among men and nations, that men could only exclaim, "This is the Lord's doing; it is marvelous in our eyes" (Ps. 118:23). So Jesus here tells us that the seed of the kingdom, in him and his first followers, is God's planting, and that no man can destroy it. Its origin is small—a Craftsman teaching a handful of followers how to pray, and himself dying on a cross—but its end result will be mighty: a home for all nations.

We are tempted to despair of the church, not least in times of skepticism and war. It would be wiser to recall that every sizable town shows some sign of Jesus and his followers. Would the disciple John, even though Jesus told him the parable of the mustard seed, have credited the possibility of the Cathedral of St. John the Divine, built above the largest American city? The cross that was once a gallows is now the saving sign set against earth's skyline.

The reference to birds holds signal import. O.T. prophecy (see Exeg.) knew that picture. The kingdom faith (such is the meaning) will provide heart's home not for Jews only, but for mankind. Thus the parable is eloquent not only of the world hunger of Jesus, but of his surety that God will fulfill it. The kingdom in Jesus' teaching is God's act: therefore it is not merely

20 And again he said, Whereunto shall I liken the kingdom of God?
21 It is like leaven, which a woman took and hid in three measures of meal, till the whole was leavened.
22 And he went through the cities and villages, teaching, and journeying toward Jerusalem.

20 And again he said, "To what shall I compare the kingdom of God? 21 It is like leaven which a woman took and hid in three measures of meal, till it was all leavened."
22 He went on his way through towns and villages, teaching, and journeying to-

3. Parable of the Leaven (13:20-21=Matt. 13:33)

20-21. The introduction in Matthew is a statement, and in Luke a rhetorical question. The parable was not in the collection used by Mark, but stood in Q as a companion to that of the mustard seed. No doubt Luke and his readers would interpret it as a prophecy of the spread of the gospel and the growth of the church. In its original application it probably illustrated the same truth as its twin: God is already asserting his sovereignty, and the mighty consequences of that fact will shortly be evident. **Leaven:** Elsewhere in the N.T. (12:1; Matt. 16:6, 11; Mark 8:15; I Cor. 5:6-8; Gal. 5:9) a symbol for evil, as often also in Jewish literature. Women did all the grinding as well as all the baking in the East. **Three measures:** A little over a bushel, which would be an enormous quantity of flour for a single baking. Perhaps the large amount was mentioned to emphasize the mighty effects of God's rule. But cf. Gen. 18:6, where Sarah is said to have used "three measures of fine meal" in preparing cakes for three guests.

K. Teaching in the Course of the Journey (13:22-35)

1. On Admission to the Kingdom of God
(13:22-30; cf. Matt. 7:13-14, 22-23; 8:11-12; 20:16)

Points of similarity with material in Matthew indicate the use of a common source, but both evangelists have dealt freely with it.

22. An editorial reminder to the reader that Jesus was still journeying **toward Jerusalem.**

of one land or time, but universal in its love. Does a profane and cruel time seem to belie the parable? The seed is still God's planting, and still carries God's life.

20-21. ***Parable of the Leaven.***—This is a twin parable with that of the mustard seed. If there is a difference, the parable of the seed promises outward growth, and the parable of the leaven the unstayable spread of unseen influence. The stress here, as in every account of the kingdom, is on the sovereignty of God. He sets his leaven in the meal of the world, and he gives it power. Notice the transformation of a word: **leaven** is usually used of evil, e.g., "the leaven of the Pharisees" (Mark 8:15); "Purge out therefore the old leaven" (I Cor. 5:7). In this parable even the metaphor used tells of redemption.

Three measures, according to most exegetes, is a large amount. Three should not be allegorized; a parable is a parable, not an allegory. Three does not represent body, soul, and spirit; or the law, the prophets, and the writings; or any other supposed parallel. Sarah (see Exeg.) used three measures to bake for her guests. If any specific meaning is to be fastened on the phrase, let it mean food enough for other nations as well as for Jewry. But safer interpretation will take it as representing the world which tries to resist the leaven life of the kingdom, but is at last totally leavened.

The promise is being fulfilled, enough at least to give foretaste of the heavenly kingdom. For the church, at the very moment when it seems to have been impotent by the inertia of the world and its own disobedience, revives in new purity and power: it has God's own life. Once the secret of Jesus is hid (e.g., in penology), it begins its slow or swift triumph. Compare this description of the cause of Christ with the then-prevalent conception of the Jewish law. The latter kept itself aloof, fearing contact with an alien world; the kingdom, conversely, invades the world in gentle might. It seems to lose its life, but actually it thus gives life and finds life. Draw the inescapable conclusion: there is no merely "individual Christianity." The leaven is hid in business and learning and statecraft, and must triumph.

23 Then said one unto him, Lord, are there few that be saved? And he said unto them,

24 ¶ Strive to enter in at the strait gate: for many, I say unto you, will seek to enter in, and shall not be able.

25 When once the master of the house is risen up, and hath shut to the door, and ye begin to stand without, and to knock

ward Jerusalem. 23 And some one said to
him, "Lord, will those who are saved be
few?" And he said to them, 24 "Strive to
enter by the narrow door; for many, I tell
you, will seek to enter and will not be able.
25 When once the householder has risen
up and shut the door, you will begin to

---

23. An introduction without any parallel in Matthew and apparently supplied by the evangelist. The question of the number of the elect was frequently debated in late Jewish literature. The author of II Esdras (late first century A.D.) gives a pessimistic answer: "The Most High made this world for the sake of many, but the world to come, for the sake of few . . . ; many have been created, but few will be saved" (II Esdras 8:1-3 Goodspeed).

24. Entrance to the kingdom of God is difficult. The metaphor of **the narrow door** is combined in Matthew with that of "the hard way," and both are contrasted with the wide gate and the easy way that lead to destruction.

25. Only a short time is left for those who wish to be admitted. Soon **the householder** will have **shut the door** and the latecomers will **knock** in vain. The words of **the house-**

23-24. ***The Kingdom: The Door Is Narrow.*** —(See also Expos., vss. 25, 25-27, 28-30). Vss. 23-30 set forth four truths concerning the kingdom: the door is narrow, the time is short, there is no favoritism, and kingdom verities overturn the judgments of earth. Interpretation may conveniently follow this sequence. So here: the kingdom door is narrow. The question about the number of the saved may have been asked in compassion. But the sharpness of Jesus' answer seems to show that the questioner was self-righteous. People then as now (see Exeg.) debated the number of the elect. Now, as then, doubtless, the debaters took it for granted that they were surely among the chosen. Jesus spoke astringently: men may peer into God's future, but they cannot see; it is a spacious land of banqueting halls and shaded gardens, but the entrance gate is narrow; a man may not enter except by the struggle of self-denial.

There is no selfishness in the counsel. Indeed, selfishness with its moneybags and full-length mirrors is precisely the baggage that a man must cast away if he would enter that narrow gate. There is no cruelty in the requirement; mystery indeed, but not cruelty. A scholar must "scorn delights, and live laborious days";[4] an athlete must eschew rich food, and subject himself to discipline; an artist must give weary hours and days to practice; a saint must pray and pray, and then deny himself so as to live as he prays. For Jesus the gate was as narrow as a cross. But there is no cruelty: faith in Christ is neither an epicureanism that would make life promiscuous, nor an asceticism that would leave life mutilated; it is rather a discipline that leads life to heaven, as the pruning of a plant gives a lovelier bloom.

While this life remains, the gate is open. Anyone who says self-righteously, as the book of Esdras says in another mood, "There be many more of them which perish, than of them which shall be saved: like as a wave is greater than a drop" (II Esdras 9:15-16), wanders from the path and may miss the gate. But the gate is now open. God precondemns no man. His heart is open. John G. Paton[5] tells of his uncle Walter who left home and, after two or three letters, disappeared. They did not know if he was indifferent or sick or dead. But the mother never gave up hoping, and every night threw the door wide open with a cry, "Come hame, my boy." A parable of God: the gate is open, but the time is short.

25. ***The Kingdom: The Time Is Short.***—Probably the reference is to the Parousia. The parable bears the marks of preaching at the turn of the first century, when the church could not understand the delay in Christ's return. Certainly he would soon come, they said, and a man must be ready. As for the Parousia, we may not dogmatize, least of all in denial; for physics and contemporary event alike hint that history is culminative rather than cyclic or evolutionary. There is no necessary permanence in man's story on this planet. As for application

[4] Milton, *Lycidas*, l. 72.

[5] *John G. Paton, Missionary to the New Hebrides*, ed. James Paton (New York: Fleming H. Revell Co., 1889), Part I, p. 15.

at the door, saying, Lord, Lord, open unto us; and he shall answer and say unto you, I know you not whence ye are:

26 Then shall ye begin to say, We have eaten and drunk in thy presence, and thou hast taught us in our streets.

27 But he shall say, I tell you, I know you not whence ye are; depart from me, all *ye* workers of iniquity.

28 There shall be weeping and gnashing of teeth, when ye shall see Abraham, and

stand outside and to knock at the door,
saying, 'Lord, open to us.' He will answer
you, 'I do not know where you come from.'
26 Then you will begin to say, 'We ate and
drank in your presence, and you taught in
our streets.' 27 But he will say, 'I tell you,
I do not know where you come from; de-
part from me, all you workers of iniquity!'
28 There you will weep and gnash your

---

holder appear to be a reminiscence of those of the bridegroom in the parable of the wise and the foolish maidens (Matt. 25:11*b*-12).

26. Many of Jesus' Jewish contemporaries will seek admission by claiming to have been his acquaintances. In the Matthaean parallel the applicants for admission will be false teachers who will claim to have been Jesus' ministers.

27. In both Matthew and Luke the words with which the unworthy are rejected are enforced by a quotation from Ps. 6:8*a*.

28-29. A vivid way of describing the dismay of the Jews who are excluded at the sight of the patriarchs and **the prophets** seated at the banquet table with non-Jews. The idea

---

of the parable to any time in any man's life, the door is always being shut. When each day ends, the opportunity of that day is gone. When each experience of joy or sorrow passes into the next, its truth, heeded or unheeded, writes finis. Meanwhile inexorable death draws an inexorable line. A thousand times God's bell tolls and ceases, and we answer the summons or disobey. "Never send to know for whom the bell tolls; It tolls for thee."[6]

25-27. ***The Kingdom: No Favoritism.***—Jewish thought pictured the reward of the faithful at history's climax as a messianic banquet or a bridal feast. That picture is the background of vss. 23-30. The Jews were children of the covenant. God had chosen them to make known to the world the good tidings of his nature and will. But the covenant could become a snare; they could construe it selfishly as a favor rather than as a mission. They often fell into the snare; they deemed themselves God's favorites, and regarded pagan lands as beyond the pale. Over and again Jesus took sharp issue with them on that score, and it did not help his popularity. For instances of this strand in his message see 4:23-29, and such sayings as "God is able of these stones to raise up children unto Abraham" (3:8).

Here the warning has an even sharper edge. Some men would plead at heaven's door that they were the contemporaries of Christ, and had heard him preach, but that plea would not save them. What use had they made of that golden chance? Was his word dwelling in them? Others would plead lineal descent from Abraham and the prophets, but that claim would be no passport. Had they lived in the power and burden of that privilege? If not, they would be strangers, for they had lived as strangers: **I know you not whence ye are.** They would be treated as **workers of iniquity,** for iniquity is iniquity under whatever name or pretense or beseeching. The modern reader of scripture should realize that no story in it is past and gone. The Book is alive; it bleeds if it is cut from any man's life. Do we not say when judgment comes, "But my parents reared me in godliness. Though I have not gone to church very much, I believe in it. At least I would not like to live in a place without a church. I have always argued that the best in our culture comes from Bible tradition, and I've lived a respectable life. I've always meant to do well, and I've given more to charity than most folks." The question then will be: What of the marrow of motive? What of very prayer and deed? Life is not an indifference or an indulgence, but the ordaining of God's holy love.

28-30. ***The Kingdom: Reversal of Earth's Judgments.***—For the chosen to be barred from the door was darkness enough; that "lesser breeds without the Law"[7] should take their place was bitterness piled on midnight. Any Jew would shrink in dismay from the mere thought of the patriarchs and prophets feasting at the messianic banquet with pagan strangers. The language is even more dramatic than translations show. **There** (vs. 28) means "There out-

[6] John Donne, *Devotions,* XVII.

[7] Rudyard Kipling, "Recessional," st. iv.

Isaac, and Jacob, and all the prophets, in
the kingdom of God, and you *yourselves*
thrust out.

29 And they shall come from the east,
and *from* the west, and from the north, and
from the south, and shall sit down in the
kingdom of God.

30 And, behold, there are last which
shall be first; and there are first which shall
be last.

31 ¶ The same day there came certain
of the Pharisees, saying unto him, Get thee
out, and depart hence; for Herod will kill
thee.

teeth, when you see Abraham and Isaac
and Jacob and all the prophets in the
kingdom of God and you yourselves thrust
out. 29 And men will come from east and
west, and from north and south, and sit
at table in the kingdom of God. 30 And
behold, some are last who will be first, and
some are first who will be last."

31 At that very hour some Pharisees
came, and said to him, "Get away from

---

of a messianic feast that would inaugurate the new age was a familiar one in late Jewish apocalyptic. Vs. 29 precedes vs. 28 in the Matthaean version, which is inserted into the story of the healing of the centurion's slave.

30. A saying preserved both in Mark 10:31 (Matt. 19:30) and in Q (Matt. 20:16). Only Luke applies it to Gentiles and Jews.

2. Warning from Pharisees (13:31-33)

31. At that very hour—the word **day** (KJV) has inferior MS attestation—an editorial prefix. It is not clear that Luke thinks of Jesus' itinerary at this time as wholly within Samaritan territory (see above, p. 181). This incident at any rate must have taken place either in Galilee or Perea, Herod's territories. Probably it was completely undated in Luke's source. It has often been associated with the narrative in Mark 6:14-16 (Luke 9:7-9), but there is no suggestion in this latter passage that **Herod** wished to have Jesus killed. Probably these **Pharisees** were friendly men who wished to warn Jesus of the danger in which he stood. It is unnecessary to think of them as commissioned by the Galilean tetrarch to deliver an expulsion order.

---

side the door from which you have been barred." **You yourselves thrust out** means "While you yourselves are being thrust out"; i.e., they would see, in one revealing glance, strangers from the ends of the earth feasting with the elect of God, and then would be thrust out to grind their teeth and weep in helpless anger of remorse.

Vs. 30 must have been a memorable and frequent saying, for it recurs in the Gospels. It should not be construed too sweepingly. **Some** of the **first**: earth's judgments are not totally blind. But the reversals will be staggering. Not only shall outcast Gentiles, believing in the light of Christ, take the place of chosen Jews, but the publican shall be justified while the Pharisee is left disconsolate (18:10-14), and the simple-minded shall receive God's secret while the brilliantly learned wander in darkness (10:21). From these instances which Jesus himself gave we may deduce others. The judge perchance shall be judged by those whom he sentenced on earth, leaders of government and trade be ruled by those whom they dismissed as "only average men," and the preacher be barred from the door while some unruly man with a hidden love for God finds welcome.

The behest in vs. 24 is thus made urgent in thunders and lightnings: a man must agonize to enter the narrow gate, and count everything else well lost to gain the kingdom joy. Likewise the question in vs. 23 is answered: The number of the elect is not arbitrarily predetermined, nor is the chosen Jew the sole candidate, but all men may come by acceptance of Christ. The inequalities of earth need not too much distress us or fetter our witness; there is a realm around our dim earth, and a throne that shall judge all our evil disparities and remold earth's brokenness into its own truth.

31-33. ***A Warning, Herod, and Jesus.***—Why not assume that the Pharisees came as friends? They were the puritans of that time; and Jesus had much more in common with them than with, e.g., the Sadducees. Nicodemus and Joseph of Arimathaea may have been representative of a considerable number of Pharisees who believed in Jesus. The reasons why Herod wished

32 And he said unto them, Go ye, and tell
that fox, Behold, I cast out devils, and I
do cures to-day and to-morrow, and the
third *day* I shall be perfected.
33 Nevertheless I must walk to-day, and
to-morrow, and the *day* following: for it
cannot be that a prophet perish out of Je-
rusalem.
34 O Jerusalem, Jerusalem, which killest
the prophets, and stonest them that are

here, for Herod wants to kill you." 32 And
he said to them, "Go and tell that fox, 'Be-
hold, I cast out demons and perform cures
today and tomorrow, and the third day I
finish my course. 33 Nevertheless I must go
on my way today and tomorrow and the
day following; for it cannot be that a
prophet should perish away from Jerusa-
lem.' 34 O Jerusalem, Jerusalem, killing the

32-33. Jews as well as Greeks could use **fox** as a metaphor for a cunning man, but it occurs more often in rabbinical literature to mean an unimportant individual—as a term of contempt. The main meaning of Jesus' words is clear: He will not interrupt his ministry because of any fear of Herod. But it has become increasingly evident that his work may lead to his death, and he intends to leave Galilee after a brief interval and meet it as a prophet in **Jerusalem. And the third day I shall be perfected** is such a specific prediction of the Crucifixion and Resurrection that it was probably added to an earlier form of the saying after the event, and the repetition of **to-day and to-morrow** might then have been considered necessary. All serious exegetical difficulties would disappear if the saying originally was as follows: "Go and tell that fox, 'Behold, I cast out demons and perform cures today and tomorrow. Nevertheless I must go on my way the day following . . .'" (Julius Wellhausen, *Das Evangelium Lucae* [Berlin: Georg Reimer, 1904], pp. 75-76).

3. Lament Over Jerusalem (13:34-35=Matt. 23:37-39)

Associated by Luke with the preceding saying only because of the recurrence of "Jerusalem." If Matthew has preserved the connection as it was in Q, these verses

---

to be rid of Jesus are not hard to guess: in Herod's eyes Jesus was a troublemaker who might be a focus of revolution; and in any event he was a friend of John the Baptist.

As to Jesus' answer, it is wise to adopt some such emendation as is suggested in the Exeg. **Fox** doubtless implies slyness, but it is probably more a term of stern contempt. Possibly the fact that the word is in the feminine gender may have implications: Herod's immorality was notorious. But Jesus' reply goes far beyond any Herod. It is the sign of Jesus' courage; no Herod or host of demons could bar him from his duty. More deeply it is the sign of his trust in God, who alone determines the times and the seasons, and who will keep his own until their word is spoken and their work is done. Thus Jesus teaches us a doctrine of providence: we may not understand God's dealings, but his hand is not shaken, and his throne is not usurped. Those who obey are in his care. They may walk undismayed.

The reference to **Jerusalem** does not mean any martyr complex; Jesus did not obdurately walk into the lion's mouth. It would seem that he planned a last appeal to his people at the center of their national life. Yet he knew the time was short; that is the meaning of **to-day, and to-morrow, and the day following.** He knew also that the appeal would probably fail, and that he might have no honorable choice but to die. Why should great cities, blessed by music and art, be also the breeding ground of crime? Why should Jerusalem, crowned by the temple, be the slaughterhouse of prophets? Ecclesiastical pride is the worst form of pride, and issues in the worst cruelty (see Expos., vss. 34-35).

I shall be perfected is probably an addition of the Gospelist reflecting the faith of the early church. We now know that Jesus shrank from such predictions, not least because ideas of messiahship in his time were cankered by earthy and nationalistic hankerings. But the phrase is not thereby falsified. On the contrary, it is confirmed by experience. The early church had learned through Calvary and the Resurrection the truth concerning Jesus: he is the atoning and regnant Lord. He did meet death at Jerusalem. But God was in him. So the brutal waywardness of Herod and the cruel pride of the temple leaders were overthrown—by the perfect sacrifice and exaltation of the Lord.

34-35. ***Lament over Jerusalem.***—No words are more poignant, except perhaps those from

sent unto thee; how often would I have gathered thy children together, as a hen *doth gather* her brood under *her* wings, and ye would not!

35 Behold, your house is left unto you desolate: and verily I say unto you, Ye shall not see me, until *the time* come when ye shall say, Blessed *is* he that cometh in the name of the Lord.

prophets and stoning those who are sent to you! How often would I have gathered your children together as a hen gathers her brood under her wings, and you would not! 35 Behold, your house is forsaken. And I tell you, you will not see me until you say, 'Blessed be he who comes in the name of the Lord!' "

---

followed the material that is now in Luke 11:49-51, part of which appears to be a quotation from a lost book about "the Wisdom of God." It has been suggested that these sayings also were originally those of the divine "Wisdom," who had called men to herself in vain, and who abandons her fruitless task until the advent of the Messiah. If Jesus spoke such words of poignant melancholy, we must assume—with the Gospel of John—an extended ministry in Jerusalem, of which the Synoptic Gospels have preserved no record.

34-35*a*. To you: Found only in Codex Bezae and a few allies (most MSS read "to her"), but justified in English in view of the Semitic preference for the third person in attributive and relative clauses dependent on a vocative. The metaphor of a bird and her young to describe God's relationship to his people occurs occasionally in the O.T. (Deut. 32:11-12; Ps. 36:7; Isa. 31:5) and frequently in rabbinical literature. **Your house** is often interpreted as a reference to the temple, but in the O.T. and in other Jewish literature the temple is almost invariably "God's house." Here probably the city—or possibly the nation. God has withdrawn his protection.

35*b*. A prediction that the inhabitants of Jerusalem will not see the speaker again until they acknowledge the advent of the Messiah. By locating the whole section during Jesus' last days in Jerusalem, Matthew interprets these words as a prediction of Jesus' return as glorified Son of man. It is just conceivable that Luke understood them as a prediction of the triumphal entry as described in 19:37-38, but in the latter account it is Jesus' disciples who acclaim him. In either case, if the preceding sayings are to be understood as utterances of Jesus, this last is almost certainly a Christian addition.

Gethsemane and the Cross. Here is a picture of divine love, not less but more if we assume with some interpreters that the words were originally deemed an utterance of "the Wisdom of God" (see Exeg.). The repetition, **Jerusalem, Jerusalem,** is like the heartbroken "O my son Absalom, my son, my son Absalom! would God I had died for thee" (II Sam. 18:33). The indifferent crowds in the city were Jesus' children, the brood whom he would fain have gathered beneath wings of love. **Jerusalem, Jerusalem** is a yearning and a sob as well. Our casual worldliness breaks his heart, yet we neither know nor care.

Here is a picture of human willfulness. Jesus' "I would" is answered by man's "I will not." Yet if God compelled our obedience he would destroy us, for we would then be but clay in his hands. Only a willed obedience is real. In that fact is the dread possibility of disobedience, to God's grief and man's desolation. **Jerusalem,** home of the temple, is here called prophet-killer. Worship can become encrusted with pride. Then it is worse pride, with more cruel weapons of selfishness, for it falls from the greatest height: Satan cast forth from heaven! There are always three groups of men within the casual crowd: reactionaries, prophets, and mutineers. The reactionaries in their greed condemn the prophet as a mutineer, and kill him; the mutineers in their bitterness condemn the prophet as a reactionary, and kill him. So Jesus was killed by the insurrectionists in the mob and by the reactionaries in temple and state. Always we must cleave to the prophets. Without them we have no standard from God and no movement toward God; life stagnates into foulness. Yet we kill the prophet. He would cure us, but we say, with sores upon us, "We are not sick." So we kill him who is more than a prophet. Calvary is always at the gates of Jerusalem.

Here is a picture of the wretchedness that always haunts the abuse of man's freedom in his denial of God. **House** does not mean temple, though temple is included in the meaning. It means home—the home of the spirit of men. **Left unto you** means left only to man's wit,

14 And it came to pass, as he went into the house of one of the chief Pharisees to eat bread on the sabbath day, that they watched him.

2 And, behold, there was a certain man before him which had the dropsy.

3 And Jesus answering spake unto the lawyers and Pharisees, saying, Is it lawful to heal on the sabbath day?

4 And they held their peace. And he took *him*, and healed him, and let him go;

14 One sabbath when he went to dine at
the house of a ruler who belonged to
the Pharisees, they were watching him.
2 And behold, there was a man before him
who had dropsy. 3 And Jesus spoke to the
lawyers and Pharisees, saying, "Is it lawful
to heal on the sabbath, or not?" 4 But they
were silent. Then he took him and healed

L. Table Talk in the House of a Pharisee (14:1-24)

1. Healing of a Man with Dropsy (14:1-6)

See on 6:6-11; 13:10-17. Matt. 12:11 is a variant of the saying in vs. 5, inserted into the framework of a Marcan passage.

14:1. Jesus dines **on the sabbath day** with a Pharisee. Sabbath feasts involved no breach of sabbath legislation. The food was prepared the day before and kept warm. **A ruler who belonged to the Pharisees:** Another interpretation of the same Greek text that the KJV translates **one of the chief Pharisees.**

2-4. Answering (KJV) : No question has preceded the statement (cf. 13:14) and the RSV omits this verbal form as a superfluous Semitism.

---

deserted by God. Destruction did overtake Jerusalem. The terrible revenge that Rome took for insurrection was thus a whip in God's hand—the outward sign of a desolation that already had blighted the soul. Thoreau's words ache and quiver with truth:

> If it is not a tragical life we live, then I know not what to call it. Such a story as that of Jesus Christ,—the history of Jerusalem, say, being a part of the Universal History. The naked, the embalmed, unburied death of Jerusalem amid its desolate hills,—think of it.[8]

Here is a picture of the ultimate triumph of God's purpose. No earthy and obstinate Jerusalem can thwart his holy will. Vs. 35*b* may refer to the triumphal entry into Jerusalem, or (as in Matthew) to Jesus' second coming, or to the victory of the messianic kingdom. By any interpretation it spells God's victory. If the comment has been added by the early church, a possibility not unlikely in view of the comparatively late date of the Gospel, it is not less true; they had already seen Christ's triumph in his resurrection. Must our disobedient Jerusalems remain forever desolate? That question we cannot answer; the future beyond death is hidden from us. Here and now the choice confronts us: to receive Jesus that his love may brood over us, or to deny him—to his heartbreak and our desolation.

[8] *A Week on the Concord and Merrimack Rivers* (Boston: Houghton Mifflin & Co., 1893), p. 84.

14:1-6. *Renewal of Controversy about the Sabbath.*—(See also Expos. on 13:14-17; also on Matt. 12:9-14.) There are several items of interest. No breach of sabbath law was made in the hospitality meal, for the food was cooked on the preceding day. The breach was in the healing; work could not be done on the sabbath, and healing was "work." In vs. 5 **ass** may be a less authoritative reading than "son" (see Exeg.). The two words are so similar in the Greek (ass is ὄνος; son is υἱός) that a scribal error would be easy to understand, especially as ὄνος accords better with parallel passages. **Fallen into a well** may refer to one of the many unprotected cisterns and wells in Palestine at that time.

Recent studies teach us that the story, though important, is here told as frame for the dictum of Jesus about the sabbath. The early church kept Sunday with far less rigor than sabbath law laid on pious Jews. Such stories as this encouraged the church; they had the sanction of the risen Christ. The sabbath was apparently a test case between Jesus and the religious leaders. They were afraid that "the hedge of the law" might be broken; he pleaded that originally the sabbath was the day on which God rested from his work of creation and saw that the work was good, and that therefore all things should be done on that day to swell man's praise for God's goodness. We should note both the courage and the authority of Jesus.

Here he argues that to leave a man uncured

5 And answered them, saying, Which of you shall have an ass or an ox fallen into a pit, and will not straightway pull him out on the sabbath day?

6 And they could not answer him again to these things.

7 ¶ And he put forth a parable to those which were bidden, when he marked how they chose out the chief rooms; saying unto them,

8 When thou art bidden of any *man* to a wedding, sit not down in the highest room; lest a more honorable man than thou be bidden of him;

9 And he that bade thee and him come and say to thee, Give this man place; and thou begin with shame to take the lowest room.

him, and let him go.
5 And he said to them,
"Which of you, having an ass[y] or an ox that has fallen into a well, will not immediately pull him out on a sabbath day?"
6 And they could not reply to this.

7 Now he told a parable to those who were invited, when he marked how they chose the places of honor, saying to them,
8 "When you are invited by any one to a marriage feast, do not sit down in a place of honor, lest a more eminent man than you be invited by him;
9 and he who invited you both will come and say to you, 'Give place to this man,' and then you will begin

[y] Other ancient authorities read *a son*.

---

5. A son (RSV mg.; cf. Goodspeed): The reading in the Chester Beatty Gospel Papyrus (p^{45}), Codex Vaticanus, Codex Alexandrinus, and a few other MSS. **An ass:** Read by Codex Sinaiticus, a few O.L. MSS, and the bulk of the late Greek MSS. Despite its less impressive attestation, the latter is preferred by the RSV editors, apparently because they believed the argument of the saying to be similar to that in 13:15 and Matt. 12:12*a*: of how much more value is a human being than an animal! But the sense could have been: If your child, or even one of your domestic animals, needs help on the sabbath you do not hesitate to give it!

6. Note 13:17*a*.

2. Rules of Etiquette for Guests at a Feast (14:7-11)

7. Editorial. It is difficult to understand the injunctions that follow as **a parable.** They appear to be practical rules of behavior that Luke has attempted to spiritualize by attaching the saying in vs. 11.

8-10. This passage is little more than an expansion of Prov. 25:6-7:

> Claim not honor in the presence of the king,
> Nor stand in the place of great men;
> It is better for you to be told, "Come up hither!"
> Than to be humbled before the noble (Amer. Trans.).

Codex Bezae and its allies have inserted a variant after Matt. 20:28 with the introduction: "Seek to increase from being little, and from being greater to be less." **A marriage feast**

---

who could be cured would not heighten, but rather destroy, the praise of God. His dictum underscores once more his sense of the preciousness of human life. If the reading (see above) is **an ass or an ox,** Jesus insists that a man is much more precious than a beast; if the reading should be "a son or even an ox," he is telling us that God yearns over his children of earth with far purer love than an earthly father over his child. God has given every man his own fingerprint, his own accent of voice, his own separateness of soul; for every man is dear in God's sight. Healing God's children is consonant with sabbath praise; to fail to heal them would be a breach in worship. Yet the dictum must not be twisted to condone any failure in reverence on the sabbath.

7-11. ***Parable of the Chief Seats.***—Is this a parable, or an example of proverb-literature giving rules on behavior? If the latter, we must assume that a piece of practical wisdom has found its way into the gospel record. Yet even in this latter event, vs. 11, which has the authentic ring of Jesus' teaching, lifts it into the light of another world. If this is a parable, Jesus is taking notice in a gentle irony of the

10 But when thou art bidden, go and
sit down in the lowest room; that when
he that bade thee cometh, he may say unto
thee, Friend, go up higher: then shalt thou
have worship in the presence of them that
sit at meat with thee.
11 For whosoever exalteth himself shall
be abased; and he that humbleth himself
shall be exalted.
12 ¶ Then said he also to him that bade
him, When thou makest a dinner or a
supper, call not thy friends, nor thy breth-
ren, neither thy kinsmen, nor *thy* rich
neighbors; lest they also bid thee again,
and a recompense be made thee.

with shame to take the lowest place. 10 But
when you are invited, go and sit in the
lowest place, so that when your host comes
he may say to you, 'Friend, go up higher';
then you will be honored in the presence
of all who sit at table with you. 11 For
every one who exalts himself will be hum-
bled, and he who humbles himself will
be exalted."
12 He said also to the man who had in-
vited him, "When you give a dinner or a
banquet, do not invite your friends or your
brothers or your kinsmen or rich neigh-
bors, lest they also invite you in return, and

(RSV) rather than **a wedding** (KJV; cf. 12:36). **Friend, go up higher,** i.e., nearer the place where the host will preside.

11. In other contexts in 18:14 and in Matt. 23:12. Luke probably understood the saying eschatologically: There will be a reversal of values in the new age.

3. Rules of Hospitality for a Host (14:12-14)

For another statement of the principle laid down in these verses see 6:32-35.

12*a*. Editorial.

12*b*. This saying should not be pressed to the point of declaring that Jesus forbade all social amenities. There is often an element of hyperbole in his utterances. Hospitality as a *quid pro quo* has no religious merit. It is paid for in this age.

---

elbowings and schemings of social ambition (vs. 15), and is using this all-too-human scene to teach by contrast the standards of the messianic banquet.

In that event we have a parable in very truth. A wedding feast is a formal occasion; a host must exercise care to honor guests according to their rank. So at a wedding, now as then, social ambition is more in evidence. J. R. Dummelow tells of "Rabbi Simeon ben Shetah, who when invited to dinner by king Jannaeus, placed himself between the king and queen, saying, 'Exalt wisdom and she shall exalt thee, and make thee to sit among princes.'"[9] B. T. D. Smith reminds us that Lucian poked fun at the same egregious pride in his day by telling of the anger of Heracles when he found Asclepius "the druggist" at a higher place at the table of the gods.[1] How few people are free from petty conceit! How many bridle as soon as their "dignity" is hurt!

Books give lists of virtues, but there is only one virtue: the lowly acknowledgment of God. Books give lists of major sins, but there is only one sin: self-worship, our attempt to set ourselves at the center of the world. Lowliness springs from gratitude: when God has given so much why should a man count himself worthy of any higher place at the table? Lowliness springs from reverence: how can a sinful man presume to approach the majesty of God? Lowliness springs from knowledge of sins forgiven: what more could a man ask? Such lowliness God honors. No one is more surprised than the lowly when they are summoned to God's nearer favor. Dante heard singing in Paradise: "Blessed are the poor in spirit."[2] The singers, being humble, doubtless could not understand why they deserved heaven. God is the host; that fact makes the parable. He has his own standard of judgment, Jesus being the test. That woman with no gift in the world's eyes except prayer, that man contrite in his sins—why should they be at the head of the table? Because at the messianic banquet in the kingdom God does not despise a broken and contrite heart.

12-14. *Hospitality in Christ.*—Notice the masterly arrangement of material in vss. 1-24, as throughout the Gospel. The whole passage might be titled "The Table Talk of Jesus." First, the presence of a sick man gives Jesus

[9] *A Commentary on the Holy Bible* (New York: The Macmillan Co., 1909), *ad loc.*

[1] *The Parables of the Synoptic Gospels* (Cambridge: University Press, 1937), p. 207.

[2] *Purgatory,* Canto XII, l. 110.

13 But when thou makest a feast, call the poor, the maimed, the lame, the blind:
14 And thou shalt be blessed; for they cannot recompense thee: for thou shalt be recompensed at the resurrection of the just.
15 ¶ And when one of them that sat at meat with him heard these things, he said unto him, Blessed *is* he that shall eat bread in the kingdom of God.

you be repaid.
13 But when you give a feast, invite the poor, the maimed, the lame, the blind,
14 and you will be blessed, because they cannot repay you. You will be repaid at the resurrection of the just."
15 When one of those who sat at table with him heard this, he said to him, "Blessed is he who shall eat bread in the

13-14. The only generosity that God will recompense is that which is extended to those who cannot repay it. The same four classes of underprivileged guests are mentioned again in vs. 21. Jesus never qualified or apologized for the Jewish doctrine of reward. He did not anticipate Paul or Luther or Kant. **At the resurrection of the just:** Luke elsewhere speaks of the resurrection of the "unjust" as well as the "just" (Acts 24:15), and it would be unreasonable to assume that this phrase excludes the idea of a general resurrection.

4. Parable of the Great Banquet (14:15-24)

There is a variant in Matt. 22:2-10, but the differences are such as to suggest that Matthew drew it from some source other than Luke's, and that Luke's version is closer

opportunity to discuss with his host and the other guests the proper use of the sabbath (vss. 1-6); next, his comment on social ambition (vss. 7-11); now, the equally incisive dictum on the right kind of guest list (vss. 12-14); finally, the parable of the great feast as splendid climax. In these verses Jesus is not rebuking social amenities. To entertain kindred and friends is an inborn instinct which he does not thwart. The verb implies "Do not habitually or exclusively call thy friends." We should remember that teaching of Jesus is often in hyperbole.

The four groups first mentioned (friends, immediate family, kinsfolk, and influential neighbors) could all return an invitation. The four groups recommended for hospitality which they rarely received (**the poor, the maimed, the lame, the blind**) could make no recompense; for the poor had no money to provide a feast, and the others were too weak. Besides, these latter may have been regarded as sinners, for the Jew was prone to regard sickness as the result of iniquity. Nehemiah says, "Eat the fat, and drink the sweet, and send portions unto them for whom nothing is prepared" (Neh. 8:10), but this remote charity is a far remove from the friendship for which Jesus here pleads.

It is a question of motive. To entertain the first group is pleasant and profitable—low motive; to entertain the second group is compassionate—high motive. To entertain the first group is to set one's own circle at the earth's center—selfish motive; to entertain the second group is to remember that God sees mankind as one family, and that his love runs most quickly to the neediest—high motive. To welcome the first group is to seek speedy reward—earthy motive; to welcome the second group is to trust in heaven's ultimate favor—faith's motive. In this issue as always God looks at the heart. How sharp a puncturing of social ambition! "Keeping up with the Joneses" is as sorry a practice as it is prevalent; the business custom of entertaining the potential buyer—with the expense added to the price of the product and the subsequent penalizing of the poor—is as greedy as it is rife. Every word of Jesus is a revolution—and a blessedness.

The doctrine of rewards (vs. 14) is unashamed in the teaching of Jesus. We are not angels, and need not pretend that our motives are so lofty that we despise rewards. Besides, if compassion issued in bitterness and chaos, the universe would be nonsense. The phrase **the resurrection of the just** should not be hardened into a dogma: it does not necessarily imply that the unjust are not raised. But it does speak of blessedness. That is a radiant word. Heaven's rewards are heavenly in nature: the hospitality which Jesus commends fills earth with love, as foretaste of a heavenly joy. Besides, it brings a man into friendship with God, who "maketh his sun to rise on the evil and on the good" (Matt. 5:45); and makes him the guest of Jesus, who feasted with "publicans and sinners" (5:30).

15. ***New Beatitude?***—Probably a hyphen provided by the author to link the dictum on hospitality with the parable of the great feast; but as such, a worthy foil nevertheless for the mind of Christ. The old law was dark with

16 Then said he unto him, A certain man made a great supper, and bade many:

kingdom of God!" 16 But he said to him, "A man once gave a great banquet, and

to the original. Allegorical elements in Matthew's account pervade the whole: The "king" who gave a marriage feast for his son is God; the "servants" are prophets and apostles whom the Jews had mistreated and murdered; and the destruction of "the murderers" and the burning of "their city" reflect a Christian interpretation of the events of A.D. 70, the capture of Jerusalem by Titus and his Roman legions and its destruction by fire. Allegory has been imported into Luke's account also, but it is clearly evident only in vss. 21*b*-22, which Luke probably added in order that vs. 23 might be understood as a reference to the Gentile mission of the church, and in vs. 24, which appears to equate the banquet of the parable with Jesus' own messianic feast.

The original parable was probably addressed to the professedly religious among Jesus' Jewish contemporaries. It is not they, but those whom they despise as sinners and outcasts, who will be admitted to the kingdom of God.

15. An interjected beatitude (cf. 11:27) effects the transition in thought from a banquet in a Pharisee's house to a banquet **in the kingdom of God.**

16-17. The custom of summoning previously invited guests is said still to prevail in the East. Matthew's version reads "servants" in keeping with the status of "a king."

prohibitions—"Thou shalt not . . ."; the new law is bright with promises—"Blessed are they that. . . ." Blessed might be freely translated "Happy and more deeply happy," for on the lips of Jesus it offers joy on earth as foretaste of joy in heaven. This beatitude, with its raising of desire from earthly tables to a messianic banquet, though not from Jesus, accords well with his mind. If someone pointed to a fishing boat, he would say, "I will make you . . . fishers of men" (Mark 1:17). If the conversation dealt with harvests, he would say, "The fields . . . are white already to harvest" (John 4:35). To him earth was a parable of heaven. So here, eyes are lifted from man's table to the hospitality of God's home. Is there not an extracanonical word of Jesus?—"The world is merely a bridge: ye are to pass over it, and not to build your dwellings upon it." [3] But the beatitude spoken by **one of those** may have been a sentimentalism, and the parable has therefore an appropriate rigor—as if Jesus had said, "Are you sure you will be there?"

16-24. ***Parable of the Great Feast.***— (See also Expos. on vss. 18, 18-20, 21-24.) Our social amenities are tagged with white lies. "Mr. and Mrs. So-and-so request the honor of your company . . .": the honor is not always deeply felt. "Mr. and Mrs. Thus-and-thus regret that . . .": the regret does not always shake them with sobs. Of course nobody would be such a fool as to decline an invitation to heaven's banquet. Yet that folly is written into the story, even in the same formal phrases: **I pray thee have me excused** means "Please present my regrets." We "regret" because we fear the banquet may be dull. Our own affairs promise much more happiness, we think, even though the promise is never fulfilled. What the world calls success is always miserable and menaced, and Jesus always comes with a hallelujah gladness; but our sight is dim, because we are locked in ourselves.

The three men who sent regrets probably repeated their excuses to themselves until they deemed them valid reasons. Matthew's version (22:1-10) says that they "made light of" the divine invitation: it did not weigh with them, it was not important. The wealth of a farm, the power of five yoke of oxen, the excitement of marriage were all vital concerns; but the voice of God could wait until sickness came or death summoned them. The body is clamantly near, while the soul is but a sound of silence; earth is hard fact, while heaven is only a hope; and God hardly stands a chance alongside investments, a car, or a wedding. Why has God set himself at such disadvantage? Is it that Love would rather wait than coerce? So men sell life for colored glass while God offers them jewels.

Then what happened at the bountiful tables empty of all invited guests? No one could have guessed the strange turn in the drama. The "nice people" having refused celestial hospitality, their places were filled by those whom they called "the wreckage of the streets." Still there was room, so God's couriers brought in also a swarm of "country folk." There can be little doubt of the meaning: God had chosen the Jews not for favor alone, but for mission; and they had refused because this world had beguiled them; and therefore their chance would now go to the "godless" and the "alien," even

[3] See David Smith, *Unwritten Sayings of Our Lord* (London: Hodder & Stoughton, 1913), pp. 71-82.

17 And sent his servant at supper time to say to them that were bidden, Come; for all things are now ready.
18 And they all with one *consent* began to make excuse. The first said unto him, I have bought a piece of ground, and I must

invited many; [17] and at the time for the banquet he sent his servant to say to those who had been invited, 'Come; for all is now ready.' [18] But they all alike began to

---

It is unlikely that Luke changed a plural to a singular in order to see in **his servant** an allegorical reference to Christ.

18-21*a*. Luke's version is more detailed and graphic at this point than Matthew's. Three examples are given of those who had accepted the invitation but who now reject the summons. **I must go out and see it:** The idea may be that the purchase would not be

---

though these had been maimed by man's cruelty and their own sin. This means today? That if the church becomes comfortable and self-righteous, God will gather in some secular movement that is lowly and contrite, baptize it with his own forgiving grace, and use it for his glad purpose.

Vachel Lindsay has caught the mood of the story in his poem, "General William Booth Enters into Heaven." In the early days of the Salvation Army the favorite hymn was "Washed in the Blood of the Lamb." That phrase recurs in the poem as it describes Booth and his followers coming into the courthouse square in heaven:

Booth led boldly with his big bass drum.
(*Are you washed in the blood of the Lamb?*)
The saints smiled gravely, and they said "He's come."
(*Are you washed in the blood of the Lamb?*)
Walking lepers followed, rank on rank,
Lurching bravos from the ditches dank
. . . .
Vermin-eaten saints with moldy breath,
Unwashed legions with the ways of death—
(*Are you washed in the blood of the Lamb?*) [4]

To be free from fear so that we can speak God's word and care not what happens to us, to grow old knowing that "the best is yet to be," to be rid of the clamor of self by the very spirit of Jesus—this would be joy. It is offered: all any man need say to God is "Jesus bade me come."

The invitation is always offered. The soul seems vague, but it is the very self. Farms can never be a real part of the self, because they fall away at last. Every man is writing his answer to the divine call. It is either, "Please present my regrets," which is but another way of saying, "My own business and home are much more important"; or it is, "Weary with my sins, pleading no merit except thy welcome, I come."

[4] *General William Booth Enters into Heaven and Other Poems.* Copyright 1913, by Vachel Lindsay. Used by permission of The Macmillan Company.

18. *Excuses.*—The word **excuse** is derived from *ex causa:* free from the charge; i.e., we know we are chargeable with some failure, so we present fictitious evidence by which we hope to win acquittal. Psychology calls it rationalizing. Milton borrowed a phrase from Aristophanes and described Satan as having a tongue that

Dropt manna, and could make the worse appear
The better reason, to perplex and dash
Maturest counsels.[5]

Everyone is prone to set a screen of lies between himself and reality. Life is a process of removing the screens so that in God's "light shall we see light" (Ps. 36:9). The excuses in the story sound reasonable in themselves: the world manifestly needs farms and oxen to provide food and clothing, and homes to provide shelter and love. But all these, without the honor that comes from God, are cisterns without water. This the three men knew. So their excuses were only excuses—plausible lies.

For excuses are never "in themselves"; they are not reasonable, but only barefaced in the context of the parable. They are plainly foolish in the light of so gracious an invitation. But the story is written with precisely that purpose—to show the folly of our refusals of God's grace. Are these excuses more foolish than ours? "I got too much religion when I was a boy." Answer: He may mean that he wishes to run away from the religion that was given him. Or he may have had too much false religion: the cure for poor religion is not no religion, but a true faith. "I am too tired when Sunday comes." Answer: Because of the very lack of religion. Every man gets tired when he tries to live in his own strength. "I must be fresh on Monday to help my family." Answer: As if any man could be fresh or help his family if he lives a godless life! "There are too many hypocrites in church." Answer: If a hypocrite must live somewhere,

[5] *Paradise Lost,* Bk. II, l. 112.

needs go and see it: I pray thee have me
excused.
19 And another said, I have bought five
yoke of oxen, and I go to prove them: I
pray thee have me excused.
20 And another said, I have married a
wife, and therefore I cannot come.
21 So that servant came, and showed his
lord these things. Then the master of the
house being angry said to his servant, Go

make excuses. The first said to him, 'I have
bought a field, and I must go out and see it;
I pray you, have me excused.' 19 And an-
other said, 'I have bought five yoke of oxen,
and I go to examine them; I pray you, have
me excused.' 20 And another said, 'I have
married a wife, and therefore I cannot
come.' 21 So the servant came and reported
this to his master. Then the householder in

---

complete until the property had been inspected. **I pray you, have me excused** translates a Latin idiom. **I have married a wife:** It is interesting to recall, in this connection, that ancient Jewish legislation excused a newly married man for one year from all military duties and other business (Deut. 24:5). **I cannot come:** The refusal sounds more impolite than the others, but probably the form has been varied only in the interests of style.

---

would you not rather see him in church? There the light of reality may strike him. Besides, can a man go anywhere in this world if he would avoid hypocrites? Not to business, certainly. Besides, are we not all hypocrites—people of strangely mixed motives? Have we right to make the charge? Besides, is that the *real* reason why the man does not go to church?

The excuses are flimsy, but the "servant" may not be blameless: the church has often presented God's invitation in a dull way to make the banquet seem dull, or even in a minatory way to make the banquet seem a threat. Excuses do not long stand. The winds of reality overturn the poor lie-shelters that we build. That is why there is no "perfect crime." The only safe place is the open sky of God's will. Why will we not see that his banquet is more joyous than the shadows of our worldly preoccupations?

18-20. ***Nothing Fails Like Success.***—The three excuses give a picture of a successful secular society. The farm might symbolize possessions and investments; the oxen and plow, our technological means of livelihood; the wife, at best our human-centered comfort, at worst our cult of sex and success. Add schools, our system of learning bereft of reverence so that it becomes pride of mind, and the list is fairly complete. All these areas are necessary to the full life, but in themselves they are means without any end—in short, an idolatry.

Plainly a man cannot live without a farm. But the farm cannot live without God. His will is written even in the land. That is why a man must honor the contour of the hill in his plowing, or his land will run away and leave him hungry; and that is why he must not cut down forests without reforestation, or dust storms will kill him. Besides, if a man gets locked within his farm (or any other possession on which he feasts his eyes and greed), he does not own it: it owns him.

Plainly a man cannot live without oxen. He needs their power for production, as he needs electricity and telephones. But as soon as he says, "This is mine," he quickens a false envy in other men to provoke strife, and he himself becomes capsuled. He worships the window glass which he makes, and forgets his dependence on the sun which he cannot make. Livelihood usurps the place of life. Then inevitably the man ceases to live.

Plainly a man cannot live without home, or even without sex. As to that latter, we now know how important it is in a full-orbed life. A man would be a misanthrope who does not rejoice in the exuberance and hope of young love. But when sex becomes the center, it is soon an obsession, then excess, then satiation, then perversity and sadness. "Homes come first" is a proverb much favored by furniture stores. It is nearly true, and therefore tragically false; for a home trying to live on itself is like a man trying to feed on his own body, a cannibalism that temporarily succeeds but finally becomes death.

Nothing fails like success, as our generation has found. There is a needs-must in our nature: we must speak truth, and must love, and must worship; or our control of nature is suicide. The needs-must, God's banquet, is joy, did we but know. In two world wars church bells were melted into cannon and carried death—because the world would not heed them when they called to worship.

21-24. ***A Wideness and a Rigor in God's Mercy.***—The attitude of the host in the story seems almost spleen: he appears to gather in **the halt and the maimed,** not in love, but in anger because of the refusal of more influential guests. But this feature is only the verisimilitude of the parable. We should not twist a parable into an allegory. Moreover, there are some items that must be attributed (see Exeg.) to the

out quickly into the streets and lanes of the city, and bring in hither the poor, and the maimed, and the halt, and the blind.

22 And the servant said, Lord, it is done as thou hast commanded, and yet there is room.

23 And the lord said unto the servant, Go out into the highways and hedges, and compel *them* to come in, that my house may be filled.

24 For I say unto you, That none of those men which were bidden shall taste of my supper.

anger said to his servant, 'Go out quickly to the streets and lanes of the city, and bring in the poor and maimed and blind and lame.' 22 And the servant said, 'Sir, what you commanded has been done, and still there is room.' 23 And the master said to the servant, 'Go out to the highways and hedges, and compel people to come in, that my house may be filled. 24 For I tell you, none of those men who were invited shall taste my banquet.' "

21*b*-22. Probably an allegorical addition. **Go out quickly to the streets and lanes of the city:** Since the Jews who prided themselves on their exemplary piety have rejected the summons, the invitation is extended first to those whom they considered to be sinners and outcasts. The four classes now to be invited are those that have already been enumerated in vs. 13. The words **still there is room** prepare the way for the third invitation that follows in the next verse. In Matthew's account only one supplementary invitation was issued and then "the wedding hall was filled with guests." No doubt the original parable ended with some such statement.

23. Go out to the highways and hedges, i.e., outside the city. In its present context an apparent reference to the Christian mission to non-Jews. **And compel people to come in:** Augustine appealed to these words in support of his argument that the Donatists should be compelled to return to the Catholic Church (*On the Correction of the Donatists* 24). Quite apart from the question whether such "proof text" use of scripture has any justification, the parable can hardly imply that one servant could make effective use of force to fulfill his commission.

24. Represented by the RSV as addressed by the householder to his servant. But **you** translates a Greek second person plural. Probably Luke thought of the verse as an interpretation of the parable given by Jesus to his fellow guests at the supper. Jesus himself will proceed as did the host in the illustration. He will cancel the original invitations to his messianic feast. The figure of speech is similar to that in 13:28-29, but in this instance Luke ascribes to Jesus a distinct messianic consciousness—**my banquet.**

Lukan authorship. Just as Matthew writes his version of the story so as to point the moral of the Jewish wars (see Exeg. and Expos. on Matt. 22:2-10), so Luke turns the story, not improperly, into an interpretation of the Gentile mission of the church. **The streets and lanes of the city** symbolize "the people of the land," that group in Jewry that neglected the law; and **the highways and hedges** betoken the wider Gentile world into which the church soon ventured. **The poor, and the maimed, and the halt, and the blind** is a phrase borrowed from vs. 13, and it stands for the unpromising "godless" crowd to whom God must turn when the chosen people fail him. Thus Luke may have added allegorical features. But they had sharp truth in his time.

Thus he has underscored rather than clouded the truth of the parable. **Yet there is room.** No man was denied welcome. Jew and Gentile were both summoned by God's grace, for his love always overleaps barriers of nationality and race. The healthy (if there are any) and the sick alike are invited to the joy of the messianic banquet; no poverty or ignorance or sin ever daunts God's grace. A man may come at the last moment, even though he has refused for a lifetime every plea of God's compassion:

> Betwixt the stirrup and the ground
> Mercy I asked, mercy I found.[6]

There *is* "a wideness in God's mercy." It *is* like "the wideness of the sea."[7]

But his love is not indulgence, or it would cease to be love. To pamper a man in obduracy would be the very opposite of kindness. Exegetes have long debated if vs. 24 is a word

[6] William Camden, *Remains Concerning Britain*, "Epitaphs."

[7] From the hymn by Frederick W. Faber.

25 ¶ And there went great multitudes with him: and he turned, and said unto them,
26 If any *man* come to me, and hate not his father, and mother, and wife, and children, and brethren, and sisters, yea, and his own life also, he cannot be my disciple.

25 Now great multitudes accompanied
him; and he turned and said to them, 26 "If
any one comes to me and does not hate his own father and mother and wife and children and brothers and sisters, yes, and even his own life, he cannot be my disci-

M. On the Conditions of Discipleship (14:25-35)

1. Renunciation as a Condition of Discipleship (14:25-27=Matt. 10:37-38)

25. Editorial introduction to a new discourse constructed by the evangelist from originally independent materials. The **great multitudes** that accompany Jesus on his journey are warned of the conditions of discipleship.

26. And does not hate: Matthew tones down the rigor of the saying, but does justice to its sense by reading: "He who loves father and mother more than me." **Wife** and **brothers and sisters** are not in Matthew's version, which preserves a parallelism characteristic of Semitic poetry. Perhaps Luke has been influenced in his wording of this saying by that in 18:29 (cf. Mark 10:29). The mention of **wife** recalls to mind the man who had been cited in vs. 20. **And even his own life:** Also missing from Matthew's version. Perhaps an amplification from some saying parallel to 9:24 (Mark 8:35). Matthew actually appends one to his account at this point (Matt. 10:39). **He cannot be my disciple** is probably more original than Matthew's unique "is not worthy of me."

that Jesus himself added to the parable, or if it is part of the story. By either interpretation we learn that real Love is not a spinelessness that coddles us in sin, but a rigor that seeks our wholeness in purity and love. Darwin confessed that his preoccupation with science ("My mind seems to have become a kind of machine for grinding general laws out of large collections of facts" [8]) had robbed him of his delight in literature and music. It is a parable: a man's preoccupation with the world may stifle in him a love for the Abiding. Is the stifling an eternal loss? The story gives no answer to the question. It is parable, not theology. But it speaks no pampering! "There's a [rigor] in God's mercy."

25-26. ***Conditions of Discipleship: (a) Discipleship and the Claims of Home.***—Great leaders have declared plainly the terms of discipleship. Garibaldi offered his followers hunger and death—and Italy's freedom. King Arthur bound his knights "by so strait vows to his own self" that they were dazed as if "half-blinded at the coming of a light." [9] But no leader asked such "strait vows," in inner and outer demand, as Jesus. Vs. 25 is probably editorial, but it gives the right setting. The multitudes were a mixed following—the revolutionary wishing to make Jesus a firebrand, the impulsive man offering him wild vows of allegiance, the self-seeking man ready to cultivate Jesus' company for gain; and only a few who saw in him the sign of heaven. Jesus never took advantage of the psychology of success. How different from some who claim to be his prophets! He never gilded the flint. These vss. 25-35 might be titled "The Conditions of Discipleship." They were so stern that the crowd was winnowed. A. T. Cadoux says that the multitudes were "atomized into thinking men and women." [1]

And hate not: the word repels. It is a staggering word. But then it was intended to stagger. *The Abingdon Bible Commentary* says that it goes back in root to an Aramaic word meaning to "love less." But in any event Jesus often used trenchantly paradoxical words, especially under deep emotion. His hearers understood him; they were not afraid of a paradox, even though some of them were afraid of its demand. The word means that they were to act *as if* they hated loved ones whenever the claims of home came into conflict with the claims of Jesus. He demanded a primary and undivided allegiance. He was not despising natural ties. He blessed little children, taught us to call God by the name of Father, and gave his own mother at his death into the care of a beloved disciple. Yet he asked an instant and unqualified loyalty —proof surely of a divine claim! We can see

[8] *The Life and Letters of Charles Darwin*, ed. Francis Darwin (New York: D. Appleton & Co., 1887), I, 81.

[9] Tennyson, "The Coming of Arthur," *Idylls of the King*.

[1] *The Parables of Jesus* (New York: The Macmillan Co., 1931), p. 174.

27 And whosoever doth not bear his cross, and come after me, cannot be my disciple.

ple. 27 Whoever does not bear his own cross and come after me, cannot be my disciple.

---

27. A negative formulation of a saying already used in 9:23*b* (Mark 8:34*b*). A criminal carrying his cross on the way to execution must have been a familiar sight to many of Jesus' hearers, but there is no evidence that "to bear one's own cross" was a metaphor for voluntary martyrdom before Christians reflected on the death of Jesus. Certainly Luke and his readers were reminded by this saying of Christ's crucifixion and the actual experiences of Christian martyrs.

---

why: ships that go by the shore lights would make the ocean ways a threat; the only chance of safety on the sea is that all ships shall take their bearings from the sky. Our human loyalties clash, and they become debased unless they are unified and purified by a supreme devotion.

Jesus practiced his own demand, for there was a day when he had to choose between home and God: "Who is my mother, or my brethren? . . . Whosoever shall do the will of God, the same is my brother, and my sister, and mother" (Mark 3:33-35). His disciples learned the seeming harshness of discipleship: the sons of Zebedee were "baptized" in their Lord's baptism of fire (Mark 10:39). Through all the years his followers have confronted a choice between home and Jesus: there have been instances in India of Moslem parents carrying a coffin through the streets to make clear to the world that their son, when he became a Christian, was dead in their love. Yet it is only in homes where Christ is guest that real peace dwells. That strange word **hate** is the one road to abiding love. An eighteenth-century prayer of Bishop Joseph Butler has this concerning "our affections": "Help us, by the due exercise of them, to improve to Perfection; till all partial Affection be lost in that entire universal one, and Thou, O God, shalt be all in all." [2]

27. ***Conditions of Discipleship: (b) Discipleship and the Cross.***—A man carrying his cross on the way to his own crucifixion was a familiar sight to Jesus' hearers. It was a cruel age, though not more cruel than one that drops atomic bombs. Hundreds had been crucified in Galilee in A.D. 6 for rebellion under a revolutionary named Judas. Scholars are fairly well agreed that this saying, however, is a fragment from preaching in the early church rather than the very word of Jesus. They claim with persuasiveness that the cross gathered divine meaning only after Jesus died on a cross; and that before Calvary a cross was a curse rather than a symbol of noblest life. Suppose the claim to be true; does it not glorify rather than dull the saying?

No man can mistake the meaning. The follower of Jesus must crucify not only his low desires, but even higher desires when they clash with the demand of Christ. Milton gave up his eyesight to write the pamphlets that kept alight the lamp of English liberty; and his motive, far from being merely political, was a dedication. Furthermore, the follower of Christ must accept crucifixion at the hands of an alien world. When the words were first written, the church was being persecuted by that same empire that had killed Jesus. The Emperor Julian said in pagan sarcasm of the church where Matthew's Gospel may have been written:

> A most admirable law, however, teaches the Christians that it is necessary to be poor to enter the kingdom of heaven; now to assist them, we command that all the property of the Church of the Edessians be confiscated and distributed to the soldiers, and the lands form part of our domain. Thus, being impoverished, they will become wise, and will obtain the hoped-for kingdom of heaven.[3]

The followers of Jesus in that day lost more than money!

Nevertheless, the carrying of a cross is final joy. **Come after me:** they had the friendship of Jesus. Besides, they shared the creativeness of his death; for the cross, so far from being a willful self-mutilation, brings forth harvest more abundant than that of sown (and dying) seed. They shared his victory—the Easter that springs from Calvary. Surely the scholars have reason on their side: only the death of Jesus and his resurrection could make the cross a sign of life's triumph! But the sharp demand remains. Does the church appeal to people after this stern fashion? There is a difference, wide as the poles, between saying, "Please join the church, and find psychological peace," and saying as Jesus

[2] *A Chain of Prayer Across the Ages,* comp. Selina Fitzherbert Fox (New York: E. P. Dutton and Co., 1943), p. 31.

[3] In a letter to Hecebolius; see Gaetano Negri, *Julian the Apostate* (New York: Charles Scribner's Sons, 1905), II, 362; see also Edward Gibbon, *The Decline and Fall of the Roman Empire,* ch. xxiii.

28 For which of you, intending to build a tower, sitteth not down first, and counteth the cost, whether he have *sufficient* to finish *it?*

29 Lest haply, after he hath laid the foundation, and is not able to finish *it*, all that behold *it* begin to mock him,

30 Saying, This man began to build, and was not able to finish.

28 For which of you, desiring to build a tower, does not first sit down and count the cost, whether he has enough to complete it? 29 Otherwise, when he has laid a foundation, and is not able to finish, all who see it begin to mock him, 30 saying, 'This man began to build, and was not able

2. Parables of the Tower Builder and of the King Preparing for War (14:28-33)

Twin parables whose original application, like that of many others in the tradition, is no longer recoverable. In Luke's context they issue a warning against any lighthearted assumption of the responsibilities of discipleship. See Epictetus *Discourses* III. 15. 1: "In every affair consider what precedes and follows, and then undertake it. Otherwise you will begin with spirit; but not having thought of the consequences, when some of them appear you will shamefully desist. . . . Consider first, man, what the matter is, and what your nature is able to bear."

28-30. A wise man considers whether his resources are sufficient to complete a building before he lays its **foundation.** Otherwise he becomes an object of ridicule. **A tower:** The Greek word can mean an expensive building as well as a simple watchtower.

---

said, "If you consider being a disciple of Christ, you must be ready to take up your cross and follow him."

28-30. ***Conditions of Discipleship: (c) Counting the Cost.***—It was an age of unfinished towers. Herod himself was a reckless builder. He thought, with many a ruler in that time, that glory comes from palaces. It is just possible that Jesus was leading the laughter against the folly of men like Herod who begin **to build** in such lavishness that they cannot **finish.** Some commentators[4] think that Jesus told the parable to justify his own caution: he could not afford to choose men who would not continue loyal. It seems likelier, in view of the fact that this whole passage concerns discipleship, that Luke related the parable believing that Jesus bade *us* count the cost. But both interpretations are valid.

There is no appeal here to fear of failure: Jesus dealt tenderly with failure. There is no poor caution: Jesus could never say, "You had better be content with a low achievement if you think you cannot build better than an average tower." But there is sharp warning against a jaunty discipleship and a merely impulsive loyalty. Can you live by the Beatitudes? They are a high tower. Can I endure loneliness for Christ's sake? Have we vision and patience enough to build the tower of the kingdom in this unruly world?

Two reasons are given why a man should **count the cost.** Failure to finish will lead to frustration in himself; he would have to say, as he looked at the stub of a tower that was intended to cleave the sky, "I am a failure." Moreover, such failure would provoke the mockery of the godless, and bring the kingdom into disrepute. Therefore a man has no right to play fast and loose with the claims of Jesus, or ever to begin a Christian life in brash confidence; he will hurt himself, and he will hurt the cause of Christ. Yet he should still follow; for if he sits down first, he will have wisdom to live in a strength better than his own: God can complete his divine plan.

Joseph Parker's insight gives the parable just that turn.[5] He asks if Jesus would ignore his own warning. Has God not counted the cost? Has he not foreseen the possible abuse of the freedom that he has given mankind? Has he no resource to carry through his own designs? Does he lack bricks and strength to finish his tower? So a man may say: "Not in my strength can I complete this allegiance. Yet it is so pure and lovely a task that I must try. Into thy hands I commend my soul."

[4] *The Abingdon Bible Commentary*, ed. F. C. Eiselen, Edwin Lewis, and D. G. Downey (New York and Nashville, Abingdon-Cokesbury Press, 1929), *ad loc.*

[5] *City Temple Pulpit* (London: Hodder & Stoughton, 1900), I, 268-74.

31 Or what king, going to make war against another king, sitteth not down first, and consulteth whether he be able with ten thousand to meet him that cometh against him with twenty thousand?

32 Or else, while the other is yet a great way off, he sendeth an ambassage, and desireth conditions of peace.

33 So likewise, whosoever he be of you that forsaketh not all that he hath, he cannot be my disciple.

34 ¶ Salt *is* good: but if the salt have lost his savor, wherewith shall it be seasoned?

to finish.' 31 Or what king, going to encoun-
ter another king in war, will not sit down
first and take counsel whether he is able
with ten thousand to meet him who comes
against him with twenty thousand? 32 And
if not, while the other is yet a great way
off, he sends an embassy and asks terms of
peace. 33 So therefore, whoever of you
does not renounce all that he has cannot
be my disciple.

34 "Salt is good; but if salt has lost its taste, how shall its saltness be restored?

31-32. A wise **king** seeks the advice of counselors before engaging **another king** in battle. He will sue for **peace** rather than invite the disastrous consequences of defeat. **And asks terms of peace:** Codex Vaticanus has a Greek reading at this point that is a literal translation (used in the LXX) of a Hebrew idiom meaning "and submits."

33. Editorial. The parables have no apparent reference to the theme of renunciation (vss. 26-27) but Luke attempts to impose it. They are more than a warning to count the cost of discipleship; they are a **summons** to **disciples** to **renounce** all their possessions (cf. 12:33-34).

3. Worthlessness of Tasteless Salt (14:34-35=Matt. 5:13)

Disciples who do not sacrifice everything in Christ's service are as useless as salt that has lost its taste. In Matthew's context (in the Sermon on the Mount) the saying

---

31-33. ***Conditions of Discipleship: (d) Measuring the Strength of the Foe.***—Again there are alternative interpretations. We may say either that Jesus is telling us that he himself must compute the power of the foe and cannot conduct his battle with poor mercenaries, or we may say that he is bidding us to size up the enemy, lest by foolhardy ventures we invite crushing defeat. Again both interpretations are warranted. But inasmuch as Luke has here clearly gathered sayings that relate to discipleship, it seems more likely that the story is addressed to impulsive followers. No essential difference need be sought in the two parables. Perhaps there is a difference of mood: the tower may be a tower of defense, the war is rather clearly a crusade. What a frank admission of desperate odds! The odds are two to one! Is Jesus telling us that his discipleship is always a minority cause, a tattered battalion? If so, the story is further token of his valor.

Again there is a plea for realism. Churches do not say to prospective members: "You propose a warfare, 'not against flesh and blood, but against principalities and powers.' Do you think you can win? Better not start than invite sure defeat to the cause of Christ!" But Jesus, whom churches profess to follow, dealt thus with men who were too ready to follow—too ready because they had not measured the power of the foe. We need not ask who is meant by **king:** a parable should not be turned into an allegory. We need only remember that a man's foes lie ambushed within himself, and are arrayed openly in an alien world.

Godet has a kindling comment, drawn from his own Switzerland: "Would not a little nation like the Swiss bring down ridicule on itself by declaring war with France, if it were not determined to die nobly on the field of battle?" [6] He has the right question; for Jesus is not advising any man to quit the field before the battle begins because he fears the odds (that is never the counsel of One who dared a lonely cross), but bravely warning us of seemingly insuperable odds which he himself is nevertheless resolved to meet. He does not want mercenaries, for they will flee when the conflict becomes stern; but he does invite crusaders, and he himself will nerve them for the strife. Vs. 33 gives the proper mood: it is invitation, not merely warning.

34. ***Conditions of Discipleship: (e) Salt as a Symbol.***—In Mark's version of this saying

[6] *A Commentary on the Gospel of St. Luke*, tr. M. D. Cusin (Edinburgh: T. & T. Clark, 1875), II, 140.

35 It is neither fit for the land, nor yet for the dunghill; *but* men cast it out. He that hath ears to hear, let him hear.

35 It is fit neither for the land nor for the dunghill; men throw it away. He who has ears to hear, let him hear."

---

declares that the disciples are "the salt of the earth." They are to keep mankind from becoming insipid or corrupt and are to be on their guard lest they lose their distinctive characteristics. A briefer variant is also preserved in Mark 9:50, where salt is said to be some undefined quality that disciples are to possess to live at peace with one another.

34. Salt was a necessity that often was heavily taxed in ancient times. It may frequently have been sold in an adulterated form that lessened its seasoning value.

35. Tasteless salt has no immediate or future use as a fertilizer. Some interpreters accept a suggestion that **for the land** is a mistranslation of an Aramaic original that meant "for seasoning": "It is fit neither for seasoning nor for manure." **He who has ears . . .** is a formula taken over in 8:8 from Mark 4:9.

(9:50) the fine quality of life indicated by **salt** is not defined. In Matthew's version (5:13) salt represents discipleship itself. But Luke intends us to interpret salt as readiness to sacrifice comfort and even life for Jesus' sake. This is the necessary and saving distinctiveness of the Christian. In the heat of Palestine salt was essential for preserving food. It was as valuable as money. So the conqueror taxed it, doubtless with the result that much diluted salt came on the market. Perhaps Jesus is echoing the remark of many a housewife when she found she had unwittingly bought adulterated salt, "This is no use."

Salt has two functions—it saves from corruption, and adds zest to the meal. The church, if it is willing to follow Christ, brings that double blessing. As to the first use, the world would become selfish, even to the decay of death, but for those who are ready to live in love. A taxi driver told of a Negro woman who hailed him late at night in a storm, when taxis were few; they had not gone far when she saw an elderly white woman who hailed the cab, and then saw that it was occupied. The Negro told the driver to stop, took the elderly woman on board, and drove her to her rather distant home. The driver's comment was, "She must have been one of these church people; it certainly taught me." As to the second use, is there any finer tang to life than that given by the brave and lowly saints? Too often the sinners give zest, but no preservation from corruption; and too often the "saints" offer a preservative, but no zest! The true church, in the self-giving of the real followers of Christ, has the double grace.

The alternative translation of vs. 35 (see Exeg.) has persuasiveness, "It is fit neither for seasoning nor for manure." Certainly that is the mood of the saying. A Christianity that has lost its readiness to carry a cross, because it has been adulterated by compromise with the world's standards, has no good use. It is worse than useless, for it brings bitterness by frustrating human hope: "This is no use." But, by gladdening contrast, even a pinch of the real article can save the whole meal—as one Cross saved the world, as ten righteous men can save a city (Gen. 18:32), as a handful of the true followers of Jesus have been the "remnant" that has rescued society from its own decay.

35. *Ears and No Ears.*—Evidently a frequent saying: **He that hath ears to hear, let him hear.** In 8:8 we are told that "he cried" (aloud) this word. If men were ready to think through his sayings, the truth was theirs; but if they refused to remove the mufflers of prejudice, they would be broken on a new Mount Sinai. The imperiousness of Jesus is here seen. His words, he implies, are the law by which men and nations rise or fall. Yet the imperiousness was so lowly that he honored human choice, though that choice might spell his death: **let him hear.** Some would refuse to hear; their ears were stopped by pride, as if they had no ears. They would say he had vicious friends (15:1); they would call his truth blasphemy. That was their freedom, though it might be his cross. Even so, his words were truth, and his truth would prevail. So we are confronted by the whole problem of our response to Jesus. Sight is not ours except by the health of the optic nerve; Jesus' truth is not ours except by the health of an inner ear.

Our ears may *miss* the truth. Familiarity may induce deafness. Preoccupation with the world may so engage us that other voices are lost, as a man fails to hear a church bell in the roar of street traffic. Though Jesus has truth for time and eternity, we shall not know his truth unless we listen: prayer is more a listening than a speaking. Our ears may *twist* the truth, for we shall hear what we wish to hear. The phrase in the parable of the great supper, "Compel them to come in," was spoken in the urgency of a great love—that God's house of grace "may be filled" (vs. 23); but even Augustine heard

15 Then drew near unto him all the publicans and sinners for to hear him.
2 And the Pharisees and scribes murmured, saying, This man receiveth sinners, and eateth with them.

15 Now the tax collectors and sinners were all drawing near to hear him.
2 And the Pharisees and the scribes murmured, saying, "This man receives sinners and eats with them."

N. On God's Love for the Lost (15:1-32)

1. Parable of the Lost Sheep (15:1-7)

There is a version in Matt. 18:12-14; but differences in detail, and the fact that the First Gospel does not reproduce the companion parable of the lost coin, suggest that the two accounts were not drawn from the same source. The brevity of Matthew's version may indicate that in respect to form it is more original, but his interpretation of the parable as teaching God's concern for those who are weak in faith—"Christ's little ones" —seems forced in comparison with Luke (vs. 7).

15:1-3. Editorial introduction to three parables on the theme of God's love for the sinner. Luke assumes that Jesus must have spoken them to **Pharisees and scribes** in

in it a command to the church to persecute heretics, because his mind was then engaged in controversy with the Donatists.[7] If we hear Jesus through a thick screen of prejudice or greed, we can even imagine him to be talking our half lies; many a group has claimed to be "Christian" in practices sharply alien from his truth. But our ears may *receive* the truth. This imperious yet lowly command is also a promise: no man need be deaf, for Jesus can open his ears. The pledge given through Isaiah, "The ears of the deaf shall be unstopped" (Isa. 35:5), was fulfilled by Jesus. Followers who were dull of hearing at the first, so that they constantly misconstrued his meaning, became interpreters, and gave us our N.T. The compassionate shock of his cross unstops ears—if we will: **He that hath ears to hear, let him hear.**

15:1-3. ***Jesus, Friend of the Lost.***—Who is **them** in vs. 3? We would like to believe that these incomparable stories were spoken directly to the "lost." Our newer knowledge of the Gospels, leading us to surmise that these verses are editorial, encourages us; we may justifiably imagine that Jesus told the story of the lost sheep to men whom the religious leaders reckoned hopeless. Yet the editorial introduction has genius, for it reveals a distinctiveness in the love of Jesus: he *sought* the lost, and vindicated the search. **Publicans** were the taxgatherers, Jews who had sold themselves to collect Roman taxes from their oppressed countrymen. **Sinners** were people careless of the religious law. Thus **publicans and sinners** were a corporation of the unholiest, as **Pharisees and scribes** were (in their own eyes at least) a corporation of the holiest. To receive sinners was bad enough; to eat with them was worse, for that meant to choose them as friends: our word companion in its origin is (*com-panis*) "with bread." We shall not properly understand the shock Jesus gave his respectable compatriots until we see him leaving some honored church "on the avenue" to take dinner with a betting tout "across the tracks" who has not been inside a church in years. Why the amazing strategy?

Because of the promise shown by "godless" men, and because of their need. "What man of you" (vs. 4) implies an axiomatic compassion in human nature. No man is rotten to the core; every man instinctively responds to God's call. There are no hopeless souls, for the soul is God's implanted hope. A Mohammedan tradition tells that Jesus came upon a crowd gathered around a dead scavenger dog; everyone was voicing disgust, but Jesus said, "Even pearls are dark before the whiteness of his teeth."[8] Humanity always holds a strain of divine gold. Indeed the "godless" are sometimes quicker in contrition and compassion than the "godly," for the "godly" can choke the inner spring by the routine of their ritual and by their self-righteous condemnation of the "godless." Jesus saw promise in his strange friends. But he was not blind to their need: a man does not live (he only exists) without prayer. If he is estranged from God and man by moral failure, he is wretchedly half dead. So **publicans and sinners** were lost in very fact—lost by folly as a sheep is lost, lost by carelessness (their own or a neighbor's) as a coin is lost, lost by willfulness as a prodigal is lost. **The Pharisees and scribes** were equally lost, the only difference being that they had wandered away by another road. So

[7] *Sermons on Selected Lessons of the New Testament*, Sermon XL and Sermon LXII.

[8] In a poem by the Mohammedan poet Nizami, quoted by David Smith, *Unwritten Sayings of Our Lord*, p. 10.

3 ¶ And he spake this parable unto
them, saying,
4 What man of you, having a hundred
sheep, if he lose one of them, doth not

3 So he told them this parable: 4 "What

defense of his ministry to **tax collectors and sinners.** If such a polemical interest is not original, they were probably words of comfort and assurance addressed by Jesus to those whom the religious elite among his Jewish contemporaries regarded as outside the pale of God's concern. "The virtues of repentance are gloriously praised in the Rabbinical literature, but this direct search for, and appeal to, the sinner, are new and moving notes of high import and significance. The good shepherd who searches for the lost sheep, and reclaims it and rejoices over it, is a new figure, which has never ceased to play its great part in the moral and religious development of the world" (Montefiore, *Synoptic Gospels,* II, 520-21).

4. A hundred sheep would constitute a large flock in the Palestine of Jesus' day. Nevertheless the loss of even one animal would be a serious matter. **In the wilderness:**

Jesus befriended sinners because of their promise and their lostness.

He went where they were. This is the only method of redemption. The Pharisees drew their robes about them to avoid contamination from the ungodly. Pharisaic righteousness was not passionate enough to provide immunity. But Jesus, defended by the very yearning of holy love, ate with sinners. Notice in the Exeg. the quotation from Montefiore, a Jewish scholar. The distinctiveness of the gospel is precisely in the fact that God became incarnate: he *seeks* us in our lostness. A doctor cannot set a broken limb from the other side of the street: Love cannot cure our lovelessness from the other side of the sky. "The Word was made flesh" (John 1:14) in seeking love, not without risk and pain! God has come to the "other side of the tracks," and voluntarily shares the prison house which remorse and defiance have built for themselves, that he may set free the prisoners. When the creature showed no reverence for the Creator, the Creator stooped in reverence before the self-disfigured soul of the creature. Such is Luke's amazing introduction to three stories that shall yet save our world.

3-5. *Parable of the Lost Sheep.*—(See also Expos. on vss. 4*a*, 4*c*, 4*e*; for Expos. on vss. 6-7 see vss. 9-10.) The farmer came down the lane. "Got a stray," he said. "How do they get lost?" asked the city man. "They just nibble themselves lost," said the farmer; "they keep their heads down, wander from one green tuft to another, come to a hole in the fence—and never can find a hole by which to get back again." The city man answered, "Like people, like every generation of foolish men." A sequence of words tells the drama.

Lost tells the tragedy of human life. Perhaps **lost** was the word Jesus used, not "sinner," still less "damned." Yet "sinner" is implied, for man is born a responsible creature; and "damnation," in its original sense of condemnation and damage, is inevitably involved. **Lost** tells the wretchedness of the stray sheep and the tender love of the shepherd. In economics and statecraft alike men keep their heads down, going from this tuft of acquisitiveness to that tuft of security to the other tuft of a "comfortable standard of living"—through a hole in the fence. Man has more intelligence than a sheep, but his wisdom is still folly unless he obeys the Shepherd. Perhaps man is always homeless in time and space. Perhaps he never understands the joy of the fold until the storm overtakes him in his wandering.

"Seek" tells the pursuing love of God. The phrase "man's search for God" is a misnomer; for no man seeks God until he has first heard the Shepherd's call. People usually seem to be unaware of God, or so intent on their own affairs as to be deaf and indifferent; but their secret heart tells a different story. Conscience in them is the footfall of the Shepherd, and pity is his Shadow falling across their wandering. Their own concern for the lost (**what man of you**), their readiness to stop a whole city's life to find one lost child, is proof of "something in us"—or rather, of Someone in us. Jesus is the incarnate Sign: we cannot forget him, because always he follows us. No man lifted him from his obscure niche in history; the truth is rather that men tried to blot him out on a Cross and then to shut him in a grave. God lifted him. He is always walking the thickets of our world—seeking us.

Until tells the unwearying persistence of God's love. **Until** is Luke's word; Matthew (18:13) says "if." Luke tells of God's concern for any lost sheep; Matthew's account says that "these little ones," Christians weak in faith, are the object of the search. Surely Luke is more

leave the ninety and nine in the wilderness, and go after that which is lost, until he find it?

man of you, having a hundred sheep, if he has lost one of them, does not leave the ninety-nine in the wilderness, and go after

---

Not sandy desert but uncultivated pasture land (cf. I Sam. 17:28). Matthew reads "on the hills."

---

centrally true! **The ninety and nine** are not on earth (are they angel flocks?), for those who are sure they are righteous are perhaps most lost: they know least about the yearning of divine love. Perhaps Matthew said "if" because demonic persecution of the church made him wonder if some people ever can be saved. Demonism enlisting human pride and cruelty always raises that question, and no man may presume upon **until.** But every man may hope in **until**—that is man's only hope. **Until** reaches as far as—Calvary.

"Joy" is the climax of the drama. Our earth is watched by an encompassing kingdom. Angels bend from the sky to mark our every step. They are not excited when a man is "successful," or when he prays to be saved from sickness and death; for perhaps they then say, "He might be nobler if death brought him nearer to our land." But they follow with intense concern the wandering sheep and the pursuit in love by the Shepherd. They say, "That man is sorry for his failure. He feels pity. He is thinking now about Jesus. Now, now he lifts his head. He is found!" Then all the bells of heaven break into joy. Jesus is that Shepherd coming down the lane—with a shepherd's crook shaped like a cross. "They nibble themselves lost," he says in tenderness. Perhaps he does not blame. Perhaps when he finds us drinking at a brackish pool of some poor clutched-at selfishness, he says, "You are thirsty; come drink at the springs of eternal life." When we are too weak through folly to walk with him, he carries us on shoulders of love. The original parable may have been less than forty words: enough on his lips to tell the whole story of earth and heaven!

4a. *The Argument from Man.*—What man of you? Jesus made his appeal to an axiomatic pity. Selfish hankerings may send a man in search of a sheep, but these do not displace an elemental compassion: we would not leave a dog out in a blizzard. By the same argument Jesus rested his case on our axiomatic sense of the true: "Why even of yourselves judge ye not what is right?" (12:57.) There is a divine flame in man amid much gloom of deviltry. The flame is only a poor candle, and dies if not fed by divine grace, but its light is derived from the central Sun. This light is far deeper than reason, for reason's logic itself rests on these primal axioms.

A man ought not to tamper with the light that is in him. Often the only and sufficient answer to "How do you know?" is "We know." To say, "The light of conscience is often obscured and even twisted by long custom," can be worthy thinking; but to say, "The light of conscience is only custom," is close to the unpardonable sin, for it calls light by names of darkness, and leaves mankind without any standard. To say, "Pity is often corroded by sentimentalism," may be true; but to say, "Pity is only a trick of the nerves," is to deliver life to chaos and cruelty. Actually we know these ultimate denials for what they are—a perverse turning against ourselves, the final cynicism, a tampering with light, an invitation to hopeless midnight. These axioms of our nature are the beachhead by which God makes his gracious invasions. We had better keep them open to his coming!

The elemental light in man is not enough of itself. For though pity for a sheep is in us, we harbor also the foolishness of sheep. Thus we are always at odds with ourselves—until God comes. Potentially every man is devil-angel. The hyphen represents a tug of war from which we are delivered only by divine reinforcements. This is but another way of saying that God has made us for himself in love. He can claim our angel axiom as his own, and either cut adrift the devilish in us or transform it. So when Jesus said, **What man of you,** he was claiming our elemental love and honor, throwing the reinforcement of his power on that side of the tug of war, and pledging the soul's victory.

4c. *The Worth of the Individual.*—One of them: A true shepherd does not say, "I have ninety-nine left" and then forget the one lost sheep. He is not satisfied with what business calls "a satisfactory percentage." Still less could a mother forget a lost child. A central stress in the story is on **one**: it tells us that every man is precious in God's sight. **The ninety and nine** may be angels in heaven, and the **one** may be our planet. But even so, each man is never merged in "the mass of men." In heaven's eyes he is always the only man. City civilization reduces the individual to an anonymous digit, totalitarian movements are concerned with totals, factories tend to whittle down the soul to "hands" that are adjuncts to machines, and wars dwarf the soldier to an expendable num-

5 And when he hath found *it,* he layeth
it on his shoulders, rejoicing.
6 And when he cometh home, he calleth
together *his* friends and neighbors, saying
unto them, Rejoice with me; for I have
found my sheep which was lost.

the one which is lost, until he finds it? 5 And
when he has found it, he lays it on his
shoulders, rejoicing. 6 And when he comes
home, he calls together his friends and his
neighbors, saying to them, 'Rejoice with
me, for I have found my sheep which was

5-6. Vss. 5*b* and 6 are vivid details that are missing from Matthew's version. Luke may have borrowed vs. 6 from vs. 9.

---

ber on a disk; but the faith of Jesus speaks age on age its protest in the thunder of love: **One of them!**

The evidence for individual worth is not far to seek. Every man is distinctive by birth. He is not a copy of his parents. He is not like any man who ever lived. He has his own fingerprint, his own accent of voice, his own turn of thought. In a profound sense he is unique. At our human best we honor this fact. Newspapers on frequent occasions tell of the search for one lost aviator, or the rescue from a landslide of one lost child. We deeply know that each life is precious, and at our best we act on that faith. So each man longs, in a valid longing, for recognition. An inferiority complex is the effect of treatment that deems a man inferior; and a superiority complex is but a more violent reaction to the same contempt. Each one of us knows that he is not inferior, but a person of unique worth. This knowledge is not conceit, for conceit is a mistaken way of overcoming contempt. Thus the conviction that the soul has abiding worth is a true and inevitable instinct. Remorse is further proof: it is the pain of a man who thinks he has wasted a divine birthright.

Jesus said that all heaven's energies are turned to find **one** lost man. Earth's only treasure is personality—the person. This faith is the wellspring of democracy, for democracy otherwise is worse than an empty form: it is clash of selfish interests and the breeding ground of demagoguery. This faith is the only warrant for philanthropy: it saves mankind from a scientific contempt for life. This faith is the answer to the soul's longing on earth: it speaks pardon and promise of fulfillment. This faith makes heaven homelike: persons are not there absorbed into some vague sea of being, as if they were worth no more than drops of water, but are recognized and loved. **One of them** is every man's name. So every man should reverence the mystery within him, and yield himself to God.

4e. Jesus, the Good Shepherd.—No picture of Jesus was more dear to the early church. It is the theme of inscriptions on Christian seals and writings, and occurs and reoccurs in the portrayals found in the catacombs.[9] Jesus has given deeper meaning to such glowing passages of scripture as Isa. 40:11, as the music of Handel's *Messiah* beautifully testifies. Jesus has captured the Twenty-Third Psalm, written centuries before his time, and made it his biography.

By Jesus the human flock finds pasturage. The grass seems greener beyond the hedge of his care, but that appearance always deceives, for man's self-will leads only to the wastelands. Our hymnals ring with the praise of Christ, not in any self-hypnotism, but because the generations of those who have loved him have found fulfillment in his shepherding care. He has kindled the mind, enriched the emotions, and nerved the will. By Jesus the human flock has found shelter. Thus he meets life's demand for both adventure and refuge. The yearning for the fold is no cowardice; those who jibe at religion as an "escape" do not choose the beating of the storm when their own door is near at hand. Pain is only slow death unless interpretation is given, sorrow is only a hopelessness unless some rainbow is flung across it, and sin is a worse despair unless there is assurance of pardon. Jesus leads the flock out of the storm of sorrow, and sin, and guides it into his fold.

But this double guidance, though it is of heaven, might not have been enough to win him the title of the Good Shepherd. Some commentators say that the sheepfold of his day was shaped like a capital letter *C,* and that the shepherd wrapped himself in his robe at nightfall and then laid himself across the opening, so that any wolf or lion trying to ravage the flock would have to cross first the shepherd's body. "I am the good shepherd, . . . I lay down my life for the sheep" (John 10:14-15). There is a fine picture, with better strength than the passive gentleness of most pictures on this theme, which shows a shepherd poised dangerously on a precipitous mountain slope, gathering in the lost sheep with a downward sweep of a strong arm.[1] The sheep is our wayward humanity, the

[9] See Jack Finegan, *Light from the Ancient Past* (Princeton: Princeton University Press, 1946), index references, especially pp. 361, 372, 384-85.

[1] Alfred Soord, "The Lost Sheep"; see Cynthia Pearl Maus, *Christ and the Fine Arts* (New York: Harper & Bros., 1938), pp. 203-5.

7 I say unto you, that likewise joy shall be in heaven over one sinner that repenteth, more than over ninety and nine just persons, which need no repentance.

8 ¶ Either what woman having ten pieces of silver, if she lose one piece, doth not light a candle, and sweep the house, and seek diligently till she find *it?*

lost.' 7 Even so, I tell you, there will be more joy in heaven over one sinner who repents than over ninety-nine righteous persons who need no repentance.

8 "Or what woman, having ten silver coins,[z] if she loses one coin, does not light a lamp and sweep the house and seek dili-

[z] The drachma, rendered here by *silver coin,* was about sixteen cents.

---

7. The shepherd's greater joy over the recovery of one sheep that had been lost than over the rest of the flock that had not been endangered formed part of the parable in Matthew's version (Matt. 18:13*b*). It is probable, therefore, that Luke has transformed the ending of the parable into this application of it. Did Jesus intend his story to stress God's concern for the **sinner** as much as God's joy at his repentance? **In heaven:** A circumlocution often used in late Jewish literature to avoid the use of God's name.

2. Parable of the Lost Coin (15:8-10)

This makes the same point as the preceding parable and is given a similar application. The fact that this parable does not occur in Matthew has sometimes been used as an argument against its authenticity, but the gospel tradition makes it clear that Jesus often used parables in pairs. As in this instance, the first sometimes revolves about a man and the second about a woman (cf. 13:18-20; 17:34-35).

8-9. Ten silver coins: The Greek drachma, a coin roughly equivalent to the Roman denarius, had a silver content worth about sixteen cents, but was much more valuable

---

slope is the wasteland that sin makes, the danger is the risk the shepherd runs, the arm is the arm of Jesus, the overarching sky is all God's love.

8-10. ***Parable of the Lost Coin.***—(See also Expos. on vss. 9-10.) These two parables, the lost sheep and the lost coin, have been called twin stories; but they may have been told at different times, and their proximity may be due only to the art of the Gospelist. We should be slow to stress the differences. One makes a man the chief actor; the other, a woman. In one the sheep is lost outside the fold; in the other the coin is lost in the house. In one the sheep's ignorance is the cause of loss; in the other, the woman's carelessness. But this emphasis on differences may be mistaken: each story may have stood in its own right at first, and we may be wrong to draw any distinction that would mar the amazing depth and simplicity of each parable. Certainly any allegorizing of this story (such as would make the house a church, the woman an evangelist, the ten coins the souls committed to her care) is artificial, and an offense against the single flame of truth in the story. The mind of Jesus moved in direct vitality, not in complicated patterns.

The accent is on the preciousness of the coin and the grief (turning to joy) of the woman. A drachma in itself had little value, but it was one tenth of her meager savings; and it was one half of the temple tax. Perhaps the coin was part of a headdress of coins; there is no law against such an interpretation. But we would be wiser to see here a memory of a cottage at Nazareth—and of its poverty, so stringent that the loss of one coin was a consternation. Each man has *that* urgent preciousness in the sight of God; each man lost to the true love of God and his neighbors is *thus* sorely missed in the house called heaven. If a barren field held radium, it would no longer be barren; it would be so valuable that armies would be sent to guard it. Man seems commonplace, like a barren field, but he holds within himself a treasure far more costly than radium. The grief of God cannot abide the loss of that treasure.

The accent is also on the search. That stress gives these two parables a deeper truth even than that of the parable of the prodigal son; for in that latter story the father did not seek the wanderer. Here the woman turns the house upside down in the eagerness of her search. Does God thus ransack his universe for one lost man? Are all our wars and the chaos of our changing systems but the dust of his search?

9 And when she hath found *it,* she calleth *her* friends and *her* neighbors together, saying, Rejoice with me; for I have found the piece which I had lost.

10 Likewise, I say unto you, there is joy in the presence of the angels of God over one sinner that repenteth.

gently until she finds it? 9 And when she
has found it, she calls together her friends and neighbors, saying, 'Rejoice with me, for I have found the coin which I had lost.'
10 Even so, I tell you, there is joy before the
angels of God over one sinner who repents."

---

than that in terms of purchasing power. A "double drachma" is mentioned in Matt. 17:24 as the annual head tax paid into the temple treasury by every adult male Jew. The money could represent the life savings of a poor woman. A **lamp** would be necessary for the search in a Palestinian house that was poorly provided with windows.

10. According to the thought of the time, a court of "angels of the presence" surrounded the throne of God.

James Stephens has a poem[2] in which a perhaps drunken man presumptuously demands that God's cosmic sweep of arm, intent on destroying mankind, should stop, because he, the intercessor, was in the way: God's reply, strictly consistent with the teaching of this parable, is, "Dear child, I feared that you were dead." So God "stayed His hand." The precious metal of the soul, the seeking God, the grief and the urgency of the search even unto Calvary: this story is a wonderment, and a heartbreak, and—redemption.

9-10. ***Angel's Joy.***—In both dramas the first act is tragedy of loss, the second act is the grief-stricken search, and the third act is joy. Our cult of the happy ending may not be after all a sentimentalism; for perhaps we deeply realize that human history is not out of God's control, and that finally his purpose of love must be fulfilled. In human life the last word is not sinning, or even the self-denial that surrender to Christ requires: the last word is joy, for Calvary is but the halfway inn that leads to Easter. *The Expositor's Greek Testament* says of these verses as they occur in connection with the parable of the lost sheep: "Every human being knows the joy of finding things lost. It is only in religion that men lose the scent of simple universal truths."[3] That is an unfortunately true comment, but it could never apply to the gospel proclaimed by Jesus. These parables are instinct with simple universal truths.

Only Jesus would dare thus to portray heaven. He said that a woman lost a silver coin, turned the house into turmoil because her poverty could not endure the loss, found the coin, and then told all the women at the well so that they might rejoice with her. Only Jesus would dare to say that God and his angels are like that woman and her neighbors. Do we understand the locale and the nature of real joy? When a man strikes oil in Texas there is not necessarily joy in heaven. It depends—on why he wanted that fortune, and how he proposes to use it. That news may bring a shadowed and averted gaze among the angels. But should the man be awe-struck in the sense of God as he looks at a child's face, or should he turn in contrition to pray, a wave of gladness sweeps through the sky. **In the presence of the angels** really means in the judgment of God. If only we would learn to judge joy according to his judgment! Perhaps we have partly learned: the professions and callings that live in genuine love for men—doctors, mothers, teachers, lowly friends in all walks of life—hold a joy which graspingness never knows. True evangelism, the seeking of the lost, shares an angel gladness. One soul coming home to God brings joy in earth and heaven, a better joy than when "the morning stars sang together, and all the sons of God shouted for joy" (Job 38:7).

Could any words more thrillingly tell the sympathy of God? He cannot rejoice alone; he needs to share his grief and joy with men and angels. "God warms his hands at man's heart when he prays."[4] This is not anthropopathism, to use a long and fear-stricken word; for an impassive God would be an idol, or less worthy than a feeling man. Man's only true joy is that which comes from God by God's sharing, the joy of finding the lost. At long last there can be no other joy than God's joy, any more than there can be light on earth without the bestowals of the sun. Are there any words in the Gospel more filled than these with morning light?

[2] "What Thomas Said in a Pub," *Collected Poems* (New York: The Macmillan Co., 1926), p. 131.

[3] Ed. W. Robertson Nicoll (London: Hodder & Stoughton, 1897), I, 578.

[4] John Masefield, *The Widow in the Bye Street* (New York: The Macmillan Co., 1912), Part VI, st. xxviii.

11 ¶ And he said, A certain man had two sons:

11 And he said, "There was a man who

3. Parable of the Lost Son (15:11-32)

The parable falls into two parts. The first (vss. 11-24) illustrates the joy with which God welcomes the repentant sinner. It is complete in itself, and teaches much the same truth as the parables of the lost sheep and the lost coin. The second (vss. 25-32) rebukes the criticism of this interpretation of the love and mercy of God that had been made by "righteous persons that need no repentance." Some interpreters have supposed this second part to be a later appendix. The elder son is said to represent either Pharisaism or Jewish Christianity. But no such direct allegory is apparent. The second part is just as parabolic in form as the first, and the whole is best regarded as a unity. The parable is left by Luke to speak for itself without any formal application.

11-12. The parable assumes that although the **younger** son requests and receives immediate possession of his **share of property**—according to Deut. 21:17 he would be

11-32. ***Parable of the Prodigal Sons.***—(See also Expos., pp. 272-80.) A country lad listened in an English cathedral to the reading of this story. Came the words **But when he was yet a great way off, his father saw him, and had compassion, and ran . . . .** The lad, quite forgetful of place and people, wishing perhaps that he had that kind of home and father, shouted, "Eh, but yon was a grand old man!" [5] The story might be called "The Parable of the Good Father." [6] Edwin McNeill Poteat's interpretation, that the father also was a prodigal—a materialist, casual and worldly in the rearing of his sons, sentimental in his forgiveness, shallow always in bourgeois mind—is a justifiable and very valuable *ap*plication, but surely not a justifiable *im*plication. Can there be any doubt of Luke's own conviction concerning the father's love: he took it to be a dim hint, which became movingly clear in Jesus, of God's love.[7] But it is still the story of two prodigals.

We need not assume that the younger son was a bad man when he left home. The division of property as described was not unusual. The younger son had initiative: he may have gone to Rome or Alexandria with resolves as high as his hopes. But he himself was the center of his dreams—**Give me . . . that falleth to me**—and he trusted his own wisdom. He was intent to win success and to be free, but had never probed the meaning of success or freedom. He was moved by pride of emotion, in sordidness at the last, for the father does not deny the scornful comment of the elder son in vs. 30. That sordidness may tempt us to believe that the younger son could never sit for our portrait. But fleshliness is a wide realm: the itch for fame, the hankering for things, the desire for popularity, even an aesthetic culture are all provinces of the far country. In Winston Churchill's novel *A Far Country* that alien land is the loss of standards and ideals. Perhaps our whole generation, like every generation, is the younger son.

The result? A famine, nature's comment on man's fleshliness. We should not scorn the lad because calamity and hunger drove him to penitence. Perhaps that is always the way. Each generation lives in pride until war and economic depression open its eyes, and many people even then are blind. Besides, the son was ashamed as well as hungry; for to a Jew the feeding of swine and the eating of their food was utter shame. Further, he knew his sin, knew even that in essence it was sin against God; and he confessed his sin. Penitence came from mixed motives, as in every man. "When he awoke from his swoon" might be a valid translation: he had realism and lowliness at last, not merely hunger.

The story of the return is all joy: if we did not smile at the gladness, we would have to cry. The father knew the son afar off: no distance could cheat the eyes of love. He kissed away the long-rehearsed confession. He gave command to bring the robe, reserved for only honored guests; and for the ring and shoes—both signs of sonship. A Buddhist story [8] on a parallel theme shows the father for twenty years hiding his identity from his son, meanwhile watching and harshly testing until penitence was fully proved and a nobility won through

[5] J. G. Greenhough, as quoted in James Hastings, ed., *The Great Texts of the Bible* (New York: Charles Scribner's Sons, 1913), X, 300.

[6] Suggested by Hugh Martin, *The Parables of the Gospels* (New York: The Abingdon Press, 1937), p. 167.

[7] See *Parables of Crisis* (New York: Harper & Bros., 1950), pp. 134-50.

[8] *The Sacred Books of the East*, ed. F. Max Müller (Oxford: Clarendon Press, 1884), XXI, 99-117. Reference is made to this same story by Martin, *Parables of the Gospels*, pp. 170-71.

12 And the younger of them said to *his* father, Father, give me the portion of goods that falleth *to me.* And he divided unto them *his* living.

had two sons; 12 and the younger of them said to his father, 'Father, give me the share of property that falls to me.' And he di-

---

entitled to one third—the **father** continues to enjoy a life interest in that portion assigned to the elder. Jesus ben Sira warns his readers against disposing of their property by gift:

> To a son or a wife, to a brother or a friend,
> Do not give power over yourself as long as you live,
> And do not give your money to someone else,
> So that you may not change your mind and have to ask for it
> . . . .
> When the days of your life reach their end,
> At the time of your death distribute your property.
> (Ecclus. 33:19-23 Goodspeed.)

---

trial. But not this father: there was no quarantine. For the younger son had been dead—death being an event of the soul, and the body's death terrible only because it is a sharp and final reminder of the judgment of the soul; but he was now alive again, restored and more than restored to home.

We almost wish the story could have ended at vs. 24. But there was another prodigal, one who stayed at home. He was as distant in spirit as his brother had been in body. Elder brothers are as numerous as younger sons. The elder son also made a good start. He said, "I will stay at home and work hard," and he kept the vow. But he also was center of his life circle, and the center grew so black in ingrowing mood that soon the whole circle was black. His was pride of temperament, which is perhaps harder to cure than pride of flesh, as a virus in the blood is harder to cure than a gaping wound. Perhaps the elder brother helped to drive the younger away from home. That is the Kipling version:

> I never was very refined, you see,
> (And it weighs on my brother's mind, you see)
> But there's no reproach among swine, d'you see,
> For being a bit of a swine.
> So I'm off with wallet and staff to eat
> The bread that is three parts chaff to wheat,
> But glory be!—there's a laugh to it,
> Which isn't the case when we dine.[9]

The elder son was always taking a sidelong glance at his own goodness, saying, "These wastrels . . . unemployables . . . foreigners." He was a leading citizen who deplored the follies of the masses. He was a prodigal.

A calamity fell also on him, worse to him than famine: he found that the universe does not honor his coldly respectable code. He could never have believed that a wastrel could be welcomed as an honored guest. He upbraided his father and the government of the world. **Lo, these many years do I serve thee:** serve, not love. **Neither transgressed I . . . :** he had kept the letter of the law, but broken all its spirit. **Yet thou never gavest me . . . :** he secretly coveted what his brother had chosen. If the younger son returning home had met his brother before he met his father, he might have turned right around and been thankful for the far country. The elder brother is sometimes the portrait of the church. Perhaps the second prodigal never returned. There is a letter written in 1861 by David Gray,[1] the young Scottish poet, after weary, lonely months in London, and after he had fallen prey to tuberculosis. "Dear Parents, I am coming home. . . . I have come through things . . . that I shall never tell to anyone but you. . . . O home, home, home!" The younger son could have written it. But the elder son? A preacher may miss salvation, while a wastrel may go straight from his doss house to the welcome of God.

This story is not the gospel within the gospel, despite pulpit claims. The father stayed at home until he saw his younger son returning in rags. In Alan Paton's novel *Cry, the Beloved Country* the Negro father searched the city of Johannesburg, up street and down street, from reform school to Shanty Town to jail, until he found his wandering son. Shall we say that he was nobler than the father in the parable? No, because a parable has one central flame of truth: it is not an allegory. The story's theme is not a careful portrayal of all heaven's ways but—two prodigals and a welcome. Jesus told the story. Had his hearers watched and listened closely, they might have heard another story:

9 "The Prodigal Son," *Rudyard Kipling's Verse,* Definitive Edition. Used by permission of Mrs. George Bambridge, Macmillan & Co., and Doubleday & Co.

1 Told by G. H. Morrison, *Sun-Rise* (New York: A. C. Armstrong & Son, 1903), p. 10.

13 And not many days after the younger son gathered all together, and took his journey into a far country, and there wasted his substance with riotous living.

14 And when he had spent all, there arose a mighty famine in that land; and he began to be in want.

vided his living between them.
13 Not many days later, the younger son gathered all he had and took his journey into a far country, and there he squandered his property in loose living.
14 And when he had spent everything, a great famine arose in that country, and he began to be in want.

---

13. Gathered all he had, i.e., after he had converted his property into money. **A far country:** Jesus' hearers would think of such lands as Italy, North Africa, Egypt, or Babylonia. **In loose living:** The phrase translates a good Greek adverb but one that occurs nowhere else in the Greek Bible. It means either "recklessly" or "in dissolute pleasures." The elder brother understood it in the latter sense (vs. 30). A papyrus from Hermopolis in Egypt, written in the late first or early second century A.D., records the complaint of the parents of a young man that their son Castor had "squandered all his own property with others in extravagant living," and now wished to waste theirs also.

14-16. Having dissipated his resources, the young man was compelled in a time of **famine** to seek employment. Jesus' hearers would consider a swineherd's occupation the most degrading a Jew could accept. A Talmudic proverb declares: "Cursed is the man who tends swine, and the man who teaches his son Greek wisdom!" He soon came to envy the **swine** the food doled out to them. He himself was not allowed even such pitiful

---

God had three sons. Two of them were sons of earth, children of his creation; and the other a Son in heaven, begotten of God's abidingness. The younger son on earth forgot his true home, and through pride of flesh sank into shame; and the older son on earth, though not unmindful of the sky in his nature, began to despise his brother, and so grew hard through pride of the mind. The Son in heaven lived always in his Father's joy, but a shadow fell on both whenever they thought of the children on earth. Suddenly one flash of resolve moved them. The Father said, "I will send the child of my abidingness to seek them"; and the Son said, "I will go, that my brothers may come home and my Father no longer grieve." So the Son took flesh, and walked the roads of earth. He found the younger prodigal, ate his husks, and shared his shame; but the prodigal was deaf: "No Brother of mine," he cried, "and God is only a name!" So the Son of God's abidingness then found the elder prodigal, who was in church; but he also was hard of heart: "Why should you seek my brother?" he asked bitterly; "for he is a wastrel: you are no better than he!" Then befell the most cruel thing earth has ever known: the two prodigals killed the Son of God's abidingness, for his light was pain to their afflicted eyes. In the hate that yearning can bring they slew him on a cross. But, but, he prayed for them as he died. The younger prodigal said: "I would return to God if I had not killed his only-begotten Son, but now. . . ." The older prodigal said: "I never knew my lovelessness until I saw his love, but I have killed him, so now. . . ." Then, then, the Son of abidingness rose from the dead, for a grave could not imprison his great love, and both prodigals knew that he was with them. What they then did, who can say? You and I must choose the answer.

11-24. ***The Younger Son.***—Had Jesus given this truth in a theology, it might have been a prison; in a science, it might have been a factory; but he gave it in a story, and the story is our home. Perhaps Jesus knew the two sons; perhaps he turned a local incident into a parable that so fills all time that every man is the prodigal, and everywhere is the far country. Consider the soul journey of the younger son.

He began in self-will. He was not wicked at first, but he was resolved to live his own life. His father might have obliged him to stay home, but could not have obliged him to be filial; and there was already one prodigal at home. If we resolve to tell a lie, no hand is clapped over our mouth. The younger son was not thinking primarily about his father or his brother, but about himself. He could not claim that he was ignorant about life: many a man before him had chosen "the primrose path of dalliance,"[2] and found that it leads "to the everlasting bonfire."[3] But self-trust always becomes blind, and the lad probably thought he could find a way where others had been lost. Self-will mars homes, trade, statecraft; and has but one terminus—the far country, so-called because it is far from home.

He continued through self-loathing. Of

[2] Shakespeare, *Hamlet*, Act I, scene 3.
[3] Shakespeare, *Macbeth*, Act II, scene 3.

15 And he went and joined himself to a citizen of that country; and he sent him into his fields to feed swine.

16 And he would fain have filled his belly with the husks that the swine did eat: and no man gave unto him.

17 And when he came to himself, he said, How many hired servants of my fa-

15 So he went and joined himself to one of the citizens of that country, who sent
him into his fields to feed swine. 16 And he
would gladly have fed on[a] the pods that
the swine ate; and no one gave him any-
thing. 17 But when he came to himself he

[a] Other ancient authorities read *filled his belly with.*

fare. **Pods** of the carob tree are frequently mentioned in rabbinical literature as fodder for domestic animals, but as food for men only in times of dire need. **Filled his belly with** (KJV; RSV mg.): The reading in Codex Alexandrinus, various O.L. versions, and the Sinaitic Syriac, as well as the bulk of the late Greek MSS.

17-20. When he came to himself: An idiom in Semitic languages as well as in Greek and Latin. In this instance it could be paraphrased: "When he realized how foolish he had been." A Talmudic proverb recalls the prodigal's predicament: "When a son [who

course he could not have hated himself unless there had been a good man in him to do the hating. That prime fact claims a separate word (see Expos., vs. 17). But self-expression, sometimes termed the new psychology but deserving rather to be named the ancient lie, brought him to the far country; and there he despised himself. Of course, for he had turned away from God, and therefore all life turned against the prodigal. **There arose a mighty famine.** Of course, for he was playing a lone hand, and therefore alienated himself even from his brother man. **No man gave unto him.** His "friends" deserted him in the time of need, for they also were playing a lone hand. Even the citizen did not really want him: the prodigal joined himself to that man in order to still the pangs of bodily hunger. The swine to a Jew were the ultimate mark of degradation. So in his self-loathing he thought of home. A poor way to turn home? Not if pain and loneliness are the only language to which a man will listen!

He turned at last through self-reverence, which is but another name for the remembrance of God. His motives were low only in part; for with the bodily pain was mixed shame, longing for home, and love for his father. Moreover, there was a true and deep realization of the nature of sin: **I have sinned against heaven, and before thee.**

> The fool was stripped to his foolish hide,
>
> . . . .
>
> So some of him lived but the most of him died.[4]

But some of him lived! He confronted his wretchedness and the cause of it. He spoke the truth out loud to himself: "Not for this shame was I born!" He arose, standing upright. He took one step homeward. Then the road almost bore him on the journey, for life helps self-reverence even as it thwarts self-will. This is the history of conversion: to face oneself, to speak the truth about oneself, to stand upright, to go. No, that is not the full history or the main history: the chief fact is that the Father himself quickens that penitence, and meets us on the homeward road in full welcome of love.

17-22. ***The Nature and Conditions of Forgiveness.***—The pardon seems at first sight all too easy. Was the father in the story a sentimentalist? Does God say to us, when we have vitiated our own life and poisoned the common life, "Oh, just forget it"? Even a sinner would despise a jaunty universe. The fact that he knows himself a sinner and suffers from remorse means that he can worship no God except a holy God. Where is the holiness of God in this story? Where is the cleansing flame of judgment? They are here if we search for them. A parable cannot be a full theology: it is a story intent to underscore one central truth. The truth here is: God welcomes the sinner. Jesus stressed it because the publicans and sinners did not believe it (it seemed too good to be true), and because the Pharisees and scribes did not wish to believe it.

Yet judgment is written across the story. The prodigal knew famine, shame that brought him as low as swine, loneliness—all the wretchedness of a soul alienated from man and God. There was no easy pardon! Besides, the marks of the far country remained on him all his life. What are euphoniously called "the social sins" (they could better be called unsocial) have consequences of physical disease and mental chaos; but subtler sins, such as those in the elder brother, have a darker aftermath, for they turn a man's temper into gall. God's holiness is like-

[4] "The Vampire," *Rudyard Kipling's Verse,* Definitive Edition. Used by permission of Mrs. George Bambridge, Macmillan & Co., and Doubleday & Co.

ther's have bread enough and to spare, and I perish with hunger!

said, 'How many of my father's hired servants have bread enough and to spare, but

has left home] has to walk barefooted [because of poverty], he remembers how well he had been treated in his father's house." **I have sinned:** There is a similar confession in a papyrus letter of a certain Antonius Longus to his mother, written in Fayûm in the

wise written across the story. For any prodigal, in the far country or at home, must confront himself (in remembrance of the Father) before he can find pardon. That awakening, that pathetic **I have sinned,** that homeward journey in rags and dejection, are not painless! Facing the light is exquisite pain to eyes that have been long closed in selfishness.

The father also was not immune. His love was no sentimentalism, but very grief so long as his son stayed in the far country. That his child should so despise his home, so rend a father's heart, so befoul the family name! The father waited because not even a prodigal must be coerced: a man cannot be saved by being robbed of manhood. But what anguished waiting! Not an hour passed without the father's gazing down the road! If we would know the full measure of that pain, we must look at—Calvary. If we do look at both the prodigal's misery and the father's grief, we shall not say the story is sentimental: we shall bow our heads in penitence, and catch some echo of angels' singing around an inviolable throne, "Holy, holy, holy, is the LORD of hosts" (Isa. 6:3).

Yet the welcome of God to the returning sinner, the truth that is the bright focus of the parable, shines with undimmed light. Pardon is no mere acquittal, no easy turn of the phrase "Thy sins be forgiven thee" (5:20, 23; Matt. 9:2, 5; Mark 2:5, 9), no mere mending of the past. It is more even than restoration. Pardon is nothing less than the welcome of home, so that day by day the love of home may work in the returned soul until he himself becomes the home of God. See now the tokens of that welcome.

17. ***Self-Discovery: When He Came to Himself.***—*The Abingdon Bible Commentary*[5] suggests that the Greek word is a medical term: when he "came to his senses after fainting." The idiom was in many languages before Jesus used it, but only he could give it heavenly light. Because of him it is in our language, for we say of a neighbor's black mood, "He is not himself today." Acts 12:11 says of Peter waking out of sleep: "And when Peter was come to himself." Our selfishness is not reality: it is an evil dream.

Suddenly the prodigal knew that he had been asleep: the life he thought was "real life" was so unreal that if he followed it further it would become death. He had no real joy, no friends, no inner peace. He had fallen so far from life that he had more in common with pigs than with men. Byron spoke his new and true realism:

My days are in the yellow leaf;
  The flowers and fruits of love are gone;
The worm, the canker, and the grief
    Are mine alone!

The fire that on my bosom preys
  Is lone as some volcanic isle;
No torch is kindled at its blaze—
    A funeral pile.[6]

A man comes to himself when he says, "What a fool I've been!" But he will not believe it even then unless, like the prodigal, he says it out loud and keeps saying it.

There are two men in us. One has the appearance of joy, but the joy is a mirage; the other wears the aspect of dullness and even distaste, but is gladness. The one seems real, but is only an evil dream; the other seems unreal, an impossible dream of goodness, but is the only vitality. The one offers promises which are never fulfilled; the other makes demands which become a paradise of fulfillment. Someone used to give this advice: "Go and shut yourself up in an empty room for the whole of one day." The prodigal was shut up in the loneliness and pain of the far country. Then he came to himself. God has his own purposes when he leads us into a wilderness.

Could any word tell more clearly the optimism of Jesus? Or the urgency? He sees the real man in us, but knows that we may choose the unreal man—to our grief. We say to one another, "Be a man!" We do not say to a clock, "Be a clock!" or to a tiger, "Be a tiger!"—for a clock and a tiger have no choice. But a man has choice between two men living in him. He makes a wise choice, the choice of the real against the unreal, when he exclaims, "My name is fool and sinner!" For then God says, "No, your name is son of God." Do the angels say of us in their clearer sight, "He isn't himself yet"? Do they weep as they comment, "He is walking in his sleep"? Is any depression or war

[5] *Ad loc.*

[6] "On This Day I Complete My Thirty-Sixth Year."

18 I will arise and go to my father, and will say unto him, Father, I have sinned against heaven, and before thee,

19 And am no more worthy to be called thy son: make me as one of thy hired servants.

I perish here with hunger! 18 I will arise and go to my father, and I will say to him, "Father, I have sinned against heaven and before you; 19 I am no longer worthy to be called your son; treat me as one of your

---

second century A.D.: "I write to thee that I am naked. I beseech thee, mother, be reconciled to me. Furthermore, I know what I have brought upon myself. I have been chastened

---

the moment when the world bumps into reality, and comes to its senses? Our only true self is that which longs for the eternal, and knows that time's prizes are but a fleeting swoon. **When he came to himself** he turned homeward to the will of his Father.

18. ***Sin and Confession: I Have Sinned Against Heaven, and Before Thee.***—The parable as a whole is a final and solving word. It is man's biography and God's answering grace. But every word and phrase is also a jewel in its own right. This verse tells profoundly the nature of sin. Sin is always antisocial: **before thee.** The prodigal's unruliness brought grief to the father, bitterness to the brother, and cast a shadow on the whole household; for we are bound by unbreakable ties to the whole human family, and any act is like purification or poison cast into a river. Sin is also self-hurt: the sinner becomes Ishmael (Gen. 16:11-16), and sinks in the scale. At the last he is obliged to say of the home fealty which he has despised:

> It surely was my profit had I known;
> It would have been my pleasure had I seen.[7]

But neither "antisocial" nor "suicidal" describes the deepest meaning and effect of sin. **Against heaven** tells sin's real nature. Suppose a man slashed a lovely canvas; and suppose that the artist forgave him, and that the people also who might have seen the originally fair picture issued a public proclamation of pardon to the vandal; and suppose that the picture was restored so that hardly a blemish could be seen. Would the man be forgiven? No, for his prime sin is against beauty, against life—as witness the gash in his conscience and memory. Thus the real offense is not against any *man,* either the sinner himself or any neighbor, but against God. The parable has penetrating truth: **against heaven, and before thee.** So sin can never prosper: the world is God's world. The outer famine was dreadful because it dramatized the inner famine. Victor Hugo has written a poem concerning the loss of the famed Spanish Armada.[8] He pictures the young infanta wondering as she watched the wind blow the petals of a rose held in her hand. Her duenna comments, "Princes rule all on earth except the wind."

The nature and saving consequence of confession are also here shown. The prodigal was wise to confess to his father, for the father stood as a worthy representative of society before whom the prodigal had sinned. Group confession is dangerous; the group may harbor some jaunty or curious people who have no power to mediate God's healing, and the whole affair may become an exhibitionism. Compulsory confession is perhaps a contradiction in terms. It holds even worse dangers if the father-confessor does his task in routine mind, or imagines that some penance is redemptive healing. That latter imagining is as shallow as if the father in the parable had sent the prodigal to work for a month in the kitchen, and then had said, "Now you are all clear." But confession to a lowly and reverent soul is wise: such a man can be in real sense the channel of God's grace, for he knows that he can never be more than a channel. If such a man is not near, the ear of God is always open. Nay, God kisses away the confession before it is half spoken, for his heart is love.

19. ***Escape from Responsibility: Make Me as One of Thy Hired Servants.***—Perhaps the plea was in humility; but since motives are always mixed, perhaps it was escape. When a man is a slave, he need make no decisions. What a relief! Ernest Psichari, grandson of Ernest Renan, enlisted in the army because (so says his biographer) "he was seeking deliverance from civil life." The industrial revolution took its "portion of goods," wasted them in an undue exploitation of the planet, came to that famine in brotherhood which acquisitiveness always brings, and now runs for refuge to totalitarian tyrannies: **Make me as one of thy hired servants.**

Every man is tempted to say, "Let someone else do my thinking for me." Every man is tempted to add, "my religious thinking"—as if anyone could be his proxy in that essentially personal realm! There can be guides in religion, as in music or homemaking, but no proxies:

[7] Tennyson, "Guinevere," *Idylls of the King,* l. 653.
[8] "The Rose of the Infanta" from *The Legend of the Centuries* (New York: G. W. Dillingham, 1894).

20 And he arose, and came to his father. But when he was yet a great way off, his father saw him, and had compassion, and ran, and fell on his neck, and kissed him.

hired servants." ' 20 And he arose and came to his father. But while he was yet at a distance, his father saw him and had compassion, and ran and embraced him and

---

even as is meet. I know that I have sinned" (Adolf Deissmann, *Light From the Ancient East,* tr. L. R. M. Strachan [2nd ed.; New York: George H. Doran Co., 1927], p. 188). The prodigal hopes for mercy, but is unprepared for the generosity of a father's love.

---

religion, by the very meaning of the word, is the bond between each man's soul and God. "My political thinking," every man is tempted to add; for true democracy is a heavy burden and it is easier to be uniform (in a uniform), at the beck and call of the demagogue or the dictator, than to be a responsible citizen. "My economic thinking," every man is tempted to add; and the corporation on the one hand or the labor union on the other is quite willing to oblige. Whenever a man or an era reaches chaos through transgression, the word springs quickly: **Make me as one of thy hired servants.** Then comes standardized opinion, then the death of liberty, then the decay of selfhood.

The prodigal was not born to be a slave; and neither were the men who served as such in that household. A man who can say, "I have sinned against heaven," can never be a slave: he has seen the throne of God. Nay, he has confessed himself the child of God, although an erring and willful child. He can come under the servitude of God's love, for that servitude is perfect freedom; and God has loved him enough to give him his own fingerprint, his own mind, his own cast of soul; and God does not drive him with a whip, but says, "I will guide thee with mine eye" (Ps. 32:8). The father in the parable waved aside the plea for servitude: "This my son" (vs. 24), he said. No man can escape responsibility, for every man is a son in his Father's house.

20. ***Recognitions: When He Was Yet a Great Way Off.***—Does a man ever deface the divine image in himself? That we cannot answer, for we do not know. The father in the story recognized his son despite the rags, the emaciation, the dejection, the head bent low in shame and tears. Had the lad remained defiantly in the far country, would he have been completely calloused at last? Again, we do not know. Homesickness is a blessedly persistent "ailment." What man can quite expunge every memory of home? No proverb could be more false or more true than our proverb "Love is blind." Love is never blind to sin; or if it is thus blind, love has ceased to be love and becomes mere indulgence. Love is never blind to the promise of goodness; or if it is thus blind, love has become only a casualness and a sentimentalism. Yet love is resolved to be blind to every transgression, that love may redeem. Jesus said, "Thou art Simon," and was not blind to the man's manifest failings. He knew Simon's reputation for headstrongness with all its unpredictable outbreaks and uncertainties. Yet Jesus was resolved to be blind, "Thou shalt be called Cephas, . . . A stone" (John 1:42).

Whoso draws nigh to God one step through doubtings dim,
God will advance a mile in blazing light to him.[9]

Jesus gave a far more wonderful pledge: he said that while a man is yet a great way off from God, with hardly more than one swift thought of home to his credit, God sees him, recognizes him for his own child, and runs down the road to meet him.

We have suggested that in one respect the parables of the lost sheep and of the lost coin hold a deeper truth even than this parable, for the former tell of the seeking love of God, while the story of the prodigal tells only of the waiting love of God. But perhaps that judgment is wrong: the father had waited only because the son must choose to return. As soon as that choice was made the father ran. Is not Jesus himself that running of God down the road of earth? "While we were yet sinners, Christ died for us" (Rom. 5:8).

20-24. ***God's Welcome to the Penitent.***—The tokens of welcome listed in vss. 20, 22, 23 are each rich in meaning. **Kissed** means in the Greek "kissed tenderly"—the more tenderly because the lad was in rags and shame. **Bring** in some of the best MSS is "bring quickly," and has almost the force of "Quick!"—because not a minute must be lost in restoring the prodigal to the love and joy of home. **The best robe** (there is no second best in the gifts of God's pardon) was a robe kept only for the most distinguished guest: it represented the most signal honor. The **ring** meant that the son was still heir: it was a sign by which the father said to the prodigal, as to the elder brother, "All that I have is thine" (vs. 31). **Shoes** were the

[9] Author unknown.

21 And the son said unto him, Father, I have sinned against heaven, and in thy sight, and am no more worthy to be called thy son.

22 But the father said to his servants, Bring forth the best robe, and put *it* on him; and put a ring on his hand, and shoes on *his* feet:

23 And bring hither the fatted calf, and kill *it;* and let us eat, and be merry:

24 For this my son was dead, and is alive again; he was lost, and is found. And they began to be merry.

kissed him. 21 And the son said to him,
'Father, I have sinned against heaven and
before you; I am no longer worthy to be
called your son.[b]' 22 But the father said to
his servants, 'Bring quickly the best robe,
and put it on him; and put a ring on his
hand, and shoes on his feet; 23 and bring
the fatted calf and kill it, and let us eat
and make merry; 24 for this my son was
dead, and is alive again; he was lost, and
is found.' And they began to make merry.

[b] Other ancient authorities add *treat me as one of your hired servants.*

---

21. The father interrupts the speech his son had carefully rehearsed. **Treat me as one of your hired servants** (RSV mg.) is regarded by most editors as an interpolation from vs. 19*b*, despite the fact that it is included in the text by codices Vaticanus, Sinaiticus, Bezae, and others.

22-23. The prodigal is clothed in finery, and his return is celebrated with feasting and merrymaking in the Oriental manner. **The best robe** was reserved for distinguished guests and special occasions.

24. Spiritually **dead** and **lost,** as in 9:60 and 19:10. The first part of the verse is repeated in vs. 32 as the conclusion to the whole parable.

---

token of sonship, for only slaves went barefoot; and the Negro spiritual has caught both the joy and the pathos of that gift:

All o' God's Chillun got shoes.
When I get to heab'n I'm goin' to put on my shoes,
I'm goin' to walk all ovah God's Heab'n.[1]

The **calf** was taken early from the mother cow, and fed against some special festival. Thus item after item tells of welcome: Jesus strained at language and imagery to assure us of the unreservedness of God's welcome to the penitent.

We need the assurance, for we are slow to believe so great a joy. Why the reluctance? Because when we become irresponsible—when we fail in response to God—we live in alienation both from God and from our fellow men; and we ascribe the alienation to God rather than to our own act. We are like men who walk with their backs to the sun: we move in shadow, and are tempted to say, "The world is by nature a shadowed world." Thus we make God in our image, and impute to him our hardness of heart: "Lord, I knew thee that thou art a hard man" (Matt. 25:24). Who among us has not said, "I can never forgive myself"? If the words mean "I will not be cavalier about sin," they are sound words; but if they mean "I refuse to believe that I can ever be forgiven," they cut across all that Jesus taught us from Bethlehem to Easter Day. A wise counselor will say to the penitent: "If Jesus were here in the flesh, he would forgive you. Therefore, and only for that reason, you can forgive yourself." Psychology wisely tells us that we must both confront ourselves and forgive ourselves. But only Christian faith can provide the light in which a man can see himself, or the ground of self-forgiveness. That light is Christ; that ground is the pardon of God made known through Jesus Christ.

[1] "All God's Chillun Got Wings," st. iv.

Once again a prime fact must be underscored: God's forgiveness is never mere pardon. It is not negative repair alone, but the grafting of the penitent soul into the tree of eternal life. We say, "I forgive you," sometimes with a casualness that betokens only a shallow mind. Or we say, "I forgive, but cannot forget," meaning actually, "I half forgive you." But God's pardon is never easy or partial. It wipes out the past (the marks may remain, but they become not penalty but discipline and the reminder of redeeming grace), and then restores the soul to God's own life. That life works in the penitent, patiently and gladly day by day, until the penitent is at home—in the Father's house and love.

24, 32. ***Dead and Alive.***—This is a new use of two words. We use them mainly of the body: when the heart stops beating, a man is dead. But the N.T. steadily insists on a far deeper meaning: "He that heareth my word . . . is passed from death unto life" (John 5:24); "We know that we have passed from death unto life, because we love the brethren" (I John 3:14).

25 Now his elder son was in the field: and as he came and drew nigh to the house, he heard music and dancing.

26 And he called one of the servants, and asked what these things meant.

27 And he said unto him, Thy brother is come; and thy father hath killed the fatted calf, because he hath received him safe and sound.

25 "Now his elder son was in the field; and as he came and drew near to the house,
he heard music and dancing. **26** And he
called one of the servants and asked what
this meant. **27** And he said to him, 'Your
brother has come, and your father has killed the fatted calf, because he has re-

---

25-28*a*. The **elder son,** coming in from his day's work **in the field,** inquires the reason for the festivities from **one of the servants.** He learns of his brother's return and refuses to enter the house. The Greek word translated by **music** may be the name of a specific wind instrument resembling the bagpipe, as it is in the LXX version of Dan. 3:5.

The rampart of the body is easily captured: a sword or a germ can win that victory. But the citadel of life, even though the rampart of the body is taken, is still intact. Real death comes only when the soul is **lost.**

Perhaps our use of the words death and life is not completely shallow: perhaps death would carry no fears or darkness but for our transgression. "The sting of death is sin" (I Cor. 15:56). Perhaps when a man says, "Death is so final," he is really saying, "It is appointed unto men once to die, but after this the judgment" (Heb. 9:27). Perhaps when he says, "Poor Bill is dead," he means, "Bill has had his chance at life; and Bill, like the rest of us, has probably left a tangle of threads instead of a tapestry; and now Bill, in the white light of Reality, must confront the snarl." Why do we always try to evade death? Why do we dismiss a funeral from memory as quickly as we can? Why do we try to disguise death? It is because judgment and death are inseparable terms. The word **lost** is the key to the Christian meaning of death, just as **found** is the key to the meaning of life. A man is dead only when he is lost to the love of God, and to the love of man within the love of God; a man is alive when he is found again by God's love.

The last note of the parable is joy. The first part of the story ends in **they began to be merry;** the second, in **is found.** The conclusion is open so far as the elder brother is concerned: we do not know if he yielded to his father's entreaties. That open conclusion is part of the supreme genius of the parable: it means that every man is offered an option. But the prodigal's choice was made, and it issued in joy. Judgment need bring no terror: "There is therefore now no condemnation to them which are in Christ Jesus" (Rom. 8:1). Sin is a breach in life. How can life be mended? Only by the Creator, in the travail of his love. The prodigal faced reality (he "came to himself"), confessed his guilt, and then his father's travail of love wrought redemption; for the father in the parable is God. Then he was saved from real death; and the death of the body, when it came, was only an entrance into real life. This is the gospel, the glad tidings. It is all joy.

25-32. ***The Prodigal Who Stayed at Home.***—The black mood of vss. 25-30 is so sharply divergent from the rest of the parable that some commentators have proposed, naturally and almost inevitably, that the story of the elder brother was originally a separate picture (see Exeg.). But who could deny that there is unity in the whole account? It is unity like that of the bright side and the shadowed side of a shield, but therefore an unbreakable unity. It is unity like that of day and night: night cannot be understood without its bright counterpart of day, and day gathers meaning by the foil of night. Yet that simile has limits: there was no necessity in the elder brother's ill-temper. He was entitled to two thirds of the estate, even though prior birth was not his merit, while the prodigal had claim on only one third; so the elder brother had little cause for complaint. Besides, the prodigal had already come under judgment, and paid a bitter penalty. How did the elder brother "get that way"?

If we deal with the story on the human level, we can regard him with sympathy. The child who stays at home is sometimes taken for granted. There was probably a certain gaiety in the prodigal, glitter rather than light, while the elder son could claim only routine gifts. The latter, therefore, may have been overlooked; and curdling resentments may have grown in him that he himself hardly understood. But the parable is a parable: it is not to be understood merely on the human level. The elder brother is the prototype of religion in the day of Jesus, and perhaps of some forms of allegedly

28 And he was angry, and would not go in: therefore came his father out, and entreated him.

29 And he answering said to *his* father, Lo, these many years do I serve thee, neither transgressed I at any time thy commandment; and yet thou never gavest me a kid, that I might make merry with my friends:

30 But as soon as this thy son was come, which hath devoured thy living with harlots, thou hast killed for him the fatted calf.

ceived him safe and sound.' 28 But he was
angry and refused to go in. His father
came out and entreated him, 29 but he an-
swered his father, 'Lo, these many years I
have served you, and I never disobeyed
your command; yet you never gave me a
kid, that I might make merry with my
friends. 30 But when this son of yours came,
who has devoured your living with harlots,

28*b*-30. His response to his father's urging that he join in the rejoicings is a bitter complaint that a life of virtue has been left without reward, while a life of dissipation and vice has been celebrated with a feast. **This son of yours:** A contemptuous repudiation of any fraternal relationship to the prodigal.

Christian faith in our day. The younger son is the publicans and sinners; the elder brother is the Pharisees and scribes. The love of God in him was only a half loyalty. In the unredeemed part of his nature he was jealous of the gaiety of his younger brother, and doubly jealous when the prodigal was welcomed with feasting. He was as self-righteous as he was jealous: **devoured thy living with harlots** is an unsparing condemnation. He was as self-pitying as he was jealous and self-righteous: **these many years** and **thou never gavest me a kid** are of the essence of self-pity. Jealousy, self-righteousness, and self-pity all come from an inward turning eye: the elder brother, while pretending to worship God, was his own god. Pride is death, whatever its form, but in a religious man it is calcined death. A novel by Susan Ertz is entitled *The Prodigal Heart.* While the younger son was prodigal in body, at least part of his heart was always at home; but the elder brother was prodigal at heart, and only his body was at home.

The elder brother is very unpopular—in the parable. He is not unpopular in society, and he has many descendants. He is sometimes an officer in the church, a leader in reform groups, a "key citizen." He thinks, or wills to think, that all other races are "inferior." A man out of work is simply unemployable: "*I* was always able to find work, and always worked hard." A prodigal like the younger son is just a wastrel: "Actually you can do nothing with them," he says. He has "no patience with people who squander time and money," especially money. Any neighbor of progressive mind is to him "a dangerous element in the community." When disaster falls on the righteous, he doubts if "it pays to be good," for he is sure that goodness ought to "pay." Friedrich W. Krummacher has an honest and penetrating comment. A questioner asked his opinion of the identity of the elder brother. He replied: "I learned it only yesterday . . . myself."[2]

The father's reply was all gentleness. He answered the son's charge of stinginess: **All that I have is thine.** He answered the harsh condemnation of the prodigal, for he quietly changed the sarcastic "This worthless son of yours" (that is the force of the phrase) to **this thy brother.** The word son is τέκνον in the Greek—a much more endearing term than υἱός, which is the usual word for **son.** One may doubt if such a father could have overlooked the child at home or ever have taken him for granted. Joseph Parker has a sermon on the revealing play of the pronouns in vss. 29-30.[3] Let the reader trace it; he will find there the selfishness of the elder brother and the selflessness of the father.

29-30. ***Perverted Religion.***—A certain sermon topic announcement caught the eye: "Attractive Sinners and Stale Saints." The title is both false and true. It is false because sin is attractive only on the surface, and because the surface is soon rubbed away; it is true because much that passes for religion is harsh in its self-righteousness and angular in its narrowness. Some people who claim to be "converted" have not been converted from bitter judgment and a capsuled mind. The Negro spiritual is right in its appraisal. "Ev'ybody talkin' 'bout heab'n ain't

[2] As quoted by J. Marshall Lang, in *The Pulpit Commentary,* ed. H. D. M. Spence and J. S. Exell (New York: Anson D. F. Randolph & Co., n.d.), *St. Luke,* II, 49.

[3] *The People's Bible* (New York: Funk & Wagnalls Co., 1881), Vol. XXI, ch. xv.

31 And he said unto him, Son, thou art ever with me, and all that I have is thine.

32 It was meet that we should make merry, and be glad: for this thy brother was dead, and is alive again; and was lost, and is found.

16 And he said also unto his disciples, There was a certain rich man, which had a steward; and the same was accused unto him that he had wasted his goods.

you killed for him the fatted calf!' 31 And he said to him, 'Son, you are always with me, and all that is mine is yours. 32 It was fitting to make merry and be glad, for this your brother was dead, and is alive; he was lost, and is found.'"

16 He also said to the disciples, "There was a rich man who had a steward, and charges were brought to him that this

---

31. The father's reply to the first part of the complaint (vs. 29).

32. The reply to the second part of the complaint (vs. 30). It is the restoration of the prodigal to the family circle that is celebrated. A recapitulation (with the necessary changes) of vs. 24*a*. **This your brother** rebukes the unbrotherly phrase used by the elder son in vs. 30.

O. On the Use and Abuse of Wealth (16:1-31)

1. Parable of the Dishonest Steward (16:1-9)

The parables of the good Samaritan and of the Pharisee and the publican commend a certain type of behavior. They are "example stories." But the parable of the dishonest steward belongs to a different category. There is nothing edifying about it. The steward's conduct was characterized in the beginning by incompetence and in the end by flagrant dishonesty. If it is a true parable, Jesus must have used it, as he did the parables of the importunate friend and the unrighteous judge, to make one truth vivid and memorable; but since we do not know its original context, we can only guess what that truth was. Whatever its original purpose, early Christian teachers used it with Jesus' authority to

---

goin' dere."[4] Yet nobody has any right to make that appraisal unless he has first asked in heart searching and prayer, "Does it mean me?" It is tragically possible to get a small injection of Christian faith, just enough to become immune from the passionate commitment that is real Christianity.

The elder brother's religion was a legalism: he kept the letter of the law, but broke its spirit. Indeed, it was less than a legalism: it was a negative legalism, the meticulous observance of a series of "thou shalt nots." Is it the fault of the church in part that so many people beyond the church have come to believe that discipleship to Christ means no more than abstaining from this and refraining from that? There was no love in the elder brother's creed: he did not love God with all his heart, and he did not love his brother in God. He was correct in an ethic, but the ethic had no root in ultimate devotion; and therefore he was as merciless as he was correct. His religion dwindled to a slavishness: **These many years do I serve thee.** He had not felt his brother's suffering in a far country or ever shared the father's grief.

Can the church be fully identified with the kingdom? The latter is God's act and invasion of love, and thereafter man's response to that pardoning and vitalizing grace. But if the response ceases to be open to the invasion, if it gets locked within itself, then the church can become a prodigal at heart. What *would* the average church do if a profligate took the church at its Lord's word? This is the question that must be asked, lest we try to exile the parable to the past, imagining that it applies only to far-off Pharisees and scribes. It is a judgment fact that Christian faith, which in essence is surrender to God's love made known in Jesus, can become self-centered; and that when it does, pride becomes worse pride, and judgment a darker judgment. What *is* the purpose of the average church—that the church shall "prosper," or that God's love shall find the lost?

32. See Expos. on vss. 24, 32.

16:1-8. ***Parable of the Dishonest Steward.***—(See also Expos., vss. 2, 9, 10.) Many people wonder if Jesus could have told this story. Would he use an arrant rascal "to point a moral, or adorn a tale"?[5] The Emperor Julian,[6] in his bitter apostasy, made great play with the

[4] "All God's Chillun Got Wings," st. iv.

[5] Samuel Johnson, "The Vanity of Human Wishes."

[6] See Richard Chenevix Trench, *Notes on the Parables of Our Lord* (London: Kegan Paul, Trench & Co., 1886), p. 441.

recommend the practice of prudence. The steward was a rascal, but a clever rascal, and Jesus' followers were invited to emulate that cleverness for better ends: **The children of this world are in their generation wiser than the children of light** (KJV). Vs. 9 limits the point to the prudent use of money, and may be Luke's own addition.

16:1*a*. Editorial introduction. If Jesus used the parable that follows, and interpreted it as Luke does in vs. 9, he may have addressed it to some such group as the "tax collectors and sinners" of 15:1. Jesus' **disciples** can scarcely have needed advice about the use of "unrighteous mammon," but no doubt the issue had become a live one in the church of Luke's day.

---

parable: he said that of course Jesus told it, and of course it proved Jesus mere man and hardly a worthy man. A score of theories have been offered, more ingenious than convincing, to avoid the impasse. The parable is here, the early church believed that it came from Jesus, and probably they found its central meaning in vs. 8*b*. It has the fascination of roguery. How the factor wasted his master's money we are not told. Perhaps he made merry with his cronies when he should have been working; there is a scapegrace camaraderie about him. The device by which he feathered his nest, just when the nest seemed to be justly doomed, is shrewd; and his lord (not Jesus) commended the shrewdness. Not even his lord, worldly-wise though he was, much less Jesus, commended the dishonesty. "Of all the swift impudence!" he cried in rueful admiration. Jesus, telling the story, sees all humanity with "larger, other eyes." Iniquity does not take him off guard or long dismay him: he has redemption.

Vs. 8*b*—**For the children of this world,** etc.—may be the comment of Jesus. He told parables, not allegories. He did not choose perfect characters for the parables: none is perfect except God. He saw with keen eyes the checkered thrust and counterthrust of human life. If the story has been preserved in something like its original form, it is no discredit to Jesus to have said in effect: "The rogue acted with prompt foresight. If only my followers would do as much—from nobler motives!" Augustus William Hare long ago made the appropriate comment: "He who chose his path like a fool, walks along it like a wise man: he who chose his like a wise man, walks along it like a fool." [7]

Look at the steward's realism. He faced facts. He did not pity or deceive himself. He sized up the situation in cold logic (see vss. 3-4). Are the children of light as unromantic? No, they trust vaguely to education (undefined), to the course of history ("The race is still young"), or to "democracy." They rarely confront the stark truth that man cannot be his own savior: In this issue he cannot **dig** into history, or **beg** from his neighbors. The persistence and poison of evil in us are their own argument for God, for plainly we would be lost without God. But does the Christian live rigorously unto God? Look at the steward's swift zeal. The worldling thoroughly cares for his senses, while the follower of Christ becomes casual about his soul. The golfer takes lessons and reads books, while the religious man forgets his prayers. The salesman becomes an evangelist for some gadget, while the disciple of Jesus rarely mentions the Savior of the world. Look at the steward's foresight. He planned an earthly future. Do the followers of Christ realize the eschatological stress in his teaching: do they look to an eternal destiny? Most men believe in savings accounts, pension plans, annuities, insurance—various forms of preparedness for this world. But what about a home in the hidden land? "I go to prepare a place for you" (John 14:2), said Jesus; but those who most profess to love him are sometimes careless about that welcome.

Let it be doubly clear that Jesus is not here praising worldliness. **The children of this world** are prisoners: they are meant for mountains and prairies, but choose to live in a narrow street. Their condemnation is that they *are* **of this world,** and therefore the victims of time's tensions. They are **children** of *darkness:* that is the clear implication. The night closes about them in hunger; they are like the starving man who opened a box in eagerness, and then exclaimed, "It is only gold." They get what they want, and find that it is not what they want. They are fools at last, despite all their shrewdness: for **in their generation** is a phrase of doom. *Pilgrim's Progress* provides the illustrations. Worldly-Wiseman feathered his nest like the steward; and planned for the future, only to find that his city had no future; and missed the Celestial City. Ignorance was something of a Christian, but with no zeal, no realism concerning the lurking evil in his nature, no urgency in prayer. He thought he had found an easier way to life, only to see the gates closed against him. But Christian sought God more eagerly than other men seek success, and followed Christ with more zeal than other men follow

[7] *Sermons to a Country Congregation* (New York: D. Appleton & Co., 1839), p. 201.

2 And he called him, and said unto him, How is it that I hear this of thee? give an account of thy stewardship; for thou mayest be no longer steward.

3 Then the steward said within himself, What shall I do? for my lord taketh away from me the stewardship: I cannot dig; to beg I am ashamed.

4 I am resolved what to do, that, when I am put out of the stewardship, they may receive me into their houses.

5 So he called every one of his lord's debtors *unto him,* and said unto the first, How much owest thou unto my lord?

6 And he said, A hundred measures of oil. And he said unto him, Take thy bill, and sit down quickly, and write fifty.

7 Then said he to another, And how much owest thou? And he said, A hundred measures of wheat. And he said unto him, Take thy bill, and write fourscore.

man was wasting his goods.
2 And he called him and said to him, 'What is this that I hear about you? Turn in the account of your stewardship, for you can no longer be steward.'
3 And the steward said to himself, 'What shall I do, since my master is taking the stewardship away from me? I am not strong enough to dig, and I am ashamed to beg.
4 I have decided what to do, so that people may receive me into their houses when I am put out of the stewardship.'
5 So, summoning his master's debtors one by one, he said to the first, 'How much do you owe my master?'
6 He said, 'A hundred measures of oil.' And he said to him, 'Take your bill, and sit down quickly and write fifty.'
7 Then he said to another, 'And how much do you owe?' He said, 'A hundred measures of wheat.' He said to him, 'Take your bill, and write

---

1*b*-2. There is no allegory in the narrative. The **rich man** is not God or the devil or mammon, and the **steward** is not intended to represent a disciple. The estate manager in this instance is an employee, not an overslave as in 12:42-48. His employer, informed that he has been wasteful in his management of his affairs, demands a final statement of his accounts before dismissing him from his service.

3-4. The steward has not been accused of dishonesty but fears that his dismissal will imperil his ability to earn a living. In his extremity he concocts a scheme by which he hopes to place a number of people under obligation to himself and thereby to assure their help when he needs it.

5-7. He summons **his master's debtors** individually and invites them to falsify their accounts. The **debtors** are either tenants who have signed agreements to pay for the rent of their land in kind (cf. Mark 12:2) or purchasers of produce from the estate who have signed notes calling for payment at some later date. They are encouraged to alter the amounts of their bills, or perhaps to draft new ones and inscribe smaller amounts. **A hundred measures of oil,** about 875 gallons. **Quickly:** Probably to be construed with **write** rather than with **sit down. A hundred measures of wheat,** about a thousand bushels.

---

fame, and built a heavenly home with closer care than other men plan their new houses; and for him as for Greatheart "all the trumpets sounded for him on the other side." [8]

2. ***An Account of Stewardship.***—The original meaning of the word steward—a ward of the sty, a keeper of pigs—goes back to a simple order of life, but still has force: man is God's agent to rule a lower level of life. He should not immerse himself in that subworld; for if he does, he sinks in the scale, becoming hardly better than a beast. We are stewards, not owners: the word "my" on any man's lips is false. That is why it has bedeviled the world. God is the only capitalist. Our job is not hoarding of wealth or fencing it for our own pleasure, but the proper circulation and use of it in God's sight. These phrases run easily from lip or pen, but if they were applied, they would be revolution—benignant revolution. That the phrases are true is hardly open to question. If we treat even forests as our own, dust storms and droughts come upon us: the universe knows its rightful Lord, and rebels against the impious usurper.

A man has a right to livelihood, but only on a commission basis, i.e., he may keep enough of this world's goods for himself provided he lives to serve the common good within the will of God. "Enough" is a measure hard to determine: mathematical equality would not make

[8] Parts I, II.

8 And the lord commended the unjust steward, because he had done wisely: for the children of this world are in their generation wiser than the children of light.

9 And I say unto you, Make to yourselves friends of the mammon of unrighteousness; that, when ye fail, they may receive you into everlasting habitations.

eighty.' 8 The master commended the dishonest steward for his prudence; for the sons of this world[c] are wiser in their own generation than the sons of light. 9 And I tell you, make friends for yourselves by means of unrighteous mammon, so that when it fails they may receive you into the eternal habitations.

[c] Greek *age*.

---

8. It is difficult to decide whether **the lord** of this verse refers to the "rich man" of the parable or to Jesus. If the former identification is accepted (with the KJV and the RSV), then we are to assume that the employer detected his steward's dishonesty but expressed admiration for his cleverness. If the latter is preferred, the first half of the verse is an indirect reference to Jesus' comment on the story and the second half is a direct quotation of his words. With vs. 8*b*, cf. Matt. 10:16*b*: "Be wise as serpents and innocent as doves." Those who belong only to this **age** (RSV mg.; cf. 20:34) are **wiser** in the attention they give their worldly interests than are **the sons of light** (cf. John 12:36; Eph. 5:8; I Thess. 5:5) in their concern for their eternal welfare.

9. Editorial interpretation. The real lesson of the parable is now said to be the wise use of money. Mammon represents the Aramaic ממונא, a word which means "money," but whose derivation is still a matter of dispute. Luke apparently believed that all money has some taint about it, and that the only redeeming feature of its possession is that it can be expended for righteous purposes. As the dishonest steward used money to make sure that people would receive him into their houses after he had been dismissed from his stewardship (vs. 4), so Christians are to use it to assure **eternal habitations** for themselves. It is the distribution of money as alms to the poor that is meant (12:33). **Make friends for yourselves:** The recipients of alms will intercede with God that the giver may be received into the heavenly dwelling places. **When it fails** (RSV): Money is

---

sense, even if it were possible. Some men, such as a physician or a judge, should be kept from livelihood anxiety; but even in these instances the exception should not be abused to become a selfishness. "To serve the common good" is also a phrase hard to construe, but parasitical work (and there is much of it) is at once condemned. Because all men are stewards, no man is better than another: his greater gifts, e.g., as judge, may entitle him to more money for training and support, but he is still a steward. His gifts are gifts—a trust, not a possession; and they lay on him the greater measure of responsibility. These truths Jesus stressed repeatedly, as witness the parable of the talents (19:11-27; Matt. 25:14-30).

Every man must give account as steward. The day of reckoning is every day; for the drawing of the curtain of night says almost of itself, "Another day! Give an account of thy stewardship!" Every crisis in life—sorrow or joy, war or peace—calls us to account: the very word crisis means in its origin judgment. It says of itself, "This is how you have lived," and of itself tots up the columns of the ledger. Death is judgment. How could so climactic an event fail to carry that meaning? The eschatological stress is always present in the words of Jesus: he told us that every act is freighted with destiny. Thus our handling of this world's goods is stewardship—a direct dealing with God, from whom we come, to whom we go.

9. ***The Proper Use of Wealth.***—(See also next Expos.) The parable of the dishonest steward is hard to interpret. One is tempted to adopt some such theory as that advanced by Edwin McNeill Poteat,[9] viz., that Jesus repeated the story as typical of the world's cynicism, and then condemned it utterly in vs. 13. But such a supposition hardly keeps faith with our newer knowledge of the Gospels. If a then popular story has here crept into the Gospels, then vss. 9-15 are Luke's interpretation of it—by means of several, perhaps originally separate, sayings of Jesus. If the story came from Jesus as we have proposed, then vss. 9-15 are a number of Jesus' sayings placed here because the parable has raised the whole question of the Christian use of possessions.

Mammon means money (see Exeg.). **The mammon of unrighteousness** may mean money

[9] *Parables of Crisis*, pp. 156-58.

10 He that is faithful in that which is least is faithful also in much: and he that is unjust in the least is unjust also in much.

10 "He who is faithful in a very little is faithful also in much; and he who is dishonest in a very little is dishonest also

useless after death, and so the clause is the equivalent of "when you die," and amounts to the same thing as the inferior reading translated by the KJV, **when ye fail. That . . . they may receive you:** The rich can help the poor in this age, and the poor can help the rich in the age to come. Or perhaps the whole clause is a circumlocution to avoid the use of the divine name. "That . . . God may receive you."

2. Faithfulness in the Administration of Wealth (16:10-12)

Luke assembles a number of sayings to guard against any misunderstanding of the parable. Jesus had not commended the steward's dishonesty, but only his prudence. The disciple must be scrupulously honest in all money matters. According to some interpreters, vs. 10 was a current proverb or maxim, and vss. 11-12 are religious interpretations of it in the light of the foregoing parable. Others believe all three sayings were suggested by the parable of the pounds, particularly the master's commendation of the servant in 19:17 (Matt. 25:21).

10. II Clement 8:5: "For the Lord says in the gospel: 'If you do not guard what is small, who will give you what is great? For I tell you that he who is faithful in a very little is faithful also in much.'" Other variants are quoted by Irenaeus and Hilarius.

that easily leads to unrighteousness; or in less likelihood, wealth with its inevitable taint. Nobody could wisely deny that wealth does provide a ready occasion for pride and greed, as nobody could deny the taint. The biography of any worn coin would turn the average drama into dullness, and the story would not lack elements of sordidness. Even a Bible in its printing and binding can involve sharp practice. A man must always be on guard against miserliness and the lure of quick money. Few men ward off the danger, as witness the fact that the word success is usually taken to mean money.

The saying singles out one centrally Christlike way of using money. We can **make friends** by means of it. Almost certainly the phrase means almsgiving to the poor. **When it fails** means when death comes. **Eternal habitations** is obviously in contrast to the earthly houses into which the steward was received by the men who profited from his dishonesty. Thus the saying sets forth a striking reversal: Help the poor now in this world, and they will help you in the next. It recommends not a shrewdly calculating charity, but a life lived in compassion and in sight of eternity. The compassion of Jesus here finds its reflection, and his awareness of a World encompassing our world. That World, he says, will resolve our distortions, provide a recompense for tears, and mend our brokenness. Notice in the Exeg. that the words **they may receive you** may be circumlocution for "God may receive you." If so, the plea is made stronger: God is the champion of the (lowly) poor, and gives to their friends his own welcome.

9. *Eternal Tents.*—Here is a remarkable linking of words. The adjective implies fixity and abidingness; the noun implies pilgrimage and the hope of the Promised Land. The adjective tells of a home on immovable foundations; the noun tells of a tent pitched at night and moved at daybreak. One is reminded of Robert Louis Stevenson's comment, "To travel hopefully is a better thing than to arrive."[1] Our earthly journeyings are not without a goal: there is a home at the end of the road. Yet that home is not stagnation: there will be finer tasks and brighter travels. There the soul finds all the joys of the road, and is yet eternally with God.

10. *The Proper Use of Money: Faithfulness in Small Issues.*—This saying may have been a current proverb. If so, it is not ruled out as a saying of Jesus. There is evidence that he used current maxims, and gave them sharper edge and application, e.g., Matt. 24:28. In another way this injunction is characteristic of the Master: he constantly stressed the momentousness of apparently trivial things—the cup of cold water, the jot of the law, the one talent. Our mood is opposite: we ask, "What can I do?" and because we seem able to do very little, we do nothing. We brag about the largest building, the largest city, the largest armaments; and we

[1] Essay, "El Dorado," in *Virginibus Puerisque and Other Papers* (New York: Charles Scribner's Sons, 1905), p. 178.

11 If therefore ye have not been faithful in the unrighteous mammon, who will commit to your trust the true *riches?*

12 And if ye have not been faithful in that which is another man's, who shall give you that which is your own?

in much. [11] If then you have not been
faithful in the unrighteous mammon, who
will entrust to you the true riches? [12] And
if you have not been faithful in that which
is another's, who will give you that which

---

11. The unrighteous mammon: see on vs. 9. **The true riches,** i.e., heavenly treasure—God's gifts in the new age.

12. That which is another's: Money is a foreign currency to those whose citizenship is in heaven. **That which is your own:** Heavenly treasure is the Christian's only true and eternal possession. "Our own" is the reading in Codex Vaticanus and some allies. Marcion reads "my own."

---

instinctively combine the adjectives "bigger and better," though there is scant evidence that larger size means more goodness. Jesus on the contrary spoke repeatedly of the cruciality of little things. Therefore his word has reality, for our life is composed of the small—small steps, small motions of the hand, small breaths. We are pygmies compared with the fixed stars, and our days are woven of tiny threads. Perhaps greatness is not possible on any other terms: a drama on the stage occupies only two or three hours, a sonnet has but fourteen lines; for genius is not revealed except within limits that at first sight seem a prison.

What makes greatness? Not the size of the means, but the nobility of the end. A liar is not great, even though he may reach a throne; but a man given to truth is great, even though he may be in rags. Pippa by her song unwittingly changed the fortunes of church and state: she was great, while a rascally steward received into wealthy houses is still a dwarf in soul. What makes greatness? Not the size of the means, but the intensity of the need to which it ministers. A lantern of itself is a small affair, but not when it shines to mark a harbor for some lost ship. A cup of cold water is almost trivial, but not to a man dying of thirst in a desert. What makes greatness? Not the measure of a man's body or even of his mind, but his willingness to work in double yoke with Jesus. Is there a church in your neighborhood called St. Andrew's? Andrew would never have been known there but for the Lord he served and in whose spirit he became great.

There is a life of Christ by Mary Austin under the title *A Small Town Man.* Jesus' land was about the size of Vermont, the Sea of Galilee was a smallish lake rather than a sea, and Capernaum was a very average-sized town. Even his cross was small: its crossbar was so close to the ground that a man holding a sponge on a reed could give the victim an opiate. Perhaps Jesus was sometimes tempted to say, "What can I do?" But he was consecrate in such utter fealty that men who follow him become great with his greatness. Perhaps the question should be not "What can I do?" but "What can I not do if I am faithful to him?"

11-12. ***The Proper Use of Money: Earth's Wealth and Heaven's Treasure.***—Vss. 10-15, perhaps vss. 10-18, comprise a chain of sayings that Luke has attached to the parable of the dishonest steward. It would appear that Luke was concerned lest the parable should be misconstrued. So he is saying in effect: "Understand clearly that Jesus was not commending the steward's dishonesty. On the contrary, listen to sayings of the Master which make it doubly clear that he required scrupulous honesty in all that concerns money and things." In considering the sayings pendant to the parable, we should consult the parallel sayings in the Synoptics, and also remember that Luke was writing from the life and problems of the early church.

There can be little doubt that Luke is here true not only to the spirit of the Lord's teaching, but perhaps also to the very word. We may have to make allowance for his frequently manifest prejudice in favor of the poor, and for some asperities against the leaders of the Jews because of the strife between synagogue and church. But when all allowance is made, the adjectives here used of earthly wealth are consonant with the mind of Jesus. Look at them. Earthly wealth is **unrighteous,** the occasion of so much greed and hardness of heart that its very nature seems tainted, while heaven's treasure partakes of the nature of God's holiness. Earthly wealth is fleeting and deceitful, like a mirage (that is the clear implication) ; for only heaven's treasure is **true,** i.e., real and of the very substance of eternity. Earthly wealth is **another man's,** for it is only on loan, and the loan may at any moment be withdrawn; heaven's wealth is **your own,** for it is of the soul and is an inalienable possession. The world scoffs at this contrast. The church does not act

13 ¶ No servant can serve two masters: for either he will hate the one, and love the other; or else he will hold to the one, and despise the other. Ye cannot serve God and mammon.

14 And the Pharisees also, who were covetous, heard all these things: and they derided him.

is your own? 13 No servant can serve two masters; for either he will hate the one and love the other, or he will be devoted to the one and despise the other. You cannot serve God and mammon."

14 The Pharisees, who were lovers of money, heard all this, and they scoffed at

---

3. Exclusive Demands of God's Service (16:13=Matt. 6:24)

13. Identical with its Matthaean counterpart except for the use of **servant** instead of "man." Incorporated by Luke at this point because of the occurrence of the word **mammon.** Devotion to money and devotion to **God** are incompatible loyalties.

4. God Knows the Hearts of Men (16:14-15)

14-15*a*. Editorial introduction. **The Pharisees,** who have not been mentioned since 15:2, are reintroduced, and we are told that Jesus now addressed himself to them. **Who**

---

upon it. But beyond doubt Jesus counseled his followers not only to lay aside covetousness, but moment by moment to sit loose to the things of time. The earth is at best a poor vesture that a man must soon doff.

Yet things and money provide a training. Imagine a woodcarver testing his son's skill. He would use clay, not fine oak. If the boy showed promise with a base medium, the father would then let him try his hand with fine wood. So if any man proves himself faithful with mammon, God will trust him with the real jewels of the heavenly kingdom. For if a man is honest with little, he will likely be honest with much, since the soul is a unity and reveals itself in little things. That is why money is important—as training ground for real living.

13. *God and Mammon.*—There is no threat or coercion in **ye cannot.** It is as much a quiet statement of fact as if the word had been, "You cannot walk east and west at the same time." A man might serve two masters by dividing his time between them, but he cannot be slave to both; and slave is the word here employed. If both demand a total allegiance, the man must choose: he can divide his time, but not his soul. So Jesus here implies that mammon poses as deity, demanding a life-and-death devotion. "Covetousness, which is idolatry," tells of the domination (Col. 3:5). Money makes a man slave indeed. It asks an absolute loyalty. It is an idol

> Before whose image bow the vulgar great,
> The vainly rich, the miserable proud.[2]

But God also asks an absolute loyalty. His command is still that no man make any graven image or worship any lesser god (Exod. 20:3-4). It is evidence of the Incarnation that Jesus required of his followers an undivided devotion. He said that a disciple must take such complete and passionate vows as to appear to hate any earthly bond (see Expos. on 14:25-26). The terms of discipleship are unqualified: no lesser loyalty can claim even one inch of ground. So of all the masters the soul can choose, there are at last only two—God and mammon. Those two are at opposites: God is everlastingly other than mammonism, for mammonism is itself rebel against the holy and loving will. All choices, however small, however the alternatives may be disguised, are but variants of this choice.

Psychology tells about split personality. A divided soul is a sick soul, robbed of the power of concentration, beset by anxiety, distraught. This cleft is a worse ill than any amputation suffered by the body. Yet many people try to live in double allegiance. They have one God on Sunday, and another god on Monday; the Father of Jesus Christ when they pray, and mammon when they work or play. They little realize that they invite a worse kind of schizophrenia. If the alternatives are clearly stated and honestly confronted, there can be no doubt of the right choice. Mammon galls even the body at last, and always leaves the spirit hungry and athirst; but God, being God, fulfills worthily every lesser loyalty, if these are gathered into the hierarchy of his grace.

14-15. *God Knows the Heart.*—Alfred Plummer[3] suggests a fuller outline for the sharply

[2] Percy Bysshe Shelley, *Queen Mab,* Part V, l. 56.

[3] *A Critical and Exegetical Commentary on the Gospel According to St. Luke* (New York: Charles Scribner's Sons, 1896; "International Critical Commentary"), pp. 388-89.

15 And he said unto them, Ye are they which justify yourselves before men; but God knoweth your hearts: for that which is highly esteemed among men is abomination in the sight of God.

16 The law and the prophets *were* until John: since that time the kingdom of God is preached, and every man presseth into it.

him. 15 But he said to them, "You are those who justify yourselves before men, but God knows your hearts; for what is exalted among men is an abomination in the sight of God.

16 "The law and the prophets were until John; since then the good news of the kingdom of God is preached, and every

---

were lovers of money is a generalization linking the saying that follows with vss. 1-13, but it does an injustice to the party within Judaism characterized by its devotion to the law. The anti-Pharisaic polemic in the Gospels is in large part a reflection of the later controversy between church and synagogue (see on 11:37-44).

15*b*. Perhaps originally a stricture on self-righteous pride. But Luke thought of it in some way as a criticism of mammon service. The Pharisees claim that their wealth is proof that they are righteous, but God's verdict is different from men's. Or the idea may be similar to that in Matt. 6:2. The ostentatious distribution of alms is **highly esteemed among men,** but is an **abomination in the sight of God.**

5. The Law and the Gospel (16:16-18; cf. Matt. 11:12-13; 5:18, 31-32)

Three scattered sayings that have little or no connection with one another or with the rest of the material in the chapter.

16. Matthew preserves a more extended, more obscure, and possibly more primitive version. **John** the Baptist marks a turning point in history. Before his time, **the law and**

---

condensed sequence of vss. 10-18, and in particular of vss. 16-18. But his proposal is conjecture, and it may be wiser to assume that Luke has here gathered together from his sources a number of sayings that bear on money. This collating is characteristic of our author; e.g., see 14:25-34, where the general theme is the conditions of discipleship. There is little evidence in the Gospels that the Pharisees were mercenary; and the harshness of vs. 14*b* may be due in part to the controversy between the church and the synagogue—joined with the empire in persecuting the Christians. Yet some Pharisees may have done what religionists are tempted to do in every generation: regarded material prosperity as the proper reward of their obedience to the law. Have we not groups in our time who tell us that they have increased their money profits by keeping the Golden Rule, the claim being blind to the prime fact that Jesus' far worthier obedience had no such issue?

We know from the Gospels what the Pharisees did to justify themselves before men. They planned to be overtaken by the three daily times of prayer (the Shema) when they were at a busy street corner, and they would then pray for a longer time than the law required, so that they would gain a reputation for piety; and they cast their gifts into the offering boxes at the temple with a loud clatter, that they might be credited with generosity. Does such ostentation seem brash and childish? Perhaps our display for the purpose of social prestige is just as much a "show off" in a poorer cause.

Notice the sharp contrast between **exalted among men** and **the sight of God.** Our life cannot escape Reality. Synthetic diamonds are soon found to be spurious: they cannot stand the cutting edge of a real stone. There is a white light of Reality: a fabric will seem to have the right color so long as it is kept in artificial light, but will appear faded when it is carried into the sun. So Reality burns through our pretenses even while we live, and shrivels them altogether when we die. This fact is judgment for those who pose in order to win the favor of men; but it is comfort, in the fine original sense of that word, for those who dare to live toward God. **God knows.** In that fact the hypocrite is condemned; in that fact the man who worries about his motives, saying, "Perhaps I am not as sincere as I think," finds his home at last. What need therefore that a man pray in utter surrender, asking God to search him through and through!

16-18. ***The Law and the Gospel.***—Vs. 16 is hard to construe, for we can only guess its original context. Perhaps **enters it violently** refers to groups who believed the kingdom of God would come by insurrection against the empire (but see Exeg.); perhaps it means that the gospel attracted the rash hardihood of shallow enthusiasts; perhaps that the

17 And it is easier for heaven and earth to pass, than one tittle of the law to fail.

18 Whosoever putteth away his wife, and marrieth another, committeth adultery: and whosoever marrieth her that is put away from *her* husband committeth adultery.

19 ¶ There was a certain rich man, which was clothed in purple and fine linen, and fared sumptuously every day:

one enters it violently. 17 But it is easier for heaven and earth to pass away, than for one dot of the law to become void.

18 "Every one who divorces his wife and marries another commits adultery, and he who marries a woman divorced from her husband commits adultery.

19 "There was a rich man, who was clothed in purple and fine linen and who

---

the prophets; since his time, **the kingdom of God.** One of several sayings in the gospel tradition that speak of the new age of God's rule as a fact of present experience, not just an event of the last days. Already **every one enters it violently.** Already men may participate in it, press their way into it, if they will run every risk, exert every effort, and make every sacrifice. Cf. Jesus' exhortations in 9:59-62; 13:24, and 14:26. No reference to political messianists, such as the Zealots, need be conjectured.

17. Used by Luke at this point to avoid the implication that the gospel has abrogated **the law.** The latter retains its validity. **Tittle:** Probably an ornamental stroke decorating the letters of the Hebrew alphabet.

18. The marriage bond is indissoluble. In addition to Matt. 5:31-32, variants are also found in Mark 10:11 (Matt. 19:9) and in I Cor. 7:10-11. Matthew is alone in introducing the clause "except on the ground of unchastity."

6. Parable of the Rich Man and Lazarus (16:19-31)

Two distinct themes are discussed. Vss. 19-26 declare that there will be a reversal of values in the life to come. The poor will be rewarded and the rich will be punished.

---

followers of Jesus seemed to their neighbors to do violence to themselves by their self-denials; perhaps (and more likely, if a guess must be hazarded) that the good news seemed to conservative minds a rending of the law, a promiscuous invitation to lawless men to enter the kingdom. That fourth interpretation certainly fits the present context: in Jesus the gates of redemption had been flung open; and godless men, such as publicans and sinners, had come pouring in (almost violently) against all the proper decorum of the law. What then would befall the manifest worth of ancient sanctions? Was the covenant of God with Israel to be torn to shreds? These misgivings must have troubled many even in the church (see Expos. on Matt. 11:12).

Vs. 17 is Jesus' answer to such misgivings. By means of the answer Luke gave assurance to the fears of the early church (see Exeg. on **tittle**). **To fail** (KJV) is well translated **become void** (RSV). The scribes maintained that every part of the law was of equal worth with every other part. Jesus endorsed them, with one proviso: that the law must be understood as the utterance of God's holy love—newly and eternally made incarnate in Jesus!—and that every item of the law must be construed in the light of that central reference. A cherry orchard wears out in a few years, and no longer bears fruit; but the new seedlings that replace the old trees are from the same seed—which the old trees have given. So Jesus seems to destroy the law; so actually he fulfills its immemorial life.

Vs. 18 gives one instance of the fulfillment (see the fuller Expos. on Matt. 5:31-32). The law permitted divorce on certain grounds, some of them flimsy and an encouragement to male irresponsibility and selfishness. But the gospel went back to the original command of God that man and woman in marriage shall be one flesh, i.e., one personality. Divorce within personality is worse than unnatural: it is death. So the gospel, while it might admit that a "writ of divorcement" is a necessary concession to the "hardness" of men's "hearts" (Matt. 19:8), upholds the original command of God's holy love. Thus the gospel fulfills the law not only by carrying its letter back to the spirit, not only by laying its yoke on men's motives rather than merely in their outward act, but also by bringing men to the love of God in whom alone they can find forgiveness and sufficient strength.

19-31. ***Parable of the Rich Man and the Beggar.***—(See also Expos. on vss. 20, 25, 27-30.) This story was the spark that touched off the

The point of view is similar to that in 6:20*b*, 24: "Blessed are you poor, for yours is the kingdom of God. . . . But woe to you that are rich, for you have received your consolation." Vss. 27-31 assert that the impenitent rich have already had ample warning of their fate in the Law and the Prophets, and would not repent even if one were to return from the dead to reiterate that warning.

Many interpreters believe that the latter section is an allegorical appendix that presupposes the conflict between early Christianity and orthodox Judaism. The rich man and his brothers represent the unbelieving Jews. Jesus is made to assert that they have stubbornly refused to repent in spite of the obvious testimony to himself in Scripture and to predict that they will fail to be impressed by his resurrection. It is conceivable that Luke and his readers imposed some such interpretation on these verses, but it is by no means clear that it is inherent. They are more readily interpreted as an attack on Sadducean wealth and worldliness. Most Sadducees were priests or members of the Jewish aristocracy—privileged and frequently wealthy people. A refusal to believe in an afterlife, or to admit that Scripture afforded any warrant for such a belief, was among their characteristic tenets. Vss. 27-31 may have been added to the parable to make it a criticism of Sadducean materialism.

In 1918 Hugo Gressmann of the University of Berlin published an elaborate monograph on the parable which has influenced much of its subsequent interpretation. According to Gressmann, the story that Jesus told was a Jewish version of an ancient Egyptian tale, still extant in a demotic papyrus of the first century A.D. The body of a wealthy man, clad in his finest attire, was carried to his grave by a large company of mourners. At the same time the body of a poor man was removed for burial, unaccompanied by attendants and covered only by a mat. An observer, impressed by the disparity in the honors bestowed on the two, commented on the advantages enjoyed by the rich man, but changed his views when he was permitted to visit the underworld. There he saw the poor man clothed in the linen garments of the rich and given a place of honor, while the rich man suffered torment for his evil deeds. The story concludes with the moral: "He who is good on earth fares well in the realm of the dead, and he who is evil on earth fares ill."

Gressmann is less convincing when he elaborates his theory to explain the apparent break in the parable at vs. 27. He asserts that the latter section was Jesus' protest against basing the doctrine of rewards and punishments in an afterlife on stories of visits to the other world. Moses and the prophets bear witness to it, and no miracle is necessary to authenticate their testimony.

---

revolution in the life of Albert Schweitzer.[4] He concluded that Africa was a beggar lying at Europe's doorstep, so he founded the Lambaréné Hospital. The parable has that kind of power. It is a drama in three acts, the first act being a tableau. Dives is richly clothed and fed; Lazarus is too hungry to refuse the pieces of bread which Dives has used for a napkin, and too weak to drive off the scavenger dogs that lick his sores. Wealth is not necessarily wicked, but it has temptations hard to resist; poverty is not necessarily virtue, but it can more easily be turned to the soul's account. Dives hardly saw Lazarus, and so was condemned.

The second act shows heaven and hell on one small stage. Each man has died: the word **buried** in regard to Dives reflects the then current belief that it was a badge of shame not to be buried: Dives' good fortune continues to the last moment of his earthly history. But in the next world the parts played by the two men are exactly reversed. Only now does the drama break into speech. Dives from his place of torment begs a drop of water, as Lazarus on earth had begged a scrap of bread. The rich man still treats Lazarus as a beggar: **Send Lazarus.** But Abraham from paradise tells him that there are two reasons why no joy can now be given: first, he has had his joy on earth; second, the time for penitence has passed and judgment is now inexorably fixed.

The third act comes unexpectedly: Dives asks that his five brothers on earth may be warned. The request hints that he himself had not been properly admonished. His brothers, he argues, will repent if one should go to them from the dead. Abraham denies the truth of the argu-

[4] *Out of My Life and Thought* (New York: Henry Holt & Co., 1933); see also Joseph Gollomb, *Albert Schweitzer* (New York: Vanguard Press, 1949).

20 And there was a certain beggar named Lazarus, which was laid at his gate, full of sores,

21 And desiring to be fed with the crumbs which fell from the rich man's table: moreover the dogs came and licked his sores.

feasted sumptuously every day. 20 And at
his gate lay a poor man named Laz'a-rus,
full of sores, 21 who desired to be fed with
what fell from the rich man's table; moreover the dogs came and licked his sores.

The parable is unique in the Gospels for its colorful description of the state of men after death. As in the LXX, Hades represents the Hebrew word Sheol. In early Hebrew thought Sheol was a gloomy subterranean pit to which the spirits of men went after death and in which they suffered some shadowy and miserable existence. When later Judaism adopted the idea of the resurrection, probably from Persian eschatology, Sheol became the temporary abode of disembodied spirits. Gradually the belief arose that there would be some separation of the righteous from the wicked even before the resurrection. In I Enoch 22 the author speaks of special places reserved in Sheol for the evil and the good "until the great day of judgment." The Lukan parable moves within a similar framework of thought. One part of Hades resembles Gehenna, the place of final punishment. In it the rich man suffers fiery torment. The other part resembles Paradise, the final dwelling place of the righteous. In it Lazarus rests on Abraham's bosom. The two men can see one another and speak to one another, but actual passage from one part to the other is impossible, for between the two **a great gulf** has been fixed.

19-21. The **rich man** is often called "Dives," the word with which the Vulg. translated the adjective "rich." The Sahidic version named him "Nineve," and the name "Phinees" also had some currency in the third century A.D. **Purple** for the outer and **fine linen** for the undergarment. **Lazarus:** The Greek form of Eleazar, which means "one whom God has helped." This is the only parable in which a proper name occurs; it is necessary

---

ment: a visitor from Sheol could not change a selfish will. His brothers already knew the way of life, or could have known it, for **Moses and the prophets** made it clear; but the brothers had not heeded, and no portent could change them. Herod was not changed, even though he thought that Jesus was John the Baptist risen from the dead (9:7; see fuller Expos. on vss. 27-30).

This parable is not theology. It is a vivid story, not a Baedeker's guide to the next world. Such stories as this were current in Jesus' day. They are found in rabbinical sources, and even in Egyptian papyri (see Exeg.). The climate of the story is almost that of the play *The Green Pastures.* But we cannot be casual with it, for its symbols are the shadows of realities. It tells us that inequalities on earth are redressed in heaven: lowliness (Lazarus means "God helps") is rewarded hereafter, and self-indulgent pride is rebuked. We all see that selfishness makes hell on earth: why should we doubt that it brings hell hereafter? The story tells us of **a great gulf.** If a man chooses a cheap heaven here, he can hardly expect to have a real heaven beyond death, for he has lost both taste and aptitude for a real heaven. If a man lives without compassion, he manifestly digs a chasm between himself and his fellow men; and by the same token he separates himself from God, for God is love. The story tells us that life here fashions an eternal destiny. Why should we call any day commonplace? Every time Dives walked past Lazarus, every time he listened to time serving speeches in which greedy men find comfort, he was building hell; and every time Lazarus refused to be embittered by the bitter bread of poverty he was building a home in heaven. Every step is destiny. The reading of this story is destiny.

20. ***Blind Casualness.***—Dives did not see Lazarus. Dives was not an intentionally cruel man. The picture painted by Giacomo Bassano,[5] and that by Gustave Doré,[6] each showing Dives' servants driving away Lazarus with their whips, are almost certainly mistaken. The likelihood is that Dives not only gave Lazarus scraps from his table, but contributed generously to charity. But he did not see Lazarus. He did not say: "This man is lonely. This man has pains of conscience and flashes of glory, and longs for God.

[5] See Anna Brownell Jameson and Lady Elizabeth Eastlake, *History of Our Lord* (London: Longmans, Green, Longman, Roberts & Green, 1865), I, 379-80.

[6] Gustave Doré, *The Bible Gallery* (New York: Cassell, Petter, Galpin, & Co., 1880).

22 And it came to pass, that the beggar died, and was carried by the angels into Abraham's bosom: the rich man also died, and was buried;

23 And in hell he lifted up his eyes, being in torments, and seeth Abraham afar off, and Lazarus in his bosom.

24 And he cried and said, Father Abraham, have mercy on me, and send Lazarus, that he may dip the tip of his finger in water, and cool my tongue; for I am tormented in this flame.

25 But Abraham said, Son, remember that thou in thy lifetime receivedst thy

22 The poor man died and was carried by
the angels to Abraham's bosom. The rich
man also died and was buried; 23 and in
Hades, being in torment, he lifted up his
eyes, and saw Abraham far off and Laz'a-rus
in his bosom. 24 And he called out, 'Father
Abraham, have mercy upon me, and send
Laz'a-rus to dip the end of his finger in
water and cool my tongue; for I am in
anguish in this flame.' 25 But Abraham said,
'Son, remember that you in your lifetime

---

for the course of the dialogue in vss. 23-25. The name is a common one, and there is no reason to suspect any connection between the parable and the story of Lazarus in John 11. **What fell from the rich man's table:** Refuse later thrown outside the gate. **Dogs** were regarded as unclean animals, and their unwelcome attentions were the climax of the poor man's miseries.

22. **Carried by the angels:** That "angels of service" and "angels of destruction" are sent to fetch the souls of the righteous and of the wicked after death is stated by a Jewish rabbi of the second century A.D., and no doubt the idea is much more ancient. **Abraham's bosom:** The poor man's relationship to the patriarch was that of a son to his father (cf. John 1:18). **The rich man . . . was buried:** Failure to receive burial could have been interpreted as an act of divine punishment on earth, but no such misfortune occurred.

23-24. The rich man craves a drop of **water,** as Lazarus had once longed for crumbs of bread. The ideas of Paradise and of Gehenna have practically coalesced with the earlier idea of Sheol—a **flame** in one part of **Hades,** and a spring of **water** in the other.

25. We are not told that the rich man had been particularly evil, and the poor man particularly good, although the story may carry that implication. Abraham's only argu-

---

This man wakes at night and asks 'Why, and whither?' " Dives spoke about the colored races, but never saw the Negro who passed his gate. Dives discussed employment statistics, but never imagined himself a man out of work. He did not see.

He was too much absorbed in himself to be able to see. He was a man of large affairs, and there were problems galore connected with his house and estate; and soon Dives was so close to himself that he could not see Lazarus, though the beggar was as near as the doorstep. His religion was only perfunctory: this we know, for had he prayed with sincerity, some measure of the life and love of God would have come to him, and he would have begun to see. So Dives became locked in Dives. A man is not meant to live alone any more than a house is meant to be shut away from the world. A man or a house shut away becomes a prison, or a place of **torments.**

There is little reason to believe that vs. 27 indicates a change of heart. It is almost an attempt at self-justification; and it is still concerned, not with any Lazarus on earth, but with the fortunes of Dives' household. King Lear, when disaster overtook him, really learned compassion: he thought of ragged men exposed to the storm:

> O, I have ta'en
> Too little care of this! Take physic, pomp;
> Expose thyself to feel what wretches feel,
> That thou may'st shake the superflux to them
> And show the heavens more just.[7]

How is any Dives changed? By tragedy on earth, by torment beyond the earth; by this story, and by the Cross of him who spoke it.

25. *Son, Remember!*—The word is almost "Child, remember." Perhaps Dives had never become an adult, for he had always regarded life as his to have and to hold: notice the personal "thy" in **thy lifetime . . . thy good things.** Yet the reminder given by Abraham almost seems like turning a knife in a wound, until we recall that no man can be saved until he does remember. For memory, by its power to

[7] Shakespeare, *King Lear,* Act III, scene 4.

good things, and likewise Lazarus evil things: but now he is comforted, and thou art tormented.

26 And beside all this, between us and you there is a great gulf fixed: so that they which would pass from hence to you cannot; neither can they pass to us, that *would come* from thence.

27 Then he said, I pray thee therefore, father, that thou wouldest send him to my father's house:

28 For I have five brethren; that he may testify unto them, lest they also come into this place of torment.

29 Abraham saith unto him, They have Moses and the prophets; let them hear them.

received your good things, and Laz'a-rus
in like manner evil things; but now he is
comforted here, and you are in anguish.
26 And besides all this, between us and you
a great chasm has been fixed, in order that
those who would pass from here to you
may not be able, and none may cross from
there to us.' 27 And he said, 'Then I beg
you, father, to send him to my father's
house, 28 for I have five brothers, so that
he may warn them, lest they also come into
this place of torment.' 29 But Abraham said,
'They have Moses and the prophets; let

---

ment is that those who enjoy **good things** in this life suffer **evil things** in the life to come and vice versa.

26. Another reason for rejecting the request: It cannot be granted.

27-28. If Lazarus cannot cross over the chasm to help the rich man, perhaps he can return to earth with a warning for the rich man's **brothers.**

29-31. Such a mission would be superfluous. **Moses and the prophets** have already spoken of rewards and punishments in a life to come. Those who do not heed Scripture would not be impressed by any miracle of resurrection.

---

restore experience, to select from experience the saving item, and to use experience for a nobler way of life, is a door of hope.

Most of the time we live in a discursive mind: we are absorbed in the flow of events. But sometimes we live in memory, in reflective mind: we stand above the flow to mark its meaning and direction. Statesmanship is reflective: when it is absorbed in the passing event it becomes mere politics. If a man is afraid to be still, his manhood disintegrates. City streets are filled with many an amateur Dives who "takes life as it comes." If only there were some Abraham to buttonhole them with "Child, remember!" For if a man would remember, he might see his name ten years hence in an obituary column, and that remembrance might turn him from mere discursiveness into the reflection that breeds sainthood.

We cannot be saved unless we remember. Yet the remembrance alone is not enough: it can reveal the shabbiness of a man's life, but cannot of itself redeem. This Augustine has said: "What shall I do then, O Thou my true life, my God? I will pass even beyond this power of mine which is called memory. Yea, I will pass beyond it, that I may approach unto Thee. . . . And where shall I find Thee? . . . And all my hope is no where but in Thy exceeding great mercy."[8] Beyond remembrance a man must pray in utter confession and in faith. We can imagine Dives from his torment thus casting himself on God, not to escape the consequence of his cruelty, but to be freed from the sin. The story might have had another ending.

27-31. ***Five Brothers and the Truth.***—At first blush this is an allegorical appendix, for the story would have been complete without it. It could be a later addition, like the story of the wedding garment, which is obviously a pendant to the parable of the great feast (see Matt. 22:11-14). Exegetically these verses are hard to construe. Several theories have been advanced,[9] among them the following: (*a*) the unlikely theory that the Lazarus in the parable is the Lazarus who rose from the dead (see John 11:11 ff.); (*b*) Hugo Gressmann's proposal (see Exeg.) that Jesus in this appendix is protesting popular endings to the story; (*c*) Rudolph Bultmann's proposal[1] that a popular story repeated by Jesus had Lazarus returning to earth to convert the brothers, and that Jesus was intent to dispute the likelihood of any such

[8] *Confessions* X. 26, 40.

[9] See B. T. D. Smith, *Parables of the Synoptic Gospels*, pp. 138-41.

[1] *Die Geschichte der synoptischen Tradition* (2nd ed.; Göttingen: Vandenhoeck & Ruprecht, 1931), p. 213.

30 And he say, Nay, father Abraham:
but if one went unto them from the dead,
they will repent.
31 And he said unto him, If they hear
not Moses and the prophets, neither will
they be persuaded, though one rose from
the dead.

17 Then said he unto the disciples, It is impossible but that offenses will come: but woe *unto him,* through whom they come!

them hear them.' 30 And he said, 'No, fa-
ther Abraham; but if some one goes to
them from the dead, they will repent.'
31 He said to him, 'If they do not hear
Moses and the prophets, neither will they
be convinced if some one should rise from
the dead.' "

17 And he said to his disciples, "Temptations to sin[d] are sure to come; but woe to him by whom they come!

[d] Greek *stumbling-blocks.*

P. On Forgiveness, Faith, God's Grace, and Man's Ingratitude (17:1-19)

1. On Those Who Cause Others to Sin; Forgiveness; Faith (17:1-6=Matt. 18:7, 6, 15, 21-22; 17:20*b*)

Three unrelated sayings abstracted from Q.

17:1-2. A general principle with a specific application. Matthew gives the verses in reverse order and there is a variant of vs. 2 in Mark 9:42. **Temptations to sin:** The plural of a noun whose basic meaning is "trap" or "snare." **Millstone:** More picturesquely

change, and so gave the story another ending; (*d*) that Luke added the "third act" to account for the dismaying fact that most Jews, such as the Sadducees or those cleaving to the Old Covenant, were not moved by the resurrection of Jesus; (*e*) that the third act is logical, and thoroughly consonant with the mind of Jesus, who again and again insisted that men are not changed at heart by "signs." The theories are here set forth as representative of many, that the reader may be aware of a problem to which no unequivocal answer can yet be given. Quite apart from exegetical problems the truth remains, and it *is* consonant with the mind of Jesus. Tennyson says in *In Memoriam* that were his friend Arthur Hallam to return from the grave, he might call the sight of his friend a "canker of the brain"; and that even were Hallam to appeal to incidents that the two had shared in friendship, even were he to make specific reference

> To chances where our lots were cast
> Together in the days behind,
> I might but say, I hear a wind
> Of memory murmuring the past.[2]

There is another instance in George Bernard Shaw's *Saint Joan.* In the epilogue of the play the maid returns. All praise her. But when she proposes to live among them again, they are almost horrified, and with one accord they leave her. The third act of this Dives drama is saving realism. "Signs" do not redeem. They pique or terrify, but are soon forgotten; and then only a more startling portent can arrest the stubborn will to evil, and that sign also is soon forgotten. Men must be **persuaded** and, in redeemed will, choose the Christlike road.

Then is the resurrection of Jesus himself of no avail? To those who are ready to follow him it is very life. It tells us in vital word that the love of the Cross is on the throne of the world. But "the devils also believe, and tremble" (Jas. 2:19); and remain devils. God gives the illumined moment. We must obey its light when it comes, and throw ourselves on the divine pardon and power. Is the great gulf forever fixed? The story is not theology. We cannot answer the question. Jesus' compassion abides, and we believe it will not be in vain; but human will abides, and it becomes hard and set. We know that here and now Dives need not remain Dives. Jesus told the story to save us from **torments.**

17:1-2. ***Offenses.***—Three sayings, comprising vss. 1-6, each held within two verses, were probably distinct at first, and spoken at different times; but Luke has joined them. In his mind they are linked as follows: **offenses** come in part by the failure to forgive, and forgiveness is so hard that it requires new access of faith. How shall we construe **sure to come?** Probably it does not refer to any doctrine of foreknowledge, but is rather another instance of Jesus' realism: the heart is wicked, and wicked men will snare the weak. But they will be held responsible. Do not we also say, "There is bound to be thieving"? But we are not so quick to say with Jesus, "But every thief is under judgment."

[2] Canto XCII, st. ii. Cf. also st. i.

2 It were better for him that a millstone were hanged about his neck, and he cast into the sea, than that he should offend one of these little ones.

3 ¶ Take heed to yourselves: If thy brother trespass against thee, rebuke him; and if he repent, forgive him.

4 And if he trespass against thee seven times in a day, and seven times in a day turn again to thee, saying, I repent; thou shalt forgive him.

2 It would be better for him if a millstone
were hung round his neck and he were cast
into the sea, than that he should cause one
of these little ones to sin.[e] 3 Take heed to
yourselves; if your brother sins, rebuke
him, and if he repents, forgive him; 4 and
if he sins against you seven times in the
day, and turns to you seven times, and
says, 'I repent,' you must forgive him."

[e] Greek *stumble.*

---

described in Mark and Matthew as a heavy one that would have to be turned by an ass. **One of these little ones:** Probably Luke understood the phrase to mean the disciples or some special group among them. The meaning is made explicit in both Matthew and Mark by the addition of "who believe in me."

3-4. Take heed to yourselves: The Greek phrase is used on several occasions in Luke-Acts but not elsewhere in the N.T. Probably Luke intended the warning to be attached to the saying in vs. 2. **If your brother sins:** Codex Bezae and its allies add "against you," which is no doubt a correct interpretation of the text. It is the individual responsibility of an injured party that is under discussion. Matthew makes the rebuke only the first step in an elaborate procedure of ecclesiastical discipline (Matt. 18:15-17). The offender is to be forgiven, no matter how often the offense is repeated, if he shows a spirit of contrition. The imperative is unconditional in Matthew's version, whose "seventy-seven times" makes the saying the converse of Lamech's cry for revenge (Gen. 4:24).

Who are described as **these little ones?** Probably here, as more often in Matthew, the phrase means disciples who are young or unsure in the Christian faith. Then to whom is the warning addressed? Luke says **his disciples.** But surely no evildoer can escape the monition.

If the caution is addressed to church leaders, the sins that snare the weak are false ambition, intolerance, assertiveness, indifference. It is an unfortunate fact that people can be alienated from the faith by the hypocrisy of believers, as many perhaps as by the outright evil of alien minds. If the caution is addressed to the world, we read here the condemnation of Jesus on those who set low standards of success or who sneer at goodness. Many a youth enters business or the professions with high motives only to find a sensual and cynical climate in which high motive cannot live. As well might a tree hope to grow in a desert as faith to flourish where men say, "Business is business."

How clear the love of Jesus in this saying! He showed no anger when he himself was hurt, but his indignation blazed when the weak were tripped. Were he to walk in the flesh through our modern world, with its oases of comfort and its desert of poverty, his speech would not be gentle. He would tell again of a judgment so searching that a man would be better off with a **millstone** around his neck, and cast, not into shallows where there might be some chance of rescue, but **into the sea.** God is not mocked. Wickedness, whether of false leaders or of an alien world, is never with impunity. God's bills are not presented every month, but inescapably they fall due; and the **little ones** are meanwhile gathered to his care.

3-4. ***Forgiveness.***—We do not know the original setting of this injunction. It seems to deal with hurts and bitterness between man and man, rather than with estrangements between groups. In a conquered land resentments probably flared often, not only between Roman and Jew, but also—because everyone was living under tension—between Jew and Jew. Perhaps **brother** points to quarrels in the church when Luke wrote; such were not unknown. This account should be compared with the Matthaean version (18:15, 21-22). The **seven** of Luke means the same as the "seventy times seven" of Matthew: the pardon is to have no limit.

What is forgiveness? So far from being a casual or indifferent attitude toward wrong, it may flame in condemnation, as witness the words **rebuke him** and **if he repents.** Only the holiest can really forgive, for only they are acutely aware of sin's hurt and shame. Only God can forgive, for the sin is against him and his creation. Yet men can and should **forgive**—within the power and grace of the divine pardon. How? By laying aside all claim to requital, by dissolving in prayer all resentment, and by

5 And the apostles said unto the Lord, Increase our faith.
6 And the Lord said, If ye had faith as a grain of mustard seed, ye might say unto this sycamine tree, Be thou plucked up by the root, and be thou planted in the sea; and it should obey you.

5 The apostles said to the Lord, "Increase our faith!" 6 And the Lord said, "If you had faith as a grain of mustard seed, you could say to this sycamine tree, 'Be rooted up, and be planted in the sea,' and it would obey you.

---

5. Probably editorial, as the use of the words **apostles** and **the Lord** suggests. **Increase our faith:** "Give us more faith so that we can carry out your command." Or the request might mean: "Add faith to the other gifts you have given us."

6. Truth made vivid and memorable by paradox. The minutest quantity of **faith**—implicit trust in God—would enable men to accomplish things that seem impossible. "This word of Jesus does not invite Christians to become conjurers and magicians, but heroes like those whose exploits are celebrated in the eleventh chapter of Hebrews (Manson, *Mission and Message of Jesus,* p. 433). "Mountain" for **sycamine tree** (a black mulberry) in Matt. 17:20*b*, and in the variant in Mark 11:22-23 (Matt. 21:21). Note also I Cor. 13:2.

---

living with the offender in healing and creative love. Men who pardon should be mindful always of their own need of pardon. Thus the judge prayed for the man whom he was obliged by law to condemn:

> O God, Thou knowest I'm as blind as he,
> As blind, as frantic, not so single, worse,
> Only Thy pity spared me from the curse.[8]

Earth's best pardon is shown when it thus brings the offender to the only and ultimate pardon of God made known in Christ. When men fail to pardon, there is an endless circle of feud breeding feud, and bitterness bringing bitterness.

Failure to pardon not only tends to make the sinner inveterate in guilt, but curdles into hate the one who should forgive, and thus unwittingly bars the door to God's grace. This Jesus repeatedly told us (see Matt. 6:12-15). But when a man tries to forgive, he opens all the doors: God can find him, and comes to dwell. Vs. 4 was binding on the early church. We turn instead to law suits, insistence on our rights, the cherishing of grudges; and in consequence our world is filled with "cold wars" and "hot wars." "Blessed are the merciful: for they shall obtain mercy" (Matt. 5:7).

5-6. ***Faith.***—The words **apostles** and **the Lord** reflect the fact that this Gospel was written almost two generations after Jesus. Vs. 5*a* is almost certainly editorial. But that fact does not diminish its truth: in any age those who would follow Christ find the demands of life too great for their measure of faith, e.g., the demand that forgiveness should be instant and repeated. What is faith? The thrust of the soul into a future always hidden. Thus the farmer has faith in the faithfulness of soil and seasons, and the doctor has faith that cures yet unknown can be found. Christian faith, itself God's gift, centers in Christ, believing that God's word in him can and will be fulfilled.

The **sycamine tree** is figurative: it could not live if **planted in the sea.** The Greek in Mark 11:23 really means "hill" and refers to the Mount of Olives. There is no encouragement here to huge sleight of hand. It would victimize life if it were possible, rather than serve the ends of faith; and Jesus himself showed no desire to practice it. William Manson[4] suggests that Mark 11:23 carries echoes of Zech. 14:4, and that Jesus was actually declaring that real faith could and would usher in the messianic age. It also draws the grace whereby men can forgive seventy times in a day. Politicians bid us "have faith in the future," meaning whipped-up excitement rather than faith. But they are right to this extent: nothing is ever accomplished except by the rallying of faith whereby men cry, "It can be done!"

How is faith increased? The quality is more important than the quantity: a tiny **seed** of **faith** is enough if the faith is real faith—faith in God revealed in Christ. The **seed** must be set in the soil of life: a man must make his venture amid the actualities of our threatening world. Then prayer will bring God's rain and sunshine, and the seed comes to harvest. Gilmour's witness in Mongolia or Elizabeth Fry's protest

[8] *The Widow in the Bye Street.* Copyright 1913, by John Masefield. Used by permission of The Macmillan Company, The Society of Authors, and Dr. John Masefield, O.M.

[4] *The Gospel of Luke* (London: Hodder & Stoughton, 1930; "Moffatt New Testament Commentary"), p. 194.

7 But which of you, having a servant plowing or feeding cattle, will say unto him by and by, when he is come from the field, Go and sit down to meat?

8 And will not rather say unto him, Make ready wherewith I may sup, and gird thyself, and serve me, till I have eaten and drunken; and afterward thou shalt eat and drink?

9 Doth he thank that servant because he did the things that were commanded him? I trow not.

7 "Will any one of you, who has a serv-
ant plowing or keeping sheep, say to him
when he has come in from the field, 'Come
at once and sit down at table'? 8 Will he
not rather say to him, 'Prepare supper for
me, and gird yourself and serve me, till I
eat and drink; and afterward you shall eat
and drink'? 9 Does he thank the servant be-

2. Parable of the Farmer and His Slave (17:7-10)

There is no apparent connection with the preceding. Jesus was not concerned in the parable with criticizing or commending the farmer's treatment of his slave. The story is not about life in the new age (as in 12:37) but about everyday rural life in the Palestine of the first century. A commonplace incident is made the vehicle of a spiritual truth.

7-9. Servant translates the Greek word for "slave." A series of questions whose answers would seem obvious to men who lived under a slave economy. The essence of the parable is in vs. 9. The slave who only carries out his master's orders has not earned any right to his thanks. **I trow not** (KJV) is added by codices Alexandrinus and Bezae, and other later MSS and versions.

---

against a brutal penology was at first less than a seed. But each came to harvest, though not without prayer and venture. The apostles came to the Lord: did he not add to their faith?

7-10. ***Parable of the Farmer and His Slave.***— There is always danger that religion may degenerate into a happiness cult, and even into beauty parlor banalities that promise shallow "peace of mind" and "winsome personality." But the word and life of Jesus are sharp corrective. This terse parable seems almost harsh in its demand. When a slave comes home tired from plowing, is he pampered at his master's table? He was not, at least in those days! He could not plead weary muscles, but perforce girded himself to serve his master's meal. Only then could the slave eat, only then drag his tired body to bed. **So likewise ye!**

This is not the whole truth about God and his dealings with men. But it is a truth, for the imperious demands of duty are never fulfilled. Milton on his twenty-third birthday realized that he must live "as ever in my great Taskmaster's eye."[5] Again, it is not a total description of God, but it has pith and point. "You ought," says a Voice. There is no respite: a man can never say, "For an hour I am not under obligation." However honorably he may live, or imagine himself to live, the only verdict he can render is, "I have done only my duty."

[5] Sonnet VII, "On His Having Arrived at the Age of Twenty-three."

The story is the cure for self-pity. The mother says, "My work is never done." The father says, "I had hoped the children would be self-supporting by this time." The patriot says, "I have sacrificed, but to what purpose?" Even the saint is tempted to ask, "What's the use? The politician still plays with marked cards, and the demagogue still incites and deceives the poor." But why the self-pity? A slave does not expect the field to stay forever plowed. He cannot quit when a rainstorm washes away the seed, but must reseed. He is not concerned with far results, but only with obedience. By the same token the story is cure for our pride and imagined sense of merit. In our contacts with children we become superior, as if there were some merit in our being forty years of age while others are only six; and in our dealings with other races we condescend, almost as if the color of our skin were our virtue. We read of thievery, and say to ourselves, "I have never failed myself and my friends in that way." Jesus told us bluntly that no man ever makes God his debtor:

> For merit lives from man to man,
> And not from man, O Lord, to thee.[6]

There is a profound sense in which it is true that no man makes a sacrifice: in the realm of duty there is no room for pride or merit.

[6] Tennyson, *In Memoriam*, Prelude, st. ix.

10 So likewise ye, when ye shall have done all those things which are commanded you, say, We are unprofitable servants: we have done that which was our duty to do.

11 ¶ And it came to pass, as he went to Jerusalem, that he passed through the midst of Samaria and Galilee.

cause he did what was commanded? 10 So you also, when you have done all that is commanded you, say, 'We are unworthy servants; we have only done what was our duty.' "

11 On the way to Jerusalem he was passing along between Sa-ma'ri-a and Galilee.

---

10. The application: Men who only carry out God's commands have no claim on any reward. "The tilt against exaggerations and perversions of the doctrine of tit for tat is a prominent and characteristic feature of the teaching of Jesus. What we receive from God is grace and goodness, and not reward. . . . The *excessive* emphasis and elaboration of the doctrine of retribution was one of the weak spots of Rabbinic Judaism" (Montefiore, *Synoptic Gospels,* II, 543).

3. The Grateful Samaritan (17:11-19)

Probably a variant of 5:12-14 (Mark 1:40-45). But in this special Lukan version the number of lepers has been increased from one to ten; the miracle is effected at a distance; a Samaritan has been included in the leper group; and the emphasis is on the fact that only a foreigner showed any gratitude for Jesus' act of healing. Possibly Luke made a place for the story in his narrative to show that an incident in Jesus' own ministry had foreshadowed the acceptance of the gospel by Gentiles and its rejection by Jews.

11. Another abrupt reminder that Jesus was still in the course of a leisurely journey **to Jerusalem. Between** (RSV)—near the border of—is preferable to **through the midst of** (KJV) as a translation of a difficult Greek phrase. Probably Luke mentions Jesus' proximity to **Samaria** only to account for the reference to a Samaritan in the story this verse introduces.

The "great Taskmaster" aspect is still not the full jewel of God's nature, but it is one facet. Our heart vibrates to this iron string in a far better joy than that of self-pity or pride.

> Stern Lawgiver! yet thou dost wear
> The Godhead's most benignant grace!
> Nor know we anything so fair
> As is the smile upon thy face.[7]

When a man is thus under duty, when the ideal light shines down in such pure and inexorable demand that he knows that in this life he can never fulfill the obligation, then he can be sure that the mark of eternity is on him. Then he is content to serve the Lord of heaven, and never ask to enter the service of some menial lord whose patch of ground is narrow and whose work is soon done. Then he can labor in quiet joy, and leave the issue in God's hands.

The parable is still only partial truth. No mention is made here of man's failure, though it is vast; or of God's love lavished on him, though the love is vaster far than the failure. The "great Taskmaster" is one name; "Our Father" is another name. Jesus told another story: "Blessed are those servants, whom the lord when he cometh shall find watching; verily I say unto you, that he shall gird himself, and make them to sit down to meat, and will come forth and serve them" (12:37). Because of that Mercy the bondservant of Christ finds that his "service is perfect freedom."

11-19. ***Ten Lepers.***—See also Expos. on vss. 17-18, where ingratitude is discussed in the light of this incident. Here we are concerned with certain general comments. There are difficulties in the story, e.g., **the nine** could hardly be condemned for not returning from an errand on which Jesus had just sent them, unless we assume that they all went first to the temple, and that then only one returned to give **thanks;** and—another instance of difficulty—the formula in vs. 19 is awkward, for all had been healed **as they went,** so that the formula applies to the nine as much as to the one. Perhaps we have here a variant of 5:12-14. Even the stanchly conservative *Expositor's Greek Testament* quotes Schleiermacher's comment that the story is "negligently told."[8] The difficulties should not be blinked.

But certain truths shine clear. Would there have been **a Samaritan** among a group of Jews but for the common misery? In leper houses

[7] Wordsworth, "Ode to Duty."

[8] I, 593.

12 And as he entered into a certain village, there met him ten men that were lepers, which stood afar off:

13 And they lifted up *their* voices, and said, Jesus, Master, have mercy on us.

14 And when he saw *them,* he said unto them, Go show yourselves unto the priests. And it came to pass, that, as they went, they were cleansed.

15 And one of them, when he saw that he was healed, turned back, and with a loud voice glorified God,

16 And fell down on *his* face at his feet, giving him thanks: and he was a Samaritan.

17 And Jesus answering said, Were there not ten cleansed? but where *are* the nine?

12 And as he entered a village, he was met
by ten lepers, who stood at a distance 13 and
lifted up their voices and said, "Jesus, Mas-
ter, have mercy on us." 14 When he saw
them he said to them, "Go and show your-
selves to the priests." And as they went they
were cleansed. 15 Then one of them, when
he saw that he was healed, turned back,
praising God with a loud voice; 16 and he
fell on his face at Jesus' feet, giving him
thanks. Now he was a Samaritan. 17 Then
said Jesus, "Were not ten cleansed? Where

12-14. There is a reference to a similar leper colony outside the gate in II Kings 7:3. For leprosy as a disease in the ancient world, and for regulations governing the segregation of **lepers** and their readmission to society see on 5:12-14 (also Vol. VII, p. 338). **Go and show yourselves to the priests:** The command precedes the actual miracle of healing in contrast to 5:14. The Jewish lepers would be required to report to the temple in Jerusalem, but what of the Samaritan?

15-16. Only a foreigner returns to give **thanks** to Jesus, as did the Syrian Naaman to Elisha (II Kings 5:15).

17-18. The story in 5:12-14 was told as an illustration of Jesus' miraculous powers as a healer. In this version the miracle has been subordinated to a series of rhetorical—and prophetic—questions.

---

today racial and creedal prejudices are forgotten, for "misery loves company." Wars are forgotten in desolation; bickerings die in a common disaster. Is that one reason why suffering comes? We learn from pain, such is our stubbornness, truths we refuse to learn from joy.

The compassion of Jesus is once more evident. The sight of a colony of lepers—hands and feet gone, faces marred by gray death—was common enough, and most men grew accustomed to it. Perhaps they said, "These things are bound to be," and took that fact as excuse for callousness; but the sympathy of Jesus was instant and redemptive. That they should have been healed **as they went** was but further proof of his power. The power did not despise wise laws of men: he directed the lepers to report to the temple.

The Gospelist's interest in the healing seems to yield place to his concern (*a*) with the whole problem of gratitude and ingratitude, expounded below; and (*b*) with the fact that the one grateful man was **a Samaritan** rather than a Jew. Luke repeatedly shows fellow feeling for the semioutcast Samaritans; and it is evident here that he, a foreigner, took delight in the grateful witness of another **foreigner.** Perhaps he stressed the story because it explained why the Christian "way" had been carried so directly to the Gentiles: the Jews, who had first chance, had despised the day of gladness. The patience of God is not without limit: if he finds no response in one man, he seeks it among others whom the one man has learned to scorn. That fact always stands as warning for any nation or any church.

Perhaps the word **whole** means whole of more than the leprosy. In Sholem Asch's *The Nazarene* there is an imaginary gospel which shows the lame and blind coming to Jesus not to be healed but "to see a new thing"; and one in particular, mocking the poverty of the Galilean rabbi, crying out, "Physician, heal thyself!" So Jesus reversed his mercy and said in effect, "Thou blind one, stay among the blind!" We may doubt if Jesus would so have acted; but perhaps we must doubt even more if the **nine** lepers were any better men because of their cure. Were they not worse off through their ingratitude? The ingratitude was a worse leprosy than the physical disease. But **the Samaritan,** because of his **praising God,** was really **whole,** in soul as well as in body, for eternity as well as for time.

17-18. ***Ingratitude.*—One** man was grateful for cure; the other **nine** quickly forgot. The

18 There are not found that returned to give glory to God, save this stranger.

19 And he said unto him, Arise, go thy way: thy faith hath made thee whole.

20 ¶ And when he was demanded of the Pharisees, when the kingdom of God should come, he answered them and said, The

are the nine? 18 Was no one found to re-
turn and give praise to God except this
foreigner?" 19 And he said to him, "Rise
and go your way; your faith has made you
well."

20 Being asked by the Pharisees when the

19. A command and a comment that were apt enough in 8:48 (cf. 7:50) but which introduce an element of confusion here. Were not the nine Jews also healed by virtue of their faith? Perhaps Luke added the verse to end the story with a familiar formula.

Q. On the Kingdom and the Son of Man (17:20-37)

1. Advent of the Kingdom of God (17:20-21)

Peculiar to Luke's Gospel, but believed by some interpreters to have stood in Q as an introduction to the matter that Luke now associates with it in the verses that follow.

one seems to us normal, in the sense that he was moving toward life's true fulfillment; the nine seem abnormal, in the sense that the movement of true life in them was thwarted. How to cure ingratitude? It is a sharp question, for grateful—or normal—people are a small company.

A man cannot become what he is not: the seed of gratitude must be in him before it can grow. It is in him: praise is native, and men give thanks for the same reason that birds sing. Praise is man's instinctive response to the creative love of God, the river's flowing back to the sea. Children are taught how to say "Thank you," but they hardly need in the first instance to be taught how to feel it. To praise, in the original meaning, means almost to shout—for joy. There is some evidence that "Hallelujah" could be translated "Hurrah for Yahweh!"

But the seed does not grow unless sunlight and rain fall on it. Sunlight and rain do fall. Sleep is a sheer miracle of renewal, and it is double miracle that the ground on which we walk seems firm; and no man is so poor that he is utterly bereft of friends, and no storm but has soon its band of light. The rain is needed for gratitude as much as the sunlight—a fact that we are slow to see. The N.T., written by men facing persecution and death, is punctuated by fountainburst of praise, e.g., "Thanks be to God" (I Cor. 15:57); and Martin Rinkart's hymn, "Now Thank We All Our God," was composed after a war, famine, and pestilence, by a minister who had buried so many victims of the plague that by the world's tests he should himself have fallen victim to morbidness. It is a safe guess that the Samaritan leper was grateful for some things even in his leprosy; only so could he have been grateful for cure.

Then how does a man become thankful? By a demonstration of God so clear that we cannot gainsay either his power or his love. This was given to ten men. Where shall we find the sign? In the grace of Jesus. Mohammedanism has little praise: it has too much self-assertion. Buddhism sings no hymns of utter joy: its symbol is an impassive idol. Incidentally, Protestantism has more outright thanksgiving than Romanism, as witness the hymns Luther sang before his conversion compared with those he wrote and composed afterward; for Romanism still trusts in part to man's works of penance, while Protestantism leans on nothing but the sheer grace of God revealed in Jesus. This demonstration, once accepted, can turn even outward disaster into praise.

But that in itself is not enough: the gift must win a man's response in worship and work. Preachers try to summon thanksgiving by the plea: "See how much more fortunate you are than other people!" a praise that is nearer selfishness than gratitude. The Samaritan gave thanks, "praising God" (vs. 15). The decay of worship makes an ingrate soul, while the practice of worship fills the land with joy. It is sure that the Samaritan's worship, day by day continued, required of him a daily life that was in keeping with worship. He shared his cure of soul with other lepers, and thus kept himself in the normality of thankfulness. Col. 3:15, 17 shows the true order. We give thanks to God for his demonstration in Jesus the Christ; and the lake of life is thus not stagnant, but flows in joy to the Sea.

20-21. ***The Kingdom Comes Not in Portents, but in Jesus.***—Religious leaders in those days debated by what "signs" the millennial age would announce its advent. By "signs" they meant such portents as the turning of the moon into blood, or "the woes" of the Messiah—

kingdom of God cometh not with observation:

21 Neither shall they say, Lo here! or, lo there! for, behold, the kingdom of God is within you.

kingdom of God was coming, he answered them, "The kingdom of God is not coming with signs to be observed; 21 nor will they say, 'Lo, here it is!' or 'There!' for behold, the kingdom of God is in the midst of you."[f]

[f] Or *within you.*

20*a*. An introduction typically Greek in its structure and possibly supplied by the evangelist.

20*b*-21*a*. A protest against speculation concerning the time when God's rule would begin. **With signs to be observed** is an interpretation of a Greek phrase, occurring here only in the N.T., which KJV translated **with observation.** From the time of the book of Daniel Jewish apocalyptic writers were more concerned with the **signs** that would mark the end of the age than with any other feature of the apocalyptic hope. They gave their imaginations free rein in their portrayal of the catastrophes—"the woes of the Messiah"—which would indicate that God was about to destroy the present world order. Wars, fratricidal strife, social collapse, natural disasters, a breakup of the cosmic order—such were the lurid events they delighted to detail and delineate. Behind this interest was the belief that the worst would have to come to the worst before God would intervene to destroy the present age and to inaugurate the new era of his rule.

21*b*. The positive half of the saying asserts the utter futility of all such popular interest in **signs.** Our interpretation of it will depend on the meaning we give to the preposition ἐντὸς. The KJV and the RSV represent two possibilities. (1) **Within** (KJV; RSV mg.) corresponds to the normal Greek use of the word, and this translation makes Jesus declare that God's rule is a new spiritual principle already operative in the lives of men. In this sense the saying can be compared with the words of Paul in Rom. 14:17: "For the kingdom of God does not mean food and drink but righteousness and peace and joy in the Holy Spirit." It has been objected that Jesus could not have spoken of **the kingdom of God** as **within** the Pharisees, but this difficulty loses its force if the introduction is secondary—i.e., in the original saying perhaps Jesus was talking to his disciples. Another objection is more serious. The thought of **the kingdom of God** as a new state of being, while similar to the concept of "eternal life" in the Gospel of John, has no parallels in the Synoptic Gospels. In the Synoptic tradition the idea appears always to have eschatological associations. It is a new age that will succeed the present world order, or that in some measure has already broken in upon it. (2) **In the midst of** (RSV) (or "among") is a translation that removes the saying from its exceptional category among the kingdom references in the Gospels. But we do not dispose of all exegetical problems by accepting

---

world-wide catastrophe and revolution. Are we much better than they? There are cults that seize on every eclipse of the moon as a token of the end of the world, and a host of people believe that the new age will come through revolution. Thus even Wordsworth said of the French Revolution,

> Bliss was it in that dawn to be alive,
> But to be young was very heaven! [9]

He changed his tune within a brief time, and saw France as a "goaded land waxed mad." Not many are as swift as he to understand that most revolutions only revolve.

[9] *The Prelude,* Bk. XI, ll. 107-8. Cf. also Bk. X, l. 336.

What did Jesus reply to the demand for a "sign"? The Greek phrase in which his answer is couched has been vigorously debated, and no man can dogmatize about its meaning. The word **within** must be suspect, however, not so much because it was addressed to the Pharisees (for vs. 20 may be Luke's introduction), but because it carries meanings neither understandable by nor consonant with the Jewish mind of that age. A vague immanentalism, not to mention "evolutionary" concepts, is not congruous with O.T. thought. So **in the midst of** seems a better translation. But what does that mean? We may surmise that Jesus was referring to himself and those committed to his gospel. The word then would find close links with

22 And he said unto the disciples, The days will come, when ye shall desire to see one of the days of the Son of man, and ye shall not see *it*.

23 And they shall say to you, See here; or, see there: go not after *them*, nor follow *them*.

24 For as the lightning, that lighteneth out of the one *part* under heaven, shineth unto the other *part* under heaven; so shall also the Son of man be in his day.

22 And he said to the disciples, "The
days are coming when you will desire to see one of the days of the Son of man, and you will not see it.
23 And they will say to you, 'Lo, there!' or 'Lo, here!' Do not go, do not follow them.
24 For as the lightning flashes and lights up the sky from one side to the other, so will the Son of man be in his day.[g]

[g] Other ancient authorities omit *in his day.*

this alternative. The verb "to be" would have been unexpressed in the Aramaic original. Is the saying predictive? Did Jesus mean to assert that the new age would arrive with such dramatic suddenness that men would have neither time nor occasion to observe its coming? Or does the saying state a fact? Does it belong with others by which Jesus declares that the new age is already **in the midst of** men, even though they may fail to be aware of it? (See on 7:28; 10:18; 11:20; 13:18-20; 16:16.)

2. Sudden Coming of the Son of Man (17:22-37=Matt. 24:23, 26-27, 37-41, 28)

Matthew combines eschatological matter from Q and from Mark 13 to form one composite discourse, much as he has already woven together the two accounts of the mission of the twelve. Luke keeps his sources separate, reproducing the Q matter at this point and the Marcan tradition in ch. 21.

22. Peculiar to Luke and possibly his own composition. Christ predicts the discouragement that would be experienced by the early Christian community at the delay in the introduction of the messianic age. The author of II Peter, writing about the middle of the second century, counseled his readers to hold fast to the hope but to postpone its realization to the distant future (II Pet. 3:3-10). **The Son of man** in this verse and throughout the paragraph is a supernatural being who will appear as God's vicegerent in the last days.

23-24. The disciples are to pay no attention to any rumors about the local advent of **the Son of man.** His coming will be as universal and unmistakable as a flash of **lightning.**

such a saying as the striking 11:20. The evidence seems clear that in the mind of Jesus the kingdom was not by human means or by slow growth, but by the act of God—an act sometimes veiled and lowly (vs. 21), as supremely in Jesus himself, sometimes sudden and vivid (vs. 24). The kingdom comes when men are confronted by Jesus Christ, a demand that they cannot long avoid. Therefore it is not **with signs to be observed.** The stock of the kingdom is not quoted on the exchange. Jesus is recognized neither in *Dun and Bradstreet* nor in the *Social Register*. He does not prop his throne on bayonets, or victimize his world with portents: he comes into our world by a lowly Bethlehem-stair. It follows that the kingdom is within, but only because it has first entered our world in Jesus: the kingdom spreads by the new nature which Christ's own receive through him, and that nature is the only "progress." Robert Morrison, busy at the translation of the Bible in his Chinese cellar, and Charles Gützlaff, stealing ashore in China to distribute the first Bibles from village to village, could have said to China, in the name of their Lord, "The kingdom is in your midst." Revolutions may result as men refuse to confront Christ and bring woes upon themselves as they flout God. But the kingdom comes when he confronts men with his quiet "Follow me."

22-25. *The Kingdom Comes Like Lightning.*—(See also Expos. on Matt. 24:27.) Vss. 22-37 are a unity, whether collated by Luke or reflecting the apocalyptic that marked the preaching of the early church. They truly reflect also the eschatological stress in the teaching of Jesus. Vss. 22-25 have separate treatment here only for convenience, because they comprise one simile. Vs. 22 holds a tragic echo of the persecutions under which the early

25 But first must he suffer many things, and be rejected of this generation.

26 And as it was in the days of Noe, so shall it be also in the days of the Son of man.

27 They did eat, they drank, they married wives, they were given in marriage, until the day that Noe entered into the ark, and the flood came, and destroyed them all.

25 But first he must suffer many things and
be rejected by this generation. 26 As it was
in the days of Noah, so will it be in the
days of the Son of man. 27 They ate, they
drank, they married, they were given in
marriage, until the day when Noah en-
tered the ark, and the flood came and de-

---

25. Note 9:22 (Mark 8:31). Missing from Matthew's version, and possibly an editorial insertion into older apocalyptic material. Jesus predicts that his passion will precede the eschatological events. Perhaps the purpose of the verse was to declare that Christ himself and none other was the Son of man of whose coming he had been speaking.

26-27. The messianic age will come upon careless men and women as suddenly and unexpectedly as the deluge **in the days of Noah** (Gen. 6:5-8; 7:6-24).

Christians then lived: so burdensome and bloody were the "reprisals" that men yearned to see even **one of the days** of the coming golden age. Truly our world lives by the travail of the saints! They yearned, and their yearning was denied: **ye shall not see it.** So unremitting was the cruelty of their foes, so fervent their own longing, that they were under temptation to say of any local catastrophe, "This is the sign of the end when God shall avenge his own" (see 18:7). But such events, so interpreted, would only dash their hopes: they must still suffer. Truly as Tertullian said, "The blood of the martyrs is the seed of the church!"

The early church believed that soon history would find climax in a world-wide judgment flash that **lights up the sky from one side to the other.** They may have been essentially right. Space and time may be infected with transience, and the death of the body a symbol of world death. The cult of the atomic bomb hardly contradicts the notion of a judgment flash. Vs. 25 may have been inserted here by the Gospelist, he knowing it from his sources to be the word of Jesus, to explain the delay in the coming Day of Judgment. The simile well describes God's word in Jesus. All men and nations recognize the light of his truth, and no sin can hide any man from his revealings. He gathers secretly (like electric power in the clouds) in the turmoil of men's thoughts, and then flashes out; and sultriness and heaviness are dispelled by the sweet, clear air of his presence. But while these comparisons are valid always, the interpreter must be true to the original intention of the words: they come from the apocalyptic hope of the early church.

26-27. ***The Kingdom Comes as in the Days of Noah.***—(See Expos. on Matt. 24:37-41.) The verbs in vss. 26-32 are in the imperfect tense: "they were eating," etc. Thus the drama is heightened: apocalypse and judgment came at the most unlikely moment of ordinary life. There is no hint here that it was wrong for people in Noah's time to eat and drink and marry. The wrong was in their carelessness. They misread life: they thought it would always move on an even tenor. They misread God and the soul: "He's a good fellow." A man would be morbid or queer to become unduly concerned with his destiny.

Doubtless these verses reflect the conviction of the early church that the consummation of history was imminent. The blinding lightning flash did not come as expected. We must confront that fact, and heed its warning lest we turn each calamity into a prophecy of the end of the world. But such a fact gives us no right to treat history as unending, still less to assume that it moves on an even tenor. Gray days are not unending; the sun breaks through. Sunny days are not unending; the storm gathers. Daylight does not endure; the night comes. No man knows what a day may bring. Nature and human nature alike carry the seeds of change and death—and of the beyond death. Our life is essentially apocalyptic, punctuated with the revealings of the judgment and mercy of God. But Noah's family, treating life as a drab and ordinary affair, missed the mercy and were condemned in the judgment.

So the truth within these verses is "Be ready, for God will come suddenly!" We have a hundred different forms of insurance by which we prepare for sickness, fire, storm, and theft; and we write wills by which our family is protected in the event of our death. Do we get ready for God? No, we live as in the days of Noah. But

28 Likewise also as it was in the days of Lot; they did eat, they drank, they bought, they sold, they planted, they builded;

29 But the same day that Lot went out of Sodom it rained fire and brimstone from heaven, and destroyed *them* all.

30 Even thus shall it be in the day when the Son of man is revealed.

31 In that day, he which shall be upon the housetop, and his stuff in the house, let him not come down to take it away: and he that is in the field, let him likewise not return back.

stroyed them all. 28 Likewise as it was in
the days of Lot — they ate, they drank, they
bought, they sold, they planted, they built,
29 but on the day when Lot went out from
Sodom fire and brimstone rained from
heaven and destroyed them all — 30 so will
it be on the day when the Son of man is
revealed. 31 On that day, let him who is
on the housetop, with his goods in the
house, not come down to take them away;
and likewise let him who is in the field

28-30. It will come upon them as abruptly as **fire and brimstone** fell upon the city of **Sodom** in the days of **Lot** (Gen. 18:20-33; 19:24-25). If this second O.T. illustration stood in the Q source, Matthew has omitted it. In both instances it is not the preparedness of the patriarch for the crisis that is emphasized, but the unpreparedness of his contemporaries. Noah and **Lot** were frequently associated in rabbinical tradition for hortatory purposes, as they are also in II Pet. 2:5-8.

31-33. Usually interpreted as the evangelist's elaboration of his source. Vs. 31 appears to have been introduced from Mark 13:15-16, which Luke does not use when he borrows other material from that chapter (following 21:21). In its Marcan context it is a warning to Judeans to flee at once when they see "the desolating sacrilege set up where it ought not to be" (Mark 13:14). Here it is advice to disciples to abandon all earthly possessions at the appearance of the Son of man. The warning **let him . . . not turn back** prompts

---

our primary dealings are with God, from whom we came, and into whose hands we fall at the last. He speaks in every change, and in the change called death; in every crisis of history, and in its climax.

28-32. ***As in the Days of Lot.***—Another illustration, peculiar to Luke, of the same truth. But this simile is sharpened by the warning against delay (vs. 29), and by the terse memorable **Remember Lot's wife** (see Gen. 19). The warning against delay hardly fits this context: a lightning flash (vs. 24) would permit neither delay nor flight. Besides, the verses have been appropriated from the Little Apocalypse of Mark 13:14-16, where they refer appropriately to the destruction of Jerusalem and the desecration of its temple. Yet the lightning is a simile ("*as* the lightning"—vs. 24) for the suddenness and irresistibility of God's judgment, so the warning has its place. The staircase of a small house in those days was on the outside. So suddenly would God come that a man would be wise not to waste the two or three minutes needed to enter the door and gather his bundle of belongings: he had better flee!

As for the terse **Remember Lot's wife**, we were told in our childhood that it is the second shortest verse in the Bible. Now the terseness can be explained: it comes of the final urgency. When the house is on fire, we do not say, "I would be obliged if someone would kindly notify the fire department"; we scream, "Fire!" We can well believe that this verse is the very word of Jesus. If it is the word of preaching in the early church in conviction of the imminent judgment, it is still the word of his Spirit. Likewise, if the story of Lot and the cities of the plain is taken as saga, its truth is not thereby lessened but heightened. Sagas are the shadows of the soul, transcripts of deepest experience. The parables Jesus told are parables, but they hold profounder verity than all our literal sciences.

That gleaming pillar of salt, where once love and life had been, seems a punishment far in excess of the crime. Her friends were in the city; and would not anyone be curious to know if the warning had been true, if flame had really seized the city? But a saga probes to the quivering center of life while literalism touches only the circumference. The story tells us that sin is a sowing of the wind, and reaps the whirlwind; and that godly folk must sometimes flee from iniquity, when effort to redeem it fails; and that the broadmindedness which becomes curious about evil could better be called pto-

32 Remember Lot's wife.
33 Whosoever shall seek to save his life shall lose it; and whosoever shall lose his life shall preserve it.
34 I tell you, in that night there shall be two *men* in one bed; the one shall be taken, and the other shall be left.

not turn back. 32 Remember Lot's wife.
33 Whoever seeks to gain his life will lose it, but whoever loses his life will preserve it. 34 I tell you, in that night there
will be two men in one bed; one will be

---

the evangelist to refer to the ill-fated indecision of **Lot's wife** (Gen. 19:26). Vs. 33 is a saying from Q that Luke has already used in a slightly different form in 9:24 (Matt. 10:39). Since there is no parallel to it in Matt. 24, it is probable that Luke himself is responsible for including it again at this point. In its present setting it declares that a man must forfeit his **life** as well as his earthly effects in the last day if he is to share in the glories of the coming age.

34-35. The closest associates will be separated by the appearance of the Son of man. **In that night** is a peculiar phrase after "on the day" of vs. 30. Luke must have been responsible for it if Matthew's "Then two men will be in the field" is the reading as it

---

maine-mindedness; and that when a man or woman chooses God, the break with the world had better be complete, since looking back on an evil past brings a divided mind, with consequent disaster. Did not Jesus say that even a plowman must not look back? (9:62.)

These verses express the belief of the early church that the end of the world would soon come. But every day is Judgment Day. A Craftsman in the streets of Galilee: who could have guessed that response to his word was eternal destiny? People knew that there was haunting loveliness and rigor of truth in him, but still decided that to get rid of the Roman yoke and to make a place for themselves in the earth were the main things. Browning has a poem about a girl student of music and a man student of sculpture who were genuinely and worthily in love, but feared a marriage of financial struggle. They looked back—to a city of fancied security. So she married a rich old lord, and he won fame; and the world credited both of them with success. But she then said:

> And nobody calls you a dunce,
> And people suppose me clever:
> This could but have happened once,
> And we missed it, lost it for ever.[1]

Were they not turned to salt? What word could better describe them? Tears are salt. They said, "What's the use of scraping along on nothing!" That thought decided their earthly destiny. There are thoughts, as seemingly tenuous as a backward glance, that decide heaven and earth. **Remember Lot's wife.**

33. *Losing Life to Find It.*—These words have already been expounded in 9:24 and in Matt. 10:39. We need ask now only why they are repeated in this context. Their truth is clear: there is a dual nature in man, and one life lives only in the death of the other. The lower comes to its own when the higher is denied; the higher thrives only by a self-discipline that says "No" to the lower. But why is the measured counsel repeated here amid the flames of judgment? Because in those flames the truth is unmistakable. Besides, a man must let everything go in the last day. In life's routine days the ultimate choices do not seem important; for then the man who makes a right choice is tempted to think he is cheating himself of joy, and the man who makes a wrong choice can comfort himself with the thought that he has plenty of time to get back on the road. But in the lightning flash the road shines clear; so does the thicket far off from the road. Then the loyal follower of Jesus can say, "By his grace I am on the road." But the other man, who in willful choice has betrayed the higher, must say, "By my stubborn folly, despite all pleadings, I am caught in briars." Judgment Day brings truth to focus: that is why the Gospelist set an earlier truth in a dramatic context.

34-36. *The Sifting and Separations of the Judgment.*—We must have care not to read too much or too little into the phrases. **Two** in vs. 34 probably means two men, as alternative illustration to **two (women)** in vs. 35; but the earlier **two** could mean man and wife. The RSV, it should be noted, omits vs. 36, which is not in some of the earlier MSS. **In that night** probably should not be given a somber meaning; it may have been in Luke's source. These details, however interpreted, do not confuse or impair the central truth, viz., that the judgment will reveal a separation as wide as heaven

[1] "Youth and Art," st. xvii.

35 Two *women* shall be grinding together; the one shall be taken, and the other left.

36 Two *men* shall be in the field; the one shall be taken, and the other left.

37 And they answered and said unto him, Where, Lord? And he said unto them, Wheresoever the body *is,* thither will the eagles be gathered together.

taken and the other left.
35 There will be
two women grinding together; one will be
taken and the other left."[h]
37 And they
said to him, "Where, Lord?" He said to
them, "Where the body is, there the eagles[i]
will be gathered together."

[h] Other ancient authorities add verse 36, *"Two men will be in the field; one will be taken and the other left."*
[i] Or *vultures.*

---

stood in Q. **Two women** would be required for the easy operation of a hand mill. **Taken**="saved." **Left**="abandoned to judgment."

36. Read by Codex Bezae, many late Greek MSS, and the Latin and Syriac versions. Probably a scribal gloss on the original text from Matt. 24:40. Its Lukan authorship has been defended on the precarious grounds that if vs. 34 refers to a man and his wife—not an improbable interpretation of the Greek text—some mention of male as well as female servants would be necessary to give a complete picture of a Palestinian household.

37. The saying is appended by Matthew—without Luke's introduction—to his counterpart to vss. 23-24, where it seems to emphasize the suddenness with which the Son of man will appear. No doubt a common proverb (cf. Job 39:30). Apparent meaning in Luke's context: "Judgment will take place wherever there is occasion for it." Possibly we should read **vultures** (RSV mg.) instead of **eagles,** for the latter are not carrion birds and are not gregarious.

---

and hell between hearts joined in life by toil or friendship. Each one of us lives in an awe-filled secrecy. No man can read his neighbor's soul. Two men may share one room, two women work as closely as at the handle of one hand mill, and still be poles asunder in motive and intent. The distance apart is unrevealed until the judgment. Then one will say, "I never knew he was so near to Christ"; and the other, "How could he have been so far from Christ!"

He has sounded forth the trumpet that shall never call retreat;
He is sifting out the hearts of men before His judgment seat,
Oh, be swift, my soul, to answer Him! be jubilant, my feet! [2]

The words **taken** and **left** are open words, the one opening on a destiny of light, the other on a destiny of doom. *The Pulpit Commentary* [3] is not convincing when it relates **taken** to I Thess. 4:17. **Taken** in its Lukan setting means saved in the final judgment; **left** means left to an overwhelming doom. The words are not dogmatic theology, and they do not prejudge the possibilities of the hereafter; but the one is daybreak and the other midnight. Two people at one bench, in one friendship; and neither knows that in the soul of one is morning, and in the soul of the other is darkness: but God knows, and judgment reveals the soul.

[2] Julia Ward Howe, "Battle Hymn of the Republic."
[3] *St. Luke,* II, 91.

37. ***The Carcass and the Vultures.***—This is probably Christ's appropriation, with the quickening of dramatic intensity such as only he can give, of a then-current proverb. It should not be allegorized, and the sometimes-held theory that the body is that of Christ on the cross, while the vultures are the saints who feed on him, is an almost repugnant idea. Vultures is preferable to **eagles,** for the latter do not flock and are not carrion birds. The more accurate translation need not invalidate the suggestion that Jesus had in mind the Roman eagles. That theory is not unlikely: Jesus sometimes suggested that the Romans, impious in themselves, could nevertheless be God's scourge.

It is a terrible picture of judgment: a sky dark with huge carrion birds which come to pick white the bones of a corpse. A. J. Grieve speaks of "morally dead hearts and of decadent nations." [4] It is an honest phrase, true to the mood of the proverb. The verse is comparable in penetrating truth with Gal. 6:7. Wherever there is irresponsibility, lack of response to God, the pride of the creature, there is spiritual death—and the gathering of black carrion birds of judgment. A certain sequence is unbreakable by man: sin, death, judgment. It is breakable only by the grace of God in Jesus. That is why Jesus quoted the proverb, giving it the dimension of his own spirit, that we might be forewarned and saved.

[4] *A Commentary on the Bible,* ed. A. S. Peake (New York: Thomas Nelson & Sons, n.d.), p. 737.

18 And he spake a parable unto them *to this end,* that men ought always to pray, and not to faint;

2 Saying, There was in a city a judge, which feared not God, neither regarded man:

3 And there was a widow in that city; and she came unto him, saying, Avenge me of mine adversary.

18 And he told them a parable, to the
effect that they ought always to pray
and not lose heart. 2 He said, "In a certain
city there was a judge who neither feared
God nor regarded man; 3 and there was a
widow in that city who kept coming to him
and saying, 'Vindicate me against my ad-

R. Parables on the Proper Practice of Prayer (18:1-14)

1. Parable of the Widow and the Judge (18:1-8)

The parable proper is restricted to vss. 2-5 and is a twin to that of the importunate friend in 11:5-8. No doubt its original moral was also the same: Persistence in prayer brings results. In the course of its transmission vss. 6-8*a* were appended to it and it became a specific injunction to the elect to pray incessantly for the Day of Judgment and for God's vengeance on their enemies. Vs. 8*b* appears to be a still later addition, perhaps reflecting a spirit of pessimism at the growth of heretical groups within the church: When Christ returns as the Son of man will there be any true community of believers on earth to welcome him? The paragraph affords an interesting glimpse into the history of the gospel tradition.

18:1. Editorial introduction. The evangelist ignores the specific application that had been given to the **parable** in his source (see general comment just above), but in so doing he may have recovered the point that Jesus had intended to make by it.

2-3. Little is known of the administration of justice at the village level in the Palestine of Jesus' day. This parable indicates that it was sometimes in the hands of a

---

The curiosity of **Where, Lord?** is not satisfied; cf. 13:23. Judgment is universal: wheresoever sin is, judgment gathers. If the **Where, Lord?** is an appeal to Jesus to draw the curtain on the next world, the proverb makes a very sharp answer. It is enough for us to know the joy of Jesus and the desolation of denying him, to trust the future to a righteous, loving God.

18:2-5. *Persistence in Prayer: The Parable of the Unjust Judge.*—Almost certainly the original parable ended at vs. 5. "And the Lord said" seems to show that vss. 6-8 are the application which the early church gave to the story. There is a difference of mood between parable and application. The parable has a touch of humor, but the application tells of persecution so cruel that the saints called on God to avenge them of their foes. Here we discuss the parable. B. T. D. Smith[5] quotes from H. B. Tristram the description of a court in Nisibis, Mesopotamia, where the parable was almost re-enacted. The woman had no money to bribe the unscrupulous judge, and no power to bully him, but she had persistence: she badgered him. Day by day he "took a beating" from her: the Greek word parallels that colloquialism. Finally she wore him down: he granted her plea not because he had any sense of justice, but simply to be rid of her.

There is no need to say that the judge is not offered as a picture of God. A parable has one central jet of truth, in this instance the need for persistence in prayer. The judge is drawn as an unworthy man that the parable may stress the "how much more" (11:13; Matt. 7:11). If a heartless judge grants a widow's prayer, surely God's heart of love will not refuse her. But this assurance only deepens the problem of the story: why should anyone, especially a widow (symbol of the innocent and helpless), have to plead and wait, and wait and plead? The pain and burden of "unanswered prayer" are in that question. We do not know the whole reason. If we did, we should be God, and we should have no need to pray. But we can partly understand; and must measurably understand, or our persistence in prayer will become blind rote and repetition.

God delays to answer in our way that our motives may be purified. Who among us has not prayed and then asked: "Is that worthy? Is it what I really want and need?" Galileo went to the tomb of St. Anthony intending to pray for money for himself, health for his children, and old age for his mother, but found

[5] *Parables of the Synoptic Gospels,* p. 150, citing H. B. Tristram, *Eastern Customs in Bible Lands* (London: Hodder & Stoughton, 1894), p. 228.

4 And he would not for a while: but
afterward he said within himself, Though
I fear not God, nor regard man;
5 Yet because this widow troubleth me,
I will avenge her, lest by her continual
coming she weary me.
6 And the Lord said, Hear what the unjust judge saith.
7 And shall not God avenge his own
elect, which cry day and night unto him,
though he bear long with them?
8 I tell you that he will avenge them
speedily. Nevertheless, when the Son of
man cometh, shall he find faith on the
earth?

versary.' 4 For a while he refused; but after-
wards he said to himself, 'Though I neither
fear God nor regard man, 5 yet because this
widow bothers me, I will vindicate her, or
she will wear me out by her continual com-
ing.'" 6 And the Lord said, "Hear what
the unrighteous judge says. 7 And will not
God vindicate his elect, who cry to him day
and night? Will he delay long over them?
8 I tell you, he will vindicate them speedily.
Nevertheless, when the Son of man comes,
will he find faith on earth?"

---

single **judge.** In the Bible **a widow** is often a typical representative of those who need to be defended against exploitation. It is taken for granted that her cause is just.

4-5. Lest . . . she weary me: "Lest she come at last and beat me" is the literal translation of the Greek text. Though the judge neither feared **God** nor felt any shame before **man,** he had a healthy respect for a widow's wrath! But most interpreters prefer the metaphorical translation of the standard English versions.

6-8*a*. An application that presupposes a period of acute persecution and whose tenor is reminiscent of the cry of the martyrs in Rev. 6:10: "O Sovereign Lord, holy and true, how long before thou wilt judge and avenge our blood on those who dwell upon the earth?" **Will he delay long over them?** The grammar and the sense of the Greek are obscure. Goodspeed's translation does justice to the present tense of the verb: "Is he slow to help them?" Many interpreters believe that the clause—and perhaps the whole paragraph—has been influenced by a passage in Ecclesiasticus. Having referred to the

---

himself asking, as he meditated on the life of the saint, for illumination of mind that he might confer some boon of new knowledge on mankind.[6] God delays also that desire may be intensified. The sculptor Randolph, in Lloyd Douglas' novels *The Magnificent Obsession* and *Doctor Hudson's Secret Journal,* when asked to reveal the secret of his life, would inquire of his interrogator: "Do you really want to know? More than you have ever wanted to know anything before?" Perhaps God speaks thus to us, and so fans true desire into a flame. God delays, according to our eyes, perchance because only by such passion of prayer can evil in the world be overcome, as the heartlessness of a venal judge was conquered only by the woman's importunity. God delays because the patience of the saints is the best weapon of the faith, for faith spreads in the earth as men persist for God despite all odds and against all disappointment.

Do we covet cheap, quick, and easy answers to our prayers? If prayer were an Aladdin's lamp, bringing by instant magic anything we might fancy, no one would pray; for the world would become a topsy-turvydom in which prayer and life alike would become impossible. Home is dearer when the journey is long; and God's gifts are more precious when we have to wait for them. Which prayer of Jesus is most life-giving? The Gethsemane prayer, thrice repeated, that seemed to find no answer! We are impatient folk. We must "get rich quick," and we must have canned music when learning music for ourselves becomes too painstaking, and we must fly in six hours the journey which our forefathers slowly compassed by covered wagon against many foes. But are we stancher in soul than they? So the parable was told lest we should weary in prayer, and to remind us that God is faithful in wisdom and love.

6-8. *Faith on the Earth.*—Probably in these verses Luke applied the parable to his own time. The synagogue reported the Christians to the empire as malcontents, and the empire too often believed the charge and punished them with imprisonment and death. Widows were numerous; they and their children were cast on a hostile world. Why did not God hear their prayers? Surely the blood of the martyrs did

[6] See Zsolt de Harsányi, *The Star-Gazer,* tr. Paul Tabor (New York: G. P. Putnam's Sons, 1939), pp. 254-56.

9 And he spake this parable unto certain which trusted in themselves that they were righteous, and despised others:

9 He also told this parable to some who trusted in themselves that they were right-

prayer of the wronged, the supplication of the orphan, and the complaint of the widow, Jesus ben Sira declares:

> . . . the Lord will not delay,
> Or be slow about them,
> Until he crushes the loins of the unmerciful,
> And takes vengeance on the heathen (Ecclus. 35:18 Goodspeed).

8*b*. It is no longer God but **the Son of man** who is judge (as in 17:26, 30). **Faith:** The noun is definite in the Greek text, and probably means "true" or "orthodox" faith.

2. Parable of the Pharisee and the Tax Collector (18:9-14)

An "example-story" like the parable of the good Samaritan (10:30-37). Not all Pharisees were like the Pharisee of this story. Talmudic literature can furnish many instances of exemplary humility. But the prayer of a rabbi of about A.D. 70, quoted in Berakoth 28*b*, is further evidence that they were exposed to the danger of spiritual pride: "I thank thee, O Lord, my God, that thou hast given me a place among those who sit in the House of Study, and not among those who sit at the street corners; for I rise early and they rise early, but I rise early to study the words of the Law, and they rise early to engage in vain things; I labor and they labor, but I labor and receive a reward, and they labor and receive no reward; I live and they live, but I live for the life of the future world, and they live for the pit of destruction."

9. Editorial introduction. Pharisees seem to be implied. **To:** The Greek preposition could be translated "against" or "with respect to," but Lukan usage is not in favor of these alternatives.

not cry to him in vain? The early church had its answer: God would come speedily in the final judgment. But by that time so many Christians might have been killed, and so many others might have lapsed from the faith through lure of pleasure or fear of persecution, that there might not be any clear witness to Christ when he returned: **When the Son of man comes, will he find faith on earth?** We ask the same question. The blight of worldliness, the threat of war, the spread of selfish propaganda make the church a beleaguered garrison in a hostile land rather than a conquering army. Perhaps faith does not find God except on the last edge of helplessness. The realism of these verses fits every age.

Suppose faith should disappear! In every area it is indispensable: medical research and new international organization would alike collapse without it. But *the* faith is doubly essential. Christ is *the* faith, not an alternative among many faiths. Imagine a world which reckons men to be marionettes of dust, and love a trick of the nerves, and conscience a convenience of custom, and God an empty name! A man who destroyed all road signs would be a fiend, but a man who concocted a fog to shut out the sun would be an archfiend, e.g., such a man who says, "Right and wrong are only relative." Suppose every memory of Christ were expunged, and every gift of Christ destroyed: earth would be worse than a morgue. The faith must be kept!

Thus these verses bid us stand fast in the faith. A Christian must endure persecution. Even if the picture he is painting may be torn to shreds by alien hands it is right and true, and the disciple must bear his witness whatever the odds. We are not asked to succeed, but only to bear our witness. If the gospel travels slowly in the souls of men, speed is no test: better a man should inch along toward God than go hell-bent in a jet plane. If a man does stand fast, though he may seem to be a voice crying in a wilderness, he is not alone. The question is not *if* **the Son of man comes,** but **when** he comes. Is not Christ himself sufficient ground of confidence? Far better than any affidavit or any promise thundered from the sky! God will **vindicate** his elect. A man should pray for power so to live that at the journey's end he can say, "I have kept the faith" (II Tim. 4:7).

9-14. ***Parable of the Pharisee and the Tax Collector.***—(See also Expos. on vs. 14.) When

10 Two men went up into the temple to pray; the one a Pharisee, and the other a publican.

11 The Pharisee stood and prayed thus with himself, God, I thank thee, that I am not as other men *are,* extortioners, unjust, adulterers, or even as this publican.

12 I fast twice in the week, I give tithes of all that I possess.

eous and despised others: **10** "Two men
went up into the temple to pray, one a
Pharisee and the other a tax collector.
11 The Pharisee stood and prayed thus
with himself, 'God, I thank thee that I am
not like other men, extortioners, unjust,
adulterers, or even like this tax collector.
12 I fast twice a week, I give tithes of all

---

10. The story has its setting in Jerusalem. **The temple** was used for private prayer and meditation as well as for public prayer at stated occasions (1:10; Acts 3:1).

11-12. With himself, i.e., "silently." Codex Bezae has the attractive reading: "The Pharisee stood by himself and prayed thus." He kept himself aloof from the main body of worshipers. In cataloguing his merits he mentions first the vices from which he abstains and then the special evidences of his piety. The latter are works of supererogation. **I fast twice a week:** Private fasts were not required by the law. Zealous Jews observed them on Mondays and Thursdays. By the second century equally zealous Christians had adopted the practice but had altered the days to Wednesdays and Fridays (Did. 8:1). **I give tithes of all that I get:** The law demanded only that agricultural products be tithed (Deut. 14:22-23). The Pharisee's reference is to the tithing of all his income, not of all his possessions (KJV).

---

a man prays alone he is revealed, or would be if we could get inside his mind. In prayer he does not pose or pretend, or at least not so easily as in his life among men. The fact that makes this story quiver is that Jesus, who knew the secret heart, allows us to overhear the secret prayers of two men. They are partly fictitious characters, for many a **Pharisee** was lowly and many a **tax collector** unrepentant. But they both live on every busy street. One of them may bear our name.

Each man described *himself,* and neither lied. **The Pharisee** was **righteous** by common tests, he did give a tenth of his income to charity and religion, and he had imposed disciplines on himself in excess of the law's requirements. Conversely, **the tax collector** was a grafter and a crook: his confession was sincere. Jesus has accented the characters, as any penetrating drama demands, but has not impaired their verity. So each man told what he thought of himself. For **the Pharisee** the key word was **I:** it repeats like a hurdy-gurdy. He thanked God, but actually his thoughts were on himself. He cited his righteous traits, and recalled that in tithing and fasting he had done more than the law required. He was a patriot and an upright man, and probably chairman both of the forefathers' day society and the temple charity fund. That, in fact, was the burden of his "prayer." **The tax collector,** on the contrary, dared not lift his eyes to heaven, kept smiting on his breast, and offered a cry rather than a prayer: he pleaded with God to cleanse a soul that was one dark blot. He was thereby **justified.** The word does not mean righteous, but rather accepted of heaven's grace. The Pharisee had everything in his favor except *the* thing; the publican nothing in his favor except *the* thing. The Pharisee's center of the world was himself, the publican's was God. Is not *our* world self-centered in its graspings and its cult of success? Our perfect punishment is that we must talk about ourselves endlessly to psychiatrists!

Each man told what he thought about his neighbors. The one man **despised others.** He looked at mankind, and thanked God that he was not like the crowd of the unworthy, such as **this tax collector.** The other man stood **afar off** from other men such as the Pharisee, because he felt himself unworthy of their friendship. All our prejudices of race and class are in the first man, the indifference to widespread wretchedness by which we provoke revolt. Comfortable people do not care how the other half of the world lives, so the neglected turn to bitter cruelty. The Pharisee preened himself by condemning others, whereas he should have said of the sinner, "There, but for the grace of God, go I." The publican said, "The blame rests on me." The Pharisee could have had many a grace if he had lived in lowliness; the publican had humility of soul, and therefore his many sins were forgiven.

So each man told half-consciously what he thought about God. The Pharisee regarded God as a corporation in which he had earned

13 And the publican, standing afar off, would not lift up so much as *his* eyes unto heaven, but smote upon his breast, saying, God be merciful to me a sinner.

14 I tell you, this man went down to his house justified *rather* than the other: for every one that exalteth himself shall be abased; and he that humbleth himself shall be exalted.

that I get.'
13 But the tax collector, standing far off, would not even lift up his eyes to heaven, but beat his breast, saying, 'God, be merciful to me a sinner!'
14 I tell you, this man went down to his house justified rather than the other; for every one who exalts himself will be humbled, but he who humbles himself will be exalted."

---

13. The **tax collector** takes up a position **far off** "from the altar." Both his actions and his words express his sense of unworthiness. He confesses that he is a **sinner** and prays for God's mercy.

14*a*. It is the contrite tax collector whom God "declares to be just," not the self-righteous Pharisee.

14*b*. A floating saying from Q (Matt. 23:12) which the evangelist has already used in 14:11. In its present context it contrasts the destinies of the Pharisee and the tax collector in the life to come.

---

a considerable block of stock, so that at any moment he might be invited to become a director. His "prayer" told God that he was waiting for well-deserved honors. If that seems an incredible attitude, we should recall that many people think God owes them something, as is shown by their question when sorrow comes, "Why has this happened to *me?*" If they can claim a respectability that has not risked jail, they think they are entitled to favors; and if favors do not come, they write letters to the celestial newspapers protesting obvious failures on the part of the celestial government. But the publican saw God as burning holiness, yet of such love that even a tax collector could be pardoned. What we think of ourselves and our neighbors stems from what we think about God.

Jesus did not justify the tax collector's way of life, but hated it. Jesus did not condemn the Pharisee's charities and honor, but would have approved them had they been rooted in true motive. But the tax collector had a soul open toward God, while the Pharisee was locked in himself. So the Pharisee was a cold hilltop where no flowers grow, while the tax collector was a valley low enough in sense of sin to hold the flowing stream of God's mercy. Is there not a story of the gift that opened heaven's gate? The first gift was a drop of patriot's blood, but the gate did not open; the second, a lover's last sigh, but the gate did not open; the third the penitent tear of an old man converted by a child's prayer, and that won entrance.

14. *Pride and Lowliness.*— (See Expos. on Matt. 23:11-12; Luke 14:7-11.) Jesus frequently used proverbial sayings, giving them by his truth a deeper thrust. **Shall be** may mean in the coming judgment. But the coming events of Christ's kingdom always cast their shadows—and light—before. Therefore our own world gives evidence of the coming reversal: the proud are brought down, and the lowly are exalted. Unworthy and worthy science provide the respective instances. The astrologer who says that stars are little lamps for a private park called earth is locked in a little mind, which nevertheless is always distraught by knockings of vaster truth upon the door; while the astronomer who studies the stars as a little child, letting them speak their own message, sees the wonders of God. But if the astronomer should then turn in pride upon the lowly follower of Christ with the demand "Prove your faith to me by logic," the astronomer might be condemned. For he would then be trying to impose his scientific tests on God, and to establish his own brain as the final criterion of Verity. Those who would know God must wait for his coming, letting him choose his own path, and must know that the path may be as lowly as at Bethlehem; and they must pray in lowliness, "Open thou mine eyes, that I may behold wondrous things out of thy law" (Ps. 119:18).

This proverb therefore does not make God a tyrant, for God himself is lowly, even to a death upon the Cross. His nature is holy love, inexorable yet long-suffering. That is why the penitent tax collector was **exalted;** that is why the Pharisee was shut off from his fellows and from God. Being capsuled, the Pharisee slowly died, as any man dies who locks himself in a little house and pretends to be self-sufficient. Christ was exalted because he descended the ladder of humiliation (Phil. 2:6-9). Any street supplies illustration of the proverb's truth; any

15 And they brought unto him also infants, that he would touch them: but when *his* disciples saw *it*, they rebuked them.

16 But Jesus called them *unto him*, and said, Suffer little children to come unto me, and forbid them not: for of such is the kingdom of God.

17 Verily I say unto you, Whosoever shall not receive the kingdom of God as a little child shall in no wise enter therein.

15 Now they were bringing even infants to him that he might touch them; and when the disciples saw it, they rebuked them. 16 But Jesus called them to him, saying, "Let the children come to me, and do not hinder them; for to such belongs the kingdom of God. 17 Truly, I say to you, whoever does not receive the kingdom of God like a child shall not enter it."

S. Conditions of Entrance to the Kingdom (18:15-34)

Luke had temporarily abandoned the Marcan narrative at 9:50 (Mark 9:40) in order to find a place in his account for a rich fund of teaching matter from other sources. He now resumes his use of his major source, almost at the point at which he had put it aside. Only the catena of sayings in Mark 9:41-50 and the teaching about divorce in Mark 10:2-12 are omitted. The evangelist had incorporated variants of two of the former in 17:2; 14:34, and perhaps he believed he had given the gist of the latter in 16:18.

1. Jesus and Little Children (18:15-17=Mark 10:13-15)

15. Infants for Mark's "little children." **Touch them:** Place his hands upon them in the course of bestowing a blessing (cf. Mark 10:16). **The disciples** wished to protect their master from requests they considered trivial.

16*a*. Both Matthew and Luke omit Mark's statement that **Jesus** was "much displeased," as well as the detail in Mark 10:16 that he embraced the children as he blessed them. They hesitated to attribute the human emotions of anger and affection to the Lord of the church.

16*b*-17. Children manifest the attitude of simple and unquestioning trust that God requires of those who will enter his **kingdom** (cf. Paul's characteristic interpretation of "faith" as man's humble and grateful response to God's grace).

---

era of statecraft writes the exposition. No scientific law is half so surely based; no morning after darkness is half so sure and radiant.

15-17. ***Jesus and Little Children.***—(See Expos. on Mark 10:13, 14; Matt. 19:13-15.) Mark's account is, of course, the probable source. See Exeg. for suggestion as to the reason why Matthew and Luke have changed the Marcan record. All accounts are needed; for Matthew and Luke adore Christ as God's self-revealing, while Mark here traces for us the fullness with which God in Jesus shared our life. This whole passage deals with conditions of entrance into the kingdom of heaven, as does the subsequent Lukan record here through vs. 34.

Why were mothers **bringing even infants** to Jesus? For his blessing. That is shown in the word **touch.** Education without that touch is without heart, and therefore without lifeblood. For education must be conducted within some faith. We cannot help making assumptions about our world. Schools may claim and pretend to be "objective," but they all make assumptions. Secular education thus has tenets, among them the following: the mind is mainly a repository for "facts," the world is secular, God can safely go unmentioned. It is said that Germany prior to Hitler was a well-educated nation. How far is the word "well" really justified? If Christ is *the* faith (such was his claim), Christ must be the cornerstone of any worthy education. The instinct of the mothers was right: their children could not enter into life without his **touch.**

Why should the disciples have **rebuked them?** Because of adult pride. It was not the disciples' merit that they were older than the children, and that therefore they had more knowledge and physical power. It was their obligation. But they deemed it merit; and like most adults, they built a selfishly adult world. How often do advertisers think of the eyes of children, or statesmen remember that they legislate for the next generation? Being older is an obligation, and one of the best tests of adult worth is its attitude toward children. Can a man play with children, not ostentatiously or with any condescension, but by glad instinct? Jesus set a child at the center of the world. Jesus said that

18 And a certain ruler asked him, saying, Good Master, what shall I do to inherit eternal life?

18 And a ruler asked him, "Good Teacher, what shall I do to inherit eternal life?"

2. A Rich Man Rejects Discipleship (18:18-27=Mark 10:17-27)

18. The man who interviewed Jesus on this occasion is usually called "the rich young ruler," a composite title from the three Synoptic accounts. All describe him as a rich man, Matthew as a young man (he has to omit the phrase "from my youth" in his version of Mark 10:20), and Luke as a **ruler,** i.e., a member of the governing body of some synagogue. Luke's title is probably an editorial inference from the fact that the questioner was rich. **To inherit eternal life:** To share the life of the age to come, i.e., of the kingdom of God.

a home is the pattern which statecraft and industry must obey.

What are the traits in children that Jesus had in mind when he said, **To such belongs the kingdom of God?** Their candor: when a child is asked, "How old are you?" he will give instant answer, and perhaps add, "How old are *you?*" The adult does not reply in the same openness as the child, for the adult has become sophisticated in defensive pride. Their seeking: a child asks endless questions, especially about God ("Who made God?"); for a child instinctively knows the real issues, whereas a man forgets, and gets sidetracked in secondary inquiries. Their trustfulness and sense of dependence: when crises come, they do not pretend to be self-sufficient. How easy it is for adults to imagine that by their science and skill they can bring heaven on earth, and how tragically they fail! As well might they expect to lift the sun into the sky as to overcome their own darkness of mind and soul!

Jesus here tells us that we need a second childhood. We cannot return to our earliest years, nor can we remain in them: that would be infantilism. Nor is there any grace in what is usually called second childhood: that comes of weakening of the mind. But it is possible for a man to pass through his self-sufficiency to a new surrender in trust to God's mercy. There is a new innocence beyond man's wisdom and guilty blundering. Confession, dependence, surrender, trust: these are the second birth, and the entrance to the kingdom.

18-27. ***The Rich Young Ruler.***—(See also Expos. on vss. 19, 25-27; cf. Expos. on Matt. 19:16-22; Mark 10:17-31.) As we try to draw the picture of this man we must remember that Mark gives the earliest account. He does not say that the questioner was young. That is Matthew's word, and he has to compensate for it later in the record by omitting the phrase **from my youth** (see RSV). Mark does not say that the man was a **ruler:** that was perhaps Luke's inference (not necessarily incorrect) because of the man's wealth and piety, for **ruler** means a member either of the local synagogue council or of the Sanhedrin. Mark's phrase, "Jesus looking upon him loved him" (Mark 10:21), is important. The man's imagination was not cluttered or unclean. He was in some measure independent and brave, or he would not have come to the new Teacher. He was eager, for he "ran up and knelt before him" (Mark 10:17). We need not assume that **What shall I do** implied an excessive dependence on rubrics or works of the law. He wished to know how he could enter the kingdom (see Exeg.).

Good Master: the word was too fulsome, too undiscerning; for **good** is an ultimate term. So Jesus brought him to a halt (see Expos., vs. 19), and then reminded him that he knew the commandments. The man was disappointed: he had kept the commandments, but still felt no assurance of entrance into the kingdom. He was not necessarily self-righteous in his claim. It was then believed that the law could be fully kept. Manson refers to a Talmud story of a rabbi who, when a hostile army was at his city's gates, went on his roof to pray as follows: "Lord of the worlds, if I have failed to follow one single word of this book of the Law, so let them come in; but if not, then let them depart." [7] In like fashion, this man asked Jesus, "What do I still lack?" (Matt. 19:20.) Of course he had not kept the law except in the sense that a musician might play with mechanical correctness any musical score set before him. He had mastered the letter of the law, but the spirit of the law—God himself—had not mastered him, for he had not made surrender to God in abandon of the soul.

So Jesus confronted him with precisely that demand. **Sell all . . . distribute to the poor, and you will have treasure in heaven.** The demand cannot be turned into a universal rule, but it must not be evaded by any man. Jesus apparently required that sacrifice of those who would be his disciples (Mark 8:34). So this

[7] *Gospel of Luke,* p. 205.

19 And Jesus said unto him, Why callest thou me good? none *is* good, save one, *that is,* God.

20 Thou knowest the commandments, Do not commit adultery, Do not kill, Do not steal, Do not bear false witness, Honor thy father and thy mother.

19 And Jesus said to him, "Why do you call me good? No one is good but God alone.
20 You know the commandments: 'Do not commit adultery, Do not kill, Do not steal, Do not bear false witness, Honor your fa-

---

19. Only **God** is entitled to the absolute predicate **good.** Matthew feared that Jesus' question might carry the implication that he was not sinless, and so he altered its phrasing to "Why do you ask me about what is good?" (Matt. 19:17*a*.) Luke was not conscious of any such christological problem.

20. Jesus refers his interrogator to the requirements of the Decalogue, the heart of the moral law. Luke's order for the sixth and seventh commandments differs from Mark's, but they are similarly quoted in Rom. 13:9 and Jas. 2:11, perhaps because of some current liturgical practice. Both Matthew and Luke omit Mark's "do not defraud," which is not numbered among the commandments in Exod. 20:12-16 or Deut. 5:16-20. No explanation is apparent for the position of the fifth commandment at the end of the list.

---

condition cannot be easily dismissed. Some temptations diminish with the years, but the temptation to riches may increase and harden. Jesus wished this man to surrender to God that God's law of love might master him, but perhaps Jesus also yearned to make him an apostle. Faith in Christ is no mere rubric however splendid, no mere abstaining from sin, no little churchiness; it is more even than the outward observance of positive righteousness: it is a launching out into the great Deep, an abandon to the love and obedience of God.

We do not know the sequel. Dante in *The Divine Comedy* describes meeting him, a man without a name:

> I looked, and I beheld the shade of him
> Who made through cowardice the great refusal.[8]

That is begging the question: the man may have been changed by the Cross or by the rapture of the Resurrection. But the story seems to hint a refusal, final so far as this world is concerned, "His countenance fell, and he went away sorrowful" (Mark 10:22). What an apostle he would have made! What a gospel he could have written! Perhaps no man ever made a poorer bargain: great possessions are tinsel compared with apostleship and a gospel.

19. ***God and Goodness.***—"Good Master" is a title occurring only in this story and, according to Plummer,[9] is nowhere in the Talmud. The title showed the speaker's charm, perhaps too much of compliment, and too little penetration of thought; for the word **good** is a profound depth. It is very important to notice that in Jesus' reply the emphasis is on **good,** not on **me.** In the second sentence of the reply the stress is on **God.** These facts make needless Matthew's obvious anxiety lest Christ's question should appear to be a denial of Christ's own purity of motive (cf. Mark 10:18; Matt. 19:17). Goodness, so far from being a tribal convention, as shallow thinking has sometimes tried to argue, is an "absolute predicate" (see Exeg.). It implies, according to Manson, "unlimited range of moral activity,"[1] and in that sense belongs only to God. Even "the Son can do nothing of himself, but what he seeth the Father do" (John 5:19). That is why man's concepts of goodness are always stricken by a discontent.

What is goodness? It must be constantly reexamined, or it becomes mere respectability or even reaction. "Good people," so-called, are not usually adventurous: they are more often circumspect and perhaps censorious. Many "good people" are good only in what they refrain from doing: they think that goodness originated in the era of Queen Victoria rather than in the holiness of God. The Pharisees were good, but their goodness became locked against the thrusts of God, and therefore hardened into an ethic and a ritual. Continuing to be selfish, it festered; and they helped to crucify Jesus. John Newton thanked God for "sweet communion," but had commanded a ship for the slave trade. Our goodness is only partly good. We condemn fleshliness, as is right; but we do not often condemn legalized avarice or the standardization of man's mind. How goodness needs to be scrutinized!

To say that none is good save God does not

[8] *Inferno,* Canto III, ll. 59-60.
[9] *St. Luke,* p. 422.
[1] *Gospel of Luke,* p. 205.

21 And he said, All these have I kept from my youth up.

22 Now when Jesus heard these things, he said unto him, Yet lackest thou one thing: sell all that thou hast, and distribute unto the poor, and thou shalt have treasure in heaven: and come, follow me.

23 And when he heard this, he was very sorrowful: for he was very rich.

24 And when Jesus saw that he was very sorrowful, he said, How hardly shall they that have riches enter into the kingdom of God!

25 For it is easier for a camel to go through a needle's eye, than for a rich man to enter into the kingdom of God.

ther and mother.'" 21 And he said, "All
these I have observed from my youth."
22 And when Jesus heard it, he said to him,
"One thing you still lack. Sell all that you
have and distribute to the poor, and you
will have treasure in heaven; and come, fol-
low me." 23 But when he heard this he be-
came sad, for he was very rich. 24 Jesus
looking at him said, "How hard it is for
those who have riches to enter the king-
dom of God! 25 For it is easier for a camel
to go through the eye of a needle than for
a rich man to enter the kingdom of God."

21. No doubt the claim was an honest one. Rabbinical teachers assumed that men were able to fulfill their obligations to the whole law.

22. Jesus issued an invitation to his questioner to become a disciple, imposing only the condition that he **sell** his possessions, **distribute** the proceeds in charity, and thereby lay up for himself **treasure in heaven.** The Marcan detail that Jesus looked on the inquirer and loved him is omitted by Matthew as well as by Luke. The story lends itself to Luke's interest in showing that Jesus had a sympathy for the poor and that he regarded wealth as an evil thing (see Intro., p. 9). But it is by no means clear that Jesus always made the renunciation of worldly possessions a condition of discipleship. In this instance he saw that a man's concern for the things of this world had become an insuperable barrier to his wholehearted devotion to the cause of the kingdom of God. He was not able to serve God and mammon. He had to free himself from one loyalty before he could accept another.

23. Jesus' appeal was in vain. The **rich** man found that discipleship would cost him too much.

24-25. Here addressed to the rich man; in Mark to the disciples, for the rich man had departed. Some interpreters have tried to weaken the rigor of Jesus' words by

necessarily express a low view of human nature. It is a realistic view; but because God has visited man in Jesus Christ and still visits man in the Holy Spirit, it is hope-filled view. It rebukes our notion that by moving the furniture we can change the soul:

They constantly try to escape
From the darkness outside and within
By dreaming of systems so perfect that no one will
  need to be good.
But the man that is will shadow
The man that pretends to be.[2]

Only by the help of God, coming near in the mercy of Christ, can man hope to be good; but God does come. Man can recognize goodness when it is presented, and he can welcome it; but he cannot invent or control it, and if unaided by God, he will always reel back into a lower life.

God is good: that is what we wish to know, and all we need to know. Our wars and hates, our greeds and griefs are not the final word. God will not refuse our uplifted face, even though our will be crumbling clay. He will not let us forget him, for he has made us for himself. Why *do* we call Jesus good? We do, despite the fact that his goodness always rebukes our pretended goodness. "That one Face, far from vanish, rather grows."[3] Why *do* we call him good? Only God is good, yet men will always call Jesus good. Who then is Jesus?

25-27. ***Impossible with Man, Possible with God.***—The proposals that have been offered to emend vs. 25 are far more ingenious than convincing. The word **camel** could be, but probably is not, a misreading for the word

[2] T. S. Eliot, *The Rock* (New York: Harcourt, Brace & Co.; London: Faber & Faber, 1934). Used by permission.

[3] Robert Browning, *Dramatis Personae,* "Epilogue."

26 And they that heard *it* said, Who then can be saved?

27 And he said, The things which are impossible with men are possible with God.

28 Then Peter said, Lo, we have left all, and followed thee.

26 Those who heard it said, "Then who
can be saved?" 27 But he said, "What is im-
possible with men is possible with God."
28 And Peter said, "Lo, we have left our

claiming that the **needle's eye** was the name of a small gate in the wall that surrounded the city of Jerusalem or that **camel** is a mistake in the Greek text for a word that means "rope" or "cable." Neither suggestion carries conviction.

26. Here the incredulous question of the whole group that was listening to Jesus; in Mark the words of the disciples.

27. A paraphrase of Mark's version. The salvation of a rich man is a miracle that only God's power can accomplish.

3. Reward of Renunciation (18:28-30=Mark 10:28-30)

28. Peter is again the spokesman for the disciples. They had fulfilled the condition that the rich man had refused to accept. **Our homes:** Inferior MSS read **all,** a harmonization of the text of Luke with Mark.

"rope"; or to cite another similar suggestion, **eye of the needle** could conceivably, but probably does not, mean the postern door through which a camel could be pushed. Why should we thus accuse Jesus of a drably literal mind, or show ourselves bereft of imagination? He was unafraid of hyperbole. He delighted in dramatic metaphor. His speech was gigantesque, and therefore unforgettable. This verse means just what it says—that riches or any other temptation represent an antagonism too strong for mere human power. Sharply Jesus told that fact, and required us to confront it.

The retort of the disciples is right and proper. For every man must ask of human helplessness, **Then who can be saved?** Man alone cannot cleanse the past or defeat death. Man alone cannot will to live in pure motive: his will itself is impure. Man alone cannot build dykes strong enough to contain the flood of demonic power that suddenly besets life. Man alone cannot overcome the temptation of riches. What we call progress is not progress, for manifestly it poses new threats of worse disasters, as witness atomic power. Man alone is weakness: realistic minds will not shy away from plain facts. But this confession does not brand man a straw on a stream. It marks him a creature required by his very nature to live with God.

Thus vs. 27, though neglected, is actually the charter of man's salvation. Manson has rightly written:

> We see here that, though Jesus appealed to human volition, he did not isolate that volition or regard it apart from energies and powers which God puts forth in order to bring His Kingdom to pass. A principle, recognized as supernatural though still ethical, enters into and operates upon the human will, so as to make it the instrument of God's purpose.[4]

But Manson sees that "principle" is hardly the right word; for he adds that this verse is a connecting link between Gospels and epistles, between "Jesus' teaching and the Pauline conception of the 'Spirit.' "[5] God can cleanse the past, overcome death, and enter the impure will to redeem and empower its energies. If there is a dark shaft below human life from which foulness rises, there is a shaft above human life down which heaven's grace pours. Thus man's life is fulfilled in God, who by Christ and his Spirit has come to make perfect man's weakness.

28-30. ***The Reward of Renunciation.***—It has become a fashion to brand **Peter** here as a brashly selfish man hankering for an instant and earthly reward. But such an interpretation is false to the climate of this Gospel. We shall be wise to remember that Luke wrote upward of two generations after Jesus, when the church was in the throes of persecution. Clearly Luke may here be bringing comfort to a hard-pressed church, by means of a saying of Jesus found in the sources. The apostles and the early church *had* met the conditions that Jesus levied on the rich young ruler. Heroically they *had* sacrificed goods and left home to follow Jesus. Our comfortable discipleship is not impressive by comparison.

Therefore they had found a present reward. There was a sharing of goods in the early

[4] *Gospel of Luke,* p. 206.

[5] *Ibid.,* pp. 206-7.

29 And he said unto them, Verily I say
unto you, There is no man that hath left
house, or parents, or brethren, or wife, or
children, for the kingdom of God's sake,
30 Who shall not receive manifold more
in this present time, and in the world to
come life everlasting.
31 ¶ Then he took *unto him* the twelve,
and said unto them, Behold, we go up to
Jerusalem, and all things that are written

homes and followed you." 29 And he said
to them, "Truly, I say to you, there is no
man who has left house or wife or brothers
or parents or children, for the sake of the
kingdom of God, 30 who will not re-
ceive manifold more in this time, and in
the age to come eternal life."
31 And taking the twelve, he said to
them, "Behold, we are going up to Jeru-

29-30. Many interpreters believe that **in this time, and . . . eternal life** is an expansion of the original saying. Jesus had promised his disciples that they would be rewarded many times over **in the age to come** for any sacrifices they had been compelled to make **in this time.** As the saying stands in Mark (and in Luke's abbreviated form) it assures them that they will be more than compensated in this life also. They will share in the common property of the Christian community (Acts 4:32) and become part of its great fellowship. Luke adds **wife** to Mark's list, omits "sisters," reads **parents** for "mother or father," and omits "lands." **For the sake of the kingdom of God:** A substitution for Mark's "for my sake and for the gospel," but one that might be justified as primitive if we were able to recover the original form of the saying.

4. Jesus Again Predicts His Passion (18:31-34=Mark 10:32-34)

In Mark this is Jesus' third prediction of his passion. In Luke it is separated from the first two (9:22, 44) by the great block of non-Marcan material (9:51–18:14), and other predictions have been added (12:50; 13:33; 17:25) to make this the sixth.

31. Luke has abbreviated Mark and has added the statement that the events of the Passion had been predicted by Scripture (cf. 9:51*a*; 22:37; 24:26-27, 44-46).

---

church: no disciple lacked for food or friendly shelter. There was a genuine fellowship in the early church: that may be the meaning of Mark's "houses and brothers and sisters and mothers," etc. (Mark 10:30; cf. Matt. 12:49). This love within the early church was so glowing in the ministries of the Spirit that its joy was **manifold more in this present time** than any worldly good sacrificed. It is worth noting that Christian faith has present gains. The worldling sacrifices his higher life, and finds that thereby his present world is cankered; the Christian sacrifices this world for his higher life, and finds that what remains to him of this world is irradiated and fulfilled. For the followers of Jesus heaven is not postponed: they have sure foretaste in this present world.

But the reward is not confined to this world. There is always an eschatological stress in the teaching of Jesus. Always he heard a "trumpet" sound "from the hid battlements of Eternity."[6] He told us that "heaven lies about us" not only "in our infancy,"[7] but always; and that every word and act of this life is determining destiny; cf. 22:28-30. Penitence on earth quickens joy in heaven (15:7); real renunciation on earth prepares an eternal home in the messianic kingdom.

31-34. ***Prediction of the Passion and Death.***—This is the sixth such prediction in Luke (see Exeg.). It lacks the drama of the corresponding passage in Mark 10:32-34, but has values of its own. Why are the Gospels punctuated by these predictions? Because they are the very core of the gospel. The events here enumerated compose the great Event of history. Good news is always an event or the announcement of an event. A neighbor running into our house to tell us of some good fortune for us would say, "The most wonderful thing has happened!" In these verses Luke reminds us that in the passion, death, and resurrection of Jesus all truth finds its interpretation and home, all history is explained and fulfilled, all life in its suffering and sin is gathered into eternal Grace. Here we have a summary of the preaching of the early church, and of true preaching in any age.

Thus vs. 31 tells of the fulfillment of history. The death of Jesus was not another tragedy. It is far more than the noblest of tragedies. Otherwise it would have been worst tragedy.

[6] Francis Thompson, "The Hound of Heaven."

[7] Wordsworth, "Ode on Intimations of Immortality," st. v.

by the prophets concerning the Son of man shall be accomplished.

32 For he shall be delivered unto the Gentiles, and shall be mocked, and spitefully entreated, and spitted on:

33 And they shall scourge *him*, and put him to death; and the third day he shall rise again.

34 And they understood none of these things: and this saying was hid from them, neither knew they the things which were spoken.

35 ¶ And it came to pass, that as he was come nigh unto Jericho, a certain blind man sat by the wayside begging:

salem, and everything that is written of the Son of man by the prophets will be accom-
plished. 32 For he will be delivered to the
Gentiles, and will be mocked and shame-
fully treated and spit upon; 33 they will
scourge him and kill him, and on the third
day he will rise." 34 But they understood
none of these things; this saying was hid
from them, and they did not grasp what
was said.

35 As he drew near to Jericho, a blind man was sitting by the roadside begging;

32-33. Luke omits the item from Mark's prediction that the Sanhedrin would condemn Jesus to death, since (in contrast to Mark 14:64*b*) his version of the passion narrative declares only that they **delivered** him to Pilate (22:66–23:1). **On the third day** instead of Mark's "after three days," as in 9:22.

34. Editorial comment. Note 9:45. The failure of the disciples to understand was in accordance with God's purpose. **This saying was hid from them** until the risen Christ should expound the meaning of Scripture (24:44-46).

T. Jesus in Jericho (18:35–19:27)

Luke omitted Mark's account of the request of the sons of Zebedee for preferential treatment in the messianic age (Mark 10:35-40), perhaps because he felt it cast some

---

No, his death together with his resurrection are the climax of man's story. In them prophecy is **accomplished.** Not even a building is explained until its fulfillment. The labor, pain, and apparent chaos when a foundation is dug, amid a medley of materials, seem senseless until walls begin to rise; and the walls enclose only a hollowness until all **shall be accomplished.** So with history. Ages prior to Christ are summed up in him; ages after him are explained as his light is shed upon them. Nothing escapes the eternal purpose of God. No unruliness of man can even cause his hand to shake, let alone defeat his plan.

Vss. 32-33 are the very sinew of Christian belief. Luke mentions for the first time the part played in the crucifixion by Roman authority: all nations are involved in the great denouement. The mocking and spite are important, not alone because the reminder of them would bring comfort to a persecuted church, not alone because they give assurance that Jesus genuinely shared the hurt of our life, but because they tell again that man's worst sin could not avail against divine grace. As for the **death,** God there came to grips with iniquity, and conquered in love-unto-death, so that his infinite sorrow becomes our cleansing. As for the words **rise again,** they tell of the breakthrough without which Calvary might have been merely tragic: Calvary without the Resurrection might have been defeat, while the Resurrection without Calvary would have given back to the world only a partial love.

Vs. 34 seems to tell why Luke omits Mark's account of the earthly ambitions of James and John (see Mark 10:35 ff.). **Hid from them** means that God withheld from the disciples the insight by which they might have understood the whole prediction. Thus Luke deals gently with the disciples' blindness. Surely he was right in this: the followers of Jesus did not and could not understand Calvary until he broke the bonds of the tomb. Only the risen Christ could interpret scripture (see 24:27). Only his finger could trace the ambiguous phrases of life and history, and win from them their heavenly meaning. The threefold repetition in vs. 34 is offset in a threefold grace: Calvary, the Resurrection, and Pentecost.

35-43. ***The Blind Beggar.***—(See also Expos. on vss. 37, 43.) Most people are ready to help a blind man across the street. He cannot see the dangers. Perhaps his worse misfortune is that he cannot see the joys—the wonder of God's world or the faces of his friends. It is not strange that

36 And hearing the multitude pass by, he asked what it meant.

36 and hearing a multitude going by, he

---

reflection on their character. He also omitted a short chain of sayings (Mark 10:42*b*-45) at this point in order to use them (or a version of them) later (22:24-27).

1. Healing of a Blind Beggar (18:35-43=Mark 10:46-52)

35*a*. Jericho was a village in Judea near an important ford over the Jordan River which travelers used when they journeyed from Galilee to Jerusalem by way of Perea. The fact that Luke follows Mark in his geographical location of this incident makes it improbable that he had any special tradition of a journey to Jerusalem by the direct route through Samaria (see above, p. 181). **Drew near to** for Mark's "as he was leaving." A necessary alteration if the story of Zacchaeus that follows was also to be located at the same Judean center.

35*b*-39. A blind man: Mark had given him the name "Bartimaeus." **Son of David:** The only occasion in Mark and Luke on which **Jesus** is addressed by this messianic title.

---

blindness wins our sympathy, but it is doubly strange that inner blindness leaves us unmoved. We do not see danger: few men were aware of the dangers lurking beneath Victorian civilization, and fewer men realize what devastation waits on selfishness. We do not see the joys: it is evident that there was joy in Francis of Assisi, but most men are blind to it though it is closer than their elbow. As proof of blindness to what is important, an encyclopedia has 4½ pages on Jesus, 10 pages on jewelry, 11 pages on lace, and 17 pages on guns.

The tragedy of blindness is that it is usually beyond cure. The Emperor Hadrian accidentally shot a servant through the eyes, and in his regret offered the man any compensation, but the man could only say, "I wish I had my eyes." The fact holds of inner blindness, at least so far as human skill goes. Who can enlighten us? Not our fellow man, for he also is blind unless God has opened his eyes. But the blind man in the story was not utterly lost. He could remember: he had heard stories about Jesus. He could cry and keep crying, **Jesus, Son of David, have mercy on me!** He could act, flinging away his garment (Mark 10:50), running toward Jesus despite the handicap of blind eyes. He could have faith (**Son of David** was a messianic title), believing despite all doubts in the possibility of cure. Likewise, we are not utterly helpless in our inner blindness. But we cannot cure our own darkness.

Why are we not cured? Perhaps our pride prevents: it is hard for us to admit our helplessness, so we cling to the vain hope that our skill in science or psychiatry can be our oculist, even though the hope is vain unless our skill is directed by One greater than ourselves. Perhaps our lack of faith prevents: we do not believe mightily in a gracious World brooding over our world. So any hope of conversion is to us "too good to be true." If we were wise we would say, "Too good to be untrue." Perhaps conventional religion prevents: it is a troubling fact that Jesus' disciples (in an officious attempt to "own" Jesus?) tried to prevent the blind beggar from reaching their Master. Perhaps we do not really wish to be cured. When Jesus asked, **What wilt thou that I shall do unto thee?** did he mean, "Do you really wish full cure?" The man, if cured, would have to earn his living by a better way than begging; and besides, sight of eyes would be a curse unless his soul also was cleansed.

The blind beggar really wished cure, and seized the swiftly passing chance (see Expos., vs. 37). The Masefield poem is a transcript of the joy that any inwardly blind man can find in Christ:

> O glory of the lighted mind.
> How dead I'd been, how dumb, how blind.
> . . . .
> Out of the mist into the light,
> O blessèd gift of inner sight.[8]

The saints are sinners who have prayed for light. The saints are those who now do the simple things with a new power: their influence is out of all proportion to their physical actions because light streams through them. They have exchanged their ponderous volumes of Braille for one tiny book—the everliving story of Jesus. There was a man who argued to himself that if he could push a button to ring a doorbell, no more than pushing a button would be needed to light a light bulb. So he simply transferred the wires, only to find that it takes five hun-

[8] *The Everlasting Mercy.* Copyright 1911, by John Masefield. Used by permission of The Macmillan Company, The Society of Authors, and Dr. John Masefield, O.M.

37 And they told him, that Jesus of Nazareth passeth by.

38 And he cried, saying, Jesus, *thou* Son of David, have mercy on me.

39 And they which went before rebuked him, that he should hold his peace: but he cried so much the more, *Thou* Son of David, have mercy on me.

40 And Jesus stood, and commanded him to be brought unto him: and when he was come near, he asked him,

41 Saying, What wilt thou that I shall do unto thee? And he said, Lord, that I may receive my sight.

42 And Jesus said unto him, Receive thy sight: thy faith hath saved thee.

43 And immediately he received his sight, and followed him, glorifying God:

inquired what this meant. 37 They told
him, "Jesus of Nazareth is passing by."
38 And he cried, "Jesus, Son of David, have
mercy on me!" 39 And those who were in
front rebuked him, telling him to be silent;
but he cried out all the more, "Son of
David, have mercy on me!" 40 And Jesus
stopped, and commanded him to be
brought to him; and when he came near,
he asked him, 41 "What do you want me
to do for you?" He said, "Lord, let me re-
ceive my sight." 42 And Jesus said to him,
"Receive your sight; your faith has made
you well." 43 And immediately he received
his sight and followed him, glorifying God;

Both evangelists assume that his true nature is now an open secret, and the reader is prepared for the story of the triumphal entry into Jerusalem (19:29-40). **And they . . . rebuked him:** Because he was giving Jesus' messianic mission premature publicity? Or because Jesus' followers wished to spare their master any unnecessary annoyance?

40. Mark's graphic details are omitted.

41-43*a*. Lord for Mark's Semitism "Rabboni." **Your faith:** Trust in Jesus' wonder-working power. **Has made you well:** It is unlikely that the KJV is correct in translating

---

dred times as much power to light a bulb as to ring a bell. How much easier it is to make a noise (e.g., with a bomb) than to create a light! That latter requires more than human power!

37. ***Opportunity Is Passing.***—Christian faith has rightly found in these words an underscoring of the fact that opportunity does not stay. There is a far deeper meaning than the pagan world knew in such mottoes as *carpe diem* ("enjoy the present day"). In any realm the pattern of our experience is this: days and weeks of dull stretches when "nothing happens," and then suddenly the passing opportunity, the breakthrough of the light. Because life is an unstayed and unstayable movement the chance that is not seized is lost. In any realm: business or friendship or art—or redemption. As for business, other cities were offered the new automobile industry, but despised the chance because "horseless carriages" would never be more than an expensive fad. As for friendship, how often we have to say, "If only I had spoken at that moment!" As for art, the mind of a poet is often like a deserted temple, with no fire burning on the altar and no banners hung, when suddenly—the Presence. As for redemption, suppose the blind beggar had said, as any man is tempted to say, "Jesus can do nothing for me: I am blind."

The story seems to show that the beggar knew that the moment had come. He cried aloud, and ran toward Jesus despite all risk of injury. Then **Jesus stopped.** For if a man does seize the chance of pardon with its renewing life, all heaven is stopped in its course. The World beyond our world is brought to attention, in all its healing power, by one cry of human need. The moment when a man says, "There is no slick external way of being rid of my blindness; I must surrender to Christ in whatever pain of a new life," is no ordinary moment: it is *the* moment. The impulse to pray is not a sentimentalism: it is destiny. So the art of life is awareness of the luminous moment. God made us aware of our need so that we may seize the joy. For the day comes when we will hear people say, "Jesus is going by!" What then shall we do? He may pass our way again, but then again he may not: Jesus was going to Jerusalem to die when a beggar seized the golden chance.

43. ***Sight and Discipleship.***—Scholars are agreed that this verse is editorial. They mean that it is Luke's comment on the story. They are probably right. But that fact, far from lessening the impact of the words, enhances their meaning. For Luke and the early church thus testify to a discovered joy. They *had* been

and all the people, when they saw *it,* gave praise unto God.

19 And *Jesus* entered and passed through Jericho.

2 And, behold, *there was* a man named Zaccheus, which was the chief among the publicans, and he was rich.

and all the people, when they saw it, gave praise to God.

19 He entered Jericho and was passing through. 2 And there was a man named Zac-chae'us; he was a chief tax col-

hath saved thee. The verb is used in this instance without any religious connotations (cf. 8:48; contrast 7:50).

43b. Editorial comment.

2. Jesus and Zacchaeus (19:1-10)

Probably a variant of the story of Jesus and Levi (5:27-32=Mark 2:13-17). Both Levi and Zacchaeus belonged to the despised class of tax collectors. In both instances Jesus scandalized pious Jews by accepting the hospitality of one whom they regarded as an outcast. The implication is that both men became Jesus' disciples. And both stories lead up to a saying that is basically the same.

19:1. Editorial. Trees frequently bordered the approaches to an Oriental village, but they rarely grew along its narrow streets. Luke's setting for the Zacchaeus story is therefore not the happiest. Probably it had no specific geographical location in his source.

2. Zacchaeus corresponds to the Hebrew Zaccai (Ezra 2:9; Neh. 7:14). The name means "pure" or "righteous," but there is no reason to believe that Luke wished to stress

healed, they *had* followed, they *had* glorified God. There are immense implications in Luke's comment. Supposing a man did receive inner sight, would he use rightly his newly given power? If not, why should he be healed? It would almost be better that he should remain blind, for then he would do less harm. Sight requires a man to walk away from his beggar's mat into the discipleship of Christ, away from racial prejudice into a new life of brotherhood, away from his money standards into active good will. When the beggar decided to follow Jesus, Jesus was on his way to Calvary.

All the people . . . gave praise unto God: if that is Luke's comment, it reflects the joy of the early church. They had followed all the way at risk of martyrdom. They had followed unto tears, or what the world about them called tears; but the tears had cleansed their eyes so that they beheld wondrous things through sorrow. The church, with all its manifest failures, has in its midst a spring of gladness. It keeps faith when the world despairs, and hopes in an assurance better than hope when other men have nought but foreboding, and can see a World beyond our world when the crowd can see only gathering shadows. Editorial comment? Call it Luke's gladness because he had been healed of inner blindness. In the Sinaitic MS of the Gospels, at the end of Luke's Gospel, the title is repeated—"Glad Tidings: According to Luke."

19:1-10. *The Guest in the House.*—In Jerome K. Jerome's *The Third Floor Back* a Stranger from the streets enters a boardinghouse in London to find his poor lodging in the only room that is vacant. As he moves in and out among the guests, an extraordinary change gradually comes over them. Suspicion, resentment, covetousness, false pride, lust, the very drab commonplaceness of weary and unillumined life disappear like fog in the morning sun, until the way back to what they had been is barred to them; only the way ahead is open.

So runs this dramatic story of Zacchaeus. Straight across his life one day a line was drawn. Rumor for him turned into fact: face to face he met Jesus of Nazareth. The whole impact of the gospel was in that meeting. It redeemed the past, transformed the present, and redirected the future. Luke alone records it for us, with a certain picturesqueness of detail, verse by verse, that fixes it indelibly in the memory. As the account runs swiftly on to the familiar saying in vs. 10, Paul's despairing cry (Rom. 7:24) finds its answer. A man "is in Christ . . . a new creation" (II Cor. 5:17). We know that there is an end; and we know with equal knowledge that the end is God's beginning. Between light and darkness (18:35-43), between life and death (vs. 8), **Jesus had entered and passed through Jericho.**

1. *A Tale of Two Cities.*—Jericho, the city of palms (Deut. 34:3, *et passim*), was a veritable

its etymology. According to the dubious testimony of the Clementine Homilies (III. 63), **Zacchaeus** later became bishop of Caesarea. **A chief tax collector:** A title that would be suitable for an official at such an important frontier post as Jericho, but one that has not yet been discovered in earlier Greek literature.

Eden (for its history read Josh. 2:1–7:26; I Kings 16:34; II Kings 2:19-22; II Chr. 28:9-16). There was a day when Mark Antony had presented it as a gift to Cleopatra, with Arabia thrown in, as if both were but the merest trifle for such a mistress.[9] Here Herod the Great had died, ordering with his last breath the slaughter of its foremost Jewish citizens, that there might be some to mourn at his passing. Here his son Archelaus had rebuilt for himself the magnificent palace, set in the most sumptuous of gardens. In the air lingered the perfume of roses (Ecclus. 24:14) and of balsam. On the streets publicans and courtiers rubbed shoulders with fanatics and wandering anchorites, with traders moving in along the great caravan route from the North and the East, with robbers and soldiers, with priests from Jerusalem and pilgrims on their way up to the yearly festivals; while now and then, in the stillness of some morning, so legend has it, the strains of temple music from Mount Moriah were borne along on the breeze in faint echoes, like "the distant sound of many waters" under the glorious summer sky.[1]

In the tiny village of squatters' huts, nestled on the still fertile plain among the scattered ruins, there is today no ghost of a whisper left of the splendor and the busy traffic of those years. Only the loneliness now and the desolation that Zacchaeus had already come to know in his heart. How little in accord with its surroundings the inmost self of a man may be! Jericho was no Eden for him; it was a wilderness. What others might well have called their paradise was his torment. Always is it true that

> The mind is its own place, and in itself
> Can make a heaven of hell, a hell of heaven.[2]

There in the motley crowd, his was the wretchedness of a man estranged from his high inheritance (vs. 9), from God and from himself. Nothing much was left him now but the futile attempt, day after dreary day, somehow to make up with all he could lay his hands on for what seemed so irretrievably lost—peace, and dignity, and self-respect.

[9] W. M. Thomson, *The Land and the Book* (New York: Harper & Bros., 1880), I, 375-89.

[1] Alfred Edersheim, *The Life and Times of Jesus the Messiah* (8th ed.; New York: Longmans, Green & Co., 1896), II, 349-55.

[2] Milton, *Paradise Lost*, Bk. I.

But

> Once to every man and nation comes the moment to decide,
> In the strife of Truth with Falsehood, for the good or evil side.[3]

For Zacchaeus it was a moment that made all the difference in the world. Jericho was no longer what it had been. There was another way now to meet enmity. Another mark had been set. There was the prize of a higher calling, of which it had been said on a hill in Galilee, "Blessed are they which do hunger and thirst after righteousness: for they shall be filled" (Matt. 5:6). It was of such a one that James Thomson the Younger wrote in "William Blake":

> He came to the desert of London town,
> Gray miles long;
> He wandered up and he wandered down,
> Singing a quiet song.

2. *What Does Your Life Add Up To?*—And there was a man named Zacchaeus. But what is there in a name? Much, every way. Paul is still for sons, and Nero for dogs. Jude it may be when a child is born, but not Judas. The prayers of a mother, tender memories of deep affection, the luster that many a stalwart soul has shed on human life—all these may be in a name, unless a man betrays it and turns it into a sneer. Zacchaeus the pure, Zacchaeus the righteous. Luke, who is sparing enough in his use of names, was at least not unaware of the incongruity. Zacchaeus the just, the good, the innocent—**chief among the publicans.** Apparently in the course of the years he had become a kind of undercommissioner of the customs, and responsible for the hated Roman tax, imposed not only on the balsam, for which Jericho was famous—still sold there in modern times, marked "Balm of Gilead"!—but as well on all the costly imports from Damascus and Arabia. The result was that in the rough judgment of his countrymen he was not to be rated among decent people, but with cutthroats and robbers, with adulterers and brothelkeepers; an informer, a traitor both to his nation and to its ancient faith in the one invisible God. And he had little enough to show for it. What but this, **and he was rich?** It reads tersely, like an epitaph (cf. 18:23). There is either death at

[3] James Russell Lowell, "The Present Crisis," st. v.

3 And he sought to see Jesus who he was; and could not for the press, because he was little of stature.
4 And he ran before, and climbed up into a sycamore tree to see him; for he was to pass that *way*.

lector, and rich. 3 And he sought to see who Jesus was, but could not, on account of the crowd, because he was small of stature. 4 So he ran on ahead and climbed up into a sycamore tree to see him, for he was

---

3-4. Details with a light touch of humor. **A sycamore tree:** A type of wild fig tree, known as the fig mulberry (cf. Amos 7:14).

---

the end of such a sentence, or sheer amazement at some reversal. So does life add itself up and come to a full stop; except God himself changes the punctuation. Of Bartimaeus it might have been written, "And he was blind." Of Lazarus, "And he was a beggar." Of Naaman, "And he was a leper." It is said of Bismarck, the "man of iron," that hour after hour at the end of the days he would sit vacant-eyed and alone by the hearth, throwing cones on the fire. With God around there need be no periods, only question marks—those unmeasured possibilities in every life that now and then turn into exclamation points, "And he was a Samaritan" (17:16)! Sometimes they turn into commas, with such a sequel as this.

3-4. ***Man in Search of God.***—**He sought to see . . . Jesus.** Why? Surely there were stories enough going the rounds to stir anybody's curiosity. But Jesus knew how to deal with curiosity (23:8-9). Was it conscience? Or was it the hunger that never had been appeased? Perhaps he wanted to be treated just once like a human being. They were saying everywhere, "This man receiveth sinners, and eateth with them" (15:2). Whatever the motive was, he seemed at first to meet with nothing but obstacles. There was the fact that he himself—or was it Jesus?—**was small of stature.** And there was the crowd that jostled him and would have brushed him aside—the crowd, large or small, which is so often a hindrance in every generation. Were they then as now the "righteous" who had no thought of repentance, the "whole" who had no need of a physician (5:31-32)? Men who scoffed and were angry; others who were sullen because they were half convinced? Sermon tasters, "rice" Christians, miracle seekers? It is hard to give only a literal meaning to those words, **but could not, on account of the crowd.** The streets of Jericho were not the likeliest place that day for a man who would take too serious a view of the odds. There was something in the very nature of the case that seemed almost ridiculous. Zacchaeus of all people, and nothing for it in the hurly-burly of the throng but the spreading branches of a **sycamore tree:** because, so he had been told, Jesus of Nazareth **was to pass that way.** Was there not somewhere a promise, "If . . . with all thy heart . . ." (Deut. 4:29)?

He sought to see who Jesus was. He wanted to know him by sight, never dreaming what would come of it. Loss (vs. 8)? Some years after, a moody Jew of Tarsus, so runs the story, stood by as the first Christian martyr fell under a hail of stones. The Jew's name was Saul, and wonderingly that day he watched the peace he had never been able to win for himself spread over Stephen's face like the dawn. Later still, near Damascus, as he was breathing out threats and slaughter against this hateful sect that seemed to him so wrong and yet so happy, the while he himself was so right and yet so miserable, there blazed a sudden glory into his eyes that made the noon seem dark. Blinded, he got to his feet, and a long and painful pilgrimage to the ends of the earth began. The rest—was loss (Gal. 2:20; Phil. 3:7-8). Gain? In John Drinkwater's play *A Man's House* is pictured scene by scene the breaking up of an old business firm in Jerusalem under the silent but mighty impact of this teacher from Nazareth and his outlandish doctrines. The senior partner, well along in years, lingers by a window, looking wistfully out on the streets, as a procession begins to form on the way to Golgotha. The son, back in the shadows, keeps turning page after page of the ledger, feverishly, gazing with set lips at the ruin written there. **To see Jesus**—no matter what may come of it! To see him still in the faces of people! One day perhaps to hear him say his "inasmuch," and not know "when" (Matt. 25:44)—because you never deliberately shouldered your way past anybody, or walked on indifferently, not caring what it was that called to you from the lives there within reach. To have his face remind you of all faces, and not be compelled to stand looking at him, trying to remember, stammering out "When saw I thee?" You will not need to worry then if he seems vaguely like someone you knew!

5 And when Jesus came to the place, he looked up, and saw him, and said unto him, Zaccheus, make haste, and come down; for to-day I must abide at thy house.

to pass that way. 5 And when Jesus came to the place, he looked up and said to him, "Zac-chae'us, make haste and come down;

5. The story is not concerned with the question: How did Jesus know the tax collector's name? In some painfully prosaic exegesis the verse is regarded as an instance of Jesus' omniscience or as evidence of careful reconnaissance by his disciples (Matt. 10:11).

5. *God in Search of Man.*—It is not primarily the issue of man's search, however, with which we have to do in this verse and the verses that follow; rather, and first, it is the issue of God's. "When first I knew Thee," wrote Augustine, "Thou didst raise me up, that I might see there was somewhat for me to see, though as yet I was not fit to see it."[4] Only by God's finding could the human soul even begin its search. In that lies the unique significance of Jesus Christ for human history (vs. 10; cf. 4:18-27). Along the ancient line of march toward the Unseen, every other trustworthy religious leader the world has ever known has taken his place among men as just another of the trudging millions—guides, indeed, but travelers too.[5] Jesus alone had the temerity to suggest that he was moving in the other direction (John 14:9). Of this the years as they passed seemed to become increasingly sure. There was One who was high and lifted up; but now with the strange and humble story of a shepherd on his lips. It was not the kind of God men were looking for, and they killed him—this blasphemer who went casting about for publicans, dragging in the dust the long glory of their King of kings. Yet nobody who has ever heard the sound of those feet has been quite able to rid himself of the haunting realization that if they mean anything at all, they mean that God is on the road. For the difference he made, set Caliban's soliloquy on the powers of the air—many a man's thought of God!—in Shakespeare's *Tempest*[6] by the side of Sidney Lanier's poem, "A Ballad of Trees and the Master." There are times when we talk about finding God in Christ. Infinitely truer is it that in him God finds us. We hardly dare lose sight of that, with the poor, fitful search we make, that cannot rightly be called a search, little more than a groping discontent, and a distant, formal, weary doffing of the hat. If anything ever happens in our lives, it will happen because wherever we hide ourselves, in what dark corner, there is a Love that whispers and prods about there with its wounded hands: walking yonder on the streets, hungry, and someone yesterday gave him food; thirsty, and someone gave him drink; a stranger, and someone took him in.

[4] *Confessions* VII. 10.

[5] Certain selections from earlier books by Paul Scherer have on occasion been incorporated in chs. 19-24. Through the kindness of Harper and Bros., permission has been granted for the use of this material.

[6] Act II, scene 2.

5. ***The Man Who Invited Himself.*—And when Jesus came to the place, he looked up and said. . . .** Nothing could have been farther from Zacchaeus' mind than that this prophet from Galilee should choose to stay the day at his home. Among all the priests of the temple "courses," among all the well-to-do and respected citizens, who was he to provide the hospitality he must have yearned to offer? Never in the world would he have summed up enough courage to extend such an invitation. Rather, with Jacob of old would he have said, "I am not worthy of the least of all the mercies, and of all the truth, which thou hast showed unto thy servant" (Gen. 32:10); or with the centurion, "Lord, . . . I am not worthy that thou shouldest enter under my roof" (7:6); or with the prodigal, memorizing his little speech, "I . . . am no more worthy to be called thy son" (15:19, 21). "Not worthy." "Not worthy." How like a refrain it sounds! "In thy sight." "In thy sight." All through Scripture. Until he whom the very search invites becomes himself the host. "Hurry and come down," as one would say in friendliest fashion. "Before they call, I will answer" (Isa. 65:24). "God is always courteous," said Francis of Assisi, "and does not invade the privacy of the human soul." But he knows where welcome waits.

5. *Invitation or Challenge?*—When Jesus wanted a disciple, he did not say, "Come and get something," or "Look, I have this to give you." He made remarkably few promises. There was much to be done, and rarely a word about anything to be had. There was not so much a bounty to be grasped as a hurdle to be leaped and a road to be traveled.

We have fallen too often into the habit of commending the Christian religion for its benefits. We have said to the life around us, as Moses once said to Hobab, "Come thou with

6 And he made haste, and came down, and received him joyfully.
7 And when they saw *it,* they all murmured, saying, That he was gone to be guest with a man that is a sinner.

for I must stay at your house today." 6 So
he made haste and came down, and received him joyfully. 7 And when they saw
it they all murmured, "He has gone in to be the guest of a man who is a sinner."

6-7. Zacchaeus . . . received him joyfully (cf. Levi, who made Jesus "a great feast" in his house [5:29]).

us, and we will do thee good." And Hobab said, "I will not go" (Num. 10:29, 30). There is that in human nature, from childhood to maturity, which almost instinctively balks at everything, from carrots to theology, when its only recommendation is that one will find it to be very good for him. A few are even convinced that whatever is good for them is bound to have a bad taste.

Human life has to be challenged. Moses said to Hobab in that ancient story, "Leave us not, . . . we are to encamp in the wilderness, and thou mayest be to us instead of eyes" (Num. 10:31). And Hobab was long remembered thereafter as one who got his things together and went along (Judg. 1:16; I Sam. 15:6). It takes more than a promise really to grip the human soul. It takes some brilliant prospect that can command its powers, take possession of them, have them, with a hold like God's (Mark 1:16-17; see also Expos. on vs. 8).

7-9. ***Man's Verdict and God's.***—Note what the people said, what Zacchaeus said, and what Jesus said. It was like being present at the Creation. "And the evening and the morning were the first day" (Gen. 1:5). They said "sinner." **Zacchaeus stood and said . . .**—but recall the apostle's word, "With me it is a very small thing that I should be judged of you, or of man's judgment; yea, I judge not mine own self. . . . He that judgeth me is the Lord" (I Cor. 4:3-4). **And Jesus said, . . . he also is a son of Abraham.** Is there not something more here than a reference to his status as a Jew? Is it not too that the outcast has entered again on his high inheritance? And are there not hints and overtones—the distant figure of one who "went out, not knowing whither he went" (Heb. 11:8-10), dissatisfied with the gods of Ur, the call of the one true God in his ears, thenceforth to be a pilgrim and a stranger on the earth, looking "for a city which hath foundations, whose builder and maker is God"?

7. ***What Do People Say About You?***—In II Cor. 6:8-10, Paul recounts the evil rumors his enemies have been spreading about him, and balances them with the facts. It was a deliberate campaign that was being carried on to undermine his influence; and he went about calmly matching all the slander with reality. **A man who is a sinner.** Sooner or later a man has to come to grips with the esteem or disesteem in which he is held. What people say about him is important. It can throw him out of any position he happens to occupy. It can hamstring a president, ruin an artist, hang an innocent victim of circumstance, unfrock a minister, or wreck a home. Bandying about careless estimates and idle verdicts may be appallingly serious. It may help to limit the sphere and narrow the horizons of somebody's life.

Yet it holds true that of all the factors which go to determine our place in the world, what people say about us is least significant. Half of it, likely enough, is not being said! Some of us have come to believe that we are the topic of conversation in thirteen homes and on seven street corners. We give ourselves great concern about what others will say of us next Thursday; and the humiliating and brutal fact is that come Thursday, they say nothing. Besides, when we have eliminated the half that is not being said, we can take a little comfort from the reflection that what is being said is said out of ignorance, out of the bias of either friendship or enmity.

Let us withdraw, then, from good report and evil report alike, and step inside, where we are saying something about ourselves, giving it the deference of our own belief, growing accustomed to the thought: puffing ourselves up or running ourselves down, until bit by bit the very stature of our souls responds to the constant suggestion. Nobody on earth can make us feel so bankrupt there as Christ will make us feel; nor can anyone so cover us over with his hand, and set us down, by the grace of God, above the stars among angels and archangels. Here is the eternal paradox of the Christian faith: it does our sufficient and lofty selves the indignity of sin; and it does these brief lives of ours on this distant planet all the honors of eternity! "It doth not yet appear . . ." (I John 3:2).

7. ***God Out of Bounds.***—**And when they saw it, they all murmured.** There was a low grumbling back and forth through the whole crowd. Zacchaeus was a **sinner**—as who is not? But to

8 And Zaccheus stood, and said unto the Lord; Behold, Lord, the half of my goods I give to the poor; and if I have taken any

8 And Zac-chae′us stood and said to the Lord, "Behold, Lord, the half of my goods

8. This resolution interrupts the sequence between vs. 7 and vss. 9-10, and is probably Luke's interpretation of the duties imposed on a tax collector by his new relationship to Jesus. It takes the place of the statement in Luke's version of the Levi story: "and he left everything, and rose and followed him" (5:28). **Behold . . . I give:** The present tense used for the future (cf. 7:27). If **Zacchaeus** could set apart **the half** of his goods for charitable purposes and still have enough left over to make ample restitution to all

them he was a sinner *because* he was a publican, "a great sinner because a chief publican."[7] On any less superficial basis their grumbling was the greater sin (cf. 15:28-30). God's white was their black. The very purpose of the gospel was its offense. Its triumph was its shame. **To be the guest of** is an interesting word in Greek. It means to remove the packs from a beast of burden; or perhaps more correctly, to loosen one's garments, bound up for the journey. Whence the word that means an "inn" (2:7; 22:11). As Edersheim comments,[8] a strange hostelry, but no stranger than at Bethlehem, and not really so strange as the house of the chief Pharisee.

Nothing but the mystery of a blindness turned fatal can account for the fact that so many of those around our Lord never did seem to understand his habit of running off among queer people, into uncharted places, to do what needed doing. Paul rings the changes on it in Rom. 15:9-12, 16, 18. That the God of Israel might conceivably be interested in the Gentiles should have been no riddle to anybody who had ever allowed himself to wonder why he should have been interested in Israel! Moses, the murderer, set out one day to explain it, and got tangled up in the most irrational sentence to be found anywhere in the Bible (Deut. 7:7-8). Before him were Abraham the liar, and Jacob the thief; after him, Rahab the harlot, Ruth the woman of Moab, and David the adulterer. Someone has suggested that the story of the prodigal son is really the story of God in swineland, always off the beaten track—because there is nobody at home but the elder brother? Queer people, odd times, and God! Surely it must mean something. Possibly a lesson in (*a*) the perils of complacence. By poll, ninety-one Americans out of every hundred, on their own representation, are honestly trying to lead a good life, though eighty-two admit that the struggle is not interfering much with either their happiness or their enjoyment. Eighteen feel that they have met with complete success in their efforts, twenty-eight are three quarters of the way along, thirty-two have got about halfway up the pinnacle of virtue, while only seven seem at the moment to be somewhat lower down! It may be we had better not settle back, even in the unexpected. This God of the unexpected may show himself in the familiar. Almost certainly in whatever it is that irks us, tramples all over our pride, upsets our prejudices. He will not be put to bed, wrapped up warm and tucked in, as was Michal's idol (I Sam. 19:13). And a lesson too no doubt in (*b*) the unreasonableness of despair. It is when something happens to make men think God has dropped them out of mind entirely that he most often breaks through the crust of self-reliance and begins to hold his serious conversations with the human soul. The worst times are his times. It would be a pity to miss him, or to suppose that any place is empty.

8. *What Shall We Have Therefore?*—(Cf. Matt. 19:27–20:16.) Zacchaeus does not enter on the Christian life by trying to negotiate a contract. Of course there are certain normal issues which one may expect (Gal. 6:7).

> In the world of the spirit . . . an eternal divine order prevails, here it does not rain both upon the just and upon the unjust, here the sun does not shine both upon the good and upon the evil, here it holds good that only he who works gets the bread, only he who was in anguish finds repose, only he who descends into the underworld rescues the beloved, only he who draws the knife gets Isaac.[9]

H. G. Wells used to wish we could believe in God without having anything at all come of it—peace or power or pearly gates. If only we could be righteous and not be paid for being righteous; or wicked, and not be punished for being wicked. If only we could be good—for nothing! And nobody can! What kind of nonsense is it to suggest that the sowing is vitiated by

[7] A. B. Bruce, "The Synoptic Gospels," *The Expositor's Greek Testament* (New York: Dodd, Mead & Co., 1910), *ad loc.*

[8] *Life and Times of Jesus the Messiah*, II, 354.

[9] Sören Kierkegaard, *Fear and Trembling*, tr. Walter Lowrie (Princeton: Princeton University Press, 1941), p. 33.

thing from any man by false accusation, I restore *him* fourfold.

9 And Jesus said unto him, This day is salvation come to this house, forasmuch as he also is a son of Abraham.

10 For the Son of man is come to seek and to save that which was lost.

I give to the poor; and if I have defrauded any one of anything, I restore it fourfold."
9 And Jesus said to him, "Today salvation has come to this house, since he also is a
son of Abraham. 10 For the Son of man
came to seek and to save the lost."

---

whom he had **defrauded,** his exactions could not have been serious; but it would be unfair to Luke to stress the mathematics of the verse. **Fourfold:** The restitution required by the Roman law for the theft (cf. also Exod. 22:1: "If a man shall steal . . . a sheep, and kill it, or sell it; he shall restore . . . four sheep for a sheep").

9. Jesus' commentary on the protests of the bystanders quoted in vs. 7 rather than his response to Zacchaeus' pledge in vs. 8. Although a despised tax collector, a "sinner" in the eyes of the pious, Zacchaeus was still a Jew—**a son of Abraham** (cf. 13:16)—and a fitting object of his care. It is strange that the text should read **to him**, for in what follows, Zacchaeus is referred to in the third person. Some O.L. MSS and some modern editors omit the phrase. Some interpreters translate "concerning him." **Salvation:** Vouched for by Jesus' acceptance of the tax collector's hospitality. **This house,** i.e., household. The solidarity of the family is taken for granted.

10. Note Ezek. 34:16. **The Son of man** corresponds to the "I" of the saying in 5:32. A variant of this verse has been inserted into the Gospel of Matthew as 18:11 by Codex Bezae and many later MSS. Other variants have been introduced into various MSS of Luke after 9:55 (see Exeg., *ad loc.*).

---

the harvest? Virtue has its rewards, and friendship has its benefits; but the benefits do not explain the friendship, and the rewards do not account for the virtue. What puzzled the author of the book of Job was that something so often seemed to go wrong. The natural sequence of piety and prosperity came apart so dreadfully, and who could say why? (Read Ps. 1:1-3, with 18:31-33 as a footnote on it; see also Expos. on vss. 17, 19, 24; 21:12-19.)

The point is that the issues arrive in parentheses. There is something you will never be without this Christ. Watch some gaunt and naked bush in the park. Under warm skies it seems suddenly to come alive. Little by little it begins to swell with the mysterious tide of the spring. Stem and twig and tendril, it pushes out one tiny bud after another. And it will keep on crowding them with life until they break open into a thousand delicate blossoms—a very burst of flame there by the side of the road (John 15:5). Call it fulfillment if you like. It is the filling full of all there is inside that is worth fulfilling, until that "intolerable compliment" which God has paid us all begins to find its way out through us into human life (John 15:12). It is a burden, living with a love like his in a world like ours, never think it anything less; but such a burden as sails are to a ship, or wings to a bird! With no fulfillment for anybody short of taking it on.

"Zacchaeus," said the carpenter gently, "what did you see that made you desire this peace?"

"Good master—I saw—mirrored in your eyes—the face of the Zacchaeus I was meant to be!"[1]

10. *What God Would Like to Do.*—Suppose we were to page through the N.T. and ask Jesus himself what it is all about. Nine or ten times he says in very simple words—most of them a child could understand—what it is he has come to do. "I am come . . . ," or "I came into the world . . . ," or **the Son of man came.** . . . And we rarely pay much attention. We would rather rub our own ideas together than to find out what his might happen to be. He did not set out to be ministered unto. It was not his purpose to destroy. He wanted to fulfill. He was born, as he told Pontius Pilate, so that the truth of God might have somebody to bear it witness. He was come to be a light in the world's darkness. Of course the light would be hard on some. Light always is. But there were others—poor folk who did not already think they knew it all; they just knew they were lost without him. These he came to **save.** "I am come that they might have life, and that they might have it more abundantly" (John 10:10). And that in a day when the literate and leisured classes in Greece and Italy were making away with themselves quite earnestly, when there were very

[1] Lloyd C. Douglas, "The Mirror," *The American Pulpit Series* (New York and Nashville: Abingdon-Cokesbury Press, 1945), Book II, p. 74.

11 And as they heard these things, he added and spake a parable, because he was nigh to Jerusalem, and because they

11 As they heard these things, he proceeded to tell a parable, because he was

3. Parable of the Pounds (19:11-27)

A comparison of this with the parable of the talents in Matt. 25:14-30 makes it possible to reconstruct its complex history with a considerable degree of confidence. Some such narrative as the following was basic to both versions: A man entrusted sums of money to three slaves and went off on a journey. On his return he demanded an account of their stewardship. Two of the slaves had greatly increased their capital and were commended. The third had carefully hoarded his money for fear of losing it and incurring his master's anger. He returned it without any increment and was severely censured. At the very least he might have deposited it with bankers so that it could have earned interest. His trust was then taken from him and given to the slave who had employed his capital most profitably. In this original form the parable appears to have criticized some group among the Jews—perhaps the scribes—who had failed to make use of the trust that they had from God.

At an early date a proverbial saying ascribed to Jesus was appended to the parable: "To every one who has will more be given; but from him who has not, even what he has will be taken away." It may have been in this form that Matthew took over the story. Several additional verses (Matt. 25:21, 23, 30) interpret it as a warning that Christ at his second advent would demand a reckoning of his followers, rewarding the faithful and punishing the unfaithful. It was given further homiletic application in the lost Gospel According to the Hebrews (quoted by Eusebius. See J. M. Creed, *The Gospel According to St. Luke* [London: Macmillan & Co., 1930], p. 233). One slave wasted his trust with harlots and flute girls and was imprisoned; one hid it and was blamed; and the third multiplied it many times and was accepted.

It is possible that the parable stood in Q in its basic form, and was elaborated by Luke, but it is more likely that the evangelist found it already combined with quite disparate material (vss. 12, 14, 27, and a few scattered phrases) in some special source. The "man" of the original parable had been transformed into a "nobleman." His de-

epidemics of suicide, because those who were sure they understood most about it had got so that they wanted to spit at life! And Jesus took it up in his hands and made men want an eternity of it! Made them see, when they began to take it seriously, that nobody had to go on forever trying to win God's pardon for the wrong he had done, trying to earn his way into heaven by washing his hands and making broad his phylacteries and measuring how far a tailor might walk on the sabbath if he left his needle at home! With the promise and the fact of God's love and God's power, he went out where the ruins were; where there was no loyalty and no obedience, and only a little hope left, sometimes none, to struggle up through the crevices of a hundred broken commandments. There he lived and sought, with his terrible compassion—make no mistake about the adjective; and there he died. Could it be that we too are **lost;** at home, though farther away than any journey could take us: until we too begin to live where he lived—and die where he died? (Gal. 2:20; see also Expos. on ch. 15; Matt. 18:11.)

11. *Parable or Allegory?*—(See Exeg.) It is possible that except for certain historical references (vss. 12, 14, 15*a*, 27) Luke in his parable of the pounds preserves the original better than Matthew. Both are impressed by the eschatological context of the saying, as in this account is made immediately obvious by the introduction, **Because . . . because.** It must have seemed to some as they looked back that the consummation of God's purpose in human history, the establishment of his universal rule in righteousness and peace, was trembling on the very edge of the days (Acts 1:6). Commonly enough, this widespread expectation, so characteristic of Jesus' time, in which many feel that he himself shared, is dismissed as little more than a pathetic illusion, unfortunately not confined to the first century. Mistaken it was. Paul had enough trouble with it (II Thessalonians). Yet in a sense it was nearer the truth than our assumption that the coming of Christ has been indefinitely postponed.

There are scholars who tell us that everything Jesus said about the pure in heart, the

thought that the kingdom of God should immediately appear.

near to Jerusalem, and because they supposed that the kingdom of God was to ap-

parture had been to "a far country" to receive a grant of "kingly power." The "citizens" had hated him and had sent "an embassy" to protest his appointment. On his return, invested with new authority, he had rewarded his faithful servants with grants of power over "cities" and had given an order that those who had objected to his appointment as king should be brought before him and put to death. This new narrative matter was probably suggested by the actual experience of the Jews with Archelaus after the death of Herod the Great. Archelaus had sailed for Rome to ask Augustus to appoint him king in his father's stead (Josephus *Antiquities* XVII. 9. 1). His petition was vigorously opposed by an embassy of fifty Jews from Palestine (*ibid.,* XVII. 11. 1-2). Caesar gave him half his father's former kingdom with the title of ethnarch and the promise of kingly dignity if he should prove a virtuous ruler. No reference is made by Josephus to any revenge taken by Archelaus after his return on those who had opposed his ambitions, but such an act would have been characteristic of a member of the Herodian family.

The addition of this new matter transformed the original parable into an allegory. The gospel story teaches that the second coming of Christ will be delayed; that Christians have specific duties in the interim; and that there will be a last judgment with rewards and punishments. Christ is to go to heaven to receive his appointment as messianic king. The Jews hate him and do not wish him to rule over them. In his absence Christians will be entrusted with responsibilities. On his return he will reward his servants according to their diligence and will punish his enemies.

11. Editorial introduction. It is difficult to determine the audience that Luke supposes Jesus to have addressed. Was it the group in Zacchaeus' house? Had **they** been led to believe that **the kingdom of God was to appear immediately** by Jesus' statement in vs. 8? Or was it—and this is more probable—the company of the twelve to whom Jesus had spoken in 18:31-33? The **parable,** which in its present form teaches that the Parousia will be delayed, would itself provide Luke with the substance of his introduction. **Because he was near to Jerusalem:** Jericho was about seventeen miles from the capital.

poor in spirit, the merciful, the meek, had the end of the world in view; that everything he did located itself not so much on the flat level of man's existence here as down the long vistas of the kingdom that was to be: the fishermen he called, the multitudes he fed, the woman he forgave; the offending eye that had to be plucked out, the dead and the dying that had to be left, the fool with his barns, the man on the housetop who should not come down, the lightning out of the east, nation rising against nation in the beginning of sorrows. So much of it looks to the casual eye to be a kind of perpetual discounting of the life that now is in favor of some life that is to come.

Nothing could be farther from the truth. The N.T. is not for the glance that only skims the surface and then is off again to the billboards and the movies. The Gospels see everything against the background of that final consummation which will bring the labored story of human life to its close, and which waits from day to day only the hidden counsels of God. Indeed, from Genesis to Revelation the end is always there. It is the context of every book, the undertone of every hallelujah. But it is not there as catastrophe; certainly not as meaningless catastrophe, canceling every item of the past and present, reducing it all to dust and nothingness. It is there as victory—that victory which the death and resurrection of Jesus Christ celebrate and, to say the whole truth, inaugurate, in the very face of life's dismal word *finished.* It is there to solemnize every beginning, to read every chapter as if there were no other, to see in all days the last days, to turn history itself into one great now of judgment, to make of each moment a moment of high decision. Where, then, are our trivialities? Is there such a word? What has become of them? With death there, and the day of the Lord like a thief in the night (20:9-18; 21), and the cry that was made, "Behold, the bridegroom cometh," and the door that was shut (Matt. 25:6, 10), and the prince that returned (vs. 15)! Across the vast panorama of Matthew's Last Judgment (Matt. 25:31-46), when all nations are gathered before God's holy angels and the throne of Christ's glory, is thrown the gigantic shadow of—a cup of cold water! In

12 He said therefore, A certain noble-
man went into a far country to receive for
himself a kingdom, and to return.

pear immediately. 12 He said therefore, "A
nobleman went into a far country to receive

12. No doubt the original parable spoke of "a man going on a journey" (Matt. 25:14).

the verses before us the shadow is thrown by the investment we make, today and tomorrow, of the trust we have from the "nobleman [who] went into a far country" (vs. 12).

12-27. ***The Use of Opportunity.***—The word "opportunity" comes from two Latin words which mean "at the gate": something that lies at the very door. In every parable that Jesus uttered there was something—that lay at the door! Surely the first thing to do about it is to see it, recognize it, and call it by name. Miracles we could help to work in this harassed world stand around waiting to happen, knocking and ringing the bell; while how many trudge on through an existence that gets duller by the hour, simply because so much of it is so unspeakably selfish and insists on carefully hoarding what it has (vss. 20-21), keeps thinking of life as a possession instead of as an investment. No wonder there are people who find even such a reeling, bewildered age as ours tiresome! They yawn when you try to talk to them about it, are aware of nothing in it but the same old story—everybody for himself, in a world filled with squabbles and graft and lust and men dying. Multitudes must have felt that way when the Renaissance was going on. And during the Reformation. One can only be sorry for them. To be on top of the earth, with arms and legs that move, breathing the clean air of heaven in some great, creative period of the human epic, and to know nothing about it! Was Jesus thinking of the scribes in his own day? To eat and sleep and stretch and plod along through magnificent years of extremity and ruin, peril and birth; and to see nothing, hear nothing, sense nothing but Monday, Tuesday, Wednesday, Thursday, Friday, Saturday, Sunday, Monday, Tuesday—how can we ever get out of this?—Wednesday, Thursday, Friday, until you could scream. **Why then did you not put my money into the bank?**

Then to quit being indifferent to it, saying that it is none of our business. The kingdom of God *is* our business. Ours or nobody's! One more retreat, one more facing of life's peremptory challenge, with one more turning of the back: and we may well have on our hands a pagan, godless, hostile world, with terrified little bands of men and women and children peeping from their underground caves, to steal out silently into the light of day from their hidden, secret altars! It was so once. It can be so again. And to quit being afraid—as the spies were, when Moses sent them over into the Land of Promise; and they came back and said, all but two of them, that it was rich, flowing with milk and honey. "Nevertheless," they added, "the people be strong that dwell in the land, and the cities are walled, and very great. . . . And there we saw the giants, the sons of Anak, . . . and we were in our own sight as grasshoppers, and so we were in their sight" (Num. 13:17-33). That little bit of cowardice cost Israel forty years in the wilderness, until another generation could rise up and go in with courage to possess the land which the Lord their God had pledged them. There is a cowardice which cannot disguise itself as the holy fear of a righteous man (vs. 21). Was he indifferent or craven? Perhaps resentful. Did it just seem too much to ask, this **Trade with these till I come** (vs. 13)? Did he from the first despair of pleasing his lord, and so from the first give up? Into the future God's laws have to go. Brotherhood has to go into it, across all the lines of color and nation, of poverty and wealth. Do we despair of that or resent it? Patience has to go into the future, if there is to be any, and tolerance: not warmongering, on one side or the other. The love of God has to go into it, pushing on to its cross, forgiving the one who smites it, healing the wound of the one who wounds. Do we resent that? No use to try? **We do not want this man to reign over us** (vs. 14).

To take whatever it is that has been committed to us, and in the moment God has given, to press it home! Never to stop halfway, discouraged with what we think are the poor results. We adventure a step or two toward allaying anger and strife, until somebody comes along and calls us appeasers. We make gestures toward fair employment practices, toward economic justice in the community, toward political decency, until somebody frowns and wants to know what religion has to do with business, or why the church keeps trying to meddle with the state. Christianity is made to appear ridiculous when we stoop with God in our hands to clear some silly thing out of our way and find that we cannot even heft it an inch! Something somebody said once, or did once; and it stands

13 And he called his ten servants, and delivered them ten pounds, and said unto them, Occupy till I come.

kingly power[j] and then return. 13 Calling ten of his servants, he gave them ten pounds,[k] and said to them, 'Trade with

[j] Greek *a kingdom.*
[k] The mina, rendered here by *pound,* was equal to about twenty dollars.

---

13. Ten of his servants: A group selected from the large retinue that would serve an Oriental prince. But only three are mentioned in the subsequent narrative (as in Matthew). In Matthew's version the master entrusts his entire property to his servants; in Luke's, only a small part of it. **Ten pounds,** one to each servant. The prince wishes to test the abilities of each. The Greek "mina" was a coin with a silver content worth about twenty dollars. In Matthew's version much larger sums are involved (a "talent"

---

there to this day in the road, grinning at us, holding us cowed. The faith that "subdued kingdoms, wrought righteousness, obtained promises, stopped the mouths of lions, quenched the violence of fire, escaped the edge of the sword, . . . waxed valiant in fight, turned to flight the armies of the aliens" (Heb. 11:33-34)—this faith come to that!

> Take my life, and let it be
> Consecrated, Lord, to thee.[2]

13. ***Having then Gifts . . .***—(Cf. Rom. 12:6 ff.) **Ten servants . . . ten pounds.** In Matthew one servant is given five talents, another two, and still another one (see Exeg. above). In this parable it is not the differences in endowment which come into view, but rather the fidelity and ability of each trustee, the rewards being distributed in proportion to their proved capacities. Jesus is certainly not to be understood as making little of life's inequalities. He makes much of them (16:19-31). Some of them may be our own fault. Moreover, we could not even begin to picture the crazy horror, the hideous nightmare, of a life without any differences, where we had struck somehow a dead level of uniformity. Jesus saw poverty shuffling along in its rags, and wealth sweeping by in its purple and fine linen. He saw the cripple and the athlete, the white and the black. But he saw beyond, and what was beyond kept all of it from being just a meaningless accident. There were glimpses of "What in hell is the difference?" So little was final about being up and in; as little as there was about being down and out. What mattered was what you did with it.

The point here is that all of us do have something. And there is not too much honesty and fair dealing in that matter. How often do we spend our time bewailing what we lack, instead of eagerly making use of what we have? Our home, our friends, our brains are not like someone else's. He has money. He ought to get along. He has had the "breaks." But just look at us. And Christ says, "To every servant his pound." What he asks of us is some truthful appraisal. The man who counts up his liabilities and leaves out his assets is ready to go out of business as soon as he lays down his pen. There was a woman who for years had been an invalid before she realized that her quiet gallantry was winning back to Christ two of the lives she loved. We have to pitch into the scales what can be done by a woman sitting in a chair. And by a man in jail, John Bunyan; and before him, Paul. Always there is the plus sign in the mind of God. See, "Lord, your pound has made ten pounds more" (vs. 16).

God's most solemn commission is that we get ourselves, with what we have, straightly and swiftly under the weight of this desperate world. There is the basis on which his last judgment of life is rendered. His interest is not in our station. Not simply in the correctness or incorrectness of our theology. The good Samaritan was not of the orthodox party. Not even in our talents. But in this: one **pound . . . pounds.** He alone can fill in the blanks. H. H. Farmer writes of a soldier during World War I.

> He was set to hoe and keep clean a vast field of turnips. For months he worked alone in that one field at that one infinitely dull task. . . . But on the horizon there lay a line of hills; . . . long, rolling contours, so strong, so peaceful, so full of distance. He did not realize, he said, how much those hills were doing to make the drudgery, if not pleasant, then at least possible and unembittered, until for a period they were veiled in mist and he could not see them.[3]

So will this God in Christ show us, if we let him, not merely the dull "turnip fields" of our own poor (?) endowments, but the clear blue distance and lofty summits of his own steady pur-

[2] Frances R. Havergal.

[3] *The Healing Cross* (New York: Charles Scribner's Sons, 1939), p. 146.

14 But his citizens hated him, and sent a message after him, saying, We will not have this *man* to reign over us.

15 And it came to pass, that when he was returned, having received the kingdom, that he commanded these servants to be called unto him, to whom he had given the money, that he might know how much every man had gained by trading.

16 Then came the first, saying, Lord, thy pound hath gained ten pounds.

17 And he said unto him, Well, thou good servant: because thou hast been faith-

these till I come.' 14 But his citizens hated
him and sent an embassy after him, say-
ing, 'We do not want this man to reign
over us.' 15 When he returned, having re-
ceived the kingly power,[j] he commanded
these servants, to whom he had given the
money, to be called to him, that he might
know what they had gained by trading.
16 The first came before him, saying, 'Lord,
your pound has made ten pounds more.'
17 And he said to him, 'Well done, good

[j] Greek *a kingdom.*

---

was worth about a thousand dollars) and responsibilities were graded. The master already knew his servants' abilities. There is no counterpart in Luke to the (superfluous) preamble in Matt. 25:16-18.

14. Part of the matter added to the original parable.

15. Having received the kingly power: Also part of the secondary tradition.

16-17. In Matthew's version each of the industrious servants doubles his trust by trade; in Luke's, each makes a different profit. **You shall have authority over ten cities:**

---

pose, all our poverty and all our wealth set in "a new context" against that splendid horizon.

15. ***What Do You Make of Life?*—That he might know what they had gained.** The Christian religion is essentially creative. The man who says he can make nothing of life—it just goes around and around toward the hole in the sink—has to reckon with all the heroes of this faith, many of them nameless now, who have made a great deal of it. They were undoubtedly puzzled by it more than once; but for them Christianity was not the answer to a riddle. It was not just a shelter or just a race. There was something for it to handle. The joy that fairly sings its way along the pages of the N.T. did not come of resisting temptation: "O the depth of the riches both of the wisdom and knowledge of God!" (Rom. 11:33)—I won a victory over myself yesterday afternoon! It did not come of being good: "Blessed be the God and Father of our Lord Jesus Christ" (Eph. 1:3)—I forgave my enemy this morning! We sing when back of all the meaninglessness there is for us—meaning (cf. W. H. Auden's Christmas oratorio, the lines beginning, "Levers nudge the aching wrist"[4]). We sing when we stand with God against some darkness or some void and watch the light come; when we are having a go where we are at shaping, by God's grace, one little corner of his eternal kingdom, chiseling out of the crude granite of the world "carved angels, eager-eyed, with hair blown back, and wings put crosswise on their breasts, . . . choir over choir, face to face uplifted."

Mark that phrase "by God's grace." What if that were the "pound"? "Trade with [this] till I come" (vs. 13). To Paul it was unthinkable that with such an incomparably great thing involved as the grace of God—the very sum total of all that God is, the depth of his wisdom, the length of his patience, the clarity of his justice, the fullness of his mercy, the gallantry of his love—anybody should set it meager tasks, and so reap from it meager harvests (II Cor. 6:1). Not the whole of God, from head to foot, to no point and no effect! That would be to harness the tides and turn a flutter wheel. Paul was not afraid that God would waste anything; he was afraid that people would waste God!

17, 19, 24. ***Rewards and Penalties.*—Ten cities, . . . five cities. . . . Take the pound from him** (cf. Matt. 21:43). Jesus deals prodigally in pictures, and the interpreter has to be careful of them. Too often devout people talk about the divine favor and the divine retribution as if they were deliberately doled out down here like so many medals, or inflicted like so many fines. As for heaven and hell, their pearly gates and flaming fires are to some no more than childish fancies. A good God would hardly make such theatrical and vindictive arrangements. Besides, they are both after a while; and after a while is time enough to worry.

The only trouble is that life has to be taken seriously, and the issues of it—or else! Right and wrong make a difference. Always men have been struggling with that difference. Always it

[4] *For the Time Being, A Christmas Oratorio* (New York: Random House, 1944). "The Vision of the Shepherds," Part II.

ful in a very little, have thou authority over ten cities.

18 And the second came, saying, Lord, thy pound hath gained five pounds.

19 And he said likewise to him, Be thou also over five cities.

20 And another came, saying, Lord, behold, *here is* thy pound, which I have kept laid up in a napkin:

21 For I feared thee, because thou art an austere man: thou takest up that thou layedst not down, and reapest that thou didst not sow.

servant! Because you have been faithful
in a very little, you shall have authority
over ten cities.' 18 And the second came,
saying, 'Lord, your pound has made five
pounds.' 19 And he said to him, 'And you
are to be over five cities.' 20 Then another
came, saying, 'Lord, here is your pound,
which I kept laid away in a napkin; 21 for
I was afraid of you, because you are a severe
man; you take up what you did not lay
down, and reap what you did not sow.'

Probably substituted for "I will set you over much" (Matt. 25:21) under the influence of the secondary tradition.

18-19. The dialogue with the first servant is repeated in abbreviated form. Codex Bezae improved the grammar by substituting "another" for **the second.**

20-21. A "mina" was small enough to be wrapped in a cloth. The "wicked and slothful" servant of Matthew's version hid the much bulkier "talent" in the ground. Translate **severe** (RSV) rather than **austere** (KJV). **You take up what you did not lay down:** Proverbial for the unscrupulous exploitation of another's labor.

---

has mattered to them whether they were good or evil. We do not live in a universe which is essentially a huge, impersonal machine, where "all things come alike to all" (Eccl. 9:2), and our codes of conduct are no more than human agreements set up for our own convenience. Only an age bewitched by the so-called "scientific method" would ever have supposed that we do. "Did God indeed say . . . ?" (Gen. 3:1.) Science is equipped to discover relations, to measure forces, to calculate speed, and to analyze matter; it is not equipped to find a person; and the Bible says we have a Person to deal with, a Person who cares. We live in the moral order which he fashioned, and that order makes his kind of sense. Not always our kind (see Expos. on vs. 8); his kind. In that order the issues of living are not held out to us as promises, or thundered at us as verdicts. They are the inevitable outcome of living in a world where law does not simply emerge; where it is a will.

Nor is there any reason to suppose that the only thing we have to do is to die, and presto, chango, everybody will be like everybody else! If good and evil, right and wrong, are only convenient labels to be distinguished from one another for the time being, our whole existence, which seems so much like a real fight and so tremendously in earnest, is not far from meaningless farce. Heaven and hell are the way the Bible has of telling us that we cannot laugh anything off because it will be over before we know it, finished, washed up. Life may make sense even in the world to come!

With the "great gulf fixed" (16:26)! The gulf that is no slight matter even here! (6:47-49; Matt. 7:24-27.) Greed and lust and crooked dealing: "Where their worm dieth not" (Mark 9:44, 46, 48)—like a sad refrain; crawling filth in the valley of Gehenna (*gê ben Hinnôm*) just outside the walls of Jerusalem, where the city's refuse was burned, with its vermin-eaten carrion. The results are not pretty. Look around. (Cf. vs. 27, the fate of the king's enemies.) Hatred and jealousy and resentment: "And the fire is not quenched"—smoldering on and on in a man's soul! The gulf right now that none can cross except Christ reach out his hand. A guide in the Alps did that once for a timid soul; and when the other hesitated, afraid, he smiled and braced himself and said, "Take it! That hand has never lost a man!"

17, 19, 24. ***Measure for Measure.***—Ten pounds, **ten cities,** *cum laude;* five pounds, **five cities,** but no praise; one pound hoarded, no pound left (cf. 6:38*b*; and Expos. on Matt. 25: 14-30). Jesus understands that there is a deep, deep sanity, a kind of ultimate decency about things, as Robert Louis Stevenson called it: a vast balance, steady as the universe itself. We never can bribe it or cheat it or dodge it. And we shake our heads. Life hardly ever works that way, we say. But our Lord is not talking about life; he is talking about God. God works that way. It scarcely means that you will get out what you put in; that after all, therefore, honesty is the best policy, and thrift pays off. These are our prudential maxims, not Christ's. To

22 And he saith unto him, Out of thine own mouth will I judge thee, *thou* wicked servant. Thou knewest that I was an austere man, taking up that I laid not down, and reaping that I did not sow:

23 Wherefore then gavest not thou my money into the bank, that at my coming I might have required mine own with usury?

24 And he said unto them that stood by, Take from him the pound, and give *it* to him that hath ten pounds.

25 (And they said unto him, Lord, he hath ten pounds.)

26 For I say unto you, That unto every one which hath shall be given; and from him that hath not, even that he hath shall be taken away from him.

22 He said to him, 'I will condemn you out
of your own mouth, you wicked servant!
You knew that I was a severe man, taking
up what I did not lay down and reaping
what I did not sow? 23 Why then did you
not put my money into the bank, and at
my coming I should have collected it with
interest?' 24 And he said to those who stood
by, 'Take the pound from him, and give
it to him who has the ten pounds.' 25 (And
they said to him, 'Lord, he has ten
pounds!') 26 'I tell you, that to every one
who has will more be given; but from him
who has not, even what he has will be

22-23. The phrasing of the master's reply carries with it the implication that the servant's characterization of him was insolent slander. If the **wicked servant** had been afraid he might lose the money, why had he not deposited it with bankers? **Interest:** Rates as high as 1 per cent per month were not uncommon.

24. The original parable has not been thoroughly revised. The gift of an additional "mina" would be of little consequence to a man who had just been entrusted with authority over ten cities! **Ten pounds:** Actually eleven, for the original sum had earned a tenfold profit. Matthew's phrasing avoids this minor incongruity.

25. Omitted by Codex Bezae and its allies; probably an interpolation into the original Lukan text.

26. A proverb ascribed to Jesus in Mark 4:25 and reproduced by Luke in 8:18. Also appended to Matthew's version of the parable (Matt. 25:29) and therefore associated with it very early in the history of its transmission.

---

him there was something large and free-handed about the gospel, but something also grim and inexorable. We dare not turn it all into a kind of idyllic loveliness, with the offense of the Cross hidden away under flowers, and Jesus himself become the mild friend of man. There is that about it too that judges, and may not be called unjust (see Exeg. on vss. 22-23) because its judgments so often reverse our own (vss. 24-25). There is that about it which, because it has little else to begin with, makes history out of trifles (**faithful in a very little,** vs. 17), turns out a civilization, spells Destiny with them—always God's minus sign in front of the evil, and his plus sign after the good (vs. 26; originally perhaps a cynicism, but here enlisted on the side of truth).

"Before Jehovah's awful throne." Have you ever noticed how incongruous the second line seems? "Ye nations, bow with sacred joy." The "awful throne" and the "sacred joy" scarcely belong together, do they? They never would have, if Christ had not moved toward us out of eternity, holding within and beyond his judgments all the mercy God had in heaven for human life!

24. ***How Much Can We Count on What We Have?***—When what we have is the covenant grace of Almighty God? The answer is that we cannot count on it even to get us through—if that is all we are counting on it to do (see I Cor. 10:1-5). It is in fact the grace of God that exposes us, for our soul's health, and all that we have, to the rigors of his justice. So does he begin, whenever he has it in mind to invade human history. Elect nothing! We are shock troops (Ezek. 9:6; I Pet. 4:17). Not saints in cellophane, but saints in overalls. Where now is the safety which we covet so much at his hand (vss. 20-21)? "In perils of waters, in perils of robbers. . . ." Read the long list (II Cor. 11:23-28). And add this, to make the toll of perils complete, "lest . . . when I have preached to others, I myself should be a castaway" (I Cor. 9:27). Paul was in peril of God!

"May the good Lord pity us for the muddle

27 But those mine enemies, which would not that I should reign over them, bring hither, and slay *them* before me.
28 ¶ And when he had thus spoken, he went before, ascending up to Jerusalem.

taken away. 27 But as for these enemies of mine, who did not want me to reign over them, bring them here and slay them before me.' "
28 And when he had said this, he went

27. Note Samuel's treatment of Agag (I Sam. 15:33). With this verse the story reverts to the secondary tradition of vss. 12 and 14. Matthew's version describes the fate of the "worthless servant" (Matt. 25:30), and Codex Bezae adds this matter to Luke's text.

VI. Jesus' Ministry in Jerusalem (19:28–24:12)

A. Jesus Enters Jerusalem (19:28-46)

1. Approach to Jerusalem (19:28-38=Mark 11:1-10)

Interpreters are agreed that there is a close connection between Mark's story of the triumphal entry and the messianic prediction of Zech. 9:9: "Rejoice greatly, O daughter of Zion; shout, O daughter of Jerusalem: behold, thy King cometh unto thee: he is just, and having salvation; lowly, and riding upon an ass, and upon a colt the foal of an ass." Matthew emphasized their relationship by quoting the prophecy in full and by changing Mark's narrative at a few points to demonstrate that the fulfillment had been exact and literal. Several hypotheses have been advanced to explain the connection: (*a*) The story is a messianic legend without any basis in fact. Zech. 9:9 had predicted that the Messiah would enter Jerusalem riding upon an ass and had summoned the people to pay him exultant homage. The early church, convinced that Jesus must have fulfilled the scriptural prophecy, wove the story out of the details provided by the prediction. (*b*) Jesus intended his entry into Jerusalem to be understood as a fulfillment of Zech. 9:9 and planned it accordingly. After long hesitation he had come to the conviction that he was the Messiah and had tacitly admitted this to his disciples at Caesarea Philippi, although at the time he had asked them not to publicize the fact. But now he casts his earlier reticence aside. He arranges with friends in the vicinity of Jerusalem to have a young ass ready for him and to release it to emissaries who could quote the password "The Lord has need of it." He mounts the animal and enters the city, acclaimed as messianic king by his disciples and the company of pilgrims. His entry was therefore a deliberate assumption of messiahship, but one that emphasized his own spiritual and nonpolitical interpretation of the Messiah's mission. He chose to fulfill a prediction that pictured the Messiah as one who would come in meekness and in peace. (*c*) Both of the preceding interpretations of Mark's narrative are open to criticism. If the story is nothing but an

we're in!" But the muddle we are in is not what God's pity is for—not unless that pity spells for us a commitment beyond all expedience and common sense. Commitment and glad stewardship (cf. Expos. on 22:24-30). Ours is a world where God in his Son met death, on an enterprise which exacted even from him blood and sweat and tears. We are not likely to carry it off without ever straining a muscle or losing a pulse beat. "I kept it" (vs. 20); but did he? (Cf. 8:18.)

28-40. ***The Triumphal Entry.***—(Cf. Mark 11:1-10; Matt. 21:1-9.) One might well entitle this whole section "The Gospel in Retrospect." The question is often asked, Why on earth do we not get back at last from all the complications of dogma to the simplicities of the earliest facts? Why not forsake all the theological implications so meticulously wrought out in the epistles and return to the kind of message which Jesus himself proclaimed—repentance, faith, the kingdom of God, the ethic of the Sermon on the Mount? Jesus said little about sin. We owe to Paul our emphasis on that. Our Lord seems rather to have been impressed by the infinite possibilities latent in the human soul. He saw in Matthew an evangelist; in the wavering, impulsive Simon a "rock"; in Zacchaeus a "son of Abraham." Why not approach life from that angle, instead of perplexing it with doctrine? We should likely make better progress if we did. People do not want to be told incessantly what a weight of sin and guilt rests on them. They are not interested in theories about

29 And it came to pass, when he was come nigh to Bethphage and Bethany, at the mount called *the mount* of Olives, he sent two of his disciples,

on ahead, going up to Jerusalem. 29 When
he drew near to Beth'pha-ge and Bethany, at the mount that is called Olivet, he sent

invention, it is curious that the early church should have chosen the particular prediction in Zech. 9:9 to develop as a legend. There is little evidence that it played any role in earlier messianic speculation. Furthermore some details of the narrative could not have been derived directly from that O.T. passage: Mark's reference to the cutting of foliage and the particular shouts of the crowd. Finally, it is only in John 12:12 that we are told that those who acclaimed Jesus had come out of the city to meet him. According to the Synoptics, the cries of homage and jubilation were uttered by Jesus' disciples and fellow pilgrims. If the entry was a staged and prearranged affair, it was out of character. It is difficult to think of Jesus as one who planned and carried out such a theatrical dramatization of his mission. And if the manner of the entry was generally interpreted as an assertion of messianic claims, it is strange that it was not cited at the trial as evidence of Jesus' treasonable ambitions. In all likelihood the story as we have it is the product both of fact and of interpretation. Probably Jesus did enter Jerusalem astride an ass—not an uncommon method of journeying—accompanied by exultant and expectant pilgrims who were looking for the speedy inauguration of the kingdom of God. At a later time messianic elements were imposed on the account under the influence of the prophecy in Zech. 9:9. An O.T. passage helped to shape the narrative as we have it, but did not create it.

28. Editorial. Luke's return to his Marcan source requires that he provide its subject matter with a new introduction. The verse is modeled on Mark 10:32.

29. The geographical details are confusing. **Bethphage** ("house of figs") appears from references in the Talmud to have been a suburb of Jerusalem on the west slope of the Mount of Olives. **Bethany** ("house of affliction" or "house of obedience") was a village on its southeast slope, two or three miles from the city and separated from it by the valley of Kidron. Perhaps **Bethany,** which is missing from Matthew's version, was added at an early date to the texts of Mark and Luke because it was a more familiar place name to Christians. According to John 12:1, it was the home of Lazarus and his two sisters. **Olivet:** A translation borrowed from the Vulg. The accent of the Greek noun differs in most MSS at this point from that in Mark 11:1 and in Luke 19:37.

the person of Christ and the nature of the Atonement. "Sir, we would see Jesus" (John 12:21). So the argument runs, and it sounds like an honest, straightforward, valid sort of appeal.

One should not be very long at a loss, however, to see how specious it is. Who is this Jesus who speaks of repentance; and if he knows less than Paul knows about sin, what is the repentance of which he speaks? "If ye then, being evil . . ." (11:13). What is the good news in which we are to believe, and the kingdom of God that is so near? Even in the Synoptics themselves the story is not quite so "simple" as some have thought it: its "simplicities" are bewildering to the disciples (9:45; 18:34). The Fourth Gospel catches them up into the ultimate mysteries. The epistles brood over them. The glory of the Resurrection illumines them. The years toil on into centuries, each bearing its own testimony to the things that have been. What faintest hope is there that we can come nearer the heart and core of the gospel by reversing the process? Instead, should we not in the very attempt be moving back out of the light into the shadow again? The street down which history marches is a one-way street. There are no "bare" facts along it: there are facts and interpretation, held now together in a bond quite inviolable. Getting back from Christianity to Jesus of Nazareth would be getting back from the British Commonwealth to Magna Charta, from the United States of America to the thirteen colonies. It is conceivable that the interpretation is wrong; but it belongs now to the fact and must be reckoned with. The union is indissoluble.

What is of utmost significance in the passage before us is the indubitable fact that the fellowship of Christ's church, looking back at this event, saw in it the fulfillment of an ancient

30 Saying, Go ye into the village over against *you;* in the which at your entering ye shall find a colt tied, whereon yet never man sat: loose him, and bring *him hither.*

31 And if any man ask you, Why do ye loose *him?* thus shall ye say unto him, Because the Lord hath need of him.

32 And they that were sent went their way, and found even as he had said unto them.

33 And as they were loosing the colt, the owners thereof said unto them, Why loose ye the colt?

34 And they said, The Lord hath need of him.

35 And they brought him to Jesus: and they cast their garments upon the colt, and they set Jesus thereon.

36 And as he went, they spread their clothes in the way.

two of the disciples, 30 saying, "Go into the
village opposite, where on entering you will
find a colt tied, on which no one has ever
yet sat; untie it and bring it here. 31 If
any one asks you, 'Why are you untying
it?' you shall say this, 'The Lord has need
of it.' " 32 So those who were sent went
away and found it as he had told them.
33 And as they were untying the colt, its
owners said to them, "Why are you untying
the colt?" 34 And they said, "The Lord
has need of it." 35 And they brought it to
Jesus, and throwing their garments on the
colt they set Jesus upon it. 36 And as he
rode along, they spread their garments on

30-34. To interpret the mysterious details of these verses as an indication that the entry had been prearranged is an unwarranted rationalization of the narrative (see above). No doubt Mark and Luke understood them to be evidence of Jesus' omniscience (cf. similar details in the story of the preparations for the Last Supper [22:8-13]). **Colt:** The young of various animals. No doubt an ass's foal is meant (Zech. 9:9). **On which no one has ever yet sat:** An unbroken animal waiting to bear the messianic king.

35-36. Oriental gestures of homage. Luke omits Mark's comment that some "spread leafy branches which they had cut from the fields."

prophecy: the sad and yet triumphant approach of the Conqueror, meek and lowly, but wearing already on his brow the victor's wreath. The revelation was not in the fact alone: the revelation was in the fact and its meaning; a meaning in part perhaps unrealized at the time, but growing ever clearer with the years as they passed. So it was certainly with the Cross. And so it was with the whole earthly life of Jesus. From our vantage point in the centuries we should be able to see, even more clearly than his first disciples, that in him, both hidden and revealed, was God, "reconciling the world unto himself." [5]

31. *God's Prior Claim.*—**The Lord has need of it.** The demands which Jesus made on human life, even while he still walked among men in the flesh, were couched in strangely absolute terms (8:22; 14:26; Matt. 16:24). On the lips of the prophet of Galilee they were sovereign words; on the lips of the risen Lord they assert God's own eminent domain, his right to all that we are and have: the God who is always near, willing and ready to come in; willing in meekness, ready in power; asking us to provide the means, always within our reach, and always pledged to us again. "The Master needs him and will return him quickly" (Mark 11:3). Is it too fanciful to add that what we lend him for his use he lays back in our hands a hundredfold? (Cf. Matt. 19:29—the reality of a fellowship that transcends even family relations!)

36. *God's Pageant.*—**As he rode along. . . .** It was a pageant, but it was God's kind: a procession at once splendid and dreary. It was something to rejoice over and something to mourn about. Like life itself. See from the first both the high lights and the shadows: Jesus, flicked off like a speck of dust by the decent people who had lionized him for a while; John the Baptist, who doubted him; Judas, whom he could never quite win; the brothers who were quite sure he was daft. Then remember that this is the man who seems to have thought of himself at last as if he had been sent of God to bring about some vast reversal in human life. And so little had been done. It had begun to look now like the end. Yet against the background of that lowly life, going out with such

[5] See H. K. Luce, *The Gospel According to S. Luke* (Cambridge: The University Press, 1933; "The Cambridge Bible"), pp. 297-303.

37 And when he was come nigh, even now at the descent of the mount of Olives, the whole multitude of the disciples began to rejoice and praise God with a loud voice for all the mighty works that they had seen;

the road. 37 As he was now drawing near,
at the descent of the Mount of Olives, the
whole multitude of the disciples began to
rejoice and praise God with a loud voice
for all the mighty works that they had seen,

37-38. Luke makes such free use of Mark in these verses that some interpreters believe he is employing another source. He stresses the site of Jesus' proclamation of his messiahship, perhaps under the influence of the prediction in Zech. 14:1-4, and declares that the disciples' praise was directed to **God,** who had been ultimately responsible for **all the mighty works** (miracles) of his Messiah. The Hebrew "Hosanna" is omitted from the disciples' cry of jubilation (see Intro., p. 4); the first part of Mark's benediction—a quotation from Ps. 118:26—is made more explicitly messianic by the substitution of **King** for "he"; the second part (Mark 11:10) is left out altogether, possibly because it is in contradiction to 19:11; and Mark's "Hosanna in the highest!" is displaced by **Peace in heaven, and glory in the highest!** This last clause is reminiscent of the angelic chorus

---

poor pomp, has been painted a glory in the skies, God's pageant of the years: until what else can a man make of him but the strange love of God walking abroad on the earth, forever hurt and despised, and forever at the last triumphant?

But there is another contrast here. What shall we say of these very disciples, all swept along for the moment at their careless, reckless best? Where were they when the vote was taken in Pilate's judgment hall? When the roar came back "Barabbas! Barabbas!" "And who for Christ?" asked Pilate. Where were they then? And yet it was of people like this that Jesus demanded everything, sure they were worth his while, offering them no bribe, making no concession, honoring them by making none, holding out a cross to them, expecting them to climb by hard paths up steep places! One might find it easy to despise them; but beyond them, God's pageant! (See Vachel Lindsay, "General William Booth Enters into Heaven.")

36. ***More or Less.*—They spread their garments on the road.** There was an abandon about it all that left its neat and careful calculations at home in the ledger, snatched off its coat, threw its hat in the air, and tossed on the road any token of devotion it could get its hands on. Part of the glory of it lay precisely in its lack of restraint. More or less would not serve: it was top to bottom now, altogether; and who was going to worry about what might happen? When we insist on being guided by reason, on figuring out just how far we should go, and just where the trouble is likely to start, we usually come to the conclusion that perhaps it would be safer not to go so far! When a man throws such caution to the winds, he is in a fair way to discover himself, and he is in a fair way to discover what it means to live—no great while, necessarily, but by the grace of God well! Long ago that prodigality was in God when he threw away all the numbers men can count and scattered his limitless bounty across the sky and over the hills; when he spread his mercy over the doomed city of Sodom ten times farther than Abraham had prayed, pressing it on through the years to pour itself out over a strange and rebellious people, to dwell at last like the unreckoned largess of the spring in the heart of a Nazarene. Life, full life, rich life, life as God intended it to be, was not something to be hoarded; it was something to be flung away in the freedom of a high and unbridled devotion.

37. ***The Drama of Life.*—As he was now drawing near. . . .** Two mighty, tragic characters enter on the wide stage of the world: man and God. Here they are in the city streets at high noon, confronting one another. Quickly they shift about, from temple court to the little village of Bethany, until on Good Friday, with dry eyes and parched lips, one comes upon Act II, "Man's Way with God." After that the hours drag by from dusk to dawn and dusk again: when there, in the dim twilight of morning, the last act opens, "God's Way with Man." We thrust him away and he comes back, like "the eager, terrible spring." And it goes on and on, as if it were timeless, with the years drawn aside one after another for curtains. Timeless and real: real as nails and blood and the grave are real, and the night, and the rising sun!

Always, late or soon, man, with the gods he makes—Baal for his crops, Venus for his lust, Mars for his anger—meets the God who made him! Never until then does he know himself for what he is: harried and hectored by gran-

38 Saying, Blessed *be* the King that cometh in the name of the Lord: peace in heaven, and glory in the highest.

38 saying, "Blessed be the King who comes in the name of the Lord! Peace in heaven

in 2:14. B. S. Easton paraphrases: "Peace is prepared by God in heaven to be bestowed on men,—may He who dwells on high be glorified!" (*The Gospel According to St. Luke* [New York: Charles Scribner's Sons, 1926], p. 286.)

deur and meanness; always halfway between heaven and hell, between the abyss of his own sin and the boldest, hungriest hopes that ever strode up and down through the human soul. Nor until then does he know what God is. This turbulent, ugly thing called humanity, princely and full of heartache, Jesus loved—and left on it forever the mark of his hand, and the seal of his unbroken dominion.

> Ride on! ride on in majesty!
> In lowly pomp ride on to die.[6]

One hardly knows what to do: whether to join the crowd here and shout "Hosanna," or to slip away into a corner somewhere and sit there for hours wondering, wondering right now what will happen!

38. *Thy King Cometh unto Thee.*—(Cf. Matt. 21:5; Acts 17:7.) We are face to face somehow with the rule of this Christ. The things he said will not lay off their royal purple and come and sit down and be at home with common words: they keep knocking at the door of the human soul. We write our recipes for chaos; and he never gives up. Even in the chaos there is his order! A majesty that keeps standing there in spite of everything, with nothing else big enough or bold enough or strong enough to take its seat on the windy throne of the world!

"There is another king, one Jesus." A grim sort of failure he was on the cross; but from that day to this it has been better to fail with him than to succeed with the people whose business it is in every generation to nail him there!

38. *Magic or Religion?*—**In the name of the Lord.** There are echoes that fling themselves back and forth in the phrase. Far off in the pagan world he who knew the name of a deity could command that deity's service. To the Hebrew, with his realization of God's awful holiness, the divine name, made known to Moses by God's act and speaking, was not to be taken on the lips—perhaps in violent revulsion from the thought that any mortal being could hold in leash the might of the Eternal. The commission laid on the disciples in his name to drive out demons (9:1); the Christian prayers that still close with the words "in the name of Jesus"; the liturgies that invoke "the name of the Father, and of the Son, and of the Holy Ghost"—in all of them is the complex of that long history: power and holiness; the grace of him who came not to be ministered unto but to minister; against whose name no evil thing can stand; whose name, above every name, is itself the symbol of the divine presence, the divine ownership, the divine protection and favor, summing up all there is of God we know, as he moves into intimate relationship with men, laying upon them his claim, and offering them himself (see Exeg. and Expos. on Matt. 6:9). Is there not here the very apotheosis of magic, the true and final exorcism, harking down from a time older than any of the records of our race, the soul's investiture?[7] **Blessed** indeed is he **that cometh in the name of the Lord.**

One comes in the name of the Lord who comes in his presence, under his authority, to make manifest his glory—the glory of that veiled Being on the other side of all created things, whose sovereignty is now over the work of his hands, whose weakness men crucified only to find it strength. "In the name of Jesus." Magic? "I, Paul, an ambassador in chains." Religion! In one, man sees himself and his little concerns at the center of God's vast providence. If anything goes wrong, he cannot understand why such an evil thing should happen to him. If he talks of faith, he thinks it means that he will be vindicated somehow, in history or beyond, his hopes, his plans, his way of life.

> Fear not, I am with thee, O be not dismayed;
> For I am thy God, and will still give thee aid.[8]

That can be the crassest kind of paganism. It is religion which understands that God is in the middle, is himself the why of all his providences. The story of the Bible is his story. The foolishness of the gospel is his wisdom (I Cor.

[6] Henry H. Milman.

[7] *S.v.* "Name," in James Hastings, ed., *Dictionary of the Bible* (New York: Charles Scribner's Sons, 1904), cf. also F. C. Conybeare, "The Demonology of the New Testament," *Jewish Quarterly Review,* VIII (1896), 576-608, and "Christian Demonology," *op. cit.,* IX (1897), 581-89.

[8] "How firm a foundation," st. ii.

39 And some of the Pharisees from
among the multitude said unto him, Mas-
ter, rebuke thy disciples.
40 And he answered and said unto them,
I tell you that, if these should hold their
peace, the stones would immediately cry
out.
41 ¶ And when he was come near, he
beheld the city, and wept over it,

and glory in the highest!" **39** And some of
the Pharisees in the multitude said to him,
"Teacher, rebuke your disciples." **40** He
answered, "I tell you, if these were silent,
the very stones would cry out."
41 And when he drew near and saw the

---

2. Jesus Justifies the Jubilation of His Disciples (19:39-40)

39. Editorial. **Of the Pharisees** is omitted by the Sinaitic Syriac, and this text is followed by some modern editors.

40. Probably a proverbial saying (cf. Hab. 2:11). There is a similar scene in Matt. 21:15-16.

3. Prediction of the Siege and Destruction of Jerusalem (19:41-44)

In marked contrast to the vengeful tone of 18:7 and 19:27. In the judgment of many interpreters a "prophecy after the event." The whole passage may be editorial. Early in the siege of Jerusalem, Titus threw some sort of earthworks around the city and sur-

---

1:23-25). What privileges we have are ours as his stewards (vss. 12-24). What evil it is that overtakes us, the will beyond it is good (Rom. 8:28). Back of things as they are is a desperate intent straining toward things as they ought to be. *In nomine Patris, et Filii, et Spiritus Sancti.* Magic? "I, Paul, an ambassador in chains." Religion!

38. ***The Angelic Chorus.***—(Cf. 2:14.) Only here, in this grim city with its cross, could that peace come of which the angels sang; only here, plumbing the lowest, could that **glory in the highest** be revealed (cf. Exod. 33:18-19).

39-40. ***Let the Redeemed of the Lord Say So.***—(Cf. Ps. 107:2.) There is a silence that is not "golden": the silence of unbelief, indifferent and sullen; the silence of diffidence, timorous and hesitating. It would have been far better to **rebuke** that, there around the edges of the crowd, than to rebuke the glad acclaim at the center. "We do not well: this day is a day of good tidings, and we hold our peace" (II Kings 7:9). Vocal life and spoken word!

40. ***The Witness of the Inarticulate.***—(Cf. Ps. 19:3-4.) There is a voice for every ear that will catch the sound of it (Rom. 1:20).

> A primrose by a river's brim
> A yellow primrose was to him,
> And it was nothing more.[9]

Compare with that Tennyson's poem, "Flower in the crannied wall," and Elizabeth Barrett Browning's "Every common bush afire with God."[1] Were men's mouths dumb, the very heavens would cry out, as indeed they do. In the midst of war's brutalities and ruin stood the mute witness of Europe's cathedrals. "We do not reach God by inferring His existence, nature, and attributes" from the noonday's splendor, or from the silent glories of a summer night; but he "comes to meet us in them."[2]

There is a truth that will not have its mouth stopped: a truth about God and life and man himself—the truth that Christ is. "O Lord, open thou my lips; and my mouth shall show forth thy praise" (Ps. 51:15).

41-44. ***Lament over Jerusalem.***—(See Expos. on 21:5-6, 20-24; 23:27-30.) According to Luke (13:34-35), Jesus had already uttered those inexpressibly poignant words, "O Jerusalem, Jerusalem, . . . how often would I . . . , and ye would not" (cf. Matt. 23:37-39, where they are quoted in the time context of the present passage). They may imply what there is no reason perhaps to doubt—though nowhere expressly set down in the Synoptics—that our Lord had on more than one occasion journeyed to the ancient city of David, tenderly and passionately hoping to ward off from his people the doom that could all too clearly be seen moving in. Here, as the verses stand, are spread out in graphic detail the terrible results of the judicial blindness which had come upon them. Again it makes little difference whether what we have before us is an accurate record of the authentic

[9] Wordsworth, "Peter Bell," Part I, st. xii.

[1] "Aurora Leigh," Book VII, l. 821.

[2] Philip S. Watson, *Let God Be God* (Philadelphia: Muhlenberg Press, 1948), p. 80.

42 Saying, If thou hadst known, even thou, at least in this thy day, the things

city he wept over it, 42 saying, "Would

mounted these "banks" with timber in the hope of cutting off the supplies and of starving the defenders into submission (Josephus *Jewish War* V. 6. 2). When this barrier proved inadequate, it was supplemented by a stone wall (*ibid.,* V. 12. 1-2).

41. Note 23:28-31; II Kings 8:11-12.

42. The apodosis of the conditional sentence is omitted. The RSV is based on a better Greek text than the KJV. **Even today:** Jesus' entry provided the city with a final

words of Jesus, or a reminiscence, colored somewhat by later events (see Exeg.), of that strange and prophetic vision which more than once seemed to flash its way from his eyes into the darkness of a man's soul. What matters is that in the midst of these hosannas, down the city streets, carpeted now as for a king, lined with welcoming throngs, judgment was drawing on: and the shadow of it, men seemed to remember, was in the very eyes of Jesus, so rarely flooded with tears; and the gloom of it fell like a pall on his spirit. Surely for him there must have been a shudder somewhere in that ecstasy.

And when he drew near and saw the city. New York? Chicago? London? Paris? Berlin? Tokyo? Or one's own city? Who else beheld it that day? And made their own appraisals? To scribe and Pharisee, to priest and Sadducee and pious Jew, it spelled out so many different things: home, pride; the legacy of a great tradition, hoary with age and memory; a rankling sore in their hearts for the tread of pagan feet; bitterness and resentment; office and the emoluments of office. To Pilate, his centurions and his cohorts: a troublesome place, and a despised people; years to be spent, away in a foreign land, with what profit and what pleasure a man could. To Jesus? **When he . . . saw the city he wept over it.** That unbelievably buoyant soul! El Greco's familiar painting of Toledo in storm might perhaps convey something of the sadness and the terror of his deep premonition.

If thou hadst known, . . . but now. . . . Paul might have whispered just such words to himself years later when as a prisoner with his guards he came for the first time in his life within sight of Rome. Jerusalem's tragic history had from the very beginning been one long dirge of radiant hopes unrealized and vast possibilities unfulfilled. What else has it been to this day—except for the cross that one morning stood just outside its walls? Few indeed would dare to sketch in that fairer picture—**If thou hadst known!** Surely there had been revelation enough, patriarch and poet, prophet and priest. Surely there had been privilege enough, mercy and judgment, blessing and curse (Deut. 30). **But now**—and the half-finished dream of all that God has prepared for them that love him is broken off. The desolate reality takes its place. Even as Jesus speaks, there is yet time in the inexhaustible patience and faithfulness of the Almighty; but man will not have it so. He seems almost to covet his own death. He himself turns the "vision of peace" (see Exeg.) into a vision of despair.

In truest sense every day is just such a day of visitation and testing (I Pet. 2:12). Every moment is a moment of crisis, of judgment or consolation (1:68), a moment for turning. The hour strikes and the soul stands before God. **Even thou, at least in this thy day:** the only bit of time that *is* thine, this fleeting shadow on the dial, where past and future meet; thine —and God's! Over here, the depth and reality of that communion with him who is the source of all life, whose service is itself the perfect peace which garrisons the inner keep and citadel of the mind (Phil. 4:7; Amos 5:18, 20): over there, eyes that have so long refused to see that they cannot (I John 2:11); ears so long attuned to the world that no sound comes now from beyond it. The wayside "bush afire with God"—of which so many years ago it was written, "And when the LORD saw that he turned aside to see, God called unto him" (Exod. 3:4)—has lost its angel. In a world where even to turn a stone may start a wing,

> 'Tis ye, 'tis your estrangèd faces,
> That miss the many-splendoured thing.[3]

It was the doom that overtook Pharaoh (Exod. 8:32; 9:35; 11:10). God, the Enemy! And man, compassed round, kept in **on every side,** laid **even with the ground!** Recall Robert Louis Stevenson's story of *Dr. Jekyll and Mr. Hyde,* or Oscar Wilde's *The Picture of Dorian Gray,* or Shakespeare's *Macbeth,* his way of life fallen at last "into the sere, the yellow leaf." [4]

42. ***The Things Which Belong unto Thy Peace.***—What are they, the things that fill life

[3] Francis Thompson, "The Kingdom of God," st. iv.

[4] Act V, scene 3.

which belong unto thy peace! but now they are hid from thine eyes.

43 For the days shall come upon thee, that thine enemies shall cast a trench about thee, and compass thee round, and keep thee in on every side,

44 And shall lay thee even with the ground, and thy children within thee; and they shall not leave in thee one stone upon another; because thou knewest not the time of thy visitation.

45 And he went into the temple, and began to cast out them that sold therein, and them that bought;

that even today you knew the things that
make for peace! But now they are hid from
your eyes. 43 For the days shall come upon
you, when your enemies will cast up a bank
about you and surround you, and hem you
in on every side, 44 and dash you to the
ground, you and your children within you,
and they will not leave one stone upon
another in you; because you did not know
the time of your visitation."

45 And he entered the temple and began

opportunity for repentance. **The things that make for peace:** Salvation was conditional on the acceptance of Jesus as Messiah. **But now they are hid from your eyes:** Possibly a play on the word "Jerusalem" is intended. The name of the city was popularly believed to mean "vision of peace."

43-44. Those who interpret the passage as an utterance of Jesus, or as a prediction of the Palestinian church before A.D. 70, point out that the details of the siege and the destruction of Jerusalem may have been borrowed from Isa. 29:1-4 and Ps. 137:9. **Your children:** The city's inhabitants. **The time of your visitation:** Jesus was God's final messenger, and the city failed to recognize him and his mission.

4. Cleansing of the Temple (19:45-46=Mark 11:15-17)

Since Luke has omitted Mark's reference to a preliminary inspection of the temple (Mark 11:11) and his story of the cursing of the fig tree (see Intro., p. 18), this incident

instead of emptying it? There are so many worn-out, impoverished, uneasy lives—people who somehow seem to grow more destitute with the years. Each day subtracts something, takes something out of them, and never seems to offer anything that can quite make up the loss. Until after a while, they will tell you so themselves, they feel much as a sucked orange must feel when it gets a chance to meditate by the side of the road!

Sin more than anything else does that to a man. It always looks at first as if it were fun; and it looks like anything else at the last. It begins with a smacking of the lips, and winds up with nausea. Hear again the cry of the psalmist (Ps. 51). Ask any psychiatrist. "You thought you were getting away with it," says the doctor in A. J. Cronin's novel, *The Citadel,* as he sits alone staring at the ruin his greed has made around him. "You thought you were getting away with it. And you weren't!" Who does?

Is there then no remedy for it? The very heart of the gospel keeps saying there is. And on the other side of it something to hope for, something to do, and Someone to love. When peace enters the human soul, it will enter by that door. Wrote a young woman whose letter tells its own story: "I haven't found Christ's way smooth. Perhaps because I had chosen so long to walk my own. Until one day quite unexpectedly I caught sight of his; and my plans for the future faded before the blaze of one great certainty: whatever the cost, I must follow him. It meant fighting through years that I had pledged to work against him. It meant losing one job after another, and one friend after another. But I couldn't turn back. I found in him a measure of life so strong, so joyous, and so unafraid that I had to keep on. He has come to mean not a dusty figure of ancient history, but a living, vibrant Presence; and the throbbing grandeur of the steady purposes of God."

There is a peace which is of this world—a spurious peace at the last. And a peace that this world cannot give. "My peace."

45. *The Divine Effrontery.*—Nobody can read the Gospels without being impressed by Jesus' undaunted courage. He heard the news of a maiden's death, so runs the story, and kept on, refusing to admit that nothing could be done (Mark 5:35-36); on the eve of the Crucifixion, away from the muttering crowds, he looked round the circle of his disciples and had but

46 Saying unto them, It is written, My house is the house of prayer; but ye have made it a den of thieves.

to drive out those who sold, 46 saying to them, "It is written, 'My house shall be a house of prayer'; but you have made it a den of robbers."

---

takes place directly after Jesus' entry into the city. The Gospel of John transposes it to the early period of Jesus' ministry (John 2:13-17). Luke has drastically compressed Mark's account.

45. Jesus' protest against the commercialization of the temple precincts. Facilities had been provided by the temple authorities for the sale of sacrificial victims to pilgrims. Mark mentions only "doves," but John adds "oxen and sheep." It is only in the Gospel of John that we are told in explicit terms that Jesus used violence to achieve his ends.

46. A combination of quotations from Isa. 56:7 and Jer. 7:11. Luke and Matthew abbreviate the former by omitting "for all the nations" after **house of prayer.** It is more probable that the O.T. texts have been attached to the account (Ps. 69:9 is quoted in John 2:17) than that the latter is a legend suggested by the texts. Some interpreters regard the incident as a further symbolical assertion by Jesus of his messianic claim. As was expected of the Messiah, he undertook a drastic reform of religious practices. It is more readily understood as a consequence of Jesus' prophetic indignation at the secular traffic which had made the temple courts resemble a market place.

---

one final charge for them as he lifted up his eyes to pray, "Be of good cheer, I have overcome the world" (John 16:33); in Matthew's Gospel, by way of a single word, stands somebody's recollection of his persistent and undefeated love the last time he saw Judas, "Friend," said he, "wherefore art thou come?" (Matt. 26:50.) The Apostles' Creed has caught it: "Was crucified, dead, and buried." Surely there is no more. Biography ends there. "The third day he rose again from the dead." The march continues. Banners still wave. The moments when life is played out, and there is no gleam of hope anywhere—God still assaults them. In the passage before us the long years of Israel's history are piling up toward swift disaster: over the door into the future the very blindness of God's own people has written "No Exit." But the procession moves on through the gates into the narrow streets. **And he went into the temple, and began to cast out them that sold therein, and them that bought** (yet cf. Mark 11:11). What difference now? Why not leave them to their traffic? Is not the difference just this, that God goes on making his bid forever? "If thou shalt hearken. . . . But if thine heart turn away. . . . See, I have set before thee this day life and good, and death and evil. . . . Therefore choose . . ." (Deut. 30:10-20).

45-46. ***The Cleansing of the Temple.***—(Cf. Exeg. and Expos. of parallel passages, Matt. 21:10-17; Mark 11:11*a*, 15-17; John 2:13-17.) There is no doubt that in the memory and mind of the early Christian community the so-called cleansing of the temple was an act of messianic significance, whether it occurred at the beginning, as in John, or at the end of Jesus' ministry. It may well have been just that in deliberate intent, with all of the strands that would inevitably associate it with the past. And this without reference to the "effect" or "lack of effect" such a protest may have had. Scripture is very hesitant about drawing the line between "success" and "failure." Nor is it possible to lay any emphasis on, or to deduce any teaching from, the "scourge of small cords" which has been so violently waved back and forth by the violent in their defense of violence. To fasten on what has often been held to be at best a suspect detail, in order either to underscore it as a *locus classicus* for Christian doctrine, or with enormous diligence to explain it away, is to cut but a sorry figure. As would equally be the case were we to lose ourselves in debate over the purpose Jesus had in view. Reform? But by this time reform was out of the question. Quite obviously nobody paid any attention. Was it the word, then, of God's wrath, set forth as by the prophets in symbolic act? Perhaps. Something certainly that was not just a "program," and not just an "outburst"; something that always happens when man's perversion of the holy comes under those eyes too pure to behold iniquity; and encounters there the judgment that is very mercy, and the mercy that is itself God's judgment.

46. ***The House of Prayer, A Den of Thieves.***—It is not necessary to suppose that Jesus intended any wholesale condemnation of the regularized transactions which took place in the Court of the Gentiles, not at least in so far as they were related to the exchange of foreign

47 And he taught daily in the temple. But the chief priests and the scribes and the chief of the people sought to destroy him,

47 And he was teaching daily in the temple. The chief priests and the scribes and the principal men of the people sought

B. Various Attempts to Incriminate Jesus (19:47–21:4)

1. Antipathy of the Sanhedrin to Jesus (19:47-48=Mark 11:18)

47-48. An editorial expansion of a single verse in Mark serves as an introduction to 20:1-8. The three groups named constituted the membership of the Sanhedrin. In addition to their functions as the court of final appeal in matters of religion, they had jurisdiction

coin for the old Hebraic money used in the paying of the temple tax, or in the purchasing of whatever was required for the sacrifices prescribed by ritual. Suffice it to say that greed and rapacity, sharp practice and sheer gangsterdom, an offense to all decent people, were there in sufficient measure to call up in the memory of any devout person the word of Jeremiah as he stood "in the gate of the Lord's house" (Jer. 7:1-14).

There is much that may be quite crude and overt, but much that may be so unbelievably subtle as for years to go unnoticed, about the process by which a holy place is profaned, turned into a bargain counter where peace of mind and health of body and very heaven itself are marked down at cut rates—formerly a cross, now a trinket—and God is blasphemed (Rom. 2:24). Any distortion, inevitably moving on toward perversion, of the true purpose for which the church exists; every secularization of her life; her prostitution to the economic order or to the state; such manipulation of her message or of her ministry as to make either of them a means to some end beyond itself (Mark 11:16); the corruption of her fellowship by class consciousness, by race discrimination, by privilege, by pride of virtue or of doctrine, self-righteous and exclusive—what is it but to change "the truth of God into a lie," to worship and serve "the creature more than the Creator, who is blessed for ever" (Rom. 1:25)? There is no very bewildering uncertainty about the answer that has to follow swiftly on the prophet's question, "Will a man rob God?" (Mal. 3:8.) Nor is there any surer recipe for turning the covenanted blessing into a curse than for all to look "to their own way, every one for his gain, from his quarter," saying "tomorrow shall be as this day, and much more abundant" (Isa. 56:1-12).

47a. The Light That Breaks Through.—**And he taught daily in the temple.** With the judgment that cleanses comes the Word that binds up and heals; then lays again the promise and the threat on the shoulders of human life (see Expos. on vs. 45). Through all the somber colors the light streams. When God wants to invade the world, his first raid is upon his own people (John 1:11). Catastrophe would not overtake the nations had it not already overtaken the church (I Pet. 4:17). "Tribulation and anguish, upon every soul of man that doeth evil; of the Jew first, and also of the Gentile." But the invasion is not by an alien and hostile force; it is by "the goodness of God" that leadeth to repentance, except for such as after their "hardness and impenitent heart" continue to treasure up for themselves wrath (Rom. 2:9, 4, 10, 5). Of them, note the instances that follow, not only in the immediately succeeding verses, but throughout chs. 20–21.

47b-48. The Will That Would Destroy and Cannot.—What began to happen now is set down by the Evangelist simply enough: **But the chief priests and the scribes and the chief of the people sought to destroy him, and could not find what they might do: for all the people were very attentive to hear him.** Under it might well be written, as a caption for all the centuries since, "The Strange Epic of the Christian Faith." For always when Christ can no longer be avoided, when it is clear that he never will be cajoled, men seek to be rid of him. His claims, they say, are ridiculous; his demands are impossible; his purity is an offense. To officialdom, sometimes in the church, far too often in the state, he is a disturber of the peace; his intolerable freedom a burden too grievous for any man to bear, or any institution. The Grand Inquisitor in Dostoevski's *The Brothers Karamazov* can think only of burning him, with all his heretical kin and kind at the stake. Some, who would force his hand, betray him. Others, who boast of their loyalty, on oath deny him. Those whom he has named his friends desert him. Away with him, into the place of dreams! Hide him behind the mummery and the pomp! Enshrine him in ritual or in doctrine! Any substitute were better! Release unto us Barabbas!

But they **could not find what they might do.** The will to evil comes promptly to wit's end. The hammer and the nails are not enough. Nor the tomb. Pilate's words are heaven's **weird**

48 And could not find what they might do: for all the people were very attentive to hear him.

20 And it came to pass, *that* on one of those days, as he taught the people in the temple, and preached the gospel, the chief priests and the scribes came upon *him* with the elders,

to destroy him; 48 but they did not find anything they could do, for all the people hung upon his words.

20 One day, as he was teaching the people in the temple and preaching the gospel, the chief priests and the scribes

over the temple and its ritual, and no doubt regarded Jesus' act of cleansing the temple courts as a challenge to their authority and prestige. **The chief priests:** Heads of the leading priestly families. **Daily:** Luke ignores Mark's apparent chronological scheme of six days from the date of the Entry to that of the Crucifixion. There are indications also in Mark that the earliest evangelist has telescoped his material (Mark 14:49).

2. The Sanhedrin's Challenge to Jesus' Authority (20:1-8=Mark 11:27-33)

No doubt the Sanhedrin had heard of Jesus' activities in Galilee and had been watching him for some time with suspicion. As long as he remained in the northern province he was under the jurisdiction of Herod Antipas and they could take no direct action against him, but as soon as he entered Judea he came into the sphere of their authority. As a religious teacher he would appear to them of little consequence, but as one whose ministry might cause a political disturbance, or lead to a messianic uprising, he would be an object of concern and distrust. This story is the first of a series that

laughter, long drawn out, at all our efforts to roll the stone and set the seal, "Make it as sure as ye can" (Matt. 27:65). The buried Christ will not stay dead. The phoenix, with a great beating of wings, soars upward from its own ashes at the heart of the flame. No sooner is the obituary read, and all the creeds quite done for, than the birth notice tumbles out on the desk and clamors for print. The Bible sits up in its coffin and grins at Voltaire. He was certain that another generation or two would finish it. Count off on your fingers as many of his works as you can recall; the others you will find in the card index at the library, under Voltaire, François Marie Arouet, Works of. "Were Cardinal de Retz," he wrote, with no little bewilderment and petulance, "to return again into the world, neither his eloquence nor his intrigues would draw together ten women in Paris. Were Oliver Cromwell, he who beheaded his sovereign, and seized upon the kingly dignity, to rise from the dead, he would be a wealthy City trader, and no more."[5] "O where are kings and empires now?" At the end of the nineteenth century Matthew Arnold was quite confident that he could hear on the shores of human life "the long, withdrawing, melancholy roar" of the sea of faith. D. H. Lawrence at the beginning of the twentieth could write to Katherine Mansfield, "Cheer up, Kate, Jesus is a back number." More recently, from the pen of an unknown disciple, comes another appraisal: "I am far within the mark when I say that all the armies that ever marched, and all the navies that ever were built, and all the parliaments that ever sat, and all the kings that ever reigned, put together have not affected the life of man upon this earth as powerfully as has that *One solitary life.*" "The word of the Lord endureth forever" (see Expos. on 21:33).

The secret of it? **For all the people were very attentive to hear him.** From that day when "certain Greeks among them that came up to worship at the feast" presented themselves to Philip, "and desired him, saying, Sir, we would see Jesus"—from that day to this, the yearning and the quest. Still he speaks with an authority unlike that of any other, waking "desires you never may forget," showing you "stars you never saw before," "dreams of the unfulfilled and unpossessed."[6] Still the same haunting radiance. Still the same mystery of release. Still the same relentless faith staring at us until the pain of it is like an iron shard in the soul.

20:1-8. ***The Question of Authority.***—Whatever occasions it (see Exeg.), it is an important question, and often enough, as here, put not by way of honest inquiry but by way of challenge, resentfully. Nor is it likely that in such a

[5] *Letters on the English,* Letter VII.

[6] Sidney R. Lysaght, "The Penalty of Love," from *Poems* (London: Macmillan & Co., 1928).

2 And spake unto him, saying, Tell us, by what authority doest thou these things? or who is he that gave thee this authority?

3 And he answered and said unto them, I will also ask you one thing; and answer me:

4 The baptism of John, was *it* from heaven, or of men?

5 And they reasoned with themselves, saying, If we shall say, From heaven; he will say, Why then believed ye him not?

6 But and if we say, Of men; all the people will stone us: for they be persuaded that John was a prophet.

with the elders came up 2 and said to him,
"Tell us by what authority you do these
things, or who it is that gave you this au-
thority." 3 He answered them, "I also will
ask you a question; now tell me, 4 Was
the baptism of John from heaven or from
men?" 5 And they discussed it with one
another, saying, "If we say, 'From heaven,'
he will say, 'Why did you not believe
him?' 6 But if we say, 'From men,' all the
people will stone us; for they are convinced

---

describes attempts by members of the Sanhedrin, or by Sadducees who controlled that body, to trap Jesus into an admission that could be framed as a charge warranting the death penalty and laid before the Roman procurator.

20:1-2. According to Mark's version, the incident took place on the day after the cleansing of the temple, and it was that act which was challenged. Luke's **one day** is vague, and according to the Third Evangelist it was Jesus' **teaching the people in the temple, and preaching the gospel** for which the deputation from the Sanhedrin demanded his **authority.** The purpose of the double-barreled question was to wrest from Jesus some explicit messianic claim.

3-4. Rabbinical debates were often conducted in the form of question and counter-question, the latter framed in some measure to convey the answer to the former. It is probable therefore that Jesus intended to do more than impale his opponents on the horns of a dilemma. He wished to suggest that there was a close connection between his ministry and John's and that his own authority also came **from heaven.** This in itself does not necessarily imply a messianic consciousness on his part.

5-8. The questioners found the counterquestion embarrassing, and their refusal to answer it freed Jesus from any need of replying to their initial challenge. Mark declares

---

case any answer the challenged can give will satisfy the challenger. In the world of personal relations true authority cannot be established either by claim or by argument. It is not deduced from facts, as in the laboratory or in the courtroom. Sir Isaac Newton's formulation of the law of gravitation acquired its authority from that which is "given" in nature and apprehended by observation and experiment: "The attractive force of bodies" does vary "directly as their masses and inversely as the square of the distances between them." Still people jump out of tenth-story windows! The traffic signal at the corner acquires such authority as it has from that which is "given" in society, the "common good," reinforced by statute and the threat of penalty. Still there are those who disregard it!

For Jesus to have asserted or argued from the evidence his messianic authority would have been misleading, it would have been meaningless, and it would have played directly into the hands of the Sanhedrin (see Exeg.). On the other hand, to have denied it, to have deprecated it, to have evaded its responsibilities, would have been unthinkable. There was no attempt at conciliation. There was no effort made to ingratiate himself with his inquisitors, or yet to side-step the issue they raised. In true rabbinical fashion he answered question with question. The implication was clear enough (see Exeg.); but by the "change of venue" from himself to John, the thrill of whose prophetic mission still tingled in the memory, its very clarity became an impossible embarrassment (vss. 5-6). The dilemma could now be seen in its real character. It was a moral dilemma. "We cannot tell" (Matt. 21:27). The appointed judges of the valid and the spurious were themselves judged. Rejection had fashioned its own dead end, where the attack that was intended to paralyze found itself paralyzed.

The only authority which is capable of establishing itself is that which derives from the Author. And never is it as helpless as it seems. It depends on no outward trappings.

7 And they answered, that they could not tell whence *it was.*

8 And Jesus said unto them, Neither tell I you by what authority I do these things.

9 Then began he to speak to the people this parable; A certain man planted a vineyard, and let it forth to husbandmen, and went into a far country for a long time.

that John was a prophet." 7 So they an-
swered that they did not know whence it
was. 8 And Jesus said to them, "Neither
will I tell you by what authority I do these
things."
9 And he began to tell the people this
parable: "A man planted a vineyard, and
let it out to tenants, and went into another

---

that the deputation hesitated to say that John's authority was "from men" because "they were afraid of the people." Luke makes them anticipate violent consequences: **All the people will stone us.**

3. Allegory of the Vineyard and Its Wicked Tenants (20:9-18=Mark 12:1-11)

C. H. Dodd interprets this story as a parable that Jesus used to illustrate his message of the kingdom of God, but his case is not impressive (*The Parables of the Kingdom* [New York: Charles Scribner's Sons, 1936], pp. 124-32). It is possible that vss. 9-12 were once part of a true parable, but the additional matter appears to make the whole an allegory that reflects the theological beliefs of the early church. The owner of the vineyard is God; the vineyard itself is Israel; the tenants are the hierarchs of Judaism; the servants are the prophets of O.T. times; the beloved son is Jesus Christ; the murder of the heir is the crucifixion of the Son of God; the dispossession and destruction of the wicked tenants are God's plan of history; and the new tenants are probably to be understood as the apostles.

9. To the people for Mark's "to them"—the deputation from the Sanhedrin. **This parable** for Mark's generalized "in parables." Israel as God's **vineyard** is a metaphorical

---

Jesus had none. His was a kingship that was not of this world (John 6:15). The authority which he had in actual and incontrovertible fact would not stand up on request and announce its name and pedigree (vs. 8). It would not confuse itself with its source (John 14:10). Savonarola made that mistake, and brought up in tragedy. It would not use its "heaven for thunder; nothing but thunder."[7] Men were at liberty to disavow it and throw it off because they did not fancy it, it was not to their taste: let every man be his own master, his own lord. "I would be as absolute king in my estate as any one would be in his," quoth Sancho Panza. "And being such, I would do what I liked; . . . I would take my pleasure, and taking my pleasure, I would be content; and when one is content, he hath no more to desire; and having no more to desire, the matter were ended."[8] It was an authority which men could reject through fear of its Cross and its crown of thorns, very much as these men *declined* to reject it through fear of the consequences. The pain of confession was on the one hand, the peril of bodily hurt was on the other.

[7] Shakespeare, *Measure for Measure,* Act II, scene 2.

[8] Cervantes, *Don Quixote,* Part I, Book IV, ch. xxiii.

Jesus' authority stemmed from the "givenness" of the kingdom of God. What else did he mean by "the sign of Jonah" (11:29-30)? It was witnessed to by the past and proclaimed by the present. "Go and show John again those things which ye do hear and see" (Matt. 11:4). It was validated by the truth that he spoke. It was incarnate in a life instinct with love (Matt. 7:29).

9-16. ***The Wicked Husbandmen.***—(See Expos. on 19:11.) For the expositor the timeless truth of the parable, instead of being obscured, is rather illumined by whatever testimony it has gathered to itself through the years. The picture is of tenants who have it in mind one day to possess the land in fee simple. What they have at present has been **let . . . out** to them by him whose vineyard it is, who has planted it, "and set a hedge around it, and dug a wine press in it, and built a tower" (Matt. 21:33; see Expos.). Everything has been done that could be done, both to provide and to protect. And they begin to treat it all as if they owned it outright. They tend it, and it brings forth its fruit in faithfulness. But on its produce they acknowledge no lien. Or is neglect to be read somewhere between the lines? Perhaps they

10 And at the season he sent a servant to the husbandmen, that they should give him of the fruit of the vineyard: but the husbandmen beat him, and sent *him* away empty.

11 And again he sent another servant: and they beat him also, and entreated *him* shamefully, and sent *him* away empty.

12 And again he sent a third: and they wounded him also, and cast *him* out.

13 Then said the lord of the vineyard, What shall I do? I will send my beloved son: it may be they will reverence *him* when they see him.

14 But when the husbandmen saw him, they reasoned among themselves, saying, This is the heir: come, let us kill him, that the inheritance may be ours.

15 So they cast him out of the vineyard,

country for a long while.
10 When the time
came, he sent a servant to the tenants, that
they should give him some of the fruit of
the vineyard; but the tenants beat him,
and sent him away empty-handed.
11 And
he sent another servant; him also they beat
and treated shamefully, and sent him away
empty-handed.
12 And he sent yet a third;
this one they wounded and cast out.
13 Then
the owner of the vineyard said, 'What shall
I do? I will send my beloved son; it may
be they will respect him.'
14 But when the
tenants saw him, they said to themselves,
'This is the heir; let us kill him, that the
inheritance may be ours.'
15 And they cast

equation at least as ancient as the parable in Isa. 5:1-7. The opening verse of Mark's account has been obviously modeled on the wording of that O.T. passage, but this dependence is scarcely noticeable in Luke's abbreviated version. Farm land was frequently owned by absentee landlords in biblical times and tenants were often sharecroppers. **For a long while:** A Lukan addition, possibly to emphasize the antiquity of God's covenant with Moses.

10-12. When the time came: According to Lev. 19:23-25, in the fifth year. In Mark's version a long series of servants attempted to collect the master's share of **the fruit of the vineyard.** Luke limits the number to three.

13-15*a*. Details that lack verisimilitude if the story is a parable based on real life, but pregnant with meaning if it is a Christian allegory. In Mark's account the wicked

simply allowed it to run to weeds. At any rate, of the owner, away in a **far country** that is yet near enough for him to disturb their peace—of him, **for a long time** which for them is all too short, they take no account. His servants, sent patiently one by one—for the debt's sake? or in mercy, lest a broken claim be their living death?—are beaten, shamefully treated, wounded, and cast out (11:47-51). From hilltop to valley the grim tale sweeps on like a highway into the dark. But not before one last counsel is taken. Could it be set over against the first in Gen. 1:26? **Then the owner of the vineyard said**—a scene of which Marcus Cook Connelly's *Green Pastures* [9] is strangely reminiscent. Gabriel suggests: "How about cleanin' up de whole mess of 'em and sta'tin all over ag'in wid some new kind of animal?" To which God replies: "An' admit I'm licked?" **What shall I do? I will send my beloved son; it may be. . . .** If only that Pauline **God forbid!** had come at the end of vs. 14! B. S. Easton says, "No man able to command force would risk a beloved son among such ruffians"—is it not precisely the point that God did?—"especially as only a question of rental was at stake" [1]—and is it not precisely the point that there was more, infinitely more? Parables may not be crowded against the wall and smothered, either by the commentator or by the interpreter; yet surely here, behind the discrepancies, it is permissible to catch some hint of that divine unreason which when it speaks for itself can only say, "For my thoughts are not your thoughts, neither are your ways my ways" (Isa. 55:8). **What then will the owner of the vineyard do . . . ? He will come. . . .** And who is there that shall say what things are "the last things"? **And destroy. . . .** By courtesy of some moral order that works very well of itself? One simply puts in a "cause," and pulls the lever hard, and gets out an "effect"? Is that the kind of world we live in? It is not the Bible's world. Perhaps we have moved to some other planet? (See Expos. on Matt. 6:9.) **And give**

[9] New York: Farrar & Rinehart, 1929, Part II, scene 1.

[1] *The Gospel According to St. Luke* (New York: Charles Scribner's Sons, 1926), p. 293.

and killed *him*. What therefore shall the lord of the vineyard do unto them?

16 He shall come and destroy these husbandmen, and shall give the vineyard to others. And when they heard *it*, they said, God forbid.

17 And he beheld them, and said, What is this then that is written, The stone which the builders rejected, the same is become the head of the corner?

him out of the vineyard and killed him. What then will the owner of the vineyard
do to them? 16 He will come and destroy
those tenants, and give the vineyard to others." When they heard this, they said,
"God forbid!" 17 But he looked at them
and said, "What then is this that is written:

'The very stone which the builders
rejected
has become the head of the corner'?

---

tenants killed the owner's son and cast him out of the vineyard. It is possible that Luke has altered the order of these events to make the narrative correspond to the Christian tradition that Jesus was crucified "outside the gate" (Heb. 13:12; cf. John 19:17).

15*b*-16. As in Isa. 5:4-6 a rhetorical question provided with an answer. The reference is clearly to God and his judgment. In real life an owner of a vineyard could scarcely take the law into his own hands after such a fashion. **To others:** Probably the Christian apostles are meant—with the implication that the church is the true Israel. The destruction of Jerusalem by Titus and his allocation of Palestinian lands to Roman veterans of the Jewish war are not implied. Luke adds to his source the protest of Jesus' listeners against the fate he prophesies: **God forbid!**

17. A quotation from Ps. 118:22 that was messianically interpreted both in late Judaism and in early Christianity (Acts 4:11; I Pet. 2:4-7).

. . . **to others,** whether to the lost and disinherited of Christ's own time, or as Luke must have thought, to the "new Israel" of the generations that followed. However the words are taken, the transfer is made, and the trust is handed on. Again and again that strange discontinuity: Seth, not Cain; Jacob, not Esau; David, not his brethren, nor yet Saul—on and on into history! How long? Does Christianity have the ghost of a chance? God's plan has. We may be sure of that! And the mercy never to be appropriated; only given, received, and shown.

17-18. ***The Stone Which the Builders Rejected.***—See the Exeg. for the source and significance of these two verses. They were widely popularized by preaching in the early church (Acts 4:11; I Pet. 2:7), and seem to have been inserted here in order to throw against the somber background of God's apparent defeat the sure and terrible light of his ultimate victory. Is Luke making up the deficit of triumph noted above (on vss. 9-16), or is vs. 17 to be regarded as actually the conclusion of the parable? In that case the stone should perhaps be understood as a symbol of all that official Judaism had **rejected,** both "the weightier matters of the law," and the very harlots and publicans who were pressing into the kingdom ahead of the kingdom's own children (Matt. 21:31). Vs. 18 associates two passages from the O.T. which were early regarded as messianic and used as an apologetic for the "new" faith. The figure of the cornerstone has apparently drawn into its orbit, without any too great attention to matters of consistency, both the "stone of stumbling" from Isaiah (8:14-15; cf. Luke 7:23; Matt. 11:6) and the stone "cut without hands" that in Nebuchadrezzar's dream "smote the image upon his feet . . . and brake them to pieces" (Dan. 2:34). We are to think not only of those who through the years find Christ to be a "scandal" (I Cor. 1:23; Rom. 9:32, 33), a cause of offense—they **shall be broken**—but also of those upon whom, for their deliberate disobedience and rebellion, his own active judgment must of necessity fall—**it will grind** [them] **to powder,** "like the chaff which the wind driveth away" (Ps. 1:4; cf. Ps. 2:9). Little wonder that in their careful search of the scriptures, confident as they were of God's eternal purpose, these first Christians fastened upon such texts and found in them "some chord in unison" with what they had heard from the lips of Jesus and his apostles.

And **he looked at them** steadily for that "God forbid," **and said, "What then is this that is written . . . ?"** What, indeed, for men whose eyes are not blinded, and whose ears are not stopped, but the threat of God's justice (vs. 18) and the assurance of his triumphant lovingkindness (vs. 17)? The pattern of the ages was already established even as he spoke. There had been a day when the very herald of the kingdom, now long since a martyr for his faith,

18 Whosoever shall fall upon that stone | [18] Every one who falls on that stone will be

18. Substituted by Luke for the quotation from Ps. 118:23 in Mark. Apparently a combination of phrases from Isa. 8:14 and Dan. 2:34. Luke may have found them already conjoined in some early Christian collection of proof texts (*testimonia*).

had seen in God's kind of Messiah scarcely more than an offense to the rigors of his own prophetic soul. All through the gospel record we catch the sound of that stumbling: Nicodemus, bewildered; a young man, sorrowful, for he was very rich; James and John, ambitious; the disciples, sullen and angry, gathered about the table with the dust of the road still on their feet; Peter, afraid in the light of the fire, swearing; Thomas, shaking his head at the news of the Resurrection. Then Paul, on the road to Damascus, "breathing out threatenings and slaughter" (Acts 9:1); and poor John Mark, who, "departing from them returned to Jerusalem" (Acts 13:13). And what for any of them but hardship and persecution, and the story of a crucified Galilean carpenter, and the "idle tale" of a life that had conquered death (24:11)? What sense did it make? To Jew or to Gentile? To the wise or the mighty or the noble (I Cor. 1:26)?

Every one who falls on that stone will be broken to pieces. Where did we get the idea of the "gentle Jesus, meek and mild"—except that we are forever intent on seeing not what is there but what we want to see there! The peace is itself a "scandal." The healing is a wound. The shelter is on "the stormy north side of Jesus Christ." Why did we ever suppose that the words he spoke, by the inherent magic which we think belongs to truth, would inevitably validate themselves to any honest, forthright mind? The world has been busy for twenty centuries twisting, adjusting, adapting what he said to make it intellectually respectable and demonstrably practical, only time and again to give over the whole sorry business, shrug its shoulders, and take off after its own devices. There is something more serious going on that does not lend itself to pastel shades. There is something more than sweet reasonableness at work in the world, something appallingly in earnest. Thoughtlessness reaps its harvest of misery. Self-pity pays the price it has to pay. Pride and stubbornness, greed and envy, bring up where they bring up. **Every one who falls on that stone. . . .**

But when it falls on any one. . . . Was such a stone in sight when he spoke? Some of them in the temple were of almost unbelievable size (Expos. 21:5-6). The destruction of Jerusalem in A.D. 70 and the fate of the Jews seemed to the rapidly growing Christian community proof enough that the God of history had at least for the time being rejected his chosen people and called another in their stead. Paul argues the case in detail (Rom. 9–11), as one struck with awe by the unsearchable judgments and the "ways past finding out." No doubt it is impossible for us so simply to equate the rise and fall of nations with the balancing up and down of God's great scales; much less the prosperity of the righteous and the defeat of the wicked with his favor and his frown. Yet could it be that in spite of all appearances there is nothing quite so safe as justice is?

With ever the hand of Christ held out to keep a man from utter ruin! "Then saith he to Thomas, Reach hither thy finger" (John 20:27). "And the Lord said, I am Jesus whom thou persecutest" (Acts 9:5). There at **the head of the corner, the very stone which the builders rejected!** It is difficult to imagine the full extent and sweep of the courage which pitted itself, with this faith in its heart, against an empire: and afterward struggled up out of the wreckage to take captive the barbarian hordes that poured down from the North. For us, in our far-off time, the assurance of Christ's final triumph, whatever the odds, should have become almost a commonplace. We have seen him emerge from the pomp and ceremony, the institutionalism and priestcraft, of the Middle Ages, stark and clear and full of majesty. We have seen him come through the intellectual and spiritual sterility of Deism and the Enlightenment, first as the Jesus of history, then as the Christ of experience, finally as man's eternal Contemporary, Christ Jesus, Lord of his church, Judge and Savior. Through slavery, through the industrial revolution, through World War I unhurt, through World War II: until not to obey him now seems only to rush down a steep place into the sea.

Before the mind's eye, as century fades into century, multitudes building: and the great block of granite there at one side, rough hewn, discarded, forgotten. Workmen stumble over it. With infinite pains they try to rid themselves of it; but the ropes break, the girders give way, and it crashes down on them. Until as in a dream it stands one day firmly in its place, and the walls hold, and "the tabernacle of God is with men" (Rev. 21:3).

18. *The Harm Jesus Risked Doing.*—Every one who falls on that stone . . . (cf. Matt. 11:6;

shall be broken; but on whomsoever it shall fall, it will grind him to powder.

19 ¶ And the chief priests and the scribes the same hour sought to lay hands on him; and they feared the people: for they perceived that he had spoken this parable against them.

20 And they watched *him,* and sent forth spies, which should feign themselves just men, that they might take hold of his words, that so they might deliver him unto the power and authority of the governor.

21 And they asked him, saying, Master, we know that thou sayest and teachest rightly, neither acceptest thou the person *of any,* but teachest the way of God truly:

broken to pieces; but when it falls on any one it will crush him."

19 The scribes and the chief priests tried to lay hands on him at that very hour, but they feared the people; for they perceived that he had told this parable against them.
20 So they watched him, and sent spies, who pretended to be sincere, that they might take hold of what he said, so as to deliver him up to the authority and jurisdiction of the governor.
21 They asked him, "Teacher, we know that you speak and teach rightly, and show no partiality, but

4. Question About Paying the Head Tax to Caesar (20:19-26=Mark 12:12-17)

19-20. Luke rewrites his Marcan source. **Spies** for Mark's "some of the Pharisees and some of the Herodians." Luke refers to the Pharisees in the phrase **who pretended to be sincere,** but never mentions the Herodians in his Gospel. He may not have known who they were or may have thought that reference to them would have little meaning for his Gentile readers. **So as to deliver him up to . . . the governor** states a purpose implicit in Mark's account.

21-22. Tribute: An annual poll tax collected by the Romans from every adult male in Judea after the deposition of Archelaus in A.D. 6. The levy was very unpopular, for it was interpreted as a mark of Jewish subjugation to a foreign power. The question was

Rom. 9:33; Gal. 5:11*b*). The gospel did indeed become a stumbling block and a "scandal." People floundered around through the words of Jesus miles away from the truth that he meant. They took left turns from his purpose, went beating about wrong corners; snatched up some poor half of a promise, with eyes all aglow, hugging it close, only to stagger off so far with it that there seemed nothing to do at last but to drag out the dry, meaningless thing, and snap it, and throw it away. But he had to run that risk.

He had to run the risk of taking the majesty away from God, leaving him forever in the eyes of men like a young Galilean, without the kingdom and the power and the glory, without any islands or stars on his mind, trailing a mystic, alien splendor through life, with common sandals on his feet, and a garment's hem that a shy woman could touch.

And he had to run the risk of taking all the blood and nails out of forgiveness, and gathering them into his own body on a cross—as if there were nothing else, and everybody could settle back with a deep sigh. He risked it all—on Calvary. And nothing but Calvary has kept him from losing!

19-21. ***Tribute—in Counterfeit.***—In Luke's account, **the scribes and the chief priests,** their hostility and anger brought now to the pitch of conspiracy both by their fear of the people and by what had been said, **for they perceived that he had told this parable against them, . . . sent spies, who pretended to be sincere, that they might take hold of what he said.** Pride and prejudice, privilege and "patriotism," combine forces. Like the outposts of an investing army, watching closely by the gates of a city, disguising themselves, pretending to be what they are not, suddenly from their place of concealment, where they have been lying in wait, they seize on their victim. The metaphor is consistent and well wrought out, as is the strategy (see Exeg.).

With a feigned and almost fawning deference they pay him their "tribute" first. It was wrung from them by the facts. Their sarcasm is sober truth: **You speak and teach rightly.** The sneer in their hearts becomes a salute on their lips. Their witness is counterfeit; but the years have reminted it and made it sterling coin. So are life's rebellious moods met and countered by God's reversal. (Ps. 2:2-6; cf. Gen. 42:36; 45:4-14; Eccl. 9:2; Matt. 5:45; Rom. 8:28; see

22 Is it lawful for us to give tribute unto Caesar, or no?

23 But he perceived their craftiness, and said unto them, Why tempt ye me?

24 Show me a penny. Whose image and superscription hath it? They answered and said, Caesar's.

25 And he said unto them, Render therefore unto Caesar the things which be Caesar's, and unto God the things which be God's.

truly teach the way of God. 22 Is it lawful
for us to give tribute to Caesar, or not?"
23 But he perceived their craftiness, and
said to them, 24 "Show me a coin.[l] Whose
likeness and inscription has it?" They said,
"Caesar's." 25 He said to them, "Then ren-
der to Caesar the things that are Caesar's,
and to God the things that are God's."

[l] Greek *denarius.*

---

cleverly framed. If Jesus were to give an affirmative answer, he would alienate all fervent nationalists. If he were to answer "No," he would lay himself open to the charge of treason (cf. 23:2).

23-24. Craftiness: An apt substitution by Luke for Mark's "hypocrisy." **A coin:** A denarius, a silver coin (of sixty grains) worth about twenty cents, minted by the Romans, and in Jesus' day bearing the **likeness and inscription** of Augustus or Tiberius. The reproduction of the head of the deified emperor violated the Jewish law against images and irritated Jewish sensibilities. The coinage issued in Judea by the procurators was made of bronze or copper and carried only such inoffensive emblems as olive branches or palms.

25. A celebrated saying often interpreted as wholly noncommittal. Jesus' answer to his enemies was a clever evasion of the trap they had set for him. But this can hardly be correct. Jesus clearly asserts that the tax is to be paid. He repudiated the position of those extremists who held that a loyal and patriotic Jew could not obey the Roman state and still serve God or regard him as King. If coins were circulating with Caesar's image on them, they belonged to the emperor and he had a perfect right to demand them. But at

---

also the curse that became a prayer, Matt. 27:25, and the grim jest in Matt. 27:37; to say nothing of Matt. 11:16-19.)

22-26. ***Caesar's and God's.***—There is no evasion here. Jesus walks into their trap with his eyes wide open, and lays himself out on both counts. In ancient times a ruler's authority was supposed to extend as far as the circulation of his coinage. Even the coinage itself was regarded as the ruler's property. **Whose likeness . . . has it?** Then give him what belongs to him! So much for the Pharisees. But he goes on, farther than anybody had asked him to go. It had not been much more than ten years since the Roman senate had voted divine honors to Caesar Augustus at his death. Temples were being built to him everywhere. Have nothing to do with that, says Jesus in effect. There is an allegiance which belongs to God alone. Give it to no other. Was this for the Sadducees? They were moving about on the world's level. No wonder they were what they were. Life had another dimension. There was an "infinite perpendicular from the stars." And men marveled: not at his cleverness in getting out of a tight place, but at the fearless and indefeasible truth he had uttered.

There is a debt we owe the state. There is a debt we owe it even when it is corrupt. Rome was not an easy mistress. Yet her claims, within bounds, were just claims. Luke no doubt would underscore it—lest the early church be thought subversive. And those claims could be met, they should be met, without surrendering that ultimate loyalty which is able to transform all of life into a sacrament of the sovereignty and presence of God. In no other way, when the final reckoning is made, can they be met. We talk about the value of the individual, and call it the keystone of democracy. It is a notion that simply cannot stand by itself. The centuries that have passed since the Renaissance have proved its inability to hold its own against science and industry. Jesus took it and set it in the context of God's creation and God's redemption. We talk about freedom, and we talk about equality: in the face of a vicious nationalism, bolstered by a spurious creed, and adorned with a spurious ritual, they become little more than political and religious window dressing.

Those who contend that the true faith can never get into politics should remember that zeal for a false faith can! National aggrandizement, private expediency, tribal doctrines of

26 And they could not take hold of his words before the people: and they marveled at his answer, and held their peace.

27 ¶ Then came to *him* certain of the Sadducees, which deny that there is any resurrection; and they asked him,

26 And they were not able in the presence of the people to catch him by what he said; but marveling at his answer they were silent.

27 There came to him some Sad'du-cees, those who say that there is no resurrection,

the same time there were duties and debts that men owed to God. The two loyalties were not incompatible. It should be unnecessary for the interpreter to point out that this saying does not support any social theory that would put our secular responsibilities in one compartment of living and our religious duties in another. Nor does it provide us with a theoretical discussion of the relationships of church and state such as Paul develops in Rom. 13:1-7.

26. An editorial elaboration of Mark's comment on the impression Jesus' answer had made on his interlocutors.

5. Question About the Resurrection (20:27-40; cf. Mark 12:18-28*a*, 32*b*, 34*b*)

27. The **Sadducees** accepted only the written tradition as authoritative. Because the doctrine of a life to come, based on belief in a physical resurrection, arose after the Pentateuch was compiled and is not reflected in it, they were justified by their premises when they declared **that there is no resurrection** (cf. Acts 23:8).

blood and soil openly take the place of morals, until man begins to lose his mind in the suppression of thought and his soul in the body politic. He shuts his eyes to what he is and begins to regard primarily what he has. Things count, and life grows cheap, ending for him in emptiness and hysteria and a ruthless bondage to his own sterile lusts. They are pictured on the sinister red walls of ancient Pompeii. Over in Rome, when you take off your hat and step into some clear, cool chapel of the early days of Christianity, you realize what freshness fell with the gospel on the jaded senses of antiquity. May it not be for God's sake that we **render to Caesar the things that are Caesar's;** and for Caesar's sake that we render **to God the things that are God's!** The Christian church has more than a nuisance value to the state; but the Word it speaks is a troublesome word, making the world angry, causing it to strike back because it never understands, but bringing it to wonder about itself!

Some refuse to listen. They still think that national elections and community housing, race riots and war, can somehow be dissociated from the passion of Christ, as secular and mundane, not quite religious; and while they stick to their knitting, many of them with what they have mistaken for the pure gospel ringing in their ears, time marches on! And God! Now and then we are told that anything we do will only make matters worse. By reason of the sin that dogs our steps, our very best efforts are bound to produce the very worst results. Whoever wants to sit down in that, let him sit down. We can manage without him. What difference does it make to proclaim a gospel to this world if that gospel can make no difference? Whoever sits down, let him at the same time, in the blunt language of the streets, shut up! There is a kingdom that God brings! To him whom we worship, the offer of the land that we love. For the land that we love, the offer of him whom we worship!

27-38. ***As on Earth, so in Heaven?***—Most of the difficulties we have with the "afterlife" can be traced precisely to this false assumption. Marie Corelli, in *The Sorrows of Satan,* satirized the golden streets and the pearly gates which at the end of the nineteenth century were the subject of so much ridicule, and in some cases no doubt quite genuine obstacles in the way of faith. Trying to read into that unknown future the conditions of time and space which provide the framework of the present is not only naïve and futile; it may be thoroughly disastrous. Will infants be infants still, and the aged still aged? H. G. Wells used to insist that an eternity of H. G. Wells would be more than distasteful to him; it would be intolerable. The people we meet, shall we know them? And shall we miss the people who are not there? With what sorrow or with what joy? Moreover, if you will, please explain to us what happens in the interval between death and resurrection. And when you are through, tell us where on earth—or in any other imaginable place—there will be room for heaven, with some two billion candi-

28 Saying, Master, Moses wrote unto us, If any man's brother die, having a wife, and he die without children, that his brother should take his wife, and raise up seed unto his brother.

29 There were therefore seven brethren: and the first took a wife, and died without children.

30 And the second took her to wife, and he died childless.

31 And the third took her; and in like manner the seven also: and they left no children, and died.

32 Last of all the woman died also.

33 Therefore in the resurrection whose wife of them is she? for seven had her to wife.

28 and they asked him a question, saying,
"Teacher, Moses wrote for us that if a
man's brother dies, having a wife but no
children, the man[m] must take the wife and
raise up children for his brother. 29 Now
there were seven brothers; the first took a
wife, and died without children; 30 and the
second 31 and the third took her, and like-
wise all seven left no children and died.
32 Afterward the woman also died. 33 In
the resurrection, therefore, whose wife will
the woman be? For the seven had her as
wife."

[m] Greek *his brother.*

---

28. The reference is to the so-called "levirate" marriage law in Deut. 25:5-6. A survival in ancient Hebrew legislation of ideas once associated with ancestor worship, the regulation appears to have been largely in abeyance in Jesus' day.

29-33. Not an attempt at cheap humor, but an effort to show that Moses could not have contemplated any resurrection. His legislation demonstrates that the doctrine leads to absurdity.

---

dates every thirty years or so, to say nothing of all the arrivals since Adam? In any case, how do you suppose we shall spend eternity, when so many of us seem unable to spend time? Even in our day there is no dearth of material at hand for those who, with an irony which so often does no more than save a man's face when he looks in the mirror—how else can he bear it?—are inclined to reduce the whole fantastic notion to wishful thinking, and beyond that to what is so manifestly a logical absurdity.

And all because we are forever bent on reducing to the familiar terms of our own experience what we do not, and in the very nature of things cannot, know very much about. It is somewhat as if the unborn child, there in the warm and sheltering dark, were able to dream of what might lie on the other side of that last convulsive shudder which is birth! The glint of the sun on water, the snow flying crazily in the wind, food, the hurly-burly of the world, the flight of planes, flowers blooming, the sound of words, rain dripping from the roof.

Some Sadducees, . . . who say that there is no resurrection. Note the argument and its implications. At best, as they saw it, the doctrine of the resurrection of the body was a popular belief that had grown up under the persecutions of the two preceding centuries. Let the philosophers among the Greeks speculate about immortality; let the Jews hold to what they always had believed from time immemorial. Read the Pentateuch. These novel and widespread ideas were nothing in the world but an unintelligent attempt to compensate for the obvious inequities of human existence; and so an abysmal waste of both the brains and the energy that might otherwise be so much more profitably devoted to politics and culture and the improvement of life as it was. In Sheol were the shadowed dead, good and bad alike, dim ghosts of their former selves. To talk about their being alive in any way that mattered was to talk sheer nonsense. It was the technique of escape, no less than the equally vague messianic hopes, which plagued the nation into idleness and sterility: "Beautiful island of somewhere"! Go back to Moses and the Law. How much of it will you find there? Besides, what would happen if we took any of it seriously? Let us say **there were seven brothers.** The trouble is that there were other assumptions, too, though unexpressed. Is it not always so? They took it for granted that what they meant by "body" was what God meant by it (I Cor. 15:12-58). They took it for granted, therefore, that the same provisions which had been made for life here would apply as well to life hereafter. And worst of all, they took it for granted that the entire question had very little practical value or bearing.

To begin with this last and deal with it first, we are surely not too wide of the mark when we find in Jesus' words, **those who are ac-**

34 And Jesus answering said unto them, The children of this world marry, and are given in marriage:

35 But they which shall be accounted worthy to obtain that world, and the resurrection from the dead, neither marry, nor are given in marriage:

36 Neither can they die any more: for they are equal unto the angels; and are the children of God, being the children of the resurrection.

34 And Jesus said to them, "The sons of
this age marry and are given in marriage;
35 but those who are accounted worthy to
attain to that age and to the resurrection
from the dead neither marry nor are given
in marriage, 36 for they cannot die any
more, because they are equal to angels
and are sons of God, being sons of the resur-

34-35. Luke rewrites his Marcan source. Some interpreters believe he is collating it with an independent tradition. Read **this age** and **that age** with the RSV. For **marry** and **are given in marriage** (vs. 34) some ancient MSS have "procreate" and "are born," and these readings are preferred by some modern editors as a better introduction to vs. 36. **Those who are accounted worthy:** Luke's version makes Jesus anticipate only "a resurrection of the just" (cf. 14:14).

36. An expansion of Mark's "but are like angels in heaven." In this age marriage is an institution necessary for the propagation of the race, but its necessity disappears when men and women become **equal to angels** and do not **die any more.** Some ancient authorities omit **and are sons. Sons of the resurrection:** A Semitism comparable to "the sons of this age" (vs. 34).

counted worthy, the note of moral relevance. Though disbelief in the life to come does not invariably have its origin in, or inevitably give rise to, moral corruption, there is nevertheless a steady, gravitational pull between them. Paul spells it out for us in Phil. 3:18-19, by way of parenthesis: "For many walk, of whom I have told you often, and now tell you even weeping, that they are the enemies of the cross of Christ." Mark this now: their "end is destruction," their "God is their belly," their "glory is in their shame," they "mind earthly things." He begins where they finish, and step by step moves back to where it all began. Their history had been a kind of pilgrim's progress headed the wrong way. It is the story of what happens to this-worldliness, not from A to Z, but from Z to A. It is the evolution of secularism in reverse. Perhaps it is not without significance that the aristocratic Sadducees, numbers of whom were priests, and rigidly conservative, were at the same time, many of them—like their counterparts among the medieval prelates of the Roman Church, and shall we add, even among the rank and file of a clergy less remote—out-and-out secularists.

Strange we scarcely ever attend to the absurdities of the proposition that "one world at a time" is enough! With an eye to this world only no man can read clearly the riddle of his own selfhood. He sees himself now as the architect of history, now as its pawn; now as the measure of all things, now as a blob of protoplasm, an automatic reflex, a cosmic accident. He is a house divided against itself, split wide open, and hopelessly split. Nor can he read the riddle of what his being here is all about: half of it looks like bread and butter, with a little decent security, and a little decent happiness on the way to it; the other half makes him think now and then that he has missed something, and perhaps ought to go to church and find out what it is. This is to secularize both the Christian doctrine of man and the Christian doctrine of man's mission under God. In the gospel we are never allowed to lose sight of the paradox of dust and divinity which we are: to forget the devil within is to become a fool, saying in his heart, "There is no God"; to forget the angel is to become a cynic, whose curse it is not even to believe in man! Nor are we allowed for a moment to lose sight of the thrust and counterthrust of human existence: the tension in which our life stands, between the actual and the possible; between what is, this week, this month, this year, in the mind of man, and what is eternally in the mind of God; between the kingdoms of this world and the kingdom of our Lord and of his Christ (see Expos. on 23:16).

Jesus would remind the Sadducees and all their kind that being is at least conceivable (*a*) on other terms than these that we know, terms whereby even the law of death is broken —**they cannot die any more**—how much, then, the law of marrying and giving in marriage;

37 Now that the dead are raised, even
Moses showed at the bush, when he calleth
the Lord the God of Abraham, and the
God of Isaac, and the God of Jacob.
38 For he is not a God of the dead, but
of the living: for all live unto him.
39 ¶ Then certain of the scribes answer-
ing said, Master, thou hast well said.
40 And after that they durst not ask him
any *question at all.*
41 And he said unto them, How say they
that Christ is David's son?

rection. 37 But that the dead are raised, even
Moses showed, in the passage about the
bush, where he calls the Lord the God of
Abraham and the God of Isaac and the
God of Jacob. 38 Now he is not God of the
dead, but of the living; for all live to him."
39 And some of the scribes answered,
"Teacher, you have spoken well." 40 For
they no longer dared to ask him any ques-
tion.
41 But he said to them, "How can they

37-38. In the passage about the bush: Exod. 3:2-6. Jesus' deduction of the doctrine of the resurrection from this O.T. passage is less direct in Luke's version than in Mark's, but in both instances its verbal exegesis is typically rabbinical. It would be nonsense for **Moses** to speak of the **Lord** as **God** of the patriarchs if they were only men who had lived and died long ago. The argument may have been adapted from Jewish sources. Interesting parallels have been cited from IV Macc. 7:19 and 16:25 (first century B.C.). **For all live to him,** i.e., "all the just" (23:43) rather than "all the patriarchs."

39-40. A conclusion constructed out of Marcan phrases (Mark 12:28*a*, 32*b*, 34*b*). Luke omits the story of the question about the greatest commandment because he has already used a variant of it (10:25-28).

6. Question About the Davidic Descent of the Christ (20:41-44=Mark 12:35-37*a*)

The Jewish hope of a Messiah arose out of an idealization of Israel under the rule of David and the longing of the nation for the return of its former glories as a united kingdom under some member of the Davidic line. Perhaps its earliest articulation in O.T. literature is in Nathan's speech to David (II Sam. 7:12-16). Micah, Isaiah, and some

---

and (*b*) among other orders of God's creation —**they are equal to angels—sons** no longer of this world but of that, **of God** and **of the resurrection.** And above all else, immeasurably more important than any of the insights that have to be deepened, or the conceptions that have to be enlarged, the fact that God is not the kind of God who would allow "the people of his pasture" to perish, "the sheep of his hand" to be swallowed up from off the face of the earth into bleak nothingness. On their own ground he would meet them (vs. 28). **That the dead are raised, even Moses showed,** there in the story of the bush that burned and was not consumed, when the Lord called unto him and said, "I am the God of thy father," **the God of Abraham and the God of Isaac and the God of Jacob** (Exod. 3:6), all of them dead long since. Why talk then of wishful thinking when it is not man who is in question anyhow, but God? It was their point of view that had to be changed. A living God meant something about the living. A loving God meant something about the dead! Were they not still his care and dear possession? It is not too distant a journey from that high lookout to the quiet and undisturbed confidence of the upper room, "In my Father's house are many mansions" (John 14:2). Not far to the breathless conviction of Paul: "For I am persuaded, that neither death, nor life, nor angels, nor principalities, nor powers, nor things present, nor things to come, nor height, nor depth, nor any other creature, shall be able to separate us from the love of God, which is in Christ Jesus our Lord" (Rom. 8:38-39).

39-40. *Victory as Dilemma.*—Master, thou hast well said. The discovery that Jesus was on their side in this long-standing controversy with the Sadducees about the resurrection brought to the scribes a certain measure of relief; but the relief was offset by the embarrassment. It was good to have an opponent defeated; it was troublesome to be hemmed in themselves by the victory, unable to set any more traps of their own! Halfhearted compliments would have to serve; and silence.

41-44. *David's Son or Lord?*—For the expositor to become involved in the questions that are raised, and properly raised, by the critic, would

42 And David himself saith in the book of Psalms, The LORD said unto my Lord, Sit thou on my right hand,
43 Till I make thine enemies thy footstool.

say that the Christ is David's son? 42 For
David himself says in the Book of Psalms,
'The Lord said to my Lord,
Sit at my right hand,
43 till I make thy enemies a stool for
thy feet.'

of the psalmists took over the popular hope, purged it of its more nationalistic and materialistic traits, and spoke of the religious, spiritual, and ethical qualities that the "son of David" would display. In postexilic times the idea of the new age came to be formulated in terms of a theocracy, and the hope of a Davidic Messiah gradually fell into the background. After the Maccabean revolt of 168 B.C. the hope was largely displaced by the expectation of a supernatural being—the "Son of man"—who would be God's vicegerent in the miraculous inauguration of the new age. But Pss. Sol. 17–18, written about the middle of the first century B.C., show that the older category of thought continued to be popular in some quarters of Judaism. They speak of a descendant of the Davidic house whom God will raise up to overthrow the rule of the Gentiles, to gather the dispersed tribes of Israel, and to establish God's kingdom with its capital at Jerusalem (cf. Matt. 9:27; 12:23; 15:22; 21:9, 15; Mark 10:47-48; John 7:42).

The early church undertook to demonstrate that Jesus had fulfilled Jewish messianic expectations by his birth at Bethlehem and his lineal descent from David, but there is little trace of this early Christology except in the opening chapters of Matthew and Luke. It was quickly discarded in favor of more adequate ways of thinking such as "Son of man," "Son of God," "Lord," and "Word of God." There are references to the earlier belief in the opening sentence of Paul's Epistle to the Romans (1:3), and in two liturgical passages in the book of Revelation (5:5; 22:16), but nowhere else in the N.T.

The passage under consideration is a forthright repudiation of the theory that the Messiah must be "David's son," and a hint that he is more properly described as "Lord," a title used in the LXX for God and in liturgical formulas of the mystery cults for various pagan deities. If the verses are based on genuine utterances of Jesus, the question remains: Was he speaking "of himself, or of some other"? More probably they reflect some early christological controversy and were intended to demonstrate from Scripture that Jesus Christ was entitled to a more adequate appellation than "son of David."

41. To them: To the scribes of vs. 39; in Mark to an audience in the temple courts. **They** for Mark's "the scribes."

42-43. The Book of Psalms was popularly ascribed to **David** long before N.T. times. The quotation is from Ps. 110:1. It is interpreted as prophetic of the Ascension in Acts 2:34-35 and of Christ's work as heavenly high priest in Heb. 1:13 and 10:12-13. In the present instance only the opening words are important for the argument.

be to manifest something of the same lack of discernment that characterized the scribes. Beneath all of the questions, and they are legion, is the deeper question; and it is as relevant today as ever it has been. Matthew preserves it for us, "What think ye of Christ?" (Matt. 22:42.) The mystery that confronts us in the person of Jesus of Nazareth is no less a mystery than it was to the scribes. If we come at it with our own prefabricated misconceptions, we are no whit better off than they. We read of him in the Gospels as of one who lived long since, and find him dealing with us as if he were strangely alive. We are happily conscious of his kinship with all our joy and sorrow; weeping over Jerusalem; standing there in the temple, far too robust a figure for many a man's taste, or here, facing his enemies with a song in his heart (read Pss. 110–118), bone of our bone, flesh of our flesh; tempted and lonely, or it may be, eating and drinking with publicans and sinners; the glint of humor in his speech, as the better people look at him askance; or weary, asleep in a boat, or trudging the roads of Palestine. Until suddenly, as in Luke's story of the miraculous draught of fishes, so carefully recorded because whatever its provenance every man knows the meaning of it, his eyes seem to flash the lightnings of Sinai; in his quiet voice sound the distant echoes of God's great

44 David therefore calleth him Lord, how is he then his son?	44 David thus calls him Lord; so how is he his son?"
45 ¶ Then in the audience of all the people he said unto his disciples,	45 And in the hearing of all the people

44. How can the Messiah be David's **son** when **David** refers to **him** as **Lord?** It has been argued that these words do not deny Jesus' descent from David; they only assert that the title "son of David," with its political associations, does not by itself do justice to Jesus' sense of mission.

7. Jesus Warns Against the Scribes (20:45-47=Mark 12:38-40)

Mark's preamble implies that this material is only an excerpt—"And in his teaching he said . . ." Since the substance of 20:46 has already been used by Luke in 11:43 as part of a discourse abstracted from Q, it is possible that Mark also knew some version of this collection of Jesus' teaching.

45. Virtually a new introduction to Marcan matter.

"I am" (John 8:58), and we too can do nothing but falter, "Depart from me; for I am a sinful man, O Lord" (5:8). Perhaps we stand one day before Michelangelo's tremendous painting of the final judgment, and see him on his throne, his great arm raised in that mighty gesture of repudiation, as from before his face the wicked stumble their way into hell (Matt. 25:41-45): and back into memory steal kindlier gestures—"And Jesus . . . put forth his hand, and touched him" (Mark 1:41); and softer words—"Come unto me, all ye that labor and are heavy laden, and I will give you rest" (Matt. 11:28); and we know in our hearts again the Word "made flesh, . . . full of grace and truth" (John 1:14), even "that which was from the beginning, which we have heard, which we have seen with our eyes, which we have looked upon, and our hands have handled" (I John 1:1). In ch. 7 of the Fourth Gospel something of this same bewilderment is tossed to and fro, from verse to verse: "When Christ cometh, no man knoweth whence he is" (John 7:27); "When Christ cometh, will he do more miracles than these which this man hath done?" (John 7:31); "Hath not the Scripture said, That Christ cometh of the seed of David?" (John 7:42.)

> Just when we are safest, there's a sunset-touch,
> A fancy from a flower-bell, some one's death,
> A chorus-ending from Euripides,
> And that's enough for fifty hopes and fears
> As old and new at once as nature's self,
> To rap and knock and enter in the soul.[2]

"Behold the man!" (John 19:5.) "Behold your King!" (John 19:14.)

Yet the last word of all is not mystery. Rather is it Pilate's question, "What shall I do then with Jesus which is called Christ?" (Matt. 27:22.) And Jesus' own question, "Why call ye me, Lord, Lord, and do not the things which I say?" (6:46.)

45-47. ***Blind Leaders of the Blind.***—Jesus' attack on the scribes or rabbis, most of them Pharisees, must not of course be regarded as directed against the whole group. It may well be that such sweeping generalizations as are placed on his lips (11:37-54; Matt. 23; Mark 12:38-40), though by no means uncommon among the prophets and reformers of all ages (cf. Luther and Wycliffe on the friars; or Erasmus' *Praise of Folly*), owe their present form in part at least to the distortions of those early years when the Christian community was subject to Jewish persecution. Even as they stand, they preserve traces of conscious hyperbole and humor (Matt. 23:4, 15, 23, 24). Certainly the seven "woes" in Matt. 23 (cf. Luke 11:42-54) cannot be summarily characterized as "maledictions"; rather are they expressions of both indignation and pity, as one should say, "Alas for the scribes and Pharisees!" Luce[3] quotes Lagrange, "Un grave avertissement sur une situation funeste" (cf. 6:24-26). Back of them one must still sense what was undoubtedly the fact, that Jesus would willingly have enlisted the support of these religious elite among his own people; but not at the cost of any compromise with the hypocritical pretensions of those who were most vocal among them. A Pharisee of the Pharisees was soon to be the foremost herald of his gospel.

In the present instance the indictment would seem to run on three principal counts (see Exeg.). Ostentation, greed, and hypocrisy are the forms which evil commonly takes when it attempts to hide itself under the cloak of piety.

[2] Robert Browning, "Bishop Blougram's Apology."

[3] *Gospel According to Luke,* on Luke 11:42.

46 Beware of the scribes, which desire to walk in long robes, and love greetings in the markets, and the highest seats in the synagogues, and the chief rooms at feasts;
47 Which devour widows' houses, and for a show make long prayers: the same shall receive greater damnation.

21 And he looked up, and saw the rich men casting their gifts into the treasury.

he said to his disciples, 46 "Beware of the scribes, who like to go about in long robes, and love salutations in the market places and the best seats in the synagogues and the places of honor at feasts, 47 who devour widows' houses and for a pretense make long prayers. They will receive the greater condemnation."

21 He looked up and saw the rich putting their gifts into the treasury;

46-47. The scribes are said to be guilty of ostentation, greed, and hypocrisy (see on 11:37-54). **Long robes:** The distinctive dress of Jewish scholars. **Best seats:** See on 11:43. **Who devour widows' houses:** Exploitation of widows (forbidden by the regulation in Exod. 22:22) is censured by Isaiah as a particularly offensive social sin (Isa. 10:2). **Greater condemnation,** i.e., than ordinary sinners. Their calling as interpreters of the law made their behavior all the more reprehensible.

8. The Widow's Gift to the Temple Treasury (21:1-4=Mark 12:41-44)

Attached by Mark to his collection of accounts of controversies between Jesus and opponents in Jerusalem, perhaps because of the reference to "widows' houses" in the condemnation of scribes with which it ends. The chapter division imposed on Luke's

---

Here are (*a*) the **long robes** of the great personage, the obsequious gestures of salutation in the market place, the "platform" **seats in the synagogues,** the positions of honor at table (14:1-11): all of it coupled in unholy alliance with (*b*) the stealthy abuse of privilege—the scribes were at times protégés or executors of rich widows—and studiously covered over with (*c*) much praying. "They have their reward"; so runs the verdict in another place (Matt. 6:2). What they seek, they get: and in the getting find that their accounts are written off, "paid in full." To that note of terror is added now **the greater condemnation:** "For unto whomsoever much is given, of him shall be much required" (12:47-48; cf. 21:1-4).

One reads this passage the more seriously, since the devil is never more to be feared than when he appears as an angel of light. His "first trick," writes Denis de Rougemont, "is his *incognito*." We "meet him in our virtues."[4] He disguises himself as a democrat. He confronts us in our gods. Tyranny, slavery, the supremacy of the white man; torture, poverty, war, and the *status quo*—all have been sanctified in the high and holy name of religion. The worship that tries to take the place of repentance, the obedience that tries to take the place of love, the charity that tries to take the place of reform: if there is ever to be any redemption for this tortured world, what chance has any of it to escape "the arrows of the Almighty"?

It is the prophet's function to tear down the façade, to strip off the sham and pretense. As Catherine the Great made her royal pilgrimages through Russia, her field marshal, Potemkin, would build along the route charming landscapes and village scenes to hide the squalor and desolation of the countryside ("Potemkin's villages"). What seems ruthlessness in Jesus, may it not be the very compassion of God, running the risk of stoking still further the murderous fires of human hate in order to break through the hard crust of man's self-esteem and rescue him from suicide? (Cf. Matt. 20:20-28.)

21:1-4. ***The Widow's Mite.***—In Mark's version, "Jesus sat over against the treasury." Where else more clearly may "the thoughts of many hearts" be revealed? **And he . . . saw the rich. . . . And he saw also a certain poor widow.** It was a moment when lives, not gifts, were in the balance; and the eyes that were looking on were eyes that nothing could escape. Each of the chests bore its own designation of the purpose it was intended to serve in the schedule of temple expenditures, the thirteen items of the current budget. There is no indication in the text that the rich were anything but gen-

[4] See *The Devil's Share,* tr. Haakon Chevalier (Washington: Pantheon Books, 1944), pp. 17, 51, 89 ff., 119 ff., 201.

2 And he saw also a certain poor widow casting in thither two mites.
3 And he said, Of a truth I say unto you, that this poor widow hath cast in more than they all:
4 For all these have of their abundance cast in unto the offerings of God: but she of her penury hath cast in all the living that she had.

2 and he saw a poor widow put in two
copper coins. 3 And he said, "Truly I tell
you, this poor widow has put in more than
all of them; 4 for they all contributed out
of their abundance, but she out of her
poverty put in all the living that she had."

Gospel is an unhappy one at this point, for the story is in no sense an introduction to the subsequent apocalyptic section. The passage is an excellent illustration of Luke's practice of abbreviating Mark, omitting his Semitisms, and improving his style. Stories with a similar moral were commonplace in Jewish, Greek, and Indian (Buddhist) literature.

21:1-2. Treasury: Probably a room in one of the porticoes of the Court of Women. Thirteen trumpet-shaped receptacles were provided, supervised by priests, and the donor had to declare the sum he was offering and the special ritual purpose for which it was intended. **Two copper coins:** A *lepton,* worth less than half a cent, was the smallest Jewish coin in circulation.

3-4. It is not the size of the gift that gives it value in the sight of God but the sacrificial generosity with which it is given. **All the living that she had:** All the money she possessed for the purchase of her next meal.

---

erous. Mark, indeed, underscores their generosity. Nor is there any reason to suppose that they made a parade of their gifts, though undoubtedly there were some who did (Matt. 6:1-4). The point is that they gave **of their abundance.** It is hinted in the word itself that they were merely drawing on what remained to them as surplus, the "over and above" after all their own needs had been fully met, and likely enough most of their desires. Perhaps to indulge the imagination further is to do violence to the simple charm of the story, which sweeps up in a single verse from wealth to **poverty,** fluttering there like a flag just broken to the breeze; from what was left of "more than enough," with the sudden flight of a bird, to the full-winged **all the living that she had,** everything she could lay her hands on at the moment. But the temptation to read a little bit more, beyond the written word, will not be so stoutly denied. Interpreters are under bond to faithfulness, not to sterility. The constant peril that stalks **the rich** is that for all their generosity God may so readily come well on toward the last of their obligations. A woman who lived quite alone in her luxurious apartment on one of the most exclusive avenues of a great city apologized for her none too miserly, yet none too handsome, gift to the church by referring to the salaries she paid her maids, her butler, and her chauffeur, to say nothing of taxes, or of the high cost of living, or of her regular seat at the opera. Insensibly such giving slithers away into the routine discharge of a routine and respectable benefaction. It may even come to serve as partial compensation for the social injustice, if nothing worse, on which great fortunes are so often built. Conscience money is not infrequent at the stated services of public worship; and perhaps should be allowed without prejudice to make what poor amends it can! Dwight Moody, the evangelist, used to say that whatever coin of the realm, long let out in the devil's use, could find its way back into the coffers of its rightful Lord, was as far as he was concerned right gladly welcome! But worse than anything else is the fact that what comes out of surplus is not missed. **Casting it into the treasury** costs nothing. There is something peculiarly depressing about the parenthood that knows no sacrificial devotion; and often enough something unlovely, because unloving and unloved, about the children of such a home. The claim that is not felt is neither acknowledged nor met. Love is a spendthrift, leaves its arithmetic at home, is always "in the red." And God is love (Rom. 8:32).

A certain poor widow. Is it any wonder that as Jesus **looked up, and saw** her he "called unto him his disciples" (Mark 12:43)? Excited was he, eagerly pointing her out? Deep was whispering to deep. Luke enhances the pathos of the story with his somewhat rare and archaic word for **poor.** It is related to our word "penury," and to a Greek root that suggests one who has to labor hard for a living. "A certain widow worn with toil and very poor." She may have

5 ¶ And as some spake of the temple, how it was adorned with goodly stones and gifts, he said,
6 *As for* these things which ye behold, the days will come, in the which there shall not be left one stone upon another, that shall not be thrown down.

5 And as some spoke of the temple, how it was adorned with noble stones and offerings, he said, 6 "As for these things which you see, the days will come when there shall not be left here one stone upon an-

C. Events That Will Mark the End of the Age (21:5-38)

1. Prediction That the Temple Would Be Destroyed (21:5-6=Mark 13:1-2)

5-6. This passage is taken over by Luke substantially as it stood in Mark. The temple was burned in A.D. 70 (Josephus *Jewish War* VI. 4. 5) and later its walls were leveled in the course of a systematic demolition of the city (*ibid.,* VII. 1). It is by no means clear that the words ascribed to Jesus were originally a "prediction after the event." It is quite possible that Jesus shared the pessimism that had led Micah (3:12) and Jeremiah (26:6; cf. also Jer. 26:18) to envisage the destruction of the first temple as a consequence of the refusal of the people to repent. This prediction may have been the basis of the charge brought by "false witnesses" against Jesus at the hearing before the Sanhedrin (Mark 14:57-58; cf. John 2:18-19; Acts 6:13-14).

been reduced even to beggary. At any rate, hers was a gift of love and gratitude and loneliness: love and gratitude for the solace and providence of the Almighty; loneliness in what bereavement and namelessness? More even than that, it was a gift of adventurous faith (see Exeg.). She was financing this "out of a deficit";[5] and with it, instead of being "left behind in the race" (derivation of the word for "poverty"), she steps out of the shadows into the light of history, where now Luke's list of great personages (3:1) is scarcely more than a roster of antiquities! Of her too, as of another, it may be said, "Wheresoever this gospel shall be preached throughout the whole world, this also that she hath done shall be spoken of for a memorial of her" (Mark 14:9). John Henry Jowett has told somewhere of a little graveyard beside a church in a tiny village, where the memory of a devoted soul who had spent herself recklessly and untiringly in the service of that small community is enshrined in a brief and touching epitaph, "She Hath Done What She Couldn't" (cf. Mark 14:8). **More than they all** (see II Chr. 29:27*b*).

5-38. *Things About To Be.*—This whole section, as the Exeg. indicates, seems to be compounded of Jewish apocalyptic ideas and many of the authentic words of Jesus, remembered in the ominous context of then current premonitions of the end. What is particularly noteworthy about it is (*a*) the sense of urgency, characteristic of so many of the parables of Jesus, heightened here by the thought of impending persecution and disaster, and coupled with the frequent injunction, "Take heed," "Take heed," "Watch ye therefore"; but also the feeling one has throughout that underneath the shifting scenes is (*b*) an eternal order of things (vs. 33), where patience has "her perfect work" (vs. 19; Jas. 1:3-4), and "the Lord God omnipotent reigneth" (vs. 15; Rev. 19:6), with (*c*) God's kind of victory at the last (vss. 18-19, 28, 36), in the darkest hour before the dawn.

5-6. *The Beginning of Judgment.*—(Cf. I Pet. 4:17; also Expos. on 19:11.) Herod's temple, begun some forty or more years before, was not yet finished; but already, with its immense wealth, it was in its own way one of the wonders of the world. Some of its huge blocks of green or white marble measured 67½ feet in length, 7½ feet in height, and 9 feet in width. The eastern front and part of the side walls were covered with gold plate, flashing in the sun; the rest of it gleaming white, so that one beholding it from a distance might think it a very mountain of snow; while within were the rich ornaments (**adorned**; akin to our word "cosmetics"!) and votive offerings (**gifts**), what we would call permanent memorials, placed there by "the great ones of the earth: a table from Ptolemy, a chain from Agrippa, a golden vine from Herod the Great."[6] What could be better calculated to stir the deepest patriotic and religious sentiment? Surely, the disciples (whether

[5] Bruce, "Synoptic Gospels," *Expositor's Greek Testament, ad loc.*

[6] Bruce, "Synoptic Gospels," *Expositor's Greek Testament, ad loc.;* cf. also on Matt. 24:1-3.

7 And they asked him, saying, Master, but when shall these things be? and what sign *will there be* when these things shall come to pass?

other than will not be thrown down." **7** And they asked him, "Teacher, when will this be, and what will be the sign when this is

2. Preliminary Signs of the Approaching End (21:7-19=Mark 13:3-9, 11-13)

To Jesus' prediction of the destruction of the temple Mark had appended a discourse on the end of the present age and the signs that would herald it. It is clear that the connection is artificial, for the discourse anticipates a defilement of the temple, not its actual destruction. There is very general agreement among interpreters that Mark's Little Apocalypse was originally a Jewish document which had been related by Christian preachers to the circumstances of the Christian mission and then lodged by the earliest evangelist in the gospel tradition. It may incorporate some genuine utterances of Jesus but they can no longer be isolated.

Luke's version differs in its detail from Mark's, but the variations are explicable as editorial and do not warrant the postulation of an independent source. They are due in the main to (*a*) the later date at which Luke was writing, and (*b*) Luke's more mature Christology. In Luke the scene is still the temple courts; in Mark, the Mount of Olives (Mark 13:3).

7. They: The "some" of vs. 5. Substituted for Mark's "Peter and James and John and Andrew."

understood generally, or in the narrower sense of the twelve; see Matt. 24:1; Mark 13:1) must have thought, "This is none other but the house of God, and this is the gate of heaven" (Gen. 28:17). "Look, Master," they said.

"You look," answered Jesus. What they saw was not what he saw. Back of all that seemed built for the ages was the ever-present specter of "change and decay."

> Like the baseless fabric of this vision,
> The cloud-capp'd towers, the gorgeous palaces,
> The solemn temples, the great globe itself,
> Yea, all which it inherit, shall dissolve
> And, like this insubstantial pageant faded,
> Leave not a rack behind.[7]

Back of it was the shadow of God's terrible left arm, lifted to strike. **As for these things . . . the days will come.** There is no reason whatever to suppose that Jesus failed to foresee the doom that was already poised, so to speak, above the temple (see Expos. on 19:41-44; and Dummelow[8] on Matt. 24).

But in the providence of God the end was not yet. Another temple was even then being fashioned, "built upon the foundation of the apostles and prophets" (Eph. 2:19-22). Another people was being called (Rom. 9:24, 26). Before ever the old was laid waste, the walls and battlements of another city were rising (Gal. 4:25-26), a freer, fairer pattern of that new Jerusalem which in the end of all the years John saw "coming down from God out of heaven, prepared as a bride adorned for her husband" (Rev. 21:2).

7. ***Times and Signs.***—Was it curiosity that prompted their questions? If it was, we may be sure there would be no disposition on the part of Jesus to satisfy it. He was no soothsayer, no fortuneteller, gazing into the crystal ball of the future, pulling aside the curtain for some momentary glimpse of the things God had hidden. In Mark 13:32, a verse that no pleasant purveyor of happy tales could ever have invented (cf. Matt. 24:36 KJV, where the reading has been altered; and notice its absence from Luke), he is represented as entering an emphatic disclaimer that any such knowledge was even in his possession. His purpose was far more serious, and as always prophetic, i.e., distinctly ethical in character. Hours never seemed to him important, except for the fulfillment of God's intent (John 2:4; 7:6; 13:1; 17:1). Days were far less significant as calendar days than as fleeting moments in eternity (see Expos. on vss. 32-33), each bringing with it its own crisis, making its own demand, carrying its own threat, holding out its own promise. No sign would be given as proof of his authority, however much he might have been tempted to do just that (4:9-12; Luke gives it as the climax of the temptations, following Q); none but God's clear word, "Repent" (11:29-32; yet

[7] Shakespeare, *The Tempest*, Act IV, scene 1.

[8] *A Commentary on the Holy Bible*, ed. J. R. Dummelow (New York: The Macmillan Co., 1936).

8 And he said, Take heed that ye be not deceived: for many shall come in my name, saying, I am *Christ;* and the time draweth near: go ye not therefore after them.

about to take place?" 8 And he said, "Take heed that you are not led astray; for many will come in my name, saying, 'I am he!' and, 'The time is at hand!' Do not go after

8-9. A warning against false messiahs and all assumptions about the imminence of **the end.** Luke strengthens the warning by ascribing the proclamation **The time is at hand** to pseudo-Christs.

cf. 21:20). Nor by the same token would any sign be given of the consummation of God's design in human history (vs. 34*b*; cf. Matt. 12:38-40). Precursors there would be, as well of the fall of Jerusalem (vss. 8-11, 12-19, 20-24), and so of the destruction of the temple, as of that vaster summing up of all things which should be the coming of the Son of man in final judgment at the end of the world (vss. 25-28). Of them he will speak. Anybody unblinded by self-deceit could read them (vss. 29-31; 12:54-56; Matt. 16:1-4); nobody whose eye was evil, his "whole body . . . full of darkness" (11:33-36, precisely in this context!), would ever so much as mark them, or "be persuaded, though one rose from the dead" (16:31; 17:26-30). To clamor **when** may well be to put off what must be done *now.* To ask **what** is likely enough to overlook *this.* Meanwhile—"Be not deceived" (vs. 8). There is much that is still true (see Expos. on vss. 5-38). Now is the time. "The day [for the Germans in World War II it was *der Tag,* and ominous; for the allies, it was D day, and after that V day, the day of decision and the day of victory!] is at hand" (Rom. 13:11-14).

7. *What Time Is It?*—And they asked him, . . . when. . . . The only time there is is God's time, and late! Shall we say that to ourselves soberly, and mean it? The Bible provides no further information. And it is God's time not because of anything we would recognize as an emergency. There are too many emergencies. Often we seem to be governed by them. There is always an emergency whenever anybody wants to do anything. God's emergencies do not look like ours. We are in the midst of one now—confronted as we are with a Truth that insists on facing us as a Person, stalking around and laying hold of us by the arm, gazing into our eyes, so that we have to say "Yes" to it or get rid of it! Christianity is not a creed, not a way of thinking about life: it is the *I* and *Thou* of a God who addresses us; a moment of meeting, a moment for hearing and becoming. The time is now—the Bible never pauses there, as the radio announcer does. It puts a period. The time is *now.*

And it is always later than we are inclined to suppose. Not wickedness so much as just silly dodges to keep from coming to grips with anything we happen not to like—this is what makes it late. With our pigeonholes for everything and everybody, our precedents, our traditions, our pride and our prejudice. The Jewish people died of what their *religion* had become! There was too little room left in it for a real God who could meet them. When he showed himself, it was blasphemy!

Could it be that before anything else we have to know that it is the end? What we have had will not serve. Paul once said a terrible thing. Back in the gospel story there was this: "Behold, . . . the Son of man . . . shall be delivered into the Gentiles, and shall be mocked" (18:31-32). A little bit farther along, "And the men that held Jesus mocked him" (22:63). Then Paul, "Be not deceived; God is not mocked" (Gal. 6:7). What shall be said of the Christianity that is familiar with all the words in the Bible, faith, and hope, and love, but does not concern itself much in this suffering world with any deeds to match them? The Christianity which assumes that the most important obligation it has is to think things through? The Sanhedrin spent much of its time thinking things through! Caiaphas at last figured out what was expedient: it was that one man should die for the people!

We have to know that it is the end. And we have to know with an equal knowledge that it is the beginning. That God is bent on rescuing his own from their misery, and all the while bent on that; planning to do it with the gospel concerning his Son, planning to do it by means of every life that will give itself away to him.

8. *False Messiahs.*—Some of them perhaps are named in Acts 5:36-37; 21:38. It was such men who became the leaders of insurrection and rebellion against Rome. Whether or not they formally proclaimed themselves messiahs, it was their political and religious fanaticism which actually precipitated the calamities of A.D. 66-70. What concerns Jesus here is not the answering of a question (vs. 7), but rather the utterance of a warning, **Go ye not . . . after them.** It is a warning timely enough in any age. Always there seems to be some other allegiance

9 But when ye shall hear of wars and commotions, be not terrified: for these things must first come to pass; but the end *is* not by and by.

10 Then said he unto them, Nation shall rise against nation, and kingdom against kingdom:

11 And great earthquakes shall be in divers places, and famines, and pestilences; and fearful sights and great signs shall there be from heaven.

them. 9 And when you hear of wars and tumults, do not be terrified; for this must first take place, but the end will not be at once."

10 Then he said to them, "Nation will rise against nation, and kingdom against kingdom; 11 there will be great earthquakes, and in various places famines and pestilences; and there will be terrors and

---

10-11. Wars, **earthquakes, famines, pestilences,** and various other evidences of cosmic disorder were part of the paraphernalia of apocalyptic and prophetic prediction (II Esdras 9:3; 13:30-32; Rev. 6:1-8; etc.); and attempts to interpret them as references to specific events in the first century A.D. are a waste of time.

---

more fruitful, some other path through the forest more certain and more secure. We will rely on reason, not on faith. We will have to do with material possessions, not with spiritual growth. Whatever love we can muster in our hearts, we will have force at our backs (see Expos. on vss. 32-33). The tragedy of Israel's history is the tragedy of a people given to running off like that, generation after generation, in pursuit of other gods. Indeed, the long record of mankind is the record of its blindness, casting about forever like a man groping in the dark, laying hold now of philosophy, now of law, today of science, tomorrow of the machine, fumbling up and down, whispering, "Art thou he that should come, or do we look for another?" (Matt. 11:3.)

Paul puts the issue of it, "What fruit had ye then in those things whereof ye are now ashamed? for the end of those things is death" (Rom. 6:21). Never was there a more terrible object lesson than Hitler's Germany. Writes Arnold J. Toynbee at the end of the whole chapter devoted to false messiahs,

> When we set out on this quest we found ourselves moving in the midst of a mighty host, but as we have pressed forward, the marchers, company by company, have fallen out of the race . . . until only gods were left in the running. At the final ordeal of death, few, even of these would-be saviour gods, have dared to put their title to the test by plunging into the icy river. And now, as we stand and gaze with our eyes fixed upon the farther shore, a single figure rises from the flood and straightway fills the whole horizon. There is the Saviour; "and the pleasure of the Lord shall prosper in his hand; he shall see of the travail of his soul and shall be satisfied." [9]

[9] *A Study of History,* Abridgement of Vols. I-VI by D. C. Somervell, p. 547. Copyright 1946 by Oxford University Press, Inc., New York. Used by permission.

For at the last, in its inmost heart the world seeks not reformation or revolution, but renewal; not forgetfulness, but forgiveness; not prosperity, but peace; not security, but strength.

9-11. ***These Things First; but the End Is Not Yet.***—Jesus—if indeed the words are his—would keep them from being deceived, and he would keep them, too, from being panic stricken. **Be not terrified.** Both of these motives appear prominently in his teaching. If he shared with others the expectation that the end would come within the lifetime of those who heard him speak, then vs. 9*b* may give evidence of Luke's reshaping of the material *ex eventu.* Certainly it would seem that the thought in vss. 8-11 may very well be of the Parousia, and not solely or primarily of the destruction of Jerusalem. Yet one cannot be sure. At any rate, "the paraphernalia of apocalyptic and prophetic prediction" must have seemed strangely apt (Exeg.). There had already been **wars** "and rumors of wars," **tumults** and massacres. Vesuvius had erupted in A.D. 63, destroying half of the city of Pompeii. There are said to have been **earthquakes** in Greece and Asia Minor and Palestine, **in divers places,** under both Claudius and Nero, **pestilences** and **famines.** The Greek words are related in sound (cf. the witches' chant in *Macbeth,* Act IV, scene 1), and the horrors of them in fact. Perhaps in much of the language and in many of the images we are simply to be made aware of the ferment of a troubled and unsteady world.

Then said he unto them (vs. 10) no doubt serves to associate what follows (vss. 10-11) with vss. 12-19, a kind of introduction ("the beginning of sorrows," Matt. 24:8; Mark 13:8) to the harrowing experiences which the apostles themselves will encounter. What is of primary significance is that the **terrors and great signs from heaven,** the nation rising against nation,

12 But before all these, they shall lay their hands on you, and persecute *you,*

great signs from heaven. 12 But before all this they will lay their hands on you and

12-13. Probably a Christian gloss on the original apocalypse, reflecting the actual experiences of such men as Stephen, Peter, and Paul. **But before all this:** A Lukan prefix which dissociates the sufferings that the disciples would have to endure from the

kingdom against kingdom, are the forerunners not of ultimate disaster, but of the breaking through of the messianic age, as the pain of a woman in childbirth is the harbinger not of death, but of life. The portents are in reality promises. They are God's judgment on the wicked and the assurance of his mercy to the upright, to those who stand in faith, not fear. The dark symbols of despair are to become the bright badges of hope. Is it not strange that when men say, "We have tried everything; we must leave the issue now in the hands of God," they say it as if matters had indeed come to a pretty pass? From the very first, where else was the issue? It is not he who is guilty of the bungling; we are. Yet we insist on thinking of him last, when all the rope is paid out, and there is nothing left but to put our fingertips together and roll our eyes heavenward. Says Mistress Quickly, reporting the death of Sir John Falstaff, "So 'a cried out, 'God, God, God!' three or four times. Now I, to comfort him, bid him 'a should not think of God; I hop'd there was no need to trouble himself with any such thoughts yet."[1] When we do at last trouble ourselves with such thoughts, perverse as we are, they bring us no peace; only the sense of utter helplessness and torturing anxiety: like a collie when we pick up one of her young to fondle it. Never is life so insecure as when we take hold of it; never is it safer than when we lay it in God's hands. That moment is a creative moment. It is not at all where we quit: it is where we may truly begin (see Expos. on vss. 12-19, 25-28).

12-19. ***How Easy Is It to Be a Christian?***—The charge is often laid at the door of the Christian faith that fundamentally it is a means of escape, both from the rigors of thought and from the harsh realities of existence. Let those comfort themselves with such excuses who can. Escape it is, not out of life, into it: from meaninglessness into meaning, from futility into purpose, from bondage into freedom, from security beset with peril into peril hedged around about by God. This whole passage seems to differ in tone from the Marcan parallel. It vibrates to the marching of feet, as if already men were getting their fingers on "the substance of things hoped for," had in front of their very eyes "the evidence of things not seen" (Heb. 11:1). There are trials to be borne (vs. 12), a word to be proclaimed (vs. 13), an instant sovereignty to be obeyed (vs. 15), hazards to be taken (vss. 16-17; note the repetition of the phrase **for my name's sake);** there is still to be a stubborn and unconquerable holding on (vs. 19, **patience):** but the goal will be reached and the haven won (vss. 18-19; cf. Hab. 2:3).

If something at least of what Jesus said they would have to face was already beginning to happen as Luke wrote, we could understand better the meaning of his words **before all this** (on vss. 12-16, cf. 12:11-12, 51-53; Matt. 10:17-22). The disciples were not to have reserved seats at the cosmic drama, watching it play itself out. They would be the first, but they would not be the last, to stand as Jesus stood before the tribunals of church and state to give an account of their allegiance. The gospel of Jesus Christ has always been a disturbing gospel. Privilege looks on it with suspicion. Power stares at it and frowns, rolling back a sleeve. The Sanhedrin was shaken by it and angry. Pilate strode in and out uneasily. Rome outlawed it. The rebellious Count of Aquitaine, surrounded by his retainers, defied it; then under the piercing eyes of Bernard of Clairvaux, as the monk moved toward him with the Sacrament, he trembled, and prostrated himself on the cold stone floor of the nave. Luther at Worms, pronouncing the words that rocked the medieval church to its foundations, "God helping me, I can do no other." Joan of Arc before her inquisitors, telling of the voices. Berggrav, bishop of Norway, before Quisling, during World War II. Shouted the angry usurper, "You should have your head struck off!" And the bishop answered quietly, "Well, here I am."

These, says Jesus, are the hours of opportunity (vs. 13). "I will tarry at Ephesus," writes Paul, "until Pentecost. For a great door and effectual is opened unto me, and there are many adversaries" (I Cor. 16:8-9; cf. II Cor. 2:12; Col. 4:3; also Rev. 3:8). Lay hold, and turn it to the advantage of the gospel. And **I will give you a mouth,** such utterance and power of speech that none shall resist it, **and wisdom** that no man shall gainsay. Of the mission on which they have embarked the risen, regnant Lord will never wash his hands, nor deny it the immediate

[1] *King Henry V,* Act II, scene 3.

delivering *you* up to the synagogues, and into prisons, being brought before kings and rulers for my name's sake.

13 And it shall turn to you for a testimony.

14 Settle *it* therefore in your hearts, not to meditate before what ye shall answer:

15 For I will give you a mouth and wisdom, which all your adversaries shall not be able to gainsay nor resist.

persecute you, delivering you up to the
synagogues and prisons, and you will be
brought before kings and governors for my
name's sake. 13 This will be a time for you
to bear testimony. 14 Settle it therefore in
your minds, not to meditate beforehand
how to answer; 15 for I will give you a
mouth and wisdom, which none of your
adversaries will be able to withstand or

eschatological portents. A similar interest impelled Luke to omit Mark's prediction (Mark 13:10) that the proclamation of the gospel to "all the nations" would be a necessary prelude to the end. **This will be a time for you to bear testimony,** i.e., "to the gospel." An interpretation of a phrase in Mark, possibly with such incidents in mind as Paul's appearances before Felix (Acts 24) and before Festus and Agrippa II (Acts 26).

14-15. A paraphrase of Mark 13:11 (cf. the Q variant in Luke 12:11-12). **Meditate beforehand:** A technical term in Attic Greek to describe the preparation of a speech for

gifts of his Spirit. Nothing untoward or unforeseen will ever disconcert him. Whatever happens, he will not be found saying, "I'm sorry, but my plans did not include that." Could it not then on that basis be with them as it had been with him? Need they ever be disillusioned, if they went into it without any illusions? What if the dearest ties that bound them to this earth were broken—**parents and brothers and kinsmen and friends?** Could forewarning alone ever forearm them? Would it be enough for them in the days to come if they should remember a night, shut away from the world, when the hand of the betrayer was on the table; and afterward the garden, and the shadows slapping back at the light of the torches, and a kiss? Would it be enough for them to remember his quiet mastery, and the strange promise he had once made: "Verily I say unto you, There is no man that hath left house, or parents, or brethren, or wife, or children, for the kingdom of God's sake, who shall not receive manifold more in this present time"—a fellowship both human and divine, transcending all other fellowships, "and in the world to come life everlasting" (18:29-30)? Is it ever enough to remember? Without a hand on the shoulder, and that whispered word, **I will give you . . .** ? On the eve of the battle of Agincourt, King Henry V moves through the English camp, from tent to tent, or as Shakespeare has it, "visits all his host,"

> That every wretch, pining and pale before,
> Beholding him, plucks comfort from his looks:
> . . . .
> A little touch of Harry in the night.[2]

[2] *King Henry V*, Act IV, Prologue.

"May God deny you peace, but give you glory."[3]

For glory there will be. Perhaps the best commentary on vs. 18 is Ps. 91 (see Exeg.). For those that dwell "in the secret place of the Most High," there may be no deliverance out of trouble; but there will assuredly be deliverance in the midst of it (cf. Rom. 8:18-39). Christianity is a religion of reward (see Expos. on 19:8). It rewards responsibility faithfully discharged with added responsibility (19:16-19). It rewards the man who is steady under tribulation: he grows patient. It rewards the man who is patient: he becomes conscious of having weathered the storm. It rewards the man who weathers the storm: his is a profound conviction. It rewards the man of profound conviction: he is never disappointed. The love of God sees to that (Rom. 5:3-5). Let him refuse to quit, keep at it (**in . . . patience**): like a wrestler who will not loosen his hold even when he is down; like Jacob, when the hollow of his thigh was out of joint, clinging fast to the angel, crying out, "I will not let thee go, except thou bless me" (Gen. 32:25-26)—and he will **possess** his soul, acquire it for his own use. (The maxim, "Possess your souls in patience," means "Don't get excited. Try to keep from flying off the handle. Put up with it awhile." It was once intended to mean "If you hold on, you will 'have' a soul worth 'having' "!) Patience is the voyage; the discovery, a soul! "Sail on! Sail on! Sail on and on!"

12. *When God Stands By.*—They will lay their hands on you and persecute you. Things had been running smoothly enough thus far;

[3] Miguel de Unamuno, *The Tragic Sense of Life* (London: Macmillan & Co., 1921), p. 330.

16 And ye shall be betrayed both by parents, and brethren, and kinsfolk, and friends; and *some* of you shall they cause to be put to death.

17 And ye shall be hated of all *men* for my name's sake.

18 But there shall not a hair of your head perish.

19 In your patience possess ye your souls.

contradict. 16 You will be delivered up even by parents and brothers and kinsmen and friends, and some of you they will put to death; 17 you will be hated by all for my name's sake. 18 But not a hair of your head will perish. 19 By your endurance you will gain your lives.

---

oral delivery. Despite his characteristic interest in the work of the Holy Spirit, Luke in this instance declares that it will be Christ himself who will provide the necessary inspiration. **A mouth:** Power of speech (Exod. 4:11-12). Luke illustrates the redemption of this promise in Acts 6:10.

16. The loyalty of individuals to the Christian faith in the impending crisis will result in the dissolution of family ties and the betrayal of Christians by their kindred. Predictions in various O.T. eschatological passages (Isa. 19:2; Mic. 7:6) influenced the phrasing of Mark's version, but this is scarcely noticeable in Luke's. **And friends** is a Lukan addition.

17. Note the exhortation in I Pet. 4:16: "If one suffers as a Christian, let him not be ashamed, but under that name let him glorify God."

18. A Lukan addition which recurs in Paul's speech to the ship's company (Acts 27:34*b*). A proverbial form has already been used in 12:7*a* (Matt. 10:30) and has O.T. prototypes (I Sam. 14:45; II Sam. 14:11; I Kings 1:52). In view of vs. 16 Luke can scarcely have meant the promise to imply immunity from martyrdom. Perhaps he had preservation from eternal destruction in mind. The alternative is to regard vss. 16-17 as addressed to a select group of martyrs, and vss. 18-19 to the Christian community as a whole.

19. A paraphrase of Mark 13:13*b*. The future tense of the RSV has somewhat better support in the MSS than the imperative of the KJV. But we must translate **souls** (KJV) instead of **lives** (RSV) if Luke meant the saying (as in vs. 18) to be interpreted spiritually.

---

soon there would be a cross, and life would start going bitterly wrong, as at a signal. It would seem like a ghastly world for such good people, with nothing much but contempt and death waiting around every corner, and God just standing by doing nothing. No matter how kind they were, putting themselves out no end to bring a little happiness on the earth, they would be slapped in the face for their pains. Many a time they would look up hurt and bewildered. Jesus only hoped they would not be unsteadied by it. Perhaps if they remembered then how he had told them of it, that would help (cf. John 16:1-4).

Certainly life does not always seem to be an arrangement with which even a human father could be well pleased; not when we reckon in its sin and its pain and all its sorrows. No need to overstate the facts. There is happiness about, and the beauty that makes for it. There are sunsets and glorious flowering trees on the grim battlefield at Gettysburg, to cover all its scars. If God does indeed give a star, as Swinburne says, only to take a sun away, we can at least be honest about the stars! There are myriads of them. Yet for all that there is still the dark. And it is real enough. A husband lying there dead, or a son who perhaps would be better off so; a poor racked body, bound with an iron grip to a chair, living on to be one long agony knocking at the doors of the mind, behind the forehead; or a job gone now, and feet that ache, trudging the streets, never catching up with anything. The evil of life, writes Abbé Ernest Dimnet, is felt in its full force by people who simply shake their heads and never say a word. God pity the man who has only something light and trivial, compounded of good health and common sense, to give humanity for its woe!

Perhaps when the plain truth is spoken, we need the hazards. There seems to be no very central concern anywhere that we should be, as we say, happy. If life is interested in anything, it is interested in what we turn out to be. Said the men at the front, in answer to a wartime questionnaire that was circulated among them, "There is something going on in the world which demands primarily allegiance.

20 And when ye shall see Jerusalem compassed with armies, then know that the desolation thereof is nigh.

21 Then let them which are in Judea flee to the mountains; and let them which are in the midst of it depart out; and let not them that are in the countries enter thereinto.

22 For these be the days of vengeance, that all things which are written may be fulfilled.

23 But woe unto them that are with child, and to them that give suck, in those days! for there shall be great distress in the land, and wrath upon this people.

20 "But when you see Jerusalem surrounded by armies, then know that its
desolation has come near. 21 Then let those
who are in Judea flee to the mountains, and let those who are inside the city depart, and let not those who are out in the
country enter it; 22 for these are days of
vengeance, to fulfill all that is written.
23 Alas for those who are with child and
for those who give suck in those days! For great distress shall be upon the earth and

3. Fate of Jerusalem (21:20-24=Mark 13:14, 17, 19*a*)

Marcan material dissociated from the immediate "signs of the end," and revised and expanded in light of the siege of Jerusalem (A.D. 70).

20-21*a*. Mark's version reads: "But when you see the desolating sacrilege set up where it ought not to be . . . , then let those who are in Judea flee to the mountains" (Mark 13:14). The "desolating sacrilege" in the book of Daniel (9:27 [LXX]; 11:31; 12:11) was the altar to Zeus that the Syrian king Antiochus Epiphanes had erected in the temple at Jerusalem in 168 B.C. In Mark it is a cryptic description of some antichrist whose appearance is to be a prelude to the coming of the Son of man (cf. II Thess. 2:3-4). For this enigmatic term Luke substitutes **Jerusalem surrounded by armies.**

21*b*-22. No Marcan base. The verses may betray a familiarity on Luke's part with events in Jerusalem just before the siege. According to Eusebius (*Church History* III. 5. 3), the Christian community in the city withdrew at that time to Pella in Perea in response to a warning given to their leaders "by revelation." **All that is written:** Cf. Hos. 9:7; Jer. 5:29; 46:10; etc.

23. Pregnant women and nursing mothers will be least able to flee. **In the land:** Palestine. **This people:** Israel.

[We] hardly know what it is. [We] only know . . . that something great and righteous wants [us] and requires of [us our] help."[4] Might they not have said even more? William James once acclaimed life as that "austere tragedy in which we relish most the bitterest it has to offer," and "heroism alone plays the great parts."

For the Christian, that heroism is no gaunt thing which simply faces the odds and outstares them. The Stoics used to manage that. It is a spirit which, leaping free against the world, has discovered that God is indeed standing by: but not as one who looks on idly and does nothing; as one who holds himself in readiness to run up at a gesture and throw in all he has! Until from that sovereign hand, out of the evil itself, not in spite of it, comes good; out of the very darkness, light; out of the pain, healing.

20-24. *The Days of Vengeance.*— (See Expos. on 19:41-44.) Did Jesus actually utter this prophecy, so accurate in detail (vs. 24 especially), of the fall of Jerusalem? Or was it shaped by the event itself? Must we think of it as Luke's rehandling of the Marcan material in the light of what had in fact already taken place, or as the form which the original words of Jesus had assumed in another "source" of which our evangelist made use? It is impossible to arrive at the very words of our Lord. What one sees here, and what Jesus saw, is God in human history. Catastrophe is not just the result of tensions that keep piling up toward the breaking point. History is a religious drama, not just a genetic process. Viewed from below, Jerusalem, with her turbulent mobs, was a thorn in the flesh of the Roman power; viewed from above, the time was drawing near when she would have to pay the forfeit of her disobedience and waywardness (20:9-16), **that all things which are written may be fulfilled.** Through the whole O.T. that bell keeps tolling; and through the N.T.

[4] Neville Talbot, *Thoughts on Religion at the Front* (London: Macmillan & Co., 1917), p. 55.

24 And they shall fall by the edge of the sword, and shall be led away captive into all nations: and Jerusalem shall be trodden down of the Gentiles, until the times of the Gentiles be fulfilled.

25 ¶ And there shall be signs in the sun, and in the moon, and in the stars; and upon the earth distress of nations, with perplexity; the sea and the waves roaring;

26 Men's hearts failing them for fear, and for looking after those things which are coming on the earth: for the powers of heaven shall be shaken.

wrath upon this people; 24 they will fall by
the edge of the sword, and be led captive among all nations; and Jerusalem will be trodden down by the Gentiles, until the times of the Gentiles are fulfilled.

25 "And there will be signs in sun and moon and stars, and upon the earth distress of nations in perplexity at the roaring of the sea and the waves, 26 men fainting
with fear and with foreboding of what is coming on the world; for the powers of

---

24. Editorial elaboration of the fate of Jerusalem. According to Josephus—whose numerical estimates are not always trustworthy—1,100,000 Jews were slain by the Romans during the siege and 97,000 were taken prisoner throughout the course of the war (*Jewish War* VI. 9. 3). **The times of the Gentiles:** Sometimes interpreted as the equivalent of Mark 13:10 (omitted by Luke)—i.e., the period during which non-Jews have the opportunity for repentance and conversion (cf. Rom. 11:25). More probably the period God has fixed for the punishment of Israel (cf. Dan. 8:13-14; 12:7, 11-12).

4. Coming of the Son of Man (21:25-28=Mark 13:24-26)

25*a*. An abbreviation of the conventional apocalyptic description in Mark of solar, lunar, and astral irregularities.

25*b*-26*a*. An editorial expansion of the Marcan source to depict the **perplexity, fear,** and **foreboding** of men in the face of cosmic disaster. **Upon the earth:** A universal judgment as distinct from the earlier judgment on Jerusalem. Probably we should translate "distress of the Gentiles" to correspond to "the times of the Gentiles" of vs. 24 (cf. Goodspeed). **The roaring of the sea and the waves:** The sea threatens to spill over its shores and engulf the world. For the phraseology cf. Ps. 65:7-8*a*.

26*b*. The Marcan source is resumed. **The powers of the heavens:** Not some demonic hierarchy but the celestial bodies referred to in vs. 25*a*.

What was it, then, in Jerusalem that was against God? To answer in any generation is to draw up an indictment of human life in every generation. Turn again to Matt. 23 and John 8. To answer is to read the handwriting on the wall of our own civilization. Yet observe the endless compassion that intrudes itself among the shadows. There is hardly a breath to be taken between the ominous sound of Rome's marching legions (vs. 20) and the urgent counsel to flee (vs. 21), as one should say in desperate concern, "There will be no refuge there where you have thought to find it." Scarcely is there warning of **vengeance** (vs. 22; cf. Rom. 12:19) before the pity of the Lord begins to brood over those for whom there can be no flight (vs. 23). No sooner is there talk of **distress** and **wrath** (I Thess. 2:16; Eph. 5:6; Col. 3:6) than there is mention of what Luke himself may very well have understood to mean the extension of God's covenant mercy to the Gentile world (cf. Rom. 11:25; yet see Exeg.).

25-28. *There Comes a Midnight Hour.*—And there will be signs in sun and moon and stars. The words take on a cosmic urgency. There is a crisis near at hand, and another more remote: so closely intertwined are they that there is almost no possibility now of separating the one from the other. Nor is there any need. Such moments do come, when we are starkly up against it, and cannot get away, and none of the old dodges will do. So it was with David, when the blazing eyes of Nathan the prophet stared up into his own. There are times when sheer loneliness brings us up short. Perhaps music, or a word read aloud; or a presence in the crowd, by his lowliness to shame our arrogance, with his industry our sloth, with his courage our cowardice. Life is like that. It does not move smoothly on and up. There is reality, and we run into it. There are facts in the broad day, when the sun is shining, that are altogether tougher than we are; and we get them naked, and we get them sharp. Nar-

27 And then shall they see the Son of man coming in a cloud with power and great glory.

28 And when these things begin to come to pass, then look up, and lift up your heads; for your redemption draweth nigh.

29 And he spake to them a parable; Behold the fig tree, and all the trees;

30 When they now shoot forth, ye see and know of your own selves that summer is now nigh at hand.

the heavens will be shaken. **27** And then
they will see the Son of man coming in a
cloud with power and great glory. **28** Now
when these things begin to take place, look
up and raise your heads, because your re-
demption is drawing near."
29 And he told them a parable: "Look
at the fig tree, and all the trees; **30** as soon
as they come out in leaf, you see for your-
selves and know that the summer is al-

---

27. The end of the present age will be marked by the dramatic and triumphant appearance of the supernatural **Son of man** of whom Daniel (7:13) and Enoch (chs. 37–71 *passim*) had spoken. Both Mark and Luke identify him with Jesus as the risen Christ.

28. In contrast to "the heathen" of vss. 25*b*-26*a* Christians may anticipate these last events with hope and confidence. Luke substitutes this word of encouragement for Mark's description of the harvest of God's elect by angels (Mark 13:27). **Redemption:** the only occurrence of the word in the Gospels. Associated here with the second coming of Christ, not, as in Paul, with his death.

5. Parable of the Fig Tree in Leaf (21:29-31=Mark 13:28-29)

In Mark's Gospel the parable introduces a new and anticlimactic series of sayings about the Second Advent. It is probable that they are of the nature of an appendix, attached by the evangelist to the discourse as he found it among his sources. In particular it is probable that the parable had no original relationship to its present Synoptic context. No doubt when Jesus uttered it he had the immediate rather than some distant crisis in mind.

29-30. Luke provides his own introduction. **And all the trees:** A rather pedantic generalization. Only **the fig tree** had been mentioned by Mark. The commonest deciduous

---

row gauge in human experience, broad gauge in human history. The world itself smashes into something: not a law, but a "No!"—"Suddenly like a snare" (vs. 34). Like a net let down on a wild beast, or the steel jaws of a trap that without warning snap fast on its leg. God has his own ways of coming; there is terror in them, and there is promise in them.

Writes Sören Kierkegaard, "There comes a midnight hour when all men must unmask." The issue will depend on whether or not we can muster enough despair to provide us with the kind of hope that will not betray us. That despair and hope belong together is the very content of the gospel. **When these things begin to take place, look up!** No silly and secular optimism can handle what is wrong. Nothing can be more fatuous than the way in which it insists, odds or no odds, on coming out at the corner of Center and Main Streets in Utopia. There is another kind of assurance that staggers to its feet at the very moment when the world is at its worst. There is something God has done that can change the climate of human history. But it is for those who have learned despair. They and they alone know where hope is. "The day of the Lord is darkness and not light" (Amos 5:18). But it is still the day of the Lord, with a cross outlined against the sky.

29-31. ***Life Out of Death.***—Here is one of God's habits. This parable, standing where it does (see Exeg.), may serve to enforce the strange counsel of vs. 28. The "signs of the end" are but the signs of God's new beginning. Where death seemed to be the only certainty, life bursts forth like the spring. The messianic woes usher in the messianic kingdom. How often do the very facts which seem to contradict a benevolent and beneficent providence validate it! Out of the womb of evil comes good. "All these things are against me," cries Jacob (Gen. 42:36); and lives to thank God for them (Rom. 8:28). "Distress" (vs. 25)—"redemption" (vs. 28): it may be that God has no other way of breaking through the crust of our pride and self-reliance.

Perhaps it should be noted that almost always Jesus has some such glad, dynamic figure as this

31 So likewise ye, when ye see these things come to pass, know ye that the kingdom of God is nigh at hand.
32 Verily I say unto you, This generation shall not pass away, till all be fulfilled.
33 Heaven and earth shall pass away; but my words shall not pass away.

ready near. 31 So also, when you see these
things taking place, you know that the
kingdom of God is near. 32 Truly, I say to
you, this generation will not pass away till
all has taken place. 33 Heaven and earth
will pass away, but my words will not pass
away.

---

tree in Palestine, its budding was a joyful harbinger of **summer. These things:** Mark and Luke have the "signs of the end" in mind, but originally Jesus may have meant the events of his own ministry. **The kingdom of God** for "he" (or "it") in Mark. Luke correctly recognized the illustration as a "kingdom" parable.

6. A Prediction and a Certification (21:32-33=Mark 13:30-31)

32. A solemn assurance that the apocalyptic events will take place in the near future. Many interpreters suspect that this formed the conclusion of the original Jewish apocalypse. But the saying is essentially the same as that credited to Jesus in 9:27 (Mark 9:1). When the later church adjusted its thinking to an indefinite continuance of the historical order, **this generation** was interpreted to mean either "the race of mankind" or "the company of the faithful."

33. Serves to authenticate the apocalyptic discourse. Jesus' prediction is reliable. Possibly a Christian revision of the saying in 16:17 (Matt. 5:18). At this point Luke omits the declaration in Mark 13:32 that the exact time is known neither to the angels nor to the Son but only to the Father. It may have offended his more advanced christological beliefs. Nevertheless he reproduces it in a modified form in Acts 1:7.

---

for the coming of the kingdom. It is the advent of the bridegroom. It is like the quiet moving of the leaven. It is the thrusting, spreading life of the seed. Again and again the sobering aspects of judgment, sudden, irrevocable, the shutting of a door, the springing of a trap; but with the gladness beyond for those that watch with eager eyes, the headiness of new wine, the marriage feast, the spring. "Stately music," as Robert Louis Stevenson once put it, getting up out of his sickbed and sitting down at his desk, "Stately music, enter God!"

32-33. ***When Nothing Is Left, What Then?***—Once more there are uncertainties to face and difficulties of interpretation that have to be met. Did Jesus expect the end within the lifetime of those who heard him speak? It seems quite certain that the early church so understood him. Or was he thinking of the destruction of Jerusalem and the dawn of the new age? (Cf. the parallel passage in Mark, and the verse there which Luke omits, in spite of the fact that it feels so authentic to the touch; for who would ever have fabricated it?)

In any case, the question *when* never seems in the N.T. to be of primary concern. Far more significant and far more urgent is the word *now* (see Expos. on vs. 7; Rom. 13:11-14, *et passim*). It may well be that the view of those who looked momentarily for the breaking in of God upon history was far nearer the truth, at deeper levels than any mere clock time could suggest, than is our view, who would indefinitely postpone that breaking in and make of it nothing more than some "far-off divine event" about which we need not at present be seriously troubled. In a real sense every day is the last day. The last things are—what things?

So are we driven back on the only ultimate resource life has to offer. One reliance after another is denied us: sometimes in very fact, always in final truth (see Expos. on vs. 8). We need not wait to find out about it—unless we insist—until everything tumbles in. Supports there are, thank God: the love of those we love; health of body, force of mind, skill of hand; bounty of sunshine and rain, winter and summer, seedtime and harvest. Until all at once, like Job's, some stricken face is lifted to an unanswering sky! And out of our daily peril the whisper comes, "When nothing is left, what then?" (Cf. Jas. 4:13-14; Luke 12:16-20.) In the lexicon of all human existence the first word is "precarious," the last is "dependence," and both mean the same!

"What then?" When nothing is left, God is left: the law that will not fail (16:17), the Presence that will not be put by (Matt. 28:20), the adventure that never disillusions (John 4:14; 6:35), the fleeting words that nevertheless outlast heaven and earth. Jesus was setting his seal to all that he had said about the end; God

34 ¶ And take heed to yourselves, lest at any time your hearts be overcharged with surfeiting, and drunkenness, and cares of this life, and *so* that day come upon you unawares.

35 For as a snare shall it come on all them that dwell on the face of the whole earth.

36 Watch ye therefore, and pray always, that ye may be accounted worthy to escape all these things that shall come to pass, and to stand before the Son of man.

34 "But take heed to yourselves lest your
hearts be weighed down with dissipation
and drunkenness and cares of this life, and
that day come upon you suddenly like a
snare; 35 for it will come upon all who
dwell upon the face of the whole earth.
36 But watch at all times, praying that you
may have strength to escape all these things
that will take place, and to stand before the
Son of man."

7. Injunction to Watchfulness and Prayer (21:34-36)

Mark's version of the apocalyptic discourse ends with the parable of the doorkeeper (Mark 13:33-37). Luke omits this, possibly because he considered it a variant to the allegory of the waiting servants (12:35-38), and composes material of similar tenor as a substitute.

34-35. Reminiscent of Pauline terminology (I Thess. 5:1-10). Isa. 24:17 may have served Luke as a model. **That day,** the Parousia. The judgment will not be localized to Judea, as the earlier one described in vss. 20-24, but will affect **the whole earth** (cf. vs. 25).

36. You may have strength has much better support in the MSS than **ye may be accounted worthy.** Christians will not be exempted from the woes of the last days, but prayer will enable them to endure, and in the end **to stand before the Son of man.**

---

has set his to everything Jesus said from the beginning (Heb. 12:26-27).

34-36. ***The Way of a Christian in a World of Change.***—An exhortation to steadfastness in a world where anything can happen. If Luke composed it, he adhered closely to the mind of Jesus, to say nothing of prophet (Isa. 24:17, 20) and apostle (I Thess. 5:1-10). Taking the passage as it stands, there are four main lines of emphasis. (*a*) Mark the importance of the disciples in the midst of this vast and cosmic disturbance. They are no pawns on some celestial chessboard, expendable, "statistics" in some divine strategy: they are central and permanent features in that kaleidoscopic scene. (*b*) Consider the terms of their peril. The heart may so easily be weighed down, made heavy with excess, until a kind of nausea overtakes it, and the drunken earth seems to reel; or caught and held fast in bitter bondage to the **cares of this life** (12:22; Matt. 13:3-9, 18-23): so that the day of Christ's appearing comes upon it **unawares** (see Expos. on vss. 25-28). (*c*) What else for it, then, but to "stay awake praying," in season and out of season, like a sentinel on guard (Eph. 6:10-20), never listless, always seeking, needy as we are (δεόμενοι), desiring as we must, to be made strong, dwelling "in the secret place of the Most High" (Ps. 91). (*d*) For in that place, and in that alone, lies our safety: not that we may escape out of life, but that we may escape into it (see Expos. on vss. 12-19), and there, before the face of **the Son of man,** having done all, "to stand"! Possibly the only additional comment that needs to be made on that word **stand** is from *Alice in Wonderland,* "You have to run with all your might just to stay where you are!" How difficult it is may appear from the experience of those who have tried to brazen it out (John 8). The assurance of such victory as Christ himself will give is for us the truest, deepest meaning of all the apocalyptic elements in the Christian gospel. The last book of the N.T. canon is devoted to it.

34. ***Your Part in God's Plan.*****—Take heed to yourselves.** Jesus sees men as they are and sees that they matter. He is never ready to accept their estimate of themselves. He will not weigh their several skills in a balance, throw in a few native talents here, add a social background there, and multiply everything, or else divide it, by the position they occupy in the city. He simply assumes, against "distress of nations in perplexity," with "the roaring of the sea and the waves," that they count. Albertus Magnus we scarcely remember: he wrote books enough to take up the first fifteen feet or so on a shelf. We remember Francis of Assisi, his modest little contemporary, who went around playing with children and birds and taking care of lepers. Look up the Crimean War, with its sabers rat-

37 And in the daytime he was teaching in the temple; and at night he went out, and abode in the mount that is called *the mount* of Olives.

38 And all the people came early in the morning to him in the temple, for to hear him.

37 And every day he was teaching in the temple, but at night he went out and
lodged on the mount called Olivet. 38 And
early in the morning all the people came to him in the temple to hear him.

8. Summary of Jesus' Life and Work in Jerusalem (21:37-38)

37-38. Note 19:47*a*. According to Mark 11:11-12, Jesus and his disciples spent the first night after their arrival at Jerusalem in Bethany, and presumably the earliest evangelist wished to imply that they continued to lodge in that village. Mark 11:19 is indefinite, but Jesus is again at Bethany in Mark 14:3-9—a scene that Luke omits because he has already used a variant in 7:36-50. Jerusalem was overcrowded at festival seasons and many pilgrims were compelled to find accommodation outside the city. It is improbable that Luke was deliberately correcting the Marcan tradition. Bethany was situated on the slopes of **Olivet** (see on 19:29). Perhaps Luke omitted the place name because it would be of little interest to the Gentile readers of his Gospel. **Lodged** in the Greek text does not necessarily mean "camped."

The similarity between the situation described in these verses and that in the introduction to the story of the woman taken in adultery (John 7:53–8:11) probably accounts for the incorporation of the latter incident at this point by the important Ferrar group of minuscules. Other MSS omit it altogether or include it following John 7:52; 7:36; or 21:24.

tling, its orders being shouted, its "charge of the Light Brigade": but not because you want to find out what it settled, if anything; rather because you want to place in her proper context a lone woman with a lantern in her hand walking through the barracks while wounded soldiers kissed her shadow where it fell on the wall. Her name was Florence Nightingale. What is a trifle? Who is obscure?

Furthermore, every man's part is essentially a creative part (II Cor. 6:1). Certainly it can be. Ask the next person you meet, "What do *you* make of life?" and the chances are good that he will answer, "I can make nothing of it, nothing at all. It seems to go around and around, in a dreadful circle—toward the hole in the sink!" But change your emphasis, and put it to him somewhat differently. Ask him, "What do you *make* of life?" If he answers you now with any such nonsense, he will be giving the lie to how much of human history and to how much of the day's real news that lies behind the headlines?

Moreover, every man's part is intended to add up to something, some magnificent whole already in the mind of God. There is a total purposefulness about life, all its varied notes fitting somehow into a sort of stirring music. Nobody is going to prove that. Any number of people will dispute it. They will fling scraps of learning at you. They will point to the chaos which waits, like the primeval dragon, while "our little systems have their day." They will ask about suffering, and the good that gets smashed into a pulp by brute force. If you try to smooth it all over with a few glib explanations, they will slam the door in your face as they go out. Who can blame them? The conviction of God's overruling providence comes of looking as steadily as a man can at Jesus of Nazareth, and the love which stands in him so squarely at the center of things that it can afford to lose, without ever for a single moment risking its own chances of victory (vs. 28).

37-38. ***The Rhythm of Life.***—Day and night, in and out, systole and diastole, morning and evening—but not routine! We take the 7:50 from the suburbs, spend our lives to weariness and near exhaustion, then the 5:45 home again: round, not rhythm; treadmill, not heartbeat! Here is a life that comes from God, and goes to God, and girds itself between (John 13:3-4). It is a stranger—far enough away to be free, close enough at hand to be involved—and a pilgrim, on the road not to its own ends but God's (22:42). Here is a crisis to be met (vss. 25-36). Here are people to be served, early and late: eager people, people hungry and athirst; angry people, people crafty and afraid (20:6, 23). Here are words to be spoken, now the flash of a sword, now the healing touch of a steady hand, while the sands of time keep running out,

22 Now the feast of unleavened bread drew nigh, which is called the passover.

2 And the chief priests and scribes sought how they might kill him; for they feared the people.

3 ¶ Then entered Satan into Judas surnamed Iscariot, being of the number of the twelve.

22 Now the feast of Unleavened Bread
drew near, which is called the Pass-
over. 2 And the chief priests and the scribes
were seeking how to put him to death; for
they feared the people.
3 Then Satan entered into Judas called
Iscariot, who was of the number of the

D. Jesus' Last Supper (22:1-23)

1. Conspiracy of the Chief Priests and the Scribes (22:1-2=Mark 14:1-2)

22:1. Luke is not quite correct when he identifies the two feasts. **The feast of Unleavened Bread** began at sundown on Nisan 14—the beginning of the fifteenth day by Jewish reckoning—and lasted for a period of seven days (Lev. 23:5-6). **The Passover** coincided only with its first day. The paschal lambs were slaughtered on the afternoon of Nisan 14, and the solemn meal itself was eaten during the evening that constituted the beginning of the fifteenth day.

2. In the process of abbreviating Mark, Luke omits the interesting note that the chief priests and the scribes wished to accomplish Jesus' **death** before the beginning of the festival. According to Luke, it was Jesus' popularity with **the people** that gave him a measure of protection (cf. vs. 6).

2. Judas' Plot to Betray Jesus (22:3-6=Mark 14:10-11)

It is scarcely conceivable that the story of Jesus' betrayal by one of his disciples should have been invented by the early church. Modern suggestions that Judas is a personification of the Jewish people fail to carry conviction.

Early in the nineteenth century Thomas de Quincey advanced the precocious theory that Judas was a high-minded individual who wished to compel Jesus to declare his mes-

and rest and friendship and the shelter of a quiet roof—and God—make up each day's spending into reserves again!

22:1-6. *Judas' Bargain.*—(See Expos. on vs. 47.) Against the background of the annual feast commemorating God's deliverance of his people from Egypt, as the first day of unleavened bread drew near, the greatest problem confronting **the chief priests and the scribes,** celebrants at God's holy altar, keepers of the law and the temple, learned men, leaders of the people now, was not *what* to do with this troublesome prophet from Nazareth—they had already made up their minds to do away with him—but *how* to do it. The Greek is much more emphatic than the English: they **sought** this, **how** they might get rid of him. The "how" has always been a nuisance. We know what we are about—or do we? We will have none of him. But we scarcely know how to manage. It is not so easy. There are many who think well of him. They still make it difficult, as they did then: impressed by his teaching, held by his authority, telling of him, looking to him for some mighty work. Life makes it difficult. He himself makes it difficult. To have done with him—but how? We can cry "Barabbas!" when the time comes. We can call out with Pilate, "I am innocent!" and wash our hands while others see to it. We can shout, if we have enough forthright malice for it, "Crucify him, crucify him!" But what occasion can we find? One of his own, perhaps, who may betray him—for a price? Some other to deny him? Will his little band of followers flee? Will the great, dumb crowd bite its lips and never lift a finger? Either that—or else we shall be as putty in his hands. Maybe it will be "or else" no matter what we do—from Julian the Apostate to the poet Swinburne:

> Thou hast conquered, O pale Galilean;
> the world has grown grey from thy breath.[5]

Pale? Or with eyes like a flame of fire? (Rev. 1:14.) Grey? Or blood red?

What a bargain it would have been if only there had been any advantage in it for anybody! For priests or scribes? "Not . . . one stone upon

[5] "Hymn to Proserpine."

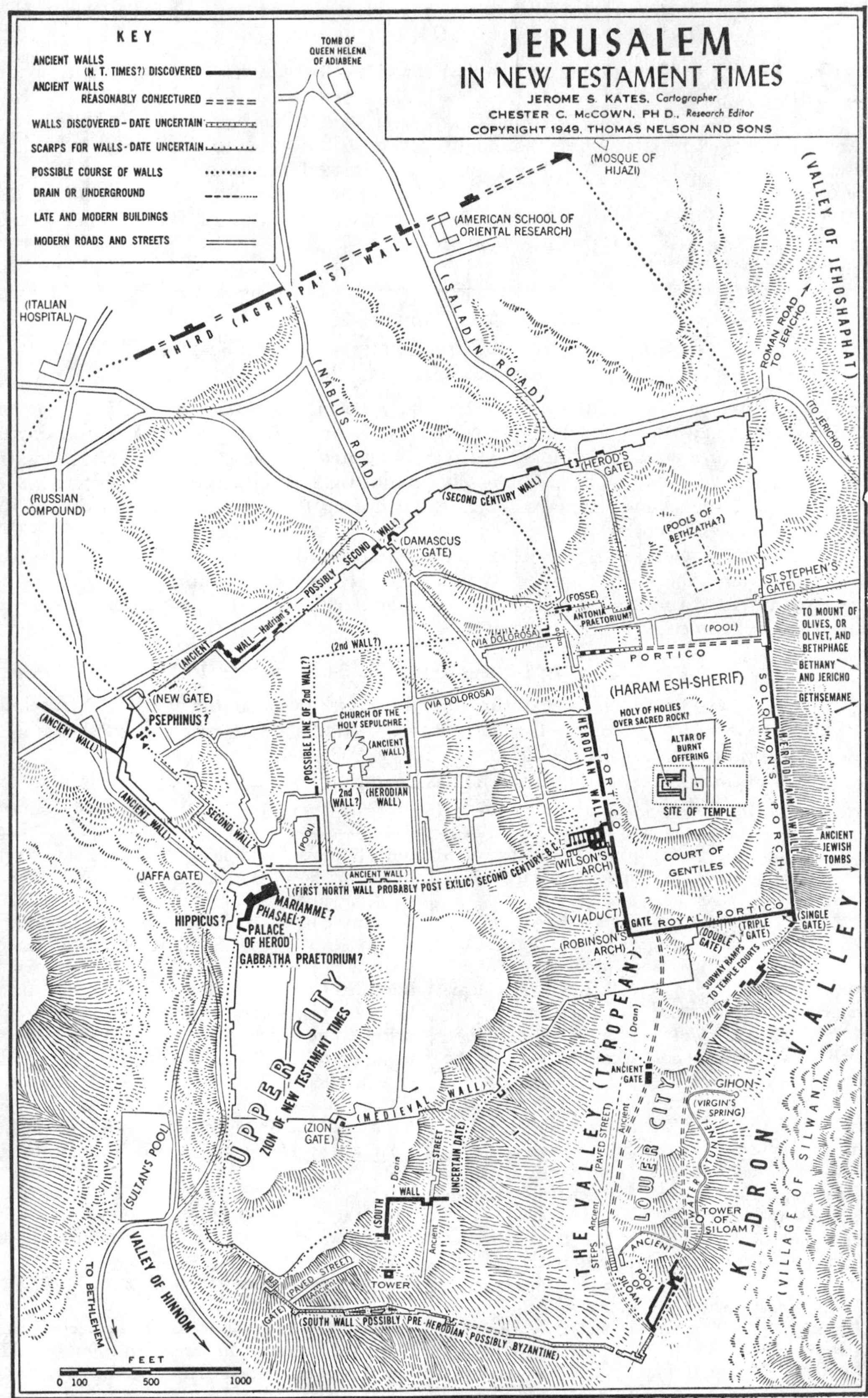
JERUSALEM
IN NEW TESTAMENT TIMES
JEROME S. KATES, Cartographer
CHESTER C. McCOWN, PH D., Research Editor
COPYRIGHT 1949, THOMAS NELSON AND SONS
KEY
ANCIENT WALLS (N. T. TIMES?) DISCOVERED
ANCIENT WALLS REASONABLY CONJECTURED
WALLS DISCOVERED - DATE UNCERTAIN
SCARPS FOR WALLS - DATE UNCERTAIN
POSSIBLE COURSE OF WALLS
DRAIN OR UNDERGROUND
LATE AND MODERN BUILDINGS
MODERN ROADS AND STREETS
TOMB OF QUEEN HELENA OF ADIABENE
(MOSQUE OF HIJAZI)
(AMERICAN SCHOOL OF ORIENTAL RESEARCH)
(VALLEY OF JEHOSHAPHAT)
(ITALIAN HOSPITAL)
THIRD (AGRIPPA'S) WALL
(SALADIN ROAD)
(NABLUS ROAD)
ROMAN ROAD TO JERICHO
(TO JERICHO)
(HEROD'S GATE)
(RUSSIAN COMPOUND)
(SECOND CENTURY WALL)
(POOLS OF BETHZATHA?)
(DAMASCUS GATE)
POSSIBLY SECOND WALL
(ST. STEPHEN'S GATE)
(FOSSE)
ANTONIA PRAETORIUM?
(POOL)
TO MOUNT OF OLIVES, OR OLIVET, AND BETHPHAGE
BETHANY AND JERICHO
GETHSEMANE
(ANCIENT WALL—Hadrian's?—
(VIA DOLOROSA)
(2nd WALL?)
PORTICO
(HARAM ESH-SHERIF)
(NEW GATE)
PSEPHINUS?
POSSIBLE LINE OF 2nd WALL?
CHURCH OF THE HOLY SEPULCHRE
(ANCIENT WALL)
HOLY OF HOLIES OVER SACRED ROCK?
ALTAR OF BURNT OFFERING
SITE OF TEMPLE
(ANCIENT WALL)
(2nd WALL?)
(HERODIAN WALL)
HERODIAN WALL
PORTICO
SOLOMON'S PORCH
HERODIAN WALL
(ANCIENT WALL)
SECOND WALL?
(POOL)
(WILSON'S ARCH)
COURT OF GENTILES
ANCIENT JEWISH TOMBS
(JAFFA GATE)
(ANCIENT WALL)
(FIRST NORTH WALL PROBABLY POST EXILIC) SECOND CENTURY B.C.
MARIAMME?
PHASAEL?
HIPPICUS?
PALACE OF HEROD
GABBATHA PRAETORIUM?
(VIADUCT)
GATE
ROYAL PORTICO
(SINGLE GATE)
(ROBINSON'S ARCH)
(DOUBLE GATE)
(TRIPLE GATE)
SUBWAY RAMPS TO TEMPLE COURTS
THE VALLEY (TYROPOEAN)
(Drain)
ANCIENT GATE
UPPER CITY
ZION OF NEW TESTAMENT TIMES
(MEDIEVAL WALL)
(ZION GATE)
GIHON
(VIRGIN'S SPRING)
LOWER CITY
(PAVED STREET)
Ancient
KIDRON VALLEY
(VILLAGE OF SILWAN)
WATER TUNNEL
(SULTAN'S POOL)
(SOUTH WALL)
Drain
STREET
UNCERTAIN DATE
Ancient
TOWER OF SILOAM?
STEPS Ancient
ANCIENT POOL
POOL OF SILOAM
VALLEY OF HINNOM
TO BETHLEHEM
TOWER
(PAVED STREET) Ancient
(GATE)
(SOUTH WALL POSSIBLY PRE-HERODIAN POSSIBLY BYZANTINE)
FEET
0 100 500 1000

4 And he went his way, and communed with the chief priests and captains, how he might betray him unto them.

5 And they were glad, and covenanted to give him money.

6 And he promised, and sought opportunity to betray him unto them in the absence of the multitude.

7 ¶ Then came the day of unleavened bread, when the passover must be killed.

twelve; 4 he went away and conferred with
the chief priests and captains how he might
betray him to them. 5 And they were glad,
and engaged to give him money. 6 So he
agreed, and sought an opportunity to betray him to them in the absence of the multitude.

7 Then came the day of Unleavened Bread, on which the passover lamb had to

---

siahship and thus to hasten the inauguration of the kingdom of God, and similar idealizing portraits of Judas continue to appear. However interesting, such theories have no evidential support. Mark's version suggests that avarice was Judas' motive, and Matthew makes that motive explicit. Luke blames it all on Satan (cf. John 13:2, 27; 14:30; and Paul's belief that the hierarchy of demonic forces who are "the rulers of this age" were the ultimate agents responsible for the crucifixion of "the Lord of glory" [I Cor. 2:8]).

The process of apologizing for Judas began at an early date. Matthew declared that the traitor, overcome with remorse, soon returned the money he had accepted and then committed suicide (Matt. 27:3-5). Luke says nothing of this. According to our evangelist, Judas used his "blood money" to buy a field, and his death was the consequence of a punitive miracle: "Falling headlong he burst open in the middle and all his bowels gushed out" (Acts 1:18). The Gospel of John was concerned about the christological problem involved: Was Jesus' judgment or foreknowledge at fault? The author guards against any such misapprehension by pointing out that Jesus was aware at the very outset (John 6:70-71) of the role that Judas would play.

What did Judas betray? Mark and the other Synoptists imply that he merely identified Jesus for the agents whom the chief priests had sent to effect the arrest, and probably we need look no further for an answer. Some modern scholars suspect that the traitor gave the Sanhedrin inside information about Jesus' secret claim to be Messiah. Our sources do not lend this hypothesis any support. There is no suggestion that Judas gave witness against Jesus or appeared at the trial.

3. Iscariot: See on 6:14-16.

4-6. Captains: As in vs. 52 (cf. Acts 4:1; 5:24, 26), the officers of the temple police.

3. Preparation for the Passover (22:7-13=Mark 14:12-16)

As in the story of the entry into Jerusalem (19:29-32=Mark 11:1-4), both Mark and Luke imply that Jesus had a prophet's foreknowledge of the course events would take (cf. I Sam. 10:2-6).

7. Both Mark and Luke ignore the Jewish custom of dividing "days" at sunset (see on vs. 1).

---

another" (21:6). For Judas, **of the number,** but not of the spirit, **of the twelve?** (See Expos. on vs. 47.) All that was left at the last was one wild vote for Jesus (Matt. 27:4), a field "to bury strangers in" (Matt. 27:7, with an infinite pathos; cf. Acts 1:18-19), and a man dead, it may be by his own choosing. It was Satan's bargain (vs. 3), entered into, ratified, and all its dividends collected. Except for the one advantage which was foreseen by nobody but Jesus himself! "In that, while we were yet sinners, Christ died for us" (Rom. 5:8; see Expos. on Luke 22:21-23, 47, 48).

7-13. ***Go and Prepare.***—(Cf. also Matt. 26:17-19.) It was the evening of the day before the Passover, the day when the water was drawn and the bread kneaded for the feast, when all leaven had to be put away from Jewish households (see Exeg. on vss. 1, 14-23). The farewell supper at which our Lord, according to Christian tradition, instituted the Eucharist, seems to have been the simplest kind of anticipatory meal (the *Kiddush,* or "sanctification" of the sabbath?), consisting of bread, blessed and broken; and wine, passed around in a common cup (not the four separate cups of the

8 And he sent Peter and John, saying,
Go and prepare us the passover, that we
may eat.
9 And they said unto him, Where wilt
thou that we prepare?
10 And he said unto them, Behold, when
ye are entered into the city, there shall a
man meet you, bearing a pitcher of water;
follow him into the house where he en-
tereth in.
11 And ye shall say unto the goodman
of the house, The Master saith unto thee,
Where is the guest chamber, where I shall
eat the passover with my disciples?
12 And he shall show you a large upper
room furnished: there make ready.
13 And they went, and found as he had
said unto them: and they made ready the
passover.

be sacrificed. 8 So Jesus[n] sent Peter and
John, saying, "Go and prepare the pass-
over for us, that we may eat it." 9 They
said to him, "Where will you have us pre-
pare it?" 10 He said to them, "Behold, when
you have entered the city, a man carrying
a jar of water will meet you; follow him
into the house which he enters, 11 and tell
the householder, 'The Teacher says to you,
Where is the guest room, where I am to
eat the passover with my disciples?' 12 And
he will show you a large upper room fur-
nished; there make ready." 13 And they
went, and found it as he had told them;
and they prepared the passover.

[n] Greek *he*.

---

8. Peter and John for Mark's "two of his disciples."

9-13. When you have entered the city: It is assumed that, contrary to custom, Jesus had spent the day elsewhere than in Jerusalem. Many interpreters arbitrarily associate the **large upper room** of these verses with that mentioned in Acts 1:13 and locate it in the house of John Mark's mother which we are told in Acts 12:12 served as a meeting place after the Crucifixion for Jesus' erstwhile followers. They are then enabled to identify the **man carrying a jar of water** as John Mark and **the householder** as John Mark's father. Sober exegesis cautions against such a dubious chain of inferences. **Furnished:** Carpeted

---

pascha). There are indications throughout the Synoptic Gospels that this view of the matter was generally taken for granted (Matt. 26:5; Mark 14:2; not to mention the carrying of arms, the trial, the preparation of spices and ointments, etc., none of which would have been permitted during the first and holiest day of the festival; note, too, that the word translated "any more" or "again" in vs. 16 is omitted by a number of important MSS). Christ himself was to be the true paschal lamb (John 18:28; 19:36; I Cor. 5:7). It is not strange that in after years this Last Supper should have been identified with the Passover, in spite of all the evidence to the contrary. And for the Christian, in truer and deeper sense than any factual correspondence could have provided, it was just that. (See also Exeg., p. 378.)

Certainly, as his ministry rapidly approached its climax, Jesus, intent as he was on being undisturbed (is this the meaning of these elaborate precautions?), is clearly represented as having regarded the events immediately to follow as of profound significance. The shadow of the mystery in which somehow they seemed to be involved fell on the mind of Luke as he wrote (see Exeg.). It was a mystery that has associated itself ever since not with a memory, but with a presence.

Over against it, all too often, stands the sheer casualness of our own long accepted observance. There have been times when the pilgrim church, under the continuing spell of it, has girded herself by fasting and prayer, in services of confession, repentance, intercession, of remembrance and dedication, unwilling except in deep and penitent awareness to hold out her hands for the sacrament of Christ's gospel, which is his gift to her. "They that were ready went in with him" (Matt. 25:10). "Be ye therefore ready" (12:40). Again and again in Scripture is that note struck. Of old, he that was to be knighted on the morrow kept until the dawn his lonely vigil before the altar. But let no man boast of his readiness (22:33). The Lord himself, and not another, must prepare his own way in the desert of our lives. "A new heart also will I give you. . . . I will put my Spirit within you, and cause you to walk in my statutes" (Ezek. 36:26-27).

10. *The Unknown Friend.*—A man carrying a jar of water. Was this a prearranged signal? At any rate, here in the background is the dim, scarcely discerned figure of a man (John Mark's

14 And when the hour was come, he sat down, and the twelve apostles with him.

14 And when the hour came, he sat at

and supplied with couches on which guests could recline at a meal. **They prepared the passover:** The purchase, slaughter, and roasting of the paschal lamb and the provision of unleavened bread, bitter herbs, and wine.

4. The Last Supper (22:14-23)

The RSV follows the so-called Western text of Luke at this point and omits vss. 19*b* and 20. There is good reason, quite apart from principles of textual criticism (see Intro., p. 20), to believe that this "short" text of Luke is original. Vss. 19*b* and 20 in the KJV are in almost verbal agreement with I Cor. 11:24*b*-25 and presumably were interpolated by early copyists.

Marcan contacts with the Western text of Luke are vss. 14 (rewritten), 18 (abbreviated), 19*a*, and 22. Some interpreters believe that Luke's account is only an editorial rearrangement and expansion of Mark's, but it is more probable that Luke had access in this instance to an independent tradition and that he has revised and supplemented it with excerpts from his primary source. If this latter hypothesis is correct, the Last Supper is attested in the N.T. by three independent accounts: I Cor. 11:17-34; Mark 14:17-26; Luke 22:14-23. John has no narrative of the Last Supper, but ch. 6 of his Gospel is an elaborate and symbolic interpretation of it.

No doubt the Christian sacrament of the Lord's Supper was influenced in its observance and interpretation by beliefs and customs current among contemporary mystery cults, many of which had sacramental meals. But the hypothesis that the early church borrowed the rite is untenable. There is every reason to accept the Christian tradition that the Lord's Supper originated as a commemoration of Jesus' last supper with his disciples.

The Pauline and the Mark-Matthew accounts of the Last Supper have much in common, and both are earlier than Luke's. Nevertheless the possibility remains that the latter rests on a more primitive tradition. It exhibits the following striking variations: (*a*) the cup comes before the bread; (*b*) the cup is not associated with the establishment of a new covenant; and (*c*) the main emphasis of the account is on the supper as a feast of anticipation (vss. 16, 18). The disciples recalled that, during Jesus' last meal with them, he had spoken solemnly of his impending death but had also confidently predicted a reunion around a banquet table in the kingdom of God. Similar traits may be noted in the regulations for the conduct of the Eucharist in the Didache (9:1-3), an early second-century book of Christian discipline.

One further preliminary question is of crucial importance: Was the Last Supper Jesus' Passover meal? This is the representation both in Mark-Matthew and in Luke, but there are grounds for believing that the meal took place twenty-four hours before that feast was to be celebrated.

---

father?—but see Exeg. Tradition would also associate the young evangelist-to-be with Mark 14:51-52, perhaps with the scene in Gethsemane, and with several of the additional details given us by Luke)[6] whose hospitality made possible the last quiet evening Jesus had with his disciples. All through the gospel record, as in some painting by Rembrandt, is the hint of those peopled shadows: shepherds and wise men, centurions, publicans, and sinners, a lad "with five barley loaves, and two small fishes," women and children whose names have never come down to us, but who moved for a moment near that central light, and by it have been etched into everlasting remembrance. The story cannot now be read without them. They have become a part of it. Unknown friends, and Jesus of Nazareth, and immortality!

14-20. *The Lord's Supper.*—The great truths of Christianity are forever simple truths, but they are not shallow truths. One is often amazed at the common assumption that everything Jesus said is easy to understand. People

[6] See *A New Commentary on Holy Scripture*, ed. Charles Gore, H. L. Goudge, and Alfred Guillaume (New York: The Macmillan Co., 1928), *ad loc.*

15 And he said unto them, With desire I have desired to eat this passover with you before I suffer:

16 For I say unto you, I will not any more eat thereof, until it be fulfilled in the kingdom of God.

table, and the apostles with him. 15 And
he said to them, "I have earnestly desired
to eat this passover with you before I
suffer; 16 for I tell you I shall not eat
it[o] until it is fulfilled in the kingdom

[o] Other ancient authorities read *never eat it again.*

The problem is created by a striking conflict between the Synoptic accounts of the date of the Crucifixion and that in the Gospel of John. All agree that Jesus died on a Friday. But Mark, followed by Matthew and Luke, says that this was the Passover while John declares that it was the day before (John 18:28; 19:14, 31, 42). In this instance John is almost certainly correct. Mark 14:1-2 looks like an excerpt from an early source that the compiler has not thoroughly revised. Here we are told that the chief priests and the scribes were anxious to bring about Jesus' death before the beginning of the festival, and there is no reason to believe that they changed their plans. Paul describes Christ as "our paschal lamb [who] has been sacrificed," and compares the Christian era to the Jewish feast of Unleavened Bread (I Cor. 5:7-8). The paschal lambs were slaughtered a few hours before the evening that marked the first part of the Passover day (see on vs. 1). Finally, since the Passover was a sacred day, it is almost inconceivable that Jesus could have been arrested, examined before the Sanhedrin, tried before Pilate, crucified, and buried during the course of it.

If Jesus died on the Cross some hours before the beginning of Nisan 15, it is clear that the Last Supper was not Jesus' Passover meal. Therefore it should not be interpreted in the light of Passover symbolism. Nevertheless the church soon came to think of it as the Christian substitute for the Jewish feast, and the passion narrative was redrafted at some pre-Marcan level to make the two coincide.

14. Editorial revision of Mark. **The apostles** is more impressive than Mark's "the twelve."

15-16. If these verses were part of some special Lukan tradition it would appear also to have identified the supper with the Passover meal. Another interpretation is possible

will cite him as the illustration par excellence of the fact that religion ought unfailingly to be set forth in terms so clear and plain as to be readily followed even by children. Just take the Sermon on the Mount, they say. What simplicity! And the prayer he taught his disciples: almost all of it in words of one syllable! Not the poorest, most ignorant, uneducated person in the world could have had the slightest difficulty with it.

But what item is there in the record more insistent than this: that Jesus was being constantly *mis*understood? Almost all men mistook his spirit. They twisted what he said to suit themselves, and failed to get at his meaning. Even those who loved him most were in a maze half the time, shaking their heads, asking him questions. And ever since then life has been taking him this way and that, sometimes quarreling about it, always wondering, like a man standing on the shores of an unknown continent, impressed by nothing so much as by a sense of measureless distance, the vast sweep of rivers and mountains waiting still to be explored.

There is a simplicity about Jesus, but we will not get to the bottom of it soon! We will not pick up his thought on anything, pack it neatly into a small, overnight bag, and make off with it under our arm. There is more here than the plain tale of a sad parting, with a lovely memorial at the heart of it in a bit of bread and a cup of wine. It is said that in those days there was a kind of solemn ritual in use among the Syrians. Whenever a man was about to leave his friends and go on a long journey, he gathered them around for one last pledge of his abiding love. He gave them food, and told them to take it; for all the leagues between, it would be as his body to theirs. And with his own hand he gave them wine to drink; it would be as the blood of his life to their life. Never would he be anywhere away; not for a moment beyond the reach of any man's heart!

Perhaps we can do no more than guess what that meant to these bewildered disciples, waiting there miserably under a cloud they could not clearly see, could only vaguely feel. He was saying good-by, they knew that. He was confirming the old, and founding a new, fellow-

17 And he took the cup, and gave thanks, and said, Take this, and divide *it* among yourselves:

18 For I say unto you, I will not drink of the fruit of the vine, until the kingdom of God shall come.

of God." 17 And he took a cup, and when
he had given thanks he said, "Take this,
and divide it among yourselves; 18 for I
tell you that from now on I shall not drink
of the fruit of the vine until the kingdom

---

but remote: Jesus' fervent desire **to eat this passover** before his death will not be realized. This latter construction is more attractive when we omit **again** with several ancient MSS —an emendation of the text favored by Westcott and Hort and RSV. **Until it is fulfilled in the kingdom of God:** The idea of a messianic feast in the new age was a familiar one in Jewish apocalyptic.

17-18. The cup is also mentioned before the bread in I Cor. 10:16, 21. The practice at a Jewish meal was for the head of the house to bless the chalice of wine, drink from it, and then pass it to each member of the company in turn. Luke's wording of vss. 17*b*-18 implies that only the disciples drank of the wine. Vs. 18 is in close agreement with Mark 14:25, but may have been taken over nonetheless from Luke's special tradition.

---

ship.[7] Beyond even that, with his soul in his eyes, was he trying to make them some stately promise that the One whose face they had seen in his was not taking his final departure from the earth? That he was leaving himself behind? Semitic to the core was his word, **This is** [from now on to be] **my body.** And as they pondered it in the years that came after, when the true Passover lamb had been slain, when the Cross was a broken tragedy and death itself something they could look at without flinching, they began to find in it not a figure of speech, not a mere gesture of the divine favor, but the very bestowal of that life which they themselves had handled and watched, as he gave himself so eagerly along the roads of Galilee: pardon beyond any they could ask, power beyond any they would be called on to use, peace that could cover their tumult with enough left over for the world to lose itself in!

When it was all done, they moved out into the night, Jesus with them, the words of a distant song still on their lips. "O give thanks unto the LORD; for he is good: because his mercy endureth for ever" (Ps. 118; Mark 14:26).

17, 19. ***From Symbol to Sacrament.*—And he took a cup. . . . And he took bread.** For the order cf. I Cor. 10:16, 21. Questions arise to which there is no certain answer. The expositor, however, need have no misgiving about the reliability of the facts out of which the Christian tradition arose (I Cor. 11:23-26; Mark 14:22-24; Matt. 26:26-28). The confusion may well have been due to the ambiguities of the situation discussed in the Exeg. and referred to in the Expos. on vss. 7-13.

[7] See Martin Dibelius, *Jesus,* tr. C. B. Hedrick and F. C. Grant (Philadelphia: Westminster Press, 1949), p. 133.

About this hour was the sanctity of Oriental custom. As men broke bread together in the East, there was set up between them a pledge of solemn affection and mutual concern to which our hurried and casual hospitalities bear little resemblance. It was the symbol of deep intimacy, unbroken by any distance, to be marred by no betrayals, nor by any forgetfulness. For people who have learned to spend so many meaningless moments around strange tables entertaining transient guests, it is scarcely possible any longer to appreciate the enormity of Judas' treachery, and Peter's denial, and the flight of Matthew and Thomas and Andrew and James, with frightened faces turned over their shoulders toward the cross. It was the breaking asunder of the holiest ties one man could bind about another with the bounty of his kindness. It was the panic-stricken tearing into shreds a covenant not yet a day old, a covenant which should have stood forever between them and this Christ who had shared with them like a host the warmth and the comradeship of food and drink. Disloyalty had no keener edge (vs. 21). It was the same breach of trust which gave to the psalmist's lament a poignant anguish that the lapse of centuries has not dulled, "Yea, mine own familiar friend, in whom I trusted, which did eat of my bread, hath lifted up his heel against me" (Ps. 41:9).

But there was more than Oriental custom to give this hour its peculiar sanctity. Around it in the busy city were gathered all the memories of the Passover, and of the God who on a night long ages ago had redeemed the children of Israel from bondage, and had led them out desperately toward the sea and the desert. That night had never been forgotten. The prophets had kept flinging their arms back toward it,

19 ¶ And he took bread, and gave
thanks, and brake *it*, and gave unto them,
saying, This is my body which is given for
you: this do in remembrance of me.
20 Likewise also the cup after supper,
saying, This cup *is* the new testament in my
blood, which is shed for you.
21 ¶ But, behold, the hand of him that
betrayeth me *is* with me on the table.

of God comes." 19 And he took bread, and
when he had given thanks he broke it and
gave it to them, saying, "This is my body.[p]
21 But behold the hand of him who betrays

[p] Other ancient authorities add *which is given for you. Do this in remembrance of me."* 20 *And likewise the cup after supper, saying, "This cup which is poured out for you is the new covenant in my blood.*

19*a*. An insert from Mark 14:22. **Bread:** "Loaf"—Moffatt. **This is my body:** The verb "to be" would not have been expressed in Aramaic, and therefore too much weight cannot be given to it in the Greek. Probably to be paraphrased: "This means my body"—Moffatt. Jesus interpreted his acted parable of the breaking of the loaf as a representation of the fate that awaited him. But it is probable that Mark and Luke and their readers understood the words in terms of the realistic sacramentalism that is already evident in Paul's references to the rite (I Cor. 10:14-22; 11:23-30). If they originally carried this meaning, the interpreter would be impelled to regard them as an early interpolation by Hellenistic Christians, for such sacramental ideas appear to have been alien to the Jewish framework of thought that Jesus shared.

21-23. Jesus' oblique reference to one of his table companions as a traitor precedes the narrative of the supper in Mark's account (Mark 14:18-21). Vs. 22 is apparently an excerpt from Mark 14:21.

---

wondering why this people ever should be afraid. When the bitter days of exile came, they sat there by the waters of Babylon, and built from that past the surest hope they had for the future. They kept taking it out, as if it were a flashing gem, and turning it over with their fingers to catch every gleam of the central, colored fires that burned within it. They sang of it in their psalms. "When Israel went out of Egypt, the house of Jacob from a people of strange language; . . . The sea saw it, and fled: Jordan was driven back" (Ps. 114:1, 3). Wave after wave of conquest had swept over them since; and now at the last Rome had marched in with her legions. But Yahweh was still governor among the nations. Doorposts marked with red, and the sound of an angel's passing. Long lines of men moving as far as the eye could see. A pillar of fire and cloud. And away beyond the wilderness, a Land of Promise. It was God forever to the rescue. There was that.

And more. This was Christ's last parable, enacted, not spoken; the bread and the wine differing from symbols in this, that they offer to men, taken into very body and very life, a presence for which no symbol is necessary (contrast Isa. 20:2-4; Jer. 27:2-11). Writes P. T. Forsyth:

> The modern symbol is but aesthetic and not energetic. It shows us, it does not act on us. The ring does not marry, it only means marriage. The symbol does not convey the thing signified. It just depicts it or suggests it. It impresses, it does not change us. It is not associated with change. The modern symbol does not do justice . . . to the present reality of God's action as the cause within our act. . . . A Sacrament is as much more than a symbol as a symbol is more than a memorial. . . . It is an act, not a lesson; . . . it is not a spectacle nor a ceremony. It does something. . . . It is an act of the Church . . . created by the eternal Act of Christ which made and makes the Church. At the last it is the act of Christ present in the Church, which does not so much live as Christ lives in it.[8]

It was to this that Luther and Calvin struck back, past all the elaborate ritual and priestly miracle of the Roman Church, which would transform Christ's inward and spiritual presence, apprehended by faith, into an outward and visible reality; yet resisting the while, in the same breath, every attempt which others might make to leave it poorer, hardly more than a sort of relic of what once had been done and suffered.

21-23. *The Betrayal Foretold.*—Behold the hand of him who betrays me. There is no hour, not the most sacred, which is secure against the inroads of evil. This passage would indicate that even Judas partook of the Last Supper (Mark 14:18; Matt. 26:23), certainly of the meal which preceded it. If so, what a mute, heartbreaking appeal—next to the last!—was the broken bread and the wine "poured out"!

[8] *The Church and the Sacraments*, 3rd ed. (London: Independent Press, 1949), p. 229. Used by permission.

22 And truly the Son of man goeth, as it was determined: but woe unto that man by whom he is betrayed!

23 And they began to inquire among themselves, which of them it was that should do this thing.

24 ¶ And there was also a strife among them, which of them should be accounted the greatest.

me is with me on the table. 22 For the Son of man goes as it has been determined; but woe to that man by whom he is betrayed!" 23 And they began to question one another, which of them it was that would do this.

24 A dispute also arose among them, which of them was to be regarded as the

E. The Farewell Discourse (22:24-38)

Note the much more elaborate farewell discourse in John 13–17.

1. True Greatness (22:24-27)

Note 9:46-48 (Mark 9:33-37). Similar in content to Mark 10:42-45, which Luke omitted at the point where we might have expected him to use it (following 18:34). Differences in phraseology and content support the hypothesis that these verses were derived from some special source. Mark's variant urges those who would be great to achieve their ambition by the way of service. Luke's tradition counsels those already in positions of leadership to demonstrate the graces of humble service (cf. John 13:2-16). In both versions Jesus enforces his advice by reference to his own example—but with diverse sayings.

24. Editorial. In Mark's version Jesus' words were addressed to the ten disciples after his reply to the request of the sons of Zebedee for places of preferment in the new age.

Love was still there, doing all even that God could do not to let him go. The eternal purpose, fulfilling itself in tragedy, could be neither stayed nor defeated; but there was nothing inevitable even now about the tragedy of the human soul which served that purpose (vs. 22). So is the mystery of evil caught up in the greater mystery of good (Acts 2:23; 4:27-28; Rev. 13:8). While around the edges, conscious somehow that they are involved in both, the disciples, unsure of themselves, and not yet suspicious of Judas, shamefacedly **question one another.** "Who could it be?" they whispered (see Expos. on vs. 64). What else for James and John but the memory of their own unseemly request that day on the road to Jerusalem? (Mark 10:35-41.) What else for Thomas but the old doubts that had kept shouldering their way into his life? For Peter, but his own sad blundering? (Mark 8:33.) "Lord," they asked, "is it I?" (Cf. I Cor. 10:12.) Until at last, motioning to John, Peter passed the word along: "Tell us who it is." And John, "close to the breast of Jesus," said "Lord, who is it?" The dread possibility was in front of every one of them, and for this moment they knew it. With what in our lives that can turn it into sudden fact? Greed or lust or envy; fear or anger or hatred: any of them can do it single-handed. And what in our lives to prevent it? Judas himself, in Matthew's account, joins the babel of those uneasy questions; and Jesus, looking upon him, answers, "Thou hast said." It was a rabbinical formula almost equivalent in meaning—though not of course in mood!—to the American slang, "You are telling me." It was a statement that was yet not quite a statement, with the knowledge it implied, and a shifting back of the responsibility to the questioner himself.

24-30. ***Who Is Greatest?***—An old debate, stirred again into life perhaps by the incident recorded in vss. 21-23; possibly even by Judas, to cover his own sense of shame and guilt, as he got up from his place at the table and made his way into the night. In 9:46-48 (cf. Mark 9:33-37; Matt. 18:1-4) the disciples may well have been thinking of their own supposed priority as a group,[9] very much as "Christians" are still inclined to do. Whereupon there followed an object lesson in humility. By the time the story moves on to the request made by (or on behalf of?) "the sons of Zebedee" (Mark 10:35-45; Matt. 20:20-28), the point at issue has resolved itself into the desire for preferential treatment inside the circle; only to bring up swiftly into the shadow of death (Mark 10:39)—the guerdon of how many who would march in the dangerous van of God's hosts, that true hospitality wherein he gives us to drink of his own cup! The verses before us

[9] See Bruce, "Synoptic Gospels," *Expositor's Greek Testament, ad loc.*

25 And he said unto them, The kings of the Gentiles exercise lordship over them; and they that exercise authority upon them are called benefactors.

26 But ye *shall* not *be* so: but he that is greatest among you, let him be as the younger; and he that is chief, as he that doth serve.

27 For whether *is* greater, he that sitteth at meat, or he that serveth? *is* not he that sitteth at meat? but I am among you as he that serveth.

28 Ye are they which have continued with me in my temptations.

29 And I appoint unto you a kingdom, as my Father hath appointed unto me;

greatest. 25 And he said to them, "The
kings of the Gentiles exercise lordship over
them; and those in authority over them
are called benefactors. 26 But not so with
you; rather let the greatest among you be-
come as the youngest, and the leader as one
who serves. 27 For which is the greater,
one who sits at table, or one who serves?
Is it not the one who sits at table? But I
am among you as one who serves.

28 "You are those who have continued
with me in my trials; 29 as my Father ap-
pointed a kingdom for me, so do I appoint

25-26. Benefactors: In Luke only. A favorite title of the Hellenistic monarchs who had ruled over Egypt and Syria. **The youngest:** The one to whom the least inviting duties would be assigned. In this instance the Greek comparative has the value of a superlative.

27*a*. It may have been this verse in Luke's source that prompted him to locate the passage after the account of the Last Supper.

27*b*. Mark's variant: "For the Son of man also came not to be served but to serve, and to give his life as a ransom for many" (Mark 10:45). Codex Bezae expands the saying as it appears in most MSS of Luke to read: "For I did not come among you as one who sits at a table, but as one who serves, and you have been happy to have me serve you."

2. The Disciples as the Future Rulers of the Twelve Tribes (22:28-30)

No doubt Matt. 19:28 is a variant, but differences make it improbable that the two versions were drawn from the same source. Rev. 3:21 may be still another phrasing. The idea of the apostles as rulers in the new age with the risen Christ is probably one that originated after the Resurrection.

28. Translate **trials** with the RSV.

29-30. The RSV should be followed in construing **kingdom** with the verb governed by **my Father,** and in regarding the clause in vs. 30 as the object of **I appoint for you.**

see this love of contention driving its wedge at last between man and man. The "strife" has become mutual, with nothing anywhere that can mortify it into decency again but this: **I am among you as one who serves** (see John 13:1-20).

Is it altogether too fanciful to suggest that in these three incidents we have a picture of the gradual but steady dissolution of Christian loyalty under the subtle encroachments of the self? What begins as a sense of exclusive privilege degenerates into the scramble for preferment and falls apart into divisiveness (14:7-11; 20:46; Mark 12:39; Matt. 23:6) and defection (vss. 31-32, 54-62; Mark 14:50; Matt. 26:56*b*). No vision of humility and the loveliness of it; no sober warning of the peril that attends both the great and the would-be great; no example of the Lord himself, with the towel that he wore and the basin that he took: nothing but the power of the Cross and Resurrection could ever have made any difference.

What the world has to say about power and privilege is obvious. The nations and races of men are ready enough with their gradations of rank and authority, scattering their titles about, in its *bellum omnium contra omnes,* its war of all against all: His Excellency, the Ambassador Extraordinary and Plenipotentiary; His Majesty, Philip the Good. Of course **the one who sits at table** is greater than the **one who serves.** Why bother to put it into words?

But not so with you. Prerogative is not the watchword in God's order (see Expos. on 19:24). Indeed, what constitutes for many the greatest religious problem is no more than their misreading of God's attempt to teach them where they actually stand. If there is a God,

30 That ye may eat and drink at my table in my kingdom, and sit on thrones judging the twelve tribes of Israel.
31 ¶ And the Lord said, Simon, Simon, behold, Satan hath desired *to have* you, that he may sift *you* as wheat:

for you 30 that you may eat and drink at my table in my kingdom, and sit on thrones judging the twelve tribes of Israel.
31 "Simon, Simon, behold, Satan demanded to have you,[q] that he might sift

[q] The Greek word for *you* here is plural; in verse 32 it is singular.

Jesus delegates privilege and responsibility in the kingdom that is to be his. **Eat and drink . . . in my kingdom** has no counterpart in Matthew's version. Possibly an interpolation suggested to Luke by the after-supper setting he has given the saying. Matthew's version reads "twelve thrones." The thought of Judas' impending defection may have prompted Luke to omit the numeral. **Judging**: probably used in the O.T. sense of "ruling."

3. Prediction of the Disciples' Desertion and a Commission to Simon (22:31-32)

According to Mark, Jesus' disciples "all forsook him, and fled" after his arrest (Mark 14:50). According to Paul, the first of the appearances of the risen Christ—on which the faith of the early Christian community was based—was vouchsafed to Cephas (I Cor. 15:5*a*; cf. Luke 24:34). The passage under discussion may reflect familiarity with both these traditions. It asserts that Jesus had foreseen his disciples' loss of faith and had entrusted Simon with the responsibility of restoring it. These verses replace Mark's prediction of the scattering of the disciples and of the Galilean appearance of the risen Christ (Mark 14:27-28).

31. And the Lord said (KJV): An introduction vouched for by Codex Sinaiticus and the bulk of the MSS but omitted by Codex Vaticanus and a few allies. The double vocative is characteristic of Luke. The role attributed to **Satan** is similar to that in the prologue to the book of Job. **You** in this verse is plural, i.e., the disciples.

---

they want to know, why does the universe take no more account than it does of life and love and beauty and tenderness? It may be because there is no other way in which we could even begin to learn that our bodies, and what happens to them, are not God's chief concern. It is a hard lesson, and he has to use tough and sinewy means to get it across. Life is not organized around us and our privileges. Neither our assets nor our liabilities are a key to the mystery. Is that why there are so many days when a closed door seems to be the only accurate symbol of reality? Pound on it ever so hard, and whoever lives there, if anybody does, will not open it. Storms come and accidents happen. Disease stalks up and down, holding hands with death. Crops grow or rot with the blight. Rain falls, or the parched earth bakes hard and cracks open under the sun. "What's the good of being good in a world like that?" asked a woman. Rather, what would be the good of being good in any other kind of world?

Preferment in God's order comes on other terms. **The greatest** shall be he who undertakes willingly the most menial of tasks; for I myself, says Christ, **am among you as one who serves.** The watchword of all true greatness is not privilege but devotion. It came as an offense to the Jews. Such a Messiah was not to their liking. It comes as an offense to us. "We do not want this man to reign over us" (19:14). Human judgments do not easily suffer themselves to be turned upside down. Yet the reversal stands, strangely in history, persistently in experience. "Alexander and I," so Napoleon is reported to have said, "both founded our empires on force. Jesus alone founded his on love. And to this day countless thousands would die for him."

It was that love which even now, as the record stands, looked around the hot little circle of its friends with no more than this soft rebuke, **You are those who have continued with me in my trials.** It was to stick fast in their memory like a barbed arrow when they fled, tug at it as they would. And this promise, grace upon grace, of a day when in spite of everything (vs. 31) they should have their appointed place in his kingdom, **on thrones judging the twelve tribes of Israel,** apostles and martyrs all!

31-34. *A Deserter's Commission.*—**Simon, Simon. . . .** History was in the name (Matt. 16:17-18). Faithful and faithless Peter, compound of every strength and weakness among

32 But I have prayed for thee, that thy faith fail not: and when thou art converted, strengthen thy brethren.
33 And he said unto him, Lord, I am ready to go with thee, both into prison, and to death.

you[q] like wheat, 32 but I have prayed for
you that your faith may not fail; and when you have turned again, strengthen your
brethren." 33 And he said to him, "Lord,
I am ready to go with you to prison and

[q] The Greek word for *you* here is plural; in verse 32 it is singular.

32. **You** represents the Greek singular. Even Simon's **faith** would be shaken, but Jesus had interceded with God to save it from utter collapse. **And when you have turned again:** Probably a reference to Simon's recovery of faith after the Resurrection. Moffatt interprets it as a Hebraism meaning "and you in turn." **Strengthen your brethren:** Cf. the similar commission in John 21:15-17.

4. Prediction of Peter's Denial (22:33-34=Mark 14:29-31*a*)

According to Mark, the prediction was uttered on the Mount of Olives. Luke shifts the scene to the upper room.

33. An editorial revision of Mark 14:29 and 31*a* that makes Peter's declaration of loyalty more positive.

the disciples—he it is that Jesus addresses directly, glancing around at those other faces for a moment, and then coming back (vs. 32). "Simon," and again "Simon"—not "Peter" now! In the repetition and in the tone of the voice "sorrow and love flow mingled down." *The crisis* is upon them all; but not suddenly, straight out of the blue. Quietly enough, through the weeks and the months "the prince of this world" had been gathering in his sieve the life of every man there at the table. What of selfishness was in this one, of jealousy in that? What quick anger could be stirred in these, what resentment? Was there weariness anywhere, slowness of heart, disappointment? Sin stalks before it leaps. It sifts gently at first, then violently back and forth, as the clouds begin to scurry, and the storm (vs. 33) sweeps up out of the night, and the trial of strength draws near: holding on as always to the chaff, trying to throw the grain away. With only One who stands opposed, that it may not be: all agony and striving his agony and striving (vs. 44; 13:24), every prayer for help his prayer (vss. 32, 44). **Behold, Satan, . . . but I. . . .** Already the power is in those steady and holding hands; the issue need not be in any doubt. Failure there would be, but not utter failure (vs. 32). The whole scene is reminiscent of the book of Job. Tears there would be (vs. 62), but after them the sound of running feet (24:12), and a man whose confidence in himself (vs. 33) had been shattered, that in weakness a strength not his own might through him find its way out into human life (cf. II Cor. 12:9). **When you have turned again, strengthen your brethren.** Follow the story of Peter through the N.T.—standing, slipping, scrambling back to his feet again, running, turning—until it comes out in the familiar legend of his flight from Rome, only to be met along the highway by a vision of the Lord. *Domine,* he faltered, *quo vadis?* "Whither goest thou?" And the answer, "To Rome, to be crucified in thy stead." Then the road back, as morning came; and the cross that was planted head downward in the earth: "Lest I," said he, "who am all unworthy, should die as my Lord died!"

Surely no premium may be set on failure; but who can say that we may not have to fail before God can get in! So like are we to those poor souls who panic-stricken tried to rush out through the narrow entrance of their air-raid shelter in London, and clogged it with themselves. Nobody could clear the struggling mass of humanity away, or keep it from hurting itself to death. "What would happen to me," asked a man of his friend, "if I should undertake to carry on my business as Christ would want me to do it?" "And what will happen if you don't?" the other answered. "What kind of ruin are you after?" There is a kind that turns sterile. Only a puny sort of prudential morality keeps threatening the sinner with the miscarriage of all his plans, saying, "Don't do that evil thing: it won't work." Jesus says, "The chances are it will!" Then he looks at you and adds, "That's the trouble. With Dives it did, and the unjust steward, and the rich fool!" But there is another kind of failure, and God builds on it (vs. 62; Matt. 16:18). Where all men deny him, each in his way, what else has he to use? Where all men desert him, each in his time, who but a deserter can be Christ's saint and apostle?

35-38. *On Guard!*—A difficult passage for the expositor; difficult, too, apparently for the disciples! And therefore, no doubt, especially as regards vs. 36*b*, highly authentic. Whatever

34 And he said, I tell thee, Peter, the cock shall not crow this day, before that thou shalt thrice deny that thou knowest me.

35 And he said unto them, When I sent you without purse, and scrip, and shoes, lacked ye any thing? And they said, Nothing.

to death." 34 He said, "I tell you, Peter, the cock will not crow this day, until you three times deny that you know me."

35 And he said to them, "When I sent you out with no purse or bag or sandals, did you lack anything?" They said, "Noth-

34. The cock will not crow . . . until, i.e., "before daybreak." **This day:** The Jewish "day" was reckoned from sunset to sunset. Contrast Luke's use of the word in vs. 7.

5. Saying About Buying a Sword (22:35-38)

35. A reminder to the disciples that they had been cordially welcomed and entertained during the course of their first mission. Luke has overlooked the fact that he had

interpretation was first put on the cryptic words which Luke is here reporting, it seems to have been a misinterpretation. If Jesus intended that his followers should now look to themselves, repelling even with force the assaults of a hostile world, there is no indication elsewhere in his teaching that such resistance might conceivably prove to be necessary, and no instance anywhere in our accounts of their having obeyed him with any literalness. For that, the **two swords** would hardly have seemed adequate. Perhaps it was for his defense, not for their own, that they made the offer (vs. 38) which was so abruptly dismissed (see Matt. 26:52-54). In any case, the situation from this time forth would not be what it had been, either in 9:3 or in 10:4. Their mission hereafter would call for all the provision they could make, all the equipment they could get together, all the skill they could summon. Doors that had been open (vs. 35) would be closed: welcome was turning into considered enmity. Precautions had to be taken, strategies worked out. The less important must yield to the more (vs. 36*b*). Christ's mission was moving on toward its fulfillment, even as God had ordained (vs. 37*b*). The gospel was coming to grips with the world.

And certain it is, when the lines are drawn, the conflict bids fair to be grim enough. By the Christian norm life is not placid, unruffled, safe; but turbulent, boisterous, rough (see Expos. on 21:12-19). "Almighty God," runs the collect, "who knowest us to be set in the midst of so many and great dangers. . . ." The N.T. came out of such an insight (see further Expos. on vss. 35-38 below). It talks of principalities, and powers, and the rulers of the darkness of this world. What confronted the men who wrote it was like a live thing, not to be shaken clear. To set about the days jauntily was the part not of a wise man, but of a fool: as if sharp temptation could be met with a flourish, choices made out of hand, peril faced; sorrow on its leaden feet, death, with always the pressure that would try to crowd God out, and the self that would keep elbowing its way in.

But they were destined to win through, these few men against the world. It was to be a fight, but it was to be an honest fight toward a real end. Life was no string of meaningless incidents. It had about it the logic of forever. That logic stood up out of a grave in the dawn one day, a day mankind will never forget. "Be of good cheer"; "Lo, I am with you." He was speaking of whom Oscar Wilde once said there was enough suffering in any London lane to show that his love is fancy, not fact. Yet toward that fancy Oscar Wilde himself came at last to stretch out his arms:

Come down, O Christ, and help me! reach thy hand,
For I am drowning in a stormier sea
Than Simon on thy Lake of Galilee.[1]

In connection with these final instructions which Jesus gives his disciples, recall Eph. 6:13-17. There, too, life is seen not as a laboratory but as a battlefield; not so much as a race, but at greater length and apparently with far more enthusiasm as the shock of armed legions, a war in the members, a panorama of fronts, flanks and reinforcements. For it men are to make themselves ready. There is armor, there is a helmet, there are a shield and a sword—with belt and breastplate and sandals. All in the knowledge of a security that runs deeper than life; because the enmities that take life away cannot touch it.

35-38. *Able to Withstand.*—Attention has already been called to the way in which the N.T. peels off like a dive bomber and heads straight for the grim realities people have to face. Nobody ever gets farther down than it

[1] "E Tenebris."

36 Then said he unto them, But now,
he that hath a purse, let him take *it,* and
likewise *his* scrip: and he that hath no
sword, let him sell his garment, and buy
one.
37 For I say unto you, that this that is
written must yet be accomplished in me,
And he was reckoned among the trans-
gressors: for the things concerning me have
an end.

ing." 36 He said to them, "But now, let him
who has a purse take it, and likewise a bag.
And let him who has no sword sell his
mantle and buy one. 37 For I tell you that
this scripture must be fulfilled in me, 'And
he was reckoned with transgressors'; for
what is written about me has its fulfill-

---

included these particular instructions in his account of the mission of the seventy (10:4), not of the twelve (9:3). See on 10:1.

36. The attitude of the Jewish people has changed. Jesus' disciples will now need money, provisions, and even means of defense. It is possible (despite Matt. 26:52-54) that Jesus contemplated the emergence of a situation in which his followers would have to resist aggression by the use of force. Most interpreters refuse to believe that Jesus was speaking literally. Some allegorize **sword** in the sense of Eph. 6:17. Others see in the saying only a vivid, pictorial description of the altered temper of the populace.

37. The quotation is from Isa. 53:12 and is usually regarded as an allusion to the whole verse. The only unambiguous reference in the Gospels to the poems of the servant

---

gets. It stands in need of no apology in any company where brains meet. Whatever goes wrong, or however badly, it will never dodge the issue. It was written from the bottom up. A man can drop right out of heaven into hell, and the N.T. will still be underneath him.

One of the grim realities which Jesus is underlining here is the terrific force of evil. (*a*) We discount it dangerously when we think of it as a kind of hangover from our brute ancestry. There is nothing primitive about any of it. It is mature: not a reversion, a development; not the petulance of a child, but the malevolence of a man (see Expos. 23:31). No use asking science to deliver us from it; "For thine is the education, and the legislation, and the evolution, for ever and ever." The farther we go, the vaster it becomes. In the temptation scene note the way in which the devil attempts to follow Jesus from lower ground to higher. It was remarked during the blitz in London that man at the top of his bent turned out the airplane; whereupon to counter it, the devil, at the top of his, checked in an ape man as pilot! (*b*) Nor can the "spiritual wickedness in high places" be simply defined as the wickedness of other people. Everybody seems to be dead certain that the chief difficulty is with somebody else. Capital says it is labor, labor says it is capital. Is it the Negro problem or the white man's problem? The Jew's or the Gentile's? Who, when he fights, is not convinced that he is fighting on the side of righteousness? At a rally day service during World War II a congregation was told by its minister that since American missionaries had been sent home from Japan, it was necessary now that another kind of missionary be dispatched, with bombs and flying fortresses. He said afterward that it made mothers and fathers feel a good deal better about the whole thing. (*c*) Bluntly, it is ourselves we are pitted against. That is part of the story the Bible tells, though not all. There is something far more tragic in the world than our nasty ways and mean dispositions. These are not enough to account for the facts, or for the commotion in heaven. Christ was too much trouble for God to take simply to keep us out of mischief and help us get along with a maiden aunt. (*d*) There is a dreadful fatality abroad. It is stupidity, and more. It is our own unwillingness to learn, and more. It is the growing, rolling pressure of the crowd, and more. It is the way life starts out after some good, and then the thing gets twisted all around until it is horrible (see Expos. on 21:8). It is the way life triumphs; and its very triumph, because God has been left out, becomes unfathomable defeat. It is the way we win freedom and turn it into anarchy. It is the way we strive for self-realization through centuries, only to be cogs at last in some monstrous mechanism. It is the way we make discoveries and destroy each other. This is what disturbs the course of history and brings us where we are.

One day a soldier sat by a window in a train and stared out at the green fields. After a while he took a drink from the bottle in his pocket, and turned to the stranger beside him. "I've come from hell," he said. "Which one?" asked

38 And they said, Lord, behold, here *are* two swords. And he said unto them, It is enough.

39 ¶ And he came out, and went, as he was wont, to the mount of Olives; and his disciples also followed him.

ment." 38 And they said, "Look, Lord, here are two swords." And he said to them, "It is enough."

39 And he came out, and went, as was his custom, to the Mount of Olives; and

---

of the Lord. At a later date the church found an answer in those O.T. passages to the meaning of Jesus' death, and it is possible that Jesus himself had also reflected on them. But the verse has little connection with what precedes and follows and may not have been an original part of the present complex. **What is written about me:** Practically a repetition of 37*a*, but the reading has much better MS support than the alternative in the KJV.

38. Two swords: Allegorized as "worldly and spiritual" authority by the bull *Unam Sanctam* of Boniface VIII (A.D. 1302). The disciples took Jesus literally and any hypothesis that they were mistaken is too subtle to be probable. **It is enough** was his comment that their resources were adequate for their immediate needs. But most interpreters regard the phrase as a Semitism meaning "Enough of this!" (Goodspeed). Jesus' metaphor had been misunderstood, and he therefore abruptly dismissed the subject.

F. The Arrest (22:39-65)

1. Jesus' Prayer on the Mount of Olives (22:39-46; cf. Mark 14:32, 35-38*a*)

One act of solitary prayer and one discovery of sleeping disciples, instead of three of each as in Mark. The story represents Jesus in doubt, even at the end of his ministry, of the course that God would have him pursue. If he were to remain in Jerusalem, it

---

the stranger, thinking of the far-flung battle lines. "Libya," he answered, and ran his tongue around his lips as if he found it quite impossible to get rid of the sand. The minutes flicked by like mileposts, as he kept gazing out across the landscape. "I was born and brought up among those hills," he muttered at last, as if to himself. "This evening I'm going to lie there, and look up into the sky, and see no planes, only clouds. And not have to run my plane behind them to hide." As the train began to slow down for his station, he staggered to his feet and shook his head. "I've got to think," he said, in a sort of daze, stumbling out into the aisle. "We've got a great enemy, and we'll not blast him out soon." And the stranger sat there wondering if he had his enemy located!

Until that happens, we shall never get back in our lives any sense of the sheer awfulness of God's might. This was the second reality which Jesus faced. And we forget it. Or we leave it out. We have said it was our only confidence; but we could hardly ever take it seriously. We have sung of it, and resorted to everything else. And it too is grim enough—witness life and witness history. It does not aim to be "kind," or to win cheaply, as we try to win. Jesus never saw it as an indulgent smile; he saw it as a Passion, fulfilling the scripture, as a strained and twisted anguish (see vs. 69; "the power" was a "Jewish euphemism for God"). But it was the secret of his peace. Everything he had given his life to do he was leaving to these few who listened, and he knew them; but they were in the keeping of that right Hand which he had seen bringing in the dawn as a very little thing (Isa. 40:10-12). It was waiting now to reach out against a world, against a cross and a grave. It is waiting still for all who have the courage to ask of it.

39-46. *The Agony in the Garden.*—Father, if thou art willing. . . . Few other scenes in the gospel story have been the source of such strength and comfort as have been drawn from this by countless multitudes, both Christians and non-Christians. Whether the words Jesus uttered were actually overheard by the disciples or the report represents their own not too difficult assumption makes comparatively little difference. Nor is the fact of anything but passing interest that at several points Luke varies from the account given in Mark-Matthew. What does matter is that the incident itself belongs quite obviously to the earliest tradition. Even vss. 43-44 enter strong claim, as do Mark 14:33; Matt. 26:37, by very reason of the difficulties to which they give rise: could it be that the Son of man was ever in such agony to begin

40 And when he was at the place, he said unto them, Pray that ye enter not into temptation.

the disciples followed him. 40 And when he came to the place he said to them, "Pray that you may not enter into temptation."

seemed certain that a violent death awaited him. He was ready to face it if that should prove his Father's will. But perhaps he should withdraw from the nation's capital and resume a less dangerous itinerant mission in Galilee. He sought by petitionary prayer to clarify his duty and resolve his doubts.

Because the only possible auditors of Jesus' prayer were overcome by sleep, and he himself was prevented by his arrest from telling his followers of his experience, many interpreters have argued that the story must be a legend. But it is probable that the disciples formed at least some impression of the crisis he faced. Heb. 5:7 is another account of it. The incident is not one that the early church is likely to have invented. The Fourth Evangelist omitted the scene altogether. It did not fit into his conception of how a divine being would have acted. "The whole story bears the hallmark of human truth. . . . The sorrow and sufferings of the solitary Son of man, profound as they are, leave on every sympathetic heart, be it the heart of the believer or unbeliever, such an impression as may never be wiped out" (Joseph Klausner, *Jesus of Nazareth,* tr. Herbert Danby [New York: The Macmillan Co., 1925], p. 332).

39-40. The place: Where Jesus and his disciples were accustomed to spend the night? This interpretation would explain how Judas knew where to find them, but would also

with; or that in it he needed the support of friends and angelic visitants? "Embellishments" usually proceed in the opposite direction! In any case, these verses embody the whole spirit and tenor of our Lord's earthly life from beginning to end, finding in his very outcry a fulfillment of the divine will (cf. Ps. 22).

Father: For all the intensity of his suffering, God is no distant, hostile being, as in Job, but intimate and close and "most wonderfully kind." Set Mark 15:34 against the background of Ps. 22 in its entirety; then hear the quiet sigh, as of a tired child, in Ps. 31:5 (turned by Luke 23:46 into a triumphant shout?). Back of that austere and dreadful scene is One who does not willingly afflict any of his children; nor is there any moment, however desolate, from which he hides his face, having nothing to do with it. Father in love, in wisdom, in strength; God of all worlds, and God still of this; great enough to care as only he can care for the work of his hands, bending down his ear to the whisper on human lips. The trouble with trouble is that so often man lets it drive a wedge between himself and God. It found Jesus where he always was—and left him there!

If thou art willing. . . . Not that God is reluctant. We are not subject to a humor, we are subject to a will—a will which does not necessarily occasion the disaster, yet is Lord of it, so that nothing falls outside the circle of the divine providence: the knowledge of God embraces it, the power of God is sovereign over it, the mercy of God holds it creatively in hand. To that will Jesus was not only subject, but eagerly subject: not in resignation, in glad surrender; not under compulsion, but as a captain of necessity, in a world that made sense (vs. 42*b*).

Remove this cup from me. Never should we attempt to hide from God the heart's desire (Ps. 139:1-12; observe how Job 1:10; 3:23 uses the thought of vs. 5, and how the psalmist uses it in vss. 10-11). What more fruitless? What less trustful? To put it simply into words (perhaps we should read, "If thou wilt remove . . ."), and then (suddenly?) to abandon it for the ultimate kindliness of that "nevertheless"! It is not likely that Jesus feared death, or faced in weakness and agony, even for a moment, what generations of men and women and children too have faced with songs and with his name on their lips (cf. Expos. on 23:27-30). Rather was it the Passion that he would have been spared (see Exeg.), with all that was involved of human sin and the world's weight. Yet he would not, except God would. The prayer may well reflect some uncertainty in his own mind about the immediate issue. What was in store for him may not have become clear, with a dreadful finality, until men took up their hammers and actually began driving the nails. But not once is any undertaking entered on or allowed that would seem to force events his way (vs. 51; cf. Matt. 26:53). We know now, if he did not, that there was to be no divine intervention. There was to be strength. There was to be calm. There was to be majesty. In the more primitive portrayals of the Crucifixion he is represented as wearing his kingly crown on

41 And he was withdrawn from them about a stone's cast, and kneeled down, and prayed,

42 Saying, Father, if thou be willing, remove this cup from me: nevertheless, not my will, but thine, be done.

41 And he withdrew from them about a stone's throw, and knelt down and prayed,
42 "Father, if thou art willing, remove this cup from me; nevertheless not my will,

require the assumption that Luke was utilizing some non-Marcan tradition (see on 21:37-38). Probably the evangelist simply chose the noun to avoid the Semitic name "Gethsemane" (see Intro., p. 4). The command to the disciples is given at the beginning as well as at the end of the incident and replaces Mark's "Sit here, while I pray" (Mark 14:32*b*).

41. Luke omits the item in Mark's version that Peter, James, and John accompanied Jesus somewhat farther than the rest of the eleven, and also Jesus' words: "My soul is very sorrowful, even to death . . ." (Mark 14:33-34).

42. Reminiscent of the opening words of the Lord's Prayer (Matthew's version): "Father . . . thy will be done." The Aramaic "Abba" of Mark's version is omitted. **This cup,** the Passion.

the very cross itself—as indeed he did. Not Pilate, but Pilate's prisoner, was both master and judge.

40, 46. ***Refuge and Requirement.*—Pray that you may not enter into temptation.** (Cf. Matt. 6:13.) At first glance there seems to be very little about such a petition that could be called heroic. But Jesus knows the hazards of the moral life, and would not have them needlessly increased. There are threats to personal integrity, as there are threats to physical well-being, which a man is in conscience bound to avoid if he can. To this end prayer is refuge, for the sake of the requirement on the other side of it. So with the Christian gospel. What shelter it offers, it offers because shelter is necessary: from the sheer futility of a godlessness that would multiply everything by zero; from the grim emptiness of an existence that cannot take with ultimate seriousness the only real difference there is in the world, the difference between good and evil. In Galsworthy's *Maid in Waiting* the daughter says one day to her mother, "I don't see the connection between beliefs and character. I'm not going to behave any worse because I cease to believe in Providence or an after life. . . . If I'm decent it's because decency's the decent thing; and not because I'm going to get anything by it." And the mother replies, "But why is decency the decent thing?"[2] The plain fact is that if we have to do without God, and everything adds up to nonsense, so does decency. The gospel is a refuge from that, as order is a refuge from disorder, and reason from insanity. But the gospel does not stop there. Neither does prayer.

Both of them have in mind not the side-stepping of anything, but the undertaking of something. We are not here to be wrapped up in the power and promises of God, as if they were cotton batting, until all our bones are jelly, and there is no flame in the soul! The "Safety First" movement had as its purpose the avoiding of those risks which might be thought of as sterile, in order that those which had some chance of being creative might be undertaken. **Pray that you may not enter into temptation.** "Count it all joy, my brethren, when you meet various trials" (Jas. 1:2; note that the nouns are the same, while the verbs differ). "Hang yourself, brave Crillon," cried Henry IV, as he greeted his tardy friend after a great victory had been won, "Hang yourself! We fought at Arques, and you were not there!"

40, 46. ***The Risk of Prayer.***—Prayer, if a man is downright in earnest about it, as Christ was in Gethsemane, is no sweet-smelling ointment, no salve for sore consciences, no pillow for infirm wills; it is rather part of the risk he has to run. It is likely enough to get him straight into trouble.

Prayer is petition; but brave petition. "Our Father who art in heaven. . . ." There is a gallantry about it. These petitions hold up their heads. They will not stoop or whine or dodge or fend off or cringe or let their teeth chatter with a beggar's fear! They march along in unbroken ranks from a name into a kingdom, with a will, through bread and trespasses and temptation and evil, to a power and a glory forever.

And prayer is communion: though scarcely for one who sentimentalizes it until it seems like a dressing gown and slippers, there by the hearth in front of the fire. God is a disturbing person to meet. Read George Matheson's hymn

[2] (New York: Charles Scribner's Sons, 1931), p. 235.

43 And there appeared an angel unto him from heaven, strengthening him.

44 And being in an agony he prayed more earnestly: and his sweat was as it were great drops of blood falling down to the ground.

45 And when he rose up from prayer, and was come to his disciples, he found them sleeping for sorrow,

46 And said unto them, Why sleep ye? rise and pray, lest ye enter into temptation.

47 ¶ And while he yet spake, behold a multitude, and he that was called Judas, one of the twelve, went before them, and drew near unto Jesus to kiss him.

but thine, be done." 43 And there ap-
peared to him an angel from heaven,
strengthening him. 44 And being in an
agony he prayed more earnestly; and his
sweat became like great drops of blood
falling down upon the ground.[r] 45 And
when he rose from prayer, he came to the
disciples and found them sleeping for sor-
row, 46 and he said to them, "Why do you
sleep? Rise and pray that you may not enter
into temptation."

47 While he was still speaking, there
came a crowd, and the man called Judas,
one of the twelve, was leading them. He

[r] Other ancient authorities omit verses 43 and 44.

43-44. Missing from Codex Vaticanus and a number of other important MSS, and probably an embellishment of the Lukan text by some Christian scribe.

45-46. For sorrow: In Luke only. **Rise and pray,** etc.: Cf. 11:4*b*, and see Exeg., *ad loc.*

2. Betrayal and Arrest (22:47-54*a*; cf. Mark 14:43, 45-49*a*)

47-48. The Synoptists give the impression that Jesus' arrest was the work of a more or less unorganized mob. In all probability it was effected by a detachment of the temple

---

about the love that would not let him go, and how he had to give it back the life he owed, and the flickering torch he carried; how he saw there a Cross, and would not ask to flee from it, but laid his dead glory in the dust. It was no quiet evening when he and God met. There were "ocean depths" and "sunshine's blaze" and "blossoms red"! A man would do well to be staggered by it!

For there he must risk seeing himself as God sees him. In one of Studdert-Kennedy's poems a cockney soldier tells of it. He has gone to church and heard a sermon on the Final Judgment; and he has not liked it. There seemed to be nothing real about it. After dinner he lay down for a nap and had a dream. He saw a figure standing beside him; and all his life came back to him. The eyes that were in those eyes! His wife's "and a million more." And they were sad. And the voice that spoke said just one word. It is not an easy word to answer —when God utters it! "Well?"[3]

Then, too, when he prays, a man must risk growing more like Jesus of Nazareth; and being like Jesus of Nazareth in a world like this is not a prospect to be viewed with composure. To love where love is crucified; to be unselfish where the crowd will take advantage of your unselfishness, cheat you for being honest, and hurt your feelings for showing yourself affectionate! It may be that God will answer your prayer as you stand naked and alone before him: risking what you are on what he is!

47. ***One Vote for Jesus.*—The man called Judas, one of the twelve.** The story of Judas' life does not seem to be just the sordid tragedy of a covetous soul. That is how it looked to the men who set it down, and they set it down often enough! He likely took none of them into his confidence, Judean as he was, lonely it may be among these men of Galilee. So they said he had the bag, and was a thief. And they kept saying it. But motives are not always so simple. Back of the record, in the dark mind of that man from Kerioth, one may vaguely envisage the gigantic, shadowy forces swaying to and fro in their silent rivalry. In his play, *The Dark Hours,* Don Marquis has Judas call himself "a city full of spirits, and they riot in the streets."[4] Nor was that all. Being what he was, the very endless love of Jesus, with its magnificent infinities, calling him "Friend," must have done him hurt, dwarfing and shriveling his soul out of its self-respect: until he began to look around furtively, trying to hide his own poverty out of sight; and at last in utter self-loathing tore his desperate way out of that awful obscurity by lifting his hand against the daily beauty that made him ugly.[5]

Whatever it was, on the bleak morning of the Crucifixion, **the man called Judas** stood in the temple court, threw his thirty pieces of

[3] "Well?" *The Sorrows of God and Other Poems* (New York: George H. Doran Co., 1924).

[4] Garden City: Doubleday, Page & Co., 1924, scene 1.

[5] See Shakespeare, *Othello,* Act V, scene 1.

48 But Jesus said unto him, Judas, betrayest thou the Son of man with a kiss?

49 When they which were about him saw what would follow, they said unto him, Lord, shall we smite with the sword?

50 ¶ And one of them smote the servant of the high priest, and cut off his right ear.

51 And Jesus answered and said, Suffer ye thus far. And he touched his ear, and healed him.

drew near to Jesus to kiss him; 48 but Jesus
said to him, "Judas, would you betray the
Son of man with a kiss?" 49 And when those
who were about him saw what would fol-
low, they said, "Lord, shall we strike with
the sword?" 50 And one of them struck the
slave of the high priest and cut off his
right ear. 51 But Jesus said, "No more of
this!" And he touched his ear and healed

---

police who acted on instructions from the Sanhedrin. In Mark's account Judas kissed Jesus to identify him for arrest. According to Luke, his intention was anticipated and frustrated by Jesus' question.

49-51. A scene that Marcion omitted from his gospel. The scuffle precedes the arrest (contrast Mark and cf. John 18:10-11). The literary history of this incident throws light on the process by which new details could be introduced into a narrative and could transform a natural event in one channel of the tradition into a miracle. According to Mark, an unnamed follower of Jesus struck off an ear of an unnamed slave of the high priest. Matthew (26:52-54) expands the account with a rebuke to the disciple. Luke identifies the severed member as the **right ear**, declares that Jesus **touched it** and **healed** the slave, and intercalates another version of Jesus' rebuke. In the Gospel of John (18:10-11), the disciple becomes Simon Peter, the slave Malchus, the ear the right one, and the rebuke still another saying, but there is no suggestion that any miracle was performed. **Suffer ye thus far:** A number of interpretations are possible (*a*) "Let me do this much!" (Goodspeed; cf. Moffatt); (*b*) **No more of this!** (RSV); (*c*) "Let events take their course—even to my arrest" (Creed and Klostermann, *ad loc.*). The last possibility merits serious consideration by the interpreter.

---

silver on the stone floor, and with them his solitary, anguished ballot for the Nazarene (Matt. 27:3-10; see Expos. on vs. 54). It was too late. The polls were closed. But he cast it in. He cast it in to the high priests and elders, the only place where it had any chance of counting. He cast it in with a courage born of his despair. The evangelists might have dealt with him more gently in their story. This much at least can be said for him that cannot be said for the others: it was not his own skin he was bent on saving that bitter day! He cast his vote!

To watch him there is like gazing out over a poor, scarred battlefield, with nothing left to show for all its once fair promise but lifeless, gaping wounds. "I have sinned." It is like a publican's smiting on his breast without being bold enough to lift up his eyes and pray. It is his *Miserere Nobis,* his litany from the farthest place to which life can get away from God. "In that I have betrayed innocent blood." His worshipful hail to the Best he has ever seen, those long sea miles yonder from this desert here! A sort of *Te Deum Laudamus* from hell! He was a betrayer, but by his very betrayal was betrayed. Sin always does that. The only thing left now was to destroy the self that had betrayed him.

So off somewhere in the distance there was a soiled and homemade gallows; while there on Calvary stood a clean cross for One who had done nothing amiss. Is not the meaning of it a mercy that can reach all the road between? There is another way to destroy the self that betrays us. The secret of it is still with Jesus of Nazareth. It is what he died to do—that carpenter whose love outstrode Judas, and from a God-lonely kiss built a symbol of hope on the world's altars; and this wistful memorial to a broken heart: "They took the thirty pieces of silver," and hypocritically washing their hands of the whole transaction, so does the story run, "bought with them the potter's field." A love that moves its hand over all the sin, and leaves behind its own fragrance: "to bury strangers in" (Matt. 27:9, 7).

48. *The Kiss of Judas.*—Would you betray the Son of man with a kiss? To the accustomed rendezvous in the garden (vs. 40) came the guards, and perhaps the stragglers who had followed them through the streets, with Judas to bring them where Jesus was. Could it be that one traitor, and one traitor alone, must stand forever in the pillory? Is betrayal then so uncommon? It can be sudden and dramatic; it can

52 Then Jesus said unto the chief priests, and captains of the temple, and the elders, which were come to him, Be ye come out, as against a thief, with swords and staves?

53 When I was daily with you in the temple, ye stretched forth no hands against me: but this is your hour, and the power of darkness.

54 ¶ Then took they him, and led *him*, and brought him into the high priest's house. And Peter followed afar off.

him. 52 Then Jesus said to the chief priests
and captains of the temple and elders, who
had come out against him, "Have you come
out as against a robber, with swords and
clubs? 53 When I was with you day after
day in the temple, you did not lay hands
on me. But this is your hour, and the power
of darkness."

54 Then they seized him and led him away, bringing him into the high priest's

---

52-53*a*. Luke adds to Mark the item that **chief priests** and **elders** as well as **the captains of the temple** came out to apprehend Jesus. This provides the evangelist with an impressive setting for Jesus' words, but it is improbable that members of the highest court of Judaism would participate personally in such a nocturnal and clandestine adventure.

53*b*. In Luke only. Probably both literal and symbolic: Evil men love darkness as a cover for their evil deeds (John 3:19) ; and the power of Jesus' enemies over him is satanic in origin.

54*a*. Jesus' arrest follows his dignified protest (contrast Mark and cf. John 18:3-12). **The high priest's house:** Annas' (John 18:13), or Caiphas' (Matt. 26:57)? See on 3:1-2*a*.

3. Peter's Denial (22:54*b*-62; cf. Mark 14:54, 66*b*-72)

The early church is not likely to have fabricated a derogatory story about its most honored apostle. While the details may be explained as literary elaboration, it is probable that the narrative has a historical nucleus in Peter's own honest admission. By attaching the introduction (Mark 14:54) directly to the body of the account (Mark 14:66*b*-72) Luke has moved the incident forward so that it precedes the hearing before the Sanhedrin.

54*b*-55. They: No doubt Luke means "the officers" (Mark and Matthew). **A fire** for warmth in the cool of a spring night. **The courtyard:** Open to the sky, surrounded by

---

be slow and almost imperceptible. It can be calculated and deliberate; it can be unpremeditated and without conscious intent. In any case, the show of comradeship and even of affection (as of pupil to master) is likely to be more than a "sign": it is likely to be in itself a symbol of the soul's warfare; for whatever is betrayed must once have been loved. And the result, in so far as the will of man can accomplish its purpose, is that the holy will of a righteous God is led away bound—toward the day of its terrible vindication! "This is your hour, and the power of darkness" (vs. 53*b*; cf. John 3:20). Though never quite, never solely "yours." God's at the last! Events took their course (vs. 54). But mercy marched on at the heart of them (vs. 51; Luce comments, "A first-century Christian [would have felt] how likely, if not certain, it was that Jesus should have blotted out the effect of His follower's act of violence";[6] see also Expos. on 23:33).

54. *Afar Off.*—And Peter followed. So much must be said for him. He was not of much use. Neither was John (John 18:15; yet see John 19:26-27). The rest of them, if anything, were of even less (Mark 14:50). Calvary could hardly be Calvary without the people who glance up and down the street, catch sight of the majority, then tiptoe quickly inside and lock the door. Or those others who stand around observing (23:35). Better to be John! Better than these others, even Peter! Better, it may be, Judas himself (see Expos. on vs. 47). Here, however, it is that phrase **afar off** which tugs at the imagination. It is of itself an interesting phrase to trace through scripture. Always there have been those who have seen the promises "afar off" (Heb. 11:13), and it kept them steady. But always, too, those whose feet have carried them "afar off" (Isa. 23:7). With somewhere between, those who have **followed**—at a distance! As who does not, even when following? And always the voice crying, "Fear thou not, . . . for . . . I will save thee from afar" (Jer. 30:10).

Franz Werfel, in *Hearken Unto the Voice,* writes of the day when Jeremiah wanted to go with the blinded king of Judah into exile; and

[6] *Gospel According to St. Luke,* p. 340.

55 And when they had kindled a fire in the midst of the hall, and were set down together, Peter sat down among them.

56 But a certain maid beheld him as he sat by the fire, and earnestly looked upon him, and said, This man was also with him.

57 And he denied him, saying, Woman, I know him not.

58 And after a little while another saw him, and said, Thou art also of them. And Peter said, Man, I am not.

59 And about the space of one hour after another confidently affirmed, saying, Of a truth this *fellow* also was with him; for he is a Galilean.

60 And Peter said, Man, I know not what thou sayest. And immediately, while he yet spake, the cock crew.

house. Peter followed at a distance; 55 and
when they had kindled a fire in the middle
of the courtyard and sat down together,
Peter sat among them. 56 Then a maid,
seeing him as he sat in the light and gazing
at him, said, "This man also was with him."
57 But he denied it, saying, "Woman, I do
not know him." 58 And a little later some
one else saw him and said, "You also are
one of them." But Peter said, "Man, I am
not." 59 And after an interval of about an
hour still another insisted, saying, "Cer-
tainly this man also was with him; for he is
a Galilean." 60 But Peter said, "Man, I do
not know what you are saying." And im-
mediately, while he was still speaking, the

---

the various rooms of the high priest's house, and approached from the street by a vestibule.

56-60. Minor variations from Mark: **a maid, some one else,** and **still another,** for "one of the maids of the high priest," "the maid," and "the bystanders"; indirect comment for direct address in the first and last quotations (and vice versa in the second); **after an interval of about an hour** in vs. 59 for "after a little while."

---

there across a gaping abyss it seemed to him he saw a luminous Figure, and heard One saying, "Thou shalt not go to Babylon, . . . I will send thee back to the Remnant." But the weary prophet rebelled. He cried out with all his might against it. Said that the longing in his heart was too strong. Insisted that the rabble back there in Jerusalem did not need him. And the blind king did!

> "Do not dispute with me," said the voice, . . . "but obey and turn back!" . . .
>
> "And if Thy servant does not turn back?" . . .
>
> "Then I will turn back. For my plan had been to journey with the blinded king and the prisoners of Zion to Babylon, and to take up my dwelling place among them. But now that *thou* art journeying with them, *I* will turn back."
>
> "No, Lord, no; . . ." cried the defeated Jeremiah in despair, "but go with them, and I will obey. . . ."[7]

And even as he spoke there seemed to be about him two strong and tender arms. What else is the deep and inward meaning of the Cross? Nor is there anything drab or tedious about the challenge it flings down with its mercy at men's feet!

54-62. ***Peter's Denial.*—Peter followed, . . . denied, . . . remembered.** (See Expos. on 31-34.) Ever the distance between Christ and the human soul tends to widen. Danger and loss, loneliness and pain, move there in the dreadful van of those who press too closely on his steps. Yet we follow, beckoned, haunted, unable to break away—as Perry said the North called to him, sleeping, waking, until he went spellbound by that white magic. But nowhere is there safety. The very light of the fire that warms, in that instant betrays. Recall Rembrandt's painting of the scene; and cf. Mark 14:54, "at the fire," with vs. 56 here, **in the light** (RSV): the same phrase in Greek. Luke's story is somewhat more gently told than the others. In Mark, two straightforward and emphatic denials are followed by a third in which Peter invokes a curse on himself and begins to swear. In Matthew, the first is followed by the second with an oath, then by the third as in Mark. Luke proceeds from a denial on Peter's part of all knowledge concerning Jesus, to a denial of discipleship, and finally to a simple disclaimer on the score of language, as one should say, "I am a Galilean, and I haven't the faintest idea of what you are talking about." The expositor can hardly fail to find in the very variations a wealth of suggestion. Until at last **the Lord turned, and looked upon Peter.** Where else in the N.T. is the mercy implicit in God's justice, and the justice implicit in his mercy, made so manifest? Most of the trouble we have in trying to administer them (!) comes of separating the one

[7] New York: Viking Press, 1938, pp. 737-39.

61 And the Lord turned, and looked upon Peter. And Peter remembered the word of the Lord, how he had said unto him, Before the cock crow, thou shalt deny me thrice.

62 And Peter went out, and wept bitterly.

63 ¶ And the men that held Jesus mocked him, and smote *him.*

cock crowed. 61 And the Lord turned and looked at Peter. And Peter remembered the word of the Lord, how he had said to him, "Before the cock crows today, you will deny me three times." 62 And he went out and wept bitterly.

63 Now the men who were holding Jesus

61*a*. A dramatic addition to the Marcan source.

61*b*-62. Mark's "twice" is omitted (cf. Matt. and John) to make the account conform to an altered version of the prediction (vs. 34). Note the omission of "the second time" in vs. 60.

4. Mockery and Mistreatment of Jesus (22:63-65=Mark 14:65)

63-65. Follows the hearing before the Sanhedrin in Mark, where it is implied that members of the court joined in subjecting Jesus to indignities. **Who is it that struck you?** One of the most interesting of the occasional agreements of Luke and Matthew against Mark. Missing from the best MSS of Mark, but well attested in Matt. 26:68.

---

from the other. "Behold therefore the goodness and severity of God" (Rom. 11:22).

61. ***Are You Able to Manage?***—Peter had been sure he would be. "Lord, I am ready to go with you to prison and to death" (vs. 33). But when life leaped upon him, as life does, all his defenses were down. Is there any defense anywhere against that? One wonders how the story would have read if three simple words which stand now at the end of it could have been set somewhere toward the beginning. They are words which have a very specific reference in the text: **And Peter remembered.** There were days and weeks and months that might have rallied to him with their memories (cf. Deut. 8; John 16:4). So often, when people go to pieces under some sudden stress, it is fundamentally because they have nothing to remember that seems worth the effort. Esau came in one day, hot and tired from the fields, and played at selling his birthright to all the sacred past, because just then it hardly seemed to amount to a great deal. David threw away his self-respect and stole another man's wife, because at the moment everything that was decent back there in the years lost its grip on him and cut no figure at all. Elijah sat disconsolately in his cave and wanted to die because he was unable to remember anything that looked like a particularly good reason for going on. All through the Bible runs that unchanging pattern. In the N.T. it is Judas who lets his precious memories go and scraps the best he has ever known for a bit of silver; or Peter, sitting by the fire and warming himself; or Demas, the poor soul that traveled for a while with Paul, then turned his back on a past which hardly seemed worth recalling. These things have I told you, that . . . ye may remember (John 16:4).

And Peter remembered. If only he could have thumbed his way back through the pages in time, so that the old, magnificent verities could have come surging in! (See Expos. on 24:35.) "So Jacob came to . . . Bethel" (Gen. 35:6), and the altar he had built in his youth. Joseph cannot forget his trust (Gen. 39:8-9). The psalmist tells over the marvelous works of God (Ps. 105). The exiles in Babylon sing to themselves in a strange land the familiar songs of Zion (Pss. 102; 119:54; cf. 137). Jesus goes forth, as was his custom, to the silence of Gethsemane, and the solemn rest of the Eternal which was waiting there (vs. 39). Paul retraces his steps, through the long corridors of the mind, to the places where light has shone through and visions have broken in (II Cor. 12:2-4).

All the old, magnificent verities, and more: one who will move with us out of the past into the living present. Joan of Arc, as she faces Dunois and the Archbishop of Rheims in Bernard Shaw's play, cries aloud: "Do not think you can frighten me by telling me that I am alone. . . . It is better to be alone with God: His friendship will not fail me, nor His counsel, nor His love. . . . I will go out now to the common people. . . . You will all be glad to see me burnt; but if I go through the fire I shall go through it to their hearts for ever and ever. And so, God be with me!" [8]

[8] *Saint Joan,* scene 5. See *The Complete Plays of Bernard Shaw* (London: Oldham Press, 1934).

64 And when they had blindfolded him,
they struck him on the face, and asked him,
saying, Prophesy, who is it that smote thee?
65 And many other things blasphemously
spake they against him.
66 ¶ And as soon as it was day, the
elders of the people and the chief priests
and the scribes came together, and led him
into their council, saying,

mocked him and beat him; 64 they also
blindfolded him and asked him, "Proph-
esy! Who is it that struck you?" 65 And they
spoke many other words against him, re-
viling him.
66 When day came, the assembly of the
elders of the people gathered together, both
chief priests and scribes; and they led him

G. The Condemnation (22:66–23:25)

1. Hearing Before the Sanhedrin (22:66-71)

A free revision and abbreviation of Mark. All preliminary details of Jewish court procedure and the charge that Jesus had prophesied the destruction and rebuilding of the temple are omitted (Mark 14:55-61*a*), and one early morning interrogation of Jesus by the Sanhedrin replaces a nocturnal sitting of the court (Mark 14:55-64) and an adjourned session at daybreak (Mark 15:1).

Various conclusions have been drawn by interpreters from the discrepancies between Mark's account and what is known of Jewish court procedure: (*a*) Jesus' appearance before the Sanhedrin was a formal trial but the gospel record is too inadequate to give us a true picture of it; (*b*) the trial was illegal from beginning to end but Mark's account reports it with fair accuracy; and (*c*) the hearing was a preliminary investigation for the purpose of preparing a charge against Jesus that could be submitted to Pilate. The last hypothesis presents the fewest difficulties. (See Vol. VII, p. 887; also quotation from Montefiore, below.) The possibility cannot be dismissed that the whole narrative is an anti-Semitic doublet of the trial before Pilate (see Intro., p. 6).

66. The scene shifts from the courtyard of the high priest's house to the council chamber—the "Hall of Hewn Stones" along one of the inner courts of the temple according to rabbinical tradition; a courthouse at the southwest corner of the temple area according to Josephus (*Jewish War* V. 4. 2).

---

64. ***Of All Questions the Two Farthest Apart.*** **—Who is it that struck you?** (Cf. I Kings 22:24-25; also Isa. 50:6; 53:3-5.) "Is it I, Lord?" (Matt. 26:22.) It was a ghastly game they were playing there just off the courtyard, a ghastly game of blindman's buff! The secret of the game, of course, is that nobody will assume the responsibility, everybody is innocent. "Lord, when saw we thee . . . ?" (Matt. 25:44.) All the distance from East to West lies between that and the quivering fear that trembles on the lips of every true disciple as he looks at the world, and at himself, and then at Christ (see Expos. on vss. 21-23).

66-71. ***Before the Council.***—(See James Moffatt, "Trial of Jesus," in James Hastings, ed., *Dictionary of Christ and the Gospels.*[9]) There is some confusion and obscurity of detail. Johannes Weiss suggests a Jewish-Christian source.[1] The possible presence of at least two eyewitnesses has been almost entirely overlooked: Nicodemus and Joseph of Arimathaea (23:50; John 7:50-51; 19:39). Montefiore comments:

> We shall never be able to tell and decide with certainty what share the Jewish, and what share the Roman, authorities had in the death of Jesus. . . . The desire of the Evangelists is clear—to increase the share of Jewish . . . to diminish the share of Roman responsibility. . . . It does not follow, [however,] because the trial of Jesus before the Sanhedrin violates Jewish law . . . , that therefore the account given of it cannot be true. There have been illegal trials at all times. . . . The Sanhedrin was convoked to draw up a charge against Jesus which could be submitted to the Roman court. . . . The balance of probability strongly inclines to the view that the Gospel narratives are so far correct in that Jesus was really put to death by the Romans at the instance and instigation of the Jewish authorities, and more especially of the ruling priesthood.[2]

[9] New York: Charles Scribner's Sons, 1908, II, 749-59.

[1] Cf. Bruce, "Synoptic Gospels," *Expositor's Greek Testament, ad loc.*

[2] *The Synoptic Gospels* (London: Macmillan & Co., 1927), I, 351-52. Used by permission.

67 Art thou the Christ? tell us. And he said unto them, If I tell you, ye will not believe:

68 And if I also ask *you*, ye will not answer me, nor let *me* go.

69 Hereafter shall the Son of man sit on the right hand of the power of God.

70 Then said they all, Art thou then the Son of God? And he said unto them, Ye say that I am.

71 And they said, What need we any further witness? for we ourselves have heard of his own mouth.

away to their council, and they said, **67** "If
you are the Christ, tell us." But he said to
them, "If I tell you, you will not believe;
68 and if I ask you, you will not answer.
69 But from now on the Son of man shall
be seated at the right hand of the power
of God." **70** And they all said, "Are you the
Son of God, then?" And he said to them,
"You say that I am." **71** And they said,
"What further testimony do we need? We
have heard it ourselves from his own lips."

67-70. Based on Mark 14:61*b*-62. But Luke divides Mark's question, "Are you the Christ, the Son of the Blessed?" To the first query Jesus refuses the answer. Any discussion of his messiahship with his interrogators would be fruitless and events would shortly speak louder than words. To the second Jesus replies with a modification of Mark's unequivocal "I am" that has been variously interpreted as an affirmative or as an evasive answer.

71. The Sanhedrists understood the answer as an affirmative, but made no declaration (as in Mark and Matthew) that the death sentence was a worthy penalty for a messianic pretender.

67-69. ***Questions Without Answer.***—**If I tell you, you will not believe; and if I ask you, you will not answer** (cf. Matt. 26:64; Mark 14:62; also Matt. 11:2-6; 15:23; Luke 16:31). Never is a question asked of God but has its answer; yet rarely is a question asked of God which is answered categorically. There were several moments in these closing chapters of the gospel story when Jesus declined to do any further talking (23:9; Mark 15:5; Matt. 27:14; John 19:9). The time for that runs out (see Expos. on 23:8-12).

But the silences of God are themselves vocal —as indeed are our own! "Why doesn't he come right out and tell us?" they asked. "Are you the Messiah? You speak of the Son of man **seated at the right hand of the power.** Are you that Son of God?" Montefiore is inclined to regard the answer in all three of the Synoptic Gospels as "intended to preclude the acceptance of the title Messiah" [3] *in the sense understood by the questioners.*

When public officials are pressed for their interpretation of events, they often decline to commit themselves. "No comment" is all that can be got out of them. God does no such thing. His silences mean either that there is something the matter with us (vss. 67-68; John 16:12)—an idea which scarcely ever seems to occur to anybody!—or that there is something in him—his wisdom? his love?—that makes waiting necessary. What was the wisdom of God doing as Paul kept praying about his thorn? Taking grace after grace and hiding it away in that wild little apostle's soul! Saying, "You'll find it enough, quite enough"; and smiling. It was so much that it has overflowed twenty centuries! What was the love of God doing the night Jesus prayed, "Father, if it be possible, let this cup pass from me"? It was taking a cross in its hands and with tense muscles holding the gaunt thing against the sky for all the ages to see!

Leslie Weatherhead tells of a day when he went with a friend to the hospital, taking that friend's three-year-old son along for an operation. The man stood holding the frightened child in his arms until the doctors came. When several of them gathered round, the boy clung desperately to his father, sobbing as if his heart would break: "Don't let them take me, Daddy. Please don't let them take me." With an indescribable agony on his face the father unclasped the child's arms and handed him over to them; then without a word turned hurriedly away. And is there nothing like that in God? The wisdom there, and the love there, piling up and up, no matter how still the heavens seem, until the day comes, or the hour, when he can answer "sharp and sudden"! It may be to thrust in our hands the very thing we have hoped for—so Elizabeth Barrett Browning put it once. But if he does, it will

[3] ***Ibid.*, II, 616.**

23 And the whole multitude of them arose, and led him unto Pilate.
2 And they began to accuse him, saying, We found this *fellow* perverting the nation, and forbidding to give tribute to Caesar, saying that he himself is Christ a king.
3 And Pilate asked him, saying, Art thou the King of the Jews? And he answered him and said, Thou sayest *it*.

23 Then the whole company of them arose, and brought him before Pilate.
2 And they began to accuse him, saying, "We found this man perverting our nation, and forbidding us to give tribute to Caesar, and saying that he himself is Christ
a king." 3 And Pilate asked him, "Are you the King of the Jews?" And he answered

---

2. Jesus Brought Before Pilate (23:1-5=Mark 15:1*b*-3)

Luke's account of Jesus' condemnation by Pilate (vss. 1-25) includes the following variations from Mark 15:1-15: the accusations against Jesus by the Sanhedrin; the threefold protest by Pilate of the prisoner's innocency; Pilate's attempt to rid himself of responsibility for the trial by referring Jesus to the jurisdiction of Herod Antipas; and the mockery of Jesus by Herod and his retinue rather than by the Roman soldiery. These striking differences have been frequently cited as evidence that Luke was employing a special source at this point in preference to Mark. While this hypothesis cannot be casually dismissed, it falls short of demonstration. That Mark's version is still basic to Luke's is clear from the reproduction of Mark 15:2 in vs. 3, the use of the Barabbas episode, and the account of Pilate's ultimate capitulation to the demands of the Jews. And the non-Marcan matter, by heightening the tendency in the gospel tradition to place the blame for Jesus' crucifixion on the shoulders of the Jews, serves one of the leading interests of Luke-Acts (see Intro., p. 6) and suggests that Luke himself has been responsible for its composition.

23:1. Before Pilate: According to one tradition, in the former palace of Herod the Great at the western outskirts of the city; according to another, in the Castle of Antonia, which overlooked the temple area at its northwest corner. The Roman procurator had his official residence at Caesarea but came to Jerusalem at the time of the great festivals to supervise the preservation of order.

2. An expansion of Mark's "And the chief priests accused him of many things." The indictment charged Jesus with seditious activity, counsel, and utterance. Since Luke has already quoted Jesus' saying about the tribute money (20:25), he must have intended the reader to regard at least the second count as a deliberate falsehood. **Christ a king:** An explanation of "Messiah" for Pilate's benefit.

3. See Mark 15:2. Pilate centers his interest on the last accusation. **You have said so:** Cf. on 22:70. Sometimes interpreted as a recognized Semitic formula for "Yes." More probably, as Luke understood it (see vs. 4), a noncommittal answer.

---

be what she called it, "A gauntlet with a gift in 't"! [4]

23:1-7. *First Appearance Before Pilate.*—The procurator of Judea had come up to Jerusalem from his headquarters at Caesarea in order to be on hand for any trouble that might develop among these despised and turbulent Jews during the Passover festival (cf. 13:1). This year there was indeed a minor commotion (see Anatole France's story, "The Procurator of Judaea," [5] the scene of which is laid at Baiae, on the southwestern coast of Italy, some years later; its climax comes with Pilate's inability to remember the name of the man from Nazareth!) A crowd pressed upon him with a prisoner accused of "stirring up the people." Such "political" agitation was likely to meet with short shrift from the Roman authorities, especially in Palestine. To it was added the charge, with no regard at all for the truth (20:25), that the accused had forbidden the payment of tribute to Caesar, claiming for himself the status of "king." Nothing could have been better calculated to bring quick action, or more serviceable, than these sinister indictments. A disturber of the peace, an aspirant to regal honors, a meddler in other men's money matters, could hardly expect to go scot free in any generation. And this is precisely what Jesus

[4] *Aurora Leigh*, Bk. II, l. 954.

[5] *Golden Tales of Anatole France* (New York: Dodd, Mead & Co., 1926).

4 Then said Pilate to the chief priests
and *to* the people, I find no fault in this
man.
5 And they were the more fierce, saying,
He stirreth up the people, teaching
throughout all Jewry, beginning from Gali-
lee to this place.
6 When Pilate heard of Galilee, he asked
whether the man were a Galilean.
7 And as soon as he knew that he be-
longed unto Herod's jurisdiction, he sent
him to Herod, who himself also was at
Jerusalem at that time.
8 ¶ And when Herod saw Jesus, he was
exceeding glad: for he was desirous to see
him of a long *season,* because he had heard

him, "You have said so." 4 And Pilate said
to the chief priests and the multitudes, "I
find no crime in this man." 5 But they were
urgent, saying, "He stirs up the people,
teaching throughout all Judea, from Gali-
lee even to this place."
6 When Pilate heard this, he asked
whether the man was a Galilean. 7 And
when he learned that he belonged to Her-
od's jurisdiction, he sent him over to Herod,
who was himself in Jerusalem at that time.
8 When Herod saw Jesus, he was very glad,

4-5. In Luke only. **And the multitudes:** For the first time we are told that the trial was open to the public. Jesus' accusers refuse to accept Pilate's pronouncement that the prisoner appears to be innocent and they renew their charges. **Judea:** Used in this instance for the whole of Palestine (see on 1:5).

3. Jesus' Examination by Herod Antipas (23:6-16)

It is not improbable that Herod Antipas was in Jerusalem at the time of the Passover festival, but Mark says nothing of any tradition that the tetrarch had been involved in the proceedings against Jesus. Furthermore if Mark (15:25) is correct when he says that the Crucifixion took place at "the third hour"—about 9 A.M.—there would scarcely have been time for this Lukan episode in addition to the meeting of the Sanhedrin and the trial before Pilate. In at least parts of the early church Ps. 2:2 was interpreted as a prediction that Herod Antipas and Pilate would act in concert against Jesus (Acts 4:27-28) and this Lukan story may have been suggested by such exegesis. As noted above, it served to heighten Jewish and to minimize Roman responsibility for Jesus' crucifixion. The extant passion fragment of the Gospel of Peter, from the first half of the second century, carries the motif a step further. Pilate is practically whitewashed and the major onus for the crime against Christ is laid upon Herod.

6-7. Pilate seizes on the reference to Jesus' Galilean activities (vs. 5) as an excuse to transfer the prisoner to **Herod's jurisdiction.**

8-9. For Herod's interest in Jesus see 9:7-9 and 13:31. Jesus' refusal to submit to cross-examination would remind Luke's readers of the behavior predicted of the Servant of the Lord in Isa. 53:7.

---

always is and does. He overturns the accepted order of things, sets a topsy-turvy world right side up—the sensation is quite as if everything were upside down!—asserts his princely claims, makes a man's conscience uneasy, costs everybody hard-earned cash, and interferes no end with business. While on the whole he does not otherwise seem particularly objectionable (vs. 4), he would no doubt better be referred, if not with carte blanche for final action, then at least for a bit of advice, to some other **jurisdiction.** Avoid all unnecessary involvements. Look around for a few suggestions from people who will appreciate whatever deference you can show them. That might conceivably be important. It would certainly be clever. And in a situation that could hardly be regarded as very critical. What if this Jesus were a king of sorts (vs. 3; cf. Expos. on 22:21-23)? His "kingdom" was not likely to prove a major threat to the kingdoms of the world (see Expos. on vs. 35). Why go further with it yourself, when others may be able to tell you exactly what to do, and none of it can matter much? One need not be troubled too seriously about justice; only about trouble—or is it the other way around?

8-12. ***Jesus and Herod.***—For the historicity of this account see the Exeg. It should be noted,

many things of him; and he hoped to have seen some miracle done by him.

9 Then he questioned with him in many words; but he answered him nothing.

10 And the chief priests and scribes stood and vehemently accused him.

11 And Herod with his men of war set him at nought, and mocked *him,* and arrayed him in a gorgeous robe, and sent him again to Pilate.

12 ¶ And the same day Pilate and Herod were made friends together; for before they were at enmity between themselves.

13 ¶ And Pilate, when he had called together the chief priests and the rulers and the people,

for he had long desired to see him, because
he had heard about him, and he was hop-
ing to see some sign done by him. 9 So he
questioned him at some length; but he
made no answer. 10 The chief priests and
the scribes stood by, vehemently accusing
him. 11 And Herod with his soldiers treated
him with contempt and mocked him; then,
arraying him in gorgeous apparel, he sent
him back to Pilate. 12 And Herod and
Pilate became friends with each other that
very day, for before this they had been at
enmity with each other.
13 Pilate then called together the chief

10-12. Omitted by the Sinaitic Syriac and by some modern editors but Lukan in language and style. The mockery of Jesus by **Herod** and **his soldiers** replaces that by the Roman soldiery after the condemnation in Mark 15:16-20. We know nothing from any other source of the **enmity** between **Herod and Pilate** that we are told was composed by this interchange of courtesies.

13-16. Pilate interprets Herod's contemptuous dismissal of Jesus as tantamount to acquittal and declares himself confirmed in his conviction of the prisoner's innocence.

however, that many are inclined to attach more weight to John 19:14 than to Mark 15:25. **When Herod saw Jesus, he was very glad.** The reasons given could well have been the most excellent of reasons: **he had heard** (cf. 9:7-9) a number of rumors—that this was John risen from the dead, that it was Elijah, that it was "one of the old prophets" come to life again; **he had long desired to see him,** ever since the apostles had gone about preaching; **and he was hoping to see some sign** [KJV, **miracle**] **done by him.** So in some sense had it been with many another: the leper of Galilee (5:12), the friends of the paralytic (5:17-26), the centurion (7:2-10), Jairus and the woman with an issue of blood (8:41-55), the ten lepers (17:11-19), the rich young ruler (18:18-23), blind Bartimaeus (18:35-43), and Zacchaeus (19:1-10). Unfortunately, good reasons are perverted into bad reasons by the personality behind them: in this case, a cunning politician, a worldling, a cynic, and a sensationmonger. The story of a great conversion could have begun exactly as this story began; but hold up the sorry figure of Herod Antipas against the conditions of discipleship laid down by Jesus himself (14:25-35), and vs. 9*b* becomes luminous (see Expos. on 22:67-68). It was not the questioning that was wrong—though from its very garrulousness one would assume the lack of serious intent. Jesus submits himself to all kinds of questioning (vs. 3; 7:18-23; 10:25-37; 18:18-23; 20:21-44; 24:18 ff.; etc.; cf. also Matt. 19:27). True, he has his own manner of response; but he welcomes the interrogation marks in every man's mind. Wrong questions were put to him his life long; but there were right questions too. Nobody can take the second step in the Christian's maturing experience of Christ without asking them. It was the questioner that was wrong—and *so* wrong as to merit no reply at all! (Cf. 13:31-32; and Jesus was not given to calling people names! The "fox" is not elsewhere in scripture the symbol of craftiness; to the rabbis it was rather "a type of general worthlessness and insignificance."[6]) In this instance the silence of suffering love (Isa. 53:7) becomes a judicial silence. And there is left nothing but a foregone conclusion. **Herod with his soldiers treated him with contempt:** dressed him up handsomely **and mocked him**—God pity us all! The **gorgeous apparel** of vestment or creed, of art and ritual, may bear its worthy testimony to deep devotion—or be the most pious and courteous of blasphemies! Better "his own clothes" (Mark 15:20) and the cross! **And Herod and Pilate became friends . . . that very day, . . . before this they had been at enmity.** What is God's Messiah between friends! Or principle—when "good fellows" can "get together" at no greater sacrifice!

13-25. ***Pilate's Effort to Release Jesus.***—Thus far both Pilate and Herod had been unable

[6] Luce, *Gospel According to St. Luke,* p. 243.

14 Said unto them, Ye have brought this man unto me, as one that perverteth the people; and, behold, I, having examined *him* before you, have found no fault in this man touching those things whereof ye accuse him:

15 No, nor yet Herod: for I sent you to him; and, lo, nothing worthy of death is done unto him.

16 I will therefore chastise him, and release *him*.

17 (For of necessity he must release one unto them at the feast.)

priests and the rulers and the people, 14 and said to them, "You brought me this man as one who was perverting the people; and after examining him before you, behold, I did not find this man guilty of any of your charges against him; 15 neither did Herod, for he sent him back to us. Behold, nothing deserving death has been done by him; 16 I will therefore chastise him and release him."[s]

[s] Here, or after verse 19, other ancient authorities add verse 17, *Now he was obliged to release one man to them at the festival.*

His proposal to **chastise him and release him** takes the place of Mark's statement (Mark 15:15) that Jesus was scourged before being crucified (in accordance with Roman criminal procedure). The RSV translation of vs. 15 has much better MS support than that in the KJV.

4. Jesus Surrendered to the Jews by Pilate (23:17-25; cf. Mark 15:11-12*a*, 13-15)

This is a free revision of Marcan matter. We are not prepared by Luke for the demand that Barabbas should be released. For a discussion of the historicity of the Barabbas incident and the claim in the First and Second Gospels that it was the procurator's custom to pardon one prisoner at the Passover festival see the commentaries on Matthew and Mark, Vol. VII, pp. 594, 895.

---

to bring in any verdict other than "Not guilty as charged." Pilate had dealt with the prisoner craftily, Herod contemptuously: neither had seen anything in him to get particularly excited about. Why not then have done with it? The only value the case had was a nuisance value. Herod made no pretense of dealing with it seriously. He was content, if he could not fully satisfy his half-superstitious curiosity, to vent his spite; Pilate was made of somewhat sterner stuff. The motives that lay back of the arrest and accusation seemed to him quite obvious (Mark 15:10; Matt. 27:18). He was in no position as a Roman to understand the deeper sources of the malice that was clear enough to him on the face of things, from the very trumped-up character of the several indictments; but he saw that on the only important matter, the matter of sedition (vs. 5), the man was certainly innocent. **I will therefore chastise him.** The suggestion seems to be that he sought thereby to save Jesus' life; and to this the Fourth Gospel apparently lends some support (John 19:1-6). Not once only, but twice, and a third time, he is represented as having attempted to provide some kind of compromise, whether in the interests of justice, or because he resented having his hand forced. There can be no doubt, however, that for all his vacillation and final cowardice (John 19:12-16) the picture given us of him is as favorable a picture as the evangelists under the circumstances could draw; it is the implacable hostility of the Jewish people and their leaders that is so insistently underscored: reflecting in some measure perhaps the history and temper of the early church, when Christianity was still in the eyes of the Roman government a *religio licita*, and the only real peril that threatened was the hatred of the "chief priests and scribes" and "elders of the people."

16. *Better This Than That.*—I will therefore chastise him. The rigid and impartial enforcement of Roman justice had already begun to yield to the pressure of the mob. The question of expediency had driven in its entering wedge: a little wrong—though scourging was no mean punishment!—to ensure a greater right. The consequence is not often so immediate, nor the process so swift. The question may well be asked and debated, What is ever gained by it?

We are all too ready to assume that compromise is necessary in the kind of world we know. God shouts no order at us. We come each day to choose how we shall live, what we shall do. And the choices are not often simple

17. KJV; RSV mg. Serves to ease the transition to the Barabbas episode, but is missing from an impressive group of Greek MSS (including Codex Vaticanus) and presumably an interpolation from Mark 15:6.

choices, black on white, or white on black, like the squares of a checkerboard. They shade off imperceptibly from one to the other, so that there are very few places where anybody whose conscience is alive can put his finger down firmly and be thoroughly happy about it. The best he can manage half the time is a preference. More than that, with human nature what it is, no choice can be a perfect choice: we lack the data, we lack the wisdom, and if we do not lack the will, we lack the purity of heart. Is it not better, then, when we cannot make up our minds and have to anyhow—is it not better to decide for the good without too much ado about the relatively evil means that seem necessary to achieve it? The atom bomb was first used, and without warning, to bring a long and bitter war to its prompt conclusion: thereby saving hundreds of thousands of lives, American and Japanese, at the price of Hiroshima and Nagasaki; and thereby losing—what moral prestige, what confidence of mankind? Carrying war itself into what atomic incineration, and history toward what anguish.

Perhaps it would be just as well to say right off that such a world, for all its difficulties, indeed because of them, is far more interesting and challenging than any other conceivable kind; far more instinct not only with peril, on which human life and the human soul seem to thrive, but also with fairly limitless possibilities for mental and spiritual growth: a God whose quiet strategy it is to be away, but not far, and silent, except for the footstep and the knocking at a man's door; a world with the sin in it that we have to fight, and the pain in it we have to suffer, and the trouble in it that comes tearing along through the days, where hardship, instead of leaving everybody flat, leaves so many people so much taller than they were before; and a life to be lived which is never willing simply to say what everyone else is saying, wrapped in a shade more pious atmosphere and tied together with but slightly devouter gestures, but is intent on making another Voice heard, ready at the drop of a hat to draw the lines so taut that they sing.

In that constant tension lies the ultimate key to the Christian ethic. The end does not justify the means; it is determined by them. From the scourging to the release of Barabbas to the final surrender, Pilate allowed himself step by step to be jockeyed into a position from which it was humanly impossible to extricate himself. On the chart under the pilot's eye, as the airliner makes her flight across the ocean, there is a "point of no return": this side of it, if anything goes wrong, there is fuel enough to get home; on the other side, nothing but to go on. The drift sets in where self enters into the choices we make.

In Shakespeare's *King Henry IV,* Part I,[7] is one of the most biting comments ever made on the way in which whole moral systems degenerate into relativism. It is the story of how Falstaff, to his own immense satisfaction, edged over inch by inch from honor to dishonor. Rationalize everything that way; become part of the evil instead of a protest against it; stop straining at what you call the *real* with what you call the *ideal;* say there are no principles that hold absolutely anyhow, that you "have to act largely in the dark," that there are no tram lines and no textbook answers, so why not relax a little; let down the lines between heaven and earth, between this world and that other; let them sag the next time some hard right stands up over against some easy wrong: and you rob life of the only meaning it has. That fat rascal on a battlefield may "conquer both space and time with his wit"; but it becomes abundantly evident to anybody who will look that "on such terms space and time are not worth conquering." Which is why Shakespeare left him; loved him to distraction, and left him pitilessly, snubbed and forgotten. For all his huge girth he would not do. There were other things about living, and the poet had to find them. It took him twelve years of climbing, through play after play, from bitter revolt to resignation to something higher and beyond: twelve years of climbing between two worlds to discover that nothing between them would serve!

What is this doubtful mood, pulled back and forth, distraught, shifting from one foot to the other, halting between right and wrong along its course to God knows what? It is not Christianity. "We are a colony of heaven." Christianity is an allegiance fixed, moving about these common streets with the stamp and seal of Forever on it, haunted by the eternal Mind, bearing itself in this its native place like a changeling, exiled from home, yet sure of its kingly state, thrusting out today and tomorrow into "some new and unclaimed and unconquered territory," going down from its rendezvous with God to have some hand with him under the shadow of a cross at the shaping of human history!

[7] Act V, scene 1.

18 And they cried out all at once, saying, Away with this *man*, and release unto us Barabbas:

19 (Who for a certain sedition made in the city, and for murder, was cast into prison.)

20 Pilate therefore, willing to release Jesus, spake again to them.

21 But they cried, saying, Crucify *him*, crucify him.

22 And he said unto them the third time, Why, what evil hath he done? I have found no cause of death in him: I will therefore chastise him, and let *him* go.

23 And they were instant with loud voices, requiring that he might be crucified: and the voices of them and of the chief priests prevailed.

18 But they all cried out together, "Away
with this man, and release to us Bar-
ab'bas" — **19** a man who had been thrown
into prison for an insurrection started in
the city, and for murder. **20** Pilate addressed
them once more, desiring to release Jesus;
21 but they shouted out, "Crucify, crucify
him!" **22** A third time he said to them,
"Why, what evil has he done? I have found
in him no crime deserving death; I will
therefore chastise him and release him."
23 But they were urgent, demanding with
loud cries that he should be crucified. And

18-23. They: the Sanhedrists and the people. As in Mark, Pilate is pictured as acting against his better judgment under the clamant compulsion of a mob. But Luke represents him as even more anxious to acquit Jesus (see Intro., p. 6). Vs. 19 (cf. vs. 25*a*)

---

18. *The Release of Barabbas.*—Away with this man, and release to us Barabbas (see Expos. on vs. 23). It is little wonder that this incident so impressed itself on the followers of Jesus that it was recorded by all four evangelists. The exchange of Jesus for Barabbas could hardly have failed to suggest, however distantly, but with what dramatic intensity, the "ransom for many" (Matt. 20:28; see A. B. Bruce, "The Synoptic Gospels," *Expositor's Greek Testament, ad loc.*) that was paid down in flesh and blood by this other (?) Jesus, son of Mary and Son of man. Of course no serious attempt should ever be made to read such an interpretation into the text. We are dealing here with one of the strange ironies of history. To Barabbas what happened was no doubt simply an odd turn of Fortune's wheel. If there was such a "custom"—possibly no more than Pilate's own, and designed to curry favor with the people, intended as it was to commemorate the "passing over" of Exod. 12:27—his luck was in, and that was that. The rest is shrouded in silence. It was the miracle that almost happened. Writes Martin Dibelius:

All four Evangelists, however, unanimously report one feature: Pilate intended to set Jesus free at the festival, i.e., to treat his case as a kind of Passover amnesty. The populace, however, rejected this, and begged amnesty for another prisoner, named Barabbas, who with others had committed murder in an insurrection. That this insurrection had any connection with Jesus' cause is not only incapable of proof but obviously counter to the meaning of the text: opposed to the King of the Kingdom of God must be set a rival, one who is most deeply involved in the world's iniquity. Even though we know nothing of any such amnesty as a custom, there is no reason to doubt the scene; the assumption of invention would mean ascribing to the earliest reporters a plastic propensity and a poetic power such as is not to be observed elsewhere in the narrative.[8]

There is a striking scene in George Meredith's *Beauchamp's Career*. The hero, Nevil Beauchamp, a youthful, aristocratic radical, having spent the years of his brief life trying to set right many an ancient wrong, plunges at last with his accustomed "dash and distinction" into the harbor to rescue a nameless urchin and is drowned.

The mother of the rescued boy sobbed . . . and dragged the urchin to Lord Romfrey's feet. . . .

All the lights . . . were turned on the head of . . . the abashed little creature.

This is what we have in exchange for Beauchamp!

It was not uttered, but it was visible in the blank stare at one another of the two men who loved Beauchamp, after they had examined the insignificant bit of mudbank life remaining in this world in the place of him.[9]

23. *Vox Populi.*—And their voices prevailed. There was the clamor of the world for one of

[8] *Jesus* (Berlin: Walter de Gruyter & Co., 1939); tr. C. B. Hedrick and F. C. Grant (Philadelphia: Westminster Press, 1949), p. 135. Used by permission.

[9] London: Chapman-Hall, 1889, p. 506.

24 And Pilate gave sentence that it should be as they required.

25 And he released unto them him that for sedition and murder was cast into prison, whom they had desired; but he delivered Jesus to their will.

26 And as they led him away, they laid hold upon one Simon, a Cyrenian, coming out of the country, and on him they laid the cross, that he might bear *it* after Jesus.

their voices prevailed. 24 So Pilate gave
sentence that their demand should be
granted. 25 He released the man who had
been thrown into prison for insurrection
and murder, whom they asked for; but
Jesus he delivered up to their will.
26 And as they led him away, they seized
one Simon of Cy-re′ne, who was coming in
from the country, and laid on him the

---

is derived from Mark 15:7. To identify the **insurrection** with that hinted at in 13:1 is pure conjecture.

24-25. Luke's narrative almost suggests that it was Jews who took Jesus away to be crucified. But Roman soldiers would execute a Roman sentence and their presence at the Cross is noted in vs. 36.

H. Calvary (23:26-56)

1. Simon of Cyrene Compelled to Carry the Cross (23:26=Mark 15:21)

26. The structure of the second half of the verse has been influenced by the form of Jesus' sayings in 9:23 and 14:27. It was Roman custom that a condemned criminal should carry the crossbeam to which his arms were to be affixed, perhaps in the hope that this indignity might serve as a further deterrent to evildoers. The Synoptic story that a certain passer-by was compelled to do this for **Jesus** was used by Basilides in the early second century to substantiate the Docetic theory that **Simon** had been crucified instead of the divine Christ. The Fourth Evangelist may have been trying to undermine this heresy when he wrote: "Jesus . . . went out, bearing his own cross" (John 19:17). **Cyrene:** A

---

its "favorite sons," the man of action, the national hero, the idol of the populace. The choice lay between him and the "harmless dreamer" of Galilee, the "friend of publicans and sinners." Which Jesus? In Mark "the chief priests," in Matthew "the chief priests and the elders," stirred up the crowd to cry out for Barabbas. It may well be that by this time they needed little prompting. So Luke implies. "That the people are now against Jesus," says Montefiore, "is—though probably not historic —not psychologically quite incredible. Jesus had disappointed them." [1] Entrenched privilege could no longer bear the sight of him. Whatever enthusiasm he had once stirred among the multitudes no longer seemed to be of much use to anybody. "Impostor." "Blasphemer." "He'll get us into trouble." "It was all right while it lasted, but look at the way things are going now." Whispers get around in a hurry, and temperatures rise. It was not likely then that any just cause would be notably served! And among us? What if between the rampant wrong and the defenseless right no high allegiance stands up to speak its word and do its battle, come life, come death? That day there was none. It was a day that was earmarked for tragedy. Heaven had no clients. The hour was getting on toward noon, and the page was turned down to the most pitiful roll call in history. *On stage:* Opposed, everybody present and accounted for—the none-too-helpless people whom the scribes and the elders had once feared! In favor, one Roman governor, testing the wind with his finger to find what way it was blowing. *Off stage:* Cowardice (Mark 14: 50); indifference (vs. 35); helplessness (vs. 48). With God behind the scenes! And with what incredible sequel? At every point along the line, defeat! **Their voices prevailed.** And at every point along the line—victory!

26. ***Conscripts of the Cross.*—They seized one Simon of Cyrene, . . . and laid on him the cross** (see Exeg.). Once more, as in the case of Barabbas (vs. 18), the early followers of Jesus must have been struck by an incident which to them seemed more and more significant as the years passed. Simon, to whose sons reference may possibly be made in Rom. 16:13 and Acts 19:33, was no more than an innocent passer-by when the Roman soldiers assigned to the Crucifixion impressed him into service, with never a by-your-leave. Their motive was not compassion:

[1] *Synoptic Gospels*, I, 375.

27 ¶ And there followed him a great company of people, and of women, which also bewailed and lamented him.

28 But Jesus turning unto them said, Daughters of Jerusalem, weep not for me, but weep for yourselves, and for your children.

cross, to carry it behind Jesus. 27 And there followed him a great multitude of the people, and of women who bewailed and lamented him. 28 But Jesus turning to them said, "Daughters of Jerusalem, do not weep for me, but weep for yourselves and for

---

North African city on the Mediterranean coast with a large Jewish population (Acts 2:10; 6:9; 13:1). It is not clear whether **Simon** was a repatriated Jew of the Dispersion or a pilgrim on the way to Jerusalem for the Passover festival. Mark's version implies that his sons later became well-known members of the Christian community, but the words "the father of Alexander and Rufus" are omitted by Luke as of no interest or meaning to his circle of readers.

2. The Road to Calvary (23:27-32)

27. Editorial. Reminiscent of—and possibly suggested by—Zech. 12:10-14. Probably Luke thought only of the **women** as stricken with grief and of the **great multitude of the people** as attracted to the scene by curiosity.

28-31. Similar in tone to 19:41-44 and possibly taken by Luke from the same source.

28. An introduction to the prophetic warning of disaster. The **daughters of Jerusalem**—to be distinguished from the Galilean women of vs. 49—have far greater reason for

---

an order was to be carried out, and if Jesus by this time was too weak to lift the heavy wooden beam of the cross (Mark 15:22 suggests that he was even unable to walk), anybody would do, best of all a stranger who was not in a position to raise any objections or give much trouble.

So may a man become involved quite unintentionally in the central drama of all the ages. Circumstances lay hold on him, and he begins as perhaps never before to understand what that lonely march to Golgotha really meant. The relentless pressure of a burden not its own shifts like the ballast of a ship in a storm to a heart that has to carry on in silence. Not just the due of pain, but pain in another's stead; not just suffering, but suffering for another's hurt; not just the routine of every day's toil, or the grim frustrations of human experience, but the weight of them taken from other shoulders, lifted from other lives. So bound up are we in the one vast bundle of life. "Every man his own" and "one another's" (Gal. 6:5, 2; cf. the scene in A. S. M. Hutchinson's novel, *If Winter Comes*[2]).

Is it altogether beside the point to remark in this connection that the world we live in is at bottom just such a world of mutual relationships and mutual responsibilities? There is a sense in which the Christian faith rests on that assumption. So does every sound economic and political system. The brotherhood of man is no fancy to be pieced together by a few idealists out of the fatherhood of God: it is a fact with a tough skin. "For the first time in history," writes one well-meaning popularizer of half a dozen departments of modern knowledge, "it is underpinned by four powerful sciences—biology, anthropology, sociology, and psychology." It always was underpinned by God! The "white man's burden" is the burden he has made the black man carry; and never on earth will either be lightened while the other is forgotten. **They seized one Simon of Cyrene, . . . and laid on him the cross.**

One would at any rate like to have heard the story he told his sons at night, when the day was done, of the rude interruption to all his plans, of his quick resentment and surly obedience; then of the face he would never after forget, and of the brutal scene that had seared its way into his memory. But what about the story he must have told—to any now who were willing to listen—in the years to come, when perhaps the far reaches of that morning's work, all undreamed of, had begun to dawn on him? What then of the old wrong? Never another had been so close to the wounded Lord as he; never another singled out of the crowd to do unwittingly so kind a thing in so great a fellowship, with generation after generation to rise up and call him blessed! (See P. Whitwell Wilson's imaginative reconstruction in *Simon the Cross-Bearer;* and Countee Cullen's poem, "Simon the Cyrenian Speaks.")

27-30. ***Via Dolorosa.*—Daughters of Jerusalem, weep not for me, but weep for yourselves, and for your children.** Luke is at pains to

[2] Boston: Little, Brown & Co., 1921, pp. 400-5.

29 For, behold, the days are coming, in the which they shall say, Blessed *are* the barren, and the wombs that never bare, and the paps which never gave suck.

30 Then shall they begin to say to the mountains, Fall on us; and to the hills, Cover us.

31 For if they do these things in a green tree, what shall be done in the dry?

32 And there were also two others, malefactors, led with him to be put to death.

your children. 29 For behold, the days are
coming when they will say, 'Blessed are the
barren, and the wombs that never bore,
and the breasts that never gave suck!'
30 Then they will begin to say to the
mountains, 'Fall on us'; and to the hills,
'Cover us.' 31 For if they do this when the
wood is green, what will happen when it
is dry?"
32 Two others also, who were criminals,
were led away to be put to death with

---

tears than the tragedy that has befallen Jesus. Luke's first readers would think of the siege of Jerusalem, and the whole passage may be colored by memories of that catastrophe.

29. Motherhood will be a curse in those days instead of a blessing, either because mothers will be torn with anxiety for the fate of their children (19:44) or because children will interfere with any attempt of their mothers to flee the city (21:21-23*a*).

30. A quotation from Hos. 10:8*b*. A prayer for death, not as in Rev. 6:16 for concealment.

31. A proverbial saying with many rabbinical parallels. Probable meaning in this context: If the innocent Jesus must suffer so terribly, what will be the fate of the guilty city? Less probable alternative: If Jerusalem in the heyday of its prosperity perpetrates such a deed as Christ's crucifixion, what horrors will it inflict in the dreadful time that is coming?

32. An editorial emendation of Mark, who mentions the "two robbers" only after telling of Jesus' crucifixion (Mark 15:27).

---

record the touch of human pity that went some little way to redeem the desolateness of Jesus' last journey of all; but it was pity that met with gentle rebuke. Pity is not what he requires of us. More often than not our pity is but a specious self-pity, made plausible and comely. It was not of himself that he was thinking (cf. Expos. on 22:39-46). It was of them. There is a self-pity that is the very "head and front" of true repentance. Let them rather weep for themselves, and for the doom that lowered even then over "the city of the great King" (Ps. 48:2; see Expos. on 19:41-44). But what matters most is this that is beyond pity: whatever else we make of that road to the Cross, the conviction comes over us that God is traveling it, not being driven, not at his wit's end, not maneuvered into a corner from which there is no escape, but with the reins of the matter in his own steady hands, dealing with something that way because there was no other way in which to deal with it (see Expos. on vss. 33, 34, 35). What is there to say at the end but that the Via Dolorosa is man's own pilgrimage? For that reason and for no other is it God's.

31. ***Sin When It Is Full-Grown.***—(Jas. 1:15; see Expos. on 22:35-38; note in the Exeg. two possible interpretations; cf. I Pet. 4:17-18 and Ezek. 20:47.) More terrible than the Crucifixion will be the horrors that follow on it, when joy itself shall be the stuff of which misery is wrought (vs. 29), and death shall be a welcome release from life. All too easily do we assume that those were "crude and cruel days."[3] No longer the cross, the oubliette, the rack, the screw, the iron maiden; no longer the Inquisition or the stake: but does it mean more than that cruelty has grown out of its callow youth and put on the refinements of maturity?

32. ***The Middle Cross.***—**Two others also . . . were led away to be put to death with him.** There were two crosses on Calvary where the wrong in human life turned on itself. It always does. We scarcely ever glance at these other crosses; but the drama of man's way with God and God's way with man would not be complete without them. They impressed themselves so deeply on the four evangelists that not one fails to speak of them. They knew that there are hours and places in this world where **malefactors** are crucified. And we need to remember that. There is far too much glib and thoughtless talk about the prosperity of the wicked. The psalmists tried to puzzle it out; and arrived no doubt at too simple an answer (Ps. 37). The balances are not so obviously struck. Yet

[3] From G. A. Studdert-Kennedy, *The Sorrows of God* (New York: George H. Doran, 1924).

33 And when they were come to the place, which is called Calvary, there they crucified him, and the malefactors, one on the right hand, and the other on the left.

him. 33 And when they came to the place which is called The Skull, there they crucified him, and the criminals, one on the

3. THE CRUCIFIXION (23:33-38)

Crucifixion was a cruel and spectacular method of execution, first employed by the Carthaginians and then taken over by the Romans as one means of imposing the death penalty. According to Christian tradition, Peter, an unenfranchised Jew, was crucified and Paul, a Roman citizen, was beheaded. The outstretched arms of the victim were nailed or tied to a crossbeam and then this plank was lashed or nailed to a vertical pole. Support was sometimes given to the naked body by allowing the legs to straddle a projection, and the feet were tied or nailed to the vertical pole. Death usually resulted from a slow process of exhaustion rather than from loss of blood.

33. Luke omits the Aramaic "Golgotha" of Mark's version and translates **The Skull. Calvary** was a translation of the Greek Κρανίον, borrowed from the Vulg. Presumably

he would be a fool indeed who would undertake to write off "the wages of sin." Evil has too fearful a way even now of piling up its own Calvary and digging the hole for its own cross.

But it did a second thing that day, and does still. It aimed the hardest blow it could at the only stalwart hope there is for it. Lies are crucified, and so is truth. The way of the transgressor is no softer than it used to be; neither is the way of redeeming love. And just there we come on the secret that unlocks the whole mystery. The cross of Christ was either a tragic incident which meant that his kind of life was futile and impotent; or it was the supreme symbol of God's conquering presence in the world that he made, a mercy and justice and peace so closely akin to the Eternal that they could be nailed down and still win!

Three crosses in all, and the issue of three lives. On one, death came down with a taunt, like the world's last grin, dark and sterile and hopeless. On another it came in a sudden shaft of light, as of the sun striking its way through the clouds to etch out of the shadows a face with a prayer on its lips and a brooding glory in its eyes. Between them, to divide the two, this way and that, as far as heaven is from hell, the Word of God, at its uttermost become deed! (See Expos. on vss. 39-43.)

33. ***Tragedy Relieved.*****—There they crucified him.** Calvary was not merely the normal outcome of a perfectly normal situation, the hill where a man far too good to be safe was put to death. This man did something by dying. The note of triumph sounds through Gospel and Epistle, again and again. Christ is himself nailing down something, showing it up (Col. 2:14-15). Swinburne once called Jesus a "pale Galilean." What pallor there was had to be found on the faces of his enemies (see Expos. on vs. 46). It was the Sanhedrin that broke up in a tumult. It was the Roman governor whose quick, startled glance swept back and forth from the crowd to that quiet prisoner who stood there talking of a kingdom. Elijah in the desert moaned his complaint, "It is enough" (I Kings 19:4). Jesus on his cross says, "It is finished," and bows his head (John 19:30).

The Cross is God's victory over sin, our sin: the old habits that keep clinging like barnacles to a ship's hull, blind, blazing prejudices, clammy indifference—all of it piling up into weird and monstrous things. Christ got into it where it was heaviest and darkest, not to wipe it out and make it as if it were not, but to do with it what only God could do: not to change the past, to change the future; to set our souls cleansed and steadied against the rush of all the evil that continually wells up from within, and from without swings like a tide across the dreary flats of human life.

God's victory and God's pattern. There is forever that about the Cross which is yet to be done. It plagues us with tasks that are too big for us, with mad, heroic things. It marched out across an empire. It leaped on the proud standards of Rome, and got itself emblazoned there. It fluttered over Europe in dark forests or lonely castles. Men have betrayed it and denied it; then bowed their heads and sworn devotion to it. It offers no argument, gives no reason, makes no exception: just presents itself as the central problem of the Christian religion by laying its incessant and solemn demands on us. The cross was Christ's. It was the only thing that *was* his. But if it was his alone, humanity is not saved. If it was his alone, humanity is not worth saving!

33. ***The Ageless Cross.*****—There they crucified him.** Who? If we should conspire against these

the place was a skull-shaped mound, although "Mount Calvary" is not a term that can be traced any earlier than the fourth century. No certain identification of the site is possible. Heb. 13:12 says it lay "outside the gate."

---

final chapters of the Gospel, and not read them again for a century, life would still come back, sure that something was missing, discover them, and feel itself oddly at home again. The Cross keeps its steady pace with the years because nothing that brought it about is dated.

Tradition was there on Calvary. And the God whose very habit it is to stand up out of the ruin of "sacred" things, of ancient and time-honored precedents—though always at the risk of getting himself lynched. Isaiah too had gone about among these people, chosen and favored as they thought they were, and told them they were doomed. They pointed the finger at him and roared. Yahweh's sword at their throat, and the hilt in the hands of Assyria? What kind of nonsense was this! Try dating that. And prejudice was there, the mood that always leaps to its conclusions and fills in the gaps with anything but the evidence; has its ready-made filing system for everything that would disturb its peace (cf. John 8:48). Try dating that. And the pride that was there. Wrote a man from Georgia during World War II, "We shall have to bash in the heads of these Nazis until they find out that they are not quite so superior as they think." It seemed to him a kind of foreign missionary enterprise, down there where a motion picture was being shown, *The Master Race,* in theaters which permitted only "the master race" to buy tickets! Try dating that, and the self-interest that was there. This Jesus had attempted to spoil too many things that the "chief priests and elders of the people" wanted—things that meant more to them than the people themselves ever had meant. As on the day he healed a maniac over in "the country of the Gadarenes" (8:26-39). It was too much. They kept swine in those parts. These healings were all very well, but what about the pigs?

We cannot even begin to fix the Cross in time or locate it in space. **There they crucified him.** Where? At the midpoint of human history and human experience, to change *before* into *after!* We may not like the language in which the doctrine of the Atonement has been expressed; but the fact inside the language is the throbbing heart of the Christian gospel. As in a detective story, we cannot read these chapters of the N.T. and then go back to pore over the others as if we had not read the end. It is different now. The timeless judgment of God, without once moving, overtakes us from that hill; and when it lays hold on us it is his eternal mercy. At deeper levels than the wailing music of the Passover, we know what the psalmist meant when he wrote, "I will walk before the LORD in the land of the living" (Ps. 116:9). And we go out dumb and forgiven and unafraid.

33. ***The Mysteries of the Cross.***—(See also Expos. on vs. 46.) The story is told quite simply, with little attempt at description, and with almost no attempt whatsoever at explanation; but it cannot be simply catalogued and simply dismissed. It keeps haunting men with the suggestion of undiscovered and untraversed meanings.

It goes on relating itself in some unaccountable fashion to the caustic, mordant mystery of sin. When Socrates drinks his hemlock, one thinks somehow of truth, and the heroism of men who are willing to die for it. When Jesus is nailed fast to his cross, one thinks somehow of human sin and the only assault that ever has been made clean at its roots. And that thought is more than just the flower of an ancient tradition: it sprang full-blown from the very inmost circle of those who saw most and heard most and loved most. The little group standing around the philosopher's bed in Athens watching a man die by inches was sure when it was over that the world was forever poorer by one great soul; death had had to do with Socrates. The death on Calvary had to do with sin, and the men who stood afar off watching Jesus die came boldly to proclaim that the world was eternally richer for it. There is no parallel for that in history: where dying has been common, that one man's death should tower like this into a refuge from the only thing that has ever harassed human life beyond endurance.

So that in some fashion equally unaccountable the Cross has got itself related to the eternal, triumphant mystery of human assurance in the face of all the odds that are piled up against it. Wrote George Matheson, "O Cross that liftest up my head." If ever there was a place on this green earth where a man's head should be bowed down, it was on Calvary. And it has come to be the one place where he has a right to lift it! In measure, no doubt, because of the bewildering confidence of Christ himself. We would have called those hours an end; he went into them as if they were really just the beginning. He was not harried, as one whose plans were being brought to exactly nothing: he was quiet and sure-footed, as one who knows his way through. He was not losing anything that day, not even his life; he was

34 ¶ Then said Jesus, Father, forgive them; for they know not what they do. And they parted his raiment, and cast lots.

right and one on the left. 34 And Jesus said, "Father, forgive them; for they know not what they do."[t] And they cast lots to

[t] Other ancient authorities omit the sentence *And Jesus . . . . what they do.*

34*a*. Forgive them: The Jews? Or the Roman soldiers responsible for executing the sentence? The omission of the prayer by Codex Vaticanus, the original text of Codex Bezae, and other important MSS makes it highly improbable that it stood from the beginning in Luke's Gospel. But the scribe who inserted it did so with a deep and true understanding of the Galilean teacher. It is one of the most typically "Christian" utterances credited to Jesus in the gospel tradition (cf. Acts 7:60).

34*b*. Jesus' **garments** became the perquisites of his executioners. No doubt the detail was recorded by the evangelists (cf. Mark 15:24*b*) because it fulfilled the messianic interpretation of Ps. 22:18.

---

winning something: something that men have gone away with in their hearts ever since, whispering it to themselves. "Clean! Clean!" As long ago a leper must have looked at his hands when Jesus had passed, and the firm, pink flesh was back.

Then there is the mystery of human response. The Cross has got itself related to that. With everything done that can be done, what man is there who can go home and put on his slippers and stay by the fire, comfortably thanking God that everything is settled? All the strange urgency that stretched out its arms on Calvary seems somehow to get down from the Cross and lay itself on our own souls. John Newton, who ran a slave ship from Africa, wrote "How sweet the name of Jesus sounds," and "Come, my soul, thy suit prepare." But read the pitiful story of his long struggle to be rid of the vicious self he had come increasingly to hate. He wrote his hymn twenty-one years after he had become a priest of the Church of England. And he set down in his own epitaph his glad and solemn confession:

JOHN NEWTON, CLERK,
Once an infidel and libertine,
A servant of slaves in Africa,
Was, by the rich mercy of our Lord and Saviour
JESUS CHRIST
Preserved, restored, pardoned,
And appointed to preach the faith he
Had long laboured to destroy.

34. *Sentiment or Beyond?*—Father, forgive them; . . . they know not. . . . It is quite conceivable that this "word," taken as referring to the Jews, dropped out of a number of "important MSS" (Exeg.) because in the light of subsequent Jewish history it seemed inept. That a persecuted church let it stand at all would seem strong evidence of its authenticity. One is inclined to be considerably more puzzled by the hypothesis that Jesus did not utter it.

Note the ignorance assigned as motive. Whether the reference is to the Roman soldiers or to the Jews, the meaning is consonant not only with the mind of Christ, but with one of the most persistent themes of the N.T. (see Expos. on 20:9-16). The ignorance of the soldiers was circumstantial ignorance; the ignorance of the Jews was "judicial" ignorance. Both are held up before the face of God with merciful entreaty. It was less the hurt, more the will that did the hurt, which clamored not for reckoning but for compassion (cf. Acts 7:60). And not by mere well-wishing: by deed done, and pain borne, and death met; not more for the pathos of the ignorance that is fact than for the tragedy of the ignorance which would masquerade as knowledge.

Nor may it be forgotten that the forgiveness of which Jesus speaks is ever creative forgiveness. Nothing else can cover the facts. Never is it a question of smiling and letting bygones be bygones: making allowances for people, excusing them for this or that, overlooking their faults. Worthiness never enters into its calculations. It gives itself to human need: that out of the chaos may come order, out of the evil, good; no matter how much one may get hurt in the process; its justice as much tangled up with love as a surgeon's knife with health.

The ultimate fact of the Christian religion is that we have to deal with a God like that; and the ultimate fact about life is that when we quit dealing with it his way, it quits holding together. Not putting up with the wrong that is done us, but matching it with something that lies far and away on the other side of what we think of as "forgiveness"; striking out toward a lost world through the very floods that have gone over us, and expecting nothing to come of anything else, either in God's world or in man's!

35 And the people stood beholding. And the rulers also with them derided *him,* saying, He saved others; let him save himself, if he be Christ, the chosen of God.

divide his garments. 35 And the people stood by, watching; but the rulers scoffed at him, saying, "He saved others; let him save himself, if he is the Christ of God, his

35. A revision and abbreviation of the mockery recorded in Mark 15:31-32*a,* which on its part may have been suggested by Ps. 22:7-8. Luke distinguishes the attitude of **the people** from that of **the rulers** (Sanhedrists), perhaps under the influence of Ps. 22:17.

35-36. ***Operation Good Friday.*—The people stood by, watching. . . . The rulers scoffed. . . . The soldiers also mocked. . . .** It is difficult, perhaps impossible, to fix the details with any accuracy. Says Montefiore:

> The statement about the priests and the Scribes [Mark 15:31] is doubtful. They would hardly have come out on purpose to feast their eyes upon the spectacle of their enemy upon the cross. That kind of thing rather befits the officers of the Inquisition than the members of the Sanhedrin.[4]

But who can say? Conduct is not always befitting! Luce remarks that such "mockery by the soldiers is unlikely," and would "scarcely have been tolerated while on duty." [5] Worse breaches of discipline have been known. There seems to be reason enough to suppose, however, that the language of the psalms had its effect in shaping the tradition (see Expos. below); though the argument *post hoc, ergo propter hoc* is not the safest argument on which to rely!

During World War II military objectives were designated by cryptic names or symbols, and the strategy designed to achieve them was labeled "Operation So-and-so." To this day no better technique can be worked out for getting rid of Jesus—temporarily!—than to have privilege scoff at him and power mock him, while the people stand by, watching! "Why call ye me, Lord, Lord, and do not the things which I say?" (6:46.) To do him the homage of praise and prayer, rendering him no obedience; to exalt his way of love, and hold on to our ways, proud, determined servants of the humble, "suffering Servant" of God: what is it but to take our place with the crowd around the foot of the Cross? While the world looks on, making up its mind that making up its mind is unnecessary. After all, if that is how things are, why become involved?

35. ***God's Weakness and Man's Might.*—He saved others; let him save himself.** Proof enough that he was not Messiah! Yet there are times in Christian experience when more downright help is to be had out of thinking about God's weakness than could possibly be got out of thinking about what we are pleased to call his omnipotence. There are many things in this queer world which he cannot do without contradicting himself and the whole wide universe. He cannot stop wars until we are ready ourselves to stop them, or make people good who do not want to be made good, or keep the wickedness of evil men from hurting the innocent, or airplanes from dropping bombs on children, or shells from bursting and killing somebody we love. Not if he is to let us be real persons, instead of ridiculous puppets with a dozen idiotic strings tied to us. In the O.T. men used to talk of the majesty of God. He covered himself with light as with a garment. He made the clouds his chariot. He bowed the heavens also and came down. Darkness was under his feet, and he walked on the wings of the wind. It was all a little naïve against the background of the God we know: reaching out through aeons of light years, through black, bleak distance, to huge, incandescent suns, and down beyond human sight to myriads of ordered worlds within the atom. Faith, to be faith, has to stretch itself now! We have found out how great God has to be in order to be God at all. Yet majesty does not consist in power. Fascinating stories used to be told about Harun al-Rashid, the caliph of Baghdad. Under him the Eastern Caliphate reached the height of its splendor and the farthest extent of its dominion. But he is best known to us in the tales of *Arabian Nights,* where in humble disguise he goes out at evening time from his palace to move unknown among his people, if by any chance he might right their wrongs or steady their hearts. It is of the very essence of majesty to lay majesty aside. There are places in the human heart where force cannot come: only weakness can get in.

Set over against that weakness our might, and you will see why God had to fly in the face of common sense before he could make any sense at all. Humanity is and always was capable of trespassing on Eternity with its towers of Babel. Man would never have tried to be God if he had not been born to it somehow, with powers that he never seems able to exhaust. We can come a great deal closer to doing what we like

[4] *Synoptic Gospels,* I, 382.

[5] *Gospel According to St. Luke,* p. 351.

36 And the soldiers also mocked him,
coming to him, and offering him vinegar,
37 And saying, If thou be the King of
the Jews, save thyself.
38 And a superscription also was writ-
ten over him in letters of Greek, and Latin,
and Hebrew, THIS IS THE KING OF THE JEWS.

Chosen One!" 36 The soldiers also mocked
him, coming up and offering him vinegar,
37 and saying, "If you are the King of the
Jews, save yourself!" 38 There was also an
inscription over him,[u] "This is the King
of the Jews."

[u] Other ancient authorities add *in letters of Greek and Latin and Hebrew.*

36-37. The soldiers joined in the derision. Ps. 69:21*b* may have influenced Luke's revision of Mark 15:23, 36. No doubt the evangelist thought of the offer of **vinegar** as an act of torture.

38. See Mark 15:26. It was a Roman custom to hang a placard—titulus—about the neck of the condemned criminal or fasten it to the cross, setting forth the legal charge against him. This gospel note is an important historical datum in any discussion of Jesus' messianic consciousness. **In letters of Greek, and Latin, and Hebrew** (KJV; RSV mg.): Missing from Codex Vaticanus and most of its allies, and probably an interpolation in codices Sinaiticus and Bezae (and later MSS) from John 19:20, where the words are intended to symbolize the universality of Jesus' kingship.

---

than God can. Call the daily newspaper as witness.

Still, for some strange reason the self-imposed weakness of God is forever stronger than all the self-achieved might we can pile up against it. Christ crucified is more than a match for the years laid end to end down the ages. His weakness is not without power. The evil which keeps getting stronger and stronger grows more and more able to cut its own throat in less and less time. Pride and anger and jealousy and lust and greed—all that any one of them can do in the end is to head into some blind alley where it can tear itself to pieces (I Cor. 1:25). Wrote a Nazi youth: "Our hearts have turned from the faith of our forefathers. There was no way out except to drive Christ from them. His is the religion of cowardly and pitiable people. It is the strong who must rule, and the weak who must be ruled. Our God is a God of power." Written in 1942, that was already out of date when Rome fell. As old as God himself, destined still to be young when our generation is nothing but a memory, is the story of an American soldier who was killed on Luzon. With some premonition of what was to happen, or so it would seem, he had written his parents that if he fell they should take his government insurance and endow a scholarship for some Japanese boy at an American college. "I want to try to make it up to them now," said that Japanese boy as he got the news in Tokyo that he had been accepted at Lafayette, "I want to repay them as much as I can for the loss of their son."

From that Hitler youth to the lad on Luzon before he died runs the tension of human life: strung taut like a wire between—that weakness and this might!

36. ***Offering Him Vinegar.***—Luke may have mistaken an act of kindness (?), the sour wine of the soldiers (*posca*), for the vinegar of Ps. 69:21*b* (Exeg.). Matthew (27:34, 48) and Mark (15:23, 36) record two potions, one before and the other during the Crucifixion. The former, in Mark, seems to be the "drink given by merciful custom . . . to deaden the sense of pain,"[6] and Jesus refuses it. Recall Browning's lines:

I was ever a fighter, so—one fight more,
The best and the last!
I would hate that death bandaged my eyes and forbore,
And bade me creep past.[7]

In Matthew the drink is wine "mingled with gall," which Jesus first tastes, then refuses (cf. Ps. 69:21*a*), as if those who offered it had from motives of cruelty made it bitter. In Luke apparently there is some confusion: unless indeed the act which he records was intended chiefly to prolong the life of the sufferer (as would seem to be the case in Matt. 27:48 and in Mark 15:36).

38. ***The Inscription Is the Truth.***—**This is the King of the Jews.** It is strange that Pilate's contemptuous jest (so Luke?) should here become "an important historical datum in any discussion of Jesus' messianic consciousness" (Exeg.)! God does not rule with a scepter; he rules from a cross.

[6] Bruce, "Synoptic Gospels," *Expositor's Greek Testament,* on Matt. 27:34. See also Vol. VII, p. 902.
[7] "Prospice."

39 ¶ And one of the malefactors which were hanged railed on him, saying, If thou be Christ, save thyself and us.

40 But the other answering rebuked him, saying, Dost not thou fear God, seeing thou art in the same condemnation?

41 And we indeed justly; for we receive the due reward of our deeds: but this man hath done nothing amiss.

42 And he said unto Jesus, Lord, remember me when thou comest into thy kingdom.

43 And Jesus said unto him, Verily I say unto thee, To-day shalt thou be with me in paradise.

39 One of the criminals who were hanged
railed at him, saying, "Are you not the
Christ? Save yourself and us!" 40 But the
other rebuked him, saying, "Do you not
fear God, since you are under the same
sentence of condemnation? 41 And we in-
deed justly; for we are receiving the due
reward of our deeds; but this man has
done nothing wrong." 42 And he said, "Je-
sus, remember me when you come in your
kingly power."[v] 43 And he said to him,
"Truly, I say to you, today you will be with
me in Paradise."

[v] Greek *kingdom.*

4. The Penitent Criminal (23:39-43)

According to Mark 15:32*b*, both robbers who were crucified with Jesus joined the bystanders and Sanhedrists in mocking him. Luke distinguishes a repentant from an obdurate sinner.

39. Are you not the Christ? The reading in codices Vaticanus and Sinaiticus and in most other ancient MSS.

40-42. But this man has done nothing wrong: Because vs. 42 shows that the speaker accepted Jesus' messianic claim, B. S. Easton argues that this clause must mean "is dying for claims that are true." But such exegesis is unnecessarily subtle.

43. The penitent criminal is promised more than he asked. His felicity will not be postponed until Jesus inaugurates his kingdom. It will begin this very day in heaven. **Paradise:** A word borrowed from the Persian. The idea that the souls of the righteous would go at death to their eternal reward gradually found a place in Jewish thought beside the earlier belief that disembodied spirits would dwell in Sheol pending the resurrection and final judgment, and sometimes coalesced with it (see on 16:19-31).

39-43. ***The Drama of the Penitent Thief.***—Montefiore summarily dismisses these verses with the words "Luke's dramatic incident can lay no claim to being historical." [8] Writes B. S. Easton, "It is difficult to argue for much historic basis in this section." [9] J. A. Findlay, on the other hand, calls this passage "Luke's greatest contribution to the Passion story, whether his informant was Simon of Cyrene, the centurion, or Paul." [1]

For all the difficulties connected with the text, there is nothing inherently impossible in the record as Luke has given it to us. The contrasts are dramatically worked out, no doubt for use by the first Christian teachers and preachers. The first to speak is the brigand on the left. He catches up the taunt of the rulers and the soldiers, and in bitter mood, fighting back at his fate with all the violence of his unbridled soul, sneers and cries out for help in the same breath: "What a Messiah you are! Get the three of us out of this! Try your hand at that! Talk later." Then the other: "Have you no fear of God even? You're dying too, man! And we deserve it. He doesn't!" Life is sometimes seen best in the light of death! Or is it rather in "the light of the knowledge of the glory of God in the face of Jesus Christ" (II Cor. 4:6)? So "godly sorrow worketh repentance . . . : but the sorrow of the world worketh death" (II Cor. 7:10). **And he said, "Jesus [when you come again as king], remember me."** The one last claim of a life with its hands quite empty, laying hold on "the grace of our Lord Jesus Christ"; forgotten of all others, the never-to-be-forgotten of God (12:8)!

And on the instant—not some far-off tomorrow, but **today;** not some bounty of an age to come, but **Paradise** itself!

[8] *Synoptic Gospels,* II, 627.

[9] *The Gospel According to St. Luke,* p. 350.

[1] "Luke," *The Abingdon Bible Commentary,* ed. F. C. Eiselen, Edwin Lewis, and D. G. Downey (New York and Nashville: Abingdon-Cokesbury Press, 1929), p. 1057.

44 And it was about the sixth hour, and there was a darkness over all the earth until the ninth hour.
45 And the sun was darkened, and the veil of the temple was rent in the midst.
46 ¶ And when Jesus had cried with a loud voice, he said, Father, into thy hands I commend my spirit: and having said thus, he gave up the ghost.

44 It was now about the sixth hour, and there was darkness over the whole land[w]
until the ninth hour, 45 while the sun's light
failed;[x] and the curtain of the temple was
torn in two. 46 Then Jesus, crying with a
loud voice, said, "Father, into thy hands I commit my spirit!" And having said this

[w] Or *earth.*
[x] Or *the sun was eclipsed.* Other ancient authorities read *the sun was darkened.*

5. Miracles That Marked the Last Hours on the Cross
(23:44-45; cf. Mark 15:33, 38)

44-45*a*. Luke omits the Marcan notice that Jesus was crucified at 9 A.M. (Mark 15:25) but reproduces the statement that **there was darkness over the whole land** from midday to three in the afternoon, no doubt to symbolize the cosmic nature of the tragedy that was being enacted. **While the sun's light failed** (RSV): Probably even Mark's version was intended to imply an eclipse but Luke makes this explanation explicit. The fact that an eclipse was astronomically impossible at the time of the Passover full moon may have suggested the inferior reading translated by the KJV: **And the sun was darkened.**

45*b*. Follows Christ's death in Mark's account. **The curtain of the temple:** The veil that separated the Holy of Holies from contiguous parts of the temple and that was lifted only once a year by the high priest when he entered the presence of God to make sacrificial propitiation for the sins of the people. This gospel miracle gives symbolic expression to the Christian faith that Christ's death made possible the direct access of men to God and is reminiscent of the argument in the Epistle to the Hebrews (cf. especially Heb. 10:19-22).

6. Jesus' Death (23:46-49)

A radical revision of Mark 15:37, 39-40.

46. A loud voice: A possible hint that Jesus' death was due to the failure of some vital organ. Luke substitutes an apt quotation from Ps. 31:5 for the one from Ps. 22:1

44-49. *The Death of Jesus.*—There are several things to note in Luke's account as it reflects *for faith* the meaning of Jesus' death. (*a*) It had cosmic significance (see Exeg.; cf. Amos 8:9). (*b*) It was therefore most surely a moment when time was invaded by eternity and heaven touched earth. (*c*) It was a fulfillment of prophecy (see Exeg. on vs. 49). (*d*) It made possible man's immediate approach to God (see Exeg.). (*e*) It was an hour not of defeat, but of victory. (*f*) It was acclaimed even by a Gentile soldier as the death of a man quite innocent—Christianity, Luke seems to insist on saying, was anything but subversive of government. (*g*) It was bewailed (Zech. 12:10) by those who looked on, and (*h*) witnessed—the men **afar off**, the women nearer?—by those who afterward found in it the heart of their gospel (I John 1:1-3). Yet it was not on the Crucifixion that the church rested its case, but on the Resurrection. The Cross in that perspective cast its lengthening shadow over all the earth.

46. *Into Thy Hands.*—(Cf. Ps. 31:5.) Here is the unashamed commitment of a trust fully discharged. Something in the past has been wrought out to the end. There are not many who are conscious of any sense of completion when death comes to them. Certainly not when they are cut off at the very threshold of life as Jesus was. Beginning in hope, but from the very beginning narrowing down toward defeat, he yet seemed increasingly aware that he bore a high commission down the Galilean roads: spotless, so that none could bring accusation against him; kind, so that the most pathetic commentary ever written on human life is the long roster of his enemies; coming out on an untimely gallows, just as he was turning into manhood, his possibilities unfathomed, his hopes unrealized, and instead of being allowed to die in solitary state, mingled there with the troubled going of two "thieves," undistinguished and obscure. Hounded from countryside to countryside, he had tried to teach a

47 Now when the centurion saw what was done, he glorified God, saying, Certainly this was a righteous man.

48 And all the people that came together to that sight, beholding the things which were done, smote their breasts, and returned.

49 And all his acquaintance, and the women that followed him from Galilee, stood afar off, beholding these things.

he breathed his last. 47 Now when the cen-
turion saw what had taken place, he praised
God, and said, "Certainly this man was
innocent!" 48 And all the multitudes who
assembled to see the sight, when they saw
what had taken place, returned home beat-
ing their breasts. 49 And all his acquaint-
ances and the women who had followed
him from Galilee stood at a distance and
saw these things.

---

that had stood in his Marcan source as Christ's last words, regarding an expression of trust and faith as more appropriate than a bitter cry of despair.

47. "Certainly this man was innocent!" for Mark's "Truly this man was a son of God." A Roman **centurion** at the Cross had admitted its founder's innocence of any crime against the state (see Intro., pp. 5-6).

48. An editorial generalization. The behavior of "the crowd," as Luke represents it in the passion story, is often contradictory.

49. And all his acquaintances: Probably Luke thought of them as including Jesus' disciples, for he had omitted Mark's earlier comment that they had all forsaken him and fled (Mark 14:50). Pss. 38:11 and 88:8*a* may have influenced the composition of this verse. Mark's list of faithful women (15:40*b*) is omitted, perhaps because Luke had already mentioned a somewhat different group by name (8:2*b*-3; cf. also 24:10).

---

handful of men to be his disciples. Of them, one had betrayed him, another had denied him, none had understood him, and all had fled. Then this: **Father, into thy hands . . . !**

It is not a surrender. The medieval artists came very near losing sight of what it was. They pictured the Crucifixion as a barbarous and ghastly thing, which of course it was; they sounded, perhaps better than Luke and John, the depths of Christ's humiliation: but they stopped there. They stopped with pathos and defeat: the pitiful issue of a tragic and unavoidable incident in the epic of human envy and human hatred and human rebellion; a limp, wan figure carved out of wood and hung over the altar, or painted in somber colors for the walls of some chapel or monastery. In early Christian art it was a crowned King on the cross: one who was fighting his last battle and driving his foes in front of him (Col. 2:14-15). Nothing had gone wrong. Something had gone eternally right. He had drained a cup to its dregs, and was hurling it from him. He was not stumbling away into death: he was climbing into it, reaching out his hand for a scepter. Some of the Fathers went so far as to cite the **loud voice** as evidence of the fact that Jesus died quite voluntarily, "breathing forth his spirit" by a free act of his own will (cf. John 10:18; but see Exeg.).

When it is asked what the commission was which had been so fully discharged, the church has been able to find but one answer, whispered all through the **O.T.**—against the background of eternal judgment stand the sure mercies of God. It is no whisper now. It is Word made flesh; nails driven through and clinched; the past and the present and all the blundering future with the mark of the Almighty on it!

But here too is the quiet confidence of a life resting in the providences of God. The whole day seems pervaded by a sense of untroubled certainty. There was none in Pilate. He went in and came out, sat down and stood up, asked questions, gave judgments, and then went back on them, like a man possessed. There was none in the frantic mob, none in the frightened little band of disciples. The Sanhedrin was disorganized and confused. Only Jesus seemed deliberate and masterful. "Thou sayest that I am a king. . . . If my kingdom were of this world, then would my servants fight. . . . Thou couldest have no power at all against me, except it were given thee from above" (John 18:37, 36; 19:11). Every step he takes is a step that no one forces on him; he takes it of himself. They offer him a drug, and he puts it aside. The executioners, and the bitter mob back of them, are all forgiven. A "thief" is made the object of a royal promise. A sorrowing mother is given over into the tender hands of a disciple. As the hours slip by, from twelve to three, he cries out into the gathering dark the first verse of Ps. 22. He could hardly have helped thinking of it; it ran so aptly with what was going on. Read the verses that follow, from the storm-

50 ¶ And, behold, *there was* a man
named Joseph, a counselor; *and he was* a
good man, and a just:
51 (The same had not consented to the
counsel and deed of them:) *he was* of Ari-
mathea, a city of the Jews; who also him-
self waited for the kingdom of God.
52 This *man* went unto Pilate, and
begged the body of Jesus.

50 Now there was a man named Joseph
from the Jewish town of Ar-i-ma-the'a. He
was a member of the council, a good and
righteous man, **51** who had not consented
to their purpose and deed, and he was
looking for the kingdom of God. **52** This
man went to Pilate and asked for the body

---

7. Jesus' Burial (23:50-56; cf. Mark 15:42-43, 46-47)

50-51. A member of the council: If Joseph was sympathetic to Jesus and his message despite his membership in the Sanhedrin, had he taken any part in the proceedings of that court against him? Luke appears to have sensed a difficulty in Mark's account at this point, for he declares that the councilor **had not consented to their purpose and deed;** cf. John 19:38, where we are told that Joseph had kept his devotion to Jesus a secret "for fear of the Jews." **Arimathea:** No certain identification is possible. Usually regarded as a corruption of "Ramathaim" (I Sam. 1:1), a Judean village near the Samaritan border. **A city of the Jews:** A geographical note inserted by Luke for the benefit of his Gentile readers (cf. 4:31; 8:26).

52-53. The Romans had no scruples about leaving a dead body on a cross over night, but it was a breach of Jewish law to do so (Deut. 21:23). **A rock-hewn tomb:** The Greek

---

tossed past of his own people. The mystery will not be probed without them. Desolation may be the word, but not despair: rather an unshaken faith making its way through the tumult to breathe its last, when the final paroxysm of pain is over, with the sure and restful sigh of a tired child, **Father, into thy hands I commend my spirit.**

The vast dimensions of sin; and the vaster dimensions of this other thing which was closing its eyes on the future! The Cross might well have seemed a black line drawn through all that Jesus had said of life. "Blessed are the poor. . . ." "He bearing his cross went forth." Canceled. "Blessed are the meek. . . ." "Into a place called . . . Golgotha." Canceled. "Blessed are the merciful. . . ." "Where they crucified him." Canceled. A thousand times over history reads like that. Did Calvary mean then that Jesus and his sort would always be so wide of the mark, so absolutely beside the point that they were bound to come out all through the ages at the little end of everything and be wiped clean off the slate at last? Why was he so confident that it did *not* mean that and never would?

It was the problem with which Paul wrestled. He too saw the odds that stood against any future at all: multiplied in his case, as in ours, by the tedious, aching slavery within; doing things still he never meant to do, wanting so much a better life than any he had ever seemed able to manage; sitting there with his head on his arms. "O wretched man that I am!" (Rom. 7:24.) When all at once he looked up. What had happened made no sense that way! God in us at Bethlehem, God for us on Calvary, God with us in the Resurrection, God beyond us in heaven, God through us at Pentecost: none of it made sense that way! And hurriedly he wrote on: "For I am persuaded that neither death, nor life, . . ."—the words kept tumbling out—"shall be able to separate us from the love of God." And where was that love? Where was it supremely, once and for all? "Which is in Christ Jesus our Lord" (Rom. 8:38-39). The counsels of the Eternal were cross-deep in the shadows when Jesus died. **Father, into thy hands. . . .**"

50-56. ***The Burial of Jesus.***—There is little about the story that calls for exposition. It is a simple, straightforward account of the kindly act of a generous and just man, **a member of the council,** and therefore of high position, a devout Pharisee who with others looked for the coming of the messianic kingdom. Whether he merely withheld his vote or actively disagreed with his colleagues in their determination to be rid of the troublesome prophet from Nazareth is not clearly stated. At any rate, from motives perhaps compounded of sympathy and the pious desire that the sabbath might not be defiled, perhaps even of disappointment and regret that his own conduct heretofore had not been more forthright, he now summons up enough courage (John 19:38) to ask of Pilate **the body of Jesus.** Hurriedly embalmed and wrapped in its linen cloth, it was laid in a

53 And he took it down, and wrapped it in linen, and laid it in a sepulchre that was hewn in stone, wherein never man before was laid.

54 And that day was the preparation, and the sabbath drew on.

55 And the women also, which came with him from Galilee, followed after, and beheld the sepulchre, and how his body was laid.

56 And they returned, and prepared spices and ointments; and rested the sabbath day according to the commandment.

24 Now upon the first *day* of the week, very early in the morning, they came unto the sepulchre, bringing the spices which they had prepared, and certain *others* with them.

of Jesus. 53 Then he took it down and
wrapped it in a linen shroud, and laid him
in a rock-hewn tomb, where no one had
ever yet been laid. 54 It was the day of
Preparation, and the sabbath was begin-
ning.[y] 55 The women who had come with
him from Galilee followed, and saw the
tomb, and how his body was laid; 56 then
they returned, and prepared spices and
ointments.

On the sabbath they rested according to the commandment.

24 But on the first day of the week, at early dawn, they went to the tomb, taking the spices which they had prepared.

[y] Greek *was dawning.*

could mean "a tomb built of stones," but no doubt Luke was simply paraphrasing Mark's "a tomb which had been hewn out of the rock." **Where no one . . . laid:** In Luke only; cf. the similar notice in 19:30 (Mark 11:2) and see Exeg., *ad loc.* Mark's comment that a stone was rolled against the door of the tomb is omitted but the detail is presupposed in 24:2.

54-56*a*. The day of Preparation, i.e., Friday (see Mark 15:42). **"The sabbath was dawning"** (RSV mg.): A Jewish idiom; in Palestine at the Passover season about 6 P.M. **Who had come with him from Galilee:** A somewhat irritating repetition of a subordinate clause in vs. 49. Because of the near approach of the Sabbath the customary embalming of the body had to be postponed. According to Mark 16:1, **the women** purchased the necessary spices after the sabbath was past.

J. Discovery of the Empty Tomb (24:1-12=Mark 16:1-6*a*)

Vss. 1-5 are a free revision and abbreviation of the narrative in Mark. Vss. 6*b*-11 are an editorial addition, but vs. 10*a* appears to be dependent on Mark 16:1.

I Cor. 15:3-8 is the most important passage in the N.T. for an understanding of the early Christian faith in Christ's resurrection. Written not more than twenty-five years after the event, it recalls the tradition that the Apostle to the Gentiles had already

near-by sepulcher—with the pathos of that repeated clause, **the women . . . which came with him from Galilee**—to await the sequel: the end that was God's beginning.

It is at least conceivable that we might catch something of the spirit of the scene, even at the cost of the letter, if we were to allow our minds some freedom with the rolling of a stone "against the door of the tomb" (Mark 15:46; Luke 24:2; Matt. 27:65-66). The Jesus who was buried was a Jesus who had been misunderstood. The God with whom life had to deal was not a God of power, answering his people's whim; or a God of privilege, guaranteeing to his favored children their ancient position. These gods we do well to bury. The God who regards not "the person of men" (Mark 12:14), yet ever is "moved with compassion toward them" (Mark 6:34)—that God will not be buried. The moment we put him away is a moment already big with his return. Men wrote "Finis" as boldly as they could. God wrote, "To be continued."

24:1-12. *Death Could Not Hold Him.*—(Acts 2:24 Moffatt.) Much is made in our time of the fact that "the idea of a bodily resurrection" is not congenial to the modern mind. The very statement itself might seem in a measure offensive. It should hardly be necessary to remind oneself that "the modern mind" is scarcely the final arbiter of truth; nor is one bound to suppose that truth will always be found "congenial" to it. From the premise, however, several inferences are drawn: (*a*) the story of the

2 And they found the stone rolled away from the sepulchre.
3 And they entered in, and found not the body of the Lord Jesus.

2 And they found the stone rolled away
from the tomb, 3 but when they went in

imparted to his Corinthian converts (I Cor. 15:5), and claims that his teaching in the matter was apostolic doctrine (I Cor. 15:9-11). In it Paul declares that the Christian conviction that Christ had triumphed over the Cross was based on appearances of the risen Lord. It asserts that the first of these had been vouchsafed to Cephas, and implies that Paul thought of his own vision of the risen Christ as similar to those of his predecessors, and as the last in the series.

There is a trace in Luke's Gospel of this early apologetic. In 24:34, when Cleopas and his companion return to Jerusalem from Emmaus to report their experience to the larger company, they are greeted with the words: "The Lord has risen indeed, and has appeared to Simon!"

Paul gives no indication that he was familiar with the doctrine of the empty tomb. There is not the remotest reference to it in any of his letters, and his own conviction that the resurrection body is not the body of this flesh but a spiritual body waiting for the soul of man in heaven (I Cor. 15:35-55; II Cor. 5:1-4) makes it improbable that he would have found it congenial. Nevertheless it appealed to Mark as the all-important fact, and in his Gospel—whose original text probably ended with Mark 16:8—it displaced all other resurrection tradition.

Both Matthew and Luke took over and revised Mark's story of the empty tomb, but both also supplemented it with a cycle of resurrection narratives. Matthew records appearances of the risen Christ to his disciples in Galilee, while the locale of Luke's stories (cf. John 20) is restricted to Jerusalem and its vicinity.

24:1-3. Of the Lord Jesus (KJV; RSV mg.): Missing from Codex Bezae and the O.L. MSS.

empty tomb can hardly be taken seriously; (*b*) the "body" of the risen Lord must therefore have been the kind of body of which Paul speaks—"spiritual," not "physical"; (*c*) the "appearances," as a result, were likely enough quite "subjective," so that the verb *to see* should properly be set off by inverted commas! Entirely apart from what Paul meant by his word "spiritual"—except for the comment that whatever he meant, he could never with his Jewish background have meant what we mean by it—there are at least three considerations that must be borne in mind: (*a*) we are dealing not with a development from within human experience—the evolution of a belief in "immortality"—but with an incursion—"God giveth it a body" (I Cor. 15:38)—from outside; (*b*) not the Resurrection but the fact of Christ is the ultimate "miracle" of the Christian faith; (*c*) the conclusion arrived at must cover the facts. The N.T. bears witness "to the force and rapidity with which the belief in the Resurrection arose among the disciples and reacted on the world."[2] The despair of Good Friday turned as at a signal into the "joy and confident activity" with which that martyred band began the long climb up "the steep ascent of heaven." The church of Jesus Christ had set out on its march across the centuries. Ask the evangelists why. Ask Paul or James or John. With one voice they will answer. And their answer has wrought mightily on human history. The only brief note that has to be added is that argument is not likely to prove conducive to faith.

2. ***The Stone in the Door of the Tomb.*—They found the stone rolled away.** As to the historical fact of the Resurrection, the Christian church is not likely to have got its start in nonsense. With regard to "immortality," it is hardly conceivable that Jesus' friends in this blazing dawn were rubbing their hands together and congratulating themselves, saying, "You see? This proves it! We shall live forever!" Adventure had not yet fallen apart into logic. What is of foremost concern is the magnificent way in which God that morning unimaginably changed life here.

He rolled away from it the stone of futility. One does not need to be told what an appalling sense of utter uselessness presses down in our modern world on the human soul: the laws and measurements of a huge order that leave little freedom and less stature; a civilization that drives men around for a while like gadgets on

[2] Luce, *Gospel According to St. Luke*, p. 367.

4 And it came to pass, as they were much perplexed thereabout, behold, two men stood by them in shining garments:

they did not find the body.[z] 4 While they were perplexed about this, behold, two men

[z] Other ancient authorities add *of the Lord Jesus.*

---

4. In Mark's version the women see "a young man . . . in a white robe" as soon as they enter the tomb. Here **two men . . . in dazzling apparel** appear only after the discovery and perplexity noted by the evangelist in vss. *3b* and *4a*. No doubt angelic appearances are implied (cf. Acts 1:10).

---

the flywheel of progress, until it smashes into some idiotic chaos called war, and everybody stands about in the peevish, petulant inadequacy of spoiled children trying to justify it. And then the little room we have: a bit of a home, a bit of a job, two children, and a few friends; that about says it. We wonder sometimes why on earth in such tiny places we should get so excited about things. Come another century, and what difference will it make? Until God flings down this glove at our feet, daring us not to be as little as we think, but as great as we are, trying to show us as best he can what poor fractions of reality we are crawling into most of the time. In Thornton Wilder's play *Our Town*[8] a little girl, leaning from a window on a moonlit night, tells of a strange letter that has come to somebody in Grover's Corners, a sort of crossroads somewhere in New Hampshire. It was addressed: "Grover's Corners; Sutton County; New Hampshire; the United States of America; Continent of North America; Western Hemisphere; the Earth; the Solar System; the Universe; the Mind of God." And the lad who listened whispered, "What do you know! . . . What do you know!" The bleak facts of every day's tiresome existence are set now where they belong, within the circle of Eternity!

And the stone of bitterness. That too lies flat against the tomb where many a life has buried its hopes (vs. 21). There is a day now beyond the pain and the failure, when God shall take it all up in his hands and shape it so that even our dull spirits can begin to catch the sheen of it. Paul says in one place (Rom. 8:18) that we cannot even see "the sufferings of this present time" clearly, such as they are; cannot see any broken plans or frayed-out hope, cannot see death itself, until we see it all against the magnificent perspective of "the glory which shall be revealed in us." Here is his list: labors, stripes, prisons, shipwreck, hunger, nakedness, cold. And here is what it came to when he added it up: "not worthy to be compared."

And the stone of injustice. Many a human heart gets buried under that before its time. God has a way of striking his own balance. There is nothing vindictive about it. The scales are weighted with his love, but they are still scales. The whole of living would make sense if we could read them. In the end he says Christ, and says it unmistakably. Men may go around as much as they please looking for thorns and reeds and purple robes and worse; but they cannot finish the story. There is One who finishes it. Nobody can hurl up into his face such a ghastly contradiction as that cross, and then go about his business as if he had won. Truth will not be treated as some treat it. The story of the Resurrection is the story of a God whose judgments are sure, saying their eternal "No" to every gleeful crucifixion, and saying it in the gospel to the sound of running feet, as people hurried about trying to lift all human faces everywhere to the face they had seen again!

4-5. ***A Tomb for Lazarus!*—While they were perplexed about this . . . and . . . frightened.** They stood, before an empty tomb, afraid! Afraid of what? Of death, or of life?

In Eugene O'Neill's stirring drama, *Lazarus Laughed,* they are afraid of life—so afraid that there is nothing to do at the last but to find a tomb again for that weird villager of Bethany, brother to Martha and Mary, who had come forth one day bound hand and foot with graveclothes, laughing softly, as out of a vision, like a man in love with God, "There is no death!" And the world, with all its pygmy people in it, could not stand him. Such laughter made their ears drunk. It was wine. And just "one terror too many." Men had to murder it.

The world that seems so big grows small on this "first day of the week, at early dawn" (vs. 1). To have our goods gone over, and the success we have been striving for pushed aside for the time being, while this Christ looks at us with eternity in his heart, to see what kind of person we are; to be meek and merciful and pure in heart; to drop our anxiety like a cloak; to love our enemies, and to give to them that ask—this is to stand on its head every man's idea of what is what! Martha and Mary looked sadly at their brother and cursed him: to greet the news of the master's death with low, musical laughter! He had become a devil. The emperor

[8] New York: Coward McCann, 1938, Act I.

5 And as they were afraid, and bowed down *their* faces to the earth, they said unto them, Why seek ye the living among the dead?

6 He is not here, but is risen: remember how he spake unto you when he was yet in Galilee,

7 Saying, The Son of man must be delivered into the hands of sinful men, and be crucified, and the third day rise again.

8 And they remembered his words,

9 And returned from the sepulchre, and told all these things unto the eleven, and to all the rest.

stood by them in dazzling apparel; 5 and
as they were frightened and bowed their
faces to the ground, the men said to them,
"Why do you seek the living among the
dead?[a] 6 Remember how he told you, while
he was still in Galilee, 7 that the Son of
man must be delivered into the hands of
sinful men, and be crucified, and on the
third day rise." 8 And they remembered his
words, 9 and returning from the tomb they
told all this to the eleven and to all the

[a] Other ancient authorities add *He is not here, but has risen.*

5*a*. An expansion of Mark's "and they were amazed."

5*b*. More graphic than its counterpart in Mark. **Among the dead,** i.e., in a tomb.

6*a*. In KJV; RSV mg. Missing from Codex Bezae and the O.L. MSS, and no doubt introduced into the archetypes of others to harmonize Luke with Mark and Matthew.

6*b*-7. Since Luke locates all the resurrection appearances of Christ in or about Jerusalem, these verses replace Mark 14:28: "But after I am raised up, I will go before you to Galilee." The reference is to the prophecies recorded in 9:22 and 44, and Luke now implies that the women were numbered among the disciples to whom they were addressed.

8-9. Instead of fleeing in terror from the tomb and saying nothing to anyone, as in Mark, the women **remembered** the prophecy after the angels had recalled it and returned

---

fled from him, and all the people who loved their solemn little affairs thrust their fingers in their ears. Are we afraid to pick up life's stuff from the counter, take it away from the glare of the artificial lights, bring it here into the "early dawn" and look at it?

The Resurrection is a vista that makes our world too small. And it makes human life too great. To turn from a world that has dwindled to a self that has grown dizzy with being a sudden giant calls for courage. **While they were perplexed about this . . . and . . . frightened.** We talk sometimes about the mean stature to which we are supposed to have shrunk under the impact of the modern, scientific view of the universe. What we need to worry about more is our manifest fear of being too great. Whenever a man comes to a huge city from the town back home, where his name was bandied about the streets, and everybody knew his uprising and his downsitting, he is inclined, almost irresistibly inclined, to scuttle in out of the limelight with a sigh of ponderous relief! Nobody knows him, thank God! And nobody cares what he does—thank God again! He can hide now from a thousand responsibilities. Perhaps the doctrine of our insignificance is a kind of wishful thinking! The Resurrection makes our dimensions too big.

This gospel is for the brave! Those who have courage to be sons of God; and if sons, "then heirs; heirs of God, and joint-heirs with Christ" (Rom. 8:17).

5. *Why Seek the Living Among the Dead?*—There is a question which has as much relevance now as it ever had. The living Lord is not to be found embalmed in creeds and ritual, or in pious ordinances (Col. 2:20-23), nor yet in "holy places made with hands, which are the figures of the true" (Heb. 9:24); but in the faith that sets its course Godward, in hope which "maketh not ashamed" (Rom. 5:5), in "love unfeigned" (II Cor. 6:6; see Expos. on 19:3-4, 5).

6-8. *Remember. . . . And They Remembered . . . and . . . Told.*—To cast the mind back over the past, instead of brooding over the desolate present, or shivering at the bleak prospect of the unknown future; to see the years again as Christ saw them, instinct with God's purpose, and with "the removing of those things that are shaken . . . that those things which cannot be shaken may remain" (Heb. 12:27); and then to proclaim it!

9. *They Told All This.*—All up and down, from Nazareth to Jerusalem, Jesus had been forbidding those whom he healed to speak of him. He had wanted people to see not the cure

10 It was Mary Magdalene, and Joanna, and Mary *the mother* of James, and other *women that were* with them, which told these things unto the apostles.

rest. 10 Now it was Mary Mag′da-lene and Jo-an′na and Mary the mother of James and the other women with them who told

to the company of disciples to report what they had seen and heard. **And to all the rest** prepares the reader for the reference to others besides the eleven in the stories that follow (vss. 13, 22-24, 33).

10. Luke had suppressed the names of the women in 23:49 and 55 (contrast Mark 15:40, 47) but now mentions three of them. The list is as in Mark 16:1, with **Joanna** (Luke 8:3) substituted for "Salome." **Mary the mother of James:** "James the younger" according to Mark 15:40. Possibly "James the son of Alphaeus" of Luke 6:15 (Mark 3:18).

but the kingdom. That was all over. Here there is breathless haste. These women stop for a moment with wild eyes, then stumble away to pour out in hot words the stupendous nonsense of a resurrection.

It meant that life now was an ineffably meaningful thing; that nobody could afford to play about on the surface of it. At first the resurrection of Jesus must have seemed to rob it of all significance (see Expos. on vss. 4-5). In fact, that is actually what did happen in the first chaos which Easter hurled into human life. Here and there people quit work (II Thess. 3:10-12). Why should they fool with such trivialities any longer? There were greater worlds in view, and many a man would gladly have leaped toward death. But gradually they came to understand that nothing of the sort would do. They were not to acquire their immortal stature by throwing this life away. They were to get into it farther than they had ever been. There were ways of being immortal now, and they were to match their step with his who had worn their homespun days like one who was "trailing clouds of glory . . . from God" who was his home.[4]

It meant that at the heart of those days there was a promise, An *x*, an unknown quantity, a mysterious factor, was flung into the equation, and it played havoc with what everybody thought was final. Life was intent on something else besides just "dying off at the top." It was not only moving, it was going somewhere. And nails could not stop it. Nor a grave. God was not ridiculous. He would not wind up everything with a jest. Easter locates us here, and locates Christ with us. It stands up out of the frightful mess where men are forever trying to live in some past which is approximately dead, or in some future which has not yet been born, and shouts, "The Lord God omnipotent reigneth" (Rev. 19:6).

[4] Wordsworth, "Ode on Intimations of Immortality."

It meant that life from now on could be steady and valorous, however put upon or sorely tried or kicked up by misfortune. No wise man lives as if living were all a holiday. Sensible people have nothing to do with the halfwitted gaiety that splashes about in the shallows, until one day it steps off a hidden ledge, and plunges away in over its head, and knows nothing at all about swimming. Inevitably we get into the deep places, and need desperately to be steadied against the facts. The Resurrection does just that. There is a distance gauge on your camera. It can be set at six feet or at fifty; or if you like, at infinity! And that makes the landscape clearer. Artists measure some object with the eye, holding thumb and forefinger at right angles to keep from mistaking its true proportions. "If only man might die and live again, I could endure my weary post until relief arrived" (Job 14:14 Moffatt).

And it meant that life could never again pitch its hopes too high. God's gauntlet was at its feet. Even a dead Jesus, no doubt, could have kept men dreaming of honor and truth and purity, sure somehow that these were not trifling, yet not really believing that much would ever come of them. It would have been like listening to eternity at a keyhole. But in a world that is all his, as life is his and death is his, there is a good deal more at work than "the gray Perhaps"[5] or "the soul's invincible surmise."[6] **They told all this to the eleven.** Then he never had been holding up in front of any man's eyes nothing but a few stray wisps of rainbow-colored fog. Soberly he had meant everything he had said: about the poor in spirit, the merciful and meek; about their own broken, beaten lives—"The works that I do shall he do also; and greater works than these shall he do" (John 14:12). The very moving power of God was pledged to it—and this spec-

[5] John Neihardt, "Let Me Live Out My Years."

[6] George Santayana, "O World, Thou Choosest Not."

11 And their words seemed to them as idle tales, and they believed them not.

12 Then arose Peter, and ran unto the sepulchre; and stooping down, he beheld the linen clothes laid by themselves, and departed, wondering in himself at that which was come to pass.

this to the apostles; 11 but these words seemed to them an idle tale, and they did not believe them.[b]

[b] Other ancient authorities add verse 12, *But Peter rose and ran to the tomb; stooping and looking in, he saw the linen cloths by themselves; and he went home wondering at what had happened.*

---

11. The implication that none of the disciples took the trouble to investigate the women's story is contradicted by vs. 24, and it may have been this apparent discrepancy that suggested to some scribe the interpolation of vs. 12.

12. In KJV; RSV mg. Missing from Codex Bezae and the O.L. MSS, and no doubt an interpolation based on John 20:3-10.

---

tacle which Christ had made of the Cross, and life had made of death.

11. *An Idle Tale.*—But these words seemed to them an idle tale, and they did not believe them. The only answer they could think of was "nonsense" (Moffatt). The women were excited. The tedious hours of grief and the sleepless nights had been almost too much for anybody to stand. Sheer exhaustion! Fevered imagination! What else could it be? Nobody was to blame. Maybe something had happened —no telling what; but not this!

Death had too long exercised its ancient dominion, lording itself around through the world, cutting folk's plans in two, leaving half-written pages, filling the valleys with shadow. Perhaps the world, to be vital and strong, to have breadth and height, could not do without it. In *If a Man Die*[7] W. Cosby Bell records a legend that in the days before men knew death, life had grown easy and selfish. Looking neither before nor after, they knew no sorrow and could wear no dignity. Until here and there one and then another laid down his tools and never took them up again. A woman was called away from home, leaving forever an empty place by the fire. And tasks began to grow out of their old proportions. Love became poignant again, marked by a strange depth and tenderness. A lad threw his own body between his friend and the leap of a beast, and courage was born. Death may be one of the ways God has of making a man, giving him a grave to keep him from being a clod! It need not be the bleak disaster we have thought it, falling sharp across the pattern of human life. Writes an unknown author, standing within its circle: "For me, death, now that it has become imminent, has changed life. . . . I have no time to spend on disliking people, on being bored, or ill-tempered, or shy. Every action assumes significance because it may be by that action that I am remembered. And the trivial things, the dull duties, the mechanical tasks, are all precious; I love them." But for all that, dominion was the word for death. It had its scepter; argue ever so bravely, none of your thimbles full of courage could take that age-old scepter from it. In the end, dying would rule, and you would be quiet! Aeschylus (*Fragment* 147) had been right about it:

> Of all the Gods, Death only craves not gifts:
> . . . From him alone of all
> The powers of Heaven Persuasion holds aloof.

The rest was the pious man's hope, and any man's guess.

Of all the tales ever told for people who wanted to keep in fettle, this tale was most incredible. There were too many things in the world that contradicted the sovereignty it disclosed. The "No" that man had shouted against God still rang so loudly in the disciples' ears that they could not hear the quiet "Yes" which God was uttering. The ugly facts of daily experience had proved too strong: no man could counter hatred with love, or power with a dream. The paltry business of living was back again on their shoulders, drab and unillumined.

Incredible perhaps; but not idle. It was too apt a tale for anybody to turn a deaf ear to it long. The text even as it stands, without vs. 12, could scarcely have been intended to convey the idea that no one of "the eleven" did anything about it from morning to night. There have been few if any since who, having heard it, have treated it with such indomitable poise and unconcern. It was too much in character, when one comes to think of it (Acts 2:24 Moffatt); too much like this "pioneer of life" (Acts 3:15 Moffatt) whom they had known. The fact of a God with whom the facts themselves had collided became more than an answer to life's riddles: in it they saw again the great Deliverer and his eternal, saving purpose; and with it they leaped at the world with a shout!

[7] New York: Charles Scribner's Sons, 1934, p. 65.

13 ¶ And, behold, two of them went that same day to a village called Emmaus, which was from Jerusalem *about* three-score furlongs.

14 And they talked together of all these things which had happened.

15 And it came to pass, that, while they communed *together* and reasoned, Jesus himself drew near, and went with them.

16 But their eyes were holden that they should not know him.

17 And he said unto them, What manner of communications *are* these that ye have one to another, as ye walk, and are sad?

13 That very day two of them were go-
ing to a village named Em-ma'us, about
seven miles[c] from Jerusalem, 14 and talking
with each other about all these things that
had happened. 15 While they were talking
and discussing together, Jesus himself drew
near and went with them. 16 But their eyes
were kept from recognizing him. 17 And he
said to them, "What is this conversation
which you are holding with each other as
you walk?" And they stood still, looking

[c] Greek *sixty stadia.*

VII. The Risen Christ (24:13-53)

A. The Risen Christ on the Road to Emmaus (24:13-35)

There are no further contacts of Luke's Gospel with Matthew, and the text of Mark that Luke used ended with Mark 16:8. Therefore interpreters have had to rely on subjective criteria in their source analysis of all but the opening verses of this chapter. Some are convinced that the Emmaus incident is an abstract from a primitive document, and that it rests ultimately on tradition stemming from Cleopas. Others regard it as Luke's own free composition. The assumption in this commentary is that the evangelist adapted earlier—and probably literary—tradition to his use by interpolating vss. 22-24. The result is a story of singular grace and charm.

13-14. That very day: Luke implies that all the events narrated in this chapter took place on the first day of the week (but see on vss. 50-53). **Two of them:** Of "all the rest" referred to in vs. 9. Included by later Christian tradition among the seventy of ch. 10. **Emmaus:** Josephus speaks of an "Emmaus" about four miles from Jerusalem that was chosen by Vespasian as the site for a colony of Roman soldiers after A.D. 70 (*Jewish War* VII. 6. 6). Often identified with the modern Qalôniyeh on the hypothesis that the latter name is a corruption of the Latin *colonia.* In Maccabean times 'Amwâs, about fifteen miles from Jerusalem on the Jaffa road, was known as **Emmaus** (later Nicopolis). **All these things that had happened:** The discovery of the empty tomb as well as the events of the Passion, but perhaps only the latter in an earlier form and setting of the story.

15-17. Jesus overtakes his disciples on the Emmaus road. Luke intends us to understand that their senses were supernaturally dulled, not that they were blinded by intense preoccupation. Mark 16:12—dependent on Luke as well as on John—intensifies the miracle: Jesus "appeared in another form."

13-35. *The Road to Emmaus.*—Once more (cf. especially chs. 1–2), in "a story of singular grace and charm" (Exeg.), its origin in the early tradition now quite beyond recovery, we have reflected for us several interesting and suggestive aspects of the faith that had laid such firm hold of the first Christian community. These two pilgrims, on their journey back home from Jerusalem, traveling in the broad daylight, were moving still in the shadow. Little more than a rumor had come whispering its way out of the night where their belief (vs. 19) and their hope (vs. 21) had come to a dead end (vs. 20). What signs there were on the horizon were still a subject for excited debate and a throwing of words back and forth in vain attempt at explanation (vs. 17, with a hint of gentle humor?). For them, as for "all the rest," "it was yet dark" (vs. 9; John 20:1. See Expos., vs. 22 below); the light had not begun to break over the hills from the east (cf. Matt. 28:1).

When suddenly a stranger **drew near and went with them;** broke into their conversation, in fact—as how often he does—so that **they stood still, looking sad.** We may be sure that they were hardly in the mood—nobody was!—to be taken in by any wanderings of the mind. Visions were not likely to be mistaken for persons. So much at least Luke is very careful to make clear (vss. 38-43). They were, however,

18 And one of them, whose name was Cleopas, answering said unto him, Art thou only a stranger in Jerusalem, and hast not known the things which are come to pass there in these days?

19 And he said unto them, What things? And they said unto him, Concerning Jesus of Nazareth, which was a prophet mighty in deed and word before God and all the people:

20 And how the chief priests and our rulers delivered him to be condemned to death, and have crucified him.

21 But we trusted that it had been he which should have redeemed Israel: and beside all this, to-day is the third day since these things were done.

sad. 18 Then one of them, named Cle'o-pas,
answered him, "Are you the only visitor to
Jerusalem who does not know the things
that have happened there in these days?"
19 And he said to them, "What things?" And
they said to him, "Concerning Jesus of
Nazareth, who was a prophet mighty in
deed and word before God and all the peo-
ple, 20 and how our chief priests and rulers
delivered him up to be condemned to death,
and crucified him. 21 But we had hoped
that he was the one to redeem Israel. Yes,
and besides all this, it is now the third day

---

18. Cleopas: A short form of "Cleopater" and possibly the "Clopas" of John 19:25. His companion was given the name "Simon" as early as the third century, perhaps because of the tradition recorded by Eusebius that "Simeon the son of Clopas" was elected bishop of Jerusalem to succeed the martyred James "the Lord's brother" (*Church History* III. 11. 1). The RSV translation of the question is preferable on grammatical grounds. The disciples are astonished that even a **visitor to Jerusalem** could remain ignorant of **the things that have happened there in these days.**

19-21. The primitive Christology of this passage is similar to that of Peter's speech at Pentecost (Acts 2:22-23). It is the **chief priests and rulers,** not the Romans or the

---

in the mood to be puzzled by such an interruption, and by the stranger's quizzical tone. That they failed to recognize him, "by his moving exposition of the scriptures" (see Exeg. on vs. 32) if by nothing else, seemed, as one looked back, much too extraordinary for anybody to account for it on the mere basis of grief or of "intense preoccupation" with **all . . . that had happened** (see Exeg. on vss. 13-14, 15-17): it seemed itself a miracle, as if their spirits had in love (vs. 19*a*) been held for a moment trembling on the brink of an unbelievable gladness. Until at last, as in sudden lightning, the whole landscape came alive: he made himself known to them in that homely and familiar, yet "solemn" and perpetual self-giving—of which the Eucharist is the active, living symbol (see Expos. on 22:17, 19). What other issue could there be but that recorded so wistfully in vs. 29 (see Lyte's hymn "Abide with me") and so eagerly in vs. 33? The "bare" facts that lie back of Luke's account are beyond our reach. There is no such thing anyhow. At deeper levels the story, in all its parts, is a transcript of human experience: a history of God's gracious dealing with the human soul.

18. ***The Only Stranger.***—"Do you live alone in these parts, by yourself somewhere, so as not to know . . . ?" (Cf. Heb. 11:9.) Surely there was never a life that seemed more lonely or more alien than the life of Jesus. It came with another language (Matt. 5:3 ff.) and moved about our common streets with the imprint on it of other and fairer customs (Mark 9:38-41). Yet whose life is it that is lonely and alien in a world of God, his or ours? And whose customs are strange? It may well be that we shall never find ourselves at home until we learn of him!

21. ***The Failures and Triumphs of Calvary.*** —**We had hoped that he was the one. . . .** Forty-eight hours had passed, and here were two of the friends of Jesus who had not found on Calvary what they were looking for. They are hardly to be blamed. Certainly not as we are. There are not many of us who are fully content with what our lives have got out of that day's transaction on Golgotha. The average result runs all the way from a vague restlessness to what at times is little less than downright discouragement.

Surely it must be said that no one will find anything at all if he has his back toward what happened there. Those who see nothing, how often is it because their most vital energies are all spent in some other direction? They keep talking of what Jesus said about living, and

22 Yea, and certain women also of our company made us astonished, which were early at the sepulchre;

since this happened. 22 Moreover, some women of our company amazed us. They were at the tomb early in the morning

Jewish people, who are blamed for Jesus' condemnation and crucifixion (cf. 21:38; 22:2, 6). **The one to redeem Israel,** i.e., the Messiah. The tragedy of the Cross had robbed the disciples of all hope.

22-24. The story of the empty tomb is not a necessary presupposition of the Emmaus incident, and these verses can be understood as Luke's attempt to integrate the Emmaus story with vss. 1-11. Vs. 24 introduces new matter (see on vs. 11).

never seem to think very long of what he did about living by dying. If God had not laid his love on us tenderly and austerely in that place where Jesus died, none of the rest would have mattered much. Here was the only final "strategy" which the mind of the Eternal could fashion. We may not take Christianity without it, or expect anything to happen unless we keep our faces toward it still.

Nor are we apt to find anything if we go peering around critically and doubtfully at everything we see. So often we are unable to think of anything else in Christ's presence but asking questions; and so often they are the wrong questions! There is a better way of coming at the cross than by sending all our uncertainties before us, as Jacob sent his messengers (Gen. 32:3), in the hope that they may provide a welcome. We can at least whisper a "Yea" and an "Amen" deep down in our souls to a passion like that, and a hope like that, great enough to be God's!

But in no case are we likely to find precisely what we are looking for. Even at a best far better than ours we should still be forever conscious that we had fallen short of what we expected. Jesus Christ is too great for our small hearts. We cannot hold him all. He shows us stars we never saw before; he wakes desires we never may forget[8]—finite souls that we are, trying to answer the call of the infinite deep.

We had hoped that he was the one. To them the Cross spelled failure. It may spell that for us. Or it may spell triumph. In it is power to cleanse every human life that will report itself there. Men have left their witness through the years that this somehow is what happens. On that bit of a mound beyond the walls they have thought of the richest, deepest word they knew, dwelt upon it with gratitude, sung hymns about it, boasted in it, taken to conquering through it: and that word was Savior.

And it called to everything that was in them of which they were not ashamed. Russell Conwell was a captain in the Civil War. One day he was leading his company in sudden retreat across a burning bridge, when he found that he had left his sword behind. A young lad from Vermont dashed through the flames and came back with it; but died a few days later of his burns. Not long after, Russell Conwell himself lay wounded all night on the field of battle; and faced there the best he had ever seen: a lad, all aflame, sword in hand, legs and arms and face blackened by the fire. And a silent vow went up that if he were spared, he would live his own life and the life of that tall young recruit. After the war he became a newspaper correspondent, a lecturer, a lawyer, now this, now that: but the vision would not fade. It seemed to him that in this queer world there was just one way to live two lives. And so he built a great church in Philadelphia, and a great university. Only at the foot of a cross could he live his own life, and the life of Johnny Ring![9]

There, too, is power to knit up a man's sorrows, whatever they are, and to heal his broken spirit. James Thomson addressed God once as

> Creator of all woe and sin! abhorred,
> Malignant and implacable![1]

Such muttering bravado has never come within sight of Calvary. Much has been said to comfort humanity. A good many things have been spun out to inspire it. But there has never been a deed like that deed of God's uttermost care for men; the Love that with wounded feet comes along the rough places with us as though it had now been long familiar with them. And its whispering is like the whisper of one who on a day bowed his head and went home, holding a thief by the hand.

22. ***On Facing God with Life.*—Some women of our company amazed us.** The evangelists try to fix for us the hour of the Resurrection (John 20:1; Matt. 28:1); and they succeed only in fixing that bewildered mood of the soul as it confronts this fact of the risen Lord. For one

[8] See Sidney Lysaght, "The Penalty of Love."

[9] See Albert Hatcher Smith, *The Life of Russell H. Conwell* (Boston: Silver, Burdett & Co., 1899), esp. pp. 71-75.

[1] *The City of Dreadful Night,* Part VIII.

23 And when they found not his body, they came, saying, that they had also seen a vision of angels, which said that he was alive.

24 And certain of them which were with us went to the sepulchre, and found *it* even so as the women had said: but him they saw not.

25 Then he said unto them, O fools, and slow of heart to believe all that the prophets have spoken:

26 Ought not Christ to have suffered these things, and to enter into his glory?

23 and did not find his body; and they came back saying that they had even seen a vision of angels, who said that he was alive.
24 Some of those who were with us went to the tomb, and found it just as the women had said; but him they did not see." 25 And
he said to them, "O foolish men, and slow of heart to believe all that the prophets have spoken! 26 Was it not necessary that
the Christ should suffer these things and

25-26. The Passion and Resurrection were in accordance with O.T. prophecy (cf. 18:31). "The words in vs. 26 almost sound as if Jesus had already entered into his glory. Does this narrative presuppose the same point of view as the saying to the repentant thief (23:43), that Jesus was exalted to heaven at the moment of his death? The supernatural appearance and disappearance of the Lord (vss. 16, 31) support this interpretation and they are not easily understood in terms of the physical resurrection that

---

split second of indecision, between things as they were before and things as they were after, these wayfaring folk, like the disciples, hardly knew whether to say that night was on the way out, or to say that morning was on the way in. More than an empty tomb (note both the fact and the skepticism in vss. 23-24), a living Presence stood at last between the two, as all the thick shadows fled together before a light which suddenly blazed around the world. They had been facing God with things and situations and circumstances; and when one added all that up, it was just living. Now they were facing God with distant dreams, deep stirrings of soul, a new yet somehow native grandeur; and when one added that up, it was life! Duration is nothing much to be excited about, or to boast of; particularly if it means that we are going on forever as we are. Such a prospect might conceivably be quite dreadful. But if living is other even now than we have thought it—not mean, nor shallow, with all the world laughing last and much the best—but great and lofty and deep; then let life let go, for Life is born!

The day returns and brings us the petty round of irritating concerns and duties. Help us to play the man, help us to perform them with laughter and kind faces, let cheerfulness abound with industry. Give us to go blithely on our business all this day, bring us to our resting beds weary and content and undishonoured, and grant us in the end the gift of sleep.[2]

[2] Robert Louis Stevenson, "Morning Prayer," from *Prayers Written at Vailima.* Used by permission of the Robert Louis Stevenson Estate, The Society of Authors, and Charles Scribner's Sons, publishers.

25. ***Slow of Heart to Believe.***—Could it be that their diagnosis was wrong? The disease was not a disease of the eyes or of the ears; it was a disease of the heart. They had had the witness of the past; in their own experience they had seen the truth and power and beauty, in word and deed, of the life that had come out of Nazareth (vs. 19): what else now but hearts that tarried elsewhere, half in shadow, half in light, dried out with trouble, with one touch and only one that could bring them at last to "burn" (vs. 32)?

26. ***Is This the Way?*****—Was it not necessary that the Christ should suffer these things and enter into his glory?** There must have been many times when Christian men and women in the first Christian centuries were not at all sure about Christianity. Some enthusiastic folk had begun to call it "The Way." But was it? They needed nobody to show them that it was not getting along very well in the world. So the apostles—remembering, it may well be, more than one word of their Lord (4:21; Mark 14:21)—undertook to make clear its relation to the long and stately history of the people of God (cf. Rom. 15:8-13; Gal. 4:28; etc.). It was part of an eternal plan, Passion and Resurrection alike. It was not something added to life, introduced from the outside as a sort of desperate remedy when things had got out of hand. It was something woven tightly into the fabric since the world began, by the Mind that had done all the weaving.

For one reason or another, some of them pretending to be scientific, men continue to look askance at the Christian faith, call it a liability,

27 And beginning at Moses and all the prophets, he expounded unto them in all the Scriptures the things concerning himself.

enter into his glory?" 27 And beginning with Moses and all the prophets, he interpreted to them in all the scriptures the things concerning himself.

---

is so strongly emphasized in vss. 39 ff." (Johannes Weiss, *Die Schriften des Neuen Testaments* [2d ed.; Göttingen: Vandenhoeck & Ruprecht, 1907], I, 524).

27. The Greek construction is awkward. Read: "From all the prophets, beginning with Moses. . . ." The risen Christ anticipates the O.T. apologetic of the early church.

---

say it is an opiate, expect less than nothing of it, cast about for something else. What if back of the nations they have built, with the ceaseless tramp of armies; back of the governments they have set up, and endowed with so much power over their own souls; back of the culture they are forever bent on defending, and the frightened order to which they grow so accustomed that they can hardly imagine any other: what if back of it all, and older than any of it, there were a purpose in the mind of God that nothing can change or replace, toward which "the whole creation groaneth and travaileth in pain together until now" (Rom. 8:22)? It was old, as time was old, when the foundations of the earth were young. It began to take shape when God resolutely set out to do the most magnificent thing even he could think of doing. He set out to fashion a life with the vistas of his own hidden in it. On and on he wrought, to give it grandeur, and to give it freedom too. And it used its freedom to wrench itself away from him. He told it by seer and martyr and book how to get up and get out in a world like this, and it spread its legs apart and stood against him. Until in this strange man of Galilee he showed it; looked steadily in its eyes and died for it: weaving the pattern whole there in eternity, with a smile shining through his tears; because he was happy with his dream. And nobody has been able since to fashion a better! **Was it not necessary that the Christ should suffer . . . ?**

With our lives heir now to a promise—and to a Presence!—whoever said that the going would not be hard? Christ said it would; that there was something about this world that could never stand Christianity. Does not Barth say somewhere that we are "like a sick man taking medicine, or a well man taking poison? We struggle with the draught to absorb it or to get rid of it forever." It is clear enough that the end is forever threatening either the world or the reality Christ came to be. Maybe a man's heart has to be where his heart was—on Calvary (John 6:15). It is said that Drake's men used to sit on the shores of Devon telling not so much of fabled lands beyond the sea as of wild hurricanes and stinging spray, the tiny ship nosing down into the huge trough of the waves, then shuddering up with the water spouting from her scuppers, shaking her bow clear and rolling on to take the next fearful dive! There is something in God like that: something willing to hazard the last precious thing it has if only it can recover the life that is lost. And in us?

When we throw in our lives with it—instead of passing it in critical review, doing what we like about it, as if somebody had made it up last week or last year, God knows why!—when we throw in our lives with it, his purpose for the world, as well as for our own souls, comes one step nearer fulfillment. Back in the days of a king whose name was Antiochus Epiphanes, when God's faithful people were being subjected to every conceivable torture in the effort to make them forswear their faith, an old, old man wrote a poem. It is Ps. 37 now—a psalm about the meek and their inheritance, which Jesus quoted one day in his sermon to a rustic crowd that had gathered on the side of a hill. Its verses keep gazing confidently at the dark, without ever expecting God to leap in and strike down the wicked. The poet, with his wealth of years, just believes that wickedness has no stability. It will fall of its own sterile, sordid weight. It makes him think of the trackless wandering of gypsies. While the upright, like peasants on some farm, shall hold their ancestral soil of the earth forever! Some of the words live again in memory as part of a contralto solo from Mendelssohn's *Elijah*. Sung in wartime, to the thunder of guns and the angry drone of planes, a thousand stinging wasps in the sky, they seem like ghastly nonsense—or the whisper of a stricken God, still stumbling toward a cross, not to lose, but to win! "O rest in the Lord; wait patiently for him."

27. *The Strange Life of God.*—He interpreted to them in all the scriptures the things concerning himself (see Exeg. on vs. 44). In the most primitive Christian tradition the Cross was undoubtedly an offense, transformed only by the Resurrection. The Messiah that was rejected had reversed the "normal" procedure of

28 And they drew nigh unto the village, whither they went: and he made as though he would have gone further.

28 So they drew near to the village to which they were going. He appeared

28-29. Stay with us: The narrative gives no reason for the disciples' journey to Emmaus, but it is a reasonable inference from these words that Luke thought of them as residents of that village who were returning to their home.

the Messiah that was expected, and had sounded another note in the world, a weird sort of note that had been there all along, but nobody had wanted to hear it.

When life sets its stubborn front against God, there are two courses of action which he never takes, and we almost always do. He never asserts himself, thrusting his will forward into the center, brushing everything else aside; never crowds up against anything or anybody; is immeasurably silent in every company, keeping out of sight, forever reluctant to bring any pressure to bear. Why is all around us here

> As if some lesser God had made the world
> But had not force to shape it as he would? [3]

He could have given any one of us a start from here to the *nova* in Hercules and outstripped us in no time at all. When Adam fell, he could have canceled Adam. And when Abraham lied, and Jacob stole, and David committed adultery. But he knew that "getting things done" that way is nothing but a futile expedient when you can't think of anything else, an idiotic stopgap that never touches the bottom of any difficulty. So, in a way of speaking, he tied his hands behind his back and came himself. He said to us, "Very well, if you will not listen, I shall not make you. I shall not use my power but put myself in yours. I shall stand in front of all your little Pilates, as helpless as can be, as poor and as friendless. And we shall see."

Nor does God ever take the short cut. He never seems to think as we do that what fails to get done now will not get done. He will not wipe out at a single stroke all the gains with all the losses of a century or two. To go about life in any such fashion—in Protestantism scrapping all our differences for the sake of uniformity, in politics shattering to bits "this Sorry Scheme of Things entire," [4] on the theory that we have only to upset what we cannot bring ourselves to like—is shallow and thoughtless and silly. We get godless tyranny out of it; we get out of it the loss of the very good we covet. In the concluding section of his epistle to the Romans, Paul instructs the members of the Christian community as to how they should bear themselves toward each other, toward the state, and toward those who are "weak in faith," putting his finger at last on the secret of it all. He had caught it from the ages past, and from Christ himself: "That we through patience and comfort of the scriptures might have hope" (Rom. 15:4 KJV). The RSV understands better the Greek. "Patience" is sticking by it, like a wrestler, even when you are down. "Comfort" is the gallantry that comes of calling Another to your side in the battle (*paraklēseōs,* paraclete). And "hope" has little to do with the synonyms given for the word in Roget's *Thesaurus:* "mirage," "fool's paradise," "castles in Spain"; the withered flowers of acre on acre of groundless, wishful, human thinking. "Hope" in the N.T. has roots. It has its roots in God (Rom. 8:24-25; 9:33; Eph. 2:12).

But note now that there are two very definite courses of action which God does take, and what little appeal on the whole they seem to have for us. He is not all self-restraint and patience. He is not just trying to "contain" the evil, hem it in, keep it within bounds. He is not merely defending himself against it, resisting its encroachments, keeping his flag flying in its face. He is creating something (see Expos. on 19:15; 21:34). Even as he waits he fashions (Mark 7:24-30). And all the joy of human life is but the shadow of the Craftsman's joy (cf. Col. 1:11). Then the hour comes, and he throws himself in. There is the supreme and final meaning of the Cross, and of this strange life that showed itself one day among men. And we have no stomach for climbing that high when the world gets to its feet flat against us. It is compassion that life needs, not censure. And compassion that costs, and thinks nothing of the scars. Not sentiment. No distant amity. A passion that trudges its way up a steep hill and gets itself face to face with the worst that can be done to it. What is there in that for us? Is there anything at all in anything else? Contrast the story which Electra tells in the first lines of Euripides' *Orestes.*

28. ***Love's Strategy?*—He appeared to be going further.** Because there were other lonely, despairing folk? It may be that for us the only way to keep him is to go with him!

[3] Tennyson, "The Passing of Arthur," *Idylls of the King.*

[4] *Rubáiyát of Omar Khayyám,* st. xcix.

29 But they constrained him, saying, Abide with us; for it is toward evening, and the day is far spent. And he went in to tarry with them.

30 And it came to pass, as he sat at meat with them, he took bread, and blessed *it,* and brake, and gave to them.

31 And their eyes were opened, and they knew him; and he vanished out of their sight.

32 And they said one to another, Did not our heart burn within us, while he talked with us by the way, and while he opened to us the Scriptures?

33 And they rose up the same hour, and returned to Jerusalem, and found the eleven gathered together, and them that were with them,

34 Saying, The Lord is risen indeed, and hath appeared to Simon.

to be going further, 29 but they con-
strained him, saying, "Stay with us, for it
is toward evening and the day is now far
spent." So he went in to stay with them.
30 When he was at table with them, he took
the bread and blessed, and broke it, and
gave it to them. 31 And their eyes were
opened and they recognized him; and he
vanished out of their sight. 32 They said
to each other, "Did not our hearts burn
within us while he talked to us on the road,
while he opened to us the scriptures?"
33 And they rose that same hour and re-
turned to Jerusalem; and they found the
eleven gathered together and those who
were with them, 34 who said, "The Lord has
risen indeed, and has appeared to Simon!"

---

30. As in 9:16 (see Exeg., *ad loc.*), the actions described were those employed by the celebrant of the Lord's Supper in the ritual of the early church. The language is too solemn to be easily understood as referring to an ordinary meal (cf. also Acts 2:42, 46). Despite the absence of wine, and despite the tradition in 22:14-23 (Mark 14:17-25) that only the twelve were with Jesus at the Last Supper, it is possible that both Luke and his source thought of the risen Christ as the host to the disciples at a Eucharist.

31. The miraculous inhibition that had prevented the disciples from recognizing their traveling companion (vs. 16) was now removed, but **he vanished out of their sight** as soon as they knew him to be the risen Christ.

32. Did not our hearts burn within us: For the metaphor cf. Ps. 39:3; Jer. 20:9. It was clear to the disciples on reflection that they ought to have recognized Christ by his moving exposition of **the scriptures.**

33-34. Despite the lateness of the hour, the disciples hurried back to Jerusalem to share their good news with the larger company, only to discover that **Simon** had anticipated their message with an account of his own vision of the risen **Lord.** A most interest-

---

Or is it that when he seems to be on the point of withdrawing, his business always somewhere farther along, farther along in truth than we have got, farther along in life than we have come, he wishes to be invited in? Not by "readying" the house for his coming: wherever he enters "he takes things as he finds them"; but takes them into his own creative hands (see Expos. on 19:3-4, and the paragraphs on 19:5). Rather by the "constraint" of deep desire, and the hospitality of a life that knows itself as guest, not host, in its own home. It is then that he makes himself known (see Expos. on vss. 13-35).

34. ***The Lord Has Risen Indeed.***—Archimedes said that if he had somewhere to stand he could with a lever lift the world. The Resurrection is not simply a fact for historians: it is a fact for people who want somewhere to stand, who want to keep on their feet when everything else seems bent on going to pieces. There are still those who tangle themselves up on the lower levels with half a dozen questions about it, wondering if it was really so. They would better face as honestly as they can the living miracle of Christ. They would better face the miracle of the Christian church through the years, and how on earth it got started and kept going in spite of a good many Christians. They would better face the prospect of life without a faith like this, and ask themselves what the chances would be of its falling away into something less than human—as indeed at times it has done, with creatures that cannot be said to

ing contact with the resurrection tradition recorded in I Cor. 15:5*a* (see on 24:1-12). Luke thinks of Simon's experience as having taken place after the departure of Cleopas and his companion from Jerusalem. Some interpreters needlessly complicate the exegesis

count ultimately, and a God who cannot be said to care ultimately, and no plans for anybody that will not be broken ultimately.

Gerald Heard[5] recounts one of the romances of astronomy. About the beginning of the nineteenth century, the Dog Star, Sirius, the brightest star in the heavens, was suspected of not behaving according to the book. Its movements were a little too irregular to pass muster. One brave soul guessed at the near presence of another body, but no one could find anything with the telescopes they had then. Years later the skies gave up their secret: a "white dwarf," bigger than a blazing sun, more wonderful than Sirius, an incredible gas so dense that a cubic inch or two would weigh a ton; and other gigantic bodies too, prodigious black objects in space, pulling away on all of us, so massive that not even light can get away from them and time itself is slowed down! They had to be there, or you could never make heads or tails of the universe. They were God's "vindication" of his order!

What happened in Palestine that first Easter dawn was God's seal on everything that went on from Bethlehem to Calvary: and the mark of a blue pencil drawn through everything else that goes on which is out of line with it. God was editing his story, all scribbled over as it had been, and with his own hand! The Christian gospel never does come to a mouthful of dust. After World War I, clever people chuckled at the way Clemenceau and Lloyd George made a fool out of President Wilson at Versailles. That was not the trouble with Versailles. The trouble at Versailles was the same trouble men had at Calvary. They tried to make a fool out of God! The movement of life is toward the gospel, not away from it, even when humanity turns its back. The saving purpose of God is over all the chaos we fashion for ourselves. Says Nels Ferré, History and Nature are God's means of creating fellowship whereby he indirectly conditions and controls the destiny of man without directly determining it.[6] The pageant is headed in his direction, and we pull it off side at our peril. Perhaps we need a new definition of realism.

The question arises at once, What is to be the relation between this moving panorama of the world we know and that huge, unchanging perspective of the world beyond our own, and infinitely more real? We can wander absentmindedly down that endless vista, telling our beads, and singing vacuously with Browning:

> Leave Now for dogs and apes!
> Man has Forever.[7]

That is one way to forget the harsh realities of the present. Or we can surrender so completely to the stirring and vicious intensity of each day's transient concerns that the future turns shadowy and impotent. In one case, with our eyes on heaven, we stub our toe. In the other, we lose the stars, and we lose our way, and we lose our soul! As a clerk behind the counter answered a prospective customer, "We have compasses for drawing circles, madam, but none for going places." The problem is fundamentally a problem of adjustment; but the adjustment has to be in the right direction. The lemmings, during their migratory period, rush down by the hundreds of thousands into the sea, struggling to follow an old land trail long since submerged! Someone has remarked that "our civilization, which stemmed in Greek philosophy, and towered high in medieval cathedrals, has at last flowered in department stores. The ends of life here become the goods of the body. Existence has been turned into a continuous bank-run, and the bank is now closing!" Bereft of Forever, living becomes an impossible experience that winds up in catastrophe. There is an adjustment the other way around: endow life with Forever, and failure itself is whipped about into victory. When the "Statendam" was bombed at her dock in Holland, during World War II, her captain was in New York. His wife and son lived in Rotterdam, which was in ruins, and no word had come from them. Talking after service one Sunday to a minister, he lapsed into a soliloquy, and then into prayer: "God help me," he said, "not to hate. Give your guidance to those who rule. Your kingdom come." The words seemed to struggle out slowly. "Watch over my wife and boy. Before they were mine they belonged to you. They are in your hands. Your will be done." Then more slowly still, as if each sentence were being pulled out of his heart by the roots: "I pray for Hitler. He has great power over the lives of men. Guide him. Help me not to hate him. And help me to mean that, O God. Amen." In it is something of the grandeur

[5] *The Code of Christ* (New York: Harper & Bros., 1941), p. 153.

[6] Cf. *The Christian Faith* (New York: Harper & Bros., 1942), ch. iii.

[7] "A Grammarian's Funeral."

35 And they told what things *were done* in the way, and how he was known of them in breaking of bread.

35 Then they told what had happened on the road, and how he was known to them in the breaking of the bread.

of vs. 34 by accepting the reading in Codex Bezae that makes the Emmaus disciples the subject of **saying** (KJV).

35. Then they told: Namely, "on their part."

which comes of shutting heaven up within the frontiers of a human soul.

The Lord has risen indeed. Relevant? We are not being particularly religious when we occupy ourselves with something that took place a long time ago. There is a critical and immediate necessity. We are like people asleep in the snow. To stay on in that state is to be doomed; to wake up is to feel the agony of coming alive again.

35. ***They Related Their Own Experience.***—So Moffatt translates the words **they told what had happened.** Entirely apart from what it was (in this case) that **had happened,** the secret of the whole Bible, from cover to cover, is wrapped up in those five words. Moses and Elijah, Isaiah and Jeremiah, none of these men were engaged in speculation, trying to set up some workable philosophy of life: they had been in the places where we have been and found every one tenanted! Read I Peter. Here is no theory of history, with a chapter entitled "The Cause and Prevention of Persecutions." Here is the road he had traveled, and hopes he had climbed, and chasms he had fallen in. It is filled with all the pathos of his plunging, stumbling course: the bitter knowledge he had won that night when his soul had slithered and cursed its way into a bottomless pit with the eyes of Jesus on it; until up out of the tears and darkness his feet had found the solid earth again, and his face with the lines on it was the face of a man who knew. He is writing on the quick parchment of his own flesh.

And there is the prime weakness of much so-called Christianity. Not that it breaks down under any intellectual demand made on it, but that it becomes so readily a twice-told tale, instead of a vital experience that can be shared by men in the street. We try to make our approach to it as if it were a system of truth that could be learned and adopted and put into practice. We spend our time asking nice questions about right and wrong, often enough the childish exercise of orphans! The pivot and center of it is what we ourselves may know of God in Christ, and there is no substitute. Not long ago a letter went the rounds: "Dear Sir, We, a band of students gathered for research upon the subject of the human soul and all its implications, address you, among the authorities. Will you give us a clear and concise definition, other than 'spirit,' of what is meant by 'soul'? We shall appreciate any light you may be able to throw on the matter. Sincerely yours. . . ." It was like going into a restaurant and asking for a definition of hunger. What those students had was a soul pain; only an experience could cure it.

The terms of that experience are not far to seek. Somewhere there is a weight of need. If you call it "sin," moralists and philosophers will demand to know what you mean, and argue with you the whole week end. Say "need," and dodge the controversy. Sin they may dismiss as an ecclesiastical fiction; the sense of guilt and utter inability are just sad facts—like lost coins, and lost sheep, and lost sons, with elder brothers who stay at home and complain. Ignore them if you like; no poet, dramatist, novelist, psychologist, can ever afford to. It is the way we take out of it that determines whether or not we are Christians. The writers of the N.T. say there is a loving, forgiving God in the world, and that they have met him in the eyes and will and bearing of a Nazarene. Whatever our word may be for what happens there, they call it freedom, and release, and power. We never have to speculate about that. We leave the dictionary at home and come up against it. It has something to do with a creed, it has something to do with a church, and men wrote of it in a book; at bottom it is a deep and inward reality. Somebody has said that when God wanted to define "oakness" he made a tree.

Nothing is left, then, save the process of growth. And that takes time. A man with no religion to speak of, or so he said, lost his wife. Every day for a month he prayed, and it seemed to him that perhaps there might be something in God and immortality after all. But gradually the feeling wore off. And gradually he quit praying. It hardly felt right any more, or sensible, or worth while. Before another month had passed he had become quite sure again that Christianity had nothing for him. With forty years on one side of the balance and two leaves from the calendar on the other, nothing very decisive happened somehow.

36 ¶ And as they thus spake, Jesus himself stood in the midst of them, and saith unto them, Peace *be* unto you.
37 But they were terrified and affrighted, and supposed that they had seen a spirit.
38 And he said unto them, Why are ye troubled? and why do thoughts arise in your hearts?

36 As they were saying this, Jesus himself
stood among them.[d] 37 But they were star-
tled and frightened, and supposed that
they saw a spirit. 38 And he said to them,
"Why are you troubled, and why do ques-

[d] Other ancient authorities add *and said to them, "Peace to you!"*

B. Appearance of the Risen Christ in Jerusalem (24:36-43)

To the Emmaus story, which belongs to the tradition that the risen Christ appeared to his followers in a spiritual, noncorporeal form, Luke appends an account that presupposes a physical resurrection and an appearance in the material body that had been buried in the sepulcher. Its original purpose may have been polemical—to allay any suspicion that the disciples had been victims of an apparition or hallucination in their resurrection faith. The striking similarity between this story and those in John 20:19-29 convinces many interpreters that the Fourth Evangelist had Luke's Gospel among his sources.

36-37. As they were saying this: While Cleopas and his companion were still speaking of their recent experience. In this way Luke links material from two different sources. **And saith unto them, Peace be unto you:** One of seven significant passages in this chapter that are omitted by Codex Bezae; almost certainly an interpolation in other MSS from John 20:19*b*. For **a spirit** Codex Bezae and Marcion read "a ghost," and no doubt this is a correct interpretation of Luke's meaning.

38-39. Christ offers visible and tangible proofs of the corporeal reality of his resurrection. An anti-Docetic motive that is manifest in the Johannine story may also

---

36-49. *When Jesus Came Back.*—**Jesus himself stood among them.** These men, who had been picked by hand to upset the world, were huddled together for fear behind locked doors. They had shut themselves up with a memory, stuck their thumbs in their ears to deaden the ugly sound of the present, and put their fingers over their eyes to keep from looking in the face of any such ghastly future as they saw whenever they took their fingers away. It is a story that has been put out in many a new edition: people in every generation climbing the rickety stairs into as much religion as they have left, just under the roof; exchanging there fond recollections, rehearsing an ancient faith that brings them precious little peace and hardly any power to speak of.

The significant thing about it, wherever we lay the scene, is that Jesus comes back. Since the Friday when they buried him they had been worse off than they had been before they started, having seen what they had seen and dreamed what they had dreamed. Nothing made sense any more; and for forty-eight hours they had been staring at it, or mumbling about it in their sleep. When there **stood one among them,** and a voice spoke! If the burden of it was anything like the burden it had borne in the days that were gone, there was in it the gift of peace, "that peace," as the collect has it, which "the world cannot give." The author of Ecclesiastes swung off after it down every road he saw, and has left us the record of his search. He looked for it in pleasure, and began to hate life. He looked for it in labor, and began to envy the dead. He looked for it in wealth, and it escaped like the wind. He looked for it in wisdom, but never a handful of quietness: only travail and vexation of spirit. Was that yesterday's experience, or is it a transcript of tomorrow's? Everywhere the bewildering turmoil of disordered minds, with a thousand and one prescriptions bandied about by bankers and politicians, authors and orators: in this at least, if in nothing else, a generation weirdly like that which stood outside Lot's house in Sodom, stricken with blindness, wearying itself to find the door (Gen. 19:11).

But the gift of peace comes, not by seeking; it comes when a purpose that has slipped out of life gets back in (vss. 45, 47-48). They were restless and uneasy, not just because they thought they were seeing a ghost (vs. 37). Luke seems to be particularly interested in providing a kind of apologetic at that point. They were restless and uneasy because with Christ gone the pattern of things was gone (vs. 44). They had had a job on their hands once, to change the

39 Behold my hands and my feet, that
it is I myself: handle me, and see; for a
spirit hath not flesh and bones, as ye see
me have.

40 And when he had thus spoken, he
showed them *his* hands and *his* feet.

41 And while they yet believed not for
joy, and wondered, he said unto them,
Have ye here any meat?

tionings rise in your hearts? **39** See my
hands and my feet, that it is I myself; han-
dle me, and see; for a spirit has not flesh
and bones as you see that I have."[e] **41** And
while they still disbelieved for joy, and
wondered, he said to them, "Have you

[e] Other ancient authorities add verse 40, *And when he had said this, he showed them his hands and his feet.*

---

have played a role in the phrasing of this one. Note Ign. Smyrn. 3:2 (*ca.* A.D. 116): "And when he came to those with Peter he said to them: 'Take me, handle me, and see that I am not a bodiless demon.' And immediately they touched him and believed."

40. Omitted by Codex Bezae and its allies; undoubtedly in other MSS an interpolation based on John 20:20.

41-43. Christ's act of eating in the presence of his disciples is a final demonstration of his corporeity. The mention of **a piece of broiled fish** leads some interpreters to suspect

---

face of the world in the company of that Galilean. It had been a great deal bigger than they could manage, but somehow it had made them happy. With that torn, mocked body there in the tomb, what could they do? What could anybody do? They were like a child on a long day indoors, not caring for his toys, the only game he wants to play quite out of the question because there is nobody to play with, standing by the window, pressing his nose against the glass, peering out on a dismal landscape. It might be worth something, against any one or all of our anxieties together, if instead of envying these apostles the mission that sent them singing through life, we actually adopted it. A woman who faced death with that in her heart spent her last months ministering to her husband with an unearthly courage that was a miracle to see. A man stared his own ruin out of countenance and kept praying for the friend who had betrayed him. A mother whose only daughter was an invalid, herself a widow, was beaten about for years by the good she tried to do for others who took advantage of her. And not one of them living for even a day in the deflated mood of people who go about trying to endure the wrong; all of them wagering their lives a dozen ways against the dark. They were not here to suffer something. They were here to win something, with a love that took life captive!

A love that never is alone or unendowed with its **power from on high.** We have our limitations, we say; they are the first troops we send into battle, and the first line of defense when we have to fall back. But our limitations are not God's. He has us on his hands. It is not the other way around! And he has made his kind of difference in and with the lives of men too long for him to be helpless when it comes to ours. A man gathered a crowd around him one evening on Mile End Waste, near Whitechapel, London, speaking and brandishing his umbrella about. Catcalls drowned out his voice, but he spoke on. Mud, garbage, stones, flew through the air. The next night he was back, only to be routed again. And the next. Fifty years later he could tell an audience which filled the vast Albert Hall that even as he stood there talking to them two hundred thousand homeless men slept under the roofs of the Salvation Army. Only the funeral of Queen Victoria herself drew a throng larger than that which shortly afterward saw William Booth borne away to rest beside his wife.[8]

41. ***Too Good to Be True.*—They . . . disbelieved for joy.** It was too good to be true. So with us does disillusion beget cynicism, and cynicism begets a proverb. Too good *not* to be true fits God's world better! It was not easy to believe in Jesus. We cannot even imagine any more what the odds were against him. We chant sentimental ditties about wishing we could have been with him then, and talk sometimes about the incredible dullness of the disciples—with the sly implication that our Lord would have been much better off if he had had us instead. But it was not easy. The Sanhedrin, which was the board of trustees and the executive committee and the court of appeals of the Church of God in Palestine, all rolled into one, would have nothing to do with him. Most of the respectable people, all the self-acclaimed patriots, despised him. And they had made him eat his words. He had died out there on that hill, just as any man would have died. These were the facts. And one had to hold with the facts. Unless they should happen to collide

[8] See Vachel Lindsay's poem "General William Booth Enters into Heaven."

42 And they gave him a piece of a broiled fish, and of a honeycomb.
43 And he took *it*, and did eat before them.
44 And he said unto them, These *are* the words which I spake unto you, while I was yet with you, that all things must be fulfilled, which were written in the law of Moses, and *in* the prophets, and *in* the psalms, concerning me.
45 Then opened he their understanding, that they might understand the Scriptures,
46 And said unto them, Thus it is written, and thus it behooved Christ to suffer, and to rise from the dead the third day:

anything here to eat?" 42 They gave him a
piece of broiled fish, 43 and he took it and
ate before them.
44 Then he said to them, "These are my words which I spoke to you, while I was still with you, that everything written about me in the law of Moses and the prophets and the psalms must be fulfilled."
45 Then he opened their minds to understand the scriptures,
46 and said to them, "Thus it is written, that the Christ should suffer and on the third day rise from the

---

that the incident was originally located by the Sea of Galilee (as in John 21:9 ff.). **And of a honeycomb** (KJV): An addition to the text, found only in inferior MSS, and possibly intended to symbolize the Christian practice in the early third century of giving honey (and milk) to the newly baptized converts.

C. Christ's Final Message to His Disciples (24:44-49)

The risen Christ declares that the apostolic message and world mission had been foretold in Scripture and promises that his disciples will be **clothed with power from on high** for their task. The passage anticipates the narrative of the Acts volume, and no literary source need be postulated.

44. These are my words: "These events (my death and resurrection) explain the words" (Creed). **Which I spoke to you, while I was still with you:** Cf. 18:31-33; 22:37. This is the only verse in the N.T. where a book out of the third division of the Jewish canon of Scripture—the Writings—is mentioned together with **the law of Moses and the prophets.** No doubt Luke referred specifically to **the psalms** because of their importance to the early church as a repository of messianic proof texts (especially Pss. 22; 69 for the Passion, and Pss. 2; 16; 110 for the Resurrection).

45. One of Luke's minor interests in the composition of his Gospel was to assert that Christ had originated the O.T. apologetic of the early church (cf. vss. 25-27). During Jesus' lifetime his disciples had not understood his references to the fulfillment of prophecy (18:34), but the risen Lord **opened their minds.**

46-47a. Scripture had foretold what had already happened (vs. 46), and what was still to come (vs. 47*a*). For another reference by Luke to the prophetic anticipation of

---

with a God who pays very little attention to any of them! What are the facts, anyhow, the real facts, with which life has to deal? Caiaphas, and Pilate, and Herod, and that Good Friday crowd? Or the Author of all things, who every time you try to alter the original text writes across the page "stet"—let it stand!

It was not easy to believe that the evil of life could ever be dislodged by the good. We shall always have poverty and graft and dirty politics and war. "Since the fathers fell asleep, all things continue as they were from the beginning of the creation" (II Pet. 3:4). Why keep fooling ourselves with pretty pictures? Nor was it easy for the disciples to believe that anything would ever be very much different as far as they themselves were concerned. No doubt it would be quite as it had always been: the same resounding failures, the same meager victories.

But life is not the cut and dried affair some people seem to think it, with everybody yawning on the front porch, or sitting around the fire in the post office, talking about how inexpressibly dull things are! And Christmas comes out of a stable, the Son of God out of a noisome little village, and twenty centuries of Christianity out of a grave! When they saw him again, they rubbed their eyes; then they stood up to be counted, and smacked into it! From what we have seen in him, God give us no rest!

47 And that repentance and remission of sins should be preached in his name among all nations, beginning at Jerusalem.
48 And ye are witnesses of these things.
49 ¶ And, behold, I send the promise of my Father upon you: but tarry ye in the city of Jerusalem, until ye be endued with power from on high.

dead, 47 and that repentance and forgive-
ness of sins should be preached in his name
to all nations,[f] beginning from Jerusalem.
48 You are witnesses of these things. 49 And
behold, I send the promise of my Father
upon you; but stay in the city, until you
are clothed with power from on high."

[f] Or *nations. Beginning from Jerusalem you are witnesses.*

---

the church's message of **forgiveness of sins** in Christ's **name** see Acts 10:43. **To all nations:** Matthew (28:19) ascribes the missionary commission of the church more directly to the risen Christ.

47*b*-48. Read: **Beginning from Jerusalem you are witnesses** with the RSV mg. Luke has in mind the story of the expansion of Christianity that he is to relate in the second volume. Acts 5:29-32 can be read as a commentary on vss. 46-49.

49. Paralleled in John 20:22 by Jesus' **gift** of the Spirit. **The promise of my Father:** The outpouring of the Spirit predicted in Joel 2:28 ff. Luke narrates the story of the

---

47. ***The Good News that Changed the World.***—**Repentance and forgiveness of sins . . . in his name to all nations.** Much that is not the gospel tries to wear its label. No statement of its content, no fixing of its center, no sweep of line to set its vast circumference could be clearer or steadier or swifter than this. Here is its sober undertaking: to deal creatively with the deepest problem of our common existence. Here lies the secret of its uniqueness: in the presence that confronts and the power that undergirds the human soul. Here, growing on the Christian conscience, constitutive, compulsive, dawns the conviction of its universality (cf. Gal. 2; Acts 15). Its nature plus its source equals its reach.

47*b*-48. ***Call the Next Witness.***—**Beginning from Jerusalem. . . .** Not from some distant scene; from this. From the place where the last flicker of hope had gone out. From the place where they had failed him and fled. **You are witnesses of these things.** The word, of course, is our word "martyrs." To tell the story. To tell it not as hearsay, but as of their own knowledge (I John 1:1). And to tell it at cost. There was no other plan. No other has yet been found, in a world grown big with plans. Nor will be (see Expos. on vs. 35).

Not dressing up the liturgy, though that may be advisable; not making pronouncements or holding committee meetings on interracial problems, though all of this is more than necessary: but the ceaseless impact on other lives of a life that has been caught and held by "the light of the knowledge of the glory of God in the face of Jesus Christ" (II Cor. 4:6). If Christianity holds the key to the future, the lock cannot be picked with a hairpin. Programs and minutes and resolutions and round tables are the readily available paraphernalia with which too many good causes, when the vitality is gone out of them, talk themselves to death! History turned once on a tax collector, four fishermen, and a tentmaker. There was no game of Button, Button, Who Has the Button? Nor any question in anybody's mind as to who was elected. "You" is a thoroughly inescapable pronoun, especially in the singular.

Still there is always some devout or earnest person to chant, "Deeds, not words! Quit talking about it, and live the right kind of life!" It is somewhat difficult to believe that the way we behave day in and day out can be so utterly startling and radiant that everybody we run into must perforce be mesmerized by it into crossing himself and muttering the Creed. They must have deeds to match, but it is *words* that burn their way into human life and leave the only indelible marks it wears. God never has discounted them. He stood them up like miracles in Galilee, with a cross beside them, to flout the centuries.

And in the midst of them the lonely soul of a man. Then another and another. He seemed to stake very little on organization. He was not impressed with the wisdom of linking zero to zero to zero, president, secretary, treasurer, and inviting a handful of other zeros to rally around at a luncheon. Somebody would have to do something. He himself would add it up and multiply it. The arithmetic was his business. A man with a word and a deed to match: that was all he asked!

49. ***The Promise of the Father.***—In Judg. 6:34 it is written, "But the Spirit of the Lord came upon [lit., "clothed itself with"] Gideon, and he blew a trumpet." (So also I Chr. 12:18; II Chr. 24:20; in Judg. 14:6; 15:14, "came

50 ¶ And he led them out as far as to Bethany, and he lifted up his hands, and blessed them.

51 And it came to pass, while he blessed them, he was parted from them, and carried up into heaven.

52 And they worshipped him, and returned to Jerusalem with great joy:

53 And were continually in the temple, praising and blessing God. Amen.

50 Then he led them out as far as Bethany, and lifting up his hands he blessed
them. 51 While he blessed them, he parted
from them.[g] 52 And they[h] returned to Jerusalem with great joy, 53 and were continually in the temple blessing God.

[g] Other ancient authorities add *and was carried up into heaven.*

[h] Other ancient authorities add *worshiped him, and.*

---

redemption of the promise in Acts 2. **Stay in the city:** Contrast the Galilean tradition of Mark 16:7; Matt. 28:7, 10, 16. **Power from on high,** i.e., from God.

D. Christ's Final Parting from His Disciples (24:50-53)

Even if it is acknowledged that the words **and was carried up into heaven** (RSV mg.; cf. KJV)—missing from Codex Bezae and its allies and also from the original text of Codex Sinaiticus—are an interpolation, there are no reasonable grounds for doubting that this is the story of the Ascension that Luke elaborates in Acts 1:6-11. One difficulty is created by the statement in Acts 1:3 that Christ's resurrection appearances continued for a period of forty days, whereas the implication of the gospel story is that the risen Lord parted once and for all from his disciples on Easter Sunday. Probably Luke was not interested in matters of chronology when he wrote his first version of the incident. At any rate he was not conscious of any discrepancy between the two accounts.

50-51. Anticipated in 9:51. **As far as Bethany:** The site is described more generally in Acts 1:12 as "the mount called Olivet."

52-53. The closing verses of the Gospel prepare the reader for the narratives in the opening chapters of the Acts volume (cf. Acts 2:46-47*a*; 3:1; 5:42). **Worshipped him, and** (KJV; RSV mg.): Omitted by Codex Bezae and its allies, and probably an interpolation based on Matt. 28:17. **Amen** (KJV): A liturgical addition found among the better MSS only in codices Vaticanus and Alexandrinus.

---

mightily," really "rushed upon"; see Acts 2.) If God should clothe himself with us! When a lone man got uncertainly to his feet, mumbling a whole baker's dozen of excuses, trying to wriggle out of doing anything, but somehow being held to it; asking for signs, begging for this to happen or that, just to be sure he was not starting out on a fool's errand; then setting his face against some wrong, and sounding his foolish trumpet: these men knew, the writers of the Book, that God was on those uncertain feet to steady them; it was his breath in that solitary blast ringing away among the hills!

We talk of history as if it were made up of movements and trends and crises in a delightfully impersonal way. They read it as if the spirit of the Lord had reached out for some trembling human flesh and drawn it on like a garment. Whenever there is something in the heart of God that needs doing, he girds himself with a living soul. He rarely chooses a great man, who is already great, for the doing of it. He never confines his efforts to the great occasion. Bodily he moves over into quiet, simple matters. And he is ready whenever we are. It is his own high and solemn word. In prose, not poetry.

50-53. ***The Ascension.***—(See Expos. on Acts 1:1-14.) The Resurrection and Ascension are the cardinal facts necessary to the understanding of the N.T. They transform the "simple" ethical concepts of the Gospels into the ethic of the new age (cf. Matt. 5:44, e.g., with I John 4:7-21). Nothing here could be more apt than Augustine's prayer:

> Be Thou exalted, Lord Jesus, who wast made flesh of her whom Thou didst make. . . . Thou who didst hunger for our sakes, thirst for our sakes, wast wearied on the road for our sakes (does then the Bread hunger, and the Fountain thirst, and the Way get tired?); Thou who didst sleep, yet, keeping Israel, dost not slumber; whom Judas sold, whom the Jews bought, yet did not possess; seized, bound, scourged, crowned with thorns, hung upon the tree; Thou dead, Thou buried, "Be Thou exalted, O God, above the heavens, . . . and Thy glory above all the earth."[9]

[9] *Sermons* CCLXII. 4. 4; 6. 5.

The Gospel According to

ST. JOHN

Introduction and Exegesis by Wilbert F. Howard

Exposition by Arthur John Gossip

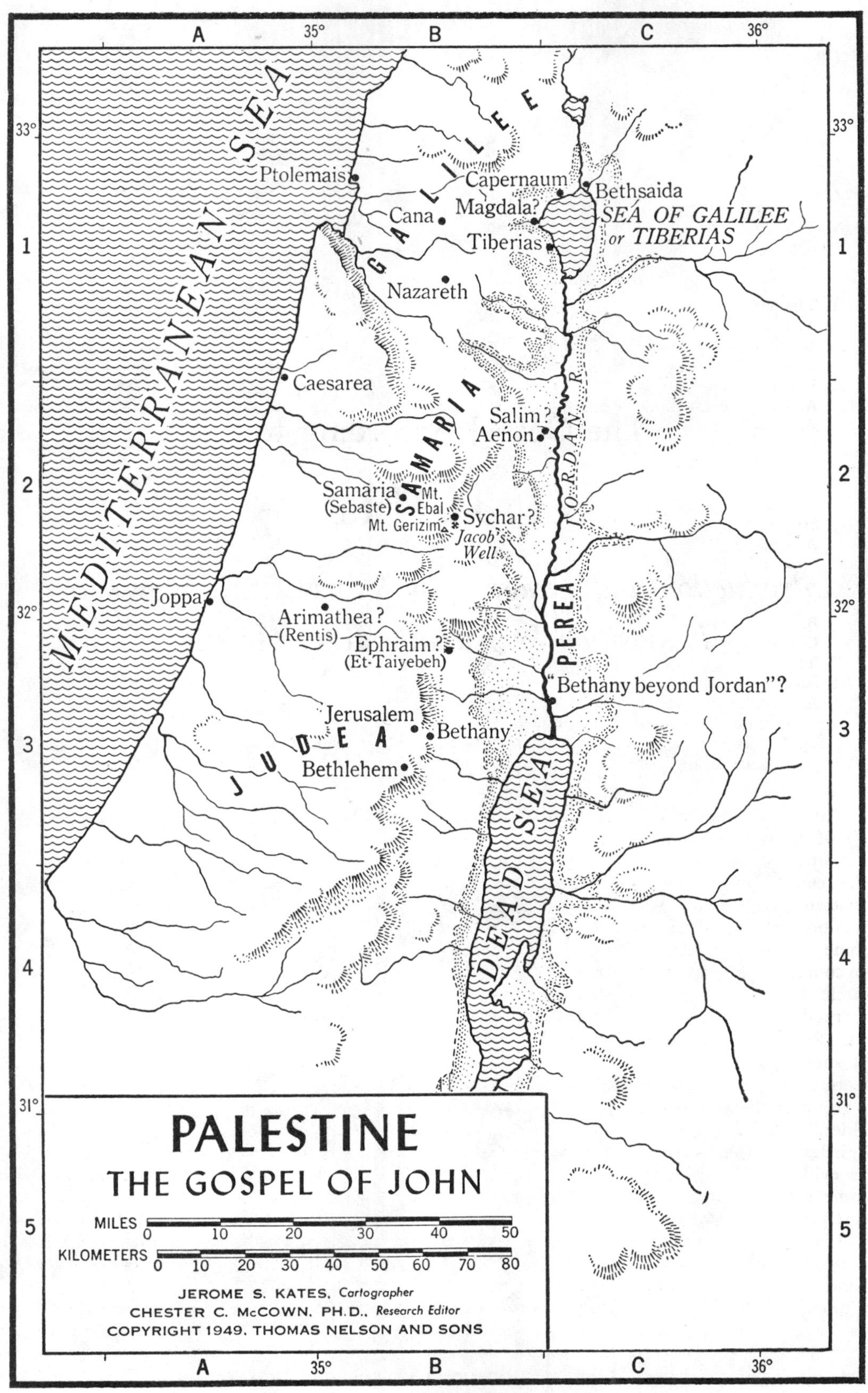
A
35°
B
C
36°
33°
1
2
32°
3
4
31°
5
MEDITERRANEAN SEA
GALILEE
Ptolemais
Capernaum
Bethsaida
Cana
Magdala?
SEA OF GALILEE
or TIBERIAS
Tiberias
Nazareth
Caesarea
SAMARIA
Salim?
Aenon
JORDAN R.
Samaria
(Sebaste)
Mt. Ebal
Sychar?
Mt. Gerizim
Jacob's Well
Joppa
Arimathea?
(Rentis)
Ephraim?
(Et-Taiyebeh)
PEREA
"Bethany beyond Jordan"?
Jerusalem
Bethany
JUDEA
Bethlehem
DEAD SEA
PALESTINE
THE GOSPEL OF JOHN
MILES
0 10 20 30 40 50
KILOMETERS
0 10 20 30 40 50 60 70 80
JEROME S. KATES, Cartographer
CHESTER C. McCOWN, PH.D., Research Editor
COPYRIGHT 1949, THOMAS NELSON AND SONS

JOHN

INTRODUCTION

The New Testament contains five writings, all of them in circulation toward the end of the first century, which found their way into the canon under the belief that they were written by the same hand and that the writer was no other than the apostle John. They have some conceptions and not a little phraseology in common and probably originated in the same circle. But critical discernment soon detected a marked difference in tone and style between the Revelation of John and the anonymous Gospel and epistles. The two shorter epistles were evidently written by a Christian leader in a group of churches where he was known as "the elder." Similarities of style between the three epistles and the Gospel are generally regarded as evidence of a common authorship, though some scholars attribute the First Epistle to a disciple of the evangelist.

The Gospel is in many ways the crown of the Scriptures. It is the simplest and at the same time the most profound book in the New Testament. History and interpretation, biography and theology, are blended in such a way that the reader, seeing the Jesus of history, yet sees him in the light of Christian experience. While intensely Jewish in the background of its thought, it is also a presentation of the Christian faith adapted to win the attention of an audience familiar with the religious phraseology of the contemporary Hellenistic world.

I. The Critical Questions

A. Purpose and General Character.—The evangelist declares his purpose in the words "that you may believe that Jesus is the Christ, the Son of God, and that believing you may have life in his name" (20:31). His aim is then theological rather than biographical, but the theological message is grounded in a historical revelation. From the prologue to the closing attestation the story is subordinated to doctrine. The Gospel is a witness to truth, or the divine reality made known in Jesus Christ. At the same time the reader becomes aware of some subordinate aims which have left their mark on the form of the message. In the region where this Gospel was written the church was faced by opposition, rivalry, and heresy. The hostility of the synagogue can be inferred from the frequent references to "the Jews" in the polemical discourses of Jesus in Jerusalem. There is evidence outside the New Testament of the existence of a sect that claimed John the Baptist as its head and made extravagant claims on his behalf. This may explain why the evangelist, though paying high tribute to the character of the Baptist, lays repeated stress upon his subordination to Christ. A third peril, as we can see even more clearly from the First Epistle of John, came from a form of religious speculation known as Gnosticism, especially in that type called Docetism. Starting from the belief that evil is inherent in matter, this type of teaching disparaged man's bodily life, and as it affected Christian thought, denied the reality of the incarnation of our Lord. This heresy is combated by the declaration that "the Word became flesh," and throughout the Gospel the genuinely human nature of the Savior is shown by his experience of hunger, thirst, weariness, sorrow, suffering, and death. These apologetic interests of the writer will be more fully discussed in section VI A of this Introduction.

The character of the Gospel becomes more evident as we compare it with the Synoptics. At first sight there is much in common. The ministry opens with the testimony of John the Baptist; disciples are called, twelve in number (6:67, 70); a successful ministry is carried on in Galilee, marked by many miraculous cures and the feeding of five thousand near the lake, after which Jesus comes to his disciples by night, walking on the sea. But popular favor declines; Peter, as spokesman of the disciples, declares his faith in Jesus as the Christ. The Gospel closes with an account of the triumphal entry into Jerusalem, the anointing at Bethany, the warning of the betrayal by Judas and the denial by Peter, the arrest in the garden, the trials before the high priest and before Pilate, the Crucifixion and the Resurrection. But there are marked differences. Whereas in the earlier Gospels only one journey to Jerusalem is related, in John a large part of the Gospel consists of visits to the capital and of long controversial discourses delivered in the temple court. The cleansing of the temple is placed in the first of these visits to the feasts, instead of in the week of the last Passover. John omits any account of the baptism, transfiguration, and agony in Gethsemane though the first and last are suggested to those who know the earlier Gospels, and the glory of the Son of God is seen throughout the incarnate life and not merely in one event. No instance is given of the cure of demoniacs, and the miracles of healing are represented not as acts of compassion, but as occasions for the revelation of divine power. The teaching of Jesus in this Gospel differs widely in subject matter and in form from that reported in the Synoptics. It is doctrinal rather than ethical; there are no parables, but several allegories which generally expand a series of "I am" sayings.

The character of the Gospel, which distinguishes it from all the others, can be seen clearly in three methods of theological emphasis which mark the Johannine narrative. They are called elsewhere[1] by the three descriptive titles, explicative, mandatory, and anticipatory emphasis. The first method makes explicit what is only implicit in the more primitive tradition of the ministry. Thus in all the Synoptics Isa. 6:9-10 is applied to the effect of the teaching of Jesus. In its parabolic form it divides his hearers (Mark 4:10-12; Matt. 13:10-15; Luke 8:9-10). John indeed gives the same citation (12:37-40), but he applies the words to the acted parables of the "signs," and throughout the narrative of the ministry emphasizes that the revelation of Christ confronted men with a crisis. It arouses either belief or unbelief, and carries with it a judgment of life or death. By mandatory emphasis is meant the way in which a title, given to Jesus and constantly repeated, gives prominence to an aspect of the ministry which is present in the earlier record but receives new significance. That Jesus was conscious of a mission is clear from Mark 1:38 and Luke 4:43 (following upon Luke 4:18). All four evangelists record the saying, "Whoever receives me receives him who sent me"; but in the Fourth Gospel the phrase "he who sent me" is spoken by Jesus twenty-six times, and a synonymous verb is used eighteen times in the Gospel for the Son's mission from the Father, as well as three times in the First Epistle. By anticipatory emphasis is meant the programmatic way in which what is represented in the earlier Gospels as a gradual revelation is boldly announced at the opening of the Johannine story. The messiahship of Jesus, with all its kindred titles, meets us before the close of the first chapter. The divine glory first seen on the mount of transfiguration in the Synoptics is to John the continuous revelation of the incarnate life. "We beheld his glory, the glory as of the only begotten of the Father, full of grace and truth" (1:14).

B. Composition and Sources.—The literary style of this Gospel combines extreme simplicity with distinct individuality. It is recognizable throughout, with the exception of the interpolated fragment containing the story of the woman taken in adultery (7:53–8:11), and a few sentences here and there where an editorial hand can be detected. The same style, allowing for difference in occasion and subject matter, is found in the Johannine epistles, but nowhere else in the New Testament. A monotonous se-

[1] W. F. Howard, *Christianity According to St. John* (Philadelphia: Westminster Press, 1946), pp. 22 ff.

quence of sentences placed side by side, with few subordinate clauses, suggests a Semitic mind, though there is seldom any breach of Greek idiom. The Hellenistic dialect spoken throughout the Mediterranean world lends itself to this representation of the Hebrew and Aramaic manner of speech. But there are personal idiosyncrasies, such as the constant use of antithetic pairs of words, the change of Greek synonyms in the same context without change of meaning, the insertion of explanatory comments, a negative statement followed by its positive equivalent. We observe how closely narrative and discourse are interwoven, so that miracles are recorded not merely as incidents in the ministry of Jesus, but rather as "signs" which are interpreted in the didactic speeches which follow. Personal encounters with Jesus are narrated with not a few descriptive details, but the story is often left unfinished as the conversation passes into a monologue. Another literary device is to report an ambiguous saying of Jesus which is entirely misunderstood by his hearers in order that some newly revealed truth may be expounded more fully. This is not to be confused with another Johannine characteristic—the subtle use of a word which has an obvious meaning in its context, but a deeper significance in the history of redemption.

This feature of the author's style is so important for the exegesis of the Gospel that a few examples must be examined here. The reply of Jesus to the challenge for a sign of authority when he had cleansed the temple—"Destroy this temple, and in three days I will raise it up" (2:19)—is interpreted by the evangelist as a reference to the body of Christ, recognized as such by the disciples only after the Resurrection. With an unmistakable twist, this saying was used as evidence against Jesus in the form "I will destroy this temple that is made with hands, and in three days I will build another, not made with hands" (Mark 14:58). But in that form it preserves a contrast which well may be part of the authentic saying, and Acts 7:48; 17:24; Heb. 9:11, 24 show that this contrast left a deep mark on the thought of the early church. If we further compare I Cor. 3:16; II Cor. 6:16; Eph. 2:21, we can see how completely the conception of the church as "the body of Christ" was established, while in I Pet. 2:5 the figure has been developed from the logion about the temple. The way was therefore fully prepared for the Johannine interpretation of the words attributed to Jesus.

The conversation with Nicodemus furnishes two examples of this method of hidden allusion. First, the Greek word (ἄνωθεν), translated "anew" (3:3), can mean either "again" or "from above." Nicodemus took it in the former sense, though the context shows that the meaning "from heaven" is intended. Vss. 13-14 refer to the descent from heaven of the Son of man, who is to be "lifted up," an expression which stands for both the crucifixion and the ascension of Jesus. In 7:39 it is said that "the Spirit had not been given, because Jesus was not yet glorified" (cf. 16:7). The insufflation (20:22) is the gift of the risen Christ, which for John means the ascended Christ. The new birth is therefore an experience which is effected by the Spirit, who is the gift of the risen and ascended Lord, coming down "from above." In the second place, in the same conversation one word is used with the meaning "Spirit" in 3:6, 8, and also "wind" in 3:8. Remembering how the symbol of wind appears in the description of the pentecostal gift (Acts 2:2; 4:31), and in that of water in John 7:38-39, we may feel that there is something in the theory that "wind" is also the meaning in 3:5. If so, regeneration is defined first symbolically—"born of water and wind" (ἐξ ὕδατος καὶ πνεύματος, 3:5), the metaphors representing baptism and pentecost—and then directly, "So it is with every one who is born of the Spirit" (ἐκ τοῦ πνεύματος, 3:8).

While the characteristics of vocabulary, syntax, and literary method are fairly evenly distributed throughout the Gospel, the section 7:53–8:11 is by every test, internal and external, a late scribal insertion in the text of the Gospel. So also is the explanatory parenthesis 5:4. Editorial comments are often recognized in 4:1, 2; 6:23; 11:2; 21:24. These additions must not be confused with the evangelist's own explanatory comments, such as 2:21; 4:9*b*; 6:61, 64, 71; 7:22, 39; 8:27; 11:13, 51; 12:6, 33, 43; 17:3; 18:14, which are marks of the Johannine idiosyncrasy.

As to sources, a comparison with the Synoptic Gospels seems to show that the writer drew upon these earlier writings to some extent, or else made use of some of the same traditions either in oral or in written form. The closest parallels in the narrative portions are the account of the feeding of the multitude and the story of the anointing at Bethany. In this latter story there seems to be a conflation of Mark 14:3-9 and Luke 7:37-38, unless we allow for an editorial retouching of these passages by one who had read the earliest Gospels. But whatever sources may have provided the evangelist with his material, he puts his own stamp upon all that he has appropriated. A tendency to heighten the miraculous element is found by some readers, who contrast the Synoptic story of the healing in Capernaum of the centurion's servant by Jesus with the Johannine statement that the officer's son in Capernaum was healed by Jesus while still at Cana. Traditional material is handled didactically. Theological conceptions color the narrative, which sometimes runs into discourse. It is almost certain that an early book of "testimonies" was used, consisting of messianic proof texts from the Old Testament. There is also some reason to think that the prologue is an adaptation of a hymn in praise of Wisdom, originally written in Aramaic, into which the evangelist has inserted prose comments about John the Baptist (see p. 445). If this is so, it can only be said that in adopting and adapting it he has made it entirely his own.

It is now generally recognized that in some places where this Gospel follows an independent line the writer is drawing upon valuable historical traditions. Thus it seems likely that Jesus carried on an early Judean ministry parallel to that of the Baptist, that he visited Jerusalem from time to time for the great annual festivals, and that John is right in his dating of the Last Supper and the Crucifixion.[2]

C. Author, Milieu, and Date.—If external evidence decided the question of authorship, a very strong case could be made out for John the son of Zebedee, one of the twelve. From the later half of the second century a consistent tradition attributes the Fourth Gospel to John —the anti-Marcionite Prologues, Irenaeus, Clement of Alexandria, Tertullian, and the Muratorian canon. These witnesses represent such different traditions as those of the provinces of Asia, Gaul, Egypt, Africa, and even of the church at Rome. Against this consensus of testimony there is only the opposition of a group of Christians in Asia about the period 160-70, who were called the Alogi because of their dislike of the teaching of the Logos. They attributed this Gospel to Cerinthus, a heretical contemporary of the apostle, and thus proved their critical incompetence. There is also some evidence, of a late and uncertain character, that Gaius, a learned and orthodox presbyter of the church in Rome early in the third century, impugned this Gospel. Further external evidence against the Johannine authorship is found by some scholars in two very late writers of the seventh and ninth centuries who allege that Papias wrote in the second book of his *Expositions of the Lord's Oracles* that the brothers James and John were slain by Jews. But Eusebius, who possessed and knew the writings of Papias, makes not the slightest reference to any such statement, even to confute it. The fact that a fifth-century Syriac calendar of martyrs celebrates on December 27 "John and James the apostles in Jerusalem" is probably due to the tendency to see in Mark 10:39 a prophecy that both sons of Zebedee would die as martyrs.

[2] See further, Maurice Goguel, *Les sources du récit Johannique de la passion* (La-Roche-sur-Yon: Imprimerie Centrale de l'Ouest, 1910), pp. 104 ff.

A more serious objection to the apostolic authorship is the silence of Ignatius, who wrote to the church at Ephesus while journeying to Rome for martyrdom. He appeals to the influence and example of the apostle Paul, but says nothing about John. Moreover, Justin Martyr seems in at least one passage to quote from this Gospel, but he does not attribute it to John, though he does speak of John as the author of Revelation, which by every consideration of style and subject matter must have been written by another hand than that of the author of the Gospel.

When we turn to the internal evidence our starting point is the attestation by some group that the Beloved Disciple is he "who is bearing witness to these things, and who has written these things" (21:24). The close association of this disciple—who must be the one also referred to as that "other disciple" (13:23; 19:26; 21:7, 20; cf. 18:15, 16; 20:2)—with Peter invites a comparison with Acts 3:1, 4, 11; 8:14; Luke 22:8; Gal. 2:9. Further, though several of the twelve are mentioned by name in this Gospel, James and John are never named; but once (21:2) "the sons of Zebedee" are included among those who were present at that last appearance of the risen Lord when special attention is drawn to the Beloved Disciple. There can be little doubt that those who gave out this Gospel to the world intended its readers to regard the apostle John as in some way its authority. One of the chief difficulties in the way of accepting that claim is that we should have expected a Gospel claiming so high an apostolic authority to have been more widely known and quoted as Johannine much earlier than seems to have been the case.

The older commentators used to argue from the nature and contents of the Gospel that the author was a Palestinian, a Jew, a contemporary, a disciple of Jesus, the apostle John. Though the last stage in the reduction of the radius of these concentric circles is uncertain, it may well be conceded that the other claims, if not for the author, at least for the authority behind the Gospel, are reasonable. More recently a popular theory postulated as the author a disciple who was not one of the twelve, but a Jerusalem adherent, and some writers went so far as to find a significant hint in the strange statement of Polycrates, a bishop of Ephesus late in the second century, that "John who leaned on the Lord's breast was a priest wearing the petalon." The Greek word πέταλον is used in the Septuagint of Exod. 28:36 for the gold plate fastened in front of the high priest's miter. It is not clear what lies behind this legendary tradition.

This Gospel, like the other three, is anonymous, and all that we can really know about the author must be derived from his writings. If, as there is the strongest reason to believe, he is the writer of the three Johannine epistles, he was evidently a venerated leader of the Christian church who claimed a spiritual authority over other churches in the same province and appealed to a tradition which goes back to Christian beginnings. He was perfectly familiar with the record of the ministry of Jesus, but he did not hesitate to interpret the record according to his understanding of the inmost mind of Christ. He stands out as a religious genius of the first order, like the apostle Paul and the unnamed author of the Epistle to the Hebrews. A sacramentalist by temperament, he yet avoided, and warned the church against, the crass materialism of the sacramental rites of pagan mysteries. He was a mystic who taught that union with God in Christ is no absorption in deity but a fellowship conditioned by obedience to the ethical demand of brotherly love. He was a theologian who looked at history *sub specie aeternitatis,* a preacher who selected incidents in the life of Jesus to illustrate the truths which the Son of God came to reveal, and cited words of Jesus in order to expand and interpret them after the manner of the Jewish Targums of the Old Testament. He translated the Christian gospel into the terms which would best win a hearing in a world that was teeming with religious speculation and was hungry for a knowledge of God.

Three places have been suggested as the center in which this Gospel originated: Antioch, Ephesus, and Alexandria. In favor of Antioch some scholars have pleaded the close resemblance to Johannine thought and phraseology in the letters of Ignatius, bishop of Antioch, and in the Odes of Solomon, which are written in Syriac and seem to have had their origin in the neighborhood of Antioch. Further evidence is appealed to in a Syriac fragment appended to the Armenian translation of Ephrem's commentary on Tatian's *Diatessaron:* "John wrote that [Gospel] in Greek at Antioch, for he remained in the country until the time of Trajan." Nearness to Palestine might account for the mystical form of rabbinical Judaism which has left so strong a mark on this Gospel. But if the writer was a Christian whose earlier thought was influenced by rabbinical discussions, Antioch was not the only center where such teaching might be heard. Jerusalem must not be ignored, nor at a later stage must Ephesus. Indeed, it is in Ephesus that the strongest tradition places the evangelist.

This great city, closely connected with Alexandria (cf. Acts 18:24), with a powerful Jewish community, the reputed home of a sect that gave special honor to John the Baptist, and a meeting place of many currents of Hellenistic thought, is the most likely center for such a presentation of the Christian message as the Fourth Gospel contains. It was there, centuries before, that Heraclitus first gave currency to the term Logos; there that a religious teacher would be most keenly aware of the syncretism of the age; there that the bitter opposition of the synagogue led to debates from the time of the apostle Paul till that of Justin Martyr; and it was in this region that Paul's most fruitful ministry was carried on, and to it that those letters were written in which, without the name, he expounded the Logos Christology.

The most recent suggestion is that the Gospel was written in Alexandria. We know that it made a powerful appeal to the Alexandrian Gnostics and that one of them, Heracleon, wrote the first commentary upon it. The marked affinity in some of the thought and language to be found in the Hermetic writings gives some support to this proposal, as does also the well-known similarity with the writings of Philo of Alexandria. Toward the end of the second century and early in the third the Christian Platonists of Alexandria found their most congenial authority in the Johannine writings. Against these arguments must be set the powerful tradition which links the Gospel with Ephesus and the lack of any such claim by the church at Alexandria.

All that can be said with certainty is that the author had come into close touch with rabbinical Judaism, both in its legalistic and its mystical aspects, with Hellenized Judaism, with Hermetism, and with Gnosticism. While combating all of them, he took spoil from them, turning their own weapons against them. Jesus, who lived and suffered and died and rose again, was none other than the Logos, sent by the Father to bring to men the true knowledge of him, to be the light and life of men, to feed them with the real bread of life, to slake their thirst with the living water, and to bring them, instead of the Mosaic code of commands, the new Torah, the abiding revelation of God as grace and truth. The Johannine Gospel was addressed to a constituency varied enough to require such a missionary message.

The late date that once found favor with critical scholars is now almost universally abandoned. Our Gospel was known in Gnostic circles by A.D. 130; it was used by the writer of the recently discovered apocryphal gospel edited by H. Idris Bell and T. C. Skeat, and dated by papyrologists as written in the first half of the second century (see p. 459); and a tiny fragment of a codex of John's Gospel has been found in Egypt, which the same experts assign to a date about A.D. 130-50. It is therefore increasingly difficult to accept a date much later than the end of the first century for the publication of the Gospel. For reasons which will be given below (see pp. 446-47) it is likely that the author did not write it all at once, but from time to time, and that the separate pieces of papyrus became disarranged before they were copied on a papyrus roll, or on the quires which were made up into a codex.

II. Leading Ideas

A. Key Words.—The word Logos, the theme of the prologue, drops out of the Gospel after 1:14, as a technical term. It was borrowed from the language of the Stoics, in which it represented the divine reason, immanent in nature and in man. Philo, the Hellenizing Jew of Alexandria, uses this term more than thirteen hundred times in his voluminous allegorical expositions of the Old Testament. Of its wide variety of meanings the nearest approach to the Johannine use is its identification with the hypostatized conception of wisdom. In the Gospel we seem to have a blend of two ideas, that of wisdom (cf. Prov. 2; 8) and that of Torah. Both are colored by the common Old Testament thought of the word of God as the expression of his creative energy. But whatever may have been the past history of this term in philosophical or religious speculation, in John's use it is solely personal and indicates Jesus Christ. Jesus is not to be interpreted by Logos; Logos is intelligible only as we think of Jesus. The universe becomes rational to men by the revelation of the divine creative principle in a truly human life. Man is redeemed, with all that belongs to his material existence, by the mediation of the Son of God, who was also Son of man—man in the completeness of our humanity.

The Logos is described as life and light. These words played a great part in contemporary Hellenistic religion, but they are also frequently found in the Old Testament. The evangelist represents Jesus as claiming to be the light of the world, and illustrates this by the story of the gift of sight to a man born blind. In the same way the raising of Lazarus illustrates the theme which runs through the Gospel, that Jesus came to give life in its abundance to those who trust in him. Eternal life is more than a future consummation of all that is hoped for on earth. It is a present experience of fellowship with God. Current movements of thought were laying stress on knowledge, faith, and wisdom as the divine gifts to esoteric groups of elect souls. Knowledge secretly imparted constituted faith and raised the initiate to a superior state of mind called wisdom. To John knowledge is not static, nor faith passive; neither is wisdom the goal of revelation. He never uses the nouns for knowledge and faith, but the corresponding verbs. The rendering, "This is life eternal, to be growing in the knowledge of thee the only true God, and of him whom thou hast sent" (17:3) gives the force of the present tense. The verb "to believe" is used nearly a hundred times in this Gospel, and stands for the exercise of the higher judgment, with a certain moral force, in taking up a personal attitude to Christ. Thus faith and knowledge are not possessions which give the Christian the status of wisdom. They are activities of the human self, in response to the divine revelation, which bring him into the realm of reality. God made known by Jesus Christ is the eternally true. So Jesus can say, "I am the way, and the truth, and the life" (14:6). He is the way to the Father, "No one comes to the Father, but by me" (14:6). While it is true that "no one has ever seen God" (1:18), yet the divine character is seen reflected in the incarnate Logos. "We have beheld his glory, glory as of the only Son from the Father" (1:14). In the prologue a word is used to describe the Father's initiative in thus visiting and redeeming the world. Grace, a word so often used by Paul for God's free and unmerited favor, is discontinued after the prologue. But grace is nothing else than love in action, and the supreme message of the Gospel is that "God so loved the world that he gave his only Son, that whoever believes in him should not perish but have eternal life" (3:16). The authority which underlies this mission of Jesus Christ is a threefold witness: the inward testimony of the Father, the audible testimony of the Baptist, and the external testimony of scripture. All these are confirmed by the "signs," the mighty works which are evidential both to the general public (10:7-8) and to the disciples (14:11).

The revelation thus attested confronts men with the responsibility of accepting or rejecting "him whom God has sent." The Incarnation brings the world of men under "judgment." This noun and its corresponding verb sound throughout the Gospel.

B. Theological Conceptions.—Under this head we shall consider (1) the Godhead; (2) human nature and destiny; (3) eschatology; and (4) the church, ministry, and sacraments.

1. ***The Godhead.***—This reality is set forth in the mutual relationship of Father and Son. "The Father loves the Son, and shows him all that he himself is doing" (5:20). "The Son can do nothing of his own accord, but only what he sees the Father doing" (5:19). The Father's love for the Son before the foundation of the world is returned with obedient trust during

the incarnate life. Therefore men are to honor the Son, even as they honor the Father. Out of this divine fellowship proceeds the Holy Spirit. The Father sends him in the name of the Son (14:26), and yet it can be said that the Son sends him from the Father (15:26). It is in this fellowship of the Spirit that the disciples of Jesus are to become one in a unity corresponding to that of the divine nature. (*a*) The evangelist writes that "God is Spirit" (4:24), as elsewhere we read that "God is light" (I John 1:5) and "God is love" (I John 4:16). He thus declares the essential being of God, so as to lift all thought of him above the earthly conditions of time and place. God seeks men to have communion with him, but his worshipers must be in spiritual harmony with God, and their worship must be based on the reality of the God whom they approach. He is the living God to whom the ancient Hebrew writers bear witness, and of whom Jesus says, "My Father is working still" (5:17). (*b*) Jesus Christ as Word and Son is the perfect revealer of God. As the commissioned envoy of the Father he speaks with full authority in the Father's name. This aspect of his nature is so far emphasized that even under the conditions of his mortal existence he is credited with omniscience. There is no limit to his miraculous powers, and he lays majestic claims in a series of "I am" sayings which recall the language used of Yahweh in the Old Testament. Yet side by side with these features in the portrait of Jesus we have glimpses of him in times of weariness and thirst, of sorrow and disappointment. It is indeed the Jesus of history and not some mythical Christ who is the subject of the Gospel, but he is viewed in the light of the Easter faith as crowned with glory and honor. (*c*) The Holy Spirit is regarded as the agent in regeneration, but as especially the gift of the risen Christ to his disciples to take his place as their counselor in personal life and in the corporate life of the church. The peculiar teaching is found in a group of sayings recorded in the farewell discourses of chs. 14–16, where the word Paraclete (παράκλητος) is used. It is a Greek word for one who is called to the side of another as intercessor to plead his cause. This conception is not peculiar to the Fourth Gospel. It is significant that in all the Synoptic Gospels a saying of Jesus is preserved which was spoken to encourage the disciples to appear before tribunals without anxious perturbation, inasmuch as in such an emergency the Holy Spirit would enable them to bear their testimony effectively. In John he is called "another Paraclete" (14:16), which recalls I John 2:1, "We have a Paraclete with the Father, Jesus Christ the righteous." There is a parallel to this in Rom. 8, where in vs. 27 intercession is attributed to the Holy Spirit, though in vs. 34 Christ is the intercessor.

2. ***Human Nature and Destiny.***—At first sight the Gospel seems to teach a rigid determinism which results from a cosmic dualism. The life of man on earth is set in the midst of a tragic conflict between opposing forces. The drama of light and darkness represents truth and falsehood contesting for victory, heaven and earth in irreconcilable opposition, mankind divided into two camps, the children of God and the children of the devil. Sometimes it seems as though no man has freedom, but that his destiny has been settled for him. Only those who have been drawn by God come to the Son and believe in him. On closer study we find that this Gospel is colored by a moral not by a metaphysical dualism, and that the writer's determinism is not carried through to its logical issue, but is rather a practical statement of the Hebraic view that foresight involves foreordination, in order to explain the otherwise incredible unbelief of the Jewish people as a whole and the treachery of Judas. There are indeed two orders of life, that which is from below and that which comes from above. Our normal life is from below. But man can break "his birth's invidious bar." Regeneration by the Spirit is a necessity if we are to enter the kingdom of God. This is birth "from above." Jesus came from above, the gift of the Father's love for the world, to redeem men, not from imprisonment in the world of matter, but from sin and the destruction which sin effects. He laid down his life freely, and was thereby "glorified," or "lifted up," that he might draw all men to himself. Raised to the world above, he sent the Spirit to the world below that men might experience the birth from above and enter into eternal life.

By this new birth men become children of God. Their original state was the darkness of sin. Their opportunity has come with the entrance of the true light into the world, Jesus who is the light of the world. He enlightens every man by his revelation of God. Active faith in him leads to the new birth. The blindness of ignorance does not count as guilt, but open-eyed refusal of the light incurs a guilt which remains (9:41) and calls down the abiding wrath of God (3:36).

3. ***Eschatology.***—The crucial importance of the Incarnation is that with the appearance of Jesus as revealer of God and savior of the world, "the age to come" is already here. Judgment is now at work, and separation is taking place between those who are destined to life and those who are heading for destruction (10:26-28). Eternal life is a present state. "He

who hears my word and believes him who sent me, has eternal life; he does not come into judgment, but has passed from death to life" (5:24). Yet one of the undeniable features of this Gospel is the appeal to a future judgment. "The hour is coming when all who are in the tombs will hear his voice and come forth, those who have done good to the resurrection of life, and those who have done evil, to the resurrection of judgment" (5:28-29). This eschatological judgment "at the last day" is rather a final manifestation of the judgment which is taking place here and now according to the nature of the human response to the divine call and demand given in Jesus Christ.

This tension between the two conceptions of the kingdom of God, or eternal life, as present and as future, runs through the New Testament. It is most noticeable in John because in the farewell discourses the culmination of the teaching of Jesus is reached in the thought of the mystical union of the disciple with the Father and the Son through the Spirit. After that any historical denouement would seem to be an anticlimax. Perhaps the tension is resolved in the Johannine saying: "Beloved, we are God's children now; it does not yet appear what we shall be, but we know that when he appears we shall be like him, for we shall see him as he is. And every one who thus hopes in him purifies himself as he is pure" (I John 3:2-3).

4. ***Church, Ministry, and Sacraments.***—On first appearance there is little that can be called ecclesiastical in this Gospel. But the evidence of the Acts and of the epistles reminds us that the whole of the New Testament must be read against the background of the life and teaching of the church. A turning point in the ministry of Jesus is marked in 6:66-70, where a separation is noted between a large and loosely attached body of disciples who "went back, and walked no more with" Jesus, and the twelve who found in his teaching words of eternal life, and confessed him as "the Holy One of God." This is the nucleus of the Christian church. The next stage is reached in the allegory of the good shepherd (10:1-18, 25-30) who lays down his life for the sheep. Here Jesus is represented as looking beyond the fold of Judaism to bring into the one flock all who will heed his voice. The unity of the Christian community is secured by the rule of the "one shepherd." The mark of the true disciple is belief, which creates obedience, so that all who follow their shepherd have eternal life and are secure in the Father's care. The metaphor is changed in ch. 15, where the church is represented in the allegory of the true vine as the branches deriving their life from the one stock, which is Christ. Fruitfulness is the test of vitality, and all unfruitful shoots are pruned away. The church is an organism, not an organization. "Apart from me you can do nothing" (15:5). This conception of organic unity is most clearly expressed in the prayer of ch. 17, where the Christian society is identified with "all whom thou hast given him" (17:2), or to give the exact meaning of the Greek, "that entire unity which thou hast given him," followed immediately by the plural, "that to them he might give eternal life."

From the high priestly prayer we learn that, in the Johannine conception, the church consists of a body of men whom the Father has taken out of the world and given to Christ. While still living in the world, they are to be kept from the evil power which rules it, and to fulfill their mission to the world by making known to others the message which they have received from Christ as the word of God. Their own faith in Christ and his divine mission is to evoke a like faith in their hearers so that these may be brought into the same unity. This unity is a fellowship of faith and love which will reflect and reveal the perfect unity between the Father and the Son. The witness of this unity in the life of the church is to convince the world of the divine mission of Jesus, and of the love of the Father for his Son and for all who are thus united in his fellowship. With a view to consecrating the church to this mission, the Son is consecrating himself in the sacrifice of the Cross, thus bringing his disciples into the reality of a life inspired by the fullness of the revelation of the Father in the Son.

The Johannine doctrine of the ministry may be inferred from passages in chs. 10; 13; 20; 21. In the allegory of the door of the fold the true pastor is distinguished from the mere hireling, whose self-interested professionalism is contrasted with self-denying devotion to the sheep of the flock. The true pastor is he who, hearing the voice of Christ and accepting his authority from him, receives eternal life himself and is able to feed the flock in green pastures and to lead the sheep beside still waters. The acted parable of the feet washing teaches the lesson of humility in service. "A servant is not greater than his master; nor is he who is sent greater than he who sent him" (13:16). The account of the insufflation, as a symbol of the gift of the Spirit by the risen Lord to his disciples, suggests a comparison with the words in Matt. 16:19; 18:18, where the rabbinical terms "binding" and "loosing" are used. The pastoral responsibility here indicated is partly that of moral instruction about the Christian way of life, and partly that of excluding from the Christian society those who will not abide in

Christ by keeping his new commandment, but who persist in sinning a mortal sin (I John 5:16-17). The final charge to Peter is that he should prove himself a faithful pastor by feeding and tending the sheep and the lambs of the flock.

The Fourth Evangelist was a sacramental mystic. We learn from the Pauline epistles that the sacraments of baptism and the Lord's Supper were a normal part of the life of the church, and it is evident that they were focal points in the instruction given to its catechumens and members. In this Gospel no word tells of their origin or institution. A confused sentence at the beginning of ch. 4 refers to an early stage of Christian baptism. In 3:22 it is said that Jesus was baptizing in the Judean territory. In 4:1 we read that a report went out that Jesus was making and baptizing more disciples than John. A parenthetic note adds the comment that Jesus himself did not baptize, but only his disciples. The long account of the Last Supper in chs. 13–17 is silent about the institution of the Eucharist, which is prominent in the Synoptics. Yet few readers fail to recognize an allusion to baptism in the conversation with Nicodemus (3:3-8) and to the Eucharist in the discourse in the synagogue at Capernaum and afterward in the explanation to the disciples (6:35-63). The evangelist is allusive and his temperament is that of one who sees a deeper reality behind the language of symbolism. In the early church baptism was the visible means of reception into the Christian society. It was the effectual sign of the change in the inner man wrought by the Spirit. In Johannine language that inward change was regeneration, a birth from above. "Unless one is born of water and the Spirit, he cannot enter the kingdom of God" (3:5). Yet the emphasis throughout this passage is upon the agency of the Spirit. Similarly, the discourse on the bread of life reaches its climax in the words, "Unless you eat the flesh of the Son of man and drink his blood, you have no life in you. . . . He who eats my flesh and drinks my blood abides in me, and I in him" (6:53, 56). No Jew could possibly take these words in a literal sense. But every reader must have been familiar with the words of institution: "Take; this is my body. . . . This is my blood of the covenant, which is poured out for many" (Mark 14:22, 24). The Eucharistic allusion is unmistakable, but any crude interpretation is guarded against in the epilogue to the disciples: "It is the spirit that gives life, the flesh is of no avail; the words that I have spoken to you are spirit and life" (6:63). The mystical union with Christ is attained through faith by appropriation of Christ's own gift of himself in his sacrificial death and in his life freely given for the life of the world. The life of the church is sustained in that sacrament which unites us in the communion of faith and love.

III. Structure

A. General Plan.—The Gospel consists of the prologue, the main narrative, and the appendix.

1. *Prologue.*—This section (1:1-18) has every appearance of being a poem, with the insertion of prose comments. C. F. Burney[3] claimed that by retranslation into Aramaic the prologue fell naturally into the form of a hymn, written in eleven parallel couplets, with comments introduced here and there by the writer. This may be represented by the following scheme.

Stanzas	*Verses in ch. 1*
1	1*a*
	b
2	*c*
	2
3	3*a*
	b
4	4*a*
	b
5	5*a*
	b
(Prose comment	6-10*a*)
6	10*b*
	c
7	11*a*
	b
(Prose comment	12-13)
8	14*a*
	b
9	*c*
	d
10	*e*
	16*a*
(Addition	16*b*)
(Prose comment	15)
11	17*a*
	b
(Prose comment	18)

Another theory is that of J. Rendel Harris,[4] who held that it is an adaptation of a hymn in praise of wisdom, in which the language of the Septuagint of Proverbs, the Wisdom of Solomon, and Ecclesiasticus can be traced. In this case we might well include vss. 9-13 and 18 in the poem. In either case, vss. 6-8 and 15 are interpolated for a polemic motive into a hymn in praise of the wisdom or word of God.

2. *Drama of Light and Darkness.*—The main portion of the Gospel (1:19–20:31) is the drama of the conflict between light and darkness. This falls into two parts. The first carries us from

[3] *The Aramaic Origin of the Fourth Gospel* (Oxford: Clarendon Press, 1922).

[4] *The Origin of the Prologue to St John's Gospel* (Cambridge: University Press, 1917).

the first public appearance of Jesus and the testimony of the Baptist to the end of the public ministry (12:50). In this part narrative is prominent, with discourses to bring out the significance of the wonderful works, or "signs," wrought by Jesus. The story begins with the call of the earliest disciples and their recognition of the messiahship and divine mission of Jesus. In Galilee and Jerusalem his works and his teaching command attention; in Samaria he makes himself known as the giver of the water of life and is hailed as the Savior of the world. In Jerusalem the healing of a cripple on the sabbath stirs up controversy; in Galilee multitudes follow and are miraculously fed. The discourse about the bread of life ends in a "hard saying" after which many of his disciples forsake him, but the twelve confess their belief in him. A series of controversies in Jerusalem lead the rulers to resolve upon his death. Jesus declares himself to be the light of the world, the good shepherd, the resurrection and the life. The raising of Lazarus brings the hostility of the chief priests to a crisis, and Jesus retires again beyond their reach. A few days before the Passover he comes to Bethany, where Mary anoints him. The next day the Galilean pilgrims come out from Jerusalem to give him a triumphal welcome as he rides into the city. Here he is sought by some Greeks and proclaims that after being lifted up, he will draw all men to himself. At the same time he announces that the judgment of the world is at hand, and declares the meaning of his rejection by the Jews.

The second part tells of the Last Supper and the promise of the Paraclete, through whom the disciples will find their true fellowship with the Father and the Son. Then follow the Betrayal, the Arrest, the Trial, the Crucifixion and the Resurrection, leading up to the beatitude pronounced upon those who have not seen and yet have believed, and closing with the statement of the purpose for which the Gospel has been written.

3. ***Epilogue.***—Ch. 21 is regarded by many scholars as an appendix added by a different hand. Others, with good reason if linguistic considerations are to count, regard it as a later addition by the evangelist himself. Vss. 24-25 are probably an attestation, written after the evangelist's death by some members of his circle. They present difficulties to the critical expositor. Their ostensible meaning is that the author of the Gospel is the Beloved Disciple, who has been in all but name identified with the apostle John. We have seen that there are strong reasons for questioning the apostolic authorship. It is possible that a close disciple of the aged apostle wrote the Gospel by embodying many of his reminiscences and meditations, while also freely handling various sources, written and oral. Other members of the Johannine circle may have so associated this church leader with his apostolic master as to regard this written Gospel as the actual work of John. However this question of authorship may be answered, it seems likely that the epilogue was written partly to remind the church that the disciple who denied his Lord was forgiven and reinstated (for this undeniable fact is not recorded in the Synoptic Gospels, though it may be inferred from Luke 24:34; I Cor. 15:5), partly to remove the false belief that the Lord's advent would come before the death of the last of the apostles.

B. Arrangement.—With the exception of the section 7:53–8:11 (the woman taken in adultery) and the parenthesis 5:4 (the legend of the angel stirring the pool), which are later additions to the Gospel, the present arrangement of the text goes back to the earliest authorities. On internal evidence alone many scholars believe that at some stage before the Gospel was published an accidental dislocation of the papyrus sheets took place. There are a number of places where there is a manifest discontinuity in either the narrative or the discourse. The clearest examples are the following: (*a*) The passage 3:22-30 interrupts the discourse of our Lord with Nicodemus. Vss. 31-36 form a natural conclusion to what has been said in vss. 1-21, and are quite out of place on the lips of the Baptist. (*b*) Ch. 5 is a scene in Jerusalem interrupting two episodes in Galilee, and ch. 6 opens with the words, "After this Jesus went to the other side of the sea of Galilee"—a strange sequel to a Jerusalem narrative. (*c*) The section 7:15-24 seems to be a continuation of the controversy that arose from our Lord's healing of the cripple described in ch. 5. (*d*) The words in 10:19-29 appear to belong to the time when Jesus spoke the allegory of the good shepherd, not during a subsequent visit to Jerusalem at the feast of the Dedication. (*e*) The closing words of ch. 14 seem to demand a time after the discourse in chs. 15–16; moreover, the statement in 16:5 seems to be contradicted by 13:36 and 14:5. These facts have led to many conjectures, the more so as it has been observed that the rearrangements which would remove these anomalies involve sections which are multiples of the same unit of length. Papyrological research, however, raises difficulties. It shows that rolls were not made up of detached sheets after they had been written upon. It also reminds us that if the Gospel was written in the form of a codex, and some of its leaves became displaced, the length of each dislocated passage, and the space between its original and its present position, would in every case have to amount to a multiple of two pages. The theory of a disarrangement of the Gospel after it had been copied out either on a papyrus roll or in the form of a codex must be abandoned, since the proposed rearrangements of the text do not conform to these arithmetical tests.

We must accordingly look for a solution of the problem of discontinuity at a time before the Gospel was copied out in a form ready for publication. Either the author wrote down his thoughts at different times with indifference to chronological sequence or to continuity of thought, or else he composed his Gospel on separate sheets at many different times, with the result that the editor or copyist sometimes failed to preserve the order. (See also, below, pp. 460-61.)

IV. Chronology and Topography

Many take for granted that it is useless to attempt to construct any chronological scheme from the Johannine story of the ministry of Jesus. The reasons generally given are: (*a*) In any matter of divergence between the Synoptics and John the former are to have the preference; the Synoptics allow for one year only, whereas John's account involves at least two years and probably three. (*b*) The Fourth Gospel is not a historical record but a series of theological disquisitions artificially arranged in a framework of festivals at Jerusalem. (*c*) All four Gospels consist of detached episodes, which for the most part are unrelated to one another and without any temporal sequence, except that some incidents inevitably belong to the beginning and others to the end of the public career of Jesus.

None of these statements is self-evident, though it must be acknowledged that any constructive scheme must be tentative and precarious. In reply to (*a*) it must be pointed out that it is by no means certain that the Synoptic Gospels limit the ministry to a single year, and that it is gratuitous to assume that John never follows a reliable tradition when his record varies from the others. As against (*b*) we shall see that John handles his material freely, but that he is not indifferent to historical tradition. P. Gardner-Smith[5] has made out a strong case for John's dependence on oral or written traditions quite independent of the other three Gospels (see further, pp. 458-59). As for (*c*) some of the exponents of form criticism have exaggerated the want of consecutiveness in the traditional course of the ministry. Mark is far more continuous and coherent than Luke, as also is John, when allowance has been made for the interruptions in order (see above, pp. 446-47). It is not in details but in the narrative as a whole that we expect to find some clear march of events. On purely internal evidence we see reason to take the sections in the following order: 1:19–2:12; 3:22-30; 2:13–3:21; 3:31-36; 4; 6; 5; 7:15-24; 8:12-20; 7:1-14, 25-52; 8:21-59; 9; 10:19-29; 10:1-18; 10:30-42; 11; 12. Reading these sections in that order, we have the meeting of Jesus with the Baptist, the call of some disciples, a Galilean ministry beginning at Cana and continued at Capernaum. Some time after, Jesus carries on a ministry in Judea parallel to the mission of the Baptist. During this period he visits Jerusalem for the Passover, cleanses the temple of traffickers, and discourses with Nicodemus. A further Galilean ministry follows, resulting in great popularity. Jesus does not visit Jerusalem for the next Passover, but with the feeding of the multitude his popularity reaches its highest point about that time. A defection ensues, but Peter makes for the disciples their confession of faith. Later Jesus goes to Jerusalem for an unnamed feast, where his action and teaching begin a long controversy with the rabbis. Their hostility sends him back to Galilee, but he returns to Jerusalem for the feast of Tabernacles. Three months later he is in Jerusalem again for the feast of Dedication. He escapes to Trans-Jordan, returns to Judea and Bethany, then retreats quickly to Ephraim, coming to Jerusalem for the last Passover.

Within this period we note three Passovers, at two of which Jesus was in Jerusalem. Before the first Passover there is an undefined period spent partly in Galilee and partly in Judea. After this first Passover a long Galilean ministry begins, which lasts until after the second Passover. Jerusalem is visited after this for another feast, which was probably Pentecost. Between this visit in the summer and his return for Tabernacles in the autumn, Jesus was in Galilee. He was in Trans-Jordan or northern Judea until the final Passover, except for a visit to Jerusalem in December for the feast of Dedication. How does this conflict with such information as we gather from the other Gospels? The main difference is that Mark's Gospel has no account of any visit to Jerusalem until the closing week of our Lord's life. But the early source known as Q reports a saying of Jesus (Matt. 23:37-39; Luke 13:34-35) in his lament over Jerusalem, "How often would I have gathered your children together as a hen gathers her brood under her wings, and you would not!" Luke also (Acts 10:36-37) preserves a primitive record of a speech of Peter's, "You know the word which he sent to Israel, preaching good news of peace by Jesus Christ, . . . the word which was proclaimed throughout all

[5] *Saint John and the Synoptic Gospels* (Cambridge: University Press, 1938).

Judea, beginning from Galilee after the baptism which John preached." A large part of Mark is believed to represent the Petrine tradition. The Johannine account depends in great part upon the memory of one who was with Jesus during his visits to Jerusalem. The outstanding contradiction has to do with the cleansing of the temple. Here again it is Mark against John, for Matthew follows Mark, and in Luke the incident is a single verse (Luke 19:45) of Marcan material inserted into a non-Marcan context. Opinion is divided, most scholars favoring the Synoptic position of this incident. But some considerations point to the Johannine position as more probable. First, if Jesus visited Jerusalem several times in his ministry, is it likely that he made no protest against the scandal till his last visit? Second, as the Synoptics describe only one visit to Jerusalem, they can insert this tradition nowhere but at the last Passover. Third, the saying preserved in 2:20 has every appearance of being part of an original tradition, and points to the year A.D. 27, too early for the final Passover of the ministry.

On another point of chronology there is a difference between John and the Synoptics—the date of the Last Supper and thus of the Crucifixion. According to Mark, the Last Supper was the Passover meal (Mark 14:2, 16), and Matt. 26:19 and Luke 22:13 follow his lead. On the other hand, John clearly held that the Supper was not a paschal meal, that Jesus died at the time when the paschal lambs were being slain, and that the Passover was celebrated on the evening of the day of his death (cf. 13:29; 18:28; 19:14, 31, 42). All four Gospels agree that Jesus died on a Friday, but according to John this was Nisan 14, while the Synoptics regard that day as Nisan 15. Even in the Synoptic Gospels there are inconsistencies (cf. Mark 14:2, where the Sanhedrin decided not to arrest Jesus during the feast, with Mark 14:43), and Luke 22:15 seems to point to an unfulfilled desire. The earliest witness we have on the subject is I Cor. 5:7-8, where Paul apparently holds the view that Jesus died as the paschal lamb, which is the Johannine interpretation of the significance of the date on which the Lord was crucified. For this reason many expositors accept the date for the Crucifixion given in this Gospel and regard the Last Supper as an anticipation of the paschal meal. Others think that in this matter doctrinal considerations have prevailed over historical accuracy for John.

As regards topography, the Fourth Gospel is remarkable for the number of references to localities, many of which are not named in the other Gospels. Such are Bethany beyond Jordan, Cana in Galilee, Aenon near Salim, Jacob's well near Sychar and Mount Gerizim, a town Ephraim "near the wilderness" to which Jesus withdrew from Jerusalem. To these may be added "the sea of Tiberias" as another name for the sea of Galilee. The writer's familiarity with the topography of Jerusalem is detailed. He describes the pool of Bethesda (or rather Bethzatha) and mentions the pool of Siloam (with a reference to the Hebrew etymology of the name). He knows that the garden to which Jesus led his disciples after the Last Supper was "across the Kidron Valley," using a word which shows that he knew this was a wadi, the dry bed of a winter torrent. He is no stranger to the temple, recalling that in midwinter at the feast of Dedication Jesus walked and talked in Solomon's portico (which was on the eastern side of the Court of the Gentiles and sheltered from the severe winds). In the trial scene Pilate is represented as coming out of the praetorium and taking his seat on "The Pavement," in Aramaic, *Gabbāthā*. It is an anachronism to suppose that an Ephesian Christian came to Palestine on a pilgrimage to identify sacred sites in the first century. The destruction of the temple and the desolation of Jerusalem during and after the Jewish War, together with the migration of the Christians to Pella at the outbreak of that war, make it almost certain that whoever provided this local information knew Jerusalem and Palestine before A.D. 65. Archaeology has verified many of these allusions, adding to the valuable section in J. B. Lightfoot's *Biblical Essays*.[6] The latest examples are L. H. Vincent's identification of the *lithostrōton* or *Gabbāthā* with the splendid early Roman pavement (recently excavated) which was the court of the Tower of Antonia adjoining the temple and the identification of Bethesda (see Exeg. on 5:2) as the result of excavations begun in 1855 and subsequently carried much further.[7]

These instances do not necessarily prove that the actual author of the Gospel was himself acquainted with these places. But they do at least indicate that the information upon which he relied, whether oral or written, came from one who was at home in Palestine and knew Jerusalem well.

V. The Value and Use of the Fourth Gospel

In the days when this Gospel was regarded as the written record of our Lord's life and work by the disciple who stood nearest to him in understanding love, its supreme value both

[6] London: Macmillan & Co., 1893, pp. 140-79.

[7] See "L'Antonia et le Prétoire," *Revue Biblique*, XLII (1933), 83-113; see also Joachim Jeremias, *Die Wiederentdeckung von Bethesda* (Göttingen: Vandenhoeck & Ruprecht, 1949).

as a historical document and as an inspired revelation was beyond challenge. When the problem of its authorship was seen to have no certain solution, there was a marked tendency to deny it any place in the historical reconstruction of the life of Jesus. Its narratives were often regarded as fictitious settings for imaginary discourses in which the writer expounded his own views about the person of Jesus Christ. That reaction has now largely spent its force, and a more reasonable estimate of the Gospel is being set forth. The Johannine tradition—in the form which it assumes in the Fourth Gospel—is recognized as one of the five streams of tradition, the others being the "Sayings" tradition (Q), the Petrine tradition in Mark, the special Lukan tradition (L), and the special Jerusalem tradition peculiar to Matthew (M). "These traditions sometimes confirm, sometimes supplement, sometimes contradict each other. None can be treated as infallible; none can be neglected. Each has its own contribution to make, a contribution which only painstaking and intelligent study can discover." [8]

One method of study, therefore, is to read John side by side with a good synopsis of the first three Gospels. This is a historical discipline, for John supplements, corrects, and is corrected by them. This keeps us from forgetting that the evangelist is writing about an actual human life lived in Palestine in the first third of the first century. At the same time he writes as a member of the Christian society to those who are members, and to others who are religiously interested but know little about the life and meaning of the founder of Christianity. To the latter group his message is that God can be known, as nowhere else, in the self-revelation which he has given in the words and acts, the teaching, example and death of one whose life was spent in an eastern corner of the Roman Empire and who died by the sentence of a Roman procurator. To the same readers, but still more to those who had been trained in the teaching of the apostle Paul, he set forth the mystical side of the teaching of Jesus. To understand this aspect of the Gospel we must study it side by side with the Johannine epistles to see how the same evangelist applied the lessons of the gospel to the members of the church, so that spiritual fellowship with God in Christ should be more than an emotional ecstasy and should perforce express itself in love of the brotherhood.

With all his sympathy for the highest forms of contemporary religious thought and aspiration, the evangelist meets this quest for God, not by allowing the truths of the gospel to evaporate into a cloudy theosophy, but by showing that all the terms of their religious vocabulary became personal in the human life of Jesus, the Logos incarnate. As he thought of every category of celestial dignity and honor, he could have said:

> The highest place that heaven affords
> Is his, is his by right.[9]

VI. Some Johannine Problems

In this section a rather fuller account will be given of some of the problems which have been sketched lightly in the previous sections, together with more detailed references for those who may wish to follow up these lines of inquiry.

A. Apologetic Interests in the Fourth Gospel.—The supreme aim of the Gospel is positive, a faith-creating witness to Jesus as the divine Son, in order that the readers may be brought into possession of that life eternal which is promised in his name. There is, however, a negative aim—the defense of the Christian message against attacks from without, or misrepresentations of the authority of Jesus Christ, or dangerous attempts to explain away the historic revelation by a vague theosophy. There is thus an implied polemic against (*a*) synagogue Judaism, (*b*) the sect of John the Baptist, (*c*) Gnosticism, especially in that form known as Docetism.

1. ***Synagogue Judaism.***—In the early days of primitive Christianity the first disciples appear to have been regular in their attendance at the services of the temple and may even have had no quarrel with the worship of the synagogue. Stephen and the Hellenists carried on their disputations within the Greek-speaking synagogues, and it was Paul's regular custom to open his mission in any town he visited in the synagogue on the sabbath. When asked to read and expound the appointed lesson from the Prophets, he lost no time in pointing to Jesus as the expected Messiah. Sooner or later this led to a breach, and the Christian preaching was continued in some hired hall or in the house of one of the wealthier converts to the new faith. Even in Jerusalem, the home of the most conservative Judaistic Christianity, the murder of James the Lord's brother in A.D. 62 showed a growing tension, and the flight of Judean Christians to Pella on the outbreak of the war with Rome in A.D. 65 marks the final severance. We know from Justin Martyr's *Dialogue with Trypho* in the middle of the next century the kind of discussion that was carried on between

[8] T. W. Manson, *The Life of Jesus, A Survey of the Available Material,* (5) The Fourth Gospel (Manchester: Manchester University Press, 1947), p. 20.

[9] Thomas Kelly, "The head that once was crowned with thorns."

the representatives of the old and those of the new religion. But a century earlier there seems to have been a book of "testimonies," perhaps several such books, in which passages from the Old Testament were collected which could be used in controversy with the Jews to prove that in the life, death, and resurrection of Jesus messianic prophecies have their fulfillment.

No reader can fail to be struck by the way in which our Lord's opponents in this Gospel are so often described as "the Jews." In the Synoptic Gospels Jesus is often found in conflict with scribes, Pharisees, or Sadducees, where he criticizes their besetting faults. Here it is a national term that covers various sects without distinction in most of the disputes, and the subject of controversy is often the very matters which were debated between church and synagogue. Jesus asserts his divinity and pre-existence, and his claim to divine sonship is rejected as blasphemous (5:18; 8:58; 10:33). Incredulity is shown toward a claim that a Galilean and a native of Nazareth is the Messiah (1:46; 7:41, 52), whereas the Scripture assigns him to Bethlehem and describes him as of Davidic descent. Yet before the publication of this Gospel these very claims had been made for Jesus (Matt. 2:1; Luke 2:4; Rom. 1:3) and are assumed by the evangelist. His enemies disputed the genuineness of his miracles (9:18), and were horrified by his sacramental language (6:52-60). Excommunication from the synagogue and even martyrdom are spoken of as trials to be endured by followers of Jesus (9:22, 34; 12:42; 16:2). Another trace of the contemporary situation when the Gospel was written may be found in the writer's attitude to the Old Testament, the supreme authority in Judaism. The inferiority of the Torah to the gospel is emphasized in the prologue, "The law [Torah] was given through Moses; grace and truth came through Jesus Christ" (1:17). Yet the Scriptures have their authority, and they testify to him (5:39; 10:34-36). The hostile attitude of the Jews to Jesus is attributed to their ignorance of the Father (5:38; 7:28; 8:39-44, 54-55; 15:21; 16:3; 17:25). Yet with all this hostility to "the Jews" the evangelist allows to Judaism its place in the providential order (4:22) and gratefully recognizes its noblest characteristics (1:47).

We must look for an explanation of these seemingly contradictory strains to some words written about the same time in the same province of Asia. In the Revelation of John there is a fierce denunciation of "those who say that they are Jews and are not, but are a synagogue of Satan" (Rev. 2:9). We may compare with this Paul's claim that the church is the true heir of the promises given to Israel, "The present Jerusalem . . . is in slavery with her children. But the Jerusalem above is free, and she is our mother" (Gal. 4:25-26). So Paul again contended: "He is not a real Jew who is one outwardly, nor is true circumcision something external and physical. He is a Jew who is one inwardly, and real circumcision is a matter of the heart, spiritual and not literal" (Rom. 2:28-29). That is the contention made again in the argument that the true children of Abraham are those "who walk in the steps of that faith which our father Abraham had while still uncircumcised" (Rom. 4:12). So in this Gospel, to those who boast that "Abraham is our father," Jesus is made to say, "If you were Abraham's children, you would do what Abraham did" (8:39). The climax of this controversy may be seen in the universalism of this Gospel (3:16; 4:42; 8:12; 9:5; 10:16; 12:20-23; 17:21). Here, as in Paul's polemic against Jewish particularism, the universal note heard in Jonah and in the Isaian prophecies is sounded out again in the Christian proclamation.

2. ***The Sect of John the Baptist.***—The attitude of this evangelist to John the Baptist compels attention. In the Synoptics John is the resurgent voice of prophecy, the leader of the national mission of repentance and hope, whose eschatological sacrament of baptism is the seal of those who are waiting for participation in the coming kingdom of God. He is also the herald of a mightier One who would baptize with the Holy Spirit. In the Fourth Gospel the historical situation is so far preserved that John's witness to Jesus is that he is the mightier One who would baptize with the Holy Spirit. It should also be noted that in agreement with the older tradition Jesus pays a high tribute to the Baptist (cf. Matt. 11:7-11; Luke 7:24-27; John 5:33-36), while recognizing that his office is preparatory and inferior. The significant difference between the Synoptics and our Gospel is that in the Fourth Gospel every mention of the Baptist emphasizes this subordinate function and status. Twice over in the prologue the hymn about the Logos is interrupted to insert words about the Baptist which can be intended only to underline this subordination (1:6-8, 15). Immediately after the prologue there are two scenes in which the Baptist testifies to the mission and messiahship of Jesus, and expressly disclaims such a title for himself (1:19-27, 29-34). In a later scene John's disciples remark upon the greater success of Jesus, to which John replies by repeating his earlier testimony, closing with the words, "He must increase, but I must decrease" (3:22-30). Again in 4:1-3 another reference is made to this superior attraction of the crowds by Jesus. In the teaching of Jesus stress is laid on the higher value of his works as a divine testimony to his mission than

the witness of John (5:36-37); and when Jesus returned late in his ministry to the region where John was baptizing at first, the crowd remarked, "John did no sign, but everything that John said about this man was true" (10:40-42). A still more striking feature of this testimony is the evangelist's silence about the baptism of Jesus by John.

All these indications led Wilhelm Baldensperger[10] to propound a theory that a main purpose of this Gospel was to refute the claims of a sect that regarded John the Baptist as the Messiah, and exalted him above Jesus and called themselves after his name. This was not altogether a new suggestion, for Hugo Grotius in the seventeenth century and G. C. Storr in the eighteenth century had drawn attention to such a possibility. But Baldensperger pushed the theory further by showing that we have evidence in Acts 18:24-28 that Apollos, before his arrival at Ephesus, "knew only the baptism of John," and in 19:1-4 that in the same city there was a group of residuary disciples of the Baptist who were led by Paul into the full Christian faith and received baptism in the name of the Lord Jesus. He carried the investigation still further by citing passages from the *Clementine Recognitions* (I. 53, 60) which preserve a tradition, going back possibly to the third century, about the disciples of John who had formed a sect and proclaimed their master as the Messiah. An interesting reference was made in a footnote to the Mandaean sect, to which Wilhelm Brandt had recently drawn attention, but Baldensperger deliberately refrained from attempting to work this possibility into his argument. (For the later attempts to use Mandaean material in illustration of this Gospel, see below, pp. 454-55.) The theory exaggerates the importance of this element in the structure of the Gospel, but we may well accept this controversy with a rival sect as supplying the evangelist with a subsidiary aim.

3. ***Gnosticism.***—About the time when Christianity was first heard of, the world of Hellenism was pervaded by a strange mixture of religious ideas combining elements from Orphic beliefs, cosmological speculations, astrological lore, and magical demonology from Babylonia, Persia, and Judea, as well as a mystical theosophy from Egypt. This religious syncretism took many forms. By the middle of the second century it had invaded the church in force, and some of its most adventurous thinkers had elaborated great speculative systems which attempted to reinterpret Christian theology in accordance with their alien presuppositions. These were essentially dualistic. There was an upper world of pure spirit and a lower world of matter. The two problems to be solved were those of creation and redemption. The upper world of light was the abode of God, who is pure spirit. The lower world of darkness is evil. How can the good God have created this evil world? To account for its existence a series of emanations from God, called aeons, are postulated; they rule over the spaces that intervene between heaven and earth, and the last of these, the most remote from God, is the demiurge, who is responsible for creating this material world. Those men in whose soul there resides a spark of the heavenly light are prisoners in this world of matter. To escape from their prison they must ascend from this dark dungeon, passing through successive stages, each guarded by one of "the world rulers of this present darkness," who are sometimes identified with the planets and the sun and the moon. Redemption means deliverance from that iron necessity which holds men in the bondage of fear. To elect souls a Redeemer comes down who reveals the secret knowledge (γνῶσις) by which the world rulers, the watchers at the several gates, can be eluded until the sphere is reached which is above the realm of the stars. Such are the main conceptions that underlie the varied forms of theosophy grouped under the common title of Gnosticism. Our fullest knowledge is derived from those systems that had incorporated Christian elements and claimed to be an accommodation of the facts of the Christian revelation to contemporary religious philosophy. (For a discussion of parallels to some Gnostic ideas in the Fourth Gospel see below, pp. 452-56.)

Forty years before this Gospel was published in Ephesus, Paul was informed that the church at Colossae, in the same part of Asia Minor, was infected with a heresy that seems to have combined an incipient Gnosticism with some Jewish ascetic practices. Later on the writer of Revelation, in the letter to the church in Thyatira, denounces some form of heresy and contrasts those "who do not hold this teaching, who have not learned what some call the deep things of Satan" (Rev. 2:24). This is a parody of a technical phrase of Gnosticism used in a letter addressed to a church in proconsular Asia. Still closer to the Gospel, we have I John, which was almost certainly written by this evangelist, but if not, then by one in closest affinity with him (see pp. 461-62). This epistle denounces some false teachers who deny that Jesus is the Christ, thereby denying the Father and the Son (I John 2:22). "Every spirit which confesses that Jesus Christ has come in the flesh is of God, and every spirit which does not confess Jesus is not of God" (I John 4:2-3). In a later develop-

[10] *Der Prolog des vierten Evangeliums* (Freiburg i.B.: J. C. B. Mohr, 1898).

ment of Gnosticism the true incarnation of Christ was denied in two ways. Docetism treated the human nature of Jesus as a mere illusion. Another speculation regarded the man Jesus as originally distinct from the heavenly Christ, who was an emanation from the Deity, temporarily connected with Jesus, descending on him at his baptism and leaving him before the passion. The writer of I John thus seems to be condemning some of the Gnostic perverters of the historical tradition which is the very core of the Christian revelation.

We have then three distinct reasons for assuming that Gnostic heresy was endemic in the district around Ephesus by the time this Gospel was written. Against the notion that matter is essentially evil, the evangelist hurls his refutation in the words "the Word became flesh" (1:14). Against the dualism of matter and spirit, which implied the eternity of matter and the belief that the world was created by the demiurge, the lowest of the aeons, he declared of the Logos, "All things came into being through him, and apart from him nothing came into being." The denial that Christ could have suffered pain and death is combated by the allusions to his thirst, his weariness, the print of the nails and the spear thrust. A negative indication may be discovered in the absence of any reference to Simon of Cyrene's bearing the cross, since one of the Gnostic beliefs was that it was Simon who went to death in the place of Jesus. So also we may account for the almost complete silence about angels and demons, in view of the prominence given to these agencies in the Gnostic view of the universe. It is also significant that the Gnostic watchwords *gnōsis* (knowledge), *pistis* (faith), and *sophia* (wisdom) are entirely absent from this Gospel, although the verbs "to know" and "to believe" are so frequent. "Wisdom" is replaced by "truth."

B. Relation of the Gospel to Contemporary Religious Thought.—We can consider here only the most important of many possible points of contact between the Fourth Gospel and its non-Christian religious environment.

1. *Philo and Hellenistic Judaism.*—We have no definite knowledge about the extent to which Hellenistic ways of thought had penetrated the Judaism of Palestine; the subject has been treated in the Schweich Lectures by Wilfred L. Knox.[11] There are a few Greek words which had already been transliterated into Hebrew or Aramaic and which survive in the Talmud. But the invasion which at one time threatened to engulf the pure monotheism of the people receded under the heroic resistance of the Maccabean patriots. At a later epoch the mad attempt of Gaius Caligula stirred up a similar fervor for the ancestral faith, while the conflict with Rome, culminating in the destruction of the temple under Titus in A.D. 70, and the obliteration of Jerusalem under Hadrian in 135, drove the Jews into a determined religious isolationism. It was otherwise in the Western Dispersion during the last two centuries B.C. and in the first part of the first century A.D. It was in Alexandria that the impact of Hellenism upon Jewish religious thought and language left its first and deepest mark. There it was that the Pentateuch was translated from Hebrew into Greek. This resulted not only in a change of language but also in a considerable change of ideas. In due course the rest of the Old Testament was turned into Greek, whether at Alexandria or in other centers of Greek-speaking Judaism. The Greek Old Testament contained other books which were never accepted into the Hebrew canon of Scripture, some of them originally written in Hebrew or Aramaic, but some, notably the Wisdom of Solomon, not only written in Greek but bearing unmistakable signs of Hellenistic culture. The outstanding example of the marriage of Hebrew religion to Greek philosophy is found in the writings of Philo. This Alexandrian Jew was a prolific author whose books were for the most part allegorical expositions of the Pentateuch, in which the thoughts of Moses were interpreted according to Platonic or Stoic teaching. Others were either philosophical dialogues or apologetic works.

The best short account of Philo's philosophy of religion is that by James Drummond.[12] Here it will suffice to mention the points in which this Alexandrian Judaism invites comparison with John. Philo used the term Logos to express that personified activity of God in creation and revelation which was represented in later Judaism by the semipersonalized figure of wisdom. With him this term, which had been current in Greek speculation about divine things from Heraclitus to the Stoics, was a bridge to span the gulf between the conception of the absolute and transcendent God of Plato and Aristotle and the idea of the divine immanence which was taught by the Stoics. For in Jewish religion the same tension was felt. Hebrew monotheism emphasized the transcendence of "the high and lofty One that inhabiteth eternity, whose name is Holy" (Isa. 57:15). Yet "in the beginning God created the heaven and the earth." The Targums emphasized the

[11] *Some Hellenistic Elements in Primitive Christianity* (London: British Academy, 1944).

[12] In James Hastings, ed., *Dictionary of the Bible* (New York: Charles Scribner's Sons, 1904), extra volume, pp. 197-208.

divine transcendence, and the Septuagint followed their method of toning down or explaining away anything in the Hebrew text that implied direct communion between God and man or attributed human action or properties to God. An intermediary agent is constantly interposed. Philo carried this tendency much further in his use of the term Logos. As it occurs thirteen hundred times in his numerous works, with a wide variety of meanings, there is room here for no more than a brief summary of the Philonic teaching about the Logos. The Logos is both the reason and the word of God; the intermediary acting in the creation of the visible world; the image of God through whom the whole universe was framed; the revealer of God who enlightens men, distributes his gifts to them, and sustains their spiritual life; the high priestly mediator and intercessor (Paraclete) for men with the Father of the world. A passage which inevitably reminds us of John 6:31-35 sees in the manna the type of the divine Logos, while another passage recalls the conversation by the well of Sychar (John 4:5-14; also 7:37-38) by the description of the Logos as "the living stream."

It would be a mistake to assume that the evangelist was a student of the writings of Philo, whose use of the term is so vague and changeful. In John the Logos is personal and incarnate. The Gospel is not an exposition of a speculative theory of creation, but the record of a life in the flesh whose explanation is a relation of eternal sonship. This was introduced to the world of Hellenism by a technical term with which the readers were already familiar. In the words of James Denney, "Though he borrows the conception, he does not borrow from it."

2. ***Hermetic Writings.***—During the present century considerable attention has been devoted to a collection of tractates consisting of religious speculation and philosophical instruction supposed to have been given by a deified sage called Hermes Trismegistus ("Hermes thrice greatest"). These tractates represent a type of speculative mysticism prevalent in Egypt in the second and third centuries of our era, in which a religious interest originating outside Judaism combined Greek philosophical ideas with material suggested by some contact with the Septuagint and with Hellenistic Jewish mysticism. The most important of these writings are the first and thirteenth. The first bears the title *Poimandres,* which was formerly explained as meaning "Shepherd of Men," but is explained by the writer himself as "The Reason of the Sovereignty." The first part contains a myth of the creation and of the origin of man, largely influenced by the cosmogony of Genesis. The second part tells how God reveals the way by which man, enlightened by knowledge, can ascend to his Father; and then how the prophet goes out into the world to preach repentance. Some reject his message, while others ask for further instruction. He preaches that knowledge (γνῶσις), especially in the sense of knowledge of God, leads to immortality, and that ignorance, displayed in self-indulgence and love of the body, leads to death. Repentance means passing from the way of death—darkness, ignorance, error, drunkenness, corruption—to the way of life—light, knowledge, truth, sobriety, salvation.

The thirteenth tractate bears the title, *Secret Discourse About Regeneration.* Tat asks his father Hermes from what womb a man can be born again, and from what seed. He is told that the womb is wisdom, the seed is the true good, the begetter is the will of God, and the ministrant is some man who is a son of God, working in subordination to God's will. To be born again a man must cleanse himself from the irrational torments of matter. Then the powers of God come and build up the body of reason. This is due to the mercy of God. These powers are described as truth, the good, life, and light. The body of reason is literally "the body of the Logos," the Logos being an organism of which the several powers of God are the constituent parts; and this organism is built up in the reborn man, as the body is built up out of the several members.

As already said, these *Hermetica* were written in Greek long after the date of the Fourth Gospel, but they probably contain elements that were current in the world of Hellenism at a much earlier time. Remote as this teaching is from that which we find in the Johannine doctrine of the divine revelation in the Logos, and of that birth from above which alone enables a man to see the kingdom of God, there are yet points of contact which show that a religious vocabulary was at the disposal of a Christian missionary who could give a historical content to these mythological speculations.[13]

3. ***Odes of Solomon.***—In the years before World War I considerable excitement was aroused by the discovery of a Syriac manuscript containing forty-two odes of Solomon. The name was already known, and five of the odes were incorporated in the Gnostic work of the third century preserved in Coptic and entitled *Pistis Sophia.* Rendel Harris, who discovered it and published the first edition of the odes, regarded it as a Jewish-Christian hymnbook of the last quarter of the first century. Adolf von

[13] See Walter Scott, *Hermetica* (Oxford: Clarendon Press, 1924-36), 4 Vols.; C. H. Dodd, *The Bible and the Greeks* (London: Hodder & Stoughton, 1935), pp. 99-248.

Harnack favored the theory of a Jewish author with a mystical bent, writing possibly in Hebrew somewhere in or near Palestine between 30 B.C. and A.D. 67, but he also detected the hand of a Palestinian-Christian editor who worked the materials over about A.D. 100. Theodore von Zahn voted for a Christian author between 120 and 150. Louis Batiffol attributed them to a Syrian Christian between 100 and 120, while J. H. Bernard thought that the odes may have been written about the year 200 for the purpose of Christian instruction leading to baptism. There are Jewish elements which show that the author was steeped in the Old Testament and adapted Hebrew poetical structures. The many references to the life and person of Christ are unmistakable. But some passages are ascribed by Hermann Gunkel to Gnostic influence. Although there are no direct citations from either the Old or the New Testament, contemporary opinion inclines strongly to the view that the odes are Christian in origin, and that they come from a region where a kind of Christian Gnosticism was prevalent. As we listen to the use of the Logos idea and the frequent reference to light, peace, and joy, to eternal life in fellowship with God, to that fellowship as the result of knowledge and of love, we seem to be breathing the atmosphere of the Fourth Gospel. Once again we are reminded of a religious world which was seeking after God, and which responded to a presentation of the Christian message in terms that suggest some kinship with the mystical side of Gnosticism.

4. ***Mystery Religions.***—We have seen that in the Hermetic writings there was a type of mysticism which offered regeneration and union with deity through the impartation of knowledge, apart from any sacramental rites. But there was another way in which the aspiration for union with God and the yearning for immortality found satisfaction throughout the Greco-Roman world. The mystery religions sprang from primitive attempts to represent the miracle of the corn of wheat that falls into the ground and dies in order that it may bring forth an abundant harvest. These ancient Greek and Oriental rites influenced one another in various ways and took a variety of forms. The common features were rites of initiation and of cleansing, rites of communion with a divinity through a sacramental meal, dramatic representations leading to a vision of an epiphany of the deity, and an assurance of immortality.

Some writers have tried to find evidence that the Fourth Gospel has been influenced by the mysteries. Naturally that is looked for in chs. 3 and 6, where allusions to baptism and the Eucharist can easily be detected. Moreover, "light" and "life" and terms closely connected with these play a prominent part in the liturgies and instructions of these cults. Initiation ceremonies for union with the deity were carried out with light effects, and the ceremony was called φωτισμός (illumination). The verb φωτίζω was also used of revelation, of imparting the knowledge of God. We know that in early Christian writers these words were often used of baptism. These initiatory rites were also described as leading to regeneration.

The discourse on the bread of life shows how easy it would be for those who had been indoctrinated with the ideas of the mystery cults to find parallels in the Christian Eucharist. The words of institution recorded in Mark 14:22-24, "This is my body. . . . This is my blood," would recur to any reader of the Fourth Gospel when he read, "Unless you eat the flesh of the Son of man and drink his blood, you have no life in you. . . . He who eats my flesh and drinks my blood abides in me, and I in him" (6:53, 56). It is true that in the higher mysteries there was no talk of eating a god, but such crude ideas found a place in the more primitive stage. The Johannine dialogue points to a Jewish repudiation of such an interpretation as horrible and incredible (6:52, 60, 66), which enabled Jesus to say, "It is the spirit that gives life, the flesh is of no avail; the words that I have spoken to you are spirit and life" (6:63). But this very disclaimer of the literal interpretation of the figure of speech seems to presuppose a tendency in Gentile communities to press too far the parallels between the Christian sacraments and the pagan mysteries.

5. ***Mandaeism.***—During the 1920's a significant group of German scholars attracted attention to a little-known literature treasured by an obscure sect which still survives in communities on the lower Euphrates and the lower Tigris, and also in scattered families farther east in Khuzistan. The Mandaeans claim a connection with John the Baptist. They have to live near running water to practice their continual baptismal rites. When they were discovered by Christian missionaries in the seventeenth century, they were found to be neither Catholic nor Protestant Christians and were called "Christians of St. John." Their books, however, show a bitter hostility to the Jews, also to the Christians, and even Christ is often alluded to as "the liar." Copies of the manuscripts of these sacred writings found their way into European libraries soon after the missionaries reported what they had discovered. But the obscure dialect of Aramaic in which they were written was not competently explored until Theodor Nöldeke published his Mandaean grammar in 1875. In the first quarter of the twentieth century Mark Lidzbarski translated into German the three

books of the Mandaean canon. These are (*a*) the Ginza, or Treasury, sometimes called the Great Book; (*b*) the Book of John (the Baptist); and (*c*) the Qolasta (Quintessence), a volume of liturgies for the annual baptismal festival and the service for the dead.

As soon as these ancient books became accessible to European scholars they were pounced upon with eagerness as evidence of a pre-Christian gnosis which threw a flood of light upon the religious environment of the writers of several of the books in the New Testament, more especially the author of the Fourth Gospel. Caution was needed, for internal evidence showed that this Book of John was compiled after A.D. 651, the date of the Mohammedan conquest, whereas in the Ginza, the most important of these sacred books and considerably earlier than the Book of John, there is only one reference to John the Baptist, except some allusions in passages bearing marks of later interpolation. At the same time it was probable that much in these curious writings of a late date might go back to a much earlier tradition. The outstanding figure in this religion is *Manda d'Hayyê* (γνῶσις τῆς ζωῆς), meaning "secret knowledge of life," and this puts the religion back into the great Gnostic movement. Wilhelm Bousset, one of the leading authorities on Gnosticism, concluded from the data supplied in these sacred books that a sect of Baptists, whose original home was near the Jordan, migrated to the lower Euphrates, bringing with them Jewish-Gnostic beliefs characterized by Phoenician polytheistic elements, garbled Jewish reminiscences, and a very slight Christian tincture. There a gradual transformation took place as this medley of ideas united with strong elements of Babylonian-Persian syncretism, in which Parsiism predominated. The older conceptions were slowly pushed out by the newer, and the highest point in the development is reached in the tractates on the doctrine of the king of light. Here we have an almost pure form of dualistic monotheism, with strong traces of Parsi influence, though Wilhelm Brandt[14] would see in this teaching also some evidence of a Judaeo-Christian gnosis. The great difficulty in attempting to read the Mandaean writings is that there is no indication of chronological order, but a bewildering variety of ideas from the most diverse sources and periods of history, all assembled with an utter disregard of internal consistency.

Two of the leading commentators of the Fourth Gospel, Walter Bauer and Rudolf Bultmann, have drawn attention to some remarkable parallels to be found in the Mandaean scriptures. Thus, the Father, the Lord of Majesty, speaks to the First, his Son, "My son, come, be my messenger; come, be my bearer, and descend for me to the mutinous earth. Go to the world of darkness, into the darkness in which is no ray of light, to the place of lions, to the abode of cursed leopards. . . ." There are many passages in which, among a formidable jumble of mythology, parallels of a kind can be extracted. Thus, the idea of the unity of the Son with the Father can be paralleled, as also the conception of the full power with which the Son is entrusted to give life, to pronounce judgment, to lead men out of darkness into light. He knows his own and chooses them, but he is hated by the world. As he has come, so will he go; as he has come down, so will he ascend; then he will be sought and not found. He will be vindicated by his ascension. Before his departure he prays for his own, for whom he has prepared a place to dwell, and he shows them the way. Parallels for all these characteristic ideas in the Fourth Gospel can be found by diligent search. The evidence is very impressive until we examine all the references in their context, noting the variety of sources from which they come. We then observe that it is by no means always one son of one father of whom these things, or something more or less like them, are said. Quite a variety of messengers are sent from the world of light to the nether world of darkness. Two of the more poetical similitudes may be cited as they recall some of the great "I am" passages in the Fourth Gospel:

A shepherd am I who loves his sheep; I keep watch over my sheep and my lambs:
Around my neck I carry my sheep, and they wander not from the village.
I bring them into the fold, the good fold, and then with me they find pasture.
From the mouth of Euphrates, Euphrates the radiant, I brought them wonderful gifts.

. . . .

No wolf leaps into our fold, and of fierce lion they need not be frightened.
Of the tempest they need not be fearful, and no thief can ever assail us:
No thief breaks into their fold, and of the sword they need stand in no terror.
When my sheep had lain down in peace, and my head on the threshold was lying,
Then opened a cleft in the height, and the thunder thundered behind me.

The true envoy am I,
In whom is no lie:
The true one in whom is no lie,
In him is no blemish nor fault.

. . . .

A vine are we, a vine of life,
A tree which cannot die:

[14] Article "Mandaeans" in *Encyclopaedia of Religion and Ethics*, ed. James Hastings (New York: Charles Scribner's Sons, 1908-27), VIII, 380-92.

The tree of praise, whose fragrance stays
All men with breath of life.[15]

The reference to the Euphrates in the first quotation proves that this song belongs to a period after the migration from the Jordan region to Mesopotamia. In that case the borrowing, if such there is, was certainly not on the part of the evangelist.

An article by F. C. Burkitt [16] brought to light the true historical situation that lies behind these curious writings. He has proved that the Mandaeans got their ideas about the Christians and their use of the Old Testament from the Peshitta, the Syriac translation made by Rabulla, bishop of Edessa in A.D. 411. Some of their terms are Mandaean transliterations of words found in that Syriac translation. Further, he shows that *Eshu mshiha* (Jesus Messiah) is a false prophet, and their hostility to him is their antagonism to the fully developed Byzantine church. In several places "Christ" is actually called "Byzantine" (*Rumaia*). There is another figure, *Anush* or *Enush,* who comes into the world in the days of *Piliatus* (Pilate), the king of the world, works miracles of healing and raises the dead. Before his ascension he unmasks the Deceiver, the Byzantine Christ, who is seized by the Jews and crucified.

Burkitt found the clew to the origin of this sect in the *Scholion* of Theodore bar Konai (A.D. 792), who tells us that its founder was one Ado, who came from Adiabene into Babylonia, and that the doctrine of the Mandaeans was borrowed from the Marcionites and the Manichees. It is probable that Mandaean history does not start in the Mediterranean world, but in lower Babylonia, some seventy years after the coming of Islam, and that a wandering ascetic from Adiabene taught doctrines drawn partly from Marcionites, partly from Manichees, both of whom were influential in Mesopotamia, while the astrological element may well have come from Bardesanes the Gnostic in the Euphrates Valley.

Except in so far as ideas and phraseology have been handed down from some later forms of the Gnostic movement, it is evidently an anachronism to look to the Mandaean scriptures for light upon the milieu of the Fourth Gospel. Indeed, it is more probable that Johannine echoes are to be heard occasionally in writings that were in part influenced by the Syriac version of the Bible.

C. Influence of the Old Testament and Earlier Christian Writings.—Having considered the relationship between the Fourth Gospel and its non-Christian religious environment, we may now turn to a brief survey of the influence of the Old Testament and earlier Christian writings.

1. *The Old Testament.*—Whatever thought forms may have been brought in from Hellenism to make the Christian gospel intelligible to the Gentile world, the Fourth Evangelist is rooted and grounded in the religion of the Old Testament. His historical sense prevents him from separating the earthly life of Jesus from the religious world of Palestine. The rules that regulate the life of the people, the customs and usages, the religious festivals, go back to the Pentateuch, or to the re-establishment of the national life in the time of Ezra and Nehemiah. The divine choice of Israel for the religious education of the race is acknowledged, "for salvation is from the Jews" (4:22). Scripture is appealed to as a final authority, its prophecies must be fulfilled; actions are regarded as predestined if the event seems to be foreshadowed by some word in the Old Testament. Jesus is set forth as the Messiah of Jewish expectations and the Son of man of Daniel's dream. The opening words of the Gospel inevitably recall the creation story at the beginning of Genesis. The allusions to baptism (if such they are) in 3:5 and 13:10 seem to be influenced by Ezek. 36:25-27. The allegory of the good shepherd with the contrasted figure of the hireling in ch. 10 is full of allusions to Ps. 23; Isa. 40:11; Jer. 23:1-4; Ezek. 34:1-15; 37:24. The allegory of the true vine carries the reader back to many passages in the prophets where this symbol is used (Isa. 5:1-7; Jer. 2:21; Ezek. 15:2, 6; 19:10-14; Hos. 10:1). Indeed, there are comparatively few chapters where quotations from or allusions to the Old Testament do not catch the eye. The following is not a complete list, but it shows the dependence of the Gospel upon the Scriptures of the Old Testament:

John 1:23 (Isa. 40:3); 1:29 (Exod. 12:3; Isa. 53:7); 1:51 (Gen. 28:12); 2:17 (Ps. 69:9); 6:31 (Exod. 16:15; Neh. 9:15; cf. Pss. 78:24, 25; 105:40); 6:45 (Isa. 54:13); 7:37 (Isa. 44:3; 55:1); 7:38 (Isa. 12:3); 7:42 (Pss. 89:3, 4; Mic. 5:2; I Sam. 16:1); 8:17 (Deut. 17:6; 19:15); 10:34 (Ps. 82:6); 12:13 (Ps. 118:25-26); 12:14-15 (Zech. 9:9); 12:34 (Pss. 89:4; 110:4; Isa. 9:7; Ezek. 37:25; Dan. 7:14); 12:38 (Isa. 53:1); 12:39-40 (Isa. 6:10); 13:18 (Ps. 41:9); 15:6 (Ps. 80:15-16); 15:25 (Pss. 35:19; 69:4); 19:24 (Ps. 22:18); 19:28-29 (Ps. 69:21); 19:36 (Exod. 12:46; Num. 9:12); 19:37 (Zech. 12:10).

2. *Wisdom Literature.*—It is in the prologue that the influence of personified wisdom is most clearly marked, as wisdom passes over into Logos. Prov. 8:22-30 carries us back to the crea-

[15] W. F. Howard, "The Fourth Gospel and Mandaean Gnosticism," *London Quarterly Review,* Jan. 1927, pp. 72-85.

[16] "The Mandaeans," *Journal of Theological Studies,* XXIX (1928), 225-35.

tion story in Genesis, but it leads on to many passages in the Wisdom of Jesus the Son of Sirach (Ecclesiasticus) and the Wisdom of Solomon. There is a verse in Ecclus. 42:15 which reads in the Hebrew (but not in the Septuagint), "By the word of God his works were formed, and what was wrought by his good pleasure according to his decree." Also, Ecclus. 43:26 declares, "By reason of him his end has success, and by his word all things consist." No doubt Ps. 33:6—"By the word of the LORD were the heavens made; and all the host of them by the breath of his mouth"—comes between Genesis and the development in the wisdom books. There is, however, another passage, Ecclus. 24—the praise of wisdom—which has striking parallels with John 1:14. Vss. 4 and 8 read: "I dwelt (κατεσκήνωσα) in the high places, and my throne is in the pillar of the cloud. . . . Then the Creator of all things gave me a commandment, and he that created me made my tabernacle (σκηνήν) to rest, and said, Let thy tabernacle be (κατασκήνωσον) in Jacob, and thy inheritance in Israel." The "pillar of the cloud" was the *shekina* of later Judaism (see Exeg. on John 1:14).

The Wisdom of Solomon is even closer to the thought of the Johannine prologue. Such sayings as "With thee is wisdom, which knoweth thy works, and was present when thou wast making the world" (9:9), and "She that is the artificer of all things taught me, even wisdom" (7:22) are near in thought to John 1:1, 3. So again, "Being compared with light, she is found to be before it; for to the light of day succeedeth night, but against wisdom evil doth not prevail" (Wisd. Sol. 7:29-30) recalls John 1:5. In the famous description of wisdom in Wisd. Sol. 7:22–8:1, the word μονογενής ("only begotten") occurs, even though its meaning is not quite the same as in John 1:18 (as an attribute of wisdom it means of a single essence, yet as the next word says, various in its modes of action). J. A. F. Gregg[17] gives a long selection of parallel thoughts between the two books.

3. ***Pauline Writings and Hebrews.***—The dominant influence on John is beyond question the factual tradition of the earthly life of Jesus. The next section will consider how far this reached the evangelist through oral sources and to what extent he shows acquaintance with the earlier Gospels. The interpretation which he put upon that historic tradition brings him into a close relationship to the two outstanding theologians of the early church whose writings have been preserved. Apart from the well-known passage in Q (Matt. 11:27; Luke 10:22), the Synoptic Gospels do not explicitly anticipate the Christology which is so characteristic of the Fourth Gospel. This, however, is found both in the Pauline letters and in the Epistle to the Hebrews, which, though later than Paul, was probably written earlier than Luke or Matthew. The significant feature of Paul's references to the pre-existence of Christ is that they do not form part of a speculative argument, but are made almost casually to support an appeal for humility and social harmony (Phil. 2:1-11), or for self-sacrificing generosity (II Cor. 8:7-9). He assumes his readers' familiarity with this cardinal doctrine of the faith. The cosmic significance of Christ and his creative activity are set forth in some fullness in opposition to some form of incipient Gnosticism which is invading the church at Colossae (Col. 1:15-20). Yet this great passage takes up thoughts which have already found terse expression in I Cor. 8:6; II Cor. 4:6, and were expressed in rather different language in Eph. 1:10. Christ is set forth as the creative agent and the final cause of the universe. The phrase "the image [εἰκών] of the invisible God" (Col. 1:15) recalls II Cor. 4:4, "the glory of Christ, who is the image [εἰκών] of God."

This term, and indeed the whole christological passage in Col. 1, is further developed in the exordium to the Epistle to the Hebrews: "[God] has spoken to us in his Son, . . . through whom he made the worlds; who being the effulgence [ἀπαύγασμα] of his glory and the very image [χαρακτήρ] of his substance, and upholding all things by the word of his power. . . ." Here it seems that both Paul and the writer to the Hebrews have transferred to Christ the language used of wisdom by pseudo-Solomon: "For she is an effulgence [ἀπαύγασμα] from everlasting light, and an unspotted mirror of the working of God, and an image [εἰκών] of his goodness" (Wisd. Sol. 7:26). The difference is that the Alexandrian author of the Wisdom of Solomon was describing an abstraction, whereas the two Christian writers are ascribing these titles and functions to him whose earthly life was the historical basis of the gospel. This is the more impressive in Hebrews, because there more than anywhere else in the New Testament, outside the Synoptic Gospels, the true humanity of Jesus is brought to the fore. We may well say that both Paul and the author of Hebrews had anticipated the Logos teaching of the prologue in all but the actual use of the term itself.

D. Sources of the Gospel.—Before New Testament scholars in the latter part of the last century devoted themselves to the critical study of the Synoptic problem, it was generally assumed that resemblances and differences between the several Gospels could be accounted for by the use of oral tradition. Where this had

[17] *The Wisdom of Solomon* (Cambridge: Cambridge University Press, 1909; "The Cambridge Bible").

assumed a stereotyped form, verbal resemblances might be expected; where it was still fluid, each writer would exercise his own freedom in the way in which he employed it. With the theories of documentary dependence in possession of the field, based as they were upon a close comparison of synoptic parallels, it was inevitable that the Fourth Gospel should be treated as a debtor to Mark and Luke at least. The prominence given to form criticism has raised the question whether the Johannine resemblance to the Marcan or Lukan parallels may not be due to independent traditions, which may or may not have been known to the earlier evangelists.

1. ***Synoptic Gospels.***—Perhaps the most closely reasoned argument for John's dependence on Mark and Luke is given by B. H. Streeter in *The Four Gospels.*[18] First, he takes six passages in which the Greek words are too closely similar to be explained as an accident. These are: 6:7 and Mark 6:37; 12:3 and Mark 14:3, 5; 14:31 and Mark 14:42; 18:18 and Mark 14:54; 18:39 and Mark 15:9; 5:8-9 and Mark 2:11-12. In all these passages there are parallels in Matthew and Luke, but without the same Greek phrases. A formidable list of parallels should be studied, in which, though Matthew and Luke show similarities, John rarely agrees with them against Mark, but constantly with Mark against them: cf. 1:19-34 and Mark 1:7-10 (the Baptist); 2:13-22 and Mark 11:15-19 (cleansing of the temple); 6:1-15 and Mark 6:31-44, also cf. 8:1-10 (feeding of the multitude); 6:15-21 and Mark 6:45-52 (walking on the water); 12:1-8 and Mark 14:3-9 (the anointing at Bethany); 12:12-19 and Mark 11:1-10 (the triumphal entry); 13:21 and Mark 14:18 (betrayal predicted); 13:38 and Mark 14:30 (denial predicted); 18:3-10 and Mark 14:43-50 (the arrest); 18:15-18, 25-27 and Mark 14:54, 66-72 (Peter's denial); 18:33 and Mark 15:2*a* (Pilate's question); 18:37 and Mark 15:2*b* (Jesus' reply); 18:39-40 and Mark 15:6-15 (Barabbas); 19:2-3 and Mark 15:16-20 (the mocking); 19:17-24 and Mark 15:22-27 (the Crucifixion); 19:38-42 and Mark 15:43-46 (the burial); 20:1-2 and Mark 16:1-8 (the empty tomb). There are also a few instances of a saying reported by both John and Mark in different contexts. These are 4:44 and Mark 6:4; 12:25 and Mark 8:35; 13:20 and Mark 9:37. On the other hand, 13:16 (15:20) is not in Mark but is found in Matt. 10:24 and Luke 6:40.

The case for Johannine dependence on Luke is not so strong. The most impressive argument in favor is that John 11:1-2 not only refers to 12:1-3 but assumes a knowledge of Luke 10:38-39. It is also difficult to deny that John's account of the anointing is a conflation of the Marcan parallel and Luke's quite different story of the sinful woman's action as told in Luke 7:36-50 (see Exeg. on John 12:1-8).

It was to rebut these deductions from the facts that lie before us that P. Gardner-Smith wrote *Saint John and the Synoptic Gospels.* He examines the Johannine narrative section by section, calling attention to the striking differences from the Synoptic records, and subjecting to a searching scrutiny those passages where the resemblances have convinced many readers of John's dependence. He looks rather to a tradition going back to an early date, which in several of the episodes has taken a different form from that followed by the ancestors of the Marcan and Lukan traditions. Thus he considers the whole passage describing the call of the first disciples irreconcilable with the Synoptic accounts. Similarly, there is a complete variation in the story of the Baptist's ministry. The story of the healing of the officer's son related the same event as the healing of the centurion's servant told with marked differences in Matthew and Luke, but it had reached John in a different form. Great stress is laid on the section John 7:40-44: "The Fourth Evangelist wrote at a time and in a circle in which the tradition that Jesus was born of the Virgin Mary at Bethlehem, the city of David, had not yet become established. If so, he did not know our Synoptic Gospels." If, as many assume, the figure of the man born blind in ch. 9 is a composite of Bartimaeus and the blind man of Bethsaida, such a confusion is more likely to have taken place in oral tradition than in following written sources. The allegory of the good shepherd in ch. 10 in no way suggests that the Fourth Evangelist was acquainted with Matt. 18:12-14 or Luke 15:3-7. Dr. Gardner-Smith denies that John 11:1 is dependent on Luke 10:38 ff., and argues that the whole conception of the story of the raising of Lazarus cannot be fitted into the Marcan framework of the ministry of Jesus. The accounts of the triumphal entry, of the betrayal, arrest, trial, and crucifixion of Jesus have elements in common with the Synoptic story, but stress is laid on the discordant features. The contention is that in these, as in the resurrection narratives, the common factors are just those which would be preserved in an oral rather than in a written tradition. The importance of Gardner-Smith's book is to be found in his argument that we must not assume that such development as took place in tradition and theology was uniform throughout the world. Early and independent traditions may have been preserved in centers where the doctrinal development was more rapid than elsewhere.

[18] London: Macmillan & Co., 1924.

2. ***Other Possible Gospels.***—In 1935 H. Idris Bell and T. C. Skeat published *Fragments of an Unknown Gospel,*[19] a transcript, with introduction, translation, and notes, of the text of some papyrus leaves which papyrological experts date about the middle of the second century. This Egerton Papyrus 2, as it is entitled in the British Museum catalogue, contains fragmentary records of some sayings of Jesus, and incidents which strikingly resemble passages in the canonical Gospels. Three of these remind us so closely of the Johannine parallels that they must be cited, with the necessary but uncertain restoration of missing letters or words. (*a*) "And turning to the rulers of the people he spoke this saying: 'Search the scriptures, in which you think you have life; these are they which bear witness of me. Think not that I came to accuse you to my Father; there is one that accuses you, even Moses, on whom you have set your hope.' And when they said, 'We know well where you are from,' Jesus answered and said to them, 'Now your unbelief is accused" (cf. John 5:39; 9:29). (*b*) ". . . to carry the stones together to stone him. And the rulers laid their hands on him to take him and hand him over to the multitude; and they could not take him, because the hour of his being delivered up had not yet come. But he himself, the Lord, going forth out of their hands, departed from them" (cf. John 8:59; 10:31; 7:30, 44; 10:39). (*c*) "Master, Jesus, we know that you are come from God, for the things which you do bear witness above all the prophets" (cf. John 3:2; 10:25).

These sentences are mingled with others which just as strikingly call to mind passages in the Synoptics. There are also touches which resemble the fantastic element in some of the apocryphal gospels. The general verdict of scholars is that the Egerton fragment is part of an early gospel of that class which has drawn material from the canonical Gospels. But the Japanese scholar, Goro Mayeda, the author of the most complete edition of this interesting apocryphon, contests this conclusion. In his book, *Das Leben-Jesu-Fragment Papyrus Egerton 2 und seine Stellung in der urchristlichen Literaturgeschichte,*[20] Mayeda tries to show, by an examination of eight passages in which the differences in style and thought between John and the Egerton fragment appears, that the writer of the latter cannot have been quoting from John. He regards the resemblances as due to a common use of the same early tradition or written source. As Idris Bell himself[21] lends a qualified support to this theory, it must not be ruled out of court. On the other hand, there is no good reason for suggesting that John has borrowed his material from the writing of which these few fragments alone remain.

[19] London: Oxford University Press.

[20] Bern: Paul Haupt, 1946, pp. 69-75.

[21] "The Gospel Fragments P. Egerton 2," *Harvard Theological Review,* XLII (1949), 53-63.

E. Unity of the Gospel.—About a century ago David F. Strauss used the famous simile of the "seamless robe" when describing the literary unity of this Gospel. Since then, many attempts have been made to prove that it was not "woven from top to bottom" but has been stitched together from a number of pieces by a variety of hands. Yet others who accept the unity of the work are impressed by internal evidence that some disturbance took place in the original order of a number of the sections before the Gospel was published, with the result that the reader is aware of some glaring discontinuities in both the narrative sections and the discourses. A catalogue of the most important theories of partition, redaction, and displacement down to 1931 is given in appendixes C and D of *The Fourth Gospel in Recent Criticism and Interpretation.*[22] Since that date interest has shifted considerably from the analytic treatment of the Gospel, but under each of these heads one representative theory of recent date may be presented.

1. ***Theory of Partition.***—In 1936 J. C. B. Mohr of Tübingen published two books by Emanuel Hirsch—*Das vierte Evangelium in seiner ursprunglichen Gestalt,* and *Studien zum vierten Evangelium.* Working on lines already followed by Wellhausen, Schwartz, and B. W. Bacon, yet differing from each of them in important particulars, Hirsch discovers an original gospel consisting of seven cycles each with five subdivisions. This, he thinks, was written about the turn of the century by a traveling merchant who visited Jerusalem, and there saw enough to provide him with those bits of local color which have led so many to infer that the Gospel was written by a Jew of Palestine. A generation later this document fell into the hands of a zealous churchman who transformed a simple dramatic story into an ecclesiastical gospel by a fourfold method: (*a*) He added ch. 21, with allusions elsewhere to the Beloved Disciple. (*b*) He enriched the book with a number of testimonies from the Old Testament to add to its apologetic value. (*c*) He added and modified passages to sharpen its use against the then prevalent danger of Gnosticism. (*d*) He brought in additions in chs. 10 and 13:34–17:26 to serve an ecclesiastical purpose—the allegory of the good shepherd and the hireling sets in contrast the Catholic bishop and the Gnostic heretic. This ecclesiastical motive is alleged to have turned the antilegal Paulinism of the

[22] 3rd ed.; London: Epworth Press, 1945.

original gospel into the proclamation of the "new commandment," and also to have set the story in a chronological framework of named feasts. Unlike Wellhausen, Hirsch attributes any use of a non-Synoptic source to the original evangelist and not to a redactor. This theory might come under the heading of "redaction," but as the editor adds so much, we may regard his work as that of a second stratum laid upon the original gospel. Without considering the transpositions which this late writer is supposed to have made in the text of the original, we may take this as a theory of partition, in which the second writer has contributed the following passages: 1:15, 24; 2:13, 17, 25; 3:5, 7, 11, 14-15, 24, 31, 32*b*; 4:2, 22-23, 36-38, 44, 45*a*; 5:22-24, 29-30, 34, 39*b*, 43; 6:8*b*, 22, 28*b*-30, 35*c*-36, 39*c*-40, 44*b*-45*a*, 51, 53*b*-56*a*, 57, 64*b*, 67-71; 7:38*a*, 39; 8:23*b*-24*a*, 36, 46; 10:9, 11*b*-13*a*, 16, 25*b*-26*a*, 28*a*, 29*b*, 34*b*-35; 11:13, 22, 42, 52; 12:14-15, 26, 42-43, 50*a*; 13:2-3, 10*d*-11, 17-20, 23*b*, 27*a*, 28-29, 34-38; 14:3, 8*c*, 11, 13-14, 18-25; 15:1-3, 6, 10-12, 14*b*, 16*d*, 20*d*-27; 16:1, 16-23*a*, 25-26*a*, 29-32, 33*bc*; 17:3, 11*d*-12*a*, 16, 20-21, 23*bc*; 18:1*c*, 5*c*-6*a*, 9, 14, 20*b*, 24*b*, 32, 39-40; 19:4-6, 23-24, 26-28, 35-37; 20:2-11; 21:1-25. In addition to these passages, a number of phrases or single words are attributed to this editor. The precarious nature of these experiments in literary analysis is exposed if one contrasts this list with the list of passages which B. W. Bacon assigns to his "redactor."

2. ***Theory of Redaction.***—Rudolf Bultmann's great commentary [23] allows most of the Gospel to the evangelist, who had drawn his material from "Revelation discourses," a "signs source," a good tradition about John the Baptist, another about the triumphal entry and the anointing, written or traditional sources dealing with incidents belonging to the passion, trial, crucifixion, and resurrection of Jesus. Sometimes these traditions are related to those followed by the Synoptists; at other times the Fourth Evangelist draws on quite independent traditions. The "Revelation discourses" provide the prologue and those sections of the teaching in which Jesus speaks of himself as "sent" from God, as well as the great "I am" sayings. Bultmann thinks that these were probably translated from an Aramaic original and were written in a rhythmic and often antithetic style. The "signs source" (cf. 20:30-31) was written in a Greek style that resembled Semitic, but was not an actual translation from the Aramaic.

Bultmann's theory of redaction postulates an editor who added to the Gospel, in an ecclesiastical interest, the section in ch. 6 (vss. 51*b*-58) which gives a Eucharistic character to the discourse in the synagogue at Capernaum, and also ch. 21. The first part of ch. 21 may have been taken from a tradition similar to that lying behind Luke 5:1-11. But the redactor introduced the figure of the Beloved Disciple to prepare for the story of the rehabilitation of Peter and the authorization of this other disciple as his equal and successor, thus giving this Gospel the authority of an eyewitness. This ecclesiastical redactor is responsible for the following among his additions: 1:22-24, 26, 33; 3:5 (the words "water and"); 3:24; 4:2, 22; 5:28-29; 6:27*b*; 7:20-21*a*, 38, 39*b*; 10:34-36; 11:2; 12:17-18; 18:32; 19:34*b*, 35; 20:9. But peculiar to Bultmann's theory is the claim that the redactor is responsible for the present disordered condition of the text, which supposedly reached him in a confused and fragmentary condition and which he tried unsuccessfully to restore. Where he failed, Bultmann attempts to recover the evangelist's original or intended order. Unlike most scholars who have essayed this task, Bultmann discards any numerical criterion of letters or words in the misplaced sections. The reconstituted Gospel is presented in this order: 1; 2; 3:1-21, 31-36, 22-30; 4; 6:1-59; 5; 7:15-24; 8:13-20; 7:1-14, 25-29; 8:48-50, 54-55; 7:30, 37-44, 31-36, 45-52; 8:41-47, 51-53, 56-59; 9; 8:12; 12:44-50; 8:21-29; 12:34-36; 10:19-26, 11-13, 1-10, 14-18, 27-42; 11; 12:1-33; 8:30-40; 6:60-71; 12:37-43; 13:1*a*, 2-30, 1*b*; 17; 13:31-35; 15; 16; 13:36–14:31; 18; 19; 20; 21. Within these sections there are smaller rearrangements; thus in ch. 6 the following sequence of verses is found: 27, 34, 35, 30-33, 47-51*a*, 41-46, 36-40.

3. ***Theory of Displacement.***—Reference has been made (pp. 446-47) to many attempts to explain breaks in the narratives and discourses by accidental dislocation of sheets before the publication of the Gospel. Many of these are based upon a close calculation of the size of the sections that have been thus misplaced and then reinserted in the wrong order. A modern and elaborate attempt is found in F. R. Hoare's *The Original Order and Chapters of St. John's Gospel.*[24] The theory of this book is that "the leaves on which the original fair copy of the Gospel was written were accidentally disarranged before they had been pasted together to form a roll and before any copies had been made." Incidentally, the author claims that "in identifying the original leaves, arithmetical tests were used that disclosed the existence in the original manuscript of a complete system of division into chapters quite different from ours." The resultant arrangement is that of the following segments: (*a*) 1:1-51; (*b*) 4:3*b*-

[23] *Das Evangelium des Johannes* (Göttingen: Vandenhoeck & Ruprecht, 1941; "Meyer's Kommentar").

[24] London: Burns, Oates & Washbourne, 1944, p. vii.

43; (*c*) 2:1–4:3*a*; (*d*) 4:44–5:47; (*e*) 7:15-24; (*f*) 6:1–7:14; (*g*) 7:25-52; 8:12-28*a*; (*h*) 12:34-50; (*j*) 8:28*b*–9:41; (*k*) 10:19–11:33; (*l*) 12:23*b*-33; (*m*) 11:34–12:23*a*; (*n*) 10:1-18; [(*o*) 7:53–8:11]; (*p*) 13:1-19; (*q*) 15:17–16:4*a*; (*r*) 13:20–14:14; (*s*) 16:15*b*-23; (*t*) 14:15-24*a*; (*u*) 16:4*b*-15*a*; (*v*) 14:24*b*–15:16; (*w*) 16:24–21:25.

It must be said that this rearrangement differs widely from most of those which are associated with the names of Friedrich Spitta, F. W. Lewis, James Moffatt, J. H. Bernard, and G. H. C. Macgregor, all of which have much in common.

F. Relation of the Gospel to the Johannine Epistles.—In the middle of the third century that acute critic, Dionysius of Alexandria, gave cogent reasons for attributing the Gospel and I John to the same author, while distinguishing this writer, on grounds of subject matter and literary style, from the writer of Revelation. This judgment, which is preserved by Eusebius,[25] has lost little of its force even today. Nevertheless, the common authorship of Gospel and epistles must still be regarded as an open question. The reader's decision depends upon a nice balancing of the various points of resemblance and of difference. These fall under the two heads of linguistic style and of subject matter. The former consideration lies outside the scope of this commentary. It turns largely upon matters of Greek grammar and vocabulary. The student who wishes to pursue this argument should examine the parallel columns in which A. E. Brooke has compared passages from the Gospel with similar ones from the epistles.[26] After this he should read C. H. Dodd's article, "The First Epistle of John and the Fourth Gospel," in the *Bulletin of the John Rylands Library*.[27] This has been examined in two articles in the *Journal of Theological Studies*.[28] Those who still favor the theory of separate authorship will at least agree that the epistles must have been written by a pupil who was profoundly influenced by the author of the Gospel, and who closely imitated his style.

Those who have no inclination to pursue this linguistic inquiry will pay more attention to the alleged differences of doctrine. Dodd claims that (*a*) I John stands nearer than the Gospel to general or popular Christian beliefs, and (*b*) there are passages in the epistle pointing to a closer connection than the Gospel with the Gnosticism against which both writings are directed. Thus, under (*a*) a contrast can be pointed out with regard to (i) eschatology, (ii) the death of Christ, (iii) the Holy Spirit. With regard to (i), it may be said that though the evangelist seems to have sublimated the more primitive eschatology in his doctrine of the coming of the Paraclete, yet the Gospel is not without traces of a futurist eschatology (cf. 5:21 ff.; 12:47 ff.). Moreover, the epistle is dealing with a specific crisis when the church is faced with a deadly peril, so that the ancient specter of Antichrist appears on the scene. It may be said further that while judgment (κρίσις) is regarded in the Gospel as a present process, in the epistle it is conceived as a manifestation (φανέρωσις) when the final doom is pronounced. As for (ii), in the epistle the death of Christ is set forth as an expiation to remove the sin which is a barrier preventing fellowship with God. This thought is not prominent in the Gospel, though 1:29 uses a figure to describe Jesus as one who takes away the sin of the world. A comparison of 1:29; 3:16 with I John 2:2; 3:5 and 4:9-10 shows that the underlying conception is the same. In the Gospel the purpose is to show that the voluntary self-sacrifice on the Cross was both an exhibition of the Father's love in saving sinners, and the means by which in glorifying the Father the Son was lifted up into the glory of the Father. In the epistle the death of Christ is considered more directly in relation to the problem of human guilt and man's broken fellowship with God. Regarding (iii), in the epistle the Spirit is thought of as a prophetic inspiration bestowed on the church; in the Gospel as a person. The Paraclete in the Gospel is the Holy Spirit, whereas in the epistle he is the ascended Christ. But in the Gospel the Spirit is "another Paraclete" who is to continue on the earthly plane what Jesus has done for his disciples during the incarnate life. In the epistle that first Paraclete is continuing in heaven the ministry of intercession begun on earth (John 17:9, 15, 17, 19-20; cf. I John 2:1), while the Spirit gives inward assurance of true fellowship with God and with the brotherhood, and also gives reality to the testimony of the church in its message and worship. There is no contrast between the farewell discourse and I John 3:24; 4:13.

As to Dodd's second contention (*b*), it may be granted that the prevalence of Gnosticism undoubtedly accounts for the use of some terms in the epistle. In such verses as I John 1:5; 3:9; 2:20, 27 it is quite possible that the writer is deliberately using language that was constantly on the lips of the heretical teachers in order to read a deeper meaning into them. Christianity was the true Gnosticism. But "God is light" is

[25] *Church History* VII. 25.

[26] See his *Critical and Exegetical Commentary on the Johannine Epistles* (New York: Charles Scribner's Sons, 1912; "International Critical Commentary"), pp. ii-xi.

[27] Vol. XXI (1937), pp. 129-56.

[28] W. F. Howard, "The Common Authorship of the Johannine Gospel and Epistles," XLVIII (1947), 12-25; and W. G. Wilson, "An Examination of the Linguistic Evidence Adduced Against the Unity of Authorship of the First Epistle of John and the Fourth Gospel," XLIX (1948), 147-56.

not a definition of God so much as a reminder that God can and must make himself known in his holiness and purity. So in I John 3:2, far from repeating the vague and formal mysticism of Hellenistic religion, the writer declares that the perfect union with God is to be attained only in the future, and that this hope is an incentive to moral effort.

II John and III John, short as they are, are bound together by several similarities in thought and language. II John 7 seems to refer to the false teachers of I John who deny that cardinal truth of the Incarnation which is the theme of the Gospel.

The question about the priority of Gospel or epistles cannot easily be solved. The First Epistle seems to presuppose a knowledge of the Gospel. This does not necessarily imply the previous publication of the Gospel. The venerable leader of the church who addresses his readers as "my little children" must have been teaching the substance of the Gospel for long years. During this time it may well have been gradually assuming written form. The epistle is the practical application to a contemporary situation of the message which constitutes the Gospel, which in its turn is "theology teaching by example."

VII. Outline of Contents

- I. The Prologue (1:1-18)
- II. The witness of the Baptist and his disciples (1:19-51)
- III. The self-revelation of Jesus in Judea, Galilee, and Samaria (2:1–4:54)
  - A. The marriage at Cana; the first sign (2:1-11)
  - B. The cleansing of the temple (2:12-22)
  - C. At the Passover (2:23-25)
  - D. Nicodemus and the new birth (3:1-21)
  - E. Testimony of the Baptist (3:22-30)
  - F. The witness from above (3:31-36)
  - G. Jesus and the Samaritan woman (4:1-26)
  - H. Jesus, the disciples, and the Samaritans (4:27-42)
  - J. Jesus, the Galileans, and the officer's son (4:43-54)
- IV. Signs and controversies (5:1–9:41)
  - A. Cure of the cripple at Bethzatha; the sabbath controversy (5:1-18)
  - B. Unity of the Son with the Father as giver of life (5:19-47)
  - C. Jesus as the bread of life (6:1-71)
    1. Feeding of the multitude (6:1-15)
    2. The crossing to Capernaum (6:16-24)
    3. Discourse in the synagogue at Capernaum (6:25-59)
    4. The testing of faith (6:60-71)
  - D. Jesus at the feast of Tabernacles (7:1-14)
  - E. A controversy section (7:15-24)
  - F. Narrative of the feast of Tabernacles resumed (7:25-31)
  - G. An attempt to arrest Jesus (7:32-36)
  - H. The last day of the feast (7:37-52)
  - J. Jesus and the woman taken in adultery (7:53–8:11)
  - K. Jesus the Light of the World (8:12-20)
  - L. Controversy about the divine commission of Jesus (8:21-59)
  - M. Healing of the man born blind (9:1-41)
- V. The shepherd and giver of life (10:1–11:57)
  - A. The Shepherd and the sheep (10:1-18)
  - B. Jesus at the feast of Dedication (10:19-40)
  - C. The raising of Lazarus and the doom of Jesus (11:1-57)
- VI. Close of the public ministry (12:1-50)
  - A. The anointing at Bethany (12:1-8)
  - B. Popularity and peril (12:9-11)
  - C. The triumphal entry (12:12-19)
  - D. Jesus and the Greeks (12:20-26)
  - E. The agony and the voice (12:27-36*a*)
  - F. Unbelief and rejection (12:36*b*-43)
  - G. Judgment by the word (12:44-50)
- VII. The Upper Room (13:1–17:26)
  - A. The Last Supper (13:1-30)
    1. The Feet-washing (13:1-20)
    2. The Betrayal foretold (13:21-30)
  - B. The farewell discourse, Part I (13:31–14:31)
    1. The new commandment (13:31-35)
    2. Peter's denial foretold (13:36-38)
    3. The way, the truth, and the life (14:1-14)
    4. First Paraclete saying (14:15-17)
    5. The threefold union (14:18-24)
    6. Second Paraclete saying (14:25-26)
    7. Peace, joy, and security (14:27-31)
  - C. Farewell discourse, Part II (15:1–16:33)
    1. The allegory of the vine (15:1-11)
    2. The fellowship of love and the call to service (15:12-17)
    3. The world's hatred (15:18-25)
    4. Third Paraclete saying (15:26-27)
    5. Forewarned is forearmed (16:1-4)
    6. Fourth Paraclete saying (16:5-11)
    7. Fifth Paraclete saying (16:12-15)
    8. Brief sorrow, lasting joy (16:16-24)
    9. The unveiling of the Father (16:25-28)
    10. The victory over the world (16:29-33)
  - D. The high-priestly prayer (17:1-26)
    1. The Father and the Son glorified—prayer for himself (17:1-5)
    2. The consecration of the disciples—prayer for "his own" (17:6-19)
    3. The unity of the church—prayer for the universal church (17:20-26)
- VIII. Gethsemane to Calvary (18:1–19:42)
  - A. The Arrest (18:1-11)
  - B. The trial before the high priest and Peter's denial (18:12-27)
  - C. Jesus before Pilate (18:28–19:16)
  - D. The Crucifixion and Burial (19:17-42)
- IX. The appearances of the risen Lord (20:1–21:25)
  - A. The risen Lord (20:1-29)
  - B. The purpose of the Gospel (20:30-31)
  - C. Epilogue (21:1-25)
    1. The appearance beside the lake (21:1-14)
    2. Peter and the Beloved Disciple (21:15-23)
    3. Conclusion (21:24-25)

VIII. Selected Bibliography

INTRODUCTION

GARDNER, PERCY. *The Ephesian Gospel* ("Crown Theological Library"). New York: G. P. Putnam's Sons, 1916.

HOWARD, WILBERT F. *The Fourth Gospel in Recent Criticism and Interpretation.* 3rd ed. London: Epworth Press, 1945.

———. *Christianity According to St. John.* Philadelphia: The Westminster Press, 1946.

SCOTT, E. F. *The Fourth Gospel.* 2nd ed. Edinburgh: T. & T. Clark, 1908.

COMMENTARIES

BAUER, WALTER. *Das Johannesevangelium* ("Handbuch zum Neuen Testament"). 3rd ed. Tübingen: J. C. B. Mohr, 1933.

BERNARD, J. H. *A Critical and Exegetical Commentary on the Gospel According to St. John* ("International Critical Commentary"). 2 vols. New York: Charles Scribner's Sons, 1929.

BULTMANN, RUDOLF. *Das Evangelium des Johannes.* Göttingen: Vandenhoeck & Ruprecht, 1941.

HOSKYNS, E. C., and DAVEY, F. N. *The Fourth Gospel.* 2 vols. London: Faber & Faber, 1948.

LAGRANGE, M.-J. *Évangile selon Saint Jean* ("Études Bibliques"). 4th ed. Paris: Librairie Victor Lecoffre, 1927.

MACGREGOR, G. H. C. *The Gospel of John* ("Moffatt New Testament Commentary"). New York: Harper & Bros., 1929.

STRACHAN, R. H. *The Fourth Gospel.* London: Student Christian Movement Press, 1941.

JOHN

TEXT, EXEGESIS AND EXPOSITION

1 In the beginning was the Word, and the Word was with God, and the Word was God.

1 In the beginning was the Word, and the Word was with God, and the Word

I. THE PROLOGUE (1:1-18)

This prologue (for structure and origin see p. 445) is an overture in which the motifs—life and light, glory and truth—are heard that recur again and again through the Gospel. The theme is the Logos (see p. 442), pre-existent, incarnate, rejected, yet revealer of God and giver of sonship to those who believe in his divine mission. The poem falls easily into stanzas, which are interrupted by prose comments (vss. 6-8, 15) concerning John the Baptist.

1:1. In the beginning recalls the opening words of Genesis, and suggests an equation between the Logos and God. Not less striking is the parallel to the hymn of wisdom in Prov. 8:22-30. Three characteristics of the Logos are named in this verse: his eternity

---

1:1-18. ***The Prologue.***—No book in literature has so breath-taking an opening as these stupendous findings on the life and character about to be described, flung down so confidently as the only possible explanation of them, given us as a kind of thesis, of which all the facts that are to follow are the proof.

It is a bewilderingly crowded preface. "I only wish," St. Teresa once complained, "that I could write with both hands, so as not to forget one thing while I am saying another."[1] This author too gives the impression of thinking much faster than he can speak or write; with the result that the reader's mind is overwhelmed by a rush of staggering assertions, at each of which he would like to be given time to pause, and try to begin, at least, to think this out; but none is allowed him, and at once he is swept on and on. The whole thing has the effect more of a piece of lofty music than of literature. It stirs strange feelings and emotions in us that surge up out of the deeps. It creates an atmosphere in which one reads, awed and tense, and with held breath. We know that we are face to face with something august, tremendous, illimitable. But the impression left upon most readers' minds,

[1] *The Complete Works of Saint Teresa of Jesus* (tr. E. Allison Peers; London: Sheed & Ward, 1946), II, 88.

2 The same was in the beginning with God.

3 All things were made by him; and without him was not any thing made that was made.

was God. 2 He was in the beginning with God; 3 all things were made through him, and without him was not anything made

---

(**in the beginning**), his fellowship with God (**the Word was with God**), his divine nature (**the Word was God**). The absence of the Greek article before the word God (θεὸς ἦν ὁ λόγος) makes it perfectly clear that θεός is predicate, not subject, of the verb. The two terms are not interchangeable; else the writer could not say **the Word was with God.** The Gospel declares that men are to "honor the Son, even as they honor the Father" (5:23), without identifying them. For the relationship cf. 14:9, 28; 5:30; 6:38; 10:30.

2-3. Vs. 2 resumes and reiterates the content of vs. 1, while vs. 3 declares, with an emphasis that is possibly polemical, the complete universality of the creative energy of the Logos. Although avoiding this term, the writers of Col. 1:16 ff. and Heb. 1:2 make the same claim for Christ. The Gnostics, with their belief in the essential evil of matter, interposed a long series of aeons, or intermediaries, between the supreme God and the creation. Here it is declared that all things without exception were made by him who from all eternity was with God. **Without him was not anything made.**

---

one fancies, is indefinite and vague; a sense of something very big and very real, but indescribable, which will not go into words. This is a passage best to be understood by that additional faculty with which the mystics credit us, which sees much farther than reason and intelligence, and knows much more accurately than they ever can; and yet it cannot tell others what it sees and experiences.

Still, for one thing, here is a lesson in how to present Jesus Christ. To do that successfully two things are required: (*a*) a big enough conception of him in our own minds; and (*b*) a medium through which we can state that conception so that it comes home to others around us.

(*a*) The Christ of the N.T. is a figure so magnific that whenever its writers think of him or name him, their minds instinctively bow down in reverence and worship. And the greatness of their Christ gives them a mighty gospel —this Christ who is the express image of God's person; in everything he does God's representative, and himself divine; the very thought and mind and word of God to us become alive here on our earth; the mighty conqueror of sin and death and hell, meeting the full shock of their power, and trampling them beneath his feet. But often nowadays all that is whittled down into a tame affair, with little thrill in it, and with only a blunted cutting edge. Many seem to belittle the wonderful figure of the N.T. into not much more than a gracious soul who generously spent himself for others; who, as a teacher on moral and religious matters, certainly takes rank among the very highest; but who was, of course, only a man of his own time—and that a much simpler time than ours; and so, in many ways and on many things, unfitted to be a guide for us among our complicated social and economic problems; and in some respects now obsolete; and who foolishly threw his life away in a quixotic enterprise, obviously hopeless from the start.

That gospel will not save the world. The very evil spirits mock at it, and settle back comfortably, knowing that this will never dispossess them. "Jesus we know; but what is this?" A pertinent question which we too might ask. For, as Paul claimed proudly, "It is no weak Christ you have to do with, but a Christ of power" (II Cor. 13:3 Moffatt). And we who have put him to the test know that the old staggering interpretation of him lies far nearest to the plain facts of our own experience—facts that cannot be ignored and that demand an explanation. It is a mighty gospel that Christ brings us, ample enough to cover every possible call upon it. **For from his fullness have we all received, grace upon grace** (vs. 16).

(*b*) Yet something more is needed if Christ is to succeed. There is only one authentic gospel, once delivered to the saints, eternal and unchangeable. But every country has its own language; and to make that single universal gospel intelligible to the inhabitants of any land it must be preached to them in their own tongue—and for the mass of them no other will do. In Britain one must use English. But cross the narrow channel, and one must take to French; over the Rhine, to German; farther east, to Polish, to Russian, to Chinese. So just as surely, every age has its own mental speech—certain conceptions that are current, certain

4 In him was life; and the life was the light of men.

that was made. 4 In him was life,[a] and the

[a] Or *was not anything made. That which has been made was life in him.*

4. The punctuation of the RSV mg. is to be preferred, since (*a*) it gives a better rhythmic structure, (*b*) the passage was so taken by commentators during the first four centuries, and (*c*) while avoiding the tautology involved in the more familiar arrangement, it yields a good interpretation. **That which has been made was life in him.** The contrast is between the perfect tense (γέγονεν) and the imperfect (ἦν), between that which has been created in time and still exists, and that which was before time began. A similar thought is found in Rev. 4:11, "For thou didst create all things, and by thy will they existed and were created." All created life is an expression of that life-giving power eternally existent in the Logos. An important group of early textual authorities substituted "is" for "was." This was probably due to a misreading of the clause on account of the unusual position of the words "in him"—"that which has come into being in him was life." Interpreting these words as meaning "the principle, which has become incarnate in him, was life," they naturally substituted the present for the past tense. But the phrase "in him" comes out of its natural position in much the same way in 3:15, where ἐν αὐτῷ is probably the right reading, and grammatical necessity determines that "in him" must go with "may have eternal life," not with "believes." Johannine usage therefore favors the attachment of the same phrase in our text to "life" rather than to "made." Inasmuch as the Logos created the natural order, there has always been the possibility of seeing in

molds into which its thinking naturally runs and sets. And as at Pentecost, so always, if the gospel is to come home to folk with power, they must hear it, "each . . . in his own native language."

This is not to suggest, of course, that a mode of thought can serve only one generation, and thereafter must be little more than useless lumber cluttering things up. Many are permanent discoveries of perennial value, and even if and when they have fallen from their centrality in men's minds, remain serviceable to all time. Many, but by no means all! Some have a limited period of usefulness, and thereafter may even darken counsel, and stumble more than help. And the church is slow to move and heavy-footed; apt to lag half a generation behind the times; still using methods and media once valuable but now grown obsolete; still speaking, so to say, in a kind of Anglo-Saxon, once the right medium when people thought and spoke in Anglo-Saxon, but now become out of date.

Not so this evangelist. As there was a day when everyone was thinking and speaking and writing in terms of evolution, so when this Gospel took shape, there was a habit of thought in the air—the Logos doctrine—which more and more were using, finding it helpful and a key to many things. It was as old as Heraclitus; but by this time it was sowing itself over the earth. One finds it everywhere among the Stoics. There is something akin to it in the Apocrypha. It was the speech of Philo and the Alexandrians. But it had escaped out of the schools, and was now being tossed from hand to hand by ordinary folk in the streets—had become common coin. And this writer seizes on it as the very medium he needs in which to state his case, and through which to bring home his tremendous facts to other minds.

It is not now the easiest conception of Christianity for us fully to follow. We have moved away from this particular point of view. For that matter, neither is it easy to follow the Epistle to the Hebrews, glorious scripture though that is. For those to whom it was written, people familiar with the Jewish sacrificial system, it must have been apt and suggestive and convincing beyond measure. But to us who know that system only vaguely and inaccurately, the great epistle has in some respects grown dimmer and less apposite. So here:

We think to-day with a totally different series of preconceptions from those of Jew and Greek of the first century. The Greek himself never thought much of the "chosen race," and it was only when he realized that Jesus was not a tribal hero that he accepted him. To the Greek the Messiah was as strange a thought as to ourselves. To us the Logos is as strange as the Messiah was to the Greek. We have really at present no terms in which to express what we feel to be the permanent significance of Jesus, and the old expressions may repel us until we realize, first, that they are not of the original essence of the Gospel, and second, that they represent the best language which Greek and Jew could find for a conviction which we share—that Jesus of Nazareth does stand in the centre of human

5 And the light shineth in darkness; and the darkness comprehended it not.

life was the light of men. 5 The light shines in the darkness, and the darkness has not overcome it.

---

this a divine revelation, as Paul clearly saw (cf. Rom. 1:20: "Ever since the creation of the world his invisible nature, namely, his eternal power and deity, has been clearly perceived in the things that have been made"). The distinctive attribute of the Logos is his life-giving power. This is now viewed in its spiritual effects in the human realm. **The life was the light of men:** These two figures are closely associated in O.T. thought. At the creation the Word of God called light into being that there might be life in the world (Gen. 1:3). So also the psalmist sings, "With thee is the fountain of life; in thy light shall we see light" (Ps. 36:9). Just as all life proceeds from God, so the possibility and the faculty of vision come from him. **The light of men** means the light which shines for men to give them the means of recognizing the giver of life. Such passages as 3:19-21 and 8:12 show how completely for this evangelist the metaphysical passes into the ethical, and the cosmological into the eschatological. So far the prologue is concerned with the relation of the Logos to the world. In the following verses the Logos is set forth as the revealer of God in history, and these abstractions take on a clearer outline until we recognize the protagonists in the life-and-death struggle between light and darkness.

5. The light shines in the darkness, and the darkness has not overcome it: This verse is further explained by vs. 9, but the climax is not reached till vs. 14, when the divine revelation is announced as the incarnation of the Son of God. The present tense—**shines**—is significant, as in I John 2:8, "The darkness is passing away and the true light is already shining." For the evangelist the Incarnation was already an event in the past, but **the light** still **shines** in the fellowship of the risen and ever-living Christ, who is identified with the eternal Logos. **The darkness** stands for the state of mind in which mankind fails to welcome the light. This spiritual blindness is expressed in the prologue by the phrases, "the world knew him not," "his own people received him not." The motif recurs throughout the Gospel. The word translated **overcome** (καταλαμβάνειν) has been variously understood. The Greek verb in the active voice can mean (*a*) "to seize" (Mark 9:18) or "lay hold of" or "appropriate" (Rom. 9:30; I Cor. 9:24; Phil. 3:12, 13); (*b*) "perceive" or "understand," a meaning not uncommon in later Greek, though in the N.T. it is found only with the middle voice (Acts 4:13; 10:34; 25:25; Eph. 3:18); (*c*) "overtake" (12:35; I Thess. 5:4). In this passage it has been translated (*a*) "apprehended" (ERV), (*b*) **comprehended** (KJV), (*c*) "overtaken." This last meaning was accepted by Origen, and is supported on the evidence of the papyri by James Hope Moulton and George Milligan (*The Vocabulary of the Greek Testament* [London:

---

history, that he has brought God and man into a new relation, that he is the personal concern of everyone of us, and that there is more in him than we have yet accounted for.[2]

Nonetheless, it was a way of stating Christ which was immeasurably effective in its day. And to this hour it enshrines a truth which cannot be so adequately stated otherwise.

1-5, 9-13. ***The Doctrine of the Logos.***—What was, what is this doctrine of the Logos? Carefully it is stated for us in vss. 1-5. Peer into the dim past as far as you may, you will never come on God alone. Always, from the beginningless beginning, there has been God. And always there has been Another with him, who is to God what a man's word and thought are to a man; through whom God acts; and by whom he expresses himself. It is the Logos who creates; and all things that exist were made by him. And so, it seems, there is no clean-cut separation between nature and grace, since nature too is grace; and the same mind that wrought our salvation for us has been working for us all the ages down, and heaping lovingkindnesses upon us. So in the early church the Eucharistic prayer was apt to take an ample sweep, thanking God for much that seems remote from the Sacrament. For all life, they felt, was of a piece, and shot through and through by the astonishing goodness of God. This life that flows from the Logos has taken many forms, even in this little earth

[2] T. R. Glover, *The Conflict of Religions in the Early Roman Empire* (London: Methuen & Co., 1909), p. 157. Used by permission.

6 ¶ There was a man sent from God, whose name *was* John.
7 The same came for a witness, to bear witness of the Light, that all *men* through him might believe.

6 There was a man sent from God, whose
name was John. 7 He came for testimony,
to bear witness to the light, that all might

Hodder & Stoughton, 1914-29], p. 328), as well as by the only occurrence of the word in this Gospel. By an easy transition from this sense the meaning (*d*) **overcome** is reached (RSV), which is substantially that of ERV mg., Weymouth, Moffatt, Goodspeed, and R. A. Knox. Among the commentators it is accepted by Westcott, Bernard, Zahn, Schlatter, Heitmüller, Bauer, and Bultmann; Loisy and Lagrange favor the interpretation which makes this verb parallel with those in vss. 10, 11, "the darkness did not appropriate" or "embrace the light." On the whole, **overcome** accords better with the moral dualism of this Gospel (see p. 443), and finds support in Wisd. Sol. 7:29-30: "Being compared with light, she is found to be before it; for to the light of day succeedeth night, but against wisdom evil doth not prevail." Light and darkness are conceived as antagonists. The Gospel is the drama of the conflict between them, issuing in the rejection by the Jews of him who is the light of the world. Yet apparent defeat led to final victory: "I have overcome the world" (16:33).

6-8. This prose comment, interjected by the evangelist into the hymn of the Logos, is the first of a number of passages in which he carefully indicates the inferiority of the Baptist to Jesus (cf. vss. 15, 24-27, 30; 3:28-30; 4:1; 5:36; 10:41; see pp. 450-51). The name John is never in this Gospel, as often in the Synoptics, distinguished by the title "the Baptist." Two things are said of him: that he was commissioned by God, and that his mission was limited to testimony. The word **sent** carries the sense of official authority, recalling the O.T. prophets, though the word is frequently used in this Gospel of Jesus, who is par excellence the emissary of God to earth (see pp. 438, 443). The immediate purpose of the mission is **to bear witness to the light**; the ulterior object is **that all might believe through him.** In this Gospel John is merely the herald and witness, bearing testimony to the nature and titles of Jesus. We should not have learned from it that the Baptist was the prophet and leader of a great movement for national repentance and hope. Some

of ours. But in men it has been fashioned into a goodly heritage—the light of reason, and memory, and conscience, and hunger for God.

These things are gifts to us from the Logos, and proofs that always he is striving to break in to us, seeking to lead us farther on, deeper in, and higher up—a conception difficult indeed to include in any Barthian view of things, but over which Justin exults, hailing it as a clear proof of his own joyous belief that wherever men are groping after God, however crudely, their efforts are God-inspired, and dear to him; and that always, always, he is seeking to dispel their darkness. For as is the way of light, he who is Light keeps feeling for an opening into each mind and soul; pouring in through every smallest chink he can find; eagerly seeking to flood every life with the glory of the noontide of the full knowledge of God.

What has befallen as the outcome of the gracious operations of the Logos? That brings us face to face with the tremendous agelong struggle between light and darkness (vss. 5, 9). There are really two chapters in this most epic of epics, before the Incarnation (vs. 5), and since then (vss. 9-13). But it is all of a piece, and the one runs on into the other.

First, then, is the fact that there is light and there is darkness. Whence comes this darkness? **All things were made through him; and without him was not anything made that was made.** So with reiterated emphasis it is laid down. It sounds absolutely all embracing. Is then the darkness, too, included? Or is it regarded not as a thing, but rather as the absence of a thing, like the hole in a stocking? Where there is no light, there is a blank that we call darkness. But where light comes, that nothingness vanishes. That seems too negative to fit the facts of our experience. Whence come the untoward things with which we have to struggle, and which maim and spoil our lives? Many philosophers, accounting hedonism as the only possible standard of values, take it for granted that the one goal that there can be before a wise Creator's eyes in his dealings with his creatures must be to secure their happiness. But that axiom the N.T. flatly denies, asserting that the

8 He was not that Light, but *was sent* to bear witness of that Light.
9 *That* was the true Light, which lighteth every man that cometh into the world.

believe through him. 8 He was not the light, but came to bear witness to the light.
9 The true light that enlightens every

commentators have applied the words **through him** to Christ, and at first sight this is supported by the context. The limited mission of the Baptist falls far short of a universal gospel. Moreover, support has been found in two other passages: "Grace and truth came through Jesus Christ" (vs. 17), and "that the world might be saved through him" (3:17, where the same phrase is used, δι' αὐτοῦ). Yet this interpretation is untenable, for "to believe through Christ" is not a Johannine expression, but always "to believe in Christ." The testimony of John, according to this Gospel, brought to Jesus his first disciples, through whom that apostolic witness went forth, which in time was to spread through all the world. So Paul can write of himself and Apollos as "servants through whom you believed" (I Cor. 3:5, δι' ὧν ἐπιστεύσατε). It is the Fourth Evangelist, and not the Synoptists, who tells us of this honorable role played by the Baptist in the drama of the world's redemption. John was the witness through whom God attested the divine sonship of Jesus (vss. 32-34).

9-11. After this parenthetic comment about John, the Logos hymn is resumed. The Logos as light, i.e., as revealer of God, is seen as entering the world, and by their response to his revelation men stand under judgment. The Greek of vs. 9 is ambiguous, admitting

great end is holiness, and that real happiness is a mere by-product of that. And we can see that very largely it has been the things which hurt that have stabbed into human nature what gives it its dignity and worth. Could there be courage without pain, or patience and endurance without disappointment? So Lucian makes Poverty declare,

> I found him suffering under Luxury's treatment, put him in the charge of Wisdom and Toil . . . , and made a good worthy man of him. . . . Have I perfected him in virtue, only to see Plutus take him, twist him to Insolence and Arrogance, make him soft and limp and silly as before, and return him to me a worn-out rag again?
> Hermes: It is Zeus's will.
> Poverty: I am off, then. Toil, Wisdom, and the rest of you, quick march! Well, he will realize his loss before long; he had a good helpmeet in me, and a true teacher; with me he was healthy in body and vigorous in spirit; he lived the life of a man, and could be independent, and see the thousand and one needless refinements in all their absurdity.[3]

But essentially the dark means what shames and soils and drags one down. Even of these things Aristotle said boldly that God is not a bungling dramatist, who lets irrelevancies slip, for no reason, into the plot. Everything in it is there for some end; and before the curtain falls, will be seen to have had its own necessary part to play in the unfolding of the story, in the working out of the predestined plan. But Plato is unhappy about that. And Zoroaster sees Good and Evil as two utterly antagonistic forces. And always in the N.T. God has set himself against the evil, throwing in his all to master it, and to eliminate it from his universe, let the cost to him be what it may. The carnal mind is enmity against God, says Paul. Upon which Calvin comments that it has chosen a great enemy! But God too has a great enemy; and often it seems to be winning. In the annals there is much to daunt and discourage and dishearten. Progress, as a rule, is slow; and there are horrible relapses; things seem to go round and round, rather than steadily up and on. Evil is noisy, blatant, self-assertive; while goodness, as Laotzu said long ago, is lowly as the dust or is like water, which, choosing the lowest places, steals along, hidden by the rushes; and you know that it is there only by the greenness that it leaves upon its banks.

All that is set down more bluntly in the N.T. than anywhere else in literature. For it is the most honest of books, facing the ugliest facts, and shirking nothing. But it is also the most hopeful—witness that glorious phrase, **The Light shines in the darkness, and the darkness has not overcome it** (vs. 5). In all this amazing world is there a more amazing thing than the invincibility of goodness? Everything seems against it, yet it refuses to be killed. Often and often it is down, and all looks over. But somehow it always scrambles to its feet again and fights on. The tide ebbs out and out; and then it turns. The night falls, and grows ever blacker; and then comes the dawn. Do not the historians tell us that long before Luther's day

[3] "Timon the Misanthrope."

10 He was in the world, and the world was made by him, and the world knew him not.

man was coming into the world. 10 He was in the world, and the world was made through him, yet the world knew him not.

of three different interpretations according to the punctuation. (*a*) **That was the true Light, which lighteth every man that cometh into the world** (KJV). (*b*) "There was the true light, even the light which lighteth every man, coming into the world" (ERV). (*c*) **The true light that enlightens every man was coming into the world** (RSV; also substantially ERV mg.). Exegesis here turns upon a point of Greek grammar. Two verbal forms, "was" (ἦν) and "coming" (ἐρχόμενον) may be taken separately, or they can be taken together as a periphrastic imperfect, "was coming." But the participle may agree with "man" or with "light." In favor of (*a*) it is said that the phrase "every one coming into the world" is a common expression in rabbinical writings, synonymous with "man." But to this there are two objections: first, there is no instance of the tautology "every man that comes into the world"; second, in Greek this would require the article before "coming" (πάντα ἄνθρωπον τὸν ἐρχόμενον). The punctuation which allows the rendering (*b*) might give a causal or a temporal meaning to the participle "coming." "By its coming into the world" would mean that the Incarnation caused light to shine on every human being; it brought a universal revelation. This gives an intelligible meaning. "When it came into the world" is not suitable, for this limits the illumination to the infancy of Jesus; or if the participle refers to "man," it suggests that spiritual knowledge

the Reformation burst into flame, here and there in Europe, time and time again? And always it was fiercely stamped out, until not a spark, it seemed, remained. But in a little while the winds of God blew over what seemed dead ashes, and once more they leaped to life; till one day they grew to a roaring fire that nothing could put out. And in our own time have not mighty nations, ruthlessly using a brutal strength, attempted to throttle religion? And it has defied them and lives on. In a most moving passage of *Pulvis et Umbra,* Robert Louis Stevenson muses in bewilderment over man, perched precariously on his little islet of this brief life, with his frail heart and his enormous difficulties, defiantly keeping the flag flying, maintaining decency and honor, and finding time and means to be kindly to others round about him.

How is it done? Because, says the N.T., this fight is not our fight, but God's; and he is in it with us. Grim, terrifying things are massed against us, principalities, and powers, and the rulers of darkness. But the best of all is God is with us. And until God's throne goes down, and unless the Almighty fail, goodness cannot be conquered; and must win in the end. So in the individual life and heart how often things die down; aye, and how often they blaze up again!

Then I saw in my dream that the Interpreter took Christian by the hand, and led him into a place where was a fire burning against a wall, and one standing by it, always casting much water upon it, to quench it; yet did the fire burn higher and hotter.

Then said Christian, What means this?

The Interpreter answered, This fire is the work of grace that is wrought in the heart; he that casts water upon it, to extinguish and put it out, is the Devil; but in that thou seest the fire notwithstanding burn higher and hotter thou shalt also see the reason of that. So he had him about to the backside of the wall, where he saw a man with a vessel of oil in his hand, of the which he did also continually cast, but secretly, into the fire.

Then said Christian, What means this?

The Interpreter answered, This is Christ, who continually, with the oil of His grace, maintains the work already begun in the heart; by the means of which, notwithstanding what the Devil can do, the souls of His people prove gracious still.[4]

When Christ came in the flesh, there was the same initial seeming failure. Everything looked down, and evil utterly triumphant. Yet Christianity survived. And today while in some places it is losing ground, in others it is leaping out across the world faster than it has ever done. Even that gross darkness upon Calvary did not master it. Nor will the difficulties by which we are faced.

But why was it that men would have none of Christ? For it is likely that it is the same reasons that keep many from closing with him still. With some of them (vs. 10) it was because the divine originality confused them. They had been expecting something utterly different. To them Christ did not look the part, and did not fit God's promises at all. It is a fearsome fact that one can brush up against Christ and never

[4] John Bunyan, *The Pilgrim's Progress,* "In the Interpreter's House."

11 He came unto his own, and his own received him not.

11 He came to his own home, and his own

is bestowed upon babes. We therefore turn to (*c*), which accords with Johannine usage. The periphrastic imperfect is quite characteristic (cf. 1:28; 2:6; 3:23; 10:40; 11:1; 13:23; 18:18, 25). In a passage that recalls vss. 9-11 it is said, "This is the judgment, that the light has come into the world, and men loved darkness rather than light, because their deeds were evil" (3:19). Finally, Jesus himself is repeatedly described as one who has "come into the world" (6:14; 9:39; 11:27; 16:28), and even says of himself, "I have come as light into the world" (12:46). This justifies completely the RSV rendering.

The true light may mean the genuine as opposed to the false, or the eternally real in distinction from the transient and illusory reflection of it. Sometimes in the Fourth Gospel, with all its Hebraic background of thought, we can detect a trace of that Platonic strain which Philo, the Alexandrian Jew, brought into Hellenistic Judaism, and which is chiefly represented in the N.T. by the Epistle to the Hebrews (cf. Heb. 8:2; 9:24, also 8:5). The statement **that enlightens every man** is potential rather than actual, and must be limited by the qualifications laid down in vs. 12. **The world was made through him** (vs. 10) refers to vs. 3. This return to the thought of the pre-existent Logos is intended to heighten the paradox of the rejection of the incarnate Word. **He came to his own home, and his own people received him not** (vs. 11) is parallel to **He was in the world, . . . yet the world knew him not** (vs. 10). **His own**

recognize him, but push on: can resent progress, not realizing that it is progress; can oppose the incoming of a better way, because it is not the way to which we are accustomed, or the way that we expected; or because this is not the road by which God used to travel, and which we assumed that he would take, was bound to take, if he came back to us again. To be open-minded and catholic-hearted, to remember that God's ways are never stereotyped, is a primary virtue. It was a masterpiece of Diabolus, when he seized Mansoul, to set old, angry, ill-conditioned Mr. Prejudice, with sixty deaf men under him, to guard Ear-gate.[5] And they tell us that this failing grows upon us with the years. Jonathan Edwards wrote in his diary:

> I observe that old men seldom have any advantage of new discoveries, because these are beside a way of thinking they have been long used to. Resolved, if ever I live to years, that I will be impartial to hear the reasons of all pretended discoveries, and receive them, if rational, how long so ever I have been used to another way of thinking.[6]

Had Annas and Caiaphas and the rest laid down that wise rule for themselves, they might have seen that Christ was Christ; and a far nobler one than they themselves had ever imagined possible. But **he was in the world, and the world was made through him, yet the world knew him not** (vs. 10).

Moreover, for us there is this warning, that what they were looking for was a leader in social reform and in political adventure. Had Christ given them that, had he allowed himself to be persuaded by them into such a course, many of them would have followed eagerly. But for spiritual things they had small taste; and in a spiritual mission they could see no hope, all which is characteristic of our generation.

And some did not receive him (vs. 11)—we are not told why. But probably it was for the usual reasons. Life was full and interesting, and he got crowded out. Or he did not appeal to them, moved altogether outside of their line of country; or if they did feel a certain pull, still, as Hawthorne put it, "The greatest obstacle to being heroic is the doubt whether one may not be going to prove one's self a fool; the truest heroism is to resist the doubt; and the profoundest wisdom to know when it ought to be resisted, and when to be obeyed."[7] They were not sure that this was the real thing; that it might not involve them in a ridiculous fiasco. And so on. They **received him not.** That is all that is set down for us here.

But the Gospels make it plain that many held aloof from Christ for more sinister reasons. They resented him; they actively disliked him; what he offered in no way attracted them; and his claims on them upset and irritated them. As Christ himself says frankly, in a pathetic scripture, "Blessed is he who takes no offense at me" (Matt. 11:6), does not find something in me that stumbles and offends and alienates him. To be offered Christ and see no beauty in

[5] John Bunyan, *The Holy War*.

[6] John Hawksley, *Memoirs of the Rev. Jonathan Edwards* (London: James Black, 1815), p. 36.

[7] *The Blithedale Romance*, ch. ii.

12 But as many as received him, to them gave he power to become the sons of God, *even* to them that believe on his name:

people received him not. 12 But to all who received him, who believed in his name, he gave power to become children of God;

---

home is a translation of a phrase (τὰ ἴδια) which has this meaning in 16:32; 19:27; Acts 21:6, and in many occurrences outside the N.T., especially in Hellenistic writers. But there is also warrant for translating it "his own possession." **His own people** (οἱ ἴδιοι) may mean those who belong to him as their creator, or the Jews, the race into which he was born, with their peculiar religious privileges (cf. Rom. 9:4-5), or the neighbors and kinsfolk of Jesus (cf. Luke 4:16-30). The term is general and must be limited by vs. 12 and by 13:1. Cf. Enoch 42:1-2:

> Wisdom found no place where she might dwell;
> Then a dwelling-place was assigned her in the heavens.
> Wisdom went forth to make her dwelling among the children of men,
> And found no dwelling-place.

12. For there are those whose response shows that they have "recognized" (or "known") him, and have acted according to that knowledge. **To all who received him,** i.e., **who believed in his name,** divine recognition is given. To believe in his name is to acknowledge his claim that he is Messiah and Son of God. It was to win acceptance of this demand that the Gospel was written (20:31). To "know," to "believe," and to "receive" the light of God in Christ, if not identical in meaning, are in Johannine thought aspects of the same spiritual activity. There are passages in this Gospel which have seemed to some readers to imply a predestinarian outlook (see p. 443). It is not so here: for privilege follows faith; it does not ensure it. To those who exercised faith in him **he gave power to become children of God.** "Right" or "authority" is better than **power,** for authorization, an imparted title to a new status, rather than an inherent ability, is the root meaning of the word (ἐξουσία, not δύναμις). It is significant that this gift is the right to **become** [γενέσθαι, not ὑπάρχειν] **children of God.** In Matthew the fatherhood of God is universal in the sense of his creative relationship (but even in Matt. 5:45 the word and the tense require the meaning "become"). The Pauline and the Johannine conceptions regard this entrance into a family relationship as a gift to be received. Paul uses a metaphor derived from the Roman law of adoption; John resorts to the Hellenistic symbolism of regeneration, the birth from above.

---

him that we should desire him; to feel no thrill at being allowed to know and serve him; to clap hands to our eyes in order to shut out this accursed light that we do not want and will not have; to shrink back into the dark, because it is our native element, and only in it do we feel really at home: that is the most terrible of conditions, and the gravest of all judgments on a soul. Yet it can happen, and does happen. Hence that heart-gripping **He came to his own home, and his own people received him not** (vs. 11).

But some did know and did receive him. And what resulted in their case? Something so amazing that only God's hands could have done it! It is not nearly enough to talk of a reformation effected in the character, whereby unworthinesses that seemed woven inextricably into the stuff and fabric of the personality disappear. Even a catastrophic word like revolution does not begin to meet the case. For what Christ effects in a soul that trusts him is something far more radical and fundamental; nothing less than the creation of a new being in place of the old, and so different from that other that a new name for it is required, because the former one no longer fits the facts, but calls up a person that is mercifully dead, and so is really libelous (II Cor. 5:17). For God has passed on to his creature some of his own nature (vs. 13), so that now it can live afar off after his fashion (vs. 12) and grow up into his characteristic ways.

When some were belauding a sermon on sanctification, old Dr. John Duncan broke in with the pertinent question, "Did he begin with regeneration?" That is the all-important point. That is the glorious possibility there is for us in and through Christ; and less than that will not do. Whatever it does, a snake can only be a

13 Which were born, not of blood, nor of the will of the flesh, nor of the will of man, but of God.
14 And the Word was made flesh, and dwelt among us, (and we beheld his glory,

13 who were born, not of blood nor of the will of the flesh nor of the will of man, but of God.
14 And the Word became flesh and dwelt

13. As later, in the conversation with Nicodemus (3:3-12), stress is laid on the necessity of regeneration. **Who were born, not of blood** [in Greek physiology the seed of the father was mingled with the blood of the mother], **nor of the will of the flesh** [sexual impulse], **nor of the will of man** [human paternity], **but of God.** The best illustration of this imagery is found in that product of Hellenistic Judaism in Alexandria, the Wisdom of Solomon, "And in the womb of a mother was I molded into flesh in the time of ten months, being compacted in blood of the seed of man, and pleasure that came with sleep" (Wisd. Sol. 7:2). A strange corruption in the text of vs. 13 can be traced as far back as the second century in some Latin Fathers, and it has made its way even into a single MS of the O.L. text of the Gospels, the fifth-century codex now at Verona. The reading "who was born" is evidently a scribe's correction to introduce an allusion to the Virgin Birth of Jesus. Apart from the fact that not a single Greek MS contains this reading, we may note that this doctrine is not part of the Johannine teaching, while the doctrine of regeneration is integral to it (cf. 3:3; I John 2:29; 3:9; 4:7; 5:1, 4, 18).

14-18. These verses crown the Logos doctrine of the prologue and contain the essential message of the entire Gospel. **The Word became flesh** is a repudiation of all Gnostic disparagement of man's physical nature, for the statement asserts the real humanity of our Lord's earthly life. **Flesh,** while sometimes used by John in contrast to "spirit" (3:6; 6:56), does not carry the derogatory sense often found in the Pauline use. Thus Paul expresses the same thought with a slight difference, "God . . . sending his own Son in the likeness of sinful flesh" (Rom. 8:3). The reference is to the birth, not to the baptism, of Jesus, though the latter was the view held by those heretics who taught that the Christ descended upon Jesus at his baptism and left him before the Crucifixion. (Vss. 32-34 show that it was the Spirit, not the Logos, whose descent was the sign to convince the Baptist that Jesus was the Son of God.) The clause **and dwelt among us** may imply far

snake; and the natural man cannot break through the limitations of his nature. But in Christ he can rise in the scale of being and become a new creature, with new aims and standards, new likes and dislikes, new possibilities and powers. The crawling insect somehow has grown wings, has entered on a higher life, in which it does with ease what had been for it utterly impossible. But so long as we remain grubs we cannot fly, try how we may. Ben Tillett used to speak impatiently of men's kindly efforts at social amelioration as a mere waste of time, like the hopeful clapping of a poultice on a wooden leg, insisting that what was needed was a new social system. Certainly our efforts to tinker and contort ourselves into something better than we feel ourselves to be must be mainly futile, till Christ gives us **power to become the sons of God.** But he can do it; and he does. C. G. Jung underlines the audacity of the claim of Christianity that it can add a further highest link to the existing chain of evolution, can lift whosoever will accept it into a nobler type of life, built on a grander scale than anything this earth knows; can make of him a new creature, able to do and be what no one else can do or hope to be. And then he adds that nobody can laugh this out of court. For it has done it! And every day we meet such new creatures on the streets.

14-18. ***The Incarnation.***—So far the evangelist would awaken little or no opposition in most of his readers. With much of what he had been saying they were familiar. But now he takes a further, a stupendous step, and calmly announces that this Logos who has always been in the world since ever there was a world, who indeed himself made the world has entered into it in a far fuller sense. For this divine Being has become flesh, has put on human nature: and he who from all eternity has dwelt with God and in God, has tabernacled among men, sharing their difficulties with them, like Yahweh dwelling in the desert with his wayward and impossible people all the long empty years which their foolishness had brought upon them. And then suddenly and without warning a name slips into the narrative, the name of Jesus

the glory as of the only begotten of the Father,) full of grace and truth.

among us, full of grace and truth; we have beheld his glory, glory as of the only Son

more than the English verb suggests. The Greek word (ἐσκήνωσεν), derived from the noun for tent, is often used without any reference to its etymology. But so allusive a writer as the Fourth Evangelist may well have been thinking of the tabernacle in the wilderness where the Lord dwelt with Israel (Exod. 25:8-9; 40:34), and more particularly of that pillar of cloud above the tent of meeting, typifying the visible dwelling of the Lord among his people. In later Jewish doctrine the word for this was *shekina,* which would suggest to a bilingual Jew the Greek word *skēnē* (σκηνή) or "tent."

In the RSV the words **full of grace and truth** are transferred to this sentence to agree with "the Word." This is probably done because the Greek word for "full" (πλήρης) is in the nominative case, and would therefore seem, in spite of its position, to refer to the Logos. But in the common Greek of this period this adjective was often used indeclinably, and its position would point rather to a connection with **glory.** The difference is not important for the **glory** was the revealed nature of God. A comparison with Ps. 85:9-10 shows that four of the key words in vs. 14 are found together there also: "glory," "dwell," "mercy," and "truth." This psalm must have been in the writer's mind. The word for **grace** (χάρις), so common in the Pauline letters, does not occur again in the Gospel after the prologue, or in I John. In the psalm just referred to, the word in the LXX, ἔλεος, "mercy," translates the Hebrew *ḥeṣedh,* a word of far richer content than

Christ; and the secret is out! (vs. 17). He is the Logos! It was the eternal Word of God whom men knew as the carpenter who carried out their orders, as the teacher so derided by the experts who surely ought to know, as the outcast crucified for blasphemy! To such lengths has he gone for us, stooping so low in unimaginable condescension, and in a humility that just will not think. If it is only a dream, how wonderful a dream! But if it is true! If there is any chance that it is true, what then? Little wonder that Dorothy Sayers [8] stares in bewilderment at people who assure her blandly that Christianity leaves them cold, as being a dull affair that bores them. Or that she is so confident that if they would read the gospel through just once and let it have its chance with them, they would be forced to admit, whatever attitude they might take up about it, that this is, out of sight, the most exciting and tremendous and amazing story that the world can ever hear.

What is the central fact of Christianity, the very heart of the religion, the wonder of all wonders in this all-wonderful faith, that has so moved and impressed and changed innumerable souls, and made so vast a difference in the world? Our Lord himself, one ventures to think, laid the main stress on the fatherhood of God. To many the gracious operations of the Holy Spirit seem the very core of any and of every authentic Christianity. In the West for centuries people have gathered upon Calvary, beside the Cross, as to the holy of holies, more moved and solemnized, nearer to God, more conscious of his presence and his lovingkindness and his claims upon us there than anywhere else. But in the Eastern Church it has always been beside the manger that hearts have grown stillest and most awed; there that the mystery of divine grace staggers men most. And there is much to be said for that. For why did Christianity survive and spread, as it has done, while other rival faiths, like Mithraism, which started with immense advantages and seemed about to sweep the earth, have vanished into nothingness? What is it in this faith that gives it its permanence, its hold on generation after generation the whole world over?

Might not this be a partial answer? Before Christ came, life for many was a desperate affair. Then too, of course, there were lighthearted folk to whom it tasted good, and many frivolous and giddy creatures. But for multitudes it was a grim holding out, and little more. And there was nothing to hope for on ahead. It was full of pain, and problems past our understanding, and sorrow upon sorrow, every kind of terrifying thing. And they were facing it alone. For God was out of it. That was the privilege, and the prerogative, and the advantage that a god possessed, that he *was* out of it, and untouched by the cold shadows that steal over us, sat smiling, as Maeterlinck once imagined he saw God doing, on a sunny mountain, high above the fog of things, looking down unconcernedly upon his troubled world, no more disturbed by it and its dark problems than we

[8] *The Greatest Drama Ever Staged* (London: Hodder & Stoughton, 1938).

ḥēn, for which χάρις was the LXX equivalent. But in the N.T. values are reversed, for mercy emphasizes man's misery evoking the divine pity, while grace stands for God's initiative in meeting the situation created by man's sin. Elsewhere John always uses "love" to describe God's character and his action toward human need. Here the reference to the conjoined attributes so frequent in the O.T. demands the use of the word by which the early church, under the inspiration of Paul, embraced all those forces which flow from the heart of God to effect man's salvation. **Truth** (ἀλήθεια or the adjective ἀληθής) is one of the watchwords of this Gospel occurring over thirty times. Its meaning in early Christian use was determined partly by its O.T. equivalent and partly from its history in the various stages of the Greek language. The Hebrew word *'emeth* stood for "faithfulness," "trustworthiness," "permanence," "sureness," while the Greek had the meaning of "truth" as opposed to "falsehood," or of "reality" as opposed to mere "appearance." The Johannine use of the word in this instance is reminiscent of the Hebrew original, but the word had undergone considerable modification as a result of the impact of Greek thought upon Judaism. Here the passage may be interpreted as meaning that from the life of God which alone has reality and permanence an activity of love has entered human history and brought the gift of eternal life into the present.

---

are by a set of puppies tumbling over each other. And suddenly men found that they were not alone. There was someone beside them; and that someone was God: not out of it, but in it, at the raw sore heart of it; touched with the feeling of their infirmities, afflicted in all their afflictions, and always there; so that, in the loneliest situation or experience, there are two of us—our own frail, foolish, frightened heart, and the all-sufficient God, upon whom it can lean, and from whom it can draw until even God's resources are exhausted. Ernest Shackleton tells us of that "long and racking march of thirty-six hours" over the ice with his two comrades. "It seemed to me often that we were four, not three. I said nothing to my companions on the point, but afterwards Worsley said to me, 'Boss, I had a curious feeling on the march that there was another person with us.' Crean confessed to the same idea."[9] All Christians know it, and it makes an incredible difference, gives hope and heartening and courage, does not remove the difficulties, but brings one through with one's head up and with one's valor rallied. "Blessed be the Lord," says the psalmist, wise before the time, "who daily beareth our burden" (Ps. 68:19 ASV). Blessed indeed!

Still more, there was sin. For people in those days were not so unconcerned about it as for the moment they are now. It drove them crazy. They rushed from religion to religion, ready and willing to try anything to be made clean. And yet, tear at it how they might, that fiery Nessus-shirt, eating into their very soul, still clung to them. All they could do was futile, ineffectual, maddeningly resultless. In Rom. 7 a strong swimmer is straining toward the shore. Yet the tides are too masterful for him, and mock and toss him in derision out to sea again. There is no hope. But in ch. 8 one comes on a very different figure—a man with quiet steady eyes, facing his enemies entirely unperturbed, knowing that he can master them, and doing it. God has come into the fight and made it *his* fight; and Christ is there; and he can lean his back against Christ's back; and they two together can do anything. And so where Paul had always fallen, he stands fast and invincible. Such difference does God's presence with us make. And does not the Incarnation mean that he has come in, and is most certainly there beside us?

Further, the Incarnation has changed, how completely, our conceptions of the two most fundamental of all things—what God is, and the meaning of holiness.

As to the former, **No man hath seen God at any time** (vs. 18). Yet he is not unknowable by us. For one has only to look at Jesus Christ to realize what God must be. A stupendous claim! And yet Christ himself endorsed it with a calm assurance which was taken aback that Philip could find any difficulty in the matter! "Have I been so long time with you, and yet hast thou not known me, Philip? he that hath seen me hath seen the Father; and how sayest thou then, show us the Father?" (14:9.) There he sat, with his work-roughened hands, quietly uttering the most staggering words in the whole range of human literature.

Putting ourselves into their place, is it any wonder that the scribes and Pharisees, and the like, were so scandalized? That any man should make such a claim was horrifying to the Jew. But that this man should impiously dare to do so was an outrage! For Christ's standards were not their standards; and his view of what goodness means was very different in many ways

[9] *South* (London: William Heinemann, 1919), p. 209.

We have beheld his glory is a simple assertion which conceals four difficulties: (*a*) the meaning of "glory," (*b*) the sense in which "behold" or "see" is used, (*c*) the force of the past tense of the verb, and (*d*) the reference in the pronoun "we." As for (*a*), δόξα is used not in the earlier classical meaning of "opinion," nor in the later meaning of "reputation" as in 5:41; 7:18, but rather represents the Hebrew *kābhôdh,* "splendor," "manifested excellence." In many O.T. passages the "glory of God" suggests a physical radiance; in others, as generally in the N.T., it stands, as here, for the revelation of the divine character in its perfection. As for (*b*) and (*c*), six different words for "see" are used in this Gospel, and the author's frequent habit of interchanging synonyms without significance warns us against a too confident discrimination. Two meanings may well be blended in this place, for the parallel with I John 1:1-3 strongly favors the testimony of eyewitnesses to certain events that took place in Galilee and Judea within the first third of the first century A.D., and at the same time the **glory** which they **beheld** was something visible to the eye of faith. The past tense rules out the thought of a mystic vision, and points to the outward aspect of a life that had long since passed out of mortal sight. Yet many who also watched Jesus in the days of his flesh failed to see what kindled faith in the hearts of the disciples. (*d*) **We** stands for the Christian witness represented by the

---

from their own. And hence to them he was bad, a moral nuisance polluting the atmosphere. You can know one by the company he keeps, they said; and you were likeliest to find this fellow among the scum of the place. The law was God-given; its regulations had been built up on the experience of generations of devoted souls. But this person largely ignored it; and here, and here, and here broke through it at will. He was a menace, a plague spot, far better away. He like God! And they came down from Calvary, well pleased, and feeling that they had been blotting out a blasphemous insult thrown into God's face.

And now everybody sees that Christ's claim was entirely justified; knows that if there is a God at all, he must be Christlike. That at least is fixed and certain and has become self-evident. In Christ's face we have seen and see God's face: through Christ's life and character we know what the divine nature must be. The Incarnation, the coming of God in among us, has achieved that.

It is indeed an extraordinary conception of Godhead to which it has brought us. Our eyes are apt to be dazzled by the attributes, omniscience and omnipotence, and such august and unthinkable qualities; to be caught and held by pomps and thrones and splendors, and metaphors which lead us far astray. For the essence of Godhead, what makes God God, is none of these, but a humility that stoops far lower than any man would stoop; and a patient kindness that bears on and on, long after every human heart would have been fretted into a passion of anger; and an unselfishness so huge that it sweeps away in whirling flood our biggest human measures as hopelessly inadequate, and bursts our human minds. Our earthly conventions and ways, our grabbiness and pushfulness and self-indulgence, are as local and parochial as a country accent. That heaven in which God's will is done is, to our eyes, a queer topsy-turvy place, where the least is the greatest and the greatest is the least; and the King is the servant of all. So Sir Oliver Lodge (see under 11:35 for passage in full):

> The Christian idea of God is not that of a being outside the universe, above its struggles and advances, looking on and taking no part in the process, *solely* exalted, beneficent, self-determined and complete; no, it is also that of a God who loves, who yearns, who suffers . . . who enters into the storm and conflict, and is subject to conditions as the Soul of it all.[1]

This, he says, whether it is considered blasphemous or not, is the truth that Christ grasped, and never let go; the truth that he has sent reverberating down the ages; and upon which man leans as upon his one real hope.

Hence the immense importance of the historicity of Christ (vs. 14). There seems to be a notion blowing about men's minds that it does not really matter whether the gospel story ever actually happened or not, whether it is history or myth. In either case, so we are told, we have gained the idea of what God must be, and the ideal of what our life should become. And that, it seems, is all that matters. No doubt much can be learned through myths. Chesterton has assured us that the deepest lessons life had taught him came to him from them. But it makes a mighty difference whether Jesus Christ really existed, whether that life was ever actually lived or not; whether that character was ever really woven out of the same stuff of life that our clumsy fingers so soil and tangle. Stand-

[1] *Man and the Universe* (London: Methuen & Co., 1908), p. 318.

15 ¶ John bare witness of him, and cried, saying, This was he of whom I spake, He that cometh after me is preferred before me; for he was before me.

from the Father. (15 John bore witness to him, and cried, "This was he of whom I said, 'He who comes after me ranks before

apostles whose knowledge of Jesus in his bodily presence was the guarantee that this was truly a revelation of the divine nature. This is further defined as the disclosure of a Father's likeness in the face of an only and well-loved Son. **Glory as of the only Son from the Father** preserves the ambiguity of the Greek. "From" may go with "begotten" (cf. the thought in 6:46; 7:29; 16:27; 17:8), or with "glory" (as in 5:41, 44).

Vs. 15 is another interjected comment about the Baptist, explaining vss. 6-8 and leading on to vss. 19-34. **John bore witness to him, and cried.** The first verb expresses the one function of the Baptist according to this Gospel, the second (κράζειν) is regularly used of an inspired utterance—by our Lord (7:28; 12:44); by those speaking under the influence of the Spirit (Luke 4:41; Rom. 8:15; Gal. 4:6); or of demons (Mark 5:7; etc.). It was often so used in classical Greek. The change of tense from present to perfect suggests that while the witness is part of the continuous testimony of the church, his actual words, spoken in the past, have an enduring significance. **This was he of whom I said** refers to the testimony given again in vss. 27, 30. **Ranks before me** (lit., "has come to be before me") gives the true meaning. The last clause, **for he was before me,** must

fast, in *The Pilgrim's Progress,* accounted for the success of his valiant life by explaining that wherever he saw the print of his Lord's shoe, therein he had coveted to set his own. That we can understand if the prints were really there. But the imagined footsteps of an imagined person, imagined to have climbed ahead of us, are surely much less helpful. One can imagine anything. But, as Carlyle used to insist, a fact is an altogether different matter, vastly more solid and dependable. As Ernest Renan said, "Humanity seeks the ideal, but it seeks it in a person, and not in an abstraction. A man, the incarnation of the ideal, whose biography might serve as a frame for all the aspirations of the time is what the religious mind sought." [2] And it finds that in a real Christ who really existed.

Emerson wrote stupidly that "every Stoic was a Stoic; but in Christendom where is the Christian?" [3] The Stoics themselves did not speak like that. In spite of their hardihood and heroism, these intrepid souls were often darkened and burdened by a sense of being baffled, beaten, cheated. It was all a stretching out of hands that came far short.

> The desire of the moth for the star,
> Of the night for the morrow,
> The devotion to something afar
> From the sphere of our sorrow.[4]

A hopeless dream! It was so remote and came no nearer, was so maddeningly shadowy, so insubstantial; never grew into fact. As Samuel Angus puts it:

> The Logos of the Stoics was a pure abstraction, the inspiration of which would touch only the enlightened, and of their ideal Wise Man Plutarch declared, "He is nowhere on earth, nor ever has been." The Logos of Philo was merely a Hypostasis, or, at best, never stepped beyond the limits of personification. But for Christians "the Logos became flesh and tabernacled among us, and we beheld His glory," an advantage which Augustine declares he could not find in any of the competitors of Christianity.[5]

Matthew Arnold tells us that it was not his father's teaching but his father's life, lived day by day beside him, that made him credit the possibility of human goodness on the great scale, which, had it not been for that, would have

> Seem'd but a dream of the heart,
> Seem'd but a cry of desire.[6]

That is what Christ has done for souls innumerable. Men rose to the Christian conception of God not so much by listening to what he said, as by watching him live among them day by day. After all, the teaching, unique though it is, was only a footnote to the main message; and that was his character and life and death. And as they watched, they became sure that God, too, must be like that. For this had been lived, been done, been achieved. And man cannot outtop God morally. And so they knew

[2] *Marc-Aurèle* (Paris: Michel Lévy Frères, 1882), p. 582.
[3] Essay on "Self-Reliance."
[4] Shelley, "To—: One Word Is Too Often Profaned."
[5] *The Mystery Religions and Christianity* (New York: Charles Scribner's Sons, 1925), p. 311.
[6] "Rugby Chapel."

16 And of his fulness have all we received, and grace for grace.

me, for he was before me.' ") 16 And from his fullness have we all received, grace upon

refer to the pre-existence of the Logos. This is strictly an anachronism on the lips of the Baptist, but is typical of the Johannine manner of anticipation (see p. 438).

Vs. 16 is a continuation of vs. 14, and **his fullness** refers to Christ, of whom Paul had written, "In him dwells the whole fullness of deity bodily" (Col. 2:9). John here is thinking of deity in the character of "gracious reality." If John, like Paul, has a side allusion to the Gnostics' use of fullness (πλήρωμα) as a technical term, he seizes the opportunity to dismiss their doctrine of the spiritual elite to whom alone the higher knowledge of God was given: **We have all received from his fullness.** (For the Gnostic use of πλήρωμα see *Dictionary of Christ and the Gospels,* ed. James Hastings [New York: Charles Scribner's Sons, 1906-08] I, 629, or more fully, *Encyclopaedia of Religion and Ethics,* ed. James Hastings [New York: Charles Scribner's Sons, 1908-27], X, 62.) And this abundance of the divine gift is never exhausted, but is continually being renewed according to our need, **grace upon grace, lit.,** "grace instead of grace." The idea is well expressed in Charles Wesley's lines:

> And who our poverty retain,
> More gifts we shall receive,
> Multiplied grace and blessings gain,
> And all a God can give.

Cf. two passages in Philo. *The Posterity of Cain* XLIII. 145: "Wherefore God ever causes His earliest gifts to cease before their recipients are glutted and wax insolent; and storing them up for the future gives others in their stead, and a third supply to replace the second, and ever new in place of earlier boons, sometimes different in kind, sometimes the same." Also *On Abraham* XLVI. 273: "Admiring the man for his faith in him, God repays him

God also must be generous with Christ's unreckoning generosity, spending himself for others in a divine glory of unthinkable unselfishness.

To all which there is a tremendous addendum. **No one has ever seen God; the only Son, who is in the bosom of the Father, he has made him known** (vs. 18). But turn to I John 4:12, and this is written, "No man has ever seen God; if we love one another, God abides in us and his love is perfected in us." So in some real sense we too ought to be revealing God to others. Shelley pictures the earth wakening in the morning, and all its myriads of creatures, great and minute, hurrying to the tasks for which they were created. And this is our august vocation. So to live that those about us will see God in us. As the Mettasutra of the Buddhists has it, "As a mother, as long as she lives, watches over her only child, so should one practice an all embracing goodwill to all beings, standing or sitting, moving or lying down. Then men will say, Here at last is the ideal life." [7] Better than that, they will feel that this is what God must be like. And how are we to do it? "I am the Light of the world" said Christ (8:12). And again, "You are the light of the world" (Matt. 5:14). In itself the moon is a dark ball, sterile and cold and dead. But it can catch the glory of the sun, and, reflecting it, make the night beautiful. But alas, in many of us the albedo, the reflecting property, is very low and desperately meager.

16-17. ***Grace Heaped upon Grace.***—The life in God is rich and ample beyond all describing. For anything and everything there is in Christ is ours for the taking and the using; is indeed pressed eagerly upon us. And God's generosity is inexhaustible and never tires; keeps heaping grace on grace upon us, far beyond reckoning up (vs. 16). All the saints have felt that; dazed by it, and uncomprehending why it should be. At the one end of things Bunyan called his autobiography *Grace Abounding to the Chief of Sinners;* and at the other, St. Teresa entitled her life story *Of the Mercies of God.* Every Christian knows that he himself is not the central figure in his own biography; and that what matters, and has mattered, in it is what God is, and what God does. So Emerson:

> The ardors of piety agree at last with the coldest skepticism—that nothing is of us or our works,—that all is of God. Nature will not spare us the

[7] See *Sutra-Nipāta,* I. 8.

17 For the law was given by Moses, *but* grace and truth came by Jesus Christ.

grace. 17 For the law was given through Moses; grace and truth came through Jesus

with faith [or faithfulness]." See F. H. Colson and G. H. Whitaker, eds., *Philo with an English Translation* (New York: G. P. Putnam's Sons, 1929, 1935; "Loeb Classical Library"), II, 413; VI, 133.

Vss. 17-18 introduce what at first sight is a new contrast. If these words were found in a letter of Paul's, we should see in them his characteristic antithesis between religious legalism and the religion of grace. That is hardly the emphasis here. In the Intro. (p. 445) it has been shown that behind this prologue there lies probably a hymn in praise of wisdom in her later aspect as the Torah. We have seen that the evangelist has interpolated comments to prevent a misapplication to John the Baptist and possibly also to guard against other current perils from false teachers. These closing verses seem to claim the superiority of the new Torah over the old. When God was about to give the tables of stone to Moses, who asked, "Show me, I pray thee, thy glory," he replied, "Thou

smallest leaf of laurel. All writing comes by the grace of God, and all doing and having. I would gladly . . . allow the most to the will of man, but I have set my heart on honesty in this chapter, and I can see nothing at last in success or failure, than more or less of vital force supplied from the Eternal.[8]

In vs. 17 there is an obvious antithesis between law and grace. Yet the law too is grace. For it was the Logos who inspired Moses to see and teach to others what a glorious thing a human life can be; to make us shrink back with a shudder from what is mean and dirty. Hence devout Jews, like Montefiore, are irritated by Paul on the law of God, and the depression it awoke in him. For their part ("O how love I thy law!" as the psalmist cried in Ps. 119:97) they exult in it as a mighty gift for which they can never sufficiently thank God. We might have been mere beasts of the field, never lifting our heads, content with our fodder and mere beastlinesses: and he has given us such lofty stars by which to steer, and has awakened in us a hunger for something bigger and better than we are, which is our letters patent of nobility; has made us see something of the infinite possibilities of such a life as ours. All which, of course, Paul knew vastly better than they do. But it is true that a religion which does not result in a passion for righteousness, and a delight in it, proves itself thereby an impostor. It is not only for his promises that we ought to thank God, but no less for his claims upon us; for his honoring estimate of what we can become, and even now can do and be.

Yet there is an antithesis. With Jesus Christ something new came into religion, which is here summed up under the two heads of grace and reality (Moffatt). This new religion was effective; it proved itself. Tested in the most drastic fashion and in the most impossible case, it worked. Here was no world of shadows and symbols, beautiful but bodiless; here was a world of solid facts, upon which one could confidently take one's stand, and know that they would not give beneath one. "I am not ashamed of the gospel," says Paul proudly, for "it is the power of God for salvation to every one who has faith" (Rom. 1:16), who will give it a chance. So the writer to the Hebrews will admit no limitations whatsoever. This is a Lord who can save, and does save, to the uttermost, when all seems lost, and right on to the end. That has always been the boast of Christianity. When Celsus jeered at Christ on the ground that while every reputable teacher naturally appeals to the wise and noble to come to him, this impossible person calls to the down-and-outs, to the scum of society, to rally to him, there came the devastating answer from a church which, so far from being abashed by the taunt, declared exultantly, Thank God, that is true! Only, he does not leave them down-and-out; but out of the material you would have tossed away as useless, he makes real men, living a life to be called life. For this thing works.[9]

And this, because in Christ religion gains a new atmosphere. For here salvation is a thing that is not earned, as elsewhere it is assumed that it must be, but given. In the N.T. the central word is grace; and that means what is granted freely, for the taking, for the carrying away; and granted to the undeserving, known to be undeserving. For Christ's bold faith is that this trust in those who have failed will shame them out of themselves, and lift them up above themselves, and make them trustworthy. If you want a man to be big, says Goethe, act toward him as if he were big, and he will rise to it. Christ staked everything on that. We are so ac-

[8] Essay on "Experience."

[9] Origen *Against Celsus* III. 59.

18 No man hath seen God at any time; the only begotten Son, which is in the bosom of the Father, he hath declared *him*.

Christ. 18 No one has ever seen God; the only Son,[b] who is in the bosom of the Father, he has made him known.

[b] Other ancient authorities read *God*.

canst not see my face; for man shall not see me and live." Now the new Torah, the living Word of God, is come. **For the law was given through Moses; grace and truth came through Jesus Christ. No one has ever seen God; the only Son, who is in the bosom of the Father, he has made him known.** The allusion cannot be missed. There is an important textual variant to **the only Son.** Three of our oldest MSS read "God only-begotten." This, the earliest form of the text, is difficult, and can best be interpreted by noticing that θεός is without the article (cf. vs. 1) and is in apposition to the noun clause: "He who is in the bosom of the Father, only-begotten, divine." From the fourth century onward the reading "Son" replaced "God," probably under the influence of 3:16, 18; I John 4:9. (The reading θεός is found in ℵ B C L 33 syp Clement of Alexandria, Origen, Epiphanius; υἱός is read in all the other uncials and cursives, O.L., syc, Chrysostom, and the Latin

customed to it that we no longer realize how daring the gospel is! There is a quite frightful risk in it. For some of us are too mean to respond to it. It is pitched too high for us and goes clean over our heads. With such, as Christ himself admits, the gospel fails, and leaves them worse instead of better. Are you never disquieted by the thought that you are less fearful of transgressing, less concerned about your unworthiness, more easy in your mind at being what you are, now that you know of God's readiness to forgive, than you would have been had you still believed him to be sternly, coldly, implacably just; so twisting the gospel awry to your own ruin? Simple, Sloth and Presumption, found asleep under the shadow of the Cross, aroused and told they were not near their journey's end, would not bestir themselves but, nodding drowsy heads in the direction of the Cross, said that would bring them through; and he who had gone so far would no doubt go a little farther; and they need not worry; and were lost upon Calvary, and because Christ died for them![1] And yet Christ felt that desperate hazard must be run. None of the big things in life are earned—our birth, our health, the love about us. "My friends have come to me unsought," said Emerson, "the great God gave them to me."[2] Who earns his wife's affections? It is given of free grace. And salvation, a bigger thing even than that, must be accepted upon these same terms—as a free gift.

From his fullness have we all received grace heaped on grace. So it is confidently stated in vs. 16. No doubt for each of us there is the practical problem to be faced. But have we? That **fullness** has been offered to us, thrust upon us. But have we accepted it? Is not Christianity, as we know it and have practiced it, a thin anemic thing, only a shadow of the solid reality which Christ has it in his heart to give us; and which many have received from him? And if in our case this is so, how have we been defrauding ourselves of all this **fullness** that is ours if we will have it?

Our Lord requires a certain responsiveness in those to whom he makes his offers, if he is not to be thwarted and disappointed. Were there not villages in which he wrought amazing things? And why? Because they gave him the right atmosphere, were eager and receptive and expectant; and so their faith and hope came true. But there were others in which, although as eager to help as ever, he could do little because faced by a blank incredulity that scoffed away their chance. "Mighty works!" so a woman might jeer. "Not he! Bless me! He was the carpenter in the town where I lived before I married. He made that chair you are sitting on now. And all the years I knew him there was never any talk of miracles. Don't you believe a word of it!" And when in that atmosphere nothing happened, they plumed themselves upon their sanity. They were not to be fooled, like hysterical folk elsewhere! "We said nothing would come of it; and nothing did!"

What was it ye went out to see,
Ye foolish folk of Galilee?
. . . .
The reeds that waver, the weeds that float?—
A young man preaching in a boat.[3]

But there was more in it than that. "Go and tell John," said Christ, "what you have seen and heard: the blind receive their sight, the lame walk, lepers are cleansed, and the deaf hear, the dead are raised up, the poor have good

[1] Bunyan, *The Pilgrim's Progress,* Part I.
[2] Essay on "Friendship."
[3] Arthur Hugh Clough, "What went ye out for to see?"

Fathers.) Some commentators regard both these nouns as a marginal comment introduced into the text as a noun complement to the isolated adjective. **He has made him known** represents two words in the Greek—an emphatic pronoun and a verb, which corresponds to the noun "exegete" (ἐξηγητής) used of the official interpreter of a divine oracle, of a dream, or of the Jewish law. The thought recalls Ecclus. 43:31, "Who hath seen him [God] that he may declare him?" Jesus is the revealer of the unseen God. In the Hellenistic mystery cults there were mystagogues who initiated candidates into the successive stages of their secret lore. In Gnosticism there were those who could impart the esoteric "knowledge" which made them "wise" unto salvation. But Jesus, the incarnate Word of God, does not only teach. In his whole life, as well as by his lips, he is the living revelation of God.

Here ends the prologue. In it we have been introduced to some of the words that are most characteristic of the Johannine Gospel: life, light, darkness, witness, the world, glory, truth, to believe, to receive, to be born of God. They will recur, but in the form of narrative or discussion as the drama of the incarnate Word is unfolded.

---

news preached to them" (Luke 7:22). All that within our reach. The pity of it if Christ comes and goes and we remain just what we were, the blind still blind, the deaf hearing nothing of God's voice, the dead stone cold, still dead!

Others cheat themselves out of the inheritance there is for them in Christ by arguing that while no limits can be set to what he can effect in the right type of person, they themselves do not belong to that type. However skillful a teacher may be, little will come of all his efforts if there is in the pupil no shadowy beginning of an aptitude to which he can appeal and on which he can work. And one must be reasonable even toward Christ, and not expect impossibilities from him. The promises are there. And they are true. In the right people they work out, and that to extraordinary lengths. "But they are not for me," so some despondent folk may say. "They are like the millions of a millionaire—for him, real and substantial, but nothing to do with me, and utterly beyond my reach." William Watson in one of his poems recounts how prisoners, learning from their warders' casual talk together that spring is once more making her triumphal progress through the land, feel dully that it means nothing for them. No roses will bloom upon the grim encircling walls that hem them in, no flowers break through the hard paving stones of the narrow court, round and round which they tramp for exercise. For them this tale of spring is but

> . . . a legend emptied of concern;
> And idle is the rumor of the rose.[4]

So many push aside this talk of the fullness that there is in Christ. "It will not happen to me," so they assume. "To such as I am it does not apply. I have immured myself within a personality from which there is now no escaping. Even Christ cannot change that for me." But they are wrong. For, says the prophet, when he comes, the Messiah will preach deliverance to the captives, and the opening of the prison to them that are bound.

But most of those who miss it lose the fullness that they could find in Christ because they do not want it, and will not have it. They may think they do. But when the test comes, they discover to their own bewilderment, that like Augustine, they have once again rejected what they were confident they desired and that "the life to which I was accustomed held me more than that other, for which I thought I yearned." Do we want, will we take, will we have this fullness that there is for us in Christ?

For some of us the Beatitudes make disconcerting reading, seeing that for us the whole thing seems to be pitched much too high and goes clean over our heads. We meet none of the conditions, and at the end are left with hands still empty. "Blessed are the meek." But I have a bit of a temper. There is nothing there for me. "Blessed are the pure in heart." But who of us will dare to claim that he satisfies that condition? "Blessed are they who are persecuted for righteousness' sake." But many of us have never lost anything worth reckoning up for Jesus Christ. And so we feel left out of this distribution of great gifts. "Well! Well!" says Christ, slipping in a beatitude for beginners, "Have you any hunger for the righteousness you have not got? For that will serve, for a start. And they too are satisfied." The grace heaped upon grace is there, ours for the accepting, for the carrying away; the most real of realities.

[4] "Estrangement," from *The Poems of Sir William Watson, 1878-1935* (London: George G. Harrap & Co., 1936). Used by permission.

19 ¶ And this is the record of John, when the Jews sent priests and Levites from Jerusalem to ask him, Who art thou?

20 And he confessed, and denied not; but confessed, I am not the Christ.

21 And they asked him, What then? Art thou Elias? And he saith, I am not. Art thou that Prophet? And he answered, No.

19 And this is the testimony of John,
when the Jews sent priests and Levites
from Jerusalem to ask him, "Who are
you?" 20 He confessed, he did not deny, but
confessed, "I am not the Christ." 21 And
they asked him, "What then? Are you Eli-
jah?" He said, "I am not." "Are you the

II. The Witness of the Baptist and His Disciples (1:19-51)

19. The Jews: A name sometimes used by John to include Galileans, especially when Jewish observances are under consideration; sometimes the inhabitants of Jerusalem and Judea; but often, as here (cf. 5:15-18; 7:13; 9:22; 18:12), the reference is to the religious authorities in the Sanhedrin. Of the two parties (cf. Acts 23:6) the Sadducean group was led by the high-priestly family of Annas. It was this section that sent priests and Levites to John. The Pharisees mentioned in vs. 24 would hardly send an embassy of priests and Levites. That would therefore be a separate deputation. The question **Who are you?** as in 8:25 refers not to identity but to status and claim in the religious life of the nation.

20-21. Three titles are disowned by the Baptist. He was not **the Christ,** the Messiah, though his baptism was an eschatological sacrament sealing men for the coming kingdom of God. He was not the **Elijah** foretold in Mal. 4:5. He was not **the prophet** whose coming was expected in fulfillment of Deut. 18:15. There is no difficulty about the first disclaimer. The second is not easy to understand in view of Mark 9:11-13; Matt. 11:14. It is best explained by Luke 1:17, where the prophecy of Malachi is applied to the Baptist, with the qualification, "He will go before him in the spirit and power of Elijah." The Jewish expectation was that Elijah himself would return in bodily form. The chief difficulty is to determine what was understood by **the prophet.** The allusion, no doubt, is to the Deuteronomic words ascribed to Moses, "The Lord thy God will raise up unto thee a Prophet from the midst of thee, of thy brethren, like unto me; unto him ye shall hearken." The reference is repeated in this Gospel (6:14; 7:40), but is absent from the Synoptics. From Acts 3:22; 7:37 it is clear that the early Christians found the promise realized in Jesus. This, however, was not due to any contemporary identification of "the prophet" with the Messiah. Rabbinical references to Deut. 18:15 are rare and never identify him with any historical figure. Popular speculation roamed freely, as the mention of Jeremiah (Matt. 16:14) shows, though he is never named either as a fore-

---

19-34. *The Witness of John the Baptist.*—The Gospel proper begins with vs. 19, with the witness of John the Baptist; and remarkable testimony, in very deed, it is (vss. 19-34; also in the prologue, vss. 6-8, 15). The center of it all is vs. 32. Perhaps the best understanding of this not easy passage comes through a worthy conception of a sacrament; from grasping the fundamental facts that always in a sacrament the central figure is not man, but God; and that what supremely matters in it is not what man does but what God does (see on 3:30).

The Baptist, with his burning sincerity, his courage, his red-hot anger against sin, had got through the nation's guard, and fairly pierced people's consciences. They flocked to him; they listened, much moved and discomfited in soul; they knew that what he said was true; they grew sick of themselves, and yearned to be quite different from themselves. And in token of this they crowded eagerly to be baptized, seeing that vivid picture wherein the man that had been up till now, plunging beneath the water, disappeared forever—that was the idea—and a new man rose up, animated by new motives, to make a new beginning in a new kind of life. All that meant much. Yet it was little to what the more spiritual of them knew was happening. For God was taking action, was accepting them; was pledging himself in their support; was individualizing his promises, and assuring them that he stood to his word toward them. Almost their hearts could hear him saying, looking straight at them, "Come now, and let us reason together, saith the Lord: though your sins be as scarlet, they shall be as white as snow" (Isa. 1:18). "Then will I sprinkle clean water upon you, and ye shall be clean.... A new heart

22 Then said they unto him, Who art thou? that we may give an answer to them that sent us. What sayest thou of thyself?

23 He said, I *am* the voice of one crying in the wilderness, Make straight the way of the Lord, as said the prophet Esaias.

24 And they which were sent were of the Pharisees.

25 And they asked him, and said unto him, Why baptizest thou then, if thou be not that Christ, nor Elias, neither that Prophet?

26 John answered them, saying, I baptize with water: but there standeth one among you, whom ye know not;

27 He it is, who coming after me is preferred before me, whose shoe-latchet I am not worthy to unloose.

prophet?" And he answered, "No." 22 They
said to him then, "Who are you? Let us
have an answer for those who sent us. What
do you say about yourself?" 23 He said, "I
am the voice of one crying in the wilderness, 'Make straight the way of the Lord,'
as the prophet Isaiah said."
24 Now they had been sent from the
Pharisees. 25 They asked him, "Then why
are you baptizing, if you are neither the
Christ, nor Elijah, nor the prophet?"
26 John answered them, "I baptize with
water; but among you stands one whom you
do not know, 27 even he who comes after
me, the thong of whose sandal I am not

---

runner of the Messiah or as connected with the messianic age (see Hermann L. Strack and Paul Billerbeck, *Kommentar zum Neuen Testament aus Talmud und Midrasch* [München: C. H. Beck, 1922-28], I, 729-30; II, 363, 479-80, 626; IV, 764-98).

23-26. Here John follows closely the words of the tradition which are found almost verbally in the Synoptics (Matt. 3:3, 11; Mark 1:3, 7-8; Luke 3:4, 16). All four cite the opening words of the great evangelic prophet of the Exile (Isa. 40:3), but John alone reports the Baptist as saying, **I am the voice of one crying in the wilderness.** He will not claim a place and a name for himself. He is but a voice—*vox clamantis in deserto.* It is noteworthy that John alone is silent about the baptism with the Holy Spirit. That is to be told in another way in "the spiritual gospel." Other peculiarities are **one whom you do not know** (vs. 26) and the local interest characteristically shown in vs. 28. The humility of the Baptist is even more marked when compared with the saying of the third-century Rabbi Joshua ben Levi, "Every service which a slave performs for his master a pupil will do for his teacher, except loosing his shoe" (cited by Strack and Billerbeck, *op. cit.,* I, 121). **One whom you do not know** is a reference to the unknown Christ, *Messias absconditus.* Even John the Baptist recognized him only by special revelation (vs. 33).

To the question **Why are you baptizing?** (vs. 25), the answer is given in vss. 31, 33. The Baptist was sent on his mission of baptism that the Coming One might be made

---

also will I give you, and a new spirit will I put within you" (Ezek. 36:25-26). And he not only said it, but he did it. Not that there is anything magical or mechanical in a sacrament. God's grace, in a sacrament as elsewhere, is like the sun which here coaxes green and growing things out of the soil, and yet, ten yards away, beating upon a stone, effects nothing at all (cf. Calvin, *Institutes* IV. 14. 9). Yet always God stands to his side of his covenant with us; and if we give him any chance at all, things happen.

And in that throng there came Jesus of Nazareth, to be baptized. Holy and pure and separate from sin, he too insisted on submitting to the rite. Why? Some, e.g., H. S. Coffin,[5] think that, himself unsullied, he may, as one of the nation, have felt himself involved in its corporate failings. In any case, he was taking our sin upon himself in a tremendous act of self-dedication to God, wherein he committed himself to the unthinkable task of taking away the sin of the world; of making an end of it, whatever the cost of that might prove to him. And what has flowed from that the whole world knows. And yet, even in Christ's baptism, what Christ himself did was not the central thing, but what God the Father did. Cyprian built up his whole conception of the sacraments upon his own experience while being baptized, when he was sure that sins, fatally characteristic and familiar, simply fell away from him and caused him no further trouble. Baptism was not only a picture of what God can do; but in it he had taken action, and had done it. And at Christ's

[5] *The Meaning of the Cross* (New York: Charles Scribner's Sons, 1936), pp. 67 ff.

28 These things were done in Bethabara beyond Jordan, where John was baptizing.

29 ¶ The next day John seeth Jesus coming unto him, and saith, Behold the Lamb of God, which taketh away the sin of the world!

30 This is he of whom I said, After me cometh a man which is preferred before me; for he was before me.

31 And I knew him not: but that he should be made manifest to Israel, therefore am I come baptizing with water.

worthy to untie." 28 This took place in
Bethany beyond the Jordan, where John
was baptizing.
29 The next day he saw Jesus coming
toward him, and said, "Behold, the Lamb
of God, who takes away the sin of the
world! 30 This is he of whom I said, 'After
me comes a man who ranks before me, for
he was before me.' 31 I myself did not know
him; but for this I came baptizing with
water, that he might be revealed to Is-

---

known. He himself did not know the one he was to proclaim, but a sign was given by which the Messiah was to be recognized (vss. 31-33). The evangelist does not record the baptism of Jesus by John. That fact was well known from the tradition already followed by the Synoptists. But whereas in the Synoptic account the vision of the dove, together with the Bath Qôl (see Mark 1:10-11; Matt. 3:16-17; Luke 3:21-22), came to Jesus alone, in this Gospel the sign was for John. Bath Qôl, "daughter of the voice," meant in later Judaism a mysterious voice by which God on occasion communicated with men after the end of prophecy. Cf. Wordsworth, *Ode to Duty:* "stern daughter of the Voice of God."

28. It is evident from 3:26 and 10:40 that there were two places named Bethany. Origen, visiting Palestine at a time when the site of Bethany beyond Jordan was lost, is probably responsible for the textual correction **Bethabara.**

29-34. On the day following the Baptism John made a threefold declaration: Jesus was (*a*) the sin-bearing **Lamb of God** (vs. 29), (*b*) the One who was to baptize with the Spirit (vs. 33), and (*c*) **the Son of God** (vs. 34).

The Lamb of God, who takes away the sin of the world (vs. 29) must probably be interpreted in the light of several references in I John, where it is said that Jesus

---

baptism John was as certain as if he had seen with his bodily eyes, as sure as if he had heard audible words, that God had accepted Christ's offering of himself, was going to use him for tremendous ends, and was promising to supply all that could be needed to bring him through the unthinkable task (vs. 29). A new era in human history was opening. Colossal and impregnable though it might seem, the sin of the world was doomed. In face of which, he felt that he himself was only a roadmaker for an infinitely greater Other (vss. 19-23). He could arouse men's consciences; he could compel them to feel the horror of their sins. But Jesus of Nazareth was the Lamb of God, who, by sacrificing himself and everything he had, could take away the sin of the world and blot it out (vs. 29).

What exactly was in the Baptist's mind when, looking at Jesus who was making his way toward him, he uttered those words of his that have embedded themselves so deeply in the human consciousness, **Behold, the Lamb of God, who takes away the sin of the world!** we do not accurately know. Many theories have been evolved, not always wisely, and not all of them helpful to every mind. It is natural that we should gaze, awed and fascinated, into the deeps of a divine generosity that we can never fathom. Does not Peter tell us that the very angels desire so to do? But we can lose ourselves in theorizing, and not press on to actual experience.

> Myself when young did eagerly frequent
> Doctor and Saint, and heard great argument
> About it and about: but evermore
> Came out by the same door where in I went.[6]

How Christ takes away the sin of the world is one thing. And the explanation of it that satisfies one mind may leave others unimpressed. But the fact that he does take it away is certain.

To be sure, it has proved a slow business. Look at the world about us even now; and at that Christ whose sad eyes on the Cross see only this after the passion of two thousand years—if one may bring Browning up to date ("Fra Lippo Lippi"). And yet how much has been accomplished! Sins, once accepted as inevitable, are dead; and others, of which people

[6] *The Rubáiyát of Omar Khayyám,* st. xxvii.

32 And John bare record, saying, I saw the Spirit descending from heaven like a dove, and it abode upon him.

33 And I knew him not: but he that sent me to baptize with water, the same said unto me, Upon whom thou shalt see the Spirit descending, and remaining on him, the same is he which baptizeth with the Holy Ghost.

34 And I saw, and bare record that this is the Son of God.

rael." 32 And John bore witness, "I saw
the Spirit descend as a dove from heaven,
and it remained on him. 33 I myself did not
know him; but he who sent me to baptize
with water said to me, 'He on whom you
see the Spirit descend and remain, this is
he who baptizes with the Holy Spirit.'
34 And I have seen and have borne witness
that this is the Son of God."

"appeared to take away sins" (3:5), that he "will forgive our sins and cleanse us from all unrighteousness (1:9), that "he is the expiation for our sins, and . . . for the sins of the whole world" (2:2), that his blood cleanses us from all sin (1:7). This language is sacrificial; yet nowhere in the Pentateuch is a lamb spoken of as bearer of the people's sin. We have probably a complex of ideas. There was the picture of the suffering Servant "as a sheep led to the slaughter, and a lamb dumb before his shearers, . . . whose soul was made a guilt offering, . . . and who bore the sin of many" (Isa. 53:7, 10, 12). There was also the symbol of the paschal lamb (cf. 19:36; Exod. 12:46; Num. 9:12; with I Cor. 5:7-8) commemorating the deliverance of Israel from its slavery. When the Gospel was written such conceptions had long been fused in the language of Eucharistic devotion. The dominant idea was the removal of the infection of sin, so that men can enter into communion with the holy God.

The Son of God (vs. 34): This title not only comprises but surpasses those which the Baptist disclaimed for himself. In the O.T. it was the title of the messianic king. To the evangelist it connotes the perfect revelation of the divine nature (cf. vss. 14, 18). The Codex Sinaiticus, with a few early authorities, reads, "the Chosen One of God" (cf. Luke 23:35 with Matt. 27:40, and Luke 9:35 with Matt. 17:5; Mark 9:7). This is not a Johannine term, and Harnack (*Studien zur Geschichte des Neuen Testaments und der alten Kirche* [Berlin: Walter de Gruyter, 1931] I, 127-32) accepts it as the original

used to think no shame, are now regarded as a break-in from a lower world; and the light grows and spreads. Or listen how, blown back to us from the other world, there comes that shout of thanksgiving from multitudes far beyond reckoning, all clean, all spotless in God's holy sight, "To him who loves us and has freed us from our sins by his blood" (Rev. 1:5). And frail and stumbling though we are, how many sins he has taken away even from us. If Christ had not come, what a different world it would have been.

There are multitudes who, because he taught and lived and died, have shaken off unworthinesses that used to beset them, sometimes with ridiculous ease, have risen above what had become an inherent part of their personality, have a peace of conscience that they did not know before they came on Calvary, are better and cleaner and stronger because Christ has taken away what had soiled and shamed them. All this at a tremendous price to him, which we cannot begin to reckon up, but the thought of which, at times at least, moves us to our soul. "He loved me, and gave himself for me." But at other times we accept it far too casually. Ours is a great salvation, won for us at a vast cost to the Savior.

But none of the ransomed ever knew
How deep were the waters crossed,
Nor how dark was the night that the Lord passed through
Ere He found His sheep that was lost.[7]

"I saw a Lamb standing, as though it had been slain. . . . Then I looked, and I heard around the throne and the living creatures and the elders the voice of many angels, numbering myriads of myriads and thousands of thousands, saying with a loud voice, 'Worthy is the Lamb who was slain, to receive power and wealth and wisdom and might and honor and glory and blessing!' And I heard every creature in heaven and on earth and under the earth and in the sea, and all therein, saying, 'To him who sits upon the throne and to the Lamb be blessing

[7] Elizabeth Clephane, "The Lost Sheep."

35 ¶ Again the next day after, John stood, and two of his disciples;

35 The next day again John was stand-

reading, attributing it to the evangelist's subtle suggestion that the Baptist could not see the full significance of the messiahship indicated by this title.

35-42. From this narrative we learn that our Lord's first disciples were originally drawn from the Baptist's circle of followers. The Synoptic story (Mark 1:16-20; Matt. 4:18-22) tells of two pairs of brothers suddenly called from their fishing craft on the

and honor and glory and might for ever and ever!'" (Rev. 5:6, 11-14.) Whereat, with "the four living creatures," our whole being cries, "Amen!"

35-51. ***How Men Find Christ.***—In these verses we are shown some of the different ways in which men find Christ.

Some of them, like John and Andrew, because they looked for him. And most of those who miss him do so because they are not interested enough in him to make a real search for him. For some indeed faith is not easy; and their quest may prove long. If so, the all-important thing for them is first to face fairly the question Browning's Bishop Blougram puts to them:

> "What think ye of Christ," friend? when all's done and said,
> Like you this Christianity or not?
> It may be false, but will you wish it true?
> Has it your vote to be so if it can? [8]

To which perhaps you answer, "But it hasn't proved itself to me. And whatever I may wish, my mind must be honest." Whereupon Bunyan, who has everything, has this:

> Then said Evangelist, pointing with his finger over a very wide field, Do you see yonder wicket-gate? (Matt. vii. 13-14.) The man said, No. Then said the other, Do you see yonder shining light? (Ps. cxix. 105; 2 Pet. i. 19.) He said, I think I do. Then said Evangelist, Keep that light in your eye, and go up directly thereto, so shalt thou see the gate.[9]

Meantime, for those who so do, even if the mists do not lift, and things do not at once clear, there is every ground for hope. For, as Oliver Cromwell wrote to his daughter, "To be a seeker is to be of the best sect next to a finder; and such an one shall every humble seeker be at the end. Happy seeker, happy finder!" [1] Only, one must not let oneself be stumbled by petty difficulties, or imagine that because an objection is new to us it is really original, and has never been faced before.

[8] "Bishop Blougram's Apology."

[9] *The Pilgrim's Progress,* Part I.

[1] Thomas Carlyle, *Oliver Cromwell's Letters & Speeches,* XXIII.

Twelve young men at Oxford wrote a book about their doubts. They asked Archbishop William Temple for a preface, and were honest enough to print it! He called their effort

> A startling childishness. . . . [The] victorious overthrow of Aunt Sallies in the belief that they are repudiating the venerable doctrines and practices of the Christian Church. . . . It is apparently never contemplated that if what Christians mean by the doctrine were so easily refuted, it would hardly have developed as a summary of Christians' experience, and would long ago have disappeared.[2]

Honest seekers have much to aid them. As the first two disciples were directed to Christ by the Baptist, friendly hands help and point and guide. "The idea of a Christian . . . as an independent, all-sufficing being, capable from the fulness of his own spirit, of satisfying all his higher wants, is a mere fiction, which all experience belies," says J. A. Moehler.[3] We are all sharers in a universal life which is carrying us on its tide, even when we think that we are moving under our own power. "Certain authors," says Pascal, "speaking of their works, say: 'My book. . . .' They would do better to say: 'Our book, . . .' because there is in them generally more of other people's than their own." [4] So is it with a man's personal faith. As Lancelot Andrewes used to pray:

> [For] teachers kind,
> benefactors never to be forgotten,
> . . . .
> for all who have advantaged me,
> by writings, sermons, converse,
> prayers, examples, for all these and all others
> which I know, which I know not,
> open, hidden,
> remembered, forgotten.[5]

In every life such make a goodly company.

Indeed, some find Christ not through their own search for him, but because those who

[2] *Be Still and Know,* ed. Keith Briant and George Joseph (London: Michael Joseph, 1936), pp. 12, 17.

[3] *Symbolism* (New York: Charles Scribner's Sons, 1894), p. 341.

[4] *The Thoughts of Blaise Pascal,* tr. C. Kegan Paul (London: Bell & Sons, 1890), p. 314.

[5] *The Private Devotions of Lancelot Andrewes,* "Fifth Day: Praise."

36 And looking upon Jesus as he walked, he saith, Behold the Lamb of God!

37 And the two disciples heard him speak, and they followed Jesus.

38 Then Jesus turned, and saw them following, and saith unto them, What seek ye? They said unto him, Rabbi, (which is to say, being interpreted, Master,) where dwellest thou?

39 He saith unto them, Come and see. They came and saw where he dwelt, and abode with him that day: for it was about the tenth hour.

ing with two of his disciples; 36 and he
looked at Jesus as he walked, and said,
"Behold, the Lamb of God!" 37 The two
disciples heard him say this, and they followed Jesus. 38 Jesus turned, and saw them
following, and said to them, "What do you
seek?" And they said to him, "Rabbi (which
means Teacher), where are you staying?"
39 He said to them, "Come and see." They
came and saw where he was staying; and
they stayed with him that day, for it was

Sea of Galilee to follow Jesus. Their prompt obedience is explained by the earlier encounter further south, described in these verses. Andrew's introduction of his brother Simon to Jesus encourages the surmise that the unnamed disciple was John, the son of Zebedee, and that he also brought his brother James, for in the Marcan tradition these four are the first disciples to be enrolled for the training of the twelve. The fact that the sons of Zebedee are never mentioned in this Gospel until 21:2, and that there is no reference to their mother Salome, is noteworthy because of their prominence in the other Gospels, and may be accounted for by the writer's intention to suggest indirectly a close connection between the Gospel and the apostle John (see Intro., p. 440, and cf. 13:23;

---

know him bring them to him. So Peter by Andrew, and Nathanael by Philip.

In this matter we are all culpably remiss, forgetting that election is not only to privilege, but to service; that we are the body of Christ, his feet that must run for him, his hands that must carry for him, his body through which his blessed will gets itself done; that if Christ is all we say he is, we cannot keep him to ourselves, but must share him with others. The whole point of Arnold's "Rugby Chapel" is that the glory of his father was that he could not be content with his own personal salvation while others around him were perishing in the storm, but took his life in his hand, and spent it unreckoningly in an eager effort to bring others along with him home to God. Yet some congregations seem to be mere religious clubs, run for the benefit of the members, not to win the world. And religions not a few are a mere spiritual selfishness, which, spiritual or not, will receive the usual wages of selfishness.

The fact that it was his brother whom Andrew found first is natural enough. Yet it is suggestive. Even now, one of the most effective portions of the church is the Christian home. Even now, one supposes that normally the God of a child has a face strangely like its mother's. Yet, in days when family ties dangle loosely, when the young are given a new independence, when people claim more and more pleasure as their right, it looks, at least, as if fewer were ardent in their pursuit of the old ideal to stand at last upon the right hand of God's judgment seat and say, "Here are we, and the children whom thou gavest us."

But some are found by Christ, like Philip, because Christ himself rose up and went to seek for them. "The Hound of Heaven," for all the splendor of its imagery and language, is a plain transcript from the lives of innumerable simple people. They are in Christ because he followed them, beset them, hedged them about with a stubborn, obstinate, untiring grace that would not be shaken off, and got its way. Paul tells us that he did not find Christ, but that Christ found him. A hand fell on his shoulder and arrested him. So too they heard Cromwell murmuring on his deathbed, "I think I am the poorest wretch that lives: but I love God; or rather, am beloved of God."

35-51. ***Christ's Faith in Ordinary People.***— Further, there is in these verses a heartening revelation of the kinds of men on whom, daringly but with confidence, Christ is content to stake his hopes. For he

> Saw into the depth of human souls,
> Souls that appear to have no depth at all
> To careless eyes.[6]

The habit of talking of Matthew and Mark gives quite a wrong impression by suggesting that these men belonged to a bigger breed than we. Yet in reality they were ordinary people.

[6] Wordsworth, *Prelude*, Bk. XIII, lines 166 ff.

40 One of the two which heard John *speak,* and followed him, was Andrew, Simon Peter's brother.

41 He first findeth his own brother Simon, and saith unto him, We have found the Messias, which is, being interpreted, the Christ.

42 And he brought him to Jesus. And when Jesus beheld him, he said, Thou art Simon the son of Jona: thou shalt be called Cephas, which is by interpretation, A stone.

about the tenth hour. 40 One of the two
who heard John speak, and followed him,
was Andrew, Simon Peter's brother. 41 He
first found his brother Simon, and said to
him, "We have found the Messiah" (which
means Christ). 42 He brought him to Jesus.
Jesus looked at him, and said, "So you are
Simon the son of John? You shall be called
Ce'phas" (which means Peter[b]).

[b] From the word for *rock* in Aramaic and Greek respectively.

19:26; 20:2; 21:7, 20). This identification of the unnamed disciple does not depend upon the precarious reading πρῶτος (א* L) for "first," though that might imply that the other disciple brought his brother to Christ. The better-attested reading gives the adverb πρῶτον, though some early versions presuppose a reading "in the morning" instead (πρωί [*mane*]: O.L. [*b e*] sy^s). There are several indications of time sequence in this chapter. Vss. 29-34 describe what happened on the day after the announcement at Bethany. Vss. 35-42 carry on the story to the third day ("the tenth hour" by Jewish reckoning from sunrise would be 4 P.M.), while vss. 43-51 cover a fourth day. If the reading "in the morning" were accepted, vss. 43-51 would point to a fifth day.

Three times in these verses the writer gives a Greek transliteration of an Aramaic word, followed by a Greek translation (cf. 4:25; 5:2; 9:7; 11:16; 19:13, 17; 20:16). The Aramaic name **Cephas** is used by Paul eight times—in I Corinthians and Galatians—but nowhere else in the N.T. apart from this passage. This surname *Petros*—"Man of Rock"—is given in Mark's list of the twelve (3:16). Its mention here, in response to the confession that Jesus is Messiah, may be an instance of John's method of anticipatory announcement (see p. 438).

Andrew, who hovers on the edges of the inner circle of the disciples, occasionally in it but usually not, has no prominence in the Gospels. But when we do glimpse him, he is always doing the same thing, bringing others to Christ; and through them at second hand effecting mighty things for Christ, which but for him would not have been done at all. Peter was our Lord's closest friend, and it was Andrew who gave Christ that signal gift. It was to Andrew that the lad shyly brought his poor little package of food; and Andrew who, somewhat shyly too, brought him and his inadequate offering to Christ. When the Greeks, wishing to see Jesus, came to Philip, the latter felt that this was Andrew's job; and he the man who would most wisely deal with the situation. And it was Andrew who gave Christ that moment of exultant happiness. So simple folk with no particular gifts of their own can do wonderful things for Christ through those they influence. It was a certain blackfriar who first turned the face of John Knox to the light: and in the books of God all the achievements of that indomitable soul are credited also to a man whose name not one in a million now remembers. There was a dispirited minister in a tiny country parish where the population and the church attendance had dwindled to nothingness, and the Bible class was no class at all; and yet it was in it one night that a little lad gave himself to Christ's service: an august service, for he was Chalmers of New Guinea. All of which is set down for us in Browning's "Pippa Passes," where the little factory lass goes singing through the town on her one holiday, and all unconsciously does mighty things, again and again, for man and God.

Then there is Peter, one of the most vividly drawn characters in literature; intensely human always and lovable even in his worst blunderings—and they were many—but the "especial marking of the man" was a queer undependability. He was as sudden and as fickle in his quickly changing moods as his own Sea of Galilee, where without warning the winds sweep down from the hills and in a moment lash the lake to fury; yet almost in another moment it may be dead calm again. And Christ looked at him and said with confidence, "You will be a strong rock of a man, upon whom I can found my church" (vs. 42). It did not look like it. And it was long in coming; and there were pitiful fallings away. But it did come. The possibilities that Christ alone saw in the man were there and became fact. And he has promised that we can

43 ¶ The day following Jesus would go
forth into Galilee, and findeth Philip, and
saith unto him, Follow me.
44 Now Philip was of Bethsaida, the
city of Andrew and Peter.
45 Philip findeth Nathanael, and saith
unto him, We have found him, of whom
Moses in the law, and the prophets, did
write, Jesus of Nazareth, the son of Joseph.

43 The next day Jesus decided to go to
Galilee. And he found Philip and said to
him, "Follow me." 44 Now Philip was from
Beth-sa'i-da, the city of Andrew and Peter.
45 Philip found Na-than'a-el, and said to
him, "We have found him of whom Moses
in the law and also the prophets wrote,
Jesus of Nazareth, the son of Joseph."

43-51. The call of **Philip** and **Nathanael** introduces the names of two disciples who are more prominent in this Gospel than in the Synoptics. Philip came from Bethsaida Julias, a town on the east side of the Jordan where it flows into the lake, in the territory of Herod Philip. It is strange that this should be called the town of Andrew and Peter, whose house (Mark 1:21, 29) was at Capernaum. In the Synoptics and Acts Philip figures merely in the lists of apostles. In this Gospel he appears again at 6:5-7; 12:21-22; 14:8-9. Nathanael is peculiar to this Gospel. In the only other reference (21:2) he is described as "of Cana in Galilee," which has been identified with either Khirbet Ḳāna, eight miles north, or with Kefr Kennā, three and a half miles northeast of Nazareth. In either case the nearness of Cana to Nazareth explains Nathanael's incredulity that the Messiah should spring from a town so familiar to him. In the apostolic lists Philip is always coupled with Bartholomew (Mark 3:18; Matt. 10:3; Luke 6:14), or grouped with Thomas, Bartholomew and Matthew (Acts 1:13); and this has led to the theory that Nathanael was the name of the disciple whose Aramaic patronymic was "son of Tolmai."

Of whom Moses in the law and also the prophets wrote (vs. 45): A comprehensive expression for the Scriptures (cf. Matt. 5:17; Luke 16:16, 29; Rom. 3:21) without any specific reference. **Jesus of Nazareth, the son of Joseph,** is a phrase which reflects the common belief about the origin of Jesus (cf. 6:42; 7:27, 28) and may be intended by the evangelist to give point to the contrast in Nathanael's exclamation (vs. 49). **An Israelite indeed, in whom is no guile!** (vs. 47): Wrestling Jacob received the new name of Israel, but his earlier name, "Supplanter," recalls Isaac's plaint, "Thy brother came with guile, and hath taken away thy blessing" (Gen. 27:35). In contrast with that, the psalmist blesses "the man . . . in whose spirit there is no guile" (Ps. 32:2). Nathanael's transparent character proves him worthy of the name Israelite. The most likely explanation of the allusion—**when you were under the fig tree** (vs. 48)—is that given by Strack and Billerbeck (*Kommentar zum N.T. aus Talmud und Midrasch,* II, 371), who cite several

---

grow into his very likeness. It is still far away; may seem more impossible than ever. Yet, says Paul, no one who believes in Christ will ever be disappointed (Rom. 10:11 Moffatt). If Christ said it, he can do it, and he will. And one day it will have come true, and the dream be the only reality.

Or Nathanael, to whom Christ gave so enviable a tribute, and yet who shows himself narrow and bigoted. "That hole of a place! Can any good come out of it?" he scoffed, despising a neighboring little town. A man once came to me in real distress of soul because his heart was set on fire by party spirit till it roared like a furnace, because so plain did things look to him that he just could not credit that those on the other side could be honest, found himself unjust to them, and hating them and all their ways. And what was he to do? Perhaps the best book in the whole world on that is Richard Baxter's honest self-review in his autobiography, in which, looking back over his life, he sets down how and where he went wrong; and better, how God corrected him; and, in especial, broadened and mellowed him till he who had once been a passionate partisan became the man of peace he was, moving unruffled through a wild day of angry and vindictive men. Or, Al Ghazzali, the great Moslem, grieved that his people should dismiss Christian teaching out of hand just because it was Christian teaching. Whereas, says he, we should consider it; and if it is true, accept it, Christian or not; and thank God for it, and them.[7]

[7] *The Confessions of Al Ghazzali,* tr. Claud Field (New York: E. P. Dutton & Co., 1909), pp. 35-36.

46 And Nathanael said unto him, Can there any good thing come out of Nazareth? Philip saith unto him, Come and see.

47 Jesus saw Nathanael coming to him, and saith of him, Behold an Israelite indeed, in whom is no guile!

48 Nathanael saith unto him, Whence knowest thou me? Jesus answered and said unto him, Before that Philip called thee, when thou wast under the fig tree, I saw thee.

49 Nathanael answered and saith unto him, Rabbi, thou art the Son of God; thou art the King of Israel.

46 Na-than'a-el said to him, "Can anything
good come out of Nazareth?" Philip said
to him, "Come and see." 47 Jesus saw Na-
than'a-el coming to him, and said of him,
"Behold, an Israelite indeed, in whom is no
guile!" 48 Na-than'a-el said to him, "How
do you know me?" Jesus answered him,
"Before Philip called you, when you were
under the fig tree, I saw you." 49 Na-than'a-el
answered him, "Rabbi, you are the Son

rabbinical references to a seat under a fig tree as the right place for the study of the Torah. Nathanael is praised as a true searcher of the Scriptures, who, unlike those referred to in 5:39, 46-47, will recognize him to whom they testify. His response justifies the praise.

Vs. 51 carries on the train of thought from vs. 47. The route from Bethany beyond Jordan to Cana would take Jesus past Jabbok, Mahanaim, and Bethel (Gen. 28:10-17; 32:2, 22-31) where heavenly dreams and mystic visions came to Jacob-Israel. Nathanael, true to his name as an Israelite, is, like Jacob at Bethel, to see **angels of God ascending and descending** on that celestial ladder. This interpretation of the ancient story was helped by the false etymology which derived the name Israel from three Hebrew words—*'îsh rô'eh 'ēl*—"a man seeing God," an interpretative derivation found in Philo's allegorizing treatment of the story of Jacob (*On Dreams* I. 27. 171). This prediction is not for Nathanael alone, to whom the promise **You shall see greater things than these** was given. The singular in vs. 50 (ὄψῃ) is changed to the plural in vs. 51 (ὄψεσθε). All who watch the incarnate Lord with the discernment of faith will discover the divine glory. "The opened heaven" belongs to the imagery of visions (cf. Ezek. 1:1; Matt. 3:16; Acts 10:11; Rev. 19:11), but the term **Son of man** in this context suggests its eschatological

46. *The Wise Way to Meet Doubts.*—In this verse is shown the wise way in which to meet doubts, whether our own or other people's. Can any good thing come out of Nazareth? Nathanael sneered, and would have summarily dismissed the matter as obviously ridiculous. And Philip did not argue with him. **Come and see,** he said; which surely is the only rational course. People have a queer idea that the claim for faith is an odd peculiarity of religion, and an unjustifiable postulate. But all progress everywhere is built up on faith; is due to an adventurous spirit that looks out ahead, and thinks it sees something, and puts it to the test. In science, to demand certainty before you will make the experiment is nonsense. It is only through the experiment, and its working out, that certainty can come. Said William James:

> So far as man stands for anything and is productive or originative at all, his entire vital function may be said to deal with maybes. Not a victory is gained, not a deed of faithfulness or courage is done, except upon a maybe; not a service, not a sally of generosity, not a scientific exploration or experiment or textbook, that may not be a mistake. It is only by risking our persons from one hour to another that we live at all.[8]

And so it is in religion. When George John Romanes had lost his faith, it came home to him that he was acting utterly unscientifically. For the first law of science is that if there is evidence for a thing, whatever I may think or wish about the matter is nothing to the point. I am bound to put it to the test. And there are heaps of at least *prima facie* evidence for Christianity; thousands of honorable folk who say it works. Therefore it behooves me as an honest man of science to give this thing its chance to prove itself, if it can. And he did. And in him also it came true.[9] **Come and see.** Test it. That seems mere common sense.

[8] *The Will to Believe* (New York: Longmans, Green & Co., 1897), p. 59.

[9] *Thoughts on Religion* (Chicago: Open Court Publishing Co., 1895), pp. 178-79.

50 Jesus answered and said unto him, Because I said unto thee, I saw thee under the fig tree, believest thou? thou shalt see greater things than these.

51 And he saith unto him, Verily, verily, I say unto you, Hereafter ye shall see heaven open, and the angels of God ascending and descending upon the Son of man.

2 And the third day there was a marriage in Cana of Galilee; and the mother of Jesus was there:

of God! You are the King of Israel!" **50** Jesus answered him, "Because I said to you, I saw you under the fig tree, do you believe? You shall see greater things than these." **51** And he said to him, "Truly, truly, I say to you, you will see heaven opened, and the angels of God ascending and descending upon the Son of man."

2 On the third day there was a marriage at Cana in Galilee, and the mother of

---

reference in such Synoptic passages as Mark 14:62; Matt. 26:64 (recalling Dan. 7:13, and reflected in Acts 7:56); and Matt. 16:27-28. The connection with some such saying of Jesus is the more obvious when the right exegesis is found for the preposition in the phrase **upon the Son of man.** It has been shown that the picture represented by this translation is not one that the Semitic mind would entertain. Matthew Black (*An Aramaic Approach to the Gospels and Acts* [Oxford: Clarendon Press, 1946], p. 85) argues that the Aramaic preposition (*'al*) which underlies the Greek (ἐπί) "upon" is regularly used with the meaning of the Hebrew preposition (*'el*) "unto" or "toward." "The picture we have then is of the heavens opened and angels from above and beneath converging on the Son of Man, the central Figure." The Johannine eschatology, however, combines allusions to a future denouement with an emphasis upon the present revelation of the glory (see pp. 443-44). The title **Son of man**—used thirteen times in John, eleven of these on the lips of Jesus—represents in this Gospel the unveiling of divine attributes in human form, and so brings to believers a fellowship of the seen and the unseen. At the same time it stands for the authority to bring into the present the judgment pronounced upon those who accept or reject him whom God has sent into the world.

III. The Self-Revelation of Jesus in Judea, Galilee, and Samaria (2:1–4:54)

A. The Marriage at Cana; The First Sign (2:1-11)

2:1. Cana, the home of Nathanael (see on 1:44), was reached on the third day after the call of Philip and Nathanael. Jesus and his disciples had been invited to a wedding feast. Among the guests was **the mother of Jesus,** who is mentioned (never by name) again in vs. 12; 6:42; 19:25. A marriage feast lasted seven days, with fresh guests arriving each day. Wine flowed freely at these festivals (Strack and Billerbeck, *op. cit.*, II, 401), and the supply may have run short (vs. 3) about the time of the arrival of Jesus and his friends toward the end of the week.

2:1-11. ***Frontispiece of the Gospel.***—Once in a group of ministers, I found myself to my surprise the only one among them who preached upon the miracles, the others feeling that it was bad tactics and unwise psychology to choose a subject likely to stumble some among the hearers, and to close their minds to anything built up on what they might consider as so insecure a foundation. With regard to the healing miracles, such an attitude is of course entirely out of date. Does not J. A. Hadfield, with his immense experience, tell us bluntly: "There was a time when people said that 'miracles do not happen,' the implication being that the narratives of miracles in the Gospels are untrue. Nowadays practically all the healing 'miracles' of the New Testament have been reproduced in shell shock hospitals over and over again."[1] Many things in the Gospels which were once scoffed out of court by confident and scornful voices are now accepted as self-evidently true; and in some sense the wonder of Christ's achievements is seemingly reduced to this, that in his own practice he antedated by a couple of thousand years the discoveries of modern science.

But some of the miracles are more difficult. And it is instructive to watch how this evange-

[1] *Psychology and the Church* (New York: The Macmillan Co., 1925), p. 190.

2 And both Jesus was called, and his disciples, to the marriage.

3 And when they wanted wine, the mother of Jesus saith unto him, They have no wine.

4 Jesus saith unto her, Woman, what have I to do with thee? mine hour is not yet come.

5 His mother saith unto the servants, Whatsoever he saith unto you, do *it.*

Jesus was there; 2 Jesus also was invited to
the marriage, with his disciples. 3 When
the wine failed, the mother of Jesus said to
him, "They have no wine." 4 And Jesus said
to her, "O woman, what have you to do
with me? My hour has not yet come." 5 His
mother said to the servants, "Do whatever

4-5. Jesus' answer to his mother seems harsh, not because of the form of address—for that is used with utmost tenderness in 19:26—but because of the words **What have you to do with me?** This translation gives the usual meaning of the Greek (τί ἐμοὶ καὶ σοί;), and the saying may deprecate fussy interference. But the words might also mean, "What have I and you to do with that?" i.e., "Never mind; don't be worried." This is rather supported by what follows, **My hour has not yet come.** In that case the evangelist seized on a phrase which simply meant, "I must wait for the right opportunity," and read into it the secondary and deeper meaning which it has elsewhere—a solemn reference to his death (7:30; 8:20; 12:23, 27; 13:1; 17:1). To this evangelist the "signs" of Jesus were a display of his power or "glory," and his complete glorification on earth was the consummation of his sacrifice on the Cross. His mother's confidence in him is shown in her instructions to the servants.

---

list has a habit of dealing with them. He never shirks them, slipping past as warily as may be. On the contrary, he lets the full light fall upon them; he makes them central; he gathers around them the Master's most characteristic teaching. And while there is no shadow of evidence that he does not accept them as literal and physical facts, he does not lay the main stress there, but uses them as evidence, very comforting to his own mind, of Christ's power to work kindred, but far more extraordinary, spiritual miracles. That the five thousand had a meal he had no doubt; but to him this is an illustration of the more glorious fact that Christ can feed the hungry souls of needy men. He was entirely sure that Lazarus rose up out of his grave. But the miracle of miracles was not even that, but that that voice of power can reach to those long dead in trespasses and sins, and startle them into newness of spiritual life and being. These incidents are, so to speak, the pictures he inserts into his book to make the gospel visible; so that at a glance we can take in what would have needed pages to describe.

In some such fashion the episode at the marriage in Cana is the frontispiece to the Gospel, summing up pictorially what is to come: how our Lord enters into people's troubles; how unbelievably he suffices in every difficulty; and above all how he enriches things for us. What water is to wine, what that embarrassing insufficiency was to the relief he wrought for his host, so is any other life compared to the fullness, the color, the adventure, the achievement that he gives.

But if that is the main lesson, many other thoughts too leap out and at us arrestingly as we move toward it. There is the fact that Christ was there; that they wanted him to be there; had no fear that he would be out of his element, or fail to fit in, or make others uncomfortable, as the Baptist, with his asceticism, would have done. And be sure there was no awkward silence at that part of the table where he sat. For Christ did not hold aloof from innocent human happinesses—a fact which many of his followers have forgotten, with tragic enough results, making his religion a more austere thing than he ever did, and by their caricatures of him scaring many from him who are his by natural right.

St. Teresa disliked "gloomy people," and prayed to be delivered from "frowning saints"; and was herself in spite of her devotion—rather because of her devotion and as a real part of it—a gay and happyhearted person. "Sometimes she would speak of the weightiest subjects; at others she would say things for our entertainment; sometimes, again, she would make up verses, and very good ones too," reports one of her nuns.[2]

And then there is the kindliness of the mother of our Lord. She appears to have been on terms of intimacy with the family. Cana was near to Nazareth—perhaps only three and a half

[2] See *Complete Works of Saint Teresa of Jesus,* III, 351.

6 And there were set there six waterpots
of stone, after the manner of the purifying
of the Jews, containing two or three firkins
apiece.
7 Jesus saith unto them, Fill the water-
pots with water. And they filled them up
to the brim.
8 And he saith unto them, Draw out
now, and bear unto the governor of the
feast. And they bare *it*.

he tells you." 6 Now six stone jars were
standing there, for the Jewish rites of puri-
fication, each holding twenty or thirty gal-
lons. 7 Jesus said to them, "Fill the jars
with water." And they filled them up to
the brim. 8 He said to them, "Now draw
some out, and take it to the steward of

6-8. The writer explains for his Gentile readers the ceremonial need for **six stone jars** of water (cf. Mark 7:3-4). The word for "firkin" (μετρητής), though used here only in the N.T., is common in the papyri, and in the LXX translates the Hebrew *bath*. According to Josephus (*Antiquities* VIII. 2. 9) this measure contained the equivalent of 8¾ gallons. The water drawn from these jars was brought to the table.

miles away (see Exeg. on 1:43-51). No doubt she noticed the whispering and growing embarrassment, understood at once that there was something wrong; that quite probably because Jesus and his party had been invited on their arrival in the town, there had been a miscalculation, and the host's hospitality was likely to be shamed. At once therefore and with confidence she appealed to her son (though what could he do in the matter? one would have asked); and whispered encouragingly to the servants, flustered over the shrinking supplies which quite obviously now were going to be hopelessly insufficient, **Do whatever he tells you.** In effect, "Don't worry, he will find some way." And indeed he himself had noticed, and was preparing to take action at the right moment (vs. 4).

But one is glad for her unconscious and instinctive tribute to him. For the silent years are very silent; and the veil that cuts us off from them is tragically thick. But this confidence of Mary in him could have come only out of long experience of one always unselfish and thoughtful and dependable, unfailing and ingenious in helpfulness.

It is a strange fact that apparently no one in his home thought of Jesus as especially religious, and that none of his friends, as boy and man in Nazareth, joined in his movement or took it seriously. It was James who was regarded as the devout member of the family; James, who belonged to an order so strict that the life of the house would in real degree have to be regulated to suit his fasts and his devotions and the like.

Yet when you came to think of it, somehow it always happened to be Jesus who was there when help was needed. Not a child in the street with a broken toy but knew that he at least would enter fully into the immensity of the tragedy; and that his clever carpenter's fingers would be sure to put things right. "Religion that is pure and undefiled before God and the Father is this: to visit orphans and widows in their affliction, and to keep oneself unstained from the world" (Jas. 1:27). Was there a tang of bitterness in James's definition of religion?—as though his memory was saying: "Fool that I was, pottering at the means leading to it; yet never recognizing the thing itself being lived out before my eyes, day in, day out, for years and years!"

That instinctive appeal of his mother, that quiet confidence of hers in Jesus, shows us much. And we had better remember that a religion which does not tell on our home life and make us thoughtful and unselfish there, in the living out of the little nothings that make up our days, is gravely suspect. No doubt when Lyman Abbott laid it down that "to be a follower of Christ is to join with Him in fulfilling His mission as He Himself defined it. And how did He define it? By His teaching. And these teachings may all be summed up in one word—Helpfulness,"[3] he lays himself open to George Jackson's indignant rejoinder that the church is more than "a sort of society of boy scouts bent on doing their daily 'good turns' ";[4] and the gospel something vastly deeper and more august than that account of it. Yet George Eliot's reminder that there are those whose celestial intimacies seem not to improve their domestic manners may well make some of us uneasy. For religion is a very practical thing. Our Lord assures us that on the Day of Judgment everybody will be taken aback by the ver-

[3] Quoted by G. A. Johnston Ross in "The Cross: The Report of a Misgiving," *Hibbert Journal*, X (1911), p. 499.

[4] *The Preacher and the Modern Mind* (London: Charles H. Kelley, 1912), p. 80.

9 When the ruler of the feast had tasted the water that was made wine, and knew not whence it was, (but the servants which drew the water knew,) the governor of the feast called the bridegroom,
10 And saith unto him, Every man at the beginning doth set forth good wine; and when men have well drunk, then that which is worse: *but* thou hast kept the good wine until now.

the feast." So they took it. 9 When the
steward of the feast tasted the water now become wine, and did not know where it came from (though the servants who had drawn the water knew), the steward of the feast called the bridegroom 10 and said to
him, "Every man serves the good wine first; and when men have drunk freely, then the poor wine; but you have kept the

---

9-10. The steward of the feast (ἀρχιτρίκλινος) may be either the head waiter or one of the guests chosen to preside throughout the series of festal suppers. If the former, then the wine was tasted before it was brought to the table; if the latter, the steward tasted the wine when it was offered to the guests. The steward's protest to the bridegroom is apparently an allusion to the custom of some hosts to reserve inferior wine to a stage

---

dict passed upon them. And some who were much in prayer and prominent in public service, but who were, if not churlish and ill-humored, at least thoughtless and self-centered and unhelpful at home, will be for that cast out. Here too our Lord gives us an example that we should follow in his steps.

Again, is there not something heartening in the fact that he brought in the servants as his fellow workers; and that still to this day he does not keep the healing and the helping and the saving of the world in his own hands, but offers a share in that to all who will accept it from him? There is an odd notion these days that you cannot serve Christ in a factory, or the like. Why? The N.T. believes that one can do it even as a slave, obscene system though slavery is. And indeed most of us can work for him in the main by little more than by the honesty and thoroughness and cheerfulness with which we carry out our daily tasks, serving no man, but the Lord Christ. This story seems to show that we can, through just such tasks, help him very really. Brother Lawrence tells us that for his part he was happy and honored if for God's sake he could pick up a straw where no straw should be. And that at his duties in the kitchen, where he was a cook—duties for which he says he had a great aversion—amid the heat and the smells and the noise and bustle, with several people calling for different things at the same time, he felt as close to God, yes even closer than when kneeling at the Blessed Sacrament.[5] Or, this was what was said of St. Teresa by those who knew her:

> Nowhere was she better than in little things. "She was never idle," says one, "and never at a loss for work to do." "She is very fond of engaging in the lowliest and humblest duties; and her companions assure me that, when it is her week to do the cooking, they never lack for anything." And how could they? For, said Teresa, . . . "the Lord walks among the pots and pans," just as much as in the Garden of Eden, "and He will help you in the tasks of the inward life and of the outward life too."[6]

One likes the mother of our Lord for her disquietude and kindly sympathy with her friends' growing embarrassment, for her appeal to Jesus, and for her wholehearted confidence in him, in all of which she seems to be a pattern for the rest of us, to be closely followed. Yet she appears to be met by a reply which, however gently it was spoken, sounds almost in the nature of a mild rebuke, and to some ears even harsh. And we had better think that out; for be sure here too there is a needed lesson for us.

We have our Lord's repeated assurances that we possess the fullest right to go to God (or to himself) and tell him with utter frankness all our problems and troubles and difficulties, or those of others, sure that in so doing we are not intruding, but are acting as we ought to do. For God has a Father's heart toward us. It matters to him what becomes of us and how we fare. Nothing that touches us but is of interest to him. And so, as Fenélon keeps urging on us, we cannot treat God with too much confidence.

Yet in our prayers we can be fussy and alarmist and unbelieving. Do not we too often speak to God as if he had forgotten, and we have to remind him of what it becomes him to be and do? Do not we at times find it difficult not to lose patience with his methods, which seem to us so incomprehensibly tardy? Do not

[5] *The Practice of the Presence of God* (New York: Fleming H. Revell, 1895), p. 20.

[6] E. Allison Peers, *Mother of Carmel* (London: Student Christian Movement Press; New York: Morehouse Gorham, 1945), pp. 159-60.

11 This beginning of miracles did Jesus in Cana of Galilee, and manifested forth his glory; and his disciples believed on him.

good wine until now." 11 This, the first of his signs, Jesus did at Cana in Galilee, and manifested his glory; and his disciples believed in him.

in the festival when the guests were less capable of judging the quality of the wine! But this would hardly apply to guests who arrived later in the week.

11. This simple story closes with a threefold climax. (*a*) It was the first "sign" wrought by Jesus; (*b*) it was a manifestation of his "glory"; (*c*) it awakened or confirmed his disciples' faith in him.

Such a narrative raises questions which cannot be shirked by a modern reader of the Gospels, but especially of the Fourth Gospel. In considering any of the miracle stories in this Gospel we must distinguish between three things: (*a*) the event as it actually happened; (*b*) the story as it reached the evangelist and as he faithfullly reported it; (*c*) the significance of the event for him in relation to the central theme of his message. With regard to (*a*), apart from those who naïvely accept the story as it stands, there are those by whom it is accepted and rationalized (i.e., Jesus told the servants to pour this water into the half-empty vessels on the table, and by his radiant presence "made glad the hearts" of the guests, so that they believed the diluted wine was a fresh supply of the finest vintage). By other interpreters, the story is dismissed as in no sense historical. In that case it is usual to look for the origin of the story in legends about Dionysus, the Greek god of wine and inspiration. It was reported (Pausanias *Description of Greece* VI. 26. 1-2; Pliny *Natural History* II. 231; XXXI. 16) that at his annual festival in his temple at Elis empty kettles, sealed the night before, were found filled with wine, and that at Andros on the fifth of January wine gushed from a spring in his temple instead of water. These legends are too remote from the Hebraic atmosphere of the Fourth Gospel to be treated seriously. A less improbable connection is to be found in

we keep running on ahead of him, or tugging at his hand, bidding him hurry, hurry, do something, in a way that is not seemly and is even ridiculous?

His mother would seem to have slipped into that error. (But see also Exeg.) To such feverish souls Clement of Alexandria said bluntly that a good man is persuaded that the affairs of the universe are managed in the best way and that God, who knows all things, supplies what will benefit, unasked.[7] "The life of a Christian is a life of paradoxes. He must lay hold on God: he must follow hard after him: he must determine not to let him go. And yet he must learn to let God alone. Quietness before God is one of the most difficult of all Christian graces." So Richard Cecil, one of England's real spiritual thinkers.[8]

But the main lesson is the glory that Christ brings with him and offers to anyone who will accept it from him—a life that is an abundant life, a peace that passeth understanding, a fullness of joy that only he can give, and that produces an astonishment in its recipients like the bewilderment of the steward of the feast (vs. 10). That is the characteristic note of the N.T. Always its people keep bursting in on us, their eyes shining, their hearts on fire, crying, "We've found it! The thing for which the whole world has been seeking, and it works! Do you go down before your temptations? So did we, but not now, with this wonderful Savior to bring us through. Do you find life too difficult for you? So did we, but not now, with the amplitudes of grace there are for us in Jesus Christ. Or is it thin and pinched and tame? With Christ, and in Christ, it grows satisfying and successful and exciting beyond measure, becomes another and a richer thing."

It was because the early Christians felt that, said that, proved that, that they drew others to the faith. It is because we are so dull and unexcited over it that others look at us, think there is nothing in it, and turn away. "They must sing better songs ere I learn belief in their Savior; his disciples must look like the saved," said Nietzsche—and surely reasonably.[9] The only way in which we shall win the world for Christ is by convincing those outside that we have something infinitely valuable that they lack. Then of themselves they will come running for a share in it. And that we do possess such a unique thing is the truth set down with vividness in this telling frontispiece.

7 Clement *Miscellanies* VII. 7.

8 *Remains*, "On the Christian Life and Conflict."

9 *Thus Spake Zarathustra*, tr. Alexander Tille (London: J. M. Dent & Co., 1933), p. 82.

12 ¶ After this he went down to Capernaum, he, and his mother, and his brethren, and his disciples; and they continued there not many days.

12 After this he went down to Ca-per'na-um, with his mother and his brothers and his disciples; and there they stayed for a few days.

Philo's allegorical treatment of the O.T. Two passages are often quoted in which the Logos is represented as the dispenser of spiritual wine. "But let Melchizedek instead of water offer wine, and give to souls strong drink, that they may be seized by a divine intoxication, more sober than sobriety itself. For he is a priest, even Reason [Logos], having as his portion Him that is, and all his thoughts of God are high and vast and sublime" (*Allegorical Interpretation* III. 26. 82 Loeb). "And when the happy soul holds out the sacred goblet of his own reason, who is it that pours into it the holy cupfuls of true gladness, but the Word [Logos], the Cupbearer of God and the Master of the feast, who is also none other than the draught which he pours—his own self" (*On Dreams* II. 37. 249 Loeb). (*b*) The artless form of the story and the little irrelevant touches make it likely that the evangelist has accepted it as it reached him. (*c*) He may well have seen in it a symbolical suggestion of the superiority of the new religion of the spirit (cf. 1:26, 33; Eph. 5:18) to the old religion with its external and ceremonial rites. But the main interest of the evangelist in the story is its evidence of the **glory** of the Son of God, now first revealed to his newly won disciples.

B. The Cleansing of the Temple (2:12-22)

12. Jesus, his family, and disciples travel down from the hill country to the plain on the northwest side of the lake, stopping at Capernaum for a few days before starting on the pilgrimage to Jerusalem. The home of Mary seems at this time to have been at Capernaum.

---

12. ***A Watershed in Christ's Life.***—Why is this verse here at all? As long ago as Aristotle's day it was a recognized literary canon that a skilled dramatist does not allow episodes and characters with no significance for the unraveling of the plot to obtrude into his play. And this evangelist is much too expert a writer to crowd his meager space with pointless irrelevancies that mean nothing and lead nowhere. If he sets down this sojourn in Capernaum, it is because something momentous must have happened there. But what? Every life has its watersheds, where things begin to run in a new direction. A youth from some remote glen sets out for a new life in a city; and when the road reaches its highest point before it dips down on the farther side, instinctively he pauses to look back at the familiar scenes that he is leaving, soaking every item of it all into his memory, and then turns and faces out into the new and unknown bigger world into which he is venturing. These few days at Capernaum were such a watershed for Jesus Christ. There the old definitely was finished. There the new just as definitely was begun.

He had his mother and his brothers with him. And with them, one supposes, there were many things to be talked out and put in train. For Jesus Christ was not one who could let a life drop from his hands and lie there forgotten. He would leave no loose ends in a task he was abandoning; and, in this too, be sure, he finished the work which God had given him to do. As even on the Cross he arranged for his mother, so at Capernaum also, one imagines, he would make final plans for her immediate future. He would remind his brothers of orders that had to be executed in the business. He would commend to their kindness this one and that one whom he had been in the habit of visiting and helping, and for whom life would be lonelier and harder because he was gone from the town.

On the other side, with his first disciples gathered there about him, he would have much to say to them; and to arrange about the spirit and methods of their opening mission, and the ways of the new life together, to which they were now fairly and openly committed. How much hung upon that being planned wisely and well!

Moreover, we can be quite sure that at Capernaum much time was spent by Christ alone with God, feeling for his hand, and listening for the guidance of his voice, that the tremendous adventure upon which he was embarking might in all things be devised according to God's holy will.

Vs. 12 is "merely an historical note," judges J. H. Bernard. Surely a little thought makes

13 ¶ And the Jews' passover was at hand, and Jesus went up to Jerusalem,	13 The Passover of the Jews was at hand,

13. The first of the annual feasts which play an important part in the chronological setting of this Gospel is described as **the Passover of the Jews,** another sign of the writer's care to explain Jewish customs to Gentile readers. Pilgrims **went up** to the religious metropolis.

plain that these few days of seeming pause were really of tremendous moment in the life of Christ.

But there is this to add, that it would seem that something grave and sinister came to a head in Capernaum. Throughout the Gospels our Lord's brothers make a sorry showing. Apparently they had no belief in him, or in his dreams and mission, were discomfited and humiliated by what they took to be a disgrace to the family hardly to be endured; and did their best to explain it away by saying that he had gone off his head, poor soul, was crazy, and not really responsible for his absurdities and worse; but they would take him home and shut him up, and keep him in safe custody, and no one would be outraged further by his lunatic ravings. It reads as if it was in Capernaum that they came into the open, and declared positively against him, telling him they had no belief whatever either in him or in his insane dreams and ongoings, that they would have no share in them, and turning their backs on him indignantly flung away.

Many are amazed that they of all people should have been so unbelieving, they who had lived with Jesus all their days; but, however pitiful, that seems too true to human nature. In time we do not see what is always there. In time we take for granted, and as a thing of course, the kindness and unselfishness of those with whom we live. It is their way. And we leave it at that; and come to think no more about it. As Browning has it,

'Tis only when they spring to heaven that angels
Reveal themselves to you; they sit all day
Beside you, and lie down at night by you
Who care not for their presence, muse or sleep,
And all at once they leave you, and you know them! [1]

So was it that the wonder of their brother dawned on these tardy minds.

None the less, a confident claim can be made out for James, the Lord's brother, as the most audacious and astonishing of all believers. For James had been brought up in the same home with Jesus. These two had played together, had shared the joys and plays and troubles of childhood, had knelt at the same mother's knee to say their prayers, had slept with one another night by night. Yet in his epistle, James proudly calls himself "the slave of Jesus Christ," speaks of his own brother as "our Lord Jesus Christ, the Lord of glory" (Jas. 1:1; 2:1); is sure that he will come again in divine power and majesty, and that we must all stand before his judgment seat (Jas. 5:7-9). Surely this is a marvelous faith in very deed.

Yet it was slow of coming. And few things can have hurt Christ more than his brothers' initial open and indignant disbelief in him, and the shame and even agony he caused them. It may well have been at Capernaum that they told him they would have no share in his daft schemes, that they were done with him; and with that went home. In this sense too, "He came to his own home, and his own people received him not" (1:11). Always it is those who stand nearest him who can stab him to the heart. Always it is by a friend he is betrayed. We who are his can and too often do work him the most grievous wrong of all. Be sure that Christ never forgot Capernaum and what happened there.

13-17. ***The Danger of Caricaturing Christ.***— The First Epistle of John ends thus: "We know that the Son of God is come, and hath given us an understanding, that we may know him that is true; and we are in him that is true, even in his Son Jesus Christ. This is the true God, and eternal life. Little children, keep yourselves from idols" (I John 5:20-21). As if to say: Here there has been revealed to you God as he really is. Hold it firmly in your mind, and do not let yourself be wiled away from it. Keep your eyes on Jesus Christ, and you will think rightly about God.

But the mind of man is ingenious in fashioning difficulties for himself and finding ways of thwarting God's gracious purposes toward him. And what if we so misread Christ that the portrait of him in our minds is not authentic, but a caricature? What if our misconception of him makes of Christ himself an idol that hides the true God from us; because we accept only such facts about him as happen to appeal to us, and blandly overlook, or stubbornly refuse to see, others no less evidently there, but which we choose to think less worthy of him, and which

[1] *Paracelsus,* Part V.

14 And found in the temple those that sold oxen and sheep and doves, and the changers of money sitting:

and Jesus went up to Jerusalem. 14 In the temple he found those who were selling oxen and sheep and pigeons, and the

---

14. The scene described in this and the following verses varies in some important details from the Synoptic narrative (Mark 11:15-19; Matt. 21:12-13; Luke 19:45-46). For the different views of its place in the ministry of Jesus, see Intro., pp. 447-48. The **temple** here is the precinct, not the temple proper. The Court of the Gentiles was a large outer enclosure, surrounded by colonnades to which Gentiles as well as Jews had access. Here it was that oxen, sheep, and pigeons, after due examination to prove their freedom from blemish, were sold for the required sacrifices. Here also were the tables of those who changed the Roman tetradrachmae and denarii for the Tyrian shekels or half shekels in which the annual head tax had to be paid into the temple treasury. The Greek words used for these money-changers, κερματιστής and κολλυβιστής refer to the small money (κέρμα) and to the fee (κόλλυβος) charged for this transaction.

---

will not fit into the conception of him to which we have come, less by diligent and humble study of the Scriptures than by excogitating for ourselves an idea and an ideal of what the Christ should be?

That is precisely what too many have done, with disastrous consequences, not for themselves alone, but for the world. The "gentle Jesus, meek and mild" idea has been so overworked that many preach and follow a Christ who has small resemblance to the Christ of the N.T.; a Christ who is not loving, but unkindly indulgent; weakly good-natured, immorally so; whose great aim seems to be to get us off. Undoubtedly he himself claimed to be "meek and lowly in heart" (Matt. 11:29). And that he was and is so, incredibly so, stares at us from a dozen passages in the Gospels; and is proved daily in our own experiences of his unbelievable patience and lack of exasperation with impossible people, impudent and inexcusable. But there are other aspects of him no less undeniable; and it is fatal to ignore them, or to pretend that they are not there. "And he looked around at them with anger" (Mark 3:5), so we read. Those who knew him best remembered that his eyes could be as a flame of fire, and spoke with bated breath of something awesome in him which they tried to describe in that strange phrase "the wrath of the Lamb." There was nothing gentle in that fierce message that he sent to Herod, "Go and tell that fox" (Luke 13:32). Nor was there any trace of mildness in him at that tremendous moment when he turned upon his best friend, who had meant only kindness, with that terrific rebuke, "Get behind me, Satan!" (Matt. 16:23). If it is true, as it is true, that nothing does he underline more heavily than the duty of forgiveness—and this not once but over and over, declaring bluntly that the salvation offered in the gospel is not unconditional, but that, as he says, if you forgive not men their trespasses, neither will your heavenly Father forgive you (Matt. 6:15)—nonetheless, he himself did not always forgive. The Pharisees did not find him gentle or meek or mild when he pursued them, ruthlessly and remorselessly, with those blistering denunciations as scorching as anything in literature. "You whitewashed tombs" (Matt. 23:27); "You serpents" (Matt. 23:33); "You make him [your proselyte] twice as much a child of hell as yourselves" (Matt. 23:15). Rather than make peace with such men acting so, he chose to go to his death. And when the traders would not cease from polluting the temple of God with their unseemliness and noise and chaffering, there came a time when he said that if they would not go then he would drive them out. And he rose up and did it.

Desperate attempts have been made by some who feel uncomfortable over it to tone down and edge out this incident. It is true that the word ἐξέβαλεν has sometimes a milder meaning in late Greek than in earlier days. But late or early, what it is in any given passage must be determined by the context. And this was a wild scene, with cowering figures clutching desperately at their tables, as these were flung here and there; or running after their spilled coins, as these rolled hither and thither; or shrinking from the lash that had no mercy till the holy place was cleansed. For though it is possible to read this account as if only the cattle were actually struck, that seems very unlikely; and in the reports as given in the other Gospels, quite impossible. If this incident had been recorded of anyone else in history, it would universally have been accepted as the scene of violence it was. And those who try to explain it away do so because they feel unhappily that it will not fit into their preconceived idea of

15 And when he had made a scourge of small cords, he drove them all out of the temple, and the sheep, and the oxen; and poured out the changers' money, and overthrew the tables;
16 And said unto them that sold doves, Take these things hence; make not my Father's house a house of merchandise.
17 And his disciples remembered that it was written, The zeal of thine house hath eaten me up.

money-changers at their business. 15 And
making a whip of cords, he drove them
all, with the sheep and oxen, out of the
temple; and he poured out the coins of the
money-changers and overturned their ta-
bles. 16 And he told those who sold the
pigeons, "Take these things away; you shall
not make my Father's house a house of
trade." 17 His disciples remembered that
it was written, "Zeal for thy house will

15-17. According to John, Jesus made **a whip of cord,** i.e., of the thongs used by the cattle drovers—sticks and weapons were not allowed within the temple precincts. The cattle traders as well as the oxen and sheep were driven out, and the tables with their heaps of coins were overturned. In Mark 11:17 the meaning of this action is explained by the quotation from Isa. 56:7 and Jer. 7:11, and a prohibition is added about fetching and carrying through the court. In John the same purpose is clear, though instead of the scripture citations, Jesus forbids **my Father's house** to be turned into a bazaar. In both narratives the indignation of Jesus is aroused by the hindrance offered to the devout worshiper, but John misses the touches that give a deeper meaning to the Marcan story. That story emphasizes the universal mission of Judaism, and hints that sanctuary was given to scoundrels within the temple. John rather lays stress on the irreverence of the traffic. The disciples recall words from Ps. 69:9, regarded as a messianic psalm and cited again at 15:25; 19:29; Acts 1:20; Rom. 15:3. The tense is changed from the past to the future, and the psalmist's metaphor of an inwardly consuming flame of energy becomes an anticipation of the doom that awaits the reforming Messiah whose attack upon vested interests will cost him his life.

what Christ should do and be; that here somehow he acted for once out of character, and fell inexplicably below himself, forgot his own law of life, lost his head and his temper. All of which is painful and regrettable. And the best thing to do is to say as little about it as one can, and look the other way, and rub this unfortunate episode out of our minds, and think of him only at the great moments when he was his real self.

But that is foolishness. Surely our understanding of what Christlikeness is must be gathered, not from such incidents as we choose to select and to regard as typically Christlike, but from the whole of his life and character and conduct. For not only now and then, but always and in every situation, Christ did the perfect thing to do. He was as Christlike here in the temple as when dying for us on the Cross. Here too he was revealing God as truly as on Calvary. For, declares Paul with assurance, in God there is kindness—and severity (Rom. 11:22). And the one is as divine and glorious as the other. For what if he were not: were only flabbily good-natured, ready to make no fuss about our sins and to pretend they do not matter greatly, and so push us through! "Ah, God," cried Luther, "punish us, we pray Thee, . . . but be not silent . . . toward us." [2] A fearsome prayer! For what if he hears and answers it? But what if he does not, and lets us sin on undisturbed! For nothing do we owe Christ more than for the magnificence of his hopes for us, and his refusal to compromise with us, and the severity that pulls us up with sharpness.

And as for ourselves, if Christ is always to be followed, it is clear that while our usual rule of conduct is a frank, free, patient forgiveness, there are times when we must not forgive; when, as Hugh Mackintosh says bluntly, "Lack of indignation at wickedness is a sign, not of a poor nature only, but of positive unlikeness to Jesus Christ." [3] We must not so misread Christ that he becomes an ugly idol, blinding our understanding, and hiding the true God from us. The wrath of God is never thought of in scripture as opposed to his holiness. It is a necessary part of it. Christ would have lost my soul if he had not refused to compromise with me.

[2] *Table Talk,* LXXXIII.

[3] *The Christian Experience of Forgiveness* (New York: Harper & Bros., 1927), p. 164.

18 ¶ Then answered the Jews and said unto him, What sign showest thou unto us, seeing that thou doest these things?

19 Jesus answered and said unto them, Destroy this temple, and in three days I will raise it up.

consume me." 18 The Jews then said to him, "What sign have you to show us for doing this?" 19 Jesus answered them, "Destroy this temple, and in three days I will

---

18-19. The Jews are the high priest's party, the Sadducean controllers of the temple revenues. They demand a warrant for the action of Jesus. So in the Synoptic narrative (cf. Mark 11:27-28, "By what authority are you doing these things, or who gave you this authority to do them?") Jesus is challenged by "the chief priests and the scribes and the elders," to whom he replies by a counterquestion about the Baptist's mission. In John the question takes the form, **What sign have you to show us for doing this?** Jesus' answer is given in the form **Destroy this temple, and in three days I will raise it up.** There is evidently a sound historical tradition behind this saying, for the Synoptists record that false evidence was borne at his trial that Jesus had said, "I will destroy this temple that is made with hands, and in three days I will build another, not made with hands" (Mark 14:58; cf. Acts 7:48-50; II Cor. 5:1). They do not report this saying in connection with the cleansing of the temple, but it may well be given its right context in John. The imperative form is equivalent to a future, and the meaning is "You will destroy this temple and I will rebuild it at once."

The purport of this saying raises many difficulties and has given rise to many interpretations. In keeping with the evangelist's style, the reply is deliberately ambiguous and was misunderstood by the hearers. The word **temple** is used both for a religious shrine and for the "body," as in I Cor. 3:16; 6:19. The word for **destroy** is used both of the demolition of houses or temples and of the dissolution of the body; so also **raise** can be used of erecting a building, and in Christian use it constantly referred to the resurrection from the dead. In the Johannine story of this episode it is evident that the Jewish authorities took the saying to mean the destruction of the temple and Jesus' claim to rebuild it immediately, while the disciples after the Resurrection interpreted it as a prophecy of his death and resurrection. It is likely that Jesus did predict the destruction

---

18-23. *Asking for Signs When Facing the Realities.*—One has a feeling of exasperation with these people bleating for a **sign.** It seems so silly. What need of a sign when no sign merely but the thing itself is there before their eyes? How can a prophet prove that he is a prophet except by doing the deeds of a prophet, by showing the zeal and passion for righteousness that make a prophet, by arousing people's consciences to feel as intolerable things they had never noticed, or which they dully assumed to be inevitable and woven into the make-up of life? Yet when this unknown Galilean burst suddenly into Jerusalem, and temporarily at least swept away bodily a pollution that had desecrated the temple for years, and which must have jarred the consciences of many of the more spiritual worshipers, the authorities buzzed around him, asking inane and yet natural questions. By what right are you doing this? What evidence have you that you are really sent by God and are commissioned by him? Some of them, be sure, were angry. For no reform was ever carried through without arousing opposition, often from men quite good in other ways. So, no doubt, it was here. Vested interests, they felt, were being hurt. Worshipers from other countries found it a very real convenience to have the money-changers actually in the temple precincts, ready to make the payment of their dues much simpler and more expeditious; while many would just not have imagination enough to see anything unseemly in the established way of things, or why what had been there so long should now be altered. In all which there is a warning for us.

And, after all, we have small right to jeer at these seekers for a sign. For we ourselves are all too apt to fall into that same foolishness, even when face to face with the marvelous works of God. J. A. Froude once remarked to Carlyle that he could believe only in a God who did things. And Carlyle, caught in a pessimistic mood, replied despondently, "And He does nothing."[4] So many seem to feel as they

[4] *Thomas Carlyle, A History of His Life in London* (New York: Charles Scribner's Sons, 1884), II, 220.

20 Then said the Jews, Forty and six years was this temple in building, and wilt thou rear it up in three days?

raise it up." **20** The Jews then said, "It has taken forty-six years to build this temple, and will you raise it up in three days?"

---

of the temple as the result of the forces at work in the religious and political state of Judaism at that time (cf. Mark 13:2). He also believed that a new and more spiritual kind of worship would replace the sacrificial system which was typified in the spectacle which had just led to his drastic symbol of reform (cf. 4:21-26). There is evidence that later in his ministry Jesus regarded his death as the means by which the old order would be condemned, and the new Israel would come into being through the new covenant sealed by his blood. The church was called in Paul's time "the body of Christ." All these ideas entered into the evangelist's mind as he retold the story of Christ's challenge to the chief priests as the leaders of the national religion.

20. Forty-six years . . . three days: The opponents of Jesus fasten upon this paradox. **In three days** may conform to the early Christian reference to Easter day. Probably the original form of the saying meant "after a short interval." **It has taken forty-six years to build this temple** correctly renders the tense which does not imply the completion of the work; cf. Ezra 5:16 (LXX), where the same tense is used: "Since that time even until now hath it been in building, and yet it is not completed" (ERV). Herod's temple was begun in 20-19 B.C. Forty-six years would bring the date to A.D. 27-28. As the temple was not finally completed until A.D. 64, this saying sounds like an early Christian tradition preserved by the evangelist, and is a point in favor of the place given to this incident in the Fourth Gospel.

---

look out on a world that has been repeatedly blasted and scorched with war. Problems that seem insoluble crowd in upon them, and unnerving doubts assail them. Why, if there is a God, they ask, is all this permitted? Why does he not do something effective about it, and make it possible and easier for us to believe in him? And this in a day to which, far down the generations, men will still wonderingly be looking back as to a time when God fairly broke in to our human affairs, and took control, and with his own arm himself wrought salvation for us! These fortunate people, they will say of us, were not asked to walk by faith. For God was there beside them, not to be overlooked, doing exceeding abundantly above all that they could ask or think; working a deliverance for them as dramatic, as staggering, as incredible as any in the O.T.—and yet not blown down to them from a far-off credulous age, but a thing through which they themselves lived and which they themselves saw with their own eyes. And we ask for a sign!

Or many seem losing faith in Christianity. It has had its chance, they say. Two thousand years is a long trial. And the old sores still remain, and it effects so little. Where is the promise of his coming? Where are the wonders that he was to work? **What sign showest thou?** And this in a day when in many lands Christianity proved to be the only thing that dared to front the powers of evil, and defied them unafraid! Did not Einstein confess how impressed he had been by the patent fact that when everything else was cowering and cringing under Hitler and his minions, or being blown away before the winds, the faith enabled men and women to stand up on their feet, and dare, and suffer, and at a great cost prevail? And men ask for a sign!

Would not most of us have made little of our Lord's enigmatic answer—perhaps spoken half to himself, as we sometimes overhear him doing—would we not certainly have understood it in the sense in which the Jews did? Naturally, so interpreted, it angered them, and hurt their national pride. For they gloried in their temple, then built for forty-six years, and still unfinished; hotly resented this saying as a meaningless and stupid boast so wounding that it stuck in their minds; and at Christ's trial they flung it at him viciously. Though indeed it is difficult to know with accuracy what Christ actually said. For the records seem overcondensed and vary quite materially. As is the way of stories, this one appears to have altered and grown as it passed from mouth to mouth (cf. this passage with Matt. 26:61; Mark 14:58). It is clear from Luke 21:6 and kindred scriptures that Christ had a presentiment and more that the temple was doomed to destruction, and that at no distant date. Yet however dear it and its services were to him, he could contemplate its passing calmly, since he himself was introducing something better and more spiritual. But if our evangelist's record of it, and still more his

21 But he spake of the temple of his
body.
22 When therefore he was risen from
the dead, his disciples remembered that
he had said this unto them; and they be-
lieved the Scripture, and the word which
Jesus had said.
23 ¶ Now when he was in Jerusalem at
the passover, in the feast *day*, many be-

21 But he spoke of the temple of his body.
22 When therefore he was raised from the
dead, his disciples remembered that he had
said this; and they believed the scripture
and the word which Jesus had spoken.
23 Now when he was in Jerusalem at

21-22. Vs. 21 is a comment by the evangelist, one of many such (see Intro., pp. 439-40). The disciples would interpret many acts and sayings of Jesus *post eventum* in the light of his resurrection (cf. 12:16; also hints dropped by Jesus, as 13:19; 14:29). **The scripture,** i.e., a particular passage in the O.T. In the primitive church much use was made of testimonies, or a catena of O.T. citations which were regarded as messianic, with their fulfillment in the life and work of Jesus. Such texts as Ps. 16:10; Hos. 6:2; Lev. 23:10-11, may have been applied to the Resurrection (cf. I Cor. 15:4, 20); also Jonah 1:17 (cf. Matt. 12:40).

C. At the Passover (2:23-25)

23-25. This brief notice refers to a period of activity during the Passover festival (vs. 13). The tense of the verb (ἐποίει) points to a continuous ministry of **signs** which

---

interpretation of it, are to be accepted, then this saying in vs. 19 is a great one indeed, splendid in its valor and undauntedness and faith. What sign? This sign—that something has come into the world that cannot be killed or thwarted. You cannot turn back the sun in midcareer; you cannot arrest the inevitable progress of the stars; and whatever you may do to me, although you hamper me, oppose me, slay me, nonetheless, I, and the truth for which I stand, must win. We had better remember that. Especially when it looks as if for a while lean times might come upon us.

Vs. 23 is a sharp reminder that the Gospels are not lives of Jesus Christ in any full sense, but merely selections made from masses of material left unused. We hear nothing whatever of these signs done in Jerusalem which proved so impressive to many.

23-25. ***Christ's Knowledge of Man.***—So far our Lord's mission seemed to be moving in the direction of success. True, an ominous opposition was beginning to take shape and become vocal. But there was interest in plenty, and even a measure of excitement. Numbers were turning to look after Christ, with a wistful hope beginning to dawn in their hearts. Could this be he? But, we read, he did not commit himself to them, not feeling the right atmosphere. Because, says the evangelist, **he knew what was in man.**

Masses of people the world over have felt that in a bewildered kind of way; felt that no one knows human nature or can read us as Christ does; that somehow all things lie naked and open to him; that nothing in us, not even the most secret places in our character and life, are hidden from him and those searching eyes of his that see us through and through, and as we are: so that, though we may fool others and may even hypnotize ourselves into believing that we are what we are not, there is no possibility of deceiving him. Indeed multitudes have come to this: they are sure that if the value of a life is to be assessed with accuracy, Christ must be upon the judgment seat. For his verdict, and his alone, is final and unchallengeable, and must stand.

And what is his reading of human nature? It might well have been a terrific denunciation, with horrible and incontestable facts crowding in as proof of every bitter word. But there came no such outburst. He speaks gravely indeed of our plight; of our inability to manage life aright in our own strength; of our need of salvation; of a slavery into which we have fallen; of a grim disease from which we suffer; of an unnecessary poverty in which we pass our days. These somber passages in the Gospels are not popular. Men ostentatiously avoid them and leave them unread. But they are there. And they are true. All the old primitive sins, says Jung, are not dead, but are crouching in the dark corners of our modern hearts, still there, and still ghastly as ever. And only Christianity, he says, holds them in check. And if it

lieved in his name, when they saw the
miracles which he did.
24 But Jesus did not commit himself
unto them, because he knew all *men*,
25 And needed not that any should testify of man; for he knew what was in man.

the Passover feast, many believed in his
name when they saw his signs which he
did; 24 but Jesus did not trust himself to
them, 25 because he knew all men and
needed no one to bear witness of man; for
he himself knew what was in man.

are not recorded in the Gospel (cf. 20:30-31), but are mentioned again (4:45) as the reason for Jesus' welcome by the Galileans who had been present at the feast. Evidently some of the Judeans recognized these wonders as tokens of his messiahship, for that is probably the meaning of **many believed in his name.** Yet their faith was not deep, but a transient excitement, and the evangelist's reason for the reserve shown by Jesus points darkly to his last week in the city and the cry of the Jerusalem mob, "Crucify him!" It is part of the Johannine dramatic method to anticipate both the messianic discovery and the tragedy of Calvary. The influence of **signs** in the creation of faith is recognized

is ever neglected, there and then the barrier that it has built against them will go down, and the old horrors rush in flood across an aghast world![5] Has not all that actually happened, and in our own time?

Yet, if there is a grave side to Christ's reading of humanity, no one had ever so honoring a conception of man as he. What promises he makes to us! What claims he confidently lays on us! What goals he dares to set before us! How staggering is his faith in us, in plain ordinary people. How huge is his trust in us. And how unshakable is his conviction that even if we are frail and blundering creatures, stumbling upon uncertain feet and muddied by many a fall, there are in us, in each one of us, enormous possibilities; something august, tremendous, divine. You and I, he says, can grow like God, can learn to live after God's fashion. You and I!

Henry Jones, the philosopher, confessed that he, born in a Welsh mining village and with no hope of anything but of spending his life there, was coaxed on to be the notable man he was by the queer faith of one woman in the little lad in whom she persisted in seeing huge possibilities no one else saw, but which proved to be really in him. And how many have risen above themselves, simply because Christ trusted them, called them, threw himself unafraid upon their loyalty, let them see he had never a thought that they would fail him, knew that there was in them what they had never so much as suspected to be there!

Our Lord's mind was amazingly original, not in one sphere only, but in many. The wonder of his revelation of God has blinded our dazzled eyes to the splendor of his teaching about man. "But Jesus Christ," says Adolf von Harnack, "was the first to bring the value of every human soul to light. . . . We may," he adds, "take up what relation to him we will: . . . [but] no one can refuse to recognize that it was he who raised humanity to this level."[6] "The modern world," agrees John Macmurray, "began with Christ's discovery of the individual." And all our progress flows from that. But is it true? At times the daring of Christ's claim for the importance of the individual breaks in upon the mind and stuns it. Watch a crowd streaming in its thousands from a football or a baseball game. If one of these multitudes, so indistinguishable from his fellows at a very little distance, were to drop out of existence, would it really make the slightest difference to the world, or to mankind, or to God? The masses of our fellow beings can produce in us a feeling akin to that awakened in General Bruce, as he stood gazing in a queerly abashed kind of way at that mighty Himalayan giant, Naga Parbat, "It gave one . . . a feeling that one wasn't there, and it gave one a feeling that if one wasn't there, it didn't matter."[7]

Surely our so-called importance is mere self-importance that has no solid basis. Thus Sarvepalli Radhakrishnan:

> In the light of our present knowledge of man's history and the vastness of the cosmos it seems anomalous, if not absurd, to imagine that the earth or the human species or any historic individuals in it form the centre of things. Our earth is parochial and our citizenship on it a triviality. Geocentrism in cosmology and anthropocentrism in philosophy and Buddhocentrism or christocentrism in religion are on a par. Man is the centre of all things only in the sense, as Professor Eddington

[5] *Modern Man in Search of a Soul* (London: Routledge & Kegan Paul, 1933), pp. 277-78.

[6] *What is Christianity?* (London: Williams & Norgate, 1901), pp. 67-68.

[7] Quoted by W. Macneile Dixon, *The Human Situation* (London: Edward Arnold & Co., 1937), p. 265.

3 There was a man of the Pharisees, named Nicodemus, a ruler of the Jews:

3 Now there was a man of the Pharisees, named Nic-o-de'mus, a ruler of the Jews.

(7:31; 10:42; 14:11), but is regarded rather as a rudimentary stage of belief, while a beatitude is pronounced upon those who have not seen and yet have believed (20:29; cf. 4:48). Our Lord's insight into the thoughts and character of men (1:47-48; 5:42; 6:61, 64; 13:11; 16:30) is taken in this Gospel as an attribute of the incarnate Logos (cf. Intro., p. 443).

D. Nicodemus and the New Birth (3:1-21)

3:1-2. Nicodemus, a figure not named in the Synoptic Gospels, a Pharisee and a member of the Sanhedrin (7:50), appears here as a furtive seeker after truth, but on his two later appearances shows considerable courage in his relation to Jesus (7:45-52; 19:38-40). He accosts Jesus as **Rabbi** on the strength of the **signs** (cf. 2:23) which attest his divine mission and the presence of God with him. A midrash on Deut. 18:19 prescribes, "If a prophet who begins to prophesy (i.e., who is still unaccredited) gives a sign and miracle, he is to be listened to, otherwise he is not to be heeded" (Strack and Billerbeck, *Kommentar zum N.T. aus Talmud und Midrasch,* II, 480). Jesus accepts the title by answering the unspoken question. Since the nation was aroused by the preaching of the Baptist, the main subject of religious discussion had been the kingdom of God, its nature and its near approach.

> has pointed out, that he stands midway in size between an atom and a star. He is almost exactly as much larger than an atom as a star is larger than a man. To those whose minds are dazed by the new knowledge of science, the orthodox theologians seem to be like men talking in their sleep.[8]

All which of course is very human thinking. To the divine mind importance is not measured by size, nor even to the thoughtful human mind. Is not the atom, with its dire possibilities, a thing tiny, yet how momentous?

Even yet, the doctrine of the value of the individual is by no means universally accepted. Far from it. It is attacked with vehemence from many quarters, by Hitler, among others, in his day:

> To the Christian doctrine of the infinite significance of the individual human soul and of personal responsibility, I oppose with icy clarity the saving doctrine of the nothingness and insignificance of the individual human being, and of his continued existence in the visible immortality of the nation.[9]

Or again in *Mein Kampf:* "The dogma according to which the individual personality has a right to its freedom and dignity can bring nothing but destruction." Or further, "There will be no license, no free space in which the individual belongs to himself."

With that last Christ agrees! Only, while Hitler and those who thought along such lines wanted the individual to belong to the state, Christ claims that he is not the state's, nor yet his own, but God's; and that he rises and can rise to the fullness of the possibilities within him only in God's service. Yet it was Christ who taught us that no one of us all, however unimpressive as we judge, is forgotten before God or lost to him in the crowd of his creation; but that each of us holds a place all his own within God's heart, and has some work which he and no one else can do for him.

3:1-21. ***Nicodemus.***—As an instance of the impression which our Lord was making in these early days, there is cited the striking case of Nicodemus.

It is indeed an arresting story, impressive from the start, and—as his figure on occasion slips in and out of the gospel narrative—growing ever more moving, till it mounts up to its dramatic and heart-gripping climax.

As I see him, Nicodemus was a great soul, possessed of enviable qualities, and bursting through difficulties to which most of us would have tamely surrendered. Bred in the schools, in a stuffy atmosphere in which very largely the conventional was regarded as the God-given, and where anything new had to fight its way to acceptance through instinctive, watchful, unfair

[8] *An Idealist View of Life* (London: George Allen & Unwin, 1932), pp. 27-28. Used by permission.

[9] Hermann Rauschning, *Hitler Speaks* (London: Thornton Butterworth & Co., 1939), p. 222.

2 The same came to Jesus by night, and said unto him, Rabbi, we know that thou art a teacher come from God: for no man can do these miracles that thou doest, except God be with him.

3 Jesus answered and said unto him, Verily, verily, I say unto thee, Except a man be born again, he cannot see the kingdom of God.

4 Nicodemus saith unto him, How can a man be born when he is old? can he

2 This man came to Jesus[d] by night and
said to him, "Rabbi, we know that you are
a teacher come from God; for no one can
do these signs that you do, unless God is
with him." 3 Jesus answered him, "Truly,
truly, I say to you, unless one is born
anew,[c] he cannot see the kingdom of God."
4 Nic-o-de'mus said to him, "How can a

[c] Or *from above.*
[d] Greek *him.*

3-4. Unless one is born anew, he cannot see the kingdom of God: This ambiguous oracle perplexed Nicodemus, and there follows the kind of dialogue so frequent in this Gospel. A term is used which can be interpreted literally or spiritually. It is misunderstood, the spiritual interpretation is given and expounded, and soon the dialogue shades off into a discourse. **Born anew** translates a Greek phrase (γεννηθῇ ἄνωθεν) which means "begotten from above." The adverb in Greek can mean "from the beginning," "anew," but the Aramaic (*millᵉʿēlā'*), which would be translated by ἄνωθεν, can mean

suspicion, he had somehow managed to preserve an open-mindedness that flung its windows wide to God's sunshine and free air. So that while his colleagues were already muttering their irritated resentment at this impudent intruder into their province, at this ignorant upstart from the north, with his strange ways and very questionable teaching and ugly disregard for authority, Nicodemus for his part felt that there was something here that could not be dismissed as lightly and as easily as they were doing—something that must be investigated with diligence and care and at firsthand. To Nicodemus, God had not fallen dumb, but was still speaking to men; and to his ears there was something in this new teaching august and true, and that might well be God's own voice. This thing must be humbly considered.

The fact that the evangelist goes rather out of his way to underline that Nicodemus came by night (vs. 2) may mean that this ruler of the Jews was at least a cautious man. (The Exeg. even says "furtive.") And why not? He was a religious leader to whom others looked for guidance, and whom they were likely to follow. It was not fair to the people, or to God, that he should plunge enthusiastically after every seeming prophet. He must find means to see for himself, to question, to meet Christ face to face, to base his decision not on carried stories, but on firsthand experience and evidence. And he did it.

Moreover, even if the phrase should betoken a certain timidity in the man, physical or moral or both, everyone who has been through a war knows that the real hero is not the bovine creature so unimaginative that no terrors ever cross his mind till he is actually struck and down, and the pain tugging at him, but the sensitive man, all nerves, who keeps foreseeing with a horrid vividness the mutilations and the like, only too apt to befall him, and yet holds on. Whatever he was feeling, there is small trace of timidity in that lonely voice raised in protest on behalf of Christ, a minority of one, facing an angry gathering of ruthless men (7:50-51). And there is nothing but gallantry in the loyalty of that last scene. Peter had denied his Lord in shameful panic; the rest had scattered or crouched more or less in hiding: for crucifixion was a frightful death, and Calvary quite dreadfully near; all seemed lost; the cause was out. But Nicodemus openly stood forth as Christ's friend still; and dared fearsome possibilities, only too likely to grow facts, in order to pay the last loving rites to the body of an executed man which was regarded as a sheer pollution. He had admired and reverenced Christ. Let the world think what it might, he admired and reverenced him still (19:39). Truly a great man.

3-10. ***A New Creature Needed for the New Life.***—Nonetheless, at that first interview, Christ, who was the most patient of teachers and characteristically sympathetic with dull people, fairly admits that he was taken aback by Nicodemus' slowness of perception, and found it difficult to moderate his own eager steps to his pupil's tardy pace. If Nicodemus was stumbled by such elementary matters, Christ could not press on to what he had really meant to say. Our Lord had brought him abruptly face to face with the central fact that

enter the second time into his mother's womb, and be born?

5 Jesus answered, Verily, verily, I say unto thee, Except a man be born of water and *of* the Spirit, he cannot enter into the kingdom of God.

6 That which is born of the flesh is flesh; and that which is born of the Spirit is spirit.

man be born when he is old? Can he enter a second time into his mother's womb and
be born?" 5 Jesus answered, "Truly, truly, I say to you, unless one is born of water and the Spirit, he cannot enter the kingdom of God.
6 That which is born of the flesh is flesh, and that which is born of the

---

only "from above," i.e., "from God." Birth can be considered either from the father's side, in which the verb is to "beget," or from the mother's side, in which the verb is to "bear." The Johannine metaphor uses the former verb, with the meaning "beget" (vss. 5, 6, 8; 1:13; I John 2:29; 3:9; 4:7; 5:1, 4, 18). It also has the meaning "bear" in 16:21, and probably in several other passages.

5-8. The term "begotten from above" is now defined as being "begotten of water and the Spirit." (For an alternate interpretation see Intro., p. 439.) If this is taken in the context of a conversation between Jesus and a contemporary Pharisee, the reference must be to the mission of the Baptist, with an emphasis upon that further gift which the forerunner predicted for the Coming One (1:33), for in vs. 8 the reference to water is dropped and the birth is simply that of one who is "begotten of the Spirit." Others, who regard this as an unhistorical allegory, see in this allusion a polemic against the disciples of John the Baptist and an insistence upon Christian baptism as the outward and visible sign of the gift of the Holy Spirit. The unpredictable nature of the wind's course illustrates the spontaneity of the divine action in renewing man's spiritual nature all the more easily since both in Greek and in Hebrew (πνεῦμα, *rûaḥ*) the same word is used both for wind and spirit. To **see the kingdom of God** (vs. 3) is the same as to **enter the kingdom of God** (vs. 5), as also is to "see [eternal] life" (vs. 36). Here alone in this Gospel is found the term **kingdom of God,** so often used in the Synoptic

---

if the new life is ever to be lived there must be a new creature, wholly new, built up in a new way; that mere tinkering at oneself is of little or no use. All the facts of life corroborate that verdict. Walter Lippmann, for instance, tells us that past experience has proved that Christ is absolutely right; and that even with the best will in the world, "the unregenerate man can only muddle into muddle." [1] We ourselves were so sure that at long last a generation had arisen, keen and eager to put this disorderly earth to rights; and fit to do it too, thank God. We meant so well; we tried so hard: and look at what we have made of it! "Can only muddle into muddle." What is required is a new kind of man. We must be **born anew.** All which is drastic teaching; and no one ever stated it so impressively as Jesus Christ. But it was not altogether novel. Nicodemus could have found adumbrations of it in his own scriptures, and fairly plain ones too. You cannot do it, so Ezekiel told his people bluntly (Ezek. 36:25-29); not as you are, not with that stony heart of yours, so hard and cold and callous, so impervious to divine influences. But God can make you a new personality, with a quite different nature and a heart of flesh, warm and sensitive, shrinking from evil as from intolerable pain; that feels and is hurt by others' sufferings, and is responsive to God's touch. So also a trapped creature in the psalms, not worrying about the consequences of his sin, but terrified by the discovery that he has done this thing, has been this thing, that this is *me;* no accidental, unaccountable happening, but this is what I am; and horrors like this can surge up out of my nature. And I, unhappy one, cannot change myself. "Create in me a clean heart, O God; and renew a stedfast spirit within me" (Ps. 51:10 ASV mg.). Make me another kind of being from what I am. Keep me another kind of being from what I am. So shall I lead a different kind of life; so, but not otherwise. Such scriptures must have been familiar to this ruler, Nicodemus. **Are you a teacher of Israel, and yet you do not understand this?**

[1] *A Preface to Morals* (New York: The Macmillan Co., 1929), p. 251.

7 Marvel not that I said unto thee, Ye must be born again.

8 The wind bloweth where it listeth, and thou hearest the sound thereof, but canst not tell whence it cometh, and whither it goeth: so is every one that is born of the Spirit.

Spirit is spirit.[e] 7 Do not marvel that I said to you, 'You must be born anew.'[c] 8 The wind[e] blows where it wills, and you hear the sound of it, but you do not know whence it comes or whither it goes; so it is with every one who is born of the Spirit."

[c] Or *from above.*
[e] The same Greek word means both *wind* and *spirit.*

Gospels. It links this narrative with the earlier tradition. Cf. Mark 10:15; Luke 18:17, "Truly, I say to you, whoever does not receive the kingdom of God like a child shall not enter it," and even nearer to the Johannine version, Matt. 18:3, "Truly, I say to you, unless you turn and become like children, you will never enter the kingdom of heaven." It is shortly after this saying that the Synoptists record a question put to Jesus by one whom Luke calls a "ruler." "What must I do to inherit eternal life?" (Mark 10:17; Matt. 19:16; Luke 18:8.) In this passage also, **flesh** and **spirit** are antithetical, though in John **the flesh** is not regarded as the fruitful source and center of sin as so often in Paul (cf. Gal. 5:17), for "the Logos became flesh." It stands merely for the physical side of our nature. The emphasis in vs. 6 is upon the need for a supernatural birth that we may have "power to become children of God, . . . born . . . not of the will of the flesh . . . but of God" (1:13).

Besides, at that very time Jerusalem had been ringing for months with the Baptist's inexorable demand that as all Israel had fallen away into unworthiness, all Israel must humbly submit to be baptized; as if they were heathen, turning out of darkness to the faith for the first time, and so beginning a new life—a demand to which multitudes agreed, though the Pharisees, disputing the premises as untrue of them, had haughtily refused; which may in part explain our Lord's insistence (vs. 5) on being **born of water and the Spirit,** through a humble acknowledgment of the shame of the past, and so to an acceptance of newness of life.

But it seems that what stumbled Nicodemus was not so much the theory of the need of a new birth as its impracticability. Almost irritably he felt that Christ was throwing about words that were easy to speak but that meant really nothing. The man was old; he had lost heart; his fight seemed over; for him things had become ruthlessly and inexorably fixed. Once on a day, everything had been possible; and the way to the heights had lain open before him. But it looked steep and tiring; and as we all do, he had turned into easier paths where the going was softer. And now the chance was gone. There is no turning back to live things over again, and this time better. What is once done cannot be undone. There is no blotting out in life. What we have written, we have written. And it stands. Slowly, unconsciously, inevitably, stone by stone, act by act, thought by thought, we have built up a personality. And now we are closely immured in it. And there is no escape. Batter as we may upon these choking walls that hem us in so straitly, there is no answer but the sound of our own futile crying.

> I am not what I have nor what I do;
> But what I was I am, I am even I.[2]

A great English preacher of the long ago says gravely that the Christ who healed the sick and cleansed the lepers and raised the dead never once made an old man young again. **How can a man be born when he is old?** "Sow a thought, and you reap an act. Sow an act, and you reap a habit. Sow a habit, and you reap a character. Sow a character, and you reap a destiny." [3] This is what I have made of life; and it cannot be changed now.

But the whole point of the gospel is that God can do just that for anyone; for you and me. And he does do it. We have seen it happening in other lives. We have experienced it in some real measure in our own. How? Ah, says Christ, that is unpredictable, mysterious, divine. The wind comes (vs. 8) who knows how, cleansing, invigorating, freshening, and then—it is gone. So does God break in—who can guess where, who can tell when?—and what was dull flesh, living dully according to the flesh, has become spirit, with high spiritual dreams and aims and deeds. Yet does it not often seem as if we were attempting to systematize the working of the

[2] Christina Rossetti, "The Thread of Life."
[3] Attributed to C. A. Hall.

9 Nicodemus answered and said unto him, How can these things be?

10 Jesus answered and said unto him, Art thou a master of Israel, and knowest not these things?

11 Verily, verily, I say unto thee, We speak that we do know, and testify that we have seen; and ye receive not our witness.

12 If I have told you earthly things, and ye believe not, how shall ye believe, if I tell you *of* heavenly things?

13 And no man hath ascended up to heaven, but he that came down from heaven, *even* the Son of man which is in heaven.

9 Nic-o-de'mus said to him, "How can this
be?" 10 Jesus answered him, "Are you a
teacher of Israel, and yet you do not un-
derstand this? 11 Truly, truly, I say to you,
we speak of what we know, and bear wit-
ness to what we have seen; but you do not
receive our testimony. 12 If I have told you
earthly things and you do not believe, how
can you believe if I tell you heavenly
things? 13 No one has ascended into heaven
but he who descended from heaven, the

9-11. To this mystical language Nicodemus listens in amazement, and Jesus replies to his bewilderment, "Are you that famous teacher in Israel [RSV misses the point in ignoring the force of the Greek definite article] and yet you do not understand this?" The difficulty in vs. 11 is that the words **truly, truly, I say to you** are found in this Gospel only on the lips of Jesus, and yet the so-called plural of majesty is never on his lips. Moreover, the second person plural is used both in this verse and in vs. 12, when the speaker reverts to the first person singular. The best explanation seems to be that the evangelist glides into a polemic against the synagogue of his own time. In the discourses of this Gospel, even when genuine sayings of Jesus are the basis of meditations, the author often applies the original attack upon Jewish unbelief in Jesus to the contemporary controversy.

12-13. The contrast between earthly things and heavenly things is common to Jewish and Hellenistic writings, and recalls Wisd. Sol. 9:16:

> And hardly do we divine the things that are on earth,
> And the things that are close at hand we find with labor;
> But the things that are in the heavens who ever yet traced out? (ERV.)

The **earthly things** may well refer to the kingdom of God (vss. 3, 5), which is God's rule over men in the present age, a kingdom into which men are to enter during their

---

Spirit; to cut man-made channels for the living water that leaps and laughs and sparkles, to change it into a tame canal soberly turning men's mill wheels in accordance with men's plans? We have tired of the old ways as too slow, and are trying to rush the saving of the world by using the world's own blatant methods, by cleverness and push, by noise and self-advertisement, by endless activities and innumerable agencies that often seem to have small trace of spiritual purpose or significance. Thomas Chalmers, once musing over the problem why his ministry with its immeasurable popularity had not more definite spiritual outcome, came to this conclusion, "I am trusting more to my own activity and animal heat than to the Holy Ghost." So may the church. But it will not do.

11-13. ***How We Can Know the Heavenly.***—Our Lord was frankly disappointed that Nicodemus fell so quickly out of step with him and lagged behind. How often he must feel that! Apparently he had much that he had meant to say; and he found himself pulled up. If we are stumbled by earthly things (see Exeg.), by matters for which there are human analogies, and which can be verified in human experience, how are we to press on to the deep things of God, to understand the heavenly? Only one with firsthand knowledge of these things can share them with us: only the Son of man, who was in heaven, and has come down from heaven; though in a very real sense, as some MSS put it grandly, he **is in heaven,** even yet and even here and even now, out in the jostle of the crowded streets, among his difficulties and discouragements. That is a very great saying. In essence heaven is not a place; it is a character, a mode of life, a kind of being. And as Christ moved about among men, he had the heavenly mind,

14 ¶ And as Moses lifted up the serpent in the wilderness, even so must the Son of man be lifted up:

Son of man.[f] 14 And as Moses lifted up the serpent in the wilderness, so must the Son

[f] Other ancient authorities add *who is in heaven.*

life on earth by a spiritual regeneration. The **heavenly things** are those mysteries which no man can declare, but which can be made known by **the Son of man,** who has **descended from heaven.** No man **has ascended into heaven** so as to bring down the divine secret. The implicit reference to 1:18 may have led to the marginal gloss (unless it is an original part of the text), **who is in heaven.** If this reading—Western, Caesarean, and Syrian—is accepted, the present tense must be taken as futuristic (cf. 7:34; 12:26; 14:3; 17:24).

14-15. The reference to ascension suggests the double sense in which the verb "to lift up" can be used of Jesus Christ. In this Gospel his exaltation on the cross is never separated from the thought of his exaltation to heaven (cf. 8:28; 12:32-34). In the same way the word for "to glorify" carries an ambiguity, for the glorification of Christ comes through the humiliation of his death (12:23). Vs. 14 finds an illustration of this "lifting up" of Christ in the story of Moses and the brazen serpent (Num. 21:9) The story had already been commented upon in Wisd. Sol. 16:6-7:

> But for admonition they were troubled for a short space,
> Having a token of salvation,
> To put them in remembrance of the commandment of thy law;
> For he that turned towards it was not saved by that which was beheld,
> But because of thee, the Savior of all (ERV).

The point of comparison here is that as healing came to the snake-bitten Israelites by looking at the brazen serpent hanging from a pole, so life is given to those who look up with the eyes of faith upon the Son of man hanging on the Cross. At this point we discover the connection of this soliloquy with the conversation with Nicodemus which gave rise to it. The theme of that conversation was the kingdom of God and the only means of entrance into it. John's synonym for the kingdom is now introduced, and

employed the heavenly standards of value, used life in the heavenly way. And people watching him were led into an understanding of the heavenly things—knew what God must be like; what our own life should be; what is the meaning of holiness; what heaven itself really is.

14. ***Looking up to Christ.***—**As Moses lifted up the serpent in the wilderness, so must the Son of man be lifted up.** On which let us say, first, this. George Eliot shows us Maggie Tulliver, in the tumult of her soul, happening upon an old thumbed copy of the *Imitation of Christ,* marked here and there in faded ink; and reading where the long dead hand directed her, she was lured into life and peace.[4] It is a moving study to consider the passages in the O.T. that made special appeal to Christ; to take, so to speak, his own copy of the Scriptures into reverent hands, and turning the pages, to note the places he has marked. This helped the Master once; against this verse he leaned in an evil hour; and this he quoted, preferring it to any words which he himself could find; through this the very voice of very God spoke to his soul.

Apparently he found the incident of the brazen serpent vividly suggestive. Here he definitely quotes it; and possibly at least it was the background out of which there came the kindred saying in 12:32, "I, if I be lifted up from the earth, will draw all men unto me." In the later passage the evangelist is quite sure Christ was foretelling the kind of death he was to face. And certainly it is above all by being lifted up upon that Cross of shame that he has won by far the most souls. Is it not a strange thing that it is the voice of a crucified man dying in agony that has convinced innumerable hearts that God is love? And that it is upon Calvary, where all seemed lost, that Christ has proved most irresistible? We can rudely shake off the warning hand of the All Wise; we can harden our faces to receive the thunderbolts of punishment of the Almighty without flinching: but what are we to do with this strange Son of God who dies for us, meeting the hugeness of our undeserving with a love still huger? It is desperately difficult to hold out against such a claimant for our hearts. For of themselves they break away from us, and run to him, and fling themselves before him, crying, "We will have this man to rule over us."

[4] *The Mill on the Floss,* Bk. IV, ch. iii.

15 That whosoever believeth in him should not perish, but have eternal life.
16 ¶ For God so loved the world, that he gave his only begotten Son, that who-

of man be lifted up, 15 that whoever believes in him may have eternal life."[g]
16 For God so loved the world that he

[g] Some interpreters hold that the quotation continues through verse 21.

---

eternal life becomes the theme to the end of the chapter—vss. 22-30 interrupt the address with a further testimony of the Baptist to Jesus. The gift of eternal life originates in the love of God; its possession depends upon the faith of the recipient (vss. 15-16). The constructions in the Greek are different in these two verses. In vs. 15 **in him** belongs to **may have eternal life,** whereas in vs. 16 these words go with the verb **believes.** In the first **the Son of man** is the source of eternal life; in the second he is the object of faith.

16-21. These verses are a reflection by the evangelist rather than part of a conversation. By this time Nicodemus has faded out of the picture, and John is pondering over the mystery of grace by which law and judgment have been superseded by gospel and forgiveness (cf. 1:17-18). The divine initiative and the divine purpose are revealed in the

---

But as to this earlier passage, what did Christ expect Nicodemus to understand by it? Is it not simplest to take it as running on from the verses that immediately precede it? Think of that desperate people in the wilderness, dying in multitudes, beset by those loathsome creatures from which there was no escape; and how the word ran through the stricken camp that if only they would keep looking at the brazen serpent lifted up for all to see, that would mean deliverance for such as still survived, and death would be cheated of its victims. So, says Christ, here is this ailing, sinful, foolish, desperate world that has lost its way, and is living like some primitive barbaric tribe which imagines that its nasty little customs are the only possible rules of life anywhere and for anyone. And if men see me, and keep looking at me, the heavenly things that are all dark to them will dawn upon them; and the glory of what God really is will come home to them; and the splendor of what a human life can be will storm their hearts, and sicken them of what they are, and bring them to their feet, whole men, ready to live a fuller life than they have ever dreamed is possible.

15. ***The Promise of Eternal Life.***—This higher mode of being is called **eternal life,** a favorite word of this evangelist. And what is that? In essence it has little to do with duration; is qualitative rather than quantitative; describes not so much the length of a life as the kind of life it is. Buddha was asked by his puzzled disciples, "But what is Nirvana? For sometimes you speak of it as if it were a present thing, and sometimes as if it lay in the future." He replied, "It is both. It is the ideal: is present, because it begins here; and future, because after death it expands into a far greater being than what we can know now, into the best that is conceivable." So with eternal life. It is present because even here and now we can have experience of it, though as yet only imperfectly and under earthly limitations. But it is also future because by-and-by it will widen into a fullness of glory that we cannot as yet even begin to comprehend. But present or future, it means to put on Christ, to use life after his fashion. Look at him lifted up, and a comprehension of how noble a thing a human life can be will dawn on you, and weary you of the poor little trivialities and worse which have been so engrossing. Keep looking at him, and a power will come from him that will enable you to rise up into a newness of life, to live in his way; most imperfectly here, but it will grow from less to more, and more to most. "The world passes away, and the lust of it" (I John 2:17). What then is to be done with those who have never an interest except in a world that has now vanished into nothingness, now that all that meant life to them, made life for them, is gone? "But he who does the will of God abides forever" (I John 2:17). It is the doing of the will, more even by far than the abiding forever, that makes it eternal life.

16*a.* ***God and the World.***—As the Exeg. indicates, scholarship seems fairly sure that the interview with Nicodemus ends at vs. 15, and that what follows is the evangelist himself, pausing in the telling of his story to brood over it and to think out its amazing implications; much as, if one may compare small things with great, Thackeray used to break into his narrative with musings upon life suggested to him by his characters and what befalls them.

In the whole Word of God there must be few if any scriptures which have appealed so irresistibly to so many as vs. 16. Deep calls to deep in it; in every phrase vistas that have no end at all, but melt into the far reaches of eternity, keep opening up before one's eyes and mind.

last and greatest of God's redemptive acts. This famous vs. 16, which Luther called "the gospel in miniature," is not content with declaring the measure of the divine love; it asserts its outcome on the plane of history. Yet the result of the Incarnation is not an arbitrary fiat in the sphere of redemption. It confronts men with a moral dilemma. Faced with the alternatives, life or perdition, man has himself the responsibility of the choice that determines his destiny. Faith is the activity of the whole personality. It is not merely

Any attempted commentary here is supremely an audacity and an impertinence, to be essayed at all only with reverence and humility.

"If I were as our Lord God," cried Luther in his vivid way, ". . . and these vile people were as disobedient as they now be, I would knock the world in pieces."[5] But God loves the world; his foolish, blundering, wayward, sin-sick world; and cannot bear to leave it in the troubles and disasters in which it has involved itself; but has unreckoningly thrown in his all, God's all, to right things for it, if it will.

How God can love us as he does, or indeed at all—he being what he is, we being what we are, why he does not shrink back from us in shuddering loathing, or blast us into annihilation as an affront he cannot have in the same universe with himself—that was a real difficulty to Paul's mind, a moral enigma over which he stumbled. He knew that it was true, that he himself had had experiences of which no other interpretation made sense. He was so sure of it that he gave his life to the spreading abroad of this the best by far of all possible good news. But why it should be, and how it could be, baffled him. And is there any explanation except that suggested to us by, say, such a passage as that remarkable chapter, Ecclus. 43, in which the writer loses himself among the immensities of the heavens, and wanders stunned and dazed amid the mysteries of creation—so vast, so many, so unthinkable—while, suddenly, stabbingly, there comes the tremendous thought, "As is his majesty, so also is his mercy" (Ecclus. 2:18). The divine is all upon that absolutely superhuman scale. God's power is not power but almightiness; that we can see. God's wisdom is not wisdom, as we know it, but omniscience; that we have proved. Yet these things are only his attributes. But God himself is love: a love that utterly breaks through our human conceptions of what love means and is; and runs out to lengths that sound incredible to our human ears, because no man could do it. But then, as the prophet heard God saying, "My thoughts are not your thoughts, neither are your ways my ways, saith the LORD. For as the heavens are higher than the earth, so are my ways higher than your ways, and my thoughts than your thoughts" (Isa. 55:8-9). If human standards are applied to it, the gospel is flatly incredible upon the face of it; but it grows possible and even likely when judged by every glimpse we catch of the divine.

How does God prove this love of his? Not by a weak indulgence which passes over what should not be as if it were not there, or which pretends it does not gravely matter even if it is. That were not love at all; but by doing all that even God can do, and giving all that even God can give to help us; stretching even divine self-sacrifice to the uttermost, and holding back nothing.

"What do you think happens at Calvary?" James Denney asked Frank Cairns. And he replied: "If I had a son, and he went wrong, dreadfully wrong, I couldn't give him up. But to redeem him a heart would need to break—my heart; and perhaps his as well. And at the Cross it comes home to me that I have broken my Father's heart; and yet that he can't give me up. And I can't bear it; grow sick of myself; and long to be quite different; and there and then begin to be it." God cannot let us go; and has tried every way to help us; has even given **his only Son** for us.

That is a phrase that reaches many a heart, especially in the wake of the world's wars, with a full and poignant meaning. Some of the past explanations of the gospel are not overhelpful to us now. Most of us, e.g., are not at home in the Jewish sacrificial system; and metaphors drawn from it can be confusing rather than illuminating. And some of the interpretations, popular in the Middle Ages, are to us incredible, and even monstrous. But many a sore if proud heart, musing on its dead, can enter far into this verse without any interpreter; and hearing it, can look toward God with a quick and instant understanding. As Dora Greenwell put it:

> When I looked upon my agonized and dying God, and turned from that world-appealing sight, Christ crucified for us, to look upon life's most perplexed and sorrowful contradictions, I was not met as in intercourse with my fellow-men by the cold platitudes that fall so lightly from the lips of those whose hearts have never known one real pang, nor whose lives one crushing blow. I was not told that all things were ordered for the best, nor assured that the overwhelming disparities of life were but apparent, but I was met from the eyes and brow of Him who was indeed acquainted with grief,

[5] *Table Talk,* CXI.

soever believeth in him should not perish, but have everlasting life.

gave his only Son, that whoever believes in him should not perish but have eternal

intellectual but moral in its nature. The antithesis to faith is not doubt but disobedience (vs. 36). God's purpose in the mission of his Son is not to condemn but to save (vs. 17); yet the reaction of men to this revelation of **light** determines their end (vs. 18), for it is a

by a look of solemn recognition, such as may pass between friends who have endured between them some strange and secret sorrow, *and are through it united in a bond that cannot be broken.*[6]

In the day of the world's desperation people gave their means, their time, their strength, even their boy on whom their hopes were centered, making no effort to hold him back, prepared to run even that risk; feeling that for the emancipation of the multitudes enslaved or threatened, and for the upholding of our tottering human liberties, even that price was not too vast. All that they paid down, unflinchingly, and having paid it, sit now in an emptied home. That, says this scripture, is the nearest human analogy to what God did to save the world.

Always the N.T. asserts that that is the background of the gospel and the origin from which it flows. He who out of the hugeness of his liberality has devised for us so many and such gracious benefits, has added this last crowning act of generosity, than which even God can do no more: has given us his only Son.

Is there a sadder fact in human history than that some have so misread the gospel that while it does draw them toward Jesus Christ, it only confirms them in their impression that God is cold and ruthless and implacable? H. G. Wells at one time gave as his reading of life this somber view, that while there is evidence that a lesser, kindly God does seek to interpose between us and the sternness and rigor of the supreme deity, his gracious effort is foredoomed to failure, since that other must and will prevail. So do many, with the Gospels in their hands, appear to see in them a lesser God giving himself to save us from the implacable fury and resentment of the great God, slow and hard to be appeased, and demanding his pound of flesh from someone. That is a hideous heresy; and the blasphemy of blasphemies. It was the eternal plan of God the Father that Jesus Christ lived out into fact: "God was in Christ, reconciling the world unto himself" (II Cor. 5:19), not standing sullenly aside, and needing himself to be reconciled. **God so loved the world, that he gave his only begotten Son.**

16*b*. *The Momentousness of Belief.*—Such is the gracious purpose of God toward his unruly world; and toward every one of us, without exception, who compose it. But if it is to work out in us individually or as a whole, it must be met by a response upon our side. God so loved the world that he sent his Son for everyone; but it is only those who believe in him that do **not perish, but have everlasting life.** Hence the momentousness of belief.

Our Lord was once asked, "What shall we do, that we might work the works of God?" and he replied, "You must begin farther back than with palpable, overt things like deeds and works, must get behind even your thoughts and motives, must start with your beliefs." For these last color everything and determine what all the rest—motives and thoughts and words and deeds—will be. "This is the work of God, that you believe in him whom he has sent" (6:29). So Buddha, four hundred years before Christ, in a land where, then as now, belief is judged to be of no primary consequence. You can be a deist, a pantheist, a theist, the worshiper of an unknowable Absolute, or of a personal deity, or of hundreds of gods, or an agnostic, or an atheist, and still be an orthodox Hindu. That, the Hindus claim, is the glory of their faith. And no one will seek to convert you to a better way of thinking. For that would only make you stumble over your own feet.[7] And Buddha flatly denied all that, holding that what a man believes is central, radical, fundamental; and sets down, as the first step in his famous eightfold path to holiness, right beliefs. That gained, everything else may follow. But without that there is no hope. So here. Even God's eager grace, stretched to its uttermost, cannot save a soul or a world unless it believes in the Son whom he has sent. If we believe in Jesus Christ and all for which he stands; if we are prepared to stake our all—our life, our soul, our destiny—on the truth of what he says, and do it; if we act on the assumption that this will bear our weight, and venture out on it, much follows of itself.

Believe in the God whom Christ reveals, and for one thing worry and carewornness and fretting must vanish away. For we are children living in our Father's house, and have no need to bother ourselves with anxious thoughts, saying, "What shall we eat? or, What shall we drink?

[6] *Colloquia Crucis* (London: Strahan & Co., 1871), pp. 14-15.

[7] See S. Radhakrishnan, *The Hindu View of Life* (London: George Allen & Unwin, 1927), ch. ii.

17 For God sent not his Son into the world to condemn the world; but that the world through him might be saved.

18 ¶ He that believeth on him is not condemned: but he that believeth not is condemned already, because he hath not believed in the name of the only begotten Son of God.

life. 17 For God sent the Son into the
world, not to condemn the world, but that
the world might be saved through him.
18 He who believes in him is not con-
demned; he who does not believe is condemned already, because he has not believed in the name of the only Son of God.

---

man's essential character that is brought under judgment (vs. 19). The test of that character is its attitude to light. The doer of worthless actions dreads and avoids the light for fear of exposure (vs. 20). **He who does what is true**—an O.T. expression, meaning to act with regard to reality rather than to pretense and display (cf. I John 1:6)—welcomes the light for the opportunity of proving that his deeds have been prompted and empowered by God (vs. 21; cf. Eph. 5:13; for "truth" see Exeg. on 1:14-18).

The word translated in this passage **condemn** means literally, "judge" (κρίνειν), as the corresponding noun (κρίμα) is translated **judgment.** The judgment is first a

---

or, Wherewithal shall we be clothed?" (Matt. 6:31). As Robert Rainy said, children "take a great deal for granted, that it will be looked after, without their looking after it—that is a child's wisdom." [8]

Believe in Christ's ennobling conception of man, and we must be lifted above ourselves; like one who has gone native, suddenly coming to himself, and with his new eyes hating the life around him and hurrying back to the more worthy one that he can have. Believe in the immortality Christ taught us is ours, and instinctively we use a new standard of measurement and scale of values, so that much that had seemed big dwindles to pettiness, and much that had meant little to us looms up, momentous, central, all important. Believe that Christ loved us and gave himself for us, and, as the KJV translates it, though wrongly, "We love him, because he first loved us" (I John 4:19); and also must live out the wider, more authentic rendering of that verse: "We love, because he first loved us" (RSV), catching from him the infection of his generous way of life, and spending ours after his fashion. What we believe means everything, and makes a mighty difference.

Hence the attempt to jettison the Christian facts as being perhaps doubtful, and the Christian doctrines as largely dust-laden lumber, much like the rickety furniture now relegated to some attic, and to concentrate on the beauty of the Christian ethic, and the living of the Christian life, is hopeless and foredoomed to failure. It is the Christian facts that have brought home to us what the ideal way of living is; it is the Christian doctrines that furnish the motive that stings us from our lethargy and gives the power to set to work upon a life after this pattern. Standing on Calvary, I want to belong to Christ. Believing that God gave his only begotten Son for me, I do not need to give my heart to him. He storms it, takes possession of it, holds it; and I wish it to be so. But without facts like these, what is to make me what I see I ought to be?

17-21. ***The Dangerousness of Grace.***—God's wish and purpose is to save all men. But there is no compulsion laid on them. They have been given their freedom of will; and it is for each, separately and individually, to determine how he chooses to react to God's gracious offer. Some close with it. And in their case it works out, here and hereafter. Some do not and will not. They are not interested in the gifts Christ has to offer them. "What would I do with these?" they ask, looking at them distastefully, and impatiently brushing them aside. But it is a grave thing to meet Jesus Christ. For we can never again be what we were before: better, please God, far better; but if not, then certainly worse, far worse. For no one can push past Christ or pretend not to see him. But each must stand, must listen, must make up his mind, must give some answer. And consciously or unconsciously, each of them does that every time. Either they accept his promises and claims, or hardening their faces, look him squarely in the eyes and answer, "I will not!" And so doing (vss. 18-21) they pass judgment on themselves; since, seeing a higher, they would have none of it, but chose a lower which made greater appeal to them—the animal rather than the spiritual, the world rather than God, their customary ways rather than the Christlikeness that they might have. And no further evidence is needed

[8] *Sojourning with God* (London: Hodder & Stoughton, 1902), p. 157.

19 And this is the condemnation, that light is come into the world, and men loved darkness rather than light, because their deeds were evil.

20 For every one that doeth evil hateth the light, neither cometh to the light, lest his deeds should be reproved.

21 But he that doeth truth cometh to the light, that his deeds may be made manifest, that they are wrought in God.

19 And this is the judgment, that the light
has come into the world, and men loved
darkness rather than light, because their
deeds were evil. 20 For every one who does
evil hates the light, and does not come to
the light, lest his deeds should be exposed.
21 But he who does what is true comes to
the light, that it may be clearly seen that
his deeds have been wrought in God.

---

decision, and this involves a separation (cf. Matt. 25:31-46) of those approved from those condemned. In both John and I John the conceptions of a present and of a future judgment are found side by side. The judgment is present in 3:18-21; 5:24, 25, 30; 12:31; 16:11; I John 3:14. It is future in 5:28-29; 12:48; I John 4:17. For a fuller treatment of this subject see Intro., pp. 443-44; cf. also vs. 36.

---

to prove what manner of folk they are. Many, says this grave passage, act so, thwarting God's grace and converting what was meant to save them into a yet greater certainty of doom. "Man is free to choose torment without God rather than happiness in God; he has a right to hell, as it were." [9]

19. *The Real Reason of Much Lack of Faith.* —We have grown chary of judging one another in these matters. We assume that those without are not there by their own free will and preference, but have been stumbled by intellectual difficulties through which they cannot as yet cut a way; that their lack of faith is not really a fault at all, but at worst only an unfortunate ailment to be treated by wise people with sympathy and kindliness; and probably enough, not even that, but rather a kind of virtue, a being honest, a manful following of truth so far as they see it, heedless of consequences. In all of which there is of course an element of fact; and in certain cases, all the facts. Yet there is at least as much of truth in this evangelist's blunt finding that a great proportion of "honest doubt" is not honest at all; that it arises not from intellectual perplexity but simply from moral perversity and an obstinate refusal to see what they do not want to see. They do not like the light. They would fain blow it out if they could. And failing that, they shrink back from it into the friendly darkness, which they much prefer, and where they feel at home, as they do not in this glaring sunshine. Because they want to follow certain ways, and this would ban them; because they have made up their minds to live after a certain fashion, and this would outlaw and condemn it, they will have none of the light, and find means of discrediting it to their minds. "Many," said Fenélon, "exaggerate their doubts to excuse themselves from action." [1] And that is little. W. E. H. Lecky, in the midst of a fierce attack upon the church for treating doubt as guilt, frankly concedes "that it would be difficult to over-estimate the number of those" who have never taken enough trouble in the matter to give them the right to have an opinion at all, whose "convictions are due to the unresisted bias of their interests," to the yielding without effort to the current, and to a lazy convincing of themselves, without any valid proof, of the truth of what they wish to believe. And still more serious, "The materials with which the intellect builds are often derived from the heart, and a moral disease is therefore not unfrequently at the root of an erroneous judgment." [2]

Of which, and of the evangelist's grave conclusions, Aldous Huxley gives corroboration from his own experience:

> I had motives for not wanting the world to have a meaning; consequently assumed that it had none, and was able without any difficulty to find satisfying reasons for this assumption. Most ignorance is vincible . . . will that decides how and upon what subjects we shall use our intelligence. Those who detect no meaning in the [world] generally do so because, for one reason or another, it suits their books that the world should be meaningless. . . . We objected to the morality because it interfered with our sexual freedom.[3]

And so these confident voices, whom some took quite seriously, tried to laugh it out of court.

[9] Nicholas Berdyaev, *Freedom and the Spirit* (New York: Charles Scribner's Sons, 1935), p. 324.

[1] *Spiritual Letters to Men*, Letter III, "To One Irresolute in His Conversion."

[2] *History of European Morals* (New York: D. Appleton & Co., 1887), II, 191, 193.

[3] *Ends and Means* (London: Chatto & Windus, 1938), pp. 270, 273.

22 ¶ After these things came Jesus and his disciples into the land of Judea; and there he tarried with them, and baptized.
23 ¶ And John also was baptizing in Aenon near to Salim, because there was much water there: and they came, and were baptized.
24 For John was not yet cast into prison.

22 After this Jesus and his disciples went into the land of Judea; there he remained with them and baptized. 23 John also was baptizing at Ae'non near Salim, because there was much water there; and people came and were baptized. 24 For John had not yet been put in prison.

E. Testimony of the Baptist (3:22-30)

22-24. After this is a vague indication of time, and since this section is an obvious interruption of the discourse on the heavenly birth, the heavenly revealer, and the divine judgment, it can mean only that after one of his visits to Jerusalem early in his ministry, Jesus left the city for the country parts of Judea, near the Jordan. Some disciples were still with him, and here Jesus carried on a parallel ministry to that of the Baptist. There is no mention of this in any of the Synoptic Gospels, nor is there any mention of Christian baptism elsewhere in the Gospels, except in 4:1-2, where an editorial note corrects an impression that Jesus himself baptized. **The land of Judea** is a vague term, but probably refers to some part of Judea to the northeast, near the borders of Samaria (cf. 4:1-4). Not far away **John also was baptizing at Aenon near Salim, because there was much water there** (vs. 23). The last clause shows that this was not on the banks of Jordan, but in some region where there were abundant sources of the streams which flowed down to the Jordan Valley. Karl Kundsin (*Topologische Überlieferungsstosse in Johannes-Evangelium* [Göttingen: Vandenhoeck & Ruprecht, 1925], p. 27) favors an identification of Aenon with Ain Farah, the well-watered district near the sources of the Wadi Farah, about two hours' journey north-northeast from Jerusalem, not far from the Wadi Selam, which suggests the name Salim; M.-J. Lagrange (*Évangile selon Saint Jean* [2nd ed.;

And this is the judgment, that the light has come into the world, and men loved darkness rather than light, because their deeds were evil.

22-30. ***He Must Increase, but I Must Decrease.***—When we look at the disciples of the Baptist, this is a natural and very human story, obviously taken straight from life. These discomfited men had been watching in bewilderment a sudden and unexpected ebbing of the tide that had been flowing in so strong and full. Angrily they had protested to some of the masses now streaming away to a newer voice and leaving yawning blanks that widened every hour, where till now there had always been a solid mass of humanity. Heatedly they had discussed and argued over the crowd's fickleness. And now, agitated and unhappy, they clustered about the Baptist, upset and shaken in themselves, hurt by the pain they felt that this must cause their master, and chagrined above everything else by the remembrance that it was his own enthusiastic eulogies of his too successful rival that had set in motion this avalanche and landslide from him to that other.

That is a situation into which life can often bring one. A statesman, by the sheer audacity of his invincible courage, saves his nation from annihilation and a doom far worse than death, as only he and not one other in his generation could have done; and within weeks of the victory the people, well knowing what they owe him, throw him over and turn to other leaders. A man we love and reverence as a prophet of the Most High God begins to grow old, and the crowded pews grow thinner and thinner, and the hearers flock elsewhere, following each other like sheep. And the resentment aroused in us is, we feel, a clean and righteous anger, the justifiable protest of outraged loyalty and of common gratitude.

But the central figure in the scene is of course the Baptist himself, with his total lack of envy and bitterness, and with his splendor of generosity and complete forgetfulness of self. Wonderingly he looked at these puzzled friends of his. For in the bigness of his nature he cannot even begin to understand their difficulty. "Did I not tell you that this is what I wanted, and that it was for this I have been working? Each of us can use only what God has given

25 ¶ Then there arose a question between *some* of John's disciples and the Jews about purifying.

26 And they came unto John, and said unto him, Rabbi, he that was with thee beyond Jordan, to whom thou barest witness, behold, the same baptizeth, and all *men* come to him.

27 John answered and said, A man can receive nothing, except it be given him from heaven.

25 Now a discussion arose between John's
disciples and a Jew over purifying. 26 And
they came to John, and said to him, "Rabbi,
he who was with you beyond the Jordan,
to whom you bore witness, here he is, baptizing, and all are going to him." 27 John
answered, "No one can receive anything
except what is given him from heaven.

Paris: Librairie Victor Lecoffre, 1925; "Études Bibliques"], p. 92) points out that Aenon is a transliteration of the Aramaic word (*'ênāwān*) for "sources." As this Gospel tells us nothing about the Baptist's imprisonment and death, this verse may be a gloss by an editor or early copyist who knew that according to the Synoptic tradition, Jesus began his ministry in Galilee after John had been delivered up (Mark 1:14).

25-30. It is difficult to see the connection between vs. 25 and what follows. At an early stage in the textual history, the reading "with a Jew" was corrected to "with Jews." But even this seems irrelevant to the context. A feasible modern conjecture would substitute "with [followers] of Jesus," or "with Jesus." A dispute between John's disciples and those of Jesus might well lead to a complaint by the former to their master of the growing success of the rival movement. The dispute was about ritual cleansing, the subject of our Lord's polemic discourse in defense of his disciples on another occasion (Mark 7:1-23). **To whom you bore witness** refers back to 1:15, 26-27, 29-34. John's reply to the jealous loyalty of his disciples means, "We must be content with what God gives." He had told them before that his mission was only that of a pioneer and healer. The marriage feast was in Oriental imagery a favorite symbol for joy; cf. the allusions in Jer. 7:34; 16:9; 25:10 to the silence of bride and bridegroom as the sign of complete desolation. In Mark 2:19 Jesus explains that wedding guests cannot fast while the bridegroom is with them. **The friend of the bridegroom** (*shôshebhîn* or groomsman)—in Judea, but not in Galilee, there were two of them, one acting for the bridegroom, the other for the bride—was responsible for arranging the betrothal, with all its commitments, and finally for leading the betrothed couple to the bridal chamber (Strack and Billerbeck, *Kommentar zum N.T. aus Talmud und Midrasch,* I, 500). Thus he had an important part to play

---

him. For any good we do comes not of ourselves, but is God working in and through us. To me he gave the privilege of being the bridegroom's friend, who makes arrangements for the wedding and sees it through; but that done, he steps back into obscurity again, with no feeling in his heart but happiness in his friend's happiness. All this that is happening is right and fitting, and as it ought to be. **He must increase, but I must decrease.** And I exult that my preliminary work has made it possible for him to come, that he has come, and that increasingly I am being forgotten and he being accepted."

It is not easy to enter fully into the Master's tremendous eulogy of John, "Verily I say unto you, Among them that are born of women there hath not risen a greater than John the Baptist" (Matt. 11:11). But this passage enables us to see something of the man's size. To be surpassed and superseded and take his own eclipse without a trace of rancor or jealousy, with nothing indeed but exultation in the other's success, is an achievement indeed. When F. W. H. Myers writes,

> John, than which man a sadder or a greater
> Not till this day has been of woman born,
> John like some lonely peak by the Creator
> Fired with the red glow of the rushing morn.
>
> This when the sun shall rise and overcome it
> Stands in his shining desolate and bare, . . .[4]

he is throwing back into the story what our smaller minds would have felt. But there is not a trace of sadness about John. **This joy of mine is now full.**

[4] *St. Paul.*

28 Ye yourselves bear me witness, that I said, I am not the Christ, but that I am sent before him.

29 He that hath the bride is the bridegroom: but the friend of the bridegroom, which standeth and heareth him, rejoiceth greatly because of the bridegroom's voice: this my joy therefore is fulfilled.

30 He must increase, but I *must* decrease.

28 You yourselves bear me witness, that I said, I am not the Christ, but I have been sent before him. 29 He who has the bride is the bridegroom; the friend of the bridegroom, who stands and hears him, rejoices greatly at the bridegroom's voice; therefore this joy of mine is now full. 30 He must increase, but I must decrease."[h]

[h] Some interpreters hold that the quotation continues through verse 36.

---

while the ceremonies lasted, but his importance pales in comparison with that of the bridegroom. The emphasis is upon **friend.** He is no rival. He rejoices in watching his friend's joy. John the Baptist meant that the hour has now struck which marks the beginning of the new age. To change the figure, his own star is sinking beneath the horizon as the star of the destined Messiah rises. As in all his references to the Baptist, the evangelist emphasizes his subordination to Jesus, but there is no belittlement of the man or his mission. He was sent by God to bear witness to a greater than himself; he faithfully discharged his commission and then, with true magnanimity, stepped aside that the Christ might have the pre-eminence.

From all of which let us draw some practical conclusions:

(*a*) Such a sane mind as Bishop Butler[5] alleges that it is greatly more difficult to rejoice with those that rejoice than to weep with those that weep. So much so that while we have many words betokening pain in others' pain—sympathy, compassion, etc.—we have none meaning to rejoice in others' joy. Which fact, he claims, must mean that we never do it, or else we would need a term to express the mood. That seems a hard saying, and an obvious exaggeration. Yet we had better examine ourselves to see how far it is true of us.

(*b*) Pascal sets it down that all that is required to be done could easily be done if only people would rise up and play their part, not bothering who gets the glory of it. Once in World War I, the battalion with which I served saved the line. Later, as the lads lay about so tired that they could speak only in small, almost inaudible voices, the papers arrived from home. By some mistake the feat was credited to a battalion which had been miles away, and ours was never mentioned. There fell a moment's somber silence, and the colonel's face flushed red. And then his head went up. "What does it matter, gentlemen, who gets the credit of it? We know we did it."

(*c*) But in some ways it is even harder to be surpassed by one who really is bigger and abler and better than ourselves; to have to fall in behind, where we had led by natural right.

[5] *The Works of Joseph Butler*, ed. W. E. Gladstone (Oxford: Clarendon Press, 1896), II, 94-97.

"Nothing delights me more," said Arnold of Rugby about one of his staff, "than to think that boys are sent here for his sake rather than mine."[6] That would have been a searching test for many a man.

(*d*) It is difficult for people getting on in life to accept with cheerfulness the fact that their way of things, their mode of thought, the world they know and in which they feel at home, must decrease; and another, alien to their mind, must increase. As Goethe says, "We readily bow to antiquity, but not to posterity. It is only a father who does not grudge talent to his son."[7]

(*e*) How are we to gain something of the Baptist's largeness of mind and soul? By the reflex action of intercessory prayer, says William Law, asserting positively that it is impossible to harbor animosity or jealousy toward one for whom we keep interceding before God. If, he declares with the assurance of experience, someone is leaving you behind, and you are becoming jealous and embittered, keep praying that he may have success in the very matter where he is awakening your envy; and whether he is helped or not, one thing is sure, that your own soul will be cleansed and ennobled, that you will grow a little nearer to the stature of the Baptist.[8]

[6] Edward Stanley, *Life of Arnold of Rugby* (Boston: Ticknor & Fields, 1860), p. 103.

[7] *Maxims and Reflections of Goethe,* tr. T. Bailey Saunders (New York: The Macmillan Co., 1893), p. 99.

[8] *A Serious Call to a Devout and Holy Life* (London: G. F. Browne & Co., n.d.), ch. xxi.

31 He that cometh from above is above all: he that is of the earth is earthly, and speaketh of the earth: he that cometh from heaven is above all.

32 And what he hath seen and heard, that he testifieth; and no man receiveth his testimony.

33 He that hath received his testimony hath set his seal that God is true.

31 He who comes from above is above
all; he who is of the earth belongs to the
earth, and of the earth he speaks; he who
comes from heaven is above all. 32 He
bears witness to what he has seen and heard,
yet no one receives his testimony; 33 he
who receives his testimony sets his seal to

F. The Witness from Above (3:31-36)

After the intrusive narrative about the rivalry of John's disciples, and of the Baptist's reiterated testimony of Christ, the closing section of this chapter resumes the meditation of vss. 16-21. Apart from the subject matter, vs. 32*b* is out of harmony with vs. 26.

The theme is the superior value of a heavenly witness spoken by One who speaks of what he has seen and heard. This testimony is given by the Son to whom the Father has entrusted full authority in his mission to earth, so that his words are God's words, and acceptance of his message brings the believer into the life that is from above, while refusal to accept it robs the unbeliever of this life, so that **the wrath,** the divine reaction against sin, is continually hanging over him (for this technical term in Jewish eschatology cf. Rom. 1:18; 2:5; 5:9; Eph. 5:6; Col. 3:6; I Thess. 1:10; 2:16; Rev. 6:16).

There are unmistakable echoes of the earlier section of this discourse. **He who comes from above** (vs. 31) corresponds to the title "he who descended from heaven" (vs. 13)—the timeless Logos who in his incarnate life speaks heavenly truth in the language of earth. The Son, whom the Father loves, **whom God has sent** (vss. 34-35), recalls the only Son whom God has given in love to the world (vs. 16). The witness he bears **to what he has seen and heard** (vs. 32) constitutes his testimony regarding "heavenly things" (vs. 12). The revelation spoken by the Son as it elicits faith or provokes disobedience (vs. 36) is the criterion of life or death, as is the coming of light in the revelation of his life (vss. 19-21).

32-34. No one receives his testimony is a comprehensive generalization which probably reflects the evangelist's judgment on the Jewish nation as a whole for its rejection

31-36. ***The Wrath of God.***—From vs. 31 onward the evangelist, it seems, again falls into a muse, revolving in his mind what has been stated, and its implications. "God, who at sundry times and in divers manners spake in time past unto the fathers by the prophets, hath in these last days spoken unto us by his Son" (Heb. 1:1), in whom "dwelleth all the fulness of the Godhead bodily" (Col. 2:9), and to whom the Spirit has been given without measure (3:34). He does not merely bring us glorious possibilities, but is a firsthand witness, telling what he himself has seen and heard and knows; he speaks to us the very words of God, as though God himself were beseeching us by him; and we can count upon it with assurance. And some do give him credence, setting their **seal to this, that God is true;** feeling that he whose word is truth is absolutely dependable, and will stand to his promises, however impossible they sound; and testifying later that they have tried this thing and it works, that God means what he says, and does it. But (vs. 32) the mass of people, frankly incredulous, will have none of it, and push it aside as obviously out of the question, or of no manner of interest to them. And on them rests **the wrath of God.**

That is a sudden, stabbing, unexpected ending to this statement of the wonderful love of God toward everyone, and of the lengths to which he has gone for each and all of us. It is a phrase not at all characteristic of this evangelist. But it, and the austere facts for which it stands, are a very marked feature of the N.T., woven inextricably into its web and texture. For if the N.T. is the happiest book in the world, and the most hopeful, it is also the gravest. Too many of us unwarrantably pick and choose in our Bible reading, returning again and again to the consolatory passages and the heartening promises, but leaving severely alone many other pages full of challenge and appeal,

34 For he whom God hath sent speaketh the words of God: for God giveth not the Spirit by measure *unto him.*

35 The Father loveth the Son, and hath given all things into his hand.

36 He that believeth on the Son hath everlasting life: and he that believeth not the Son shall not see life; but the wrath of God abideth on him.

this, that God is true.
34 For he whom God has sent utters the words of God, for it is not by measure that he gives the Spirit;
35 the Father loves the Son, and has given all things into his hand.
36 He who believes in the Son has eternal life; he who does not obey the Son shall not see life, but the wrath of God rests upon him.

---

of its own Messiah (cf. 1:11). As in 1:12; 8:16, the sweeping negative is modified by the exception (vs. 33) which proves the rule. The man whose insights are conditioned merely by his nature "in the flesh" cannot discern the meaning of that which originates in the realm of the Spirit (I Cor. 2:9-12). The man of faith can receive the witness, for he recognizes in Jesus one whose life and teaching are identical; they are both self-authenticated as a true disclosure of the character and purpose of God (cf. I John 5:10). Without searching for further evidence, the believer attests that the divine revelation of love in the Incarnation is worthy of acceptance as coming from the God who is real and reliable. Other prophets have come with fleeting and fugitive inspiration. There is a rabbinical saying, "The Holy Spirit which abides on the prophets does not abide except by measure" (Rabbi Acha in the Rabba on Lev. 15:2, quoted by Strack and Billerbeck, *op. cit.* II, 431). On the other hand, it is here (vs. 34) said of Jesus, **For it is not by measure that he gives the Spirit,** i.e., the Father does not bestow the Spirit upon Jesus except in its fullness, as a constant endowment. Some authorities omit the object (**the Spirit**), and many do not express the subject, but in any case those MSS which supply the name of God give the obvious meaning.

35. For the love of the Father toward the Son—a characteristic idea in this Gospel—cf. 5:20; 10:17; 15:9-10; 17:23-24, 26; and for the Johannine thought of the delivery of authority by the Father to the Son, cf. 5:22, 26-27; 6:37; 12:49; 14:31; 17:2, 4, 11, 21.

---

of warning and even threatening, of an awed shuddering of fear. These we will not see, ostentatiously ignore them, carefully looking the other way, pretending that they are not there. But they are there. And the facts behind them are eternal verities which mercifully will not pass away. But how, men confidently ask, if God is love, can there be wrath in his heart toward anyone? Such an idea surely is the surging up, out of the deeps, of crude and primitive conceptions of him, which Christ's revelation of him as he really is has made obsolete and proved untrue.

But in the N.T. men hear no clash between divine wrath and divine lovingkindness; are sure both of the goodness and the severity of God; sure that his severity is a part of his goodness, and that, were it absent, he would not be good: and the moral foundations of the world would rock and buckle and collapse. There is of course no conceivable antithesis between God's holiness and his love; for his love is part of his holiness. But if it were possible to differentiate between the two, or if one had to choose the one and do without the other, better a thousandfold that the love should go rather than that God's holiness should falter: for in that case his love would not be love, to be called love; but only a weak, flabby, sentimental, immoral indulging of us to our ruin.

Yet that is what too many fondly imagine that he is; or that they want him to be, to their vast hurt. Says James Denney:

> Nothing is commoner than the denial that the revelation of the divine wrath is real. The wrath of God, it is constantly asserted, is an idea which is ultimately inconsistent with the Christian conception of God as a loving father. It is an illusion, a misunderstanding, the natural mistake of a bad conscience; and, like other mistakes, it is removed by explanation. Sin, against which it is supposed to be the divine reaction, has no such reality for God as this terrible word implies. It does not create a problem for Him the solution of which is costly and awful. The wrath of God, in short, is not a revelation but a bugbear. Well, this is a question of fact.[9]

And the N.T. has no doubt whatsoever about what is the fact.

[9] *The Christian Doctrine of Reconciliation* (London and New York: Hodder & Stoughton, 1917), p. 144. Used by permission.

4 When therefore the Lord knew how the Pharisees had heard that Jesus made and baptized more disciples than John,
2 (Though Jesus himself baptized not, but his disciples,)
3 He left Judea, and departed again into Galilee.

4 Now when the Lord knew that the Pharisees had heard that Jesus was making and baptizing more disciples than John
2 (although Jesus himself did not baptize,
but only his disciples), 3 he left Judea and

G. Jesus and the Samaritan Woman (4:1-26)

4:1-6. The introductory verses explain the reason for our Lord's journey from Judea to Galilee, and for his contact with the people of Samaria. The Pharisees were jealous of the popularity of the new movement, which exceeded even that of the Baptist in the Judean territory. The Synoptic Gospels are silent about baptism as an accompaniment of the ministry of Jesus, and an editorial note here limits this function to his disciples (see on 3:22). The direct route from Judea to Galilee lay through the region of Samaria, which, though forming part of the subprovince of Judea under the rule of the Roman procurator, was inhabited by the mixed population separated sharply from the Jews since the time of Ezra and Nehemiah. The bitter rivalry between Jews and Samaritans led to violent attacks upon stragglers in the trains of pilgrims journeying from Galilee to the temple feasts at Jerusalem. Luke 9:51-56 illustrates the inhospitality shown to Jesus and his disciples on one of these journeys. For this reason the alternate route by way of Perea was more popular. The Samaritan religion was based upon the Pentateuch, and its cultus had been centered in the temple on Mount Gerizim. Indeed, where the Hebrew text of Deut. 27:4 records the divine command that after crossing the Jordan into the Promised Land, the Israelites were to build a stone altar on Mount Ebal for burnt

Or Percy Gardner:

> The ordinary Christian teaching about God needs infinite stiffening. . . . The sterner side of God is quite as prominent, even in the New Testament, as the more humane side; it is only that preachers have fallen into the way of dwelling on the latter to the exclusion of the former, whence the sickly onesidedness of our current religion. . . . Men have come to think of God as a weak and indulgent parent, who will not be hard on them in any case, who will think more of their happiness than of their perfection, and give them the things which they want, or think they want, . . . and veneration is drowned in a sickly flood of talk about divine love.[1]

Have not we ourselves proved many a time that Christ is never kinder than when his eyes, as he looks at us, are as a flame of fire, and he speaks to us terrible words; when he will make no compromise with us, but demands instant obedience, here and now, on pain of parting with him. If he had not loved us enough to be severe with us, he would have lost our souls. With awe and humility we need to give God thanks no less really for his wrath than for his mercy.

4:1-3. *The Necessity of Controversy.*—Now when the Lord knew that the Pharisees had heard that Jesus was making and baptizing more disciples than John . . . he left Judea and departed again to Galilee. Why? Probably to avoid the storm of controversy he saw blowing up. For since the authorities had become aware of the extent of this new and to them disquieting menace, they would shift their main suspicion from the Baptist to Christ as plainly now the more dangerous of the two. And he felt that in a noisy clamor around him the people might be distracted from the true ends of his mission and might be only too likely to lose their way in a mist of angry disputation, and never reach religion at all. So he went north. Would that his church had always been as wise as he! For if the Scriptures are final and conclusive witnesses that there is a real and necessary place for controversy (of which in this particular Gospel there is not a little), if often enough one must ring out the truth and stand to it unflinchingly, nevertheless, would not much more have been accomplished for Christ and his kingdom down the ages if all the time and energy and passion and enthusiasm expended in disputes around and about the gospel had been thrown into and spent upon the proclamation of that gospel? To which there comes the immediate question, "But what is the gospel? How can we know it, and be sure of its authenticity, and differ-

[1] *The Practical Basis of Christian Belief* (London: Williams & Norgate, 1923), pp. 136, 135. Used by permission.

4 And he must needs go through Samaria.

5 Then cometh he to a city of Samaria, which is called Sychar, near to the parcel of ground that Jacob gave to his son Joseph.

6 Now Jacob's well was there. Jesus therefore, being wearied with *his* journey, sat thus on the well: *and* it was about the sixth hour.

departed again to Galilee.
4 He had to pass through Sa-ma'ri-a.
5 So he came to a city of Sa-ma'ri-a, called Sy'char, near the field that Jacob gave to his son Joseph.
6 Jacob's well was there, and so Jesus, wearied as he was with his journey, sat down beside the well. It was about the sixth hour.

offerings, the Samaritan Pentateuch substitutes Gerizim for Ebal. The reason is to be found in Deut. 11:29; 27:12, where Ebal is the mount of cursing and Gerizim the mount of blessing (for a defense of the Samaritan claim see Moses Gaster, *The Samaritan Oral Law and Ancient Tradition* [London: The Search Publishing Co., 1932], I, 221-29, 270-77). **Sychar** (vs. 5) is generally identified with the modern 'Askar, a village in the valley about halfway between the two mountains, and about a mile north of Jacob's well (George Adam Smith, *The Historical Geography of the Holy Land* [26th ed.; London: Hodder & Stoughton, 1935], pp. 367-74; see further, Intro., p. 448). About halfway between them is the traditional site of Joseph's tomb (Gen. 33:19; 48:22; Josh. 24:32). Although Jacob's well is not mentioned in the O.T., there can be little doubt about the place described in this narrative. There must have been some reason for a well having been dug out to a depth of more than a hundred feet in a locality where rills run down from the mountain slopes in such abundance. The shaft is seven and a half feet wide and is cut through a thick bed of soil and lower down through soft rock. The

entiate it from the shams that masquerade in its name?" Which seems to bring us back once more to the necessity of controversy!

Still, Christ's example proves that there is "a time to every purpose; . . . a time to keep silence, and a time to speak" (Eccl. 3:1, 7).

Is there not real truth, though not all the truth, in that judgment of Lord Lindsay, the master of Balliol: "You ministers are making a mistake. In your pulpits you are arguing for Christianity. And no one wants your arguments. You ought to be witnessing. Does this thing work? Then share it with the rest of us." For the gospel proves itself, and is its own best evidence. God's word, as Luther used to say, has hands and feet. It runs after a man; it grips him. Let it loose, and things will happen. But many are so busy contending for the gospel that they forget to preach the gospel. And that spells disaster.

Moreover, are we ourselves entirely sure that we have not been mistaking the outer courts for the sanctuary, and that we have not been dwelling there contentedly, never pressing on and in, imagining that an interest in religion is religion? And are we certain that we are free of the besetting sin of controversialists, that once having declared themselves and taken up a position, they contend thereafter not for truth but for the validity of their own expressed view, seeing only what tells in its direction, while blind to all the facts that challenge it; going far to justify that clever gibe of old John Duncan, "Orthodoxy is my doxy; heterodoxy is the other man's doxy."

6. *The Tired Christ.*—It was high noon, and hot at that. The little group of men had been for several hours on the dusty road. And some of them were hungry, and had gone to seek for such food as might be available (vs. 8). But this was Jacob's well; and Christ elected to remain there in that place of memories, alone with God. Moreover he was wearied, and glad to rest.

Hearing that last, many look up and turn toward him with a quickened interest and a new sudden hope. The popular conception of the coming Messiah was of a mighty conqueror, ruthlessly crashing his way to irresistible victory. But there are multitudes for whom a tired Christ means far more. For they themselves are tired, are always tired, and see no prospect of ever being anything else. And a tired Christ must understand, might help, as no other could. It is so easy for one outside of a trouble, himself wholly secure, to toss good advice from the safe distance of his own immunity to poor souls struggling desperately with what is like to overwhelm them; so easy—and unhelpful! Did not Carlyle once protest that Emerson, shut in that quiet nook of a life of his, into which no breath of the tidings of the

7 There cometh a woman of Samaria to draw water: Jesus saith unto her, Give me to drink.

7 There came a woman of Sa-ma'ri-a to draw water. Jesus said to her, "Give me a

water filters in through the sides, so that it is both a "spring" (πηγή, vss. 6, 14) and a "rain pit" (φρέαρ, vss. 11-12). The track that Jesus would probably take runs to the east of Ebal, avoiding the steep gradients of the road through Shechem (Nablus) and Samaria (Sebaste), as well as the unfriendly population of these large towns—for Samaria was largely Greek and Shechem strongly Samaritan (cf. Matt. 10:5-6). While he rested by the well at the fork of the roads, weary with travel and the heat of the midday sun, his disciples went to Shechem to buy provisions for their journey (vs. 8). From Jacob's well Mount Gerizim towered to the southwest of the valley, while to the east stretched for miles the valley fertile with fields of wheat.

7-26. Two questions have been raised about the conversation with the Samaritan woman: why a woman should come in the heat of midday rather than in the evening to draw water, and why she should come so far when she must have passed several running streams on the way. The second question overlooks the sacred character of the well; the first assumes that she came from Sychar, whereas she may have come to fetch water for men working in the fields close by. Such questions had no interest for the narrator. The descriptive context supplies a setting for a typical Johannine dialogue. The themes are the living water (vss. 7-15), and spiritual worship (vss. 16-24), leading to Jesus' self-disclosure as Messiah (vss. 25-26).

7-15. The request for **a drink** was natural, since the traveler had neither the skin bucket (ἄντλημα, vs. 11) nor the rope needed for drawing water from so deep a well, and Oriental courtesy never refused such a demand (cf. Job 22:7; Prov. 25:21). The woman's

world's unhappinesses was allowed to blow, lest that might ruffle the placidity of his existence and vex him, seemed to him like a complacent person, himself keeping well out of the least touch of spray, throwing chatty and cheerful remarks to a swimmer battling for his very life in huge and angry waters, and with the breath being battered out of him? [2]

If a homely illustration is in order, to one of the three or four best people I have known, suddenly without warning there came a day of disaster when her whole life was disorganized. She said no word, made never a whimper of complaint, but bent everything in her being to a valiant attempt to straighten things. There dropped in a pious person, clad in soft furs, and with not one wrinkle in her luxurious existence; who, hearing how things were, murmured comfortably out of her own immense security, "Isn't it sweet to know that it is all in the plan?" My friend knew it was in the plan, and had with steady eyes accepted it as such. But she confided to me later, "That good soul will never know how nearly it was also in the plan that I should fairly slap her!"

Hence the N.T. takes pains to bring home to us Christ's oneness with us; and people recognizing that will listen to him, feeling that he has the right to speak. Thus those who labor and are heavy laden can see for themselves that he is carrying burdens far heavier than their own, and might well be able to show them how to bear theirs with something of his own unfaltering courage and quietheartedness. Since he himself has been tempted in all points like as we are, but with evil flinging itself against him with a ferocity of fury which we who go down so cheaply before its lesser efforts have never experienced, it is likely that he can show us how to stand fast where he himself has stood. And seeing that it is a voice rising out of a bleak and wintry-looking life that assures us that God is love, it does not irritate us; it convinces us.

7. ***Christ's Most Successful Appeal to Our Day.***—As Christ sat on the wellhead, there appeared a woman coming to draw water. Which was odd. For the natural time for that was of course the cool of the evening, when all the women gathered about the well and heard and told the news. The Exeg. suggests a possible explanation. Or perhaps we are to suppose that not only her life as a whole was disorderly but not less her daily putting of it through as well. It may be that this was a trachled, futile creature always behindtime, and always running after duty. Or perhaps her unsavory reputation had made her unpopular in the town; and the other women pointedly shrank from

[2] *The Correspondence of Thomas Carlyle and Ralph Waldo Emerson* (Boston: J. R. Osgood & Co., 1883), II, 81.

8 (For his disciples were gone away unto the city to buy meat.)

drink." **8** For his disciples had gone away

surprise was due to something in the dress and accent of the stranger, for, as the evangelist explains for his Gentile readers, **Jews have no dealings with Samaritans.** The feeling of Jews toward Samaritans is well illustrated by the son of Sirach:

For two nations doth my soul feel abhorrence,
Yea, and for a third, which is not a people;
The inhabitants of Seir and Philistia,
And that foolish nation that dwelleth in Sichem

(Ecclus. 50:25-26, Oesterley's text in R. H. Charles, ed., *The Apocrypha and Pseudepigrapha of the Old Testament in English* [Oxford: Clarendon Press, 1913], I, 511). Strack and Billerbeck give many citations from the rabbis to illustrate the repugnance felt on the Jewish side. Of special pertinence is the saying of R. Eliezer ben Hyrcanus (early second century), "He that eats the bread of the Samaritans is like to one that eats the flesh of swine" (Shebiith 8:10; cf. *The Mishnah,* tr. Herbert Danby [Oxford: Clarendon Press, 1933], p. 49). Small wonder, then, that the woman, in giving Jesus water, indulged in this ironical question (vs. 9).

her and ignored her. And rather than be so slighted and publicly ostracized, she had formed the habit of slipping out to the well at a time when it was reasonably certain no other would be there. Anyhow, there she was. And it was Christ who took the first step, and opened this famous incident. He did it by throwing himself upon her courtesy, and asking something from her, **Give me a drink.**

There is no shadow of doubt that what draws most people to him is not so much what he gives as that he asks. Many have no great appetite for the spiritual, for the deep things of God he offers us. But it does move them that he looks to them to help him, and throws himself frankly on their assistance, offering them a share in his tremendous enterprise. And not a few do hear the call, do thrill to it, and to the measure of their ability do respond. There results a winsome but shallow Christianity which does not reach the deeps nor surge out of the deeps. It is the type which in the main is being offered Christ today.

Yet shallow or not, it looks as if it might pass muster at that judgment seat where the tests are to be so uncomfortably practical and homely, better than some other kinds that seem by far more profound and deeply rooted. What did you do for the down-and-outs? For the needy? For the lonely? "Inasmuch as ye have done it unto one of the least of these my brethren" (Matt. 25:40), I accept it from you gratefully, as a personal kindness shown to very me. So that we too can hold our pitcher to Christ's lips, make him less tired, be helpful to him.

Buddha, shocked one day at coming on a grumpy and cantankerous brother, left unattended in an attack of dysentery, cleaned up the mess with his own hands and lovingly waited on the man, and the next day he told the others with a grieved heart how they had failed, and added, "Always remember that what you do for helpless folk I take as kindness done to me."

8. ***No Unnecessary Miracles.***—But this too is to be noted, that whereas in ch. 6 we are given the strange story of the feeding of five thousand people, Christ made no use of his powers to meet his own requirements or those of his friends. If and when they were hungry, they had to go and seek food, and pay for it in the usual way. We need not fancy that Christ will do for us what with a little ordinary pains and trouble we can and should do for ourselves. Yet many expect him to lift them, miraculously and without effort on their own part, to the goal, and are chagrined to find that the entire long road must be traveled, foot by foot, and one step at a time. Thus, for example, they imagine that he will enable them to become experts in prayer for the mere wishing, and without themselves giving the time and thought and pains to it which they would devote as a matter of course to the learning of a language or the growing proficient in a game. But though the Holy Spirit is the Comforter—which is a strong, not a soft title—the Friend in need, who can brace us in every possible way and according to our ever-varying requirements, he will not spoil or mollycoddle us. And Christ will not use his powers to make good what is lacking to us only because of our own crass laziness and nothing more.

9 Then saith the woman of Samaria unto him, How is it that thou, being a Jew, askest drink of me, which am a woman of Samaria? for the Jews have no dealings with the Samaritans.

10 Jesus answered and said unto her, If thou knewest the gift of God, and who it is that saith to thee, Give me to drink; thou wouldest have asked of him, and he would have given thee living water.

11 The woman saith unto him, Sir, thou hast nothing to draw with, and the well is deep: from whence then hast thou that living water?

into the city to buy food. 9 The Samaritan
woman said to him, "How is it that you, a
Jew, ask a drink of me, a woman of Sa-
ma'ri-a?" For Jews have no dealings with
Samaritans. 10 Jesus answered her, "If you
knew the gift of God, and who it is that is
saying to you, 'Give me a drink,' you would
have asked him, and he would have given
you living water." 11 The woman said to
him, "Sir, you have nothing to draw with,
and the well is deep; where do you get that

The dialogue that follows conforms to a pattern frequent in chs. 3, 4, and 6, and is paralleled in Mark 7:15-23 and 8:15-20. J. H. Bernard (*A Critical and Exegetical Commentary on the Gospel According to St. John* [New York: Charles Scribner's Sons, 1929; "International Critical Commentary"], I, cxi-cxii) compares six instances of this pattern: John 3:3-9; 4:10-15, 32-39; 6:27-41, 41-48, 51-60. In each of these discourses Jesus utters a profound saying which is misunderstood. The misunderstanding is expressed in a stupid question to which Jesus replies with a slightly modified repetition of the saying before explaining and applying its meaning. **Living water** is understood to mean running water, as opposed to rain water. The woman understands this as a slight upon the gift of the patriarch who had this well sunk centuries before. Jesus replies that the water of which she is thinking can assuage only bodily thirst, and then explains that he refers to a spiritual gift. This is (*a*) a direct **gift of God** (vs. 10); (*b*) the **living,** i.e., "true" to type, "eternal," spiritual water; (*c*) a spontaneous energy of unfailing interior grace (vs. 14). The **gift of God** (*a*) is Jesus Christ himself. Water, as a symbol of the satisfaction of man's highest need, is a frequent metaphor in the O.T. (cf. Pss. 23:2; 36:9; 42:1-2; 65:10; Isa. 12:3; 44:3; 55:1-2). God himself is "the fountain of living waters" (Jer. 2:13).

9-10. *The Pathos of the Lost.*—Simple though it was, the woman was a little taken aback by Christ's request (vs. 7). **For Jews have no dealings with Samaritans.** And our Lord, looking pityingly at this faded creature so avid for what she took to be a vivid and colorful life, yet with only this drab tashed thing to show for it, said, "If you knew who I am and what I can give, it is you who would be asking me for living water." **If you knew!** How much of the pathos and the tragedy of lives innumerable lies in that little phrase! If they knew! But they do not know; in Christ's kindly words they are lost, have strayed, have missed their way, go blundering blindly into foolishness. If only they had a sane standard of values and could see things as they are! If they knew how unsatisfying are the world's best and biggest gifts, and how fleeting, seen and gone, could they be duped and fooled into paying down their life only for that? If they knew where that road they are taking ends, by the swine troughs, and among the trampled mud, in that gnawing hunger and that loneliness and that envy of the very pigs, could they go swinging down it so jauntily, whistling as they go, and feeling big and manly because they have cut the apron strings that tied them, and are free men at last? If they knew how rich and splendid and exciting is the life in Christ, could they ignore and despise it as they do? But they neither know nor suspect, imagine they are clever and far seeing, and—like the traders in *Vanity Fair,* who thought that men who had no interest in their paltry wares were plainly crazy—they dismiss those who choose spiritual things as soft or thin-blooded, and indeed contemptible. If they knew, if they had a sane standard of values, if they saw things as they are!

11-14. *A Great Claim.*—Naturally enough, the woman could not see how this confessedly thirsty stranger sitting there with never a pitcher could possibly give her water from a deep well; and perhaps with a flicker of the old archness of long ago she attempted to rally him as one talking boastfully or without meaning. To which Christ answered; **Every**

12 Art thou greater than our father Jacob, which gave us the well, and drank thereof himself, and his children, and his cattle?

13 Jesus answered and said unto her, Whosoever drinketh of this water shall thirst again:

14 But whosoever drinketh of the water that I shall give him shall never thirst; but the water that I shall give him shall be in him a well of water springing up into everlasting life.

15 The woman saith unto him, Sir, give me this water, that I thirst not, neither come hither to draw.

living water? 12 Are you greater than our
father Jacob, who gave us the well, and
drank from it himself, and his sons, and
his cattle?" 13 Jesus said to her, "Every one
who drinks of this water will thirst again,
14 but whoever drinks of the water that I
shall give him will never thirst; the water
that I shall give him will become in him
a spring of water welling up to eternal
life." 15 The woman said to him, "Sir, give
me this water, that I may not thirst, nor
come here to draw."

Wisdom is described as "a stream from a river" (Ecclus. 24:30), and Philo, in a passage which comes near to the saying of the Johannine Christ, writes: "The man who is capable of running swiftly it bids stay not to draw breath but press forward to the most high divine Logos, who is the fountain of Wisdom, in order that he may draw from the flowing stream and, instead of death, find life eternal as his prize" (*On Flight* XVIII. 97). That **living water** (*b*) is equivalent to "the real water" is seen by the synonymous expressions "the living bread" (6:51), "the bread of life" (6:35, 48), and "the real bread" (6:32). The evangelist, or an editor, interprets this water as "the Spirit, which those who believed in him were to receive" (7:39). This spiritual gift, like the "real bread" (6:32), brings eternal satisfaction. The gift of God is Christ (*c*); the gift of Christ is the Spirit, that "other Counselor," who "dwells with you, and will be in you" (14:16-17). This indwelling Spirit, creative and energizing, not only brings back to the memory of his disciples "words of eternal life," but also becomes in them a self-renewing force constantly ensuring fellowship with Jesus Christ, whom to know is life eternal (cf. 17:3)—**a spring of water welling up to eternal life** (cf. 7:38). Vs. 15 shows that the woman has not yet grasped the hidden meaning.

---

one who drinks of this water will thirst again, but whoever drinks of the water that I shall give him will never thirst. That is a bold claim—to be able permanently to satisfy a soul. But Christ makes it constantly and with assurance.

In one sense, indeed, what he does in us is to arouse a yearning that is unappeasable. "All my stock of Christ is some hunger for Him," declared Samuel Rutherford.[3] Incited by Christ, we stretch out our hands, and they find and grasp and hold, yet still keep reaching out farther and farther. Every new achievement forms the starting point of new endeavor. However much we have been given, always there is infinitely more ahead. Did not the men of the N.T. really gain their faith in their own immortality by having it brought home to them that, marvelous as were the unbelievable possessions they had already gained in Christ, these did not exhaust his grace to them, but were a mere foretaste of the fullness of his kindness toward them; and that eternity itself would not bring them to the end of that?

But there is no growing tired of Christ, no thought of seeking elsewhere for a fuller satisfaction than he gives. Whoso lives with Christ and in Christ has in his heart **a spring of water** perennial and inexhaustible; a peace that passes understanding; a joy deeper and more real than any other joy; a life far more abundant than anyone else can know; a power that can meet every call upon it—a perpetual fountain, clear and clean, cooling and refreshing.

15. *The Danger of Christ's Lesser Gifts.*—Still understanding too prosaically, the woman responds eagerly enough, feeling that if there were any kind of truth in the odd things this man was saying, here was a possible end to her perpetual daily trudges through the glare of the hot sunshine, and to her weary carrying of heavy waterpots. **Sir, give me this water, that I may not thirst, nor come here to draw.** We are inclined, unfairly, wonderingly, to despise her for the obtuse literalness of her interpreta-

[3] *Letters* (Edinburgh and London: Oliphant, Anderson & Ferrier, 1891), Letter LXXXI, p. 169.

16 Jesus saith unto her, Go, call thy husband, and come hither.

17 The woman answered and said, I have no husband. Jesus said unto her, Thou hast well said, I have no husband:

18 For thou hast had five husbands; and he whom thou now hast is not thy husband: in that saidst thou truly.

16 Jesus said to her, "Go, call your husband, and come here." 17 The woman answered him, "I have no husband." Jesus said to her, "You are right in saying, 'I have no husband'; 18 for you have had five husbands, and he whom you now have is not your husband; this you said truly."

16-24. The transition to the next stage in the dialogue is made by a favorite Johannine device to evoke a recognition of Jesus' supernatural knowledge (cf. 1:42, 48; 2:24–3:2). For this reason it is futile to ask how our Lord knew the details of this woman's private life. It is not less futile to try to find an allegorical significance in the mention of the **five husbands.** Since the time of D. F. Strauss many commentators have seen here an allusion to the five deities worshiped by the five nations which were settled in Samaria from Babylon after the Assyrians had destroyed the northern kingdom (II Kings 17:24-34; Josephus *Antiquities* IX. 14. 3). But these gods were seven, not five; they were worshiped together, not in succession; Yahweh, whom the Samaritans were

tion, and for the crude materialism of the interests that alone seem to appeal to her. But as a generation have we the right so to do? For if we face the facts, must not we, with our far fuller knowledge of Christ's aims and offers, range ourselves along with her, as being in the same condemnation?

Again and again Christ was plainly disappointed that people, eager enough for his physical cures and material benefits, had so little appetite for and interest in the spiritual gifts he offered them, and which he knew to be so vastly more worth while. "You seek me for the loaves and the fishes," he once said sadly (6:26). Or on another occasion it was as though he said, "Your only interest in me is that you think I might be a judge and divider, redistributing material things, and giving you a bigger share in them" (Luke 12:13-14). And is not that precisely the mood of the hour? We are hugely interested in the by-products of Christianity—and they are most important—but in Christianity itself scarcely at all. If Christ can help us to bring in a new social order; if he can give us shorter hours, and bigger wages, and better houses, and such like amenities, ah! these things are real and solid and substantial; and we will gladly work with him, and under him, for them. But those spiritual nebulosities of which he speaks—who wants them? And what would one do with them? And what better would we be for them? We believe, as Barth says, in a civilization of things; Christ believes in a civilization of persons.[4] A man's life, Christ assures us, consists not of the abundance of the things that he possesses (Luke 12:15). But we hold that it does, that most certainly it surely does. Give us more things, and still more things, and we shall have a full and ample life. That is the leading axiom of the day. Even Bertrand Russell, found unexpectedly among the prophets, protests that that confident assumption of the leaders of the popular movements that are impressing men's minds that the most important thing in a man's life is the size of his income, and that the sure road to happiness is for him to find means to increase it, is an insulting libel upon human nature and a palpable untruth:

> I believe this involves too passive a conception of what constitutes happiness. It is true that, in the industrial world, large sections of the population are too poor to have any possibility of a good life; but it is not true that a good life will come of itself with a diminution of poverty. Very few of the well-to-do classes have a good life at present, and perhaps socialism would only substitute the evils which now afflict the more prosperous in place of the evils resulting from destitution.[5]

16-23. ***How Religiosity Can Choke Religion.*** —And so Christ brought the woman sharply up against the facts of her own life, facts which might have told her that something more is needed than a mere change in circumstance or in environment. **Go, call your husband, and come here.** She hesitated, but answered honestly enough, so far as it went. But when Christ pressed her further, she, feeling that things were growing much too searching and uncom-

[4] Cf., "Let a civilization of the spirit take the place of a civilization of things" in Karl Barth, *The Word of God and the Word of Man,* tr. Douglas Horton (Boston: The Pilgrim Press, 1928), p. 160.

[5] *Principles of Social Reconstruction* (London: George Allen & Unwin, 1916), p. 130.

19 The woman saith unto him, Sir, I perceive that thou art a prophet.
20 Our fathers worshipped in this mountain; and ye say, that in Jerusalem is the place where men ought to worship.
21 Jesus saith unto her, Woman, believe me, the hour cometh, when ye shall neither in this mountain, nor yet at Jerusalem, worship the Father.

19 The woman said to him, "Sir, I perceive that you are a prophet.
20 Our fathers worshiped on this mountain; and you say that in Jerusalem is the place where men ought to worship."
21 Jesus said to her, "Woman, believe me, the hour is coming when neither on this mountain nor in Jerusalem will you worship the Father.

---

now worshiping, would not be represented as an irregular lover living in adulterous union with the Samaritan community. The writer is concerned only to elicit from the woman an acknowledgment that Jesus is a prophet, and a question to open up a dialogue about true worship.

The burning question discussed between Jews and Samaritans was about the divinely appointed site for the central worship and sacrifice of the religion of Israel. The quarrel started with the building of a temple on Mount Gerizim as a rival to the temple at Jerusalem, but it had been destroyed by John Hyrcanus in 128 B.C. As we have already seen, the Samaritans could point to passages in the Pentateuch which gave them a strong case over against Jerusalem. G. F. Moore (*Judaism* [Cambridge: Harvard University Press, 1927], I, 25-26) seems to favor the reading "Gerizim" in the Samaritan Pentateuch at Deut. 27:4, and to regard the reading "Ebal" both here and at Josh. 8:30 in the Jewish text as a defensive textual corruption. Shechem was one of the most venerable religious sites in the land, with its patriarchal associations. It was here that after the conquest Joshua had made the final covenant with the people, "and set them a statute and an ordinance in Shechem. . . . And [he] took a great stone, and set it up there under an oak, that was by the sanctuary of the LORD" (Josh. 24:25-26). The Samaritan Pentateuch also, immediately after the Decalogue (Exod. 20:17; Deut. 5:21), has a command to erect great stones on Mount Gerizim, and to build an altar to the Lord and offer sacrifices upon it. But most scholars regard this as a tendentious addition to the original Hebrew text. In the time of our Lord both Jews and Samaritans firmly believed that their own form of the text was the right one, and the vested interests on either side were fiercely defended. The woman states the case and appeals to the "prophet" for a decision (vs. 20).

The sublime answer of Jesus lifts the conception of true worship far above the rival claims of local cults. Yet at first sight this declaration of the "pure, universal love" of the Father, drawing to him true spiritual worshipers, seems to be mingled with Jewish sectarianism. To avoid this contradiction in terms some expositors have interpreted **you worship** (vs. 22) as applying to Jews and Samaritans, and **we worship** as referring to Christ and the Christian religion. But the last part of the verse forbids this interpretation. Others regard either the whole of vs. 22, or else its last clause, as a gloss. But it is unlikely that a later scribe would attribute salvation to the Jews in an age when the breach between church and synagogue was complete. It seems better, then, to take the successive verses as they stand. In vs. 21 Jesus accepts the role of prophet and declares that the hour will soon strike to usher in the new age of the messianic kingdom. When that time comes, this woman and her compatriots will know a higher order of worship than the national rites of Mount Gerizim or Mount Zion. They will know God in his universal fatherhood, and will worship him accordingly.

In Judaism (vs. 22), with its fuller revelation through the prophets, some hints of this worthier ideal have already been proclaimed. Thus Solomon's prayer at the dedication of the temple (I Kings 8:27) asked: "But will God indeed dwell on the earth? behold, the heaven and heaven of heavens cannot contain thee; how much less this house that I have builded?" So in the closing chapter of Isaiah (66:1-2) the Lord deprecates the building of a house for him to dwell in, whose throne is the heaven. Rather, "to this

22 Ye worship ye know not what: we know what we worship; for salvation is of the Jews.
23 But the hour cometh, and now is, when the true worshippers shall worship

22 You worship what you do not know;
we worship what we know, for salvation
is from the Jews. 23 But the hour is com-
ing, and now is, when the true worshipers

---

man will I look, even to him that is poor and of a contrite spirit, and trembleth at my word." The same chapter closes with a description of the assembling at "my holy mountain Jerusalem" of "all your brethren . . . out of all nations" for "an offering unto the LORD" (Isa. 66:18-23). Even more striking is the message of the last of the prophetic books: "For, from the rising of the sun even unto the going down of the same, my name shall be great among the Gentiles; and in every place incense shall be offered unto my name, and a pure offering" (Mal. 1:11). The Samaritans rejected all of the O.T. except the Pentateuch. Further, the evangelist must have intended to convey the thought that he who was Messiah and incarnate Word, and was bringing salvation to the world, was sprung from Israel (cf. Rom. 9:3-5). It is true that "he came to his own home, and his own people received him not" (1:11). But it was among the Jews that he found some who were "waiting for the consolation of Israel" (Luke 2:25), and they received him, and from them came his first disciples and apostles. The eschatological **hour** (vs. 23) has brought the dawn of the day of the Lord. The men of Samaria will soon be flocking to hear the good news from Jesus the Christ. Possibly there is also a veiled reference to the mission of Philip, when numbers of Samaritans were to receive the Christian gospel. But the reference widens out at this point, and true worship is required from all who recognize the true nature of God.

God is spirit (vs. 24): This is one of the three Johannine affirmations about the divine nature; cf. I John 1:5; 4:8: "God is light," "God is love." This conception is

---

fortable, tried cleverly to escape by starting a discussion about sects and religions—hers and his.

Newman maintains that it is quite a common thing for people to use their religion as a shield between them and God. That was what this woman was attempting. And many do it successfully. They may be keen churchgoers, immersed in church affairs, diligent among the organizations of the congregation, interested in its services and sermons, well versed in doctrines and theology; and yet with no more than a theoretical knowledge that never brings them into any vital relationship to God, and indeed makes it harder for them to break through to him and reach him. It is possible to know about Christ so well that, satisfied with that, we never come to know him; possible to haunt the holy place, and bustle about its precincts, yet catch no vision of the Holy One.

Christ, not to be deflected by side issues, answers briefly, if pointedly, and passes on to the epoch-making pronouncement in vss. 23-24.

23. *The Worshipers God Wants.*—That is an arresting phrase which our Lord uses, **For such the Father seeks to worship him;** such eager, ardent, expectant souls, on tiptoe for his coming, and sure that he will come; and, coming, do exceeding abundantly above all that they can ask or think. God, says Christ, wants such worshipers, is always seeking for such worshipers. Even when we are apathetic and half-hearted, only partially attentive, dully putting through a formal weekly routine, or very little more, God, with huge liberality in his heart and vast gifts in his hands, is searching for those who will accept them, and allow him to save them, help them, hearten them.

The central fact in a time of worship is not that we are seeking God, but that he is seeking us. Often he contrives to find means of breaking in to us. "Ready was I to answer men who never asked me, ready to be found by men who never sought me. I cried out, 'Here am I,' to folk who never called to me. . . . Ere ever they call to me, I answer, and while they speak I hear" (Isa. 65:1, 24 Moffatt).

But when God's willingness to give is met by responsive and receptive hearts; when what the liturgical experts call the descending type of service in which God comes to our aid with all the grace that we can need, intermingles with the ascending type, in which man climbs and reaches out toward God in adoration and thanksgiving, in confession and intercession and petition, with eager hearts that long for him and watch for him—things happen.

Barth, after speaking of the expectancy with

the Father in spirit and in truth: for the Father seeketh such to worship him.

24 God *is* a Spirit: and they that worship him must worship *him* in spirit and in truth.

will worship the Father in spirit and truth, for such the Father seeks to worship him.
24 God is Spirit, and those who worship him must worship in spirit and truth."

---

common to Jewish and to Greek thought. Isa 31:3 brings out the Hebraic opposition between flesh and spirit. Yet in relation to the conditions of worship more than this is implied. Moore (*Judaism* [Cambridge: Harvard University Press, 1927], I, 223) warns us against a possible confusion of thought: "The principle that God cannot be seen in any natural object nor imaged by man's hands in any likeness is frequently called a doctrine of the 'spirituality' of God. If 'spirit' were taken in the biblical sense, there would be no other objection to the phrase than its abstractness; but in modern use spirit is the contrary of matter, and 'spiritual' equivalent to 'immaterial.' In this sense the spirituality of God is a philosophical theory derived from the Greeks, not a doctrine of Judaism in biblical times or thereafter, any more than Jewish monotheism is a doctrine of the unity of God in the metaphysical sense." The main thought here is that the highest part of man's nature should be attuned to God, who is spirit, and that his worship must be based upon the reality of the God whom he approaches in devotion. The sense of the divine reality arises from God's own initiative. He it is who seeks such worshipers, and bestows the spirit of truth.

---

which the people should assemble in the house of God, says that they are met by an expectancy greater than their own.

> The Bible is expectant of people who have eyes to see what eye hath not seen, and ears to hear what ear hath not heard, and hearts to understand what hath not entered into the heart of man. . . . *God* expects, *God* seeks, such people. The expectancy brought to the situation by the congregation, intense as it may be, is in truth small and insignificant in comparison to that expectancy which comes from the side of the open Bible. If the awakening of the people is significant and striking, it is so only in the light of what God expects there. The reason the human expectancy is to be taken seriously is because it is an adumbration of the great expectancy with which God arrives first upon the scene.[6]

24. ***Reality in Worship.***—Really to worship, one must get past the symbols to the realities they typify, and of which they are meant to remind us; past conventions and the formal or thoughtless putting through of the accepted rites in the accepted manner, to an open vision of God, breathlessly real and near, or at least to a sure knowledge that whether we see and feel it or do not, he is here, in this place now, and we are in his presence, and he is stooping to listen and take action, *is* taking action upon our behalf, if we will give his gracious purposes toward us a chance to mature.

How worship can most fully become spiritual varies from case to case. For some the presence of God is most evident in and through a type of service pruned to a lean and naked austerity, in which there is nothing to distract the mind, or to catch and hold the eyes, or to tempt one to lose oneself in merely secondary and auxiliary things, and so miss the ending end of worship. As Browning says:

> I then, in ignorance and weakness,
> Taking God's help, have attained to think
> My heart does best to receive in meekness
> That mode of worship, as most to his mind,
> Where earthly aids being cast behind,
> His All in All appears serene
> With the thinnest human veil between.[7]

But others feel that every gate must be thrown wide open that the King of glory may come in; that every art ought to be brought to the service of the Creator, and that he can make appeal to us through every sense that he has granted us. And so they heap up majesty on majesty, and even pomp on pomp.

Well, there are twelve gates into the holy city, and they all really lead into it. But a wise man will choose that one among them which brings him surest and quickest and deepest into the presence of the King. For worship is not worship unless our spirit holds communion with him who is Spirit, face to face, and—what is far more essential—unless he in his divine condescension stoops to us with the lovingkindness his wisdom sees we need.

[6] *The Word of God and the Word of Man*, tr. Douglas Horton (Boston: The Pilgrim Press, 1928), pp. 121-22. Used by permission.

[7] "Christmas-Eve," st. xxii.

25 The woman saith unto him, I know
that Messias cometh, which is called Christ:
when he is come, he will tell us all things.
26 Jesus saith unto her, I that speak
unto thee am *he*.
27 ¶ And upon this came his disciples,
and marveled that he talked with the wom-

25 The woman said to him, "I know that
Messiah is coming (he who is called
Christ); when he comes, he will show us
all things." 26 Jesus said to her, "I who
speak to you am he."
27 Just then his disciples came. They

25-26. The woman's rejoinder is not an evasion, but rather an acknowledgment that this thorny question will be settled finally when the Messiah, expected by both Jew and Samaritan, comes to **show us all things.** From the Samaritan literature of a later period it seems that there was an expectation of such a Messiah, called in their language *Tā'ēbh* ("he who returns"). As they did not accept the prophetical books with their wealth of messianic prediction, the Samaritans probably based their hopes on the fulfillment of Deut. 18:15, for they looked for a second but inferior Moses, who would be a prophet, but at the same time a temporal conqueror and king. It may have been a pretender to this title who promised to recover the sacred vessels which Moses had buried on Mount Gerizim, and whose rising was ruthlessly repressed by Pilate (Josephus *Antiquities* XVIII. 4. 1). This remark by the woman opens the way for the announcement by Jesus, **I who speak to you am he.** This self-revelation contrasts with the secrecy about this claim which Jesus observed according to the Synoptic Gospels. Lagrange explains this by pointing out that the danger of a messianic revolt in Samaria was far less than in Galilee. Others regard this whole narrative as colored by the remembrance of the first Christian mission beyond Judaism (Acts 8:4-25). As elsewhere, John regards the earthly mission of our Lord in the light of the later recognition of his nature and person.

H. Jesus, the Disciples, and the Samaritans (4:27-42)

27-30. On their return the disciples **marveled that he was talking with a woman,** not because of her nationality, nor of her character. There is a rabbinical saying, "A man

---

25-26. *Christ's Confidence in Unlikely People.* —The woman was impressed, and looked at Christ, and looked again; and a half thought began to gather and form in her mind. This man with his clear-sighted eyes that looked so deep and saw so far was certainly a prophet, that was sure; but might he not be something even more? **I know,** she said—surely speaking slowly and almost hesitatingly, and all the time watching his face—**that Messiah is coming . . . ; when he comes, he will show us all things.** And Christ said, **I . . . am he.**

Which was a clearer revelation of himself than he had as yet granted anyone. And it was made to one faded failure of a soul! But then all history is full of instances of how Christ often feels that he can trust himself far farther to some most unlikely-looking people than he can to the mass of us. There was once a giddy-headed youth, a man about town, playing the fool, likely to go straight to the devil, you and I would have said. But Christ, looking at him, felt that he could trust him, and gave him such a knowledge of himself that the lad became Francis of Assisi. Or he looked at the brutal captain of a villainous slave ship, of all people! "I can open my whole heart to this man," he felt; and did so in such measure that John Newton, in his experience and in his preaching and in his hymns, waded far farther into the deeps of the gospel than most of us can. And with this woman, too, Christ's daring justified itself. At least more than half convinced, and so excited that she left her waterpot, she ran for the town and panted out her story to the men, no doubt lounging in the shadows during the noontide heat. "Can this be the Christ?" (Vs. 20.) She was a most unlikely person to bring any authentic tidings about the matters of which she was talking, but she impressed them enough to make them stream out through the glare to see for themselves if there was anything in it (cf. vs. 39).

27. *What Woman Owes to Christ.*—There is a suggestive addendum to the story in this verse, where we are told that the disciples marveled that Christ was talking to a woman, which no rabbi would have done without breaking the regulations by which his life was ruled. Rabbinical religion was not happy in its treatment of woman; nor was it singular in that. For do not all the main faiths of the world

an: yet no man said, What seekest thou? or,
Why talkest thou with her?
28 The woman then left her waterpot,
and went her way into the city, and saith
to the men,
29 Come, see a man, which told me all
things that ever I did: is not this the
Christ?
30 Then they went out of the city, and
came unto him.
31 ¶ In the mean while his disciples
prayed him, saying, Master, eat.

marveled that he was talking with a wom-
an, but none said, "What do you wish?"
or, "Why are you talking with her?" 28 So
the woman left her water jar, and went
away into the city, and said to the people,
29 "Come, see a man who told me all that
I ever did. Can this be the Christ?" 30 They
went out of the city and were coming to
him.
31 Meanwhile the disciples besought

---

should hold no conversation with a woman in the street, not even with his own wife, still less with any other woman, lest men should gossip" (Strack and Billerbeck, *Kommentar zum N.T. aus Talmud und Midrasch,* II, 438). But the disciples wisely kept their surprise to themselves. Now that the conversation is interrupted, the woman leaves Jesus and reports to the citizens of the neighboring town her suspicion that the stranger is the Messiah. She leaves her water jar (ὑδρία) beside the well, since to carry it full on her head would prevent speed. She interprets the insight of Jesus as a sign that he is a prophet. Can he be the prophet par excellence, the Messiah? She conveys enough of his deep impression on her to the townspeople to bring them in a troop to the well.

31-38. Meanwhile a conversation goes on between Jesus and his disciples. Jesus declines an offer of food with the cryptic saying, **I have food to eat of which you do not**

---

stumble sadly there? Perhaps nowhere was woman's status worthier than in ancient Egypt. Confucianism has many glories; but it left woman more depressed than it found her. Mohammed did something for her; but the whole trend of his thinking was that she is a much inferior creation to a man. The Hindu longs for a son; but the birth of a daughter is a very second-rate affair. There are notable woman philosophers in the Upanishads, and at the start of Buddhism there was a remarkable woman's movement; wherein, bursting out of the stuffiness of their cramped life, they entered freely into many spheres as teachers, philosophers, and much else—and often rose to eminence in them. But that glory faded. And Buddha himself was not enthusiastic on some aspects of the movement. Indeed, while some of his sayings on woman are wise and noble, he seems to have regarded her in the main as a dangerous creature, to be watched with vigilant care. Thus he advised Ananda to keep out of their company as much as possible, and, if he had to meet one, to be sure to "keep wide awake."[8] In Christ's own day it was being debated in the schools whether woman had a soul at all or not. And in the paganism around him, the horrid figures of the numbers of female infants exposed at the father's whim reveal how little woman, as woman, was regarded—though individual women were admired and honored. A. W. Verral wrote bluntly that its low conception of woman was one of the main diseases from which pagan civilization died. Compared to all that, the sheer sanity and cleanness of Christ's thinking about woman are extraordinary, and not the least of his glories. So remarkable was it that even yet his people, who made a fine start in this matter, have not climbed up into the fullness of it.

It was Christ who gave woman her chance, who saw her possibilities, who discovered her value. And as a sex she has repaid him with a loyalty of devotion that has had illimitable consequences. So long as the mothers are Christian, there is not much to fear. But if they too in the mass should give themselves to selfishness and worldliness and pleasure-seeking, what would become of the next generation, and of the church it ought to form in its day?

It was Christ who discovered and emphasized the worth of woman. It was Christ who lifted her into equality with man: not, indeed, into sameness of duty, for nature itself precludes that. Yet as Paul has it, in Christ there is neither male nor female in the sense that both alike are dear to God, and both alike are called to the service of the kingdom, and both alike can and should reach the same lofty spiritual goals.

31-38. ***Certain of Christ's Characteristics.***—Meantime the disciples had arrived back with

[8] *Dialogues of the Buddha,* tr. T. W. and C. A. F. Rhys Davids (London: Oxford University Press, 1910), II, 154.

32 But he said unto them, I have meat to eat that ye know not of.

33 Therefore said the disciples one to another, Hath any man brought him *aught* to eat?

34 Jesus saith unto them, My meat is to do the will of him that sent me, and to finish his work.

him, saying, "Rabbi, eat."
32 But he said to them, "I have food to eat of which you do not know."
33 So the disciples said to one another, "Has any one brought him food?"
34 Jesus said to them, "My food is to do the will of him who sent me, and to

---

know. The disciples as usual take these words literally. In explaining their deeper meaning, Jesus then utters a series of sayings in which it is not easy to trace the connection of thought. A paraphrase is therefore offered: "My real food consists in carrying out to the end the purpose for which my Father sent me into the world. You have a saying, 'Four months to harvest.' As you look on these whitening fields, you see that harvest is close at hand. There is another harvest approaching, swifter than any that you have known. It is a spiritual harvest. There, too, sower and reaper has each his appointed toil. The reaper is now to receive his wages and to gather the harvest to eternal life. The sower shares in his joy, for he now knows that his own labor has not been in vain. Their kinds of work are distinct, as your proverb has it, 'One sows, another reaps.' It is into this harvest field that I am sending you as reapers. The first fruits of Samaria are already waiting to be gathered. You must not congratulate yourselves that the garnered crops will stand to your credit alone. There would be no harvest for you to reap if others had not sown the grain."

My food (vs. 34) recalls our Lord's answer to the first challenge of the tempter in the wilderness (Matt. 4:4; Luke 4:4). Three phrases in this verse represent three of the

---

the food they had been seeking, and urged Christ to eat. But he would not. **I have food to eat of which you do not know,** he said; and again, **My food is to do the will of him who sent me, and to accomplish his work.** About which three things may be said:

First, the unreckoning generosity with which Christ used his life. There is, no doubt, a very real exhilaration in spiritual work, especially if it is being crowned with a measure of visible success. This can be deceptive to the point of danger. For the nervous strain is severe; and one is using up one's capital of strength and vigor. And so full were Christ's days that it makes one tired even to read of them. Mark's rapid narrative brings home vividly to the mind how endless were the appeals that kept breaking in to him. And every one of these importunate applicants felt that his case was all-important and must be attended to, whatever else was set aside. And always—sometimes without waiting for the end of the plea—Christ was up and on his feet, and "Let us go at once," he said, and went; to the consternation of the disciples, who felt that he was wearing himself out before the time. Almost never was there any respite. He said, "Come ye yourselves apart into a desert place, and rest a while" (Mark 6:31). Yet there was to be no resting. For the crowds surged into their privacy. And Christ, laying aside his planned retreat, spent himself willingly and eagerly to meet their clamorous needs. We too have a will of God to live out; and a work that he has given us to do. But we are grudging and niggardly with our lives; and claiming large margins of time for ourselves, dole out small bittocks of them to God and our fellows—like William Law's Flavia, who if asked for something for the church will, if she likes the person, toss him half a crown or so, "and tell him if he knew what a long milliner's bill she had just received, he would think it a great deal for her to give."[9] To be allowed to serve God and his fellow men was all Christ asked from life. And a Christian is a man who has caught something of his spirit, and is growing up into his likeness.

Second, there is the hopefulness so characteristic of Jesus Christ; his certainty that in the same world as God anything is possible, and the best is the likeliest. A handful of Greeks ask to see him, and before his eyes there rises a whole world golden and heavy with the harvest. The seventy return, excited over their successes. It was a very little dent they had made in the solid mass of evil; but Christ was exultant over it. "I was watching Satan toppling from heaven," he told them (Luke 10:18). A trapped partisan was dying in agony, and turned to his fellow sufferer with a strange but dim and inchoate half faith. And the cloud that

[9] *Serious Call to a Devout and Holy Life,* ch. vii.

35 Say not ye, There are yet four months, and *then* cometh harvest? behold, I say unto you, Lift up your eyes, and look on the fields; for they are white already to harvest.

36 And he that reapeth receiveth wages, and gathereth fruit unto life eternal: that both he that soweth and he that reapeth may rejoice together.

accomplish his work. 35 Do you not say,
'There are yet four months, then comes
the harvest'? I tell you, lift up your eyes,
and see how the fields are already white
for harvest. 36 He who reaps receives wages,
and gathers fruit for eternal life, so that
sower and reaper may rejoice together.

leading ideas of this Gospel. **To do the will** of the Father (cf. 5:30; 6:38; 14:31) is also a watchword in the Epistle to the Hebrews (10:6-10), where Ps. 40 is cited to explain the true nature of the sacrifice of Christ. **Of him who sent me** is a designation of God used on the lips of Jesus twenty-five times in John, with other variations of the verb, which all emphasize the mission of the Son in the world. **To accomplish his work** (cf. 5:36; 9:4; 17:4; 19:28), an aim that reaches its triumphant culmination in the cry from the cross, "It is finished" (19:30).

The proverbial saying in vs. 35 was probably current in Galilee, where to this day the sowing is often delayed till the end of December and the harvest is reaped at the beginning of May. It has sometimes been erroneously inferred that we have here a chronological datum for the length of our Lord's ministry. The proverb emphasized the interval between sowing and reaping. Jesus was looking at the waving fields of wheat and barley in the rich plain of Mahneh, already ripening for the sickle, and this suggests the imminent harvest of souls in the neighboring town, though the sowing has been so recent. Note the contrast between **yet four months,** and **already white for harvest.** For the

had been brooding heavily above the Master cleared from his spirit; and he died with the shout of a conqueror, "It is finished; it is working, and will work." A faded woman who has made a mess of life half believes in him, and persuades her neighbors to judge of him for themselves; and as he watches them approaching, Christ feels that summer is breaking in before the time.

Contrast that with the gloom and dejection too often met with in the pulpit and in the religious press and in the minds of many Christian people. Epictetus has a witty portrait of a so-called philosopher he knew, a melancholy creature, as depressed and hangdog in his mind as his own drooping mustache. "He does not look like a conqueror to me," he said.[1] Or Nietzsche of us Christian folk, "I will never believe in the Christian Redeemer until they show me that they themselves have been redeemed." Jesus Christ really believed in God and in the faith; and used large standards of measurement for what might be expected from them. Do we?

Third, there is that saying how some have the glory of the harvest, and some the labor of sowing barren fields that keep looking no less barren for all that we can do. Yet the one is no less needed than the other. And in the end sower and reaper will rejoice together. There is a message from the Master to those who are discouraged because their lot has been cast in a day when more than usual spiritual things are neglected and unpopular, and are impatiently pushed aside as irrelevancies that get in the way of real and practical progress. The laborious plodding up and down the furrows in the bleakness of winter, and the patient sowing in the spring, though for long months not even one blade will show through to encourage one, are every whit as vital, if there is to be a harvest, as the creaking of the laden carts on their way to the bulging stackyards.

> There have been long periods of the Church's history when there were no revivals, and no Christian work but that of the steady teaching and preaching of the truth, and (what is vastly more important) the influences of Christian personalities, and the deep and well-nigh irresistible stream of the training and love of the home. . . . With the majority of men development is slow. It is accomplished in the unrecorded, unromantic work of the home or the class-room or the study, . . . without struggle or passion or tragedy,

says George Steven,[2] and the facts are with him. If a man has been called to such quiet, undramatic work, let him fulfill his task with loyalty and thoroughness; well assured that his labor is

[1] *Discourses* IV. 11. 25-30.

[2] *The Psychology of the Christian Soul* (New York: Hodder & Stoughton, 1911), pp. 26-27, 28.

37 And herein is that saying true, One soweth, and another reapeth.

38 I sent you to reap that whereon ye bestowed no labor: other men labored, and ye are entered into their labors.

39 ¶ And many of the Samaritans of that city believed on him for the saying of the woman, which testified, He told me all that ever I did.

37 For here the saying holds true, 'One
sows and another reaps.' 38 I sent you to
reap that for which you did not labor; others have labored, and you have entered into their labor."

39 Many Samaritans from that city believed in him because of the woman's testimony, "He told me all that I ever did."

---

evangelist these words and those which follow have a wider and deeper reference. The language is eschatological. The kingdom of God is at hand. In the O.T., harvest is the figure under which the judgment that is to usher in that great event is represented. In the Synoptic setting Jesus was preaching the gospel of the kingdom, and when he saw the crowds he said to his disciples, "The harvest is plentiful, but the laborers are few; pray therefore the Lord of the harvest to send out laborers into his harvest" (Matt. 9:35-38). C. H. Dodd (*The Parables of the Kingdom* [New York: Charles Scribner's Sons, 1936], pp. 175-87) has argued that the three parables of the seed growing secretly, the sower, and the tares, all illustrate in various ways the coming of the kingdom of God in the ministry of Jesus, under the figure of harvest. In John, as in Matthew and Luke, Jesus is sending his disciples, not to sow, but to reap. They are to gather **fruit for eternal life** (vs. 36), which is the Johannine equivalent for the kingdom of God. Vs. 38 recalls Matt. 11:13; Luke 16:16, the prophets who "prophesied until John," after whom "the good news of the kingdom of God is preached, and every one enters it violently." In this eschatological harvest that marks the coming of Jesus and the mission of his disciples there is an eternal "now," in which the separation of sower and reaper is lost in the common joy of harvest.

39-42. These verses resume the narrative interrupted after vs. 30. Our attention now turns from the disciples to the Samaritans. They illustrate two types of faith. An

---

not in vain in the Lord, though it may look as if it were, and that if not his own hands, then other hands will gather a rich harvest from what he has sown.

Here too is a warning to those who have a full tide running strongly beneath them, and sweeping them to triumphs and successes that are denied to many. Yours is the easier task, which needs a steady head indeed, but calls for far less faith and courage than is asked of those who work on and see nothing. Yet it was they who sowed what you now reap; and to them very largely falls the credit of your harvest.

39-42. ***Why People Believe in Christ.***—Some, like these Samaritans, because while they themselves have not as yet had personal experience of him, they credit and accept the emphatic and unhesitating witness concerning him of others who have had that firsthand knowledge of him, and so have the right to an opinion on him and his claims (cf. vss. 46-54).

Most of those who are Christians are so not because with panting effort they have hacked a slow laborious way to a hard-won faith through a jungle of doubts and intellectual difficulties and the like, but simply because those whom they trusted believed in Christ, declared they had made proof of him and had found him entirely dependable; and so hearing, their own faces turned naturally in Christ's direction, and with them too he had his chance and took it.

To dismiss that attitude of mind as blind credulity is senseless. In every department of life one must and does so act habitually. No one individual has the capacity to test things for himself in every sphere. In most of them he must accept, and does accept, the findings of the experts, of those who have knowledge which he does not have, and who have made experiments he cannot make. So here, for a start. It is mere common sense to assume that, say, the men chosen to represent their country in any game know that game better than the mass of us who may be interested in it but do not actually play it; or that the saints, the people who know Christ and who live with him, can give us the most authentic information about him.

Hence the immense importance of the church, and the hugeness of the debt we owe it. Had we been thrown purely upon our own resources, upon the puny efforts of our single

40 So when the Samaritans were come unto him, they besought him that he would tarry with them: and he abode there two days.
41 And many more believed because of his own word;

40 So when the Samaritans came to him, they asked him to stay with them; and he stayed there two days.
41 And many more

invitation to stay in that town is given by a group whose faith rests on the unsupported testimony of the woman, **He told me all that I ever did.** After a stay of two days, Jesus received the believing trust of many more, who were first attracted to him by the woman's witness, but went on to test his words for themselves until they could make their confession of faith. The avowal that Jesus **is indeed the Savior of the world** may be the evangelist's own adaptation to Christian ends of a title that was widely used in the Hellenistic cults of the contemporary world, and which also in the imperial cult was applied to Roman emperors. But the word **Savior** was a title often given to God in the O.T. (Isa. 43:3, 11), and the removal of national conceptions of worship (vss. 21-24) would inevitably lead on to the recognition that God's saviorhood is universal. The woman had learned from Jesus his claim to be Messiah. Jesus had transcended the distinction between Samaritan and Jewish conceptions of messiahship. John represents Jesus as saying to the Samaritans

and unaided mind, how thin and inadequate our conception of Christ would have inevitably been. But we are born into an enormous inheritance in Christ, slowly and painfully won for us by the church, by others generously sharing with us what they themselves have found. Had the church not adopted and authorized the Gospels, would we have known of Christ at all, save in the dimmest fashion? And how the meanest of us now can profit from the daring experiments in Christ, and the marvelous experiences through Christ, of intrepid pioneers like Paul all down the Christian centuries! Other men labored; and we have entered into their labors. My faith comes to me, not through my individual effort, but largely as a gift bestowed on me by others who made it possible, imperative, inevitable. J. A. Moehler, the Roman Catholic, writing of Calvin and his conception of the church, says that "he had not overlooked the fact that the idea of a Christian as an independent, all-sufficing being, capable from the fulness of his own spirit of satisfying all his higher wants, is a mere fiction, which all experience belies." [3] And indeed the reformers laid emphatic stress on the privilege and advantage of being in the visible church, even though as yet one might not belong to the real church of God at all. For to associate with those who know him, to breathe that atmosphere, to be constantly played upon by these gracious influences, makes it far more likely that one will come to meet God, and to close with him, and be really his.

For in order to be vital, faith must be much more than a mere credence given to tidings blown to us from other lives; must be something by far more personal and individual and practical than that. The Roman Catholic Church, really defining faith as intellectual assent, declares that by itself faith is not nearly enough. And on that definition of it, it certainly is not. But the reformers think of faith as something very different, as a reckless banking on the truth of what Christ says, and as an intrepid testing of it where the pinch lies for each of us. Inevitably that involves initial risk; for we are staking everything on what has not been proved as yet in our experience. But such risk cannot be avoided. "Do not think, try," as Hunter, the scientist, used to keep urging on his pupils. Only through such trying can one reach assurance, one way or the other. As to Jesus Christ, the thing justifies itself, and at an ever-quickening pace. A little while, and we are walking no longer by pure faith but almost by sight; or at least with much to hearten and encourage us, visibly and obviously there. No longer do we simply believe: in part at least, we know. Ours has become firsthand evidence, culled from our own experience. And as Pringle-Pattison insisted, "No supposed result of speculative theory can override a certainty based on direct experience"; and again, "In no sphere of our experience is the implication of objectivity —the 'truth-claim' as it has been called—more insistent, one might say more overwhelming, than just in the moral and religious life." [4]

A miner once interrupted John Hutton when he was preaching, by leaping to his feet and leading the whole congregation in the doxology.

[3] *Symbolism*, p. 341.

[4] *The Idea of God* (Oxford: Clarendon Press, 1920), p. 252.

42 And said unto the woman, Now we
believe, not because of thy saying: for we
have heard *him* ourselves, and know that
this is indeed the Christ, the Saviour of the
world.
43 ¶ Now after two days he departed
thence, and went into Galilee.

believed because of his word. 42 They said
to the woman, "It is no longer because of
your words that we believe, for we have
heard for ourselves, and we know that this
is indeed the Savior of the world."
43 After the two days he departed to

---

what has been affirmed in the report of the dialogue with Nicodemus, and the comments made upon it (3:16-17; cf. I John 4:14).

J. Jesus, the Galileans, and the Officer's Son (4:43-54)

43-45. The journey to Galilee (vs. 3) is now resumed. It is, however, difficult to see the point of the saying in vs. 44 in this context. The proverb is quoted in similar form in all four Gospels (Mark 6:4; Matt. 13:57; Luke 4:24), and in an expanded form in the sayings of Jesus found at Oxyrhynchus in 1897, "A prophet is not acceptable in his own country, neither does a physician work cures upon those who know him." In all the Synoptics the words are our Lord's comment upon his rejection by his unbelieving fellow townsmen. Here the Galileans welcome Jesus because of all that they have seen him do in Jerusalem during the feast. The words may have been inserted at this point in the narrative because they were spoken in Galilee, and probably in Nazareth, according to the common tradition. But John seems to have changed the meaning of **his own country** and applied it to Jerusalem, the city of the Messiah, the place of the final rejection (cf. 1:11, "He came to his own home, and his own people received him not").

Later he explained that he had been a Christian only for some months, and that it was all so gloriously different that he could not sit still in his place. For, said he, "I was a bad lot; I drank; I pawned the furniture; I knocked my wife about; and now life is real life, and splendidly worth while." Asked how he fared among his fellows down the pit, he laughed and replied, "Today they asked me, 'You don't seriously credit that old yarn about Jesus turning the water into wine?' " To which, it appeared, he had made the devastating answer, "I know nothing about water and wine, but I know this, that in my house Christ has turned beer into furniture; and that is a good enough miracle for me!"

Those who really believe in Christ do so because they can say, "But it happened to me; and unless you are prepared to set me down as a consummate liar, you will have to think things out again." "We are not *living* members of the external Church, until we belong to the interior one," says J. A. Moehler. "What hath been imparted to us from without, must be reproduced by and within us; the objective must become subjective, ere we be entitled to consider ourselves true members of the Christian Church."[5] "And many more believed because of his own word; and said unto the woman, Now we believe, not because of thy saying: for we have heard him ourselves, and know that this is indeed the Christ, the Saviour of the world" (vss. 41-42). Assuredly he does heal; because from this and this he has healed me. I know he is the Savior, because through him I am saved. Beyond all question he does raise men up to a newness of life. How do I know it? Because "my name is Lazarus, and I live." "There is nothing more real than what comes in religion. To compare facts such as these with what is given to us in outward existence, would be to trifle with the subject. The man, who demands a reality more solid than that of the religious consciousness, seeks he does not know what."[6]

43-54. ***An Object Lesson on How to Pray.***—The transition (vss. 43-46) is puzzling. Many, not without reason, regard this story as merely another version of that told us even more vividly in Matt. 8. Among those who do not, it seems to be the custom somewhat to belittle this official in comparison with that bluff centurion whose servant was healed and whose robust faith so impressed the Master. But that is less than fair. We are expressly told that Christ was astonished by the daring and hardihood of the soldier's attitude to him: and said roundly that in his entire experience of men it stood out unique and alone; that hungry though he was to meet with faith, such faith as this amazed him; that he had not expected

[5] *Symbolism*, p. 336.

[6] F. H. Bradley, *Appearance and Reality* (New York: The Macmillan Co., 1897), p. 449.

44 For Jesus himself testified, that a prophet hath no honor in his own country.

45 Then when he was come into Galilee, the Galileans received him, having seen all the things that he did at Jerusalem at the feast: for they also went unto the feast.

46 So Jesus came again into Cana of Galilee, where he made the water wine. And there was a certain nobleman, whose son was sick at Capernaum.

Galilee. 44 For Jesus himself testified that a prophet has no honor in his own country.
45 So when he came to Galilee, the Galileans welcomed him, having seen all that he had done in Jerusalem at the feast, for they too had gone to the feast.

46 So he came again to Cana in Galilee, where he had made the water wine. And at Ca-per'na-um there was an official whose

46-54. The story of the healing of the officer's son seems to be a variant tradition of the episode of the centurion's servant told by Matthew and Luke from a source other than Mark. A comparison of Matt. 8:5-13 and Luke 7:1-10 shows that even in the Synoptic tradition there are slight divergences. But the common matter is that when Jesus had entered Capernaum, a centurion asked him to heal his paralyzed servant, but begged him not to come to his house, as he was unworthy of such honor; he knew the military principle of delegated authority, so that a word spoken by Jesus at a distance would effect the cure. Whereupon Jesus declared that he had not met with such faith in Israel. The differences are that Matthew speaks of a boy (the Greek word παῖς might mean either son or servant), while Luke uses the regular word for servant or slave (δοῦλος). Matthew speaks of the centurion as coming to Jesus in person. In Luke he

it, and did not get it. Against that shining but trying background anyone else must look somewhat dwarfed. But as Bunyan has it, not all the king's servants, though real and loyal in their allegiance, can be the king's champions. And one can have an impressive faith without attaining to the topmost pinnacle of it. Surely a candid reading of his story makes it clear that this officer's faith also was noteworthy and remarkable, and a humbling rebuke to most of us.

He was a man of importance in that countryside, living a busy life. But his laddie was desperately ill, seemed to be dying; and he could think of nothing except how the boy might even yet be saved. Strange rumors about one Jesus of Nazareth were blowing to and fro. They sounded incredible. And yet there might be something in them. There was a chance of that at least. It was worth trying; better that than sitting still, watching that life so precious to him drifting out. So he set off to search for Christ, and came upon him at Cana, some twenty-five miles from his own home town of Capernaum.

Immediately he reaches him, he blurts out his eager plea. The answer he receives is not encouraging, sounds chilly and detached from the man's heartache, coldly unsympathetic. But if Dods is right about the meaning of the puzzling vss. 1-3, that difficulty vanishes. Christ had withdrawn from Judea because he found himself surrounded by a growing popularity which was largely the result of misapprehension as to his aims, and which was awakening such a hot resentment in official religious circles as boded ill for his mission at this early stage. **A prophet has no honor in his own country.** And in Galilee there was little likelihood of such noisy public demonstrations as were becoming common in the south. And so to Galilee he went.

But there he found an even more unhappy situation. For many of the Galileans had been in Jerusalem at the feast, and had been mightily impressed and flattered by the sensation which their countryman had created there. They had never themselves seen much in him. But the capital had taken him really seriously, and made no end of a fuss about him; and so they looked at him with new eyes, the capital's eyes. And thus he found himself surrounded by a constant buzzing of excitement and empty enthusiasm. They kept flocking to him; they gaped at him; they listened to him, not seeking for some word from God, but only because they must hear the man of whom people were talking, and not be left out of whatever was going on; they hung about, waiting for him to do some of these queer things of which they had heard. It was, at most and best, mere local pride in the man of the hour, their man: it was not faith, had nothing spiritual in it. And it hurt Christ. So when this new claimant burst in to him with his request, and no doubt the others present gathered nearer, feeling that now something would happen, Christ, sad and disappointed, said, **Unless you see signs and**

47 When he heard that Jesus was come out of Judea into Galilee, he went unto him, and besought him that he would come down, and heal his son: for he was at the point of death.

48 Then said Jesus unto him, Except ye see signs and wonders, ye will not believe.

49 The nobleman saith unto him, Sir, come down ere my child die.

50 Jesus saith unto him, Go thy way; thy son liveth. And the man believed the word that Jesus had spoken unto him, and he went his way.

son was ill. 47 When he heard that Jesus
had come from Judea to Galilee, he went
and begged him to come down and heal
his son, for he was at the point of death.
48 Jesus therefore said to him, "Unless you
see signs and wonders you will not believe."
49 The official said to him, "Sir, come down
before my child dies." 50 Jesus said to him,
"Go; your son will live." The man believed
the word that Jesus spoke to him and went

---

sends elders of the Jews to plead with Jesus, and then as Jesus and the elders draw near to the house, he sends other friends deprecating Jesus' personal entry. Matthew speaks of paralysis; Luke says merely that the servant was at the point of death. Matthew closes the story with the words, "And to the centurion Jesus said, 'Go; be it done for you as you have believed.' And the servant was healed at that very moment." Luke simply tells us: "And when those who had been sent returned to the house, they found the slave well." In the Johannine version of the story Jesus was at Cana, and a king's officer, whose son was ill, hearing at Capernaum **that Jesus had come from Judea to Galilee, . . . went and begged him to come down and heal his son, for he was at the point of death.** Instead of commending his faith, Jesus said to him, **Unless you see signs and wonders you will not believe.** But he added, **Go; your son will live.** The man went away believing the promise and was met by his servants who told him, **Yesterday at the seventh hour the fever left him,** the very time when Jesus assured him of the boy's recovery. The man and all his

---

wonders you will not believe. That, he implied, was all they seemed to care about. But when the father cried out, "I don't want any signs or any wonders! But my boy is dying! Come, help, before it is too late!" Christ's heart ran out to him. "Your lad will live," he said.

And the amazing thing is that the man credited it, and was entirely satisfied, and at once went his way, with his heart and mind at rest, implicitly believing that what Christ had promised would assuredly come true. Most of us would have been hurt and indignant, feeling that our trouble was not being taken seriously, and that this casual offhandedness was nothing less than a wounding insult. "Go and wash in Jordan seven times," said Elisha to Naaman, in that extraordinarily human story; and the great man was angry. "Behold, I thought, He will surely come out to me, and stand, and call on the name of the LORD his God, and strike his hand over the place, and recover the leper. . . . So he turned and went away in a rage" (II Kings 5:10-12). "Come down," this officer had pleaded. It was a long way—twenty-five miles or more—and it was asking a good deal of Christ. But he was a big man in that countryside. And in any case, important or not, his need was desperate, and calling aloud for vital remedies. He had thought Christ would go home with him, and pray to God over the boy, and lay his hand on him, would do something visible, tangible, worth while. And to be dismissed with a word was too cavalier. Yet no such thought entered the man's mind. At once, entirely content and reassured, he went his way, and did not even hurry home; there was no longer need for that, nor any reason for further anxiety. So that when sudden improvement plucked the lad back from death to an obvious recovery, and the servants were sent to tell the father the glad news, they came upon him next day still far from home, apparently going about his ordinary duties with a completely easy mind.

That seems to me an amazing faith that may well shame the puny thing we call ours. The promises given us concerning prayer are staggering. And in their fullness they have not worked out in the experience of most of us. What we have received is wonderful. Yet it looks thin and meager compared to what we are confidently told will come of it—and does come, given any chance! It is no doubt extraordinarily difficult for us to know when to pray the prayer of bold petition that knocks, and keeps knocking, and will not desist; and when to pray with much more diffidence, and willing to be taught

51 And as he was now going down, his servants met him, and told *him*, saying, Thy son liveth.

52 Then inquired he of them the hour when he began to amend. And they said unto him, Yesterday at the seventh hour the fever left him.

53 So the father knew that *it was* at the same hour, in the which Jesus said unto him, Thy son liveth: and himself believed, and his whole house.

54 This *is* again the second miracle *that* Jesus did, when he was come out of Judea into Galilee.

his way.
51 As he was going down, his servants met him and told him that his son was living.
52 So he asked them the hour when he began to mend, and they said to him, "Yesterday at the seventh hour the fever left him."
53 The father knew that was the hour when Jesus had said to him, "Your son will live"; and he himself believed, and all his household.
54 This was now the second sign that Jesus did when he had come from Judea to Galilee.

---

household became believers. Whereas Matthew writes "boy" John says **son** (υἱός). John's term **official,** "king's officer" (βασιλικός), would suit the position of a Roman centurion in the service of Herod the tetrarch. John agrees with Luke in saying that the boy was at the point of death, but speaks of a fever, thus disagreeing with Matthew as to the nature of the illness. It may well be that the words of rebuke were addressed to the bystanders, for the verbs are in the plural, **Unless *you* see . . . *you* will not believe;** and this recalls sayings reported in the Synoptics (cf. Mark 8:11-12; Matt. 16:1-4; Luke 11:29) condemning the sign-seeking Jews. The man himself accepted the word of Jesus with faith. The **sign** followed when his servants informed him that the turn for the better was noticed at the very hour (one o'clock) when Jesus announced his recovery. Credence (vs. 50) now becomes faith (vs. 53). For the second time a miracle is recorded as having been wrought in Galilee after a journey from Judea (vs. 54). No detailed account is given of those which took place in Jerusalem (vs. 45; 2:23).

---

of God, and ready to withdraw our request if it grows clear to us that it is not his will—what is called the prayer of resignation or of "suspended desires." Yet if we prayed believingly, as this man did; and if, having prayed, we went our way sure that God has heard us and will stand to his word, what would there not result? "Whatever you ask in prayer, believe that you receive it, and you will" (Mark 11:24). So Christ himself assures us. But as things are with us, how often the answers to our prayers must have come and knocked for entrance on a locked door that did not open! Because we never imagined anything would really result; and prayed merely because it is the thing to do, and without hope or expectation. In *Grace Abounding* Bunyan sets down as one of the seven abominations still extant in his heart that he had not watched for the answers to his prayers. And Wilson, in the *Sacra Privata,* declares only too truly that it is a monstrous discourtesy to ask a man for a favor, and then turn away, not waiting for his answer. And yet continually we treat God with such shocking rudeness, and so doing, cheat ourselves out of how much that he had eagerly sent to us!

As to how the cure was effected, modern medicine of course constantly uses suggestion, etc., to produce very remarkable and blessed results in many types of illness. But always, I suppose, or at least practically so, patient and physician are face to face. Yet present-day science seems to claim that one mind can influence and tell upon another even at a distance; in some cases with surprising outcomes. Years ago Arthur James Balfour, the British prime minister, wrote confidently:

> Who is there, reflecting on the mental epidemics which may afflict a whole generation, on the eager subservience commonly shown to the fashion of the hour, on the swaying humours of a crowd, on the overwhelming waves of national emotion, on the influence silently, even unconsciously, exercised by certain individuals, . . . who is not haunted by the suspicion that something more is happening between human souls than even the most admirable system of external signalling will wholly account for? . . . Consciously or unconsciously we are all . . . capable of telepathically affecting others.[7]

The Buddhists, or most of them, have no prayer; but the devout among them practice

[7] *Theism and Thought* (New York: George H. Doran Co., 1924), pp. 246, 202.

5 After this there was a feast of the Jews; and Jesus went up to Jerusalem.
2 Now there is at Jerusalem by the sheep *market* a pool, which is called in the Hebrew tongue Bethesda, having five porches.

5 After this there was a feast of the Jews, and Jesus went up to Jerusalem.
2 Now there is in Jerusalem by the sheep gate a pool, in Hebrew called Beth-za'tha,[g]

[g] Other ancient authorities read *Bethesda,* others *Bethsaida.*

IV. Signs and Controversies (5:1–9:11)

A. Cure of the Cripple at Bethzatha. The Sabbath Controversy (5:1-18)

5:1. The journey to Jerusalem and the events described in this chapter are thought by many scholars to find their proper order after the events recorded in ch. 6 (see pp. 446, 459-60). In that case the feast referred to here was the Passover (cf. 6:4). **A feast of the Jews** is indefinite and contrary to Johannine usage in mentioning these festivals (cf. 2:23; 6:4; 7:2; 11:55; 13:1). Evidence from MSS is divided between this reading and "the feast of the Jews." If the latter reading is correct, and if ch. 5 is in its right position, then the feast would mean the feast of Tabernacles. Pentecost is more likely.

2-5. The right text is probably "Now there is in Jerusalem by the sheep pool [a place] called in Aramaic Bethesda, having five porticoes." RSV follows a reading **by the sheep gate a pool, in Hebrew called Bethzatha.** In either case a noun must be supplied. "Sheep gate" is suggested by Neh. 3:1, 32; 12:39. But the pool would not be called a house (*bêth*). Recent excavations below the ruins of the basilica of St. Anne, a little to the north of the temple site, have disclosed a large trapezium-

a daily exercise, the Brahma-Viharas. Primarily this is a species of moral hygiene whereby one cleanses his own nature from humors that ought not to be there, so expediting one's own moral progress. But certain modern Buddhist scholars assert with confidence that there is more in it than that; and are emphatic that when these people are thinking of all sufferers the whole world over they are not only fortifying their own hearts to meet the suffering that must inevitably come to them in turn, but are exercising a species of televolition on behalf of present sufferers, are putting their own wills alongside these others to buttress and rally and steady them, and so bring them through with honor. And so with the other classes of men over whom they brood. That seems not only a seemly and a gracious exercise but a practical one as well, likely to have results. But if these things are so, given a personality like Jesus Christ, how likely it grows that he even at a distance could rally and inspire to the new effort that meant life and health, a tired and spent boy who had lost heart and stopped trying!

5:1-9*a*. *Christ's Real Difficulty With Us.*—Had you been in Jerusalem when Christ was there, where would you have looked for him? An obvious answer is the temple. Yet almost the first place I would have tried would have been the porches at Bethzatha, with their pathetic crowd of broken humanity. Surely it was like him to be there; and once there, how characteristically he acted. For he did not cure some rich neurotic woman, whose ailment was the outcome of sheer ennui through having nothing much to do; so winning a cheap reputation and an easy fame. With resolution he threaded his way through that mass of suffering to the most desperate case in the whole place, and "If my powers cannot avail for this man here," he practically said, "then there is nothing in them." But there is! He proved it then; and he keeps proving it day after day in souls innumerable whose plight is desperate, and who have lost all hope until he comes. For it is hope that most people need; a new hope that will arouse them from the lethargy of a dull, crushed acceptance of what they are, as the one thing now possible; a realization that their case has not been finally closed, and that the issue for them has not been already definitely decided. It is so easy to accept the gospel as a theory; to have never a doubt as to its truth in other lives, and with the right kind of people. But we say we are not of the type to whom it can happen; and we do not really expect it will. One must be reasonable even toward Jesus Christ, we tell ourselves, and not ask obvious impossibilities from him. And so, Christ or no Christ, we remain what we are, and settle down in that as the only thing left us to do. **Rise, take up your pallet and walk,** said Christ. That was the very thing that the man could not do, except pitifully, stumblingly; the very thing he

3 In these lay a great multitude of impotent folk, of blind, halt, withered, waiting for the moving of the water.

4 For an angel went down at a certain season into the pool, and troubled the water: whosoever then first after the troubling of the water stepped in was made whole of whatsoever disease he had.

5 And a certain man was there, which had an infirmity thirty and eight years.

which has five porticoes. 3 In these lay a
multitude of invalids, blind, lame, paralyzed.[h] 5 One man was there, who had been

[h] Other ancient authorities insert, wholly or in part, *waiting for the moving of the water;* [4] *for an angel of the Lord went down at certain seasons into the pool, and troubled the water: whoever stepped in first after the troubling of the water was healed of whatever disease he had.*

---

shaped double pool divided in the middle by a broad wall. This corresponds to the description—given by Origen early in the third century, and a century later by the Bordeaux Pilgrim and by Cyril of Jerusalem—of the sheep pool with four porticoes surrounding it and a fifth in the middle. Remains of pillars and balustrades further support the identification, and votive inscriptions suggest that ancient superstition ascribed healing virtue to the water. The early variant "Bethzatha" is probably due to confusion with Bethzetha, the name of the northern suburb, according to Josephus *Jewish War* II. 15. 5; 19. 4; V. 4. 2; 5. 8. Bethsaida is perhaps a corruption due to confusion with the well-known town in Galilee. After vs. 3 words are added in some later and less reliable MSS (see KJV; RSV mg.), preserving a fragment of folklore. The disturbance of the water caused by an intermittent spring was in primitive times attributed to the action of a local divinity. Jewish superstition substituted an angel, and healing virtue was supposed to cure the first to bathe in the pool after this movement of the water. The comment (vs. 4) was inserted later to explain the man's answer (vs. 7).

---

had been trying to do for years past counting now, without any success. But looking at Christ, he found that he could do it. Thus, when we are asked impatiently, even irritably, "But how does Christ help? What difference does he make?" here is an indication of what happens. Of itself our will won't will what we know it ought to will; of itself our heart won't choose what we really wish it to choose: As Peer Gynt has it, "Think of it—wish it done—*will* it to boot,—but *do* it—! No: that is past my understanding!"[8] And yet, looking at Christ, somehow we find that we can do what we have always failed to do, can be what we could never be, can master what has consistently baffled us, can reach and grip and hold and use what had been utterly beyond us. The scriptures are crowded with impressive and even staggering promises that seek to bring home to our dull minds that no one is beyond the reach of Christ's helping hand. But this dramatic picture of it, this symbol and proof of it, sets it before the mind with a vividness that words cannot do.

Christ's opening question, **Do you want to be healed?** takes us aback, sounds curiously callous, even cruel. The poor soul had been there for eight and thirty years—a bleak and wintry life indeed! And every day he had tried, hirpling desperately on his impotent feet and useless limbs, to reach the pool, and sometimes almost made it. A little more, a very little more and—but no! For always someone else, with friendly hands to help him, pushed past him, or in the jostle he was brushed aside. And once more he had to crawl back to the too-familiar place where he had lain so long. And all this every day for eight and thirty years, some fourteen thousand times in all! And Christ stood and looked down at him and asked, "Would you like to be healed?" "Would I like! I, shut into this horrible, living death! I, who know nothing of real life in its glamour and its fullness. I, who day after day see someone joyously escaping back to that! For always they keep coming: and always they keep going: but always, always, I am left behind. And you ask, Would I like to be made whole!"

Yet Christ stands to his question, and puts it to all of us. For his real difficulty with us, what hampers his gracious purposes toward us, lies precisely there. We hear his promises, and our hearts run out to them and claim them. And we believe that we mean what we say. Yet this has happened time on time, with some of us for far longer than thirty-eight years; and this is all we are, and this all that has come of it! And why? Because we do not really want what we say that we want and think that we want. "Men often mistake their imagination for their heart; and they believe they are converted as soon as they think of being con-

[8] Henrik Ibsen, *Peer Gynt*, Act III, scene 1.

6 When Jesus saw him lie, and knew that he had been now a long time *in that case,* he saith unto him, Wilt thou be made whole?

7 The impotent man answered him, Sir, I have no man, when the water is troubled, to put me into the pool: but while I am coming, another steppeth down before me.

8 Jesus saith unto him, Rise, take up thy bed, and walk.

9 And immediately the man was made whole, and took up his bed, and walked: and on the same day was the sabbath.

ill for thirty-eight years. 6 When Jesus saw
him and knew that he had been lying there
a long time, he said to him, "Do you want
to be healed?" 7 The sick man answered
him, "Sir, I have no man to put me into
the pool when the water is troubled, and
while I am going another steps down be-
fore me." 8 Jesus said to him, "Rise, take
up your pallet, and walk." 9 And at once
the man was healed, and he took up his
pallet and walked.

6-16. The account of the cure has points of resemblance with the story of the paralytic in Mark 2:1-12. The command **Rise, take up your pallet, and walk,** and the result, **He took up his pallet and walked,** are substantially common to both incidents. But whereas in the Marcan story it was the vicarious faith of the bearers which moved Jesus to his healing act, the lame man at Bethzatha was appealed to, **Do you want to be healed?** Possibly another connection is to be found in the relation between the physical and spiritual evil in both stories. In Mark, Jesus says to the paralytic, "My son, your sins are forgiven." In the Johannine story Jesus says afterward, **See, you are well! Sin no more, that nothing worse befall you** (vs. 14). On the other hand, in the Marcan story

---

verted."[9] Because, while Christlikeness at a little distance does attract us, on a nearer view of it we are not so sure. This, we feel, would make a sorry upset of our little comforts, and be something of a bore. So we drop what Christ has just put into our hands, and turn back to continue as we are, as on the whole the more to be preferred; like Augustine, finding again and again to his bewilderment that the life to which he was accustomed held him more than the life for which he really longed.

There was something to be said for the porches at Bethzatha. In time one grew accustomed to that way of putting in the days, came at last almost to like it. It was not unpleasant to lie there in the coolness of the shadow, while hale men, poor unfortunates, were toiling and perspiring out in the heat and glare. No doubt health is a great matter; yet, on the whole, this will do well enough for me. So, we can clearly see that Christlikeness is the gallant mode of living. But to secure it we have to pay down so much we value. Selfishness is, no doubt, a disease; yet it does bring us a bigger share of things than we could get without it. And temper is a childish ailment; but it pays. To be free of our noise and disagreeableness, folk give us what we wish. Do we want to be made whole? In theory of course, yes. But in reality and at the pinch, when we might gain it, we decide that the accustomed way of things will do. This is no idle or unnecessary question

[9] *The Thoughts of Blaise Pascal,* p. 307.

that Christ puts to us; but central, all-important, radical. And everything depends upon our answer.

9b*-15. *What Some of Us Cost Christ.—What manner of person was this man whom our Lord healed? If some appear to be captiously severe in their reading of him, nonetheless he seems to have been at best and most something of a poor creature. We are told that he had brought his long and fearsome disability upon himself by foolish excesses in his youth (vs. 14). Further, one gathers that there was little of winsomeness about him; or else surely, on occasion at least, someone would have paused to lend him a helping hand in his desperate struggles toward the pool. Everyone else had friends eager to assist them. But he was always left alone. It seems odd, and yet perhaps it was quite natural that in the excitement of his sudden and wholly unexpected cure he should have allowed Christ to slip away unthanked, and even without learning who his benefactor was. Perhaps it was even more natural that when, as he was joyously making his way out of the porches, at long last a healed man, he was roughly challenged for carrying his mat upon the sabbath, he should have answered, **The man who healed me said to me, "Take up your pallet, and walk";** so saying, not in the mean attempt of a badly frightened man to get himself out of trouble by throwing the blame on another, but rather stoutly replying, "The man who healed me told me to do this. And

10 ¶ The Jews therefore said unto him that was cured, It is the sabbath day: it is not lawful for thee to carry *thy* bed.

11 He answered them, He that made me whole, the same said unto me, Take up thy bed, and walk.

12 Then asked they him, What man is that which said unto thee, Take up thy bed, and walk?

13 And he that was healed wist not who it was: for Jesus had conveyed himself away, a multitude being in *that* place.

Now that day was the sabbath. **10** So the
Jews said to the man who was cured, "It
is the sabbath, it is not lawful for you to
carry your pallet." **11** But he answered
them, "The man who healed me said to
me, 'Take up your pallet, and walk.'"
12 They asked him, "Who is the man who
said to you, 'Take up your pallet, and
walk'?" **13** Now the man who had been
healed did not know who it was, for
Jesus had withdrawn, as there was a crowd

---

the paralytic was not healed on the sabbath. The dispute on that question arose from the plucking of the ears of corn and the healing of the man with the withered hand on the sabbath (Mark 2:23–3:6).

The question in vs. 6 was addressed to a cripple who after thirty-eight years might well have lost the desire to be sound. The warning (vs. 14) raises a difficult question. Later on (9:3) Jesus rejects the disciples' suggestion that a man's blindness was due to his parents' sin, although as he was born blind, his own sin could not be the cause (cf. Luke 13:1-5). Possibly the evangelist regards this as an instance of the insight of divine knowledge (cf. 1:42, 48; 2:24–3:2; 4:19, 29, 39), tracing the man's physical infirmity to his past sin (cf. Intro., p. 443). The **pallet** (κράβαττος) was the poor man's bed, a light and flexible mat which could easily be rolled up and carried. It was this act which provoked the censure of the Jews (i.e., the strict Pharisees who opposed Jesus), who gave a strict interpretation to Jer. 17:21; Neh. 13:19. In the Mishnah there is a list of thirty-nine works forbidden on the sabbath. Here it is allowed to carry a living man on a couch, since the couch is secondary, i.e., the bed is regarded as necessary for a man's conveyance. But to carry the bed itself is not permissible (see Danby, *The Mishnah,* p. 109; Strack and Billerbeck, *Kommentar zum N.T. aus Talmud und Midrasch,* II, 461).

---

what he says is good enough for me. If he had not said it, I should still be lying in my customary place, a useless hulk of a thing." For, though it sounds ugly, is there anything necessarily sinister in the fact that on learning who Jesus was he reported it to the authorities (vs. 15)? They had no doubt told him so to do. On the credit side of his account is the fact that he was in the temple; surely there, one hopes, to bless God for his recovery. Yet it is ominous that when Christ made time to seek for one who was not looking much, it seems, for him, and ultimately found him, it was to give him a solemn warning. Apparently Christ was less than sure that this misguided creature might not perversely twist awry the grace bestowed on him to his own further and fuller ruin; and given the chance, plunge back into his old follies. **See, you are well! Sin no more, that nothing worse befall you.** On which Marcus Dods says, with a stabbing succinctness, "There is, then, some worse consequence of sin than thirty-eight years' misery and uselessness."[1] In short, the man reveals himself as for the most part weak and stupid, with little in him to attract. Yet it was to benefit such a drab personality that Christ brought upon himself the open and declared hostility of the religious leaders. Not that they founded on this one isolated case alone. Vs. 16 makes it plain that it was an accumulation of such incidents that had upset and infuriated them. But it was over this man's case that the breach suddenly yawned wide open. And it was here that Christ's road turned sharply in the direction that led straight to Calvary.

Judging by human standards, the man was just not worth it. The price Christ paid to give him back his health was far too vast—immeasurably so.

But what about ourselves? For the furtherance of his own interests it looks sheer folly that Christ should ever have called us at all; and inexplicable that having given us our chance, and having learned how futile and undependable we are, he has not broken with us and dropped us. For we are poor advertisements for him, and must be stumbling blocks to others

[1] *The Gospel of John, Expositor's Greek Testament* (London: Hodder & Stoughton, 1897), I, 238.

14 Afterward Jesus findeth him in the temple, and said unto him, Behold, thou art made whole: sin no more, lest a worse thing come unto thee.

15 The man departed, and told the Jews that it was Jesus, which had made him whole.

16 And therefore did the Jews persecute Jesus, and sought to slay him, because he had done these things on the sabbath day.

17 ¶ But Jesus answered them, My Father worketh hitherto, and I work.

in the place. 14 Afterward, Jesus found
him in the temple, and said to him, "See,
you are well! Sin no more, that nothing
worse befall you." 15 The man went away
and told the Jews that it was Jesus who
had healed him. 16 And this was why the
Jews persecuted Jesus, because he did this
on the sabbath. 17 But Jesus answered them,
"My Father is working still, and I am

When the Jews discovered that Jesus was responsible for the man's breach of the sabbath law, they turned their attack upon him. The rabbis allowed necessary works of mercy on the sabbath, but the critics of Jesus felt that a man who had waited thirty-eight years for a cure might easily have waited till the following day (see on 7:23). The translation of RSV, as of KJV, fails to bring out the force of the imperfect tenses (ἐδίωκον . . . ἐποίει); it is rather, "This was why the Jews used to persecute Jesus, because he did things like this on the Sabbath" (Goodspeed).

17. It is clear from Mark 3:1-6 and Luke 14:1-6 that this (vs. 16) was a constant ground of complaint against Jesus, whose principle of action is stated here, **My Father is working still, and I am working.** The point of this reply lies in its relation to contemporary Jewish teaching. The sabbath rest was based upon the divine example (Gen. 2:1-3; Exod. 20:11; 31:17). Yet it was recognized that the living God must still be active. Two illustrations of this thought may be given. In the second century B.C. the story is told in the Letter of Aristeas (ch. 210) that when one of the translators of the Pentateuch was asked by King Ptolemy to tell him in what piety consisted, he replied: "In the belief that God is working in the Universe, and has knowledge of all things at all times, and that no unrighteous deed or evil action of man can escape his eyes; for as God is benefactor of the whole world, so wouldst thou, by imitating him, be void of offense." So also

---

rather than helps. For far from being open epistles, known and read of all men, proving Christ's power and efficiency beyond gainsaying, rather must our glib profession and our very ordinary, perhaps even shabby, characters demean and lower their conception of what a Christian is, and tempt them to conclude that there is not much in this thing. For they can see nothing in us that requires any explanation; and so assume that Christ can be safely neglected, since we with him seem in no way markedly different from themselves without him. "Have you taken the name of Christ on purpose to dishonour him?" asked Robert Leighton in a sermon. Long ago Clement of Alexandria set down vividly his bewilderment as to why Christ could want to do it, "The Lord pities, instructs, exhorts, admonishes, saves, shields, and of His bounty promises us the kingdom of heaven as a reward for learning; and the only advantage He reaps is, that we are saved."[2] He does not seem to get much out of his kindness toward us. It was not only on Calvary that we cost Christ dearly. We do so day by day. And yet unflinchingly he pays down the full price of our salvation, all he loses through it; and seems to count it well worth while.

16-19. ***Christ and Sabbath Observance.***—It was on the worthy keeping of the sabbath that there came the open clash between the authorities and Christ, and that same problem kept recurring, with an obstinate insistence, time on time. The rabbis had evolved an immense and complicated legislative code of minutely particularized regulations, designed to meet every possible situation in which one could find oneself. So that one had only to turn up the book of the words to find set down with exactness what one ought to do; what in these circumstances was permissible, and what was not. The thing had developed into a huge system of often monstrous casuistry. Thus it was solemnly debated in the schools whether a man with a wooden leg might walk on the sabbath at all or not. By no means, certain of the authorities maintained. For the leg is a burden he is carry-

[2] *Exhortation to the Heathen* I.

18 Therefore the Jews sought the more to kill him, because he not only had broken

working." 18 This was why the Jews sought all the more to kill him, because he not only broke the sabbath but also called

Philo wrote in the first century A.D.: "For God never leaves off making, but even as it is the property of fire to burn and of snow to chill, so it is the property of God to make: nay more so by far, inasmuch as He is to all besides the source of action. Excellently, moreover, does Moses say 'caused to rest' not 'rested'; for He causes to rest that which, though actually not in operation, is apparently making, but He Himself never ceases making" (*Allegorical Interpretation* I. 3; Loeb). To reconcile the thought of continuous divine activity with the texts in the Pentateuch the rabbis discriminated between God's

ing, and one may not carry burdens on the sabbath. Not so, held others. For the leg is no burden, but a part of the man. Such childishness and prosaic literalness Christ resented as utterly unworthy.

Always in considering his ethical teaching on any matter, we have to bear in mind that he was never interested in rules, and flatly refused to lay down rules. What he taught us was principles, a very different matter. Apparently what many people want, and think he should have given us, is a kind of railway timetable through life, in which every possible journey is detailed for us, and exact information furnished as to what we do at every stage of any we may have to take; where we change and where we sit still, and all the rest of it. And when, looking up the index of Christ's moral teaching to consult him on something about which they are keen—say, the ideal form of government—they find nothing definite upon this subject at all, nor even that heading, they fling down the book, declaring hotly that it is obsolete and out-of-date and of no manner of use in our modern world. And yet, any set of rules, constructed however cleverly for a particular day, must largely become out-of-date with the passing of that generation. But Christ's principles will last, unalterable, to the end of time. Only there is this to add, that loyalty to a principle means that it may have to be applied quite differently in differing situations. To keep it really, and in its spirit, one may have to break it in the letter. This of course involves us all, blundering and foolish as we are, in a grave risk. But Christ cannot spare us that responsibility. He offers us the Holy Spirit to counsel and guide us. But we ourselves have to apply his principles in the circumstances in which we are placed.

So here in this particular instance. Christ gloried in the sabbath as preserving the freedom of men, of necessity immersed in material things and living in a jam of mundane duties that must fill their minds. On the sabbath they can lift themselves up from their tasks, and straighten their stiff shoulders, and see past the cobwebs on the rafters of the workshop of life, and catch a glimpse of the eternal stars, and remember the big things that matter, and feel that they themselves are not machines but souls, and hold communion with the God in whose likeness they were fashioned. But human perversity can mistake the mere means for the end, and the helps to religion for religion itself; can twist this glorious thing, designed to free us for a little from the temporalities that might otherwise choke us, into a new type of slavery. "The sabbath was made for man," said Christ, "not man for the sabbath" (Mark 2:27).

Moreover, he is clear that not all God's demands on us are equally imperative. Some take precedence over others. The duty of kindness and of helpfulness is a much bigger thing than a meticulous sabbath observance. Hence, when he had cured that woman (Luke 13:10-16), bowed almost to the ground with "a spirit of infirmity for eighteen years," and the "ruler of the synagogue, indignant because Jesus had healed on the sabbath, said to the people, 'There are six days on which work ought to be done; come on those days and be healed, and not on the sabbath day,' . . . the Lord answered him, 'You hypocrites! Does not each of you on the sabbath untie his ox or his ass from the manger, and lead it away to water it? And ought not this woman, a daughter of Abraham whom Satan bound for eighteen years, be loosed from this bond on the sabbath day?' " And when he cured the man with the withered hand, "and they watched . . . whether he would heal . . . on the sabbath, so that they might accuse him, . . . he looked around at them with anger" (Mark 3:2-5). Men never forgot that look in his eyes. But nowhere does he take so high a line as here. Epictetus avers in a noble passage that once we realize our kinship with God, the sense of it forms a rule and standard for our lives. If God is faithful, we also must be faithful. If God is beneficent, we also must be beneficent, doing and saying whatever we do and say, in union with and

the sabbath, but said also that God was his Father, making himself equal with God.
19 Then answered Jesus and said unto
them, Verily, verily, I say unto you, The Son can do nothing of himself, but what

God his Father, making himself equal with God.
19 Jesus said to them, "Truly, truly, I

---

work as creator and as judge. He rests from physical work on the sabbath, but is externally active in works of judgment, condemning the wicked and conferring life. The answer of Jesus is that such works of healing are part of his mission as giver of life in fulfillment of the Father's will. The defense of works of healing on the sabbath is contained in the argument of 7:15-24, which may originally have followed immediately after ch. 5. Meanwhile, the Jews fasten upon the blasphemous claim to equality with God (vs. 18).

B. Unity of the Son with the Father as Giver of Life (5:19-47)

To this charge Jesus makes a formal reply (ἀπεκρίνατο instead of the informal ἀπεκρίθη). His words had been misinterpreted as a claim to independence of God, for

---

imitation of him.[3] And Jesus here declares with confidence that it is his realization of his kinship with God that causes him to act as he has done; that in healing on the sabbath, in his whole use of the day, in everything indeed, he is doing **what he sees the Father doing,** and following closely in the steps of the holy and loving God. For God knows no sabbath rest, works on uninterruptedly, weekday and sabbath day alike, spending himself unstintedly for his needy creatures (vs. 17).

Evidently our conceptions of God and of the heaven wherein he dwells, and of the type of life they have yonder, are still crude and rudimentary. Each of our human metaphors can only hint at one aspect of truths that are many-sided. When Milton tells us

> His state
> Is kingly: thousands at his bidding speed
> And post o'er land and ocean without rest,[4]

it is beyond question true. Yet by itself that calls up to the mind one served by countless multitudes, while himself sitting otiose and at ease upon his throne. Whereas, says Philo, God never stops working; for, as it is the property of fire to burn, and of snow to be cold, so of God to work. Francis Bacon quotes a strange pronouncement of Pythagoras, who, being asked by Hiero what was his function in life, replied that as people flock to the games from different motives, some to contend, and some to sell, and some to meet their friends and enjoy themselves, and some merely to look on, so he for his part was one of those who came to look on at life. And then Bacon adds the still more singular comment of his own, "But men must know that in this theatre of man's life it is reserved only for God and angels to be lookers on."[5] God, whose very being is a divine, unthinkable unselfishness; whom we see clearest and learn to know best on Calvary!

"There remaineth therefore a rest to the people of God," runs a much-befingered scripture (Heb. 4:9). And many a tired soul, just barely holding on and nothing more, looks forward to it keenly. And yet there is another side to the beyond. Browning once allowed a mood by no means characteristic of him, indeed the very opposite of that, to blow across his mind.

> There's a fancy some lean to and others hate—
> That, when this life is ended, begins
> New work for the soul in another state,
> . . . .
> Only the scale's to be changed, that's all.[6]

But for the moment he shrinks from that. When we have grown up and learned our lesson,

> The uses of labor are surely done;
> There remaineth a rest for the people of God;
> And I have had troubles enough, for one.[7]

Yet another scripture tells us that yonder his ministers are a flame of fire; and that their whole existence is an eagerness of happy and unselfish and untiring service (Heb. 1:7). **My Father is working still, and I am working,** said Christ. This that you resent in me means that I am using life in the heavenly way, and after God's own fashion.

19-29. ***The Tremendous Claims of Jesus Christ.***—For tremendous indeed they are! Looking back at them, and reading them in the light of all that he has done in and for the

[3] *Discourses* II. 14. 13.
[4] "On His Blindness."
[5] *Advancement of Learning,* VII. 1.
[6] "Old Pictures in Florence," st. xxi.
[7] *Ibid.,* st. xxii.

he seeth the Father do: for what things soever he doeth, these also doeth the Son likewise.

20 For the Father loveth the Son, and showeth him all things that himself doeth: and he will show him greater works than these, that ye may marvel.

21 For as the Father raiseth up the dead, and quickeneth *them;* even so the Son quickeneth whom he will.

22 For the Father judgeth no man, but hath committed all judgment unto the Son:

23 That all *men* should honor the Son, even as they honor the Father. He that honoreth not the Son honoreth not the Father which hath sent him.

say to you, the Son can do nothing of his
own accord, but only what he sees the
Father doing; for whatever he does, that
the Son does likewise. 20 For the Father
loves the Son, and shows him all that he
himself is doing; and greater works than
these will he show him, that you may mar-
vel. 21 For as the Father raises the dead
and gives them life, so also the Son gives
life to whom he will. 22 The Father judges
no one, but has given all judgment to the
Son, 23 that all may honor the Son, even
as they honor the Father. He who does not
honor the Son does not honor the Father

---

that is the meaning of the rabbinical phrase "making himself equal with God." The Pharisees acknowledged God as Father of his people, and, in a creative sense, of all men. For any man to claim personal divine sonship was to set himself above God's law and to repeat the arrogance of the Seleucid kings and Roman emperors. The only possible relationship of the pious to God was unswerving obedience to the written law.

19-23. The Son does not claim independence, but derives all his authority from **the Father,** whose example he follows and whose purpose he carries out (cf. 3:35). His actions are not those of a rebellious son, but display the Father's love in revealing to him his own actions. The deed (vss. 5-9) at which they **marvel** (7:21) will be surpassed by even greater works in which his observers will see further evidence of the Father's continued activity. This is especially shown in his action as judge, pronouncing sentence upon men, but also in withholding doom by preserving and conferring life (vs. 21). In delegating authority to the Son, the Father allows him to give **life to whom he will.** Yet this does not mean the arbitrary exercise of power by **the Son,** but that **the Son** is to receive the same **honor** as **the Father** while he is exercising his delegated authority in the Father's name and according to his purpose. Those who dishonor **the Son** by disputing his right to dispense this saving strength to enfeebled bodies and inert souls are dishonoring **the Father.** This is the function of the eschatological judge. Cf. Enoch 69:27,

> And he sat on the throne of his glory,
> And the sum of judgment was given unto the Son of man.

---

world, we can now see that they are true, and no whit overstated. But at the time how staggering they must have been! We are all extremely severe in our strictures upon the people who were stumbled by them; not realizing how hidebound and conventionalized we are all apt to be. The absolute unity of mind and will he claims with God (vs. 19); the emphatic declaration that to reject him is to turn one's back not on him only but on God (vs. 19); the calm assertion that it is God's wish "that all may honor the Son, even as they honor the Father" (vs. 23): all that is staggering enough. But it only leads on and up to what is even more breath-taking (vs. 26). "This incident," says our Lord in effect, as I understand him, "is allegorical and typical, sums up the possibilities I bring, and what comes of them, in the case of those who accept them and those who do not. As this poor broken creature has, simply through coming into contact with me, regained a full and rounded human life in place of the drab existence which he had endured, so as I pass to and fro among mankind I can and do offer, to anyone and everyone who will accept it, life that is life indeed. And I can really give it; not only, as your own eyes have seen, in the physical sphere, but in the mind and soul and spirit—a far fuller and ampler and richer life than can be had apart from me, incomparably so." These are bold words. Yet no claim has ever been more often proved and

24 Verily, verily, I say unto you, He that heareth my word, and believeth on him that sent me, hath everlasting life, and shall not come into condemnation; but is passed from death unto life.

25 Verily, verily, I say unto you, The hour is coming, and now is, when the dead shall hear the voice of the Son of God: and they that hear shall live.

26 For as the Father hath life in himself; so hath he given to the Son to have life in himself;

27 And hath given him authority to execute judgment also, because he is the Son of man.

who sent him. 24 Truly, truly, I say to
you, he who hears my word and believes
him who sent me, has eternal life; he does
not come into judgment, but has passed
from death to life.
25 "Truly, truly, I say to you, the hour
is coming, and now is, when the dead will
hear the voice of the Son of God, and those
who hear will live. 26 For as the Father has
life in himself, so he has granted the Son
also to have life in himself, 27 and has
given him authority to execute judgment,

---

24. The coming age is already present. The criterion is the kind of response made by men to the revealer of God, who is also commissioned by him to execute **judgment.** Jesus now changes from the third to the first person. **He who hears my word and believes him who sent me, has eternal life; he does not come into judgment, but has passed from death to life.** Here we listen to the evangelist's "realized eschatology." The powers of the coming age are in some sense already in occupation. In Jesus Christ, the revealer, the crucial test is found. By the coming of the Logos, "the only begotten of the Father, full of grace and truth" (1:14), men are given the opportunity of listening to a human voice which yet speaks the message that comes from God. Those who receive that message believe the King who sent the revealer. They thus enter into the kingdom of God, they share in the life eternal, and this is transition **from death to life,** from the realm of the prince of this world (14:30) into "the inheritance of the saints in light," from "the dominion of darkness" into "the kingdom of his beloved Son" (Col. 1:12-13).

25-29. In these verses realized and futuristic eschatology are mingled. **The hour is coming, and now is** introduces a statement about the result of the coming of the Son of God, who is already present as the revealer and judge. The spiritually dead—those who live the unreal life of "the world," which "is in the power of the evil one" (I John 5:19)—

---

justified. Millions of souls the whole world over testify that it is true, as they themselves know from experience.

And yet the grace of God has, and must always have, a grave obverse side. For if we will not accept it, then inevitably we involve ourselves in judgment. No one can meet with Christ and go his way exactly as he came. He may be better; but if not, he must be worse. Our attitude toward what he is and what he offers reveals with accuracy the manner of folk we are. If we see nothing in his gifts, and push them peevishly away; if we do not want them, and do not like them, and will not have them, we are preferring the lazy boredom of the porches of Bethzatha to the glow of health, and the happy activities of a real life. So true is it that **the Father judges no one, but has given all judgment to the Son,** that Christ is set for the fall as well as for the rising of many generations (Luke 2:34), that he is the sufficient touchstone by which we are not so much tried as try ourselves. What we do with Jesus Christ, how we react to him, that is enough to make plain whose we are and whom we serve. And so the judgment day is going on now, and some of us are choosing the left hand, keep moving toward it, have drawn perilously near it; while others (vs. 24)—**He who hears my word and believes him who sent me, has eternal life; he does not come into judgment, but has passed from death to life.** That also here, that also now. For indeed the final scene of vss. 25-29 is not strictly speaking judgment, but rather registration. When we **who are in the tombs . . . hear his voice and come forth;** when in that awful silence our case is called, and we stand forth alone, the books are to be opened. It is all written down, all settled, all recorded. Sheep and swine, wrote John Watson, may feed in the same field. But in the evening when the gate is thrown wide, the sheep make for the fold; but the swine, squealing happily, rush for the mucky pigsties. "One is afraid," he adds,

28 Marvel not at this: for the hour is coming, in the which all that are in the graves shall hear his voice,

29 And shall come forth; they that have done good, unto the resurrection of life; and they that have done evil, unto the resurrection of damnation.

30 I can of mine own self do nothing: as I hear, I judge: and my judgment is just; because I seek not mine own will, but the will of the Father which hath sent me.

because he is the Son of man. **28** Do not
marvel at this; for the hour is coming
when all who are in the tombs will hear
his voice **29** and come forth, those who
have done good, to the resurrection of life,
and those who have done evil, to the resurrection of judgment.

30 "I can do nothing on my own authority; as I hear, I judge; and my judgment is just, because I seek not my own will but the will of him who sent me.

---

will now **hear the voice** of God's vicegerent, and those who attend to that voice will receive that power to live the real life which issues from the Son out of that endowment of essential life **(life in himself)** which the Father has granted him. He is to hold assize immediately **(execute judgment)** under the warrant which the Father has given to him in virtue of his identity in experience and trial with his fellow men—i.e., in virtue of all that is involved in his title **Son of man** (the absence of the Greek article emphasizes quality rather than title). This present and spiritual awakening is a presage and foretaste of that general and final assize when the dead will hear the voice that summons them to their ultimate fate. There will be those whose actions have fitted them for rising to fullness of life; also those whose evil practices fit them for condemnation (cf. Matt. 25:31-46). This is an echo of the futuristic eschatology which dominated the primitive thought of the church. The judgment which is being formed by man's present attitude to Christ will be manifested in the great event with which the present order will be brought at last to its end.

30. This passage (vss. 30-47) in the self-defense put upon the lips of Jesus reverts to the claim made in vs. 19. The **judgment** by Jesus is valid because the Father has invested him with divine **authority; it is just,** because his loyalty to the Father's will rules out any possibility of caprice. Next the question of **witness** is raised. **Witness** by himself is inadmissible (as the Jews urge later on, 8:13). **Another who bears witness to me** is the Father (vs. 32; see vss. 34, 37). This first witness is internal. It is not of such a nature that the

---

"that some will inherit Hell and be content." [8] "What shall I do with Jesus who is called Christ?" (Matt. 27:22.) Everything hangs on our answer to that.

30-47. ***Christ Calls His Witnesses.***—First, John the Baptist, whose adherence meant much to that generation, and told heavily upon their minds. Yet this is to be noted, that while as always our Lord speaks of the Baptist with warm admiration (vs. 35), he prefaces his eulogy, and indeed his citation of him at all, with the words (vs. 34), **Not that the testimony which I receive is from man; but I say this that you may be saved**—as likely to impress you and be helpful to you. His church would do well to remember that and imitate it—in both ways. Sometimes, when, say, a prominent scientist or a former opponent of the faith declares in whole or in part for Christ, there is a flutter of excitement and a rather stupid cackling; as if it was felt that now that this great figure in the public eye is backing him, Christ has a real chance at last, has obviously become more intellectually respectable! It is well for the man that he has come to see the light, in whole or in part. But with him or without him, truth will prevail and Christ will conquer. He does not require testimony from man. Yet as this passage proves, we have the right to lay stress on the witness of memorable people for the Master. And the list of those who have testified for him and humbly believed in him is enormous. For the complacent assumption that the intellectual giants will have none of him is laughed down by the facts. As Bacon put it, "It is true that a little philosophy inclineth man's mind to atheism, but depth in philosophy bringeth men's minds about to religion." [9]

"But," says Christ, "I have greater and more striking testimony by far to advance than that.

[8] *The Mind of the Master* (New York: Dodd, Mead, & Co., 1896), pp. 201-21.

[9] Essay, "Of Atheism."

31 If I bear witness of myself, my witness is not true.

32 ¶ There is another that beareth witness of me; and I know that the witness which he witnesseth of me is true.

33 Ye sent unto John, and he bare witness unto the truth.

34 But I receive not testimony from man: but these things I say, that ye might be saved.

35 He was a burning and a shining light: and ye were willing for a season to rejoice in his light.

31 If I bear witness to myself, my testi-
mony is not true; 32 there is another who
bears witness to me, and I know that the
testimony which he bears to me is true.
33 You sent to John, and he has borne wit-
ness to the truth. 34 Not that the testimony
which I receive is from man; but I say this
that you may be saved. 35 He was a burning
and shining lamp, and you were willing to

Jews can receive it, for it is invisible; but it is the consciousness of a divine revelation in the heart of the Son. Next there was the testimony of John the Baptist. Then there was the evidential value of the works which the Father enabled the Son to do (cf. 3:2, "No one can do these signs that you do, unless God is with him"). Finally, there is the testimony of the Scriptures, those sacred writings to which the Jews appeal, but which condemn their attitude of unbelief and self-seeking.

31-40. The inadmissibility of such **witness** is laid down in several rabbinical sayings (see Strack and Billerbeck, *Kommentar zum N.T. aus Talmud und Midrasch*, II, 466, 522). **I know that the testimony which he bears to me is true.** There is a variant reading, "you know." This was a correction made by a scribe who thought that the reference was to the Baptist, whose answer to those who were sent to him is given in 1:19-28. **You sent to John, and he has borne witness to the truth. . . . I say this that you may be saved;** cf. 1:6-7: "John . . . came for testimony, to bear witness to the light, that all might believe

---

The works that I do are final proofs of all I claim." To this day the main evidence for Christianity is what it effects; that this thing works, and such wonderful works! It heals, it helps, it saves, it changes and ennobles character, it carries kindness and mercy to all kinds of need the whole world over, it has brought into being and maintains that huge and many-sided structure we call charity—which is the creation of Christianity, and practically speaking not really found elsewhere—it has taught us to carry one another's burdens in a way that is not natural to man. So much so that those outside the faith, who are now following slowly and afar off along these lines, learned their desire to help from Christianity. They may resent such a suggestion; but it is unchallengeable. It was not from Hinduism, which is curiously callous in these matters, that Gandhi learned such limited sympathy as he had with the downtrodden. It blew to him from Christianity. The early church fathers kept stressing the works of Christianity as unanswerable proof that here was a new people, living their lives in a new way. And the enemies of the faith admitted it was so. Lucian has witty pages in which he jeers at the inconceivable folly of these crazy folk who actually spend themselves for others, and that so ungrudgingly that of course they get fooled by sanctimonious rogues, as their daft mode of life deserves: while others point out jeeringly that they so give themselves not only for their own people, but for outsiders, and even for their enemies! Did any body ever hear of such midsummer madness? [1] "But," says Christ, "if you have any adequate conception of God's nature, you must feel that in what I am doing and am teaching my people to do there is something divine and that reminds of God; something that has his touch upon it and about it. The difficulty is that you do not know him as he is, and so are shocked and scandalized by what is characteristic of him." **These very works which I am doing, bear me witness that the Father has sent me.**

But Christ goes still further. Browning tells us that when he read Bunyan he saw past the author to the God who obviously had inspired him and whose own very voice kept breaking through to the reader out of the wonderful pages. "'Tis my belief, God spoke: no tinker has such powers." [2] So Christ says confidently that in what he did it was not really he who was acting, but God who was working through him;

[1] "The Death of Peregrine."

[2] "Ned Bratts."

36 ¶ But I have greater witness than
that of John: for the works which the
Father hath given me to finish, the same
works that I do, bear witness of me, that
the Father hath sent me.
37 And the Father himself, which hath
sent me, hath borne witness of me. Ye have
neither heard his voice at any time, nor
seen his shape.
38 And ye have not his word abiding in
you: for whom he hath sent, him ye be-
lieve not.

rejoice for a while in his light. 36 But the tes-
timony which I have is greater than that of
John; for the works which the Father has
granted me to accomplish, these very works
which I am doing, bear me witness that the
Father has sent me. 37 And the Father
who sent me has himself borne witness
to me. His voice you have never heard,
his form you have never seen; 38 and you
do not have his word abiding in you, for
you do not believe him whom he has sent.

---

through him. . . ." Vs. 35 would be better rendered, "He was that burning and shining lamp," i.e., the one man who deserves to be called "Elijah" who must "come first" (Mark 9:11-13). Cf. Ecclus. 48:1,

> Also there arose Elijah the prophet as fire,
> And his word burned like a torch.

Throughout the Gospel Jesus appeals to his **works** (vs. 36) as evidence of his divine mission (cf. 10:25, 38; 14:11; 15:24), even though a belief resting upon these "signs" is inferior to that which springs from insight into his person and message (cf. 14:11; 20:29). The same claim of Jesus is attested in the early collection of sayings known as Q (cf. Matt. 11:2-6, 20-24; 12:28; Luke 7:18-23; 10:13-15; 11:20). The reproach of Jesus (vs. 37) is not that his critics have never seen the invisible God (cf. 1:18; 3:13; 6:46), but that (vs. 38) they have not appropriated his message spoken of old by seer and prophet. They have ransacked the Scriptures (vs. 39), but missed their inner meaning. They have fondly imagined that their minute examination of the letter of the law would give them

---

corroborating what he did, making it possible, and so bearing witness to him (vs. 37). We are too apt to explain away Christ's triumphs and to excuse our own spiritual ineffectiveness by telling ourselves that he had certain unique powers which we have not. But Christ walked by faith, as he asks us to do, and how huge a faith his was! Christ too was utterly dependent upon God; and without him could do nothing. The fact that he was enabled to do the works that he was doing was accepted by him as proof that God was with him, and acknowledging him, and working through him. And if we believed, as Christ believed, what might not God be able to accomplish through us too!

And so Christ calls the scriptures as a further witness (vss. 39-47). "You pore over them," so he allows, "you study them with zeal, feeling that it is in them alone that you can find life that is really life, and worthy of the name. And yet, though they point straight at me, you do not see it, will not believe it."

It was a constant source of wonder to the early Christians that the Jews did not perceive how perfectly Christ fulfilled the promises of the O.T., and met and answered the longings of the generations of the saints; how obviously this was he who had been foretold, dreamed of, and waited for, really come at last. For as F. W. Faber says, he was the brightness of innumerable lives, and the sweetness of innumerable sorrows, when he was but the expectation of longing Israel. Paul can explain it only by declaring that "to this day whenever Moses is read a veil lies over their minds" (II Cor. 3:15), and that a spirit of drowsiness, of stupor, of insensibility (Rom. 11:8) has for the time being overwhelmed them. "The Bible beguiled the Pharisees," says Samuel Rutherford boldly.[3] And these men, with all their ardent studying of the scriptures, had been led by them to expect something so different from Jesus—a conqueror bursting in to work national deliverance, or the like—that as they saw things he did not fit the part at all, was not in the least like what the Messiah would be when he did come. Even the Baptist was in the end staggered and completely puzzled. For this was not what he had confidently expected.

In all of which there is nothing unusual, and few generations have the right to jeer at these

[3] *Letters,* Letter CVI, p. 219.

39 ¶ Search the Scriptures; for in them ye think ye have eternal life: and they are they which testify of me.

40 And ye will not come to me, that ye might have life.

41 I receive not honor from men.

42 But I know you, that ye have not the love of God in you.

43 I am come in my Father's name, and ye receive me not: if another shall come in his own name, him ye will receive.

44 How can ye believe, which receive honor one of another, and seek not the honor that *cometh* from God only?

39 You search the scriptures, because you
think that in them you have eternal life;
and it is they that bear witness to me; 40 yet
you refuse to come to me that you may
have life. 41 I do not receive glory from
men. 42 But I know that you have not the
love of God within you. 43 I have come
in my Father's name, and you do not re-
ceive me; if another comes in his own name,
him you will receive. 44 How can you be-
lieve, who receive glory from one another
and do not seek the glory that comes from

eternal life. Rabbi Hillel had said ironically of some Pharisees, "Who has gained for himself words of Torah has gained for himself the life of the world to come" (Pirke Aboth 2:8; see Charles, *Apocrypha and Pseudepigrapha,* II, 696). Yet they failed to see the witness which these same scriptures bore to him who has "life in himself" and in his message (vs. 40). As a result, they **refuse to come** to him who is the giver of life. This is the tragedy announced in the prologue (1:11). For a further discussion of vs. 39 see Intro., p. 459.

41-47. In these verses the word **glory,** or rather **honor,** replaces "witness." His opponents have demanded a testimonial from some human source to accredit Jesus, who declares that he cannot submit to their standards. They cannot truly love God, or they would not be indifferent to the honor **that comes from the only God,** and value the honor which a man can gain from his fellows. They are "of the earth and speak of the earth" (cf. 3:31). The evangelist illustrates this eagerness to "receive honor from one another" later in the Gospel: "Nevertheless many even of the authorities believed in him, but for fear of the Pharisees they did not confess it, lest they should be put out of the synagogue; for they loved the praise of men more than the praise of God" (12:42-43). In contrast with these, Paul describes the true Jew as a Jew "who is one inwardly. . . . His praise is not from men but from God" (Rom. 2:29). Though "the Jews" have rejected Jesus who came in his Father's name (vs. 45), he will not be their accuser. That role will be filled by the very one upon whom they confidently rely as their advocate. Rabbi Eliezer ben Jacob, a second-century teacher, said, "He who does one precept gains for himself one advocate; and he who commits one transgression gains for himself one accuser" (Pirke Aboth 4:13; see Charles, *Apocrypha and Pseudepigrapha,* II, 705). The Jews put their trust in the security which was guaranteed to those who kept the law of **Moses** (vs. 46); but that is a false confidence.

men's blindness. It is one of the sorriest of facts how often scientific advances have been ruthlessly opposed by the scientific orthodoxy of the time, which would have none of them, derided them as absurdities, and did its best to laugh or crush them out of being.[4] In like manner, well-meaning Christian people have often been incredibly obtuse, as later generations judge, failing to recognize Christ when he came among them, and hotly resisting what proved to be God's Holy Spirit, because what happened did not look to them like God, and was not in the least what they had imagined he would do.

Expecting Him, my door was open wide:
Then I looked round
If any lack of service might be found,
And saw Him at my side:
How entered, by what secret stair,
I know not, knowing only He was there.[5]

So does the God whose ways are never stereotyped bewilder us by the immensity of his inexhaustible originality. Too often, indeed,

[4] Cf. Robert H. Murray, *Science and Scientists in the Nineteenth Century* (London: The Sheldon Press, 1925).

[5] T. E. Brown, "Praesto," *Poems* (London: Macmillan & Co., 1912), p. 137.

45 Do not think that I will accuse you to the Father: there is *one* that accuseth you, *even* Moses, in whom ye trust.

46 For had ye believed Moses, ye would have believed me: for he wrote of me.

47 But if ye believe not his writings, how shall ye believe my words?

6 After these things Jesus went over the sea of Galilee, which is *the sea* of Tiberias.

2 And a great multitude followed him, because they saw his miracles which he did on them that were diseased.

3 And Jesus went up into a mountain, and there he sat with his disciples.

4 And the passover, a feast of the Jews, was nigh.

5 ¶ When Jesus then lifted up *his* eyes, and saw a great company come unto him,

the only God? 45 Do not think that I shall
accuse you to the Father; it is Moses who
accuses you, on whom you set your hope.
46 If you believed Moses, you would believe
me, for he wrote of me. 47 But if you do not
believe his writings, how will you believe
my words?"

6 After this Jesus went to the other side
of the Sea of Galilee, which is the Sea
of Ti-be'ri-as. 2 And a multitude followed
him, because they saw the signs which he
did on those who were diseased. 3 Jesus
went up into the hills, and there sat down
with his disciples. 4 Now the Passover, the
feast of the Jews, was at hand. 5 Lifting up
his eyes, then, and seeing that a multitude

This controversy started with their zealous concern for the sabbath regulations in the Pentateuch. They have failed to see the significance of such a prophecy as Deut. 18:15, "The LORD thy God will raise up unto thee a Prophet from the midst of thee, like unto me; unto him ye shall hearken." Their blindness to the deeper meaning of the Torah prevents them from recognizing the true nature of Jesus and accepting his message. The same argument is expressed rather differently in the closing words of the parable of Dives and Lazarus (Luke 16:31).

Much discussion has revolved round the saying **If another comes in his own name, him you will receive** (vs. 43). At one time the popular interpretation was to identify this figure with Bar Cocheba, that messianic claimant who gained the support of Rabbi Aqiba, the foremost rabbi of his age, and whose disastrous rebellion in the years A.D. 132-35 was put down by the Emperor Hadrian. It is now generally recognized that the Fourth Gospel was published a generation before that event. In the Synoptic Gospels there are predictions of false messiahs and false prophets who would come in the name of Jesus, and this saying probably goes back to some such word of Christ.

The controversy is continued in 7:15-24.

C. Jesus as the Bread of Life (6:1-71)

1. Feeding of the Multitude (6:1-15)

6:1-15. This story, with a few significant variations, follows the tradition of the feeding of the five thousand recorded in Mark 6:31-44 (=Matt. 14:13-21; Luke 9:10-17), of which the story of the four thousand in Mark 8:1-9 (=Matt. 15:32-39) is probably a

---

when he comes, people staring at him insist this is not God at all, is not anything like him; resent him, actively resist him, and imagine that in so doing they are offering him service.

And so Christ boldly calls as his last witness against these Jews—whom but Moses, their own Moses, to them the final word, and the ultimate authority! "If," said Christ, "you would read your own scriptures with seeing eyes and open minds, you could not fail to acknowledge that this is he who was to come (vss. 45-47). I do not accuse you, but Moses will and does, for your crass unbelief in what he wrote." And is it not a puzzling thing that people eager to bring in a better world do not see that their dreams can come true only in Jesus Christ?

6:5-6. ***Teaching and Examination.***—As we make our way toward the unfathomable passage (vss. 35-40) in which the evangelist records what Jesus himself declared to be central and of supreme importance in the dramatic incident

he saith unto Philip, Whence shall we buy bread, that these may eat?

was coming to him, Jesus said to Philip, "How are we to buy bread, so that these

doublet. Since the story of the walking on the sea follows immediately, as in Mark and Matthew, John has either made use of Mark, or they are both indebted to an early source. The position of this narrative in the Johannine Gospel points either to a

of the five thousand, we keep being halted by things not a few that, laying hands upon us, arrest the mind and claim attention.

At vs. 5, e.g., **Seeing that a multitude was coming to him, Jesus said to Philip, "How are we to buy bread, so that these people may eat?"** Why to Philip, who does not figure largely in the Gospels? Vs. 6 seems to make it plain that it was not simply because at the moment he happened to be standing near, but for a weightier reason.

The fleeting glimpses of him that the Gospels vouchsafe us leave the impression that Philip was not the quickest minded or the most adventurous of the disciples. In the initial fact that while some of the twelve themselves sought out Christ and asked for an interview Philip took no such step, but Christ himself went after him, and found him, and called him, there is signal testimony to the essential worth of the man, but also something indicative of a lack of drive and initiative in him. Christ's dealings with him suggest a steady, sober-minded, dependable personality; but one pictures him as often listening to the Master with a blank face and a mind that was not following all the way. Certainly his question in the upper room fell on Christ almost like a blow. It staggered him that one should have been with him "so long," and have picked up so little of the very essence of his teaching. Perhaps what Lascelles Abercrombie says of Thomas is fully more apt of Philip:

> The Lord knew
> What a frail soul he gave me, and a heart
> Lame and unlikely for the large events.[6]

Such a one may have many virtues, but the audacities of faith, the heroism that ventures and takes risks, are not natural to him, nor easy for him.

And it would seem that discerning such a temperament in his disciple, our Lord was taking pains to train him where his need lay, to help him to evade the dangers into which his type of mind might lead him. **This he said to test him, for he himself knew what he would do.** Certainly he often does that with most of us. Looking back at life, it falls into a pattern. What at the time seemed dark and inexplicable, perhaps even hard and cruel, tends to gain meaning and significance. It becomes clear that one who knows us very thoroughly, far better than we know ourselves, is taking trouble to train us, to correct our faults, to grant us chances to rise above our natural weaknesses.

Moreover, as there comes a time when a teacher, having done his best for the pupil, has to subject him to some kind of an examination to make sure whether or not he is following and understanding and really making progress; and during it cannot write his answers for him or give him any hints, but must stand back and leave him to himself and allow him to make of things what he can—so life brings us up against such ordeals, such chances to prove ourselves, such tests designed to show whether we are learning or are not. And during them Christ too may have to stand a little farther off, and seem to leave us to our own inadequate resources.

Perhaps, like Philip here, who came from the district and knew its possibilities and felt that what was suggested just could not be done, we may answer despondently. Perhaps the experience we are asked to face may seem to us too drastic, even cruel. But really it is wise and kind and necessary. **This he said to test him.** If it appears that we have made some real advance, let us thank God and take courage. For there is still much to attain. If we break down in the old way, well, it is better to be made to realize our weaknesses, and so no longer be able to deceive ourselves as to the true state of affairs. And all we have to do is to get closer to Jesus Christ, to listen to him more attentively, and this time really take it in. For he is a marvelous teacher, patient beyond belief, who gets incredible results out of the most unpromising material.

5. *Christ and the Social Gospel.*—But it is not only the person to whom it was addressed, but the question itself that grips the attention and makes one think. Today there are many who are unhappy in their minds because they feel that the church, swept away by the currents of the time, is laying the stress far too heavily on material and economic improvements, which after all are secondary, while pushing the spir-

6 "The Sale of St. Thomas," *The Poems of Lascelles Abercrombie* (London: Oxford University Press, 1930). Used by permission.

6 And this he said to prove him: for he himself knew what he would do.
7 Philip answered him, Two hundred pennyworth of bread is not sufficient for them, that every one of them may take a little.

people may eat?" 6 This he said to test him,
for he himself knew what he would do.
7 Philip answered him, "Two hundred denarii[h] would not buy enough bread for

[h] See on Mt. 18. 28.

displacement of sections or to a remarkable indifference on the evangelist's part to historical sequence. Ch. 5 left Jesus in Jerusalem. Ch. 6 begins, **After this Jesus went to the other side of the Sea of Galilee.** Ch. 7 opens with a statement that "Jesus went about in Galilee" rather than Judea because the Jews were trying to kill him (cf. 5:18). The

itual, which is primary and fundamental, and the core and essence of its message, more or less into the background as a matter which it is unwise these days too obviously to emphasize. And as this very chapter will remind us gravely, Christ himself was at times uneasy and disturbed because the people of his day were making that same mistake. "Let us beware," warns Maurice Maeterlinck, "lest we act as he did in the fable, who stood watch in a lighthouse, and gave to the poor in their cabins about him the oil for the mighty lanterns that serve to illumine the sea."[7] That is a caution much required when what many call their Christianity is not easily differentiated from mere humanism, and not a few are preaching social reform instead of the salvation of men's souls. Dostoevski was of the opinion that humanitarianism is the form of atheism most to be dreaded, the greatest antireligious force in Europe; so he confidently laid it down.

Nonetheless, we must keep a balance and sense of proportion. To speak and act as if Christ were not touched by and sympathetic toward people's material disabilities is to fly in the face of the facts which the Gospels set down plainly for us. It is true that poverty and even pain seemed to him small matters compared to the horror of sin. Yet day after day he spent himself ungrudgingly to heal physical ailments, tiring himself out for that, accounting it well worth the strength and time. Indeed he was so acutely conscious of the economic hardships of the masses that for a while he seriously considered giving himself to a career of social reform. We are expressly told that that was one of the ideas which at the beginning had to be thought out in what he came to feel was his temptation, and which he ultimately put aside as an attempt of the evil one to lure him from his real and vastly deeper task. His own hunger after his long fast helped him to realize what many a pinched life had to face day after day. Yet when the suggestion followed, "If you are the Son of God, command these stones to become loaves of bread"—use your powers and life to ease men's economic pressure and meet their material wants—he answered, "Man shall not live by bread alone, but by every word that proceeds from the mouth of God" (Matt. 4:3-4). And that, and that alone, will really reach down to the sore and heal it.

[7] *Wisdom and Destiny*, tr. Alfred Sutro (13th ed.; London: George Allen & Unwin, 1915), p. 178.

But to seek to limit Christ's interests and sympathies to spiritual things, in any narrow interpretation of that word, is just unreal. Has he not covered with eternal scorn the man who can shut himself into his own religion and pass by on the other side, going on his clean but unhelpful way, unperturbed by the troubles of other people and doing nothing to assist them? Are not the tests of the N.T., by which men stand or fall, uncomfortably practical? So James, in his blunt fashion, tells us that he thinks nothing at all of pious talk that does not end in action. "If a brother or sister is ill-clad and in lack of daily food, and one of you says to them, 'Go in peace, be warmed and filled,' without giving them the things needed for the body, what does it profit? So faith by itself, if it has no works, is dead" (Jas. 2:15-17). And the questions which Christ assures us are to be put to us at the judgment seat have nothing directly to do with prayer and doctrine and spiritual things at all, but only with the helpfulness and the unselfishness that ought to flow from them. So here, in lesser matters as in greater. The people had tracked him far up among the hills. They looked, and were, tired and hungry. They were a long way from towns and shops. And Christ's first thought for them was not about their souls, but how to meet their clamant physical requirements. **How are we to buy bread, so that these people may eat?** Time enough after that to seek to help their souls. That too is a real part of the Christ we serve; and we must seek to grow up into his whole likeness.

7-9. ***The Importance of Unimportant People.***—Philip, casting his eyes over the crowd and making a rough calculation, answered, **Two**

8 One of his disciples, Andrew, Simon Peter's brother, saith unto him,
9 There is a lad here, which hath five barley loaves, and two small fishes: but what are they among so many?

each of them to get a little." [8] One of his disciples, Andrew, Simon Peter's brother, said to him, [9] "There is a lad here who has five barley loaves and two fish; but

scene opens in ch. 6 just before the feast of Passover. Ch. 5 opens with a visit to Jerusalem for an unnamed feast. Ch. 7 describes a controversy in Jerusalem during the feast of Tabernacles. It seems probable that ch. 6 relates events that took place before those narrated in ch. 5 (see Intro., pp. 446, 459-60).

hundred denarii, say forty dollars, some dozen pounds or so, would hardly buy sufficient bread to give all these people even a bite. And as they possessed no such sum, and even if they had, could have done nothing with it in those mountainous solitudes, there seemed no more to be said. But then Andrew intervened. Whenever we come upon that likable soul, he is unostentatiously but most efficiently doing something helpful to someone, and through him to Jesus Christ. **There is a lad here,** he volunteered, **who has five barley loaves and two fish; but,** very reasonably, added almost shamefacedly, **what are they among so many?** The boy sounds as if he were too young to have been there with any very serious purpose. Likely enough there was not much more in his mind than to see and hear the man of whom everyone was speaking. One may suppose that he had begged his mother for permission to make a day of it; and that she had no doubt told him that he was too young to understand or to enjoy what he would find. But he had pestered her, as a boy will. Until in the end she had given him his way; and making up a little bundle of food, enough to see a boy through the day, had let him go. Perhaps, standing as near to the great man as he could get, he had overheard Christ's question and the subsequent dilemma, and had generously offered his little store to Andrew. In any case, is it not fairly certain that that night he burst into his home, with his eyes shining and his cheeks on fire, to tell them of the miracle that "I and Jesus" wrought! And his bold claim was true.

In the parable of the talents our Lord makes it plain that in his experience he has proved that it is the one-talent people who are most likely to falter and fail him; and this on the ground that anything they could do is so trivial as to be not worth doing. If it were done, it would make no appreciable difference; and being left undone, it will never be missed. That, says Christ, is a fallacy that has disastrous consequences. And it continually robs and hampers him. If this world is ever to be won for him, it will have to be done largely through the undistinguished services of simple folk, one-talent people with no outstanding opportunities, each throwing in what seems a very unimportant effort, yet which in the mass, and often individually, can have far-reaching results. Useless though it looks, put into Christ's wonder-working hands the offering that we can make, the little bit of time or means that we can spare, the service, such as it is, that we can bring to him, and nobody can tell what he may effect through us and it.

One's thoughts, too, wander farther—to that mother who, as we would say, had made the sandwiches for her laddie; and who probably was not herself among the five thousand, but busy at home among her ordinary household tasks. These seem to us quite remote from Christ and his tremendous mission. And yet through one of them, put through in the bygoing among the rest, she all unconsciously gave Christ his chance, and helped him mightily.

There is much talk these days of the right of woman to express herself; and many, indeed most, spheres now lie wide open to her. In not a few she has attained to eminence and real distinction. But in none of them will she find an influence so deep and vital and effective as that which nature offers to her in the making and the running of a home. Her daily duties there may look tame and uneventful and prosaic. But she is inevitably telling upon the children and molding their characters: and when they pass out into the world, she will through them influence endless people that she never saw, and bring about results, often remarkable, in far-off places that she never knew. As Robert Louis Stevenson put it:

And as the fervent smith of yore
  Beat out the glowing blade,
Nor wielded in the front of war
  The weapons that he made,
  But in the tower at home still plied his ringing
    trade;

So like a sword the son shall roam
  On nobler missions sent; [8]

[8] "It Is not Yours" from *Underwoods.*

10 And Jesus said, Make the men sit down. Now there was much grass in the place. So the men sat down, in number about five thousand.

what are they among so many?" 10 Jesus said, "Make the people sit down." Now there was much grass in the place; so the men sat down, in number about five thou-

The significant variants from the Marcan story are (*a*) Jesus' initiative (vss. 5-6); (*b*) the disciples' embarrassment (vss. 7, 9); (*c*) the naming of two disciples, with Greek names (vss. 5, 8; cf. 1:44, 48; 12:21-22; 14:8-9); (*d*) the stress upon the magnitude of the miraculous supply (vss. 7, 11). Even more striking is the sequel. According to the Johannine narrative, the people on seeing the sign said, **This is indeed the prophet who is to come into the world** (vs. 14; cf. 1:21, 25; 7:40). But they misunderstood the nature

but it is the mother who fashioned him, who made his exploits possible.

10. *The Common Sense of Jesus Christ.*—Lady Hosie tells us of that remarkable man, Timothy Richard, that he was grievously hampered in his splendid and untiring efforts to relieve the desperate famine-stricken folk in China by the sheer unmanageableness of the starving crowds that would not be held back, but kept breaking in upon him, jostling him, impeding him. Till one day at morning worship he happened to read the verse in which Christ said, **Make the people sit down;** and at a flash he saw the way out of his problem and perplexities. Sitting people do not shove or crush! Lady Hosie adds that for the whole of his life afterward, Timothy Richard held the highest opinion of the common sense of Jesus of Nazareth.

Common sense is not a word that rises naturally to the mind in relation to Jesus Christ; and indeed one feels a little shocked by it when used in connection with him. Yet how true it is that this also formed a real part of our Lord's perfection! How often great and good men, and perhaps even more, great and good women, have not attained to all that was within their reach, have wasted not a few of their gifts, and thrown away not a little of their chance and influence, because with all their other rich endowments they lacked common sense: and so egregiously failed to understand their fellows, or allowed themselves to be swept away by some erratic fanaticism, or lost touch with reality. But Jesus Christ possessed it in full measure.

Here he sees at a glance how with extreme simplicity twelve men can feed five thousand. Make them sit down! Again, when Jairus' daughter was restored to life, the parents in the room were so amazed that apparently they did nothing but stand there staring at what could not be true. And while Christ had enjoined that no one else was to be told what had happened, the news soon leaked out that something extraordinary had taken place, that the lassie was alive and better; and as Christ had foreseen, the whole house was soon buzzing with excitement. And only he remained calm and wise, seeing what to do, and with his feet planted firmly on the solid ground. "Give her something to eat," he said (Mark 5:43). The sheer common sense of it!

And that is typical. Smetham wrote once to a friend:

> Every believer realises by experience that Christ is the only perfect sympathiser. "I'm not perfectly understood," says everybody in fact. But if you are a believer you are perfectly understood. Christ is the only one who never expects you to be other than *yourself*. . . . He takes your view of things, and mentions no other. He takes the old woman's view of things by the wash tub, and has a great interest in wash powder; Sir Isaac Newton's view of things, and wings among the stars with him; the artist's view, and feeds among the lilies; the lawyer's, and shares the justice of things. But He never plays the lawyer or the philosopher or the artist to the old woman. He is above that littleness.[9]

All of which he puts down, truly enough, to the perfection of Christ's sympathy. But is it not due, not a little, to his gracious and most blessed common sense? He has vast ambitions for us; he startles plain humdrum people, who had never supposed that they had anything in them, by the loftiness of his hopes for them. But he does not set them to impossible tasks outside their particular province; and is not vexed with us if we cannot offer the services and help which others, differently endowed from us, can bring him. And this, we say, is because he is too kindly and generous and gracious for that. But is he not too sensible as well? The common sense of Jesus Christ!

The account of this incident given by the Synoptists differs in some radical respects. It is the disciples who become disturbed in mind about the people, tired and hungry after a long and exhausting day, and who beseech Christ to

[9] *Letters of James Smetham*, ed. Sarah Smetham and William Davies (London: Macmillan & Co., 1902), p. 297.

11 And Jesus took the loaves; and when
he had given thanks, he distributed to the
disciples, and the disciples to them that

sand. 11 Jesus then took the loaves, and

---

of the sign. It was indeed, as Jesus was to show on the following sabbath in the synagogue at Capernaum, a symbol of the heavenly food which gives life to the world, and is

---

send them away that they may reach the villages and buy food. For night was ready to fall, and it is emphasized how lonely was that solitude among the hills where the darkness was about to catch them. "You give them something to eat," says Christ. "We!" they exclaim, "We have only five barley loaves and two small fish! Where are we to get food for all this people unless we buy it? Two hundred denarii's worth of bread, even if we had it, would give each of them only a bite!" Moreover, there is no word of the boy; rather the impression is left that it was their own store of food they brought to Christ on his demand—and that this is what he began distributing, with the result, so some explain it all, that others in the crowd handed up their provisions too, and ultimately it was found that there was more than sufficient for a simple communal meal. The lesson being that if we would use such resources as we do possess, hopelessly inadequate though they may seem, others will come to our assistance; we shall discover that we can draw on far bigger resources than we had realized could be available, and the thing we thought impossible and obviously out of the question will get done.

But as the Fourth Evangelist sets it down, no such interpretation is possible. For there it is explicitly underlined that all that Christ had to work with was the meagerness of the boy's gift. And Jesus took it, "and when he had given thanks," according to the gracious custom of the blessing before meals now growing obsolescent if not obsolete, he began to distribute to that hungry mob.

11. ***An Audacious Grace Before Meat.***—It is surely a pity, and no good sign, that this seemly little rite is growing so unusual and out of date. No doubt we have all felt, as Charles Lamb did:

> I own that I am disposed to say grace upon twenty other occasions in the course of the day besides my dinner. I want a form for setting out upon a pleasant walk, for a moonlight ramble, for a friendly meeting, or a solved problem. Why have we none for books, those spiritual repasts—a grace before Milton, a grace before Shakespeare? [1]

Many graces in the course of the day were indeed advisable and fitting. But to have dropped the one we had betokens that humanity is in a churlish mood, and that ours is an apathetic and ungrateful generation.

> . . . If morning skies,
> Books and my food, and summer rain
> Knocked on my sullen heart in vain: [2]

that strikes Stevenson as nothing less than shocking, and a sure indication of a spirit dying, if not dead. And how much more meaningful and rich life becomes to those for whom the daily comforts never just happen, and are not chance-blown, but are accepted as sure evidence that our Father has been thinking of us, working for us, supplying our legitimate needs; that our happinesses are gifts thought out for us by him, and put into our hands by his.

There is something tremendous in the picture, in the fact of Christ facing that hungry crowd, seated, as Mark 6:40 puts it vividly, by fifties and hundreds on the green grass, with those thousands of eyes intently watching him; and he starting to distribute his so hopelessly inadequate supplies. The thing is preposterous, we feel; is courting certain failure, and a ridicule surely not undeserved. For in this prosaic world things do not really work out in the fairy tale fashion he seems to expect. But obstinately five small barley loaves remain five barley loaves, and nothing more; and two small fishes two small fishes, however much we pray over them. That sounds reasonable. And yet is it? For it is the simple fact that there are audacious people who live their lives upon this very principle and in this very spirit; and with them too, however incredible it sounds, and indeed frankly fantastic, the thing works. Some seventy years or so ago a simple soul with no means, no position, no influence of any kind, felt it borne in upon him that he must give his life to doing something for the orphaned, needy, friendless children of his countryside. And with nothing at his back, he started; and that upon this basis—that he would appeal to no one for financial help, but get on with the work, believing that if God saw that it was good, he would arouse men and women to send the needed aid unasked. And he did. For from small beginnings Quarrier's famous homes have grown to an enormous enterprise; and far

[1] "Grace Before Meat," in *Essays of Elia.*

[2] Robert Louis Stevenson, "The Celestial Surgeon."

were set down; and likewise of the fishes as much as they would.

when he had given thanks, he distributed them to those who were seated; so also the

brought by the true Messiah in the eschatological age. Quite wrongly they thought of a political deliverer whose kingdom was of this world (18:36). Josephus gives two instances of charlatans who deluded the populace by claiming to perform signs to prove their leadership in delivering them from the Roman dominion. One is the story of Theudas (*Antiquities* XX. 5. 1), who persuaded a multitude to follow him to the river Jordan, saying that he was a prophet, and would by his own command divide the river and give them an easy passage over it. The procurator Fadus shattered this mad attempt.

more than five thousand have been fed, and clothed, and started out in life, and made good citizens, and been surrounded by a Christian atmosphere. And all this, so to speak, from five barley loaves and two small fishes, if even that.

But most of us do not trust God like that; and as a consequence, live much more timidly, and so with no such dramatic outcome. If this is what Christ means by faith, little wonder that what we are accustomed to call ours effects so little. If we really trusted God as Jesus trusted him, what might there not result?

11. *The Place of Thanksgiving in Prayer.*— (See also on 10:22-23.) Very notable is the place that thanksgiving holds in the devotions of our Lord. It is true that there is one inexplicable fact, that in the Lord's Prayer there is no thanksgiving at all. Is that not an indication that this model was never meant to be used in the mechanical and formal manner that it is? But in his own private prayers, whenever up and down the Gospels we overhear Christ communing with his Father, how often he is giving thanks—for life and the best thing life gives, fellowship with Almighty God (cf. 17:25). For the friendship of the disciples, and all that that had meant to him; for the common mercies, as we insolently call them—common indeed to us who have them, and too little regarded, but each of them how wonderful to those who are denied them—for the disappointments that would have soured or at least sadly disheartened most men, as when it grew clear that the influential people would have none of him; "I thank thee, O Father, . . . that thou hast hid these things from the wise and prudent, and hast revealed them unto babes: even so, Father; for so it seemed good in thy sight" (Luke 10:21). The thing is striking; and a settled mood of Jesus Christ in prayer. And the early church caught the same spirit. In the services of those first days thanksgiving had by far the largest place in their approach to God, edging the other main categories of prayer into a minor and subsidiary place. Apart from intercession there was not much petition; and even more striking, a relatively small place was thought sufficient for confession. These people were bewildered by the amazing beneficence of God in nature, but especially in the grace that had reached them through Christ. They knew that they were needy sinners. But they were saved sinners; or at least sinners being saved. That is what held their minds. And when they came to God, their natural inclination was to give thanks.

Nowadays the joyousness and sunshine of these first halcyon times seem dulled into a far tamer and less happy communing with God. Evelyn Underhill indeed points out that

> the Western Church from the earliest times, has put the *Venite* at the beginning of the great Office of Matins which opens her daily cycle of prayer, to give straightaway the colour and accent of her worship. All her ministers are required to adore God under this formula every day; to come before His presence with thanksgiving, and show themselves glad in Him with psalms.[3]

Which is undoubted. But when she continues, "The Church of England . . . seems specially to have desired to emphasize this note of worshipping joy,"[4] she has to break a lance with Newman, who even in his Anglican days held that the Prayer Book had completely lost the characteristic praise and gladness of primitive Christianity, and had replaced that with a sob of penitence, and the bitter cry of a returning prodigal.[5] And he seems nearer to the facts.

Whether it is that we have not really experienced that saving power of Christ which his first disciples knew so well, or that having grown accustomed to it by long familiarity, even the redeeming love of God in Christ no longer astonishes us, but has come to be accepted by us as a thing of course, the old adoring note of praise has largely died away. We would do well to revive it. For if we did, it

[3] *Collected Papers* (London: Longmans, Green & Co., 1946), p. 151. Used by permission.

[4] *Ibid.*, p. 152.

[5] *Tracts for the Times,* LXXXVI (London: J. G. & F. Rivington, 1839), Part I, sec. 8, pp. 19-23.

12 When they were filled, he said unto his disciples, Gather up the fragments that remain, that nothing be lost.

13 Therefore they gathered *them* together, and filled twelve baskets with the fragments of the five barley loaves, which remained over and above unto them that had eaten.

14 Then those men, when they had seen the miracle that Jesus did, said, This is of a truth that Prophet that should come into the world.

15 ¶ When Jesus therefore perceived that they would come and take him by

fish, as much as they wanted. 12 And when
they had eaten their fill, he told his disci-
ples, "Gather up the fragments left over,
that nothing may be lost." 13 So they gath-
ered them up and filled twelve baskets
with fragments from the five barley loaves,
left by those who had eaten. 14 When the
people saw the sign which he had done,
they said, "This is indeed the prophet who
is to come into the world!"

15 Perceiving then that they were about
to come and take him by force to make

The other story is told twice (*Antiquities* XX. 8. 6; *Jewish War* II. 13. 5) about an Egyptian who gave himself out to be a prophet. He assembled a crowd on the Mount of

---

would be not only salutary for our own soul's health, but we would be immeasurably more likely to attract others to the Master. We shall never get them to think seriously of him until we prove to them that through him we possess something worth the sharing. Once they have seen that, they will, of themselves, come hurrying for it.

But are we likely so to convince them if our faces are long, and our services in the main an abashed confession that Christ or no Christ, our accustomed sins still have dominion over us and our religion effects little for us?

12. ***One's Place in One's Own Life.*—And when they had eaten their fill, he told his disciples, "Gather up the fragments left over, that nothing may be lost."** And this apparently for their own use. A striking illustration of how to spend life. Hoard it, as Christ once said, and you will lose it. It will go bad on you. Throw it away for others, and you will find how rich and interesting and exciting a thing life, any life, can be. And here we are assured that if we so do, God will see to it that we have enough for our legitimate needs. As Evelyn Underhill has put it:

> When all were fed, when the job was done, they gathered up twelve baskets full; one basket for each Apostle. As you know, the word translated basket is the little satchel in which the travelling Jew carried enough food for one day's journey, not more. No waste, but no stinginess. God does not starve His staff; He always leaves them, if they follow His plan for them and give without reserve to His children, with enough food in hand for the day. Give without reserve, and you will gather up enough to fill your own lunch basket.[6]

[6] *Collected Papers,* p. 212. Used by permission of Longmans, Green & Co.

Yet one notices that there was no basket for Christ. The great Giver kept back nothing for himself at all. In which one seems to read a kind of parable and a lesson for us all. In the living of our lives we are too apt to adopt the order of things given us in the grammar book. And that is the exact opposite of Christ's order. As we judge, it is the all-important I that is the first personal pronoun: that comes first, that holds the center of the stage, that must be primarily considered. Those round about us only come second, while those farther off occupy an even more subordinate place. I, you, he: so it is that we range them in our minds. All the saints warn us about this, accounting it a major error. The author of the *Theologia Germanica* speaks bitingly about the devil's pronouns, I, me, mine. And if that is too savage, it is well to listen to T. E. Brown, musing on the beach one day over an empty shell:

> If thou couldst empty all thyself of self,
> Like to a shell dishabited,
> Then might He find thee on the Ocean shelf,
> And say—"This is not dead,"—
> And fill thee with Himself instead.
> But thou art all replete with very *thou,*
> And hast such shrewd activity,
> That, when He comes, He says—This is enow
> Unto itself—'Twere better let it be:
> It is so small and full, there is no room for Me.[7]

15. ***Attempted Emendations of Christ's Gospel.***—The impression made, for the time being at least, upon the volatile people was such that they had some crazy notion of compelling Christ, whether he wanted it or not, to become their king, leading them back to national free-

[7] "Indwelling," *Poems* (London: Macmillan & Co., 1912).

force, to make him a king, he departed again into a mountain himself alone.

him king, Jesus withdrew again to the hills by himself.

Olives, declaring that at his word the walls of Jerusalem would collapse, upon which he would lead them to the capture of the city. This rising was also crushed. The flames of fanatical nationalism were easily fanned into a blaze, and it was evident to Jesus that the populace of Galilee wished to hail him as the head of a messianic rising. Therefore **Jesus withdrew again to the hills by himself** (vs. 15).

---

dom and the other glories they felt he could work for them.

Throughout his ministry all kinds of people kept trying to induce him to lay aside his own plan and adopt others which they urged upon him as far likelier to succeed. However they differed from each other, they all agreed that his way of it was quite hopeless and just would not do; as surely he must see for himself, now that they had shown him their own vastly more effective program for him. Even John the Baptist lost heart at what seemed to him the futility of Christ's ineffectual methods; while Peter characteristically burst into open protest, if not indignant anger, over his simply preposterous suggestions; even his own family told him to his face that he was making a sad mess of things, and added bluntly that if he must play the fool, as he was doing, he might at least give himself some dim kind of a half chance; and here the mob tried to rush him into a line of conduct they felt might have real results, whereas his present course was merely throwing away his opportunities and must end in little. But Christ, wiser than their confident foolishness, managed to evade their noisy clamor and withdrew to be alone with God among the hills, in the hush and brooding solitude which his soul seems to have loved and found so healing.

Unhappily, his people have not been nearly as wise as he. Down the centuries they have allowed themselves to be rushed and concussed into many a foolish and unwise adventure that has lured them from the path that Christ laid down for them. True, the guidance of the Holy Spirit, promised to them, has been a very real and wonderful fact; in many ways quite extraordinarily effective, in spite of their waywardness and heedlessness and unteachable obstinacy.

But how we have adulterated the faith that was committed to us, toning it down and altering it to suit the moods of those who did not like it as it stood, or imagining we were bettering it. We have allowed elements of sheer paganism to filter into it. We have substituted a queer doctrinaire unintelligibility for the terrible simplicity there is in Christ. Is the church, as it exists today, anything like what Christ meant it to be? Is the Athanasian Creed, with its emphatic assertion that "Whosoever will be saved, before all things it is necessary that he hold the Catholic Faith. Which faith except every one do keep whole and undefiled, without doubt he shall perish everlastingly. And the Catholic Faith is this: . . ."—and with that there follows for many what Jeremy Bentham would have called deliberate "incognoscibility"—is that a fair and recognizable account of the gospel in the heart of Jesus?

Well indeed is it for us that our Lord steadfastly refused to be sidetracked into what others kept assuring him were far shorter and straighter roads to much bigger results than the hard uphill way that he was taking would or could ever reach. And how much better had it been for him and for the world if we had imitated him in that! Kierkegaard seems to me often to exaggerate his facts, screaming them at us at the full pitch of his lungs. Yet how much sobering truth there is in his austere and challenging message! Again and again he comes back, with a hammering iteration, to the charge that we have grossly adulterated the faith and preach "a cheap edition" of it; easy, where the reality is desperately difficult; and completely able to serve many masters, whereas a genuine discipleship cannot be combined with any other major aim, and leaves no room for it in the mind.

> We extol our age for the fact that Christianity is no longer persecuted. That I can well believe, for Christianity does not exist. . . . We have transformed it into something quite different. That which we call Christianity is not Christianity, but a very much softened interpretation of Christianity, a something remotely related to Christianity. . . . We chatter as nearly as possible in imitation of the truth; heard cursorily, it is as though we were saying the same thing. [But in reality we follow] that "common sense" which thinks the requirement must be altered to suit men; and not Christianity which maintains that man must be altered to suit the requirement.[8]

[8] Cf. "Christ as the Pattern," in *For Self-Examination and Judge for Yourselves,* tr. Walter Lowrie (Princeton: Princeton University Press; London: Oxford University Press, 1941), pp. 166-68. Used by permission.

16 And when even was *now* come, his disciples went down unto the sea,

17 And entered into a ship, and went over the sea toward Capernaum. And it was now dark, and Jesus was not come to them.

18 And the sea arose by reason of a great wind that blew.

19 So when they had rowed about five and twenty or thirty furlongs, they see Jesus walking on the sea, and drawing nigh unto the ship: and they were afraid.

20 But he saith unto them, It is I; be not afraid.

21 Then they willingly received him into the ship: and immediately the ship was at the land whither they went.

16 When evening came, his disciples
went down to the sea, **17** got into a boat,
and started across the sea to Ca-per′na-um.
It was now dark, and Jesus had not yet
come to them. **18** The sea rose because a
strong wind was blowing. **19** When they
had rowed about three or four miles,[i] they
saw Jesus walking on the sea and drawing
near to the boat. They were frightened,
20 but he said to them, "It is I; do not be
afraid." **21** Then they were glad to take
him into the boat, and immediately the
boat was at the land to which they were
going.

[i] Greek *twenty-five or thirty stadia.*

---

2. The Crossing to Capernaum (6:16-24)

16-24. Here again John and Mark (followed by Matthew) are drawing upon the same tradition, but with marked variations. In Mark (6:45-56) the disciples are making for Bethsaida, and the impression left upon a modern reader is that they were coasting along by the shore and were nearing the head of the lake when a strong northerly wind drove them back to a place not far from where they had left Jesus. Here they took Jesus on board and finally landed in the district of Gennesaret, not far from Capernaum. In the Johannine story there is the perplexing statement (vs. 17), **It was now dark, and Jesus had not yet come to them,** and at the close the mysterious announcement that when Jesus had come on board, **immediately the boat was at the land to which they were going** (vs. 21). In both accounts Jesus is described as **walking on the sea.** The Greek phrase (ἐπὶ τῆς θαλάσσης) could mean, as in 21:1, "by the sea." But Mark (6:47) clearly says that the boat was in the middle of the sea ("out on the sea"), and the same miraculous feeling pervades the story in John. Whatever may have been the actual occurrence, there can be little doubt of the numinous air which surrounded Jesus in the eyes of his disciples. To John, Jesus is from the beginning of his ministry the incarnate Logos whose power knows no limit.

In short, our clever and worldly-wise amendments of the Master's original plans have made a sad mess of things!

16-21. ***Belittling the Authentic Christ.***—This account of what happened on the lake is less vivid and dramatic than that of the Synoptists. There is no record at all of Peter's impulsive adventure; and the whole incident is somewhat telescoped. Yet as it stands it is tremendous indeed! Its spiritual lessons, or some of the most obvious of them, thrust themselves upon the mind and can hardly be missed. (*a*) How often in life people are badly scared and frightened by what is really Jesus Christ drawing near to them in helpfulness and kindness. And (*b*) what a difference his presence with us makes, both in the serenity it gives to our own minds, and in the effectiveness of efforts that without him were tiring and largely futile. For the rest (*c*) religions not a few hold it to be a proved axiom, repeatedly verified, that a full measure of saintliness is apt to bring along with it, in certain folk at least, unusual powers over the forces of nature. Thus barefooted they can walk unscathed over a bed of glowing embers, etc. And a number of little circumstantial corroborative touches that slip into his narrative (vss. 22-25) make it clear that this evangelist will have no talk of vision or hallucination, but is certain that what he sets down is fact. Perhaps the main lesson to be gleaned from the passage is that these first Christians felt and saw certain elements in Christ which have grown dimmer to the most of us, if not largely lost. "Is it not a shame," says Luther, "that we are always afraid of Christ, whereas there was never in heaven or earth a more loving, familiar, or milder man, in words,

22 ¶ The day following, when the people, which stood on the other side of the sea, saw that there was none other boat there, save that one whereinto his disciples were entered, and that Jesus went not with his disciples into the boat, but *that* his disciples were gone away alone;

23 (Howbeit there came other boats from Tiberias nigh unto the place where they did eat bread, after that the Lord had given thanks:)

24 When the people therefore saw that Jesus was not there, neither his disciples, they also took shipping, and came to Capernaum, seeking for Jesus.

22 On the next day the people who re-
mained on the other side of the sea saw
that there had been only one boat there,
and that Jesus had not entered the boat
with his disciples, but that his disciples
had gone away alone. 23 However, boats
from Ti-be′ri-as came near the place where
they ate the bread after the Lord had given
thanks. 24 So when the people saw that
Jesus was not there, nor his disciples, they
themselves got into the boats and went to
Ca-per′na-um, seeking Jesus.

Meanwhile, those of the crowd who remained near the scene of the feeding were waiting for Jesus. They had seen the disciples sail away in their **boat** without him, and there was no other boat by which he could have escaped them. When on the following day they could not find Jesus, good fortune brought some **boats** across the lake **from Tiberias.** They embarked and made for Capernaum. The significant note is the description in vs. 23. The boats put in **near the place where they ate the bread after the Lord had given thanks.** (The last six words, however, are omitted by D 69 O.L. [a e] sys c.) In the Marcan account of the five thousand, Jesus "blessed, and broke the loaves" (Mark 6:41). In the doublet which tells of the four thousand, we read "and having given thanks he broke them" (Mark 8:6), though he "blessed" the fish. John follows the story of the five thousand in most of the details, but he uses the word for giving thanks, not that for the blessing (vs. 11). The significance of this is emphasized by the use of the same word again (vs. 23), where we might expect simply, "where they ate the bread." The Greek word for giving thanks is *eucharistein* (εὐχαριστεῖν), and thanksgiving is *eucharistia* (εὐχαριστία), words which soon became technical terms for the celebration of the Lord's Supper (Ign. Phila. 4; Ign. Smyr. 7:1; 8:1; Did. 9:5; 10:1, 2; 14:1; Justin *Apology* I. 65-66). It is almost impossible to escape the inference that the discourse on the bread of life, which follows in the synagogue at Capernaum, has a Eucharistic reference. Its

---

works, and demeanour, especially towards poor, sorrowful, and tormented consciences." [9] These aspects of the Master have come home to us, and fill our minds—too exclusively. We serve a very gracious yet very human Christ. But the Scriptures make it plain that those who lived with him were conscious that, along with all that, there was also in him something awesome, tremendous, superhuman, something that awoke in them what was a kind of dread. That is too apt to be forgotten. We lack fitting reverence toward the wonderful Christ. It helps us to think of him somewhat less inadequately if we try to picture that lonely figure in the darkness that wild night, coming down from the hills, and setting out where the waves were breaking in white foam and the winds were howling.

24-27. ***The Substance and the Shadows.***—Determined not to lose touch with him, the crowds made shift on the next day to follow him to the other side of the lake. But Christ was not impressed by their eager enthusiasm. And here emerges a much-needed lesson. Too many today give the impression that to them numbers and popularity and packed pews and the like are all important and sufficient in themselves; seem to be willing to accept people on any terms, if only they will come at all; whereas Christ would accept them only on his terms, and did not want them upon any other. It hurt him that they were interested in him only insofar as through him they might find some easing of material difficulties and some increase in their comforts. "You seek me only for the chance of loaves and fishes," he said sadly (vs. 26).

That is a disappointment which meets him upon every side these days. People are hugely interested in the by-products of Christianity, but hardly at all in Christianity itself. If he will be

[9] *Table Talk,* CCXII.

25 And when they had found him on the other side of the sea, they said unto him, Rabbi, when camest thou hither?

26 Jesus answered them and said, Verily, verily, I say unto you, Ye seek me, not because ye saw the miracles, but because ye did eat of the loaves, and were filled.

27 Labor not for the meat which perisheth, but for that meat which endureth unto everlasting life, which the Son of man shall give unto you: for him hath God the Father sealed.

25 When they found him on the other
side of the sea, they said to him, "Rabbi,
when did you come here?" 26 Jesus an-
swered them, "Truly, truly, I say to you,
you seek me, not because you saw signs,
but because you ate your fill of the loaves.
27 Do not labor for the food which perishes,
but for the food which endures to eternal
life, which the Son of man will give to
you; for on him has God the Father set

relation to the Last Supper (which is not associated with the Eucharist in this Gospel) is subtly suggested by vs. 4, which has no obvious relevance to the story of the feeding of the multitude.

3. Discourse in the Synagogue at Capernaum (6:25-59)

25-27. The discourse is partly discussion, as in ch. 4 in the discourse on the living water. The remnant of the crowd which had been fed, those who had followed after Jesus and had at last found him at Capernaum, wanted to know when he arrived there. The question in their minds was probably, How had he reached the place? Jesus ignores their question, but charges them with failure to discern the "sign" in the miraculous meal. Their bodily appetite was satisfied; hence their eagerness to see him again. But to seeing eyes that meal illustrated the power of the Son of man to meet the hunger of the soul. These Galilean peasants toiled hard for their farmers and landowners, and in return earned just enough to keep their bodies alive. But there was one who could give them in return for their service food in abundance, and not merely perishable food, but food that nourishes the life which is life indeed, the life eternal. He is the Son of man, who has come down from heaven (1:51; 3:13), bearing the credentials **(seal)** of God the Father.

a judge and divider of material things, increasing our share in them; if he will give us loaves and fishes, better houses, shorter hours, bigger wages, gadgets to lessen work and add to our leisure—these are real things well worth the having, and we will follow him for them. But who wants his spiritual gifts? What would we do with them? What difference would they make? And so Christ's supreme offers to us—the power to conquer selfishness and temper, and so be no longer the helpless playthings of temptation, to be masters in our own lives, putting them to high and worthy ends—are peevishly pushed aside as stupid irrelevancies and nothing to the point.

"A clever European," says C. G. Jung, "is convinced that religion and such things are good enough for the masses and for women, but are of little weight compared to economic and political affairs."[1] What vexes Christ the most in the economic situation is not that material things are so badly distributed, but rather that they are so grossly overvalued. In his standard of measurement they rank very low indeed. And he looks in amazement at a world pressing and jostling like swine about their feeding troughs, paying life away for what to him are trifles at the best. Augustine has a fascinating passage in which he describes how most of us never grow up, but to the end of life keep strenuously playing the old nursery games, with slightly different toys and counters, to be sure—lands and shares instead of the original sand castles, and gold and money for the earlier marbles—but the old games, with the old rules, and the old ends and aims and marks of failure or success.[2] "There are those," says Seneca, "who have nothing to prove their age, except the number of their years"![3] **Do not labor for the food which perishes, but for the food which endures to eternal life.** There are far bigger and more satisfying things within our reach than we have realized.

[1] *Modern Man in Search of a Soul*, p. 252.

[2] *Confessions* I. 30; cf. the impression made by this passage on Robert Louis Stevenson, *Letters* (ed. Sidney Colvin; New York: Charles Scribner's Sons, 1911) II, 200-1.

[3] *Minor Dialogues* IX. 3.

28 Then said they unto him, What shall we do, that we might work the works of God?

29 Jesus answered and said unto them, This is the work of God, that ye believe on him whom he hath sent.

30 They said therefore unto him, What sign showest thou then, that we may see, and believe thee? what dost thou work?

his seal." 28 Then they said to him, "What
must we do, to be doing the work of God?"
29 Jesus answered them, "This is the work
of God, that you believe in him whom
he has sent." 30 So they said to him, "Then
what sign do you do, that we may see, and
believe you? What work do you perform?

28-34. The transition to vs. 28 is explained by the metaphor used in 4:34, "My food is to do the will of him who sent me, and to accomplish his work." So here a connection is traced between divine food and doing the will of God. His questioners ask Jesus, **What must we do, to be doing the work of God?** This translation, however, misses the distinction between the plural of the noun in the question and the singular in the reply (ἔργα, ἔργον). Jesus answers that what God desires is not the multitudinous legal works

---

28-29. ***A Fundamental Question and Christ's Answer.*—Then they said to him, "What must we do, to be doing the work of God?"** A central, indeed a tremendous, question, reaching down to the roots of things, and proving that they who put it had some depth of earth in their mind and nature. Many drift through life seeing no serious purpose in it; flinging it away, lightly and flippantly, anyhow. For what can it matter? But how much anxious, even tortured, thought has been given to this problem! Why are we here? What are we meant to be and do? How should we use this strange and fundamental gift of life, of which we find ourselves possessed? And what diverse answers have been hazarded! Few of them probably are nobler than the familiar august opening to the Shorter Catechism: "What is the chief end of man? Man's chief end is to glorify God, and to enjoy Him forever." True. But how? How are we to glorify God? How does one enjoy him? How are we to fulfill the main purpose and object of our being? **Jesus answered them, "This is the work of God, that you believe in him whom he has sent."**

Always and everywhere a man's beliefs color and shape his personality. Really to know him or to change him one must get behind such overt things as conduct and speech, even thought and motive, to the beliefs from which they flow. If a man thinks of woman as a toy and plaything, he will act accordingly; but if she is to him a great creature of God, then whole departments of his life will take another color and be lived upon a different plan. So in a hundred things. But most momentous of all is how a mind reacts to the things for which Christ stands.

If it has allowed all taste and appetite for them to atrophy, like Darwin with his early love of poetry; if it is not daring enough to hope that they may be true, and big enough to live on the assumption that they are true, and by so doing help to make them true, inevitably it consigns itself to a lean, starved type of being, bleaker and emptier by far than its natural birthright and inheritance. Even pathologically the results may be terrible. Says C. G. Jung:

> During the past thirty years, people from all the civilized countries of the earth have consulted me. . . . Among all my patients in the second half of life—that is to say, over thirty five—there has not been one whose problem in the last resort was not that of finding a religious outlook on life. It is safe to say that every one of them fell ill because he had lost that which the living religions of every age have given to their followers, and none of them has been really healed who did not regain his religious outlook.[4]

And spiritually it means a hideous impoverishment. For to believe in Christ and the things for which he stands, the way of life he teaches us, the God whom he reveals to us, the grace and help he came to offer us, the victory which he makes possible for the least likely of us, is to have the doors flung open, and infinite possibilities keep crowding in. But it all starts with believing in him whom God has sent. Given that, the rest follows. That is the fundamental and foundational thing.

30-34. ***The Uniqueness of Jesus Christ.***—To which they answered, "But why should we believe in you? What is there in you to call out such devotion and allegiance as you claim from us? Where are your credentials? You have indeed fed a crowd mysteriously in a desert place from no visible supplies. But what of it?

[4] *Modern Man in Search of a Soul* (New York: Harcourt, Brace & Co.; London: Routledge & Kegan Paul, 1933), p. 264. Used by permission.

31 Our fathers did eat manna in the desert; as it is written, He gave them bread from heaven to eat.
32 Then Jesus said unto them, Verily, verily, I say unto you, Moses gave you not that bread from heaven; but my Father giveth you the true bread from heaven.

31 Our fathers ate the manna in the wilder-
ness; as it is written, 'He gave them bread
from heaven to eat.'" 32 Jesus then said to
them, "Truly, truly, I say to you, it was not Moses who gave you the bread from heaven; my Father gives you the true bread

---

required by Judaism, but the one **work** which consists in an obedient attitude to his will. It is the obedience of faith, and its test is their response to **him whom he has sent** (cf. 3:17). Their rejoinder is a demand for a **sign** (cf. 2:18; 4:48). The significance of the meal on the other side of the lake had been lost on them. There was a rabbinical rule that if a prophet who was not yet recognized as such should give a sign or wonder, he must be listened to; otherwise no heed need be given to him (see on 3:2). There was also a rabbinical tradition that the Messiah when he came would bring down manna from

---

Wonderful though that may be, it is not unique. **Our fathers ate the manna in the wilderness; as it is written, 'He gave them bread from heaven to eat.'** Since you have done no more than Moses did, why should we turn from him to you?"

That is a popular argument—to allege that there is nothing unique in Jesus Christ; that he is merely one among the many masters and prophets who have been given to the world; and that his teaching can be and is closely paralleled by that of other sages; that strictly speaking there is nothing original in the revelation of God he brings us, or in his message of salvation, or in the Christian standards and way of life; that while Buddha and Mohammed and the rest may and do differ from him in detail, their message is essentially the same as his and has the same results. So Matthew Arnold:

Children of men! the unseen Power, whose eye
For ever doth accompany mankind,
Hath look'd on no religion scornfully
That man did ever find.

Which has not taught weak wills how much they can?
Which has not fall'n on the dry heart like rain?
Which has not cried to sunk, self weary man,
Thou must be born again! [5]

So Ernst Troeltsch argued that while Christ is the only moral and spiritual teacher at all likely to hold dominion over our minds, for other people other prophets may be even more serviceable than he. These had therefore better be left to the leader and guide natural to them; since by our so doing, it seems, they will lose nothing.[6]

[5] "Progress."

[6] "The Place of Christianity Among the World Religions," in *Christian Thought* (London: University of London Press, 1923), pp. 26-28.

"Moses gave our fathers bread from heaven as certainly and as efficiently as you have fed this crowd."

Faced by that type of reasoning, Christ replied, "In the manna Moses, or rather, God through Moses, did give your fathers something real and wonderful that helped and sustained them in their time of need, and brought them safely through." In which saying it is surely not stretching things unduly to see a sanction from Christ for studying the classics of the other great religions humbly and reverently; hearing in them not only the human voice of a brother man seeking to point out the road, but divine grace trying to break in to the minds of men so far as they were able and willing to receive it, using of course the mental language of the time, the only language in which they could think. But what Christ underlines is that though in a very real sense the manna too was a gift direct from God, and impossible without his kindness, still what came to men through Moses was not **the bread . . . which comes down from heaven,** the bread he is now offering—as even God, even through Moses, could not do!

That is a claim which Christ makes with assurance; and we must stand to it. For the facts completely justify it. Elsewhere indeed one is thrilled and gladdened by coming on glorious adumbrations of what he brings to us; on approximations to it, more or less close, and sometimes splendidly close; on parallels, often moving and impressive. What else would one expect? For, says Leibnitz, "The criterion of a true philosophy is that it would at once explain and collect fragments of truth scattered through systems apparently the most incongruous." [7] Which is precisely what Christianity does do.

[7] See, e.g., a finely worded footnote on Christianity as the synthesis of all the higher religions in B. H. Streeter, *Reality* (New York: The Macmillan Co., 1926), pp. 47-48.

33 For the bread of God is he which cometh down from heaven, and giveth life unto the world.
34 Then said they unto him, Lord, evermore give us this bread.
35 And Jesus said unto them, I am the bread of life: he that cometh to me shall

from heaven. 33 For the bread of God is
that which comes down from heaven, and
gives life to the world." 34 They said to
him, "Lord, give us this bread always."
35 Jesus said to them, "I am the bread

---

heaven. Words from Pss. 78:24 and 105:40 were accordingly cited, recalling the gift of manna in the wilderness. Jesus parries this challenge by telling his hearers that **it was not Moses who gave** the children of Israel that heavenly **bread** in the distant past, but God, who as Father is giving in the living present the real (i.e., **the true**), the eternal bread **from heaven,** and this **gives life** not to the Jews only but **to the world.** Like the Samaritan woman who said, "Sir, give me this water, that I may not thirst, nor come here to draw" (4:15), these Galileans now exclaim, **Lord, give us this bread always** (vs. 34).

35-40. The bread from heaven (vs. 32), **the bread of God** (vs. 33), is now identified with Jesus himself in the first of the great I am sayings of this Gospel: **I am the bread of life** (vs. 35), **I am the living bread** (vs. 51), **I am the bread which came down from heaven** (vs. 41). Not his message only, but all that he is in himself, gives life and

---

When Schleiermacher makes his confident assertion that Christ is never a prolongation, but always a break, he has many facts to face; among them our Lord's attitude to Moses and the O.T. dispensation. It is a poor tribute to Christ to feel that in order to ensure his pre-eminence the other teachers must be belittled and their glories minimized. Rather state them at their highest, and Christ will still tower above them like the mighty Himalaya dwarfing their foothills, stately and august although these latter be. Radhakrishnan grows irascible and peevish at the claim of something distinctive and unique in Christ; but, for all his fine scholarship and sensitive mind, he is mistaken in thinking that it is "imperialistic" insolence and nothing more that finds in Christianity "the highest manifestation of the religious spirit," and "the moral standard of the human race while every other religion is to be judged by it." [8] In spiritual things as elsewhere there are stars of differing magnitudes, and some excel others in glory. And the greatest must be ranked as greatest because it is greatest; and because truth is truth. Montefiore, Jew though he remained, frankly concedes an amazing originality to Jesus Christ. And this along many lines. As thus, "It was left to Jesus to turn this picture of divine activity into an ideal of human activity; and it is amazing to think what marvelous and fruitful results have followed the dozen or score of verses in which this ideal is set forth and driven home." Or again, "Through the mists and miracles a character seems to emerge unlike that of any Old Testament and rabbinic

[8] *East and West in Religion* (London: George Allen & Unwin, 1933), p. 24.

hero." [9] As Irenaeus put it, when they asked him what new thing has Christ brought that others do not give us, "He brought himself." [1] So Rudolf Otto, in his sympathetic, even enthusiastic, study of the Indian religions, frankly admits that the whole axis around which life turns, both thought and action, is entirely different in Christianity from that of these other faiths.[2] Moses was Moses, a mighty servant of the most high God. Yet "What Moses gave you was not **the bread from heaven;** it is **my Father** who **gives you the true bread from heaven;** and he is offering that to you in me." In answer to which mighty promise comes the cry of human need and human longing, here too as at that wellhead in Samaria, **Lord, give us this bread always.**

35-40. ***The Good News Christ Brings to Whoever Will Accept It.***—Here it becomes us to walk softly and to speak humbly. For even in the Scriptures, search where you will, there is no more central passage than this "concentrated gospel" as Dods called it. And what a full and satisfying gospel! How ample in its sweep, how generous in its terms, how difficult to evade; answering every doubt and countering every objection; making us see that it was looking straight at us that the promises were given, and that it is for us that they are meant, that no one is excluded from them who will take and use them. This is a kind of innermost citadel, a last trench into which we may retreat in evil

[9] So often, in *Some Elements of the Religious Teaching of Jesus* (London: Macmillan & Co., 1910).

[1] *Against Heresies* IV. 34. 1.

[2] *India's Religion of Grace* (tr. F. H. Foster; London: Student Christian Movement Press, 1930), ch. iv.

never hunger; and he that believeth on me shall never thirst.

of life; he who comes to me shall not hunger, and he who believes in me shall never

---

sustains life in such abundance that no unsatisfied desire remains to frustrate the believer. Indeed, the message to the Samaritan woman (4:14) is recalled in the parallelism of vs. 35, with its implication, "and I am the water of life." Later in the discourse unmistakable allusions to the Eucharist will be found. The metaphor is preserved from any

---

hours, and out of which nobody has ever been shelled. Little wonder that many, e.g., Bunyan, cling to this passage, like a drowning man to the spar on which he tosses in wild seas. With this there is still hope, still infinite hope. But were this swept out of his clutching grasp, there would be none.

I am the bread of Life, says Christ. So we have found. He is as necessary to us as our food. In sober fact he is our food, enabling us to meet life's calls upon us and to keep hale and healthy. A man is tired; and because tired, irritable and impossible. But let him have a meal and likely enough, throwing aside his gloom and ill humor, he will become his usual equable self again, kindly and unselfish and companionable. And why? Because the strength that was in the food has passed into him and become his strength, has made a stronger and a better man of him. So in Christ there is that which feeds, which sustains, which restores spent vigor and exhausted energies, a strength we can appropriate and make our strength, doing and being what apart from him we could not do and be.

That is a fact which many will not realize. They are impressed by certain elements in Christ's standards of life. This, they agree, is what we ought to work out day by day. And optimistically they set out to carry it through, accepting from Christ only his ideal for us; never realizing that, besides that, we need to receive from him the power to live it out, a power that springs naturally and of itself from an acceptance of the Christian verities, and from the gratitude and love and willingness of service they inspire. But apart from these, the needed power just is not there. And all their well-meant efforts to obey Christ's calls upon us is but a hopeless tugging at oneself, in a vain effort to lift oneself up from the muddy ground. Says C. G. Jung:

> It is well known that Freudian psychoanalysis is limited to the task of making conscious the shadow-side and the evil within us. It simply brings into action the civil war that was latent, and lets it go at that. The patient must deal with it as best he can. Freud has unfortunately overlooked the fact that man has never yet been able single-handed to hold his own against the powers of darkness. . . . Man has always stood in need of the spiritual help which each individual's own religion held out to him. . . . Man is never helped in his suffering by what he thinks for himself, but only by revelations of a wisdom greater than his own. It is this which lifts him out of his distress.[3]

So C. E. M. Joad, in an article in which he gives his three reasons for abandoning his rationalist attitude to religion, sets down as one of them that the growing realization of the facts of sin, and of the helplessness of human nature face to face with it, had forced him to belief in the need and the fact of divine grace, without which, as he now sees, no man can achieve salvation. Hence, as so many do, to neglect regular seasons of devotion, to fall out of step with Christ, to lose touch with him, is to deny oneself one's necessary meals. We must have the living bread or perish.

But then, whosoever wills can have it for the asking. The one and only requirement Christ stipulates is that we have some appetite for the things he offers. Bring him that, and eagerly he will do the rest. But what Christ especially emphasizes here is the satisfying fullness of the life he gives to men. **He that cometh to me shall never hunger; and he that believeth on me shall never thirst.** There is an end to craving and to discontent. To quote Jung again:

> I have a Red Indian friend. . . . When we were once speaking confidentially about the white man, he said to me: "We don't understand the whites; they are always wanting something—always restless —always looking for something. . . . We can't understand them. They have such sharp noses, such thin, cruel lips, such lines in their faces. We think they are all crazy." [4]

So did the wisest of men feel as they looked around them at the bustling, fidgety, greedy world. Always people were hungering for something; always thirsting after something more; never were they at peace and satisfied. Buddha declared roundly that the root of all our evils is desire, the itch for possessing; which, like drinking salt water, does not quench thirst, but

[3] *Modern Man in Search of a Soul* (New York: Harcourt, Brace & Co.; London: Routledge & Kegan Paul, 1933), pp. 277-78. Used by permission.

[4] *Ibid.*, p. 246.

36 But I said unto you, That ye also have seen me, and believe not.

thirst. 36 But I said to you that you have

possible crude materialism borrowed from heathen cults by this verse. The promise is given to any who **comes to me** and **believes in me.** But that raises a difficulty. This **bread of life** has **come down from heaven** to give life to the world. How, then, is it that the Jews as a whole do not share in the gift of eternal life? Jesus has already (vs. 26) convicted some of his hearers of their lack of spiritual vision. He now (vs. 36) returns to this charge. They have indeed seen without perception; they have heard without

increases it, keeps leading on and on interminably. And Christ said bluntly that the mass of us seem not to understand the bigness of the nature God has given us, or we would not attempt to satisfy it by such futile trivialities as we do; as if some immense and yawning abyss could be filled by the pebbles which idle hands toss into it, and which tinkle faintly far down in its hollow emptiness.

> All earth's full rivers can not fill
> The sea, that drinking thirsteth still.[5]

Or as old Joseph Hall put it vividly, the heart of man, which is too small to make a meal for a kite, can be satisfied with nothing less than the Lord God Almighty! But in Christ one is given even that; has found what matters: fever and restlessness are over; there are peace and fullness of life.

It is true that in one very real sense Christ awakes and keeps intensifying a hunger of desire which, though given vast things, remains unappeasable and reaches out after still more. But the experts warn us to be cautious how we seek to outrun God. There is something paradoxical in the Christian life. We must have faith, hugeness of faith, and eager spiritual ambitions; and yet we must be content to remain good-temperedly where and what and as we are, with all our zealous efforts to advance seemingly foiled and fooled, until God's good time. As F. W. Faber has it:

> We must wait for God, long, meekly, in the wind and wet, in the thunder and lightning, in the cold and the dark. Wait, and He will come. He never comes to those who do not wait. . . . When He comes, go with Him, but go slowly, fall a little behind; when He quickens His pace, be sure of it, before you quicken yours. But when He slackens, slacken at once and do not be slow only, but silent, very silent, for He is God.[6]

But we have found the meaning and the end of life. If we were given our choice, a single choice, of one thing out of all that life can bring us, our hands might let go their hold on many glorious gifts and possibilities lingeringly and grudgingly. And yet surely we could not hesitate. But of themselves our hearts would cry out, "Give us Jesus Christ!" Whatever else we miss, we must have him! And since we have that greatest, we are past hungering and thirsting in the fundamental sense, are happy and content. So Wesley:

> By this faith we are saved from all uneasiness of mind, from the anguish of a wounded spirit, from discontent, from fear and sorrow of heart, and from that inexpressible listlessness and weariness, both of the world and of ourselves, which we had so helplessly laboured under for many years; especially when we were out of the hurry of the world, and sunk into calm reflection.[7]

Still, Christ allows that there are those who see no beauty in him that they should desire him; who have no interest at all in what he is and brings, and so look at him coldly and pass by (vs. 36). As Bertrand Russell: "My own view on Religion is that of Lucretius. I regard it as a disease born of fear and as a source of untold misery to the human race." [8] Or that pathetic creature, H. G. Wells, who writes:

> Why do people go on pretending about this Christianity? At the tests of war, disease, social injustice and every real human distress, it fails—and leaves a cheated victim. . . . Jesus was some fine sort of man perhaps, the Jewish Messiah was a promise of leadership, but Our Saviour of the Trinity is a dressed-up inconsistent effigy of amiability, a monstrous hybrid of man and infinity, making vague promises of helpful miracles for the cheating of simple souls, an ever absent help in time of trouble.[1]

The only explanation of such findings is that these folk are ill, and have no appetite, and so turn from their natural food. If the

[5] Christina Rossetti, "By the Sea."

[6] *Growth in Holiness* (4th ed.; London: T. Richardson & Son, 1872), p. 120.

[7] "Earnest Appeal to Men of Reason and Religion," *Works* (London: John Mason, 1830), VIII, 5.

[8] "Has Religion Made Useful Contributions to Civilization?" *The Rationalist Annual for the Year 1930* (London: Rationalist Press Association), p. 3.

[1] *Experiment in Autobiography* (New York: The Macmillan Co., 1934), p. 46.

37 All that the Father giveth me shall come to me; and him that cometh to me I will in no wise cast out.

seen me and yet do not believe. 37 All that the Father gives me will come to me; and him who comes to me I will not cast out.

belief. But the divine initiative is at work. It is by the grace of God that men are able to exercise faith, and it is his **will** that all who see his glory revealed in **the Son** and who make the surrender of faith should possess that real life which is offered now and which abides forever. As the will of the Son is in unison with the Father's will, he will carry it out by receiving all who come to him.

world looks with wonder and a pitying contempt at religious people, as at strange folk who dwell in a world of shadows and waste their lives in dreaming insubstantial dreams or in chasing tenuous, thin nebulosities; if the traffickers in *Vanity Fair* are "not a little amused" at men who are not interested in the solid and colorful merchandise they have to sell—we on our side cannot understand how reasonable beings can bring themselves to miss so much and for so little! They are offered the bread of life; and they prefer to starve, or to try to satisfy the cravings of their royal nature with the half-eaten husks the swine have mouthed and left!

37. ***God's Gift to Christ.***—But, says Christ, **All that the Father gives me will come to me.** So Christ regards us as a gift to him from God! We speak of Christ himself as God's "unspeakable gift" to us, as something that breaks through language and cannot be described, as the last and crowning proof of divine grace and kindness toward us. And that is natural enough. But surely it is very wonderful that Christ should regard us, and the saving of us in our incorrigibility and obstinate perverseness, not as a trying and all but impossible task, but as a thing to be joyously accepted as a token of God's trust in him and kindness toward him. Something of what is in his mind toward us can be seen in the attitude of parents to their children. These mean for them continual labor, and self-sacrifice, and thought, and care. Yet they esteem them a marvelous gift of God to them; feel that without them life would be a vastly poorer and emptier thing. So, but far more, it seems that our Lord thinks of us. We are a gift of God to him, to be prized and treasured, making his life fuller than it would have been without us.

But what does this giving of us by the Father to Christ actually mean? It was on texts like this that the Calvinists built up their doctrine of election. And beyond all questioning the texts are there; cf. the even stronger statement of vs. 44. And what interpretation can be given if their explanation and exegesis are not to be accepted? Always it is God who takes the first step; God and not we. When the gospel came originally to the world, it was, so we are told, because while we were dead in trespasses and sins, God in his mercy took action. And so it is always in the individual soul. If we are in Christ at all, it is not as the result of our own hard-breathing efforts, but because God pitied us, and called us, and came seeking us, and drew us to him, and gave us to Jesus Christ. What possible quarrel can anybody have with that fact, taken straight from the experience of an innumerable company who have no doubt about it? But difficulty arises when people try to tidy things up into neat and compact bundles, with no loose ends or threads.

So long as it is taken from experience, a doctrine is valid and dependable. But the moment it passes beyond that it is challengeable, and possesses no self-evident authenticity, often little truth; e.g., when Cyprian laid it down that saving grace comes through the sacraments, he was founding solidly on the memorable things that indisputably happened to himself when being baptized, as he had every right to do; and his doctrine cannot be refuted. But when it is claimed that such grace comes and can come only through the sacraments, one has passed from experience to logic. And there are truer things in life than that. So here. It was the unsought grace of God that found me and made me Christ's. That is experience; and that cannot be shaken. But to move on from that to form a syllogism that sounds grimly logical, as thus:

> **All that the Father gives me will come to me.**
> There are those who do not come to me.
> Therefore the Father did not give me these.
> And they are outside of his plans of grace—

that is to leave experience behind, and launch out on wild seas of thought. The doctrine of election does not of necessity imply belief in reprobation, and grave tenets of that kind. All that it says is—and it says it, dazed, confused, bewildered by a grace which has blinded it through excess of light—all that it says is that if we are Christ's at all, then we are his not

38 For I came down from heaven, not to do mine own will, but the will of him that sent me.

39 And this is the Father's will which hath sent me, that of all which he hath given me I should lose nothing, but should raise it up again at the last day.

38 For I have come down from heaven, not to do my own will, but the will of him who sent me; 39 and this is the will of him who sent me, that I should lose nothing of all that he has given me, but raise it up

---

I will raise him up at the last day sounds as a refrain in this discourse (vss. 39, 40, 44, 54). It has often been regarded as an erratic boulder in this Gospel, inconsistent with

---

because of anything that we have done, and not through any native worth in us, but solely because God set himself to win us, ringed us about, and would not let us be; was resolute, persistent, obstinate, and had his gracious way. That is all that can be said and ought to be said; and it comes directly from experience.

And as if that were not wonderful enough, Christ, heaping grace on grace, adds the emphatic promise, **And him that cometh to me I will in no wise cast out—in no wise,** for no possible reason, for no statable cause. That seems fairly to shut the door behind us with a right comfortable sound, shutting us in and shutting the dark out. It is true that while in the Greek there is a strong and assured negative, the vital phrase **in no wise** is not there. And there are modern versions which account "never" (Moffatt, Goodspeed), and even a mere **not** (RSV), as a sufficient translation. But the emphasis of the KJV is a touch nothing short of genius, catching with exactness the Master's meaning, and stating it in a way that has brought hope and heartening to innumerable souls, e.g., John Bunyan:

> This scripture did also most sweetly visit my soul: "And him that cometh to me I will in no wise cast out" (John vi.37). Oh the comfort that I have had from this word "in no wise." As who should say, by no means, for nothing whatever he hath done. But Satan would greatly labour to pull this promise from me, telling of me that Christ did not mean me and such as I, but sinners of a lower rank, that had not done as I had done. But I should answer him again, Satan, here is in this word no such exception; but him that comes, him, any him —him that cometh to me I will in no wise cast out. . . . If ever Satan and I did strive for any word of God in all my life, it was for this good word of Christ,—he at one end and I at the other. Oh, what work did we make! It was for this in John, I say, that we did so tug and strive; he pulled, and I pulled; but, God be praised, I got the better of him.[2]

And how many have built their hopes upon that same foundation! At the beginning it is this that gives us courage to make the initial venture. "I am willing with all my heart [said Goodwill], and, with that, he opened the gate. . . . We make no objections against any, notwithstanding all that they have done before they come hither, they in no wise are cast out."[3] And how often, turning back from some far country, we have found again that "he is not ashamed to call [us] brethren" (Heb. 2:11), but comes out eagerly to meet the shabby figure creeping hesitatingly home, and hopefully begins afresh, still confident and undiscouraged by our many failures. And what plea can we have at the end of life, with our chances over and so little to show for them but what is disappointing and unworthy, except that we are trusting to his promise: **him that cometh to me I will in no wise cast out.** And what is this coming but a hungering and thirsting for what he has to give us; a hungering that takes, a thirsting that accepts?

38-40. ***The Will of God.***—But still more heartening even than these tremendous facts are the reasons that Christ gives us for the facts; they seem to clinch things finally. For we are definitely told that Christ's own honor is bound up in getting us safe home. We may falter and forget and fail, prove disobedient and unruly; but Christ will not fail. With loyalty, and to the last jot and tittle, he will carry out the will that God has given him to do; and part of that will is that we must not slip through his guard. "I have received my instructions from him who sent me, and they are that of **all which he hath given me I should lose nothing**—not you. And those instructions are going to be carried out. When evening comes, you also must be in the fold, with the gate closed behind you on all danger and all sin; or God will look at me and ask. 'But where is that other I committed to your keeping?' " Behind us we have not only our own futile efforts and insufficiency, but the will of God—that wonderful will which has achieved such sheer impossibilities, as we should judge—and the obedience to God of the Lord Jesus Christ.

[2] *Grace Abounding to the Chief of Sinners,* par. 215.

[3] Bunyan, *The Pilgrim's Progress,* Part I.

40 And this is the will of him that sent me, that every one which seeth the Son, and believeth on him, may have everlasting life: and I will raise him up at the last day.

41 The Jews then murmured at him, because he said, I am the bread which came down from heaven.

42 And they said, Is not this Jesus, the son of Joseph, whose father and mother we know? how is it then that he saith, I came down from heaven?

43 Jesus therefore answered and said unto them, Murmur not among yourselves.

44 No man can come to me, except the Father which hath sent me draw him: and I will raise him up at the last day.

at the last day. 40 For this is the will of my
Father, that every one who sees the Son and
believes in him should have eternal life;
and I will raise him up at the last day."
41 The Jews then murmured at him, be-
cause he said, "I am the bread which came
down from heaven." 42 They said, "Is not
this Jesus, the son of Joseph, whose father
and mother we know? How does he now say,
'I have come down from heaven'?" 43 Jesus
answered them, "Do not murmur among
yourselves. 44 No one can come to me un-
less the Father who sent me draws him;
and I will raise him up at the last day.

---

the Johannine doctrine of eternal life. But the Johannine eschatology is both realized and future. The "now" and the "shall be" are related but distinct (see Intro., pp. 443-44).

Some commentators find a trace of predestinarianism in vs. 37 (cf. vs. 44), and regard this teaching as the church's answer to the problem of the rejection of the Jews which Paul worked out in Rom. 9–11 (see Intro., p. 443).

41-52. In vss. 41-59 two objections are raised by **the Jews,** and in replying to them, Jesus elaborates his teaching about **the living bread.** The first muttered protest is that the parents of Jesus were known to many (cf. 7:27-28) and that this fact disproved the claim, **I have come down from heaven.** As the doctrine of the Virgin Birth has no place

---

And as life goes on, a gracious sense of helplessness steals over us, a conviction that keeps deepening, that not God's power alone but his love too is an immeasurable and even awesome thing; that his grace toward us is more patient and persistent even than our sinfulness toward him; that his determination to save us looks as if it must have its way, seems inescapable. **For I have come down from heaven, not to do my own will, but the will of him who sent me; and this is the will of him who sent me, that I should lose nothing of all that he has given me, but raise it up at the last day. For this is the will of my Father, that every one who sees the Son and believes in him should have eternal life; and I will raise him up at the last day.** "Any him," as Bunyan says, can have the glory of the life in Christ here and now; and the fullness of it yonder.

We have an odd way of speaking of the will of God in sad and resigned voices, as if it were something that must be accepted, but which no one can like or would ever dream of choosing. Yet how rich and generous is God's will for us: how liberal are the gifts he has granted us already; and how majestic are his hopes and plans for us! In this passage, for example, we are told that God's will for us is (*a*) that we should have the glory of fellowship with Jesus Christ, to whom he gives us; (*b*) that all the skill and care of Christ should be ours to shepherd us safely through this dangerous world; and (*c*) that we should know life at its highest, even here, even now; and later enter into a fullness of it which is indescribable, and which as yet we cannot even imagine.

41-66. ***Being Drawn by God.***—Anderson Scott affirms, and with truth, that nothing hurt Christ more than a stupid obtuseness that kept interpreting his metaphors with a wooden literalness.[4] Few things have cost him dearer down the centuries; and as this passage makes only too clear, he was dogged by it from the very first. "Even the gods," said Schiller, "fight in vain against stupidity."[5] And Christ is met by much of that. First of all, prosaic people, staring at him in a bewildered fashion, objected that they knew his parents, and were neighbors of his, living in a near-by street, and had all their lives seen him moving about his affairs. What then could he mean by "coming down from heaven," as he claimed to have done? And they were irritated and stumbled; as dull

[4] *New Testament Ethics* (Cambridge: University Press, 1930), pp. 13-15.

[5] *The Maid of Orleans,* Act III, scene 6.

45 It is written in the prophets, And they shall be all taught of God. Every man therefore that hath heard, and hath learned of the Father, cometh unto me.

46 Not that any man hath seen the Father, save he which is of God, he hath seen the Father.

47 Verily, verily, I say unto you, He that believeth on me hath everlasting life.

48 I am that bread of life.

49 Your fathers did eat manna in the wilderness, and are dead.

50 This is the bread which cometh down from heaven, that a man may eat thereof, and not die.

51 I am the living bread which came down from heaven: if any man eat of this bread, he shall live for ever: and the bread that I will give is my flesh, which I will give for the life of the world.

45 It is written in the prophets, 'And they
shall all be taught by God.' Every one who
has heard and learned from the Father
comes to me. 46 Not that any one has seen
the Father except him who is from God;
he has seen the Father. 47 Truly, truly, I
say to you, he who believes has eternal life.
48 I am the bread of life. 49 Your fathers
ate the manna in the wilderness, and they
died. 50 This is the bread which comes
down from heaven, that a man may eat of it
and not die. 51 I am the living bread which
came down from heaven; if any one eats of
this bread, he will live for ever; and the
bread which I shall give for the life of the
world is my flesh."

---

in the Johannine theology (cf. Exeg. on 1:13, 45), the reference to **Joseph** is not countered. Jesus deprecates this sort of literal interpretation (cf. 3:5-6) and takes up again the thread of the discourse from vs. 40. It is the gracious leading of the Father that draws men to Jesus. (The same word ἕλκειν is used as in the LXX of Jer. 31[38]:3, "With lovingkindness have I drawn thee.") Isaiah writes (54:13; cf. Jer. 31:33-34), "All thy children shall be taught of the LORD." Divine instruction should lead those who have the teachable disposition to the only one who speaks out of direct knowledge which comes from the vision of God (cf. 1:18). **Eternal life** is the possession only of those who have passed beyond reliance upon the physical senses into the experience of spiritual perception, i.e., faith. Life in that higher sphere is sustained by spiritual food, unlike the manna which lasted but for a day and was food merely for perishable bodies. The **living bread . . . from heaven** is no other than the very life of Jesus given up that **life** may be given to the world.

---

creatures, with no glint of poetry in them, often are by Christ.

To that he replies by reiterating what he has already said: that only divine grace can draw a man to him, which "drawing" seems to be the method of the "giving" of vs. 37. Certainly as we look back at life this drawing is a major fact in it, indeed, the fact of all facts. For we too must say, with Miguel de Unamuno,

> I believe in God as I believe in my friends, because I feel the breath of His affection, feel His invisible and intangible hand, drawing me, leading me, grasping me; because I possess an inner consciousness of a particular providence and of a universal mind that marks out for me the course of my destiny.[6]

And his will is to give us to Jesus Christ, so that we too may inherit and appropriate all there is in him. Again, he declares with assurance that only in and through him can anyone know life in its fullness (vs. 47). And again, and with a deepened emphasis, he claims that he, and what he is, and what he teaches, is the true food of the soul, keeping it in life, sustaining it, enabling it to do and be all it is meant to be and do (vs. 48). Other good gifts from God can help us for a little (vs. 49): but the grace of God there is for us in him is inexhaustible, whatever our calls on it may be; and it will last forever (vs. 50).

51-67. ***A Crucial Metaphor.***—Then there comes a saying which alienated many who had been drawn to him, and sadly thinned the ranks around him: **I am the living bread which came down from heaven; if any one eats of this bread, he will live for ever; and the bread which I shall give for the life of the world is my flesh.** That is a metaphor which has had immeasurable consequences for good and for evil. Souls without number have found in it a perfect statement both of the meaning of real

[6] *The Tragic Sense of Life*, tr. J. E. C. Flitch (London: Macmillan & Co., 1921), p. 194.

52 The Jews therefore strove among themselves, saying, How can this man give us *his* flesh to eat?

53 Then Jesus said unto them, Verily, verily, I say unto you, Except ye eat the flesh of the Son of man, and drink his blood, ye have no life in you.

54 Whoso eateth my flesh, and drinketh my blood, hath eternal life; and I will raise him up at the last day.

55 For my flesh is meat indeed, and my blood is drink indeed.

56 He that eateth my flesh, and drinketh my blood, dwelleth in me, and I in him.

57 As the living Father hath sent me, and I live by the Father; so he that eateth me, even he shall live by me.

52 The Jews then disputed among them-
selves, saying, "How can this man give us
his flesh to eat?" 53 So Jesus said to them,
"Truly, truly, I say to you, unless you eat
the flesh of the Son of man and drink his
blood, you have no life in you; 54 he who
eats my flesh and drinks my blood has eter-
nal life, and I will raise him up at the last
day. 55 For my flesh is food indeed, and my
blood is drink indeed. 56 He who eats my
flesh and drinks my blood abides in me,
and I in him. 57 As the living Father sent
me, and I live because of the Father, so
he who eats me will live because of me.

52-59. This raises the second objection, **How can this man give us his flesh to eat?** In the words that follow we have the Johannine interpretation of the "words of institution" spoken in the upper room, but detached in this Gospel from their original setting (cf. I Cor. 11:23-26; Mark 14:22-25; Matt. 26:26-29; Luke 22:17-19). The paradox **Unless you eat the flesh of the Son of man and drink his blood, you have no life in you** is the more striking when we remember how repulsive the thought of drinking blood would be to any Jew. The metaphor stands for dwelling in constant union with Christ, as the allegory of the true vine will show in ch. 15. That which is symbolized in the Eucharist by the act of eating the bread and drinking the wine is that the believer in Christ, as he says (vs. 56), **abides in me, and I in him.** This mystical union with Christ is not subject to the temporal chances and changes of this our mortality. "Because I live, you will live also" (14:19). The contrast between the physical and the spiritual is again emphasized in vs. 55: "For my flesh is real food and my blood is real drink" (Moffatt). In vs. 57 the preposition translated **because of the Father, . . . because of me,** could be taken in two ways. (*a*) The rendering given means that as the Son owes his life to the Father, so he who appropriates the Son and dwells in union with him owes his experience

---

discipleship and of the secret of Christian faith and Christian living. But it has rent the church, as few things have done, into angry factions. And it has received interpretations which to many seem grossly pagan and incredibly obtuse. The crude material meaning which the original hearers read into the words is gone; but it has widely been replaced by only more refined forms of it. The holders of the doctrine of transubstantiation, e.g., appeal with confidence to this passage as a plain dominical justification of their view of the sacrament. The "accidents" of the bread—i.e., what is visible and tangible about it—remain indeed unaltered. But "the substance" of the bread—i.e., the intangible and invisible something to which the tangible and visible accidents are supposed to adhere—becomes the substance of the body of our Lord. And of this, literally, we are said to partake, eating his flesh, and by this sacred food our souls are kept alive and strengthened.

But surely what has to be remembered is that this is a metaphor, to be understood and used like every other metaphor. When Luther chalked on the table, "This is my body," as if that were final and conclusive—Christ said it, and Christ meant it, and that is that—someone else might have inscribed, "I am the door"—Christ said it, and Christ meant it, and it must be believed. No doubt! But no human being because of that saying thinks of Christ as a literal door, swinging on its hinges. Why should one metaphor be read with such prosaic woodenness, while all the rest are not? Understood as a metaphor, the saying is arrestingly vivid and lays down what is precisely and exactly the plain truth. Really to receive from Christ what he has to give us, really to have experience of his saving power, we must feed on him—there is no other word that expresses it with a like accuracy—must absorb his teaching, his character, his mind, his ways; must appropriate the

58 This is that bread which came down from heaven: not as your fathers did eat manna, and are dead: he that eateth of this bread shall live for ever.

59 These things said he in the synagogue, as he taught in Capernaum.

60 Many therefore of his disciples, when they had heard *this,* said, This is a hard saying; who can hear it?

61 When Jesus knew in himself that his disciples murmured at it, he said unto them, Doth this offend you?

62 *What* and if ye shall see the Son of man ascend up where he was before?

63 It is the Spirit that quickeneth; the flesh profiteth nothing: the words that I speak unto you, *they* are spirit, and *they* are life.

58 This is the bread which came down from
heaven, not such as the fathers ate and
died; he who eats this bread will live for-
ever." 59 This he said in the synagogue, as
he taught at Ca-per′na-um.
60 Many of his disciples, when they
heard it, said, "This is a hard saying; who
can listen to it?" 61 But Jesus, knowing in
himself that his disciples murmured at it,
said to them, "Do you take offense at this?
62 Then what if you were to see the Son
of man ascending where he was before?
63 It is the spirit that gives life, the flesh
is of no avail; the words that I have spoken

---

of eternal life to the Son. This recalls the teaching of 5:26. (*b*) Others translate this preposition (διά with the accusative) "for the sake of," "in the interests of," and claim that here the mission of Christ links this passage with the recurring thought of 4:34; 5:30; 6:38-40, but applies it to the motive which should inspire the life of the believer in Christ. This thought is found again in 15:9-10, and is put in reverse order in I John 2:17. While both interpretations accord with Johannine teaching, perhaps the former is a little closer to the context.

4. The Testing of Faith (6:60-71)

60-65. Some from the larger circle of disciples, as distinct from "the Jews," took offense at this **hard saying.** They were repelled by the crass materialism of the words in their literal sense. Jesus removes any ground for this misunderstanding by two reminders. (*a*) He has been speaking throughout of a higher order of life than the world known only to the physical senses. His true home is in that higher realm from which he has come and to which he will return. When they have the spiritual discernment to see him

---

virtue there is in him, till his mind becomes our mind and his ways our ways; till we think somewhat as he would do if he were in our place; and can be and do what without him we could not be or do: and this because his power has passed into us and become our power. As Paul has it, "I can do all things through Christ which strengtheneth me" (Phil. 4:13). **He who eats my flesh and drinks my blood abides in me, and I in him.** Indeed, so intimate and vital is the relationship between Christ and a real believer in him, that he compares it to that which exists between God and himself (vs. 57); and claims that while other aids, even though God-sent and serviceable for a time, are left behind, what he does for a soul, what he gives to it, is no transitory thing, but a permanent help, lasting and deepening to all eternity, enabling it to live forever (vs. 58). All which, he adds, is of course to be understood in a spiritual sense (vs. 63). Which, alas! too often it has not been. Certainly to many of those who first heard it, all this seemed crazy talk; so meaningless, if not positively repulsive, that forthwith they flocked away from Christ, done with so unbalanced a creature (vss. 60, 66).

Evidently, then, it is unsafe to gauge the faithfulness and spiritual value of a ministry by its popularity. That glib assertion, thrown about from hand to hand, that if only ministers would preach the real gospel their pews would be crowded out, has to face and account for ugly facts such as this in the experience of Christ himself. Consistently, unswervingly, he stood to his policy that the deep facts and doctrines must be preached, whether the people liked it or not, whether they were alienated or attracted, whether folk thronged to hear or would not listen. And he did preach them, at the cost of losing his crowd. Whether we can be cleverer than he and, as he could not and did not do, can maintain both our faithfulness to

64 But there are some of you that believe not. For Jesus knew from the beginning who they were that believed not, and who should betray him.

65 And he said, Therefore said I unto you, that no man can come unto me, except it were given unto him of my Father.

66 ¶ From that *time* many of his disciples went back, and walked no more with him.

67 Then said Jesus unto the twelve, Will ye also go away?

68 Then Simon Peter answered him, Lord, to whom shall we go? thou hast the words of eternal life.

69 And we believe and are sure that thou art that Christ, the Son of the living God.

to you are spirit and life. **64** But there are
some of you that do not believe." For
Jesus knew from the first who those were
that did not believe, and who it was that
should betray him. **65** And he said, "This
is why I told you that no one can come
to me unless it is granted him by the Father."

66 After this many of his disciples drew
back and no longer went about with him.
67 Jesus said to the twelve, "Will you also go
away?" **68** Simon Peter answered him,
"Lord, to whom shall we go? You have the
words of eternal life; **69** and we have believed, and have come to know, that you

---

with the eyes of faith, after his life on earth is completed, they will understand what it is to assimilate the living bread, to enjoy eternal life. (*b*) Only **spirit . . . gives life.** It is the life-giving quality of his message as the Word of God which Jesus has symbolized as food and drink. But it is not only his **words** that give life, it is himself in the life laid down for the world, his body and blood freely given for all. His spirit liberated from the conditions of this earthly life will be a quickening power in all who believe in him. Unbelief robs **some** of them of this promise of life. Probably the word "ascend" (vs. 62) suggests a double meaning, like the words "lift up" and "glorify." The ascension implies the preceding passion and death. Vs. 65 reiterates the principle that conjoins God's initiative and man's responsibility.

66-71. As in Mark 4:10-12, the hard sayings of Jesus serve to sift the disciples. Many of these **drew back and no longer went about with him.** Whereupon Jesus turned to the **twelve** (here named for the first time in this Gospel) and asked whether their loyalty could stand the strain. The reply given by Peter is the Johannine equivalent for the

---

God and the truth on the one hand, and on the other our popularity with men—that is a problem which ministers with crowded churches must think out and answer for themselves.

W. E. Orchard once went with his wife to worship in the church of a clergyman who passed his days in a buzz of excited and adoring people, and noticing that she was looking around her somewhat contemptuously at a crowd that showed no visible mood of worship, he whispered to her, "It is all very well, my dear, but I could not fill this place." "No," she replied; "but you could empty it"![7] And there are places where, in order to obtain any spiritual outcome from what is being carried on, that is the first and the most pressing step required. So here (vss. 62-65) where Christ says, "Are you stumbled by what I have said?" And far from withdrawing or modifying any of it because of their bewilderment, he tells them frankly that things yet more amazing will have to be faced and thought out.

> How very hard it is to be
> A Christian!

So Browning begins his "Easter Day." And Christ will not tone down the faith and make it easier for us by emasculating it. We must remember that side of things too, when we talk with truth about the simple gospel.

So sadly thinned were the ranks around him, with wide gaping spaces opening everywhere, in place of the customary serried rows of rapt listeners; so many kept streaming away, that Christ felt far from certain of the continued allegiance even of the twelve. **Will you also go away?** he asked.

68-69. ***Peter's Great Moment.***—No one in history is more vividly photographed than Simon Peter. No character in literature stands out before the reader's eyes more visible and

[7] *From Faith to Faith* (New York: Harper & Bros., 1933), p. 142.

70 Jesus answered them, Have not I chosen you twelve, and one of you is a devil?

71 He spake of Judas Iscariot *the son* of Simon: for he it was that should betray him, being one of the twelve.

are the Holy One of God." 70 Jesus answered them, "Did I not choose you, the twelve, and one of you is a devil?" 71 He spoke of Judas the son of Simon Iscariot, for he, one of the twelve, was to betray him.

Synoptic account of the confession at Caesarea Philippi (Mark 8:27-30). The ERV, following the Greek, rightly omits the definite article before **words of eternal life.** It is the characteristic of the message of Jesus that is emphasized; it explains and offers **eternal life.** His words have kindled faith and led to the knowledge of his secret. He is **the Holy One of God,** a messianic title (Mark 1:24; Luke 4:34). Jesus is also called **the Holy One** in I John 2:20. The choice of the **twelve** (vss. 70-71) is dwelt upon again in 13:18; 15:16, but the scene closes with the reminder that not even divine election overrules the responsible freedom of sinful man. The mention of Judas' treason in this connection points to a knowledge of the tradition preserved in the Synoptic Gospels. Luke 9:18-20 places Peter's confession immediately after the feeding of the multitude, as John does here. John brings in the first reference to the treachery of Judas in this version of the Eucharistic discourse. Later, in 13:21-30, the announcement of the betrayal takes place in the Upper Room, where it is placed by the Synoptists (Mark 14:17-21; Matt. 26:20-25; Luke 22:21-23) at the Last Supper. The description of Judas as a **devil** is explained in 13:2.

---

knowable than he. "A man of extremes," as Samuel Rutherford said of himself, there were unexpected heights and depths in him, a queer unaccountability. For he was passionate, impulsive, affectionate, apt to dare and risk more than his faith could carry through. Yet it was he, not John, who was Christ's closest friend; he upon whom Christ leaned the most; he who was the natural spokesman for the others. So it was here. And a right worthy answer he made. "Going away? But **to whom shall we go?** For there is no one else who can teach us as you can teach us, and give us what you can give us, and be to us what you have been and are. Already you have made life a new and far fuller thing for us; and always other and exciting vistas keep opening up before us, not to be seen apart from you. **We have believed and have come to know, that you are the Holy One of God.**" That is the natural and inevitable order. First, faith that ventures on a possibility that it may be true! Then, in a little, something surer and steadier than faith: faith grown to knowledge, a knowledge built out of the solid facts of personal experience. But it is only that first daring leap that can land us there!

Is anyone in history more to be envied than Peter during this episode? There was a day (12:12-19; Matt. 21:1-11; Luke 19:28-40) when Christ passed through cheering throngs. And one would like to have been of them, and among them. But there was this other day when many, done with Christ, as they said disgustedly, were pouring away from him. And the very disciples were swithering, as the Scots say; were hesitating whether they too would go. And Peter strode across the opening and quickly widening blanks, and set his back against Christ's back. "Go?" he said. "No! Whoever else may go, there will always be two of us at least!" Who would not rather have been Peter then than one of the cheering crowd? It is not all loss that we have been set in a day when for the moment the tides of religion are ebbing. "Do not you love me best," wheedled Ayesha, the young and beautiful wife of Mohammed. "No, by Allah," he cried out, "for Kadijah" (now old and withered) "believed in me, when no one else believed. She will always come first." [8]

70-71. ***Judas.***—(See also on 13:26-30.) Yet Christ's answer is grave and awesome, even terrible. As elsewhere, so here he has to pull up Peter's too glib assurance, and meet his overconfidence with the cold douche of reality. **Did I not choose you, the twelve, and one of you is a devil?** From which this at least is plain, that there are occasions where and when not to use bluntness of speech is to be un-Christlike. There is no trace here of the soft amiable Christ who is so popular. There was at times a terrible anger in Christ's heart; and wounding, scathing, searing words were then on his lips. And if there is no sign of these things in our preaching and our representing of him, then without any doubt ours cannot be the authentic Christ of the N.T., but is a sham and a deceiver of our own contriving.

For the rest, the evangelists hardly give us a

[8] Carlyle, *On Heroes, Hero-Worship, and the Heroic in History,* "The Hero as Prophet."

7 After these things Jesus walked in Galilee: for he would not walk in Jewry, because the Jews sought to kill him.

2 Now the Jews' feast of tabernacles was at hand.

7 After this Jesus went about in Galilee; he would not go about in Judea, because the Jews[j] sought to kill him. 2 Now the Jews' feast of Tabernacles was at hand.

[j] Or *Judeans.*

D. Jesus at the Feast of Tabernacles (7:1-14)

7:1. After this, i.e, after the events recorded in ch. 5. The events related in ch. 6 probably took place before the incident described in ch. 5. Internal evidence suggests also that vss. 15-24 in this chapter, and possibly 8:12-20 as well, are part of the controversy which followed the healing of the cripple at Bethzatha (or Bethesda). Jesus avoided Judea **because the Jews sought to kill him** (cf. vs. 19; 5:16, 18). **The Jews' feast of Tabernacles** (for this way of referring to "the Jews" see on 1:19 and 5:10) is described in Lev. 23:33-43; Deut. 16:13-17; Num. 29:35. See also Josephus *Antiquities* VIII. 4. 1, "The feast of Tabernacles is considered especially sacred and important by the Hebrews." It began on the fifteenth of the seventh month, Tishri (September-October), and in the time of Christ lasted eight days.

fair chance with Judas. From the beginning, and all through the Gospels, they hang round his neck that damning phrase, "who also betrayed him," till unconsciously we get the impression that like the villain in a medieval play, whose very name reveals the role he is to fill, Judas was chosen for the part of the betrayer. But that is to miss the horror and sheer terror of the tragedy. For Judas was one of Christ's best friends. And Jesus did not choose his friends at random, but after long prayer and communion with his Father. This was a man whom our Lord liked and trusted; one of those whom he chose out, wanting to have him with him; and assured that he possessed aptitudes and capacities for usefulness to the cause that almost no one known to him could rival. So he called Judas. And Judas responded, felt the thrill of the adventure, rose up, left all, and followed, as really as Peter or John. And then something went wrong, so tragically wrong that of all the dense masses of humanity he is ranked absolutely last; the most horrible blot upon our human records, so men judge. Did not Dante see him in the very lowest place in hell, farthest from God and any gleam of hope? Is not his name a synonym for utter infamy? Certainly the judgment that Christ passes on him here sets the heart shuddering. But is it final? When Christ came upon Judas on the other side, did he look at him with cold eyes and say, "You are a devil," and pass by? All through the N.T. the loyalty of Christ to the most hopeless and impossible is underlined. "If we are faithless, he remains faithful—for he cannot deny himself" (II Tim. 2:13). Ah, Judas, sinful brother Judas! Had you turned to him upon this side of the grave you would have found that true even for you. And that utter blackness of despair that overwhelmed you, that inability to bear yourself, or to live with yourself, or to become accustomed to the horror you had done, is proof that there was still something in you that hated it and shrank from it and loathed it. Even "if we are faithless, he remains faithful—for he cannot deny himself." Try it, man! Try it even yet! Go to him, saying only this:

> O Savior, I have naught to plead,
> In earth beneath, or heaven above
> But only my exceeding need,
> And Thy exceeding love.[1]

He may still have mercy even upon us.

7:1-44. ***A Confusion of Opinion.***—A great and good man was assailed in his public life from some quarters by a ferocious persistence of misrepresentation and dislike that was nothing short of venomous. So much so, that one asked him how he could stand it. He replied, "I am happy at home; and given that, a man can face anything." After the opening of his ministry, our Lord was denied that solace too. **Even his brothers did not believe in him.** And indeed we read elsewhere that at one point they and the mother apologized for him on the ground that he had gone off his head, poor crazed soul; but they would take him home, and sane folk would not be outraged any longer by his wild conduct and preposterous talk—a grim experience for anyone; and how much more for a heart as sensitive and generous as Christ's.

Yet though they had no belief in his so-called mission, it seems that they were all in favor of Christ's going up to the feast of Tabernacles and repeating the sensation he had caused in

[1] Jane Crewdson, "O Savior, I have naught to plead."

3 His brethren therefore said unto him, Depart hence, and go into Judea, that thy disciples also may see the works that thou doest.

4 For *there is* no man *that* doeth any thing in secret, and he himself seeketh to be known openly. If thou do these things, show thyself to the world.

5 For neither did his brethren believe in him.

6 Then Jesus said unto them, My time is not yet come: but your time is always ready.

7 The world cannot hate you; but me it hateth, because I testify of it, that the works thereof are evil.

3 So his brothers said to him, "Leave here
and go to Judea, that your disciples may see
the works you are doing. 4 For no man
works in secret if he seeks to be known
openly. If you do these things, show your-
self to the world." 5 For even his brothers
did not believe in him. 6 Jesus said to them,
"My time has not yet come, but your time
is always here. 7 The world cannot hate
you, but it hates me because I testify of it

3-9. His brothers (see vs. 10; cf. Mark 3:31; 6:3) seem to have become believers only after the Resurrection (cf. Gal. 1:19; Acts 12:17; 15:13-21; I Cor 9:5; 15:7). The brothers of Jesus did not dispute that Jesus had done mighty works, but they felt that if he was really what he claimed to be, he should make a public demonstration before the whole nation at the greatest festival of the year. This may have been prompted by the same misplaced solicitude which their mother had shown at Cana, for the reply of Jesus recalls the words spoken then (2:4). If the falling away of many halfhearted disciples mentioned in 6:66 took place before this, it is easier to understand the challenge put forward by the brothers of Jesus. His insistence upon following the chronometry of the inward call is in keeping with a principle repeatedly alluded to in this Gospel (vs. 30; 2:4; 8:20; 12:23; 13:1; 17:1; the same thought appears in Matt. 26:18; Luke 13:32-33).

Jerusalem at the Passover—apparently (unless indeed they were merely scoffing and jeering) willing enough to walk in the light of a glory reflected on them by their brother, the man of the hour (vss. 1-9). It hurt Christ; and he shrank back from the insult. Always it is those who are nearest to him who have it in their power to hurt him most. And we, who are his, have done so many a time.

Later he did go to the capital, but privately, and with no blare of publicity, such as he had been advised would be wise and politic (vs. 10). That is a fact that might be pondered with advantage by some would-be prophets of our day, by not a few of the confident planners of what they allege is the policy needed to win the modern world, and the only one that will do it. They have no faith at all in the still small voice. Whatever it may have effected among the simple unsophisticated souls of the times of the prophets or of Christ himself, that is of no use to us up-to-date people now. The fire, the earthquake, the mighty rushing wind, these are what tell, and impress, and gain results! If the world is ever to be won, it can be done only by the wise world's own blatant, noisy self-advertising methods. Precisely as his brothers said so long ago: **Leave here and go to Judea, that your disciples may see the works you are doing. For no man works in secret if he seeks to be known openly. If you do these things, show yourself to the world.** But Christ would not do it then. Nor will he do it now, however they suggest it to him.

Ch. 7 has nothing like the spiritual appeal for most people of the wonderful ch. 6. Yet it too is a masterly piece of writing. As we read it, the ancient Eastern city rises up and takes shape round us. We are in it, mingling with the throngs upon the streets, jostling and being jostled. For there is something electric in the air; and everybody is excited, inflammable, on edge. Everywhere there are groups, or couples, their heads close together, their voices low and guarded—for there are listening ears and watchful eyes, and the officers and spies of the authorities were who knew where, perhaps unsafely near (vss. 12-13). And so one had to be cautious what one said. But all alike were discussing the one topic, and risk or no risk, no one seemed able to get away from it. There was much arguing, and there were heated differences of opinion. Some were pro-Christ. **He is a good man,** they said (vs. 12), but whispering

8 Go ye up unto this feast: I go not up yet unto this feast; for my time is not yet full come.

9 When he had said these words unto them, he abode *still* in Galilee.

10 ¶ But when his brethren were gone up, then went he also up unto the feast, not openly, but as it were in secret.

11 Then the Jews sought him at the feast, and said, Where is he?

12 And there was much murmuring among the people concerning him: for

that its works are evil. 8 Go to the feast
yourselves; I am not[k] going up to the feast,
for my time has not yet fully come." 9 So
saying, he remained in Galilee.
10 But after his brothers had gone up
to the feast, then he also went up, not pub-
licly but in private. 11 The Jews were look-
ing for him at the feast, and saying, "Where
is he?" 12 And there was much muttering

[k] Other ancient authorities add *yet*.

8-14. From early times vss. 8-10 caused perplexity. Porphyry, the Neo-Platonist of the third century, used this inconsistency in his attack upon the Gospels (see Jerome *Against the Pelagians* II. 17), and this probably led to the textual variant **not yet** for

---

it below their breath. Some were against him. Frankly, they did not like the look of his mission and works, or of the so-called prophet himself, so they declared—though at this stage they too thought it best not to commit themselves too openly to an opinion, one way or the other (vs. 13). There was amazement in plenty at his gifts (vs. 15). Though some were unimpressed, and said bluntly that the fellow was insane and spouting nonsense (vs. 20); others, noting the freedom with which he moved about and taught at will, concluded that the authorities must have gone over to his side, and become convinced that this was indeed the Christ, really come at last (vs. 26). Still others held to it that he in no way conformed to the required conditions laid down in Scripture as the marks of the authentic Christ (vs. 27). Yet many were assured that this was certainly not only a prophet but the forerunner long foretold. And many more went further, and announced definitely, "This is the very Christ himself" (vss. 40-41). For what more could one do to prove himself the Christ than this man was actually doing (vs. 31)? But others remained unconvinced (vss. 27-28). There was division, confusion, a crisscross of opinion—with not a few, angry and indignant about it all, who kept insisting that the whole thing should be put down resolutely, and Christ taken into custody as a menace and disturber of the peace, and an impudent heretic (vss. 30, 44). And the authorities, to whom something of all this muttering and murmur was duly reported, evidently came to the conclusion that the time for decisive action had arrived—either because the opposition to Christ had grown vocal enough for them to hear it distinctly and be encouraged by it, or, on the contrary, because things were swinging too far the other way, and something must be done about it swiftly and ruthlessly. In short, things were uncertain, and swayed to and fro. Sometimes it looked as if Christ was winning; at others, that he was plainly doomed—a man marked out for a horrible end that was drawing ominously near.

12, 15, 31, 41-42. ***Nothing New under the Sun.***—It is interesting and a little daunting to note with what curious exactness the opinions about Christ held by differing sections of that old-world throng are reproduced among men still. Now as then, those who believe in him do so largely for the reasons which some of these people kept expressing.

(*a*) **He is a good man,** they said. The character of Christ, his personality, the use he made of life, his sheer unselfish goodness, have made an immense impression on innumerable minds—a goodness and unselfishness, be it noted, lived out where we have to live, and when immersed in the tasks we have to do, and worse.

> Let Me have your tools, the little stage of your workshop, surround Me with your identical temptations, add the malice and suspicion of man, narrow the stage to the dimensions of a dirty Eastern village, handicap Me with poverty, weight the scales, crib and cabin Me in a little Eastern land, and there, at the point where you have failed in the flesh, I will produce the fairest thing earth has seen; I will give the world the dream come true.[2]

So A. E. Whitham imagines Christ as throwing down his challenge to life and to humanity, and justifying it up to the hilt. In face of this new ideal, and of the fact that this has been done with a life like mine, that this shining glory has been woven out of the selfsame chances which I so soil and tangle, multitudes have grown utterly dissatisfied with what had con-

[2] *The Pastures of His Presence* (London: Hodder & Stoughton, 1939).

some said, He is a good man: others said, Nay; but he deceiveth the people.

about him among the people. While some said, "He is a good man," others said, "No,

not which is found in many MSS and versions. The most feasible explanation of the words as they stand is that Jesus would not make his messianic entry at this feast. He went up after the caravans of Galilean pilgrims, when the festival was half over, and

tented them well enough; and sick of themselves have resolved to put on Christ, to follow in his footsteps, to catch, please God, the infection of his mind and ways. Even now, admitted J. S. Mill,[3] by no means a witness prejudiced in his favor, one cannot even think of a character better than that of Jesus. After all these centuries of slow climbing toward him, he is still as far above us as the how vastly distant stars.

(*b*) Further, these people kept urging, **When the Christ appears, will he do more signs than this man has done?** That is indeed a pertinent question. It was forced upon them by watching Christ and what he effected; not what he promised only, but what he did. So people beyond numbering, in every age and land, still feel. Here is one whose teaching, unlike others', does not grow obsolete, but remains true to all eternity; who rouses, and helps, and heals, and saves, as no other can; who has done far more for the needy world than all its other benefactors put together. (And blessed be God's name, these last are almost without number.) Is not this he who was to come, the answer to man's dreams, the fulfillment of his hopes, aye, and of the bigger and braver hopes which he himself awakens in us, and then meets and satisfies; the living out to us of all God's most divine and overflowing promises? If this is not the Christ, what is he? And what can the Christ do which can surpass this record?

On the other hand, the objections raised against Christ then have a familiar ring. For to this day there are those who, imagining themselves to be bravely original and as uttering something quite new and decisive, repeat them triumphantly, or something much the same.

(*a*) **He is leading the people astray,** they said. So they do still; holding that any and every type of religion, and especially Christianity, is largely an irrelevancy, a turning men aside from what ought to be their main interest, upon which they should be concentrating their attention and their powers. This concern about one's soul, this unhappiness over one's moral and spiritual state, this absorbed effort to improve them, is, so they tell us, pathological, is a disease, is simply selfishness and rank stupidity as well. If only men would avoid this side road leading nowhere, down which they have let themselves be enticed too long; if only they would really do what they ought to be doing, giving all that is in them to build up a better political and social order—that would be carrying through something really remedial and practical and worth while. Once that were done, as it could and should be done, everyone would be happy to the end of the story.

(*b*) Again, there were those who refused to take Christ's claims seriously because their familiarity with him had dulled their minds to his majesty and wonder. That is no doubt usual enough. Montaigne sets it down with a half-humorous, half-cynical smile: "In my climate of Gascoigne they deem it a jest to see me in print. The further the knowledge which is taken of me is from my home, of so much more worth am I. In Guienne I pay printers; in other places they pay me!"[4] So, because they read the Gospels in their youth, many think they know them, and leave them alone. As the rage is all for the most recent songs, and those of three months ago are already out of date, so our Lord's teaching is too old and too well known to have any thrill in it for them, and they abandon it, and run eagerly after any new voice, however strident and superficial its message may be. Thus F. R. Barry:

> For centuries, almost up to living memory, it was the prerogative of the Christian Church to be the custodian of the world's values, whether moral, aesthetic or intellectual. To-day . . . this task has been entrusted to other hands. The most crucial function in our civilization is now discharged by novelists and critics, dramatists, editors, and wireless publicists.[5]

And G. K. Chesterton: "Nothing more strangely indicates an enormous and silent evil of modern society than the extraordinary use which is made nowadays of the word 'orthodox,'" which by many is regarded as a synonym for old-fashioned, out of date, impossible. A man, Chesterton goes on, "says, with a conscious laugh"—and who of us has not heard it?—"'I suppose I am very heretical,' and looks round for applause. The word 'heresy' not only means

[3] *Three Essays on Religion* (New York: Henry Holt & Co., 1874), p. 255.

[4] *Essays* III. 2.

[5] *The Relevance of Christianity* (London: Nisbet & Co., 1931), p. 4.

13 Howbeit no man spake openly of him for fear of the Jews.

14 ¶ Now about the midst of the feast Jesus went up into the temple, and taught.

he is leading the people astray." 13 Yet for fear of the Jews no one spoke openly of him.

14 About the middle of the feast Jesus

---

with no public display of authority. The contrast between vs. 10 and 12:12-15 is explained by the difference between vs. 8 and 12:23. But though Jesus went to Jerusalem unobtrusively, he **taught** in **the temple** as before.

---

no longer being wrong; it practically means being clear-headed and courageous." [6]

(*c*) Yet again, some were stumbled and would not even consider Jesus as a prophet because he came out of Galilee (vs. 41*b*); their prejudice was sure that that despised province had nothing to teach them. Today in India, e.g., national pride presents a real difficulty—as where in measure does it not? The leaders of a great land with a long and mighty past just will not credit that mother India needs any help in spiritual things, or that any imported prophets can surpass her prophets, or that a little land like Palestine can have anything better than their own native classics. Besides, always and everywhere there are those who, holding too naïvely Browning's overconfident saying that

> The first of the new, in our race's story
> Beats the last of the old,[7]

speak quite patronizingly of this old-world Teacher from Galilee, that quiet corner of a world where things were vastly simpler than they are today, and life slipped along placidly, and, so it is supposed in blank defiance of all the known and palpable facts, there were no huge and puzzling social problems crowding in on men as there are now. And so they speak loftily about Jesus' teaching as being little likely to be helpful to us where we live amid the whirring of machinery he never knew, and in a din and bustle and confusion very different from his placid times. All of which a very elementary knowledge of his day proves to be sheer and utter nonsense. The fact is that in essentials his age was quite startlingly like our own, with insistent problems clamoring for solution often queerly similar to ours now; cf. T. R. Glover's description of the world in which Christianity was born and cradled and grew up, a world which had

> had too much of war and waste, the sheer destruction of human life, the loss of home and gear and all that makes life livable. Very generally it had lost heart and hope, it had ceased to believe in anything but blank endurance, but acceptance of whatever the selfishness of rulers and adventurers and the malice of irrational fortune might bring upon them.[8]

That sounds strangely familiar.

(*d*) Still others were confirmed in their opinion against Christ by a too-literal reading of the Scriptures. These were fulfilled, but not in the precise manner that they had expected; and rigidly they would not admit that any interpretation of them other than their own was possible or thinkable. The Christ was to come from Bethlehem (vs. 42). And they took that to mean that he would be one of its permanent inhabitants, which this Jesus was not, and so his claim fell. And down the centuries how much damage has been wrought, and how many have misled themselves, by a too-literal handling of God's Holy Word! The Bible is a dangerous book which we can twist to our ruin. As the Roman Catholics remind us, it may be inerrable, but we who read it certainly are not, and we may misunderstand it grievously, with sinister results. Well may we cry for the Holy Spirit, who alone can lead us into all the truth.

14-17. *How a Real Creed Is Fashioned.*—From all the hum and buzz of many voices, only half heard, certain things swell out into greater distinctness, carrying plainly to our ears. Thus, when that murmuring of amazement reached him, **How is it that this man has learning, when he has never studied?** Christ replied that though he had never been at the rabbinical schools, he was not simply self-taught, but had received his message from God himself; and added that if any who heard him were really in earnest about their religion, and would resolutely set themselves to live out the divine will, they would find that his teaching authenticated itself as unchallengeably true, and beyond questioning God-given. **If any man's will is to do his will, he shall know whether the teaching is from God or whether I am speaking on my own authority.**

That is the way in which a real creed is

[6] *Heretics* (New York: John Lane Co., 1912), pp. 11-12.
[7] "Old Pictures in Florence," st. xx.
[8] *The World of the New Testament* (New York: The Macmillan Co., 1931), p. 16.

15 And the Jews marveled, saying, How knoweth this man letters, having never learned?

went up into the temple and taught. 15 The Jews marveled at it, saying, "How is it that this man has learning,[l] when he has

[l] Or *this man knows his letters.*

E. A Controversy Section (7:15-24)

15-24. Whether or not the Gospel as we have it represents the form in which the evangelist intended to arrange his narrative (see Intro., pp. 446-47), this section seems to be a continuation of the controversy described in ch. 5. The closing words of Jesus there are, "If you do not believe his writings, how will you believe my words?" This section opens with the words **The Jews marveled** [omit **at it,** not in the Greek], **saying,**

fashioned. At the start we may passively accept certain propositions held by the church—in the sense that we do not actively challenge them, or, in truth, think much about them; they are as yet mere notions, still unproved by us personally at first hand, and for ourselves. But a real creed cannot be slipped on like a suit of ready-made clothes. For a creed or a doctrine is an attempt to put into words the facts that life has taught us, what our experience has proved to us, and the deductions which flow from that. It is true that in a way we can believe what is guaranteed to us by the experience of those farther on than we. But this last does not as yet belong to us in the full sense.

Hence, probably, a very simple declaration is all that can be fairly asked of young communicants and catechumens. In the early church the confession "Jesus is Lord" would seem to have been held sufficient to give one the right to be accounted a Christian. James Denney argued with great force that while of course the church as a church, in order to declare its tenets and position, must have a much more ample and exhaustive statement, perhaps enough to ask from a beginner, and as the essential, might be no more than, "I believe in God through Jesus Christ His only Son, our Lord and Saviour."[9] The beginner will grow into vastly more than that. But till he has experienced it for himself, while it is for him only a carried story, a rumor blown to him from other lives, does he really believe it in any vital sense at all? As Keats wrote in a letter, "We find what he [Wordsworth] says true as far as we have experienced, and we can judge no further but by larger experience—for axioms in philosophy are not axioms till they are proved upon our pulses. We read fine things, but never feel them to the full until we have gone the same steps as the author."[1] The Roman Catholic, indeed, declares that he who says, "This is my faith," has none: for it is the part of every believer to accept the church's findings; and his own subjective reactions are a lesser and comparatively unimportant matter. But the Protestant maintains that until one can say, "This is my faith," he has no faith, or at least no creed, in the true sense at all. For as Pascal says, "To love man, you must know him; to know God, you must love Him."

In any case, our Lord guarantees that if a man sets out determinedly to do God's will, he will find that Christ's teaching will be corroborated by his experience, and will prove itself to the full. As thus: try how he may he will find himself largely beaten and baffled; that his searching hands come short and cannot reach what he is groping after; that something persistently drags him down and back; that he cannot attain to be what, in his better moments he earnestly desires to be; in short, he will discover that sin is a horrible and a humiliating fact from which, if we are to have any chance at all, one must somehow be saved, precisely as Christ teaches. But he will find this also: that the whole business is not simply a struggle between this loathsome thing and our own insufficiency against it, but that there is something else in this, something as real as sin, and stronger than sin; something that hurries to our aid, and does aid, in the strangest and most effective and often unexpected ways; that the grace of God too is a fact, ever present and entirely dependable. So also in the difficulties and perplexities of life: if we will dare to believe in the fatherhood of God, we shall find that in very deed there is Someone to whom it matters what becomes of us and how we fare; who thinks of us, and plans for us, and spends himself on our behalf, and brings us through what we could never have managed by ourselves. So in a hundred things. "Give my teaching a chance," claims Christ with confidence, "and you will find it is not mine alone, but the very word of very God, that God whose word is truth."

15. See Expos., vss. 12, 15, 31, 41-42.

[9] *Jesus and the Gospel* (New York: A. C. Armstrong & Son, 1908), p. 350; but see the whole chapter.

[1] *Works*, ed. H. Burton Forman (Glasgow: Gowan & Gray, 1901), IV, 107.

16 Jesus answered them, and said, My doctrine is not mine, but his that sent me.

17 If any man will do his will, he shall know of the doctrine, whether it be of God, or *whether* I speak of myself.

18 He that speaketh of himself seeketh his own glory: but he that seeketh his glory that sent him, the same is true, and no unrighteousness is in him.

19 Did not Moses give you the law, and *yet* none of you keepeth the law? Why go ye about to kill me?

never studied?" 16 So Jesus answered them,
"My teaching is not mine, but his who sent
me; 17 if any man's will is to do his will, he
shall know whether the teaching is from
God or whether I am speaking on my own
authority. 18 He who speaks on his own
authority seeks his own glory; but he who
seeks the glory of him who sent him is true,
and in him there is no falsehood. 19 Did
not Moses give you the law? Yet none of
you keeps the law. Why do you seek to

"How is it that this man has learning, when he has never studied?" The marginal translation in the RSV is **How is it that this man knows his letters?** and many commentators take the words in this literal sense. It is then a taunt at the presumed illiteracy of Jesus (cf. Acts 4:13). But the same Greek word (γράμματα) is used for **learning** or "letters" (vs. 15), and for "writings" in 5:47. The sequence seems convincing, and the point of the question is bewildered admiration rather than disdain. The instruction in reading given in the synagogue schools was based upon the Scriptures, which were read and committed to memory. It was the insight as well as the knowledge displayed by Jesus in his interpretation that impressed his hearers (cf. Mark 1:22). Even those versed in rabbinical exegesis were surprised. A great rabbinical authority has written: "My own general impression, without asserting an early date for the Fourth Gospel, is that that Gospel enshrines a genuine tradition of an aspect of Jesus' teaching which has not found a place in the Synoptics" (Israel Abrahams, *Studies in Pharisaism and the Gospels* [Cambridge: University Press, 1917], 1st Ser., p. 12).

In reply to this tribute to his appeal to the Scriptures Jesus sums up the argument already given and applies it to the test case of the cripple who had been healed on the sabbath. In 5:31-40 the subject was the witness of Jesus; in 5:41-47 it was rather the kind of honor which is in the mind of the bearer of witness. In vss. 16-24 the order is reversed. Jesus reiterates that his **teaching** comes from the Father who commissioned him. Therefore anyone who is resolved to do the **will** of the same Father will recognize the divine origin of this **teaching** (vss. 16-17). Self-seeking after honor is the mark of the man **who speaks on his own authority.** The true witness comes from the man whose sole concern is for the honor of his commissioner (vs. 18; cf. 5:41-44). Now this dispute about the **authority** of Jesus, and his claim to be seeking only the honor of God in all that he says and does,

---

18-24. ***The Rule of the Road.***—The connection between vs. 18 and what follows seems obscure. As the Exeg. points out, much can be said for the suggestion that this passage has somehow slipped out of its true place at the end of ch. 5. But taking it as it stands, are we to conceive of Christ as catching up and answering not only the bewildered admiration of some in the crowds (vs. 18), but also the growling anger against him of others around about him, which he sensed, and perhaps even overheard? **Why do you seek to kill me?** he asked. Whereat, voices not a few answered indignantly, "Don't be daft! Who wants to kill you?" But he had diagnosed the tense situation much more accurately than they had. Apparently the old sore of that healing on the sabbath at Bethzatha was still rankling and raw in many minds, which could not get over it, or forgive what struck them as monstrous. Turning defense into attack, our Lord shows them (and us, for we too often sadly need his guidance in these matters) how illogical and unreasonable was their position. "You yourselves do not keep the law in certain cases with the wooden literalness upon which you insist in others. In point of fact, there are circumstances in which the whole law cannot be kept [vs. 19], but one must choose between obedience to a greater or a lesser element in it, since the two clash. To keep the law of Moses you circumcise upon the sabbath, although that law lays it down that no work should be allowed to break in on the sabbatical rest and calm. Why then are you

20 The people answered and said, Thou hast a devil: who goeth about to kill thee?

21 Jesus answered and said unto them, I have done one work, and ye all marvel.

22 Moses therefore gave unto you circumcision; (not because it is of Moses, but of the fathers;) and ye on the sabbath day circumcise a man.

23 If a man on the sabbath day receive circumcision, that the law of Moses should not be broken; are ye angry at me, because I have made a man every whit whole on the sabbath day?

24 Judge not according to the appearance, but judge righteous judgment.

kill me?" 20 The people answered, "You
have a demon! Who is seeking to kill you?"
21 Jesus answered them, "I did one deed,
and you all marvel at it. 22 Moses gave you
circumcision (not that it is from Moses,
but from the fathers), and you circumcise
a man upon the sabbath. 23 If on the sab-
bath a man receives circumcision, so that
the law of Moses may not be broken, are
you angry with me because on the sabbath
I made a man's whole body well? 24 Do not
judge by appearances, but judge with right
judgment."

---

arose out of the healing of a lame man on the sabbath. The argument is therefore clinched by proving that the appeal to the Torah vindicates that action (vss. 19-24). **Moses** is their accuser (cf. 5:45), for they profess to observe the legislation that bears his name. The rite of **circumcision** is even older than Moses. It was the sign of the covenant made with Abraham. The Mosaic law enforces sabbath observance. It also prescribes circumcision on the eighth day after birth. If, then, the child is eight days old on a sabbath, circumcision takes place whatever breach of the sabbath is involved. Can they say, then, that to heal a limb and make the whole body sound on the sabbath is contrary to the sabbath law? Circumcision may happen again and again on the sabbath, and yet they want to put Jesus to death for one healing act on a sabbath! What a superficial judgment on the part of men who are supposed to be responsible for binding and loosing, for determining when to enforce and when to relax a legal requirement!

The rabbinical regulations relating to circumcision on the sabbath are given in Shabbath 18:3–19:5 (see Danby, *Mishnah,* pp. 116-17). Abrahams (*Studies in Pharisaism and Gospels,* 1st Ser., p. 135) has a striking comment: "It is interesting to note that John vii. 22 reports Jesus as defending his general position from the analogy of circumcision. Here we have yet another instance of the Fourth Gospel's close acquaintance with Hebraic traditions, for the most notable relaxation of the Sabbath law was just in cases of circumcision. In *Yoma* 85 b the very words of John vii. 23 are paralleled . . . from the rite of circumcision." The difference, however, is that Jesus went further than the Pharisees. They gave a humane interpretation of the law when life was in danger, or when acute pain could be alleviated. But they did not allow such acts where postponement could be safely made. Jesus contended that no act of mercy was to be delayed for the sake of the sabbath, even though the need was not urgent.

---

angry with me, because in exercising the right of discrimination between a less and a more, as you yourselves habitually do in that matter of circumcision, I have judged that to heal a suffering fellow man, to give him back fullness of life upon the sabbath, is a thing far nearer the heart and will of God, a much more real and vital obedience to his demands upon me, than to preserve a rigid and immaculate abstinence from work upon that day?" And so he lays down the abiding general principle, **Do not judge by appearances, but judge with right judgment.**

No doubt at all that is the ideal. Only how are we to do it? We are so blind, so foolish, so hidebound by convention, so at the mercy of a hundred partialities of which we ourselves are often unaware, so prejudiced by our upbringing, and indeed by the whole set of our minds. We are the children of our time, are swept along by the currents of the prevalent thought, our minds are colored by the atmosphere in which they live. There is no one, said Emerson, who would not have been an entirely different being had he been born ten years earlier or later than he was. Well may we pray for that Holy Spirit, promised to guide us; and that of his mercy he will grant us the priceless gift of a

25 Then said some of them of Jerusa-
lem, Is not this he, whom they seek to kill?
26 But, lo, he speaketh boldly, and they
say nothing unto him. Do the rulers know
indeed that this is the very Christ?
27 Howbeit we know this man whence
he is: but when Christ cometh, no man
knoweth whence he is.
28 Then cried Jesus in the temple as
he taught, saying, Ye both know me, and
ye know whence I am: and I am not come
of myself, but he that sent me is true,
whom ye know not.

25 Some of the people of Jerusalem
therefore said, "Is not this the man whom
they seek to kill? 26 And here he is, speak-
ing openly, and they say nothing to him!
Can it be that the authorities really know
that this is the Christ? 27 Yet we know
where this man comes from; and when the
Christ appears, no one will know where
he comes from." 28 So Jesus proclaimed, as
he taught in the temple, "You know me,
and you know where I come from? But I
have not come of my own accord; he who
sent me is true, and him you do not know.

F. Narrative of the Feast of Tabernacles Resumed (7:25-31)

25-31. This section takes up the story from vs. 14. The teaching of Jesus leads to a division among the Jerusalemites. One section opposes him on the ground that his origin is well known, whereas the Messiah's emergence will be mysterious. They cannot understand why the authorities, who must be aware of this flaw in the credentials of Jesus, have not carried out their intention of putting him to death. To this Jesus replied that they knew only his earthly family home, whereas his ultimate origin was unknown to them because they did not know him from whom he had received his commission. Thereupon they tried **to arrest him,** but failed in their attempt **because his hour had not yet come** (cf. vss. 6, 8; 8:20). Another section believed in him because his **signs** were equal to those predicted of the messianic age.

The purpose **to kill** Jesus has been mentioned in vs. 1; 5:16, 18. **We know where this man comes from:** Galilee, and perhaps Nazareth, would be understood. **When the**

discerning, honest, open mind, so that we may not be misled into mistaking our prejudices and customs for principle, and our conventions for the eternal and unalterable laws of God.

To help us to keep our footing in these slippery places there is this to be said: Life is not like a chessboard, made up of white squares and of black, plainly differentiated from each other; nor is our business simply to keep upon the white, and to avoid the black, though indeed even that is hard to manage. There are twilight patches in between, in which we are confronted by many puzzling problems and confusing dilemmas, where there seems to be no one obvious categorical imperative universally applicable, but we have to feel our way, and duty varies with differing circumstances, so that what is right in one situation is quite wrong in another. Paul tells us of a problem common in his day by which sensitive consciences were often much disturbed and made unhappy. When a member of the Christian community was asked out to a meal, it was likely enough that the meat set before him had been offered to some idol, and later sold in the market place. To the apostle's own sturdy common sense there was no difficulty. An idol was nothing. Paul accepted what was set before him as a good gift from the living God. Eat with a grateful heart, so he advises, and without scruple. Such is his general rule. But he admits that there are circumstances in which it will not do, and must be laid aside. If someone with a too-scrupulous conscience is hurt by your freedom and cannot do as you do with any liberty of spirit, never stumble your poor brother for what is after all a matter of indifference to you, but for the time being lay aside your own liberty. So the rule of the road is entirely altered and now runs: Refrain from eating, for the sake of your oversensitive brother. So in many problems that confront us. Christ's cardinal principle is that he will not and cannot give us a code of rigid and unalterable rules, applicable in all circumstances in which we may find ourselves. What is needed, he declares, and what he offers to us, is a spirit, a kind of tact, a feeling in our finger tips for the right thing to do here and now, as each occasion arises; a loyalty to the law that will sometimes break the letter in order to maintain the spirit, ignoring for the moment a lesser ordinance in order to carry out a higher.

25-29. ***Where Do We Come From?***—There were of course some literalists who were

29 But I know him; for I am from him, and he hath sent me.

30 Then they sought to take him: but no man laid hands on him, because his hour was not yet come.

31 And many of the people believed on him, and said, When Christ cometh, will he do more miracles than these which this *man* hath done?

32 ¶ The Pharisees heard that the people murmured such things concerning him; and the Pharisees and the chief priests sent officers to take him.

29 I know him, for I come from him, and
he sent me." 30 So they sought to arrest
him; but no one laid hands on him, be-
cause his hour had not yet come. 31 Yet
many of the people believed in him; they
said, "When the Christ appears, will he
do more signs than this man has done?"

32 The Pharisees heard the crowd thus muttering about him, and the chief priests and Pharisees sent officers to arrest him.

Christ appears, no one will know where he comes from: At first sight this seems inconsistent with vs. 42. But the words refer to the Jewish expectation of a sudden appearance of the Messiah (Mal. 3:1) from some place of concealment. This belief is attested by the Jew Trypho in Justin's *Dialogue* (VIII. 4; cf. CX. 1): "But Messiah, if indeed he has ever been and now exists anywhere, is unknown, and does not even know himself at all, nor has any power, until Elijah shall have come and anointed him, and shall have made him manifest to all." A later legend is preserved in the Jerusalem Talmud (Berakoth 5*a*), that the "comforter" (i.e., Messiah) was born in Bethlehem on the night when Jerusalem was destroyed, and was carried off by a storm wind (see Moore, *Judaism,* II, 348, n. 5). Vss. 28-29 state a recurrent theme in this controversy (vs. 16; cf. 5:30, 37; 8:18-19, 26, 42, 55).

G. An Attempt to Arrest Jesus (7:32-36)

32-36. The cross fire of popular discussion reached the ears of **the Pharisees,** who brought the matter to the Sanhedrin, and the temple police were ordered **to arrest** Jesus. He met the challenge with one of his enigmatic sayings which puzzled his opponents, who put a fantastic meaning on his remark. **The chief priests and Pharisees** is another way of saying "the Sanhedrin," as in vs. 45; 11:47, 57; Matt. 21:45; 27:62. The fuller title was

---

stumbled. Though mightily impressed by Jesus, they still felt that he could not really be the Christ, as their minds kept suggesting he must be; because, while no one was to know where the Christ came from, it was in everybody's mouth that this figure now attracting such attention hailed from Nazareth. And Jesus answered, "But do you know me? And do you know where I have come from? It was not in the carpenter's shed at Nazareth this enterprise was planned; not there, as I stood ankle-deep in shavings, and executed the orders of some of you now present, that the idea of it first took form. I come to you from God. And he it was who sent me." So Emerson reports of John Brown, the champion of the slaves:

> His enterprise . . . was not . . . a plot of two years or of twenty years, but the keeping of an oath made to Heaven and earth forty-seven years before. Forty-seven years at least, though I incline to accept his own account of the matter at Charlestown, which makes the date a little older, when he said, "This was all settled millions of years before the world was made."[2]

And indeed of us too that is true. For when, to speak humanly, the thought of us first rose up in the mind of God, for us also he had a will, a plan, a work that he wished done. And of all possible beings we were the likeliest to do it. And therefore we are here.

That the crowd well understood the tremendousness of his claim is evidenced by the fact that many, infuriated beyond further endurance, were all for arresting him forthwith, as an intolerable person, no longer to be borne. Yet for the moment the crisis passed, and the tide of anger ebbed again, and nothing decisive actually happened. For there was a party in his favor to be reckoned with; and many were still hesitating, not at all convinced that this was not the Christ.

31. See Expos., vss. 12, 15, 31, 41-42.

[2] "John Brown: Speech at Salem," *Miscellanies* (Boston: Houghton Mifflin & Co., 1888), p. 260.

33 Then said Jesus unto them, Yet a
little while am I with you, and *then* I go
unto him that sent me.
34 Ye shall seek me, and shall not find
me: and where I am, *thither* ye cannot
come.
35 Then said the Jews among themselves,
Whither will he go, that we shall not find
him? will he go unto the dispersed among
the Gentiles, and teach the Gentiles?
36 What *manner of* saying is this that
he said, Ye shall seek me, and shall not
find *me:* and where I am, *thither* ye can-
not come?

33 Jesus then said, "I shall be with you
a little longer, and then I go to him who
sent me; 34 you will seek me and you
will not find me; where I am you cannot
come." 35 The Jews said to one another,
"Where does this man intend to go that we
shall not find him? Does he intend to go to
the Dispersion among the Greeks and teach
the Greeks? 36 What does he mean by say-
ing, 'You will seek me and you will not
find me,' and, 'Where I am you cannot
come'?"

"chief priests, elders, and scribes" (Matt. 27:41; Mark 11:27; 14:43, 53; 15:1). (For the constitution and powers of this high court in Jerusalem see Emil Schürer, *A History of the Jewish People in the Time of Jesus Christ,* tr. S. Taylor and P. Christie [Edinburgh: T. & T. Clark, 1910], Div. II, Vol. I, pp. 165-95.) From this time onward Jesus speaks of his earthly life as near its end (vs. 33). The determined hostility of his enemies makes that certain, but his final challenge will not be flung down at this feast. When his mission ends with his death, this will not mean defeat but a return to his Father, where his foes cannot follow him. This saying was explained to his disciples as a message of comfort (cf. 13:33; 14:19; 16:16-19). To his opponents it was a message of doom. Deut. 4:29 had spoken of a possible recovery of the nation in its dire need if it would search after the Lord. Hos. 5:6 gave warning of a condition in which Israel and Judah would seek the Lord with their sacrifices but not find him, "He hath withdrawn himself from them." Isaiah (55:6) pleads, "Seek ye the Lord while he may be found, call ye upon him while he is near." Even so, a time will come when the Jews will seek their Messiah, but he will be beyond their reach. In their blindness they have failed to recognize him when in their midst. **The Dispersion among the Greeks** (vs. 35) is a rendering of a phrase which might also mean, less probably, "the dispersed Gentiles." Long before this Gospel was written, the Christian mission, starting from Antioch, had followed this very method, preaching to the Jews of the synagogue and then to the Gentiles in the western **Dispersion.** To our Lord's opponents the thought that he would escape out of their hands for such a mission was fantastic.

33-36. ***Spiritual Atrophy.***—The Pharisees, made aware of the muttering in the crowds, felt that the time to strike had come, so they sent officers to arrest our Lord. But Jesus, seeing them mingled among the people, and knowing why they were there, was not intimidated into silence; rather he warned the people that their time of opportunity was running out. **A little while, he said, ye shall seek me, and shall not find me** (vss. 33-34). It was a terrible saying, yet tragically true; as indeed the pathetic history of Jewry since Christ's day makes plain —a seeking and a seeking, and a not finding one to help; because he came, and they not recognizing him rejected him. "And the door was shut," says the patient Christ. That echoes eerily through the heart with an awesome finality. And yet experience and psychology corroborate it solemnly. Each time that Christ makes appeal to us, and especially each time we are moved, and convinced, and drawn to him, and nothing positive happens, but it all ends in stubborn refusal or evaporates in empty feeling and emotion; each time that we leap to our feet, meaning to clinch things here and now, and then sit down again—each time it grows less and less likely that anything will ever come of it in us. Theseus and Pirithoüs went boldly into the underworld on a gallant adventure; but sitting down to rest, they dallied, to discover to their horror that they could not rise, for they had grown fast to the rocks. It was a real saint of God who cried to him in agony that he could not repent, could not make progress in the spiritual life: "Now I can not, because once I would not." The eyes of fishes that elect to live in darksome caverns in time grow dimmer and dimmer, and at last go out.

37 In the last day, that great *day* of the feast, Jesus stood and cried, saying, If any man thirst, let him come unto me, and drink.

38 He that believeth on me, as the Scripture hath said, out of his belly shall flow rivers of living water.

39 (But this spake he of the Spirit, which they that believe on him should receive: for the Holy Ghost was not yet *given;* because that Jesus was not yet glorified.)

37 On the last day of the feast, the great day, Jesus stood up and proclaimed, "If any one thirst, let him come to me and drink. 38 He who believes in me, as[m] the scripture has said, 'Out of his heart shall flow rivers of living water.'" 39 Now this he said about the Spirit, which those who believed in him were to receive; for as yet the Spirit had not been given, because Jesus was not yet glorified.

[m] Or *let him come to me, and let him who believes in me drink. As.*

H. Last Day of the Feast (7:37-52)

37-39. As the festival was closing, Jesus proclaimed to the crowds in Jerusalem the promise made to the woman of Samaria. The words of warning and appeal, echoing Isa. 55:6 just uttered (vs. 34), recall the great promise with which that prophecy began. The same division appears in the crowd as earlier in the festival. The temple police excused their failure to arrest Jesus by declaring that his utterance was without parallel, whereupon the Pharisees taunted them with accepting a judgment worthy of the ignorant crowd but rejected by the religious leaders of the nation. Nicodemus (vss. 50-52) protested against judging a man before hearing his evidence, only to be taunted with the sneer that he must be a Galilean to forget that no prophet was to rise from Galilee. In vss. 37-38 the punctuation favored in the RSV mg. alone makes sense. The figure called chiasmus can be recognized if we translate, "If anyone thirst let him come to me, and let him drink who believes in me." The scripture **"Out of his heart shall flow rivers of living water"** cannot be traced in the O.T., though such texts as Isa. 12:3; 44:3; 55:1 may well have been in mind. In any case, it is Jesus, not he who believes in him, who is the source of living water (cf. 4:10). The evangelist adds one of those interpretative comments which are a feature of the Gospel (see Intro., p. 439), and sees in this living water an

And the faculties in us to which Christ can appeal, stimulated resultlessly time after time, atrophy and ultimately will no longer respond.

37-39. ***Privilege and Service.***—Part of the symbolism of the feast of Tabernacles was a reminder of the water given to the fathers from the rock in the desert in their time of need. On each of the seven days of the festival a full golden pitcher was carried in procession to the temple. But on the last and great day that rite was dispensed with; for now they were celebrating the entrance into Palestine with its springs and water courses. It was in such a setting that Christ promised, not symbolism merely, but reality, a **living water,** abundant, satisfying, overflowing. What he offers is (*a*) the assuaging of our own thirst, the satisfying of our needs, of our legitimate desires, of the spiritual longings that disturb and harass us. But (*b*) better than that by far, he promises that through him we shall be a strength and inspiration to others round about us; no longer a stumbling block to them, no longer something that must be explained away if God is to have a chance with them, but a proof to which Christ can point and claim, "Show me anything like that apart from me." "All unconsciously, those who believe in me," says Christ, "as they move about among their fellows, will help and hearten and inspire them. Life will be a bigger thing to them, and man a nobler creature, and God nearer and more efficient than he had seemed to be." So senseless is the stupid allegation of a self-centered selfishness brought against Christianity! In Christ people are called not only to enormous privileges, but to service. This is a kind of patriotism that claims a man's all for the kingdom. It is an incitement to learn to use life not for ourselves, but to throw it away for others. And so fundamental is this that in his arresting judgment parable Christ tells us, as bluntly and as frankly as it can be done, that if, however innocently and cleanly, we pass through this needy world, so full of folk in desperate straits, self-absorbed and unsympathetic, then our religion is a self-deception and a sham.

Now this, adds the evangelist, **he said about the Spirit, which those who believed in him**

40 ¶ Many of the people therefore, when they heard this saying, said, Of a truth this is the Prophet.

41 Others said, This is the Christ. But some said, Shall Christ come out of Galilee?

42 Hath not the Scripture said, That Christ cometh of the seed of David, and out of the town of Bethlehem, where David was?

43 So there was a division among the people because of him.

44 And some of them would have taken him; but no man laid hands on him.

45 ¶ Then came the officers to the chief priests and Pharisees; and they said unto them, Why have ye not brought him?

40 When they heard these words, some
of the people said, "This is really the
prophet." 41 Others said, "This is the
Christ." But some said, "Is the Christ to
come from Galilee? 42 Has not the scripture
said that the Christ is descended from Da-
vid, and comes from Bethlehem, the village
where David was?" 43 So there was a divi-
sion among the people over him. 44 Some
of them wanted to arrest him, but no one
laid hands on him.

45 The officers then went back to the
chief priests and Pharisees, who said to
them, "Why did you not bring him?"

---

allusion to the gift of **the Spirit,** which could come only after the "glorification"—i.e., the Crucifixion and Resurrection (12:16, 23; 13:31)—of Jesus (cf. 16:7; 20:22). **The last day of the feast, the great day:** This may refer to the seventh day, the day on which the procession with willow branches and special prayers was made seven times around the altar of burnt offering. Others think that the eighth day was meant, though that was observed as a sabbath, as was the first day of the feast, because that was a day of solemn assembly (Lev. 23:36; Num. 29:35). The ritual of this feast is given in the Mishnah (see Danby, *Mishnah,* pp. 170-81). A full discussion is furnished by Strack and Billerbeck (*Kommentar zum N.T. aus Talmud und Midrasch,* II, 490-91, 774-812) together with all available material regarding the feast of Tabernacles.

40-44. The prophet: see 1:21, 25; 6:14; Deut. 18:15-18. **Descended from David:** cf. Ps. 89:3-4; Isa. 11:1; Jer. 23:5. **Comes from Bethlehem:** cf. Mic. 5:2; I Sam. 16:1. **There was a division among the people over him:** cf. vs. 12, also 9:16; 10:19. **Some of them,** i.e., of the people (vs. 40); not of the authorities, who are mentioned in vss. 25-26, 30.

45-52. The officers: The temple police as in vs. 32. Their testimony to the supremacy of the teaching of Jesus was an affront to the Pharisees, who were specialists in religious instruction. **Any of the authorities,** lit., "rulers" (ἄρχοντες), as in vs. 26, also 3:1; 12:42. **But this crowd, who do not know the law, are accursed:** The term "people of the land" (Amhaarez) goes back to Ezra 4:4, where it is used of the mixed population with which

---

were to receive; for as yet the Spirit had not been given, because Jesus was not yet glorified. And certainly that Spirit has produced in and through the church a mass of unselfishness and eager service for others, which is not natural to man, and to which our human annals can show no parallel. But probably Weymouth comes near the heart of the central meaning of the evangelist's interpretation of this passage when he says:

> So it may be that individual men do not receive from God the fulness of spiritual blessing expressed in the N.T., as "the gift of the Holy Spirit" until they cease to regard Jesus as a mere teacher, example and friend, and glorify Him by accepting Him as their Saviour and the absolute Lord and Ruler of their hearts and lives! [3]

[3] *The Modern Speech New Testament* (New York: Baker & Taylor Co., 1904), John 7:39 n.

41-42. See Expos., vss. 12, 15, 31, 41-42.

45-52. ***No Man Like This Man.***—Apparently the Sanhedrin had convened a meeting at which Christ was to be interrogated, and perhaps something more. Hence their anger when their officers returned without the expected prisoner, explaining frankly that so impressed and moved had they been that they had not been able to bring themselves to lay hands upon Christ, for **No man ever spoke like this man!** Which recalls the admiration of Alcibiades for Socrates, wrung from him, so he said, almost against his will.

> When we hear any other speaker, even a very good one, he produces absolutely no effect upon us, or not much, whereas the mere fragments of you and your words, even at second-hand, and however imperfectly repeated, amaze and possess the souls of every man, woman, and child who comes within

46 The officers answered, Never man
spake like this man.
47 Then answered them the Pharisees,
Are ye also deceived?
48 Have any of the rulers or of the Pharisees believed on him?
49 But this people who knoweth not the
law are cursed.

46 The officers answered, "No man ever
spoke like this man!" 47 The Pharisees answered them, "Are you led astray, you also?
48 Have any of the authorities or of the
Pharisees believed in him? 49 But this
crowd, who do not know the law, are

Ezra forbade the Jews to intermarry. In the first century A.D. it stood for the ignorant elements in the nation that showed no interest in or respect for the ceremonial law. The Pharisees despised them, and even the gentle Hillel said, "A rude man fears not sin; and no Amhaarez is pious." This term of contempt is applied to those who were favorably impressed by the teaching of Jesus. It must have been exasperating, therefore, when a member of the Sanhedrin intervened with a plea for fair treatment of the accused. **Nicodemus, who had gone to him before**: cf. 3:1; 19:39. The principle referred to in

hearing of them. . . . I have heard Pericles and other great orators, and I thought that they spoke well, but . . . my soul was not stirred by them, nor was I angry at the thought of my own slavish state. But this Marsyas has often brought me to such a pass, that I have felt as if I could hardly endure the life which I am leading . . . ; and I am conscious that if I did not shut my ears against him, and fly as from the voice of the siren, my fate would be like that of others,—he would transfix me, and I should grow old sitting at his feet. For he makes me confess that I ought not to live as I do, neglecting the wants of my own soul . . . ; therefore I hold my ears and tear myself away from him.[4]

How strange it is, and sad, and tragic, that while scribblers of no importance have their ephemeral stuff printed in full, so little of the Master's teaching (e.g., so little of what these men heard) has been preserved. Some recollections of the disciples, a story or two gathered from some auditor's memory, no book or writing from Christ's own hand, "mere fragments of . . . your words, even at second-hand, and . . . imperfectly repeated"—these have made a far deeper impression on the world than all its crowded literature. But how much of incalculable value has been lost to us, blown irretrievably into oblivion! Stevenson once, in a letter to Henley, pretended the discovery of some exciting literary finds—the autobiography and journal of Shakespeare, a new novel by Fielding, the journals and private correspondence of David, king of Israel; and as he writes, he grows greedily wistful that it could really be. But what would we not give for it, if a fifth authentic and accredited gospel of further sayings of Jesus Christ could be discovered? Years of his teaching; and we have only four slim pamphlets as the record of it all!

[4] See the whole passage in Plato *Symposium* 215-16.

There was nothing judicial about the atmosphere of the Sanhedrin: only a fierce prejudice against the accused, and a contemptuous anger toward those who had been impressed by him, and an overstatement that twisted the facts to make decision simpler (vs. 52). That is too commonly the way in theological disputes, to the grave discredit of the church and of religion. Samuel Johnson, indeed, argued with some plausibility that their very heat and passion was a proof that these were men in earnest, fighting for momentous things that mattered immeasurably to them; that while a Gallio-like unconcern about what seems of little consequence either way may be cool and calm enough, those who are out for truth, and nothing less than truth, and who will not be fobbed off with mere travesties and simulacra, are apt to become hot and indignant, as, said Johnson, a man can listen without emotion to the vilifying of some woman of whom he has never heard; whereas, insult his wife, and he will knock you down. All of which is only half a truth. Bigotry and party spirit and many another ugly trait have all too commonly burst in and filled men's hearts and minds. Says W. E. H. Lecky:

To love truth sincerely means to pursue it with an earnest, conscientious, unflagging zeal. It means to be prepared to follow the light of evidence even to the most unwelcome conclusions; to labor earnestly to emancipate the mind from early prejudices; to resist the current of desires, and the refracting influence of the passions; to proportion on all occasions conviction to evidence, and to be ready, if need be, to exchange the calm of assurance for all the suffering of a perplexed and disturbed mind. To do this is very difficult and very painful; but it is clearly involved in the notion of earnest love of truth.[5]

[5] *History of European Morals*, II, 189.

50 Nicodemus saith unto them, (he that
came to Jesus by night, being one of them,)
51 Doth our law judge *any* man, before
it hear him, and know what he doeth?
52 They answered and said unto him,
Art thou also of Galilee? Search, and look:
for out of Galilee ariseth no prophet.
53 And every man went unto his own
house.

8 Jesus went unto the mount of Olives.
2 And early in the morning he came
again into the temple, and all the people
came unto him; and he sat down, and
taught them.

accursed." 50 Nic-o-de'mus, who had gone
to him before, and who was one of them,
said to them, 51 "Does our law judge a man
without first giving him a hearing and
learning what he does? 52 They replied,
"Are you from Galilee too? Search and you
will see that no prophet is to rise from Gali-
lee."[n]

[n] Other ancient authorities add 7. 53–8. 11, either here or at the end of this Gospel or after Luke 21. 38, with variations of the text.

8 [53] *They went each to his own house,* [1] *but Jesus went*
to the Mount of Olives. [2] *Early in the morning he came*
again to the temple; all the people came to him, and he

---

vs. 51 is implied in such passages as Deut. 1:16; 17:4, 6. If (in vs. 52) the Pharisees were thinking of the past, they must have overlooked Jonah (cf. II Kings 14:25; Jonah 1:1), who was from Gath-hepher in Zebulon, and have forgotten Isa. 9:1. Very different was the judgment of Rabbi Eliezer (*ca.* A.D. 90), "You have no single tribe in Israel out of which prophets have not come forth."

J. Jesus and the Woman Taken in Adultery (7:53–8:11)

This story is not part of the Gospel According to St. John, but is rather a piece of floating tradition which centuries later came to be inserted at this place in some late

---

And he proceeds to argue that the church violates every one of these axioms and principles, stigmatizes doubt as criminal, and seeks to lock the mind into a cell. All of which we, who have no reason to fear frank examination of the facts, must, by our candidness and love of truth, prove to be wild statements.

Only Nicodemus, by nature it would seem a timid man (yet see on 3:1-21), stood up and spoke out in honest and indignant protest against animosity and foregone conclusions, jostling aside the deliberate and careful processes of justice (vs. 51)—only to be assailed by cheap and personal abuse (vs. 52). A lonely voice left unsupported! Lack of such moral courage in men often costs Christ dear. It is so easy to keep silent; either because we cannot be bothered to speak out, or else because we want to avoid misunderstanding or some clever gibe. And so, in yet another company, Christ or truth is left undefended. "It is easy," says Emerson, "in the world to live after the world's opinion; it is easy in solitude to live after our own; but the great man is he who in the midst of the crowd keeps with perfect sweetness the independence of solitude." [6]

7:53–8:1. ***A Main Cause of Our Failures.*—They went each to his own house, but Jesus went to the Mount of Olives.** Apparently to be alone with God; to think things out with him, as he always did; and very specially to feel for his hand to steady him, now that the clouds were gathering black and threatening, and the storm was blowing up. Is not the real root of the difficulties that beset us simply this—that so largely as a generation, and so often as individuals, we have lost touch with God, and no longer turn to him, appeal to him, consult him, wait upon him for counseling and guidance, as Christ did, or even as our fathers did. The road to God, once much frequented, has become grass grown and largely deserted. The times of public worship are invaded by other claimants for them who filch them away from God. Family prayers, which daily brought one within sight of the eternal hills and let a breath of clean air straight from their heights into musty lives, have become nearly obsolete. In how many of us nowadays is there this instinct of Christ to take our difficulties and problems and lay them at God's feet, looking to him for light and leading, careful to be ruled by that? Yet, declared William Law, "He who has learned to *pray,* has learned the greatest Secret of a holy and happy Life." [7]

2-11. *A Judgment Scene.*—This dramatic incident has no place in a number of the best

[6] Essay on "Self-Reliance."

[7] *A Practical Treatise Upon Christian Perfection,* ch. xxii.

3 And the scribes and Pharisees brought unto him a woman taken in adultery; and when they had set her in the midst,

4 They say unto him, Master, this woman was taken in adultery, in the very act.

5 Now Moses in the law commanded us, that such should be stoned: but what sayest thou?

6 This they said, tempting him, that they might have to accuse him. But Jesus stooped down, and with *his* finger wrote on the ground, *as though he heard them not.*

7 So when they continued asking him, he lifted up himself, and said unto them, He that is without sin among you, let him first cast a stone at her.

8 And again he stooped down, and wrote on the ground.

9 And they which heard *it,* being convicted by *their own* conscience, went out one by one, beginning at the eldest, *even* unto the last: and Jesus was left alone, and the woman standing in the midst.

10 When Jesus had lifted up himself, and saw none but the woman, he said unto her, Woman, where are those thine accusers? hath no man condemned thee?

11 She said, No man, Lord. And Jesus said unto her, Neither do I condemn thee: go, and sin no more.

sat down and taught them. [3] *The scribes and the Pharisees*
brought a woman who had been caught in adultery, and
placing her in the midst [4] *they said to him, "Teacher, this*
woman has been caught in the act of adultery. [5] *Now in*
the law Moses commanded us to stone such. What do you
say about her?" [6] *This they said to test him, that they*
might have some charge to bring against him. Jesus
bent down and wrote with his finger on the ground.
[7] *And as they continued to ask him, he stood up and*
said to them, "Let him who is without sin among you
be the first to throw a stone at her." [8] *And once more*
he bent down and wrote with his finger on the ground.
[9] *But when they heard it, they went away, one by one,*
beginning with the eldest, and Jesus was left alone with
the woman standing before him. [10] *Jesus looked up and*
said to her, "Woman, where are they? Has no one condemned you?" [11] *She said, "No one, Lord." And Jesus*
said, "Neither do I condemn you; go, and do not sin again."

MSS of the Gospel. In one important group of cursives (the Ferrar group) the passage is found after Luke 21:38. If it is authentic history, that is a suitable place for its insertion, as a comparison of John 7:53 with Luke 21:37-38 will show. The vocabulary is not Johannine, and several words characteristic of the Lukan writings may be noted. It is found in no Greek MS earlier than the sixth-century Codex Bezae, and is absent from the earlier Syriac and Coptic versions. It is found in a few O.L. texts, though not in others. It is significant that no Greek writer for a thousand years after this Gospel was written comments upon this story.

8:4-5. According to Lev. 20:10 and Deut. 22:22, in the case of adultery both guilty parties are to be put to death. In Deut. 22:23-24 death by stoning is appointed for a

MSS. But it is well indeed that it has been preserved for us. Its main points thrust themselves upon the mind and cannot be missed. The callousness of the Pharisees toward this wretched creature caught in the act of sin; the ruthlessness with which they drag her and her shame into the staring light of day; the horrid subtlety with which they seek to trap Christ into a declaration they could use against him—for the law of Moses was inexorable that death by stoning was the penalty for such a lapse; and Jesus had established a reputation which made them think he would be slow to condemn, and so quite likely to give them a handle against him on the score of his unorthodoxy; the strangely arresting touch of Christ stooping and writing on the ground; till, when the glib accusations had at last come to an end, and they stood triumphantly waiting, thinking he had no escape, he raised himself, and with a level look straight in their eyes, said quietly, **Let him who is without sin among you be the first to throw a stone at her,** and so, once more stooping, resumed that mysterious writing with his finger in the dust. What was it that he wrote? It is the only time we hear of him so doing.

special case of adultery, when the woman is a virgin betrothed to another man. Presumably the charge that his opponents hoped to bring against Jesus was either that of illegally inciting others to kill the woman, a charge that might be brought before the Roman authorities; or else a charge of condoning so heinous a sin according to the Jewish law, an attempt to discredit Jesus in the eyes of religious people. The reference in vs. 7 is to the procedure prescribed in Deut. 17:7, "The hands of the witnesses shall be first upon him to put him to death." This is elaborated in the Mishnah, Sanhedrin 6:4 (see Danby, *Mishnah,* p. 390). **Who is without sin:** The Greek word (ἀναμάρτητος) is quite general in meaning, and does not suggest that these accusers were themselves adulterers. The saying recalls Matt. 7:1. It may be illustrated by Rom. 2:1, and is itself an application of Matt. 5:28. The refusal to **condemn** does not mean palliation of sin. There are two Greek words which may be so translated: one (κρίνειν) means to give the verdict, the other (κατακρίνειν) to pass sentence. It is the latter which is used in these verses. Jesus would not endorse the harsh sentence of the salacious accusers, who paraded the woman's shame in public, but he bade her give up forever her sinful life.

Perhaps something that broke through their guard, and reached and aroused their consciences. In any case they slipped away, **beginning with the eldest,** till not one remained.

Some will have it that the younger men stood back, deferentially giving precedence to their elders. Likely enough there was nothing so formal in the order of their going, but something deeper. Age is said to harden, and experience to make one cynical. Few pages in literature are more depressing than that in which Aristotle, casting aside his customary calm, savagely depicts old men as human nature fallen into ruin, selfish and unenthusiastic, knowing and mean. But is it true? Often age mellows and experience broadens. The cocksureness of youth gives place to a more catholic heart, and to a mind that is slower to judge and quicker to understand. As Goethe has it, "One need only grow old to become gentler in one's judgments. I see no fault committed which I could not have committed myself."[8] So perhaps was it that the eldest went out first.

In any case, Christ and the woman were left there alone; the soiled plaything of men facing his perfect holiness. It is a situation which makes one watch with an intensity of painful interest. For a day is coming when each of us must stand, as she stood then, as if there were no other in the world—just Christ, just I; and for me life here will be finished and over and past amendment, and everything will hang upon his verdict on it. One gathers from the experience of these Pharisees that our past sins will rise up out of their graves, and press in upon us with a frightful disconcertingness. De Quincey held that there is no such thing as forgetting; that the brain is a palimpsest; that "everlasting layers of ideas, images, feelings" keep falling upon it "softly as light. Each succession has seemed to bury all that went before.

[8] *Maxims and Reflections of Goethe,* p. 86.

And yet, in reality, not one has been extinguished."[1] These are the books that will be opened at the last, and whose evidence is irrefutable and final. As Mohammed said: "Every man's fate we have fastened about his neck. And we will bring to him on the day of Resurrection a book which shall be offered open; 'Read thy book; thou thyself art accountant enough against thyself this day.'"[2]

A glimpse of it seems to have been caught by these men here, each of his own; and they fell silent, and stole out and away. But the attitude of the woman gives a glimmering of hope. For if it betokens shame and awe, there is no sign of terror in it. And Christ's attitude to her gives vastly more; extricating her, as he does, from the natural consequences of her sin, and contriving for her, hopefully, another chance. **"Woman, where are they? Has no one condemned you?" She said, "No one, Lord." And Jesus said, "Neither do I condemn you; go, and do not sin again."**

What is to be made of that? For at times Christ was by no means so tolerant and kindly in judgment, but spoke terrible words, and condemned with a dreadful finality. Perhaps this woman had somehow slipped into a lapse that was not characteristic of her, and was ashamed and miserable over it, giving good hope that she was done with it and wishful with all her heart that it had never happened. And there is this also to be said: that certainly Christ ranked sins in a different order of heinousness from that we use, accounting faults of passion less ominous and dangerous and deplorable than other cooler faults we tend to minimize. At any rate, here, as so often elsewhere, he acted in his daring way, frankly forgiving where others would have condemned; not paying by results, and doling out forgive-

[1] Essay on "The Palimpsest of the Human Brain."
[2] Koran, ch. 17.

12 ¶ Then spake Jesus again unto them, saying, I am the light of the world: he that

12 Again Jesus spoke to them, saying, "I am the light of the world; he who

K. Jesus the Light of the World (8:12-20)

After the interpolation (7:53–8:11), the controversy with "the Jews" is resumed. Possibly this section continues the argument found in ch. 5 and in 7:15-36. Some of the sayings in this passage point back to the discussion at the unnamed feast of ch. 5; others closely resemble words that belong to the debate at the feast of Tabernacles in ch. 7. The following comparisons are instructive: 8:13 with 5:31; 8:14 with 7:28-33; 8:15 with 7:24; 8:16 with 5:30; 8:18 with 5:37; 8:19 with 7:28.

Such a comparison, while showing a connected train of thought, brings to light an apparent contradiction. The theme of the discourse in 5:19-30 was "judgment" (κρίσις), followed by the discourse in 5:31-40 in which "witness" (μαρτυρία) was the theme. Now in this section there seems at first sight to be a complete *volte-face*. In the earlier dialogues Jesus disavowed any intention of bearing witness to himself, as self-witness is by law invalid. He also declared that the Father had handed over his functions as judge to the Son "that all may honor the Son, even as they honor the Father" (5:23). In the present dialogue both assertions seem to be reversed. Jesus claims to bear witness to himself, and in doing so, to be speaking the truth. He also declares that he judges no man. The opposition disappears, as Bultmann has shown in his commentary (*Das Evangelium des Johannes* [Göttingen: Vandenhoeck & Ruprecht, 1941], pp. 210 ff.), if we remember that vss. 13-20 must be read in the context of ch. 5. Vs. 14 harks back to 5:31, "If I bear witness to myself, my testimony is not true." Then 8:14*a* will mean **Even if** [κἂν] **I do bear witness to myself** [in a different sense of self-witness] **my testimony is true.** The kind of self-witness repudiated in ch. 5 is that concerned with gaining a personal reputation. Self-glorification can have no place in the message of Jesus. But the witness he bears about himself is that, unlike his critics, he is aware of his origin and destiny (vs. 14*b*). This gives his self-witness a different character from that of others. A man's knowledge of himself depends upon his knowledge of the Revealer. But it is just because the Revealer

ness piecemeal in response to growing amendment, but blotting out the whole debt, and trusting to the honor of the other to respond to that and rise above the evil. And if the mystery of divine forgiveness toward us does not create in us a new horror of sins to which we had grown accustomed, or which we liked too well to renounce, and a new power to resist them and a new cleanness of life and nature, then in us God's tremendous plan of salvation has as yet entirely failed, and even his willingness to forgive us cannot save us from our doom.

12-20. ***Christ's Claim to Be the Light of the World.***—In common fairness to the Pharisees it must surely be admitted that it is not surprising that they were stumbled and incensed by Jesus. For so enormous and breathtaking are his claims that if they were not true, he would be an impossible person, crazy beyond words, or inordinately swollen-headed, without any parallel. Millions of people now know that they are true; have proved it and experienced it. But what wonder that his original hearers, looking at a carpenter from Nazareth, that unimportant provincial town in a forgotten corner of the world; and listening to a man who spoke, it may be, with the broad slurred vowels of the rather uncouth Galilean accent, which always excited a measure of ridicule in polite and cultured circles; [3] to one at least certainly unversed in the learning of the schools; and hearing such a one of all people announce, **I am the light of the world; he who follows me will not walk in darkness, but will have the light of life**—what wonder if they pushed such claims aside as a preposterous throwing about of words without sense or meaning, flatly incredible on the face of them!

There is nothing like it elsewhere. Buddha believed he had a marvelous and beneficent gospel to offer men, but for himself he claimed to be only the rediscoverer of an old and forgotten path; and urged his followers not to think of him, but to concentrate upon the teaching. Confucius, with a winsome humility, declared that as often as he walked with others three abreast he was sure to find a teacher; and asked, "How dare I lay claim to holiness or

[3] Cf. Ad. Neubauer, "On the Dialects Spoken in Palestine in the Time of Christ," and his citation from the Talmud, in *Studia Biblica* (Oxford: Clarendon Press, 1885), I, 41-42.

followeth me shall not walk in darkness, but shall have the light of life.

follows me will not walk in darkness, but

is so strange and remote in the eyes of the world that his self-knowledge is different from that of others. He has a true knowledge of himself. As this results in another standard of witness, so it leads to another standard of judgment. In ch. 5 the astonishing claim of Jesus to be judge (vss. 19-30) led to the theme of "witness" (vss. 31-40). Now the explanation of the sense in which Jesus is bound to bear witness about himself leads to a clearer definition of "judgment." The Pharisees understood judgment as they exercised it themselves. They judged **according to the flesh** (κατὰ τὴν σάρκα, vs. 15), i.e., "by material standards" (Goodspeed), "by the outside" (Moffatt), "according to appearances" (Weymouth), "after your earthly fashion" (Knox). As Jesus had said to them already (7:24), "Do not judge by appearances [κατ' ὄψιν], but judge with right judgment." Human judgment is easily limited by sense impressions and earthly experience. The Revealer of God has not come to dispense that kind of judgment. "For God sent the Son into the world, not to condemn the world, but that the world might be saved through him" (3:17). "If any one hears my sayings and does not keep them, I do not judge him; for I did not come to judge the world but to save the world" (12:47). Yet in another and higher sense the Revealer is judge. As **the light of the world,** he exposes all that belongs to the darkness of this world (cf. Eph. 5:13). If he has refrained from judgment, that is due to his forbearance. He has every qualification to judge. Thus Jesus continues (vs. 16), **Even if I do judge, my judgment is true, for it is not I alone that judge, but I and he who sent me.** This is judgment worthy of the name (ἀληθινός; cf. δίκαιος, 5:30), dispensed according to the rules of justice. He acts conjointly with his Father, whose emissary he is.

12. I am the light of the world: This is another of the great "I am" sayings so characteristic of this Gospel (cf. 6:35, 41, 51; 10:7, 11; 11:25; 14:6; 15:1). Jesus gives light to the

love? A man of endless craving, who never tires of teaching, I might be called, but nothing more."[4] Mohammed, with all his lofty claims, once, covering his head, cried out that unless God cast the cloak of his mercy over him, there was no hope for him at all. "This he said thrice."[5] And indeed these mighty spirits have been in part left behind, both in teaching and in conduct; have in places become out of date and obsolete. But Jesus Christ is still the light of the world, and whoso follows him does not walk in darkness, but can see to find his way. Always our wisdom is to look to him, and to absorb his spirit, and to apply that to the circumstances in which we may be.

Indeed, with so sure a guide provided for us, it is strange that the world, and we as individuals, have not made progress much faster and farther than we have. But however reliable the guidance offered us may be, we can neglect or fumble it. Too often, consciously or unconsciously, we will not have the light, preferring the darkness because our deeds are evil; because this teaching seems to be asking too much from us, or clashes with our comforts and wishes; and so we resent it, resist it, thrust it away, as ideal, perhaps, but out of the question. Too often, though the light shines straight in our faces, we seem not to see it. Looking back, it is hard for us to understand how honest Christian people, with the teaching of Christ before them, could have endured many things that were woven into the texture of their way of living—slavery, children of five or so sent down for long hours into the mines, women denied some of their primary rights as human beings. And future generations will gaze back at us with the same astonishment at our failure to live out what to them will seem the plainest and most obvious applications of the spirit of the Christ whom we too professed to follow. Too often again we keep twisting our Lord's teaching awry, to our own confusion; mistaking our prejudices for love of truth, our anxious keeping in step with what is customary for loyalty toward God. "Christ," said Tertullian, "did not call himself the conventions, but the truth."[6] Nonetheless, if only we would keep our eyes fastened steadily on the light that shines from him, and steer straight toward it, we could meet every difficulty that confronts us, and make port through any seas.

To the Pharisees this astonishing claim seemed mere wild talk and heady nonsense

[4] *The Sayings of Confucius,* tr. Leonard A. Lyall (London: Longmans, Green & Co., 1909), p. 35.

[5] *The Speeches and Table-Talk of the Prophet Mohammed,* tr. Stanley Lane-Poole (London: Macmillan & Co., 1882), p. 182.

[6] *On the Veiling of Virgins* I.

13 The Pharisees therefore said unto him, Thou bearest record of thyself; thy record is not true.

14 Jesus answered and said unto them, Though I bear record of myself, *yet* my record is true: for I know whence I came, and whither I go; but ye cannot tell whence I come, and whither I go.

15 Ye judge after the flesh; I judge no man.

16 And yet if I judge, my judgment is true: for I am not alone, but I and the Father that sent me.

17 It is also written in your law, that the testimony of two men is true.

18 I am one that bear witness of myself, and the Father that sent me beareth witness of me.

will have the light of life." 13 The Phari-
sees then said to him, "You are bearing
witness to yourself; your testimony is not
true." 14 Jesus answered, "Even if I do
bear witness to myself, my testimony is true,
for I know whence I have come and whither
I am going, but you do not know whence
I come or whither I am going. 15 You judge
according to the flesh, I judge no one. 16 Yet
even if I do judge, my judgment is true, for
it is not I alone that judge, but I and he[o]
who sent me. 17 In your law it is written
that the testimony of two men is true; 18 I
bear witness to myself, and the Father who

[o] Other ancient authorities read *the Father*.

---

world. He is himself the life, the life-giving power, which is "the light of men" (1:4). The revelation of the divine nature makes men partakers of that nature, so that fellowship with Christ is a way of life. The moral implication of the announcement made in vs. 12 is brought out more fully in I John 1:5-7 (cf. 9:5; 12:35, 46).

13-19. The ensuing dialogue may be paraphrased as follows:

The Pharisees: You are giving yourselves a testimonial. As you yourself said once (5:31), a man's evidence about himself is not accepted if unsupported. Besides, what you are saying is in itself incredible (vs. 13).

Jesus: In the courts it is the rule that a man's unconfirmed testimony to himself cannot be accepted. But what a man says about himself is not necessarily false. That depends upon the character of the man. Being such as I am, it is not possible that I should speak untruly about myself. This does not appeal to you because you do not really know me. You estimate people by external appearance. I do not now come to a final decision about anyone; though if I did, I have that inner knowledge of men's hearts that would qualify me to judge rightly. And further, my witness to myself is not without support, for I am never alone; my Father who sent me is with me, and stands by me (vss. 14-18).

---

sprung from colossal vanity. They had Moses, given of God, to guide them; who was this ignorant upstart to try to oust him, making himself the polestar by which men should steer their way through life? To which Christ replied that although he was bearing witness to himself, his testimony was reliable; for he was speaking with all the facts before him, as they were not. He knew whence he came, and whither he was going (vs. 14). They were judging according to the flesh, and by appearances. All that they saw was a countryman from the north, the validity of whose mission they challenged because it did not fit into their expectations. But there is more here, said Christ, than that. And then he adds, "You are fond of judging by the dim lights that you have; but **I judge no one.**" A surprising statement indeed, had it stood alone! For the Gospels hold many instances of scathing judgments from Christ's lips in burning words that to this day still blister and sting. "Go and tell that fox." "You brood of vipers!" "Whited sepulchers!" Or in this very chapter, "your father the devil." Evidently if we are to be Christlike, a genial amiability is not in itself anything like enough. And there are times and places when we must oppose and denounce and castigate: must make a clear distinction between good and evil, right and wrong; not slurring over what ought not to be there, or pretending that it is not there, or that it does not matter if it is. So necessary and true is Bengel's commentary on that curt command of Christ, "*Judge not,*—without knowledge, love, necessity. Yet," he adds, "a dog is to be accounted a dog; and a swine a swine." [7]

[7] *Gnomon of the New Testament,* tr. C. T. Lewis (Philadelphia: Perkinpine & Higgins, 1860), *ad loc.*

19 Then said they unto him, Where is
thy Father? Jesus answered, Ye neither
know me, nor my Father: if ye had known
me, ye should have known my Father also.
20 These words spake Jesus in the treas-
ury, as he taught in the temple: and no
man laid hands on him; for his hour was
not yet come.
21 Then said Jesus again unto them, I go
my way, and ye shall seek me, and shall die
in your sins: whither I go, ye cannot come.

sent me bears witness to me." **19** They said
to him therefore, "Where is your Father?"
Jesus answered, "You know neither me
nor my Father; if you knew me, you would
know my Father also." **20** These words he
spoke in the treasury, as he taught in the
temple; but no one arrested him, because
his hour had not yet come.
21 Again he said to them, "I go away,
and you will seek me and die in your sin;
where I am going, you cannot come."

The Pharisees: **Where is your Father?** (Vs. 19.)

Jesus: If you really knew me, you would not ask. You cannot know me, in the full sense of that word, without knowing God; for he and I are inseparable.

20. This section closes (cf. 6:59) with a localizing comment: **He spoke in the treasury, as he taught in the temple.** Better, "near the treasury," unless the name is given here to the Women's Court as a whole. It was in this court that the strong rooms of the temple, and the thirteen trumpet-shaped money chests (cf. Mark 12:41) were built. The last half of the verse repeats 7:30.

L. Controversy About the Divine Commission of Jesus (8:21-59)

A summary paraphrase is given before the comments on special points:

Jesus: I am here for only a little longer. After I have gone away you may begin to seek me, but it will then be too late; I shall be where you cannot come, and your case will then be desperate; for, as Ezekiel said, those who do not heed the warnings of the watchman will die in their sins (vs. 21; cf. Ezek. 3:18; 33:8).

And so here Christ immediately adds, **Yet if,** and when, **I do judge, my judgment is true** (vs. 16): for it is not my own alone; **he who sent me** corroborates it in all things. (Alas! in our case, how often God of his mercy has to overturn what seemed to us so wise and certain and indeed God-given!) Granted, says Christ, that in law a man's testimony on his own behalf is often not much accounted unless it is substantiated by another, still in this instance that necessity too is fully met. For my Father guarantees all that I claim (vss. 17-18). To which one might have expected some such irritated retort as, "You are begging the question! You are assuming as proved facts the very things that we dispute. Did God send you? We much doubt it. Have you his countenance? For our part, we just do not believe it. Prove these matters if you can; but do not expect us to accept them without valid evidence."

But their actual reply, **Where is your Father?** gives Christ the opening to say what is the simple fact, that it is only through Christ, and knowing Christ, that anyone can understand what God is really like and is (vs. 19). Before Christ came, others had had adumbrations, some of them very glorious, of what they felt must be the truth about God's character and nature. But it is in Christ that it came home to us, proved itself, convinced us, stormed men's hearts, and won a place among their settled convictions. Whereas in the days of his flesh men clapped horrified hands to affrighted ears to shut out what they held to be his blasphemous claims, it has for long grown absolutely certain that if there is a God at all, he must be Christlike; and that in very deed our Lord is the express image of his person. It is through Christ that we have come to know the Father. But at the time these words were spoken, they seemed so audacious that the evangelist can explain Christ's immunity from immediate violence only on the ground that **his hour had not yet come** (vs. 20).

21-26. ***The Patience of Christ.***—Christ himself, however, felt the shadow of the approaching end creep nearer and fall cold and dark across his path only a little way ahead. But characteristically it is not of himself that he thinks, but of those who, disillusioned and despairing, will in a while be seeking help and not finding it, the very help he is now offering them (vs. 21) and they will not have. Some thought that he spoke of an approaching suicide, and asked in bewilderment, **Will he kill himself?** So he explains that he and they belong to different worlds. **You are from below, I am from above; you are of this world, I am not of**

22 Then said the Jews, Will he kill himself? because he saith, Whither I go, ye cannot come.

23 And he said unto them, Ye are from beneath; I am from above: ye are of this world; I am not of this world.

24 I said therefore unto you, that ye shall die in your sins: for if ye believe not that I am *he,* ye shall die in your sins.

22 Then said the Jews, "Will he kill himself, since he says, 'Where I am going, you
cannot come'?" 23 He said to them, "You
are from below, I am from above; you are
of this world, I am not of this world. 24 I
told you that you would die in your sins,
for you will die in your sins unless you be-

The Jews: Where is he going that we cannot come? Is he going to put an end to himself? (Vs. 22.)

Jesus: Your question shows how completely opposite your whole outlook is from mine. Your thoughts and motives are from the lower world; mine are from above. That is why you are in deadly peril unless you put your trust in me (vss. 23-24).

The Jews: Who, then, are you? (Vs. 25.)

Jesus: I have been telling you all the time. (Or, What need is there that I should say any more to you than what I have already said?) And yet there is much more to be said, even though it condemn you; and it will be said, with the authority of him who sent me (vs. 26). [They did not notice this reference to the Father (vs. 27). So Jesus added:] When you have lifted me up you will know who I am, and will perceive the intimacy that is between me and the Father, whose words I speak, who is always with me, and whom I please in all that I do (vss. 28-29). [Many believed (vs. 30); some put their trust in him, and followed him; others merely accepted the truth of his words. To the latter he said:] If you make my word the guiding principle of your lives, you will indeed be my disciples; you shall know the truth; the truth will make you free (vss. 31-32). [Note the moral condition of both knowledge and freedom.]

The discussion then turned (vss. 33:52) upon their claim to be descended from Abraham (and therefore free!), whereas their conduct showed that they were slaves of sin and children of the evil one (cf. the previous note on the father-son relationship). Finally they argued (vss. 53-58) that Jesus was putting himself above Abraham. He said: **Before Abraham was, I am.**

21-29. Again he said to them: cf. 7:33-34. On that occasion they explained this prediction as a mission to the Dispersion. Now they suspect suicide!—in one sense an unconscious prophecy, for Jesus did voluntarily lay down his life (10:17-18). **From below**

this world. And each will pass to his own proper place, and abide in the sphere native to him; **for you will die in your sins unless you believe that I am he.** Certainly that has been proved true in the experience of multitudes. Only their faith in Christ—in what he is and what he does—gives them the power to rise above themselves, to shake off their unworthiness, to live what may be called life. But the word, when first it was spoken, was met by vacant faces and a blank lack of comprehension. **Who are you?** they asked, puzzled and irritated, "you who make such confident claims?"

Very different translations have been offered of Christ's answer (see Exeg.). The most familiar runs. **Even what I have told you from the beginning;** i.e., "what I keep repeating over and over." But the Greek fathers preferred the reading of the RSV mg., **Why do I talk to you at all?** As if, for once, the patience of Christ was all but exhausted; as if he wondered if it were worth while to try any longer to make anything of people so obtuse. In the Gospels that strange patience of the Master with slow, dull, impossible folk is constantly underlined. And our experience corroborates that day by day. How often he repeats lessons which we keep forgetting or find difficult to grasp; how uncomplainingly he moderates his pace to our slow, stumbling, uncertain steps. Even Confucius, for once almost ruffled out of his accustomed kindly equanimity, one day snapped out that he could not keep on repeating the same simple lessons, that he expected a disciple, having been put on the right road, to do something for himself. But Christ, after a thousand failures on our part, begins again, and tries once more, still patient, still kind, still encouragingly hopeful. And so perhaps what he says here might be rendered, **Why do I talk to you at all?** Because

25 Then said they unto him, Who art thou? And Jesus saith unto them, Even *the same* that I said unto you from the beginning.

26 I have many things to say and to judge of you: but he that sent me is true; and I speak to the world those things which I have heard of him.

27 They understood not that he spake to them of the Father.

28 Then said Jesus unto them, When ye have lifted up the Son of man, then shall ye know that I am *he*, and *that* I do nothing of myself; but as my Father hath taught me, I speak these things.

lieve that I am he." 25 They said to him,
"Who are you?" Jesus said to them, "Even
what I have told you from the beginning.[p]
26 I have much to say about you and much
to judge; but he who sent me is true, and
I declare to the world what I have heard
from him." 27 They did not understand
that he spoke to them of the Father. 28 So
Jesus said, "When you have lifted up the
Son of man, then you will know that I
am he, and that I do nothing on my own
authority but speak thus as the Father

[p] Or *Why do I talk to you at all?*

---

means **of this world**—human life organized in hostility to the will of God (cf. 3:31; 17:14; I John 4:5). This sinful order is doomed to destruction for want of faith which, according to this Gospel, is the fundamental sin (cf. 16:9). **I am he** (vs. 24), "I am," as in vs. 28; 13:19, where we seem to have a cryptic formula, recalling Exod. 3:14; Deut. 32:39; Isa. 43:10, and suggesting unity with God. This bold assertion led his hearers to challenge Jesus to declare his identity (vs. 25). His reply is a famous *crux interpretum*. The text and margin of RSV give the two main lines of interpretation. The Greek adverbial phrase τὴν ἀρχὴν can mean either "from the beginning," or "at all." This is followed by a word which could be either a relative pronoun (ὅ τι) "that which," or an interrogative

---

I have much to say about you—things that you do not like and will resent. But God himself has given it me to tell you; and tell it I must, and will. There is a message for ministers. They are to preach not what the people want to hear, but what God bids them say; and for that they must listen, long and closely; and having heard it, ring it out—like it or mislike it as men may. For if it is part of their duty, and it is, to keep in step with their own generation, and to speak to them in their own mental language about the problems that are pressing in upon their minds, that is only one side of what is required. For there are fashions in preaching and in believing, as in everything else. In each new day certain portions of Christ's teaching are underlined and emphasized and thrust into the foreground, while others no less surely there are overlooked and forgotten, and indeed deliberately avoided. A preacher cannot have Paul's ease of conscience when parting from the Ephesian elders, unless like the apostle he can declare, "I testify to you this day that I am innocent of the blood of all of you, for I did not shrink from declaring to you the whole counsel of God" (Acts 20:26-27). If anything in Christ is being toned down and ignored, that too must be boldly stated if our hands are to be clean and we true followers of the Master.

28. *Christ's Death More Potent Than His Teaching.*—Still met by that same look of puzzled lack of understanding, Jesus takes a further step. Apparently it was being borne in on him that he must die for this people; that while his teaching might not impress them, and his life might fail to win them, somehow his death would do what nothing else could do; and through that God's gracious purposes toward them, which they were so impeding, would work themselves out. **When you have lifted up the Son of man, then you will know that I am he, and that I do nothing on my own authority.** Is it not an amazing thing that a wayside cross, set up on a hillside where somebody was always being crucified, has proved far and away the most central and momentous thing in human history; that that symbol of shame and utter failure has stormed men's hearts the whole world over; that what ought to have ended the whole enterprise in utter fiasco has given Christ an irresistible power, and convinced multitudes that this is he; and that as they stand there on Calvary, looking at him dying for them, burningly it comes home to them that there is more here than a noble and indomitable spirit giving itself for truth, and paying down its life rather than compromise or falter—that this is an eternal and divine plan finding its way to its fulfillment, God's grace to man proving the length to which it is prepared to go to save us from ourselves and from the difficulties into which we have blundered? In the light that

29 And he that sent me is with me: the Father hath not left me alone; for I do always those things that please him.

30 As he spake these words, many believed on him.

31 Then said Jesus to those Jews which believed on him, If ye continue in my word, *then* are ye my disciples indeed;

taught me. 29 And he who sent me is with me; he has not left me alone, for I always do what is pleasing to him." 30 As he spoke thus, many believed in him.

31 Jesus then said to the Jews who had believed in him, "If you continue in my

pronoun (ὅτι—as in Mark 2:16; 9:11, 28) "why?" The marginal reading, **Why do I talk to you at all?** is a possible translation, but it does not suit the context well. The first meaning given for the two Greek expressions may be taken in three ways. (*a*) "From the beginning I am even what I tell you." (*b*) "I am even what I have told you from the beginning." Or, taking "from the beginning" in a slightly different sense, (*c*) "I am essentially even what I am telling you." The word "lift up" in vs. 28 (ὑψοῦν) is used in its double sense (see note on 3:14 and Intro., p. 439). Crucifixion leads to exaltation to the Father.

30-31. Many believed in him . . . the Jews who had believed in him: A difficulty arises from the swift change from belief to vehement hostility. Within a few verses these believers are denounced by Jesus as those who seek to kill him (vs. 37), and they declare that Jesus "has a demon." Though most expositors ignore the different constructions as having no significance, it would solve the problem if we allowed the grammar to represent the meaning. In vs. 30 the words (ἐπίστευσαν εἰς αὐτόν) mean **believed in him.** In vs. 31 the literal translation is "who had believed him" (τοὺς πεπιστευκότας αὐτῷ). If we observe this distinction in meaning, the previous paragraph ends with the report that many of our Lord's hearers put their faith in him. The next paragraph refers to a section who had accepted his words, but had not made the full surrender of faith. These, like those disciples (cf. 6:60, 66) who were repelled by a "hard saying" and withdrew from his company, failed to **continue in** [his] **word.** Their simple acquiescence in his teaching was not deeply rooted faith, and therefore quickly withered. Discipleship involves constancy as learners, and that gains the promise of knowledge of the truth and freedom. If, however, this distinction of meaning cannot be maintained, then we should have to assume that the **many** who **believed in him** were easily shaken in their faith. **Continue in my word:** cf. 15:7 for mutual relationship, and see on 6:56. **You are truly my disciples:**

streams from Calvary, how clear it grows that through everything Christ said the voice of God is speaking to us, that in everything Christ did there is a reliable revelation of how God thinks and feels and acts toward us.

29. *The Nearness of God.*—Christ himself knew that at the time. **He who sent me is with me; he has not left me alone, for I always do what is pleasing to him.** Even we who are not pure in heart, and have no right to the open vision, have had amazing experiences of the nearness and the graciousness of God. (As my Scottish forefathers put it in their original confession: We profess that in the sacrament we "have had such conjunction with Christ as the natural man could not comprehend.") But how unthinkably close and intimate and wonderful must the communion have been between God and Jesus Christ, with never a cloud of any kind between them. And we, poor fools, lose that—for what? And let ourselves be tricked and cheated into paying away God for ugly little sins which we account worth that tremendous price—we who like Christ might walk with God in open vision!

30-33. *All Scripture Is Given by Inspiration of God.*—**As he spoke thus, many believed in him,** says the evangelist, pausing to chronicle a marked and notable impression made by these reasonings and words of Christ. Yet many other of his sayings storm and hold and haunt the heart far more than these. It makes an interesting study to take the Bible into our hands, and as we turn the pages, to recall how this one and that one was born here; how through this passage God's voice broke in and arrested one of his great servants; how in this verse a fellow man once met God face to face, and could no longer evade him, or push past him, or pretend not to see him, but had to give his answer and decision there and then. To take such instances as first come to mind—Augustine, har-

32 And ye shall know the truth, and the truth shall make you free.

33 ¶ They answered him, We be Abraham's seed, and were never in bondage to any man: how sayest thou, Ye shall be made free?

34 Jesus answered them, Verily, verily, I say unto you, Whosoever committeth sin is the servant of sin.

word, you are truly my disciples, 32 and you will know the truth, and the truth will make you free." 33 They answered him, "We are descendants of Abraham, and have never been in bondage to anyone. How is it that you say, 'You will be made free'?"

34 Jesus answered them, "Truly, truly, I say to you, every one who commits sin

---

The Greek word ἀληθῶς, translated "truly," is parallel to the word ὄντως, translated "indeed" in vs. 63. In each verse there is a contrast between the real and the false. Real discipleship alone leads to the real freedom. (For the relation between faith and knowledge see Intro., p. 442.) The Pharisees, unlike the Zealots, did not look for political freedom for they agreed with Jesus that God's gift of freedom came from obeying his will. But they regarded this freedom as their birthright, as Abraham's descendants who kept their national privilege of studying the Torah.

34-37. The words **to sin** are omitted by some important authorities and are a gloss which destroys the balance of the sentence. The **slave** (vs. 36) is contrasted with the **son.**

---

assed and desperate, hearing a child's voice crying over and over, no doubt at some game, "Take up and read," opened the Scriptures

> and in silence read that section on which my eyes first fell: *Not in rioting and drunkenness, not in chambering and wantonness, not in strife and envying: but put ye on the Lord Jesus Christ, and make not provision for the flesh.* . . . No further would I read; nor needed I: for instantly at the end of this sentence, by a light as it were of serenity infused into my heart, all the darkness of doubt vanished away.[8]

Cowper, the poet, had a very similar experience. But for him the all-important passage that brought light was this, "Whom God hath set forth to be a propitiation through faith in his blood, to declare his righteousness for the remission of sins that are past, through the forbearance of God" (Rom. 3:25). Or John Knox, who when he lay dying said to his wife, "Read where I cast my first anchor." So she read in John 17. There must be few passages in the N.T. that have not proved to be the holy of holies for some soul. And many who believed in Christ looked back to this scripture as the place where their eyes were opened and God found them.

But if the evangelist was impressed, Christ, as he confesses, was much less so—apparently not a little doubtful of the reliability of their faith (but note in the Exeg. a possible distinction between two kinds of faith). **If you continue in my words, you are truly my disciples, and you will know the truth, and the truth will make you free.** Many of us must grievously disappoint him there. We cross the border into his kingdom and then we settle down in it—but no more; never press on to win the fullness that there is for us in him; never grow up in Christ, but remain crude, immature, undeveloped, childish. Yet as the rabbis used to say, the reward of keeping a precept is to be given another precept to keep. The life in Christ is like climbing a mountain which seems constantly to draw back its head, so that each top gained reveals another, and that in turn another we had not seen from farther down, nor realized that it was there. "If you abide by what I say, more and more you will understand the truth, and the truth will set you free."

34-36. ***Christ the Emancipator.***—Whereupon our Lord's misgivings concerning them were at once justified. Their national pride took umbrage; and they grew critical, captious, angry, these new believers. "We have never been in bondage to anyone," they declared hotly. "What do you mean by saying, 'You will be free'?" This odd account of their history, and of their own position as the vassals of Rome, will be read by some as obstinate blindness and by others as an indomitable independence, not to be cowed or broken. In either case Christ pushes aside their political interpretation and presses further into things more central by far even than these.

Perhaps even the Gospels have no more arresting sayings than those of vss. 34 and 36, notable indeed—the one because of the gravity of its diagnosis of the human situation, the other because of the confidence of Christ that he can meet and cure and satisfy it.

Truly, truly, I say to you, every one who

[8] *Confessions* VIII. 12. 29.

35 And the servant abideth not in the house for ever: *but* the Son abideth ever.

is a slave to sin. 35 The slave does not continue in the house forever; the son con-

The **Son is free** and the giver of freedom. **My word finds no place in you:** This rendering follows the KJV; but the intransitive use of the Greek verb (χωρεῖν), especially in the

commits sin is a slave to sin. How much of the tragedy of life is crowded into that one succinct sentence! Yet all experience corroborates it. "Show me," says Seneca, "anyone who is not a slave. One is a slave to lust, another to avarice, a third to ambition; all alike to fear." "No one," as Goethe put it, "is more of a slave than he who thinks himself free without being so." That poor fool, swaggering down the road to the far country, is not really his own master but is the slave of his passions, and has to come to heel at call, and slink there, cowed and obedient, like the beaten cur he is. Have you ever tried to help some unhappy soul firmly enmeshed in a settled evil habit? It is a painful and pathetic business that makes one sick. Often the man wants to be free, and is eager to set about it. But sometimes his will has become so pulpy that it will no longer function. Any passing pair of fingers can squeeze him into any shape they choose. But sometimes he does pull himself together, does try, and does break free. And it is over, and the victory attained! But often not! Something, anything, nothing, and he is down once more; and the ground gained is lost again; and not seldom in the reaction he is swept back farther than he was before. The house swept and garnished, in the Master's dreadful metaphor, is now inhabited by seven raging devils in place of the original one. "Sin," says Browning, "which steals back softly on a soul half saved." [9]

Who of us can meet Christ's eyes without our own falling before them when he takes up our silly human boast, "Free! You free! You who are not masters in your own life! You, not so much men as things at the disposal of this other that lords it over you! **Every one who commits sin is a slave to sin.** Break free from yours, if you can. Try it, and you will see how free you are; rather how mercilessly bound and shackled!" Moreover, as time goes on, the more inexorable do things grow. For the oftener one surrenders to a failing, the more difficult does it become to do anything else. As Schiller said,

> This is the very curse of evil deed,
> That of fresh evil it becomes the seed.[1]

Once we begin, normally we are carried down the hill faster and faster by our own impetus. Where one has once passed through the meadows, others are apt to follow, till a path is beaten broad and bare and hard. And a deed, once done, tends to repeat itself, to harden into a habit, to grow in time almost automatic. The thing that we are doing may distress and humiliate us, yet it carries us away, like a swimmer helpless in the raging waters that toss him where they will. We may hate it and resist it, yet we cannot will what we want to will, or choose as we would like to choose; but too often at the moment of decision find ourselves once more breaking our sturdy resolutions and making the accustomed tame surrender.

It is a miserable servitude, photographed once for all in Rom. 7:14-24. But literature is full of striking parallels, all drawn from life, all taken straight from the experience of desperate souls. So Francis Quarles:

> I like, dislike, lament for what I could not;
> I do, undo; yet still do what I should not,
> And, at the selfsame instant, will the thing I would not.[2]

Like enemy troops quartered on a conquered people, habits we loathe loll at their ease in our personality. And though we may glower at them, we have to do their bidding, and fetch and carry at their call.

But blessed be God, there is the other side of things; not only vs. 34 but also vs. 36, **If the Son makes you free, you will be free indeed.** It is the sense and the realization of that which give the N.T. its atmosphere. And thus it is far and away the happiest book in literature. When at long last the day of their emancipation was breaking, the slaves in Jamaica, who had climbed to the summits of the highest hills that they might miss no moment of it, no sooner saw the sun's rim rise above the horizon than they laughed, and wept, and sang, and danced, and threw their arms about each others' necks, and fell upon their knees in prayer. But all alike kept crying in a kind of dazed and happy ecstasy, "Free! Free! Free!" That is the N.T. note. These people are always exulting in their new-found incredible liberty—incredible yet true. "Where the Spirit of the Lord is, there is freedom" (II Cor. 3:17). And this, "the glorious liberty of the children of God" (Rom.

[9] "Pauline."

[1] *Piccolomini,* Act V, scene 1.

[2] "O how my will is hurried to and fro," in *Emblems Divine and Moral* (New York: Robert Carter & Bros., 1857), p. 202.

36 If the Son therefore shall make you free, ye shall be free indeed.

37 I know that ye are Abraham's seed; but ye seek to kill me, because my word hath no place in you.

38 I speak that which I have seen with my Father: and ye do that which ye have seen with your father.

39 They answered and said unto him, Abraham is our father. Jesus saith unto them, If ye were Abraham's children, ye would do the works of Abraham.

tinues forever.
36 So if the Son makes you
free, you will be free indeed.
37 I know
that you are descendants of Abraham; yet you seek to kill me, because my word finds no place in you.
38 I speak of what I have
seen with my Father, and you do what you have heard from your father."

39 They answered him, "Abraham is our father." Jesus said to them, "If you were Abraham's children, you would do what

---

Hellenistic age, favors the ERV, "hath not free course in you," or Moffatt's "makes no headway among you," or Weymouth's "gains no ground within you."

8:21). That is the main point of Galatians. As Marcus Dods used to say, "You can hear Paul's heart dancing and exulting at the thought of it; and, still more, in the experience of it. The Son had made him free."

And many others down the ages have been delivered from hard bondage by the great Emancipator; have with amazement seen the heavy iron prison gates, so long inexorably shut, open before them of themselves; have felt the shackles that had bitten deep into their wrists snap and fall off; have found that they were free. When Celsus jeered and gibed at Christ, declaring scornfully that this was the strangest of teachers—for, said he, while all the others cry, "Come to me, you who are clean and worthy," this singular Master calls, "Come to me, you who are down and beaten by life"; and so, being taken at his word by these impossible people, he is followed about by the rag, tag, and bobtail of humanity trailing behind him—Origen answered devastatingly, "Yes; but he does not leave them the rag, tag, and bobtail of humanity; but out of material you would have thrown away as useless, he fashions men, giving them back their self-respect, enabling them to stand up on their feet and look God in the eyes. They were cowed, cringing, broken things. But the Son has made them free."[3] One can of course go back from Christ. In the old Jewish dispensation there were slaves who were afraid of liberty and shrank from it; who, given their chance of it, pushed it away, and with deliberation chose a perpetual, lifelong servitude in preference to it. That seems inexplicable. Yet who of us has not at times acted on similar lines and gone back to weaknesses from which Christ had delivered us? "It is said," says Samuel Butler, "when Andromeda and Perseus had travelled but a little way from the rock where Andromeda had so long been chained, she began upbraiding him with the loss of her dragon, who, on the whole, she said, had been very good to her."[4] Yet it is no idle boast, but actual fact, authenticated over and over in lives beyond numbering, that if we continue in his word, we shall know the truth, and the truth will make us free.

But if the general sense of the passage is plain, vs. 35 is not easily fitted in. **The slave does not continue in the house forever; the son continues forever. So if the Son makes you free, you will be free indeed.** What house? The fact that the Son lives in it permanently and has authority within it makes it clear that it must be God's. But in what sense? And what is the slave of sin doing in it? The report of what Christ said seems here to be so succinct and compressed as to be not readily followed. Are they right who would interpret thus: The promises made to Abraham are valid and reliable; but those of his descendants who are the slaves of sin have a precarious hold on them, and may easily lose their rights in them, while those whom the Son makes free are permanently and securely settled in the inheritance designed for them—those, but those only?

37-41*a*. *The Visible and the Invisible Church.*—The general sense of our Lord's teaching here would seem to be what the theologians have sought to sum up for us in the doctrine of the visible and the invisible church. To belong to the former, to be brought up in its atmosphere, to be played upon day after day by its gracious influences is in itself an immense advantage which ought to predispose one to become a member of the real church (called invisible because only God knows with accuracy who belongs to it), i.e., to the body, not merely of traditionalists and conformists and outward adherents, but of genuine believers, of those

[3] See Origen *Against Celsus* III. 59.

[4] *Life and Habit* (London: Jonathan Cape, 1923), p. 112.

40 But now ye seek to kill me, a man that hath told you the truth, which I have heard of God: this did not Abraham.

41 Ye do the deeds of your father. Then said they to him, We be not born of fornication; we have one Father, *even* God.

42 Jesus said unto them, If God were your Father, ye would love me: for I proceeded forth and came from God; neither came I of myself, but he sent me.

43 Why do ye not understand my speech? *even* because ye cannot hear my word.

Abraham did,
40 but now you seek to kill me, a man who has told you the truth which I heard from God; this is not what Abraham did.
41 You do what your father did." They said to him, "We were not born of fornication; we have one Father, even God."
42 Jesus said to them, "If God were your Father, you would love me, for I proceeded and came forth from God; I came not of my own accord, but he sent me.
43 Why do you not understand what I say? It is because

---

41. We were not born of fornication; we have one Father, even God: The Jews resent Jesus' reply to their claim of pure descent, that their actions betray their paternity. Unlike the Samaritans, their lineage is indisputable. But they see the drift of the argument, and claim now that God is their father. For centuries their ancestors have been loyal to his commands. They have not been guilty of apostasy (for which the metaphor of adultery was used in the O.T.).

---

who have accepted God's offers of salvation, and have put on the Lord Jesus Christ, and are learning to grow up into his mind and ways. Apart from that, membership in the outward church is not nearly enough.

So, says Christ, to be able to claim Abraham, that mighty spiritual hero, as your ancestor, to have his blood in your veins, is a glorious privilege indeed. Yet of itself it will not automatically avail for you, or in you; but only if the blood tells, if you catch and reproduce something of the spirit of that audacious believer who trusted God and continued so to do, though life was running out and not one of the promises had as yet come true; who died indeed, as others held, tricked, cheated, empty-handed, fooled, but himself still obstinately and undauntedly believing that what God had promised God would do. **If you were Abraham's children, you would do what Abraham did.** He heard God's voice and followed trustingly. But you have nothing of his spirit of faith and adventure in you. I come to you from God: I tell you what he sent me to declare to you. And you remain cold, suspicious, unresponsive. **This is not what Abraham did.**

And then, with what later is seen to be a terrible home thrust, he adds, **You do what your father did.** To which they answered, **We have one Father, even God.**

41*b*-47. *The Fatherhood of God.*—(See also on 14:6.) Assuredly the fatherhood of God as we know it was a discovery of Jesus Christ; the greatest and most fruitful of them all. But foreshadowings of it, more or less dim, can be discovered here and there, elsewhere, and before his day. If in the O.T. God is the Father of the nation more than of the individual soul, nonetheless the writer of the superb Ps. 103 had an understanding of this central truth amazing in its depth and insight.

Max Müller, lecturing in Westminster Abbey, had this striking passage:

> Five thousand years ago, or, it may be earlier, the Aryans, speaking as yet neither Sanskrit, Greek, nor Latin, called [God] *Dyu patar,* Heaven-father.
>
> Four thousand years ago, or, it may be earlier, the Aryans who traveled southward to the rivers of the Penjâb, called him *Dyaush-pitâ,* Heaven-father.
>
> Three thousand years ago, or, it may be earlier, the Aryans on the shores of the Hellespont, called him Ζεὺς πατήρ, Heaven-father.
>
> Two thousand years ago, the Aryans of Italy looked up to that bright heaven above, . . . and called it *Ju-piter,* Heaven-father.
>
> And a thousand years ago the same Heaven-father and All-father was invoked by our own peculiar ancestors, the Teutonic Aryans, and his old name of *Tiu* or *Zio* was then heard perhaps for the last time. . . .
>
> And when we here in this ancient Abbey, . . . if we want a name for the invisible, the infinite, that surrounds us on every side, the unknown, the true Self of the world, and the true Self of ourselves—we, too, feeling once more like children, kneeling in a small dark room, can hardly find a better name than: "Our Father, which art in Heaven."[5]

Which is eloquent and true; and yet misleading. For as our Lord used it of Almighty God, the word Father has a content and a connotation infinitely richer than anything to

[5] *Lectures on the Origin of Religion* (London: Longmans, Green & Co., 1878), pp. 216-17.

44 Ye are of *your* father the devil, and the lusts of your father ye will do: he was a murderer from the beginning, and abode not in the truth, because there is no truth in him. When he speaketh a lie, he speaketh of his own: for he is a liar, and the father of it.

45 And because I tell *you* the truth, ye believe me not.

46 Which of you convinceth me of sin? And if I say the truth, why do ye not believe me?

you cannot bear to hear my word. 44 You
are of your father the devil, and your will
is to do your father's desires. He was a
murderer from the beginning, and has
nothing to do with the truth, because there
is no truth in him. When he lies, he speaks
according to his own nature, for he is a
liar and the father of lies. 45 But, because
I tell the truth, you do not believe me.
46 Which of you convicts me of sin? If I
tell the truth, why do you not believe me?

---

44. You are of your father the devil: Like father, like son. Their desire to kill Jesus proves their devil's pedigree. **He was a murderer from the beginning,** cf. I John 3:8. Moreover, he is essentially false, and his native tongue is falsehood. His children cannot welcome the revelation sent by the only true God. The Greek could be strictly translated, "You are of the father of the devil, . . . for he is a liar and so is his father." Some writers find an allusion here to Gnostic speculations about the devil's father. But there can be little doubt that the usual translation (e.g., RSV) gives the right meaning.

Bultmann points out (*Theologisches Wörterbuch zum Neuen Testament,* ed. Gerhard Kittel [Stuttgart: W. Kohlhammer, 1933], I, 245): "Though John goes so far in agreement with Hellenistic-Gnostic dualism, yet there is a distinction between them. The antagonism between ἀλήθεια (truth) and ψεῦδος (falsehood)—as the divine power and its opposite—is not cosmological, in spite of the mythological dress in which it occasionally appears (John 8:44). For ἀλήθεια and ψεῦδος are understood not as 'substances,' but rather as actual possibilities of human existence."

45-47. Jesus asserts that his hearers do not believe him because he speaks the truth. Presumably they showed their indignation at this charge which follows on his indictment

---

be found elsewhere. Yet one is glad that these Jews had gained some conception of the glorious truth.

Nonetheless, Christ's answer to them is grim indeed. **You are not of God. You are of your father the devil,** and his nature shows itself in you. **He was a murderer from the beginning;** and you seek to kill me; he **has nothing to do with the truth,** and true to your blood and ancestry, when and because **I tell you the truth,** you do not believe it, resent it, fling it from you.

What are we to make of this terrible accusation? Are not all of us God's children? Many of us no doubt wayward, provoking, heartbreaking; yet each of us with his own secure place in God's heart and plans, a place that nobody can fill except himself. That seems to be the plain meaning of many passages in the N.T.—a meaning emphasized and underlined. And yet there is another graver side; and there are passages like this, as really a part of the record, which make some believe that it is only Christ who gives us the right to say "Abba, Father"; that what he does for us is to introduce us into a closer and more intimate relationship with God than others know or can know. Those others at the best are subjects; but in Christ men are God's children. In any case, one may assume that this graphic passage is a telling instance of Christ's characteristic way of flinging down a truth so daringly and vividly that the dimmest eyes must see it, and the slowest mind must take it in; but with the risk that literalists may misinterpret or be stumbled.

46. ***Some Modern Attacks upon Christ's Sinlessness.*****—Which of you convicts me of sin?** The words leap at one out of the page, a bold challenge indeed! Yet after all these centuries it stands and still remains unanswered. Even Socrates condoned and indulged in practices impossible to any decent person now. Even Mohammed, with all his noble and winsome qualities, degenerated sadly toward the end; so that the Mohammedan modernist agrees that he cannot in all things be accepted as the standard for life now. But Jesus Christ remains our ideal of what goodness means; and to become good is to learn in all things to put on his nature. Holiness is Christlikeness. And Christlikeness is holiness. So for two thousand years a vast and ever-growing proportion of the human race has held. Coming on Christ, they have

47 He that is of God heareth God's words: ye therefore hear *them* not, because ye are not of God.

47 He who is of God hears the words of God; the reason why you do not hear them is that you are not of God."

---

of their father the devil. So Jesus replies to their signs of protest with the challenge, "Does any of you convict me of falsehood? If not, why refuse assent to the truth which I

---

caught their breath, feeling, with a new understanding of life's possibilities, that this is what life ought to be, is meant to be, can be; the thing lived out; and, without any qualification whatsoever, taking his character as it is recorded for us, they have adopted that as the ideal, as the headline given us to reproduce; and have judged the standing of themselves and others by their likeness or unlikeness to Jesus Christ. To live according to his spirit, that is goodness. To fall out of step with him is sin. A huge mass of mankind has met the Master's question, **Which of you convicts me of sin?** by answering, "No one, Lord."

But nowadays in many quarters all that is being confidently challenged. Even Nicolai Hartmann says despondently that "we do not yet know what good is."[6] Many of us have thought that we have only to look at Jesus Christ to learn that. H. G. Wells, for what his opinion may be worth upon such matters, declared, "There is no creed, no way of living left in the world at all, that really meets the needs of the time."[7] Many of us have thought that Jesus Christ shows us, and leads us in the way that runs both straight and sure through all the problems life can set us. But many seem now much less sure of that.

(*a*) Some—such as certain pacifists, and certain fanatical temperance reformers, and certain soft and amiable creatures—feel uncomfortably that there are features of his portrait as it stands which are unfortunate and must be eliminated if he is to be our pattern. "Who convicts you of sin?" they seem to ask, and answer, "That ugly scene in the temple, when you lost your temper; the marriage in Cana, and how you acted there; your harsh words to the Pharisees; your terrible answer to Peter—a well-meaning if blundering friend. Surely some kindlier methods might have been found and used, not breaking your own law of love?" All this, not hearkening to Ecclus. 5:6, where it warns us, "Say not, His compassion is great; he will be pacified for the multitude of my sin. For mercy is with him—and wrath." And we can bless his name for that.

(*b*) Some, quick to admit the perfection of his personal character and the finality of his teaching for the individual, feel that goodness as he defined it and lived it out was much too circumscribed a thing to touch and regulate life at all points as we know it and have to live it; and that he does not give us guidance where we sadly need it, where our consciences are teased and troubled, and our problems press in upon us most insistently. Some Moslems think that this is true even about personal ethics. According to a catechism published at Lahore: "What we need is the guidance of one who has lived in all branches of life. Jesus never conquered his enemies, never married, never had little ones. He is no guide to us there. The only guide is the prophet with his rounded life." And many in the West these days hold something of the same view, but upon broader lines. For it is social and economic and political wrongs that most shame and harass us nowadays. And many tell us impatiently that Christ has far too little interest in these; that while we may still learn from him how to pick our own way through life and keep from stumbling, for help in the larger issues, for guidance about patriotism and civic and national duties, we must turn to the Greeks. And that, so they maintain, is a serious defect in Christ, a lamentable one-sidedness, a lack of sympathy, a callous passing by upon the other side; whereas Marx and Lenin come to grips with the real problems of real life.

That is a curious criticism of the teaching which beyond question has incited more men and women to self-sacrifice for others than anything else in the whole world. Accept and apply and live out Christ's principles of self-restraint, of unselfishness, of brotherhood, of service, which he kept underlining; take it in, that goodness as he claims it from us is not a negative thing, a not doing this, a not being that, a keeping out of actual wrong, but that it is intensely positive, a zeal, a passion, an enthusiasm, a giving of life away with both hands for others—as J. R. Seeley has it, that "no heart is pure that is not passionate, no virtue is safe that is not enthusiastic. And such an enthusiastic virtue Christ was to introduce."[8] Take that in, and we shall find that though we have no book of the words, with an elaborate index and everything required of us neatly arranged

[6] *Ethics*, tr. S. Crit (London: George Allen & Unwin, 1932), II, 173.

[7] *The Fate of Man* (New York: Alliance Book Corp., 1939), p. 230.

[8] *Ecce Homo* (Boston: Roberts Bros., 1886), p. 14.

proclaim?" **Of God . . . not of God** (vs. 47) : The same acid test as in vs. 23, where action attests origin.

---

under the appropriate heading, we have something hugely better and more serviceable, a spirit that can and ought to be universally applied, and principles that will work and guide us in every conceivable situation in which we can find ourselves.

(*c*) But there are others much more aggressive in their onslaughts, who say bluntly that Christ has led us astray, that acquiescence in his teaching has landed us in disaster, that "to have bound up [the] New Testament along . . . with [the] Old Testament into one book . . . is perhaps"—so thinks Nietzsche—"the greatest audacity and 'sin against the Spirit' which literary Europe has upon its conscience." [9] Some of them, Nietzsche himself for one, do not doubt or question that good untold has come to many through the pity and self-sacrifice Christ set in motion. But on the whole, say they, his influence even there has been pernicious, and unless checked, must bring ruin upon the race. For it too is covered by Freud's confident dictum, "What the world calls its code of morals demands more sacrifices than it is worth, and its behaviour is neither dictated by honesty nor instituted with wisdom." [1] What Christ held to be virtues are, it would seem, not virtues at all, but weaknesses, diseases, stupid repressions heading straight for far worse things, and often landing us in them. So Nietzsche declares with heat that for far too long the so-called Christian virtues have been taken at their own valuation, and accepted as such; but that the time is more than come when they must be summoned to the bar of reason and compelled to prove their case. And once there, he maintains, it becomes evident that they are impudent impostors with no case at all, to be hooted with derision into the oblivion from which they should never have been allowed to emerge.[2]

No doubt this "slave morality" is well enough for slaves; this meekness and humility and self-sacrifice upon which Christ lays such stress. These suit the slavish nature. But for virile people they are an insult, and "the danger of dangers." Moreover, he thinks, they are an absurdity. Why should the weaklings be allowed to fix the rules of the game of life to suit themselves and to their own advantage? As if a team of Rugby footballers, noticing that their opponents are burlier and swifter than themselves, should have it ordained that there must be no tackling, for that might hurt a bit; and that no one shall be allowed to run faster than at a fixed and very moderate speed. Why should the strong not use their strength even if the weak do get hurt in the jostle? So to Nietzsche the pity that Christ brought into the world is an absurdity and a sheer evil. No doubt at all, poor, hurt, broken things innumerable have profited by it. But what of the race? Had Christ no thought of it? The weaklings should have been allowed to go to the wall, as is nature's wise and really kindly way. The individual may perish, but the race as a whole is by their elimination saved from degeneration, as it ought to be. Christ's law of love has done wonders for our brothers and our neighbors. But has he not been sadly remiss in his failure to keep the law of "Love to the Remote"? These weaklings, saved now at his command, will in the years to come breed far more weaklings, and increase the difficulties of the coming generations. Better, on the long view, to have let them perish. "I realized that the morality of pity . . . was the most sinister symptom of our modern . . . civilization." Moreover, the standards which Christ gave us are all wrong.

> Weakness is turned to merit. . . . The impotence which requites not, is turned to "goodness," craven baseness to meekness. . . . The inoffensive character of the weak, the very cowardice in which he is rich, . . . gain here fine names, such as "patience," which is also called "virtue"; not being able to avenge one's self, is called not wishing to avenge one's self, perhaps even forgiveness.[3]

In fact, when one looks at "the European Christian" of the present day, that "dwarfed, almost ludicrous species, . . . does it not . . . seem that some single will has ruled over Europe for eighteen centuries in order to make a *sublime abortion* of man?" [4]

Well! We have seen what happens when a nation turns away from Christ, and repudiates his teaching, and thinks that it knows better than he. The bestialities and unbelievable enormities which rose up out of their graves and shocked and shamed us showed us how much we owe to him; and how wise are the ways in which he bids us walk. And if any individual or generation differs from him, life will prove how wrong they are; nor will they know real peace of mind, or attain to what is fully worthy, ex-

[9] *Beyond Good and Evil,* tr. Helen Zimmerer (Edinburgh: T. N. Foulis, 1909), p. 71.

[1] *Introductory Lectures on Psycho-Analysis* (London: George Allen & Unwin, 1923), p. 362.

[2] *Beyond Good and Evil,* p. 48; cf. also preface to *Genealogy of Morals,* tr. H. B. Samuel (Edinburgh: T. N. Foulis, 1910), pp. 9-10.

[3] *Genealogy of Morals,* p. 48.

[4] *Beyond Good and Evil,* p. 84.

48 Then answered the Jews, and said unto him, Say we not well that thou art a Samaritan, and hast a devil?

49 Jesus answered, I have not a devil; but I honor my Father, and ye do dishonor me.

50 And I seek not mine own glory: there is one that seeketh and judgeth.

51 Verily, verily, I say unto you, If a man keep my saying, he shall never see death.

52 Then said the Jews unto him, Now we know that thou hast a devil. Abraham is dead, and the prophets; and thou sayest, If a man keep my saying, he shall never taste of death.

53 Art thou greater than our father Abraham, which is dead? and the prophets are dead: whom makest thou thyself?

54 Jesus answered, If I honor myself, my honor is nothing: it is my Father that honoreth me; of whom ye say, that he is your God:

55 Yet ye have not known him; but I know him: and if I should say, I know him not, I shall be a liar like unto you: but I know him, and keep his saying.

48 The Jews answered him, "Are we
not right in saying that you are a Samaritan
and have a demon?" 49 Jesus answered, "I
have not a demon; but I honor my Father,
and you dishonor me. 50 Yet I do not seek
my own glory; there is One who seeks it and
he will be the judge. 51 Truly, truly, I say
to you, if any one keeps my word, he will
never see death." 52 The Jews said to him,
"Now we know that you have a demon.
Abraham died, as did the prophets; and
you say, 'If any one keeps my word, he
will never taste death.' 53 Are you greater
than our father Abraham, who died?
And the prophets died! Who do you
claim to be?" 54 Jesus answered, "If I
glorify myself, my glory is nothing; it is
my Father who glorifies me, of whom you
say that he is your God. 55 But you have
not known him; I know him. If I said, I do
not know him, I should be a liar like you;
but I do know him and I keep his word.

48. You . . . have a demon, cf. 7:20; 10:20, where the interpretation follows that he is mad. **You are a Samaritan,** therefore baseborn and not one of the children of God. Some scholars see in this a reference to the Samaritan magician, Dositheus (an older contemporary of Simon Magus), who claimed to be the Messiah, foretold by Moses, and the Son of God. If the allusion is to this mad claim, we need not ask why Jesus replied to the charge of madness and said nothing about the accusation of being a Samaritan.

51-54. Another way of saying that obedience to Christ is the way which leads to eternal life. On keeping **my word** cf. 14:23-24; 15:20; 17:6; I John 2:5. On **see death** cf. Ps. 89:48; Luke 2:26; Heb. 11:5. Cf. 7:18 for Jesus' refusal to seek honor for himself (vs. 54) and 13:32; 16:14; 17:1-5 for the Father's glorification of the Son.

cept by obedience to Jesus Christ, and by putting on his likeness. For in very deed he has given us an example that we should follow in his steps (I Pet. 2:24). And though heaven and earth will pass away, his words will not pass away (Luke 21:33). They stand; they last; they remain true, "yesterday and today and forever" (Heb. 13:8).

48-55. ***False Humility.***—But these Jews answered him with revilings; hurling at him angry and contemptuous words—Samaritan, and madman, and demon-possessed. Especially were they infuriated by his claim, **If any one keeps my word, he will never see death.** That, they said, clinched things, and made them sure he was insane and worse. Abraham died, and the prophets died: **Who do you claim to be,** that you and yours should not die? Enough of such meaningless and crazy mouthing. Whereat, calmly and without hesitation, he who was meek and lowly in heart makes the tremendous claim that he knows God as no one upon earth had ever done; adding, **If I said, I do not know him, I should be a liar like you; but I do know him and I keep his word.**

There is a much-needed lesson for the church in that—the church which through a false humility has too often allowed itself be jostled out of the leadership in its own sphere which belongs to it by right; and many a time listens with silly deference to pronouncements in its own province from self-confident people who

56 Your father Abraham rejoiced to see my day: and he saw *it,* and was glad.

57 Then said the Jews unto him, Thou art not yet fifty years old, and hast thou seen Abraham?

58 Jesus said unto them, Verily, verily, I say unto you, Before Abraham was, I am.

59 Then took they up stones to cast at him: but Jesus hid himself, and went out of the temple, going through the midst of them, and so passed by.

56 Your father Abraham rejoiced that he was
to see my day; he saw it and was glad."
57 The Jews then said to him, "You are
not yet fifty years old, and have you seen
Abraham?"[q] 58 Jesus said to them, "Truly,
truly, I say to you, before Abraham was, I
am." 59 So they took up stones to throw
at him; but Jesus hid himself, and went
out of the temple.

[q] Other ancient authorities read *has Abraham seen you?*

56-59. Abraham rejoiced that he was to see my day: The reference is to Gen. 17:17. It is important to notice that the Aramaic Targum of this passage renders the Hebrew word for "laughed" by "rejoiced"; and in the pre-Christian Book of Jubilees, with its expansions of the stories in Genesis, it is repeatedly said that **Abraham rejoiced.** In one passage the writer adds, "For he knew and perceived that from him would arise the plant of righteousness for the eternal generations, and from him a holy seed so that it should become like Him who had made all things" (E. Nestle, "Abraham Rejoiced," *Expository Times,* XX [1909] 477). Strack and Billerbeck (*Kommentar zum N.T. aus Talmud und Midrasch,* II, 525-26) cite rabbinical expositions of Gen. 24:1 (where the Hebrew reads, "he came into the days") as meaning "he came to the veil of this world," i.e., the curtain which separates this world from the future world; or "he came to the days," i.e., the absolute sense, "into all the days there are." After many other such quotations they conclude, "These passages show that the old synagogue was often concerned with

---

have no right to an opinion, who speak with little knowledge, and no thought. "Everything," as Lawrence Hyde complains, "tends to be dragged down to the level on which it is comprehensible or emotionally satisfying to the man who has neither purified his perceptions, disciplined his will, nor cultivated his mind."[5] And the church allows herself to be dazed and unsettled and in certain ways overwhelmed by these amateur findings; forgetful that she possesses deeper knowledge of the things of God, and surer oracles, and the final revelation, compared to which these vaporings mean little—as indeed those who make them often themselves come to see. In measure the church, too, not only can but ought to say with boldness, **If I said, I do not know him, I should be a liar like you; but I do know him;** though alas! we cannot say, as our Lord could with truth and with assurance, **and I keep his word.**

56-59. ***Man's Dream Come True.*****—Your father Abraham rejoiced that he was to see my day; he saw it and was glad.** "All the hopes and dreams and longings and dim aspirations of the soul of man, reaching out blindly after something other and deeper and better than they knew, find in me their fulfillment. It was of me that they were dreaming. It was toward me that they were climbing; even the biggest of them."

[5] *The Prospects of Humanism* (New York: Charles Scribner's Sons, 1931), p. 10.

That sounds an unthinkable claim! Yet put it to the test, and judge of it for yourself. What sane spiritual aspiration for the world or for oneself is not fully met in Jesus Christ, if only we would take what in him we are offered, and would follow his guidance right through to its end? And where else can we find a like satisfaction? The facts show that this is simply the plain truth.

The Jews then said to him, "You are not yet fifty years old, and have you seen Abraham?" Jesus said to them, "Truly, truly, I say to you, before Abraham was, I am."

There are those who feel that such a saying as that in vs. 57, spoken to a man of perhaps thirty-three or so, is a further proof of how obviously Christ's sympathy and unselfishness were telling on him. Constantly he was entering deep into other people's troubles and sorrows; constantly he was carrying the burdens of men and women whom he would never see again; constantly virtue kept passing out of him, leaving him tired, making him old before the time. For nobody could spend himself for others as he did without paying the price of it. And no one ever felt so keenly as he that, as Browning says,

> This life of mine
> Must be lived out and a grave thoroughly earned.[6]

[6] *Paracelsus,* Part IV.

9 And as *Jesus* passed by, he saw a man which was blind from *his* birth.
2 And his disciples asked him, saying, Master, who did sin, this man, or his parents, that he was born blind?

9 As he passed by, he saw a man blind from his birth. 2 And his disciples asked him, "Rabbi, who sinned, this man or his

---

the revelations of the future granted to Abraham. Jesus must thus have been able to count upon his hearers' understanding of his claim in this verse." **My day:** cf. "the day of the Lord" O.T. *passim.* This eschatological day has dawned with the coming of the Son of man. **And have you seen Abraham?** The reading of the RSV mg., **has Abraham seen you?** agrees better with the previous verse, and has strong and ancient support (ἑώρακέν σε: ℵ 0124 sys Sahidic); but the overwhelming weight of authority supports the text. **Before Abraham was, I am:** cf. 1:1-2, 18. The incarnate Logos is speaking. As in 10:31, the Jews attempted to inflict the penalty for blasphemy (vs. 59), but Jesus, as on a later occasion (12:36), **hid himself.** His "hour" had not yet struck.

M. Healing of the Man Born Blind (9:1-41)

This story is the sign to illustrate the theme, Jesus **the light of the world,** for vs. 5 carries us back to 8:12. The narrative is told with vivid strokes, which bring before us in succession (*a*) the healing and the interest aroused among Jesus' neighbors (vss. 1-12); (*b*) the division of opinion among the Pharisees (vss. 13-17); (*c*) the Jews' examination of his parents (vss. 18-23); (*d*) the recall of the healed man and his debate with the Jews (vss. 24-34); (*e*) Jesus leading the man to fullness of faith, but condemning the willful blindness of the Pharisees (vss. 35-41). For the didactic handling of traditional material in these "signs" see Intro., p. 439. Yet the evangelist's closeness to contemporary Jewish thought is evident (see on 7:15-24).

9:1-12. The scene is Jerusalem at the feast of Tabernacles. The disciples' question in vs. 2 turns upon ideas about the relation between physical suffering and sin, which were

---

Against such a background, and tested by such a standard, how shabby and greedy are our lives; how selfish in their planning; how niggardly even in their generosities!

Whatever else lies in Christ's unfathomable answer (and who can even begin to plumb its deeps?) can there be anything greater even in it than this—that Christ's coming made no change in God, or in his attitude and bearing toward us; that though men did not realize it, and for long enough formed crude conceptions of him, and had slowly to climb up through these to worthier and truer thoughts of him, nonetheless from all eternity God, as he really was, was always Christlike, was always what his self-revelation in our Lord has shown us that he is. It was not something that Christ did that made God loving and forgiving toward us. It was because God was loving and forgiving even to us that our Lord came at all. What we see God to be through him, God always was. **Before Abraham was, I am.**

As Baxter put it long ago:

> It is not God but man that is changed by our Saviour's death; it is not necessary for our reparation that a change be wrought upon him, but upon us, seeing that it is not God but man that has lost his goodness. Christ came into the world, not to make God better, but to make us better; nor did he die to make him more disposed to do good, but to dispose us to receive it.

Although it is our only hope, this saying seemed to its first hearers so horrible a thing that they picked up stones, eager to silence such a blasphemous mouth forever, which shows the difference that Christ has made.

9:1-3. ***The Problem of Suffering.***—If in ch. 8 the reporting of what our Lord said seems at places to be so condensed that the meaning is not always easy to follow, ch. 9 is a piece of writing so graphic and detailed that the scene rises up of itself before the reader's eyes and seems to take place in his very presence. We do not so much read, as ourselves see and hear.

The question put by the disciples, **Rabbi, who sinned, this man or his parents, that he was born blind?** has a long history behind it, stretching far back into the dim beginnings of human thought. The moment man began to think at all, problems dreadfully pertinent and demanding solution kept pressing in upon him. Why sin? Why pain and suffering? Why has this

3 Jesus answered, Neither hath this man sinned, nor his parents: but that the works of God should be made manifest in him.

parents, that he was born blind?" 3 Jesus answered, "It was not that this man sinned, or his parents, but that the works of God

touched upon in the Exeg. on 5:6. Here it is noteworthy that Pharisees come into special prominence, for while both Pharisees and Sadducees found the will of God revealed in the Torah, they held different views about the way in which a man's destiny is determined. The Sadducees laid all the stress upon man's responsibility, as he acted with wisdom or folly. The Pharisees taught that the divine will was the determining factor in a man's

wretchedness befallen me? How many centuries ago it is since that puzzled soul, oppressed and bewildered by the baffling enigmas of life, cried out to the heavens and whoever dwelt in them,

> Pity our eagerness to know
> Whence we have come, and whither go,
> How came into the world, and why,
> Sin, and her daughter misery.[7]

And the old problems still confront us to this day. It is all very well for Browning to write,

> I say, the acknowledgement of God in Christ,
> Accepted by thy reason, solves for thee
> All questions in the earth and out of it.[1]

Eventually, no doubt, that is true. But at the start the new faith only adds acuteness to some problems that were already hard enough in themselves. If he is love, if what Christ says is true, why sin at all in the universe of such a God? Why suffering, under his governance? Why this loss or agony that has stricken me, or some one dearer even than self to me?

One of the boldest of the many attempted solutions of these perennial enigmas is summed up in the doctrines of karma and transmigration, which to a vast proportion of the human race have seemed axiomatic, and, when once grasped, almost self-evident, and have been held and preached by not a few of the wisest and the greatest of mankind. In such a view there are no enigmas and no baffling problems of providence to puzzle and confuse the mind. It is all clear, and understandable, and absolutely just. We are here, imprisoned in another of a normally really infinite sequence of lives, running on and on, like an endless chain. And what we are today, our circumstances, what befalls us in our present existence, and the like, these are not chance-blown, but are the fruit of what we were and did in some of our previous careers, the inevitable consequence of which has now overtaken us and come home to roost. "What we have been makes us what we are." All the disabilities that beset us arise from

[7] Ancient Greek saying.

[1] "A Death in the Desert."

our own mistakes and wrongdoings in the past existences. We have no possible grievance against anyone or anything. It is all self-inflicted. Sin a sin, and there is no possible evasion even thinkable of the inescapable results. For in life there is no favoritism, no letting off; no grace, no forgiveness; nothing but a calm, inexorable, automatic justice. If now we are poor, or diseased, or blind, look for the reason of it in our conduct in some former life. All which is worked out in detail in not a few of Buddha's discourses. But in none of them with such elaboration as in his reply to Mallika's questions on this very matter, as given in the Anguttara.[2]

There is something majestic in this conception of a fundamental justice woven into the very web of life, running through all things, and working itself out in everything that happens to us: a conception which leaves no room in the mind of those who accept it for whimpering, or whining, or self-pity, or railing against fate, which asks for no quarter and is very sure it can get none. Yet surely it is much too crude and easy a solution, an attempt to squeeze the facts into a mold that just cannot hold them all. It is unduly fatalistic; it forgets that it is not justice only that one finds in life, but grace as well, something that hurries to our help; it ignores the fact that not all suffering is penal, nor all disability and sorrow retribution; that it may be and often is a glory of self-sacrifice, a gallant and deliberate choice of loss for others' benefit. Our Lord went to his Cross not because of some failure of his in the past that had to be expiated, but willingly giving his life a ransom for others; no man taking it from him, but laying it down of himself. Moreover, the ethical and practical consequences of the doctrine are as a rule disastrous, inciting to indifference and callousness, or at least to a dull and helpless apathy to others' pains. Why should I help? For they have brought it on themselves. How can I help? For here or elsewhere it has got to be borne to the last jot and

[2] See *The Book of the Gradual Sayings*, tr. F. L. Woodward (London: Oxford University Press, 1933), II, 214-18.

4 I must work the works of him that sent me, while it is day: the night cometh, when no man can work.

might be made manifest in him. 4 We must work the works of him who sent me, while it is day; night comes, when no one can

fate, but this was exercised according to his relationship to God. Rabbinical teaching dwelt upon the O.T. warning that the sins of the parents bore heavily on their descendants (cf. Exod. 20:5; 34:7; Num. 14:18; Deut. 5:9). From the O.T. Apoc. cf. Wisd. Sol. 4:6:

> For children unlawfully begotten are witnesses of wickedness,
> Against parents when God searcheth them out.

Also cf. Ecclus. 41:5-7:

> The children of sinners are abominable children,
> And they frequent the dwellings of the ungodly;
> The inheritance of sinners' children shall perish,
> And with their posterity shall be a perpetual reproach.
> Children will complain of an ungodly father,
> Because they shall be reproached for his sake.

tittle. And my interfering kindness cannot save them from what ultimately has to be. As well for them to bear it now as later. And so they stand by and do nothing. Nonetheless, the theory has gained and kept a firm hold on enormous masses of mankind, has seemed to them entirely plausible and likely and true. And even where it has not been accepted, or even known in its entirety, elements of it are apt to rush the mind, and are not readily dislodged. These disciples, in spite of the poignant agony of Job's protest in their own scriptures, assumed instinctively that this man, blind from birth, sitting in the sunshine at his house door, was blind because of sin—his parents' or his own. That, they took for granted. And all they asked was, "But which was it, theirs or his?"

But Jesus will have none of it. "Neither," he says. And so saying, lifted what a weight of unhappiness from poor souls burdened enough already without having the misery of that hard interpretation added to what they were suffering. No doubt at all, sin does have penal consequences; and sometimes some of them are physical. Any doctor will tell us that this very case of blindness from birth is sometimes the direct result of the father's or the mother's misdemeanors. Sometimes. But there are many other possibilities that may account for such catastrophes; and to read the sinister interpretation into every case would be monstrously unjust.

"This man," said Christ, "was born blind in order that God's works might be openly shown in him" (vs. 3). That is a bold interpretation of the untoward things in life by which so many are afflicted. And yet how true it is; and how often it proves itself so, in one way or another! In this case the man, just because of his grievous disability, became a striking symbol and proof of what Christ can effect, bringing that home to many as no other could have done. A whole man would have been of no use to Christ in this particular way. For it was his blindness, his cross as men say, that gave him his chance to be of such signal service to the Master. And so it often is. Who of us but must be moved and shamed and heartened and inspired by the sheer gallantry that his faith calls out in a really Christian man when evil comes upon him, some hideous pain, some ruinous loss, some daunting providence; by his childlikeness and meekness when sorrow knocks at his door and enters, cold and shivery, into his home. And that is justified. I know a poor soul whose wife was taken from him without warning, in a second of time; and to rally his own heart he wrote a sermon which was published long ago. From that day to this, hundreds of letters have reached him from all over the world, all telling him it was not for nothing that his heart was broken. "It had to break," two who had been through deep and icy waters wrote to him, "that God, through you, might help, and steady, and save our stunned, lost souls." Without the loss and emptiness, that healing ministry would have been quite impossible. So if tragedy or suffering comes to us, in any case we shall have to bear the pain; but what inexpressible folly not to accept the high vocation it was sent to offer us, and which it puts within our reach! In us too, through our loss, our pain, our sorrow, our particular disability, whatever it may be, **the works of God might be made manifest.**

4-5. ***Christ's Work and Ours.***—And Christ expects that of us. For note that gracious "we" in vs. 4. **We must work the works of him who sent me, while it is day; night comes, when no**

5 As long as I am in the world, I am the light of the world.
6 When he had thus spoken, he spat on the ground, and made clay of the spittle, and he anointed the eyes of the blind man with the clay,

work. 5 As long as I am in the world, I am
the light of the world." 6 As he said this, he
spat on the ground and made clay of the spittle and anointed the man's eyes with

There are also sayings in the Targums and in the Talmud (see Strack and Billerbeck, *op. cit.*, II, 527-29) which seem to show that some rabbis thought it possible that a child could sin while in its mother's womb. It is hardly likely that belief in the pre-existence of souls had penetrated into Palestinian Judaism, but since it is found in Philo's writing

one can work. And the day is so short, so swiftly over. Scarcely have we begun to correct a few of our initial blunderings, and to gather together some small smatterings of experience, than the dark is falling around us, and we must down our tools. Our chance, taken or missed, is over. Horace Walpole declared peevishly that life has been badly planned, seeing that experience comes at the wrong end of it; and so tardily that once gained, there is no time to use it. It is, he thought, like a light upon a vessel's stern, illuminating what is past, only when it is past.

No doubt the Christian faith tells us that we are being shaped and fashioned here into beings whom God can use in some lofty service in the eternities that lie ahead. But we feel, and our Lord here fully agrees, that we cannot live only in the future tense, that here and now we should be offering God loyal and eager service. As William Watson put it,

> Let me learn
> . . . .
> on this world no more
> To cast ignoble slight,
> Counting it but the door
> Of other worlds more bright.
> Here, where I fail or conquer, here is my concern.[8]

If we belittle and ignore this world in which we have been set to play our part and tell for righteousness, neglecting the prosaic daily duties that keep calling to us now to rise and help, contemptuously dismissing them as mundane and material, dreaming of another world and of another nobler type of service, ours proves itself thereby to be a false religion, and is self-condemned. Certainly it has no dimmest resemblance to Christianity as Christ conceived it or as Paul taught it. **As long as I am in the world, I am the light of the world,** said Christ. But then, as Matt. 5:14 tells us, he claims that august office and title not for himself alone, but for his followers as well, "You are the light of the world." So here. **We must work the works of him who sent me**—all of us. No doubt he is self-luminous; and we shine only by the light reflected upon us by him. Yet the moon, dark and sterile in itself, lights the sky at night for multitudes. And is there not another luminary in the heavens, a star larger by far than the moon, and of a lovely blue-green color? So does our stolid earth look to the neighboring planets, reflecting from its native dullness a radiance that is not natural to it, catching a glory from the sun, and, itself transfigured by it, sharing it with others. And in and through Christ we are meant to be the light of the world, letting others see their road, changing night to day for them, enriching and beautifying life.

6-7. ***Christ's Different Methods in Different Cases.***—Various cures of complete blindness by Christ are recorded in the Gospels; and his methods vary in each case. And so it is in spiritual things. And if his treatment sometimes seems to our impatience to be less speedy and successful with us than it has proved to be with others, we must trust him, unafraid, sure that he knows best what is required.

That intrepid creature who violently pushed his way through the crowd, deaf to indignant protests from those whom he was jostling, refusing to be kept back or to cease from that frenzied crying to attract Christ's attention which was completely hindering those in his neighborhood from hearing and following what was going on, was healed by a mere word, at once, completely, and without any delay. And there are those who in spiritual things are saved by Christ with a like dramatic suddenness. All in a moment the light breaks in upon them and they see. One instant they are the slaves of some passion that they cannot resist, far less master; and the next they are free: the thing has dropped away from them, out of their lives; they have no further inclination to it. Like Dostoevski, that pitiful plaything of gambling, who made hot vows and broke them, sturdy

[8] "The Hope of the World," st. xv, *The Poems of Sir William Watson, 1878-1935* (London: George G. Harrap & Co., 1936). Used by permission.

7 And said unto him, Go, wash in the pool of Siloam, (which is by interpretation, Sent.) He went his way therefore, and washed, and came seeing.

the clay, 7 saying to him, "Go, wash in the pool of Si-lo'am" (which means Sent). So he went and washed and came back seeing.

(On the Giants III. 12-15) and at a later period in the Hermetic tracts, it may have been known in the world for which this Gospel was written. (For a full discussion of Wisd. Sol. 8:19-20, which has been thought to teach pre-existence, see F. C. Porter, "The Pre-Existence of the Soul in the Book of Wisdom and in the Rabbinical Writings," in *Old Testament and Semitic Studies in Memory of W. R. Harper* [Chicago: University of Chicago Press, 1908], I, 207-69, who concludes that "the Platonic doctrine of the pre-existence of the soul is not to be found in the *Book of Wisdom*.") Jesus dismisses (vs. 3)

---

and determined resolutions which at the very first temptation were swept bodily away; who simply and literally could not refrain from what had grown to be a settled habit and an essential part of his nature. And one day, quite suddenly and without warning, he knew that his long servitude was over. And it was. So that although for years he lived above a gambling den, and passed its door each time he went out, never so much as once did he feel the least desire to turn in and resume his folly. So, as Paul says, are some made more than conquerors. They do not need to struggle, but are lifted clean above themselves into a new life that has no place in it for the old uglinesses. They live beyond the range of the enemy's artillery, in a secure and settled peace.

But there was another to whom sight came more gradually, even with Christ to help him (Mark 8:22-26). At Bethsaida some kindly folk brought a blind man to him "and begged him to touch him." On that occasion our Lord preferred to use a more elaborate method, and then asked, "Do you see anything?" "And he looked up and said, 'I see men; but they look like trees, walking.'" And only after further treatment could he see "everything clearly." So it is only gradually that some are healed of their spiritual ailments, even by Christ, and only slowly that they grow out of their weaknesses. And sometimes they are taken aback by that, become despondent and depressed. That something comes of it, they readily acknowledge. They owe much to Christ. But in them as yet his promises have not worked out in full. And what results there are look meager against the background of the expectations he himself raised in them. They may be, they are, better. But they are still invalids, and far from spiritual robustness and health. A cold wind may at any time cause a setback. And a temptation is still dangerous. And sometimes they lose hope and heart. But one must be patient with Christ, as he is amazingly patient toward us, still striving with us, undismayed when we ourselves have long ago stopped really trying. He will not fail nor be discouraged. This bruised reed also will be coaxed to uprightness and strength again. But even for his skill it takes time and pains to change our natural uncouthness into his likeness.

This man, however, had an even harder test and method of cure prescribed for him. To have his face daubed with dust and clay and spittle, and then to be sent in such a messy state tapping his way through the public streets to the pool of Siloam, feeling himself no doubt a ridiculous spectacle: what good could come of that? Or why could not he be healed, as others had been, with a quick touch of Christ's hand? What wonder if this man had told himself indignantly that Christ was mocking his misery, as Naaman so long before had said of Elisha; that he for one was not going to let himself be fooled, and would take no part in such idiotic and absurd ongoings. But there came no such outburst. There was obedience, when obedience was not easy; there was faith, where faith looked fantastic and grotesque. Resolutely the man carried through what he had been told to do. And though at first there was nothing to show for it, in the end he too came back seeing.

"God is the great Physician of souls," says Origen.[4] But the process of cure takes in some cases an almost illimitable time. For God is long suffering; and to some souls, as to some bodies, a rapid cure is not beneficial. But in the end all souls will be thoroughly purged. So even if the time is long, the thing is sure.

> When the shore is won at last,
> Who will count the billows past?[5]

"Therefore, my beloved brethren, be steadfast, immovable, always abounding in the work of the Lord, knowing that in the Lord your labor is not in vain" (I Cor. 15:58).

[4] Cf. *On First Principles* III. 6. 6.

[5] John Keble, *The Christian Year*, "St. John the Evangelist's Day."

8 ¶ The neighbors therefore, and they which before had seen him that he was blind, said, Is not this he that sat and begged?

9 Some said, This is he: others *said,* He is like him: *but* he said, I am *he.*

10 Therefore said they unto him, How were thine eyes opened?

11 He answered and said, A man that is called Jesus made clay, and anointed mine eyes, and said unto me, Go to the pool of Siloam, and wash: and I went and washed, and I received sight.

12 Then said they unto him, Where is he? He said, I know not.

8 The neighbors and those who had seen
him before as a beggar, said, "Is not this
the man who used to sit and beg?" 9 Some
said, "It is he"; others said, "No, but he is
like him." He said, "I am the man."
10 They said to him, "Then how were your
eyes opened?" 11 He answered, "The man
called Jesus made clay and anointed my
eyes and said to me, 'Go to Si-lo'am and
wash'; so I went and washed and received
my sight." 12 They said to him, "Where is
he?" He said, "I do not know."

---

any such explanation of this man's blindness. He sees in this occasion an opportunity for God's gracious purpose to be displayed.

The mission of Jesus, vs. 4 reminds us, is continually to reveal not only the judgment of God but also his creative and restoring power. The better-supported text reads, **We must work the works of him who sent me.** Here, as in vs. 31; 3:11 the plural seems to include the disciples, who as apostles were to carry on this work after his death and resurrection, through the Spirit (cf. 14:11-17). In all Christ's manifestations he gives light, so to this blind beggar he gives sight (vs. 5). The symbolical means used to give eyesight (vss. 6-7) recall the story in Mark 8:22-26, though at Bethsaida clay was not made of the spittle. The healing virtue of saliva was a matter of widespread belief in the ancient world. By making a paste of dust and spittle, Jesus may have symbolized the creative act of Gen. 2:7. He sealed the eyes and then sent the man to the pool of **Siloam** to wash away the clay. Modern excavations have shown that **Siloam** was an extensive reservoir which drew its water through a subterranean canal running from northeast to southwest from Gihon. Hence the Hebrew name which meant "Sender," originally given to this canal. The evangelist has taken the word as a passive participle, **Sent,** and sees in it a cryptic allusion to the name so often used of Jesus, "He who was sent" (see Intro., pp. 438, 442).

8-38. ***The Man Born Blind.***—The rest of the chapter consists almost entirely of five vignettes which tell their own story vividly and dramatically. The buzzing of the neighbors' wonder and excitement and discussion, as they stared unbelievingly at what their own eyes told them (vss. 8-12); the man's interview with the Pharisees, who were still worried and tormented by the old sore (for this cure also had been wrought on a sabbath day, and so some were stumbled and indignant, but others, in spite of their prejudices, confessed themselves to be much shaken and impressed [vss. 13-17]); the incredulous summoning of the parents, sure that they would explode an impudent imposture or kill a ridiculous mistake; and their confident testimony (wrung as it was from a timidity that is not pleasant to contemplate, but which had very grievous things to fear) that beyond all possibility of doubt this most certainly was their son (vss. 18-23); the second interrogation of the man himself with its sinister ending (vss. 24-34); and last, Christ seeking for him in the sore trouble that had come upon him, that he might help and hearten him (vss. 35-38). All through, it is the man himself who catches and holds our eyes. And the more we see of him, the better do we like him—this plain fellow mortal, with his sturdy independence, and his refusal to be cowed or browbeaten; with his loyalty to his benefactor, **If this man were not from God, he could do nothing** (vs. 33); with his blunt and direct mode of speech, **He said, "I am the man"** (vs. 9), **He said, "He is a prophet"** (vs. 17), **He said, "Lord, I believe"** (vs. 38); with his daring and intrepidity which face the terrible prospect of excommunication, of being cast out and treated like a leper, entirely unafraid; with his shrewd common sense that by sheer honesty and downrightness discomfited men skilled in argument and trained to debate (vss. 30-33), till conscious of it they blazed up

13 ¶ They brought to the Pharisees him that aforetime was blind.

14 And it was the sabbath day when Jesus made the clay, and opened his eyes.

15 Then again the Pharisees also asked him how he had received his sight. He said unto them, He put clay upon mine eyes, and I washed, and do see.

16 Therefore said some of the Pharisees, This man is not of God, because he keepeth not the sabbath day. Others said, How can a man that is a sinner do such miracles? And there was a division among them.

17 They say unto the blind man again, What sayest thou of him, that he hath opened thine eyes? He said, He is a prophet.

18 But the Jews did not believe concerning him, that he had been blind, and received his sight, until they called the parents of him that had received his sight.

19 And they asked them, saying, Is this your son, who ye say was born blind? how then doth he now see?

20 His parents answered them and said, We know that this is our son, and that he was born blind:

13 They brought to the Pharisees the
man who had formerly been blind. 14 Now
it was a sabbath day when Jesus made the
clay and opened his eyes. 15 The Pharisees
again asked him how he had received his
sight. And he said to them, "He put clay on
my eyes, and I washed, and I see." 16 Some of
the Pharisees said, "This man is not from
God, for he does not keep the sabbath."
But others said, "How can a man who is
a sinner do such signs?" There was a divi-
sion among them. 17 So they again said to
the blind man, "What do you say about
him, since he has opened your eyes?" He
said, "He is a prophet."

18 The Jews did not believe that he had
been blind and had received his sight, until
they called the parents of the man who
had received his sight, 19 and asked them,
"Is this your son, who you say was born
blind? How then does he now see?" 20 His
parents answered, "We know that this is
our son, and that he was born blind;

13-17. The next stage in the story tells how his friends brought the healed man to the Pharisees, who promptly pointed out that the preparation of clay for use on the sabbath was forbidden. The seventeenth-century rabbinical scholar, John Lightfoot, shows that "it was prohibited amongst them to besmear the eyes with spittle upon the sabbath day upon any medicinal account, although it was esteemed so very wholesome for them" (*Horae Hebraicae et Talmudicae,* new ed. by Robert Gandell [Oxford: Oxford University Press, 1859], III, 342). The ranks of the Pharisees were divided. Some declared that a sabbath-breaker could not have been sent from God. Others were embarrassed by the evidence that a miracle had accredited Jesus as a prophet to be received (see on 3:2). It was much the same principle as separated the two Pharisaic schools of Hillel and Shammai. The former in regulating life looked carefully at the actual conditions in judging a particular case; the latter considered only the strict letter of the law.

18-23. The Jews, i.e., the opponents of Jesus, disputed the fact of the cure, and summoned the parents for examination. They testified that the man was their **son,** that he had been **born blind,** and that now he could see. But for fear of expulsion from the synagogue they disclaimed any knowledge of the healer or of the manner of the cure.

---

into ugly temper (vs. 34), reviling him, and they too accepting as their own the view that his blindness was a proof of unusual sin—this was no ordinary person, but a real man.

At least one of his sayings is immortal. **One thing I know, that though I was blind, now I see** (vs. 25). That is the final and conclusive argument for Christ which can never be met or refuted. Science beseeches us to deal with facts, and not with mere dreams and imaginings. That is precisely what we as Christians do. We cannot ignore our own experience. We must in honesty face its facts too. We are scientific enough to insist that no theory which does not take account of them has or can have much value. We know that Christ does save, for the very best and most irrefutable of reasons, because he has saved us. Whereas we were blind,

21 But by what means he now seeth, we know not; or who hath opened his eyes, we know not: he is of age; ask him: he shall speak for himself.

22 These *words* spake his parents, because they feared the Jews: for the Jews had agreed already, that if any man did confess that he was Christ, he should be put out of the synagogue.

23 Therefore said his parents, He is of age; ask him.

24 Then again called they the man that was blind, and said unto him, Give God the praise: we know that this man is a sinner.

25 He answered and said, Whether he be a sinner *or no,* I know not: one thing I know, that, whereas I was blind, now I see.

26 Then said they to him again, What did he to thee? how opened he thine eyes?

27 He answered them, I have told you already, and ye did not hear: wherefore would ye hear *it* again? will ye also be his disciples?

21 but how he now sees we do not know,
nor do we know who opened his eyes. Ask
him; he is of age, he will speak for himself."
22 His parents said this because they feared
the Jews, for the Jews had already agreed
that if any one should confess him to be
Christ, he was to be put out of the synagogue.
23 Therefore his parents said, "He
is of age, ask him."

24 So for the second time they called the
man who had been blind, and said to him,
"Give God the praise; we know that this
man is a sinner." 25 He answered, "Whether
he is a sinner, I do not know; one thing
I know, that though I was blind, now I
see." 26 They said to him, "What did he
do to you? How did he open your eyes?"
27 He answered them, "I have told you
already, and you would not listen. Why
do you want to hear it again? Do you too

They therefore advised that as their son was **of age** he should give the answer. **The Jews had already agreed that if any one should confess him to be Christ, he was to be put out of the synagogue.** This is often taken as evidence that the Gospel was written after the final breach between the synagogue and the church. But this passage may refer to the exercise of the milder discipline, the *niddui* or *shammatta,* which meant exclusion from the community of the synagogue for thirty days (Strack and Billerbeck, *op. cit.,* IV, 293-333).

24-34. This **second** summons of the healed man suggests that we have a description of a formal investigation. The courage of the former beggar in browbeating his examiners infuriates them. The phrase **Give God the praise** was a technical term in appealing for truthfulness, especially for confession of sin. Thus Joshua said to Achan, "My son, give, I pray thee, glory to the LORD God of Israel, and make confession unto him" (Josh. 7:19);

---

now we see; that is the basal fact which has to be met and explained. We take our stand upon it, and are unassailable. So Evelyn Underhill:

> [There] is now added the consciousness of a Living Fact which includes, transcends, completes all that you mean by the categories of personality and of life. Those ineffective, half-conscious attempts towards free action, clear apprehension, true union, which we dignify by the names of will, thought, and love are now seen matched by an Absolute Will, Thought, and Love; instantly recognized by the contemplating spirit as the highest reality it has yet known. . . . None who have had [this experience] have ever been able to doubt its validity. It has always become for them the central fact, by which all other realities must be tested and graduated. [By God the mystics] mean, not a notion, however august; but an experienced Fact so vivid, that against it the so-called facts of daily life look shadowy and insecure.[6]

And one can safely substitute throughout that passage "authentic Christian" for the too-narrow "mystic."

The man was excommunicated, a grave matter indeed, involving severe and even dreadful penalties and disabilities—at first for thirty days, but with more permanent consequences if

[6] *Practical Mysticism,* pp. 133-35. Copyright 1915 by E. P. Dutton & Co., New York. Used by permission.

28 Then they reviled him, and said, Thou art his disciple; but we are Moses' disciples.

29 We know that God spake unto Moses: *as for* this *fellow,* we know not from whence he is.

30 The man answered and said unto them, Why herein is a marvelous thing, that ye know not from whence he is, and *yet* he hath opened mine eyes.

31 Now we know that God heareth not sinners: but if any man be a worshipper of God, and doeth his will, him he heareth.

32 Since the world began was it not heard that any man opened the eyes of one that was born blind.

33 If this man were not of God, he could do nothing.

34 They answered and said unto him, Thou wast altogether born in sins, and dost thou teach us? And they cast him out.

want to become his disciples?" 28 And they
reviled him, saying, "You are his disciple,
but we are disciples of Moses. 29 We know
that God has spoken to Moses, but as for
this man, we do not know where he comes
from." 30 The man answered, "Why, this
is a marvel! You do not know where he
comes from, and yet he opened my eyes.
31 We know that God does not listen to
sinners, but if any one is a worshiper of
God and does his will, God listens to him.
32 Never since the world began has it been
heard that any one opened the eyes of a
man born blind. 33 If this man were not
from God, he could do nothing." 34 They
answered him, "You were born in utter
sin, and would you teach us?" And they
cast him out.

---

cf. II Esdras 10:11, where the Greek is "give praise," and the ERV translates "make confession." The meaning here is that the authorities required the man to agree with their condemnation: **We know that this man is a sinner.** He stands firmly by the one fact of which he is sure. They taunt him with being a disciple of Jesus, and contrast with his obscure authority their adherence to Moses, who spoke what God had proclaimed to him (Num. 12:2, 8). **As for this man, we do not know where he comes from** seems to contradict their claim to know the origin of Jesus (7:27). But Jesus had told them (7:28-29) of his heavenly origin and commission, and this they deny as unauthentic. This the healed man refutes by citing the principle that had already led some of their number to look favorably on Jesus (cf. on vss. 13-17). Unable to meet this argument, his examiners express their indignation that one who was not only a sinner (cf. Pss. 51:5; 58:3) but **born in utter sin** (as his blindness from birth proved) should dare to instruct them—purists whose eyes were devoted to the study of the Torah!

---

one proved obdurate; in which case one was ostracized and hounded from human society, became a lonely outcast. And Christ, hearing of it, laid everything else aside, and sought for him until he found him. It was a characteristic act, and very like the Christ we know. Whoever fails us, he abides faithful. In any loneliness or trouble we can be quite sure that we are not forgotten; that he is thinking of us, planning for us, coming to us with the very help we need.

> One friend in that path shall be,
> To secure my step from wrong;
> One to count night day for me,
> Patient through the watches long,
> Serving most with none to see.[7]

And Christ and you together can face even that which scares you.

[7] Browning, "A Serenade at the Villa," st. vii.

Vss. 35-38 make clear two things. First, that a very elementary and inchoate faith in a Christ, but little understood as yet, can effect mighty and glorious results. And second, no less surely, that our Lord will not be satisfied to leave us in the dim twilight in which we first met him, but will be at pains to lead us into fuller light and truer understanding, and that the wise soul responds so that Christ should be continually looming up before us, ever greater and more wonderful; and this on to life's end, and indeed through all eternity. It was a far less amazing Christ to whom we gave ourselves long ago than is the Christ that we know now. He is the same, yesterday and today and forever; but our understanding of him deepens, and keeps deepening with the years.

So here. **Do you believe in the Son of man?** he asked.

35 Jesus heard that they had cast him out; and when he had found him, he said unto him, Dost thou believe on the Son of God?
36 He answered and said, Who is he, Lord, that I might believe on him?
37 And Jesus said unto him, Thou hast both seen him, and it is he that talketh with thee.
38 And he said, Lord, I believe. And he worshipped him.

35 Jesus heard that they had cast him
out, and having found him he said, "Do
you believe in the Son of man?"[r] 36 He an-
swered, "And who is he, sir, that I may
believe in him?" 37 Jesus said to him, "You
have seen him, and it is he who speaks to
you." 38 He said, "Lord, I believe"; and

[r] Other ancient authorities read *the Son of God.*

35-41. The chapter closes with an example of the principle of **judgment** that runs through the Gospel. This sign has proved a test to show the presence of faith and of unbelief in those who saw the result of the cure. The blind man has already testified to his judges, **If this man were not from God, he could do nothing** (vs. 33). Before that, he had recognized in Jesus a prophet (vs. 17). Jesus now seeks him out and asks him the general question, **Do you believe in the Son of man?** The man had heard the title and knew that it referred to some supernatural revelation. But a vague belief in some eschatological expectation meant little to him. He asked for a personal knowledge, and received it when Jesus disclosed his true nature to him, as he had done to the Samaritan woman (4:26). Recognition now passes over into faith, and faith to worship (vs. 38).

Jesus came into the world for judgment (vs. 39). To those who received him he gave the right to become children of God, to those who believe on his name (1:12). But those who rejected him and persisted in their spiritual blindness were doomed to perpetual

35-41. ***The Son of Man.***—One supposes that the healed man must have been quite familiar with this phrase—for it was an old and current one—and that in his reply he was asking (vs. 36), "The Son of man! Has he really come? **Who is he?**"

Yet the incredible ignorance nowadays of very many in so-called Christian lands of the first facts and elements of Christianity, their complete indifference to that whole line of things which apparently simply does not exist for them, raises doubts in the mind. Then too, so one imagines, masses of people lived in a world into which the hopes and dreams, the phrases and disputings of the theologians and of religious laymen never blew, or were mere soundless sounds, meaning little or nothing.

In any case, the phrase **the Son of man** has to this day no one fixed connotation that is universally accepted. To some the title is an expression of lowliness and humility; to others, of a majesty without a rival under God. To some it is a synonym of the Messiah; to others not quite that, but something different and something more. Our Lord's use of it calls up to the mind an august figure to whom the first place belongs of right. Hence the full significance of that saying, "Even as the Son of man came not to be ministered unto, but to minister" (Matt. 20:28). No doubt in essence what Christ asked the man was, "Do you believe in me? Can I count on you?" But why did he use this particular title which at first did not help the other, but confused him?

Perhaps there is a lesson for us here. That in a very real sense the man had proved that he believed in Christ was already certain. He had faced the religious authorities as Christ's stout-hearted and unbreakable supporter; his loyalty to his benefactor had proved unshakable; he utterly refused to compromise. "This man," he held to it, "is a wonderful man. You tell me that he is a sinner; but that is utterly impossible. God does not listen to sinners; but he listens to this man. God does not work through sinners; but through this man he has wrought an incredible, an unprecedented, an unheard-of thing: and that to me. If this man were not from God, he could do nothing" (vss. 31-33). And no revilings and ugly threats of hideous consequences could move him. "Excommunicate me if you will, but I am this man's man; and at all costs I stand behind him." All of which is fine and noble. Yet Christ, recognizing in him an apt pupil, asks from him even more! Today many believe gladly and eagerly and gratefully in Jesus Christ, the Friend, the Teacher, the Leader, the Helper. But there is more in Christ by far even than that. Ask them if they believe in Jesus Christ the Savior, and they are more doubtful. Press them to say if their whole beings bow down in reverence before him, feeling the

39 ¶ And Jesus said, For judgment I am come into this world, that they which see not might see; and that they which see might be made blind.

40 And *some* of the Pharisees which were with him heard these words, and said unto him, Are we blind also?

41 Jesus said unto them. If ye were blind, ye should have no sin: but now ye say, We see; therefore your sin remaineth.

10 Verily, verily, I say unto you, He that entereth not by the door into the sheepfold, but climbeth up some other way, the same is a thief and a robber.

he worshiped him. 39 Jesus said, "For
judgment I came into this world, that those
who do not see may see, and that those who
see may become blind." 40 Some of the
Pharisees near him heard this, and they
said to him, "Are we also blind?" 41 Jesus
said to them, "If you were blind, you
would have no guilt; but now that you say,
'We see,' your guilt remains.

10 "Truly, truly, I say to you, he who
does not enter the sheepfold by the
door but climbs in by another way, that

---

separation from the light of the world. This warning Jesus gave in public, and some of the Pharisees who heard him asked, **Are we also blind?** Jesus' reply makes it clear that it is not honest doubt which he condemns, but self-satisfied prejudice (vs. 41). As in 3:36, the antithesis to belief is disobedience, "He who does not obey the Son shall not see life, but the wrath of God rests upon him." Now Jesus says, **If you were blind, you would have no guilt; but now that you say, "We see," your guilt remains.**

V. The Shepherd and Giver of Life (10:1–11:57)

Here again a strong case has been made out for the theory that some dislocation has disturbed the order of the sections. Those who favor this theory are agreed that after

---

majesty and awe that there are in his personality, confessing that in him there is nothing less than the express image of God's person, and they are happy who can say truthfully and with meaning, **Lord, I believe** (vs. 38), and who give him, not their friendship only, not their loyalty alone, but worship.

Finally our Lord sums up the whole matter in two gravely impressive sayings (vss. 39-41). **For judgment I came into this world.** Not that he wishes to condemn (cf. 3:17); but the thing is inevitable. For whenever people come into contact with Christ, they judge themselves. **That those who do not see may see;** that poor souls who feel their limitations and their failures, and who thrill at the hope of an escape from them, and are willing to do what they are told will have that happy issue, may gain their heart's desire; while others who vaingloriously imagine that they already know all that there is to know lose the fuller revelation offered them and lag behind, become themselves the blind, in comparison with those whose once-dead eyes are opened, and who now see what those that formerly outdistanced them cannot see. So true is it that there are first who will be last, and last who will be first.

Some of the Pharisees were standing near, and overhearing, saw an innuendo in this saying directed against them. **Are we also blind?** they asked. To which there came the sobering answer, **If you were blind, you would have no guilt; but now that you say, "We see," your guilt remains** (vs. 41). In some respects that is a right heartening verdict, bringing hope where there had seemed to be no ray of it. **If you were blind, you would have no guilt.** Does that cover the peoples who have never heard of Christ, with their minds impregnated from birth with customs and conventions and ethical standards, crude and primitive, as we judge, but all that they have ever known, and which to them seem final and inevitable and God-given; or dwellers in the uglier of the slums, cradled in poverty and dirt, inured to sights and sounds of sin, given how base a view and conception of life by say a drunken and quarrelsome father, or a mother lustful and undisciplined? Will account be taken of handicaps that weight things so heavily against one?

But on the other hand, knowledge means responsibility to use that knowledge, and a more drastic test before the judgment seat. For, says Thomas à Kempis (and who can challenge the justice and the truth of it?), "The more thou knowest, and . . . the better thou understandest, the more strictly shalt thou be judged, unless thy life be also the more holy." [8]

10:1-42. ***The Shepherd and His Flock.***—Whatever may be thought about possible dislocations in ch. 10, that chapter seems to connect closely

[8] *The Imitation of Christ* I. 2.

2 But he that entereth in by the door is the shepherd of the sheep.
3 To him the porter openeth; and the sheep hear his voice: and he calleth his own sheep by name, and leadeth them out.

man is a thief and a robber; 2 but he who
enters by the door is the shepherd of the
sheep. 3 To him the gatekeeper opens; the
sheep hear his voice, and he calls his own

ch. 9 the true order of sequence is 10:19-29, 1-18, 30-42. The reasons for this are that 10:21 would naturally come immediately after the healing of the blind man and the discussion to which it gave rise; and that the allegory of the **good shepherd** and the allusions to **my sheep** obviously belong to the same discourse. As the sections have come down to us in the normal text, the allegory of the good shepherd was spoken at the feast of Tabernacles, whereas 10:26-29 belong to an address spoken at the feast of Dedication two months later. This Exeg. must follow the order of the transmitted text, but the reader will do well to remember the rearrangement suggested above.

A. The Shepherd and the Sheep (10:1-18)

10:1-6. The Greek word (παροιμία) translated by KJV and ERV **parable** here and "proverb" in 16:25, 29, and by RSV **figure** in all passages, stands for an enigmatic saying. The old distinction holds good: "A parable is a picture; an allegory is a transparency."

with the incidents of ch. 9. The connection is not perhaps obvious. Yet surely it is a moving thing that these immortal sayings which have meant so much to souls innumerable were spoken in the first instance to hearten and steady one poor soul whose connection with Jesus Christ had landed him in a grave and terrifying situation. To follow the metaphor fully we must think of an Eastern sheepfold, surrounded by high and strong stone walls, and with a formidable door, no mere flimsy hurdle, but a much more massive thing, designed for protection. The whole picture as originally painted is unhappily blurred and spoiled for us by our rough forcible Western ways of shepherding. Even among ourselves a shepherd worthy of the name is the most patient of men. And yet what rises up before our minds is a huddled mass of scurrying and uneasy creatures, chivied by wheeling dogs, with amazing craft and skill indeed, yet the whole scene suggesting compulsion and force. But the relationship between an Eastern shepherd and his flock is much more intimate and affectionate and personal. And that of course was what was in the mind of Christ when he used the figure.

1-5. ***The Marks of the Real Shepherd and of the True Flock.***—In these verses our Lord challenges the action, and indeed the authority in more than name, of those who had excommunicated the once-blind man; claims that he himself is the real shepherd of God's flock; and that it is those who recognize his voice and follow him who are the true heirs of the promises and the genuine people of God. Disreputable folk, out for their own ends, may steal into the sheepfold, evading the vigilance of the keeper of the gate, climbing in over the walls, and make havoc among the flock. But the real shepherd can be recognized at once by certain facts about him: (*a*) that he makes no surreptitious entrance, but uses the door; (*b*) that its keeper knows him, and so opens to him; and (*c*), most convincing proof of all, that the shy sheep that would be thrown into panic by a stranger, or at the best would treat him with indifference, hearing the shepherd's voice, come hurrying to him, docile and eager.

One spares a thought for the underling who keeps the door, on guard all through the night, and until the shepherd returns—putting through a tiring task that calls for watchfulness and patience, a task involving real anxiety, and at times some measure of danger. Those called of God to watch over his flock must be faithful and vigilant—lest some intruder break into the fold to work evil there—so that when the chief shepherd shall appear, the sheep that he committed to their care may be all there, none missing. Though indeed, even here and now, no underling but the shepherd himself seems to be continually spending himself upon our behalf.

With confidence Jesus lays it down that those who are really his respond in certain ways. And how do we meet these tests he gives us, by which we can try ourselves? **A stranger they will not follow, but they will flee from him, for they do not know the voice of strangers.** That is a saying that may well disquiet. For mankind in its instability is so greedy for something new, so quick to tire of what it has already heard, of what has grown familiar. Are not very many streaming away from a Christ whom they feel

4 And when he putteth forth his own sheep, he goeth before them, and the sheep follow him: for they know his voice.

5 And a stranger will they not follow, but will flee from him; for they know not the voice of strangers.

sheep by name and leads them out. 4 When
he has brought out all his own, he goes before them, and the sheep follow him, for they know his voice. 5 A stranger they will
not follow, but they will flee from him, for they do not know the voice of strangers."

In these verses we have a general description of a **sheepfold,** with **door** and **gatekeeper,** enclosing the sheep, intruders climbing the wall to steal, and the shepherd, who is recognized by the gatekeeper, and whose voice is known to the sheep as he calls them **by name and leads them out** for pasturage. This is clear enough in itself; the obscurity lies in the confused identity involved in any interpretation. The explanation is found in the evangelist's purpose. He is thinking of the Christian church, of the difference between

has had a long chance and made little of it, to substitutes for the gospel which they imagine will work more quickly and more effectively? And alas! are there not half a dozen weaknesses to which each of us is prone, which have only to whistle and we come to heel, slinking obediently after them, often despising ourselves for doing so even while we do it? Yet this has to be added, that as sheep start and turn their heads, and come running when they hear one whom they know and trust, so when Christ's voice really breaks through to us, we do thrill to it, do respond; suddenly sickening of what had enticed us from him, knowing again with assurance that he is what we need, and he is what we want, and nothing else will do. And there is hope for us in that.

But there is something better even than that, far better. For they who are wise build their confidence not on anything subjective, which is shifting and unstable, but on the great objective verities which do not change: relying in the last resort not on their faith, which is a fickle thing, but on God's faithfulness, which is most sure and certain; not on their love to him, which flows and ebbs, but on his love to them, which is from everlasting to everlasting; not on their own crumbling efforts after something better, but upon his eternal purpose set upon our salvation, which has gone the length of Calvary for us. The shepherd, says Christ (vs. 3), **calls his own sheep by name;** for they are not just one of an indeterminate flock to him, but individually known to him, and individually precious. That is the final test—not how we act toward Christ but how he acts toward us. And there is not a doubt that he has called us, and keeps calling, misses us when we wander, waits for us when we loiter in the fold, until we too have come (vs. 4); seeks for us when we stray and lose ourselves, until he finds us. All of which must surely mean that he acknowledges that we are his—wayward, perverse, provoking, but still his—and that he has accepted the responsibility of bringing us safe home. So Samuel Rutherford: "How often I play fast and loose with Christ! He bindeth, I loose; He buildeth, I cast down; He trimmeth up a salvation for me, and I mar it; I cast out with Christ, and He agreeth with me again, twenty times a day."[1]

When he has brought out all his own, he goes before them (vs. 4). Once in France, during World War I, I had a bonnie experience. We had come out from the unbelievable desolation near Paschendaele, the worst place by far in the whole line, for five days' rest, and had got back to human and lovely things again, houses, and trees, and flowers, and kindly people. But the day after our arrival, word came that the line was broken, that the Germans were clean through and heading for the Channel ports, and that we, with others, were to be thrown in anyhow to try to stem the racing tide. The lads were young, with all their lives before them. And as I looked at them, so soon to be sacrificed, my heart grew sore and hot and resentful. Waiting for the time at which we were due to fall in, I turned down an enticing little lane, winding and twisting between fields ablaze with flowers, golden and blue. And suddenly I came upon a shepherd lad, not driving his flock, and with no dog, but walking on ahead of them, they willingly following. And every now and then he paused to call to a laggard, which hearing its name, came at once, running, and affectionately rubbed itself against him. So they moved on, and over a little ridge, and out of my life. And standing there, as plain and clear as if they had been spoken first to very me, I heard, **And when he putteth forth his own sheep, he goeth before them;** and turned, and went into the valley of the shadow, with a heart quieted and stilled.

That is a truth with innumerable applications, each of them more steadying than the last.

[1] *Letters,* Letter CCLIV.

6 This parable spake Jesus unto them; but they understood not what things they were which he spake unto them.

7 Then said Jesus unto them again, Verily, verily, I say unto you, I am the door of the sheep.

8 All that ever came before me are thieves and robbers: but the sheep did not hear them.

6 This figure Jesus used with them, but
they did not understand what he was say-
ing to them.
7 So Jesus again said to them, "Truly,
truly, I say to you, I am the door of the
sheep. 8 All who came before me are thieves
and robbers; but the sheep did not heed

---

fold and flock, between Judaism and Christianity, between the Pharisees and Jesus, and of the relation between Christian pastors and the Good Shepherd.

7-10. The interpretation falls into two parts. (*a*) Jesus is the **door** in relation to the fold (vss. 7-10). "The gate" may be an allusion to words in Ps. 118:20, a psalm quoted messianically several times in the Gospels. Vs. 8 has perplexed commentators from the beginning, and the omissions of the words **before me** by three of our oldest authorities (p^{45} ℵ* sy^{s}, *et al.*) and of the word **all** by another important MS (Bezae) were probably attempts to remove the difficulty. There is no disparagement of Moses, or the prophets, or of John the Baptist (cf. 5:39, 45-47; 12:41; 1:6-9). These thieves and robbers may correspond to those teachers who had prejudiced the people against the words and works

---

The time is drawing near when the happy family circle must be broken up, and the young folk go their several ways, out into an alien and unknown world. And the mother's heart grudges the coming parting, would fain keep things as they are. Or already one or more have gone, are far away where her hands, that itch to help them, cannot reach them. How well to know that **when he putteth forth his own sheep** Christ **goeth before them;** and that he is as near them, and as watchful over them, and as ready to spend himself on their behalf yonder, as when they were at home.

Or a life that had flowed gently, with still and quiet waters, is broken into white and tortured agony by rocks and falls. Pain comes, or disappointment, or some crippling sorrow. So is it men are made, and strength of character is fashioned at a fearsome price. But what a difference it makes to know that in these bleak places we are not alone, and left to make such shift for ourselves as we can; that Christ too learned obedience by the things he suffered, and was in all points tempted like as we are, though without sin; that **when he putteth forth his own sheep,** out of the security of the fold, **he goeth before them.**

And most striking of all, when death comes into a Christian home, what a tremendous tribute it is to Jesus Christ that the one who is taken away is given so confidingly! We know so little about the beyond. But Christ is there; and where he is, we feel, all must be well with us and ours. And so we watch them passing out, without a fear for them. For **when he putteth forth his own sheep, he goeth before them.**

6-7*a*. ***Christ's Patience with Us.***—It was a very vivid figure that Christ used, and one that should have been familiar and understandable through their own scriptures. Yet they did not follow, but listened uncomprehendingly and lost. Well, it is not for us, with our incredible slowness in spiritual things, to jeer at them. But how pathetic is Christ's patience with us, and his condescension to our tardiness and dullness. So it was in his lifetime. They could not take in what he taught; and so he took to telling stories, wonderful stories that must surely break through to their minds: and when even these sometimes puzzled them, he slipped in the pictures of the sacraments, teaching them, like children, through their eyes, if their ears could not grasp and hold. And with what tolerance he bears with our thoughtlessness and inattention and inability to grip the simplest matters, though he is eager to press on to bigger things. "I have yet many things to say to you, but you cannot bear them now," he said, with his time swiftly running out (16:12). Yet undiscouraged by our lack of aptitude he starts again, trying some other way to bring home to us the truth which is self-evident to him, but which our perplexed mind and soul just cannot follow. So here. **So Jesus again said to them,** we read; putting it in another way that might succeed.

7*b*-9. ***Christ as the Door.***—To begin with, he varies the metaphor. **I am the door of the sheep,** he says; and again with emphasis, **I am the door.**

Perhaps in the first instance this was said to encourage the excommunicated man. He might

9 I am the door: by me if any man enter in, he shall be saved, and shall go in and out, and find pasture.

10 The thief cometh not, but for to steal, and to kill, and to destroy: I am come that they might have life, and that they might have *it* more abundantly.

them. **9** I am the door; if any one enters by me, he will be saved, and will go in and out and find pasture. **10** The thief comes only to steal and kill and destroy; I came that they may have life, and have it abun-

---

of Jesus. The evangelist may have in mind those heresiarchs whose erroneous teaching had threatened the churches in Asia in his time, as we know from I John. In either case, the words **before me** would be understood in some sense other than the purely temporal which the aorist tense of the verb (ἦλθον) seems to require.

The most probable reference, however, is to such men as Judas the Gaulonite (or Galilean; cf. Acts 5:37). Josephus gives an account of this insurgent in *Jewish War* II. 8. 1 and in *Antiquities* XVIII. 1. He also tells that at the beginning of that century "Judea was full of robberies; and, as the several companies of the seditious light upon anyone to head them, he [Judas] was created a king immediately, in order to do mischief to the public. They were in some small measure indeed, and in small matters, hurtful to the Romans; but the murders they committed upon their own people lasted a long while" (*Antiquities* XVII. 10. 8). In this Gospel we are told that the Jerusalem mob howled for the release of Barabbas, described in Luke 23:19 as "a man who had been thrown into prison for an insurrection started in the city, and for murder." John 18:40 says simply, "Now Barabbas was a robber." His word "robber" or "brigand" (λῃστής) describes one who would be described by many Jews as a popular patriot. The same word is used here (κλέπται καὶ λῃσταί). **But the sheep did not heed them.** The true

---

be thrown out of the organized religion round about him. But through Christ he had access to a sure place in the true flock of God. Now happily it has a far wider application. Life is lavish with its benefits, and has many gifts to offer us. For was it not planned for us by the huge liberality of God? Yet nothing is more certain than that it is through Christ that we gain what matters to us far the most; and that much of it cannot be had at all apart from him. He is the door that leads to it. What he himself instances here (vs. 9) are (*a*) safety from prowling and marauding dangers; and (*b*) a full life (**he . . . will go in and out**); and (*c*) all we need to keep us fit and healthy (**and find pasture**). But Christ throughout the Gospels is constantly claiming that he can and does give us what the world, with all its specious and seductive promises, cannot give; nor can anything else. It is through Christ one enters into and enjoys the peace which passes all understanding—when others are flurried and harassed and careworn. It is through Christ one gains that joy of the Lord that is our strength. It is through Christ that one attains to life that is life indeed. So he himself promises. And the apostles are entirely sure that through him they have come upon innumerable glories, which without him were as inaccessible and distant as the stars. All of which is summed up in that triumphant shout of Paul, "Thanks be to God, which giveth us the victory through our Lord Jesus Christ" (I Cor. 15:57)—a door that opens on how much; and without which we would be left how poor and emptyhanded!

But as A. B. Davidson put it:

> That figure of a door is worth dwelling on. Christ uses it in a sort of absolute way. There is a door, an entrance, a way in,—He does not say in from where nor into what. It is a way in, in where and in from what, our own hearts will suggest to us. . . . Sometimes, when one comes in youth from a distant home to a great city where he is unknown and alone, he walks through the streets beholding the lighted windows and hearing the sounds of music and joy within. The sounds but intensify his own sense of solitude, and he is fain to hurry away to his own room, lest he should have to confess to himself his own weakness. . . . Surely, there is a door out of this outer darkness. Is there not an open door leading in to where there is light and joy? [2]

There is. **I am the door,** says Christ; and multitudes have found it even so.

But then Christ drops that figure and returns to this of the shepherd.

10. ***Abundance of Life Through Christ.***—"All who came before me" (vs. 8) must not be taken too literally; as the Exeg. says, the phrase cannot include, for instance, John the Baptist, whom Christ himself so eulogized, or Moses, or

[2] *Waiting Upon God* (Edinburgh: T. & T. Clark, 1904), pp. 337-38. Used by permission.

Israel was not duped by such false messiahs. The friends of Jesus did not yell for Barabbas with the hirelings of the chief priests on the morning of the Crucifixion. It was then that the Good Shepherd laid down **his life for the sheep.** Later on, as the evangelist remembered, neither Theudas nor the violent Zealots, who plunged the Jews into the hideous and hopeless war against Rome, succeeded in seducing the Christians to follow their banner.

The harsh change in the figure from **shepherd** to **door** (vs. 9) would be easier to understand if we might think of the Oriental shepherd as sometimes lying in the narrow entrance to the fold to guard against intruders. But the meaning points to a future situation, when the under shepherds will derive their authority to care for the flock from the chief shepherd (cf. I Pet. 2:25). First, they must be saved through him. Then with his commission they will be free to guide the flock and find rich pasture for the sheep. The phraseology recalls Num. 27:16-17. Unlike the intruders who avoid **the door,** they will be listened to by the sheep, for like their chief, they are free from self-interest and greed, and seek life in its fullness for those under their care.

---

the prophets. Probably in **the thief** [who] **comes only to steal and kill and destroy** there is a reference to the authorities who had just excommunicated a poor soul; and that in the end merely to revenge their own hurt pride and offended dignity. In contradistinction to that kind of thing, **I came that they may have life, and have it abundantly.**

There is no manner of doubt that a first law of the kingdom is that of self-denial; and that means a resolute cutting off of much that is unworthy. In laying emphasis on that requirement, Christ is at one with all the moral and spiritual masters everywhere the whole world over. As Walter Lippmann says:

> It is a fact and a most arresting one, that in all the great religions, and in all the great moral philosophies from Aristotle to Bernard Shaw, it is taught that one of the conditions of happiness is to renounce some of the satisfactions which men normally crave. This tradition as to what constitutes the wisdom of life is supported by testimony from so many independent sources that it cannot be dismissed lightly. With minor variations it is a common theme in the teaching of an Athenian aristocrat like Plato, an Indian nobleman like Buddha, and a humble Jew like Spinoza; in fact, wherever men have thought at all carefully about the problem of evil and of what constitutes a good life, they have concluded that an essential element in any human philosophy is renunciation.[3]

But while that is so, to those who have tried both ways of it, or who have any practical experience of the living of the Christian life, there is something inexplicable and even grotesque in the assumption which many so complacently and ignorantly make that the Christian mode of life must be an intolerably dull and boring affair, a repressing of everything one wants to do, a forcing of oneself to comply with what nobody could wish or choose, a shivering with chattering teeth in the gloom of a chilly monastic twilight, out of the sunshine and free air that God made for us and means us to enjoy. On the contrary, it is an abundant life—happy, adventurous, exciting; more so than any other. Had we come upon Paul the apostle, and asked what he was doing, he might have answered, "Wrestling with principalities and powers, and mastering them through Jesus Christ." That seems a way of life with much more call in it upon a man who is a man than the tame and colorless round of trivialities which some term living.

While as for those who fling their lives away in an avid questing for sensation, is there a more scathing passage anywhere than that in which C. E. Montague points out that many, seeking to make a collection of experiences as others do of stamps, and esteeming every new experience of any kind an addition to their store, will get drunk simply for the experience, and touch unholy things that they may taste the whole of life: not realizing, poor duped fools, misled by some hobbledehoy thinkers, so-called, who have cooked these immature ideas into a kind of messy philosophy, that in life as in arithmetic there is a minus sign as surely as a plus; and that certain experiences do not add to, but subtract from, what we had and were before, each new indulgence in forbidden things leaving us poorer, leaner, emptier, and at length beggared.

It is only the pure in heart who see God. And whatever else others may gain, if they miss that vision and experience, surely their life has been a futile failure. It is in Christ that one has life abundantly. Or ought to have, and can have. But alas! too many of us have only a thin-blooded and anemic type of Christianity,

[3] *A Preface to Morals,* p. 156. Copyright 1929 by Walter Lippmann and used with the permission of The Macmillan Co. and George Allen & Unwin.

11 I am the good shepherd: the good shepherd giveth his life for the sheep.

12 But he that is a hireling, and not the shepherd, whose own the sheep are not, seeth the wolf coming, and leaveth the sheep, and fleeth; and the wolf catcheth them, and scattereth the sheep.

13 The hireling fleeth, because he is a hireling, and careth not for the sheep.

14 I am the good shepherd, and know my *sheep,* and am known of mine.

15 As the Father knoweth me, even so know I the Father: and I lay down my life for the sheep.

dantly. 11 I am the good shepherd. The good
shepherd lays down his life for the sheep.
12 He who is a hireling and not a shepherd,
whose own the sheep are not, sees the wolf
coming and leaves the sheep and flees;
and the wolf snatches them and scatters
them. 13 He flees because he is a hireling
and cares nothing for the sheep. 14 I am
the good shepherd; I know my own and
my own know me, 15 as the Father knows
me and I know the Father; and I lay down

11-18. This is the second part of the interpretation introduced in vss. 7-10. (*b*) Jesus is the shepherd in relation to the flock. He is the model shepherd because he is essentially good and, since he is mindful of his own, he will risk his life for the sheep. The O.T. is rich in pastoral symbolism. Ps. 23; Isa. 40:11; Ezek. 34:11-15 apply this figure to Yahweh. In the Ezekiel passage the divine care for the sheep of the flock follows a description of false shepherds, and in Jer. 23:1-4 good shepherds are contrasted with those who "destroy and scatter the sheep of my pasture." These marauders have their counterpart in the figures of vss. 1, 8, 10. The goodness of the true shepherd is now set out in opposition to the indifference of the **hireling.** Jesus states three aspects of his mission in relation to the flock. He establishes a community of understanding and purpose between himself and

---

know little of the vigor of its health, and the splendor of its adventure, and the exciting possibilities it puts within the reach of anyone.

11-15. ***The Good Shepherd.***—Christ claims to be the good shepherd; and that really upon three grounds, as the Exeg. in a somewhat different way suggests. First, because he **lays down his life for the sheep.** This every day, and all the day. For the whole life of a shepherd, with the many other possibilities that it contains, must be completely sacrificed to meet the wants of the dependent, needy, hungry, foolish creatures that have been put into his keeping. And what might not Christ, with his amazing gifts, have made of his life or done with it? But with determination he chose to give it for us, all of it, holding back nothing of it for himself and his own interests.

A hireling, says our Lord with contempt, will do something for the sheep; but he will not risk himself for them. If danger threatens, he will make his own escape and leave them to their fate. But the good shepherd sets himself between the flock and peril. Evil and doom can reach them only over his dead body. If it is necessary, he will die to save them. And Christ did that for us.

Further, a good shepherd has intimate knowledge of each of his flock. To others the sheep may be practically indistinguishable. But he knows them at a glance, their characters and idiosyncrasies; can pick them out at once from a mass of other sheep among which they have mingled. That, and that, and that, he claims, is mine. Augustine says that often enough Christ's sheep do not know themselves; are not at all sure that such wandering creatures as they are can really belong to a flock from which they are so often missing and from which they so frequently keep straying. But, says Christ, with confidence, **I know my own.** And that is what supremely matters. And the next best is also true, that they know him: know that they have about them a watchful and unselfish care which they have proved day after day and never found to fail; know that they are not alone, left to make such shift as they can, but are in the keeping of one whom they can absolutely trust.

So close and intimate is this relationship between Christ and his own that in as staggering a metaphor as can be found in literature he dares to compare it to that which exists between the Father and himself, than which nothing can be more intimate or close. And because he knows us so thoroughly, and sees how helpless we are without him, he devotes his whole life to us day by day, and finally throws it away in a supreme act of that constant self-sacrifice.

Again, being the good shepherd, his heart goes out to other sheep who need him, proved to be his by their very needs and by his power

16 And other sheep I have, which are not of this fold: them also I must bring, and they shall hear my voice; and there shall be one fold, *and* one shepherd.

my life for the sheep. 16 And I have other sheep, that are not of this fold; I must bring them also, and they will heed my voice. So there shall be one flock, one shep-

---

his disciples after the likeness of his unity of will with the Father (cf. 1:1, 18; 6:57; 15:9; 17:11, 21-23). He will bring into his flock those who are not within the fold of Judaism (cf. 6:37; 11:52; 12:32). He means of his own free will to lay down his life, not in futile self-sacrifice, but in a victorious act of obedience to the Father's command. This emphasis upon the death of Christ calls attention to its vicariousness (vs. 15), its voluntariness (vs. 18), its fulfillment of the Father's loving purpose (vss. 17-18). In vs. 18 the three oldest MSS (p^{45} ℵ* B) read "has taken" (ἦρεν), though all other authorities read **takes.** If that reading should be correct the verse refers to the various unsuccessful attempts already made by the Sanhedrin to arrest Jesus. The present tense would mean that Jesus

---

to meet and satisfy these needs; to men and women not actually his as yet, but scattered over the Gentile world, who, when they hear his voice, will heed it and will follow. Them too he will gather in, and lead, and tend. How well for us that our Lord's heart was so catholic: that he broke through those national limitations of which he sometimes spoke as if he felt that he was confined within them; that he reached out in yearning for those dim masses of the Gentiles—each one of them an immortal soul; each one of them facing the difficulties of his lot, and often puzzled and perplexed by what life had brought on him; each one of them betrayed by his own foolish heart into unworthiness and sin; all of them strayed and lost, and in desperate need of someone who could shepherd them.

16. ***One Flock, One Shepherd, but Not One Fold.***—**So there shall be one flock, one shepherd.** But be it noted that he does not add one fold. And that gives food for thought. In a natural and belated recoil from the disruptive and fissiparous tendencies of past days, which often, as it seems to many now, unnecessarily broke Christ's church into a jumble of innumerable jarring sects, there is throughout the church something of a crusade, almost a clamor, for organic union and a healing of wounds, which crusade sounds wiser than it is, may indeed be only a particular form of a tendency of the day which has still to prove itself. Everywhere more and more it becomes the fashion to seek to squeeze and concuss all men into the one particular mold that the majority for the time being happen to prefer; to frown upon and actively discourage all individuality and all variety. Which, if it is not a hopeless endeavor, and if it could succeed, would mean the impoverishment of human nature, which can be so regimented only at the cost of many of its glories, and of a sad loss to the general good.

In religion as elsewhere it is a vain dream to force all men into a single pattern which may suit some of them but be unnatural to others. There is no one type of church government laid down for us in the N.T. Rather and plainly, as B. H. Streeter argues,

> the greatest obstacle [to union] is the belief . . . that there is some one form of Church Order which alone is primitive, and which, therefore, alone possesses the sanction of Apostolic precedent. Our review of the historical evidence has shown this belief to be an illusion. In the Primitive Church no one system of Church Order prevailed. Everywhere there was readiness to experiment, and, where circumstances seemed to demand it, to change. . . . It may be that the line of advance for the Church of to-day is not to imitate the forms, but to recapture the spirit, of the Primitive Church.[4]

There is no one type of service which all Christian people ought to see to be the Christian type, and so seeing, adopt and practice it. Men are built upon different lines. For some, grandeur and ceremony, even a measure of pomp are required if they are to feel themselves in the presence of God and be able really to worship him. But others draw far closer to him through the medium of the simplest of services, with nothing in it to catch and hold and, as these folk feel, distract the mind and eyes. To endeavor to contort the one or the other into the opposite, and for them unnatural, type is futile. And indeed, why should it be attempted? There is **one flock,** and **one shepherd.** There is one Lord, one faith, one baptism. There is "one army of the living God." But an army may have many regiments. And it is questionable if that army would be more efficient if they, with their honors and traditions, were obliterated in one unbroken and mechanical unity.

[4] *The Primitive Church* (New York: The Macmillan Co., 1929), p. 268.

17 Therefore doth my Father love me, because I lay down my life, that I might take it again.

18 No man taketh it from me, but I lay it down of myself. I have power to lay it down, and I have power to take it again. This commandment have I received of my Father.

herd. 17 For this reason the Father loves me, because I lay down my life, that I may take it again. 18 No one takes it from me, but I lay it down of my own accord. I have power to lay it down, and I have power to take it again; this charge I have received from my Father."

is waiting for the destined hour to strike (cf. 7:30; 8:20; Luke 13:32-33). **I have power to take it again** recalls 5:21. The confidence rests upon the assurance revealed in 8:29 ("... he who sent me is with me ...").

Behind the sublime allegory it is possible to trace a polemic and apologetic note, which is explained if this section is read together with vss. 24-30. John, in reconstructing a scene in the temple court, has in mind the skeptical opposition of the synagogue of his own time to the claims of the church and its message about the crucified and risen Christ.

17-18. ***He Suffered Because He Willed to Suffer.***—These verses are a superb example of the strange majesty of Jesus Christ. The rest of us, even at the best, pant and strain and contort ourselves; and with it all too often fumble and fail and blunder. But he is so sure, so calm, so obviously sufficient for every call upon him that everything he does seems simple, inevitable, automatic, in the sense that we feel that though very man of very man, and tempted in all points like as we are, it is inconceivable that he should fail. Always he is so completely master of the situation. When we read the terrible story of the Crucifixion with its horrors, and in a way even more testing, its demeaning circumstances, the impression grows and deepens that this victim, bruised, jostled, dragged about, spat upon, nailed down to a cross which was then roughly jolted into its socket, is not a victim, the mere plaything of circumstance, or the sport of his enemies, but that, as a monk carved on the walls of Melrose Abbey long ago, "He suffered because He willed to suffer." His life was not filched from him. He gave it. **No one takes it from me, but I lay it down of my own accord. I have power to lay it down, and I have power to take it again.** That is exactly what one feels, put into perfect words for us, as one stands awestruck upon Calvary.

17-18. ***The Christian Conception of Goodness.***—**This charge I have received from my Father.** The fundamental originality of Christian ethics, of Christ's teaching upon how we are to use our lives, is that it is all built up upon the will of God. Other teachers would make the ideal for our conduct the seeking of the greatest happiness of the greatest number, or the resolute obedience to the categorical imperative, etc. But Christ bids us, first and last and in everything, take this as our guiding star: to seek the will of God; to choose it, and to enjoy it, and to live it out. As Emil Brunner puts it:

> There is no Good save obedient behaviour, save the obedient will. But this obedience is rendered not to a law or a principle which can be known beforehand, but only to the free, sovereign will of God. The Good consists in always doing what God wills at any particular moment. . . . Human conduct can only be considered good when, and in so far as, God Himself acts in it through the Holy Spirit.[5]

It is because when watching Jesus Christ we feel that always he is obeying the free sovereign will of God, that always God himself is acting through him, that we call him good as we call no other. And it is for that reason that God himself has given him a name that is above every name. **This charge I have received from my Father. For this reason the Father loves me, because I lay down my life, that I may take it again.** Perfect obedience to God's will, that is the Christian ideal, what it means by the word goodness. And Christ lived it to the full.

Most of us find it very difficult at times to accept with equanimity and trust the charges that God lays upon us. We start back from them; we feel that here there is some hideous mistake; that this cannot be meant; not this, not now, not yet, not for me. We burst into God's presence with angry or aggrieved expostulations. We tell him to his face that his ordering of things will never do at all, as he must see for himself, now that we have pointed it out to him. We make suggestions and propose amendments; and are surprised and hurt if he will not be convinced.

All of which is sufficiently foolish. For if we are teachable at all, life as it runs on proves to us that to differ from God is always to be

[5] *The Divine Imperative,* tr. Olive Wyon (New York: The Macmillan Co., 1937), pp. 83-84.

19 ¶ There was a division therefore again among the Jews for these sayings.
20 And many of them said, He hath a devil, and is mad; why hear ye him?
21 Others said, These are not the words of him that hath a devil. Can a devil open the eyes of the blind?

19 There was again a division among the
Jews because of these words. 20 Many of
them said, "He has a demon, and he is
mad; why listen to him?" 21 Others said,
"These are not the sayings of one who has a demon. Can a demon open the eyes of the blind?"

B. Jesus at the Feast of Dedication (10:19-40)

19-30. Vss. 19-21 seem to follow our Lord's charge of willful blindness with which ch. 9 closes, for the reference to the cure of the blind man is closely connected with 9:32 and appears to belong to the same occasion. Vss. 22-29 mark a new situation. Jesus is again in Jerusalem, this time for the feast of the Dedication, which was instituted to commemorate the purification of the temple by Judas Maccabaeus on Chislev 25 (November-December), 165 B.C., after its desecration by Antiochus Epiphanes (I Macc. 4:36-59). Because **it was winter, Jesus was walking in the temple, in the portico of Solomon**—the covered-in colonnade on the east side of the outer court of the Gentiles (cf. Acts 3:11; 5:12). Vss. 24-29 introduce the discourse about the good shepherd, which was then elaborated in the allegory to be found in vss. 1-18 (see Intro., p. 446). The

---

wrong. As time goes on and experience lengthens, even we become less sure of our own judgment and more trustful of him. The saints ahead of us are all possessed of a most enviable imperturbability and equanimity and calm. They are not hot and flustered and peevish, as we are. They look and are so strong and unafraid. And it all comes of their faith in God, their certainty that what he wills for them must be and always is the best that can befall them. O Lord, my God, thou art very great, and very, very wise. Hence Epictetus' prayer, "Give me what thou choosest for me. . . . For I know that what thou choosest for me is far better than what I can choose."[6] So indeed in a hundred places in the Stoics, with the splendid valor of their outlook upon life; e.g., "Dare to look up to God and say, deal with me for the future as thou wilt. I am of the same mind as thou."[7] Or Seneca, "I am not God's slave, I am his willing servant."[8]

But no one has ever attained to such oneness of wish and will and spirit with God as the Lord Jesus Christ. Already in this passage the shadow of the Cross was falling dark across his path. Already he felt certain that events were moving steadily, surely, inexorably, to a grim ending, which to our eyes looks sheer ruin, and the crashing of everything, and hope out. For not one soul as yet believed, to be called believing. We would have said that time must be given him, or else there was no chance at all for him or for the world. So Christ himself thought, even in the garden. Yet feeling what was coming, what already was drawing tragically near, our Lord moved on to face it with his head up and his eyes steady, in an audacity of glorious faith and trust and courage. If this was God's will, it was right. **For this reason the Father loves me, because I lay down my life, that I may take it again. No one takes it from me, but I lay it down of my own accord. I have power to lay it down, and I have power to take it again; this charge I have received from my Father.** The splendor of it! How the best in us, hearing, leaps to its feet in instinctive and admiring homage.

But Christ expects us to do more than offer such emotional enthusiasm, expects that we shall catch and reproduce his spirit of contented obedience. And that even where the pinch lies for us, and where God's will is not our own natural and instinctive will, that there too we shall not simply let what is dear to us be wrenched out of our grasp, but since it has to go, give it as a free gift. Well may we pray with Bishop Thomas Wilson of the long ago:

> O Heavenly Father, give us light to see, an heart to close with, and a power to do Thy will at all times.
>
> Grant that we may cheerfully accomplish those things which Thou wouldest have done, through Jesus Christ.
>
> Let it ever be the desire of my soul to do Thy will, and to be pleased with all Thy choices for myself and others.
>
> May I ever sacrifice my will to Thine, to do in me and with me as to Thee seemeth most meet. . . .
>
> Subdue in us that natural aversion which we have to Thy holy will, O God. . . .
>
> Keep our minds in such a temper, that we may

[6] Cf. *Enchiridion* IV. 7.
[7] *Ibid.*, II. 16.
[8] *Minor Dialogues* I. 5.

22 ¶ And it was at Jerusalem the feast of the dedication, and it was winter.

23 And Jesus walked in the temple in Solomon's porch.

22 It was the feast of the Dedication at Jerusalem; 23 it was winter, and Jesus was walking in the temple, in the portico of

---

hostile Jews who have heckled Jesus on his previous visits for the festivals open their attack with a challenge. **How long will you keep us in suspense? If you are the Christ, tell us plainly** (vs. 24). They were correct in saying that so far Jesus had thrown out hints, but had not declared himself publicly to be Messiah. Jesus had revealed his person and mission to the Samaritan woman (4:26) and to the man born blind (9:37), but not in his discourses in the temple. How, then, can Jesus reply (vs. 25), **I told you, and**

---

close with Thy will whenever it is made known to us.

May this be the constant practice of our lives, to be pleased with all Thy choices, for ourselves and others. . . .

What are we, that we should make exceptions against the will of a God infinitely wise, and just, and good? [9]

22-23. ***A Jewish Day of Remembrance.***—It was a happy celebration, held annually (see Exeg.), that our Lord attended in Jerusalem—a kind of day of remembrance, in which the Jews called to mind the exploits of their forefathers who had won and kept their freedom for them, and in especial the goodness of God, through which alone the victory and their liberty had been secured.

But as our own experience teaches all too quickly, such a rite, though nobly conceived and very seemly, can soon become formal and mechanical. When after World War I such a day of remembrance was instituted in Great Britain, it was so near to the events it celebrated that the service was one of vivid, poignant, almost unnerving emotion. But a few years, and a new generation was growing up, men and women who had not actively lived through it all, to whom what was being celebrated lay in the past, before their time, meaning little or nothing to their minds. So no doubt it was also in Jerusalem at the feast of the Dedication. But that year there was one worshiper at least who threw his whole heart and soul and being into his thanksgiving. For Jesus Christ was there. And when he was with God, thanksgiving was his native language.

22-23. ***On the Place of Thanksgiving in Worship.***—(See also Expos., 6:11.) Is there enough thanksgiving in our worship and religion? The type of service to which we are accustomed was designed for us by the Reformers, who in such matters agreed largely with the Roman Catholics; and they for centuries have drawn near to God in their public worship with a sob of penitence and a cry of confession; and have taught us also so to do. And one can see the meaning and the truth in that. We are not pure in heart, and have no right to the open vision. We must be cleansed in mind and soul and conscience; and then we shall be able to see God face to face, and hold communion with him. Indeed, so natural and fitting and instinctive does that manner of approach appear to many that they cannot conceive of any other as even thinkable. Yet in the early church they drew near by quite a different route, in quite another mood. To them worship meant in the main a dazed and bewildered thanksgiving to Almighty God for his patient and incredible kindness toward their wayward and provoking souls. On that note it began. To that it kept returning. That gave its atmosphere to the whole period of worship. Hence to Ignatius,[1] as to Luke in the Acts before him, a sufficient definition of a Christian service is a meeting for thanksgiving, in which he says the congregation, assured of its salvation, with one mind and mouth sings praise to God as one great choir.

In part they had inherited this view of things from their forefathers. "Enter into his gates with thanksgiving, and into his courts with praise: be thankful unto him, and bless his name" (Ps. 100:4). So a psalmist had advised his fellow countrymen. To him *that* was the natural and seemly mood in worship. For his part, when he thought of God, he wished to bless and praise him—that first, that most, that all in all. And to this day the Jewish service opens with a noble act of adoration and thanksgiving. But the Christians had far more for which to give God thanks than their fathers ever knew. For they had Jesus Christ; and in him they had been redeemed and uplifted and ennobled. They knew that they were sinners; yes, but they were saved sinners, or at least sinners being saved. That was for them the fundamental and foundational fact. They were very conscious that in themselves they were frail, and undependable, and constantly beset

[9] *Sacra Privata:* "Tuesday." *Works* (Oxford: John Henry Parker, 1860), V, 122-23.

[1] Ign. Eph. 4.

24 Then came the Jews round about
him, and said unto him, How long dost
thou make us to doubt? If thou be the
Christ, tell us plainly.
25 Jesus answered them, I told you, and
ye believed not: the works that I do in
my Father's name, they bear witness of me.

Solomon. 24 So the Jews gathered round
him and said to him, "How long will you
keep us in suspense? If you are the Christ,
tell us plainly." 25 Jesus answered them,
"I told you, and you do not believe. The
works that I do in my Father's name, they

---

you do not believe? The answer is found in 5:36. In the dispute that took place after his healing of the cripple on the sabbath, Jesus declared that the Father bore witness to the Son whom he had sent, by means of the works which he enabled him to do. He now repeats this, adding that the unbelief of his hearers shows that by nature and disposition they were disqualified from recognizing him. This is illustrated by the figure of the shepherd. Those who are spiritually capable of recognizing the true Messiah will follow him as the flock follows the shepherd. The Messiah inaugurates the kingdom of

---

by many and grave dangers. But every day they lived made them more certain that they were surrounded by a watchful grace set upon their salvation and more than sufficient for every call upon it. That was what caught and held their eyes. And so, said Clement of Alexandria, "the prayer of a Christian man is a thanksgiving. . . . The very function of such an one is thanksgiving, and a pleading for the conversion of his neighbors. . . . He rejoices in the good he has, and in what is promised, as if it were already present; . . . and is well pleased with all that happens, persuaded that the affairs of the universe are managed in the best way, and so has little or no petition."[2] While Origen lays it down that public prayer should open with thanksgiving. Indeed, in those days praise and thanksgiving and happiness in worship were taken as the characteristics and sure marks of a real Christian, by which he could be differentiated from others.

All this has largely changed. That first excited exultation has died down into a much soberer type of worship; whether it is that many of us have not had the vivifying experience of Christ which the first Christians knew, or that the usual deadening effect of repetition comes into play here too, so that nowadays we have listened to the gospel so often that we take it, as we do sight and hearing and the other natural gifts, as a thing of course, as God's way, as what he is for, and think no more about it. I well remember when the first airplane passed over Glasgow, how everyone ran out into the streets and stood gazing excitedly upward; and now who ever notices an airplane flying overhead? Whatever the cause of it, the note of gratitude to God, of thanksgiving to Jesus Christ, is much more muffled in our services than it once was. Yet, though strangely enough there is no thanksgiving in the prayer that he taught to his disciples, our Lord himself was constantly thanking God for something, his daily bread, his friends, sometimes even for what would have daunted and indeed broken many men. And the great saints have learned that from him. "Our very confession," wrote Baxter, "is a thanksgiving."

And rightly so. For we are coming to a Father whose heart is with us even in our failure; and to a Savior who can save, does save, will save us now from this which we confess to him. And we must learn again to come to God in that spirit. It is the very least we owe to him. Faber says somewhere that nothing hurts like ingratitude, and yet that is the daily and the hourly portion that we offer God. And do we not owe something in this matter to those around about us also? Clement of Alexandria assures us:

> They say in the traditions that Matthew the apostle constantly said, that "if the neighbour of an elect man sin, the elect man has sinned. For had he conducted himself as the Word prescribes, his neighbour also would have been filled with such reverence for the life he led as not to sin."[3]

Moreover, if our public worship were as happy and thankful and exultant as it ought to be, would not others be much more likely to be attracted to it, drawn to this faith which manifestly works, than they are by the grave color of services which keep moaning out the same ever-recurring tale of the same ever-recurring failure, leaving the impression that Christ makes little or no difference in one's spiritual struggles and can safely be neglected?

24-26. ***Under Solomon's Portico.***—Since it was winter, our Lord was teaching, not in the open as his custom was, but under cover, in Solomon's portico. There his enemies found him; and feeling that he could not escape them this time, closed around him in a threatening

[2] *Miscellanies* VII. 7, 12.

[3] *Miscellanies* VII. 13.

26 But ye believe not, because ye are not
of my sheep, as I said unto you.
27 My sheep hear my voice, and I know
them, and they follow me:
28 And I give unto them eternal life;
and they shall never perish, neither shall
any *man* pluck them out of my hand.
29 My Father, which gave *them* me, is
greater than all; and no *man* is able to
pluck *them* out of my Father's hand.
30 I and *my* Father are one.

bear witness to me; 26 but you do not be-
lieve, because you do not belong to my
sheep. 27 My sheep hear my voice, and I
know them, and they follow me; 28 and I
give them eternal life, and they shall never
perish, and no one shall snatch them out
of my hand. 29 My Father, who has given
them to me,[s] is greater than all, and no one
is able to snatch them out of the Father's
hand. 30 I and the Father are one."

[s] Other ancient authorities read *What my Father has given to me.*

God, which is a spiritual gift—eternal life (cf. on 3:3). So (vs. 28) **I give them eternal life, and they shall never perish, and no one shall snatch them out of my hand.** The ground for this assurance is that as those who are his own are the Father's gift to him, they are not only in his care, but also in the care of the Father; and he is all-powerful.

There is a well-known textual problem here in vs. 29: two alternative readings with some minor variations. They are represented by the translations given in the text and in the margin of RSV. The marginal reading has the stronger support, but the reading followed in the text yields a meaning which better fits the context (ὅς A B^{2} Γ Δ Θ sy Sahidic; μείζων ℵ D L Γ Δ W sy^{s} Sahidic; ὅ ℵ B* L W; μεῖζον A B Θ).

In vss. 1-18 the metaphor of the shepherd and the flock is developed into the allegory of the good shepherd. The perfect devotion of the shepherd is proved by his self-sacrifice to the utmost limit of death. The reciprocal relation between the shepherd and the

ring, and kept plying him with questions which they assumed must force the issue and bring matters to a head. For they thought, no doubt, that while it was all very right and fitting to be celebrating deliverances from grim dangers in the past, here was a new menace threatening God's cause; and the best way for them to serve that God, and to show their gratitude for all that had been, was to deal with it firmly and at once. And so they said, "Why dilly dally? **Tell us plainly,** Are you the Christ, or are you not? (vs. 24).

There are some questions that cannot be answered with a simple "Yes" or "No." Terms must first be defined, or else there is certain to be grave misunderstanding. "Am I the Christ? If by that you mean the Christ of your expectations, No. But if you mean the real Christ, judge of me for yourselves. Do not my works and words seem to you to be credentials that make good my claim? But if these do not convince you, what more is there to say? In that case evidently you have no manner of kinship with me, or with anything for which I stand; and I no method of appealing to you or convincing you." As Paul puts it bluntly, "The unspiritual man does not receive the gifts of the Spirit of God, for they are folly to him, and he is not able to understand them because they are spiritually discerned" (I Cor. 2:14)—a grave judgment indeed, yet unchallengeable.

27-30. *An Ocean Fullness of Grace.*—Few scriptures are so crowded with encouragement and heartening as these verses. Wave upon wave, wave upon wave, God's grace to us comes flowing in until the brain grows dizzy and the eye is tired. And still out of the fullness yonder, still as full as ever, wave upon wave upon wave comes, breaking into whiteness at our feet.

The sheep hear and follow; the shepherd knows his flock, and provides for them a full and satisfying life both here and in even greater measure in the hereafter; there is no fear of a final disaster, or of the whole thing flickering out; they shall never perish, guarantees Christ confidently, because they are not dependent merely on their own poor efforts, but are surrounded by a strong and watchful grace, set upon their salvation, able to effect it, and not to be turned back: **no one shall snatch them out of my hand.** And there is better even than that. For unless the Almighty can fail and the plans of the All Wise miscarry, this thing is going to work out. It is God himself who has committed these souls so dear to him to Christ's safekeeping. It is God himself who has thrown in upon their behalf all his divine resources. So that unless all God's all proves insufficient, nothing can snatch them from his hand.

So Christ promises with assurance. And so Paul found—witness his ringing challenge,

31 Then the Jews took up stones again to stone him.

32 Jesus answered them, Many good works have I showed you from my Father; for which of those works do ye stone me?

33 The Jews answered him, saying, For a good work we stone thee not; but for blasphemy; and because that thou, being a man, makest thyself God.

34 Jesus answered them, Is it not written in your law, I said, Ye are gods?

35 If he called them gods, unto whom the word of God came, and the Scripture cannot be broken;

36 Say ye of him, whom the Father hath sanctified, and sent into the world, Thou blasphemest; because I said, I am the Son of God?

31 The Jews took up stones again to
stone him. 32 Jesus answered them, "I have
shown you many good works from the Father; for which of these do you stone me?"
33 The Jews answered him, "We stone you
for no good work but for blasphemy; because you, being a man, make yourself
God." 34 Jesus answered them, "Is it not
written in your law, 'I said, you are gods'?
35 If he called them gods to whom the
word of God came (and scripture cannot
be broken), 36 do you say of him whom
the Father consecrated and sent into the
world, 'You are blaspheming,' because I

---

sheep corresponds to the reciprocal relation between the Father and the Son. This discourse finds its climax in vs. 30: **I and the Father are one.** The theme has been heard before (5:17-24; 7:29); it will be heard again in ch. 17. This is the clearest and most succinct expression of the Logos doctrine of the prologue. But the declaration is now found on the lips of the incarnate Christ.

31-42. As before (cf. 8:59), Jesus' opponents were infuriated by what they regarded as blasphemy, and prepared to carry out the penalty prescribed for that offense (Lev. 24:16). Jesus met their attack by a twofold argument. First, he parried their thrust with

---

"Who shall separate us from the love of Christ?" And with that, running through the possibilities that might conceivably sweep us away from him, he at once dismisses them and reaches his happy persuasion that "neither death, nor life, nor angels, nor principalities, nor powers, nor things present, nor things to come, nor height, nor depth, nor any other creature, shall be able to separate us from the love of God, which is in Christ Jesus our Lord" (Rom. 8:35, 38-39). God's love has gripped us, and will hold us fast. **My Father, who has given them to me, is greater than all, and no one is able to snatch them out of the Father's hand.** How do we know? Only because, as Jesus says so boldly, **I and the Father are one.** Looking at Christ we know what God must be, and how he bears himself toward us. If Christ is so kind and self-sacrificing and resolute and wholehearted and effective for our salvation, then God must be so too; or else human nature, at its highest in our Lord, would dwarf even deity. And that cannot be. Hence, as Christ says elsewhere, "He that hath seen me hath seen the Father" and knows what God is like, knows what God is. And what a marvelous vision it is that flashes in upon us! Christ's is indeed a very ample gospel.

31-42. *The Courage of Jesus Christ.*—How many times was Jesus face to face with imminent death, and that in a violent and ugly form? Far oftener than people in the main remember. Here once more it drew perilously near. **Then the Jews took up stones again to stone him.** And here, as usual, our Lord, entirely unafraid, fronted it and outfaced it. His meekness, his gentleness, his kindness, are constantly being emphasized. But read through the records of his story, and nothing is more striking or more obvious in it than the sheer gallantry with which time after time he looked death in the eyes without a flicker of fear in his own.

On this occasion it was because they had been shocked by what they took to be his intolerable blasphemies that their outraged feelings swept them to within an inch of murdering him: true to their ancestry—"O Jerusalem, Jerusalem, thou that killest the prophets" (Matt. 23:37)—and true to themselves, who had been upon the very verge of such action before. It was an ugly and unnerving situation, to be circled about by angry men who had already in their hands the stones by which they meant to batter him to death. But Christ remained entirely calm and undisturbed. He replied by quoting Ps. 82. It is an out-of-the-way scripture, not much frequented and difficult in itself, in which God challenges those who had been called to be the judges over his people for their

37 If I do not the works of my Father,
believe me not.
38 But if I do, though ye believe not me,
believe the works; that ye may know, and
believe, that the Father *is* in me, and I
in him.
39 Therefore they sought again to take
him; but he escaped out of their hand,
40 And went away again beyond Jordan
into the place where John at first bap-
tized; and there he abode.
41 And many resorted unto him, and
said, John did no miracle: but all things
that John spake of this man were true.
42 And many believed on him there.

said, 'I am the Son of God'? 37 If I am not
doing the works of my Father, then do not
believe me; 38 but if I do them, even though
you do not believe me, believe the works,
that you may know and understand that
the Father is in me and I am in the Fa-
ther." 39 Again they tried to arrest him, but
he escaped from their hands.
40 He went away again across the Jor-
dan to the place where John at first bap-
tized, and there he remained. 41 And many
came to him; and they said, "John did no
sign, but everything that John said about
this man was true." 42 And many believed
in him there.

---

a weapon that they were bound to respect, for it was quite sound reasoning on principles of rabbinical exegesis. He quoted Ps. 82:6, where God says to the judges of Israel, "I said, Ye are gods, and all of you sons of the Most High." If an inspired scripture allowed that title to mere men to whom God entrusted a message, how much more can he, **whom the Father consecrated and sent into the world,** claim to say **I am the Son of God** (vs. 36), without incurring the reproach of blasphemy? But the second line of defense was a repetition of the contention that his works were of a character to reveal the presence of God with him (cf. 5:20-23, 36). Jesus is the revealer of God. In all that he says and does God is speaking through him. If they have not the spiritual perception to read the revelation in his whole conduct, if they cannot hear the divine voice in his message, at least they ought to be able to know and understand the "signs" discernible in his

---

failure to carry out with impartiality and justice the duties of their high office. "It was I who appointed you gods, sons of the Most High—all of you." "If," says Christ, "he so speaks of those who had been lifted up out of the ruck of men and summoned to that honorable task, do you accuse me of blasphemy **because I said, 'I am the Son of God'?** [vs. 36]. I who have been sent into the world by God on this high mission, for which he chose me? Let my works be called as witnesses. If they are not what God himself would do, then I am discredited; but if they strike you as divine and Godlike, even if something in me stumbles you, believe the works, and credit what they tell you."

That dangerous moment passed. But Christ withdrew to Bethabara beyond Jordan, and there remained for some three months or more. That was for Christ a place of holy memories. There John, his herald and forerunner, had exercised his memorable ministry (1:28); there he himself had finally felt himself called, and had committed himself to his tremendous mission; there he had won his first successes. And now that the sky was gray and threatening he went back.

Too often it is with shame and in contrition that most of us return to the sacred places in our lives. Like Jacob, who had forgotten, who had been enticed aside, over whose soul the world had spread like rust, and who had pushed away his early dreams like childish toys that he had outgrown. And suddenly one day there came upon him a homesickness for what he had once been in his purposes at least, and had lost; the old dead dreams of youth rose up out of their graves and beckoned to him; something that he felt to be none other than the voice of God himself said to him clearly and unmistakably, "Go to Bethel and stay there; make an altar there to the God who appeared to you when you fled from your brother Esau." So Jacob said to his household and all his people, "Put away your foreign gods, wash yourselves clean, and change your clothing; and let us go to Bethel. There I shall make an altar to the God who answered me in the day of my distress, and accompanied me on all my journey" (Gen. 35:1-3).

But sometimes it is much moved and with gratitude that we go back; like Thomas Boston, who tells us that often and often, on to life's end, he returned in thought to an orchard in Kennet, where once in his youth under a certain tree he had committed himself to God and been accepted by him. So even Christ went back to Bethany, where God had wrought wonderful things for him; and, it seems, found new heartening and inspiration there.

11 Now a certain *man* was sick, *named* Lazarus, of Bethany, the town of Mary and her sister Martha.

11 Now a certan man was ill, Laz'a-rus of Bethany, the village of Mary and

mighty **works.** These tell that **the Father is in me and I am in the Father** (vs. 38). This same argument was to be pressed upon the disciples in the upper room (14:11). It did not convince his enemies and another unsuccessful attempt was made to arrest him, but he eluded their grasp.

As the time was not yet ripe for surrendering his life, Jesus left Jerusalem and retired to a district in Trans-Jordan, where John had once baptized early in his mission. In this remote region there were many who remembered the Baptist's ministry and his testimony to Jesus. They flocked to see and to hear Jesus. The report went around that John's testimony had proved true. The signs that Jesus wrought proved his superiority to John. The Baptist was a prophet pure and simple, who did no miracles as some of the prophets had done. Jesus was much more than a prophet. Amidst such popular recognition Jesus won many disciples there.

C. The Raising of Lazarus and the Doom of Jesus (11:1-57)

This story is the climax in the series of signs, and it sets forth the supreme gift of the Logos to men. He has been exhibited as the fountain of living water, as the light of the world, as the good shepherd; he is now to be seen as **the resurrection and the life** (vs. 25).

11:1-5. The household at Bethany has not yet been mentioned, but the evangelist assumes familiarity with the tradition recorded in Luke 10:38-42, and also with the

Yet he was working too for others. **Many came to him** and **many believed in him there.** For, said they, **John did no sign, but everything that John said about this man was true.** There is a word of encouragement for ordinary preachers with no particular or special gifts. They do no miracles, but if what they proclaim concerning Christ proves itself true, theirs is indeed a God-accredited ministry.

11:1. ***Unknown Friends of Jesus Christ.***—Even Boswell, with all his ruthless honesty and conscientious wealth of detail, gives us only a sectional view of Johnson's life. For as we learn from other sources, many who meant much to him, and who were regularly in his company, never appear at all in the biography; or, like bodiless ghosts, slip in and out of it again, mere names, casually mentioned almost by accident.

So even the Gospels are at best and most only little bunches of incidents collected out of the crowded fullness of Christ's days. And it would seem that many near and dear to him are given no place in them at all. If it had not been for the sorrow that shadowed their home, all we should have known about the family at Bethany would have been that vivid little incident recorded in Luke 10:38-42, which by itself gives us no inkling of how close was the relationship between Jesus and them. Once he does mention them, our own evangelist keeps underlining how intimate and affectionate were the terms on which they stood to him, and he to them: e.g., that moving message in vs. 3, "Lord, he whom you love is ill." Just that! But he would understand, and to a certainty do everything that was possible. They could be sure of that. Or the emphatic declaration of vs. 5, "Now Jesus loved Martha and her sister and Lazarus." Or in vs. 36, the impression made upon the Jews by his emotion over his friends' sorrow, "See how he loved him!" Obviously if these people have but a little place in scripture, they had a large and sure one in Christ's heart. And so it would seem that he had unknown friends, of whom we hear nothing at all. Yet he was drawn to them, and felt at home with them, and looked toward them with confidence.

So it was in the days of his flesh. So it is still, in a world that seems to have small room for him and little interest in him. The unknown friends of Jesus Christ! We never hear of them. Yet they love him; and he loves them.

A woman has no place in the headlines, lives her retired and, as men judge, uneventful life. But she brings up her children in the fear of God and in an atmosphere of spiritual things; turning their faces in God's direction, making Christ real and near to them, so that they cannot wander from him, and forget about him, and be satisfied for long. For a homesickness chases them back to their real place beside him. And does anyone do anything more vital and telling for Christ than that? Strange, mused

2 (It was *that* Mary which anointed the Lord with ointment, and wiped his feet with her hair, whose brother Lazarus was sick.)

her sister Martha. 2 It was Mary who anointed the Lord with ointment and wiped his feet with her hair, whose brother Laz'a-

---

story which is told in the next chapter (12:1-8). Presuming on the special friendship which Jesus had shown to this family, the two sisters sent word that their brother was ill.

Luther, that every twenty years or so God builds himself a new church out of little children.[4] And no one helps him so to do so much as the mothers hidden away in their homes. The unknown friends of Jesus Christ!

Or a man gives his life to the Master, eager to help in the furtherance of the kingdom. And he is settled in some lonely rural parish where things are on a very tiny scale, with a sparse congregation thinly sown about the empty pews, and little, if anything, visible to encourage him, where his enthusiasm seems to spend itself without result. "Forty years of preaching," said Cardinal Manning once in a mood of depression, "look like forty years of beating the air." Yet a statistically-minded friend of mine once made a kind of census of the church leaders, of the folk foremost in all good works and evidently telling for righteousness in his own Scottish city. To his amazement he discovered that a remarkable portion of them hailed not from the great and flourishing congregations in the cities, but from little churches lost in the forgotten country places. These proved to be the springs from which there flows the power that turns the wheels of the church's activities where all can see them. The unknown friends of Jesus Christ!

Or more prosaically, the church's funds include large and sometimes magnificent donations. Yet in the main they are composed of quite small sums, intrinsically trifling, yet often the outcome of real sacrifice and self-denial. And still, as on that day when he sat over against the treasury, and with enthusiasm watched that audacious creature casting in her all, amounting to a farthing, it is these loyal, unreckoning givers of what costs that interest and that excite Christ most. The unknown friends of Jesus Christ!

1-2. *A Plea for Martha.*—Although in these verses Mary is mentioned first, as if she were the more important, everywhere else throughout the narrative precedence is given to Martha, who would appear to have been the eldest of the family, as Lazarus almost certainly was the youngest; and indeed, in Luke 10:38 we are told that the house was hers.

As the records unfold themselves in the N.T., it seems that we are obviously meant to regard Mary as the finer of the sisters. Yet, obstinately and distinctly, may not one prefer Martha as being both the stronger character and the more likable as well? She looks at us out of the pages, a curiously vivid personality; downright, honest, practical, unselfish; a little flustered at times, it may be, by the lesser rubs of life, but in a major crisis splendidly and unshakably calm and steady-eyed. While Mary is of a softer and much more emotional type, apt to be swept away into extravagances of mood and action, a little trying surely for those round her. Thus, although Martha is obviously deeply wounded by her brother's death, an iron self-restraint allows no outward show of feeling; which terrible silence is as a rule the sign and proof of the most poignant grief of all. "I tell you hopeless grief is passionless." When Manning lost his dearest, "Do not speak to me," he said, "I can just bear it when I keep quite quiet." [5] But Mary's weaker nature could and did find relief in recurrent bursts of passionate weeping (vss. 31, 33).

Again, Martha is much the abler of the sisters. When she meets Christ (vss. 20-27), there is something vastly impressive in the stanchness of her loyalty, and the depth and reach and stability of her faith. Whereas Mary says nothing, except to repeat that cry of the heart, "Lord, if you had been here, my brother would not have died," which Martha had already used; making one feel that the two desolate souls had often said to one another in the days of waiting, "Oh, if only he were here!" Martha it is who does things needing to be done, who takes command of sudden situations, who meets emergencies and sees them through, who spends herself for others. And if, in Luke 10:40, distracted with much serving, with half a hundred things to see to, hot and rushed and bustled that their guest might lack for nothing, she allows herself to be irritated because her younger sister, cool and at her ease, seems to have no wish to lend a hand in what she must know has to be done, but sits there drinking in what Christ was saying, oblivious of the fact that her sister was missing it all, had she not a right to be annoyed? She too would have preferred to listen. But someone had to get the

[4] *Table Talk,* CXXIX.

[5] E. S. Purcell, *Life of Cardinal Manning* (New York: The Macmillan Co., 1896), I, 123.

3 Therefore his sisters sent unto him, saying, Lord, behold, he whom thou lovest is sick.

rus was ill. 3 So the sisters sent to him, saying, "Lord, he whom you love is ill."

The comment of Jesus (vs. 4) recalls his words about the blindness of the man whom he healed (9:3). This illness would be the occasion for a display of God's glory. But twice over an ambiguity conceals a deeper meaning. **This illness is not unto death** refers to the

meal prepared and think of the guest's comfort. And so Martha forgot herself and did it. Yet she was surprised at her sister; and so are we.

No doubt our Lord's surely smiling half rebuke implies that this willing energetic soul was almost fussy in her kindness, as such good people can be, and a little overwhelming in her determination to give her very best and do all that was in her power. Still, in comparison with Martha's thoughtfulness for others, Mary seems selfish, or at least self-absorbed, now in her own grief, now in her own spiritual profiting. And one can be as selfish about spiritual things as about anything else. And Martha was not selfish. Neither at home nor at Simon the leper's, could she sit still, letting others serve, but had to be up and about, in and out of the kitchen; again, one thinks, perhaps a little fidgety and fussy, but actively helpful. And when the Master reached her house of mourning and she went out to meet him, much as it mattered to her to be with him, she did not keep him to herself, but broke away to call her sister, that Mary too might miss nothing of Jesus Christ, the sister who, on her side, could sit so absorbed in listening to him that she forgot Martha altogether!

In any case, it is Martha, and not Mary, who is the patron saint of this generation; she, and not the other, who represents the type of goodness which we can understand and which we would like to reproduce. To our shame be it spoken, we have small aptitude for contemplation, and not much liking for communion with the Master in the hush and secret of his presence; and, compared with our forefathers, not much zeal in prayer. But we would fain be helpful to our fellow men, and long to leave a saner and more brotherly world behind us. If Christ can accept that from us, we are ready to offer it. All of which may to some appear rootless and superficial. Yet the tests Christ gives us, whereby the value of our faith and lives is to be assessed at his judgment seat, are dreadfully practical. Not how much time we spent in prayer, but what came of our prayers in actual unselfishness and helpfulness to others; not simply what did we believe, but did these beliefs of ours compel us to spend our lives for those who needed kindliness and succor. That is the note that constantly rings out in the N.T., e.g., in the epistles of John, "We know that we have passed out of death into life, because we love the brethren. He who does not love remains in death. . . . If any one has the world's goods and sees his brother in need, yet closes his heart against him, how does God's love abide in him? Little children, let us not love in word or speech but in deed and in truth" (I John 3:14, 17-18). "He who does not love his brother whom he has seen, cannot love God whom he has not seen. And this commandment we have from him, that he who loves God should love his brother also" (I John 4:20-21).

In any case, it is written that Jesus loved Martha. And no more is said of Mary. And indeed what better could be said?

3. ***A Lesson in Prayer.***—This verse arrests one and tugs at the heart. **So the sisters sent to him, saying, "Lord, he whom you love is ill."** Surely it is a moving and impressive fact that for two thousand years the whole world over, multitudes incalculable of frightened, hard-pressed people, in suffering and sorrow, and indeed every conceivable calamity, have thus instinctively felt for the hand of Christ, and made just such appeal to him. They want him to know about their trouble. Their first thought is to tell him. They feel that somehow he will be able to help. They have experienced that there are rigorous limitations to Paul's gracious law of life, "Bear ye one another's burdens"; that in the last resort, often very quickly reached, each of us must carry his own burden; and loving hearts around us find themselves cut off from us, and able to do little more than watch and pray that grace be given us to carry ours with honor to the end. For every man must bear his own pain; every man must endure his own sorrow; every man must face his own death—alone. Yet somehow Christ is not shut out, as others are; but can come in; and does come in, as others cannot do.

That in itself means more than we can calculate—to know that we are not alone, that there are two of us in this, that it matters to Jesus Christ, that he is thinking of us, and will surely help us. But in addition is there not given us here something of a lesson on how to make our appeal to him? The Master's teaching upon prayer is far from simple. For there are two distinct sides to it, both of them stressed

final issue, not to the immediate result. In the same way, a deeper meaning lies behind the words **So that the Son of God may be glorified by means of it.** In this Gospel the "glorification" of Jesus is achieved by his being "lifted up" on the Cross. The very act by which the divine power over death is to be displayed will cause the doom of Jesus by crucifixion.

---

with urgency and emphasis. Yet if they are not actually antagonistic, and even contradictory, they are not easily coalesced into a single working plan. So that in actual practice it is sometimes difficult to be sure what he would have us do in the particular circumstances in which we now find ourselves.

For, on the one hand, while continually underlining how amazing is the huge and untiring generosity of God, that as Plato has it[6] there is nothing of the dog-in-the-manger about the divine nature, that to God the joy of possessing is to be able to share, to keep heaping benefits on our gross undeserving, so that everything that really matters to us is ours at all only because God willed to give it to us, nonetheless Christ bids us ask, and keep on asking at the mercy seat; laying it down that there are circumstances in which such persistency alone gives us a chance of receiving; using vivid and daring and even staggering metaphors—like that about the sulky, sleepy neighbor, ruthlessly knocked up at midnight; or that about the unjust judge, harassed and badgered by an insistent claimant who would not let him alone, till finally for his own peace and comfort he surrendered and let her have her rights—teaching so bold, and written in such large letters for our dim eyes, that unless we are careful, stupid souls may misinterpret it into the idea that prayer is a noisy clamoring for our own desires; an effort not, as the mystics say, to "one" us with God, but to one him with us; a passionate attempt to argue and cajole and wheedle the All Wise out of his blessed will and into ours.

But then there is the other side of Jesus' teaching on the subject, as really there, as heavily underlined: what has been called "the prayer of resignation," which Friedrich Heiler claims as a discovery of Christ—and that only with some exaggeration. For no one ever practiced it as did our Lord—in the Garden of Gethsemane, and in other places not a few, recorded for us here and there throughout the Gospels. This is the prayer of "suspended desire," as Calvin called it. We go to God, certain that something is imperatively needed if we are to have a chance at all, say, of real service to the Master, and urge that it be granted us. But as we pray, we grow less and less sure that we are right, and feel increasingly that God in his wisdom has another plan and will for us.

[6] *Timaeus* 29E.

And with that, like Paul, we desist from our petitioning, and leave ourselves with confidence and quiet minds to God's ordering and disposal. For we never had the insane idea of bending God's will to ours; and having learned what his will seems to be, we accept it willingly and gratefully.

But when are we to use the one method of prayer and when the other? When is what we take to be the required energy and persistence of faith not really faith at all, but merely an obstinate holding to our own way, and an attempt to force it upon God? And when is what we take to be childlike submission only a fainthearted slackening in prayer which, if carried a little farther, would have gained its end? That is a real and at times a dreadfully practical problem not easily solved. Wilhelm Herrmann, indeed, spending all his spiritual genius on it, finally admits that no rule can be set down as to which method of prayer ought to be used in any given case.[7] Apparently this is an instinct that is gained only by long and arduous practice, like the skill of a cricketer or the like.

The key to the enigma that is offered us is the phrase "for Jesus' sake." If and when we can pray for something, not for ourselves merely, but for Christ's glory, as a gift from God to him, or for the furtherance of his kingdom, we can do so with passion and insistence and wholeheartedness; though indeed even there we can make sad mistakes. But in other cases we shall come to God boldly, indeed, as we have every right to do, and opening our hearts with frankness, make known our requests to him. For is he not our Father, and are we not his children, sure of his interest in us, and of his affection toward us? But we shall speak to him with a seemly humility, remembering that our childish minds are very foolish, and often ask to our own hurt what

> . . . the wise powers
> Deny us for our good; so find we profit
> By losing of our prayers.[8]

Enough perhaps, and often at least best perhaps, to act as these wise women acted; to lay our trouble at Christ's feet, and trustfully leave it at that. He knows; he is thinking about us; he will not forget, nor fail us.

[7] *The Communion of the Christian with God,* tr. J. S. Stanyon (London: Williams & Norgate, 1895), Bk. III, ch. vi.

[8] Shakespeare, *Antony and Cleopatra,* Act II, scene 1.

4 When Jesus heard *that,* he said, This sickness is not unto death, but for the glory of God, that the Son of God might be glorified thereby.

5 Now Jesus loved Martha, and her sister, and Lazarus.

6 When he had heard therefore that he was sick, he abode two days still in the same place where he was.

7 Then after that saith he to *his* disciples, Let us go into Judea again.

4 But when Jesus heard it he said, "This
illness is not unto death; it is for the glory
of God, so that the Son of God may be
glorified by means of it."
5 Now Jesus loved Martha and her sis-
sister and Laz'a-rus. 6 So when he heard that
he was ill, he stayed two days longer in the
place where he was. 7 Then after this he
said to the disciples, "Let us go into Judea

6-10. This fact explains his deliberate delay in starting on the journey (vss. 6, 15). Then the announcement that they were to return to Judea aroused the disciples' apprehension: that was to put their heads into a noose (cf. 8:59; 10:31). Their Master calmed their anxiety with a proverb. While daylight lasts, duty can be performed in safety. Until the hour strikes, Jesus must work the works of him who sent him (9:4) while it is day. Before that appointed hour his foes will be powerless to hinder him. Lazarus must be brought to life before "the night comes."

4-16. ***The Strange Tardiness of Jesus Christ.*** —Met by such confident loyalty and faith, our Lord's reaction to it is so unexpected that it takes us aback. **So when he heard that he was ill, he stayed two days longer in the place where he was.** All through the Gospels one is struck by his eagerness to help. However tired he was, no new claimant was ever turned away. Often before the petitioner could state his case and make his plea, he was already on his feet suggesting, "Let us go at once." That was his nature. Such was his way. And so when we read, **Now Jesus loved Martha and her sister and Lazarus,** we assume with confidence that, hearing of their sore trouble, he will put everything else aside and hurry to their help. "My friends need me, and I must go to them at once." And yet it was not so. **He stayed two days longer in the place where he was;** till we look at him in surprise. This is so wholly out of character. At Bethany the pale-faced anxious women kept stealing out to look, again and yet again, along the road by which he would come. "He must have heard by this time! It cannot be much longer! He must be here any moment now!" And still he did not come, and the loving hearts he loved were tortured by that futile waiting, and the flickering life sank lower and lower, and went out. Christ did not come.

Why? What is the explanation of that unaccountable delay? Well, to begin with, not a few have to pass through similar experiences. A man's dearest dies; and in a little a cure is discovered which saves multitudes from the disease which proved fatal to her. Why did God dally? Why was the discovery not made a few months earlier? Why does he help so many others, but let my heart break? But that apart, in spiritual matters, so the experts tell us, it is a common experience to have to learn to wait for God, who often seems to our hot impatient hearts so slow that we grow peevish and querulous toward him, and cannot believe that he is really trying upon our behalf, or surely he would be swifter and accomplish more than these meager results.

"If the vision tarry," says the prophet, "wait for it, for it will come, and it will not be late" (Hab. 2:3).

The function of religious people, so this tired man heard God saying to his heart in dark and trying days when there was not much to encourage, what is it? What do I set them in the world to do? What is it that I ask of them? Is it not largely this—to keep cool and unfidgety when other folk are growing flustered about things; to look out upon this confusing life with steady eyes, when those around them, badly scared, have taken to glancing back across their shoulders, and there is that ominous feeling of panic in the air; to trust Me, not only when that is easy and the sun is shining, but when there is most need for faith, yes, and some valour in the offer of it? Suppose the times are disappointing and disquieting, that I seem to have forgotten, appear not to care; that in spite of all your efforts nothing, so you judge, is happening. Still, don't get nervy and irritable, fussy and on edge. Don't toss your dream impatiently away, as something that evidently can never come to pass in this dusty workaday world of drab realities. Still hold to it, work for it, believe in it, expect it. If the vision tarry, wait for it: grant Me some loyalty, and some tenacity of purpose, and some common courage. Give Me that—long enough—and we win.[9]

[9] A. J. Gossip, *The Hero in Thy Soul* (Edinburgh: T. & T. Clark; New York: Charles Scribner's Sons, 1929), pp. 212-13. Used by permission.

8 *His* disciples say unto him, Master, the Jews of late sought to stone thee; and goest thou thither again?

9 Jesus answered, Are there not twelve hours in the day? If any man walk in the day, he stumbleth not, because he seeth the light of this world.

10 But if a man walk in the night, he stumbleth, because there is no light in him.

11 These things said he: and after that he saith unto them, Our friend Lazarus sleepeth; but I go, that I may awake him out of sleep.

again." 8 The disciples said to him, "Rabbi,
the Jews were but now seeking to stone you,
and are you going there again?" 9 Jesus
answered, "Are there not twelve hours in
the day? If any one walks in the day, he
does not stumble, because he sees the light
of this world. 10 But if any one walks in
the night, he stumbles, because the light is
not in him." 11 Thus he spoke, and then
he said to them, "Our friend Laz′a-rus has
fallen asleep, but I go to awake him out of

11-16. Another instance of the omniscience of the incarnate Logos according to John (cf. 1:42, 48; 2:25; 4:16, 49-53; 5:6; 6:64), also of the enigmatic saying misunderstood by the hearers (cf. 3:3-4; 4:10-15; 6:5-7, 32-34; 11:23-26; 14:7-9, 21-22; 16:16-22; see Intro., p. 443; also p. 438). **Thomas** is given special prominence in this Gospel (cf. 14:5; 20:24-29; 21:2), as in the second series of sayings of Jesus, found at Oxyrhynchus

---

Or as F. W. Faber puts it:

> We must wait for God, long, meekly, in the wind and wet, in the thunder and lightning, in the cold and the dark. Wait, and He will come. He never comes to those that do not wait. He does not go their road. When He comes, go with Him, but go slowly, fall a little behind; when He quickens His pace, be sure of it, before you quicken yours. But when He slackens, slacken at once: and do not be slow only, but silent, very silent, for He is God.[1]

Still, why did Christ delay? The records make it plain that to return to Judea was courting practically certain death. So the disciples felt; and they proved to be right. When ultimately Christ told them of his decision so to do (vs. 7), they protested in dismay that it was madness; that only too surely they had learned to their cost that the authorities were set upon destroying him; that only a few days before he had narrowly escaped violent and horrid death (vs. 8). So they sought to dissuade him from an insane foolhardiness that they felt must be fatal. In particular Thomas, that honest realist, whose mind never evaded ugly facts because they were unpalatable, but faced them squarely, emerges from his customary silence and obscurity by reason of the strength of his bleak conviction that this impossible scheme, if really carried out, spelled sheer disaster. If Christ insisted on returning, then everything was over, and the dream was out; the end had come in irretrievable and utter failure. **Let us also go, that we may die with him** (vs. 16).

Ah! if only they had held to that—he and the rest—how hideous a blot upon our human records would not have been there! But when Christ died on Calvary, they did not die with him. Peter, in a sudden panic, for all his confidence in his own loyalty, scared by a servant lassie, hotly denied his Lord; and Thomas did not break through the guard of soldiers around the cross, crying, "I am Christ's man, and I will die with him." "They all forsook him and fled." Only two strangers, "partisans," as we would call them now, were crucified along with him. For Thomas, all his brave resolutions scattered to the winds of heaven, was not there.

Still, one's heart runs out to the man for his generous intention. And perhaps Christ in his mercy may pronounce over him what God said of another whose brave dream came to absolutely nothing, and whose bold plans never even were begun, "Whereas it was in thine heart. . . . , thou didst well that it was in thine heart" (I Kings 8:18). But no danger would have made the Master hesitate and dally. The sheer courage of our Lord has not been nearly sufficiently emphasized and underlined. Again and again, so the records tell us, he faced the ugliest perils, and a threatening death dreadfully near, with a superb indifference, and even contempt, that thrills the heart. And in this very passage, as elsewhere, he reveals the secret of that imperturbability and valor so characteristic of him. For when the anxious disciples expostulated with him, giving expression to their fears—fears that were justified to the letter, and that proved tragically true—and arguing that to go back to where hostile eyes were searching for him and hostile hearts plotting his doom was nothing less and nothing other than deliberate suicide,

[1] *Growth in Holiness* (4th ed.; London: T. Richardson & Son, 1872), p. 120.

12 Then said his disciples, Lord, if he sleep, he shall do well.

13 Howbeit Jesus spake of his death: but they thought that he had spoken of taking of rest in sleep.

14 Then said Jesus unto them plainly, Lazarus is dead.

15 And I am glad for your sakes that I was not there, to the intent ye may believe; nevertheless let us go unto him.

16 Then said Thomas, which is called Didymus, unto his fellow disciples, Let us also go, that we may die with him.

sleep." 12 The disciples said to him, "Lord,
if he has fallen asleep, he will recover."
13 Now Jesus had spoken of his death, but
they thought that he meant taking rest in
sleep. 14 Then Jesus told them plainly,
"Laz'a-rus is dead; 15 and for your sake I
am glad that I was not there, so that you
may believe. But let us go to him." 16 Thom-
as, called the Twin, said to his fellow dis-
ciples, "Let us also go, that we may die
with him."

---

and published by Grenfell and Hunt in 1904. The introductory words of that fragmentary collection of agrapha are: "These are the [wonderful ?] words which Jesus the living [Lord] spoke to . . . and Thomas, and he said to [them], Every one who hearkens to these words shall never taste of death." The name Thomas is a transliteration of the Aramaic word for **twin,** for which **Didymus** is the Greek equivalent.

---

and a foolish throwing away of his life, he quietly put that aside in the calm saying of vss. 9-10: **"Are there not twelve hours in the day? If any one walks in the day, he does not stumble, because he sees the light of this world. But if any one walks in the night, he stumbles, because the light is not in him." Thus he spoke**—meaning thereby, so we may understand it, that each of us is set here in the world with a work to do which God created for him, assigned to him; that so long as he pursues this task, and seeks to know God's will, and tries to live it out, no evil or disaster will prematurely cut him down; but if, shrinking from trouble or danger or unpleasantness he seeks to prolong his life, and refusing what he realizes is God's will turns into some softer and easier path, then indeed danger threatens, and disaster has drawn perilously near. As Dods put it, he may prolong his life, but his day is done. And so, though well aware of what the end of it must be to him, our Lord rose up, and resolutely set his face toward Bethany.

The fact is that not for one moment did he delay to help his friends. It is quite clear from the narrative that he sensed and knew that Lazarus was dead before the message reached him. Self-evidently that was so before he set out. Thus in vs. 11, **Our friend Lazarus has fallen asleep, but I go to awake him out of sleep.** And when naturally the disciples, misunderstanding him, replied, **Lord, if he has fallen asleep, he will recover,** he said bluntly, **Lazarus is dead** (vs. 14). But from the beginning he had felt that this was so. And so it actually was. For it was after two days that he started upon what was no great journey, measured in miles. And yet when he arrived, Lazarus had been buried for four days (vs. 17). Without doubt, the moment he heard of his friends' sorrow, his instinct and his purpose were to hasten to their aid, whatever the costs. **When Jesus heard it he said, "This illness is not unto death; it is for the glory of God, so that the Son of God may be glorified by means of it"**—words which cannot be twisted into meaning that he looked forward with pleasure to an astonished buzz of admiration around him, and a blaze of popularity won at the cost of his friends' pain. Far otherwise! For that phrase, recurring in the same or similar words here and there throughout the Gospel, is a grave and solemn one, betokening that terrible end to which Christ felt with an increasing assurance that his following God's will must bring him. Lazarus was to be given back his life, but at the price of our Lord's own.

That was his immediate reaction to the news. And yet before he could set out on his errand of self-sacrificing mercy, two things had to be done. And hence that strange seeming delay. And first, so one imagines, the Christ who claimed, "For I have come down from heaven, not to do my own will, but the will of him who sent me" (6:38), had to make absolutely sure that in this matter he had read God's will aright. Many philosophers assure us that no two virtues can possibly conflict. To which the ordinary man listens respectfully, but remains well aware that not the least of life's practical difficulties is precisely that so often one finds oneself in situations where they do clash noisily; when indeed, though both are desirable, one of them must be taken and the other must be left:

17 Then when Jesus came, he found that he had *lain* in the grave four days already.
18 Now Bethany was nigh unto Jerusalem, about fifteen furlongs off:
19 And many of the Jews came to Martha and Mary, to comfort them concerning their brother.

17 Now when Jesus came, he found that
Laz'a-rus[t] had already been in the tomb four
days. 18 Bethany was near Jerusalem, about
two miles[u] off, 19 and many of the Jews had
come to Martha and Mary to console them

[t] Greek *he.*
[u] Greek *fifteen stadia.*

17-27. The story describes the arrival of Jesus at Bethany, where Lazarus had died four days earlier. Embalming and burial in the rock-hewn sepulcher would take place on the day of death. According to a rabbinical tradition, dating in written form from early in the third century A.D., the soul hovers by the grave for three days in the hope of reunion with the body, but at the first sign of decomposition it departs finally (cf. vs. 39; see Strack and Billerbeck, *Kommentar zum N.T. aus Talmud und Midrasch,* II, 544; Adolf Schlatter, *Der Evangelist Johannes* [Stuttgart: Calwer Vereinsbuchhandlung, 1930], pp. 250-51). Attention is drawn to the fourth day to enhance the magnitude of the miracle which follows. The nearness of **Bethany** to **Jerusalem** explains the large number of mourners from the city and the speed with which the news of the astounding sign reached the authorities. The behavior of the two sisters deserves attention. Martha went to meet Jesus; Mary stayed in the house (vs. 20), but went at once when summoned by

---

horrid dilemmas, yet we cannot shirk them. So here. Our Lord's instinct was to hurry to his friends' relief, even though it meant death to himself. But he had a whole world to save. Its last hope lay in him. If he were rash or premature, that hope would go out. Was it God's will he should die now, with so little as yet accomplished; with so much, as it seemed, still to do? Surely throughout these two days of delay our Lord was praying about that, and feeling for God's hand to guide him, with all the passion and the agony we see and overhear in the Garden of Gethsemane.

And further, and this time quite certainly, once he had learned it was God's will he should return, he lost himself in prayer for Lazarus; prayer so audaciously believing that it burst through the usual limitations and brought him from the dead again. At the grave Christ spoke no prayer, only gave thanks that God had already heard him, and had granted his request (vs. 41). When? During these two days of "waiting," when far from forgetting the circle at Bethany or ignoring their sorrow, he was wrestling in prayer uninterruptedly on their behalf. So foolish is it to doubt Jesus Christ! So loyal is he toward us, even when we cannot understand and seem to be left alone.

17-27. ***I Am the Resurrection and the Life.***— How many of the central and most fundamental sayings of the gospel which have brought new hope and courage to a hard-pressed world were given in the first place to single, and sometimes as we might esteem them, unimportant individuals, e.g., to the woman of Samaria, to the man born blind, to Nicodemus, or here to Martha in her hour of sorrow. True, for that last, our admiration grows, and that increasingly, as the interview with Christ proceeds. Her quietness, her self-restraint, her strength of mind and faith and character awaken a respect for her in us that deepens into reverence. Obviously she had been hoping against hope that in answer to her mute appeal Christ would come in time. But there is not a whisper of reproach or murmuring over his failure to appear. Only that sad, heart-gripping, wistful, **Lord, if you had been here, my brother would not have died.** If! If! But that was not to be. Just that. And then that strangely trustful saying, **And even now I know that whatever you ask from God, God will give you.**

What did she mean by that? Probably she herself hardly knew. And yet her attitude was very natural, is often reproduced in other troubled, confused souls, who yet in this are wise indeed. For those who know Christ at all well come to give him a blind trust. They do not know what he will feel it right to do, nor what they themselves ought to ask from him; but they are entirely sure of his interest in them, and his compassion toward them, and his power to carry through what no one else could do for them. And they leave it at that, with quiet and contented minds. Is it not an extraordinary tribute that we pay to Christ when we leave our dead so confidently in his keeping? They are so dear to us; we know so little of the other world; peer how we may, our eyes can make out next to nothing; and we are given only some vague

20 Then Martha, as soon as she heard that Jesus was coming, went and met him: but Mary sat *still* in the house.

21 Then said Martha unto Jesus, Lord, if thou hadst been here, my brother had not died.

22 But I know, that even now, whatsoever thou wilt ask of God, God will give *it* thee.

concerning their brother. 20 When Martha
heard that Jesus was coming, she went and
met him, while Mary sat in the house.
21 Martha said to Jesus, "Lord, if you had
been here, my brother would not have
died. 22 And even now I know that what-
ever you ask from God, God will give you."

---

her sister at the bidding of Jesus (vs. 29). Both accost him with the same words of implied reproach (vss. 21, 32). But it is to Martha's energetic assurance of her Master's ability to prevail with God that Jesus replies with the declaration that Lazarus would rise again (vss. 22-23). Martha accepts this as a consolatory platitude. Schlatter (*Der Evangelist Johannes,* p. 252) says that this kind of statement, **Your brother will rise again,** had become so conventional that in the Palestinian dialect of Aramaic the word for "consolation" had acquired the meaning "resurrection." She, like a pious Pharisee, could say: **I know that he will rise again in the resurrection at the last day** (vs. 24). These words with their tone of disappointment evoked from Jesus the supreme announcement of his many "I am" sayings, **I am the resurrection and the life** (vs. 25). (The words **and the life** are omitted by p^{45}, O.L. [a 1], sy^{s}, *et al.,* but they are required by the context.) Jesus

---

metaphors to indicate what lies ahead. And yet we let them go without a fear for them into that dim unknown. And why? Because Jesus is there; and they are his; and he will not forget them; and whatever he asks of God for them, God, we feel, will give him. Such faith in Christ have those who know him. **Your brother will rise again,** said Jesus. To which Martha answered bravely, **I know that he will rise again in the resurrection at the last day.** That in itself is an august faith which transforms these human lives of ours, and puts new sense and meaning and depth and glory into them.

To be assured that we are more than mere ephemerids, and the mere passing creatures of a day, seen for a moment and then forgotten, utterly and forever; that what we loved and love in our dear dead has not ceased to be, but is as real as ever; and that one day we shall find our lost again; to have the heartening and inspiration of knowing that all the struggle and endurance of the individual and of the race are not futile and fatuous and doomed; but that whatsoever a man sows here, that shall he also reap not only here but hereafter; to have outgrown that bleak and chilling creed

> No motion has she now, no force;
> She neither hears nor sees;
> Rolled round in earth's diurnal course,
> With rocks, and stones, and trees.[9]

And that was all that was left, or that would ever be, of what had once been Lucy; to escape from that somber and shadowed faith is in itself a mighty thing.[8] Yet the last day is so far away, so very far. And meantime, here and now, there are the blank, the ache, the emptiness: the blank where loving hearts keep forgetting, and listening for a footstep that never comes; the ache of those who move through life as in a dream, with what had been momentous to them suddenly faded into bodiless shadows of no manner of importance, and to them scarcely real; like Walter Scott, when his wife died, "A kind of cloud of stupidity hangs about me, as if all were unreal that men seem to be doing and talking"—a terrible picture taken straight from life; the emptiness of useless arms that yesterday held a baby that is gone.

And so Christ gave to Martha that august saying which has been recited at innumerable funerals to poor souls stunned and agonized, lowering their dear ones into the dull, senseless earth. And hearing it their heads went up, and their hearts rallied. **I am the resurrection and the life; he who believes in me, though he die, yet shall he live, and whoever lives and believes in me shall never die.**

It is stupid and futile to attempt to comment upon a passage so majestic and unfathomable; which indeed has the quality of music rather than of words, in that it suggests and brings home to the mind truths too deep and profound to be bluntly expressed in our stammering human speech. But fumbling clumsily around

[9] Wordsworth, "A slumber did my spirit seal."

[8] On this point see many arresting quotations in Pringle-Pattison, *The Idea of Immortality* (Oxford: The Clarendon Press, 1922).

23 Jesus saith unto her, Thy brother shall rise again.

24 Martha saith unto him, I know that he shall rise again in the resurrection at the last day.

25 Jesus said unto her, I am the resurrection, and the life: he that believeth in me, though he were dead, yet shall he live:

23 Jesus said to her, "Your brother will rise again." 24 Martha said to him, "I know that he will rise again in the resurrection at the last day." 25 Jesus said to her, "I am the resurrection and the life;[v] he who believes in me, though he die, yet shall he

[v] Other ancient authorities omit *and the life.*

does not repudiate the Jewish doctrine of a final resurrection of the righteous, but according to the Johannine representation of his teaching, the eschatological age had begun with the ministry of Jesus. Not only is Jesus the bringer of life, but he *is* essential life in his own person. **He who believes in me, though he die, yet shall he live, and whoever lives and believes in me shall never die** (vss. 25-26; cf. 14:18). The raising of Lazarus is but a symbol of this general and abiding truth. To the challenge **Do you believe this?** Martha responded with the confession of faith, **Yes, Lord; I believe that you are the Christ, the Son of God, he who is coming into the world** (vs. 27).

It is significant that Martha, instead of answering the question directly, avows her personal trust in one whom she describes by three messianic titles. This is the fifth confession of faith in Jesus recorded so far in this Gospel. Nathanael hailed Jesus as "Son of God" and "King of Israel" (1:49); the Samaritans acknowledged him to be

its outer edges, one sees to begin with that here is a striking instance of the Fourth Evangelist's habit of using Christ's physical miracles as so many parables and pictures and proofs of those spiritual exploits and achievements which are his main work, and which astonish this writer more by far even than the others.

Even in this present life Christ has been for untold multitudes **the resurrection and the life.** Through him and in him dead souls can and do rise up out of the sleep of death, become alive, grow sensitive, active, purposeful, endowed with powers they did not have before. That is a claim made confidently everywhere in the N.T. Of the fact of it, apostles and evangelists are entirely sure. But their astonishment over the wonder of it never so much as begins to dim or lessen. Thus Paul, in that magnificent passage in Ephesians in which he exults in the unthinkable power and sufficiency of God as these are proved in the resurrection of our Lord, does not scruple to add, with no sense of anticlimax, but rather adding mystery to mystery, and heaping marvel upon marvel: "And you he made alive, when you were dead through the trespasses and sins in which you once walked. . . . But God, who is rich in mercy, out of the great love with which he loved us, even when we were dead through our trespasses, made us alive together with Christ" (Eph. 2:1, 4-5). In that sense it has been proved beyond gainsaying that **he who believes in me, though he die, yet shall he live.** Explain it how you will, this thing has actually taken place times without number. And the one possible solution, the only key to the mystery, is Christ. When men believe in him, this happens. Without him, it does not.

But Jesus was speaking to a woman whose brother was dead, and whose heart was sore and lonely. And what he said leaped out across the barriers of death, giving us a tremendous promise for the future life. **Whoever lives and believes in me shall never die.** Quite certainly it was along that road of thought that the church in the beginning reached its assurance of the fact of immortality. Men found themselves surrounded by a divine love in Christ that even now and even here had done and kept on doing for them far more than they could express. And yet, marvelous though their experiences of it had already been, they had the feeling that far from exhausting itself in these, all that they had received thus far was only a preface and a foretaste of what that divine grace had set itself to accomplish for and in them.

Cowper declared that seventy little years give certain of our human relationships no time in which to come to their full fruition; and so ended a letter: "For you must know that I should not love you half so well, if I did not believe you would be my friend to eternity. There is not room enough for friendship to unfold itself in full bloom in such a nook of a life as this. Therefore I am, and must and will be, Yours for ever."[4]

Much more, so these men felt, the love of God to us in Jesus Christ was not a passing

[4] William Hayley, *The Life and Letters of William Cowper* (London: Saunders & Otley, 1835), III, 175.

26 And whosoever liveth and believeth in me shall never die. Believest thou this?
27 She saith unto him, Yea, Lord: I believe that thou art the Christ, the Son of God, which should come into the world.
28 And when she had so said, she went her way, and called Mary her sister secretly, saying, The Master is come, and calleth for thee.

live, 26 and whoever lives and believes in
me shall never die. Do you believe this?"
27 She said to him, "Yes, Lord; I believe that you are the Christ, the Son of God, he who is coming into the world."
28 When she had said this, she went and called her sister Mary, saying quietly, "The Teacher is here and is calling for you."

"the Savior of the world" (4:42); Simon Peter confessed him as "the Holy One of God" (6:69); the man born blind believed in him as "the Son of man" (9:35-38). By the third title in Martha's affirmation John teaches us that the Messiah's reign has begun on earth already; the powers of the age to come are present and even now are at work.

28-36. Mary's confidence in Jesus is shown only by her eager answer to his question, and by prostrating herself at his feet. Jesus asked her no test questions, for her grief moved

---

thing, but would require a whole eternity in which to express itself with adequacy, and work out for us and in us all he has in his heart to give us. Calvary itself was only a beginning. There is infinitely more for us in Christ even than that. The longer they knew him, the more wonderful and in all ways sufficient did he grow. And each height gained revealed new peaks still to be won. Here too, as Tennyson put it,

> . . . all experience is an arch wherethro'
> Gleams that untraveled world whose margin fades
> For ever and for ever when I move.[5]

And they could not believe that all this was cut off abruptly with one's death. Rather, they watched their loved ones slipping out and out, until they lost them in the glory of a sunset which was not the end but only the dawn of a new and fairer day. And for themselves, they lived their lives with diligence and with thanksgiving; and yet waited for death with an eager excitement, knowing that it would lead them into something vastly better still than all that they already had.

> The streams on earth I've tasted,
> More deep I'll drink above:
> There, to an ocean fulness
> His mercy doth expand.[6]

Already they could feel its mighty tides plucking at them, and enticing them from these tame inland waters, out and still out, until they lost themselves in that divine love which they knew to be illimitable and unending, the length and breadth and height and depth of which pass our poor groping human understanding. Only they are entirely sure that Christ's grace toward them does not end at death; that on the contrary, eye hath not seen, nor ear heard, neither hath it entered into the heart of man to conceive the things he has prepared farther out, and farther on, for them who love him.

Do you believe this? Christ asked of Martha. And she answered bravely that she did. Yet her understanding of it all was no doubt dim and inchoate, a twilight faith at best. And so at most is ours. Yet what an incalculable difference it makes to hold this faith however crudely—to dare to credit God's strange love to us, and the salvation he has wrought for us in Christ; and that in him our dreams are not only dreams, but rather audacious prophecies of what one day will really be.

28-37. ***Why Did Jesus Weep?***—Apparently Christ had asked for Mary; and Martha, with her usual unselfishness, broke away from him to summon her, and to whisper the news that he had come. It would seem that Mary, more emotional than the other, had slipped away from time to time to weep beside her brother's tomb. And those about her, seeing her rise up and hurry out, supposed that she was going there again, and followed her. But she found Christ, and flung herself before him with that same wistful cry, **Lord, if you had been here, my brother would not have died.** And with that she broke into a passion of weeping, in which those about her joined. Our Lord was greatly moved. For once his iron fortitude deserted him. And we read, awed, and with a tense stillness suddenly fallen around us, **Jesus wept.**

Why was our Lord so deeply moved? He knew he was about to give her brother back to Mary; that her sorrow in a moment or two at most would be over, replaced by a half-incredulous happiness. Why then should he weep? Was it that, looking at the sorrowful little group, there rushed in upon him an overpower-

[5] "Ulysses."

[6] Mrs. A. R. Cousin, "The sands of time are sinking." See *Letters of Samuel Rutherford*, p. 742.

29 As soon as she heard *that,* she arose quickly, and came unto him.

30 Now Jesus was not yet come into the town, but was in that place where Martha met him.

31 The Jews then which were with her in the house, and comforted her, when they saw Mary, that she rose up hastily and went out, followed her, saying, She goeth unto the grave to weep there.

32 Then when Mary was come where Jesus was, and saw him, she fell down at his feet, saying unto him, Lord, if thou hadst been here, my brother had not died.

29 And when she heard it, she rose quickly
and went to him. 30 Now Jesus had not yet
come to the village, but was still in the
place where Martha had met him. 31 When
the Jews who were with her in the house,
consoling her, saw Mary rise quickly and
go out, they followed her, supposing that
she was going to the tomb to weep there.
32 Then Mary, when she came where Jesus
was and saw him, fell at his feet, saying to
him, "Lord, if you had been here, my

---

him profoundly, and the evangelist describes his sorrow in the tenderest description of his human nature to be found in all the Gospels, **Jesus wept.** The grief of human friendship impressed the crowd, **See how he loved him!** But others asked the question (vs. 37)

---

ing sense of the crowding sadnesses there are in life; always so many hearts broken or breaking, always so much of suffering and pain and loss? As A. B. Davidson once confessed about himself, shy and reserved man though he was:

> Do you ever, . . . without any special reason for grief, fall into uncontrollable weeping? . . . The other day that came upon me in great strength. I was alone; and there came such a sense of the mystery, the uncertainty, the loneliness, the pathos of life, that I was for a long time shaken with sobs which I was unable to control.[7]

Had Christ such an experience, and that carried to an intensity that no other can feel?

Or was it that his heart smote him because he must recall Lazarus—in view of all that Lazarus, poor soul, must lose thereby? "Now upon the further shore, lands the voyager at last," we sing exultantly at the funerals of our Lord's friends, thinking of all the glory that they have attained, and rejoicing in their triumph.

> Sleep after toil, port after stormy seas,
> Ease after war, death after life does greatly please.[8]

Yet scarcely had Lazarus' hands closed upon the heavenly glories, really his very own at last, than they were withdrawn from him again, and he himself sent back to sea again to face once more the storms and dangers of this difficult and uncertain life. A strange providence!

No doubt Dante (*Paradise,* Canto 3) tells us that when he asked an angel, stationed at the outermost confines of heaven, whether she did not envy those who stood much farther in and face to face with God, she smiled at such a very human question and answered, "In his will is our peace." Where God wishes me to be, there, out of all his universes, would I choose to live and work for him. And Browning thinks that Lazarus, having attained to heaven, had acquired the heavenly mind, and so was utterly content to be wherever God might choose to send him. Nonetheless, and whatever our Lord felt about his friend's recall, is there not a truth here to remember in our times of loss and sorrow? For are we not apt to be too selfish, too self-centered, in our grieving? If we took in all it must mean to those who have passed on, would we desire them back with us? Or could we grudge them their glory? Would not our very love for them compel us to exult in it, choosing our own lonesomeness, since it means that to them?

But the main truth pressed home upon us by this passage is its proof of how really our Lord is one with us. Everywhere indeed, throughout the Gospels we can feel that this glorious message of hope and heartening is not spoken from the outside, by one himself untouched by what life brings upon the rest of us. It is no young and radiant Greek god, himself well out of the storms that buffet us, who throws easy cheering words to us wrestling with huge and thunderous billows that toss us to and fro and leave us spent and breathless. Mysteriously enough, it is the voice of one dying in agony upon a Cross that has convinced innumerable souls that God is love. And that fact, brought home so vividly to us in this scripture, that we have not a high priest who cannot be touched with the feeling of our infirmities, but was in all points tempted

[7] *The Called of God* (Edinburgh: T. & T. Clark, 1902), p. 44.

[8] Spenser, *Faerie Queene,* Bk. I, Canto 9, st. xl.

33 When Jesus therefore saw her weeping, and the Jews also weeping which came with her, he groaned in the spirit, and was troubled,

34 And said, Where have ye laid him? They say unto him, Lord, come and see.

35 Jesus wept.

36 Then said the Jews, Behold how he loved him!

37 And some of them said, Could not this man, which opened the eyes of the blind, have caused that even this man should not have died?

brother would not have died." 33 When
Jesus saw her weeping, and the Jews who
came with her also weeping, he was deeply
moved in spirit and troubled; 34 and he said,
"Where have you laid him?" They said to
him, "Lord, come and see." 35 Jesus wept.
36 So the Jews said, "See how he loved him!"
37 But some of them said, "Could not he
who opened the eyes of the blind man
have kept this man from dying?"

---

which so many have since asked on reading vss. 4-6. Many commentators (e.g., Bauer, Bultmann, and Hoskyns) interpret vs. 33 as an expression of indignation at the unbelief of the Jews. It seems, however, better to regard this deep disturbance of the soul of Jesus as part of the Johannine equivalent of the Synoptic record of the agony in Gethsemane (cf. 12:27).

---

like as we are, though without sin, makes us by far more sure, both that he can really undertake for us what is required if we are ever to come through, and that he will not fail us.

There are, it seems, those who regard Christ's fullness of sympathy even to tears as a sign and proof of weakness—a strange verdict! Everyone knows that the very heart of Islam, the core of Mohammed's teaching, is an immediate and unmurmuring acceptance of whatever life may bring upon us, as being the will of the wise God. Yet when Seid, his old slave died, Seid's daughter came upon the prophet, broken and in tears. And when in bewilderment she asked, "What do I see?" he answered with moving simplicity, "You see a friend weeping over his friend." [9] And one likes him the better both for the honesty of his words and for the tenderness of his heart.

Which takes us a farther step. And as sometimes a sloping beach shelves sheer into vast deeps, so suddenly we find ourselves among unfathomable things. For Christ, so the N.T. keeps assuring us, is the express image of God's person, the perfect showing forth in human form of the very character of God. And this not merely now and then, or in general; but always, and in everything he did and everything he was. Hence these tears also are a revelation, an authentic revelation of the divine: granting us insight into God's mind and nature; bringing home to us some inkling of the wonder of his compassion; of the depth and the sureness of his sympathy with his needy, desperate world, and for hurt minds and hearts. Hence **Jesus wept** is not a blot upon the records, a slip, a weakness, something to be uncomfortably explained away. But through that also we can learn what God is really like and is, and how he bears himself toward us.

[9] Carlyle, "The Hero as Prophet," *On Heroes*, p. 82.

So Sir Oliver Lodge, in his *Man and the Universe:*

> The Christian idea of God is not that of a being outside the universe, above its struggles and advances, looking on and taking no part in the process, *solely* exalted, beneficent, self-determined, and complete; no, it is also that of a God who loves, who yearns, who suffers. . . . It is a marvellous and bewildering thought, but whatever its value, and whether it be an ultimate revelation or not, it is the revelation of Christ. Whether it be considered blasphemous or not—and in his own day it was certainly considered blasphemous—this was the idea he grasped during those forty days of solitary communion, and never subsequently let go. This is the truth which has been reverberating down the ages ever since; it has been the hidden inspiration of saint, apostle, prophet, martyr; and, in however dim and vague a form, has given hope and consolation to unlettered and poverty-stricken millions:—A God that could understand, that could suffer, that could sympathise, that had felt the extremity of human anguish, the agony of bereavement, had submitted even to the brutal hopeless torture of the innocent. . . . This is the extraordinary conception of Godhead to which we have thus far risen.[10]

See how he loved him! So the Jews said, watching his emotion, and themselves deeply impressed by it. And as we also look, vividly it comes home to us how God loves the world.

[10] London: Methuen & Co., 1908, pp. 318-19. Used by permission.

38 Jesus therefore again groaning in him-
self cometh to the grave. It was a cave, and
a stone lay upon it.
39 Jesus said, Take ye away the stone.
Martha, the sister of him that was dead,
saith unto him, Lord, by this time he
stinketh: for he hath been *dead* four days.
40 Jesus saith unto her, Said I not unto
thee, that, if thou wouldest believe, thou
shouldest see the glory of God?
41 Then they took away the stone *from
the place* where the dead was laid. And
Jesus lifted up *his* eyes, and said, Father, I
thank thee that thou hast heard me.

38 Then Jesus, deeply moved again,
came to the tomb; it was a cave, and a
stone lay upon it. 39 Jesus said, "Take away
the stone." Martha, the sister of the dead
man, said to him, "Lord, by this time there
will be an odor, for he has been dead four
days." 40 Jesus said to her, "Did I not tell
you that if you would believe you would
see the glory of God?" 41 So they took away
the stone. And Jesus lifted up his eyes and
said, "Father, I thank thee that thou hast

38-44. The miracle is so recorded as to remind us that the writer is a dramatist who handles the tradition with the interest of the theologian rather than that of the strict historian. Again we are not allowed to forget that **four days** have passed since the death of Lazarus (vs. 39), so that the magnitude of the miracle may be evident to all. The prayer refers to the words spoken to Martha, to emphasize the thought that the mighty deed was a revelation of the glory of God. It was wrought in the name and power of the Father, who had sent him (cf. 6:29; 17:3). At the resounding call, **Lazarus, come out,** the dead man is described as coming out, **his hands and feet bound with bandages, and his face wrapped with a cloth.** This is surely the language of symbolism, as also is the command which ends the story, **Unbind him, and let him go.**

It is useless to ask what was the event in the early tradition which John has adapted and retold in his own way and for the purpose declared in 20:31. The primitive tradition of the sayings of Jesus reported an answer to the Baptist's embassy, "Go and tell John what you have seen and heard: the blind receive their sight, the lame walk, lepers are cleansed, and the deaf hear, the dead are raised up, the poor have good news preached to them" (Luke 7:22; Matt. 11:4-5). All three Synoptists record the raising of Jairus' daughter (Mark 5:22-43; Matt. 9:18-26; Luke 8:41-55), and Luke tells the story of the restoration of the widow's son at Nain (Luke 7:11-17). The difference between revival

38-44. ***The Raising of Lazarus.***—Told with consummate skill throughout, the story of Lazarus, as it proceeds, keeps deepening till finally it reaches an intensity and climax of drama. About the actual raising, three things leap out upon us and arrest us.

First, that order and requirement of the Master, **Take away the stone.** "Could not he who opened the eyes of the blind man have kept this man from dying?" the Jews asked themselves (vs. 37). So, puzzled a little, we object, Could not he who was about to raise the dead to life, and actually did it, have effected this infinitely lesser matter for himself? But we had better grasp what the spiritual experts tell us, that Christ will not and does not do for us what we can and should do for ourselves. Divine grace, free though it is, will not coddle and pet and spoil us, does not permit us to loll back lazily at our ease, expecting Christ to manage for us. Innumerable instances make that quite plain. Take one of them in illustration.

"He who has learned how to pray," claims William Law with confidence, "has learned the greatest secret of a holy and a happy life."[1] Yet, as a rule the gift of prayer is not a natural aptitude, but has to be won by hard toil and often by prolonged endeavor. St. Teresa, that authority in all this region, confesses that there was a time when God's company bored her; and that at the stated seasons of devotion she kept glancing wearily at the hourglass, feeling time dreadfully slow-footed.[2] Brother Lawrence, who admits that he had reached such a constancy of communion with God that it would be as difficult for him not to live with him, as once he had found it hard, says that it took him ten years of effort and failure and renewed effort before he attained. Christ did not put it in his idle hands. And neither will he do so for anyone, for you or me. **Take away the stone**, he says. And if there

[1] *Christian Perfection*, ch. xiv.

[2] Peers, *Works of Saint Teresa of Jesus*, **I, 51.**

42 And I knew that thou hearest me always: but because of the people which stand by I said *it,* that they may believe that thou hast sent me.

43 And when he thus had spoken, he cried with a loud voice, Lazarus, come forth.

44 And he that was dead came forth, bound hand and foot with graveclothes; and his face was bound about with a napkin. Jesus saith unto them, Loose him, and let him go.

heard me.
42 I knew that thou hearest me always, but I have said this on account of the people standing by, that they may believe that thou didst send me."
43 When he had said this, he cried with a loud voice, "Laz'a-rus, come out."
44 The dead man came out, his hands and feet bound with bandages, and his face wrapped with a cloth. Jesus said to them, "Unbind him, and let him go."

immediately after death, and resurrection after four days, is so great as to raise doubts about the historicity of this story, especially in view of the unimaginable details in vs. 44. Yet there are features in the story which have the marks of verisimilitude. The portraiture of the sisters is in keeping with the story in Luke 10:38-42, and the grief of Jesus as he drew near to the tomb has impressed itself upon the imagination of successive generations of readers.

Some commentators have found in this narrative an allegorical development of the parable of the rich man and Lazarus in Luke 16:19-31. The name Lazarus (an abbreviated form of Eleazar, "God has helped") is common to both, while the climax of the parable is the assurance that if the rich man's brothers will not give heed to Moses and the prophets, neither will they be convinced if someone should rise from the dead. The sequel to the miracle in John 11 is the unbelief of the Jewish religious leaders, to whom Jesus had already said, "If you believed Moses, you would believe me, for he wrote of me. But if you do not believe his writings, how will you believe my words?" (5:45-47.) One objection to this solution of the difficulty is that John's first words after the report of the raising of Lazarus are, **Many of the Jews . . . who had seen what he did, believed in him** (vs. 45).

The dominant thought throughout the narrative is that Jesus is **the life** essential and eternal, that such life is not withheld until "the last day," but becomes a present possession where Jesus is. But in order that he may become **the resurrection** as well as **the life,** he

is to be a miracle, we must bend our backs and strain our muscles and heave, playing our little part.

Second, there is that natural shrinking of spirit and quick involuntary protest of poor Martha, fearful that something dreadful was about to happen. For her brother had been buried four days; and in the East decomposition comes on swiftly. Besides, for some reason, Lazarus, it seems, had not been embalmed. Surely Christ was forgetting! Surely he was not about to bring upon them this new, crowning, unendurable horror. **Lord, by this time there will be an odor, for he has been dead four days. Did I not tell you,** Jesus made answer, **that if you would believe you would see the glory of God?**

We had better remember that. For to us too at times Christ may appear to act strangely, unaccountably, woundingly. But it is only seeming, as later, looking back, we ourselves shall see and confess, ashamed that we could ever have doubted him. But meantime we must make shift, although we do not understand, to hold to our belief in him, or he cannot work out for us all he has in his heart to give us. **So they took away the stone.** And Martha made no further protest, but watched silently, uncomplainingly, trustfully.

Third, and most of all, always our eyes come back to Jesus as he stands ringed about with watchful eyes fastened immovably upon him: some of them unbelieving, not giving him the needed atmosphere; some of them frankly hostile, hopeful of seeing a disconcerting failure and a complete and ridiculous collapse. Yet with the miracle still unaccomplished, still indeed to be begun, with the dead man still dead, Christ lifted up his eyes and heart to heaven in thanksgiving for what he knew that God would give him. **Father, I thank thee that thou hast heard me.** When? For at the graveside Christ had uttered no word of petition. During those days of apparent delay, that seemed so

45 Then many of the Jews which came to Mary, and had seen the things which Jesus did, believed on him.
46 But some of them went their ways to the Pharisees, and told them what things Jesus had done.
47 ¶ Then gathered the chief priests and the Pharisees a council, and said, What do we? for this man doeth many miracles.
48 If we let him thus alone, all *men* will believe on him; and the Romans shall come and take away both our place and nation.

45 Many of the Jews therefore, who had
come with Mary and had seen what he did,
believed in him; 46 but some of them went
to the Pharisees and told them what Jesus
had done. 47 So the chief priests and the
Pharisees gathered the council, and said,
"What are we to do? For this man per-
forms many signs. 48 If we let him go on
thus, every one will believe in him, and
the Romans will come and destroy both

---

must be exalted on the Cross. Anticipations of this twofold principle have occurred in 5:25-29 and 10:17-18. This story is thus the preface to the passion of our Lord. The earlier gospel tradition brings clearly before us the deep anguish of soul with which our Lord advanced to the appointed hour of his death. Luke 19:41-44 reveals the profound emotion of Jesus at the thought of the doom which Jerusalem was bringing upon itself. The agony in Gethsemane is recounted by all the Synoptists (Mark 14:32-42; Matt. 26:36-46; Luke 22:39-46). John does not describe that scene, but sums it up in the victorious assurance that followed, "Shall I not drink the cup which the Father has given me?" (18:11.) In the story of the miracle at Bethany a triple emphasis is laid on the deep sorrow of Jesus in the presence of death. **He was deeply moved in spirit and troubled** (vs. 33); **Jesus** "burst into tears" (vs. 35); **Jesus, deeply moved again, came to the tomb** (vs. 38). The same deep-toned cry of anguish is heard again: "Now is my soul troubled. And what shall I say? 'Father, save me from this hour'? No, for this purpose I have come to this hour. Father, glorify thy name" (12:27-28). So here, immediately after his frame was shaken with grief, he said to Martha, **Did I not tell you that if you would believe you would see the glory of God?** (Vs. 40.) The passion is part of the unveiling of the glory of God, the divine character of love in its redemptive activity for all mankind.

45-53. As before (cf. 7:43; 9:16; 10:19), the wonder-working power of Jesus created a division. Many of the Jews were moved to belief; others reported to the Pharisees, who induced the chief priests to summon the Sanhedrin. Whatever they themselves thought

---

incomprehensible, Christ had felt that God had heard him; and he counted on that now with absolute conviction. And that is what Christ means by faith! And these are the conditions needed for the complete fulfillment of his staggering promises concerning prayer, which often sound to us so exaggerated and impossible in this drab workaday world, and seem to shoot out far beyond the facts of our experience, and so monstrously far ahead! "Whatever you ask in prayer," so he once said, "believe that you receive it, and you will" (Mark 11:24).

And that was not a counsel of perfection. He himself did just that and, since he did it, prayer for him became immensely potent. And if we learn to pray as he prayed, and to believe as he believed, prayer for us also will become a mighty thing.

So Lazarus came forth. It is a great story, greatly told! Though for us too it will be well if, like the evangelist, we see in it, above everything else, a symbol and a proof of the spiritual powers that Christ can use on our behalf. Over us too there has rung out that voice of authority, saying, **Come forth.** And some of us have started up to a newness of life and being. But others of us, hearing, have only stirred a little, and dropped off into the sleep of death again; choosing, poor fools, corruption and the cramped darkness of the tomb to the interest, the color, the fullness of life Christ offers them—a sorry choice indeed!

45-53. ***The Gospel According to Christ's Enemies.***—News in the East travels fast and mysteriously. And so it was not long before tidings of these amazing happenings were carried through the city by the excited spectators of the miracle as they scattered far and wide. It sadly flustered the Jewish authorities, filling them with a sense of helplessness. For some-

49 And one of them, *named* Caiaphas, being the high priest that same year, said unto them, Ye know nothing at all,

50 Nor consider that it is expedient for us, that one man should die for the people, and that the whole nation perish not.

51 And this spake he not of himself: but being high priest that year, he prophesied that Jesus should die for that nation;

52 And not for that nation only, but that also he should gather together in one the children of God that were scattered abroad.

53 Then from that day forth they took counsel together for to put him to death.

our holy place[w] and our nation." 49 But
one of them, Ca'ia-phas, who was high
priest that year, said to them, "You know
nothing at all; 50 you do not understand
that it is expedient for you that one man
should die for the people, and that the
whole nation should not perish." 51 He did
not say this of his own accord, but being
high priest that year he prophesied that
Jesus should die for the nation, 52 and not
for the nation only, but to gather into one
the children of God who are scattered
abroad. 53 So from that day on they took
counsel how to put him to death.

[w] Greek *our place.*

about the report, they recognized that the populace was greatly impressed, and that the increasing reputation of Jesus as a worker of signs was in danger of stirring up the excitement of a messianic movement which would attract the notice of the Roman authorities (cf. 6:15; 12:13; 18:33; 19:12). So long as riots and patriotic insurgence were avoided, the high priestly clique held virtual control of Jerusalem, with the rich revenues of the temple. This arrangement suited the convenience of the Roman overlord, for any undue military display might easily inflame the constantly smoldering fanaticism of the Jewish Zealots. But the one thing that Roman tolerance would not brook was insurrection. Naturally the chief priests deprecated anything that would compel the Romans to **come and destroy both our holy place and our nation.** (This seems to be the meaning of the Greek word τόπος, which is literally **place,** but is used of the temple in 4:20 as also in Acts 6:13-14; 7:7, and in II Macc. 5:17-20.) It was therefore decided on the advice of **Caiaphas** that steps must be taken immediately to silence Jesus once for all. This crafty ecclesiastic was the son-in-law of Annas, and after Annas had been deposed and three other high priests had been removed after holding office for no more than one year, he retained his post during the whole of Pilate's procuratorship. His diplomatic counsel of security (vs. 50) is taken up by the evangelist as an unconscious declaration of the spiritual principle of vicarious suffering adumbrated in Isa. 53. In view of the writer's evident familiarity with Jewish ways and customs it is unnecessary to suppose with some commentators that he was ignorant that the high priest held his office for life, unless deposed

thing, they felt, must be done; and yet what could be done; and yet again, to do nothing at all spelled ruin. The people would be swept away by their enthusiasm into some stupidity; and Rome would grow suspicious, and would crush them with its iron heel; and they would lose everything that was left to them. In this nervous opinion they were probably quite honest and sincere. For progress and truth are always impeded and resisted by timid souls who, frightened by the possible price that may have to be paid for them, prefer, as they say, to let well enough alone, and allow matters to run on as they are.

But Caiaphas at least had no doubt whatever as to what their course must be—no doubt at all, and never a scruple. The only adequate policy, he said, was to take steps to rid themselves of this awkward and upsetting person once and forever. It was a cold-blooded and deliberate incitement to murder; but it carried the day. And from that moment Christ was doomed. The smoldering hostility that had sporadically leaped up into a flame of open violence toward him had now adopted that as its fixed and settled policy. This nuisance was to be destroyed. How it was to be done they did not see as yet. But they could wait. Their opportunity would come.

But what interests and arrests the evangelist is how aptly the malevolent words of Caiaphas sum up what myriads the whole world over have felt about Christ's death. In the N.T. there are not four Gospels only, "according to" Matthew and Mark and Luke and John. There is a fifth, "according to" Christ's enemies, from which the four others on occasion quote. And these fragments, culled from that hostile source,

54 Jesus therefore walked no more openly among the Jews; but went thence unto a country near to the wilderness, into a city called Ephraim, and there continued with his disciples.

55 ¶ And the Jews' passover was nigh at hand: and many went out of the country up to Jerusalem before the passover, to purify themselves.

56 Then sought they for Jesus, and spake among themselves, as they stood in the temple, What think ye, that he will not come to the feast?

54 Jesus therefore no longer went about openly among the Jews, but went from there to the country near the wilderness, to a town called E'phra-im; and there he stayed with the disciples.

55 Now the Passover of the Jews was at hand, and many went up from the country to Jerusalem before the Passover, to purify themselves. **56** They were looking for Jesus and saying to one another as they stood in the temple, "What do you think? That he

---

by the Roman authority, and imagined, on the analogy of the annual election of the asiarchs in the imperial cult, or of the high priests of a Syrian goddess, that the high priest at Jerusalem was appointed for one year only. It is an instance of the writer's tragic irony that he points to Caiaphas, high priest in that fateful year, and invests him with the gift of unconscious prophecy, as at the same time the spokesman of the doctrine of selfish expediency and of the truth of universal atonement through the Lamb of God. This was the man whose carnal policy procured the sacrifice of the Son of God.

54-57. But the hour had not yet struck; so Jesus with his disciples withdrew to the seclusion of **a town called Ephraim.** This is generally identified with the modern Eṭ-Ṭaiyibeh, some fourteen miles to the north of Jerusalem and four miles to the east of Bethel. G. Adam Smith (*Historical Geography of the Holy Land,* pp. 350-51) agrees with this identification and refers to II Sam. 13:23; II Chr. 13:19. With the approach of the Passover (vs. 55) the stream of pilgrims began to flow to Jerusalem in good time for the purification required according to Exod. 19:10-15; Num. 9:9-14; II Chr. 30:17-18; cf. John 18:28. There was the same curiosity as before (7:11), when the pilgrims speculated whether Jesus would be present at **the feast.** Long since efforts had been made to arrest Jesus with a view to his removal from the scene (cf. 5:18; 7:1, 19, 25, 32, 45; 8:40, 59; 10:31; 11:8, 16). Now the Sanhedrin, ruled by Caiaphas, had not only resolved upon his death but had also given it out that anyone who knew his whereabouts must report this to the authorities.

---

have stormed the heart of mankind fully as much as anything written about him by Christ's friends. It was men who loathed him and were seeking to discredit him who shouted after him in open derision, "Friend of publicans and sinners." Yet how many, hearing that name meant to be an insult, have plucked up heart (for they were sinners), and have stolen to him, and have found that it is graciously and gloriously true. Or upon Calvary, as the long hours dragged past, and their fears that he might baffle them by some incredible miracle subsided, and death drew near our Lord, those around his cross exulted over him, and threw their triumphant gibes into his face. He saved others; well, he cannot save himself: no tricks will avail him here, as he is finding to his cost. But how many quote the jeering words with a great awe in their hearts. He loved me and gave himself for me. One died for all, in order that these others might not die. He saved others; and to win them their salvation could not save himself. And these cold words of Caiaphas have rung for all these centuries in innumerable hearts, but with a depth and spirituality of meaning of which he never dreamed. **He prophesied,** says the evangelist, **that Jesus should die for the nation, and not for the nation only, but to gather into one the children of God who are scattered abroad.** "For," as he puts it elsewhere, "God so loved the world, that he gave his only begotten Son, that whosoever believeth in him should not perish, but have everlasting life" (3:16).

54-57. ***Christ Abides Faithful.***—This notable chapter ends with a vivid picture of the buzz of excitement in men's minds concerning Christ as they gathered for the Passover, with groups everywhere whispering their speculations as to whether he would dare to come or not. The feel of danger for him was in the very air; and it had become noised abroad that the authorities had

57 Now both the chief priests and the
Pharisees had given a commandment, that,
if any man knew where he were, he should
show *it,* that they might take him.

12 Then Jesus six days before the pass-
over came to Bethany, where Lazarus
was which had been dead, whom he raised
from the dead.

will not come to the feast?" 57 Now the
chief priests and the Pharisees had given
orders that if any one knew where he was,
he should let them know, so that they
might arrest him.

12 Six days before the Passover, Jesus
came to Bethany, where Laz'a-rus
was, whom Jesus had raised from the dead.

VI. Close of the Public Ministry (12:1-50)

A. The Anointing at Bethany (12:1-8)

This story is told in some dependence on Synoptic narratives. A comparison with Mark 14:1-9 (followed closely in Matt. 26:1-13) shows that the scene took place at Bethany shortly before the final Passover, that a woman brought some costly nard and anointed Jesus while he was reclining at a meal, that this extravagance provoked a complaint that the ointment could have been sold for **three hundred denarii** in the interests of **the poor.** Jesus deprecated this criticism, saying that the poor are always here, but he would not always be present. He also referred to his burial and embalmment. The most striking resemblance is in the use of an identical phrase for this ointment in Mark and John, in which the Greek adjective (πιστικῆς) is so unusual as to baffle all the commentators and to give rise to a great variety of explanations (Mark: ἔχουσα ἀλάβαστρον μύρου νάρδου πιστικῆς πολυτελοῦς; John: λαβοῦσα λίτραν μύρου νάρδου πιστικῆς πολυτίμου). But whereas Mark says that the nard was poured on the head, John describes the ointment as poured on the feet, which the woman then wiped with her hair. This is obviously borrowed from the entirely different tradition recorded in Luke 7:36-50. Luke's story is about a sinful woman who came to the house of Simon the Pharisee where Jesus was dining, and stood behind him to anoint him. When her tears fell on his feet, she hastily wiped them away with her hair, and then poured her ointment on his feet. That is a coherent account of another incident. But John tells us that this incident took place in the house where Lazarus was, that Martha was serving, and that Mary her sister brought the ointment. The unbound tresses, appropriate for the harlot, would be regarded as shameful on the part of a lady of the house. The pouring of the ointment by Mary on the feet instead of on the head would be strange, but the wiping it away with her hair would be unthinkable. Either John has mingled two traditions maladroitly, or an editor has introduced some phrases from Luke as well as

---

grown implacable toward him. **What do you think? That he will not come to the feast?** So they surmised. But Christ was there. This is a text that must have been used times without number at services in preparation for the sacrament of the Lord's Supper. For we have failed him so often that it is little wonder we speculate if it is really possible that he should deign to meet with us again, and to renew his covenant once more with creatures so unstable and so undependable. Yet Christ always comes. He never fails us. For if we are faithless, he abides faithful, and cannot deny himself. And he never does.

12:1-50. ***Christ's Failure and Success.***—At this point the Fourth Gospel ends its account of Jesus' public ministry with a frank avowal that judged by the test of immediate and popular success, he had failed (vss. 36-40). At the same time, it was not all failure. Far from that. And in this chapter there are gathered together and set down representative instances and proofs of the impression he had made on many. First, a vivid example of the love and gratitude he had awakened in numbers of individuals. Then an outstanding instance of the enthusiasm he had awakened in numbers of his own countrymen. After that, a first indication and prophecy of the enormous kingdom he was to win in the Gentile world. And finally, God's own full approval of this life that seemed so largely thrown away and lost (vs. 28).

1-8. ***Judas and Christ on Mary of Bethany.***—Mary of Bethany is granted the honor of being chosen as the representative of the many grateful hearts which in his lifetime ran out to

2 There they made him a supper; and Martha served: but Lazarus was one of them that sat at the table with him.

3 Then took Mary a pound of ointment of spikenard, very costly, and anointed the feet of Jesus, and wiped his feet with her hair: and the house was filled with the odor of the ointment.

4 Then saith one of his disciples, Judas Iscariot, Simon's *son,* which should betray him,

5 Why was not this ointment sold for three hundred pence, and given to the poor?

6 This he said, not that he cared for the poor; but because he was a thief, and had the bag, and bare what was put therein.

2 There they made him a supper; Martha
served, but Laz'a-rus was one of those at
table with him. 3 Mary took a pound of
costly ointment of pure nard and anointed
the feet of Jesus and wiped his feet with
her hair; and the house was filled with the
fragrance of the ointment. 4 But Judas Is-
cariot, one of his disciples (he who was to
betray him), said, 5 "Why was this oint-
ment not sold for three hundred denarii[y]
and given to the poor?" 6 This he said, not
that he cared for the poor but because he
was a thief, and as he had the money box

[y] See on Mt. 18. 28.

from Mark into John's independent record. Other Johannine touches are the name of Judas as the grudging critic, and the sordid motive attributed to him, the symbolical mention of the fragrance which filled the house, and the form of our Lord's defense of Mary.

12:1. Six days before the Passover: The date is therefore either Nisan 8, 9, or 10, according to our dating of Good Friday on Nisan 14 or 15, and treating the six days as inclusive or exclusive. The Johannine dating seems to be that Thursday, Nisan 13, was the day before the feast (13:1); the sixth day before the Passover would be Saturday the eighth (the last sabbath before the Passion); and the triumphal entry would take place on Palm Sunday the ninth. The indefinite phrase **there they made him a supper** (vs. 2) means "a supper was given there in his honor," and does not necessarily contradict the Marcan statement that this took place in the house of Simon the leper. Lazarus was one of those reclining at the table. Martha, as usual, was in charge of the service (cf. Luke 10:38, 40).

4-6. The complaint of the disciples (Matt. 26:8), or of some people (Mark 14:4), is here laid to Judas' account. His treason has already been anticipated (6:70-71). Now

Christ with an adoring affection that could not sufficiently express itself.

Matthew tells us that this supper took place in the house of Simon the leper. Yet our evangelist never so much as mentions him, good man; but apart from Christ himself, concentrates our attention upon Martha, as usual helpful and unselfish; on Lazarus, a fellow guest with Christ; and especially on Mary, as in her emotional way she allowed her heart to spill over in a gratitude which she could not hold back. Without a doubt her impulsive anointing of Jesus' feet was a well-meant act of love, and a thing so spontaneous as to be almost involuntary; but, as we Westerners judge by our shy, reserved, self-conscious standards, surely almost intolerably trying for Christ, or at least for anyone but Christ. For here too he leaves us far behind. To be able graciously to accept is often a more difficult thing than to give. But always the great Giver was the most grateful of receivers; and in this instance he saw past what to us would have been the embarrassment of the situation, and thought only of the affectionate heart so full of thankfulness. "She has done a beautiful thing," so Matthew tells us he said (Matt. 26:10).

And we may all be grateful for his kindness. For not a doubt much of the well-meant offering we bring him seems foolish and unnecessary and exaggerated to the world's cold and unsympathetic eyes; and indeed not a little of it may often be less than wise. Yet our Lord does not refuse it and in irritation push it away. He sees that we mean well, and thanks us frankly and heartily.

But even in the East, where of course they are more demonstrative than we are, one at least of the company was startled, and even shocked, by Mary's conduct. To Judas Iscariot, looking on, the whole thing seemed such sheer tomfoolery, such culpable and senseless waste, that the man could not contain himself, but blurted out in angry indignation, **Why was**

7 Then said Jesus, Let her alone: against the day of my burying hath she kept this.
8 For the poor always ye have with you; but me ye have not always.

he used to take what was put into it. 7 Jesus
said, "Let her alone, let her keep it for the day of my burial. 8 The poor you always
have with you, but you do not always have me."

a special factor in his moral deterioration is indicated. He was treasurer of the common purse and was in the habit of pilfering from it. John does not record the financial bargain between Judas and the chief priests which the Synoptics record at this point (Mark 14:10-11; Matt. 26:14-16; Luke 22:3-6).

7. Let her alone, let her keep it for the day of my burial: This translation is in keeping with Hellenistic idiom, and interprets the Greek construction (ἵνα . . . τηρήσῃ) as a permissive imperative. Contrary to the Synoptic statement that the box had been broken and all the nard poured out, the implication is that some of the ointment remains and is to be used in the preparation of the body of Jesus for burial. Others, according to another Johannine idiom, treat the sentence as elliptical and supply the thought, in answer to the complaint of Judas, "She has not sold it, in order that she might keep it for this anticipation of my death and burial." However this sentence is taken, the story is linked up with the events related in ch. 11. In boundless gratitude for the restoration of her brother Lazarus this lavish gift is offered without consideration of cost. There is no waste in love! As in Wordsworth's sonnet, "Inside of King's College Chapel, Cambridge":

> Give all thou canst; high Heaven rejects the lore
> Of nicely-calculated less or more.

this ointment not sold for three hundred denarii—about sixty dollars—**and given to the poor?**

The evangelist, perhaps a little prejudiced against Judas because of his subsequent fall, sees nothing at all in the man's open and hot annoyance except that a chance of pilfering was being denied him. Yet Judas had a case. In fact, Matthew tells us that all the disciples sided with him (Matt. 26:8). The poverty in Palestine in those days was a grim and dreadful fact. For what we call our modern problems are in essence not modern at all, but run back far into the past, as far indeed as we can see. There was gross overcrowding and horrible housing and fierce competition for a job and not a little unemployment, as Christ's parable makes plain, with men hanging about in enforced idleness all day. And there were many poor; some of them so poor that they had only one farthing, and when that was given away, quite literally, just nothing at all. Sixty dollars may not be a mighty sum; and not much could be effected with it. Yet something could be done. And here was this fool woman wasting it for no end or point at all, and in a simply idiotic fashion. So it seemed to Judas.

That is an argument with which the church is constantly confronted. For to many people, hot and eager about social reform, and impatient for the betterment of the material conditions round them, the church seems nothing more or less than an irritating irrelevance: its labors a sheer nuisance, distracting people and turning them aside from the real things requiring to be done, inciting them to lose their way among, and waste their time upon, what does not really count or matter one way or the other; while its worship seems to them an absurdity that gets one nowhere. "Religion," wrote Marx, "is the opium of the poor. . . . To suppress religion, which provides an illusory happiness, is to establish the claims of real happiness."

As a matter of fact, these confident critics have no understanding of what the church is doing; of the inspiration it gives to many which sickens them of mere self-centeredness; of the powerhouse it is, generating far more generosity and brotherliness than anything else in the world. All that they do not know; or to all that they resolutely shut their eyes. And for the moment, more and more are deserting Christian worship, seeing no sense in it, and frankly angered by it. Do something material for the poor! That is practical and helpful and worth while! But all that the church stands for ends in nothing, and is simply silliness. So Judas Iscariot thought confidently in his day.

But Jesus Christ did not. **The poor you always have with you,** he said, throwing his protecting kindness around Mary, who must have been sadly taken aback by Judas' attack upon her; **but you do not always have me.** "Let Mary keep such of her ointment as is left. She may help to prepare me for my burial with it." Such honor did Christ offer her, although, **in**

9 Much people of the Jews therefore knew that he was there: and they came not for Jesus' sake only, but that they might see Lazarus also, whom he had raised from the dead.

10 ¶ But the chief priests consulted that they might put Lazarus also to death;

11 Because that by reason of him many of the Jews went away, and believed on Jesus.

9 When the great crowd of the Jews learned that he was there, they came, not only on account of Jesus but also to see Laz'a-rus, whom he had raised from the
dead. 10 So the chief priests planned to put
Laz'a-rus also to death, 11 because on account of him many of the Jews were going away and believing in Jesus.

B. Popularity and Peril (12:9-11)

9-11. In the Synoptic narrative it was the cleansing of the temple that precipitated the crisis. In the Johannine account this took place at the beginning of the ministry, and the raising of Lazarus is substituted as the provocative cause of the final clash between Jesus and the chief priests (see Intro., p. 448). Immediately after the miracle and the popular excitement that it aroused, the Sanhedrin had taken steps for the arrest of Jesus (11:53, 57). This plan had been foiled by the escape to Ephraim (11:54). Meanwhile, at the approach of the Passover a crowd of pilgrims had come to Jerusalem in good time to allow for the prescribed quarantine, lest any ceremonial defilement should prevent them from sharing in the festival. Many were speculating about the probable appearance of Jesus in Jerusalem for the Passover (11:56). When they heard that he

---

point of fact, it was two men to whom it fell. And indeed does she not teach us a much-needed lesson? It is so easy in time to forget the wonder of Christ's gifts and benefits, to take them casually and for granted, to accept them without thought as his way, and to leave it at that. Well for us if Mary's gratitude infects us, and saves us from such callousness.

> What can I give Him,
> Poor as I am?
> If I were a shepherd,
> I would bring a lamb;
> If I were a wise man,
> I would do my part;
> Yet what I can I give Him—
> Give my heart.[3]

9-11, 17-19. ***The Chief Witness for Christ.***—Of the manner of man that Lazarus was we know nothing at all, except the one important fact that him too Jesus loved; that there was something in him that attracted Christ to him; something that Christ found likable and hopeful. Yet so far as we can judge, he was a very ordinary mortal, much like the mass of us. He does nothing notable; he says nothing worth recording, not even about his own remarkable experiences. For as Tennyson says:

> He told it not, or something seal'd
> The lips of that evangelist.[4]

Browning indeed has a fascinating study of him in which he sets it down that

> . . . the especial marking of the man
> Is prone submission to the heavenly will.[5]

It may be so. It very likely was so. But there is not a trace of evidence for it in Scripture. Yet this simple soul became Christ's most unanswerable witness. So that our Lord's enemies in desperation took seriously to plotting **to put Lazarus also to death,** feeling that there was no refuting him, and so he also must be got out of the way. Christ's most unanswerable witness! And this not because of anything he did for Christ, but simply and wholly because of what Jesus had done for him. As a modern poet puts it, our Lord had many witnesses whom he could call, who could and did give prompt and first-hand evidence for him. "He opened my blind eyes." "He cleansed my leprosy." "He gave me back my health after long years of helplessness." But far the most convincing of them all was the quiet man who said just this, "My name is Lazarus, and I live."

So even though we may possess not the faintest trace of genius, and have nothing we can bring to Christ, yet if we too lay long dead in trespasses and sins; if over us there has rung out that voice of power saying to us, "Come forth"; if we did wake out of the sleep of death and have risen into a newness of life:

[3] Christina Rossetti, "A Christmas Carol."

[4] *In Memoriam*, st. xxxi.

[5] "An Epistle."

12 ¶ On the next day much people that were come to the feast, when they heard that Jesus was coming to Jerusalem,

13 Took branches of palm trees, and went forth to meet him, and cried, Hosanna: Blessed *is* the King of Israel that cometh in the name of the Lord.

14 And Jesus, when he had found a young ass, sat thereon; as it is written,

12 The next day a great crowd who had
come to the feast heard that Jesus was com-
ing to Jerusalem. 13 So they took branches
of palm trees and went out to meet him,
crying, "Hosanna! Blessed be he who comes
in the name of the Lord, even the King
of Israel!" 14 And Jesus found a young ass
and sat upon it; as it is written,

---

was at Bethany, they went across the Kidron Valley and over the Mount of Olives to the village, partly to see Jesus but even more to see the man who had been brought back from the tomb. The chief priests were alarmed at this recrudescence of popular fanaticism and added the name of Lazarus to the list of the condemned.

C. The Triumphal Entry (12:12-19)

12-19. The next day reverses the order of events in Mark. Here it is the crowd of Galileans already in the city who come out to give Jesus a royal welcome. Vss. 14-16 should come logically before vs. 13, which is a slightly different form of Ps. 118:25-26 from the quotation given in Mark 11:9-10. **Hosanna,** i.e., "Save now," is rightly used, whereas in Mark 11:10 "Hosanna in the highest" is evidently used in the sense represented by "glory in the highest" in Luke 19:38. **Jesus found a young ass and sat upon it:** The Synoptic Gospels all describe the way in which Jesus sent his disciples expressly to bring

---

and if, though we were bound about hand and foot with grave clothes, so that we could only shuffle helplessly, to us also he has said, "Loose him, and let him go," and we are free—then we too are arguments for Christ that there is no refuting; and we too, poor things in ourselves though we may be, are of real value to him. "You are the proofs of my discipleship," claimed Paul to those whom he had won and changed. And Christ ought to be able to point at you and me and say, "Show me anything like that apart from me." You and I, obviously through him living a new life in a new way, should be our Lord's last and unanswerable evidence.

12-19. ***The Entry into Jerusalem.***—But, claims the evangelist, more than individuals like Mary or Lazarus had been won. People in masses had welcomed Christ with a wild rapture of enthusiasm. **The next day a great crowd who had come to the feast heard that Jesus was coming to Jerusalem. So they took branches of palm trees and went out to meet him, crying, "Hosanna! Blessed be he who comes in the name of the Lord, even the King of Israel!"**

The account of the entry into Jerusalem given in this Gospel is curiously curt and undetailed compared with the vividness of Luke's or Mark's report. All that is here emphasized is the delirium of eager welcome that surrounded Christ as he rode into the city; an excitement which is here ascribed very largely to the raising of Lazarus, and to the astonishing reports of that tremendous happening spread abroad by those who had themselves witnessed it and who kept declaring that there could be no possible doubt about the fact of it. For they had been quite close, and had seen the whole thing with their own eyes; with the result that the streets were lined with dense mobs of excited and enthusiastic folk. So much so indeed that the Pharisees looked at each other in consternation, feeling that they had been too late in taking action against Christ, since the day seemed to be already lost. **The Pharisees then said to one another, "You see that you can do nothing; look, the world has gone after him."**

According to Luke there was much more in it than that. For he seems to claim the whole of that shouting crowd as definite adherents of the cause. "As he was now drawing near, at the descent of the Mount of Olives, the whole multitude of the disciples began to rejoice and praise God with a loud voice for all the mighty works that they had seen, saying, 'Blessed be the King who comes in the name of the Lord! Peace in heaven and glory in the highest!' And some of the Pharisees in the multitude said to him, 'Teacher, rebuke your disciples.' He answered, 'I tell you, if these were silent, the very stones would cry out'" (Luke 19:37-40). Such enthusiasm was there in the air.

Looking back, comments our own evangelist, Christ's disciples came to link the whole episode

15 Fear not, daughter of Sion: behold,
thy King cometh, sitting on an ass's colt.
16 These things understood not his dis-
ciples at the first: but when Jesus was
glorified, then remembered they that these
things were written of him, and *that* they
had done these things unto him.
17 The people therefore that was with
him when he called Lazarus out of his
grave, and raised him from the dead, bare
record.

15 "Fear not, daughter of Zion;
behold, behold, thy king is coming,
sitting on an ass's colt!"
16 His disciples did not understand this at
first; but when Jesus was glorified, then
they remembered that this had been writ-
ten of him and had been done to him.
17 The crowd that had been with him when
he called Laz'a-rus out of the tomb and
raised him from the dead bore witness.

---

this mount for the triumphal entry (Mark 11:2; Matt. 21:2; Luke 19:30). The quotation from Zech. 9:9 in vs. 15 is abridged and introduced by a phrase that may be a reminiscence of Isa. 44:2; Zeph. 3:16. A comparison with Matt. 21:5 suggests that this was an early messianic testimony (see Intro., p. 440). The significance of this symbolical act was that it established a claim to messiahship, but at the same time transposed this theme into the key of the song of the suffering Servant in Deutero-Isaiah. Vs. 16 is the evangelist's comment, as in 2:22; 7:39; 20:9; 21:19. According to a reading with inferior MS support, vs. 17 would be translated, "The crowd that was with him was bearing witness that [ὅτι] he had called Lazarus out of the tomb and raised him from the dead." This would avoid the confusion made by referring to two crowds. But there is overwhelming support for the reading translated in the RSV, **The crowd that had been with him when** [ὅτε] **he called Lazarus out of the tomb and raised him from the dead bore witness.** The story told by the crowd of vs. 17 and 11:42—many of whom accompanied Jesus from Bethany to Jerusalem—had already reached the city and aroused the crowd of vss. 9, 12, 18 to acclaim the royal hero as they came out to meet him with **branches of palm trees.**

---

in their minds with a wistful verse or two, slipped into a fiercely primitive chapter in the prophet Zechariah, which dreams of a new type of king who should one far-off day really appear in Jerusalem:

> Here comes your King,
> triumphant and victorious,
> riding humbly on an ass,
> on the foal of an ass!
> He banishes all chariots from Ephraim,
> war-horses from Jerusalem,
> and battle-bows;
> his words make peace for nations,
> his sway extends from sea to sea,
> from the Euphrates to the ends of earth (Zech. 9:9-10 Moffatt).

That was a prophecy which had lingered in the Jewish mind; and the fulfillment of which they imagined, indeed took for granted, that they of course desired. Yet it describes a quite new type of king, with no proud trappings of royalty, heralded by no fanfare of trumpets, surrounded by no pomp and circumstance. "You say that this is what you want: but would you like him if he really came; and would you even recognize that it is he at all?" So Jesus challenged them.

W. M. Macgregor, looking at this scripture with those shrewd eyes of his, commented on it thus:

> On this occasion Jesus did what He never did before or after. He was surrounded by men who talked and thought a great deal about Messiah's coming, and who professed enthusiasm for it. The words were often on their lips; the hope, they said, was in their hearts; but Jesus, who knew the snare and the delusion of words, searched their profession to the bottom. Like an actor, but in deep and sorrowful solemnity, He dressed Himself to play His part before their eyes. He was close to the city and did not need a beast to ride on; but He halted on His way, and sent two of the disciples to borrow a young ass from a friend. And then, on His sober beast, with the crowd growing denser about Him, He paced up the slopes and in at the gate. "You say you are longing for the Messiah's coming; you say that you look for Him to come to His capital riding on an ass; it has a good sound in the words of it, but here is the thing—such a King as the prophet spoke of—how do you like it now?" And what had seemed fascinating and credible, when it was found on the page of a sacred book, lost all its charm when it was seen in flesh. They discovered that such a power was ineffectual for setting up a reign of God, though they had liked the words about it. That was Christ's challenge and its result. . . . We nearly all trust in some degree in an arm

18 For this cause the people also met him, for that they heard that he had done this miracle.

19 The Pharisees therefore said among themselves, Perceive ye how ye prevail nothing? behold, the world is gone after him.

18 The reason why the crowd went to meet
him was that they heard he had done this
sign. 19 The Pharisees then said to one
another, "You see that you can do nothing; look, the world has gone after him."

This popular ovation increased still further the anxiety of his opponents, already reported in vss. 10-11; 11:47-48, 53, 57. The repeated emphasis upon the result of the miracle at Bethany is to account for the determination of the religious leaders to put Jesus to death. The mention of **the Pharisees** goes back to 11:47, 57, where they are named, as also in 7:32, as part of the Sanhedrin. They appear in this Gospel in 1:24 as interested in the movement of the Baptist, in 4:1 as concerned in the growing success of the Judean ministry of Jesus, in chs. 7 and 9 as the stern critics of Jesus for his lax observance of the sabbath law, also in ch. 8 for his claim to divine sonship. Nicodemus belonged to their party in the Sanhedrin (3:1). Their powerful allies in this coalition to dispose of Jesus were "the chief priests," the family of Annas, several of whom had held the office of high priest. These were the leaders of the party of the Sadducees, whose disbelief in the story of Lazarus was required by their creed (cf. Acts 23:8), and who were infuriated by the young reformer's attack upon the temple revenues (2:16) and alarmed at the possibility of a messianic riot which might cost them their virtual control of the city if it came to the notice of the Roman authority.

of flesh, and find our comfort in a Church which is a kind of second-rate world, with supporters amongst the learned and the mighty. It is natural to ask for something looking like dominion, not a peasant riding on a borrowed beast, with a mob of pilgrims shouting round Him. . . . Jesus of Nazareth, on His borrowed farm-beast, . . . and yet offering Himself to His nation as the King of prophecy, is the speaking reminder of the powers which lie behind our sight. I wonder when we, in the Church of Jesus, will learn from Him to trust these powers and to cease from man.[6]

It is not altogether easy to fit that interpretation with literal exactness into the Scriptures. For Christ rode through the crowded streets amid a delirious whirlwind of enthusiasm. Some of the people, at least when they saw him, did find beauty in him; and momentarily at any rate did desire him. But of the authorities, the big people, those whose opinion counted, that reading seems undeniable.

And do we not all, too often, need this sharp reminder, lest we too deceive ourselves with words that little though we realize it are only words? We think we are sincere lovers of truth, that we want progress, that we are ardent for the coming in of our Lord's way of life. And yet how often truth and progress and Christ himself offer themselves to us; and we fail to recognize them; frankly do not like the look of them and will not have them. Not seldom we look God himself full in the face and say with complete confidence, "No, no, this is not God, is not the least like God"; and will not give him welcome, but turn him away. Often God's thoughts in very deed are so unlike our thoughts that many a time they seem to us just futile and preposterous and silly.

They were all looking for a king
  To slay their foes and lift them high:
Thou cam'st, a little baby thing
  That made a woman cry.[7]

So in a hundred matters. In theory we are all wholehearted in our acceptance of Christ's teaching about forgiveness and unselfishness and the like. But when an actual call is made upon us for one or the other, we push the thing away. For this, we feel, is not unselfishness but simply weakness; and this is not forgiveness but abject cowardice: both obviously quite out of the question for a man who is a man. We listen to Christ's promises about the Holy Spirit. But in an emergency do we not often find that something prosaically earthly and material feels more solid underneath our feet than what we then dismiss as nebulosities? Think, says Christ; prove yourselves; do you really believe

[6] *Jesus Christ, the Son of God* (Edinburgh: T. & T. Clark, 1907), pp. 87-89. Used by permission.

[7] George MacDonald, "That Holy Thing," from *Poetical Works*. Used by permission of the author's executors and Chatto & Windus, publishers.

20 ¶ And there were certain Greeks among them that came up to worship at the feast:

21 The same came therefore to Philip, which was of Bethsaida of Galilee, and desired him, saying, Sir, we would see Jesus.

20 Now among those who went up to
worship at the feast were some Greeks.
21 So these came to Philip, who was from
Beth-sa'i-da in Galilee, and said to him,

D. Jesus and the Greeks (12:20-26)

20-23. The Pharisees have just complained, "The world has gone after him." The evangelist now sees a prophecy of the universal spread of Christianity in an incident at the festival. Some proselytes, or at least "God-fearers" (cf. Acts 10:1, 22, 35; 13:16, 26, 43, 50; 16:14; 17:4, 17; 18:7), who were accustomed to visit Jerusalem at this festival for **worship** (so the present participle—ἀναβαινόντων—may be translated), approached Philip asking for an introduction to Jesus. **Philip** and **Andrew** are the two disciples with Greek names, and they both came from Bethsaida, which was just outside Galilee, on the east side of the Jordan where it flows into the Lake of Gennesaret (cf. 1:44). This fact may

---

what you confidently take for granted that of course you believe?

20-26. ***Some Greeks Ask to See Jesus.***—The evangelist next puts forward, as a proof of the impression Christ had made, certain Greeks who stopped Philip—perhaps choosing to approach him rather than the others because he had a Greek name, perhaps because he came from Bethsaida, a cosmopolitan town with not a few Greeks among its population—and asked him if they could see Jesus. We are assured in the Acts that the Greeks were characteristically an inquisitive people, with minds that, like hounds, kept questing after anything novel and up to date. But Philip felt that there was more in this request than that; that these were serious seekers after truth and God. Yet he was not prepared singlehanded to lay their request before the Master—evidently being dubious how it might be received. And after all, he had probably heard Christ saying to another Gentile claimant, and she in sore straits, "I am not sent but unto the lost sheep of the house of Israel." Happily he bethought himself of Andrew, and consulted one who seems to have been the kind of man that people in difficulties can and do consult: and apparently on Andrew's advice they went together and told Jesus of the request.

Seldom was our Lord so deeply moved. Huge tides of thought and feeling raced each other through his mind—exultation, gravity, a measure of uncertainty, utter and absolute and happy resignation to the will of God, whatever that might cost him; and then, as the clouds that had blown up scattered and the sun broke through again, once more and finally exultation. And all this because a handful of Gentiles were impressed by him, and wanted to go further in the matter and know more about it! Yet that was characteristic of Christ. For if he had the most resolutely honest of minds, which evaded no grim facts, but stated things frankly and as they really were, however grievous, along with that he possessed such a sense of the reality, the nearness, the sufficiency of God, that nothing, he felt, was too wonderful to happen in the same world as God. Always Christ had a happy expectation that it all might burst in at any moment. So that events which seem to us no very great affairs, and trivial enough, were to him not the little matters for which we dismiss them, but momentous; the opening of a door on something huge, tremendous, incalculable, and actually begun. Thus, when the seventy returned from their first missionary tour—though, as we judge, it was at most and best only a tiny dent that they had made in the mass of evil in the world—Christ met them with a cry of triumph. "I saw Satan fall like lightning from heaven," he declared (Luke 10:18). It had begun; it was effective; it would go on increasingly until Satan was down and evil overthrown.

Or when the thick darkness around the Cross had stolen cold and numbing into his very soul, and he seemed to be forgotten and left unbefriended even by God, that strange unexpected cry from a neighboring sufferer, that dim, groping, inchoate faith that yet was faith, lifted the oppression heavy on his soul, and scattered it to nothingness. And he died with the shout of a conqueror, "It is finished." "It is working, and will work! I have not failed in the task that God gave me to do."

So here. A few Greeks, of small consequence so far as numbers go, ask to be brought to him; and Christ sees past them to the dim Gentile peoples, masses of them down the centuries, following these forerunners into his church and

22 Philip cometh and telleth Andrew:
and again Andrew and Philip tell Jesus.
23 ¶ And Jesus answered them, saying,
The hour is come, that the Son of man
should be glorified.
24 Verily, verily, I say unto you, Except
a corn of wheat fall into the ground and

"Sir, we wish to see Jesus." 22 Philip went
and told Andrew; Andrew went with Philip
and they told Jesus. 23 And Jesus answered
them, "The hour has come for the Son of
man to be glorified. 24 Truly, truly, I say

---

explain why Philip and Andrew were the intermediaries. It is possible that the evangelist implies more than this. Just as the Greeks represent the world outside Judaism, so the Gentile mission of Paul and his successors shows the call for missionaries with a sympathetic understanding of the wider quest for God. Those who have never seen with their own eyes Jesus the revealer of God must come to the knowledge of him through those who can transmit the living witness (cf. I John 1:3-4, "That which we have seen and heard we proclaim also to you, so that you may have fellowship with us. . . . And we are writing this that our joy may be complete"). Jesus saw in this request the sign for which he had been waiting. Time after time we have read that "the hour has not yet come" (2:4; 7:6, 30; 8:20). Now at last (vs. 23) Jesus exclaims: **The hour has come for the Son of**

---

kingdom. It had begun! His lifework had not been in vain. **The hour has come for the Son of man to be glorified.**

And with that he lays down the law of life, and of success in life, to be called success. **Truly, truly, I say to you, unless a grain of wheat falls into the earth and dies, it remains alone; but if it dies, it bears much fruit.** Immortal words, which somehow haunt the memory and will not be forgotten. One supposes that when he so spoke, he had turned and was looking back along the road he had traveled, and at his labors in the past. For he did not lay down his life only upon Calvary. Always and in all things he had given it away for God and others, retaining for himself only the necessities needed to enable him to continue such service. And sometimes it had looked as if it had been futile, as if little had come of it, as if it had been thrown away and lost. But here was proof that it was not so, the first shimmer of living green showing through the bare fields that foretold the gold of coming harvest.

24-26. ***The Loneliness and the Futility of Selfishness.***—Very memorable is the warning we are given of the loneliness of selfishness and of its futility. The loneliness of it! For **unless a grain of wheat falls into the earth and dies, it remains alone.** The man who lives immersed only in his own interests and ploys and pleasures and sorrows—for is not Cowper near the mark when he asserts, reading partly from his own experience and partly from that of others, that the miserable are nearly always selfish?—such a one maroons himself upon a narrow spit of a life, a mere islet, far more cramped than the human inheritance that falls to kindlier folk. He may plume himself upon his wisdom, asserting that the wider one's sympathies the bigger target does one offer to the arrows of fate. Have children, and you have given hostages to fortune, and peace of mind is largely gone. Make friends, and you are wounded by their wounds and hurt by their misfortunes. Shut yourself into your own life, and nothing can touch you but a trouble that is definitely personal. But that is to mistake for wisdom what is really abject poverty. He who would have friends, says a shrewd scripture, must show himself friendly. Else he has no vital relationships, no living part in the community, drops out of it at last, and his absence is scarcely noticed; makes no difference to anybody; not missed. It is recorded that a king of Israel died without being desired; a lonely, eerie epitaph.

And the futility of it! For **He who loves his life loses it.** Often indeed it seems that the shortest, some feel the only, way to the top of the tree and to the things that count is to be self-centered, pushful, concentrated utterly on winning what one has set out to attain. But as Christ judges, one can gain what the natural man assumes are the solid and substantial prizes, yet throw away one's life. For the big things may all be missed; the others are so transient!

> The Worldly Hope men set their Hearts upon
> Turns Ashes—or it prospers; and anon,
> Like Snow upon the Desert's dusty Face,
> Lighting a little hour or two—is gone.[8]

That is a grave and somber end Sir Walter Raleigh sets down to his long *History of the World,* a gallant breathless tale of human struggle and effort and adventure; of hot and soaring

[8] *The Rubáiyát of Omar Khayyám,* st. xvii.

die, it abideth alone: but if it die, it bringeth forth much fruit.
25 He that loveth his life shall lose it; and he that hateth his life in this world shall keep it unto life eternal.

to you, unless a grain of wheat falls into the earth and dies, it remains alone; but if it dies, it bears much fruit.
25 He who loves his life loses it, and he who hates his life in this world will keep it for eter-

man to be glorified. This glorification of the Son of man means much more than the coming of the Gentiles into the knowledge of Jesus. As Loisy says: "The hour for the glorification is not the hour of the glorification; it is the hour upon which this glorification depends as its condition and principle. In the following discourse 'this hour' will be spoken of again, and it will be the hour of death" (*Le Quatrième Évangile* [2nd ed. revised; Paris: Émile Nourry, 1921], p. 371). Here as in vs. 16 (cf. 7:39; 13:31) "glorification" (δοξασθῆναι), just as "exaltation" (ὑψωθῆναι), refers to death as the condition for rising again and heavenly triumph. But in all this Jesus as the revealer of God is declaring through his passion the divine purpose of saving the world (see on 3:13-17). This paradox of the Cross is illustrated in the next three verses.

24-26. The **grain of wheat** sets out the mystery of life through death. This is the secret of fruitfulness, which is repeated in vs. 32. Sacrifice (vs. 25) is the salvation of life,

ambitions, of proud conquests, of honors daringly sought and won:

> O eloquent just and mighty death! Whom none could advise, thou hast persuaded; what none hath dared, thou hast done; and whom all the world hath flattered, thou only hast cast out of the world and despised; thou hast drawn together all the far stretched greatness, all the pride, cruelty, and ambition of man, and covered it all over with these two narrow words, *Hîc jacet.*[9]

And they must face the judgment seat of God, to give account of what they have made of the life that he entrusted to them, empty-handed, empty-hearted, empty-souled; tricked, cheated, fooled. For **he who loves his life,** laying it up as a personal treasure and possession, **loses it** thereby; and only **he who hates his life** —not of course in the sense of despising this lordly heritage which God has planned for us and given to us, but using it for others and for God, throwing it away with generosity—only **he who hates his life in this world will keep it for eternal life.**

So Christ assures us. And he ought to know. For no one ever made anything like so much of a human life as he. And indeed many of us have ourselves gone far enough to have experienced that no life is so full as that which has no place in it for self. And that is the characteristic of eternal life. A. E. Taylor, after remarking that it is the life of the flesh which must be surrendered if eternal life is to be won, points out that in Scripture the flesh means much more than carnality. "To live to the flesh is . . . to take 'I want it' as a last and final legitimation of any pursuit." That way, he argues, there is no possibility of permanent satisfaction. And so, as evidence of the existence of a better way open to all of us, he summons as his witness the experience in World War I of many of those who were listening to him.

> There are probably among my audience some who, as young men rejoicing in their youth and all its promise of a full and varied life, then made, from sheer loyalty to a higher good, the surrender of hazarding all they prized most to play a man's part in their country's struggle, and made it with the full sense of the preciousness of all they were setting on hazard, and yet gladly and ungrudgingly. I take it that if any man can recall, as perhaps it is hardly possible he should, what the quality of his life was when he was making the choice, he knows by analogy what is the abiding character of eternal life, as a life in which . . . one has ceased to be one of the world's takers and become finally a giver, and so, in fact, has found the good part which nothing can take away, because one has no longer anything which is a mere private possession to be shared with no one, but lives wholly by bestowing.[1]

Certainly Christ expects those who claim to be his to follow in his steps, to adopt his standards of value, and to put their lives to the same uses he did. For the whole point of Christianity is a reaching out toward Christlikeness; and its end and goal is such Christlikeness attained. **If any one serves me, he must follow me; and where I am, there shall my servant be also; if any one serves me, the Father will honor him.** "Do you believe all this?" Rainy once interrupted himself in a sermon. "Do you take in these promises given to very you? Do you credit

[9] Bk. V, ch. vi, sec. 12.

[1] *The Faith of a Moralist* (London: Macmillan & Co., 1930), I, 314-15. Used by permission of the representatives of the author.

26 If any man serve me, let him follow me; and where I am, there shall also my servant be: if any man serve me, him will *my* Father honor.

nal life. 26 If any one serves me, he must follow me; and where I am, there shall my servant be also; if any one serves me, the Father will honor him.

---

as selfishness is its stultification (cf. Mark 8:35; Matt. 10:39; 16:25; Luke 9:24; 17:33). Service (vs. 26) involves discipleship; following Christ and serving him brings its reward in sharing the honor which the Father bestows on the Son (cf. Mark 8:34=Matt. 16:24=Luke 9:23; Mark 10:45=Matt. 20:28; cf. also Luke 22:27). These three verses suggest that the Cross is the symbol not only of man's salvation, but also of the Christian way of life.

---

that a day is coming when you will stand before the throne of God, and the angels will whisper together and say 'How like Christ he is'?" There are those, thank God, of whom it is not difficult to credit even that. For already they remind us of Jesus Christ; so that we look at them, and look again, and then from them to him, seeking an explanation of them there; feeling that they possess something they could not have had apart from him.

But of the mass of us is it not too true that our Christianity is a theory to be accepted, rather than a life to be daily and actively lived out? Apparently we have some vague idea that what Christ does for us and offers us is to enable us, while and though remaining what we are, to evade the consequences of being what we are, and to reap a destiny that is not naturally ours. Such people, naming the name of Christ, and not wishing to break with him, yet living after the world's fashion, are the greatest of all stumbling blocks to the progress of his kingdom. As Tennyson put it:

> For good ye are and bad, and like to coins,
> Some true, some light, but every one of you
> Stamp'd with the image of the King.[2]

So Nicholas Berdyaev looks at us oddly and tells us bluntly that our manner of it will not do. "There is no longer any room in the world for a merely external form of Christianity based upon custom. . . . The world is entering upon a period of catastrophe and crisis when we are being forced to take sides and in which a higher and more intense kind of spiritual life will be demanded from Christians." [3]

We have not grasped the meaning of this scripture **If any one serves me, the Father will honor him.** But how? And with what kind of honor? By giving us a place beside our Lord, the place that falls by right to one who has put on his nature and has learned to spend life after his way! It is, says Paul, because "he humbled himself, and became obedient unto death, even death on a cross" that "God has highly exalted him and bestowed on him the name which is above every name . . . in heaven and on earth and under the earth" (Phil. 2:8-10). If we wish to be where he is, or anywhere in his neighborhood, we can reach that only by traveling—a vast way behind the Master—in the same direction and by the same road. But in actual fact, do we want Christlikeness? And when we think out what it really means, are we willing to accept it? His may be the gallant use of life. That we can see. But it is so much cozier to shut ourselves into our familiar comforts. Sympathy hurts. Why then develop it, when with eyes averted, or that seeing do not see what we do not care to notice, we can pass by on the other side without such discomfort? If we do not care for Christlikeness, we do not need to take it. But we can gain it only by following Christ and using life after his fashion.

> If a man serve Me, him will My Father honour. Only by that He does not mean what lesser spirits mean. In the Old Testament, for instance, many even of the saints take it for granted that you can judge of a man's spiritual standing by the state of his bank book; and can safely assume that the good man will be rich, and that the rich man must be good; must be, they felt, for God is over all, and will, no doubt, shelter and shield and heap His benefits upon His own, and put to shame those who resist Him. As an exultant Psalmist sums it up, "Because he hath set his love upon me, therefore will I deliver him: I will set him on high, because he hath known my name." Yes, agrees the New Testament and leads us again to that little slope, and climbs it, and stands there with awed heart in the darkness, and looking up says solemnly, Because He hath set His love on Me and known My name, I have set Him on high.
>
> The honour that God offers us is this—that He will condescend to use us, lean upon us, call for our poor help, give us a real share in His own agony and saving of the sinful world. And Christ expects that that will, not scare us away, but thrill us, win us, . . . draw us irresistibly. Such faith has He in you and me.[4]

[2] "The Holy Grail," ll. 25-27.

[3] *Freedom and the Spirit*, p. 268.

[4] A. J. Gossip, "How Christ Won Through," *Expository Times*, XXXVII (1926), 504. Used by permission of T. & T. Clark, publishers.

27 Now is my soul troubled; and what shall I say? Father, save me from this hour: but for this cause came I unto this hour.

27 "Now is my soul troubled. And what shall I say? 'Father, save me from this hour'? No, for this purpose I have come to this

E. The Agony and the Voice (12:27-36*a*)

27-28. Neither the agony in Gethsemane nor the Transfiguration is recorded in this Gospel, but these verses offer the Johannine equivalent. **Now is my soul troubled** (cf. Pss. 31:9; 42:5; 55:4; Lam. 2:11) is closely parallel to Mark 14:33-34, and the question **What shall I say? "Father, save me from this hour"?** recalls Mark 14:35. The anguish is caused by the thought of approaching death, but the very conviction expressed in vss. 24-26 gives the answer to this question, **No, for this purpose I have come to this hour,** which is immediately followed by the prayer, **Father, glorify thy name** (vs. 28). This is essentially the same as the Marcan, "Yet not what I will, but what thou wilt." For the

When Ignatius died, so we are told, his followers in their grief were granted three visions of him. In the first he moved about among themselves, and took their hands in the familiar fashion they had known so long. In the second he had risen above them, and his hands were spread over them in blessing and intercession. But in the third they saw him farther off, sweat-bedewed, and in an agony, standing beside his Lord.[5]

27-36. ***Christ Thinks Aloud.***—But if as Christ looks back his heart exults and praises God, when he turns to meet what lies ahead the shadow of the Cross falls dark and forbidding on his path and on his mind. And with that there breaks from him a saying as profound and helpful to hard-pressed souls as almost anything even he ever uttered. And for this reason.

Charles Reade has a striking passage in which he reminds us that we see the great figures in human history only when, their minds made up, and their course set, and their resolution hardened and tempered, they move from triumph to triumph. It is not given us to witness their hesitations and uncertainties, or to overhear the mental struggles through which they passed in secret before they saw their way, and found their feet, and gained the insight and the courage they required.

But one of the characteristics of the Gospels, and that not the least helpful of them, is that from time to time we do come upon Jesus Christ in the privacy of his own soul; do overhear him thinking aloud, as if he had forgotten those around him, and were alone with God, feeling his way to the course required of him by the Father, and bracing and steadying himself to face it. All of the passages in which this is recorded are memorable. But this one much the most of all. For Jesus' courage is so calm, so sure, so seemingly inevitable, that we cannot even imagine him or it breaking down or failing. Even where we succeed, it is as a rule with much hard-breathing effort and desperate contorting of ourselves; but our Lord's triumph is so certain, looks so effortless and without any strain, that it seems easy and almost automatic. So that we might very well dismiss it as no doubt glorious, but as largely meaningless for us. For he is he, and we are only we; and between him and us there is a great gulf fixed. Where he can climb, sure of foot and firm of tread, we slither, and slip, and fall. And it is well and blessed to be made to realize that with him too it was a case not of *non posse peccare,* but of *posse non peccare;* that he had a heart human as our own; and had to fight what we must fight, where we must fight; and that too, using only the same weapons we are offered; that he came through with his unsullied honor only by reason of his faith in God and the indomitable gallantry of his own heart. For the glory of all glories in his victory, and what awakens hope in us in very deed, is that Jesus was no Achilles, dipped in the waters of immortality, invulnerable, and so easily rushing unafraid into the thickest of the fighting; but that, thank God, we have not a high priest who cannot be touched with the feeling of our infirmities; but "was in all points tempted like as we are, yet without sin" (Heb. 4:15).

There is a type of valor which, impressive though it may be, is largely animal, and that flows, mainly at least, from a source no higher than a dull insensitiveness of nature that cannot even imagine pain and mutilation until these horrors have actually struck one down; and even then feels them less acutely than does a more delicate spirit. Far nobler and more staggering is the courage of that last—shrinking, sensitive, foreseeing, and forefeeling all the grim and ghastly possibilities with a dreadful vividness, yet holding on indomitable. It was a man who had been mad, and in whose skies these black and threatening clouds kept gather-

[5] *Martyrdom of Ignatius* 7.

revelation of the Father's nature and purpose is the true meaning of the Incarnation, and this life is to culminate in the death on the Cross. It is this assurance which enables Jesus to bid his disciples, "Let not your hearts be troubled" (14:1, 27). To those familiar with the tradition of the Transfiguration preserved in the Synoptics, the Bath Qôl (see on 1:26), the **voice . . . from heaven,** might suggest the voice which said, "This is my beloved

---

ing again, who horribly though he feared them still faced them with his head up, and still entered them with this amazing feat of faith,

> Blind unbelief is sure to err,
> And scan his work in vain.
> God is his own interpreter,
> And he will make it plain.[6]

That is a faith beside which anything that has been asked of us and that we can show looks trivial.

So here, in this tremendous passage which sets down for us the very heart and soul of religion, and also that something in Christianity which inspires one to it, and enables one to reach it if he will. **Now is my soul troubled. And what shall I say? "Father, save me from this hour"? No, for this purpose I have come to this hour. Father, glorify thy name.** Supreme and final words that echo and re-echo through the heart! What deeps calling to deeps are in them! The natural shrinking of the human spirit; the quick resolute curbing of that, and the quiet laying of it aside; the certainty that in this appalling providence beginning to loom up, in it too there were meaning, and love, and God; the wholehearted committing of himself to God's purposes, keeping back nothing, asking only that God will deign to stoop and use him for his glory; and the rest he leaves with him. Is not that the very essence of religion? And is it not Christ's revelation of what God is really like, of how entirely trustworthy he is even where we cannot see and do not understand at all, and Christ's own example at such times in his own life, that enable us in some degree to climb toward it in our evil days, as we are wont to call them? Even so, it is sore and difficult for the mass of us. And Christ is not vexed with us for that: that when death threatens to break up our circle, the heart clings to its own; or that when health is taken, we let it go with fingers that relax their grip on it reluctantly. For his own soul was troubled on occasion, and he himself was sometimes for a moment staggered and less than sure what he should ask. But only for a moment.

And we must learn to pray his prayer, and mean it; begging not that we may escape what threatens us, but that we may see it through with honor; and may so bear ourselves that whatever befalls us, God may be glorified. And as Browning reminds us:

> We are his glory; and if we be glorious,
> Is not the thing achieved?[7]

For this purpose I have come to this hour. Grim though it looks, there is meaning in it, plan in it, love in it, God in it. When Philip Doddridge lost his little lass, he set down honestly:

> This day my heart hath been almost torn in pieces by sorrow; yet sorrow so softened and sweetened, that I number it among the best days of my life! . . . Doest thou well to be angry for the gourd? God knows I am not angry; but sorrowful He surely allows me to be. . . . Lord, give unto me a holy acquiescence of soul in Thee; and, now that my gourd is withered, shelter me under the shadow of Thy wings.[8]

Read again with thankfulness and reverence the noble letters[9] in which Samuel Johnson, with never a whimper of complaint or bleating of self-pity, faced the horrors of paralysis suddenly come upon him, and you will feel, as Augustine Birrell put it, "This is indeed tonic and bark for the mind."[1] Better still, turn to the entry Carlyle made in his diary that dreadful night when John Stuart Mill told him that the manuscript of *The French Revolution* Carlyle had lent him was burned to ashes.

> Oh, that I had faith! Oh! that I had! Then were there nothing too hard or heavy for me. Cry silently in thy inmost heart to God for it. Surely He will give it thee. At all events, it is as if my invisible schoolmaster had torn my copybook when I showed it, and said, "No, boy! Thou must write it better." What can I, sorrowing, do but obey—obey and think it the best? To work again; and, oh! may God be with me, for this earth is not friendly. On in His name![2]

We come of a great breed who faced their difficulties staggered but unbroken. And we

[6] William Cowper, "God moves in a mysterious way."

[7] "Paracelsus," Part IV.

[8] Cf., *The Correspondence and Diary of Philip Doddridge* (London: Colburn & Bentley, 1831), V, 361-63.

[9] Letter to Mrs. Thrale, dated June 19, 1783, in Boswell, *Life of Johnson.*

[1] *Obiter Dicta*, 2nd Ser. (New York: Charles Scribner's Sons, 1900), p. 117.

[2] J. A. Froude, *Thomas Carlyle, A History of His Life in London* (New York: Charles Scribner's Sons, 1884), I, 25.

28 Father, glorify thy name. Then came there a voice from heaven, *saying,* I have both glorified *it,* and will glorify *it* again.

hour. 28 Father, glorify thy name." Then a voice came from heaven, "I have glori-

---

Son; listen to him" (Mark 9:7). It now says, **I have glorified it, and I will glorify it again.** Thus past and future are united, even as the Father and the Son are one. Hitherto God has glorified his name through the works of the Son (cf. 5:36; 9:3-4; 11:4). He will now do so through the death and resurrection of the Son, and the mighty works which will follow in the power of the Spirit (cf. 13:31-32; 14:12; 5:20).

---

must not fail or shame it, whining and sniveling when some grave call is made upon our faith and courage. And if we ask him, the Lord Christ, who faced more than all the others had to do, will give us of his spirit, that we too may play our part with gallantry.

28. ***God's Judgment on Christ's Mission.***—As the fourth and final witness for the essential success of Christ's mission, even though the mass of men had held aloof, indifferent and unconcerned, or at least unwon, the evangelist dares to call the Lord God himself. **Then a voice came from heaven, "I have glorified it, and I will glorify it again."**

No conception of God has so stormed the heart of man as that we gain by looking steadily at Jesus Christ and taking in that he is the very image of God's person, the open expression of his word and thought and mind, the surest indication of how he feels toward us, and what in himself he is, in his essential character and nature. **I have glorified it;** and indeed it is so. What Christ had been and taught even up to this point has revolutionized our human understanding about God. Yet if in John 12 Christ had died peacefully in his bed, and there had been no Calvary, how much would have been lost to us. Already God had glorified his name through Christ, bringing home to us, to an extent of which no one had ever dreamed, the mystery of the divine sympathy and generosity. For men felt confident that they could safely argue from Christ to God. If Christ so spent his life for others, then so must God; or else humanity at its highest in Christ would excel deity —which did not stagger the Greek mind, but which to the Jew was a thought unthinkable. Yet after all that, there was more to come; more, and still better. **I will glorify it again,** said God. And so it has proved. What as yet lay ahead—the upper room, the Agony, the Cross and Passion and rising—these have almost infinitely deepened and brought home to us what we had glimpsed in our Lord's character and teaching.

For what is it in Christianity that has made so immense an impression on countless minds? Why has it survived when other mighty faiths which at one time raced across the earth and seemed destined to world dominion are now dead and buried and forgotten, and mean nothing whatever to the most of us, like a word of some obsolete language, only a soundless sound, conveying no idea to the mind? It is of course because Christianity had Christ and the others had not. True. Yet what is it in Christ that has proved so effective? Everything about him has added its quota to his influence. The Incarnation, with its stunning revelation of the unthinkable magnanimity and generosity of God; the healing ministry, with its proof of the divine sympathy and understanding; the words he spoke, blowing away the thick and choking fogs of our grievous misunderstanding, and bringing us out into the sunshine of the glorious reality and truth. But does not the chief power and appeal of Christianity lie in the twofold discovery it made through Christ?

First, that discomfited men and women, set down in what looks to them to be a wild and disorderly world, discouraged by their endless struggles with difficulties that they never fully master, and hurt by sufferings and sorrows that they cannot evade, and assuming that the God who set them in this stress and strain is himself out of it all, and far above their troubles, suddenly found that he was not out of it all, but in it with them, bearing and suffering along with them, till things are righted; and whereupon, fortified by their realization that they have a great Companion, they turned and faced their problems with a new courage and a new success?

As Pringle-Pattison put it:

> It must be confessed that the speculative truth expressed in the central doctrine of the new religion has seldom been taken seriously—taken in bitter earnest. . . . [Yet] what was the secret of Christianity, the new interpretation of life by which it has conquered the world? . . . It was the lesson of self sacrifice, of life for others, precisely through which, nevertheless, the truest and intensest realization of the self was to be attained—in the Pauline phrase, dying to live, in the words of Jesus, losing one's life to find it. . . . It is the final abandonment of the hedonistic ideal, through the recognition of the

29 The people therefore that stood by, and heard *it,* said that it thundered: others said, An angel spake to him.

fied it, and I will glorify it again." 29 The crowd standing by heard it and said that it had thundered. Others said, "An angel

---

29-36*a*. Three interpretations were given to this voice. Some dismissed it as a natural phenomenon. Others, remembering such O.T. stories as Gen. 21:17; 22:11, thought that an angel had spoken to Jesus. Jesus himself declares that the voice was not spoken to comfort him, but was for the sake of the people. The hour is one of crisis for him, but no less for the world. This is the hour of judgment and of salvation. (*a*) **Now shall the ruler of this world be cast out.** That title (cf. 14:30; 16:11) refers to the devil, as the personification of evil, for in later Judaism, especially through the apocalyptic writers, an

---

inherent emptiness of the self centered life. . . . If this is the deepest insight into human life, must we not also recognize it as the open secret of the universe? . . . No God, or Absolute, existing in solitary bliss and perfection, but a God who lives in the perpetual giving of himself, who shares the life of his finite creatures, bearing in and with them the whole burden of their finitude, their sinful wanderings and sorrows, and the suffering without which they cannot be made perfect.[3]

Secondly, even more, that souls, unhappy about a sinfulness and moral failure which they might hate and against which they might struggle, but which they could not master nor shake off, and who felt miserably that because of this unworthiness of theirs God in his holiness must be estranged from them, and hostile toward them, found with a wondering amazement that their sorry plight, so far from hardening God against them, had touched him to a divine pity for them, a pity ready and eager to go any length, and to make any sacrifice, and to meet any cost, if thereby he can help and save them.

And is it not the cross of Christ that above everything else has made us sure of this that sounds too good to be true? So Browning thought when he made David say of God,

Would I suffer for him that I love? So wouldst thou —so wilt thou!
So shall crown thee the topmost, ineffablest, uttermost crown—[4]

So Christ himself felt when he said with confidence, "And I, when I am lifted up from the earth, will draw all men to myself" (vs. 32; see Expos., vss. 31-33).

29-30. ***The Mystery of Common Things.***—Of all which there is no immediate evidence in the reaction of his first hearers to these profundities that Christ was uttering. When the voice came from heaven, **The crowd standing by heard it and said that it had thundered. Others**—apparently a minority—**said, "An angel has spoken to him."** For my part, to be honest, I imagine that had I been there, I too would have assumed that there had been a stray peal of thunder, and have left it at that. Yet—.

Everywhere there are always these two types of mind—the one quick and ready with easy surface explanations, proud of its logic and its balance and what it calls its sturdy common sense. This causes that, it says; and there is nothing more to it than that; and so saying, puts the thing aside as fully grasped and understood. That is a mental attitude, the sheer stupidity of which maddened Keats.

There was an awful rainbow once in heaven:
We know her woof, her texture; she is given
In the dull catalogue of common things.[5]

The other type moves about this common earth of ours with an awed heart and marveling eyes that grow worshipful as they look. For always mystery envelops them; and always wonders beyond fathoming keep leaping out of the most ordinary things and stare them in the face; till the most marvelous explanations seem the likeliest, and what is needed to account even for the most common and prosaic facts. A weed springs up by the roadside. And you and I look at it, and pass on. We see no mystery at all. A seed was borne here on the wind, happened to lodge, took root, sprang up, and that is all. Yes, that is all! Yet Tennyson, looking at what to our crass minds is so prosaically simple, found himself carried out into vast deeps in which his feet could find no bottom at all.

Flower in the crannied wall,
I pluck you out of the crannies,
I hold you here, root and all, in my hand,
Little flower—but *if* I could understand
What you are, root and all, and all in all,
I should know what God and man is.[6]

Some said, "It's thundering," and went their way, and thought never another thought about

[3] *The Idea of God* (Oxford: Clarendon Press, 1920), pp. 409-11. Used by permission.
[4] "Saul," st. xviii.

[5] "Lamia," Part II.
[6] "Flower in the Crannied Wall."

elaborate demonology corresponded to a developed angelology. The Pauline teaching saw in the cross of Christ the instrument by which the empire of evil in the supraterrestrial sphere had received its mortal injury (I Cor. 2:6-8; Col. 2:14-15). This was not without precedent in the teaching of Jesus (Matt. 12:25-28; Luke 10:18), who saw in his works of exorcism a sign that the kingdom of God was already present. (*b*) **I, when I am lifted**

---

it. Yet others plainly heard an angel speaking to him; had no doubt of that at all. And surely if this latter explanation is the true one, if the world is really full of miracles for those with eyes to see, it is pathetic enough to miss it all, and go trudging stolidly on our dull way without a suspicion that they are there; to mistake angel voices for the growl and rumbling mutter of a distant storm; to have God himself beside us, and see nothing except empty air!

Yet is it not the true explanation? Can we not hold it as an axiom that so amazing is this life of ours that a simple explanation of anything at all rules itself out as at least suspect, and probably hopelessly inadequate and wrong? "A fine starry night," one man says with a casual, unlingering glance at the broad skies above him, and with that plunges into chatter about mundane things—last Saturday's game or some spicy bit of social news. Yet the man at his side perhaps hears not one word of it. For he is far away, out in infinite reaches of unthinkable space, amid mighty suns heaped upon suns, and systems piled upon systems, and endless wastes of nebulae, those humming workshops of Almighty God, where tonight and every night, from the beginning to the end of time, the mind and hands of the Eternal are fashioning new worlds, new suns, new universes, hour by hour. To the one it is only some gleaming spots of light; but to eyes that can see, all these immensities and tremendousnesses lie hidden away in and behind the familiar sight. So peer beneath the surface of the simplest thing, and before you understand it, it will lead you straight as an arrow to the feet of God, will need him to account for it.

> Seeing, hearing, feeling are miracles, and each part and tag of me is a miracle,
>
> . . . .
>
> And the narrowest hinge in my hand puts to scorn all machinery,
>
> . . . .
>
> And a mouse is miracle enough to stagger sextillions of infidels.[7]

Just thundering? No. There is more in it than that; always much more. A little soul begins its life. And who except a fool is satisfied with the poor stuttering explanations of that marvelous phenomenon that science gives? Beside a cradle, mystery engulfs us, sucks us down and down, till we are overwhelmed and drowned. Looking at this new personality, shut in there alone within itself, at this new character already partly formed, from its first hour a thing distinct, and by itself, who can help musing over what strange unknown seas, from what far and adventurous voyaging, this little vessel has drawn to shore; awed by the feel of God's own fingers touching ours as his own hands lay this new life tenderly in our keeping? Thunder? Ah, no! There is far more in it than that. And, standing there, some hear the angels plainly.

Or we look down upon our dead; all in a moment cut off from them by that impassable gulf; all in a moment shut out from what had been ours for years and years; all in a moment in a chilly desolate place. For the heart that loved us is cold now; the brain that thought and planned for us is still. And science tells us briskly what has happened. But who is willing to accept its superficial explanation? It is not just thundering; and death is not just death.

As with the stars, so here. The eyes that see and the heart that knows find hidden away in it marvels on marvels, other worlds, eternities, infinities. And this thing, like a glass, brings them all very near. And blown back to us, we can hear the song of the redeemed, quite clearly, standing here.

And this whole life of ours, that begins in mystery and ends in mystery, that comes from God and goes to God, is full always both of it and him. Take your daily round, what is it? Why, not much, you say. Only the usual run of little nothings—teaching the rudiments to restless children, bustling to and fro about the house, off to the office of a morning, and so home again at night. That is my life! Not much excitement in it, is there? Day just follows day; and one jogs on, contentedly and happily enough.

That is your reading of it; that is all you see in it. It is not Jesus Christ's. These matters of which you speak are to him only the stage on which a tremendous drama is being played out to its consummation. Something, for instance, goes wrong in the office; or at home you are flustered and irritated and upset. A stupid clerk annoys you; or you yourself, the stupid clerk, exasperate your employer. A careless shopkeeper or tradesman gets on your nerves, and

[7] Walt Whitman, "Song of Myself," sts. xxiv, xxxi.

30 Jesus answered and said, This voice came not because of me, but for your sakes.

has spoken to him." 30 Jesus answered, "This voice has come for your sake, not

up from the earth, will draw all men to myself. The evangelist's comment (see Intro., p. 439) explains this as referring to the Cross (see also 3:14; 8:28). The **all men** corresponds to the "much fruit" of vs. 24. Yet in this work of salvation the principle of judgment operates (cf. 6:37-40). The gift of eternal life is conditioned by faith. (Two important MSS, א and D, with some support in Latin authorities, read "all things" for **all men,** but the thought here is of the universal range of the Atonement, not of the cosmic significance of Christ, as in Col. 1:16-17.) The crowd meanwhile is perplexed by this utterance. Catching at the words **lifted up** they object that according to **the law**—i.e., the scriptures—**the Christ remains forever. How can you say that the Son of man**

you are tempted to grow irritable, to let your temper have its head. The words indeed are all but out. But you restrain yourself, say nothing, and the little gust blows past. And that night, when they ask you if anything special happened today, "No," you say, "nothing." Yet Jesus, watching, saw principalities and powers fling themselves upon you, resolute to rush your soul. But God was there, there in your room, throwing his grace about you in defense, and meeting power with power, and strength with greater strength. Some said that it was only thundering. Yet think it out, and it was that that happened. When you go back to the familiar spot, might you not well tread softly, as on holy ground? As R. L. Stevenson once wrote to his friend Baildon in Edinburgh, from the far South Seas, "Go the first grey east-windy day into the Caledonian Station, if it looks at all as it did of yore. I met Satan there."[8]

Or a joy blossoms in your life. It was not chance-blown. It was God's gift to you. Or trouble comes. You are not fit, are ill and laid aside. And we have ready our glib explanations. You have been overworking, we say; you are tired out; a chill has settled down on you. And no doubt these are grim realities and very genuine secondary causes. Yet Al Ghazzali, the great Moslem, tells us how he was wont to listen smilingly to the physicians and the learned chemists with their reasons for each of his ailments.

> They are doubtless right, each in his own particular branch of knowledge. Yet it does not occur to them that the Almighty has a concern for the welfare of my soul, and has produced in me a condition such that I may turn away from the world to him, my Maker. They do not see that illness is a cord of love, by which God draws his saints nearer to himself. For illness itself is one of those experiences by which men arrive at the knowledge of God; as saith the prophet, "sicknesses also are my servants, and are attached to my chosen."[9]

[8] *Letters,* III, 284.

[9] *Confessions.*

Yet some said, "It thundered." Shallow fools! And only one here and one there saw deeper and knew better.

Or take it of our sins. Nowadays they do not vex us much. No doubt there are tremendous sayings in the Gospels that regard them very seriously. But either we pass these by or else frankly we do not credit them, do not believe that they are true for us, that sins like ours can bring such dismal retribution on us. Spurts of temper, hot words, and a lack of thoughtfulness—to relate such trivialities as these to those grim passages about the outer darkness and the like were surely wild exaggeration and an abuse of words. So we say complacently. Yet are these things as trivial as we think? Judge for yourself! Yonder is the Cross. You see how the Lord hangs upon it; how tired, and hurt, and wounded, and heartbroken. And that is the perfect revelation of how the Almighty's heart is affected every hour and every day by those so-called trivial sins of ours. Trivial? When they hurt and break God's heart like that! Never an evil thought is harbored but a shadow gathers around the throne. Never an angry word escapes us but God is stabbed by it. It is not the little thing we thought it, but grim and horrible and full of terror. Let it go! If not for your own sake, then for God's. For surely, surely we will not knowingly cause him such pain as that.

Or take it of forgiveness. How lightly we esteem the pardoning grace of God, how indifferently we stretch out our hands and take it as the merest thing of course. We sin; impudently, flagrantly, deliberately. And then we come to ourselves, and kneel in prayer, and ask forgiveness. And God gives it every time. And we rise up, and go our way, not in the least surprised, and but little grateful or impressed. And yet look at it more closely. Free though it is to you, do you not see what it costs God—that gift of his we take for granted—his all, his Son—God's all, God's Son! Look at it more closely and you will cherish it more jealously,

31 Now is the judgment of this world: now shall the prince of this world be cast out.

32 And I, if I be lifted up from the earth, will draw all *men* unto me.

for mine. 31 Now is the judgment of this
world, now shall the ruler of this world
be cast out; 32 and I, when I am lifted up
from the earth, will draw all men to my-

must be lifted up? Who is this Son of man? There is no place in the O.T. where it is said expressly that the Messiah will reign forever upon earth. It is rather an inference from such passages as Pss. 89:4; 110:4; Isa. 9:7; Ezek. 37:25; Dan. 7:14. It is to be observed that Jesus said, **When I am lifted up** (vs. 32), but his hearers substitute **the Christ, the Son of man.** This assumes that the words in vs. 23 had been heard by the crowd, or that

with an awed heart, and something like fear in your eyes. No. They are wrong who tell us it is only thundering. For life is full of mysteries. And not one thing, when we examine it, but leaves us on our faces at the feet of God.

31-33. ***The Attractive Power of the Cross.***—About this daring saying of the Master (vs. 32) one fact stands out in bold relief: that this is no longer theory. It has become history. And Christ's impossible-looking faith has been astonishingly justified.

Whether it is an authentic saying of his as some, e.g., Newman thought, or not (and some, e.g., Rosebery, have questioned it), Napoleon has been confidently quoted as having said at St. Helena, looking back over his life, that Alexander, Caesar, and he had founded mighty empires upon force, and they had vanished; whereas Christ had built his upon love, and today millions would die for him. Which, whether Napoleon said it or not, is true and undeniable.

For that ghastly scene on Calvary, that horrible death with every aggravation of agony and contempt of one hanging there naked, tortured, pitilessly taunted by remorseless and exultant enemies, ought to have been the sorry, even the sordid, ending of the gallant if quixotic adventure of a brave heart that had dared everything and yet had utterly and absolutely failed. Yet somehow it has not been so. Far otherwise! And here too Christ was right.

It is not for nothing nor by accident that the Christian faith has adopted as its symbol that cross of shame, that hangman's gibbet, around which at the first a few faithful souls clustered, stunned and in despair, with not even the feeblest star showing so much as the faintest glimmering in the utter blackness of their skies; and all hope out and dead, stone dead. For is it not through it supremely that Christ has conquered and keeps conquering? No doubt it is around the manger rather than the Cross that the Eastern Church gathers with awed and grateful hearts; that comes first for them, that most fills them with amazement. No doubt it is the open grave that marks Christ's triumph, and that gives the final proof of his sufficiency as a Savior. But multitudes standing with Paul on Calvary, feeling that this was undergone for very them, that "he loved me and gave himself for me," have not been able to hold back their hearts, which broke away from them and ran to Christ crying out with decision, "We will have this man to rule over us."

So it is that in the main Christ's kingdom has crept and run and leaped out and still out, farther and farther, till it has reached the very edges of the world. And what can halt its progress, or challenge that exultant tribute, "Thy kingdom is an everlasting kingdom, and thy dominion endureth forever"? Or even begin to refute this daring verdict of the Master, when with everything still to do, and nothing as yet, so it seemed, accomplished, he declared with confidence, **Now is the judgment of this world, now shall the ruler of this world be cast out.** For a new power and spirit has come into the world, which will oppose that ruler face to face, and will alienate his subjects from him, detaching more and more, till what today looks so impregnable, immovable, eternal, will sway and totter and crash in a rumble of ruins.

For while, impudently, men can refuse the will of the All Wise, and shaking off his restraining hand, can fling stubbornly on their own way; and petty creatures though they may be, can face the thunderbolts of the Almighty, still rebellious and uncowed and defiant—what are we to do with this strange God who meets our sin with grace, and added sin with added grace; who gives his all, even himself, for us? It is desperately hard for self to hold its own against such a claimant for our hearts as that. And so in heaven and on earth a multitude uncountable keeps crying, "To him who loves us, and has freed us from our sins by his blood, . . . to him be glory and dominion for ever and ever" (Rev. 1:5-6). "Believe me," said Christ with assurance, "men and women may listen to my teaching and not be much impressed; they may accept my gifts and quite forget the Giver;

33 This he said, signifying what death he should die.

34 The people answered him, We have heard out of the law that Christ abideth for ever: and how sayest thou, The Son of man must be lifted up? who is this Son of man?

self." 33 He said this to show by what death he was to die. 34 The crowd answered him, "We have heard from the law that the Christ remains forever. How can you say that the Son of man must be lifted

---

his hearers remembered the prediction of 8:28. The reader remembers 3:14, and the equation of **lifted up** and "glorified." Jesus closes the discussion with an appeal to his audience to seize the day of their opportunity. The language echoes the discourse given at the feast of Tabernacles (8:12) and of words already spoken to his disciples (9:4-5; 11:9-10). This is the crisis, the short testing time, and the warning is summed up in the pregnant words, **While you have the light, believe in the light that you may become sons of light.** So far Jesus has not directly answered the crowd's questions. His opponents were quoting ironically titles that he had applied to himself. Jesus therefore takes up another title he had claimed, "the light of the world" (8:12), and gives warning that this light will not shine in their midst indefinitely. Now is the day of opportunity while it is still possible for them to see the truth revealed in him, and after accepting

---

but if they see me dying for them, I win. **I, when I am lifted up from the earth, will draw all men to myself."**

Yet musing over this confident prophecy, it grows disquietingly clear that there are bleak facts in plenty which would seem to disprove and deride it, which would bring us almost to dismiss Christ's optimistic outlook as only a dream of the heart with little substance and reality in it. Has he not gravely overestimated the nobility of human nature? Has he not pitched his appeal to us much too high, so that it goes clean over the heads of most of us? For look out on the world around us, untiringly busy and eager over so many things that it accounts momentous, and what place has Christ in most people's lives? **The ruler of this world** has gifts to offer they find more attractive and compelling—solid, substantial, worth-while things; and they choose him, and follow after him, remain unshaken in their allegiance to him. Whereas Christ and the things for which he stands have little interest for them. The story of his cross no longer holds, or stabs, or thrills; it has become "a twice-told tale," heard by "the dull ear of a drowsy man," with a wandering half-attention, or with positive boredom. And when Christ calls to them from his cross, "Is it nothing to you, all ye that pass by?" they pause a moment, and consider; and looking up into his face they answer, "Well, really, not much," and turn upon their heels and stroll away. Such facts are facts. And each of us had better consider how we stand to them.

Yet there are others, proving that the old power is not lost; but that the Cross is as attractive and effective as ever. More so indeed. Tertullian boasted that in his day the faith was sweeping everywhere to victory. Then too they had much to dismay and daunt them. Yet "Even the islands have heard of it," he claimed triumphantly. And so they had. But never in the whole course of its long history has Christianity spread so fast and far into new territory as in the last century, and the pace is still quickening.

Many things around us are disquieting and grievously disappointing. look, indeed, as if much of the world had tired of Christ and flung away from him. For the tides flow; and the tides ebb. But

> . . . while the tired waves, vainly breaking,
> Seem here no painful inch to gain,
> Far back, through creeks and inlets making,
> Comes silent, flooding in, the main.[1]

The Cross still triumphs. And Christ still rides on, irresistible as ever.

34-36. ***The Only Road to Spiritual Progress.***—Later, when Christ was speaking to them of his death, the crowd, apparently not much moved or impressed, brought things back to earth with a dunt by questions which no doubt seemed to them momentous, but which to us now have no great weight, and appear, if not irrelevant, at least somewhat prosaic. Yet they were natural enough. For we are all straitly imprisoned in our particular and customary modes of thought. Rarely can we escape from them, or even see out past them. Jesus kept speaking of dying, and of a horrible and accursed death at that; yet he seemed to be claiming to be the

[1] Arthur Hugh Clough, "Say Not the Struggle Naught Availeth."

35 Then Jesus said unto them, Yet a little while is the light with you. Walk while ye have the light, lest darkness come upon you: for he that walketh in darkness knoweth not whither he goeth.

36 While ye have light, believe in the light, that ye may be the children of light. These things spake Jesus, and departed, and did hide himself from them.

up? Who is this Son of man?" 35 Jesus said to them, "The light is with you for a little longer. Walk while you have the light, lest the darkness overtake you; he who walks in the darkness does not know where he goes. 36 While you have the light, believe in the light, that you may become sons of light."

When Jesus had said this, he departed

this revelation, to take their bearings and follow the direction as he points the way. Otherwise the night of lost opportunity and of blank despair will suddenly surprise them. By trusting themselves to this guiding light, their own character will take on the quality of light. That is the meaning of the Hebrew idiom, **sons of light,** as "sons of God" means those who bear their Father's likeness (Matt. 5:9), or "sons of disobedience" (Eph. 5:6) means men who disobey the commands of God, in contrast to "children of light," whose whole manner of life can bear the searchlight of truth.

F. Unbelief and Rejection (12:36*b*-43)

36*b*-43. As in 8:59, Jesus **departed and hid himself from them.** This marks the close of the public ministry of Jesus. Henceforth the evangelist describes the closing stage of the intimate relationship with the disciples before the last tragic scenes of the Betrayal, Trial, and Crucifixion. But this chapter closes with two brief statements. The first explains the unbelief of most of those who should have accepted his message. The other gives a summary of the doctrine of the crisis, the theme of many of the temple discourses.

The problem of the unbelief of the Jewish leaders and their rejection of the Christ was a cause of perplexity to the faithful and a weapon in the hands of the critics of the early church. The Christian apology can be traced in Mark 4:12 (cf. Matt. 13:13-15; Acts 28:25-27), and still more in Rom. 9–11. Neither the number nor the character of the signs which had marked the ministry of Jesus evoked faith. Why not? The answer was found in two passages in the prophecies of Isaiah. The last of the songs of the suffering Servant (Isa. 53:1) was interpreted messianically by the primitive church: **Lord, who has believed our report?** So also was the account of the call of Isaiah, with its stern charge to the prophet. But whereas Isaiah was commanded, "Make the heart of this people fat, and make their ears heavy, and shut their eyes; lest . . ." (Isa. 6:10)), these words are

Christ. And everybody knew that the Christ would abide forever. **Who is this Son of man?**

That is a question which is still debated. For scholars are not clear about the answer even yet. Some, founding upon certain passages, see in the phrase a figure of lowliness; some, who are perhaps nearer the truth, basing themselves upon other scriptures, find in the words a title of august dignity and honor. On this much might be said. But at the time Christ would not let his hearers turn aside to theological discussions, to hanging about on the environs of religion, but spoke with gravity and a blunt directness straight to their individual consciences. And us too, no doubt, he would wish to keep to the main point.

It is indeed a first law of life, of the utmost gravity and moment, and one which all experience corroborates, that he enunciates for us in vss. 35, 36. Primarily he was speaking of himself, and of the urgency of at once closing with him, since dallying and delay can mean that the opportunity for that may fade away and at last go out. But the same law holds good in many things—the pursuit of truth, sensitiveness of conscience, fellowship with the Lord God. Use such light as you have, walk in it (and, as it has been said, the dark ages were not so wholly dark but that those dwelling in them could always see their next step!), believe in it, be loyal to it and that dim light that you have will grow and brighten, till, the darkness past for you, you will be **sons of light,** living in the sunshine, and in yourselves grown luminous by a reflected radiance, illuminating others round about you. But stubbornly refuse or neglect a duty which you know to be a duty; or keep on committing, consciously and with deliberation, what you are well aware is for you sin; and in time conscience will lose heart, grow tamed and

37 ¶ But though he had done so many miracles before them, yet they believed not on him:

38 That the saying of Esaias the prophet might be fulfilled, which he spake, Lord, who hath believed our report? and to whom hath the arm of the Lord been revealed?

39 Therefore they could not believe, because that Esaias said again,

and hid himself from them. 37 Though he
had done so many signs before them, yet
they did not believe in him; 38 it was that
the word spoken by the prophet Isaiah
might be fulfilled:

"Lord, who has believed our report,
and to whom has the arm of the Lord
been revealed?"

39 Therefore they could not believe. For
Isaiah again said,

---

written here as God's action: **He has blinded their eyes . . ."** (vs. 40). This unbelief was the fulfillment of prophecy (vs. 38), **Therefore they could not believe** (vs. 39). Further (vs. 41) this prophecy was given as the result of a vision which accompanied Isaiah's consecration: **Isaiah said this because he saw his glory and spoke of him.** (This is the better-attested reading. For **because** [ὅτι] some authorities read "when" [ὅτε].) The evangelist declared "No one has ever seen God" (1:18). He was probably well aware of the rendering in the Targ. of Isa. 6:1, "I saw the glory of the Lord." He would therefore regard this theophany as a vision of the pre-existent Logos, who in his incarnate life revealed the divine glory. In the N.T., words which in the O.T. were written about the Lord are without embarrassment applied to Jesus. This whole passage seems to suggest again the Johannine doctrine of predestination. Yet vs. 42 shows that **many even of the authorities believed in him.** The Johannine doctrine carries on the O.T. teaching that in the historical chain of cause and effect every result follows a divine purpose. In the historical revelation of God in Christ his life and death confront men with the demand for a decision for or against him. The refusal to recognize him is sin. "That sin causes a

---

broken; until gradually its imperious authority will die to a mild, almost apologetic, whisper, hardly to be termed a protest, and then to silent acquiescence in what it has learned it cannot prevent. At which people may smile complacently, seeing in all this merely a proof that they have wisely laid aside their first impossible ideals, like childish toys that they have outgrown now that they have learned to know the world and to deal with it as it is. And yet, often may it not rather be the fulfillment in them of that eerie foreboding of the prophet, when with assurance he tells us that he heard the Lord God himself saying over a people with whom he had mercifully striven long and hard to hold them from the ruin they insisted upon courting, "Ephraim is joined to idols: let him alone" (Hos. 4:17)?

Walk while you have the light, lest the darkness overtake you; he who walks in the darkness does not know where he goes. While you have the light, believe in the light, that you may become sons of light. That is the road that leads from less to more; and in the end to the heights. And there is no other. As Bunyan has it:

> Then said Evangelist, pointing with his finger over a very wide field, Do you see yonder Wicket-gate? (Matt. vii.-13, 14). The man said, No. Then said the other, Do you see yonder shining light? (Ps. cxix.105; 2 Pet. i.19). He said, I think I do. Then said Evangelist, Keep that light in your eye, and go up directly thereto, so shalt thou see the gate; at which, when thou knockest, it shall be told thee what thou shalt do.[2]

37-41. ***But Does God Blind Men's Eyes?***—Finally the evangelist, summing up the outcome of Christ's ministry, sets it down with a blunt frankness that in spite of the wonder of his words and his innumerable kindnesses and the many signs that he had done for them, **they did not believe in him**—a fact so staggering to the author himself that he accounts for it by an explanation even more staggering, quoting from Isaiah the audacious words,

> **He has blinded their eyes and hardened their heart,**
> **lest they should see with their eyes and perceive with their heart,**
> **and turn for me to heal them.**

So that those who so glibly criticize Calvin have to deal not only with him but with this evangelist, and with Isaiah, and with many another scripture writer who dared to face the grim and puzzling facts in this difficult life of ours; facts which do not disappear because others, resolutely shutting their eyes tight

[2] *Pilgrim's Progress,* Part I.

40 He hath blinded their eyes, and hardened their heart; that they should not see with *their* eyes, nor understand with *their* heart, and be converted, and I should heal them.

41 These things said Esaias, when he saw his glory, and spake of him.

42 ¶ Nevertheless among the chief rulers also many believed on him; but because of the Pharisees they did not confess *him,* lest they should be put out of the synagogue:

40 "He has blinded their eyes and hardened their heart,
lest they should see with their eyes and perceive with their heart,
and turn for me to heal them."
41 Isaiah said this because he saw his glory
and spoke of him. 42 Nevertheless many
even of the authorities believed in him, but
for fear of the Pharisees they did not
confess it, lest they should be put out of the

---

blindness of the soul, a moral insensibility to spiritual truths, is a law of the natural, that is of the Divine, order" (Bernard, *Gospel According to St. John,* II, 451). As in the days of Isaiah, so during the lifetime of Jesus, the divine message was spurned. **They could not believe** (vs. 39). **Nevertheless many . . . believed in him** (vs. 42). Even those who did believe, like Nicodemus (3:1; 7:50; 19:39) and Joseph of Arimathea (19:38), were daunted by the Pharisees, and the threat of excommunication (cf. 9:22). The severe judgment of vs. 43 is an echo of 5:41, 44. Once more (as in 8:30-31; see Exeg.) we are reminded of the two kinds of belief. There is an inward conviction, a mental judgment,

---

against what they do not want to see, maintain doggedly that they are not there.

This is not an awkward, outgrown, uncomfortable scripture to be kept hidden and well in shadow, a thing to be explained away. It is an honest facing of the realities, of which account must be taken. Why are the mass of Hindus Hindus at all? (Or for that matter, why are the mass of Christians Christians?) Is it not because they were set down in a Hindu atmosphere, where of necessity they breathed in from their earliest years the Hindu view of life, of God, of what makes holiness; absorbed it, took it for granted, perhaps never even realized that any other was held or could be held by a reasonable mind: so that only those among them who possess a more than ordinarily adventurous spirit are the least likely to be able to see out beyond their own familiar doctrines and conventions, or to want to do so; and even fewer to be willing to close with a new, alien, unaccustomed way of life and thought?

They did not choose the environment in which they find themselves; God set them there, the very God who wills not that any man should perish, as this evangelist is foremost in declaring; and so setting them,

> **. . . blinded their eyes and hardened their heart,**
> **lest they should see with their eyes and perceive with their heart,**
> **and turn for me to heal them.**

Do not the words fit with a literal exactness?

Or, Emerson tells us that every one of us would have been markedly different from what we are if we had been born ten years earlier or later than we were. This startling sounding saying—not to haggle over a year or two more or less—is absolutely and most surely true. Each generation finds itself in a new world of its own, in many ways quite different from that of any other generation that has ever been or ever will be; a world that has its own habits, ways, ideals, standards, to which those who live in it conform without thinking, as a matter of course, almost automatically. And not one in a hundred, born then, does not come true to the prevalent type, or fails to reproduce in great degree the spirit of the day. God, by setting them in a particular age, has largely determined how the mass of them will live and think. For they will nearly inevitably be carried along by the crowd around them, instinctively keeping in step with them, doing what they do, being what they are, using their molds of thought.

So this evangelist can account for Christ's failure to sweep the land and storm all hearts only by assuming that the habits of the time, the doctrines in which these people had been reared from infancy, the religion they possessed—God-given though that was, however much men might have mutilated and contaminated it—seemed good enough to them, and blinded them to the value of the vastly better things Christ offered them.

42-43. ***Being Praised by God.***—Still, **Many even of the authorities believed in him; but**

43 For they loved the praise of men more than the praise of God.

44 ¶ Jesus cried and said, He that believeth on me, believeth not on me, but on him that sent me.

45 And he that seeth me seeth him that sent me.

46 I am come a light into the world, that whosoever believeth on me should not abide in darkness.

47 And if any man hear my words, and believe not, I judge him not: for I came not to judge the world, but to save the world.

synagogue; 43 for they loved the praise of
men more than the praise of God.
44 And Jesus cried out and said, "He
who believes in me, believes not in me but
in him who sent me. 45 And he who sees
me sees him who sent me. 46 I have come
as light into the world, that whoever be-
lieves in me may not remain in darkness.
47 If any one hears my sayings and does not
keep them, I do not judge him; for I did
not come to judge the world but to save

---

which is good so far as it goes; but it has not yet become an act of faith, which ventures wholly in the sphere of obedience. We have already seen (3:36) that in the Johannine teaching the opposite of "believing in the Son" is "to disobey the Son." Intellectual assent is not enough.

G. Judgment by the Word (12:44-50)

This section opens with the statement **And Jesus cried out and said.** But as the previous section (vs. 36*b*) opened with the formula "When Jesus had said this, he departed and hid himself from them," we may conclude that these verses consist of the evangelist's brief summary of the public teaching of Jesus. The main thoughts are given, together with the parallels in this Gospel.

44-50. Belief in Jesus is belief in the Sender (cf. 5:36-37; 7:16; 8:19, 42; 13:20). The vision of Jesus (vs. 45) is the vision of the Sender (cf. 1:18; 6:40; 8:19; 10:30, 38; 14:9). The **light** of the world (vs. 46) has come to rescue men from darkness (cf. vss. 35-36; 1:4-5; 8:12; 9:5). Jesus did not come as **judge** (vs. 47), but rather as Savior (cf. 3:17; 5:21, 45; 8:15, 50). Rejection leads to judgment (vs. 48; cf. 3:18; 5:45). The **word** as the content of the preaching of Jesus will be the judge (cf. 4:41; 5:24; 8:31, 37, 43, 51; 14:23-24; 15:3, 20). On **the last day** cf. 5:28; 6:39-40, 44. Jesus does not speak on his **own authority** (vs. 49), but obeys the Father (cf. 5:30; 6:38; 7:16-17; 8:26, 28, 38; 10:18; 14:10). God's commandment, the divine message obediently uttered by Jesus, issues in eternal life (vs. 50; cf. 6:63; I John 2:25).

---

secretly, fearing, so the evangelist judges, the grave risks of open discipleship, and in particular the lonesomeness of excommunication, the being shunned as a polluted and contaminating thing; but even more, one gathers, in his view, because **they loved the praise of men more than the praise of God.**

Set down in cold print that seems an obviously impossible choice. And yet how often it is made. For human praise is audible, noisily vocal, and its heady roar is apt to be intoxicating; whereas the commendation of one's own conscience is a still small voice that can easily be lost and smothered in the hubbub of things.

Yet all literature and history are crammed with proofs and instances of the instability of anything founded on popular favor, of the incredible fickleness of man, of the essential worthlessness and fleetingness of any praise from him. Whereas to be praised by God—! Is the thing thinkable? That he should grant us his forgiveness is amazement enough; that he should thank us is a thing very difficult to credit; but that being what he is, and with his holy standards, he should praise us! There was once a shy Scottish saint who confessed that if ever he could bring himself to question the Lord Christ, it would be if he should hear him say, and that to him, "Well done, good and faithful servant!"

44-50. ***The Essence of the Gospel.***—We have here a swift recapitulation of some of the main features of the message which Christ had proclaimed. Wave upon wave it surges into the mind, each phrase of it, unfathomable, inexhaustible.

He who believes in me, believes not in me but in him who sent me. So it should be; and

48 He that rejecteth me, and receiveth not my words, hath one that judgeth him: the word that I have spoken, the same shall judge him in the last day.

49 For I have not spoken of myself; but the Father which sent me, he gave me a commandment, what I should say, and what I should speak.

the world. 48 He who rejects me and does not receive my sayings has a judge; the word that I have spoken will be his judge on the last day. 49 For I have not spoken on my own authority; the Father who sent me has himself given me commandment what to

---

This summary focuses attention on the two aspects of the Christian message, the person of our Lord and his teaching. Faith in Jesus is demanded because through him God is known. Just as in the controversy that followed the healing of the cripple at Bethzatha (ch. 5), it is here made clear that Jesus claims no independent **authority.** He is the Father's envoy, who as Son exemplifies the true spirit of filial trust and discloses the nature of the invisible God. He has come with no tyrannical purpose of enslaving men, but to bring them into the freedom of the truth. It is in their own interest to receive his revelation, which can become theirs only by the exercise of faith. The light which shines from him is sent to dispel the darkness of ignorance, fear, and despair which overshadows the world of men. In the same way, obedience to his teaching is demanded in their own interest, as that will prove the crucial test at doomsday. As he has not claimed exclusive faith in himself, but a trust which will bring his hearers into a living knowledge of God, so now the importance of his words lies in their saving virtue. He came not as judge but as Savior. If this seems to contradict 5:27 (the Father "has given him authority to execute judgment, because he is the Son of man"), it need only be noted that that passage points to the result of the mission of the Son; this declares its purpose. It will be noted that the practice of the teaching of Jesus as the judicial test is brought out strongly in the Synoptics (cf. Matt. 7:21-27; 25:31-46; Mark 10:17-19; Luke 10:25-37; 11:28). In John the ethical teaching is not given in detail, but is all comprised in "the new commandment" (13:34; I John 2:7-8; II John 5). Some commentators would excise vs. 48*b* on the ground that **the last day** is an editorial concession to primitive Christian eschatology. But this is to misunderstand the Johannine eschatology, which combines the mystical with the traditional. The judgment which is present and continual will be revealed in the final assessment of human character and work. The summary closes with the emphatic assertion that the message of Jesus is the uttered word of God. If his hearers denounced this claim as presumptuous, or even worse, the evangelist recalls the prophecy in Deut. 18:18-19:

---

so it often is. Yet is there not a too common unitarianism the other way round? Do not at least some appear to have no real God at all but Jesus Christ? And must not that grieve One who again and again stands back in order that we may see past even him to the Father, who thought out our salvation for us, who gave his Son, and to whom belongs the supreme glory? **And he who sees me sees him who sent me.** How daring a saying! And yet how literally true. For if in the days of his flesh they hounded him to death because a creature like him claimed likeness to the God whom they felt he did not at all resemble, now the wheel has come full circle; and we are sure that if there is a God at all, he must be Christlike. **I have come as light into the world, that whoever believes in me may not remain in darkness.** And is it not Jesus Christ who has taught us, slow scholars though we have proved to be, how to think of God, and of man, and of what holiness means and is, and of the world around us, and of immortality—of everything, in truth, that really matters? **If any one hears my sayings and does not keep them, I do not judge him; for I did not come to judge the world but to save the world.** The church has never had a doubt that at the end of things there is a judgment seat; and that Christ is to be the judge; and that each one of us who has come into contact with him must and will be tested according to our attitude toward him and all for which he stands. Yet he has come to save whosoever among us will accept salvation. That was the whole end of his incarnation; that the purpose of his mission; that the dream of his heart: that we might all be with him in his glory—not one missing.

He who rejects me and does not receive my sayings has a judge; the word that I have spoken will be his judge on the last day. Every

50 And I know that his commandment is life everlasting: whatsoever I speak therefore, even as the Father saith unto me, so I speak.

13 Now before the feast of the passover, when Jesus knew that his hour was come that he should depart out of this world unto the Father, having loved his

say and what to speak. 50 And I know that his commandment is eternal life. What I say, therefore, I say as the Father has bidden me."

13 Now before the feast of the Passover, when Jesus knew that his hour

"I will raise them up a Prophet from among their brethren, like unto thee, and will put my words in his mouth; and he shall speak unto them all that I shall command him. And it shall come to pass, that whosoever will not hearken unto my words which he shall speak in my name, I will require it of him." That prophet has been referred to several times in this Gospel (1:21, 25; 6:14; 7:40). But a greater than "the prophet" is here. He had a mandate from the Father to give to men a command which is the condition of life eternal.

With ch. 12 the record of the public ministry is brought to a close. Chs. 13–17 take us away from the crowded temple court and its polemics into the calm atmosphere of the feast of fellowship and the last words of warning and hope.

VII. The Upper Room (13:1–17:26)

A. The Last Supper (13:1-30)

Whatever view may be held about the relation of this Gospel to the Synoptics, there can be little doubt that at a very early stage in the formation of the tradition the events in the last days in the life of our Lord were recorded in a fixed framework. John gives some of these in a different sequence, but from the time when Jesus led his disciples into the upper room, there is little scope for variation in the order. This makes it the more remarkable that John says not a word about the institution of the Eucharist, which is not only related in the three earlier Gospels but is fixed in the still earlier tradition of Paul. As early as A.D. 55, in writing to the Corinthians, the apostle recites the tradition which goes back to the actual event (ἀπὸ τοῦ κυρίου), which he himself had handed on to them, viz., "that the Lord Jesus on the night when he was betrayed took bread, and when he had given thanks [εὐχαριστήσας], he broke it, and said, 'This is my body which is broken for you. Do this in remembrance of me.' In the same way also the cup, after supper, saying, 'This cup is the new covenant in my blood. Do this, as often

idle word that we have carelessly uttered, so we are warned, will have to be accounted for when they meet us again before the judgment seat (Matt. 12:36)—a sobering thought indeed. But even more ominous, surely, is it that every gracious invitation which Christ ever made to us, every appeal of his which reached us and moved us for a little until we forgot again, or which we thrust aside—these too will meet us on the day of testing, and confront us with their deadly accusations. And what answer can we make? It is a fearsome thing to come upon Christ in some narrow place where we cannot push past him, or pretend that we do not see him; where we must pause, must listen to his claims upon us; must make up our minds upon them, must answer one way or the other; must either accept his call, or look him in the eyes and tell him flatly, "I will not!" All these rejected offers of his are not dead. They will crowd in upon us at the judgment seat. And then, what then? **For I have not spoken on my own authority; the Father who sent me has himself given me commandment what to say and what to speak. And I know that his commandment is eternal life. What I say, therefore, I say as the Father has bidden me.** All wise believers have been sure of that, and so speak not even of the gospel of the love of Christ, but rather of the gospel of the grace of God.

And with that, these records of the public ministry of Jesus Christ take end.

13:1. ***The Beginning of the Passion.***—This chapter marks the beginning of the Fourth Gospel's presentation of the passion of our Lord and Savior Jesus Christ (13:1–19:42).

Abruptly and with little introduction it brings us at a step straight into the upper room, that holy of holies, where multitudes have met

as you drink it, in remembrance of me.' For as often as you eat this bread and drink the cup, you proclaim the Lord's death until he comes." The entire silence in John about this important incident demands an explanation. The omission is the more perplexing because a comparison with the Synoptic tradition shows how much the two have in common. Thus Luke relates (*a*) the preparation for the paschal supper, (*b*) the Last Supper, (*c*) the declaration of Judas' treachery, (*d*) the dispute about precedence, (*e*) the prediction of Peter's denial. In John we have (*a*) the feet washing, (*b*) the lesson of humility, (*c*) the declaration of Judas' treachery, (*d*) the prediction of Peter's denial. The silence about the Eucharist cannot be accidental. It is often urged that the Eucharistic language of 6:35-65 made any reference to the Eucharist at this point in the narrative unnecessary. Others think that the evangelist deliberately omitted the institution to correct an extravagant sacramentalism, or because the Christian Eucharist was impossible until after the death of Christ. It is quite possible that because of sacramentarian controversy John wished to remove the subject from the hallowed memory and serene atmosphere of the upper room. Yet others (including Goguel and Loisy) interpret this story of the feet washing as a symbolic representation of the Eucharist. In support of this they point to the solemn words in vs. 1, after which the description of the feet washing would be an anticlimax if it meant nothing more than a simple act of humble service. Moreover, the words of Jesus seem to command the repetition of the rite (vs. 15), and there is no evidence that the *pedilavium* was an annual observance before the time of Augustine. Jesus himself assures Peter that this symbolic action will be understood only after his death (vs. 7). The conclusion which has been drawn by these scholars is that John has taken the institution of the Eucharist from the older tradition, but has substituted another rite which gives a concrete form to the Lukan logion, "I am among you as one who serves" (Luke 22:27), thus blending the two conceptions in this "neglected sacrament." It is quite unnecessary to derive this story from the saying recorded in Luke. Those who regard I Peter as containing apostolic teaching, as well as those who accept its Petrine authorship, will see an allusion to this incident in I Pet. 5:5, "Be clothed with humility as with a slave's apron" (an expansion of the metaphor contained in the word ἐγκομβώσασθε). As it is quite in keeping with the Johannine method to relate an incident in its original occurrence and with its obvious meaning, and at the same time to suggest a deeper symbolic interpretation, we can combine the obvious lesson of humility shown

---

God face to face, and felt him nearer to them there than anywhere else, even in the Scriptures.

Bengel, in the preface to his famous commentary, expresses a seemly diffidence about his right to attempt his task at all. No one, he says, can enter on a work such as this without asking himself, "By what right am I doing this?" That is an awkward question not easily answered! And if that is true of the N.T. as a whole, is it not even more pertinent and uncomfortable about these chapters, which to many are uniquely sacred. In such a place as the upper room surely it is a gross impiety for any other voice to break in upon Jesus Christ. The occasional questions of the disciples, which are recorded here and there throughout the narrative, are apt and natural and human, and open the way to profound answers of eternal value. Does not Bacon tell us that "a faculty of wise interrogating is half a knowledge"? [3] Yet even their interjections jar a little. And for a commentator to push in must surely be merely disturbing and distracting, like the maddening gabble of a guide shattering the spell cast upon the spirit by some august sanctuary. Rupert Brooke has a savage poem in which he tells how once, rapt out of himself by the beauties of nature, and with a solution of many of the enigmas of life breaking in on him, drawn indeed very close, and coming nearer, all but within his reach, he was suddenly brought back to earth again and the revelation lost to him by a flat clear voice beside him, quacking cheerful clear flat platitudes, hopeless inanities about how good the view was and how pretty the sunset, and how nice it was to be alone a bit; and with that the glory and the mystery were gone.[4]

So, dangerous everywhere, commenting in a place like this may merely goad exasperated people into crying out, "In common decency be quiet here, and let me hear Christ speaking; you with your flat voice interrupting him with even flatter platitudes!"

[3] *Advancement of Learning* XIII. 9.

[4] "The Voice."

own which were in the world, he loved them unto the end.

had come to depart out of this world to the Father, having loved his own who were in

in self-forgetful service with a sacramental allusion. As the Exeg. will show, this reference may be to baptism and the Eucharist, but only as these serve to express the self-humiliation of him who "emptied himself" of all but love, and was "obedient unto death, even the death of the cross." The church was already familiar with the Pauline teaching that "all of us that have been baptized into Christ Jesus were baptized into his death. We were buried therefore with him by baptism into death, so that as Christ was raised from the dead by the glory of the Father, we too might walk in newness of life." (Rom. 6:3-4; for further discussion of the nature of the Last Supper in the Fourth Gospel see below, on 17:24-26.)

1. The Feet Washing (13:1-20)

13:1-5. The date of the Last Supper is definitely fixed as Nisan 13, by the words **Before the feast of the Passover,** whereas Jesus died on Nisan 14 according to 18:28, "They themselves did not enter the praetorium, so that they might not be defiled, but

1-3. *Certain Key Phrases in the Narrative.*—With only four august phrases to preface it, the evangelist begins his tale. But these four phrases strike the note of the whole narrative and give us a key how to read what otherwise we might be stupid enough to misunderstand. For what is to follow seems to be a sorry story of defeat and ignominy; of a life thrown away, and that for nothing; of a cause broken and shattered into fragments far past any hope of ever being pieced together again; of a circle of adventurous spirits who dared, and then drew back in shocking failure, in inexcusable dishonor. It is tragedy unrelieved, a colossal and complete collapse. So it might seem. And yet that Figure, beaten, bleeding, surrounded by guffaws of mockery, jostled and dragged from court to court, denounced, derided, execrated, buffeted, spat upon, is not the plaything of his enemies, but remains somehow through it all majestic, imperial, even awesome. Always he is the center of each scene in his long agony; never belittled by anything that they could do to him, but dwarfing everyone else around him. Pilate and Herod sink into insignificance beside him. Always he seems the master of the situation. This is a life not snatched away but a life given.

All this is cunningly foreshadowed in these introductory words, **When Jesus knew that his hour had come to depart out of this world to the Father,** and **Jesus, knowing that the Father had given all things into his hands, and that he had come from God and was going to God.**

Again, what is to be recounted is as ugly a blot as ever disgraced our human annals, splashing them with a shame that will not wash out, but remains down the ages, staring, black, hideous, damning, indelible. The gloom is not entirely unrelieved. Peter impulsively drawing his sword in his Master's defense against impossible odds; the women in the streets weeping as Christ staggered past them underneath his cross; that strange cry from a dying outlaw; the splendid loyalty and daring of Joseph of Arimathaea and Nicodemus—for these facts we are grateful, gleaming out against how dark a background. For at Calvary human nature sank surely to its lowest and its most humiliating. There are the shilly-shallying and weakness of Pilate, the flippancy and callousness of Herod, the buffoonery of the rough soldiers, the fickleness of the crowd, the passionate hate of the accusers seething red hot out of their hearts. And on the other side, treason and treachery, failure and denial, flight and desertion. And for the rest, only a stunned, numb grief that watched helpless and impassive. Not one voice spoke up for Christ; no one was ready to die with him or for him; no one even attempted to do anything at all—a miserable showing! And yet Christ passed through it all not only unbroken by his terrible experiences, but unsoured by them; still kindly and considerate and thoughtful for others; still somehow believing in those who had so tragically failed him; still finding something likable and hopeful in poor creatures who had been lamentably false, not to their friendship and discipleship alone, but to their common manhood. All this is hinted and slipped into the reader's mind by that haunting phrase with which the foot washing is prefaced, **having loved his own who were in the world, he loved them to the end.**

This is true to life, as all those who know Jesus Christ have proved, with an experience that keeps increasing and deepening. Nothing in this astonishing world is more amazing than Christ's faithfulness; than the persistence of that loyal, stubborn, obstinate love of his that will take no refusal, and accept no defeat; but in

2 And supper being ended, the devil
having now put into the heart of Judas
Iscariot, Simon's *son,* to betray him;
3 Jesus knowing that the Father had
given all things into his hands, and that
he was come from God, and went to God;

the world, he loved them to the end. 2 And
during supper, when the devil had already
put it into the heart of Judas Iscariot,
Simon's son, to betray him, 3 Jesus, know-
ing that the Father had given all things
into his hands, and that he had come from

---

might eat the passover." The struggle is over, and Jesus looks forward with confidence. Death henceforth is merely **his hour . . . to depart out of this world to the Father** (14:12-28; 16:5, 10, 28; 17:11, 13; cf. 7:33). Public proclamation and debate are now at an end. Jesus devotes himself to **his own who were in the world,** delivering to them his last charge, as he **loved them to the end**—or to the utmost—in complete fulfillment of the trust into which they had been committed to him by the Father. Words recorded in the older tradition (Mark 10:45; Luke 22:27) are here illustrated by an acted parable. The Greek syntax of vss. 2-5 is the most complicated in this Gospel. There are also two textual problems: (*a*) The reading **during supper** (γινομένου: ℵ* B L W) is better attested, and makes better sense than "after supper" (γενομένου: ℵc A D F Δ Θ). It was the slave's duty, as the guests reclined at table before the meal began, to come behind the couch and lave their feet. As none of the disciples would compromise his claim to eminence by undertaking a servant's task, Jesus left the table and performed the menial duty. He then resumed his place as host at the supper. A more difficult question arises out of the other variant reading in vs. 2: (*b*) **When the devil had already put it into the heart of Judas Iscariot, Simon's son, to betray him,** makes good sense; but many editors follow a small group of important MSS in reading "having put it into his heart that Judas . . ." (ℵ B L). This might mean that it entered into Satan's heart that Judas

---

face of impossible treament that would have sickened every other and made them fling away in angry indignation, somehow still loves on. In very truth, where sin abounds his grace yet more abounds. However often we break through the hedges and wander away, this Good Shepherd patiently follows us, and finds us yet again, and heads us once more into safety. As Samuel Rutherford witnesses:

> How often I play fast and loose with Christ! He bindeth, I loose; He buildeth, I cast down; He trimmeth up a salvation for me, and I mar it; I cast out with Christ, and He agreeth with me again twenty times a day; I forfeit my kingdom and heritage, I lose what I had; but Christ is at my back, and following on, to stoop and take up what falleth from me.[5]

Until a sense of happy helplessness steals over us; a comfortable feeling that Christ, with a determination that will never give, is set upon bringing us through; and that he is going to have his way. **Having loved his own who were in the world,** he holds to them with a magnanimity that, knowing all that they have done and the many times that they have failed him, loves on **to the end.**

2-5. ***The Background of the Foot Washing.***—What is the background of the moving incident of the foot washing? What was it that induced our Lord to carry through that act which has so gripped the imagination of his church? Quite evidently there was something wrong that had to be put right. "With desire I have desired to eat this passover with you," our Lord said (Luke 22:15). He had so much to say to them, so much to do for them! But he felt something in the mental atmosphere about him that kept thwarting and hindering him. What was it?

Some hold that on the road the disciples had been arguing about points of precedence in the more or less material kingdom which, in spite of the apprehensions that kept blowing across their minds, they still seemed to think was opening before them, was already more or less at the door. They had been questioning the pretensions put forward by their fellows, and stating and urging their own claims. And that had resulted in ruffled tempers, and such sore feelings that they had trooped into the upper room like a set of sulky schoolboys, not one among them willing to see the pitcher and basin and towel set there, as was customary, for their use. One supposes that, as a rule, on arriving at their destination, it was their practice to take turns at washing off the dust of the roads from the sandaled feet of the little brotherhood; and that they did it willingly, as a matter of course, and thought nothing about it. But tonight all of them sat stubbornly in their places and would have none of the menial duty.

[5] *Letters,* Letter CCLIV.

4 He riseth from supper, and laid aside his garments; and took a towel, and girded himself.

5 After that he poureth water into a basin, and began to wash the disciples' feet, and to wipe *them* with the towel wherewith he was girded.

God and was going to God, [4] rose from supper, laid aside his garments, and girded himself with a towel. [5] Then he poured water into a basin, and began to wash the disciples' feet, and to wipe them with the

---

should betray Jesus. But syntax and intrinsic probability point the other way. The latter reading is doubtless the right one, but for the sake of emphasis the name of Judas comes at the end of the sentence. **The heart** means Judas', and so the two readings are identical in meaning. The word **already** points to tentative steps taken even then by the traitor, while the last chance of withdrawing from his treason was not lost until the final surrender to the tempter, as told in vs. 27. A subtle allusion to the action recorded in vs. 5 is to be found in the Greek word ἐγκομβώσασθε in I Pet. 5:5 (see above), which probably refers to the knotted towel of the slave.

"The right hand and the left, indeed! They with their bits of tarry boats! And not a thought about what I gave up! What have they done that I cannot match? Why should they claim precedence in the kingdom over me? They will sit there long enough before I wash their feet!"

And so for once the customary little courtesy was not carried out, and they began their meal with feet still travel-stained. Until our Lord, feeling hampered and baffled by the sullenness and anger in the atmosphere around him, saw that until and unless this childishness was cleansed out of their hearts, he could do nothing for them; that all that he had planned to say to them that night to help them through the horrors he sensed looming up before them, and dreadfully near at that, could simply not get through to them; that even his words would dash themselves to nothingness against this dour dead wall by which he found himself confronted. And so, not **supper being ended,** as the KJV reads, but **during supper,** as in the RSV, feeling that he could bear it no longer, breaking in upon the meal, he rose and carrried through his dramatic action, all of which seems a likely reading of the situation, and with some scriptural warrant behind it.

Yet does not the wording of vs. 2 (and other things also in the narrative) suggest that there was something else, if not other, then further, in our Lord's mind? It looks, in part at least, as if the foot washing was a crowning appeal to Judas Iscariot; as if it were designed to save that unhappy man from the infamy with which he was dallying and in which he sank. According to the Synoptists, the die was already cast, the deal was closed, and the thirty pieces of silver in the poor wretch's possession. They suggest that he was only waiting for a favorable time and place at which to strike his murderous blow. But John's account leaves the impression that things had not yet gone so far; that it was actually in the upper room and at the supper that Judas finally made his tragic decision.

And during supper, when the devil had already put it into the heart of Judas Iscariot, Simon's son, to betray him. These words seem to imply that while ugly ideas of betrayal had found a lodgment in his mind, nothing as yet was settled. The man was slipping, losing grip upon himself, was perilously near the edge; another foot, and he was over. He had been in contact with the authorities; he had made certain base suggestions, and had listened to theirs. No doubt they had said to him, corroborating his own gloomy estimate of how things now stood, "This insane enterprise of yours is doomed. Nothing can come of it. If you choose to go down with it, that is your own affair; but if you can show us where and when we can lay hands on this mad master of yours—and you are too sensible a man, as your presence here shows, not to have realized that he is mad, and his whole enterprise a sheer imbecility—if, we say, you can show us where and when we can arrest him quietly and without risk of disturbance, if you can engineer that for us, well, we shall remember it in your favor when the collapse comes. Meantime there will of course be something for your trouble. Think it out." So they had said. And Judas kept thinking; sat there brooding over the proposal, fingering it, reckoning up the pros and cons of it, inclining more and more toward acquiescence in it. The game was obviously lost, that much seemed certain; the adventure had proved a ridiculous fiasco. It was time to think of his own safety, how he could scramble out of the mess with a whole skin. And Jesus, sensing what was hovering in the balances in his mind, knew that here was something far worse and more soiling than the dust of the roads, something that must be

6 Then cometh he to Simon Peter: and Peter saith unto him, Lord, dost thou wash my feet?
7 Jesus answered and said unto him, What I do thou knowest not now; but thou shalt know hereafter.

towel with which he was girded. 6 He came to Simon Peter; and Peter said to him, "Lord, do you wash my feet?" 7 Jesus answered him, "What I am doing you do not know now, but afterward you will under-

---

6-11. In the Greek of Peter's protest (cf. Matt. 3:14) and the answer of Jesus the pronouns are emphatic. **Lord, do *you* wash *my* feet? What *I* am doing *you* do not know now.** The promise **afterward you will understand** may refer to the explanation that follows in vss. 12-17, but more probably to the lesson which time and experience alone will teach the apostle. It is a Johannine thought that many things became clear to the disciples only after the Resurrection and the gift of the Paraclete (cf. vss. 19, 36; 2:22; 12:16; 14:29; 16:12, 22. The immediate lesson of self-denying humility is obvious, but the warning **If I do not wash you, you have no part in me,** points to a deeper meaning. This impression is strengthened by vs. 10. For after Peter's impulsive demand that his hands and head, as well as his feet, should be washed, Jesus replies, **He who has bathed does not need to wash, except for his feet, but he is clean all over.** This metaphor is drawn from the social custom by which the visitor after a long journey was taken by a slave to a room where a bath was prepared. If he had come but a short distance, the slave unfastened his sandals and carried them away, and then laved his feet as he reclined at table (cf. Matt. 3:11; Luke 7:44). What is the hidden meaning in the distinction between being bathed and the washing of the feet? Many commentators find a reference

---

cleansed away if the soul of a man he loved, and in whom he had believed, who had unusual possibilities in him, was not to be lost. And a great part of this chapter seems to be the record of our Lord's persistent and moving attempts to save him.

However that may be, and whatever was the specific reason for his action, he **rose from supper, laid aside his garments, and girded himself with a towel. Then he poured water into a basin, and began to wash the disciples' feet, and to wipe them with the towel with which he was girded.**

6-10. ***Peter and the Foot Washing.***—As they followed these preparations and realized what he was going to do, they must have watched him with a growing discomfort and uneasiness. Yet curiously no one spoke. No one cried out, "No! No! You must not do that! Let me do it for you!" Yet surely it must have been with hot faces, contrite and miserable, that they saw Christ kneeling to each of them in turn; and that they watched him drawing nearer and nearer to themselves, until they felt the touch of his hands on their own feet. But it was all in a tense silence. For still no one spoke.

Until he came to Simon Peter, always impulsive, never tongue-tied, apt to blurt out everything in his mind. And this was more by far than he could stand. At first he stared in a kind of stunned amazement at what could not be real; like a man faced by some incredible happening, who shuts his eyes to dispel the illusion, and opens them to find it all still there. He gasps out, no doubt plucking them well out of the way, **Lord, do you wash my feet?** And one likes him for the outburst. But Jesus answered gravely, **What I am doing you do not know now, but afterward you will understand.**

Often in life we have to be content to leave it at that, sometimes for a long time. Things burst in on us that do not look like love and make no sense seen from our angle. And we must learn to trust Christ in the dark, to accept his ordering of matters for us as right and wise and kind, however incomprehensible and sinister these may seem to our hearts, hurt and confused by them, and so remain quiet and uncomplaining. It helps us in such seasons to be told, as we are here, that he knows that sometimes we must be and are completely puzzled; and that he is not vexed with us for that; knows that it is not easy for us to grasp why this dear one should be taken; or why this pain or infirmity should be allowed to hamper us; or why a door of opportunity should open invitingly before us, without our opening it, and then be slammed shut in our faces, leaving us outside, with our life, it would appear, condemned to run henceforth in shallow channels, and without possibility of any large or evident results.

And even more does it help to be assured that one day all that now staggers and daunts us will grow plain; that the pattern which is being woven in our lives will stand out then, patent and self-evident, and we shall say,

8 Peter saith unto him, Thou shalt never wash my feet. Jesus answered him, If I wash thee not, thou hast no part with me.
9 Simon Peter saith unto him, Lord, not my feet only, but also *my* hands and *my* head.

stand." [8] Peter said to him, "You shall never wash my feet." Jesus answered him, "If I do not wash you, you have no part in me." [9] Simon Peter said to him, "Lord, not my feet only but also my hands and

to baptism. In view of the allusive sacramentalism of the evangelist that must not be ruled out as impossible. The meaning would then be that the regenerate man (whose rebirth had been symbolized by baptism) had not need for any cleansing but that from the small, everyday stains of this earthly life. This might be the thought of I John 3:9. There is, however, another reading (RSV mg.) which omits **except for his feet** (so **א**, some O.L. witnesses, Origen [often], Tertullian, Jerome). If this is the true reading, we get rid of the supposed contrast between the bath and the washing of the feet. The latter is symbolical of total cleansing.

The incident must be read in the context of the Passion because of the solemn introduction in vs. 1. According to Mark 10:35-45, Jesus, in reply to the request of the two disciples for special honor in his kingdom, said, "With the baptism with which I am baptized, you will be baptized." After declaring that the path to greatness was that of service, he concluded, "For the Son of man came not to be served but to serve, and to give his life as a ransom for many." Luke 22:24-27 records a similar conversation closing with the words, "But I am among you as one who serves." In one of the anticipations of his passion Jesus said, "I have a baptism to be baptized with; and how I am constrained

understanding it all at last, "That is why it was sent!" When, looking back, we shall see for ourselves that nothing that was so sent us could have been omitted without loss to us. Meantime, we must just have faith in Christ, and trust him where we cannot see. And why not? For has he not proved himself to be trustworthy?

At first, however, and often for long enough, we are apt to be slow to believe all that. For what has befallen us, or what is asked of us, seems to us monstrous, unreasonable, impossible. So here Peter replies with stubborn emphasis, "**You shall never wash my feet.** I will not have it, and cannot bear it! This thing is just not going to be!" And once more one likes him for his very vehemence. But again it is gravely that Christ answers, **If I do not wash you, you have no part in me.** If the gospel, if our fellowship with Christ and our faith in him, if our glib professions of allegiance, our prayers and religious exercises, are not cleansing our characters from what soils them and healing our natures from what maims them; if we drift on from day to day much what we have always been, and not markedly different with Christ from what we would have been without him: then for us the gospel has failed. We have missed the point and end of the whole business and are not really Christ's at all. So Christ himself told his best friend.

Whereat Peter, shocked and panic-stricken at the mere thought of being disowned by Christ and separated from him, of being thrown aside as one with whom even the Master could do nothing, swung in his impulsive, affectionate way to the other extreme. **Lord, not my feet only but also my hands and my head!** But it is as unwise to seek to outrun Christ as it is to lag trailing behind him. No doubt we are to go the second mile; are not to be parsimonious and grudging in our obedience, doling out the bare minimum that may just be sufficient, like a grocer or chemist guardedly shaking into the bag the last grains that will bring down the scales. But there is an exaggeration of obedience that is not asked of us, and that is unwise. We are enjoined to train for the spiritual life, to discipline our body and our desires. And how many as a result have plunged headlong into orgies of asceticism, that have missed their end and told adversely, and the wrong way. So Francis of Assisi frankly confessed about his maltreatment of his body. And many a saint has set it down with contrition that his austerities made him irritable, querulous, bad-tempered, less Christlike than he would have been under a saner scheme of life.

Nonetheless, our Lord's answer in vs. 10, **He who has bathed does not need to wash, except for his feet, but he is clean all over; and you are clean,** is a right gracious and heartening saying. And we must believe it, and walk in the sunshine of it: must try to credit that the forgiveness of God—and that toward us, if we have any real claim to be Christians!—is not

10 Jesus saith to him, He that is washed needeth not save to wash *his* feet, but is clean every whit: and ye are clean, but not all.

11 For he knew who should betray him; therefore said he, Ye are not all clean.

12 So after he had washed their feet, and had taken his garments, and was set down again, he said unto them, Know ye what I have done to you?

my head!" 10 Jesus said to him, "He who has bathed does not need to wash, except for his feet,[z] but he is clean all over; and you are clean, but not all of you." 11 For he knew who was to betray him; that was why he said, "You are not all clean."

12 When he had washed their feet, and taken his garments, and resumed his place, he said to them, "Do you know what I

[z] Other ancient authorities omit *except for his feet.*

until it is accomplished!" (Luke 12:50). There is yet a further contribution to the elucidation of our text. According to I John 1:7, "The blood of Jesus his Son cleanses us from all sin." The death of Jesus is a baptism with which all his disciples must be baptized. That death is the culmination of a life of self-denying love and service. Through faith in their Master and Savior, shown by obedience to his spirit and example, his disciples share in his baptism and are cleansed from sin. **You have no part in me,** accordingly, does not refer in this passage to the life of mystical fellowship with Christ, promised in I John 1:3, 6, and described in the allegory of the vine (15:1-11), but to fellowship with the suffering Servant, in that passion which is the way to glory. The acted parable of the feet washing is a symbol of this cleansing. Not that the physical act cleanses by itself, **You are clean, but not all of you.** The traitor submitted to the Master's act of lowly service, but it did not cleanse his heart from the sinful purpose on which it was bent.

12-20. These verses supply the ethical application of the doctrine implicit in vss. 1-11. This acted parable has a meaning which the disciples can understand only "hereafter"

merely a dim hope which may conceivably come true in some far-off future, but is a present fact; that here and now there is no condemnation to those who are in Christ Jesus; that God has already blotted out the past, has put it out of mind and pardoned it so freely and eagerly and fully that, as Isaiah declared in a daring phrase, the Omniscient no longer even remembers it any more. As if, when we begin our confession to him, he interrupted us saying, "Sins! Sins! Were there sins? I have forgotten about them!" **He who has bathed,** says Christ, **is clean.** Those who are troubled at being what they are, and who reach out toward something better and look to Christ to help them to it, such are clean already, except for the dust gathered in the day's traveling and marketing and bustling to and fro. And that too Christ will cleanse away if with seemly humility we allow him to work out his generous purpose toward us.

11. See Expos., vss. 18-30.

12-15. ***The Imitation of Christ.***—Vs. 15 sweeps us out into great waters. What is the ideal that the Christian faith offers us and lays upon us? There is no doubt about the answer to that question. And it is sufficiently startling. For it is God himself. That sounds impossible. For he is he, and we are only we; and between him and us there is a great gulf fixed. Here are we, frail creatures, seen and gone, filling our little stock of years with the petty nothings of our trivial lives. And we are to take him as our model, to live out our lives upon the plan of his eternal being! And nothing else will do!

In the main, that is a startlingly original suggestion. True, the Hebrews, even when their ideas of God were crude and primitive, always looked up to him, as to One far above themselves; whereas the Greeks and Romans, in the mass, looked down upon their gods from a superior moral height which the gods themselves never attained. The average Greek would not have dreamed of taking them as his standard, well knowing that, did he and his neighbors do so, society could not hold together, but must fall into chaos. Indeed, to be a god meant to be free from those bothersome and restraining moral laws which they laid upon others but never dreamed of practicing themselves. So Terence makes one of his characters exclaim in hurt, indignant tones, "May I, a lad, not do it, when Jupiter does it?" [6]

The greatest minds had of course left such crudities behind. So Plato, "Now God ought to be the measure of all things, and not man. . . . And he who would be dear to God must, as far as is possible, be like Him and such as He is." [7] And, as he saw things, that was a noble aim.

[6] *The Eunuch* III. 5. 36.

[7] *Laws* IV. 716.

13 Ye call me Master and Lord: and ye
say well; for *so* I am.
14 If I then, *your* Lord and Master, have
washed your feet; ye also ought to wash
one another's feet.
15 For I have given you an example,
that ye should do as I have done to you.

have done to you? [13] You call me Teacher
and Lord; and you are right, for so I am.
[14] If I then, your Lord and Teacher, have
washed your feet, you also ought to wash
one another's feet. [15] For I have given you
an example, that you also should do as I

(vs. 7), i.e., they must first be baptized into the passion of their Lord, or as Paul would say, "be crucified with Christ" and rise again with him into newness of life. But the meaning of discipleship in its humble-mindedness and its life of mutual service is clear from the example of their Master (cf. I Pet. 2:21). We have Synoptic parallels to vs. 13 in Luke 22:27; to vs. 16 in Matt. 10:24 and Luke 6:40; to vs. 20 in Matt. 10:40 and

And so, too, Aristotle laid it down that our goal was likeness to God. Yet the masses trailed so far behind them, and lived in so different a world of thought, that Samuel Dill is not one bit too strong when he asserts that the world "demanded a moral God,"[8] and it was Jesus who gave that to man, who showed us that God is bound by his own moral laws, that as Whittier said:

> By all that He requires of me,
> I know what God Himself must be.[9]

If he lays on me the law of love, I can be sure that he himself is love. Since he insists that I must forgive unto seventy times seven, he also will and does forgive persistently, obstinately, endlessly.

But if God is our standard, how can we be sure what he is like and is? To this Christ answers, "Look at me." Again and again he offers himself as our ideal. "As I," "as I," "as I"—the phrase runs through the Gospels. "As I act, so do you act; accept that as your model."

Not a few, e.g., the Stoics, have urged men to take some lofty, outstanding moral figure of the past, and make of him a kind of external conscience; keeping him in mind, and doing only what they would like to do if he were in the room along with them, and they under his very eyes. So Seneca advises, "We ought to choose some good man and always have him before our eyes that we may live as if he watched us, and do everything as if he saw."[1]

But all the figures they suggested have been dimmed by time; have in part become morally obsolete, and been left behind. But after nearly two thousand years of climbing toward him, Christ, so far from being overtaken and surpassed, is still as high above us as the stars. Not "even now would it be easy, even for an unbeliever, to find a better translation of the rule of virtue from the abstract into the concrete, than to endeavour so to live that Christ would approve our life."[2]

Hence the imitation of Christ is a very real and central part of Christianity. Our business is to put on Christ; to grow into his character and mind and ways; to think what he would have us do, and do it; to take him as our model and goal, and press toward it. **I have given you an example, that you also should do as I have done to you** has a far wider application than the original and immediate one there in the upper room. Kant, indeed, lays it down that "imitation finds no place at all in morality, and examples serve only for encouragement, *i.e.* they put beyond doubt the feasibility of what the law commands, they make visible that which the practical rule expresses more generally."[3] It is of course true that we must possess something within ourselves, some faculty more or less developed, to which goodness, new to us, can make its appeal and be approved; or else we should not recognize that it is goodness. But that faculty at the start is not full grown in us. It begins as a rudimentary and far from infallible thing. It must be taught. It has to grow, and learn to see farther and better and more accurately, to rise above its past mistakes, to perceive and approve and adopt better and better things.

And how is this effected in an individual, or in a generation, or in mankind as a whole?

Always advance comes because some great soul, going on ahead of the mass of us, makes discoveries and then shares them with the lesser folk. And with that a new virtue, or a new application of an old one swims into view, a new star has been added to the sky. So Nicolai Hartmann, "It is the great individuals who

[8] *Roman Society from Nero to Marcus Aurelius* (London: Macmillan & Co., 1905), p. 621.

[9] "Revelation."

[1] *Epistles* II. 8.

[2] John Stuart Mill, *Three Essays on Religion* (New York: Henry Holt & Co., 1874), p. 255.

[3] *Kant's Theory of Ethics*, tr. T. K. Abbott (London: Longmans, Green & Co., 1889), p. 25.

16 Verily, verily, I say unto you, The servant is not greater than his lord; neither he that is sent greater than he that sent him.

have done to you. 16 Truly, truly, I say to you, a servant[a] is not greater than his master; nor is he who is sent greater than he

[a] Or *slave.*

Luke 10:16; also in Mark 9:37; Matt. 18:5; Luke 9:48. The beatitude in vs. 17 recalls the moral of the parable of the builders (Matt. 7:24-27). A further mention of the traitor (vs. 18; cf. 6:64, 70-71) serves both as a Christian apology and as a warning to forearm the disciples against the shock which the betrayal will bring to their faith. Ps. 41:9, with its description of a guest's treachery to his host, is used as a messianic testimony (see Intro., p. 440; also on 2:21-22) to show that even this act of treason falls within the scope of the

first give light and splendour to the life of the community, who open up a higher order of value which spreads to the rest, singly and collectively." It is, he feels, the function of what he calls "the noble" to pioneer ahead of the rest of us, and keep "laying hold of the untried and uncommon." [4] And so Browning:

'Tis in the advance of individual minds
That the slow crowd should ground their expectation
Eventually to follow; as the sea
Waits ages in its bed till some one wave
Out of the multitudinous mass, extends
The empire of the whole, some feet perhaps,
Over the strip of sand which could confine
Its fellows so long time: thenceforth the rest,
Even to the meanest, hurry in at once,
And so much is clear gain.[5]

And no one was ever so rich a discoverer as Jesus Christ; nor has anyone shown us so many glorious and unsuspected constellations. Nonetheless, this imitation of Christ has to be done with care, since what he asks of us (as in vs. 14) is not slavish obedience to an unalterable set of hidebound rules, but the growing up into a spirit, his spirit, which acts sometimes in one way, and, in differing circumstances, it may be, in quite another. The Christ who tells us that we must forgive unendingly spoke about Herod with hot and open scorn, even with contempt. And if we are to imitate him with correctness, we shall have to act sometimes forgivingly and sometimes with a clean and resolute anger. And that means in not a few situations difficulty and uncertainty as to what he would have us do. But we have this to help us, that whereas wistful souls in the ancient world kept dreaming of an ideal, it was only an abstraction—nothing more. So Plutarch, "He is nowhere on earth, nor ever has been." But we have for our guidance not a mere dream, but a real life that was really lived, not an imaginary thing but a fact. Some say that makes no difference; since whether Jesus ever existed or not, at least we have now the idea of the thing to guide us. It makes a vast difference. One can dream anything; but will it work? This has worked. As Renan has it: "Humanity seeks the ideal; but it seeks it in a person, and not in an abstraction. A man, the incarnation of the ideal, whose biography might serve as a frame for all the aspirations of time, is what the religious mind sought." [6] And it finds it in Jesus Christ, whom Martineau called "the realized ideal."

As William Adams Brown has summed it up:

To us, as to the first disciples, he is not only true man, but ideal man. This is the fact of experience which underlies the doctrine of the incarnation. When we say that Jesus is God incarnate, it is our way of reminding ourselves that, in Jesus, God is teaching us by example. To tell me what I ought to think or what I ought to do is insufficient. I need some one to show me how to think and act as I ought. It is not enough to tell me how I ought to feel or what I ought to be. I want some one who will be the kind of a person that he wants me to be. . . . We must see the ideal life realized in the person of one who has lived it. We must see sin conquered in the person of one who has defeated it. It is example, not words, which inspires us to make the effort for ourselves and gives us confidence that the struggle will not be in vain.[7]

16-17. *The Impression Made on Peter by the Foot Washing.*—At the time, Peter was obviously deeply moved, and he never forgot it. He was not the kind of man who does forget. In that first epistle that bears his name and which we may hope is his, he

does not argue much. Rather, faced by some moral problem, he flashes a vision of Jesus Christ before the mind, and says no more, leaving Him to make His own appeal. When the younger men, and indeed the whole community, strike him as somewhat pushful and over ambitious, he does not rail at them, nor complain, nor protest, but simply says, "put on

[4] *Ethics,* II, 113.

[5] "Paracelsus," Part III.

[6] *Marc Aurèle,* p. 582.

[7] *Beliefs that Matter* (New York: Charles Scribner's Sons; London: Hodder & Stoughton, 1928), p. 106. Used by permission.

17 If ye know these things, happy are ye if ye do them.

18 ¶ I speak not of you all: I know whom I have chosen: but that the Scripture may be fulfilled, He that eateth bread with me hath lifted up his heel against me.

19 Now I tell you before it come, that, when it is come to pass, ye may believe that I am *he*.

20 Verily, verily, I say unto you, He that receiveth whomsoever I send receiveth me;

who sent him. 17 If you know these things,
blessed are you if you do them. 18 I am not
speaking of you all; I know whom I have
chosen; it is that the scripture may be fulfilled, 'He who ate my bread has lifted his
heel against me.' 19 I tell you this now, before it takes place, that when it does take
place you may believe that I am he.
20 Truly, truly, I say to you, he who receives

---

divine providence (see on 12:36-43). Some commentators (e.g., J. H. Bernard) have discovered in vs. 18 a deep significance in the unusual Greek word for "eat" (τρώγειν), which is also used in the Eucharistic discourse of 6:54-56. But a comparison of Matt. 24:38 (τρώγειν) and Luke 17:27 (ἐσθίειν) completely disposes of this imaginary distinction.

---

the apron of humility," quite obviously back in the Upper Room among that angry group of irritated men, seeing Christ rise and gird Himself with a towel, beginning with a reddening face to take in what He proposed to do, watching Him drawing nearer and still nearer, with a sick dismay; feeling the agony of that touch on his soiled feet, hearing that quiet voice, "I have been giving you an example, that you should do what I have done to you." . . .

Or, the elders in the church are growing slack, and Peter drops a single phrase, "When the chief Shepherd shall appear." And, face to face with that good Shepherd, who gives His whole life for the sheep, and will not lose one of His flock, but follows it through all its wayward wanderings until He finds it, careless of the cost to Himself, how shabby and unworthy their own efforts look, though but a moment since they had thought them quite adequate, and all that could be reasonably asked of anyone. Or there were men with a grievance, a just grievance, as we judge. They were not whining, they explained, knew they themselves were far from perfect, and were quite prepared to face the consequences of their own slips and mistakes. But this was something very different, the unbearable surliness of utterly unreasonable people who were giving them no chance, grossly denying them that barest justice which is a human birthright. And Peter does not argue their particular case, but of a sudden they are looking at Christ staggering beneath His cross to Calvary, upon His way to die, "the just for the unjust." And with that, somehow, their own grievance, which had filled their universe, has shrunk into a vastly lesser thing. So it is always. Paul for faith, and John for love, but Peter for remembrance. Keep within sight of Christ, and let His influence tell upon you, and allow nothing to break your fellowship with Him, and all the rest must follow, so he holds.[8]

[8] A. J. Gossip, "The Religious Message of the General Epistles for the Present Day," *Study Bible* (London: Cassell & Co., 1930), pp. 19-20. Used by permission.

18-30. ***Judas in the Upper Room.***—But if our Lord's bold experiment succeeded with Peter, with Judas Iscariot it entirely failed. And Christ himself felt that at once. Before Judas also he had knelt; and his feet too he had washed and dried; praying no doubt that this semi-sacrament might prove efficacious; that the unhappy man might see past the symbols to the realities that lay in them and behind them; that through the visible sign the invisible grace might break through to him and reach him; and that the cleansing forgiveness of God, which he so needed, and which was offered him so eagerly and freely for the taking, if he would have it, might be accepted; that Judas would amend that cry of Peter so as to meet his own worse case, "Not my feet only, but my heart, and my mind, and my soul!" Instead, the man sat there, stolid, impervious, still all but set upon his purpose. And still Christ sought to hold back his friend from the ruin upon which he was rushing.

First, he kept dropping sayings which apparently the others did not follow, but which must have let Judas realize that Christ knew what he, or someone in the circle, had in mind. "You are not all clean" (vs. 11). And again, **I am not speaking of you all** (vs. 18). And once more, **He who ate my bread has lifted his heel against me** (vs. 18). And when his friend's face never softened, and showed never a sign of change of heart, Christ was much moved. **He was troubled in spirit** (vs. 21) and said openly, casting aside in great degree the reserve with which he had tried to shield his friend, **One of you will betray me.**

That wholly unexpected announcement fell among the startled disciples like a bombshell. Its effect on them is very moving. Through it,

and he that receiveth me receiveth him that sent me.

21 When Jesus had thus said, he was troubled in spirit, and testified, and said, Verily, verily, I say unto you, that one of you shall betray me.

22 Then the disciples looked one on another, doubting of whom he spake.

23 Now there was leaning on Jesus' bosom one of his disciples, whom Jesus loved.

any one whom I send receives me; and he who receives me receives him who sent me."

21 When Jesus had thus spoken, he was troubled in spirit, and testified, "Truly, truly, I say to you, one of you will betray
me." 22 The disciples looked at one another,
uncertain of whom he spoke. 23 One of his
disciples, whom Jesus loved, was lying close

---

2. The Betrayal Foretold (13:21-30)

21-23. The dark hints now give way to a definite prediction. This passage opens with words that recall the announcement of the passion (12:27), **He was troubled in spirit.** One bitter ingedient in the cup of his suffering was the knowledge of the moral breakdown of a friend and chosen comrade. The disciples are plainly told, **One of you will betray me.** To relieve their misgivings Peter signaled to the disciple who was reclining on the right of Jesus on the same couch, and who, by turning his head slightly, could ask a question without being overheard by the rest. This disciple is described here for the first time as one **whom Jesus loved** (vs. 23; cf. 19:26; 20:2; 21:7, 20; see Intro., p. 440). The modern reader who is familiar with Leonardo da Vinci's painting, "The Last Supper," may easily misconceive the relative position of Jesus and his disciples. The Oriental custom was to recline on a couch, with the left arm resting on a cushion upon the table and the right arm free. Sometimes two reclined on the same divan; the one on the right would have his back turned to his neighbor, with his head resting at the level of his neighbor's breast. That was the position of the Beloved Disciple. Where was Peter placed? It is often assumed that he would lie in the place of honor above Jesus, i.e., on his left. But in that case his communication with the Beloved Disciple would be extremely difficult, and it is more likely that Judas occupied that place. This would explain the

---

indeed, one gains a far truer understanding of the relations that subsisted among the members of the little fellowship than that which certain thin-sown and unhappy but colorful episodes of quarreling and pushfulness are apt to leave on our minds. For not one of them dreamed of suspecting any of his comrades. They had lived together intimately for months and years and they could think of no one in the least likely to do this horrible thing. According to Matthew, they gazed at one another in consternation; and then, so sure was every man's confidence in all the others, that pathetically enough each of them felt that if this dastardly wrong was really to be done, then he himself was the least impossible for the doing of it! "Can it be I?" they asked themselves with a shock of horror; and then in faltering voices put it to the Master, "Lord, is it I?" The account here is different. But there are the same bewilderment and the same inability to credit such enormity in any of their fellows. Be it noted particularly that no one suspected Judas. All eyes did not turn instinctively in his direction, as if everybody were sure it must be he; nor were they carefully averted from him, an act that would have been as telltale as the other. No one, it seems, so much as thought of Judas. In 12:6 we are told that "he was a thief." Whether that was common knowledge at the time, or as one suspects, was discovered later; whether or not they were already aware that he was a pilferer, no one dreamed of him as being capable of an infamy like this. Even when he had been unmasked and was making for the door, set on his purpose, they had not taken in the truth, but still remained entirely unsuspicious of him, supposed that he was going out because he had remembered something which he had to do as the treasurer and mess president of the group. Even John, after he had been definitely told (vs. 26), apparently remained incredulous of Christ's own judgment. All this we must seek to remember in a fair estimate of that tragic figure—Judas.

Incidentally, a moving semi-parallel to this abashed lack of confidence in themselves which surged up so uncomfortably in each of the eleven is to be found in *Faith of a Moralist,* where A. E. Taylor, discussing with humility

24 Simon Peter therefore beckoned to him, that he should ask who it should be of whom he spake.

25 He then lying on Jesus' breast saith unto him, Lord, who is it?

26 Jesus answered, He it is, to whom I shall give a sop, when I have dipped *it*. And when he had dipped the sop, he gave *it* to Judas Iscariot, *the son* of Simon.

27 And after the sop Satan entered into him. Then said Jesus unto him, That thou doest, do quickly.

28 Now no man at the table knew for what intent he spake this unto him.

to the breast of Jesus; 24 so Simon Peter
beckoned to him and said, "Tell us who it
is of whom he speaks." 25 So lying thus,
close to the breast of Jesus, he said to him,
"Lord, who is it?" 26 Jesus answered, "It is
he to whom I shall give this morsel when
I have dipped it." So when he had dipped
the morsel, he gave it to Judas, the son of
Simon Iscariot. 27 Then after the morsel,
Satan entered into him. Jesus said to him,
"What you are going to do, do quickly."
28 Now no one at the table knew why he

---

action in vs. 26 and the whispered words in vs. 27*b*. Probably Peter was on the right of the Beloved Disciple. If he was reclining on another divan, we can more easily account for the signal as well as for the whispered appeal.

24-30. Simon Peter beckoned to him and said, "Tell us who it is of whom he speaks" follows the best textual authorities. The KJV reading (A D W Γ Δ Θ [א] sy^s), not Johannine in style, arose from the difficulty of understanding why the Beloved Disciple should be asked to tell what only Jesus knew. Vs. 25 makes the situation clear. It is not certain whether our Lord's reply to the Beloved Disciple (vs. 26) was intentionally obscure or whether it supplied the clue. The Marcan narrative (14:19-20) says that in answer to the announcement that treachery lurked within the fold, all the disciples in turn asked, "Is it I?" to which Jesus replied, "It is one of the twelve, one who is dipping bread in the same dish with me." Such a general remark would explain John's statement that **no one at the table knew why** Jesus said to Judas, **What you are going to do, do quickly.** But in this Gospel the answer is more explicit, **It is he to whom I shall give this morsel when I have dipped it,** and the morsel was then dipped and given to Judas. Why, then, did not the Beloved Disciple recognize the traitor and pass on the information to Peter? By Oriental custom, to dip a morsel of bread or meat into the dish and hand it to a guest is a token of friendship (cf. Ruth 2:14). The remark that **after the morsel, Satan entered into him** must not be interpreted in the light of I Cor. 5:5; 11:29.

---

and lowliness of mind the tremendous problem of whether or not any are lost finally and forever, ends thus:

> A living divine was recently reported, correctly or not, to have declared that "if there are really diabolical men, no doubt, their destiny is perdition, but I should hope that such men are very few". I should like myself to hope that there are none such, but there is just one man, of the many whom I have known, about whom I feel it is salutary not to be over-sanguine, myself.[9]

But there was an unhappy tension in the room, and Peter acted characteristically. Raising himself, he made signs, with eyes or face or gesture, urging John to find out who the traitor was. Christ's reply to this question was one more last attempt to save Judas. **"It is he to whom I shall give this morsel when I have dipped it."** **So when he had dipped the morsel, he gave it to Judas**—a courtesy more or less reserved for honored guests and for particular friends. As he did so, Christ's eyes must have looked frankly into his, asking, "Can you do it? Will you do it? After all that there has been between us?"

But with that suddenly the trap snapped tight about the wretched man. "He knows. And I have gone too far for drawing back. If I fail the authorities, who can tell what may befall me? I must act. I must act now." And **he immediately went out.** And Christ, knowing that even he could do no more, uttered words so terrible from him that they send a shuddering through the spirit. **What you are going to do, do quickly.** He can save to the uttermost: And yet here was a soul, and a soul dear to him, that was being swept out into roaring waters; and it would not grip his hand, and would not let itself be saved, and it was going down! And there was nothing more that Christ could do!

[9] London: Macmillan & Co., 1930, I, 331. Used by permission of the representatives of the author.

29 For some *of them* thought, because Judas had the bag, that Jesus had said unto him, Buy *those things* that we have need of against the feast; or, that he should give something to the poor.

30 He then, having received the sop, went immediately out; and it was night.

31 ¶ Therefore, when he was gone out, Jesus said, Now is the Son of man glorified, and God is glorified in him.

said this to him.
29 Some thought that, because Judas had the money box, Jesus was telling him, "Buy what we need for the feast"; or, that he should give something to the poor.
30 So, after receiving the morsel, he immediately went out; and it was night.

31 When he had gone out, Jesus said, "Now is the Son of man glorified, and in

---

Vs. 2 lets us know that satanic temptation had been working in the mind of Judas before this. The crowning infamy was that at the very moment of accepting this pledge of friendship Judas made his final resolve to betray his Master. Jesus, seeing in his eyes that Judas had yielded to the base suggestion, bade him carry out his intention **quickly.** Some commentators (e.g., Loisy, Lagrange, Bauer) read in these words (vs. 27*b*) John's intention to show that Jesus himself took the initiative in this first act of his passion, which could be accomplished only by his own will (cf. 10:17-18). As so often, the words of Jesus were misunderstood. John refers again to the position which Judas held as treasurer of the common fund (cf. 12:6). Once more it is placed on record that **after receiving the morsel, he immediately went out.** The tragedy of a lost soul is packed into the closing comment: **and it was night.** Yet the paschal moon was shining at the full.

B. The Farewell Discourse, Part I (13:31–14:31)

These last words of Jesus to "his own," and the high priestly prayer in which he dedicates himself to his last act of sacrifice and intercedes for his disciples that they may continue his work, form a unity. They continue the narrative which opens in 13:1. Yet there are questions raised by an apparent disorder in the sequence. The final words of ch. 14 ("Rise, let us go hence") seem to mark the close of the farewell address as Jesus and the disciples rise from the supper to make their way to Gethsemane. If the prayer of ch. 17 followed immediately, there would be no difficulty. But chs. 15–16 intervene, with many thoughts and phrases that recall the substance of ch. 14. Some commentators

---

Except surely to follow him to the door, and through the door with eyes full of a tragedy of pain, not for himself, but for this soul he loved that was flinging itself away. Once in a town where I was a minister, a big man in the place, rough and insensitive as one might judge, looked after my old colleague as he passed, and, "Do you know," he said, "what keeps me straight? If I threw away my soul and were cast into hell, I think I could make shift to face my punishment, but I could not bear the pain that there would be in Mr. Cumming's eyes."

But Judas unflinchingly bore the pain in Jesus' eyes, closed the door behind him resolutely, and was gone; to sell his Lord and Master for a trifle to a hideous doom. **And it was night.** There is a dreadful finality in that. So terrible is the responsibility which our high prerogative of free will lays upon us. For when the Lord God, almighty and all merciful, and a human soul front each other in conflict, face to face and foot to foot, so far as our peering human eyes can see, it is the stubborn soul that has its way. Christ can love on to the very end, and yet the soul he loves goes out into the dark. "One of the most convenient Hieroglyphicks of God," says John Donne, "is a Circle; and a Circle is endlesse; whom God loves, hee loves to the end: and not onely to their own end, to their death, but to his end, and his end is, that he might love them still." [1]

31-38. ***The Intimacy of Christ.***—See Exeg. for a proposed rearrangement of the text. According to this sequence, immediately after the departure of Judas in vss. 31*a*, we should read chs. 15–16, and only then return to the remaining vss. 31*b*-38. If that is accepted, it implies that when the door closed behind Judas, Christ, following in thought his lost friend as he slipped through the darkness, has no hot words of reproach for him, but at once gives the eleven the parable of the vine; as if what had immediately suggested it to him was that here was a branch which ought to have been, could

[1] *Donne's Sermons*, selected passages by Logan Pearsall Smith (Oxford: The Clarendon Press, 1919), p. 134.

assume an accidental displacement and attempt to secure an ordered progress of thought by placing chs. 15–16 before ch. 14. This would remove the objection that the assertion in 16:5 ("None of you asks me, 'Where are you going?' ") ignores Thomas' question in 14:5. But it would still leave Peter's direct question in 13:36. A further dislocation must then be allowed for, and accordingly the rearrangement generally proposed is as follows: 13:1-31*a*; 15–16; 13:31*b*-38; 14; 17. For Bultmann's intricate reconstruction see Intro., p. 460. He would insert the prayer of ch. 17 after 13:31*a*, introducing it with words that form part of 13:1: "When then he had gone out, Jesus, knowing that his hour had come to pass from this world to the Father, having loved to the uttermost his own who are in the world, rose from the supper and lifted his eyes to heaven and said, 'Father, the hour has come. Glorify thy Son.' " Ch. 17 is then followed by 13:31-35; 15–16; 13:36–14:21. This carries us beyond the theory of accidental displacements, for Bultmann allows for considerable redaction.

A close study of the farewell discourses leads to the suggestion that they contain meditations upon sayings of Jesus, composed at different times and strung together without any organic unity. Thus in chs. 14–16 there are five groups of sayings about the Paraclete, side by side with other sayings which refer to the appearances of the risen Lord. The climax of those meditations is reached in the great prayer of ch. 17, where the mystical union of the church with its Lord, and the unity of its members severally with one another are rooted in the fellowship within the Godhead.

In this commentary we must take the text in the order known to us in all surviving MSS.

1. The New Commandment (13:31-35)

The impending hour of the Passion was eagerly heralded in 12:23. Now it is exultantly welcomed. **Now is the Son of man glorified.** Note this use of the term **Son of man,** as

---

have been, abundantly fruitful, but somehow it had become detached from the parent tree, and so was withering and dying—a kindly, pitying judgment on a friend turned into an enemy and a traitor.

But taking the text as it stands, some find in vss. 31 and 32 a palpable sense of relief; as if a weight had been lifted from Christ's spirit, as if he found that he could breathe more freely, and could now open his heart in a way and to a degree he could not do even to his best friends so long as a mind grown unsympathetic and hostile remained among them. But now that what had caused restraint was gone, he heaped his gifts eagerly upon them. And certainly he did open his heart to them in full measure "I pray for them," he said himself, "as I cannot pray for the world" (17:9). And he spoke to them more intimately, and much further in, than he could do to others.

Yet he did not seem to have much to encourage him in what was left: eleven men about to scatter in ignominious panic—they did not know it; but he did. And his chief friend upon the verge of making the most abject failure of them all. When Christ tells them that he is going away where they cannot immediately follow him, though they will in time, Peter protests hotly and almost angrily at being kept out and separated from a Master for whom he knows—aye, and that Master knows—he would do anything. **Lord, why cannot I follow you now? I will lay down my life for you.** And most of us, had we been reading the story for the first time, would have said to ourselves with complete confidence, "And he will." He was the very type of man to throw away his life in an act of passionate devotion. And yet Christ looked at him and said, **Will you lay down your life for me? Truly, truly, I say to you, the cock will not crow, till you have denied me three times.** And so, as we know, it proved.

"But they were not yet at their journey's end," says Bunyan, looking thoughtfully at the pilgrims, rejoicing, perhaps a little headily and boastfully, over their progress and successes. It becomes us to walk softly, and to speak low, set as we are in this perilous world, with these frail and undependable wills of ours, and with so many flying sparks of temptation blown to us upon every wind; and if one of them lights in our inflammable hearts, what then? We have grave need of that twofold assurance Peter gives us so confidently, that the prize at which we aim is being "kept" for us by a power stronger than our own; and that meantime it "keeps" us too, so that we may not fall away nor fail (I Pet. 1:4-5).

31-32. *The Selflessness of Christ.*—What seems most arresting in the whole chapter is the

32 If God be glorified in him, God shall also glorify him in himself, and shall straightway glorify him.

33 Little children, yet a little while I am with you. Ye shall seek me; and as I said unto the Jews, Whither I go, ye cannot come; so now I say to you.

34 A new commandment I give unto you, That ye love one another; as I have loved you, that ye also love one another.

him God is glorified; 32 if God is glorified
in him, God will also glorify him in himself,
and glorify him at once. 33 Little children,
yet a little while I am with you. You will
seek me; and as I said to the Jews so now
I say to you, 'Where I am going you cannot
come.' 34 A new commandment I give to
you, that you love one another; even as I
have loved you, that you also love one an-

---

so often in the Synoptics, instead of the first person singular. The Cross is the way to exaltation with the Father. But further, God, who has been glorified in the works of Christ (14:13; 15:8; 17:4), will now be glorified by the passion of the Son (cf. 12:27-28), in which the perfect obedience of him who said, "Lo, I have come to do thy will, O God" (Ps. 40:8; Heb. 10:7) is to be consummated. Nor is that all, for in the N.T. the Cross is never the last word. It is always viewed in the light of the Easter revelation. **God will also glorify him in himself, and glorify him at once.** The meaning of these words is most clearly revealed in the prayer of 17:5, "And now, Father, glorify thou me in thy own presence with the glory which I had with thee before the world was made."

---

selflessness of Christ. While Judas is present, so absorbed is he in his efforts to save him, that no thought of the horrors in which his treachery must involve his own person appears to have gained an entrance into Christ's mind at all. And what surely leaps out at one in vss. 31-32 is that when the door had closed upon a man hurrying through the night to bring about his destruction, Christ, unable to do more for him, and at last facing what it meant for himself, has not one word of murmuring or complaint; only a paean of thanksgiving that God should be granting him this opportunity of glorifying him so fully and so signally.

Against such a background our whimperings over the frets and rubs of life look small and mean indeed! And no less foolish. For all experience corroborates Paul's bold assertion that in all things, literally all things, even the most unlikely, that seem to score themselves out as palpable exceptions to the rule, "God works for good with those who love him" (Rom. 8:28). Fraser of Brea, that fine old Covenanter who suffered many things for his Lord and for his cause, set down in his diary that he had come to this: that whenever an untoward happening or cruel-looking providence broke into his life, he had learned to look at it with interest, and to greet it hospitably, asking himself, "Now what good does this bring me? [2] The messenger is certainly harsh-featured, but it too has a love token from the King." Christ saved us by his cross, thought a minister long ago, because he took it "lovingly." And if we too were dedicated spirits, taking lovingly what is sent to us and is asked of us, claiming only to be used of God, laying down no conditions, making no exceptions, praying, as Baxter prayed in grim pain on his deathbed, "It is not fit for me to prescribe—when thou wilt, what thou wilt, how thou wilt," [3] we too should know that peace of God that passes all understanding; and even through us he would accomplish incredible things.

34-35. *Christ's New Commandment.*—After warning them that in a little he must leave them for a time, Christ explains what he requires of them (and us), and how we can help him in the world. It is all gathered up in one little word. What Christ asks of us is to be unselfish, generous with ourselves, using our lives for others, and not merely for personal interests and our own ends. "Give yourself royally," were Cromwell's last words to Tyndale. Whoever does so, not in a vague purpose that comes to nothing definite and real, but actually, practically, day by day, is keeping Christ's commandment, living in accordance with his law, showing forth the characteristic spirit of his kingdom; and to produce that in us is the aim and point and end of Christianity. Fail there, and we fail altogether; and have missed what is distinctive, characteristic, original in this teaching. For Christ himself claims that what he lays upon us in this matter is **a new commandment.** And so it literally is.

There are of course prophecies of it, and real gleams of the thing itself, in his own literature

[2] *Memoirs of James Fraser of Brea,* ed. W. K. Tweedie (Edinburgh: Wodrow Society, 1847), pp. 241, 264.

[3] *Autobiography of Richard Baxter* (London: J. M. Dent & Sons, 1925), p. 266.

35 By this shall all *men* know that ye are my disciples, if ye have love one to another.

other. 35 By this all men will know that you are my disciples, if you have love for one another."

There are two textual variants which affect the interpretation of vss. 31-32. (*a*) A group of authorities omit the conditional clause, **If God is glorified in him.** The group is weighty, ℵ B C D L W and many MSS of the ancient versions. But this omission is probably due to homoeoteleuton (i.e., an omission due to the copyist's eye leaping from one word or clause to another with a similar ending). (*b*) Vs. 32*b*, καὶ ὁ θεὸς δοξάσει αὐτὸν ἐν αὐτῷ. Some MSS read ἑαυτῷ. ℵ B Origen have εν αυτω, which must be accented as in the two previous clauses. Both Zahn and Lagrange argue that even if the pronoun were reflexive (αὑτῷ), it would refer, not to the subject ὁ θεός, but to the object αὐτόν. If this is so, the thought is that just as the Son has glorified the Father by doing his works according to his will, so the Father will glorify the Son in his own earthly life, by allowing the glory which he had before the world was, to shine forth for men to see. Then καὶ εὐθὺς δοξάσει αὐτόν would refer to the Resurrection, when the eyes of the disciples were fully opened to what they had dimly seen before the Passion.

of the O.T.—kindly regulations in the law, curbing the selfishness into which men are so prone to fall, and enjoining remembrance of others' needs and rights; and shining out here and there in the annals of his own people, there are noble examples of how life ought to be spent—the forgiveness and generosity of Joseph toward his brothers; the moving magnanimity of Moses, that great soul indeed, beseeching that he himself be blotted out if thereby his people can be spared; the gallant epic of Jonathan's wholehearted friendship, when a smaller man would have been jealous and resentful. And in other religions too one does come on not a few right thrilling sayings, some of which go far in the direction to which Christ points us, and one or two of which keep step with him to the end. And yet the plain fact remains that Christ has altered the whole moral landscape in a way we had not even begun to realize till in World War II many of the Germans, turning their backs upon his teaching, reverted to what was natural to man before he came, and astonished us with their bestiality. Even on the heights things are entirely different. In Hinduism holiness is not what Christ has taught us to think of as holiness, is not a generous giving of one's self for others, is not the eager loving of one another which he claims from us, but is an anxious, jealous, self-absorbed guarding of ourselves from evil. The goal it sets before men is not service. It is blamelessness. And Christ has no interest in blamelessness. It is too tame, too vague, too colorless for him. He demands as a minimum something much more daring and generous, more adventurous and positive. What he claims from his followers is not that they should do no evil but that they should "do good" (Luke 6:35). Neutrality, says a tremendous scripture, makes him sick (Rev. 3:16). A mere nonentity, not evil yet not good, doing no actual harm yet not telling for righteousness, is of no manner of use to him, he says; and that over and over. No charge is entered against Dives as to his personal character, which may have been notably clean, or as to his business methods, which so far as we learn were unchallengeable. The man spent his life harmlessly enough; but he did nobody any good. He did not love, did not run out in service to the needy, did not, as Browning tells us Herakles did, hold "his life out on his hand, for any man to take."[4] And for that he is cast out. Christ's heart warmed to the rich young ruler, who had no actual guilt upon his record, and who had, so he claimed, kept the commandments. But that was nothing like enough. He had hurt nobody. But whom had he helped? That was the major point.

Because, as J. R. Seeley puts it, Christ added a new hemisphere to the moral world.[5] Beside negative morality, in and above it, he set positive morality. One could keep the Ten Commandments perfectly, and yet not be within sight of real Christianity. There are for us not ten commandments but eleven. And the last is, "Thou shalt love." In the one little word "love," says Christ, there is summed up the whole duty of man. In all this he manifests far more originality than we realize. So T. R. Glover, in *The Influence of Christ in the Ancient World,* a fine little study of Christianity and its nearest rivals: "Epicurean and Stoic had laid stress on 'undisturbedness' and 'freedom from emotion'—in each case an essentially

[4] "Balaustion's Adventure."

[5] *Ecce Homo* (Boston: Roberts Bros., 1886), pp. 201-2; but see entire chapter, "Positive Morality."

36 ¶ Simon Peter said unto him, Lord, whither goest thou? Jesus answered him, Whither I go, thou canst not follow me now; but thou shalt follow me afterward.

36 Simon Peter said to him, "Lord, where are you going?" Jesus answered, "Where I am going you cannot follow me now; but you shall follow afterward."

This glorification of the Son involves separation from the disciples (vs. 33). Jesus had told the Jews (7:33-34; 8:21) that they could not come where he was going. So now he tells his **little children** that his time with them can only be short. There must be a separation. Later on (14:3) they are to learn that the separation is not permanent. Meanwhile the Christian society, represented by these disciples, is to bear its witness to the world by keeping the new commandment of mutual love. How central this was in the ethical teaching of the churches where this Gospel first circulated may be seen from I John 2:7-10; 3:11, 23; II John 5. The distinctive feature of this love of the brethren is that it is the natural outcome of the love of Christ for them, which it is to resemble in its sacrificial devotion (cf. I John 3:11, 14; 4:7-11).

2. Peter's Denial Foretold (13:36-38)

Peter presses for information about this departure foretold in vs. 33. Jesus qualifies the bare statement just made by saying, **Where I am going you cannot follow me now;**

selfish canon of life." He allows that in the case of the Stoic it was always modified by the memory of the rest of the cosmos. Still, " 'Freedom from emotion?' The Greek word was, and is, letter for letter, *apathy*. 'I do not hold,' wrote the gentle Plutarch, 'with those who hymn the savage and hard Apathy.' "[6] It was no ideal of Christ's. Like the Master, the Christian must expose himself "to feel what wretches feel."

> There lay one of the secrets of Christian morality; its keynote was not self-protection, but the utmost of self-giving help for others, and the dynamic was the love of Christ, "who loved me and gave himself for me." The Christian does here exactly the opposite to the Stoic; the Stoic emphasized the self . . . and strove to protect that self in tranquillity from the emotions that other selves would awake in it. The Christian emphasized the personality of others . . . and forgot the claims of his own self.[7]

But on this showing is it not evident that Christ is nothing more or less than a great, or the great, moral teacher; and that those are right who tell us to stop worrying about theology, advising us to dismiss that as useless lumber cluttering up the mind, and to stick to the Sermon on the Mount, and such practical teaching, which they acclaim as being level with life, and not losing itself in the mists but really getting somewhere? Yet this very passage shows the folly and impracticability of such rootless ideas.

For says Christ, "My commandment to you is nothing less than this, **that you love one another; even as I have loved you,**" i.e., he is the measure against which we are to be tested. The Cross, affirms Clement, is our standard; and we must live right up to that boundary. So it makes a difference what Christ means by love. For that word has been tossed about with varying meanings; and some of them are cool and tepid compared to what is required of us. The sound is the same, but the content is much meagerer and thinner. After all, it is not so much even Christ's teaching as his character, his life, his death, all that he was and did, the sacrifices that he made, the lengths to which he went, that have brought home to us something of what he meant by love. And to grasp that we must have the facts concerning him before us. No doubt, thank God, there are prophecies and adumbrations of his spirit to be found elsewhere; as on the dark part of the moon one can see through a telescope spots of light, which are the reflections of the sunshine, caught first by the highest peaks among the lunar mountains and flashed back, while the valleys at their feet still lie in somber and unbroken shadow. That glorious offer of self-sacrifice by Moses, "Blot me, I pray thee, out of thy book" (Exod. 32:32), if thereby the people can be spared and saved. Or Hiuen-Tsiang, the Buddhist, fallen among bandits in The Himalaya, using his last moments in dedicating himself to use all his future existences, in the endless chain of transmigration which he believed to lie before him, for the reclaiming of these wild spirits now about to murder him—life after life ungrudgingly—till the last of them is changed, is saved.[8]

[6] Cambridge: University Press, 1929, pp. 76-77.

[7] *Ibid.*, p. 77.

[8] Shaman Hwui Li, *The Life of Hiuen-Tsiang* (London: Kegan Paul, Trench, Trübner & Co., 1911), pp. 86-88.

37 Peter said unto him, Lord, why cannot I follow thee now? I will lay down my life for thy sake.

37 Peter said to him, "Lord, why cannot I follow you now? I will lay down my life

but you shall follow afterward. It is the same lesson that Peter had already been taught about knowledge (vs. 7), "Not . . . now, but afterward." This is another instance of deliberate ambiguities in the sayings of the Johannine Jesus (see Intro., p. 439). The promise to all the disciples was that Jesus would return and take them to himself when a place had been prepared (14:3). But here there is also an allusion to the martyrdom

Much lesser things indeed than such supreme examples. For some of the mountains that have caught the sunlight were not unusually high. An ordinary lad giving his life for his country; a mother spending herself for her children; even a bird, shamming lameness and a broken wing, that, the alarming intruders being diverted from the fledglings by that ruse, the threatened brood may be given time to scatter and find cover.

Nonetheless, Christlikeness in its fullness is an amazingly original thing. And it is that, and not less, that is claimed from us. And to offer less is, for us, sin. And how are we to realize what this Christlikeness is, sufficiently to aim at it at all, unless the facts are given us?

But further, the facts concerning Christ not only give us a new and loftier conception of what a human life should be, not merely make us want to reproduce it, they also provide the inspiration needed to push us over into definite action, enabling us to will what we know that we ought to will, yet could not bring ourselves to will. And that is where many a brave scheme has broken down. There are noble and eloquent statements of the brotherhood of man to be found here and there throughout the past, e.g., in Cicero. Apparently in those days too, as in our own times, there was a reaching out in the minds of many after something bigger, broader, more wide flung than sect, or party, or mere nationalism; something that, overleaping all such barriers and limitations, would embrace all mankind in a universal brotherliness and charity. It reads well; and yet nothing came of it. Because it was a theory that remained only a theory; and evaporated in a cloud of beautiful words and notions, nothing more. But realize the love of Christ and one has to do something about it, must respond to it, must catch the infection of it, must reproduce what one can of it in one's dealings with his fellows. And it happens! We love, so John explains in his epistle, we seek to bear ourselves unselfishly and helpfully toward those about us, because God has first loved us; and we cannot accept all that from him and yet drift on ourselves in the old hard, self-centered way.

To that, too, of course, there are analogies thick-sown in life. A youth plays the fool at college or elsewhere; loses control of himself and plunges into ugly courses. And though in his better moments he may despise and loathe himself for the way he is living, he cannot stop it, but is carried down the hill faster and faster by his own impetus, and nothing lies ahead but ruin. Yet let a fine girl come into his life, and often everything is changed. Somehow the man can now do what formerly he could not do; both can and does resist what had grown for him irresistible, both can and does rise above what had become his very nature. Dishonoring things that had him firmly in their grip have no more dominion over him. This new and greater interest, this clean love stooping to him in his unworthiness, has altered the whole situation. As Tennyson's lover puts it,

> If I be dear to someone else,
> . . . .
> Shall I not take care of all that I think,
> Yea ev'n of wretched meat and drink,
> . . . .
> If I be dear to someone else?[9]

But it is standing upon Calvary, awed, humbled, astonished by the lengths that Christ's love has gone for us, that multitudes have murmured with Paul, incredulously and yet sure that what cannot be true is true, that he "loved me, and gave himself for me" (Gal. 2:20); and in view of this I cannot, dare not, will not live as I have been doing; this and this and this must go—and have found that it had given them the power to rise above them. But without the love of Christ to sting them into action they would have remained poor, wingless, crawling creatures to the end; helpless to do what they wanted to do, and yet could not begin to do, to be what they saw that they ought to be—only it was completely out of reach.

"This is my commandment, **that you love one another; even as I have loved you."** If the claim made upon us here is staggering, the power offered to us here is enough, even for that.

[9] "Maud," st. xv.

38 Jesus answered him, Wilt thou lay down thy life for my sake? Verily, verily, I say unto thee, The cock shall not crow, till thou hast denied me thrice.

for you." 38 Jesus answered, "Will you lay down your life for me? Truly, truly, I say to you, the cock will not crow, till you have denied me three times.

in which Peter would follow in the steps of his Master (cf. 21:18-19). Unconscious of this deeper meaning, Peter impatiently avows his eagerness to follow immediately. He would follow the Good Shepherd in laying down his life for him. But his character had not yet been tempered for this ordeal. Now he will deny his Lord three times over. Afterward, in the unknown future, he is to make good his claim.

And so Christ lays it down that what he wishes to be the distinguishing mark of his people, what is inevitably to differentiate real believers from outsiders, the something extra and special that he gives which others cannot show, is the kindly, unselfish, generous way they have of using life, a way that simply does not occur to non-Christian folk, but which, when seen, strikes and arrests them. That is to be the characteristic of a Christian, giving him the one valid claim to rank as such, the only title deeds to the name that will be honored and accepted. **By this all men will know that you are my disciples, if you have love for one another.** A self-centered, crabbed, unforgiving person will rule himself out even in the eyes of unbelievers. For anyone can see that he is not at all the type. And if relying upon other evidence which we confidently adduce, saying "Lord, Lord, did we not prophesy in your name, and cast out demons in your name, and do many mighty works in your name?" (Matt. 7:22), we appeal to Christ to own us, he on his judgment seat will himself corroborate their unfavorable verdict. For there, so he has warned us, everything will turn on this all-decisive question, "Did your Christianity compel and enable you, within the limits of your powers and opportunities, to be thoughtful and compassionate and helpful and unselfish toward others around about you? Your whole case stands or falls by that." And everything else is merely subsidiary to that, or else irrelevant.

In the beginning Christianity did effect precisely the result that our Lord wants in us. Outsiders turned and looked at these odd Christian people, openly astonished at their unheard of mode of spending life, not in their own interests or for their own ends, as others naturally did, but in a reckless generosity toward people with no claim on them whatever. Not only the fathers, but those without, bear evidence to that, e.g., Lucian holds his sides, sore with laughter, through whole pages of merry japes over these impossible innocents, who will make any sacrifice for those of whom they know nothing at all, if only they claim to be Christians; and indeed showing that same openhandedness to those who could not advance even that shadowy qualification for their bounty. Here was a new type of people, living their lives in a new kind of way.

No doubt, unhappily since then there has been another and right ugly side to the story—long annals of bigotry, persecution, cruelty, murder. It is surely a gloomy thought that after all the Nazis were only a few hundred years behind the Christian church itself in those obscene devilments of theirs that make us sick, though indeed their ruthlessness was more wholesale, and was given a sharper cutting edge by the discoveries of modern science. But it is well to remember that slaughter in the name of reason has exceeded in a few years all that was done in the name of religion in two thousand, that under recent totalitarian regimes more were killed than under the Inquisition in three centuries. But all this apart, many feel that the characteristic Christian spirit has been lost; that those who hold the faith have fallen back into step with the world round about them, living as they live, not manifestly more unselfish than they; that often their very religion, as they have used it, has made them too self-centered and cautious and unadventurous. So John Stuart Mill read the average Christian, though admitting that in this the so-called follower had fallen away from Christ.

> Christian morality has all the characters of a reaction. Its ideal is negative rather than positive; passive rather than active; Innocence rather than Nobleness; Abstinence from Evil, rather than energetic Pursuit of Good: in its precepts . . . "thou shalt not" predominates unduly over "thou shalt."[1]

That seems a one-sided judgment calling out for rethinking. After all, it is Christianity that has created and chiefly maintains this enormous, world-wide, multisided thing that we call charity, which was almost unknown till Christ taught people to be hurt by others' sufferings and to rise up and hurry to their aid. And to

[1] *On Liberty* (New York: P. F. Collin & Son, 1909) p. 253.

14 Let not your heart be troubled: ye believe in God, believe also in me.

14 "Let not your hearts be troubled; believe[a] in God, believe also in me.

[a] Or *you believe.*

3. The Way, the Truth, and the Life (14:1-14)

14:1. Let not your hearts be troubled: The connection is not with the warning addressed to Simon Peter in the closing verses of ch. 13, but Jesus is calming the minds made anxious by the announcement in 13:33. His own heart has been troubled by the

this day it is the Christians who cheerfully bear the main burden of what is being done for those in every kind of trouble and difficulty and disability, not feeling it to be a burden, but wanting to come in and lend a hand, as others do not. Because instinctively a real Christian plans and lives his life more generously, helpfully, lovingly than does the average outsider. But if there is any substance in Mill's allegation, then we must indeed bethink ourselves, and get closer to the Master, and catch the inspiration of his spirit, and not fail him in what he has underlined as central. When Donald Fraser, the distinguished missionary, finally came home from Africa, the native session sent after him a moving minute of thanks for all that he had done for them, he who had found them heathen and wild men, leading an uneasy life, and had brought among them peace, and education, and the glory of the Lord Jesus Christ. And their noble expression of gratitude ends with this haunting and memorable sentence, "We are ashamed that we have not caught the infection of a like heart." [2] So surely should we feel and say to the Master who has done so much for us, and given so much to us; making life for us a different and better thing, and who expects that we shall learn to use our lives after his fashion, and to follow in his steps.

14:1. ***How to Be Untroubled.*—Let not your hearts be troubled,** so Christ said, looking around on that little company growing bewildered by his staggering warnings. And in truth, as we judge, they had plenty to trouble them. There was this mysterious departure of the Master which they did not grasp or understand. He kept saying that he was going away. But where? If he meant that he was about to die, their minds recoiled from that as obviously the end of everything. Further, if indeed the horror of that had begun to come home to them as yet, there was the fall of Judas, one of themselves. In any case, there was that ugly saying that one of their circle was ready to betray the Master; and even more daunting still, that other utterly incomprehensible one about Peter, of all people, their second in command, and the stanchest of them all—that he was on the very eve of failing his Lord! Everything seemed to be shaking and collapsing. Yet Christ told them, faced by facts as grim as these, not to worry, not to allow themselves to become alarmed and disquieted, inciting them toward his own gallantry of spirit, and sharing with them the secret of how to gain it.

That is a rallying cry much needed in this world so full of troubled, alarmed, desperate folk, with disquieting, even disastrous possibilities always crowding in upon them and hardly to be held off; with their lives cut so narrowly that there is never an inch of margin, so that tugging hard, they can barely get the ends of things to come together. And they are growing older, or illness threatens, or a sudden unforeseeable change in taste and fashion has reduced the value and the appeal of the goods that they produce and of the work that they can do; or those dear to them hurt them, or fail them, or make shipwreck—the thing is endless. In troops the troubles that beset men and women all around us come flocking and jostling into the mind. Moreover, there are the fears that clutch at us with their cold hands. They may never come true, never grow into actual realities, may be only nightmares; but in the dark, to some minds, they are frightening beyond describing. "Imaginary grievances have always been my torment more than real ones," confesses Keats.[3] Is not the world as a whole losing its nerve because human science is outrunning human morality, and growing scared at the thought of hideous disasters that may never happen?

So J. A. Hadfield, with his wide experience: "If fear were abolished from modern life, the work of the psychotherapist would be nearly gone. It was not without cause that the Master of the soul so often reiterated 'Fear not,' 'Be not afraid,' 'Be not anxious.'" [4]

John Macmurray, the philosopher, argues that many are hag-ridden by fear, "by the feeling of being alone in a hostile world," and that a false religion tries to steady them by asserting that what they dread will never really happen—

[2] Agnes R. Fraser, *Donald Fraser of Livingstonia* (London: Hodder & Stoughton, 1934), p. 273.

[3] Letter CXX.

[4] *The Spirit* (ed. B. H. Streeter: New York: The Macmillan Co., 1919), p. 97.

thought of impending betrayal, separation, and death (11:33; 12:27; 13:21), but victory has come with the assurance that his death was but a homecoming to the Father, and that the cup which he was to drink was given by the Father's hand (cf. 18:11). His word of comfort to the distressed disciples is that they should exercise faith—belief in God and in himself. Faith in Jesus is the only true faith in God (cf. 8:19; 10:30, 38; 12:44). Grammatically these two verbs can be taken either as indicative or imperative. Four renderings are thus possible: (*a*) **Ye believe in God, believe also in me;** (*b*) "You believe in God, you believe also in me"; (*c*) **Believe in God, believe also in me;** (*d*) "Believe in God, you believe also in me." The choice is between (*a*) and (*c*), with a strong preference for (*c*). The full force of this interpretation is well brought out by F. J. A. Hort (*The First Epistle of St. Peter* I. 1–II. 17 [London: Macmillan & Co., 1898], p. 83): "The sense is, 'Believe, on God and on me believe'; the first suggestion being of constancy opposed to troubling and fearfulness (exactly as in Isa. vii. 9; xxviii. 16), and the second of the ground of that constancy, rest in God, itself depending on rest in Christ."

---

which, says he, is a lie. But a real religion rallies them by convincing them that, if the worst does come, "there is nothing to be afraid of." And he ends thus:

> If you ask me, now, where is there a religion that has ever taken that line, which has refused to offer its adherents an escape from the reality of evil and suffering, the answer is "The religion of Christ". . . . The solution of our dilemma is to be found, I am convinced, in Christianity and only there.[5]

Long ago Buddha, that wise man, looking out upon his fellows with those shrewd eyes of his, laid it down over and over that the futility of most lives is due to one or other or all of five main "hindrances" that keep men back or pull them down. These vary very slightly in different places. But he has no doubt at all that among the chief dangers that beset us, a foremost place is held by "worry and flurry." And if we watch our fellows, or better, if we watch ourselves, we shall see that that is an accurate diagnosis. If anyone can make an end of trouble in these unquiet hearts of ours, that were a boon indeed!

"I can," says Christ. **Believe in God,** he says. Believe that there is a God; that you are never alone, are never asked to manage somehow for yourself and by yourself; that you can always go to him and be helped by him; that even when you forget about him, he comes to you and finds ways to steady and bring you through with honor. Believe in God as we do in a man to whom we have often turned, and he has never failed us, so that now we are entirely certain that he never will. **Believe in God.**

So Christ himself came through. Because he really did believe in God, "with no if's and but's," as George Macdonald said; because he really did believe that God means what he says, and is wholly dependable, and will assuredly stand to it; and went forward upon that assumption. In some real measure he has taught us also to believe; and that often almost instinctively. So that we do not realize the enormous difference which that faith makes, the sense of security and of stability it gives us. There was a time when this world of ours was a wild, uneasy place in which to live. For it seemed to be a sheer chaos in which anything might happen; and that for any or no reason. Till science reassured men by its revelation that this is an orderly universe, subject to definite laws on which one can rely; and that this world is not a welter of confusion, but that effects have causes which can be learned and stored in memory; so that one can plan ahead with a real measure of assurance; and since there is seen to be sense and meaning in it, life becomes thinkable and livable. So, to believe in God shuts out much that otherwise would have been frightening enough: gives us the feeling of a child, living in its father's house, or of a passenger who, once he has committed himself to a long sea voyage, gives himself no uneasiness about the navigation or the like, but leaves that to the captain, who is wise and skilled and trustworthy —and knowing this, he himself feels no need to worry, sees no sense in it, and does not do it.

Believe also in me, says Christ; in all that I have told you about God, and man, and life, and sin, and salvation, and immortality. And, especially and specifically here, in me. For much will soon crowd in upon you which will tempt you to doubt me; to make you think I have deceived you, have led you out by false promises which I cannot keep, on an impossible adventure that has come to nothing; and that I have deserted you, leaving you to scramble out of the mess and muddle in which I have landed you, as best you can, and with no help from me—like Napoleon, in that ghastly retreat from Moscow, making off, and securing

[5] *Freedom in the Modern World* (London: Faber & Faber, 1932), pp. 59-60.

2 In my Father's house are many mansions: if *it were* not *so*, I would have told you. I go to prepare a place for you.

2 In my Father's house are many rooms; if it were not so, would I have told you

2-3. The **many mansions** (KJV), **rooms** (RSV), "resting-places" (Weymouth), "abodes" (Moffatt), may be thought of in two ways. One possible interpretation is that in the **Father's house** there is room for all. Another interpretation of the Greek word (μονή) regards it as a hospice where weary pilgrims of eternity rest before continuing their journey in the endless realm of "coming to know . . . the only true God" (17:3). On the whole, the former view is preferable. In vs. 23—the only other occurrence of the word in the Greek N.T.—it means "abode" or "home." Two ways of punctuating vs. 2*b* lead to

his own safety, while leaving his troops to perish miserably in that bitter cold. But, says Christ, I am not deserting you, and I will not forget you. You have a sure and permanent place in my heart; and wherever I may be, I shall be thinking of you, working for you, expecting you. He tells them frankly that they have a steep and stony road before them; but that as Samuel Rutherford put it, the worst that there can be is "a tired traveller, and a joyful and a sweet welcome home."[6] And that he guarantees to whosoever will accept it.

2. ***The Argument from Christ's Silence.***—There are few things more self-revealing than one's conception of heaven. Some niggardly souls have cramped and narrow thoughts of it; appear to wish and to expect only a stuffy little corner of a place, where they and a few kindred spirits are to gather, and all the rest are to be left outside. But in the N.T. heaven is a gloriously spacious place, with twelve gates opening in every direction (Rev. 21:12-13), and multitudes pouring in through them from all nations and peoples and kindred and tongues (Rev. 7:9). **In my Father's house are many rooms,** says Christ. Yet in all that mass of happy people the individual is not overlooked or forgotten or lost in the throng. "Say not," demands the author of Ecclesiasticus, to people discouraged by a depressing sense of their own insignificance, "Say not I shall never be missed in a boundless creation" (Ecclus. 16:17). You will, says Jesus Christ, with absolute assurance. For each one has his own distinctive, personal, exclusive place in the Father's heart, and in the Father's house, and no one else can ever fill it. **In my Father's house are many rooms; if it were not so, would I have told you that I go to prepare a place for you?**

So the RSV renders it; though some of us perhaps cling a little wistfully to the old and familiar KJV translation, **If it were not so, I would have told you. I go to prepare a place for you.** That is admittedly so spacious a saying that unless used with caution and humility and reverence it might easily become a danger to us, seeming to sanction individual and fanciful whimsies. Simply because he did not explicitly and in set words repudiate them, the Lord Christ is not to be held as having acquiesced in everything that these foolish hearts of ours choose to desire and claim. But there are yearnings in us which seem to be essential to and a part of our nature, that keep welling up out of its deeps, which might seem to be covered and met by this assurance. Are we, for instance, really only "Ships that pass in the night, and speak each other in passing";[7] and so fall apart—forever? Or shall we find and know again those we have lost, once we too reach the beyond? Does it not seem at least that in such a case we might apply the rule, **If it were not so, I would have told you?** Ignatius, for one, was sure that "He who possesseth the words of Jesus is able to hear his very silence."[8] That is a saying which has many possible applications; some of them wise and some of them less so.

Yet the RSV rendering also is a bonnie metaphor, or rather, a moving fact. **In my Father's house are many rooms; if it were not so, would I have told you that I go to prepare a place for you?** When an honored and loved guest is coming, preparations are made which are designed to meet his tastes and likings. The books that will appeal to him are laid where he can find them; flowers which we remember as favorites of his are set about the rooms. These preparations are not merely general, but are thought out for very him. And yonder Jesus Christ is so lovingly making ready for our coming; arranging a place, our place; and that with such an exact remembrance of our particular needs and likings that it cannot fit anybody else. It is your place. And it is waiting for you, yonder. We must not fail the Father; leaving him to all eternity with that room designed for us still empty. For God wants all his family to gather home, not one among them missing.

[6] *Letters*, Letter LVI.

[7] Longfellow, "Elizabeth," st. iv, in *Tales of a Wayside Inn*.

[8] Ign. Eph. 15:2.

3 And if I go and prepare a place for you, I will come again, and receive you unto myself; that where I am, *there* ye may be also.
4 And whither I go ye know, and the way ye know.

that I go to prepare a place for you? 3 And
when I go and prepare a place for you, I will come again and will take you to myself, that where I am you may be also.
4 And you know the way where I am go-

two different meanings: (*a*) **If it were not so, I would have told you** (KJV). (*b*) **If it were not so, would I have told you that I go to prepare a place for you?** (RSV.) In reply to the objection that Jesus had not told his disciples that he was going to prepare a place for them, we may refer to 12:26, though as in 10:25; 11:40; 12:34, the reference to a past statement is not perfectly clear. **I will come again and will take you to myself, that where I am you may be also.** This promise is definitely eschatological, and must be taken, as in 21:22-23; I John 2:28, as the basis of the advent hope of the church (cf. Rev. 22:20, and in its apocalyptic setting, I Thess. 4:17).

4-6. The disciples **know the way** (vs. 4) that Jesus is going—death. To this Thomas replies that they know neither the goal nor **the way.** Jesus replies (vs. 6), **I am the way, and the truth, and the life.** He does not merely point **the way,** he is **the way.** Union with Christ is the one way to God and to the Father's home. This saying may have given rise

3. *The Master Is Come, and Calleth for Thee.*—And when I go and prepare a place for you, I will come again and will take you to myself, that where I am you may be also. The coming of our Lord has a great place in the N.T., but has become much dimmer and less vivid and dramatic in our minds. Yet in one sense to all of us he will certainly come. Robert Bridges speaks drearily of the time, so surely nearing,

> . . . when in the dark,
> Unwilling, alone we embark,
> And the things we have seen and have known and have heard of, fail us.[9]

But that is pagan thinking. For a Christian does not embark alone, nor do the things upon which he has founded give or vanish. And when for him it is the end here, and those watching around the bed say softly, "It is over. Death has come," it is not really death that takes his hand, and leads him out, or rather in, but Jesus Christ himself. For said he, **I will come again and will take you to myself, that where I am you may be also.** He keeps his word; that is all we know about the Christian heaven. Yet it is enough.

Minds wise, and not so wise, keep listening in hope of catching further tidings blown to us from the other world. But what they think they hear seems for the most part self-condemned as unauthentic and plainly incredible, by reason of its utter silliness. They are with Christ, so the plain Christian says, and leaves it contentedly at that, admitting that Christ has a claim on his dear ones far superior to his own, agreeing that he would never dream of wishing them to come back—to what? To be with him again, whereas yonder they are with Christ? And so they are not dragged out of his hands, but given freely and thankfully by one exulting in the glory that has come to them, though his own heart is sore and lonesome.

[9] "On a Dead Child," from *The Poetical Works of Robert Bridges.* Used by permission of the Clarendon Press, Oxford.

This is certainly one of the most gracious passages in Scripture; and few can have been so much read and befingered, especially in times of loss. How often at a funeral has one watched a mother, numbed by the blow, listen to scripture after scripture by which others have been comforted, with her face still stony, unmoved, impervious; and yet, at the first words of this passage something seemed to melt within her and there came the healing tears.

And have any other verses been so much to so many at the hour of dying?

> John Watson, that consummate preacher, used to tell us that, sometimes, when one of his flock was dying, and seemed gone, he would kneel down and whisper into the quickly dulling ears, "In My Father's house are many mansions." And, with that, the soul, three-quarters through the river, turned, and came back to listen (and you could see the soundless lips making the motions of echoing the familiar "Father's house," "many mansions"), and waited till there came the words of invitation and of welcome, "I go to prepare a place for you. And if I go and prepare a place for you, I will come again, and receive you unto Myself; that where I am, there ye may be also." And at that, with a contented little sigh, it was gone, entirely unafraid.[1]

4-7. *How Christ Is the Way.*—And, adds Christ, **You know the way where I am going.** Whereat Thomas, who always liked the feel of

[1] A. J. Gossip, *Experience Worketh Hope* (Edinburgh: T. & T. Clark, 1944), p. 188. Used by permission.

5 Thomas saith unto him, Lord, we know not whither thou goest; and how can we know the way?

ing."[b] 5 Thomas said to him, "Lord, we do not know where you are going; how can

[b] Other ancient authorities read *where I am going you know, and the way you know.*

---

to the earliest name by which the Christians were known (for the Way, cf. Acts 9:2; 19:9, 23; 22:4; 24:14, 22). **The truth** is the divine reality, the goal of all thought and effort. In the syncretistic Gnosticism of his age the evangelist was aware of all the speculations about the heavenward journey of the soul after death and the need of a guide. The key to all was imparted in an esoteric knowledge—gnosis—to favored souls. In this Gospel the noun "knowledge" is avoided (see Intro., p. 452), but Christ declares himself to be the ultimate reality—**truth.** Thus Jesus is the only **way . . . to the Father.** Because he and the Father are one (10:30) in the perfect relationship of Father and Son, no other can lead men to God as Father in the way that Jesus can. The way leads through death to life eternal. Jesus is **the life.** This characteristic of the Logos is one of the dominant notes of the Gospel (see 1:4; 5:21, 26; 11:25). The connection between the ideas of truth and of life is best studied in the discourse on the bread of life in ch. 6. Some expositors following John Lightfoot (*Horae Hebraicae,* III, 398) take this threefold claim as a single idea with two qualifying adjectives—so Moffatt, "I am the real and

---

solid facts beneath his feet, and perhaps had not much poetry in his nature, blurts out, **Lord, we do not know where you are going; how can we know the way?**

What did he mean by that? In 11:16 he had been quite sure that if Christ returned to Jerusalem, that was certain death for him; so certain that, rising to his feet, he had said stoutheartedly, "Let us also go, that we may die with him." Was he now somehow less confident that this must be the end? Or was he staring fixedly out into the beyond, and in his honest way admitting that he could see never a trace or vestige of this Father's house of which Christ had been speaking? "What lies ahead? What kind of life, if any, awaits us there? It is all dark and blank to me." To which Christ answered, "I am going to my Father."

And indeed what else could be done with one who had lived as he had lived—human and yet divinely unselfish and kind—except that he be set in his natural element, with God, and in God? For there is nothing arbitrary in the destiny that awaits us. Each of us will receive that for which we have fitted and prepared ourselves. And so Christ must be seated at the right hand of the Father, far above every name that is named in heaven or on earth; though as Calvin reminds us, he reigns far more for us than for himself, here, too, seeking nothing for himself; but using his pre-eminence, like everything else, for the glory of God, and to help our need and frailty.

"Where am I going? To the Father. And the way to him? **I am the way.**" Other teachers have used that same symbol, e.g., Buddha, claiming to be the rediscoverer of an old path, long lost, into the reality of things; or Lao-tzu, calling his dark teaching "the Way." So Christ, **I am the way,** he claims. And multitudes have found that the aptest of symbols. Thus Chesterton, in the notebook out of which came all his works, once set down:

Xmas Day
Good news: but if you ask me what it is, I know not;
It is a track of feet in the snow,
It is a lantern showing a path,
It is a door set open.[2]

The way to what? To many things. But here specifically to the Father. And that is literally true. **No man cometh unto the Father, but by me.**

Which might seem difficult to prove or credit. For one would claim that the writer of Ps. 103 knew quite a deal about the fatherhood of God. Or when a Negro woman in Jamaica first heard the gospel, and turned to her neighbor sitting beside her, crying out, "I knew it! Did I not tell you that it must be so? My mother's heart was sure God is like that!" There was a spiritual genius who had seen deep and far into the heart of the ultimate things.

Nonetheless, Christ's teaching of the fatherhood of God is amazingly original. In a thin, attenuated sense the mere word is to be found more or less openly in several religions (see on 8:41). Yet when under the stress of World War I, people of differing faiths in India felt they would like to meet together in an act of united worship and self-dedication, the idea had to be abandoned because they could find no

[2] Maisie Ward, *Gilbert Keith Chesterton,* p. 65. Copyright 1943 by Sheed & Ward, Inc., New York.

6 Jesus saith unto him, I am the way,
the truth, and the life: no man cometh
unto the Father, but by me.
7 If ye had known me, ye should have
known my Father also: and from hence-
forth ye know him, and have seen him.

we know the way?" [6] Jesus said to him, "**I
am the way, and the truth, and the life;
no one comes to the Father, but by me.**
[7] If you had known me, you would have
known my Father also; henceforth you
know him and have seen him."

---

living way." But while the context draws out the implications of **the way, truth** and **life** (11:25; 17:3) are substantive and not merely attributive conceptions. **No one comes to the Father, but by me:** cf. Wisd. Sol. 7:28, "For nothing doth God love save him that dwelleth with wisdom." But the Johannine Jesus demands far more than intellectual or moral affinity for approach to God. Here as elsewhere in this Gospel a claim is made for the absoluteness of Christianity. This saying gathers up the three announcements and interprets the Way by the Life; cf. F. J. A. Hort, *The Way, the Truth, the Life* (London, Macmillan & Co., 1893), p. 124: "Translated into any language but that of the aspiring life of love, 'coming to the Father' is a hollow and dangerous phrase; as pronounced by the Son, it proclaims the ultimate source of life in the Father's eternal Fatherhood."

---

common standing ground. And when the Christians innocently suggested that at least they could all repeat the Lord's Prayer, with its "Our Father," that was at once turned down, not without indignation, as involving a Christian belief by no means acceptable to others.

It is Jesus Christ who brought home to men how fatherly God is, and with what childlike confidence we can draw near to him; who has given us the happy feeling that to turn to God is a going home.

I am the way to God, claims Christ, because in me men at last come upon **the truth** about him; learn to know him as he really is, have their misconceptions of him dissipated, like mists when the sun shines down on them in strength; and their misunderstandings which like thick fogs had deceived and caused them to wander are blown clean away. Formerly, because they knew that God was holy and of purer eyes than to behold iniquity, and that they themselves were soiled and sin-stained, they did not dare to come to him, assuming that that would be an act of sheer effrontery, asking for doom. For they had not taken in that an essential part of the divine holiness is a divine pity for poor souls who have lost themselves, and a divine self-sacrifice—divine, and so immeasurable, deeper than our vastest human molds of thought, overflowing, breaking, sweeping these away; a divine pity that cannot rest till it has done to the uttermost all that even God can do to save and rescue them.

But, seeing all this in Christ, with a new hope and heart they can and do come boldly by that new and living way which Christ has consecrated for them, to what they now are sure is not an alarming judgment seat as they had supposed, but a throne of grace where things are given for nothing, for the taking, for the carrying away; and to One who is not cold and hard and implacably just, as they had feared, but a Father, wise, understanding, tender, and most gracious of all, set upon helping them to grow up worthily. "The main cause of Christ's coming," says Augustine, "was that men might know how much God loves them." Hot-tempered Tertullian felt that men should have recognized that Christ was God; his patience, he thought, should have proved that to them. And heaping up his instances, he concludes, "Such longsuffering as his is an example to all men, but is found in God alone." [8] Yes, but it was precisely the longsuffering of Christ that made men certain and convinced that God too is like that. Christ is the way that leads us to the truth. He himself is the truth.

Further, Christ claims, I am the way to the Father because it is through me that men attain to that **life** in and with God, to that communion and closeness of fellowship with him which alone enables them really to know him better and better, and ever more surely and as he actually is. For the way to know God is not merely to assemble correct thoughts and notions of him in one's mind, which remain mere intellectual concepts: it is to live with him; to have firsthand experience of him; to put this whole matter to the proof, testing it for one's self; to let what we have been told about him have its chance to do for us and in us what it can. Do that, says Christ, and you will find the most audacious of my promises, which look stupidly impossible, working themselves out and coming true for you; till by and by you will

[8] *Of Patience* III.

8 Philip saith unto him, Lord, show us the Father, and it sufficeth us.

9 Jesus saith unto him, Have I been so long time with you, and yet hast thou not known me, Philip? he that hath seen me hath seen the Father; and how sayest thou *then*, Show us the Father?

8 Philip said to him, "Lord, show us the
Father, and we shall be satisfied." 9 Jesus
said to him, "Have I been with you so long, and yet you do not know me, Philip? He who has seen me has seen the Father; how

9-14. The relation between Jesus and the Father is further unfolded. Imperfect knowledge of Jesus has blinded the disciples to the true nature of the Father; this blindness will now be removed. In answer to Philip's bewilderment and his plea for the all-sufficing vision of God, Jesus declares that the vision of God is granted to those

accept what I have assured you that God is, not for my saying, and no longer by pure faith at all, but basing your judgment upon solid facts in your own life which cannot be confuted or explained away.

To such a life of adventure and experiment and discovery Christ keeps inciting us, patiently correcting in us what would blur the open vision for us. For as Plotinus warned us, it is only the Godlike who can see God; or as Christ said, only the pure in heart.

That sounds a daunting judgment, which would seem to rule most of us out. But the thing is reciprocal. The purer we become, the clearer we see God. But the clearer we see God, the purer do we grow. Does not a scripture tell us that one day we shall be like him, for we shall see him as he is? And that open vision of him will burn up everything that is unworthy in us clean away? As Donne put it, with a breathtaking audacity, in one of his tremendous sermons: "I shall be so like God, as that the devil himself shall not know me from God, so farre as to finde any more place to fasten a temptation upon me, then upon God; not to conceive any more hope of my falling from that kingdome, then of Gods being driven out of it." [4]

I am the way to God, says Christ, the way that leads you to the life through which you can attain to know God better and better. But you must walk it for yourself. And the farther that you travel in it, the surer will you know that, as I told you, God's heart is a Father's heart.

I am the way. Some of us have a long way to travel before we can reach journey's end. Still, as Alice Meynell put it:

> Thou art the Way.
> Hadst Thou been nothing but the goal,
> I cannot say
> If Thou hadst ever met my soul.[5]

[4] Logan Pearsall Smith, *Donne's Sermons*, p. 228.

[5] "I Am the Way," in *Poems* (New York: Charles Scribner's Sons, 1913), p. 28. Used by permission.

And though it is steep and straight, it is a good way in which Christ leads us. It is only the lazy flesh, says Samuel Rutherford, that raises a word against it, and that whimpers and complains about it.

> Does the road wind uphill all the way?
> *Yes, to the very end.*
> Will the day's journey take the whole long day?
> *From morn to night, my friend.*[6]

Well, where else would we rather be than in the way with Christ? And what else can life offer us to be compared to that through which and into which it leads us day by day?

8-10. ***The Most Staggering Saying in Literature.***—But there Philip breaks in, not satisfied, nor seeing clearly. "The Father! Yes; but is there really such a Father? And if so, how are we to get to him and know him? **Show us the Father, and we shall be satisfied."** It seems a natural enough interruption. Yet our Lord was plainly taken aback by it. He was the kindliest and most understanding of teachers, never flustering his pupils by seeking to hurry minds faster than they could go, but patiently moderating his own pace to suit slow, stumbling steps; repeating and repeating, till something of it all had at last come home to them and in part they had grasped it.

Confucius was a lovable and gracious soul. Yet once, irritated by a scholar's unreceptive dullness and lack of initiative, he protested that he could not always be saying the same things over and over; but that once he had shown one corner of a subject, he expected the pupil to see the other three for himself. But Christ was far more tolerant than that. Yet Philip startled him. One can almost see him looking at him queerly as he answered, **Have I been with you so long, and yet you do not know me, Philip? He who has seen me has seen the Father; how can you say, "Show us the Father"? Do you not believe that I am in the Father and the**

[6] Christina Rossetti, "Uphill."

10 Believest thou not that I am in the Father, and the Father in me? the words that I speak unto you I speak not of myself: but the Father that dwelleth in me, he doeth the works.

can you say, 'Show us the Father'? **10** Do you not believe that I am in the Father and the Father in me? The words that I say to you I do not speak on my own authority; but the Father who dwells in me

---

who have had the revelation of the Father in the life of the incarnate Son. The truth has already been declared (8:28-29; 10:38) that the works of Jesus are the works of the Father, because of the indissoluble unity of Father and Son. The disciples must now recognize this relationship, if not because of the nature of his teaching, then at least by the self-evident quality of his works. Where there is this faith in Christ, the same power that has been at work in him will show its presence in his disciples. Two reasons for this are given: (*a*) **Because I go to the Father** (vs. 12); (*b*) "In that day you will know that I am in my Father, and you in me, and I in you" (vs. 20). This threefold relationship will enable the disciples to do such works as Jesus has done through the Father who dwells in him (vs. 10). Indeed, their works will be still greater, for the Son will then be freed from the physical limitations of his life on earth. They will not be confined to

---

Father in me? As if to say, "Surely you have not lived with me for years and have not grasped that if you want to know what God is like, you have only to look at me!"

That is, without exception, surely the most staggering saying to be found in human literature, search where you will. There Christ sat, with his work-roughened hands, and calmly made that astounding claim as if it were a thing too self-evident to require to be proved. Yet it is true. And half the world has come to know that it is true. Once one has come on Jesus Christ and learned to know him he cannot think of God except in terms of Christ. Everything else has become superseded and hopelessly inadequate. But this will serve. This makes us see God as he is. And that without exception, and no reservations. For the whole of Christ, all that he was and did and said, all parts of it, are an authentic and dependable revelation of the nature of God. And nothing has to be omitted, nothing explained away, nothing hurriedly passed by as uncomfortable episodes, in which unaccountably he fell below himself. For when with violence he cleansed the temple, when he turned on Peter in that terrible anger, when he set his face like flint against sham and unreality and would make no peace with those who practiced them, he was as Christlike and as Godlike as when he wrought his kindly works of healing or proclaimed his gracious gospel. In all he said and did and was, he was the express image of God's very person, the Word that conveys to us God's very thought and mind and heart. Nothing can be left out without grave risk of spiritual peril, and the likelihood of God being grievously misunderstood.

But what a gospel it is to be made sure that the God with whom we have to do is the God we see in Jesus Christ! "Abraham believed God, and it was counted unto him for righteousness," says Paul (Rom. 4:3). Surely a strange saying! We all believe each other; we all assume that what a man says, he will do; that if he makes an appointment, he will keep it; that if he gives his word, he will abide by it. Without such an assurance society would fall to pieces. And why should it be regarded as a major virtue and a real spiritual triumph that the God whose word is truth can be believed, that he means what he promises and will fulfill it. And yet God's grace and kindness are so huge and patient and inexhaustible that judged by our largest human standards they sound incredible; and it is difficult for us to bank on them. Yet, says Christ, you can safely trust them. Is there not something extraordinarily moving in the Father's kindness, not only to the prodigal, poor, broken, ashamed soul, but to the elder brother also, and in a way even more? For when that most unprepossessing figure, so churlish and ill-humored and unnatural, growls out his angry and snarling complaints, the Father answers, "Laddie, all that I have is yours." "Laddie"! That gets right to the heart!

It is worth noting that in the two parables, in which a father directly addresses his son, it is with the tender word τέκνον which is more like a pet name. It adds to the meaning of the parable of the prodigal, when the father calls the elder brother by the little name that has come down from childhood. The heavenly Father does not cease to be a father because his children are ungracious and bad. He sends rain and sun—and all they mean—to evil and to good. The whole New Testament is tuned to the thought of Jesus—the philanthropy of God our saviour.[7]

[7] T. R. Glover, *The Conflict of Religions in the Early Roman Empire* (London: Methuen & Co., 1909), p. 135. Used by permission.

11 Believe me that I *am* in the Father, and the Father in me: or else believe me for the very works' sake.

12 Verily, verily, I say unto you, He that believeth on me, the works that I do shall he do also; and greater *works* than these shall he do; because I go unto my Father.

does his works. 11 Believe me that I am in the Father and the Father in me; or else believe me for the sake of the works themselves.

12 "Truly, truly, I say to you, he who believes in me will also do the works that I do; and greater works than these will he

---

Jewish territory, nor to so short a period as his earthly ministry. Such works will be wrought through prayer "in the name of Jesus." The appeal to the glorified Christ in all the majesty of heaven will be answered, so that by such works **the Father may be glorified in the Son.** The nature and the name of God will be further revealed by this continued activity of the Son in the faith and life of the consecrated community. **If you ask anything**

---

11. *Two Types of Faith.*—There are two types of faith, so our Lord tells us. One can believe in him **for the sake of the works.** An honest mind comes to consider this whole matter, asking itself, "Is it effective? Does it work?" and finds that it is and does. For undeniably this Christ who claims to be a Savior does save. At his touch broken lives are mended, sores in the social polity get healed, characters that had fallen into pitiful decay right themselves and become clean and strong. These things are facts, staring one in the face, brooking no question. And in themselves they can create a kind of faith which has its value, and which may produce striking and beneficent results.

But Christ seeks from us something much deeper and more fundamental than that: nothing less indeed than the recognition of his own oneness with God; that what he does is in reality God himself working in and through him; that his birth was an incarnation, whereby the divine, which has always sought to hasten to man's assistance, has fairly come in among us, unable to stay out of it all while his creatures were in trouble; that Christ's works are the proof of how God bears himself toward us, so lovingly, generously, unstintedly; and that Christ's sufferings mean, as Denney wrote like Calvin before him, that God "was quite prepared to take all the consequences" of this confused world of his with its tangles and enigmas, "and He took them in Christ"; [8] that in short one can safely argue from Christ to God—and indeed there is no step to take between them. For looking at Christ, we can say not only that this is what God is like, but that this is what God is; this is how he feels toward us, this is how he spends his life, this is what it means to be God.

12. ***A Breath-taking Promise.***—The confident promise of this verse seems on the face of it incredible. If this is even remotely possible, then we have never taken in what Christ has in his heart for us, and have been satisfied with much less than what he has planned to give us. For Christ has made a far deeper mark in human history than any other. And to assure us that we can do what he has done, and even greater things, sounds a mere throwing about of idle words that have no manner of connection with the reality of things. Even if we believe in Christ and seek to serve him, it looks as if most of us can do but little. We are plain and ordinary folk with one talent, if that; our sphere is cramped and limited; do it as thoroughly as we may, our work seems to make little difference; we fall out in the end and nothing stops; things just go on; someone else fills our office; and in a little we are never missed or so much as remembered; have been at once and easily replaced.

> Most men eddy about
> Here and there—eat and drink,
> Chatter and love and hate,
> Gather and squander, are raised
> Aloft, are hurl'd in the dust.
> Striving blindly, achieving
> Nothing; and then they die—
> Perish—and no one asks
> Who or what they have been,
> More than he asks what waves
> In the moonlit solitudes mild
> Of the midmost Ocean, have swell'd,
> Foam'd for a moment, and gone.[9]

S. R. Crockett assures us that in his beloved countryside there is a churchyard in which lie buried whole generations of a family; and on the tombstone there are cut the names, and then this, as the summing up of their endeavors and achievements: "They keeped shop in Wigtown —and that's all." [1] Worthy folk, not a doubt! But greater works than Christ's? The Christ who

[8] *Letters of Principal James Denney to His Family and Friends*, ed. James Moffatt (London: Hodder & Stoughton, n.d.), p. 188.

[9] Matthew Arnold, "Rugby Chapel."

[1] Preface to John Galt, *Annals of the Parish* (Edinburgh: J. Grant, 1936), p. xvii.

13 And whatsoever ye shall ask in my name, that will I do, that the Father may be glorified in the Son.

14 If ye shall ask any thing in my name, I will do *it*.

do, because I go to the Father. 13 Whatever you ask in my name, I will do it, that the Father may be glorified in the Son; 14 if you ask[c] anything in my name, I will do it.

[c] Other ancient authorities add *me*.

---

in my name, I will do it (vs. 14) appears to be a later gloss, for (*a*) it is a repetition of vs. 13*a*, and is superfluous after 13*b*; (*b*) the text itself is uncertain. Some important authorities omit it altogether, some have **ask me** (RSV mg.), others add "this" after "do."

---

has saved a world of men, who finished the work that God gave him to do, who has been crowned with the glory and honor that are his right?

Yet Christ means what he says. Take out of our human story all that has been effected since he died by those whom he inspired and helped, and how its glory would be dimmed, and what a mass of heroism, devotion, gallantry, endurance, achievement would be lost to us! And the tale runs on and on and on. In his own day Christ made only a passing impression on his own little atomy of a land, and almost none on the great world beyond it. But followers of his have swept across the earth like the conquerors they are, winning masses for the Master, far more than he ever gained himself. And they all tell us that it was not they who did it: that the inspiration, the power, the endurance that made it possible all came from Jesus Christ; that if he had passed out of being on Calvary, if he had not gone to his Father (vs. 12), had not remembered them, and planned for them, and stood by them, and supplied all their need, all the achievements that men credit to them would have been utterly impossible. So they all say, the men and women who were in it, and who did it. And who else has the right to an opinion?

Things are not collapsing, so Christ told them boldly. But, together, you and I will see this through. And remember there are two of us; that you will never be sent out or left alone; that always it will be you—and I; and together what can we not accomplish—you and I? The grace you saw for yourselves to be so effective in my hands is not withdrawn from the world. It lies at your disposal. Draw on it; draw on me; ask of me; lean on me; look to me; and there is no limit to what we can accomplish.

13-14. *On Prayer.*—And with that he commits himself to a promise about prayer, tremendous in its amplitude and its assurance; but which he reiterates and emphasizes, telling us we can confidently count upon it. **Whatever you ask in my name, I will do it, that the Father may be glorified in the Son; if you ask anything in my name, I will do it.**

That is the kind of scripture by which many people have been stumbled. For the promises are so big, and sweeping, and emphatic, and illimitable. And yet often, upon trial made, the actual results seem in comparison meager and disappointing and not at all what they had been led to expect. Ask, they were told, and you will receive. And they did ask, and were left empty-handed. Seek, so it was said to them, and you will find. And they did make appeal to God, and nothing came of it. Usually the first religious problems and perplexities that break in on the mind are likely to meet us there or thereabout. Nor does it always help such people to point out to them that their difficulty often has its roots in naïve, crude, and indeed barbaric conceptions of what prayer is and does. "What else can the words upon which I founded mean," they ask, "except what I took out of them? Whereas you are now, if not denying them, at least thinning them down, explaining them away, leaving me after all with nothing."

There are passages of scripture where that difficulty does seem to arise, and where it must be faced, and can be answered. But it simply does not meet us here at all. For wide flung and much embracing though they are, the promises here given are not unconditional; on the contrary they are explicitly and strictly limited. It is only what we ask for "in Christ's name," what we can pray for "for his sake," as a gift from God to him; only what will advance his cause, and so enhance God's glory, that in this passage is so certainly guaranteed to us. **I will do it,** he says. And again, **I will do it. If you ask anything in my name, I will do it.**

Even that does a little stumble us. Anything? For so foolish are we and ignorant, that we know not what to pray for as we ought; and often ask what we imagine would prosper Christ's cause, though later we may clearly see that it would not have done so. God is too wise and kind to grant such foolish and imbecile prayers. But surely Christ's words here must and do mean that nothing that can further his great ends is too big for him to do for us; that we have at our back all the resources of Jesus Christ and all the grace and power of the Lord God Almighty and All Merciful; and that unless these can fail and these run dry, we are well

15 ¶ If ye love me, keep my commandments.

16 And I will pray the Father, and he shall give you another Comforter, that he may abide with you for ever;

15 "If you love me, you will keep my commandments. 16 And I will pray the Father, and he will give you another Coun-

---

4. First Paraclete Saying (14:15-17)

In chs. 14–16 a group of sayings about the promised presence of the Holy Spirit occur. Four of them (14:15-17, 25-26; 15:26-27; 16:5-11) are characterized by the use of the word Paraclete or **Counselor** (RSV), and the fifth (16:12-15), though not using this term, speaks of **the Spirit of truth,** who is equated with the Paraclete (vs. 17; cf. 15:26; see Intro., p. 443). The unity of the disciples with Jesus will be shown by their keeping the Father's commandments (15:10), and especially the "new commandment" (13:34). This is the test of love, and forms one of the main themes of the Johannine epistles (I John 5:3; II John 6).

15-17. For those who exhibit this obedience of love Jesus will pray to the Father, who will give **another Counselor.** This **Counselor** is the alter ego of Jesus—another Paraclete. So in I John 2:1, "Jesus Christ the righteous" is called "an advocate [Paraclete] with the Father." Unlike the transient presence of their Master, the disciples will have this **Counselor** with them **forever.** He is called **the Spirit of truth,** for he comes forth from God, expressing his essential reality, which found embodiment in the life of the incarnate Logos (vs. 6), and truth is the mark of his witness to the world. When the

---

able, if we draw upon them, to do anything and everything that God may ask of us.

15-16. ***On Christ's Praying for Us.***—But we have more wonderful things even than that to bring us through with honor. Pray "in my name," so Christ promises, and you will certainly be heard. He pledges himself to that. But, better by far, he promises that he himself will pray for us. And that gives one a hope indeed! For what may not result from that? For he is wise, and knows our needs as we ourselves do not; he makes no blundering in his petitioning on our behalf, as we ourselves too often do. And who can set a limit to what his prayers for us have accomplished, are accomplishing, and will accomplish? There have been strange happenings in our experience. Habits broke; light dawned on us; suddenly for no visible reason we leaped forward. And we ourselves did not know why. Yet may it not have been that Christ's prayers for us had prevailed, and had received an answer? Surely it is a strangely moving thought that he does pray for you and me. "Jesus Christ," says Ignatius, speaking of the ascended Lord in glory, "who is always mindful of you in his prayers." [2] "He ever liveth," says the scripture, "to make intercession" for us (Heb. 7:25); with his whole life and being devoted to getting us safe home. Calvin points out that whereas in one place in the N.T. we are told that he has sat down on the right hand of God, in another he is not sitting but standing there; as if he had sprung to his feet in the urgency of his prayers to God for us. Here of a truth is something to hearten and steady us.

And yet there are conditions to the granting and the success even of Christ's prayers for us. In the days of his flesh he was often thwarted by the spirit of the people whom he longed to help, and could have helped if they had given him a chance. And here Christ warns us that while for those who love him and keep his commandments everything is possible and nothing too good to come true, if of set purpose and conscious of and knowing what we are doing we are harboring and practicing thoughts and desires and purposes which are contrary to his will, even his prayers for us will fail. It is dreadful enough by such impudence and folly to throw away the answers to our own prayers; like St. Teresa, clinging for eighteen years to a sin which she knew was arresting her progress and inhibiting her from that union with God, for which with one side of her mind she longed.[3] But to prevent the answers to Christ's prayers from reaching us, who can begin to reckon up the imbecility of that?

16. ***The Promise of the Spirit.***—What he promises here specifically and particularly to ask for us is the **Counselor,** as the RSV has it. The old familiar name in the KJV, the **Comforter,** is etymologically a fine and sufficient word. But to modern ears it suggests something softer than the real connotation of the Greek equivalent. No one is so tender as the Holy

[2] Ign. Eph. 21:1.

[3] Peers, *Complete Works of Saint Teresa of Jesus,* I, 48-49.

17 *Even* the Spirit of truth; whom the world cannot receive, because it seeth him not, neither knoweth him: but ye know him; for he dwelleth with you, and shall be in you.

selor, to be with you forever, 17 even the Spirit of truth, whom the world cannot receive, because it neither sees him nor knows him; you know him, for he dwells with you, and will be in you.

Logos "came to his own home, . . . his own people received him not (1:11); the same lack of discerning sympathy prevents the world, dominated by the spirit of error (I John 4:6), from receiving the Spirit (cf. I Cor. 2:14). By contrast, **you know him, for he dwells with you, and will be in you.** For the Christian disciple the obedience of love brings the discernment of truth. Knowledge of Jesus involves the welcome of his Spirit, and will lead to his abiding presence in the inner council chamber of the soul. The bodily presence of Christ is an external manifestation of that Spirit whose indwelling presence will be the characteristic of the new dispensation. Believers will recognize the Spirit because his ministry will be a continuation of the life and teaching of Jesus (15:26; 16:14). An important variant reads the present for the future: "and is in you" instead of **and will be in you** (ἔσται: ℵ A D2 L Θ; ἐστί: B D* W 1 22 69 565 O.L. syc syp). The future tense is perhaps a correction, for the present is at first sight inconsistent with 7:39; 20:22, as well

---

Spirit—so tender or so patient. And yet he comes to rally us, to bring us to our feet again, to help us to face life still unafraid. Beaten today we may have been, perhaps dishonorably enough.

> But tomorrow,
> By the living God, we'll try the game again.[4]

And this time with his help will hold our ground!

It is here that the Christian ministry often breaks down. Phillips Brooks, in what is probably the best book on preaching yet published, says all too truly of the pastoral work of the average minister:

> It is pitched in too low a key. It tries to meet the misfortunes of life with comfort and not with inspiration, offering inducements to patience and the suggestions of compensation in this life or another which lies beyond, rather than imparting that higher and stronger tone which will make men despise their sorrows and bear them easily in their search for truth and nobleness, and the release that comes from forgetfulness of self and devotion to the needs of other people. The truest help which one can render to a man who has any of the inevitable burdens of life to carry is not to take his burden off but to call out his best strength that he may be able to bear it. The pastorship of Jesus is characterized everywhere by its frankness and manliness. [But ours, he thinks,] tries to soothe with consolation more than to fire with ambition or to sting with shame.[5]

[4] John Masefield, "Tomorrow," from *Salt Water Poems and Ballads*. Copyright 1916, 1944. Used by permission of The Macmillan Co., The Society of Authors, and Dr. John Masefield, O.M.

[5] *Lectures on Preaching* (New York: E. P. Dutton, 1877), pp. 79-80.

But, blessed be his name, God will not so pamper and mollycoddle us. The Spirit whom he sends us is a strong Spirit, with rousing calls upon us. He braces; he revives; he reinvigorates; he puts new heart and courage into those who were dispirited; and rallying the broken ranks, enables us to snatch victory out of defeat. So it was with the first disciples. So, please God, is it with us still.

17. *The Spirit of Truth.*—But more especially in this passage Christ promises that the Spirit will give us guidance where things are difficult, and the crossroads puzzle, and our hearts are at a loss. **The Spirit of truth,** he calls this Counselor. Many get irritated with religious people on the ground that they are disloyal to truth and will not face facts; that they live in an unreal world of dreams; believe in what they want to believe, and not at all in things as they actually are. But on their side religious people have real difficulty in crediting that these others do not see what is so self-evident to them. They cannot understand how anybody can honestly deny what are the obvious facts of their own daily experience, things staring at them, solid, palpable, undeniable. Once on a day a Christian man talking to Thomas Huxley stressed this: observing that while he in no way wished to impugn the other's sincerity, might it not be that mentally the great scientist was color blind, as some folk see no trace of green where normal eyes cannot help seeing it. Huxley, admitting that it was quite possible, added that if it were so, he himself, of course, could not know or recognize it. He was a man whose honesty in all things claims respect. But it is difficult not to become incensed by some flippant spirits who have never given any serious consideration to

18 I will not leave you comfortless: I will come to you.

19 Yet a little while, and the world seeth me no more; but ye see me: because I live, ye shall live also.

18 "I will not leave you desolate; I will come to you. 19 Yet a little while, and the world will see me no more, but you will see me; because I live, you will live also.

as with vs. 16. But the three verbs **you know, he dwells with, will be in,** might have the present of the impending future, or else may represent the realization of the promise in the time of the evangelist. The change of prepositions is significant. **With** (παρά) is appropriate for the Intercessor (Παράκλητος), who dwells beside us in the church. **In** (ἐν) brings out the thought of the indwelling Spirit in the heart of every disciple. We may legitimately detect an implied contrast between the abiding presence of the Paraclete in the postresurrection church (**with you forever** [vs. 16], **dwells with you** [vs. 17]) and the occasional character of his help in the Synoptic representation—"in that hour" of special need (Mark 13:11; Matt. 10:19-20; Luke 12:11-12).

5. The Threefold Union (14:18-24)

Between the first two Paraclete sayings the theme of vs. 3 is resumed—the return of Jesus to his orphaned disciples. The brief interval of their bereavement will end with the Resurrection, when Jesus will manifest himself to his disciples but not to the unbelieving world.

19-20. Yet a little while: For the meaning of this phrase see on 16:16-24. **Because I live, you will live also.** The vision of the risen Christ will bring assurance of enduring life to those who are his own. Some commentators (e.g., Lagrange, Loisy, Bauer) punctuate differently, connecting the last clause of the verse with the preceding words, "But you will see me, because I live and you also will live." It is the fact that Jesus is the

---

these matters and yet blandly and loftily dismiss as silly, childish fairy stories which they have outgrown, what we have tested and proved true. "There are a few intellectual snobs with whom it is a sign of accomplishment to ridicule religion. To care for religion is to be old-fashioned; to be critical of it is to be in the movement." [6]

There is a **Spirit of truth** who leads whosoever will listen to him into the truth. But many pay no heed to him, and slam the doors of their minds against what they do not want to hear. And though in so doing they imagine themselves to be daring thinkers, and advanced beyond the stupid mass of us, they are not the wise men that they count themselves. After all, there is point and a barb in Joseph Parker's merry gibe that when a man plumes himself on his agnosticism, he is only confessing in Greek that he is an ignoramus, as the Latin renders it. The higher mathematics may be all dark to us; yet we would not on that account presume to question its findings, or try to laugh it out of court, simply because in our stupidity we cannot grasp what others can. The facts of religion are solid and verifiable and entirely obvious to those gifted with the faculty that can pick them up. And a man's failure to do so in no way invalidates them or disproves their reality. As F. H. Bradley says with an impressive emphasis:

> We can see at once that there is nothing more real than what comes in religion. To compare facts such as these with what is given to us in outward existence, would be to trifle with the subject. The man who demands a reality more solid than that of the religious consciousness, seeks he does not know what.[7]

There is a **Spirit of truth;** but **the world cannot receive** him, **because it neither sees nor knows him;** but **you know him, for he dwells with you, and will be in you.** Or as Paul puts it, "Although they knew God they did not honor him as God or give thanks to him, but they became futile in their thinking and their senseless minds were darkened. Claiming to be wise, they became fools" (Rom. 1:21-22).

18-21. ***The Living Christ.***—Further, Christ assures his disciples that not only will they have the presence and the guidance of the Spirit, but that he himself, far from deserting them, will come to them and dwell with them. That is not poetry or fancy; it is simple fact. The enemies of Christ came down the hill of Calvary when all was over, well satisfied with their day's work. For they had made an end of this upsetter

[6] Radhakrishnan, *Idealist View of Life*, pp. 49-50.

[7] *Appearance and Reality*, p. 449.

20 At that day ye shall know that I *am* in my Father, and ye in me, and I in you.
21 He that hath my commandments, and keepeth them, he it is that loveth me: and he that loveth me shall be loved of my Father, and I will love him, and will manifest myself to him.
22 Judas saith unto him, not Iscariot, Lord, how is it that thou wilt manifest thyself unto us, and not unto the world?

20 In that day you will know that I am in
my Father, and you in me, and I in you.
21 He who has my commandments and
keeps them, he it is who loves me; and he
who loves me will be loved by my Father,
and I will love him and manifest myself
to him." 22 Judas (not Iscariot) said to him,
"Lord, how is it that you will manifest
yourself to us, and not to the world?"

---

life, and that when he has risen, he will impart this life to his disciples, which will enable them to see him when he is no longer visible to the eyes of the flesh. **In that day** (vs. 20) is an eschatological term. It means first the period of the Easter appearances; but this is a foretaste of the new era of the reign of God. The discovery of the new era is that God in all his fullness dwells in the believing disciple who enters into mystic communion with Christ. This is further described as a triple relationship. In vs. 10 it was said, "I am in the Father and the Father in me." That life of divine fellowship is to be extended to embrace the fellowship of believers as well, **You will know that I am in my Father, and you in me, and I in you.** In 17:20-23 a vision is opened of a yet wider fellowship, including also those who will come into the faith through the disciples' testimony, "That they may all be one; even as thou, Father, art in me, and I in thee, that they also may be in us, so that the world may believe that thou hast sent me."

21-24. This mystical communion is also an ethical fellowship, no mere emotional ecstasy. Obedience and love are the conditions that rule this new life of the church. Just

---

of the people. That, thank God, was all over! There would be no more of him. But they were wrong. For today millions, not in heaven only, but on earth, live in daily communion with him. They speak to him; they listen to him; they consult him; they are guided by him; they draw their inspiration from him. It is because he lives that they live; as the mill wheel is turned by the rush of living water, and cannot turn without it.

> Loud mockers in the roaring street
> Say Christ is crucified again:
> Twice pierced his gospel-bearing feet,
> Twice broken his great heart in vain.
> I hear and to myself I smile,
> For Christ talks with me all the while.[8]

So Le Gallienne; and summing up the noisy views that Christ is now obsolete, and left behind, is out of things, ends with the quiet and yet confident rejoinder:

> So in the street I hear men say,
> Yet Christ is with me all the day.[9]

If we have no experience of that, it is the price of sin. For here too there are conditions. Really to love Christ is to try to be obedient to his mind, to reproduce his ways, to live our life after the pattern of his. And whoso attempts so to do **will be loved by my Father,** declares Christ. God's heart will run out to this loyal soul, blundering and falling many a time, but always picking himself up, and still keeping his face to the light; will make to very him, in a private and personal sense, his unspeakable gift; and Christ himself will not only be near to help, but will enable such a one to see that he is near, that he in his need is not alone, for Christ is with him.

22-24. ***Our Hearts God's Home.***—Whereat, out of the background there comes the voice of **Judas (not Iscariot),** as for once breaking his accustomed silence he bursts out impulsively, "But how? But how are you to **manifest yourself to us** in a way that others cannot share?" And patiently, perhaps more slowly, Christ repeats almost verbatim what he has said; but with one amazing addition. **If a man loves me, he will keep my word, and my Father will love him**—all that we had had before. But then there comes the staggering announcement, **and we will come to him and make our home with him.**

Our heart the home of God! The door into which Christ turns with the restful feeling that he is in his own place, where love will meet him and surround him, where he is at home. So

8 "The Second Crucifixion." Reprinted by permission of Dodd, Mead & Co. and the Society of Authors as the Literary Representative of the Estate of the late Richard Le Gallienne.

9 *Ibid.*

23 Jesus answered and said unto him, If a man love me, he will keep my words: and my Father will love him, and we will come unto him, and make our abode with him.

24 He that loveth me not keepeth not my sayings: and the word which ye hear is not mine, but the Father's which sent me.

25 These things have I spoken unto you, being *yet* present with you.

23 Jesus answered him, "If a man loves
me, he will keep my word, and my Father
will love him, and we will come to him
and make our home with him. 24 He who
does not love me does not keep my words;
and the word which you hear is not mine
but the Father's who sent me.

25 "These things I have spoken to you,

---

as Thomas and Philip have been used to voice the difficulties felt by the disciples, so now **Judas** (otherwise Thaddaeus or Lebbaeus; cf. Mark 3:18; Matt. 10:3) asks why this manifestation is not to be given with convincing force to the unbelieving world. The answer is that this manifestation is granted to the discernment of love. He who does not love Jesus disregards his words, which are indeed the words of God (cf. 7:16-17; 8:26; 12:49). A moral affinity is needed for the reception of a divine revelation (cf. 1:12).

6. Second Paraclete Saying (14:25-26)

25-26. The spoken teaching of Jesus is coming to an end with his departure. But **the Counselor,** the Spirit of truth, will come from the Father to continue the work of the Son. This will consist in recalling the vital truths which have been heard and almost

---

much do these broken bits of faith and affection which we are half ashamed to offer him mean to our Lord. For it is still true that he comes unto his own, and they receive him not. And he is lonesome in a world that cannot be bothered with him or make room for him. "Behold, I stand at the door and knock." And many never hear him; and others pay no heed. "It is only Jesus Christ," they say, and do nothing about it. And some think, "Plenty of time. There is no need, happily, to worry about him for a long while yet"; like that miserable comforter at the deathbed of Falstaff, who, when "a' cried out 'God! God! God!' three or four times, Now I, to comfort him, bid him a' should not think of God; I hoped there was no need to trouble himself with any such thoughts yet." [1]

And it matters to Christ that when you know he is at the door, you run to it and throw it open; that when you remember, you do choose him.

It is a poor place that we have to offer him, not worthy of his entering it. Yet the upper room too was a shabby little garret, up under the roof. There were some couches and a table, and a waterpot and a towel and a basin set behind the door; but not much else. Yet Christ had dreamed about that simple room, had chosen it, asked for it, planned to be with his followers there alone. And a believing heart, however simple, means much to him too. And if remembering our many failures and disloyalties, our hearts misgive us, Zacchaeus also had a sorry record. Yet Christ asked for his hospitality. **Our home,** says Christ, speaking of himself and God. **Our home!**

25-26. ***The Sea Grows Always Greater.***—These verses give us a much-needed lesson which to our cost we keep forgetting, so shutting ourselves into a much leaner and more meager life than Christ has planned for us and means us to enjoy. Already we owe him more than we can tell, more than we ourselves realize. But we have not come to the end of what he has in his heart and mind for us; have indeed as yet waded only a very little way out from the shore; and before us stretches, illimitable, all the inexhaustible fullness of the ocean of God's grace, reaching out to the far horizon, and much farther still beyond it. All that is unexplored by us, untraveled, inciting us to new adventures. Yet so many miss it. They close with Christ; they have their initial experiences of him; and then they settle down and go no farther—in the kingdom, but no more; never press on to possess the amplitude of the inheritance there is for them if they will take it. For there are those who will not credit that there can be even in Christ anything better than what they have already received from him. They even plume themselves on that belief as a proof of their loyalty to him, not realizing that they are insulting and belittling him. For in spiritual things as elsewhere there ought to be not only birth, but growth and manhood. To remain a babe in Christ is a monstrosity. We are meant to grow up in him.

[1] Shakespeare, *Henry V,* Act II, scene 3.

26 But the Comforter, *which is* the Holy Ghost, whom the Father will send in my name, he shall teach you all things, and bring all things to your remembrance, whatsoever I have said unto you.

while I am still with you. 26 But the Counselor, the Holy Spirit, whom the Father will send in my name, he will teach you all things, and bring to your remembrance

forgotten, and in interpreting them to the church according to the contemporary need (cf. e.g., 2:22; 12:16; 13:7). As Jesus is the truth (vs. 6), the Spirit of truth will confirm and expound the teaching of Jesus. **Whom the Father will send in my name:** So in vs. 16, "I will pray the Father, and he will give you another Counselor." Yet in 15:26 we read, "Whom I shall send to you from the Father," and in 16:7, "But if I go, I will send him to you." In the light of vs. 10 there is no contradiction in attributing the mission of the Spirit, now to the Father, then to the Son. As in vs. 16, the Father sends "another Counselor" to take the place of the first Paraclete, and to speak in his name. This phrase **in my name** does not here mean "in answer to my prayer" (cf. vs. 16), but must be interpreted in the light of 5:43 ("I have come in my Father's name") and 10:25 ("the works which I do in my Father's name, they bear witness to me"); i.e., he is the Father's envoy,

No creed is final, or can be. For a creed is the setting down in words what loyal hearts have found in Jesus Christ. But no man can take this wonderful gospel into his hands and say, "I have looked over it, and under it, and measured it with accuracy—its length and breadth and depth—and this is all there is to say about it." Far on in his discipleship Paul felt that all he knew of Christ—and who ever knew him better?—was merely a glimpse of him, a first chapter; felt that there was far more in Christ than he had thus far grasped and appropriated. "That I may know him" was his hope and prayer, "really know him as he really is; may get past these shadowy suggestions of him to the fullness of the truth." And so he kept ever pressing on, wading deeper and deeper, farther and farther, into the knowledge and experience of an inexhaustible Lord.

The promised Holy Spirit did not come and help us only until Nicaea, or Dort, or Westminster, and then withdraw—there being nothing further left for him to teach us. But he is in the world today. And those who will consent to listen he still teaches, and still guides, and still leads deeper and deeper into all the truth. But many will not credit that. F. D. Maurice said of Carlyle, "He believes in a God who lived till the death of Oliver Cromwell."[2]

"I have made a beginning with you," so Christ says. "But there is still much for you to learn. And the Holy Spirit will teach you all things, and will lead you on and on and on, far further than I have been able as yet to take you" (see also on 16:1-12).

26. *The Holy Spirit a Remembrancer.*—And yet how much our Lord has already given us! But, then, as the Westminster Shorter Catechism says, "That the Word may become effectual to salvation, we must attend thereunto with diligence, preparation, and prayer; receive it with faith and love, lay it up in our hearts, and practice it in our lives."[3] Samuel Johnson thought we need more frequently to be reminded, rather than to be informed. How often Christ has spoken to us, but the seed fell upon stony ground, on preoccupied minds, on insensitive consciences, and nothing came of it; or we did thrill to it, leaped up and took action—until we forgot. The people were much moved, so Wesley noted once, adding that if they did not take great care, they might remember—for a week. "The heedless world," so Emerson laid it down with a comfortable assurance, "has never lost one accent of the Holy Ghost." On which L. P. Jacks pertinently muses, "How, I wonder, did Emerson find that out?"[4] It seems a judgment that flies in the face of many ugly and indisputable facts. How vastly farther on we should have been if only we had listened and paid heed! Yet, blessed be his name, this promise of the Master keeps fulfilling itself. For the Holy Spirit does bring to our remembrance much that we had let slip.

A Sunday-school teacher, faced by her row of little inattentive, even bored and restless, urchins, wonders if anything at all is coming of her work, and grows discouraged; yet some of the seed which she is sowing will lodge in the crevices of these odd little minds, and will spring up and bear after long years. Once in my congregation there was an old woman, all but a hundred, quite blind, and three-parts deaf, who was left alone in her cottage for long hours each day. "How do you pass the time?"

[2] *Life of Frederick Denison Maurice*, ed. F. Maurice (New York: Charles Scribner's Sons, 1884), II, 277.

[3] Answer to Question 90.

[4] *From the Human End* (London: Williams & Norgate, 1916), p. 137.

27 Peace I leave with you, my peace I give unto you: not as the world giveth, give I unto you. Let not your heart be troubled, neither let it be afraid.

28 Ye have heard how I said unto you, I go away, and come *again* unto you. If ye loved me, ye would rejoice, because I said, I go unto the Father: for my Father is greater than I.

all that I have said to you. 27 Peace I leave
with you; my peace I give to you; not as
the world gives do I give to you. Let not
your hearts be troubled, neither let them
be afraid. 28 You heard me say to you, 'I
go away, and I will come to you.' If you
loved me, you would have rejoiced, because
I go to the Father; for the Father is greater

---

with full authority to declare his mind. So now the Father will send this other Paraclete with full authority to declare under fresh conditions the message which Jesus taught within the terms of the incarnate life.

7. Peace, Joy, and Security (14:27-31)

27-28. The closing verses of this part of the farewell discourse return to the note of the opening verse. The legacy of Jesus is not trouble but **peace.** He does not counsel peace; he gives it. He gives the peace which was his own possession with death overhanging him. How unlike the superficial talk of peace on the lips of worldlings! Where this peace dwells there can be no foolish regrets and misgivings—not even sorrow at the

---

I shouted into her dulled ears. And she laughed and said, "My teacher would not believe it, for I did my best to spoil her class. Yet though she has been in her grave for eighty years, I lie here repeating to myself the texts and psalms she taught me!" And how often we ourselves, when flustered or depressed, have been steadied and given the necessary strength of will by some forgotten scripture which, rushing out of nowhere in the nick of time, sufficed to bring us through. So really does the Spirit bring to our remembrance all that Christ has said to us.

Roman Catholics have a notion that whatever that church teaches, and whatever doctrine it may formulate, it is founding on the direct teaching of Christ, which, though it may not be in scripture, has been preserved in the tradition, and at need, like writing in invisible ink held to the fire, flames out into distinctness. It had been forgotten. But the Holy Spirit in his mercy has now brought it to the remembrance of the church. Hence that church cannot err. For all it teaches is Christ's own teaching, happily remembered. Upon which one need only say what Robert Rainy did about a somewhat kindred matter, "There can be no question [of] the ecclesiastical efficiency of the principle laid down. Also it is simple, and saves a world of discussion." [5] The only question that remains is whether it is true! We too can deceive ourselves and mistake another voice for Christ's.

27-31. ***Christ's Legacy.***—And then looking around on that little group of men very near his heart, so soon to be bereft of his visible presence, and swept away in a roaring flood of disaster threatening to batter the breath out of their bodies and the very life out of their souls, Christ tells them of his legacy to them. He had little to leave. Even his clothes would soon be the property of the crucifixion squad of soldiers. But there was one thing he could give—**Peace I leave with you; my peace I give to you**—a mighty gift indeed!

Not as the world gives do I give to you. What did he mean by that? In those days the ordinary salutation at parting from a casual meeting, the usual greeting thrown to a passer-by, was "Peace be with you." But as the meaningful ancient prayer which we still use, "May God be with you," has been shortened to the curt "Good-by," which nowadays often means little more than "Well, I must be going," so in the world of men the peace they flung to one another had little substance or significance.

Christ too was going away. But the peace he offered his disciples to bring them through what lay before them was very real, and incalculably worth the gaining. **My peace,** he says. "Trust God wholeheartedly, as I have trusted and do trust him; accept unquestioningly his ordering of your life; lay your whole being at his absolute disposal, holding back nothing, making no reservations: and you will have a peace that passes understanding, garrisoning your heart, and you will come through with honor and in quietness of spirit—calm, steady, unafraid.

Too many have an insane idea that the road to contentedness and peace runs through self-indulgence and the satiating of one's passions

[5] *The Ancient Catholic Church* (New York: Charles Scribner's Sons, 1902), p. 194.

29 And now I have told you before it come to pass, that, when it is come to pass, ye might believe.

30 Hereafter I will not talk much with you: for the prince of this world cometh, and hath nothing in me.

than I. 29 And now I have told you before it takes place, so that when it does take place, you may believe. 30 I will no longer talk much with you, for the ruler of this world is coming. He has no power over me;

---

words of farewell and promise (vss. 2-3). The disciple who loves his Master rejoices at the thought of his homecoming, **because I go to the Father.** He rejoices for the sake of the joy that this will bring to Jesus. But he should rejoice for his own sake, because of the greater power available for the disciple. **For the Father is greater than I:** The earthly life of humiliation has placed restrictions upon the activity of the Son, which will be removed on his return to the Father. Now the disciples' faith and hope will be strengthened, for "greater works than these will he do, because I go to the Father" (vs. 12).

29-30. The shock of the final separation may unsettle the disciples' faith, but this warning is given in advance that faith may not yield to fear (cf. 13:19; 16:4). The time for further talk is short, for the struggle with the supreme foe will soon be engaged. The **ruler of this world is coming**—the embodiment of the spirit of worldly craft and power is on his way. But **he has no power over me** (lit., **hath nothing in me,** i.e., "there is no traitor within the citadel of my soul," or to change the figure to one suggested by the Hebrew phrase behind the Greek, "he has no claim against me"). The death of Jesus is

---

and desires. Unanimously the experts are against them. But they, poor fools, will not believe that they are experts. "The only way to get rid of a temptation is to yield to it," said Oscar Wilde.[6] The ugly facts of his own shameful life are a sufficient and a damning answer. Augustine had tried all ways of it. And there is a mass of human experience packed into that famous prayer of his, famous because so many can corroborate it from the facts of their own lives, "Thou hast made us for Thyself and our hearts are restless till they rest in Thee." [7]

And so Christ ends by repeating the rallying cry with which he began, **Let not your hearts be troubled, neither let them be afraid.** How real and many-sided an encouragement he had given them—that though unseen, he would be working for them in the other world; that they now knew God as he really is, and so could trust him utterly; that though they were about to scatter and fail tragically, they must not lose heart about themselves, for he himself still trusted them, was sure that they would do for him works even more signal than his own had been; that they had in their hands the wonderful gift of prayer, which, if rightly used, is of illimitable power; that they would have the Holy Spirit as their Counselor, and be led by him farther and farther into all the truth; that Christ himself would make his home with them, he and the Father; and that if they would believe all that and walk in the strength and sunshine of it, they would have his peace to steady them and bring them through with honor.

In vs. 28 he gives us a lesson to which all those to whom there has come sorrow and loss ought to pay heed. **If you loved me, you would have rejoiced, because I go to the Father**—a crushing loss to them; but think what it means to Christ and to his cause! So with our loved ones also. They are with Christ, which is far better for them, though lonelier for us; and just because we love them, we cannot begrudge them their glory.

And so this chapter ends with a renewed reminder that things were not crashing in about their ears in hideous ruin; that his life was not being snatched away out of his hands by a force which he could not resist, but that he was about to give it freely. That was what gave the Cross its value and its glory. R. L. Stevenson, looking out on death drawn very near, bade them cut upon his tombstone, after he was gone,

> Glad did I live and gladly die,
> And I laid me down with a will.[8]

Christ laid himself down on the Cross with a will: not struggling, clamoring, cursing, as other victims did, but making it a voluntary sacrifice for a lost world. And we must learn to face the sorrows, disappointments, losses that life brings us with something of his magnanimity of spirit; not having what is taken from us wrenched away, but since it has to go, making it a free gift.

[6] *The Picture of Dorian Gray* (New York: The Modern Library, 1926), ch. ii.

[7] *Confessions* I. 1.

[8] "Requiem."

31 But that the world may know that I love the Father; and as the Father gave me commandment, even so I do. Arise, let us go hence.

15 I am the true vine, and my Father is the husbandman.

2 Every branch in me that beareth not fruit he taketh away: and every *branch*

31 but I do as the Father has commanded me, so that the world may know that I love the Father. Rise, let us go hence.

15 "I am the true vine, and my Father is the vinedresser. 2 Every branch of

---

no defeat. He lays down his life in obedience to the loving will of the Father. That is the final evidence to the world of his unity with the Father. B. F. Westcott connects the clauses rather differently: "But though the prince of the world has no claim upon me, I freely offer myself to the uttermost powers of evil, to death the last punishment of sin, that in me the world itself may see the greater power of love, and so learn (if God will) that the kingdom of Satan is overthrown" (*The Gospel According to St. John, the Greek Text with Introduction and Notes* [London: John Murray, 1908], II, 187).

31. I love the Father: This is the only place in the Gospel where Jesus speaks of his love for the Father. The Father's love for him is dwelt upon in 10:17; 15:9; 17:23, 24, 26. Nevertheless, the thought is implicit in those passages where Jesus speaks of his delight in doing the Father's will. For him love and obedience are inseparable. **Rise, let us go hence** may have been inserted from Mark 14:42. Others, thinking that it marks the close of the farewell discourse, transpose chs. 15–16 to come before ch. 14 (see Intro., pp. 446, 459-60).

C. The Farewell Discourse: Part II (15:1–16:33)

1. Allegory of the Vine (15:1-11)

The figure of the vine is often used in the O.T. for Israel (cf. Isa. 5:1; Ezek. 15:1-6; 19:10-14; Ps. 80:8-19), but here it is used in the second allegory of the Gospel (cf. 10:14), and is introduced with one of the great "I am" sayings. **The true vine** means the genuine vine, i.e., the vine which corresponds perfectly to its name. Israel, once a noble vine (Jer.

15:1-8. ***The Vine, the Branches, and the Vinedresser.***—There is nothing for it but to throw oneself bodily into this unfathomable parable, to feel one's feet plucked from beneath one, and oneself swept helplessly far out into great waters, with mighty billows breaking over one, and on all sides, farther than human eyes can see; to be made to take it in that this wonderful gospel of ours is not a measurable thing that we can take into these little hands of ours and say, "This is the length of it, and this the breadth of it; and I have looked over it and under it and on all sides of it, and that is all there is to say about it"; that it is not a shallow pond around which we can stroll, but that there are the surgings of eternity in it, and deep calling to deep! Here every verse arrests us, and every phrase calls to us to pause and consider, and almost every word offers us more than we can carry away. **I am the true vine, and my Father is the vinedresser. . . . You are the branches** (vss. 1, 5).

And for a beginning let us start with what are surely the most hopeful words in Scripture, **Apart from me, you can do nothing.** For it is on the basis of that frank recognition of our utter fecklessness apart from him that Christ enters into his covenant with us, and gives us his tremendous promises, and makes his honoring claims upon us. There is no fear that when he comes to us he may draw back, saying that though his grace is an all but illimitable thing, he had not realized that anyone could be so futile as we are; and that we can scarcely expect it to cover such a case as ours. Knowing all there is to know, the very worst, he is not daunted in the least, is sure that he can manage for us. Meantime he is not surprised that apart from him, or using him only sporadically, we have not done better. He knew that without him we could do, not something fairly good though insufficient, but just nothing at all. **I am the vine, you are the branches.** And the vine does and must do everything for them. It is the vine that draws the sap from the kindly earth; the vine that passes it to the needy branches; the vine that enables them even to hold on, in order that they may get more. Apart from the vine, the branches are mere withering sticks, soon ready for the burning; and there comes a puff of smoke, a crackle of fire, and then nothing at all. **"But I," says**

that beareth fruit, he purgeth it, that it may bring forth more fruit.
3 Now ye are clean through the word which I have spoken unto you.

mine that bears no fruit, he takes away, and every branch that does bear fruit he prunes, that it may bear more fruit.
3 You are already made clean by the word which

2:21; the LXX uses the same word as here, ἀληθινός), had become degenerate. The choice of the figure may well have been determined by the "fruit of the vine" (cf. Mark 14:25; Matt. 26:29; Luke 22:18), and is John's one hint of the place of the Eucharist in the teaching of the upper room (see also other summary remarks below, pp. 752-54).

15:1-3. These verses describe the action of the Father as the vinedresser. He removes the unfruitful branches, and prunes (lit., "cleanses") the rest to make them more fruitful. The disciples do not need this treatment because of the teaching of Jesus which they have accepted, which is "spirit and life" (6:63) and which has made them "clean" (13:10).

Christ, "can make you green and living things, heavy with fruitfulness, laden with usefulness toward God and man."

There is a heartening message for any day, but especially for ours, when tremendous problems that refuse to wait are crowding in upon us and demanding a solution. Some years ago we would have accepted the situation with a measure of complacency. For then we imagined we were on a moving staircase, and had only to stand still, and the progress of the suns would lift us automatically up to God's feet. We laughed at the scripture warning that that which is crooked cannot be made straight. "Can't it!" we said with confidence. "Let us get our hands upon it, and a little social and political and economic pressure will soon straighten it." For we had the comfortable feeling that at long last a generation had arisen, determined to put this disorderly earth into some kind of shape and well able to do it! And look at the world after our efforts!

And why has all this come upon us? Because the branch thought that it could **bear fruit of itself.** And it cannot; and it never will. We are full of schemes for social betterment and human brotherhood. But as a generation, we have little use for Christ, see no need for him, push him impatiently aside! "We are a great breed," we claim. "Faced by any problem and given a little time, we shall ultimately solve it. Have we not harnessed the lightning, gained a new empire in the air and another underneath the sea; are we not eliminating space, and dragging nature's jealously guarded secrets into the light of common day? A Savior? A Savior from what? What do we need to take from Christ?" And so, many ignore him as a useless irrelevance. "This is the most irreligious age since Christ was born," wrote Earl Baldwin, the British Prime Minister. And Aldous Huxley [9] jeers at that. Since Christ was born! Search the annals of humanity since man was man, and we will find no age in which religion was so slighted and ignored! And C. E. M. Joad, "For the first time in human history there is coming to maturity a generation of men and women who have no religion and feel no need for one." [1] And Walter Lippmann thinks that unbelief is more radical today than it ever was.[2]

And look at what, striving so valiantly but, on the whole, along these lines, the world has made of things. All my life, confessed Seneca,[3] I have been trying to climb out of the pit of my besetting sins—in vain. And I never can, and never will, unless a hand is let down to me to draw me up. If we are being forced back to that, to see that what we need is a Savior, there is hope for us. For the hand is there. For, says Seneca again, the gods are not jealous. If a man will climb up eagerly they stretch out a hand to him. But **the branch cannot bear fruit of itself,** try how it may.

So of the church. Perhaps the ministry was never busier than it is now. Hundreds of men are hoarse from continual speaking, and are wearied out with running here and running there. If things slow down, we evolve yet another type of meeting. And when this new and added wheel is spinning merrily with all the other wheels, there may be no spiritual outcome whatsoever, but there is a wind blowing in our faces; and we hot and sticky engineers have a comfortable feeling that something is going on.

Yet Thomas Chalmers, musing over the problem why there were not more spiritual results from his deliriously popular ministry, came to this explanation of it—that he was trusting more to his own animal heat and activity than to the Holy Spirit. **The branch cannot bear fruit of itself,** and never will.

[9] Cf., "The Decay of Religion," in *Proper Studies* (New York: Doubleday, Doran & Co., 1928).

[1] *The Present and Future of Religion* (New York: The Macmillan Co., 1930), p. 121.

[2] *Preface to Morals,* p. 12.

[3] Cf. *Epistles* LXI. 1.

4 Abide in me, and I in you. As the
branch cannot bear fruit of itself, except
it abide in the vine; no more can ye, except ye abide in me.
5 I am the vine, ye *are* the branches.
He that abideth in me, and I in him, the same bringeth forth much fruit; for without me ye can do nothing.

I have spoken to you. 4 Abide in me, and
I in you. As the branch cannot bear fruit by itself, unless it abides in the vine, neither
can you, unless you abide in me. 5 I am the
vine, you are the branches. He who abides in me, and I in him, he it is that bears much fruit, for apart from me you can do

---

4-11. The allegory of the vine and the branches is the most complete expression of the mystical union between Christ and the Christian in this Gospel. It combines the thought which Paul expressed in the figure of the body and its members with the

---

So in our individual lives. It is so difficult to work out our ideals. We see them; we long to achieve them; but they elude our clutching hands. Against the tremendous background of the promises, what Christ has effected in us looks meager and insignificant. May it not be that the branch has got detached from the vine, and hangs loose and limp and withering? Life is rushed and bustled; and in the jostle of competing interests always twitching at our sleeve and attracting our attention, spiritual things can easily get overlooked and lost. Seasons of devotion are shortened or crowded out, God's Word is not seriously or regularly studied, and the like. Get closer to Jesus Christ! And he will do the rest for you. But **the branch cannot bear fruit of itself.**

When our Lord asked Zacchaeus if he might stay with him that night, the roar of welcome in the streets died away into an ominous and outraged silence through which the two moved on in tense stillness. And Christ said not a word. But suddenly Zacchaeus stopped. "I am done with it," he said. "I promise you I am done with it. I thought that it was clever. I set out to make my fortune, and I have made it. And when they jeered at me, the jingle in my moneybags was answer enough for me. But I am done with it. The half of my goods I give to the poor. And if I have defrauded anyone of anything, I will restore it four times over. For I see clearly that if I am to be your friend, the old life will not do." Get closer to Jesus Christ, and he will do the rest for you. For the vine does cause the branch to bear.

And Christ wants us to bear. For after all, we are the branches, and apart from the branches, the vine can have no harvest. Is it not a moving thing that Christ has trustfully committed his cause, in our day and generation, so largely to our keeping? Aristotle says that the high-minded man, his ideal character, will give to anyone; but he will not take from any. For that would be to demean himself.[4] But Christ is high above that pettiness; and leans plans that are very near his heart against our frail loyalties, and stoops to take from our soiled hands. The vine bears through its branches. And Christ's cause, if it is to spread, must spread through you and me.

But what can we ordinary people do? Well, to begin with, amending Carlyle, It is not what we have, nor even what we do, but what we are, that gives us our kingdom. A neutral personality is unthinkable and does not exist. Inevitably, unconsciously, as we move about among our fellows, we are either like the sun coming through on a gray day, and because we have passed by, somehow men look nobler, and God seems nearer, and the great dreams much more than dreams; or else we are a wet and clammy mist, soaking into men's spirits, depressing and disheartening, chilling their very souls; and God seems far away, and men have surely shrunk, and life is a mere scuffling of crows over some gobbets of meat.

> Every life is a profession of faith, and exercises an inevitable and silent propaganda. . . . It tends to transform the universe and humanity into its own image. . . . Every man is a centre of perpetual radiation like a luminous body; . . . a beacon which entices a ship upon the rocks if it does not guide it into port. Every man is a priest, even involuntarily; his conduct is an unspoken sermon, which is for ever preaching to others;—but there are priests of Baal, of Moloch, and of all the false gods. Such is the high importance of example.[5]

Moreover, it is not of these first disciples alone that our Lord speaks in that wonderful vs. 16, in which he returns to this metaphor, "You did not choose me, but I chose you and appointed you that you should go and bear fruit, and that your fruit should abide." In measure that is true of every Christian.

C. G. Jung declares that the bold claim of Christianity really is that it adds a new rung to

[4] *Nicomachean Ethics* IV. 3-24.

[5] *Amiel's Journal,* tr. Mrs. Humphrey Ward (London: Macmillan & Co., 1890), pp. 24-25.

6 If a man abide not in me, he is cast forth as a branch, and is withered; and men gather them, and cast *them* into the fire, and they are burned.

7 If ye abide in me, and my words abide in you, ye shall ask what ye will, and it shall be done unto you.

nothing. 6 If a man does not abide in me,
he is cast forth as a branch and withers;
and the branches are gathered, thrown into
the fire and burned. 7 If you abide in me,
and my words abide in you, ask whatever

peculiar emphasis which John lays on love as the chief mark of this inward fellowship. Continued dependence upon Christ is the condition not only for fruitful service, but even for continued life. Vs. 6 harks back to vs. 2. For the evangelist there may be a reference to those who must be removed from church membership as so much dead wood. This warning is followed by the promise of vs. 7, **If you abide in me, and my word abide in you.** We might expect the second clause to read, "and I abide in you," but the thought

the ladder of evolution, producing a new creature who lives in a new way to which the natural man can no more attain than a crawling thing can fly (though birds, they tell us, were evolved from reptiles); a creature whose way of life is different from what it has now left behind, with new desires, new possibilities, new powers, new achievements. And, adds Jung, this daring claim cannot be laughed out of court. For it has done it. And we meet such new creatures every day upon the streets. And we are meant to be one of them; are intended so to live that others, meeting us, will look at us, and look again, and then from us to Jesus Christ, seeking the explanation of us there. And that perhaps is the most signal way in which we can help Christ. Yet in some fashion so to do is open to us all. **You are the branches;** and it is through them that the vine bears. You are the body of Christ. His feet that must run for him. His hands that must carry for him. His body through which his blessed will gets itself done. "Come, help me in my saving of the world! You have it in you; and I need you so. Come! Come!"

And my Father is the vinedresser: The **vinedresser** gives his whole life to the vines, tending them, feeding them, coaxing them toward fruitfulness. And looking back over a life nearing its ending, what strikes one most of all about it is what a mass of divine grace it takes to bring an ordinary person through a very ordinary life with some show of decency and honor. We have an odd way of speaking about the will of God in sad and resigned voices, as if it were a thing that must be borne, but which no one could possibly be expected to enjoy. And yet how ample, generous, ungrudging, lavish is the will that God has toward us. As the writer to Diognetus put it long ago, looking around on the wonderful provision God has made for us—Who could have expected any of these things. And yet they are all ours; simply because God willed to give them to us.[6] "It is your Father's good pleasure to give you the kingdom" (Luke 12:32). He has huge liberality and goodness in his heart toward us, and keeps heaping more on more.

Yet in this passage only one operation out of the whole year's working is even mentioned. There comes a day when the trailing greeneries and prettinesses are ruthlessly cut away, and the vine, pruned back drastically, is left a mere maimed and disfigured stump. And there are lives like that, so bleak and bare and wind-swept that one wonders how they are possible under God's governance, and if he is really Love. And in this scripture Christ gives us a daring explanation of the grim and untoward things in life. They are not chance-blown, do not just happen. But there is meaning in them, love in them, plan in them, God in them. The Cross was set up through the malice and the sin of man. Yet, say the Scriptures, through these things the eternal purpose of God's heart was working itself out. And whatever are the secondary causes for it that may leap to the eye—foolishness, blundering, unkindness—if the calamity that came through these is taken lovingly, it will work out for good to them that love him.

Nor is the calamity necessarily punishment. Though there is nothing daunting in being punished by God. "Ah God, punish, we pray Thee, . . . but be not silent . . . toward us," cried Luther.[7] A tremendous prayer. For what if God hears and answers? But what if he does not! If in our lives there is heard only the retreating footsteps of a God beaten by the works of his own hands. "Ephraim is joined to idols: let him alone" (Hos. 4:17). One of the most tremendous sermons in English is by John Donne on the text, "It is a fearful thing to fall into the hands of the living God." Yes.

[6] Epistle to Diognetus 8:11.

[7] *Table Talk*, p. 39.

8 Herein is my Father glorified, that ye bear much fruit; so shall ye be my disciples.

9 As the Father hath loved me, so have I loved you: continue ye in my love.

you will, and it shall be done for you. 8 By
this my Father is glorified, that you bear
much fruit, and so prove to be my disci-
ples. 9 As the Father has loved me, so have

---

is the same as that in 6:63. Three results follow from this inward union with Christ: (*a*) effectual prayer (vs. 7); (*b*) the glorification of the Father through our fruitfulness in character and service (vs. 8); and (*c*) fullness of joy flowing from Christ into every soul united with him (vs. 11). Prayer is answered because he who abides in Christ will ask for nothing that is not in accord with the will of Christ, i.e., because he prays in Christ's

---

But what must it be to fall out of his hands, he asks; to be ignored and let alone as past hope of amendment, as no longer worth bothering about, "to be secluded eternally, eternally, eternally from the sight of God"? [8]

Yet it is not always punishment. Sometimes it is promotion and the proof of approval. **Every branch of mine that bears no fruit, he takes away; and every branch that does bear fruit he prunes, that it may bear more fruit.** Because it bears, he prunes. The pupil who does well is put into a higher class, with heavier tasks. In that terrible day for Charles Lamb, when in a fit of madness his sister murdered their mother, Coleridge wrote: "I look upon you as a man called by sorrow and anguish and a strange desolation of hopes into quietness, and a soul set apart, and made peculiar to God."

We can see that that is so on the big scale of humanity as a whole. For what a flabby, backboneless, unattractive creature man would be, had he not had to face the difficult things in life! One cannot have courage if there is nothing to fear; or unselfishness if there is more than enough for all, and no one need stand back and do without. All that is noble in us has been hammered into us by the hard things we would eliminate, against which we angrily protest. "Trial," says Amiel, "only stops when it is useless: that is why it scarcely ever stops." [9]

And so it is with the individual; though it is difficult to believe that when trouble comes upon oneself. Montaigne declares that the saints assert that they have been mellowed and deepened by such things. But he pushes that claim of theirs aside as most unlikely. "All I know is that they only make me curse." [1] That is human and natural. Often enough we have lost our temper with God; have told him bluntly and with anger that his way of it just will not do, is indeed perfectly ridiculous, as any half-reasonable God would have seen for himself without our having to point it out to him! And yet the saints are right. No doubt, as Bunyan says, there are those who grow ill and well again like beasts, learning nothing from it. And as Caliban says to Prospero in the play, "You taught me language, and my profit on't is I know how to curse." [2] So one can be not better but worse for the discipline of life—hardened, rebellious, sullen, unbelieving, all our faith thrown to the winds, like Niobe, turned to stone by the sorrows that befell her. Nonetheless, if rightly met and used, these sorrows and trials through which we have to pass do open up new ministries of helpfulness, and do endow us with the sympathy, the understanding, the fellow feeling, the knowledge of what will help, which those who have not been so exercised are unlikely to possess. For Robert Burns was right. "Misery is like love; to speak its language truly, the author must have felt it." As Fraser of Brea set down: "I am learning to read love in the greatest of evils . . . ; and to put good constructions on all God's dealings; and when anything comes, though never so cross, I first inquire, What love can I see in this?" [3] The pruned branch does bear more and better.

We need not be afraid of life. It is often puzzling. Its ways can be steep and slippery, and the crossroads very confusing. But **I am the vine,** says Christ. "I guarantee to give you everything you can require. And **you are the branches,** which can do great things for me if you so choose. **And my Father is the vinedresser.**" And God is very wise. And we can trust him even in the darkness when we do not understand at all.

9-12. ***A Staggering Parallel.***—Staggering words, not easily credible. No doubt Christian people keep experiencing that in very deed they can apply to their Master's attitude to them the greatest of the assertions which the prophets made about God's goodness toward his wayward people; have found that Christ's love for them is a divine love in its wholeheartedness, in its depth and fullness, in its

[8] Smith, *Donne's Sermons*, p. 210.

[9] *Journal*, p. 53.

[1] *Essays*, Bk. III, ch. ii.

[2] Shakespeare, *The Tempest*, Act I, scene 2.

[3] *Memoirs*, p. 241.

10 If ye keep my commandments, ye shall abide in my love; even as I have kept my Father's commandments, and abide in his love.

I loved you; abide in my love. 10 If you keep my commandments, you will abide in my love, just as I have kept my Father's commandments and abide in his love.

---

name (cf. 14:14). The thought now revolves around two points—love and the observance of commandments. In both of these the relation between the Son and the Father is to be

---

persistency in face of every obstacle; have felt that it is God's own love to them that reaches them in and through Christ.

But the breath-taking parallels in this passage sound impossible! It is natural that God the Father should love Jesus Christ. For nothing came between them to mar the perfection of their union. Montaigne once declared that were he asked concerning his best friend, "How is it that we were so much to one another, you and I?" he could come only to this answer, "It was because you were you, and because I was I."[4] Apparently they fitted into one another. So God and Christ were one in heart and mind and will; and nothing hindered the fullness of their communion. But how can Christ love us like that—us, surely so uncongenial to him, and with so much in our soiled ways that must offend and alienate the pureness of his mind? "Can two walk together, except they be agreed?" (Amos 3:3.) And our whole way of life, our ideals, our likes, our dislikes, are so different from his. Pity, and compassion, and a willingness to spend himself to save us from being what we are, that one can partly understand. But **as the Father has loved me, so have I loved you.** How can that be? G. K. Chesterton claimed that Francis of Assisi was a real lover of men. Not merely a philanthropist toward them, interested in their case, so he explains; but one who somehow really loved them, utterly unlovable to one like him though they might seem.[5] And life has proved that for some utterly inexplicable reason Jesus Christ finds something lovable in us, and meets it with a love so wonderful that he himself can find no comparison for it, except the love of God's own heart for him.

And we must try to believe that, to accept it as a fact, and to walk in the sunshine of it. For it is there. Yet some miss it all, and shiver through life on the shadowy side of the street. **If you keep my commandments, you will abide in my love, just as I have kept my Father's commandments and abide in his love.** "Sin . . . falls like a blot upon all my evidences," admits Fraser of Brea.[6] It does more. For if we knowingly, deliberately, willfully harbor an ugly habit, we cannot keep in step with God. Something comes between us, and we fall apart from him, lose touch with him. We have to pay away our communion with him as the price of that which we have chosen. It is a madman's bargain. For life has nothing to offer which can even be compared to peace of conscience and the fullness of joy that comes from fellowship with Jesus Christ.

But our Lord does not leave things in the general; he lays his hand on what in particular is required of us if we are to walk with him. **This is my commandment, that you love one another as I have loved you.** Again a staggering comparison, and a standard set us that seems utterly beyond our reach. For who can love as Christ has loved, or give as he has given? But the same spirit must be there. Be loving, unselfish, generous with ourselves, using our lives not merely for our own ends and aims and interests but on behalf of those around us. Such people, says the Master, walk with me, and I with them. And naturally so. For as Burns has it:

> But deep this truth impress'd my mind—
> Thro' all His works abroad,
> The heart benevolent and kind
> The most resembles God.[7]

And they can fit into one another—God and they. As Aristotle has it, "The perfect kind of friendship is that of good men who resemble one another in virtue."[8] And surely even more between a good man and God.

11. *The Happiness of Christianity.*—These things I have spoken to you, that my joy may be in you, and that your joy may be full. So peace is not Christ's only legacy to his people. For to that he adds fullness of joy, and his own joy at that. And if we do not accept and appropriate this that he offers we are defrauding ourselves of a major part of the gift that he intends for us and are not adequately Christian.

Confessedly the N.T. is a grave and even a stern book; never shirking ugly facts, but facing them with honesty and frankness. Yet could we read it for the first time, what would strike us most in it would surely be that this is the hap-

[4] *Essays,* Bk. I, ch. xxvii.
[5] *St. Francis of Assisi* (London: Hodder & Stoughton, 1923), p. 14.
[6] *Memoirs,* p. 229.
[7] "A Winter Night."
[8] *Nicomachean Ethics* VIII. 3. 6.

11 These things have I spoken unto you, that my joy might remain in you, and *that* your joy might be full.

11 These things I have spoken to you, that my joy may be in you, and that your joy may be full.

the pattern for the reciprocal relations between the disciples and Jesus (cf. 3:35; 5:20; 10:17; 14:20-21, 23; 17:24, 26). Just as Jesus imparted his peace to the troubled hearts of

piest book in the whole world. It thrills with joy; its message is a gospel, a shout of good news; it is the breaking through of midday sunshine on a morning that had been bleak and gray. So Christ himself quite certainly meant it to be. When he had started on his ministry, but was back for a time in his own Nazareth, they asked him to take part in the service of the synagogue. "And he stood up to read; . . . and found the place where it was written, 'The Spirit of the Lord is upon me, because he has anointed me to preach good news to the poor. He has sent me to proclaim release to the captives and recovering of sight to the blind, to set at liberty those who are oppressed, to proclaim the acceptable year of the Lord.' And he closed the book, . . . and sat down," and said, "In this the prophet speaks of me. And today all this has come to pass" (cf. Luke 4:16-21). Or when John, brooding in his prison, lost heart and wavered in his faith in him, what were the signs and proofs that he sent back to rally him? "Go and tell John what you hear and see: the blind receive their sight and the lame walk, lepers are cleansed and the deaf hear, and the dead are raised up, and the poor have good news preached to them" (Matt. 11:4-5). And indeed one could trace Christ's progress through the country by the happiness that he had left behind. Where he had passed, sorrows were healed and diseases cured, and shadows lifted from strained minds, and souls restored to health and strength and cleanness. The early Christians were the happiest of people. The note of that first Christianity is joy.

And they caught the infection of that happiness from their Master. For with his unsullied conscience, his uninterrupted communion with God, his perfect trust in him, his unselfish spending of himself for others, Christ must have been the happiest of men. As Spinoza put it in his closing proposition, "Blessedness is not something added to goodness, it *is* goodness."[9] And Christ offers to share his own fullness of joy with anyone who will accept it from him, using arresting metaphors to bring home to us something of how immeasurably he can enrich and amplify our life. A peasant, tired with toil that has absorbed his days and strength, and yet has just sufficed to make ends barely meet, if even that, happens to plow somewhat deeper than his wont and comes upon a hidden treasure. And with that his penury is over, and he has entered on an affluence of which he had never even dreamed as possible for him. "So," claims Christ, "I can enrich your life, making it a new thing, crowded with interests and full of color where it had been tame and drab and little more than emptiness and failure."

[9] *Ethics*, Part V, Proposition 42.

And in the epistles and the Acts those who have tried him keep telling us it is all gloriously true; so true that it just cannot be described, will not go into language. They do their best. They coin new words. They invent superlatives and supersuperlatives. But in the end they frankly confess that they have given no idea of it; and that one must experience this thing for himself before he can begin to understand how wonderful it is. Always their eyes are shining; always their hearts dance and exult in the sheer happiness of this that they have found. Paul, for instance, in that royal metaphor of his bids us think of this earth of ours as finished indeed but still rolling through space—dark, sterile, dead—and then light found it out, and bursting through the vapors, played on it. And with that everything followed—color and life and endless interests. "Look at that dead ball turning in the darkness. Look at this world we know, teeming with joys and beauties. That is the difference Christ made to me!" "For it is the God who said, 'Let light shine out of darkness,' who has shone in our hearts to give the light of the knowledge of the glory of God in the face of Christ." (II Cor. 4:6.) The splendor and the joy of it!

So Clement, "All life has become a song"; and again, "Ploughing, we praise; sailing, we sing."[1] And Barnabas speaks of the Christians as "the children of joy."[2] And Hermas talks about the Holy Spirit as "a happy Spirit." That note runs on and on, down to this day. "The Christian ethics is the ethics of inexpressible joy," says Theodor von Haering.[3] And William James gives nearly the whole of his second lecture in his *Varieties of Religious Experience* to a consideration of the unique happiness of

[1] *Miscellanies* VII. 7.

[2] Barn. 7:1.

[3] *The Ethics of the Christian Life*, tr. James S. Hill (London: Williams & Norgate, 1909), p. 253.

his followers (14:27; 16:33), so now he inspires them in the hour of gloom with his own radiant joy (vs. 11; cf. 16:20, 22, 24; 17:13). Joy is henceforth a note of the true church (cf. I John 1:4; II John 12; III John 4).

religion, but most of all of Christ's religion; of which happiness nothing else in the whole world, so he maintains with emphasis, holds the secret. And T. K. Abbott, that delicate scholar, witnesses that to turn from the greatest of the classical teachers to the N.T. is to pass from the cold bracing austerity of a mountaintop into the warmth and security of home.

Have we been misrepresenting Christ? For enter a church during the time of worship, and one finds gravity and seemliness and a feeling of reverence. But would anyone, stumbling in, sense that here are people who have made a glorious discovery, and are thrilled and joy-possessed? Or do the mass of us who claim to be Christians so live that we give the impression to outsiders that we have found something so worth the having, and bringing such happiness, that they feel that they too must seek it, and from Christ himself? Have we been misrepresenting him by concentrating, as the West has done, upon the suffering Savior and the Man of Sorrows? Campanella, in one of his sonnets, said bluntly that art has failed to give a worthy and authentic picture of our Lord. Why, he protested, is he always depicted hanging on the Cross, where he was only for a few hours, and not rather risen, with his foot set upon the stone that could not hold him, the triumphant conqueror he is, and that forever?[4] The conception of Jesus Christ to be found in the pictures in the catacombs, painted by refugees crouching there for safety, is a far more joyous one than ours is apt to be. As Dean Arthur P. Stanley wrote:

> It represents to us the joyful cheerful side of Christianity. . . . Look at that beautiful, graceful figure, bounding down as if from his native hills, with the happy sheep nestling on his shoulder, with the pastoral pipes in his hand, blooming in immortal youth. . . . That is the primitive conception of the Founder of Christianity. . . . The popular conception of Him in the early Church was of the strong, the joyous youth, of eternal growth, of immortal grace.[5]

And they had warrant for their view. For the N.T. makes plain that those who saw Christ in the flesh were struck almost first by a certain sunnyheartedness about him which prim minds did not easily associate with religion. The thing indeed became a scandal. "Now John," they said, "with his lean austere life in the desert, is patently a saint of God. But this other, mingling in people's happinesses, going to weddings and the like, is he a religious man at all?" And they called after him along the streets, "Hie! friend of publicans and sinners!" And Jesus admitted he was happy. "What else can we be?" he asked, knowing what we know, believing what we do believe, experiencing what we are experiencing day by day of the goodness of God. He likened his little company to a wedding party on the wedding morning; talked of my joy. And indeed he was always giving thanks for something; found life a good thing; gazed in astonishment at the mass of folk making so little of it, throwing away for nothing that with which they might have won so much; looked at them in bewilderment, so hot and fussy and eager about trivialities, and missing all that matters. "Can they be satisfied with only that?" he used to muse, looking after them in amazement. "They look satisfied, yet can they be? And are they never bored by that dull uneventful thing which they mistake for life?" And bluntly he called them dead; not really living at all, to be called living; implored them to believe that he could give them a life that is life indeed, far more abundant, satisfying, exciting than the tameness of their drab existence. "You are poor slaves," he used to say, "and I can make you free; you are ill, and I can grant you strength and health again, and all the fullness of real life instead of that decrepitude of yours. You find life much too difficult for you, are really unfit for its tasks, feel miserably that arrears of duty left undone are ruthlessly accumulating, and that one day the avalanche will roar down on you and sweep you bodily away; and I can make you fit for your job and competent to see it through." And he does. "He is able; we are able"; that happy confidence runs everywhere through the N.T. And if it is not so with us, are we not caricaturing Christ to the great damage of his cause? For even in the upper room, with the thick darkness gathering about them, Christ could and did say, **These things I have spoken to you, that my joy may be in you, and that your joy may be full.** "We are the children of joy," and the first Christians literally were so. And if that is no natural or fitting definition of us now, then we are less than fully Christian, and are missing something that Christ has to offer us that would make us so.

[4] Sonnet XXI, "The Resurrection."

[5] *Christian Institutions* (New York: Charles Scribner's Sons, 1881), pp. 284-85.

12 This is my commandment, That ye love one another, as I have loved you.

13 Greater love hath no man than this, that a man lay down his life for his friends.

14 Ye are my friends, if ye do whatsoever I command you.

12 "This is my commandment, that you love one another as I have loved you.
13 Greater love has no man than this, that a man lay down his life for his friends.
14 You are my friends if you do what I

2. The Fellowship of Love and the Call to Service (15:12-17)

12-17. The principle which is to bind in one the new community in Christ is the new commandment (13:34; cf. I John 3:11, 23; 4:21). Its members are to love one another in the way that Jesus has loved them. He is laying down his life for them (10:14-15). The highest test of love is that a man is willing to risk his life for his friends. If the disciples are loyal to his instructions he gives them the rank of **friends.** The relationship has been that of **master** (κύριος) and **servant** (δοῦλος, lit., **slave**), as they are twice reminded in these discourses (vs. 20; 13:16). It is now transformed into that service which is perfect freedom, for the disciples are taken into their Master's confidence as **friends** to share all that he has heard from the Father. With **you are my friends** (vs. 14) cf. Wisd. Sol. 7:28 ("Wisdom makes men friends of God") and the description of Abraham as the friend

13-17. *What Christ Means by Friendship.*—"Friend" is a word that is tossed about from hand to hand with very varying meanings. Often it has no depth of earth in it, and signifies no more than an acquaintance. But the foremost teachers, seeing much farther than that, have been at pains to try to enlarge and perfect our conception of what friendship is, and to make us realize its possibilities. So Cicero[6] and Aristotle;[7] Buddha not seldom, here and there. Among the marks of a true friend the latter notes that "he guards you when you are off your guard and does not forsake you in trouble; he even lays down his life for your sake; he restrains you from doing wrong; he enjoins you to do right; . . . he reveals to you the way of heaven."[8]

But in this succinct passage, brief though it is, Jesus Christ has given us a reading of friendship beside which the others, noble though they may be, pale like the stars when the sun rises. For this too, like everything else he touches, he has deepened and glorified. Real friendship between any two, he tells us, involves a certain drawing to each other, a kinship of spirit more radical than the surface differences there may be between them, obvious and even startling though these last may be. That is essential, or else there can be no friendship at all (vs. 14). But given that, in what does the thing itself consist?

Characteristically, Christ puts first a willingness to spend oneself for the other; and this not only ungrudgingly, without reckoning up the cost, but eagerly, and so ready to help that he will give and give, his very life if need be, to aid and save his friend (vs. 13). "Friendship," says Aristotle, "seems to lie in the loving rather than in the being loved."[9]

Friendship also consists in a frank unhesitating opening of one's heart and whole mind to the other, without shyness or secretiveness. That is where many an acquaintanceship falls short of friendship and never reaches it. For to practice friendship worth the name, we must allow the other to see right in and know us as we really are, unstintedly sharing with him what we ourselves have learned (vs. 15).

Finally, in real friendship there is a trust in the other that believes in him, risks on him, never doubting his loyalty, but looking toward him with confidence.

It is to this intimate and wholehearted relationship that Christ calls us. Mere obedience is less than what he asks. That is a slave's part; and we are summoned to something warmer and more spontaneous, are to be Christ's friends (vss. 14-15).

Certainly he himself meets, with exactness and overflowing fullness, his own lofty definition of what a friend is. As Aristotle has it:

> We need friends when we are young to keep us from error, when we get old to tend upon us and to carry out those plans which we have not strength to execute ourselves, and in the prime of life to help us in noble deeds,—"two together" [as Homer says]; for thus we are more efficient in thought and in action.[1]

All that, innumerable souls have found in Christ as in no other.

The Cross is only the last crowning proof and

[6] *Concerning Friendship.*

[7] *Nicomachean Ethics* VIII, IX.

[8] See, e.g., Sigālovāda Suttanta in *Dialogues of the Buddha* (Oxford: University Press, 1921), III, 177-79.

[9] *Nicomachean Ethics* VIII. 8. 3.

[1] *Ibid.*, VIII. 1. 2.

15 Henceforth I call you not servants; for the servant knoweth not what his lord doeth: but I have called you friends; for all things that I have heard of my Father I have made known unto you.

16 Ye have not chosen me, but I have chosen you, and ordained you, that ye should go and bring forth fruit, and *that* your fruit should remain; that whatsoever ye shall ask of the Father in my name, he may give it you.

command you. 15 No longer do I call you servants,[d] for the servant[e] does not know what his master is doing; but I have called you friends, for all that I have heard from my Father I have made known to you.
16 You did not choose me, but I chose you and appointed you that you should go and bear fruit and that your fruit should abide; so that whatever you ask the Father in my

[d] Or *slaves.*
[e] Or *slave.*

of God (Isa. 41:8; Jas. 2:23). This friendship is costly, for such love involves a sacrifice. In the perils and difficulties that will confront the disciples their strength will lie in the knowledge that their mission is not of their own choosing, but of divine initiative and appointment. This selection and commission have a purpose and a result: the purpose, that they should go out upon a mission fruitful in its effects on their own character, and yielding for eternity a harvest of gains to the Christian cause; the result, that the Father will hear and answer their prayers. This note sounds again and again in these farewell discourses (cf. 14:13-14; 16:23, 24, 26). **All this** (ταῦτα) is involved in the one comprehensive command (vs. 12) **that ye love one another** (cf. vs. 17). A contrast has sometimes been drawn between the wider command to love one's neighbor (Mark 12:31; Matt.

instance of his unstinted giving of himself throughout his whole life, keeping back nothing; and, say the Scriptures, that same generosity runs on into eternity and the other world, where he is thinking of us and working for us still. Everything he has is ours to draw upon. "It is yours," he says, "because it is mine. That is what I mean by friendship."

Buddha claimed that in his teaching he never selfishly kept a closed fist tight upon what he had discovered, but with an open hand shared everything he had learned with whoever would accept it. And, says Christ, setting it down as a proof of his friendship for us, **All that I have heard from my Father I have made known to you.** And what a marvelous difference it has made that Christ was not content with thinking things out in his own mind, but shared with us what he had found concerning God, and man, and life, and salvation, and a dozen other central matters. How bare and bleak and incomprehensible life would have been had he not given us his guidance, and heaped upon us discoveries which we could not have made.

Life is full of mysteries, but as it proceeds, surely the most amazing thing in it is Christ's unshaken trust in ordinary people; and this after we have repeatedly faltered and failed him. **You did not choose me, but I chose you and appointed you that you should go and bear fruit and that your fruit should abide.** That is the bewildering fact! It was not that you came upon Jesus Christ, and that, seeing him, your heart broke away and ran to him and clung to him, beseeching him to lift you up out of the drabness that you are toward all the glory that he is; but that he came on you, turned and looked after you and said, "Now there is one to whom my heart is drawn, and out of whom I know that I can fashion something of permanent worth; through whom I can effect something that will be not merely of transitory value but that will abide, and keep telling for good far down the centuries, long after the man himself is utterly forgotten; one in whom I see infinite possibilities, if he will come to me and lean on God, and claim and use what God and I can give him" (vs. 16). And often though we fail him, to that he holds: "I chose you; and, knowing all there is to know, the very worst, I choose you still."

Here is a Friend indeed "that sticketh closer than a brother." But on our side how do things stand? And how have we responded to Christ's friendship for us? But shabbily at best! We take so much and give so little; we are so eager over our own interests and so lukewarm about his. "To me to live is Christ," claimed Paul (Phil. 1:21). And he could say it truthfully. But for us it would be a wild exaggeration. Once our own interests are served, once our own ends are met, we will share some of the surplus with Christ, if there is a surplus; give something to him, and do something for him. But against the background of his friendship for us, ours toward him is a poor and stunted thing. Apply to it that rule that he suggests so often, "As I, so you," and how thin it looks and is!

Nor are we frank and open with him, as he is toward us. Our prayers are often stiff and

17 These things I command you, that ye love one another.
18 If the world hate you, ye know that it hated me before *it hated* you.

name, he may give it to you. 17 This I command you, to love one another.
18 "If the world hates you, know that

22:39-40) and this narrower injunction of brotherly love; also between the witness of God's mercy described in Rom. 5:6, 8, 10, and this restricted expression of sacrificial love. In the Pauline conception Christ died for "the ungodly," for "sinners," for "enemies." The Johannine Christ dies for his **friends.** The antithesis is unreal, as 3:16 shows. The Christian fellowship is the school of Christian character. It is to work as leaven (Matt. 13:33), influencing all human relationships, setting before the world a revelation of Christ in the brotherly love that marks his community (13:35).

3. The World's Hatred (15:18-25)

Two Johannine characteristics are prominent in this section: the writer's moral dualism, and his habit of expanding and expounding traditional sayings of Jesus in the light of the experience of the church during two generations.

18-21. If the world hates you: The disciples had not yet incurred this hostility, but from Pentecost onward the world's hatred was displayed. Christ's presence and teaching were a touchstone of character. His life fulfilled the prophecy of the aged Simeon (Luke 2:34): he was "set for the fall and rising of many in Israel, and for a sign that is spoken against, . . . that thoughts out of many hearts may be revealed." The division between

formal, less than honest. Moreover, we soon grow bored in his presence and find nothing more to say. And this because we do not seem to realize how intimate our prayers can be and ought to be; that we are with a Friend to whom we can speak frankly and freely, and with the happy confidence that nothing that touches us is without interest to him. As Fénelon put it:

> Tell [God] all that is in your heart, as one unloads one's heart to a dear friend. . . . People who have no secrets from each other never want subjects of conversation; they do not . . . weigh their words, because there is nothing to be kept back. Neither do they seek for something to say; they talk out of the abundance of their heart—without consideration, just what they think. . . . Blessed are they who attain to such familiar, unreserved intercourse with God.[2]

Nor do we trust Christ as he trusts us; are often quick to doubt him, easily grow suspicious of him, lose heart, fear that he surely has forgotten us, or is not really trying, or is unequal to the task of shepherding us safe home; are ready to suspect and blame. Yet he has never failed us; and still trusts us who have failed him countless times.

As things are, our discipleship has brought us more than we can begin to reckon up. But if we entered fully into the relationship Christ offers us, what would there not result? And has life anything to give to be compared to this, that when we pass into the other world, Christ should come out to meet us, and draw us in—poor, shambling, shabby figures though we are—and present us to God saying, "Father, this is a dear friend of mine, to whom I have owed hugely." That sounds incredible. Yet there are those who one day will hear that spoken of them by him. To such lengths does his friendship go. And he asks of us that we should reproduce this spirit that we find in him, not only toward himself, but to all among whom we live. **This I command you, to love one another.**

18-21. ***Warning and Encouragement.***—Having given them so much to cheer and hearten and bring them through, Christ warns his friends of grave troubles already at their door; a warning which more or less runs on to the close of ch. 16, but which is very definite in these verses, verses, nonetheless, in which the disciples find something amazingly encouraging for them in the very unpopularity and hardships and the like so soon to come upon them. Erskine of Linlathen remarks in one of his letters, "How consoling to receive tribulation as the fulfilment of a Father's promise—as the private cipher agreed on between the Saviour and the saved!"[3] That is a truth; but one that must be used with caution. For often enough mistaking prejudice for principle, and their own obstinacy and stupidity for loyalty to Christ, people involve themselves and him in troubles and ill will that are quite unnecessary.

[2] *Spiritual Letters to Men,* Letter LXXXVIII, "To the Vidame D'Amiens: On Prayer and Meditation." See also Letter XXIV, "To One Who Had Recently Turned to God."

[3] *Letters of Thomas Erskine,* ed. William Hanna (Edinburgh: David Douglas, 1878), p. 55.

19 If ye were of the world, the world would love his own; but because ye are not of the world, but I have chosen you out of the world, therefore the world hateth you.

20 Remember the word that I said unto you, The servant is not greater than his lord. If they have persecuted me, they will also persecute you; if they have kept my saying, they will keep yours also.

21 But all these things will they do unto you for my name's sake, because they know not him that sent me.

22 If I had not come and spoken unto them, they had not had sin; but now they have no cloak for their sin.

it has hated me before it hated you. 19 If
you were of the world, the world would
love its own; but because you are not of
the world, but I chose you out of the world,
therefore the world hates you. 20 Remem-
ber the word that I said to you, 'A servant[f]
is not greater than his master.' If they per-
secuted me, they will persecute you; if they
kept my word, they will keep yours also.
21 But all this they will do to you on my
account, because they do not know him
who sent me. 22 If I had not come and
spoken to them, they would not have sin;
but now they have no excuse for their sin.

[f] Or *slave.*

God and the world appeared more clearly whenever he delivered his word. The world is partial to those who share its standards, but hates those who testify against its accepted code (cf. 7:7, "The world cannot hate you, but it hates me because I testify that its works are evil"). Those who hated and rejected Jesus will act in the same way to his followers because they have been chosen and called to leave the world's ways. Persecution once directed against him will now be turned against those who carry on his mission. How can they expect anything else in view of the warning already given (13:16; cf. Matt. 10:24)? On the other hand, just as some responded to the words of Jesus, so some will accept his message from the lips of his disciples. The spirit of refusal originates in ignorance of God. Hostility to the church has its roots in enmity to Christ, **because they do not know him who sent me.**

22-25. This ignorance is culpable on the part of those who had the opportunity of seeing and hearing the commissioned representative of the Father and of watching his significant acts, which had no parallel in their experience. Blind prejudice repudiated this evidence with a hatred of Jesus that was equivalent to hatred of the Father. The disciples may take comfort from two considerations. Their being hated by the world proved that

---

But wisely used, it is a right comfortable and steadying word which must have helped and rallied innumerable hard-pressed souls.

Perhaps, however, face to face with Christ's prophecy of violence and dislike to be incurred for his sake, what we ought to ask ourselves is, Are we hated enough? Is this church which we know and see around us the kind of church that our Lord planned and desired to create? Or is it much too acquiescent and complacent, far less dynamic and alarming to the world than it was meant to be? To be hated is uncomfortable, and may mean terrible things. But even that surely is better than to be blandly ignored and overlooked, contemptuously dismissed as a set of children playing their futile childish games—doing no good, of course, but not much harm, and so left to amuse themselves with their innocuous pastimes. Are we sufficiently like Christ to draw the world's fire? There can be no truce between him and it. They front each other, Christ and the world, foot to foot, in deadly enmity. But many of his followers seem to imagine that they have contrived a clever and most satisfactory compromise by which, without breaking with either, they can meet the demands of both these claimants for their loyalty. This, said Christ bluntly, is impossible.

22-25. ***To Meet Christ Is a Fearsome Thing.***—The saddest words in Scripture are surely vss. 22-24. Christ was so eager to help mankind. And the Scripture interpretation of his life and death and resurrection is sufficiently astounding: they were the working out of God's eternal plan for the deliverance of a lost world. Yet with all that in his heart and in his Father's, Christ feels that some are the worse for his coming, and not the better, dreadfully worse; that through their perverted misuse of what has such infinite possibilities in it, he who came to save them must be for some the final and conclusive witness against them, whose evidence must close the case, and settle the issue, and make their condemnation certain. That was a sorrow that lay cold and heavy upon the

23 He that hateth me hateth my Father also.

24 If I had not done among them the works which none other man did, they had not had sin: but now have they both seen and hated both me and my Father.

25 But *this cometh to pass,* that the word might be fulfilled that is written in their law, They hated me without a cause.

26 But when the Comforter is come, whom I will send unto you from the Father,

23 He who hates me hates my Father also.
24 If I had not done among them the works
which no one else did, they would not
have sin; but now they have seen and hated
both me and my Father. 25 It is to fulfill the
word that is written in their law, 'They
hated me without a cause.' 26 But when the
Counselor comes, whom I shall send to you

---

they were on God's side in his judgment of the world. Moreover, the astounding failure of the enemies of Jesus to recognize and receive him had been foreseen in God's plan for the future. The psalmist had twice borne witness to this groundless hatred (Pss. 35:19; 69:4). This use of scripture to prove that God is not taken by surprise, but has every situation completely in his hands, is a favorite thought of the evangelist (cf. 12:37-38; 13:18; 17:12), whose language suggests that he looked upon such events even as inevitable because foreseen. This use of the O.T. is not confined to the prophetic writings. **Their law** includes any part of the Scriptures. It is spoken of as theirs with no thought of disparaging the Scriptures, but to lay stress on their boasted study of the very book whose warnings they failed to read.

4. Third Paraclete Saying (15:26-27)

26-27. The mission of **the Counselor** is described in this passage in a way that unites the apparent differences in two of the other sayings. According to 14:16, in answer to the prayer of the Son, it is the Father who will give the Paraclete; according to 16:7, it is Jesus who sends him. Here it is written, **whom I shall send to you from the Father.** The Paraclete is the alter ego of Jesus, continuing his work on earth, **who,** as **the Spirit of truth, proceeds from the Father.** This is the basis of his authority in witnessing to Christ. The disciples **also are witnesses, because you have been with me from the beginning.** The early church, according to Eph. 2:20, was being "built upon the foundation of the apostles and prophets, Christ Jesus himself being the chief cornerstone." The apostolic testimony witnessed to the truth of the historic facts about which their

---

heart of Christ. **If I had not come and spoken to them, they would not have sin; but now they have no excuse for their sin.** His revelation of what human life can rise to be, and of the helps accessible to us in him and God, has made the old standard of things, once thought sufficient, obsolete and woefully inadequate. And if we shrink back from the high adventures to which he summons us, do not want and will not take what he has put within our reach, but turning our backs upon such possibilities, run squealing greedily to the accustomed swine troughs, our failure is now a far worse failure, and our doom a darker doom.

Again, **If I had not done among them the works which no one else did, they would not have sin; but now they have seen and hated both me and my Father.** For us who have seen in other lives the evident proofs of his sufficiency for every possible call upon him, for us who in our own lives have experienced that in very real degree, for us who have found that he does help, does heal, does save, to let go his hand and turn back to the sordid things from which he has delivered us is a far more shocking trespass than were our original wrongdoings. For then we surrendered because we could not resist. But now that we have found that in him we can rise above our weaknesses, if we knowingly return to them, ours is a blacker sin because deliberate and voluntary.

To meet Christ is a fearsome thing. We may be the better for it, in the end infinitely better. But if we are not, then we must be the worse, far worse. Never again can matters be with us just what they were before we came on him. And all Christ's grace cannot spare us from the decision as to what we are to do with it. We must choose. And we do choose. And not all of us in the same way.

26-27. ***Christ's Witnesses.***—"Still," says Christ, "if many will reject me, I have my witnesses

even the Spirit of truth, which proceedeth
from the Father, he shall testify of me:
27 And ye also shall bear witness, because ye have been with me from the beginning.

from the Father, even the Spirit of truth, who proceeds from the Father, he will bear witness to me;
27 and you also are witnesses, because you have been with me from the beginning.

---

long and close intimacy with Jesus made them reliable witnesses. The prophets were those through whom the inspiration of the living Spirit came to the church. But the historic revelation and its inspired interpretation both depended upon the Spirit for effective witness to the world (cf. 3:11; 7:39; I John 1:2; 4:14; 5:7; III John 12; Acts 1:21-22; 13:31).

In vss. 1-25 there is a thread of continuity in the thought, though the paragraphs may be expansions of separate sayings of Jesus. The allegory of the vine represents the living union which unites Christ and the members of his church. Separation from him in thought, feeling, and purpose is fatal. The vinedresser looks for fruitfulness (vss. 2, 8), the *raison d'être* of every vine. With this end in view he not only cuts away withered branches, but at the end of the fruiting season he uses the pruning knife, so that during the winter little of the vine is left but the trunk and a few principal branches. The result is seen in the spring, when the new shoots are more vigorous and bear better fruit. There are thus two main thoughts in the allegory: (*a*) The health and vitality of the vine depend on the free flow of the sap from the parent stock into every branch and shoot; (*b*) to secure this end the vinedresser prunes both for destruction and for renewal of life. As the evangelist ponders these facts, and sees them applied to the church of his time, he recognizes in (*a*) the need for unity. This is imperiled by certain teachers of error, who disregard the revelation given in Jesus so that his word does not dwell in them. "They went out from us, but they were not of us; for if they had been of us, they would have continued with us; but they went out, that it might be plain that they all are not of us. . . . No one who denies the Son has the Father. He who confesses the Son has the Father also. Let what you heard from the beginning abide in you. If what you heard from the beginning abides in you, then you will abide in the Son and in the Father. And this is what he has promised us, eternal life" (I John 2:19, 23-25). The excommunication of these errorists seems to be implied in vs. 6. The internal unity is endangered when brotherly love wanes. This also is a recurrent theme in I John. But this love of the brotherhood issues from and is maintained by the divine love itself (vss. 9, 12, 17), for the initiative is always with God (cf. I John 4:19, "We love, because he first loved us"). So here: "You did not choose me, but I chose you" (vs. 16). The outward expression of our love to man must be obedience to the royal law of sacrificial service (vss. 12-14). Our love to God is to be shown by the prayer of confident trust (vss. 7, 16). It should be observed that there is one word (μένειν) in the Greek which is variously rendered in the Gospel and I John by the words "dwell," "abide," or "continue." It is one of the characteristic terms in the Johannine vocabulary. The pruning knife (*b*) in God's hand is the discipline of the word of truth, but also the discipline of loss and persecution. The world's hatred of Jesus will be suffered by his followers. If they are united with him they must be prepared to suffer with him (vss. 18-21). But persecution will not enfeeble; it will invigorate the church. The thought that links this paragraph (vss. 18-25) to the section about the vine is that of the vinedresser's knife, even when it is exercised through the hatred of the unbelieving world. The poet Horace (*Odes* IV. 4. 59), after describing

---

by which many will be convinced. There is **the Spirit of truth;** and he will prove effective. For with all its follies, blunderings, indifference, evasions, the mind of man loves truth; and when it sees it, is inclined to follow and adopt it. And **the Spirit of truth** will bring it home to many that this gospel works, does things, fulfills its promises; and so will induce others to give it its chance with them. And you also are my witnesses; you who have been with me, have tried me, have put me to the test; you who are not credulous enough not to believe what you yourselves have seen and heard and experienced. And through your witness for me others will be drawn to me." And indeed that is in the main how the faith has spread.

16 These things have I spoken unto you, that ye should not be offended.
2 They shall put you out of the synagogues: yea, the time cometh, that whosoever killeth you will think that he doeth God service.
3 And these things will they do unto you, because they have not known the Father, nor me.

16 "I have said all this to you to keep you from falling away.
2 They will put you out of the synagogues; indeed, the hour is coming when whoever kills you will think he is offering service to God.
3 And they will do this because they have

---

the disasters which almost overwhelmed the Roman state in its wars with Carthage, puts upon the lips of its inveterate enemy, Hannibal, a comparison of that sturdy and invincible race with a broad oak on Mount Algidus, lopped by the woodman's ax:

> Its loss its glory makes,
> And from the very steel fresh strength and spirit takes.

The church is cleansed by the words that Jesus spoke, so exacting in their moral demand (vs. 3); it is also cleansed and vitalized by the final word which this whole discourse is leading to, the word of the Cross.

5. Forewarned Is Forearmed (16:1-4)

16:1-4. These verses are an obvious continuation of the section 15:18-25, thus supporting the theory that the evangelist inserted the Paraclete sayings into the farewell discourses, which are consecutive and complete without them. The hatred of the Jews, already mentioned in general terms, is now described in detail. It will involve excommunication from the synagogue (cf. 9:22, 34) and even death (Acts 7:57-58). In their fanaticism they will regard even such murder as a proof of their loyalty to God (cf. Num. 25:13). Its real cause is their ignorance of the Father and the Son (cf. 15:21). Their rejection of Jesus has robbed them of their opportunity of learning what God is like.

16:1-15. ***Growing and Maturing in Spiritual Things.***—What leaps at us out of this whole passage is the fact that there is plan, method, sequence in Christ's training of us. He is too good a teacher to overwhelm us with an avalanche of facts which we cannot as yet assimilate. Patiently, and moderating his pace to ours, he leads us on bit by bit, here a little and there a little, as we are able to follow. **I did not say these things to you from the beginning;** for, at that stage it would have been premature. **I have said these things to you now, that when their hour comes you may remember that I told you;** so that you may not be staggered by what otherwise would have been unexpected, and would have seemed inexplicable, and surely finally disastrous. **I have yet many things to say to you, but you cannot bear them now.** You are not ready for them yet.

So the Christian life should be a gradual growth and training; a wading deeper and deeper into the truth. To walk with Christ ought to mean that every turn of the way opens up new views and vistas to us, vistas and views for which all our experience of him thus far had not prepared us. To be born again is very well—as a beginning. But it is only a beginning. One must grow up and mature in spiritual things, and reach one's full stature in Jesus Christ. Life as it passes ought to be deepening our Christianity, enabling us to see far more in it than we originally did, offering us helps in it against the new perils and difficulties that confront us at new periods; as J. A. Froude thought that at forty pleasure ceases for most people to be the main menace and is replaced by ambition, against which new trenches have to be cut. And so wise pupils keep attentive, letting their Teacher lead them on and on, and in and in, and up and up.

In this connection is there not something surprising in the marked preference of many congregations for younger ministers over their older brethren? A partial justification of the practice may be that inexperienced Christians, finding themselves on much the same level as the inexperienced minister, are not confused by studies in that higher Christianity which they have not yet reached. At any rate, however gifted in mental and spiritual things these youthful preachers are, almost of necessity theirs must be a partial, immature, not fully

4 But these things have I told you, that
when the time shall come, ye may remember that I told you of them. And these things I said not unto you at the beginning, because I was with you.
5 But now I go my way to him that sent me; and none of you asketh me, Whither goest thou?
6 But because I have said these things unto you, sorrow hath filled your heart.

not known the Father, nor me. 4 But I
have said these things to you, that when their hour comes you may remember that I told you of them.

"I did not say these things to you from the beginning, because I was with you.
5 But now I am going to him who sent me; yet none of you asks me, 'Where are you going?'
6 But because I have said these things to you, sorrow has filled your hearts.

This warning was unnecessary while he was with his disciples, but in a little while he will leave them (vs. 16) ; he therefore prepares them in advance for such persecution as might shake their faith and crush their courage, **I have said all this to keep you from falling away** (cf. 13:19; 14:29).

6. Fourth Paraclete Saying (16:5-11)

None of you asks me, "Where are you going?" sounds strange after 13:36; 14:5, but the diffiulty is removed on the supposition that these sayings were written separately from the discourses of chs. 13–16, and inserted by the evangelist later. Two things are said about **the Counselor:** (*a*) He cannot come while Jesus is still with his disciples (vss. 6-7). (*b*) He will be counsel for the prosecution in the arraignment of the world (vss. 8-11).

6-7. (*a*) The two Counselors cannot both minister on earth at the same time. It is to the advantage of the disciples that their Master should leave them, however sorrowful that prospect may make them. So long as he was visibly with them as companion and helper they would never rise to full manhood. They would rely upon him to settle all their difficulties and to answer all their questions. Neither would they be able to exercise to the utmost their faith and obedience until the visible companionship had become an

---

rounded gospel. Christ has still many things to tell them, but they cannot bear them yet. In a classical passage Bunyan confesses how his preaching grew and expanded and matured; how it was only slowly, and step by step, that he won and made his own province after province of the faith. At first his whole message was the terror of the law: "I went myself in chains to preach to them in chains. . . . I preached what I felt, what I smartingly did feel." This for two whole years. But then, given some staid peace and comfort through Christ, "Now I altered in my preaching, for I still preached what I saw and felt; . . . I did much labour to hold with Jesus Christ in all his offices. . . . After this, God let me into something of the mystery of the union with Christ; wherefore that I discovered and showed to them also."[4] The gospel which he preached in the end was a much richer and fuller and truer one than the hearers of his youth had had offered to them.

But not all of us are intrepid adventurers like Bunyan. Some of us close with Christ; and so pitch our tent and settle down for life there, where we first met with him; will not credit that even in him there can be anything more or better than that first initial gift. God, says Luther, "has given us a whole sea full of his word." But we never venture out into its immensities; and so never discover the wide new lands that lie waiting for us, that might be ours, and should be ours, and are meant to be ours; but potter to and fro about the inland waters of the faith, never feel the rush and heave and irresistibility of the whole gospel, with its far horizons that keep receding as we make for them, luring us on and on. "The sea grows always greater, nobody can paint it," declared Tintoretto, throwing down his brushes in despair. W. M. Macgregor was fond of using that as an apt summing up of a faithful and industrious Christian's experience in Christ. There is no getting to the end of him. Range rises behind range, and peak towers above peak. What any one mind grasps of him, thought Paul, is a mere segment, woefully inadequate, compared to the whole fullness to be gained through him. It takes all the saints, so he maintains, all pooling their experiences of him, all throwing in what each of them has seen from his particular and limited angle, to provide us with an inkling of what Christ is, and

[4] *Grace Abounding*, pars. 276-80.

7 Nevertheless I tell you the truth; It is expedient for you that I go away: for if I go not away, the Comforter will not come unto you; but if I depart, I will send him unto you.

8 And when he is come, he will reprove the world of sin, and of righteousness, and of judgment:

9 Of sin, because they believe not on me;

10 Of righteousness, because I go to my Father, and ye see me no more;

11 Of judgment, because the prince of this world is judged.

7 Nevertheless I tell you the truth: it is to
your advantage that I go away, for if I do
not go away, the Counselor will not come
to you; but if I go, I will send him to you.
8 And when he comes, he will convince the
world of sin and of righteousness and of
judgment: 9 of sin, because they do not be-
lieve in me; 10 of righteousness, because I
go to the Father, and you will see me no
more; 11 of judgment, because the ruler of
this world is judged.

---

inner communion, and they were developing a new sense of responsibility in their individual and corporate life.

8-11. (*b*) The Paraclete is more than advocate and protector of the disciples; on his arrival he will also counterattack the world. By convicting the world on three counts he will reverse its erroneous judgment passed upon Jesus in his crucifixion. He will **convince it of sin** by showing the Jews that their claim to righteousness, based upon external conformity to a code of laws, would not stand trial. Unbelief, blindness to revealed truth, spiritual pride and prejudice had led to the rejection of the long-expected Christ. That was essentially sin (cf. 3:19-20; 7:7; 8:47; 15:22). He will **convince it of righteousness,** for whereas his enemies thought that Jesus was discredited by the shameful death on the Cross, it would become evident that his death was a return to the Father, who had welcomed him as "the Holy and Righteous One" (cf. Acts 3:14; 2:36; 5:30-32).

---

what there is for us in him (see also on 14:25-26).

7-15. ***How We Are the Better for Christ's Going Away.***—All of us must have thought upon occasion, sometimes a little peevishly, how much easier it would have been if we had known Christ in the flesh, had lived with him and listened to him, had felt his hand laid upon very us in healing; if it had all been visible, and tangible, and obvious, and there: whereas we seem to move in a world of shadows, where we cannot see, cannot hear, cannot feel or touch, must just believe. Christ does not think that there is much in that. **It is to your advantage that I go away.**

For one thing, when he was here upon earth, it was in the main merely a local influence that he could exert; whereas now, the whole world over, he keeps telling on innumerable souls. Thomas à Kempis, musing upon the sacrament of the Last Supper, imagines to himself how it would be prized if it were possible to receive it only once a year, and that only at one place. Its very freeness, he thinks, blinds us to its value.[5] And that is true. Yet who would question that things are better as they are? And is it not a blessed thing that wherever they may be, souls in a second can be face to face with Christ?

More definitely, **the Spirit of truth,** says Christ, **will glorify me,** "will take the things that are mine and declare them to you, pressing them home upon you, enabling you to grasp and appropriate them, leading you into all the truth." For as yet only a constellation or two have swum into our ken, out of the vast overreaching heaven of the love of God to us in Christ. There is far more; and after that has been seen and appropriated, far more still in him for us than we have understood. Old John Duncan used to resent the habit we have of talking about the earliest Christian writers outside the canon as the fathers, holding that theirs was a very rudimentary knowledge of Christianity—and indeed, as Robert Rainy says, "Elementariness is the signature of all the early literature. . . . What the apostles and some others of their generation taught is one thing; what the Church proved able to receive is quite another."[6] So that, in reality *we* are the fathers: we, born into the goodly birthright of the fruit of all the toil and thought and faith of those who went before us; of those who labored, and we have entered into their labors; of those who made daring experiments in Jesus Christ, who brooded over him, and learned to know him better than their predecessors did, and handed on to their successors

[5] *The Imitation of Christ* IV. 1. 13.

[6] *Ancient Catholic Church,* pp. 67, 66.

12 I have yet many things to say unto
you, but ye cannot bear them now.
13 Howbeit when he, the Spirit of truth,
is come, he will guide you into all truth:
for he shall not speak of himself; but whatsoever he shall hear, *that* shall he speak:
and he will show you things to come.
14 He shall glorify me: for he shall receive of mine, and shall show *it* unto you.

12 "I have yet many things to say to you,
but you cannot bear them now. 13 When
the Spirit of truth comes, he will guide you into all the truth; for he will not speak on his own authority, but whatever he hears he will speak, and he will declare to you the things that are to come. 14 He will
glorify me, for he will take what is mine

The Resurrection cancels the shame of the Cross and vindicates the righteousness of Jesus. He will **convince the world of judgment** by showing that the invisible rulers of this evil world overreached themselves in crucifying the Lord of glory (12:31; 14:30; cf. I Cor. 2:8), and by exposing as impotent folly the statecraft of those who had been their tools.

7. Fifth Paraclete Saying (16:12-15)

12-15. In the farewell discourse Jesus speaks of the frankness with which he has shared with his friends all that he has heard from his Father (15:15). Yet their spiritual immaturity has unfitted them to learn immediately much that Jesus had in store for them (cf. I Cor. 3:1-2). This incomplete form of the incarnate revelation will be continued by the Spirit of truth until they can receive it in its fullness. The Spirit's authority is the same as that on which Jesus has relied in all his teaching (3:32; 7:16-17; 8:26; 12:49; 14:10). The substance of his instruction will be the same as that of Jesus, for **he will take what is mine and declare it to you.** In this **he will glorify me.** For just as the Son's words and works glorified the Father (12:28), i.e., revealed his nature and purpose, so the glory of the Son (11:4; 12:23; 13:31) will be made known after his earthly life is over by the ministry of the Paraclete. Jesus has already declared that his passion and death are the supreme evidence of his complete obedience to the Father's will, the climax

---

what they had found in him. And that process is not over. It is a blasphemous delusion to assume that we have plumbed the deeps of the greatest and most characteristic thought of God. Later generations looking back at us will wonder how we failed to see in him what will have grown obvious to them by then. For each age as it passes is meant not only to appropriate what had been grasped before, but to make new discoveries in this inexhaustible Christ, and hand them on as henceforward part of the common possession in him. On to the unending end of an endless eternity, new astonishments will keep breaking in on us in Jesus Christ. "That I may know him," prays Paul. "Something of it I have grasped. But how much there is in this wonderful gospel that I can only faintly glimpse as yet, if even that! That I may really know him as he really is!" And those who will listen, the Holy Spirit, slowly, patiently, unendingly, step by step, does lead into all the truth.

Moreover, our Lord promises that it is not only with believers that the Counselor is to succeed. The world too is to be convicted and convinced by him of three fundamental matters. And this through Christ's going away.

First, **of sin.** Surely that is literally true. For the fact that it rejected Christ, did not want him, would not have him, nor anything else he had to give, but rose up angrily and cast him out as a nuisance much better away, is the last and crowning proof of the world's sin, stands out as the most appalling blot on our human annals, as the world itself often feels uncomfortably—staring, hideous, indelible. When a tourist remarked in the Bargello that he did not think much of what he was being shown, the custodian answered crushingly, "Sir, these pictures are not on trial; you are." So, to be offered Jesus Christ and turn indifferently away, to see no beauty in him that we should desire him, to be irritated and offended by him, is the sin of sins, the most damaging of revelations of what we ourselves are; the clearest of all evidences of our need for the Savior whom we can so summarily reject. Once we have come face to face with Christ, the final test of what we ourselves are is the attitude that we adopt to him; and by that we stand or fall.

Second, **of righteousness.** How does Christ's going to the Father convince the world of that? For the crucifixion scene on Calvary and that grim death of his look like the overthrow of

15 All things that the Father hath are mine: therefore said I, that he shall take of mine, and shall show *it* unto you.

16 A little while, and ye shall not see me: and again, a little while, and ye shall see me, because I go to the Father.

17 Then said *some* of his disciples among themselves, What is this that he saith unto us, A little while, and ye shall not see me: and again, a little while, and ye shall see me: and, Because I go to the Father?

and declare it to you. 15 All that the Father has is mine; therefore I said that he will take what is mine and declare it to you.

16 "A little while, and you will see me no more; again a little while, and you will see me." 17 Some of his disciples said to one another, "What is this that he says to us, 'A little while, and you will not see me, and again a little while, and you will see me'; and, 'because I go to the Father?' "

---

of the revelation of the incarnate Logos. That truth has yet to be fully grasped by the disciples, and through them proclaimed to the world. The Spirit will continue and complete the unfinished training of the twelve. Yet one more office of the Paraclete is to be named: **He will declare to you the things that are to come.** The Spirit of Christ is also the Spirit of prophecy. Amid all the gloomy forebodings in days of persecution and apostasy the Spirit would inspire Christian seers with the vision of the Lamb seated upon the throne, the symbol of the victory of the Cross (Cf. Rev. 4:1-2; 5:12-13; 19:10; 22:3).

8. Brief Sorrow, Lasting Joy (16:16-24)

16-22. A little while, and you will see me no more; again a little while, and you will see me: One of the puzzling sayings which baffled the disciples until Jesus gave the explanation. The words quoted by the perplexed disciples contain a clause from vs. 10: **because I go to the Father,** which belongs to the fifth Paraclete saying. This must have been added when these sayings were incorporated in the farewell discourses. It plays no part in the explanation which follows. Before their murmured remarks have been framed

---

righteousness and the triumph of evil. Yet in point of fact it is Christ's death and rising that have made it clear as nothing else has done that righteousness is a far stronger thing than evil, blatant and noisy though that evil may be. There at the Cross God and the devil, righteousness and sin, joined in one final all-determining conflict, flinging in everything they had; and good seemed to go down, and God to be worsted. And if Christ's death had been the end, the last hope would have been out. But it was not the end. **Because I go to the Father, and you see me no more**—there is the crowning evidence that righteousness cannot be broken, that God is over all, and that this wild confused world is his world and not the devil's. It is in the thick darkness upon Calvary that light has broken in upon innumerable souls who had found none elsewhere. It is where Christ seemed crushed and broken that his disciples gather to be rallied and reinspired, to see again with their own eyes that God is over all, that righteousness must win. And in its heart of hearts the world too knows it.

Third, **of judgment, because the ruler of this world is judged.** Certainly that is the impression made upon the mind by the story of our Lord's trial and passion. As the tale proceeds, by a queer inevitable reversal the positions of the participants in the drama are transposed. It is not Christ who is condemned, but they who condemn him. And every insult heaped upon him enhances his majesty. While those who exultantly wreak their malice and vengeance upon one, seemingly in their power, only dwarf themselves thereby, and reveal their own futility and smallness. It is at Calvary that the meanness of evil comes home to one most overpoweringly; and there, that Christ most storms the heart.

Such unexpected convictions has **the Spirit of truth** forced in upon how many minds, all culled from what had seemed at first to be the utter ruin of a sheer debacle!

17-18. ***Conference or Communion?***—Not following the whole way through, the disciples, or some of them, took to discussion among themselves as to what it all might mean. **Some of his disciples said to one another, "What is this that he says to us, 'A little while, and you will not see me, and again a little while, and you will see me'; and, 'because I go to my Father?' " They said, "What does he mean by 'a little while'? We do not know what he**

18 They said therefore, What is this that
he saith, A little while? we cannot tell
what he saith.
19 Now Jesus knew that they were desirous to ask him, and said unto them, Do ye inquire among yourselves of that I said, A little while, and ye shall not see me: and again, a little while, and ye shall see me?

[18] They said, "What does he mean by 'a little while'? We do not know what he
means." [19] Jesus knew that they wanted to
ask him; so he said to them, "Is this what you are asking yourselves, what I meant by saying, 'A little while, and you will not see me, and again a little while, and you will

---

into a question, Jesus answers the disciples. Just as a woman in **travail** is in **anguish,** and then forgets her agony when the child is born, so his friends have a season of sorrow to pass through before their **sorrow** is turned into **joy.** The immediate reference is to the Resurrection, for seven times over in these verses the phrase **a little while** is used. But there is probably a remoter reference to the Parousia, the return of Christ to consummate

---

means." And they got nowhere at all until Christ broke in and brought them light (vss. 19 ff.).

Here there seems to be a much-needed lesson for our times. For as an age we are obsessed by an insatiable passion for conferences. That seems to this generation to be the broad, beaten, obvious road to the solution of every problem that confronts and baffles us. Let us lay our heads together and confer about it; and light, we think, is sure to come. Yet at the best by such means we do not get outside the circle of our own human limitations and infirmities. Can we not say of conferences what Carlyle once snapped out about the public? "The public! The public! And how many fools does it take to make a public?" And often do we not seem to be gathering together simply to tell each other once again what we already know perfectly well; to lay down what we ought to be doing, instead of staying each in his own place and doing it? And that last is not by any means so popular these days. The older method —now, it would appear, considered out of date, or at least old-fashioned—was to turn to God and humbly seek his guidance by waiting upon him in prayer and closer communion; not founding upon our own wisdom but listening for his voice.

Conference or communion? The two methods are of course not of necessity mutually exclusive, though the latter sounds the more likely to succeed, while the former has been dreadfully overworked. A modern Soviet poet seems to have had enough of it, and ends a scornful satire on the craze by crying to whoever will hear this latest slogan, "Let us have another conference; still one more; in order to discover how to make an end of conferences!"

Here certainly it was not conference among themselves, but sitting at the feet of Christ and listening to him that worked and brought results.

18-22. ***The Alleged Eudaemonism of Christ's Teaching.***—Certain curious minds are fond of loftily dismissing our Lord's teaching as mere eudaemonism: asserting that so far from taking the high line, that

> . . . because right is right, to follow right
> Were wisdom in the scorn of consequence,[7]

he stoops to bribing us to goodness with promises of reward, or to frightening us into it by threats of dire punishment; with the result, say they, that Christianity is essentially immoral in its very morality.

"Why should I be moral?" asks F. H. Bradley, and answers:

> To ask for the Why? is simply immorality; to do good for its own sake is virtue, to do it for some ulterior end or object, not itself good, is never virtue. . . . And the theory which sees in virtue, as in money-getting, a means which is mistaken for an end, contradicts the voice which proclaims that virtue not only does seem to be, but is, an end in itself.[8]

Does our Lord contradict that voice? Does he seek to induce us to be good and faithful by guaranteeing to compensate us for the bother and unpleasantness of being good and faithful, even to scare us into the choice of good by assuring us that to choose evil means a fearsome retribution, inescapable here and inevitable in the beyond?

With the Gospels in our hands we are at once struck by Christ's constant underlining of the difficulties of discipleship and of the cruel cost of faith. So much so that he shocked the twelve, who protested that he was giving people a wrong impression, and painting in the shadows much too heavily. Yet Christ would not desist,

[7] Tennyson, "Œnone," l. 147.

[8] *Ethical Studies* (New York: G. E. Stechert & Co., 1911), pp. 56-57.

20 Verily, verily, I say unto you, That ye shall weep and lament, but the world shall rejoice; and ye shall be sorrowful, but your sorrow shall be turned into joy.

21 A woman when she is in travail hath sorrow, because her hour is come: but as soon as she is delivered of the child, she remembereth no more the anguish, for joy that a man is born into the world.

22 And ye now therefore have sorrow: but I will see you again, and your heart shall rejoice, and your joy no man taketh from you.

see me'? 20 Truly, truly, I say to you, you
will weep and lament, but the world will
rejoice; you will be sorrowful, but your
sorrow will turn into joy. 21 When a wom-
an is in travail she has sorrow, because her
hour has come; but when she is delivered
of the child, she no longer remembers the
anguish, for joy that a child[g] is born into
the world. 22 So you have sorrow now, but
I will see you again and your hearts will
rejoice, and no one will take your joy

[g] Greek *a human being.*

---

his kingdom on earth. The "messianic woes" were regarded in Judaism as the birth pangs of the new creation. The short bliss of the Easter fellowship with Christ would be a foretaste of the joy which **no one will take . . . from you.**

---

but kept on warning those who thought of throwing in their lot with him that discipleship is a costly business, with the wind in one's face, and the tide against one, and a heavy price to be paid down. "I send you out as sheep in the midst of wolves" (Matt. 10:16); or as Luke puts it even more vividly, "as lambs in the midst of wolves" (Luke 10:3); "You will be hated by all" (Matt. 10:22); "Whoever kills you will think he is offering service to God" (John 16:2). It will be like going to the gibbet and hanging there amid the guffaws of men's open derision.

It was a right gallant call Christ made upon the valor of daring men prepared to lose their all for him—like Garibaldi's to the young Italy of his day, "Come to me; for I have such gifts to offer you—forced marches, nights on the hard ground, wounds perhaps, or, it may be, even death itself for Italy!" And Christ so emphasized all that, that Bacon said bluntly that while "prosperity is the blessing of the Old Testament; adversity is the blessing of the New." [9]

Nonetheless, it is true that frankly, openly, undisguisedly, Christ claims over and over that he has something to give worth all the sufferings in which it may involve us; that something here; that something now; that something even in the midst of the foretold trials and far more in the great beyond; does say that he bestows a peace, a joy, a fullness of life such as no one apart from him can ever know.

But what is it that Christ offers? Not something other than goodness, promised us in compensation for having swallowed with a wry face an unappetizing draught which no sane man would choose for itself, but which unfortunately is the price that must, however unwillingly, be paid down for this other thing that we desire. What Christ promises is goodness. And that goodness is the joy and the peace and the fullness of life he guarantees to us all, as Spinoza put it in his well-thumbed saying.

There are those who seem to think that happiness is a blackguardly kind of thing, of which we ought to be almost or quite ashamed. But there are happinesses and happinesses. One man loves jazz and is bored stiff by the classical concert which delights his neighbor. And does not virtue consist very largely in being made happy by the right things? Or to put it otherwise, happiness by nature is shy and elusive. Go seeking it and it will evade you. Forget about it, put yourself out of mind, live for others, serve God, walk with Jesus Christ, and you will have it as your daily companion. It was not happiness that you were seeking. It was goodness, duty, Christlikeness. But happiness adds itself on to these as their companion; nor can it be excluded. For with Christ life tastes better. Beside him it is fuller and more adventurous and interesting than elsewhere. As Seneca put it, "Happiness is not a reward given us for being virtuous, nor is it the reason why we are virtuous. But it is a concomitant of virtue. We do not love virtue because it gives us pleasure; yet, because we love it, it does give us pleasure." The eye, said Marcus Aurelius, does not claim a reward for seeing. The seeing is itself the reward. So goodness, Christlikeness, the knowledge of God, are what we seek as Christians. But happiness is thrown in as an extra, and cannot be kept out.

So in the metaphors Christ uses. "You are slaves," he says, "and I can make you free." Well, being freed means a huge happiness. "You are sinsick, and I can make you hale in soul." And every normal person hates the

[9] Essay, "Of Adversity."

23 And in that day ye shall ask me nothing. Verily, verily, I say unto you, Whatsoever ye shall ask the Father in my name, he will give *it* you.

from you. 23 In that day you will ask me no questions. Truly, truly, I say to you, if you ask anything of the Father, he will give it

---

23-24. Two difficulties of translation and interpretation occur in vs. 23. First, there are two Greek verbs meaning "to ask." In classical Greek αἰτεῖν meant "to make a request" and ἐρωτᾶν, "to ask a question." In Hellenistic Greek the words were used interchangeably. The RSV follows the ERV mg., and most modern commentators and translations, by rendering, **In that day you will ask me no questions.** The main reason for this is that a contrast is implied between the past and the future. So far many questions have been asked but no requests have been made. But there is strong reason to follow the ERV text, "shall ask me nothing." The reasons in favor of this rendering are (*a*) in the Greek the emphatic word is **me,** in contrast with **the Father** in the next sentence. (*b*) A marked mannerism of this evangelist is to ring changes in the use of synonyms in the same context. (*c*) The Vulg. translates, *Et in illo die me non rogabitis quicquam,* i.e., "you will not ask me for anything." Second, the next sentence may be translated as in

---

cramped life, and the pain and discomforts and boredom of invalidism. Yet who would dream of saying that a doctor bribes his patients because with the health that he restores to them, there come fullness of life and half a hundred happinesses that were completely out of reach until health came and brought them back along with it?

Tyndale and Wycliffe both translate Christ's saying concerning Zacchaeus, "This day is health come to this house." And again in the Acts we read, "To heathen men this health is sent." Goodness is health. And it is goodness that Christ offers us. But goodness does not come alone.

Thus far many may agree. But some may allege that all this talk about the future life spoils everything, seeing that goodness is offered not for its own sake, and is chosen, it would seem, merely to escape the penalties of hell, or else to gain the rewards of heaven; is simply a long-headed bargain, a cleverer deal than the worldling can pull off, but essentially irreligious and just immoral. To F. H. Bradley's question, "Why should I be moral?" comes the crude answer, "Why? To escape the dreadfulness of hell; to win the beatitudes of heaven." Is Spinoza not right? "There are those who expect to be decorated by God with high honors for their virtue, as for having endured the direst slavery. As if virtue and the service of God were not in itself happiness and perfect freedom."[1] Does not Paul's "I reckon that the sufferings of this present time are not worthy to be compared with the glory which shall be revealed in us" (Rom. 8:18), or his "For our light affliction, which is but for a moment, worketh for us a far more exceeding and eternal weight of glory" (II Cor. 4:17), or the advice "to pay the tax of suffering" (I Pet. 5:9) come under this condemnation? And does not a little of the teaching of the Master himself? As here in this passage (vss. 20-22), or in his judgment parable, or in his saying that no one who gives even a cup of cold water in his name will lose his reward? Are these passages so many incitements to pursue goodness not for the sake of goodness, but for that of the rewards that goodness earns? Would it not have been cleaner and more gallant if no such hopes and fears had been set before us and we had been called on to follow goodness for itself alone?

Thus some have looked back almost wistfully to the O.T.,[2] before men had begun to dream of immortality in our sense of that word, when they chose God and goodness for the sake of fellowship with him in this brief life of ours here and here alone; since after death there were no right and left hands, but all, good and evil, were alike herded into a dim, bleak, dusty, silent place, toward which God never looked, of which he never thought.

Certainly there is no doubt that it was Christianity that made the masses of the Western world believe in immortality, and in moral retributions and rewards in the beyond, e.g., as Gibbon emphasizes. For good or evil Christianity must carry the responsibility of that. But whether it is good or evil depends on the conception of heaven and of hell that Christianity gives us. And indeed nothing more clearly reveals either a man or a religion than just that. Plato waxed indignant over the fools around him who looked forward to drunken carousals in the afterlife. And some of the Moslems have done their faith sad damage by their ugly con-

[1] Cf. *Ethics,* Part V, Proposition 42.

[2] Cf. G. A. Smith, *Modern Criticism and the Preaching of the Old Testament* (New York: A. C. Armstrong & Son, 1901), pp. 177-78.

24 Hitherto have ye asked nothing in my name: ask, and ye shall receive, that your joy may be full.

to you in my name. 24 Hitherto you have asked nothing in my name; ask, and you will receive, that your joy may be full.

the ERV and the RSV, or as in the KJV, the phrase **in my name** being placed by one group of authorities after **Father** (A C[3] D N W Γ Θ Sy. Lat.), and by another group after **give . . . you** (א B C* L Δ Origen). If we follow the RSV, the meaning is "he will give you as my followers" (Goodspeed). On the whole, the context and the Johannine use of the phrase favor the alternate position: **If you ask anything of the Father . . . in my name. In that day** refers to Easter, and the future era, when the majestic reunion of

ceptions of reward and punishment in the beyond. And it is true that there are so-called Christians who in the main seem out to escape the left hand, and so constrain themselves to pay the price of that escape; who exercise some measure of self-restraint and self-denial simply because God has the last word. Otherwise they would not act as they do act. For they are not good people; they are simply anxious to avoid the foretold penalties of evil-doing, or to win the rewards promised to goodness. To them heaven is essentially something added to goodness, more than goodness, different from goodness; and hell essentially something added to badness, more than badness, different from badness.

On the other hand, some reach a somewhat similar belittling of the promises of final triumph from another angle. They throw about truculent sayings, like that of R. L. Stevenson, that it is the traveling that counts, and not the arriving; or that of G. E. Lessing, that if he were offered truth with the one hand and the search for it with the other, he would choose the latter. Which sounds athletic and manly and has some point; yet is essentially just silly. We are not playing a game in life, the result of which does not matter. As William James said, we are not taking part in private theatricals;[3] we want really to put down evil, really to acquire goodness, really to reach what we have dreamed of reaching. And all the great religions offer us not only a road but a goal; something that not only ought to be attained but that will be attained by faithful souls. For Christianity heaven means the putting on of Christ, the growing into his likeness. As Robert Rainy said, it is to stand before the throne of God, what time the angels whisper together and say, "How like Christ he is!" For heaven is not really a place so much as a character. And so is hell. As Milton heard Satan admitting,

> The mind is its own place, and in itself
> Can make a heaven of hell, a hell of heaven.[4]

[3] *The Will to Believe*, p. 61.

[4] *Paradise Lost*, Bk. I, ll. 254-55.

Or again,

> Which way I fly is hell; myself am Hell.[5]

Heaven means to live for God and for Christ and for others. And if you ask, "But where do I come in?" you do not come in at all! For heaven is to have outgrown selfishness and self-seeking. And for those who have not done so, heaven would prove intolerable. They would batter upon the door, demanding, "Let me out of here! This whole place bores me stiff!" And they would be let go.

Long ago Clement of Alexandria summed up this matter.

> Could we then suppose anyone proposing to the Gnostic whether he would choose the knowledge of God or everlasting salvation; and if these, which are entirely identical, were separable, he would without the least hesitation choose the knowledge of God, deeming that property of faith . . . desirable, for its own sake. This, then, is the perfect man's first form of doing good, when it is done, not for any advantage in what pertains to him, but because he judges it right to do good. . . . He who obeys . . . , neither from fear, nor for enjoyment, is on his way to knowledge. For he does not consider whether any extrinsic . . . gain . . . follows to him; but drawn by the love of Him who is the true object of love, . . . practises piety. So that not even were we to suppose him to receive from God leave to do things forbidden with impunity; not even if he were to get the promise that he would receive as a reward the good things of the blessed, . . . not even if he could persuade himself that God would be hoodwinked . . . (which is impossible), would he ever wish to do anything contrary to right reason. For he makes his choice of what is truly good and worthy for its own sake. . . . Whereas let the predicted promise be taken away, and the threatened dread be cancelled, and the impending danger be removed, and the disposition of such people will be revealed. . . . Whenever, then, one is righteous, not from necessity or out of fear or hope, but from free choice, this is called the royal road, which the royal race travel. But the byways are slippery and precipitous.[6]

[5] *Ibid.*, Bk. IV, l. 69.

[6] *Miscellanies* IV. 22; VII. 12.

25 These things have I spoken unto you
in proverbs: but the time cometh, when I
shall no more speak unto you in proverbs,
but I shall show you plainly of the Father.
26 At that day ye shall ask in my name:
and I say not unto you, that I will pray
the Father for you:

25 "I have said this to you in figures; the
hour is coming when I shall no longer
speak to you in figures but tell you plainly
of the Father. 26 In that day you will ask
in my name; and I do not say to you that

the Son with the Father in the heavenly places has given the disciples a fresh conception of the power of prayer, and of the place of Christ in their thoughts when praying to God as Father. To act on this discovery is to find a fullness of **joy** never experienced before (vs. 24; cf. 15:11).

9. The Unveiling of the Father (16:25-28)

25-28. So far, not only in his allegories but also, especially in this discourse, in his references to God, Jesus has spoken in **figures** (παροιμίαι), i.e., in parables, **proverbs,** and enigmatic sayings (cf. 10:6), whereas he will now speak **plainly of the Father** (cf.

25-27. ***What We Owe to Christ's Parables.***—**I have said this to you in figures**—which seems to belittle the figures. And yet how much we owe to our Lord's parables, to the cunning and vivid metaphors he used to make his message seeable by our dim eyes and get it home to our slow, uncomprehending minds. As Chesterton, musing alone with himself, once put it in his private papers:

> There was a man who dwelt in the east centuries ago,
> And now I cannot look at a sheep or a sparrow,
> A lily or a cornfield, a raven or a sunset,
> A vineyard or a mountain, without thinking of him;
> If this be not to be divine, what is it? [7]

Luke tells us that he went here and there gathering materials for his Gospel, asking any likely persons he could find if they had ever heard Christ teaching. And plainly nearly all Christ said had been forgotten. For in the main it was only the illustrations he had used that remained embedded in his hearers' memories: that apt and moving one about the foolish, headstrong laddie who went wrong; that other about the sheep that strayed and lost itself; that third about a woman seeking distractedly for her missing coin—these were remembered. But all the rest of what Christ had poured out that day had vanished into thin air.

Take away the parables from the Gospels and what a blank would be left, like the staring gaps on the walls of the British galleries during World War II, when the masterpieces had been taken down and hidden away. It is through the figures that the gospel has come home to us. How can Christ speak to us more plainly of the Father than he has done in them? And indeed some of us can think only in pictures, must see before we can understand. And so, if he should abandon his pictorial method, we should be lost, and unable to follow even thus far. True, the contemplatives and certain of the mystics speak loftily even of our Lord's teaching, dismissing it as a mere primer suitable for infant souls, but to be left behind by those who have grown up in spiritual things. All this talk of a Father and the like must give place in adult minds, so they hold, to a bowing down before an unknown Absolute who cannot be described in human language or even be apprehended in human thought at all. But plainly Christ has no part in such notions, because he is not to discard the idea of God the Father as outworn and no longer useful, but to tell us of him more plainly. And when these same higher experts, as they claim to be, assure us that prayer too is left behind, lost in such an utter acquiescence in the will of God as allows no room for petition and intercession, or even confession and thanksgiving, they have again fallen out of step with Christ, who here as everywhere assumes that we shall ask, must ask, should ask.

Our Lord assures us that he can help us to know God better even than as yet he has enabled us to do. **I do not say to you that I shall pray the Father for you; for the Father himself loves you, because you have loved me and have believed that I came from the Father.** There are phrases in scripture that may be, and, as one suspects, not seldom are, sadly misused. Verses such as "We have an Advocate with the Father," or "Who liveth to make intercession for us," may create the impression in unwary minds that Christ has to interpose between God and us, has to intervene on our behalf with One less willing than he is himself to pity and forgive and help us. Again and again Christ is

[7] Maisie Ward, *Gilbert Keith Chesterton*, p. 66. Copyright 1943 by Sheed & Ward, Inc., New York.

27 For the Father himself loveth you, because ye have loved me, and have believed that I came out from God.

28 I came forth from the Father, and am come into the world: again, I leave the world, and go to the Father.

I shall pray the Father for you; 27 for the Father himself loves you, because you have loved me and have believed that I came from the Father. 28 I came from the Father and have come into the world; again, I am leaving the world and going to the Father."

11:14). **The hour is coming** is a frequent phrase in this Gospel, but here, as in vs. 2; 4:21, 23; 5:28, the definite article is not present in the Greek, and it means no more than "a time is coming." That time is defined more clearly in vs. 26, **in that day,** which refers to the new era when the visible presence of Jesus is withdrawn, and under the guidance of the Spirit our Lord's teaching about the Father will be more completely understood (cf. vss. 14-15). In that more perfect understanding of God the disciples will pray as Jesus has taught them to pray, and there will be no need of his intercession on their behalf. The loyalty of the disciples to their Master, and their acceptance of his claim to be the Son and revealer of God, ensure his loving interest in their petitions. On vs. 28 Bernard (*Commentary on Gospel of John,* II, 520) says, "Here, in four short phrases, we have the Pre-existence of Christ, His Incarnation, His Death, and His Ascension."

---

at pains to root out such blasphemies from our minds; again and again he stands back, bidding us look past him to the God who thought out our salvation for us and whose grace alone makes it possible. So here. **I do not say to you that I shall pray the Father for you; for the Father himself loves you.** Doubtless God loves everyone; for he is love. And he cannot deny himself or be false to his nature. "God so loved the world," this crazy, difficult, impossible world. God loved us even when we were dead in trespasses and sins, and surely most unlovable. But he has a particular affection for those who love Jesus Christ and all for which Christ stands, who are drawn to him and who close with him; for those who believe that Christ came from the Father; who, getting past their wounding and dishonoring misconceptions of God, know him as he really is because they have realized that Christ is the express image of his person, his Word that reveals his heart and makes us sure of how he thinks of us, of how he feels and acts toward us.

28. ***The Gospel and the Power of God.***—A succinct verse indeed, crowded with great words that have august facts behind them. This is the gospel that has proved to be the power of God to everyone who believes it, as pale attenuated versions of it have never been and can never be. Because they have been eviscerated of what gives the authentic gospel its appeal and power. Take away the Incarnation and the Ascension of the risen Lord, and you have left a moving and a gallant story that can thrill and inspire; and much true and helpful spiritual teaching: but not a gospel that can save lost souls, and a needy, desperate, chaotic world.

Nonetheless, one has difficulty in understanding why it was just there and then that suddenly light broke in on the disciples' minds. For much said here seems to have been urged on them before, and many times. Yet theirs was a natural and very human experience. William Temple set down [8] half humorously and half wryly, but yet seriously, how very often a teacher has old pupils coming about him to pour out excited accounts of the immense impression made on their minds and outlook by some course of lectures they have taken elsewhere; and how he listens, trying to enter into their enthusiasm, and yet not a little puzzled, because what they are acclaiming as so novel and epoch-making is plainly only a repetition of what he himself had told them time and time again, and that without catching their attention, or producing even a ripple of interest on the surface of minds left placid and unimpressed, even perhaps a little bored. He accounts for it by observing that in the days gone by they were not ready for what, when they were ready for it, made a revolution in their thinking. And that is true. Paul may plant, and Apollos may water, and Christ himself may teach; but only God can give the increase. And it is not until God says "Let there be light" that there is light.

All this we have ourselves experienced many times. We take up a book much like numbers of other books, or we read a passage of scripture which we have often read before, we hear an ordinary sermon, and somehow a new truth bursts in on us, like the sun suddenly appearing over the gray morning hills. And for us a new

[8] *Readings in St. John's Gospel,* 2nd ser. (London: Macmillan & Co., 1940), pp. 289-90.

29 His disciples said unto him, Lo, now speakest thou plainly, and speakest no proverb.

30 Now are we sure that thou knowest all things, and needest not that any man should ask thee: by this we believe that thou camest forth from God.

31 Jesus answered them, Do ye now believe?

32 Behold, the hour cometh, yea, is now come, that ye shall be scattered, every man to his own, and shall leave me alone: and yet I am not alone, because the Father is with me.

29 His disciples said, "Ah, now you are
speaking plainly, not in any figure! 30 Now
we know that you know all things, and
need none to question you; by this we be-
lieve that you came from God." 31 Jesus
answered them, "Do you now believe?
32 The hour is coming, indeed it has come,
when you will be scattered, every man to
his home, and will leave me alone; yet I
am not alone, for the Father is with me.

10. The Victory over the World (16:29-33)

29-30. The disciples misunderstood the allusion to the time when all would be plain to them, and assumed that they had already grasped his meaning in its fullness. They felt assured that he interpreted their unspoken thoughts, so that there was no need for them to question him to elicit what they wanted to know. Once again (cf. 1:48-49; 4:18-19, 29; 6:61; 13:11), but not for the last time (cf. 21:17), this insight into men's inmost thoughts is recognized. So they acknowledged their belief that Jesus had come from God. This was true as far as it went, but it did not cover all that had just been affirmed (vs. 28). For that reason they would not recognize that his arrest was necessary for him to return to the Father.

31-33. The reply of Jesus may be a challenging question, **Do you now believe?** or a statement, "You believe at this moment." But that very night they would be put to the test. Mark 14:27 tells that as the little band was on its way to the Mount of Olives, Jesus said to them, "You will all fall away; for it is written, 'I will strike the shepherd, and the sheep will be scattered'" (Zech. 13:7). It is strange that John should here put on the lips of Jesus the warning that the disciples would **be scattered, every man to his home,**

day has dawned. So true is it that God is never far from any one of us, and is always feeling for an entrance into our hearts and minds.

30-32. ***The Danger of Spiritual Complacency.*** —**Now we know that you know all things, and need none to question you; by this we believe that you came from God.** So they said in happy confidence. Once, when the pilgrims were excited and perhaps a little vainglorious over their progress and successes, Bunyan dropped a grave reminder to his readers and to the pilgrims too, if they would take it, "But they were not yet at their journey's end." They had many a testing time still to be faced, and many a river, swift and dark and deep and treacherous, to cross before they could win home. So here. Christ breaks in on his friends' premature self-congratulations with a warning, terrible in its solemnity. **Do you now believe? The hour is coming, indeed it has come, when you will be scattered, every man to his home, and will leave me alone.**

That must have seemed impossible to them —just unthinkable. They could not do it; and of course they would not do it. As Browning makes John say,

> "Forsake the Christ thou sawest transfigured, Him
> Who trod the sea and brought the dead to life?
> What should wring this from thee!"—ye laugh and ask.
> "What wrung it? Even a torchlight and a noise,
> The sudden Roman faces, violent hands,
> And fear of what the Jews might do! Just that,
> And it is written, 'I forsook and fled.'"[9]

So wise is that grave admonition, "Let him that thinketh he standeth take heed lest he fall" (I Cor. 10:12). For indeed the ways of life are slippery and our hearts are frail and undependable. A man may run well and far and yet stumble to ruin. A sin may be vanquished only to rise up out of its ancient grave and regain its dominion. A slip, and we are down. So it becomes us to walk softly, and to keep our hand upon our mouth, eschewing boastfulness, and leaning hard on Jesus Christ, who is our sole hope. For Samuel Johnson is reading from

[9] "A Death in the Desert."

33 These things I have spoken unto you, that in me ye might have peace. In the world ye shall have tribulation: but be of good cheer; I have overcome the world.

33 I have said this to you, that in me you may have peace. In the world you have tribulation; but be of good cheer, I have overcome the world."

---

and would **leave** him **alone.** For in this Gospel they remain with him until Jesus, upon his arrest, asked for them to be allowed to go, and even Peter made his ineffectual resistance. Moreover, two disciples followed him into the high priest's court, and one was present at the Crucifixion. The evangelist characteristically emphasizes the Father's presence with Jesus when no visible friend was left at his side (vs. 32). This may be his way of removing a false impression left by the quotation of the first verse of Ps. 22 in the older tradition of the Crucifixion (Mark 15:34). He knew that the psalm, which opens with a cry of dereliction, ends on a note of confident hope. The closing verse of the discourse is a glorious paradox. The prophecy of disaster carries within it the promise of peace. **Tribulation** lies ahead, but "Courage!" **I have overcome the world** (cf. I John 5:4-5).

---

experience when he tells us in the *Rambler* that a habit opposed and victorious is more than twice as strong as it was before the contest.

33. *How Peace in Christ Through Failure?*—But what did Christ mean by that strange addendum to this prophecy of failure and shame, **I have said this to you, that in me you may have peace?** "That I may forewarn you and arrest you; that I may cause you to think in time; that I may induce you to be careful and so enable you to avert what otherwise is certain; that you may be chastened and rid of a complacency for which there is no adequate reason"—these we could understand. But to tell them of their coming ignominy and desertion **that in me you may have peace,** what can that mean? Confusion of face, bitter repentance, abashed humility, but peace!

Is it perhaps that we may understand, and wonderingly take in, that these inexcusable failures of ours which so daunt and dishearten us are no surprise to him, and that they do not daunt him or his faith in us or his hopes for us; that knowing us at our weakest and blackest, he has no thought of tossing us away as weapons that have snapped in his hand and are of no further use to him, but that he still believes in us, is still sure that we shall rally, and still dares to trust us. So loyal is Jesus Christ to those who are not loyal to him at all. Peter is going to deny him, but Christ is praying for him; and because of these prayers the fallen man will make shift to get to his feet again. The whole circle of the disciples is on the point of scattering in an ugly panic that has brought discredit on mankind. But they will rally and reform. Christ still believed in them and still stood to his choice of them. Let them remember that in the dark days of their shame. A wise soul builds in the last resort not on its love to Christ, which is a feeble thing that flows and ebbs, but on Christ's love to it, which is from everlasting to everlasting.

33. *The Most Gallant Words in Literature.*—As for our Lord himself, left utterly alone he knew that he was not alone. "For the Father is with me" (vs. 32). There is the secret of the majestic serenity of Jesus Christ, in contradistinction to our uneasy fussiness and swift discouragement. We build so largely upon secondary things which give and crash and let us down; and standing ruefully among the ruins of what we had assumed to be so stable and dependable, we think all is over. But Christ's hope was really set on God. And so whatever befell him he remained calm, unshaken, indomitable; as so notably here. For God and he together could face anything. And so he met the disappointments crowding in upon him, and the horrors on horrors already crouching for their spring, with his head up and his eyes steady and his heart unafraid.

Hence the superb words with which he ends his communing with his followers in the upper room, words which reduced Carlyle to tears for the sheer valor of them, with everything for which Christ had striven giving or down, with his best friends about to fail him and make his long training of them seem ridiculous, with every conceivable humiliation and agony on agony ready to heap themselves upon him. **In the world you have tribulation; but be of good cheer, I have overcome the world.** No hiding of the cost, no minimizing of the dangers of discipleship, but a frank warning that serried ranks of enemies are massing themselves to hurl themselves against them, in an attempt to rush them down. "God," said a Scottish plowboy-martyr to a fellow sufferer, a little scared as the horrid end drew ghastlily near, "never guaranteed to keep us out of troubles, but he did promise to bring us through the worst of

17 These words spake Jesus, and lifted up his eyes to heaven, and said, Father, the hour is come; glorify thy Son, that thy Son also may glorify thee:

17 When Jesus had spoken these words, he lifted up his eyes to heaven and said, "Father, the hour has come; glorify thy Son that the Son may glorify thee,

D. The High Priestly Prayer (17:1-26)

This title has often been given to this prayer, for in it the Son of God consecrates himself before offering his life as the one perfect sacrifice for the sins of the world. He then consecrates his disciples that they also may be offered in the service of perfect obedience which will win the world to God. The meditation falls into three parts, in which Jesus prays (*a*) for himself, (*b*) for his own disciples, (*c*) for the universal church.

1. The Father and the Son Glorified—Prayer for Himself (17:1-5)

17:1-5. Father: The keynote of every prayer of Jesus (cf. vss. 5, 11, 24; 11:41; 12:27-28; Matt. 11:25; Luke 22:42; 23:34, 46; also the primitive Christian echo, Rom. 8:15; Gal.

---

them. And he will do it." So Christ to these men who he knew would fail him, "Courage, courage"—that favorite word of his—"This is not everything collapsing in utter defeat." And then he adds—and is there anything in literature or history to equal it for sheer audacity of gallantry?—he about to be rejected and forsaken, he left alone, one facing all the exultant hordes of evil, **I have overcome the world.** That is a faith that cannot be beaten. That is a Master worth the following. And not in heaven only, but there in the gross darkness gathering around him, "a royal diadem adorns the mighty victor's brows."

17:1-26. *A Prayer of Adoration and Thanksgiving.*—Before they left their sanctuary to face what was to come, now dreadfully near, Christ lifted up his heart in prayer to God.

Our prayers are often gloomy and sad-colored. We beg; we complain; we even reproach God, as surely doing for us less than his most and best, or why is there not much more to show? But desperate though the setting of it seems to us, these notes have no place whatsoever in Christ's prayer, which is shot through and through by adoration and thanksgiving and something even deeper and warmer, something that can only be described as exultation. Eight separate times the word glorify, or glorified, or glory, occurs in it, runs through it indeed like a thread of gold that holds it all together. When the sun is about to set, the birds pour out their very being in a passion of song. And as he went out to face his appalling end, Christ put his whole soul into an adoration of thanksgiving to the Father for allowing him to suffer for the world. As he once said, "No man takes my life from me, but I lay it down of myself." That is the atmosphere of this whole prayer. Here is no unwilling victim dragged to the altar; but one who offers himself freely, holding back nothing, making no conditions.

1-26. *The God to Whom Christ Prayed.*—In the opening of his prayer (vs. 1) and three times later (vss. 5, 21, 24) Christ calls God **Father;** that and nothing more, as he has bidden us to do.

And that name gives the atmosphere to the whole prayer. Listening, we learn how natural prayer is, how simply we can turn to God, sure of his interest in us and his lovingkindness toward us; in the happy assurance that he will certainly do for us all that even God can do, and that gladly and willingly. Christ spoke to God with open face, as a man to his friend, as a child to its father, reverently and humbly, and yet with an utter confidence to which we cannot attain—we, sin-stained in conscience and foolish in mind, too liable to ask for what, had it been granted to our unwise pleading, would have injured and not helped us. And yet we too in prayer come to a Father, our own Father, sympathetic, understanding, kindly, slow to anger, eager to help and guide and give and do. And we should treat him with all frankness, opening our mind to him wholeheartedly and with absolute sincerity and honesty. As Fénelon advised:

> Tell [God] all that is in your heart, as one unloads one's heart to a dear friend. . . . Tell Him your troubles, that He may comfort you; tell Him your joys, that He may sober them; tell Him your longings, that He may purify them; tell Him your mislikings, that He may help you to conquer them; talk to Him of your temptations, that He may shield you from them; show Him all the wounds of your heart, that He may heal them. Lay bare to Him your indifference to good, your depraved tastes for evil, . . . your instability. . . . If you thus pour out to Him all your weaknesses, needs, and troubles, there will be no lack of what to say; you

2 As thou hast given him power over all flesh, that he should give eternal life to as many as thou hast given him.

3 And this is life eternal, that they might know thee the only true God, and Jesus Christ, whom thou hast sent.

2 since thou hast given him power over all
flesh, to give eternal life to all whom
thou hast given him. 3 And this is eter-
nal life, that they know thee the only
true God, and Jesus Christ whom thou hast

4:6). **The hour has come** (cf. 12:23, 27; 13:1; 16:32). **Glorify thy Son** (cf. 7:39; 12:16). **That the Son may glorify thee** (cf. 12:27-28; 13:31-32; 11:4). This glorification of the Father consists in the giving of **eternal life** (vs. 2) to his own disciples. He will do this after his heavenly exaltation, out of the even greater authority with which he has been invested, i.e., over all mankind. **Eternal life** (vs. 3), the *summum bonum* in this Gospel, as the kingdom of God is in the Synoptics, consists in the knowledge of God—yet not the

---

will never exhaust this subject, it is continually being renewed. People who have no secrets from each other never want subjects of conversation; they do not . . . weigh their words, because there is nothing to be kept back. Neither do they seek for something to say; they talk together out of the abundance of their heart—without consideration, just what they think. . . . Blessed are they who attain to such familiar, unreserved intercourse with God! [1]

But in vs. 11 Christ calls God **Holy Father,** appealing not to his love only, but to his holiness; by reason of which he feels God cannot and will not allow these men for whom he is praying to be soiled and besmirched by the world.

That is a name we are forgetting; a divine characteristic which we are allowing to fall out of sight. We talk much about the love of God. But we are apt to interpret it as little more than mere indulgence, too soft to be firm with us, too weak to smite us for our good. We are not blinded these days by the blazing whiteness of God's holiness. Rather we can turn to him nonchalantly, shoving the door open with a careless shoulder, and speaking to him as if he and we were almost on a level. And the results are disastrous. For we can make an idol even out of the fatherhood of God; can so misread that as to be deceived by it—to our doom. If it were possible, which it is not, to separate the holiness from the love of God, if we were offered either of them, one or else the other but not both, it were better by far to choose that God be holy rather than that he be love. But there is and can be no such distinction. For God's love is a holy love. And God is holy largely because he is loving.

In vs. 25 Christ appeals to the righteousness of God. **O righteous Father,** so he prays, claiming that because God is righteous he will not and cannot let human endeavor after truth and righteousness fade out without result, but will justify and crown it. "Shall not the Judge of all the earth do right?" That happy assurance is felt, dimly or more clearly, by most men. They believe that somehow in spite of appearances to the contrary that thrust themselves upon us, in spite of grave facts which there is no denying, nonetheless this is a moral world in which righteousness comes to its own—at last—and evil, however strong and blatant, goes down—in the end. But no one is so sure of that as Jesus Christ. And he has passed on something of his certainty of it to his people. It is a faith that makes a mighty difference and has had incalculable results in bringing men to their feet again in grave and terrible days when all seemed lost; in keeping souls, on whom the dark had fallen, and who could not begin to understand God's ways with them at all, quiet, and brave, and hopeful, and expectant of the solution of it all, which they are sure will come.

1-3. ***Two Petitions.*****—The hour has come,** an hour of appalling happenings for him. Yet it never occurs to him to beg to be spared the coming horrors. For himself he makes only two petitions: first, that he may so meet and use the hour that God may be glorified through him; and second, that he may so bear himself through it that he may **give eternal life to all whom thou hast given him.** And that is all that he asked for himself; and, for the rest, he forgot himself in thinking of and interceding for his friends. God grant that when our hour comes, of pain, or disappointment, or sorrow, or loss, or death, we may face it with a touch of Christ's unselfishness and gallantry, and quiet and unshakable trust in God.

No prayer has ever been so abundantly answered as these requests of Christ. As to the first of them, while there are innumerable things in life that incite us to give God the glory due to his name, nothing awakes in souls beyond reckoning so deep and awed and dazed a gratitude toward him as the cross of Christ;

[1] *Spiritual Letters to Men,* Letter LXXXVIII, "To the Vidame D'Amiens: On Prayer and Meditation."

4 I have glorified thee on the earth: I have finished the work which thou gavest me to do.

5 And now, O Father, glorify thou me with thine own self with the glory which I had with thee before the world was.

sent. [4] I glorified thee on earth, having accomplished the work which thou gavest me to do; [5] and now, Father, glorify thou me in thy own presence with the glory which I had with thee before the world was made.

---

static knowledge of the Gnostics, but a progressive knowledge, "learning to **know thee**" (note the force of the present tense, ἵνα γινώσκωσίν σε). **The only true God:** In contrast with the unreal gods of the pagan world (cf. Rom. 16:27; Jude 25; Rev. 15:4). **And Jesus Christ whom thou hast sent:** Obviously the evangelist's addition, not spoken by Jesus. Yet the supreme message of this Gospel is that God as Father is made known only through Jesus. The Son glorifies the Father by completing the work given him to do (vs. 4; cf. 5:36). Pre-existence is implied in the prayer (vs. 5) that the Father will restore the glory partly hidden during the earthly life (as in vs. 24; 1:1; 8:58).

---

or makes us realize so vividly what God means by loving and forgiving and self-sacrifice and grace, how glorious a thing it is for us and in itself that God is what he is, all that he is, and only what he is.

And as to that second petition of Christ, what is eternal life? Sometimes in the N.T. it is spoken of in the present tense as something to be had now; at other times it is thrown into the future, is something that still lies ahead of us. For it is both. It begins here and now. And one can know and live it in this world. But it comes to its fullness only in the other life. As Percy Gardner put it, eternal life is spoken of not strictly in the present, or in the future, but rather in "the mystic tense." [2] As Christ describes it here, it means and is to know God as he really is; and all that flows from that. For to take in what God is, to grasp something of his unselfishness, his generosity, his patience, his humility, must give one a new standard of measurement, a new scale of values, a new idea of how life should be used. And with that one must begin to try to live it in that fashion. That is eternal life. It is to live after God's way, as life is lived in the eternities. It is to break away from the rude tribal conventions of mankind and rise to worthier ways and ampler possibilities; beginning here, but reaching in eternity to something that will not be defined and cannot be described except as the best possible and thinkable come true.

The difference between eternal life and the existence of the natural man is indicated vividly in a passage of Walter Lippmann.

> It is possible to drift along not too discontentedly, somewhat nervously, somewhat anxiously, somewhat confusedly, hoping for the best, and believing in nothing very much. . . . But it is not possible to be wholly at peace. For serenity of soul requires some better organization of life than a man can attain by pursuing his casual ambitions, satisfying his hungers, and for the rest accepting destiny as an idiot's tale in which one dumb sensation succeeds another to no known end. And it is not possible for him to be wholly alive. . . . These are the gifts of a vital religion.[3]

And also no bad definition of the ingredients of eternal life. **That they know thee the only true God;** then, as it is set down for us, the prayer adds **and Jesus Christ whom thou has sent.** This, as the Exeg. reminds us, is probably an addition, and not our Lord's own exact words. In any case, the two clauses of the prayer are so intertwined that they are not really two but one. We know the true God only through Jesus Christ: and to know Christ is to be given that revelation. Everything about him has helped us to it. But it is his death that has convinced and made us sure: as he himself prayed that it might do.

4-8. ***A Great Claim.***—So far from being shaken and shattered by the ruin of all his hopes, as one might have expected him to be, Christ blesses God with a full heart for enabling him to carry through the task with which he had been entrusted: **having accomplished the work which thou gavest me to do.** So he reports with confidence; and counts on his recall from an adventure hazardous beyond words, but carried through fully and thoroughly (vs. 5).

It is a great claim indeed! For it is shamefacedly enough that the rest of us go back to God, able to bring him so little of what we had intended, of what he himself had planned when he designed our life and its possibilities; only a child's pathetic little bunch of withering weeds; only some broken purposes and hopes;

[2] *The Practical Basis of Christian Belief* (London: Williams & Norgate, 1923), p. 168.

[3] *A Preface to Morals,* pp. 7-8. Copyright 1929 by Walter Lippmann and used with permission of The Macmillan Co. and George Allen & Unwin.

6 I have manifested thy name unto the
men which thou gavest me out of the
world: thine they were, and thou gavest
them me; and they have kept thy word.
7 Now they have known that all things
whatsoever thou hast given me are of thee.

6 "I have manifested thy name to the
men whom thou gavest me out of the world;
thine they were, and thou gavest them to
me, and they have kept thy word. **7** Now
they know that everything that thou hast

---

2. The Consecration of the Disciples—Prayer for "His Own" (17:6-19)

6-8. The incarnate Logos is the revealer of God. The work of Jesus was twofold: to reveal the **name** (i.e., the true nature) of God to those who were willing and able to receive his teaching, and to bring deliverance to the world. The first part has now been

---

only some dreams that faded and went out; only some efforts that can show small result. Here is our life as God planned it; and alas, this is what we have made of it, how we have lived it out! But Christ could look God in the eyes and say, "What thou didst ask of me, that I have done."

Futile at the time though his efforts might appear, with everything that he had sought to build rumbling to ruin round him, he boldly claims to have effected three things; and these so fundamental and foundational that if his claim is true, the whole face of the world is changed and life become another thing.

First, **I glorified thee on earth.** Who is going to challenge that, or question that God is to us men an infinitely greater, dearer, more adorable Being because Christ has lived and taught and died? It is Christ who has brought home to us how good God is, how unthinkably lovable; that if his wisdom is unsearchable, and his ways past finding out—and who but God could have planned Calvary, or thought out a salvation that leaves our human minds bewildered and stunned?—what of his love revealed in and through Jesus Christ, its length, its breadth, its depth, its height, which pass our human knowledge? We cannot understand it, but we can believe it, and can try it, and can prove it true. And how the heart runs out to such a God! If, said Epictetus, I were a nightingale, I would sing to God like a nightingale. But I am a rational being, and it is my part to praise and bless him. And this I will do; nor will I desert my post so long as I am allowed to hold it.[4] And if he felt that about God, what must we feel, standing upon the slopes of Calvary? So has Christ made God glorious in the minds of men by revealing to us what he always was, and is, and will be, everlastingly.

Second, claims Christ, **I have manifested thy name to the men whom thou gavest me out of the world.** What is the core and essence of Christ's teaching, its center, what makes it a gospel? Surely above everything else it is his revelation of the fatherhood of God. If that goes, everything goes with it. But if that is true, all the rest can follow from it. That is the name of God that Christ has manifested to us. What he kept seeking to bring home to our minds is this—that what our little ones are to us, not less than that are we to God; that each of us holds his own secure place in God's heart, a place that nobody except himself can ever fill; that it matters to God what becomes of us and how we fare, matters the length of Calvary; that if all the rest were safely gathered home and only we were absent, still there would be a shadow around the throne, and still an ache and longing in the Father's heart for the one child still lost to him, and still out in the cold and dark and rain; that we need not worry, that it is senseless to worry, because we have one who will certainly take care of us in our foolishness and weakness, who will think for us when we cannot think, and do for us what we cannot do—and who, if we are stupid, is very wise; if we are disobedient, is divinely understanding and patient and forgiving; that as a baby, just because it is so small and helpless, is the center of the home, comes first, so do we hold a central place in the heart of the great God whose property it is to be able to give himself to all of us, to each of us, as if there were no other in the world—just God and you, just God and I. Believe that, and the whole incredible gospel becomes possible, and thinkable, and likely. And it was Jesus Christ who made us sure that it is really true.

Third, claims Christ, **I have given them the words which thou gavest me;** and again, "I have given them thy word" (vs. 14). So it is there, upon the word, that our Lord himself lays the main stress; the word that he accounts to be the center of his message, and the chief medium by which he reaches minds and hearts and souls.

There are those who would put the first emphasis upon the sacraments. Not so this writer; and as he narrates things, not so Jesus Christ. And surely it must be self-evident, how-

[4] *Discourses* I. 16.

8 For I have given unto them the words which thou gavest me; and they have received *them,* and have known surely that I came out from thee, and they have believed that thou didst send me.

9 I pray for them: I pray not for the world, but for them which thou hast given me; for they are thine.

10 And all mine are thine, and thine are mine; and I am glorified in them.

given me is from thee; [8]for I have given
them the words which thou gavest me, and
they have received them and know in truth
that I came from thee; and they have be-
lieved that thou didst send me. [9]I am
praying for them; I am not praying for the
world but for those whom thou hast given
me, for they are thine; [10]all mine are thine,
and thine are mine, and I am glorified in

---

completed in the training of the twelve. The disciples had been given **out of the world** into his care (cf. 6:37). Now Jesus can rejoice in the fruit of his instruction. **They have kept thy word.** They have received his teaching, recognizing that both he and his message had come from God (vs. 8). Their receptive hearts were the soil in which faith and knowledge could grow. His word was abiding in them (cf. 5:38; I John 2:14).

9-10. The prayer that Jesus is now offering is for them, as distinct from **the world** from which they have been separated (vs. 6). He prays especially for the disciples for three reasons: (*a*) Because they are God's—God's gift to Christ, returned to the Father by the Son, in that reciprocal relationship (cf. 16:15) which is the essence of the divine unity (vss. 11, 21). (*b*) Because Jesus is **glorified in them;** he has brought them to the

---

ever vivid and helpful the sacraments may be, that it is the word that is the basic and essential thing. For what is a sacrament? It is a sign and seal. Yes, but of what? Only the word can answer that. A little bit of bread, a sip of wine —what does it mean? In itself little or nothing. But given the word, and the meaning of the symbols leaps into distinctness. "This is my body broken for you." "This is my blood, shed for many, for the remission of sins." And then we see and understand. It is the word that gives content to what otherwise would be an empty circle; or at most only a vague indefinite thing, who can tell what? And so, says Augustine, bring the word to the water, and you have a sacrament. But the word comes first. And the sacrament is only (*a*) a visible sign of what the word has promised us; (*b*) a personal assurance that God stands to it, and that toward very us; and (*c*) a proof that what the word has promised us is true.

9-19. ***Christ's Prayer for His Disciples.***— What strikes one first and most in our Lord's prayer is not even his moving loyalty to his friends (and they upon the point of breaking and deserting him, as he well knew), though that is wonderful enough, but rather his unmistakable pride in them—**I am glorified in them,** he says; though to us they look poor bungling blunderers that make us feel ashamed—his pride in them, and still more, his gratitude to God for them. For all through the prayer he keeps speaking of his disciples as a gift of God to him. **Those whom thou hast given me:** that phrase keeps recurring over and over throughout the prayer: vss. 6, 9, 11, 12, 24. Again and again he acknowledges God's goodness to him in that God had himself thought out this wonderful thing for him and, with his own divine hands, put it into his. He cannot get away from that; keeps coming back to it time after time. We speak of him as God's unspeakable gift to us. Christ on his side, incredibly enough, seems to regard us as an amazing gift from God to him. That sounds impossible. That Christ should bother about us at all is wonderful enough. Why should a shepherd squander the fullness of his human life on lowly creatures such as sheep, thereby drastically limiting the possibilities open to himself? And why should Christ devote his life to our salvation; and for all his self-sacrifice, at most and best get only us? And yet unaccountably he seems to esteem that more than a fair bargain!

"The Lord," mused Clement of Alexandria, "keeps pitying us, instructing us, exhorting us, admonishing us, saving us, shielding us; and of his bounty promises us the kingdom of heaven as a reward for learning; and the only advantage he reaps is, that we are saved."[5] "There is a friend more loyal than a brother" (Prov. 18:24 Moffatt). So a wise man set down in wondering gratitude long ago. But no friend is so loyal as is the Lord Jesus Christ.

And does not that loyalty of his, and his gratitude to God for what his friends have meant to him, make us ashamed of our own carelessness about the beautiful gift of friendship which God has thought out for us and put

[5] *Exhortation to the Heathen* I.

11 And now I am no more in the world, but these are in the world, and I come to thee. Holy Father, keep through thine own name those whom thou hast given me, that they may be one, as we *are.*

them. 11 And now I am no more in the world, but they are in the world, and I am coming to thee. Holy Father, keep them in thy name which thou hast given me, that they may be one, even as we are one.

---

knowledge of God; the power of his character is reflected in their faith, and will be continued in their lifelong service. (*c*) Because they will soon be left without the guidance and protection of the Son on his return to the Father.

11. Therefore Jesus prays first that the Father will protect them by his gracious providence that they may be kept in unity of heart and mind after the pattern of the divine unity. **Holy Father:** only here and in vs. 25 is the name Father qualified by an adjective. Here the holiness of God is what separates him from the sinful world; and therefore Jesus prays for the disciples that they may be kept undefiled by the sin of the world in which they must continue to live (vs. 15). **Keep them in thy name which thou hast given me.** This is probably the right reading, though some authorities have: **Keep through thine own name those whom thou hast given me** (KJV). The **name** stands for the personal power and character of God. The meaning of the former rendering is, "Protect them with the power which thou hast given to me, and bind them in that unity which is ours."

---

into our hands? We take our friends so casually; we accept them without thinking; we seldom even begin to realize what they have been to us, and done for us, and given us, how they have filled and enriched life for us. It was no wonder that the disciples were drawn to Christ. But that our friends somehow like us, believe in us, and judge us kindlily, and hold to us, and hearten us, that surely is a very moving thing! Yet how often do we go to God, as Christ did in the upper room, and thank him for our friends?

But what, out of all the possibilities, does Christ ask for these men so near to his heart? Lovingly and trustfully he commits them to the Father's watchfulness and care. **While I was with them, I kept them . . . ; I have guarded them. . . . But now I am coming to thee;** and they are to be left alone in this dangerous world. **Holy Father, keep them,** so he asks. "Watch over them" (Temple). From what, and for what?

(*a*) His first prayer is for the little company as a company: guard them against disunity and falling apart; keep them that they may hold together, and be one in heart and mind and purpose. **That they may be one,** he prays, so utterly and wholly one that he dares to compare what he has in mind for them with the completeness of the unity between God and himself. **Holy Father, keep them in thy name which thou hast given me, that they may be one, even as we are one.**

How right he was we can now see for ourselves in the sorry records in the Acts and the epistles of how nearly at the start the church came to disintegrating into a mob of little angry, snarling sects, condemning one another, opposing one another, excommunicating one another! Borne to us down the ages there comes even yet a clamor of violent most unbrotherly disputings between the conservative Judaizers and the more liberal minds who seemed to them not liberal at all but deliberately disobedient to God-given truth; much bitterness, hot debates, a most unseemly clash of parties, with even apostles differing from each other, and at times publicly denouncing one another, and with new and further difficulties constantly cropping up. Looking back we can all see now how wise was Christ our Master in praying for them first of all, "Hold them together; help them to preserve their unity."

It is a blessed thought that for us too he is praying, with a like wisdom and perfect knowledge of us and our needs. **Keep them in thy name which thou hast given me.** That name, as the Exeg. points out, is the Father. And it implies that we his children are all members of one family. "Help them," prays Christ, "to keep in mind their relationship to thee, and so to one another." And indeed, in the early days of the faith, for all the quarreling and contending, it was largely the obvious affection and ungrudging practical help which the Christian community instinctively and as a matter of course gave to its members, especially to such of them as were in any kind of trouble, that impressed outsiders and convinced them that something new and real and vital had come to birth among them. So literally and so fully was Christ's petition heard and answered, "I in

12 While I was with them in the world, I kept them in thy name: those that thou gavest me I have kept, and none of them is lost, but the son of perdition; that the Scripture might be fulfilled.

13 And now come I to thee; and these things I speak in the world, that they might have my joy fulfilled in themselves.

14 I have given them thy word; and the world hath hated them, because they are not of the world, even as I am not of the world.

12 While I was with them, I kept them in thy name which thou hast given me; I have guarded them, and none of them is lost but the son of perdition, that the scripture might be fulfilled. 13 But now I
am coming to thee; and these things I speak in the world, that they may have my joy fulfilled in themselves. 14 I have given them
thy word; and the world has hated them because they are not of the world, even as

---

12-14. Throughout their continuous training, the disciples were held together in the unity of the divine fellowship and preserved from harm with one exception. The man who prated about "waste" (12:4; Mark 14:4) was the one waste product of the Lord's ministry. Here again (cf. 13:18) an explanation is sought in scripture (Ps. 41:9; cf. Ps. 109:5-8; Acts 1:20) for the apostasy. Jesus on the eve of his departure from the world prays secondly (cf. on vs. 11) that the joy which has been his may be fully theirs (15:11; 16:24). This will compensate for the world's hatred, which they must encounter because of their loyalty to Christ, whose refusal to accept worldly standards has incurred the hostility of the world. **The world has hated them** (vs. 14): The evangelist, writing long afterward, uses the past tense by anticipation.

---

them and thou in me, that they may become perfectly one, so that the world may know that thou hast sent me" (vs. 23). In some degree it is so even yet; though again unhappily there is much on the other side—among the sects silly disputes, and narrow-minded contentions that those who differ from them are not in the true sense Christ's at all; and among individuals such selfishness and such failure to notice and be hurt by the sores and sufferings of others, such inability to see over the barriers that we have raised between each other, such cooping of our minds in some little corner, such unwillingness to overleap our differences and reach our essential oneness in and with our Lord, that the light of the world which Christ meant should shine in and through us has grown dim indeed.

And so Christ's first prayer for his people is that they may be perfectly one in heart and mind and will among themselves.

(*b*) But that little company of his was set down in a hostile world, surrounded and pursued by its bitter antagonism. And how are they to bear themselves toward it?

In his characteristically generous way—for his was ever the most grateful of hearts, much moved by any faith in him, by any kindness shown him—Christ pays a splendid tribute to his followers; so splendid that to us it is a little difficult to understand. **They are not of the world,** he claims, speaking to God, **even as I am not of the world;** and repeats it with a confident assurance (vss. 14, 16). That startles. That sounds by far too generous; more generous than true, we should have said. For Christ was hardly even tempted by the world. Its gifts that so intoxicate so many held no appeal at all for him. When the suggestion came to him in the wilderness that the easiest and surest way of furthering and carrying out his God-given mission was to seize political power and eminence, he thrust that from him. And for himself he did not even have to reject the world. Such pettinesses as it has to offer had no interest for him whatever. "The prince of this world cometh," so he said, "and hath nothing in me" (14:30). But the disciples, as we judge, had not attained as yet to more than the first beginnings of that spirit, if even that. They had clung to their material dreams of an earthly kingdom and of their own prominence in it. They were ambitious; on occasion pushing their own claims against each other and jostling for the first places; carefully reckoning up their sacrifices (within earshot of Christ, so one gathers), and the rewards to be expected—all in the world's own fashion. Yet our Lord makes a clean-cut distinction between them and that world, differentiating them from it as belonging to another type and category of being altogether. **They are not of the world, even as I am not of the world.** So kindlily, in spite of his huge dreams for us and his insatiable ambitions for our spiritual progress, does he judge foolish and blundering men; so much do our dim

15 I pray not that thou shouldest take them out of the world, but that thou shouldest keep them from the evil.

16 They are not of the world, even as I am not of the world.

17 Sanctify them through thy truth: thy word is truth.

I am not of the world. 15 I do not pray
that thou shouldst take them out of the
world, but that thou shouldst keep them
from the evil one.[h] 16 They are not of the
world, even as I am not of the world.
17 Sanctify them in the truth; thy word

[h] Or *from evil.*

15-19. The third prayer for the disciples is that, not evading the risks of life in the present evil world, they may be kept out of the clutches of the ruler of this world. May he have no power over them, as he had none over their Master (14:30). A final petition for the disciples is that God may **sanctify them in the truth.** Sanctification is more than separation from the sinfulness of the world—that is already assumed (vs. 16). It means dedication and equipment for their service of God. They are equipped by being brought into the truth, which is "the word of God" (Ps. 119:142 LXX—א reads: καὶ ὁ λόγος σου ἀλήθεια), conveyed to them not only by the lips, but also by the life of their Master. Their mission is to continue the mission of the Son of God (vs. 18; cf. vs. 3). Yet this does not exhaust the meaning of consecration, for ἁγιάζειν (to **consecrate**) is a sacrificial term, and in vs. 19 it refers to the self-offering of Jesus (cf. 1:29; 10:17-18). His sinless life is offered in perfect obedience to the will of God. In this passage the sacrifice is viewed in relation to the disciples as an offering on their behalf, to enable them to serve God as those who have been dedicated and made fit to continue the revelation of the Father in the Son. But whereas Jesus alone could consecrate himself, the disciples are consecrated by

---

inchoate longings after better things count with him; so does he value men by the direction in which they are facing, rather than by their actual present position on the road. Essentially these men were different, and he knew it, and gave them credit for it.

And he knew too that that must make their position difficult. For they, not of the world, were in the world, surrounded by its malign enmities and influences. And what does he ask for them concerning that? He has no fear for them at all, given the aid and grace of God; does not propose or wish that they should shrink back into a secluded corner of life, refusing to take part in the game, fearing its rough and tumble, and keeping anxiously out of the heat and dust of things. Milton had little admiration for "a cloistered virtue." Neither had Jesus Christ. He wants his followers to live in the world. **I do not pray that thou shouldst take them out of the world, but that thou shouldst keep them from the evil one.** It is not release that he asks for them, whether by death or by a tame withdrawal through fear of the press of battle. In face of this definite pronouncement it is difficult to see how those who, meaning only complete loyalty to Christ, have withdrawn into nunneries and monasteries, justify their conduct. Don't coop your soul up in a corner, urged St. Teresa to the young women whom she was training.[6] Yet were they not doing precisely that? Christ means us to live in the world, although not of the world; means us to take life in its fullness as a gift from God and to use it for his glory.

All down the ages there have been two ways of it for serious-minded people, calling to them and enticing them to follow: the Puritan view of life, a right noble endeavor, ruthlessly and unhesitatingly cutting off everything touched with defilement, and valiantly living out the law of self-denial on which Christ lays such stress, caring nothing in their loyalty that life is left bare and pruned, if may be that the soul, escaping from the dust of things, can breathe and is not choked and smothered. Yet others no less loyal feel that these first have cut too close and deep, and have despised and thrown aside what are good gifts of God, thought out for us by him, however men may have misused them. Art, music, literature, the drama, business and work, the ordinary round of things—we should not be afraid of these, nor yet neglect them, but ought to use them in God's service. "Why," asked General Booth, "should all the best tunes be left to the devil?" "It is better," said Christ solemnly, "to enter into life with one hand or one eye, rather than, having two, to be cast into hell." Better! Far, far better! But best of all surely if we can bring both hands, and use them for God's glory.

It is not easy to find and to follow the wise mean between the two extremes. In our day there seems little visible self-denial in the mass

[6] Peers, *Complete Works of Saint Teresa of Jesus,* III. 25.

18 As thou hast sent me into the world, even so have I also sent them into the world.

19 And for their sakes I sanctify myself, that they also might be sanctified through the truth.

20 Neither pray I for these alone, but for them also which shall believe on me through their word;

is truth.
18 As thou didst send me into the
world, so I have sent them into the world.
19 And for their sake I consecrate myself,
that they also may be consecrated in truth.
20 "I do not pray for these only, but also
for those who are to believe in me through

this offering of himself. They are **consecrated in truth** because their Savior's sacrifice gives them an inward quality of life in contrast with the symbolical cultus of the O.T., and the unreal sacrificial ritual of the pagan world.

3. The Unity of the Church—Prayer for the Universal Church (17:20-26)

20-23. After this exclusive prayer for the disciples Jesus prays for the church of the future, the whole company of the faithful won from the world by the apostolic preaching. He prays for its unity in God, that it may share that fellowship which the

of folk. The reins have been thrown upon the neck of their passions and their self-indulgings and their every passing desire. And chaos is resulting. How to live in the world and use it, and yet not bow down to it or be swept away headlong by its conventions, that is our problem. And, says Christ with assurance, with the help of God it can be done. As Lord Rosebery, the British prime minister, wrote of the purposeful and striking saintliness of the great Thomas Chalmers:

> Again, it should be said that this saintliness was not that of an anchorite brooding in religious solitude. Here was a man, bustling, striving, organising, speaking and preaching with the dust and fire of the world on his clothes, but carrying his shrine with him everywhere.[7]

(*c*) But our Lord goes much farther even than that. For in his plan his little group existed not merely for itself, but to tell on the world, to go to it, to influence it, to save it, changing it from what it is into what it is meant to be. For it too God loves. And as he gave his only begotten Son to help it, so, says Christ, "I am sending you for that same high end." And what these men were to accomplish was not merely a dull appendix in small print, after the really momentous happenings are over. They were to carry on and out his enterprise and mission. "The works that I do shall [you] do also; and greater works than mine shall [you] do; because I go unto my Father" (14:12).

It is with Christ's commission, Christ's authority, Christ's trust in them, Christ's hopes centered upon them under God, that they are set to their immense and hazardous and impossible-looking task. And he is sure that given the help of God, they are well able to see it through, if they themselves are zealous and wholehearted in the business. And so he prays, "Help them to devote themselves to it without reservation, and as the end and purpose of their lives; accept them as men dedicated to thy service, to the spreading of the truth, and the sharing with others what I have brought to them from thee. I myself **consecrate myself.** Not least for their sakes, that they may catch the inspiration of my spirit; so that they may be utterly unable to keep out of this adventure, but will have to fling themselves into it." Given that, he felt, anything and everything is possible.

It was a bold faith. For look at these eleven wavering men, upon the point of deserting him; and then at this huge immovable crowded impervious world, so set in its ways: what chance is there of anything worth reckoning coming out of this pathetically futile little effort? "Yet," said Christ with assurance, "they can do it: they, and I, and God." How ridiculous it must have seemed to the wiseacres at the time! Yet how marvelously has our Lord's daring faith been justified!

And today he looks at us, faced by our problems that seem unsurmountable, with the same hope and trust and confidence, risking everything upon our loyalty. "If they are zealous and wholehearted and united, and lean hard on me, and look to God, they can do it," he says. "They can surely do it—they, and I, and God."

20-26. ***Christ's Prayer for Us.***—For it is not only for these eleven men that Christ prayed

[7] *Miscellanies, Literary and Historical* (London: Hodder & Stoughton, 1921), I, 246-47.

21 That they all may be one; as thou, Father, *art* in me, and I in thee, that they also may be one in us: that the world may believe that thou hast sent me.

22 And the glory which thou gavest me I have given them; that they may be one, even as we are one:

23 I in them, and thou in me, that they may be made perfect in one; and that the world may know that thou hast sent me, and hast loved them, as thou hast loved me.

24 Father, I will that they also, whom thou hast given me, be with me where I

their word, 21 that they may all be one;
even as thou, Father, art in me, and I in
thee, that they also may be in us, so that
the world may believe that thou hast sent
me. 22 The glory which thou hast given me
I have given to them, that they may be
one even as we are one, 23 I in them and
thou in me, that they may become per-
fectly one, so that the world may know
that thou hast sent me and hast loved them
even as thou hast loved me. 24 Father, I
desire that they also, whom thou hast given

Son has with the Father. This spirit of unity in the church is to convince the world that Jesus was indeed commissioned by God (cf. vss. 3, 8, 18; 3:17; 5:36, 38; 6:29, 38, 57; 7:29; 8:42; 10:36; 11:42; 20:21; I John 4:9-10, 14). The incarnate life was a revelation of the nature of God (1:14), "full of grace and truth," the shining forth of the filial love of the Logos. This the disciples had received from their Lord, and had shared in the unity of the divine fellowship, in the gift of eternal life (vs. 2). This unity is not that of a human organization, but is a gift of divine love. The unity of the Godhead demands the unity of the entire Christian communion. This can be perfectly consummated only as its members have fellowship with the Father and with his Son Jesus Christ (I John 1:3). Such fellowship is possible to those who know that the Father's love for his Son proves his love for them (cf. 3:16; I John 3:1).

24-26. The closing verses pass from faith to hope in the eschatological vision of the glorified church. The Father's love was shown to the Son **before the foundation of the world.** It will now be revealed to all who are united with the Son in faith and love. **Righteous Father** (cf. "Holy Father," vs. 11): This descriptive attribute is an appeal to divine justice against the world's hatred of the church. The believers have received

---

thus daringly; and not from them alone that he expected so much. Very moving are these verses. Barrie tells us that sometimes when his mother was upon her knees at her devotions, her children stole about the house in a hush of spirit, knowing that she was praying for them. And here we come on Christ praying for us. **I do not pray for these only, but also for those who are to believe in me through their word.** Christ praying for very us! And what does he ask for us? What does he feel that we must have from God if we are to be faithful to his trust in us?

Again he lays his hand upon that all-important oneness. As the ages come and as the ages go, Christ singles out as the supreme requirements of his church (*a*) that we should live near, and with, and in God; that first, that all-important. But (*b*) out of that must flow the second essential—that we shall thereby draw nearer to one another. Two points on the circumference of a circle can be far apart. But let them both come closer to the center, and they cannot avoid approaching one another. It is because we live too far from God that we are alienated from each other, sect from sect and church from church. However we may squabble with each other, the moment that we worship God we are apt to find ourselves drawing together; e.g., all singing the same hymns, culled from all kinds of churches, our differences forgotten.

When Benjamin Jowett of Balliol was fiercely attacked for so-called heresy, he made no reply, except that he ends his essay on "Atonement and Satisfaction" thus:

> As a measure of the value of such disputes, which above all other interests seem to have for a time the power of absorbing men's minds and rousing their passions, we may carry our thoughts onward to the invisible world, and there behold, as in a glass, the great theological teachers of past ages, who have anathematized each other in their lives, resting together in the communion of the same Lord.[8]

"And why not here," prayed Christ, "why not here?" Get closer to God and it will happen. And out of all the possibilities that is what he asked for us. So only, he was sure, can we con-

[8] *Theological Writings*, ed. Lewis Campbell (London: John Murray, 1902), p. 94.

am; that they may behold my glory, which
thou hast given me: for thou lovedst me
before the foundation of the world.
25 O righteous Father, the world hath
not known thee: but I have known thee,
and these have known that thou hast sent
me.

me, may be with me where I am, to be-
hold my glory which thou hast given me
in thy love for me before the foundation
of the world. 25 O righteous Father, the
world has not known thee, but I have
known thee; and these know that thou hast

---

the revelation about God which the world has rejected. Jesus will continue his revelation through the Spirit in order that knowledge and love may be one in the fellowship of the life eternal.

As we conclude our consideration of this section, an additional note on the Last Supper is appropriate. We have already seen (Intro., pp. 445, 448) that the Johannine account of the Last Supper varies in several important particulars from that given in the Synoptics. Apart from John's silence about the institution of the Eucharist, the main divergence is in respect of the date and the character of the meal. The general impression derived from Mark and Matthew (and to some extent also from Luke) is that the Last Supper was the paschal meal held on the evening of Nisan 14/15, the first day of the Passover (i.e., from Friday 6 P.M. to Saturday 6 P.M.). In this fateful year the first day of the Passover fell on a sabbath; but the feast took precedence of the sabbath. According to John, the Last Supper took place on Nisan 13/14 (the day beginning at 6 P.M. on Thursday, Nisan 13, and closing at 6 P.M. on Friday, Nisan 14). This was the day of Preparation, on the afternoon of which the paschal lambs were sacrificed, and on which the Crucifixion took place. It was the day before the first day of the feast. Jesus met with his disciples for supper on the evening that began this day of Preparation, twenty-four hours before the Jewish families sat down to celebrate the Passover. In John, therefore, we have the Last Supper on Thursday evening, the Crucifixion on Friday, and the Resurrection on Sunday, Nisan 16. But in the Synoptics the supper was taken on Friday evening of Nisan 14/15, the Crucifixion followed on Saturday morning, Nisan 15. Now Nisan 16 (Saturday 6 P.M. to Sunday 6 P.M.) was the second day of the Passover, yet it is spoken of as "after the day of Preparation" (Matt. 27:62), "the day of Preparation, that is, the day before the sabbath" (Mark 15:42), "the day of Preparation, and the sabbath was beginning" (Luke 23:54). The Resurrection must therefore have taken place on Nisan 17 (Sunday 6 P.M. to Monday 6 P.M.). Nevertheless, all three Synoptics place the discovery of the Resurrection on the morning of "the first day of the week" (Mark 16:2; Matt. 28:1; Luke 24:1). This confusion in the Synoptic chronology raises such difficulties that the words of Jesus, "I have earnestly desired to eat this passover with you before I suffer" (Luke 22:15), may well be interpreted as the expression of an unfulfilled wish. Moreover, in the Synoptic accounts of the Supper there are two puzzling features. Neither Mark nor Matthew (nor Luke except indirectly in 22:7) refers to the roasted paschal flesh—the central feature of the Jewish Passover meal—and the

---

vince the world that something divine has come in among us, that we have the love of God in us and about us (vs. 23).

Although the past tense of the phrase **they . . . whom thou hast given me** might seem to limit it in the first instance to his original circle of friends, the prayer in vss. 24-26, blessed be God, covers all Christ's people down the centuries. It is a petition that tugs strongly at the heart. Samuel Rutherford, that saint of God, with his immense gifts, spent his ministerial life in Anwoth on the Solway, quite a small church and parish. But when his eloquent tongue was silenced by the government, and he himself exiled to Aberdeen, his homesick heart still dwelt among the people he had left, and whom he could not forget.

> Oh! if one soul from Anwoth
> Meet me at God's right hand,
> My Heaven will be two Heavens,
> In Immanuel's land.[1]

Father, prays Christ, **I desire that they also, whom thou hast given me, may be with me**

[1] Mrs. A. R. Cousin, "The Sands of Time Are Sinking." See *Letters of Samuel Rutherford,* p. 742.

26 And I have declared unto them thy name, and will declare *it;* that the love wherewith thou hast loved me may be in them, and I in them.

sent me. 26 I made known to them thy name, and I will make it known, that the love with which thou hast loved me may be in them, and I in them."

---

word for ordinary bread (ἄρτος) is always used, never ἄζυμα, the word invariably used for unleavened bread, which was the other distinguishing feature of a Passover meal.

Accordingly, there is a strong presumption in favor of the Johannine suggestion that the Last Supper was not the Passover, but a supper which Jesus took with his disciples on the previous day. The fullest and most convenient explanation is that given by W. O. E. Oesterley in *The Jewish Background of the Christian Liturgy* (Oxford: Clarendon Press, 1925). He reminds us that we have evidence in pre-Christian times of a custom by which certain groups of friends called *ḥabhûrôth* (singular *ḥabhûrāh*) met together in one of their homes for a meal on Friday afternoon, which was carried on with religious conversation till dusk told that the sabbath was about to begin. This meal was known as *qiddûsh,* or "sanctification" (of the sabbath). This meal, and the sanctification which followed it, ushered in not only the weekly sabbath, but also the great festivals. Jesus and the twelve formed a *ḥabhûrāh* to which Jesus refers in the words, "Ye are my friends, if you do whatsoever I command you" (15:14). They met for their meal on the afternoon of Thursday, Nisan 13, and as Nisan 14 drew near at dusk, Jesus began the ceremony of sanctification. It was the eve of the Passover, so the *qiddûsh* combined the commemoration of the sabbath with that of the deliverance from slavery in Egypt. He took the cup, spoke the usual benediction, and passed it around for all to drink. He then passed around the bread. In the Synoptics only one cup is spoken of, and all drank from it, whereas in the Passover ritual each person present had his own cup and drank from it four times during the meal, celebrating with joy the four benefits granted in their nation's historic deliverance—freedom, release, redemption, election. Oesterley suggests that though only one cup was drunk at the Passover *qiddûsh,* the theme of Passover would be in the minds of all present. It is not too fanciful to trace some association of ideas in words attributed to Jesus in the farewell discourses. Seven thoughts that were emphasized in the Passover *qiddûsh* are enumerated in Oesterley's book: (*a*) the completion of the work of creation, culminating in the sanctification of the sabbath; (*b*) the words, "Blessed art thou, O Lord our God, the King of the Universe, who created the fruit of the vine"; (*c*) the redemption from Egyptian bondage; (*d*) the election of Israel and its sanctification among the nations; (*e*) the words "Blessed art thou, O Lord, King of the Universe, who bringest forth bread from the earth"; (*f*) freedom, suggested by the season of Passover; (*g*) joy brought by this season. With (*a*) cf. 17:4-5; with (*b*) cf. 15:1-6; with (*c*) cf. 14:1-2; with (*d*) cf. 13:18; 15:16, 19; with (*f*) cf. 15:15; with (*g*) cf. 15:11; 16:22; 17:13.

The fact that from the beginning the Eucharist was celebrated as a weekly, not as an annual, feast favors the theory that the Last Supper was the culmination of many weekly meals for the sanctification of the sabbath and not merely a commemoration of the Passover. Of course the special associations of the Last Supper would help toward

---

where I am, to behold my glory which thou hast given me in thy love for me before the foundation of the world.

And this for two reasons. Partly for his own sake. For heaven will not be quite heaven to Christ unless his friends are with him there. So real and intimate and lasting are the ties that bind us to him. But partly also for their sake. **O righteous Father, the world has not known thee, but I have known thee; and these know that thou hast sent me. I made known to them thy name, and I will make it known, that the love with which thou hast loved me may be in them, and I in them.** As if to say, "They have dared to believe my message in a world of indifferent or scoffing unbelievers; and many things will seem to prove it all a dream of vain desire, an unsubstantial fantasy, mere wishful thinking, nothing more. In justice to them, righteous Father, give them at last to know it is all true; that I did come from thee; and that the name I gave them for thee is no mere poetry

18 When Jesus had spoken these words, he went forth with his disciples over the brook Cedron, where was a garden, into the which he entered, and his disciples.
2 And Judas also, which betrayed him, knew the place: for Jesus ofttimes resorted thither with his disciples.

18 When Jesus had spoken these words, he went forth with his disciples across the Kidron valley, where there was a garden, which he and his disciples entered.
2 Now Judas, who betrayed him, also knew the place; for Jesus often met there with his

---

the identification of Jesus with the paschal lamb (cf. 1:29), but the command "Do this in remembrance of me" would also be an appeal to the disciples to continue the fellowship of the *ḥabhûrāh*.

It is right to say that such eminent authorities as Gustaf Dalman (*Jesus-Jeschua* [Leipzig: J. C. Hinrichs, 1922; Eng. tr., London: Society for Promoting Christian Knowledge, 1929]) and Joachim Jeremias ("The Last Supper," *Journal of Theological Studies,* L [1949], 1-10) accept the identification of the Last Supper with the Passover meal. But the light thrown by Oesterley and others on this subject helps to explain the divergent traditions about the Supper, while strongly reinforcing the claim that the Fourth Gospel is often based upon an early and true tradition, however free a hand the evangelist allows himself in dealing with his material.

VIII. Gethsemane to Calvary (18:1–19:42)

In this section John follows more closely the tradition preserved in the Synoptic narrative. He also draws upon an independent tradition, for it is unlikely that an evangelist who so constantly lays upon the Jews the blame for the rejection and death of Jesus would have introduced the squad of Roman soldiers into the story of the arrest, unless it was already mentioned in his special source.

A. The Arrest (18:1-11)

Cf. Mark 14:26, 43-50; Matt. 26:30, 47-56; Luke 21:37; 22:39, 47-53. There are some striking differences between the Johannine and the Synoptic record having to do with (*a*) those who were charged with the arrest of Jesus; (*b*) the part played by Judas in this episode; and (*c*) the attempt at resistance. (*a*) According to Mark, Judas was

---

but fact; and that thy love is really around about them."

> Is it a dream?
> Nay but the lack of it the dream,
> And failing it life's lore and wealth a dream;
> And all the world a dream.[2]

But this is true! But this is *surely* true!

18:2. ***The Mystery of Judas.***—At this point the Fourth Gospel grows curiously bare and full of unexpected, staring, inexplicable gaps. There is nothing about the Sacrament of the Lord's Supper—which seems to mean that this author was not a sacramentarian, with the corollary that one can live unusually near to Jesus Christ and have intimate knowledge and experience of him without laying the stress upon the sacraments that many give them; nothing about that moving hymn they sang before going out to the Mount of Olives; nothing about the long agony in Gethsemane. And though the betrayal of our Lord as it is set down for us here is an ugly story, it has little of the terrible vividness of the Synoptists' account of it and is much less heart gripping.

Here there is no mention of the kiss which has so shocked mankind, inured to horrors though it is, that it has as a rule been in full agreement with Dante when he puts unhappy Judas lowest of all men, in the deepest depth of hell. In some ways this report is too abrupt, too summary, and as a result, unsatisfying, particularly with regard to Judas. When he, poor wretch, in his desperate remorse, went back to the authorities, they treated him with a cool, aloof, contemptuous unconcern, as a tool that had served its purpose, and in which they had no further interest. And something of that same impression is left by this narrative on the reader's mind. Here are no hints of the man's agony of despair and miserable end. Once his fell part is played, the writer shows no further interest in Judas. He fades out of the story. We look for him, and he is not there. Nor are we given any

[2] Walt Whitman, "Song of the Universal," st. iv.

accompanied by "a crowd with swords and clubs, from the chief priests and the scribes and the elders," i.e., the officers of the Sanhedrin. Matthew agrees, but omits "and the scribes." Luke simply mentions "a crowd" under the leadership of Judas. John tells that Judas brought a band of soldiers, and some officers from the chief priests and the Pharisees, with lanterns, torches, and weapons. (*b*) All three Synoptists speak of the sign which Judas had given the temple police. Mark writes: "The one I shall kiss is the man; seize him and lead him away safely." Matthew leaves out the last five words. Luke writes: "He drew near to Jesus to kiss him; but Jesus said to him, 'Judas, would you betray the Son of man with a kiss?' " According to John, Jesus stepped forward to meet the band of soldiers and police with the challenge, "Whom do you seek?" The only reference to the traitor is that "Judas, who betrayed him, was standing with them." (*c*) The incident of the ineffectual attempt at rescue shows as great a variation among the Synoptists as between Mark and John. Mark and Matthew tell of an unnamed disciple who slashed off the ear of the high priest's slave. Matthew adds a rebuke to the disciple, and a reminder from Jesus that he could appeal for a reinforcement of twelve legions of angels. According to Luke, it was the right ear that was struck, and Jesus checked the disciple and healed the slave's ear. John is explicit. It was Peter who brandished the sword; it was the right ear that was severed. Peter was rebuked with the words, "Put your sword into its sheath; shall I not drink the cup which the Father has given me?"

18:1-2. Across the Kidron valley: This name was derived from the Hebrew word "to be dark," "gloomy," "turbid." In Greek, both in the LXX and in this passage, some readings show a confusion with the genitive plural of the word for "cedar" (τῶν Κέδρων:

---

indication whatsoever of what became of him. Surely too summary, too abrupt, and so unsatisfying. For the character of Judas will always be a puzzling, sobering, terrifying mystery. As we watch this goodly vessel putting gallantly out to sea, and running far and swift and straight, yet going down in appalling disaster, cold fears steal into the heart. Life is so perilous. We are so frail. This actually happened to a real man like us. And it is with low voices and a trembling heart that we whisper the ghastly, dread, "Lord, is it I?"

In some respects the Gospels seem unfair to Judas. From the beginning, when they mention him they are apt to add, "who also betrayed him," hanging that hideous superscription around his neck like the placards carried by the primitive actors in some old-world miracle play, or like the names which Bunyan gives his characters, which at once reveal the part that they are there to play, all as if Judas had been assigned the part of villain in the mighty drama of Calvary. But that is to miss the tragedy and to refuse to face the facts.

One must begin by realizing that Judas was one of Christ's closest friends; that Christ believed in him; saw immense possibilities in him; chose him out as likely to be really helpful to the cause, more so than others who suggested themselves to his mind, and yet were put aside to make way for a likelier man, and that man Judas of Kerioth. Moreover, he was a personality, a man of gallant hopes, of daring, of adventure, ready to sacrifice his all for a big dream. In fact he actually did that, just as truly as the rest of them; rose up, left all, and followed.

Further, he was a man of parts, of more business capacity perhaps than any of the others. And so he was appointed the treasurer and mess president of the little company, was given the worry of looking after their bits of affairs, and of making provision for their needs. For three years more or less he lived with Christ, and in the circle of the disciples; and so bore himself that when our Lord suddenly announced that one of them would betray him, nobody apparently suspected Judas; and even when he rose and set out on his terrible errand, not one of them even then began to take in what was happening. Each of them, we read, had earlier in a kind of panic suspected himself. But no one attributed the sudden departure of Judas to its real and sinister cause—not even after Christ's open denunciation of him to some or to all of them. That seemingly struck them as out of the question. He was not the man for that.

True, this evangelist lets slip almost casually that Judas had taken to pilfering what could only be small sums out of the common purse they had entrusted to him. He could do that, and look Christ in the eyes! A fact sinister enough. Yet conscience tells us how often we too fail Christ in our own way, and how little concerned we are about it; can indeed soon forget it altogether.

Yet with all his good qualities Judas betrayed Jesus Christ. How? And why? How did this day

B C L Θ; τοῦ Κέδρου: ℵ D W abdr; τοῦ Κεδρών: A S Δ cefgq vg sy^s). The original reading, which accounts for both the others, is τοῦ Κεδρών. This was a likely instance of false etymology. The **valley** (χείμαρρος) was a wadi or the bed of a winter torrent that was dry in summer. John alone speaks of a **garden**, which Mark and Matthew name Gethsemane (i.e., "oil press"). Judas knew this as a frequent resort of Jesus, who went there expecting betrayal and arrest. It was no doubt for this reason that Judas had been

---

that broke so bright and had so fair and promising a forenoon close in such utter darkness? "And it was night," so this evangelist dismisses him with an irrepressible shudder. A. B. Davidson, in a consummate study of King Saul, says that when we come upon his mangled form, instinctively we look up at the height from which he fell.[3] So here. How did the tragedy happen? Nobody knows. But many have conjectured.

Some, e.g., De Quincey, think that Judas grew impatient with what he judged to be Christ's dilatory methods. Time, he felt with an ever-increasing anxiety, was running on, and Christ was doing little with it, seemed to him to be frittering it away. The chance was passing; if it were not to be lost, it must be seized forthwith. Opposition was consolidating. Now was the hour to act. And yet as Judas saw things, Christ was effecting nothing to the point: And so this theory runs, Judas resolved that he would force our Lord into a position where he would have to act with decision, and drawing upon all his powers, scatter his enemies, and come into his own. That was the plan. And when with horror it came home to the unhappy man how tragically he had bungled and miscalculated, and how the scheme he thought so clever had dissolved into sheer and utter ruin, his heart broke; he could not bear it, or himself, but went and hanged himself, having no more to live for. It may be so.

Others suppose that Judas saw the game was up; that Christ had failed; that the authorities were certain, before many days were over, to bring the crazy structure of their brave enterprise crashing to ruin about their ears; and that feeling it was now a case of *sauve qui peut,* each man for himself in an effort to escape what was coming, Judas incontinently threw the cause overboard in a panic that was cunning enough to think out an ugly way to his own personal safety. Again, it may be so.

In any case, were it not for that charge of petty pilfering which keeps rising up in the mind accusingly, one would have said with absolute assurance that by no possibility could the man have been tempted by the insignificant bribe that he was promised. For according at least to certain scholars' computations, thirty pieces of silver might amount to something

[3] *Called of God*, pp. 154-55.

like twenty-five dollars. To betray Christ for anything, for the whole round world and all that it contains, were monstrous. But for so paltry a sum! Yet how often we too fail Christ, betray Christ, barter Christ, for trifles of no moment whatsoever! So once again, even that may be so.

AE, the poet, is of opinion that the real cause of the tragedy is to be sought far back in some temptation to which Judas succumbed in his early life, and which, finding a lodgment in his mind—at first a very little thing and accounted of no moment, perhaps forgotten even by himself—rooted and grew and spread until it blossomed into that final hideous infamy.

In ancient shadows and twilights
  Where childhood had strayed,
The world's great sorrows were born
  And its heroes were made
In the lost boyhood of Judas
  Christ was betrayed.[4]

What, then, are we to think of Judas and his destiny? Are we to

Blot out his name, then, record one lost soul more,
  One task more declined, one more footpath untrod,
One more devil's-triumph and sorrow for angels,
  One wrong more to man, one more insult to God?[5]

This Fourth Evangelist tells us explicitly that Jesus Christ, claiming that he had lost none of his flock, sadly and explicitly excepted Judas (17:12). And what Christ says is true. And yet was that the ending end of all Christ's hopes for Judas? For one thing, such despair and agony as Judas knew requires real depth of character and soul in which to root itself. Is there not a half hope for him in the man's unbearable horror of himself and of his deed? Is there not something true in Tennyson's verdict that might seem applicable even to this case?

The sin that practice burns into the blood,
And not the one dark hour which brings remorse,
Will brand us, after, of whose fold we be.[6]

[4] "Germinal," from *Vale and Other Poems* (London: Macmillan & Co.; New York: The Macmillan Co., 1931), pp. 28-29. Used by permission of Diarmuid Russell.

[5] Browning, "The Lost Leader."

[6] Tennyson, "Merlin and Vivien," ll. 760-62.

3 Judas then, having received a band *of men* and officers from the chief priests and Pharisees, cometh thither with lanterns and torches and weapons.

4 Jesus therefore, knowing all things that should come upon him, went forth, and said unto them, Whom seek ye?

5 They answered him, Jesus of Nazareth. Jesus saith unto them, I am *he*. And Judas also, which betrayed him, stood with them.

6 As soon then as he had said unto them, I am *he,* they went backward, and fell to the ground.

7 Then asked he them again, Whom seek ye? And they said, Jesus of Nazareth.

8 Jesus answered, I have told you that I am *he:* if therefore ye seek me, let these go their way:

disciples. 3 So Judas, procuring a band of
soldiers and some officers from the chief
priests and the Pharisees, went there with
lanterns and torches and weapons. 4 Then
Jesus, knowing all that was to befall him,
came forward and said to them, "Whom do
you seek?" 5 They answered him, "Jesus of
Nazareth." Jesus said to them, "I am he."
Judas, who betrayed him, was standing
with them. 6 When he said to them, "I am
he," they drew back and fell to the ground.
7 Again he asked them, "Whom do you
seek?" And they said, "Jesus of Nazareth."
8 Jesus answered, "I told you that I am he;

---

bribed by the high priest's agents, who were anxious to make the arrest at some place and time at which there would be the least danger of popular resistance.

3-8. John alone mentions **a band of soldiers and some officers** (cf. vs. 12). This cannot mean that a cohort from the garrison quartered in the tower of Antonia and led by the military tribune (ὁ χιλίαρχος) was detailed for the arrest, but that in view of the charge of high treason planned by the chief priests, the military authorities were asked to send a detachment of auxiliaries to support the temple police in case of serious resistance. The moral majesty of Jesus astonished the captors, who recoiled in amazement, and some **fell to the ground.** The dramatic description, completely Johannine, must not be interpreted literally. It corresponds to the Synoptic tradition of the withering scorn with which Jesus accosted his adversaries: "Have you come out as against a robber, with swords and clubs to capture me? Day after day I was with you in the temple teaching, and you did not seize me" (Mark 14:48-49). Luke 22:53 adds the contemptuous comment, "But this is your hour, and the power of darkness." Peculiar to John is the appeal, **Let these men go.**

And one remembers that when Mary Magdalene, poor soul, grief-stricken and distracted, had lost all faith and hope, a voice said to her, "Mary!" And with that, Christ, speaking to her through her faithlessness and hopelessness, had found her again. Remembers too that special message which the angel at the tomb sent to Peter, poor unhappy Peter, fallen, shamefaced, disgraced. "Go, tell his disciples and Peter" (Mark 16:7); as if to say, "You must remember Peter. More than any of them he needs to be assured that Jesus has not turned from him nor lost heart about him." Remembering acts like these, would it not have been like the Master, when he reached the other world, to seek out this lost soul, this Judas who had been his friend? What if sunk in the horror of his sin, he too heard a voice saying, "Judas!" and was found again by that faithful heart who, having loved his own, loves them on to the end! The love of Christ is very wonderful. And my experience of it makes me still harbor hopes for Judas—and for me.

3-9. ***The Betrayal.***—The chapters that lead up to Calvary leave on the mind an overpowering impression of the majesty of Jesus. They laid violent hands on him; they bound him; they dragged him here and there and to and fro; they hustled him from court to court and trial to trial; they struck him in the face; brutally they scourged him; they mocked him, surrounding him with guffaws of laughter: yet they could not demean him; but on the contrary, he towers above them ever greater and greater. All through what was meant to humiliate him he gives one the sense that it is he who is master of the situation.

So here in the garden. When the soldiers, or as Matthew says, the gang of roughs with swords and staves, were led by Judas to a place where he knew that Christ was likely to be found, our Lord stepped out at once from among the trees

9 That the saying might be fulfilled,
which he spake, Of them which thou gavest
me have I lost none.
10 Then Simon Peter having a sword
drew it, and smote the high priest's servant,
and cut off his right ear. The servant's name
was Malchus.
11 Then said Jesus unto Peter, Put up
thy sword into the sheath: the cup which
my Father hath given me, shall I not drink
it?

so, if you seek me, let these men go." 9 This
was to fulfill the word which he had spoken,
"Of those whom thou gavest me I lost
not one." 10 Then Simon Peter, having a
sword, drew it and struck the high priest's
slave and cut off his right ear. The slave's
name was Malchus. 11 Jesus said to Peter,
"Put your sword into its sheath; shall I not
drink the cup which the Father has given
me?"

9-11. This fulfillment of the Lord's own word (17:12) hardly does justice to the thought of 6:39 and 10:28. We owe the names **Malchus** and **Peter** in this incident to this Gospel alone. **Shall I not drink the cup which the Father has given me?** This

---

into the glare and flicker of the torchlight, with something so majestic in his mien and attitude that momentarily they fell back (vss. 4-6). "Since it is I whom you are seeking," he said, "let these others go" (vs. 8). A characteristic thought and act. That was a stupid jibe which they exultantly flung into his dying face as he hung on the Cross, "He saved others; himself he cannot save." Of course he cannot. For he saves others only by his own self-sacrifice for them. Always, to the alarm of the disciples, he kept spending his strength that others might be healed. And he gave up his life that our souls might be saved. So here. **Let these men go,** he said, offering himself freely. That is Christ's character and nature. And since the whole point of Christianity is to enable us to rise into his likeness and to put on his ways, if we are not gaining his mind and entering into his spirit of self-sacrifice, in us the divine plan is breaking down and failing. "In Christianity," says Berdyaev, "the central idea is that of transfiguration, not justification. The latter has occupied too prominent a place in western Christianity." [7]

10-11. ***The Strange Problem of the Swords.***—Rightly or wrongly, there are those who are glad that Peter made his flustered, futile, dangerous gesture of defiance, and struck out, wildly and to small effect although it was. No doubt at all it was a daft thing to do; and Christ at once arrested what might easily have incensed the authorities into blotting out the whole little company, thereby destroying the infant church at birth—a hideous possibility, but at that moment perilously near. And yet, incorrigibly and unrepentantly the mind may be glad that one blow at least was struck for Jesus; that not all men stood quiescent and inactive as Christ was dragged here and there.

However that may be, what strikes one with wonder in this whole episode is the fact that Peter was armed! Did our Lord know of it? Did he approve of it? Did he agree to it? Or were things of which he was unconscious happening behind his back in his own little circle, things of which, had he known of them, he would not have approved? That last seems unlikely.

But the problem is bigger than this one incident. For according to Luke 22:38, there were at least two swords among them, and these had been shown to Christ. Indeed, as A. B. Bruce pointed out long ago, the article before μάχαιραν might suggest that the whole band were going about armed, each disciple having his own sword. "The fear that they might be explains the largeness of the band following Judas." [8] Moreover, Christ's reproof to Peter, while it is reproof, is a singularly mild one. Would we not have expected him to ask his overzealous and rash disciple, sternly and even angrily, what he was doing with a sword at all? Did he not understand the spirit of the movement he had joined? And so, bid him be done with such crude and unseemly things forever. Yet all he said was, **Put your sword into its sheath.**

If people carry weapons, it is presumably because upon due and fit occasion they propose to use them. Did our Lord sanction that? Or if not, why were his followers—all or some—moving about the city armed? These are facts that must be faced and taken into account in honestly considering Christ's attitude toward physical resistance to evil. They do not seem to fit easily into the pacifist position.

11. ***The Untoward Things in Life.***—There are vociferous voices these days that will have none of the doctrine of an all-embracing providence, that resent the idea that everything

[7] *Freedom and the Spirit*, p. 176.

[8] "The Synoptic Gospels," *Expositor's Greek Testament*, ed. W. Robertson Nicoll (London: Hodder & Stoughton, 1897), on Matt. 26:51-54.

12 Then the band and the captain and officers of the Jews took Jesus, and bound him,

12 So the band of soldiers and their captain and the officers of the Jews seized

sublime saying sums up in a sentence the unrecorded story of the agony in the garden (for the symbol of the cup, cf. Pss. 23:5; 75:8; 116:13).

B. The Trial Before the High Priest and Peter's Denial (18:12-27)

Cf. Mark 14:53-72; Matt. 26:57-75; Luke 22:54-71. A comparison shows that John agrees with the Synoptics that the arrest was followed by a trial before the high priest, and that Peter's denial took place then. He agrees with Mark and Matthew in recording a nocturnal session, whereas in Luke the trial takes place the following morning. John is silent about the horseplay which in Luke took place before, and in Mark and Matthew after, the trial, but he records the blow on the face given by an officer of the court (vs. 22). The main differences relate to the name of the high priest, the questions asked, and the result of the trial. As the text of John stands, the trial took place before Annas. Jesus is merely sent to Caiaphas, who hands him over to Pilate. No questions are asked of Jesus except about his teaching and his disciples (vs. 19), neither about his messianic claim nor about his alleged threat to destroy the temple. No charge is formulated and no judgment is pronounced.

From Luke 3:2 we know that Annas and Caiaphas were regarded conjointly as high priests, and from Acts 4:6 that Annas was regarded as still leader of the high priestly family. His son-in-law, Joseph Caiaphas, was actually in office in this fateful year (see on 11:49-51). As John refers repeatedly to Caiaphas as high priest, he probably intends the hearing before Annas to be regarded as a preliminary investigation, followed by a meeting of the Sanhedrin with Caiaphas as president. The Sinaitic Syriac version of the Gospels corrects the sequence of events as follows: vss. 12-13, 24, 14-15, 19-23, 16-18, 26-27. As this may possibly depend on the text of Tatian's Diatessaron, it may be taken as reflecting an attempt to harmonize the Johannine story with that of the Synoptics rather than as preserving the original order of the verses. Lagrange, however, calls attention to a small but significant textual indication that some disturbance occurred in the original order of the verses. He points out that some important authorities give vs. 24 in the

that befalls us comes upon us of God's ordering or with his permission, dismissing that as an insult to him, and indeed a sheer blasphemy against him, impossible to fit into the belief that he is love. According to this theory the calamities that overtake mankind—sorrow and pain and loss, etc.—are not God's will for them at all; but either are so shallow-rooted that none of them runs back farther than to what are customarily called their secondary causes, and are due only to human folly and stupidity and malice and sin; or else are the bursting in on us of an eruption of evil things out of the abyss, which breaking through the guard that God has thrown about men work a havoc for them which had no part in God's plan.

Superficially this may seem to relieve the tension of enigmas, dark and incomprehensible to us, by which at times we are confronted, if not in our own lives, then in those of certain others around about us whom we know or of whom we hear; enigmas that shock and stagger every sensitive and sympathetic mind.

But that way lies no road to a solution, or to peace of mind. To believe that the harsh happenings and untoward things in life are part of a divine plan for us which as yet we do not understand, but which will one day justify itself even to us, may sometimes seem to be asking for the incredible. The infamous, unthinkable atrocities of the concentration camps at Belsen, and the like, do they too fall within God's ordering of things? And yet that brave, audacious faith has rallied and steadied and brought men and women through appalling things with minds still unbroken and indomitable. Whereas, to be told that God's care around about us is not really effective, and that horrors can hoodwink him, and evade his watchfulness and strike us down, does not that destroy all sense of security and fling us back into a world of chaos, where anything may happen, and the worst seems the likeliest? And certainly it is not scriptural, and was expressly rejected by Christ over and over and over again; never even occurred to him as a possible explanation.

13 And led him away to Annas first; for he was father-in-law to Caiaphas, which was the high priest that same year.

Jesus and bound him. 13 First they led him to Annas; for he was the father-in-law of Ca'ia-phas, who was high priest that year.

form, "But Annas sent him bound to Caiaphas . . ."; others read, "And Annas" or "Then Annas"; and some omit the conjunction altogether. "Then" (οὖν or τότε) suits the sentence well where it stands. "But" (δέ) is out of place here while fitting the position after vs. 13. There is thus good textual reason to suspect that a disturbance has taken place. The conjunction "so then" (οὖν) is in place in vs. 28, especially if this verse follows an account of the process before Caiaphas, of which nothing has been said in the text as it stands. Internal evidence supports the suspicion of a change in the primitive order of vs. 24, for two reasons: (*a*) Peter's denial takes place in the house of Caiaphas according to the Synoptics. As the text stands in John, two of Peter's denials take place after Jesus has been led away to Caiaphas. It is unlikely that he would have remained in the place of danger when his presence there was due to his desire to follow Jesus. (*b*) John does not call Annas high priest; indeed, he emphasizes the fact that in that very year Caiaphas bore the title. Vss. 15, 19, 22 would more naturally refer to Caiaphas than to Annas.

13-16. High priest that year: Cf. on 11:49. On vs. 14 cf. 11:50. **Another disciple . . . the other disciple** (vss. 15-16). For the identity of the unnamed disciple with "the disciple whom Jesus loved" (13:23) see Intro., p. 440. **Known to the high priest** (γνωστός)

When the people of moment and importance scoffed at his claims and turned away, he did not put it down merely to human prejudice and obstinacy. He accepted it as part of the divine plan for him. "Even so, Father; for so it seemed good in thy sight" (Matt. 11:26). When the shadow of the Cross fell dark and ominous and shivery across his path, this too he felt came to him from God. "My Father, . . . thy will be done," he said (Matt. 26:42). So here. When the soldiers or their rabble following seized and bound him, he saw past and through the human ignorance and passion around him, and felt with confidence that God's own hand was in it all. **The cup which my Father hath given me, shall I not drink it?** And has not that faith of his been abundantly justified? And looking back over life, can we not see even now that God was in what, at the time it came upon us, looked to us to be nothing less than his desertion and abandonment of us? And if some things still remain dark and mysterious as ever, is not experience teaching us to be quiet and submissive under the discipline of life, more teachable and trustful, because we are learning that even the bleakest happenings are not chance-blown; that they too come from God; and that at the sore heart of them we can meet him face to face?

Clearly any understanding of the ways of God with men must rest upon some awareness of what the divine purpose is seeking to achieve in human life. If God is seeking one thing, and man believes He is, or ought to be, seeking something else, there can be nothing but estrangement, misunderstanding, and cross-purpose. . . . It is fatally easy . . . to measure the goodness of God by the extent to which pain and trouble are escaped. [But] God's purpose is to conform men to the image of His Son, and His Son died on the Cross. To conform them to that image and save them from trouble, even great trouble, are two contradictory ends which not even the providence of God can encompass at one and the same time.[9]

The loss of this belief in the overriding providence of God, so characteristic of the present day, has proved to be a major disaster. As Walter Lippmann puts it,

In the old order the compulsions were often painful, but there was sense in the pain that was inflicted by the will of an all-knowing God. In the new order the compulsions are painful and, as it were, accidental, unnecessary, wanton, and full of mockery. The modern man does not make his peace with them. For in effect he has replaced natural piety with a grudging endurance of a series of unsanctified compulsions. When he believed that the unfolding of events was a manifestation of the will of God, he could say: Thy will be done . . . in His will is our peace. But when he believes that events are determined by the votes of a majority, the orders of his bosses, the opinions of his neighbors, the laws of supply and demand, and the decisions of quite selfish men, he yields because he has to yield. He is conquered but unconvinced.[1]

[9] H. H. Farmer, *The World and God* (London: James Nisbet & Co.; New York: Harper & Bros., 1935), pp. 235-36. Used by permission.

[1] *A Preface to Morals,* p. 10. Copyright 1929 by Walter Lippmann and used with permission of The Macmillan Co. and George Allen & Unwin.

14 Now Caiaphas was he, which gave counsel to the Jews, that it was expedient that one man should die for the people.

15 ¶ And Simon Peter followed Jesus, and *so did* another disciple: that disciple was known unto the high priest, and went in with Jesus into the palace of the high priest.

16 But Peter stood at the door without. Then went out that other disciple, which was known unto the high priest, and spake unto her that kept the door, and brought in Peter.

14 It was Ca'ia-phas who had given counsel to the Jews that it was expedient that one man should die for the people.

15 Simon Peter followed Jesus, and so
did another disciple. As this disciple was
known to the high priest, he entered the
court of the high priest along with Jesus,
16 while Peter stood outside at the door. So
the other disciple, who was known to the
high priest, went out and spoke to the maid
who kept the door, and brought Peter in.

---

does not necessarily carry the idea of intimate friendship, still less of family relationship (συγγενής); cf. Luke 2:44, "kinsfolk and acquaintances" (συγγενεῖς καὶ γνωστοί).

15-27. ***The Tragedy of Peter.***—Nothing in literature is told more graphically than the tragedy of Peter's fall. So vivid is it that one feels as if he were not merely reading an old-world incident of the very long ago but as if he himself were actually present, watching uneasily an unhappy fellow man who has ventured farther than his courage can follow and dared more than he can carry through, caught off his guard by a sudden question, and flustered and frightened, stammering out his shameful denials, growing quite truculent about it, heaping up lie on lie and noisy oath on noisy oath; once started on that fatal slope, unable to stop himself, but carried downward faster and faster by his own impetus, until too tardily there come the terrible awakening and bitter shame. A pitiful scene indeed! But a marvelous piece of writing. And a grim warning of the unreliability of these unstable hearts of ours.

How did it happen? And to Peter of all men? It all began with that **other disciple** (vs. 16). He had the right of entrance to the high priest's house. They knew him at the doors and let him in without challenge. And apparently noticing Peter hanging about outside, he came out and agreed or offered to pass him in. The man meant nothing but friendliness, and was seeking to be helpful. Yet had it not been for him, Peter would not have fallen! So easily, and without knowing what we are doing, can we set stones of stumbling before other people's feet, over which they trip and stumble. A mother spends herself for her son, with nothing but kindness toward him in her heart; and thereby spoils him, and stunts his soul, so that he grows up selfish and intolerable. Or casually we happen to introduce one friend of ours to another; and as the direct result of what we did, thinking nothing about it, a life is spoiled, perhaps two lives are ruined. May God have mercy on us, blundering so ignorantly through this life of ours, so perilous often to ourselves, and unknowingly bringing danger upon others around about us.

But not a little of the trouble came of Peter's own foolhardiness, for which indeed one likes him; and yet it was not wise, and invited disaster. It was a fatal instance of that habit of misreading himself, to which he was prone; of that supreme self-confidence which often did not justify itself. On the Sea of Galilee that night of storm nothing would satisfy him except walking to Christ on the angry waters—quite unnecessarily. But he must do what Christ was doing. Characteristically, he began bravely, even audaciously; but losing nerve and confidence, was soon going down, and had to be snatched back from imminent death. So in the upper room. He had been taken aback by Christ's wholly unexpected warning that he was on the eve of denying him publicly and persistently; had pushed it from him vehemently as ridiculous nonsense; just did not believe it; could not think of himself in the part of a deserter; felt he was not the man for that, whatever his faults might be. He had said so at the time with a loud-voiced, offended, almost truculent assurance. And later when he ventured into the lion's den, it may in part, and perhaps only half consciously, have been with some idea in his mind of proving that he was no coward, as it had been more than hinted that he was. Moreover, presumably he was confirmed in his action by the fact that that other disciple was doing with safety what he too now proposed to do.

From this two lessons can be learned and stored in memory. First, if Christ has warned us—and he often speaks to us through our consciences—that we are in danger, it is folly not to be upon our guard and to walk warily, even though we ourselves see no sign of any special

17 Then saith the damsel that kept the door unto Peter, Art not thou also *one* of this man's disciples? He saith, I am not.

18 And the servants and officers stood there, who had made a fire of coals, for it was cold; and they warmed themselves: and Peter stood with them, and warmed himself.

17 The maid who kept the door said to
Peter, "Are not you also one of this man's
disciples?" He said, "I am not." 18 Now the
servants[i] and officers had made a charcoal fire, because it was cold, and they were standing and warming themselves; Peter also was with them, standing and warming himself.

[i] Or *slaves.*

17-18. Peter's first challenge came from **the maid who kept the door** as he was admitted into the court (αὐλή) where **the servants and officers . . . were standing and warming themselves.** The **officers** (ὑπηρέται), as in vss. 3, 12; 7:32, 45-46, are the temple police who were left in charge of the prisoner, now that the military detachment was seen to be no longer required.

risk. And second, the fact that others can do with impunity what Christ tells us is dangerous for us gives us no right to ignore his warning, and we do so at our peril. Others may move to and fro among the high priest's servants, others may practice this and that without harm to their souls. But if what they do strains our consciences or leaves a bad taste in our mouths or gives us an uneasy sense of being alienated from God, whatever it may be for them, to us it is sin.

Peter's ordeal leaped out upon him through a girl's sudden question, with an unexpectedness common enough in life. According to this evangelist, she was the maid at the door. In which case it may have been her duty to allow through only such people as were known, and to challenge all others. But according to Mark's account, she was drifting through the hall, idling among the men folk, when her eyes happened to fall on Peter; "You are one of them," she said. And even when he denied it, she was not satisfied, but came back and looked at him again. "But you *are* one of them," so she insisted, pointing him out to others. Maliciously, as it sounds to us now. But probably, being a servant of the house, she sided naturally enough with her masters, and so was against Christ and his following, regarding them as a dangerous lot because her masters, the constitutional authorities, who, she would feel, were bound to know, were taking rigorous action against them. Not without reason, she would say; and this man was one of them, and had better be watched.

It is easy to scoff at Peter and say jeeringly that he, so braggartly sure of his own loyalty to Christ, was scared into denying him by a chit of a girl. But that girl had only to call out to bring ugly possibilities crowding in on him. And she looked hostile. But perhaps hers was only the idle question of a pert and chattering woman, not meaning much by it, and really speaking only for speaking's sake. Joseph Butler, in his famous sermon, "Upon the Government of the Tongue," [2] warns us, and with truth, what incalculable harm and damage is constantly being caused, thoughtlessly and with no conscious malice in one's mind, by that itch for talking from which most of us suffer. The particular evil consequent on this, which he underlines, is that legitimate subjects of conversation being exhausted, people, in order to indulge their insatiable propensity for talking, have to betake themselves to the discussion of their neighbors and other folk in general, and to the giving of characters, often maliciously and with little or no knowledge. But a more fundamental danger even than that is "talkativeness," which, thinks Butler, is "an original disease in some minds, a disposition to be talking, with very little or no regard to, or thought of doing either good or harm. And let not any imagine this to be a slight matter, till he considers the bad effects that follow from it." Unhappy Peter's fall for one. "Study to be quiet, and to mind your own business," urges Paul to the Thessalonians, according at least to the old translation. And, whether that is an accurate version of what he said or not, it is a rule to be remembered carefully. If it were kept, how much mischief would be avoided. If that persistent maid had known and practiced it, Peter would not have denied his Lord.

But however it was occasioned, Peter's was not only a gross sin but a stupid one as well. Once he was noticed and watched, there was no possibility of concealing that he was a Northerner. His Galilean accent inevitably gave him away. And the Synoptists tell us that it did, as surely as his rolling r's proclaim a Scotsman, or his clipped Cockney speech a Londoner, or his nasal twang an American. We know that in the capital the Galileans were held to be uncouth

[2] *Works,* ed. W. E. Gladstone (Oxford: Clarendon Press, 1896), II, 77-91.

19 ¶ The high priest then asked Jesus of his disciples, and of his doctrine.

20 Jesus answered him, I spake openly to the world; I ever taught in the synagogue, and in the temple, whither the Jews always resort; and in secret have I said nothing.

21 Why askest thou me? ask them which heard me, what I have said unto them: behold, they know what I said.

19 The high priest then questioned Jesus
about his disciples and his teaching. 20 Je-
sus answered him, "I have spoken openly
to the world; I have always taught in syna-
gogues and in the temple, where all Jews
come together; I have said nothing secretly.
21 Why do you ask me? Ask those who
have heard me, what I said to them; they

19-21. In this preliminary inquiry Jesus is questioned **about his disciples and his teaching.** Annas tries to find out if Jesus has founded a sect whose heretical teaching will survive his death. No details are given. Jesus in reply appeals to the openness of his teaching—**openly** [cf. 7:4, 26] **to the world, . . . nothing secretly,** but both **in synagogues and in the temple, where all Jews come together,** thus covering the Galilean and the Judean ministry. As in 5:31 (see Exeg.), Jesus cites the principle (Tosephta Ketuboth 3:2, quoted by Schlatter, *Der Evangelist Johannes,* p. 153) that no one gives witness about himself.

---

and rustic in their speech because of their habit of slurring their gutturals and swallowing certain syllables. That in itself betrayed Peter as he mingled with the knot of cold men shivering around their charcoal fire that bitter night, and no doubt keeping himself well in the shadow and hoping to escape attention, warmed himself with the rest. Quite obviously this man beyond all question was a Galilean; and the fact that he had pushed in where he was betokened that he must have some special interest in the prisoner now being questioned.

So he was challenged, once and again. At first, so Thomas Hardy thinks, in a not unjovial fashion, by men half friendly, though boisterously incredulous of Peter's vehement denials.

"O come, come!" laughed the constables. "Why, man, you speak the dialect
He uses in his answers; you can hear him up the stairs.
So own it. We sha'n't hurt ye. There he's speaking now! His syllables
Are those you sound yourself when you are talking unawares,
As this pretty girl declares."

"And you shudder when his chain clinks!" she rejoined. "O, yes, I noticed it.
And you winced, too, when those cuffs they gave him echoed to us here." [8]

The thing was plain to all. Yet matters were not yet quite desperate.

But there was worse to come. For by and by a man in passing looked at Peter, paused, and peered closer, and asked, **Did I not see you in the garden with him?** Of all unfortunate encounters! For who was this but a kinsman of that Malchus, whom Peter had wounded in that brief scuffle in the darkness a few hours before! Here was no joviality, no friendliness, but hard eyes, and a heart out for revenge and punishment. And with that, Peter, sadly scared, lost the last remnants of his self-control and tried to bluster his way out of the trap closing upon him, with loud-voiced oaths and curses and passionate denials. "I tell you I know nothing about the fellow, nothing at all." Until suddenly the wretched man realized what he was doing, came to himself, and faced by the shame and horror of his conduct, his heart broke. According to this evangelist, it was a cock crowing in the new day that did it. Suddenly with that sound there flashed into his mind Christ's solemn warning which he had tossed aside. And yet it had come true! Unbelievably, it had come true! Openly, repeatedly, he had denied his Lord; he, Peter, had done that!

There is no pain known to man like the agony of remorse. "Fool that I was! How did I bring myself to do it! If only, oh, if only it were given back to me, that chance I threw away; that hour, that moment that I so mishandled, how differently would I live it now!" But down the ages the grim Greek saying holds inexorably true, that even the gods cannot undo what is once done. So this evangelist. But Luke adds a touch to the narrative so unbearably poignant that it is all but unendurable to read it. The rough fellows who were guarding Christ passed the time of waiting in baiting their prisoner.

[8] "In the Servants' Quarters," *Collected Poems* (London: Macmillan & Co.; New York: The Macmillan Co., 1940), p. 360. Used by permission of the Trustees of the Hardy Estate.

22 And when he had thus spoken, one of the officers which stood by struck Jesus with the palm of his hand, saying, Answerest thou the high priest so?
23 Jesus answered him, If I have spoken evil, bear witness of the evil: but if well, why smitest thou me?

know what I said."
22 When he had said this, one of the officers standing by struck Jesus with his hand, saying, "Is that how you answer the high priest?"
23 Jesus answered him, "If I have spoken wrongly, bear witness to the wrong; but if I have spoken rightly, why do you strike me?"

22-24. With our Lord's dignified rebuke of this highly irregular assault in a judicial inquiry contrast Paul's explosive retort on a similar occasion (Acts 23:3). Some critics have denied that such an outrage as this, or the worse acts of violence reported in the other Gospels, could have been committed before the Sanhedrin, as the strictest judicial procedure is laid down in the tractate about this court in the Mishnah. But along with the

They blindfolded him; they struck him on the face crying, "O great prophet of God, tell us which of us struck you!" There was much merriment and a roar of laughter. But perhaps when they were looking for a cloth to put about his eyes, and the noise had died down for the moment, there carried plainly to Christ's ears the voice of a man he loved, who was his best friend indeed, calling down vehement curses on himself if ever he had known the prisoner. So he kept shouting with a frenzied emphasis. And that caused Christ a stabbing wound, far sorer and far deeper than the ruffianly fools about him were able to deal him. "And the Lord turned and looked at Peter" (Luke 22:61).

May God forgive us for the pain we have all given to Jesus Christ! And may he help us to remember that so sorrowfully will he look at us from the judgment seat, if we too fail him and go out into the dark. Yet is not Elizabeth Barrett Browning right when she sees not infinite pity only but infinite hope in our Lord's look?

I think that look of Christ might seem to say—
"Thou Peter! art thou then a common stone
Which I at last must break My heart upon.
. . . .
The cock crows coldly.—Go, and manifest
A late contrition, but no bootless fear!
For when thy final need is dreariest,
Thou shalt not be denied, as I am here—
My voice to God and angels shall attest,
Because I KNOW this man, let him be clear."[4]

But of that whole moving incident the Fourth Evangelist says nothing.

22-23. ***What Is Christian Forgiveness?***—When the court official smote Jesus in the face (vs. 22), the man was guilty, according to our standards of justice, of an intolerable outrage. For no one in a civilized land is allowed so to mishandle a prisoner. Yet our Lord received the blow with an unruffled calmness and no shadow of loss of temper or of self-control (vs. 23). When Paul was subjected to a like outrage at the instance of the high priest, his vehement nature, even after years of strenuous self-discipline, blazed up in uncontrollable anger: "God shall strike you, you whitewashed wall! Are you sitting to judge me according to the law, and yet contrary to the law you order me to be struck?" (Acts 23:3.) But Christ said only, **If I have spoken wrongly, bear witness to the wrong; but if I have spoken rightly, why do you strike me?** It was a perfect living out of a whole side of his teaching on forgiveness—of one side of it; for there are two, and they are not easily reconciled or fitted together into one rounded whole. For they seem to clash noisily.

Upon the one side, nothing in his ethical teaching does he so emphasize and underline as the absolute necessity of a frank and free and unconditional forgiveness; and this, time on time, in the face of repeated injuries or insults; not waiting for the wrongdoer to confess his fault; but oneself, although the injured person, taking the first step toward reconciliation.

Widely different was the teaching and practice of the great classical moralists. No doubt thin-sown sayings with a real approximation to the Christian ethic in this matter can be found among them. Thus Seneca advises that if a man injures you, pay him back by doing him a kindness. For, he explains, it takes two to make a quarrel; and if one of them will not play, the thing will gutter out like a lamp when its oil is exhausted. But that was not the characteristic attitude. Rather, quite simply, to injure one's enemy was accounted a virtue, and as real and estimable a virtue as to help one's friends. Thus Plutarch, that attractive soul, describing an extraordinary instance of conversion whereby a notorious creature was transformed—everyone around him being witness—into an eminently pious and good man, puts down among the unanswerable proofs of

[4] "The Meaning of the Look."

24 Now Annas had sent him bound unto Caiaphas the high priest.
25 And Simon Peter stood and warmed himself. They said therefore unto him, Art not thou also *one* of his disciples? He denied *it,* and said, I am not.

24 Annas then sent him bound to Ca'iaphas the high priest.
25 Now Simon Peter was standing and warming himself. They said to him, "Are not you also one of his disciples?" He

---

argument of Herbert Danby ("The Bearing of the Rabbinical Criminal Code on the Jewish Trial Narratives in the Gospels," *Journal of Theological Studies,* XXI [1920], 51-76) that this second-century tract is an ideal reconstruction drawn up by rabbis at a time when the institution was no longer in existence, there are other considerations which make the story quite probable. Joseph Klausner (*Jesus of Nazareth,* tr. Herbert Danby [New York: The Macmillan Co., 1925], p. 337) quotes from a street ballad preserved in the Talmud, which was written about the Bethusian high priests (among them Annas of the Gospels), complaining of their "clubs" and "staves," their secret denouncements, their "fists," as well of the violence done by their servants. Those who remember Macaulay's description of Richard Baxter's treatment by Judge Jeffreys will not imagine that such things cannot happen even in a country which prides itself upon its judicial code. The meeting of the Sanhedrin in the house of Caiaphas is probably referred to in this verse (cf. Matt. 26:57), but its proceedings are not described unless we may assume that this verse belongs properly to a place immediately following vs. 13.

25-27. As the scene is still the same as in vs. 18, we must regard this narrative as a resumption of vss. 15-18; we have then a continuous narrative of Peter's conduct in one

---

this that all his neighbors were agreed that no one did more good to his friends or more ill to his enemies.

In Buddhism, indeed, lofty teaching is to be found, worthy even of being put alongside that of Christ; e.g., in the parable of the saw Buddha, using memorable and arresting illustrations, declares that one must test his keeping of the law about harboring no resentment, not when life runs smoothly for us, but when we are being unjustly, even villainously treated; and bluntly maintains that if a tyrant were to gouge out one's eyes, saw off one's limbs, tear out one's tongue, and one were not able to declare or make signs indicating that one still had no ill will toward him, one would not be a real Buddhist at all.

If that is theory, then here is fact. Hiuen-Tsiang, about to be massacred by bandits in The Himalaya, asked for a few moments ere the end, and spent them begging that he might not be granted his nirvana, but might be sent back to this earth, life after life, to work for these murderers of his and to lead them to the truth, till there was not one left among them still unsaved.[5]

Such splendors must not be forgotten or dimmed down. And yet nothing in Christ's ethical teaching has seemed to men so original as his insistence on forgiveness. If we are to be his at all, that is a *sine qua non,* so he assures us over and over in the plainest words. People

[5] Hwui Li, *Life of Hiuen-Tsiang,* pp. 86-88.

are wont to talk of "the unconditional freeness of the gospel." But in one real sense that is a mere empty phrase. "If you do not forgive men their trespasses, neither will your Father forgive your trespasses" (Matt. 6:15). There is a condition, bluntly stated. "Of him that hopes to be forgiven, it is indispensably required that he forgive. . . . On this great duty eternity is suspended; and to him that refuses to practice it, the throne of mercy is inaccessible and the SAVIOUR of the world has been born in vain." [6]

Yet on the other hand, while he laid such stress upon forgiveness under injury, Christ himself did not always forgive; e.g., he pursued the Pharisees with red-hot scathing denunciations that still blister and scald and burn. "You hypocrites," "you whited sepulchers," "you children of hell." And he would make no peace with them, nor cease to pursue them with his vehement denunciations. And in the temple he took violent action, crying out, "Stop making my Father's house a den of thieves, or I will throw you out of it"; and did it in a scene of wild disorder and confusion, with the traders clutching at their toppling tables or cowering to escape the whip, with their money rolling here and there, and the stampeding cattle plunging and lowing. He did not "forgive" them. He did not say, "They are mistaken; no doubt they mean well; and in any case one must be patient with them." He rose up in

[6] *Selections from Dr. Johnson's 'Rambler,'* ed. W. Hale White (Oxford: Clarendon Press, 1907), p. 112.

26 One of the servants of the high priest, being *his* kinsman whose ear Peter cut off, saith, Did not I see thee in the garden with him?

27 Peter then denied again; and immediately the cock crew.

denied it and said, "I am not." 26 One of the servants[i] of the high priest, a kinsman of the man whose ear Peter had cut off, asked, "Did I not see you in the garden with him?" 27 Peter again denied it; and at once the cock crowed.

[i] Or *slaves*.

court, viz., that of the house of Caiaphas. The second challenge came from the servants and temple police, the third from a kinsman of Malchus, who thought he recognized Peter as one of those with Jesus in the garden. If he had identified Peter as the assailant of his relative, Peter's position would have been one of dire peril. **At once the cock crowed** (cf. 13:38). The interesting suggestion has been made that this refers to the *gallicinium,* the signal given on the bugle when the change of guard took place in the Roman garrison at the end of the third watch of the night called the "cock crow," ἀλεκτοροφωνία (cf. Mark 13:36, where the word is followed by "morning" [πρωΐ]; so John 18:28). But it is unlikely that Pilate would be aroused so early as 3-6 A.M.

anger and he cast them out. What, then, of his law "until seventy times seven," his insistence on a dogged, illimitable forgiveness?

The way to truth for us is clear. It will not do to fasten on certain parts of our Lord's teaching and action that happen to appeal to us, ignoring the rest. It is the whole of Christ that is our standard; all that and nothing less than that. It is futile and dishonest to belaud his conduct when the court official struck him, or his cry from the Cross, "Father, forgive them; for they know not what they do"; to say, "Ah! That is the real Christ whom we must heed and follow"—while turning resolutely away, with eyes tightly closed, from the scathing message he sent to Herod, "Go and tell that fox," or from the violent cleansing of the temple: with the uncomfortable feeling that in such incidents our Lord unaccountably fell far below himself, broke his own laws, simply lost his temper, and to speak frankly, judging him by his own standards, made a fool of himself in a way that is incomprehensible. "It is unfortunate," we say, "but there it is. And we had better look the other way and forget these unhappy episodes."

That will not do! In every situation Christ did, and did to the full, what in such circumstances ought to have been done. He was as Christlike when he so hotly denounced the Pharisees or drove the money-changers from the temple as when he overlooked this angry official's blow and insult, or when he asked for forgiveness for his enemies, as he hung on his Cross, to which they had nailed him down.

What, then, are we to do? What in this matter does he claim from us and insist upon having? Taking Christ as our standard, the real Christ, and not a man-made caricature of him, the whole Christ as he stands before us in the Gospels, does it not come to this of it—that the usual working rule, required of us in practice and in the living of our daily life, when under provocation, is to be endlessly patient and forbearing and forgiving; but that there are occasions when, if we are to follow in his footsteps, it becomes us to be angry, with an anger that is a clean and wholesome and Christlike anger, and to refuse to make peace with the evildoer until he has desisted from the evil thing. There are times, said Hugh Mackintosh, when not to be angry "is a sign . . . of positive unlikeness to Jesus Christ." [7]

At which we ask confusedly enough, "But when are we to use the one side of Christ's teaching on forgiveness and when the other?" This is an instance of a characteristic of all his ethical teaching. He will not lay down rules for us. He gives us general principles which we must apply for ourselves in differing ways in differing circumstances. That irks us. What we wish is a railway timetable through life, with explicit instructions of what we have to do in every situation as it arises; a book of the words, furnished conveniently with an elaborate index which we turn up and find what is required of us, all explicitly set down. People who are keen on social amelioration turn up the index under social order and to their chagrin find in the Gospels very little about that at all. On which many cry out indignantly that Christ is hopelessly out of date; well enough doubtless for the simple type of life he knew, but of no value for us, set down in our complicated social system with its elaborate social problems and quandaries; not realizing that it is for us to take his general principles and apply them wisely to our own particular

[7] See the whole passage in *The Christian Experience of Forgiveness*, p. 162.

28 ¶ Then led they Jesus from Caiaphas unto the hall of judgment: and it was early; and they themselves went not into the judgment hall, lest they should be defiled; but that they might eat the passover.

29 Pilate then went out unto them, and said, What accusation bring ye against this man?

30 They answered and said unto him, If he were not a malefactor, we would not have delivered him up unto thee.

28 Then they led Jesus from the house
of Ca'ia-phas to the praetorium. It was
early. They themselves did not enter the
praetorium, so that they might not be de-
filed, but might eat the passover. 29 So
Pilate went out to them and said, "What
accusation do you bring against this man?"
30 They answered him, "If this man were
not an evil-doer, we would not have handed

C. Jesus Before Pilate (18:28–19:16)

This Gospel, so meager in its narrative of the trial before the Jewish authorities, compensates by giving an extended, if in parts an imaginative, description of Pilate's hearing of the case. The description is in six stages.

28-32. (*a*) Pilate is dissatisfied with the validity of the charge. **The praetorium:** Originally a praetor's quarters in a camp, is used of a provincial governor's official residence (cf. "Herod's praetorium" at Caesarea, Acts 23:35; i.e., the palace built by Herod the Great and now the procurator's residence). It is generally believed that the official residence during the feast was Herod's palace on Mount Zion (see, however, Intro.,

---

case. That is a risk indeed for bunglers, such as we are. Yet even Christ cannot spare us that responsibility.

So in this matter of forgiveness. The fact is that while on reading them, the great classical moralists seem to move in another universe from Jesus in this whole sphere of things, the more we study Christ, the clearer does it grow that these others are not far from the kingdom; and that their teaching approximates far more closely than at first it seems to do, to our Lord's own.

Thus Plato:

> The unrighteous and vicious are always to be pitied in any case; and one can afford to forgive as well as pity him who is curable, and refrain and calm one's anger, not getting into a passion like a woman, and nursing ill-feeling. But upon him who is incapable of reformation and wholly evil, the vials of our wrath should be poured out; wherefore I say that good men ought, when occasion demands, to be both gentle and passionate.[8]

And so Aristotle:

> He then who is angry on the right occasions and with the right persons, and also in the right manner, and at the right season, and for the right length of time, is praiseworthy. But it is not easy to define how, and with whom, and at what, and for how long one ought to be angry. . . . For it depends upon the particular circumstances of each case, and can only be decided by immediate perception.[9]

[8] *Laws* V. 731.

[9] *Nicomachean Ethics* IV. 5. 3, 13.

But blessed be God, we have the Holy Spirit, who in his lovingkindness, and if we will take his leading, will guide us in this matter also!

28-32. *How Men Can Lose Their Sense of Proportion.*—These verses are a striking instance of how strangely these curious minds of ours can work. Here are men set upon compassing the death of a fellow mortal, so determined on it that nothing but his immediate execution will satisfy them. Their hearts are ablaze with a roaring prairie fire of party spirit and rancor and undisguised hatred willing to go any length. Yet these same men are so scrupulous not to violate the ceremonial regulations, and so careful not to pollute themselves by entering the Gentile praetorium, that it is standing afar off, thronging the doors but not crossing the threshold, that they gesticulate and clamor and shout their bloodthirsty demands. And this with no sense of any incongruity in their conduct in their own minds. Which seems a monstrous thing! Yet do we not all take pains to walk with accuracy according to the recognized conventions and to abide by the accepted standards while blind to patent social evils crying out for redress? Can we not be keen and zealous about church attendance or early Communion and the like, yet be as raw in temper, and as blatantly selfish, and as wounding and unguarded with our tongues, as are the rest of folk? And we too seem to feel no uneasiness about it, which looks as if we had lost our way.

Paul prayed that his converts might be given

31 Then said Pilate unto them, Take ye
him, and judge him according to your law.
The Jews therefore said unto him, It is
not lawful for us to put any man to death:
32 That the saying of Jesus might be fulfilled, which he spake, signifying what
death he should die.
33 Then Pilate entered into the judgment hall again, and called Jesus, and said
unto him, Art thou the King of the Jews?

him over." 31 Pilate said to them, "Take
him yourselves and judge him by your own
law." The Jews said to him, "It is not
lawful for us to put any man to death."
32 This was to fulfill the word which Jesus
had spoken to show by what death he was
to die.
33 Pilate entered the praetorium again
and called Jesus, and said to him, "Are you

---

p. 448). The refusal of the Jewish leaders to **enter the praetorium, so that they might not be defiled, but might eat the passover,** is clear evidence that in the Johannine tradition the Last Supper took place the evening before the Passover. Pilate demands the charge brought against the prisoner (vs. 29). The Jews avoid a specific accusation, so Pilate directs them to try Jesus according to their own procedure (vss. 30-31). They reply that they have no power to carry out a death sentence. The one exception to this jealously guarded *jus gladii* was the Jewish right to kill any Gentile trespasser beyond the marble barrier of the inner courts of the temple (see G. A. Deissmann, *Light from the Ancient East,* tr. L. R. M. Strachan [new and revised ed.; New York: George H. Doran, 1927], pp. 79-81). On the "fulfillment" of a word of Jesus in vs. 32, cf. 12:32-33. The Jewish method of execution was by stoning, the Roman by crucifixion.

33-38*a*. (*b*) Pilate interrogates Jesus. Evidently the Jews had brought a vague accusation against Jesus as a messianic pretender. All the Gospels make it clear that his

---

"a sense of what is vital" (Phil. 1:10 Moffatt)! No gift is more to be desired than to be able to discern which things are primary and which only secondary; and to rank them in their due order in the living of our lives and in the working out of our faith. "These," said Christ, "are the things you ought to have done—and not to have left the others undone"; thereby dismissing matters which too often are accounted central and all-important, as the small dust of the balances—no more. Yet one fears that too many concern themselves in the main with little else than such lesser things.

33-38. *What Is Truth?*—Pilate's first interview with our Lord reveals him as a man puzzled by an unusual case, and even more by an unusual prisoner. Obviously he is not impressed by the accusations brought against Jesus, and is inclined to dismiss them as self-evidently baseless, as only one more of these endless squabbles forever boiling up among the hotheaded and impossible people whom he had been set to govern, squabbles that no civilized man could be expected to follow (vs. 35). But there was some talk about the prisoner having made some claim to sovereignty over his own people. It was, so Pilate felt, probably a lying accusation. For these Jews would say anything. But for safety's sake the thing had better be investigated. And so, telling his prisoner what was being said, "Are you a king?" he asked him. To which in effect Christ replied, "Not in the sense in which you use the word. But in a deeper sense, yes, I am. Only, my kingdom is a dominion not over people's bodies but over their minds and souls; and is maintained and extended not by violence and force of arms but by persuasion of the truth finding its way from heart to heart and winning for me willing subjects."

Whereat Pilate, satisfied that there was nothing in the charge, broke in, "Truth! Truth! But **what is truth?**" And turned away to tell the accusers that their charge failed, had broken down. Francis Bacon, with less than his customary shrewdness, thinks that Pilate was jesting when he put his question.[1] There is no evidence of that. There may have been the cynicism of a disillusioned man of the world, or the uncertainty of one who had seen life from many angles and heard many differing opinions on most subjects confidently held.

But is his not a right pertinent question? For **what is truth?** Are we not told that Charles Kingsley resigned his chair of history on the ground that there is no such thing as history, no dependable knowledge of past events as they actually happened, but only inaccurate accounts of them colored by prejudice and bias? Have we not, as life lengthens, read statements, and seen them unquestioningly accepted, of happenings in which we ourselves played a part, and which we knew from the inside, which ac-

[1] Essay, "Of Truth."

34 Jesus answered him, Sayest thou this thing of thyself, or did others tell it thee of me?

35 Pilate answered, Am I a Jew? Thine own nation and the chief priests have delivered thee unto me: what hast thou done?

36 Jesus answered, My kingdom is not of this world: if my kingdom were of this world, then would my servants fight, that I should not be delivered to the Jews: but now is my kingdom not from hence.

37 Pilate therefore said unto him, Art thou a king then? Jesus answered, Thou sayest that I am a king. To this end was I born, and for this cause came I into the

the King of the Jews?" 34 Jesus answered,
"Do you say this of your own accord, or
did others say it to you about me?" 35 Pilate
answered, "Am I a Jew? Your own nation
and the chief priests have handed you over
to me; what have you done?" 36 Jesus an-
swered, "My kingship is not of this world;
if my kingship were of this world, my
servants would fight, that I might not be
handed over to the Jews; but my kingship
is not from the world." 37 Pilate said to
him, "So you are a king?" Jesus answered,
"You say that I am a king. For this I was

---

enemies charged Jesus with what could be condemned as blasphemy before the ecclesiastical, and as high treason before the political, tribunal. Pilate asks Jesus if he claims to be **King of the Jews.** Jesus parries the question with another: Is Pilate speaking out of personal knowledge, or repeating a Jewish accusation? The Roman procurator replies with a sneer, **Am I a Jew?** The **chief priests,** representing the Jewish nation, have delivered Jesus up. What has Jesus done to provoke this? Jesus does not deny his **kingship,** but shows that it is not of earthly origin or political in character. Earthly kings have servants to fight for them. But the kingship of Jesus belongs to the realm of **truth.** Those who recognize the royal authority of **the truth** acknowledge him. To this Pilate can reply only with a shrug, **What is truth?** The **truth** of which the Johannine Jesus speaks is the true knowledge of God (cf. 1:14; 8:46-47), and it is his mission to

---

counts bore no resemblance to the facts which we ourselves saw, lived through, and showed no understanding of the motives of the actors in them? Is it not true, as Aristotle says, that as the years pass one becomes much less strident and assured in his opinions; that, as he puts it, whereas the young man says "I know," the old man is content with a more modest claim, "I think"? [2] For while in youth one lives in a flat world where things have only one side—that which we see—as time goes on, it is recognized that most things are puzzlingly many-sided; that there is almost no opinion but has some facts behind it; that at best and most, as even science now humbly admits, all human knowledge can be nothing better than empirical; that we with our limited equipment cannot know things as they really are—only God can do that. Had Pilate tarried, Christ might have answered him, "I am the truth." Which in all likelihood would have meant little or nothing to the haughty Roman. Yet it is strictly true. For if Browning's bold claim,

> I say, the acknowledgment of God in Christ
> Accepted by thy reason, solves for thee
> All questions in the earth and out of it,[3]

may be too generally stated—for indeed the Gospel raises a further question: if God is really love, then how? then why?—nonetheless, Christ is the only key to the mysteries of life. And it is he alone who, unlocking the doors, leads on to the solution.

It is a heartening study to watch Paul, as the years pass over him, wading his way from his first daring faith to certainty; finding all the enigmas that life raised for him answered in Jesus Christ; leaving behind such phrases as, "I think," and "I believe," and contrary to Aristotle, attaining to an assured "I know"; walking at last not by pure faith at all but by experience, almost indeed by sight. If sin besets him, "I know whom I have believed, and am persuaded that he is able to keep that which I have committed unto him against that day" (II Tim. 1:12). If trouble presses in on him, "We know that all things work together for good to them that love God" (Rom. 8:28). If death draws near, "We know that if the earthly tent we live in is destroyed, we have a building from God, a house not made with hands, eternal in the heavens" (II Cor. 5:1). So all problems are solved in Jesus Christ. "I am the truth," he said. And multitudes have found that it is so.

[2] *Rhetoric* II. 13.

[3] "A Death in the Desert."

world, that I should bear witness unto the truth. Every one that is of the truth heareth my voice.

38 Pilate saith unto him, What is truth? And when he had said this, he went out again unto the Jews, and saith unto them, I find in him no fault *at all.*

39 But ye have a custom, that I should release unto you one at the passover: will ye therefore that I release unto you the King of the Jews?

40 Then cried they all again, saying, Not this man, but Barabbas. Now Barabbas was a robber.

born, and for this I have come into the world, to bear witness to the truth. Every one who is of the truth hears my voice."
38 Pilate said to him, "What is truth?"
After he had said this, he went out to the Jews again, and told them, "I find no crime in him. 39 But you have a custom that I should release one man for you at the Passover; will you have me release for you the King of the Jews?" 40 They cried out again, "Not this man, but Bar-ab'bas!" Now Bar-ab'bas was a robber.

---

bear witness to this (3:32). Affinity with the truth is a mark of membership of Christ's kingdom (cf. 3:21; 8:47; 10:26-28).

38*b*-40. (*c*) Pilate attempts to evade judgment by appealing to the custom (not attested outside the Gospels) of releasing a prisoner at the Passover (cf. Mark 15:6-11; Matt. 27:15-21; Luke 23:18-19). He tells the Jews that he can **find no crime** in the prisoner, but he infuriates them by calling him **the King of the Jews.** John and Luke tell this episode more tersely than Mark and Matthew. In the dramatic climax, **Now Barabbas was a robber,** readers can recognize the irony which runs through the Johannine narrative of the Passion and Crucifixion.

39-40. ***Christ and Barabbas.***—It seems clear that when he remembered the annual custom of releasing a prisoner at the time of the feast, Pilate had never a doubt that Jesus would be liberated, since only the other day there had been such wild enthusiasm all along the streets for this Galilean. And he was patently taken aback by the result of what he had thought to be his adroit move. Yet it was not so wonderful that the vote went as it did. **Barrabbas was a robber,** says the Fourth Gospel bluntly. But Luke lets us see that the man was likely to appeal to the crowd. He was a patriot after his lights, indomitable and uncowed, who chafing against the Roman yoke had been captured with blood on his hands in a futile splutter of insurrection such as was constantly flaming up, like a bonfire seemingly out but blown back into life again by every passing puff of breeze.

And in our own times are not the mass of people making the same choice? **Not this man,** they keep crying, **but Barabbas;** pinning their faith and hopes to something economic and political; turning impatiently away from Christ's insistence upon spiritual things; openly incredulous of his belief that a mere change of environment is not enough, that man too must be changed.

One wonders what happened to Barabbas. Did he on his release go home forthwith, uninterested in that other whose death had brought about his own salvation, sparing never a thought for him, as so many do? Or did he stand among the rest on Calvary, looking up at the man hanging where but for him he himself would have hung, and dying there literally in his place? And how did he react to it? Did he drift back again to the old wild life? Or did Christ's death for him sober and change him? However that may be, how many have stood on Calvary awestruck, arrested, feeling of Jesus what Barabbas surely must have felt,

> Bearing shame and scoffing rude,
> In my place condemned he stood;
> Sealed my pardon with his blood.[4]

For in his remarkable experience there is something closely akin to what many Christians feel they owe to Jesus Christ. With reason and truth scholars keep pointing out that when the Scriptures tell us that Christ died for us, the preposition used is ὑπέρ, "on behalf of," and not ἀντί, "in the place of." For Barabbas at least there was no such distinction. And it is never clean cut. Ὑπέρ keeps merging into ἀντί, do what you will.

The men who faced the hardships of the front, and in especial those who laid down their lives there, did it for us, on our behalf. That certainly. That undeniably. But many feel that even that is an inadequate account of what they did and what we owe them; that ὑπέρ

[4] Philip P. Bliss, "Man of Sorrows."

19 Then Pilate therefore took Jesus, and scourged *him.*
2 And the soldiers platted a crown of thorns, and put *it* on his head, and they put on him a purple robe,

19 Then Pilate took Jesus and scourged him. 2 And the soldiers plaited a crown of thorns, and put it on his head,

---

19:1-7. (*d*) Foiled in his attempt, Pilate now tries to work on the pity of the Jews. He has Jesus **scourged,** and when the soldiers have tricked him out in the mock regalia of the **King of the Jews,** he leads him out in the torture of his humiliation as an object of pitiable contempt. The exclamation **Behold the man!** was probably a rough jest, meaning, "That poor fellow is the dangerous rebel you bring to me for judgment!" But the Johannine irony may well have suggested to the readers a deeper meaning, "This is indeed the Word become flesh!" The Jews had no pity. Their leaders shouted the more,

---

flows into ἀντί; that they bore and died not merely upon our behalf but literally in our stead; that because they endured, we were not called on to endure the horrors that befell the peoples who were overrun and beaten down, and that because they suffered and died, we escaped the sufferings and death which but for them would to a certainty have overwhelmed us. So many feel with a humble and ashamed gratitude as they stand beside the Cross. Their mood is what Barabbas' mood ought at least to have been. As James Denney puts it,

> The conception of [Christ's death] as in some sense substitutionary, [covers] the truth that there is something from which Christ's death saves the sinner. It does not save him unconditionally, or apart from any relation he assumes to it. . . . But it does save the sinner from something. There is something from which he is exempted—the due conditions being fulfilled—by the death of Jesus. In other words, Jesus died *for* him, in an irreducible sense of the words; He died for him in a sense and with a potential result which can never be ascribed to any action or experience of his own or of others, but only and for ever to the death of Jesus itself. If the question is put, What, then, is it which we are spared or saved from by the death of Jesus—what is it that we do not experience because He died?—the answer is that He saves us from dying in our sins. But for His death, we should have died in our sins; we should have passed into the blackness of darkness with the condemnation of God abiding on us. It is because He died for us, and for no other reason, that the darkness has passed away, and a light shines in which we have peace with God and rejoice in hope of His glory.[5]

In trying to think out what the Cross means for us it is wise to keep our eyes upon Barabbas.

19:1. ***The Scourging.***—Nothing in history or in literature has made such an indelible impression even on our heedless world as the passion of Jesus Christ. Once read, it can never be forgotten. The effect produced upon the mind is increased immeasurably by the reticence and iron restraint with which it is recorded. Even as it stands it is a dreadful tale of horror heaped on horror throughout its long-drawn agony. And there is hardly one redeeming feature to palliate the shame with which it has disgraced humanity, except the majesty of bearing of the suffering Savior under the insults and ruthless brutalities through which he had to pass.

In vs. 1, set down almost in the bygoing as a mere incident far surpassed by other things to follow, we read, **Then Pilate took Jesus and scourged him.** Just that, no more. Yet a scourging with the terrible iron-tipped and iron-weighted Roman lash was a fearsome ordeal, tearing the lacerated flesh to ribbons and often causing death. But of that not a word.

And we had better imitate the reverent reticence of Scripture. Enough perhaps to say that stout old Samuel Johnson could never hear or read the noble Latin hymn without breaking down when he came to the words, "It was seeking me that Thou didst sit wearied; and for me that Thou didst bear the cruel pains of crucifixion. Grant that such labor may not be all thrown away." "With a great sum bought I my freedom," so the tribune said to Paul. But our salvation cost far more. And it was Jesus Christ who paid it.

2-3. ***The Mocking of Christ.***—Sick and dizzy with pain as he must have been, our Lord found no touch of sympathy among his guards. Rough soldier men, made callous and brutalized by knocking about the world from garrison to garrison and camp to camp, they saw nothing unmanly or unseemly in taunting and jeering at a helpless prisoner. It was a merry jest. It whiled away the time. Until one lively humorist thought out a vastly better joke which won instant approval and was duly carried out amid delighted roars of laughter. They had all heard, of course, of the charge that Jesus had claimed

[5] *The Christian Doctrine of Reconciliation* (London and New York: Hodder & Stoughton, 1917), pp. 282-83. Used by permission.

3 And said, Hail, King of the Jews! and they smote him with their hands.

4 Pilate therefore went forth again, and saith unto them, Behold, I bring him forth to you, that ye may know that I find no fault in him.

5 Then came Jesus forth, wearing the crown of thorns, and the purple robe. And *Pilate* saith unto them, Behold the man!

6 When the chief priests therefore and officers saw him, they cried out, saying, Crucify *him,* crucify *him.* Pilate saith unto them, Take ye him, and crucify *him:* for I find no fault in him.

7 The Jews answered him, We have a law, and by our law he ought to die, because he made himself the Son of God.

and arrayed him in a purple robe; 3 they
came up to him, saying, "Hail, King of the
Jews!" and struck him with their hands.
4 Pilate went out again, and said to them,
"Behold, I am bringing him out to you,
that you may know that I find no crime in
him." 5 So Jesus came out, wearing the
crown of thorns and the purple robe. Pilate
said to them, "Here is the man!" 6 When
the chief priests and the officers saw him,
they cried out, "Crucify him, crucify him!"
Pilate said to them, "Take him yourselves
and crucify him, for I find no crime in
him." 7 The Jews answered him, "We have
a law, and by that law he ought to die,
because he has made himself the Son of

Crucify him! Pilate lashed them to fury by saying the third time (cf. vss. 4, 6; 18:38) that as he can **find no crime** they had better crucify him themselves, thus reminding them of their political impotence. Then they blurt out the real reason for their insistence. Their charge is not political but religious. **He has made himself the Son of God** (cf. 5:18; 10:33, 36).

---

to be king of the Jews; and this wit's fancy saw in that a golden chance of endless merrymaking. They decked Christ in a faded tunic which might pass for the royal purple. They wove some thorns into a crown and forced it down upon his brow. They cried, "The King! The King! Down on your knees, man! Don't you see him?" They made mock obeisance. And then, their mood changing, they struck him over and over, as each man willed. It was immensely funny, so they felt. Their humorist had fairly surpassed himself. And no doubt far down the years, when in a jovial mood and in congenial company, they would cap other men's tales and bring down the house by telling, "As fine a jest as ever I saw. Once in Jerusalem . . ."—and out again it would come.

And yet humanity, watching that blackguardly scene, does not join in the laughter, and never has so done; but falls silent and stands awed and very still; and then gets to its knees in very deed, owning allegiance to One worthy of sovereignty. "Here is the man!" said Pilate, bringing him out, still wearing the emblems of his bogus royalty. And if the priests and their followers, when they saw him, burst into shouts of "Crucify him! Crucify him!" multitudes the whole world over have murmured with awe-struck conviction, "My Lord and my God!"

How would that witty humorist look now if he could come back on earth and hear masses in every nation and people and kindred and tongue acclaiming Jesus Christ as sovereign over all? And listen, how blown back to us from the other world there comes that shout from multitudes no man can number, acclaiming King of kings and Lord of lords that same Jesus whom these fools once mocked, thinking his claim ridiculous.

4-16. *Pilate and His Dilemma.*—"Suffered under Pontius Pilate," so run the familiar words of the Creed. To the end of time the unhappy man will fill that unenviable niche in history. Yet there are those who hold that Pilate did, if not well, at least the best that was possible for him in the terrible dilemma in which he found himself. And his advocates have this evidence behind them—that while Jesus Christ had open scorn for Herod—"Go and tell that fox"—and scathing denunciations for the Pharisees in plenty, for Pilate he shows only pity, as for some lordly creature, trapped, uncomprehending, plunging wildly to and fro, but doomed. Everyone must feel how, as the narrative proceeds, the roles of judge and prisoner are reversed; and that it is really Pilate who is being tried. While Christ—so absorbed in it that he seems to forget his own desperate situation—watches with compassion and pain in his eyes a soul, not without worthy instincts, losing its footing like some climber on a dangerous ridge, clutching wildly at anything and everything within his reach, only to find them give beneath his hand; and with that he has slipped, is being carried down and down,

8 ¶ When Pilate therefore heard that saying, he was the more afraid;

9 And went again into the judgment hall, and saith unto Jesus, Whence art thou? But Jesus gave him no answer.

10 Then saith Pilate unto him, Speakest thou not unto me? knowest thou not that I have power to crucify thee, and have power to release thee?

11 Jesus answered, Thou couldest have no power *at all* against me, except it were given thee from above: therefore he that delivered me unto thee hath the greater sin.

12 And from thenceforth Pilate sought to release him: but the Jews cried out, saying, If thou let this man go, thou art not Caesar's friend: whosoever maketh himself a king speaketh against Caesar.

God." 8 When Pilate heard these words,
he was the more afraid; 9 he entered the
praetorium again and said to Jesus, "Where
are you from?" But Jesus gave no answer.
10 Pilate therefore said to him, "You will
not speak to me? Do you not know that
I have power to release you, and power to
crucify you?" 11 Jesus answered him, "You
would have no power over me unless it had
been given you from above; therefore he
who delivered me to you has the greater
sin."

12 Upon this Pilate sought to release
him, but the Jews cried out, "If you release
this man, you are not Caesar's friend; every
one who makes himself a king sets himself

8-12. (*e*) Pilate returns to the praetorium, disturbed by superstitious uncertainty, and asks the prisoner **Where are you from?** Whether exhausted by his brutal treatment, or disdainful of a question from such a worldling, Jesus kept silent. Pilate with offended dignity asked him if he did not know that he had power of life and death over him. This aroused Jesus to remind him that his power was only delegated authority, entrusted to him by high heaven, for which he was therefore answerable to the righteous God. Since this was so, Caiaphas and the Jews, in handing Jesus over to Pilate, were degrading the powers that be, ordained of God (cf. Rom. 13:1-2), into an instrument of malice and injustice, and were adding to the tale of their sins.

---

till there comes the last sickening fall to certain death.

Christ has no word of blame for Pilate. Nor have the evangelists, who set down the facts with a terrible simplicity and without comment, leaving them to speak for themselves. True, the naked austerity of their record is to most minds appallingly damning. But there are no denunciations, no vehement and angry criticisms, such as one would have expected, and such as we actually have in the bitter Jewish accounts of Pilate in Philo and Josephus. It is almost as if the authors of the four Gospels half sympathized with this unhappy fellow man caught in a cruel dilemma so terribly real and almost impossible to handle wisely.

Pilate gives the impression that by nature he was a just man. He is at once convinced that there is no substance in the charges leveled against Jesus. And the increasing fury with which they are urged makes him only the surer of it. Quite evidently his instinct and intention was to dismiss the accusations and let Christ go. But he was in a difficulty. There had been trouble before in this restless city in his time. On more than one occasion Pilate had already aroused the Jews to an almost unbelievable passion of patriotic and religious fury and determination before which he had had to bow—once on the direct orders of Tiberius himself, to whom the Jews had successfully complained. There was no love lost between the procurator and his touchy and impossible people. Blood had been spilled at Pilate's orders in the outer courts of the temple itself—some new orgy of national feeling having broken out during a religious feast which he had ruthlessly suppressed. And Philo tells us that there was always tension in the air. For Pilate knew that these Jews were ready upon any or no provocation to take their grievances, real or alleged, to the emperor; and any further trouble there spelled doom for him. Tiberius was quite capable of siding with the Jews again and publicly humiliating him. Things, he felt, were uncomfortably near the edge. Hence the first fixed rule he had to keep in mind was at all costs to avoid violence against this impossible people and to refrain from exasperating them, never an easy matter when dealing with that proverbially excitable race. And by ill fortune at the worst possible moment in the whole year, when

13 ¶ When Pilate therefore heard that saying, he brought Jesus forth, and sat down in the judgment seat in a place that is called the Pavement, but in the Hebrew, Gabbatha.

against Caesar." 13 When Pilate heard these words, he brought Jesus out and sat down on the judgment seat at a place called The Pavement, and in Hebrew, Gab'ba-tha.

13-16. (*f*) Stung with a momentary pang of shame, Pilate made one last attempt to release Jesus. But the Jews threatened him with a charge of indulgence to Caesar's rivals. To condone high treason was a capital offense on the part of a Roman governor. These shouts sent him back to the judgment seat, placed on an elevated dais of tessellated pavement. (On τὸ λιθόστρωτον and its Aramaic original *Gabbāthā'* see Intro., p. 448.) The Greek verb ἐκάθισεν can be either transitive or intransitive. The apocryphal Gospel of Peter, as also Justin Martyr (*First Apology* 35), interpreted it as transitive, suggesting that Pilate made Jesus sit in mock majesty on the procurator's throne. But it is unlikely that a proud Roman official would debase the symbol of authority by such buffoonery. He resumed his judicial pose and said for the last time, **Here is your King!** To the renewed shrieks of **Crucify him!** he retorted, **Shall I crucify your King?** The chief priests answered in words that abandoned both their boast of freedom and their messianic hope with the fateful cry, **We have no king but Caesar.** Pilate's last feeble resistance was at an end. He capitulated to the priest-ridden mob of Jerusalem. This is the gospel of the rejection.

The chronological discrepancy between John and Mark is notorious. Mark 15:25 gives 9 A.M. as the hour of the Crucifixion, with darkness overshadowing the earth from noon till 3 P.M. Most attempts to reconcile the two statements are unsatisfactory. A useful discussion may be found in Sir William Ramsay's article "Numbers, Hours, and Years" in *A Dictionary of the Bible,* ed. James Hastings (New York: Charles Scribner's Sons, 1904), Extra Vol., pp. 477-79. John says that about noon on Friday in the final week

---

from all over the then-known world, Jewry had flocked back to Jerusalem for the feast that meant so much to them—perhaps a million of them, crowded somehow into the packed city and camped around it wherever a tent could be pitched—with their national spirit, always too intense, always inflammable, fanned by the mood and excitement of the hour to danger point, so that year after year during the feast the religious authorities had the right at need to call upon the cohort—i.e., six hundred soldiers—quartered in the castle Antonia to help them to put down such riots and disorders as were only too likely to burst out; at such an inauspicious moment there had cropped up this unfortunate business, Jew against Jew, with the ecclesiastical authorities hot on the scent of one they had determined to hunt down, one who only a few hours ago had been hailed with acclamation by enthusiastic crowds lining the streets. Here palpably were all the elements of further trouble and more tragedy. Where indeed was there even a loophole of escape? Did he let the man off, there would be a passionate outcry from those in high places, which might work their followers and adherents into a frenzy and incipient rebellion. While did he condemn the prisoner, what of those cheering multitudes who had thronged the roads? They too might lose their heads. Either course seemed to lead to further killings in an excited city. And with the eyes of Tiberius already turned on him, that must not be. Naturally a proud man, used to giving bluff orders, he must on this occasion be adroit, and find some compromise which might, if not satisfy all parties, at least keep them quiet. That was the problem by which he was confronted. And there are those who hold that face to face with it, he did all that he could have done and should have done; and that there is no blot upon his record.

Those who adopt the full-blown pacifist position seem almost compelled to hold that Pilate was justified in what he did. For if peace is the first essential, if above everything else we must see to it that there is no violence or bloodshed, if no cost is too great that ensures that, if Belsen and Dachau and the other infernal camps with their unthinkable brutalities to multitudes are indeed frightful facts which sicken one, but facts which must continue for multitudes more rather than that we should take arms and bomb the accursed system that maintained them out of being; if peace must be kept even at the price of the continuance of such atrocious bestialities—then where is ground left to us from which we can condemn

14 And it was the preparation of the passover, and about the sixth hour: and he saith unto the Jews, Behold your King!

14 Now it was the day of Preparation for the Passover; it was about the sixth hour. He said to the Jews, "Here is your King!"

Jesus was delivered up for crucifixion. It was usual for the condemned felon to be scourged as the preliminary to crucifixion, and so Mark 15:15 (followed by Matt. 27:26) records the scourging as part of the death sentence. John and Luke (23:22) report it as an earlier attempt to placate the Jews.

It is clear that the evangelist assumes that his readers know the general tradition about the various stages of the trial from the arrest until the death sentence was finally pronounced. Thus nothing is said about the formulation of a charge before the high priest, or the examination of witnesses. If we take the text as it stands, a preliminary inquiry before Annas is an attempt to secure from Jesus some compromising claim that could be used in the formal investigation by the Sanhedrin. There is no mention of the Sanhedrin, and not a word is said about what happened in the trial before the high priest. If we follow the order of verses in the Sinaitic Syriac palimpsest of the Gospels, the impression is equally vague. Jesus is brought to Annas, who sends him at once to Caiaphas, and after an unsuccessful attempt to get Jesus to compromise himself, Caiaphas sends the prisoner to Pilate. Pilate immediately asks for the terms of the indictment, but the accusers of Jesus have no charge to bring forward—merely a vague assertion that he is an evildoer. On being told to settle the matter in their own court, they reply that they have no authority to carry out a death sentence. As Pilate then conducts a private examination within the residence, and asks Jesus whether he was really the King of the Jews, we must infer that the evangelist presupposes a knowledge of the intermediate process, which is so fully told in the tradition followed in the earlier

---

Pilate with any confidence? As Sir James Fitzjames Stephen maintained, in his wholehearted defense of him,

> Was Pilate right in crucifying Christ? I reply, Pilate's paramount duty was to preserve the peace in Palestine, to form the best judgment he could as to the means required for that purpose, and to act upon it when it was formed. Therefore if and in so far as he believed in good faith and on reasonable grounds that what he did was necessary for the preservation of the peace of Palestine, he was right.[6]

In any case, that was his problem, as it seems. The pity is he was not big enough to meet it. He began well. Philo tells us that Pilate was "by nature stubborn and obstinate." And at the start and for a long time he threw, not his sense of justice only, but his stubbornness and obstinacy on the side of Christ. "These people are determined to force me into condemning an innocent man to death. I will not do it. I will take no compulsion at their hands." So he thought doggedly. And he kept seeking means, trying now this way and now that, to liberate our Lord.

Asking of what they accused the prisoner, he is met with the insolent answer, "If this man were not an evil-doer, we would not have handed him over" (18:30), and he replies, glad to be rid of the case, "You know your rights in the matter as well as I do. Take him yourselves and judge him by your own law, as you are well aware you are entitled to do." "But you know," they countered, "that we are not allowed to try a case that involves a capital charge, that we cannot condemn to death; and that is what we demand in this instance; and so have brought the man to you" (18:31). So that door of escape was closed. As later was that other, when he tried to pass the dangerous problem on to Herod and was foiled by that gratified but astute monarch (Luke 23:6-12). Things, so Pilate felt, were certainly ominous. There was a thundery feeling in the air; there were whitecaps upon the waves, and darkened patches on the waters, which at any moment might lash themselves into fury and a fearsome storm. Luke tells us that the accusers alleged, "We found this man perverting our nation, and forbidding us to give tribute to Caesar, and saying that he himself is Christ a king" (Luke 23:2). It was a serious and telling charge, none more so under Roman law. So Pilate interviewed our Lord upon that matter too, quickly saw that there was nothing material in the accusation, and announced bluntly, "I did not find this man guilty of any of your charges" (Luke 23:14).

So far so good. And with that surely he ought to have released his prisoner. But it was there

[6] *Liberty, Equality, Fraternity* (New York: Henry Holt & Co., 1882), p. 87.

15 But they cried out, Away with *him*, away with *him*, crucify him. Pilate saith unto them, Shall I crucify your King? The chief priests answered, We have no king but Caesar.

15 They cried out, "Away with him, away with him, crucify him!" Pilate said to them, "Shall I crucify your King?" The chief priests answered, "We have no king but

---

Gospels. Just as 18:11 is an allusion to the agony in Gethsemane (not recorded by John), so 18:33, 39 assume a knowledge of the charges brought against Jesus. Earlier narratives in the Gospel show the hostility of the religious authorities because Jesus claimed to be "Son of man" (8:28; 9:35), "the Christ" (10:24), "the Son of God" (10:36). Another sign of compression can be detected in the word "again" in 18:39-40, "They cried out again, 'Not this man but Barabbas!'" Yet this is the first mention of the offer to release Jesus in accordance with their custom. It is noticeable again that John does not report the release of Barabbas, which in the Synoptic story is closely associated with the death sentence to Jesus, but he continues the narrative of the trial.

Maurice Goguel (*Les Sources du Récit Johannique de la Passion* [La Roche-sur-Yon: Imprimerie Centrale de l'Ouest, 1910], p. 84) has pointed out an interesting contrast between the Synoptic and the Johannine emphasis in the two trial scenes. In the Synoptics Jesus replies to the high priest and is condemned by the Sanhedrin. When he comes before Pilate for the confirmation of the Jewish sentence he keeps silence, as the sentence is already determined. In John, on the contrary, Jesus refuses to plead before the high priest, knowing that the blind hatred of his enemies has settled his doom beforehand. But before Pilate, who is open to reason, he speaks at length. Indeed, Pilate makes no secret of his conviction that Jesus is innocent of any political offense, though he surrenders at last to the pressure of the Jewish leaders and their crowd, who are

---

he made his fatal error. Things had grown dangerous, and he felt that he must be wary. He knew those accursed Jews, had had experience of their wild fanaticisms and maniacal hatreds, loathed and despised them. "Am I a Jew?" he had asked Christ indignantly. "What interest have I in the eternal squabbles of your impossible people?" Yet there was too much tenseness and bitter anger among them for him to goad them much further. Their self-control, already frayed, might snap, and then, what then? He had better make some compromise with them. And with that there came into his mind what the man took to be a heaven-sent inspiration (18:39-40). Thankfully he remembered the annual custom of releasing a prisoner at the feast. That was the very thing to meet the situation. There was no doubt in Pilate's mind who would be liberated. Only a few hours ago Jesus had had a long ovation in the crowded streets. "He will be chosen. The high priestly party can attach no blame to me. Christ will be freed, as I am determined he must be; and the peace will be kept." Adroit, and, it seemed, reasonable, and certain to succeed. And Pilate was quite plainly taken aback by that unexpected shout of voices for Barabbas. So that plan also had gone wrong.

Well, he would have unwillingly to concede something. Still, this man must not die. He was determined about that and would see to it that he did not die. So he ordered that Jesus should be scourged (vs. 1), a fearsome ordeal, under which men often died; but better, at any rate, than certain death, thought Pilate, still struggling to save Jesus' life. And indeed it seems to have been inflicted not seldom on prisoners who were then released, apparently on the principle that though they were not guilty of this particular offense, they would be all the better for a sharp lesson. Nor was Pilate angered on discovering how the soldiery had been maltreating and mocking their prisoner. That, he conceived, played exactly into his hands. And so he had our Lord, still wearing the ridiculous trappings of his sham royalty, led out before the crowd. According to the KJV, **Behold the man** he said. And down the ages men have gazed at him with an awe and sudden stillness in their minds, immeasurably shaken and impressed. But as the newer renderings make clear, the words were in reality contemptuous. "Here is the fellow! You cannot seriously think that such a figure as this is really claiming to be your king!"

It was an appeal addressed to their compassion, to their national pride, almost to their sense of humor. But the Jews have little humor; and that gathering had no touch of compassion. And so there came that roar of **Crucify him!** Another failure! And by this time the Jews had seen that for all his bold front Pilate was

16 Then delivered he him therefore
unto them *to be* crucified. And they took
Jesus, and led *him* away.

Caesar." 16 Then he handed him over to
them to be crucified.

animated by hatred. In the earlier Gospels there may be an undertone of apologetic, to show that Christianity was not born of high treason against the Roman imperium. In John the emphasis is rather upon the obdurate refusal of "the Jews" to acknowledge the divine mission of Jesus, and their hatred in hounding him to his death.

John's dramatic close in the story of the trial (vs. 16) has caught the attention of most of the commentators. **Then he handed him over to them to be crucified.** This is often taken to mean that the Jews were given the responsibility for carrying out the execution. It must be noted that Mark and Matthew simply record, "And having scourged Jesus, he delivered him to be crucified," though an important group of authorities insert "to them" in Matthew, and a small group insert these words in Mark. Luke, however, writes, "But Jesus he delivered up to their will." This means that Pilate in yielding to the pressure of the Jewish leaders made them morally responsible for the Crucifixion, as but for them he would have released Jesus. It no more suggests that the Jews literally executed Jesus than Peter's attack on the Jews does in Acts 3:14-15, "But you denied the Holy and Righteous One, and asked for a murderer to be granted to you, and killed the Author of life." The apocryphal Gospel of Peter took the expression literally, and offers a highly developed picture of the actions of the Jews: "And he delivered him to the people on the day before the unleavened bread, that is their feast. And they took the Lord and pushed him as they ran, and said: 'Let us hale the Son of God, now that we have gained authority over him.' And they put on him a purple robe, and made him sit on the throne of judgment, saying: 'Give righteous judgment, thou King of Israel.' And one of them brought a crown of thorns and set it on the Lord's head; and others stood and spat in his eyes, and others buffeted his cheeks; and others pricked him with a reed, and some of them scourged him, saying: 'With this honor let

afraid of them; that they had only to exert more pressure upon him and he would give. Still, even yet he was not beaten. Well knowing that they could not do it, nettled and baited, he exclaimed angrily, "If this is to be done, then it must be by your act, and not mine. I find no charge that lies and holds against the prisoner, none at all" (vs. 6). Whereat, falling back on their own verdict against Christ in the court of Caiaphas, they urged, **We have a law, and by that law he ought to die, because he has made himself the Son of God.**

Startled and frightened, Pilate then sought to interrogate his prisoner yet again. But this time Christ remained silent. It was evident to him that this unhappy weakling had slipped down so far that he could not right himself, was doomed. Even he who can save to the uttermost felt that he could do nothing further for this miserable soul caught in the toils. He would not turn back now.

And even yet Pilate, stubbornly, obstinately, hating to be mastered, fought on and made one further effort. Whereupon the priestly party played their last decisive card. **If you release this man, you are not Caesar's friend; every one who makes himself a king sets himself against Caesar** (vs. 12). Every governor and official throughout the empire dreaded that accusation and was haunted by it as by a perpetual and fearful nightmare. Whenever the people of a province wanted to be rid of their ruler, they trumped up this charge among the rest, well knowing that whatever else failed, this was almost certain to succeed.[7] For Tiberius was moody, jealous, suspicious, ferocious. And, indeed, in the end of the day Pilate himself was recalled and disgraced. Hence what occurred to him, faced by their threat, was that if these abominable people could say in Rome that they in their loyal zeal had brought before him an impostor impudently claiming to be their king —they who had no king but Caesar—and that in spite of their appeals, in spite of their indignant rejection of the insolent claimant, he had insisted on turning the fellow loose, there could be but one outcome. And so at last, and in the end, to save himself from a trumped-up charge, sullenly he let the accusers have their way and passed the dreadful sentence on one whom he knew was innocent, *Ibis ad crucem:* "You will go to the cross."

Anatole France has a strange story that long

[7] Tacitus *Annals* III. 36-38.

17 And he bearing his cross went forth into a place called *the place* of a skull, which is called in the Hebrew Golgotha:

17 So they took Jesus, and he went out, bearing his own cross, to the place called the place of a skull, which is called in

us honor the son of God.' And they brought two malefactors, and crucified the Lord between them." Here we see the length to which a later writer could go in trying to transfer to the Jews completely all that is attributed in the canonical Gospels to the Roman procurator and soldiers. Indeed, in the Gospel of Peter it is Herod rather than Pilate who is said to have delivered Jesus to "the people." The soldiers are called in only to guard the tomb.

In the Johannine story the construction is certainly confused, but the subject of the verb translated "they took" (vs. 17) and of the verb translated "they crucified" (vs. 18) is made perfectly clear in vs. 23. It was the soldiers who crucified Jesus.

D. The Crucifixion and Burial (19:17-42)

17-24. Jesus went out, bearing his own cross: So every condemned prisoner went to the place of execution. John is silent about Simon of Cyrene, who was requisitioned to carry the load that was too heavy for Jesus (Mark 15:21), perhaps because the incident

years later someone was reminding Pilate of this difficult case, but it awoke no echo whatsoever in his mind:

> "His name was Jesus; he came from Nazareth, and he was crucified for some crime, I don't quite know what. Pontius, do you remember anything about the man?"
>
> Pontius Pilate contracted his brows. . . . Then after a silence of some seconds—
>
> "Jesus?" he murmured, "Jesus—of Nazareth? I cannot call him to mind." [8]

That is hard to believe. He was a proud man. And he had been mastered. And all his life the sore would fester. For essentially he was just.

But what a ghastly tale it is, and how cruel to read! Helplessly we stand and watch this fellow man of ours caught fast in a quicksand, sinking deeper and still deeper the more that he struggles to free himself, lower and lower before our horrified eyes, till at last he is gone! Well, we too have failed Jesus Christ; have seen the right, and yet hesitated ourselves into situations from which we could not extricate ourselves; have chosen our self-interest, not caring what became of him; have crucified our Lord afresh, and put him to an open shame; and often for a very little thing.

> Thy weak self-love and guilty pride
> His Pilate and His Judas were.[9]

May God have mercy upon them—and us!

17-18. *Taking Up the Cross.*—Compared to those of the Synoptists, the account which this evangelist gives us of the Crucifixion is disappointingly meager and niggardly and bald. Here there is no reference to the dramatic episode of Simon of Cyrene, or to the women of Jerusalem, or more surprising still, to the moving incident of Christ's two fellow sufferers. In two curt verses we read: **So they took Jesus, and he went out, bearing his own cross. . . . There they crucified him, and with him two others, one on either side, and Jesus between them.** And that is all.

It was a grim custom whereby a condemned man on his way to execution carried his own cross. Yet our Lord could find no apter metaphor for a genuine discipleship than that. "No one," he says bluntly, "can be a disciple at all, to be called such, unless daily he denies himself and takes up his cross and follows me." One can see the fitness of that symbolism in the case of the first Christians. Quite literally, by the declaration of their faith, they took their lives into their hands; did face imminent and horrid trouble and persecution and opprobrium and outlawry; and likely enough, death itself. And recent history has shown that the same demand in all its naked completeness can, on occasion, still be made on modern Christians also; that for them too loyalty to Christ may mean the loss of everything—but Christ.

But anything that could require this dreadful picture to describe it seems a thousand miles away from that easy and comfortable thing which we call our discipleship. So much so that one wonders if Christ can regard what we offer him as coming under that august name at all; and also whether if we lived out what he expects from us thoroughly and wholeheartedly, we too might not have to face a cross. As things

[8] *Mother of Pearl* (tr. Frederic Chapman; London: John Lane, 1922), p. 26.

[9] Frederick W. Faber, "O come and mourn with me awhile."

18 Where they crucified him, and two others with him, on either side one, and Jesus in the midst.

19 ¶ And Pilate wrote a title, and put *it* on the cross. And the writing was, JESUS OF NAZARETH THE KING OF THE JEWS.

20 This title then read many of the Jews; for the place where Jesus was crucified was nigh to the city: and it was written in Hebrew, *and* Greek, *and* Latin.

21 Then said the chief priests of the Jews to Pilate, Write not, The King of the Jews; but that he said, I am King of the Jews.

Hebrew Gol′go-tha.
18 There they crucified him, and with him two others, one on either side, and Jesus between them.
19 Pilate also wrote a title and put it on the cross; it read, "Jesus of Nazareth, the King of the Jews."
20 Many of the Jews read this title, for the place where Jesus was crucified was near the city; and it was written in Hebrew, in Latin, and in Greek.
21 The chief priests of the Jews then said to Pilate, "Do not write, 'The King of the Jews,' but, 'This man said,

was unimportant to him, possibly because Gnostic heretics were already suggesting, as Basilides did a generation later, that Simon and Jesus changed places, so that Jesus did not actually suffer death (see Irenaeus *Against Heresies* I. 24. 4). There is a strongly anti-Docetic strain in the Johannine Gospel and epistles. The word **Golgotha** is a transliteration of the Aramaic *galgaltā'* or *gulgultā'*, "skull" (κρανίον). Presumably the name was given because of its skull-like appearance, and it was this striking resemblance which led Otto Thenius in his identification of the site in 1849. John follows the same tradition as the Synoptics in recording that Jesus was crucified between two others, that Pilate put an inscription on the cross, **the King of the Jews,** and that the soldiers cast lots for the clothing of Jesus. Peculiar to John is the information that the inscription gave

are, we use the word too indiscriminatingly of any trouble or untoward happening we have to meet. "This is my cross," a man will say, meaning thereby some sore that hurts or handicaps him and yet has to be borne. But Christ limits the phrase to what is suffered for his sake. Certain it is that we are saved not by one Cross but by two—Christ's and our own. Ruthlessly we must nail down our selfish nature to the hard wood with resolute unrelenting blows; and like the crucifixion squad, must sit and watch it with hard eyes, writhe and plead how it may, until it die. We must be crucified with Christ, must die with him, and rise with him into a new way of life and being.

As to the startling brevity of this account, and its reserve and reticence—there is no dwelling on the physical agonies. "It is excruciating!" men cry out of pain hardly to be endured. And excruciating means the pains of crucifixion. But all that is left in shadow. We are told nothing of the being laid upon the wood, of the nails driven home into the feet and hands, of the intolerable shock as cross and victim were lifted and dunted into the socket, of the long crawling hours of shame and pain—of all that there is hardly a hint in the whole narrative. And did not God's own hand draw a veil of thick darkness round about the Cross? It is not wise for us to attempt to peer through it. Because for one thing, to the Scriptures the physical horrors were by far the least part of our Savior's passion. Something much more tremendous than that had to be faced; something that Paul attempts to depict for us in the dark, awful phrase of his, "He was made sin for us, who knew no sin"; something that is carried to us in that heart-shaking cry, "My God, my God, why hast thou forsaken me?"

For the rest—when an assistant once complained to R. W. Dale of Birmingham, "I wanted to preach on 'Christ died for our sins,' and I thought that if I could only show how through the death of Christ it was made possible for God to forgive sin, many whom I knew might be led to believe," Dale replied, "Give up troubling . . . about *how* it was possible for God to forgive sin, and go straight and tell the people that God *does* forgive sin, and tell them straight that Christ died for their sins. It is the fact the people want most to know, and not your theory, nor mine, as to how it was or is possible."[1] That is a truth, and a vital one; even if not the whole truth.

19-22. *What I Have Written I Have Written.* —**Jesus of Nazareth, the King of the Jews,** so ran the superscription that Pilate put on Christ's cross. His curt refusal to alter it sounds like the stubbornness and obstinacy of a weak man who, worsted in the main issue,

[1] A. W. W. Dale, *Life of R. W. Dale* (London: Hodder & Stoughton, 1898), pp. 643-44. Used by permission.

22 Pilate answered, What I have written
I have written.
23 ¶ Then the soldiers, when they had
crucified Jesus, took his garments, and made
four parts, to every soldier a part; and also
his coat: now the coat was without seam,
woven from the top throughout.
24 They said therefore among themselves,
Let us not rend it, but cast lots for it,
whose it shall be: that the Scripture might
be fulfilled, which saith, They parted my
raiment among them, and for my vesture
they did cast lots. These things therefore
the soldiers did.

I am King of the Jews.'" 22 Pilate answered,
"What I have written I have written."
23 When the soldiers had crucified Jesus
they took his garments and made four
parts, one for each soldier. But his tunic
was without seam, woven from top to bot-
tom; 24 so they said to one another, "Let
us not tear it, but cast lots for it to see
whose it shall be." This was to fulfill the
scripture,

"They parted my garments among them,
and for my clothing they cast lots."

---

the name **Jesus of Nazareth,** and that **it was written in Hebrew, in Latin, and in Greek.** The Jewish leaders would be infuriated by the suggestion that their king was a Galilean, though there is no reason to suppose that this was intended by Pilate as an insult. He had been informed by the chief priests that Jesus was a Galilean (Luke 23:5-6), and they charged Jesus before Pilate with being a messianic claimant. This reason for the death sentence was inscribed on the headboard, called in Latin *titulus,* a technical term preserved by John alone among the evangelists in its Greek form, τίτλος. The mention of the three languages, a detail peculiar to John, is probably a correct tradition. Josephus tells us (*Jewish War* V. 5. 2) that the slabs placed at regular intervals on the balustrade protecting the holy place from alien intrusion bore an inscription of warning, some in Latin, some in Greek. Moreover, Julius Capitolinus, a biographer of the fourth century A.D., records that when the emperor Gordianus Pius was murdered in Persia, the soldiers erected a sepulcher for him "and added a *titulus* in Greek, Latin, Persian, Aramaic, and Egyptian, to be read by all." A trilingual inscription would be necessary in Jerusalem, for Latin was the official language of the administration, Greek the language of international commerce and culture, and Hebrew (i.e., Aramaic) the language spoken by

---

salves his hurt pride by scoring a petty point against his enemies. Yet what he snapped out to the chief priests, who, wounded in their national feelings, had hurried to protest, remains eternally and fearsomely true—of him and us. **What I have written I have written.** Of him, since all down the centuries to the end of time people will keep reciting, "suffered under Pontius Pilate, was crucified, dead, and buried." And of us no less. For life is a terrible, inexorable thing.

> The Moving Finger writes; and, having writ,
> Moves on: nor all your Piety nor Wit
> Shall lure it back to cancel half a Line,
> Nor all your Tears wash out a Word of it.[2]

What we have written, we have written; and it stands. Mohammed tells us that there will be nothing arbitrary about the Day of Judgment, but that each of us will appear there with our life story written by our own hand hanging about our neck; and that it will be said to us, "Read thy Book: thou thyself art accountant enough against thyself this day."[3] It is all in the records, says the Revelation. And one day the books will be opened. There is no blotting out in life. And what is done can never be undone. What we have written, we have written. And it stands.

23-25. ***Power Only Through Christ.***—The clothing of executed criminals became the property of the soldiers, unlucky enough to be detailed for crucifixion duty, with its labors, and worse, its long and boring wait. Hence Jesus' garments were the perquisites of the four men who formed the execution squad on that particular day. As a Jew's clothing in those days consisted of five articles—the headdress, the outer garment, the shoes, and the girdle, there was something for each of them, and in addition there was a tunic, in this case woven all in one piece. Agreeing that it was too good to be divided and so ruined, they resolved to draw lots for it. And one of them no doubt

[2] *The Rubáiyát of Omar Khayyám,* st. lxxi.

[3] Lane-Poole, *Speeches and Table-talk of Mohammed,* p. 59.

25 ¶ Now there stood by the cross of Jesus his mother, and his mother's sister, Mary the *wife* of Cleophas, and Mary Magdalene.

26 When Jesus therefore saw his mother, and the disciple standing by, whom he loved, he saith unto his mother, Woman, behold thy son!

25 So the soldiers did this; but standing
by the cross of Jesus were his mother, and
his mother's sister, Mary the wife of Clo′-
pas, and Mary Mag′da-lene. 26 When Jesus
saw his mother, and the disciple whom he
loved standing near, he said to his mother,

Palestinian Jews. But for the evangelist this polyglot inscription signified the universal mission of Christ crucified (cf. 12:32). John also reports the procurator's refusal to alter the inscription, and that **lots** were **cast** for the seamless tunic. Here again this trivial incident has deeper meaning for John. We need not look for an ecclesiastical interpretation! It is a "fulfillment" of Ps. 22:18—that psalm in which the earliest Christians found so many anticipations of the passion of the Savior.

25-30. Those standing near the cross are **Mary** the **mother** of Jesus, her **sister, Mary the wife of Clopas,** and **Mary Magdalene.** From Mark 15:40 and Matt. 27:56 we learn that **Mary Magdalene,** Mary the mother of James and Joses, and Salome the mother of the sons of Zebedee were present. If identification of these lists is allowable, **Salome** appears to have been the sister of Mary the mother of our Lord; and **Mary the wife of Clopas** must have been the mother of James and Joses. The mother of Jesus is

---

considered himself lucky when it fell to him. One wonders what became of it. Once on a day a timid creature at the end of her resources and very desperate put out a shy hand and touched it. For, said she to herself, "If I may but touch his garment [this very garment], I shall be whole" (Matt. 9:21). And so it proved. And down the ages it has wrought how many similar cures! For Whittier sings truly,

> The healing of His seamless dress
> Is by our beds of pain;
> We touch Him in life's throng and press;
> And we are whole again.[4]

But without Jesus Christ it has no virtue in it, becomes merely a soldier's property, nothing more.

Are we not apt to forget that; and so to blunder into error upon error? Some speak as if the most thoughtless participation in Holy Communion were automatically, magically, efficacious: forgetting that thougn God every time stands to his promises and presses his gracious gifts upon us, we can thwart his purposes of mercy toward us; that as Calvin put it, here the sun, streaming down upon fertile soil, coaxes out of it green living things that spring up and grow and bear; and yet, yonder only a few yards away, beating down upon hard rock, can there accomplish nothing; so, not only unless Jesus Christ is present, but unless we meet him face to face, a sacrament loses its potency, cannot work out for us all it has in it. Or we appropriate some of our Lord's moral teaching, "This is true," we say, "and we must work it out." And with that we set about trying so to do. For the most part, and often enough, in vain. For without Christ it is a hopeless dream—beautiful, but impossible. And our most strenuous attempts to realize it frequently only land us in new difficulties. "There is nothing radical about revolutions," thinks Berdyaev. "They are, to a big extent simply masquerades in which nothing is changed but the outward dress of the performers. Revolutions do not so much overcome evil as give new birth to it by provoking fresh evil."[5] John Morley, the British statesman, once said that political life is a daunting affair. For years, he said, we labor to eradicate some social evil; and at long last persuade the people, and the evil falls. Yet, too often, a worse evil grows up in that clearing where the other had flourished.

[4] "Immortal Love, forever full."

26-27. ***On Christ's Thoughtfulness for His Mother.***—Epictetus, that disciplined soul, asked little or nothing from life, but took contentedly what it sent him. But he had very definite wishes about his dying. "I should like best," he said, "that it should find me busy at something noble and beneficent and for the good of all mankind. But, since that is little likely to befall me," adds the wise philosopher, "I should choose next to go out, rendering what is due to every relation in life."[6]

Christ in his dying lived out both these as-

[5] *Freedom and the Spirit,* pp. 186-87.

[6] *Discourses* IV. 10. 12-13.

27 Then saith he to the disciple, Behold thy mother! And from that hour that disciple took her unto his own *home*.

"Woman, behold your son!" 27 Then he said to the disciple, "Behold your mother!" And from that hour the disciple took her to his own home.

---

mentioned only once before in this Gospel (2:1-5), and her presence at the Crucifixion is recorded by no other evangelist. The only mention of her name after the Crucifixion in the whole N.T. is in Acts 1:14, when we are told of those who "devoted themselves to prayer, together with the women and Mary the mother of Jesus, and with his brothers."

John reports three sayings from the cross. The first entrusts his mother to the care of the Beloved Disciple; the second "fulfills the scripture" (Ps. 69:21) with the cry **I**

---

pirations. He died for the whole world in an act of supreme self-sacrifice for it which has lifted it up bodily far nearer holiness and God. And yet, so doing, even in the excruciating agony of crucifixion, and with the salvation of this great world hanging in the balances, dependent on his faith, the faith of one from whom even God had hidden his face, or seemed so to have done, of one with nothing left to clutch at, or to cling to, even then, and even there, in that appalling responsibility, he had a mind lifted above himself, serene and calm enough to think, and pray, and plan, for others. "Father, forgive them." "To-day shalt thou be with me in paradise." **Woman, behold thy son! Son, behold thy mother!**

God grant that when the dark is falling round us in that last scene of all, when the poorest of us, for once, holds the center of the stage, we may face death with a like unselfishness and thoughtfulness for others, not fidgeting about ourselves, not hurriedly making last minute and feverish preparations, but packed and ready and waiting for the tide, may smother the pain, and be able to enter eagerly into the happiness and interests of those around us on to the very end, thinking and planning for them after Christ's gallant fashion, that for us too death may be no squalid thing, but big and brave and enviable.

> The primal duties shine aloft—like stars;
> The charities that soothe, and heal, and bless,
> Are scattered at the feet of Man—like flowers.[7]

If it was in the thick darkness upon Calvary that there flamed out the mighty constellations by which ever since humanity has steered, the homely virtues too flower bravely on that bleak hillside. They also are a real and essential part of Christlikeness.[8] Long ago Philo said a pertinent thing, for, noticing how both generations and individuals sway between a passion for social amendment and a zeal for individual righteousness, he gave a warning fitted for most ages, and certainly for ours.

> There are some who have attached themselves to one of these devotions, and neglected the other. For, being filled with a sense of piety, they have preferred that to all other interests, and devoted the whole of their lives to the service of God; while others have adhered simply to their connection with men in social zeal, affording all alike the use of their possessions, and, also, as far as possible alleviating their woes. The latter you might call philanthropic persons, the former devout. For those alone are perfect who have a reputation in both departments.[9]

Wherever you come on Christ, and whatever test you apply to him, he far outdistances the rest of us. He did, he was, what the next greatest to him only dreamed, and hoped, and longed to do and be. It is difficult to gain proficiency in either of these provinces of Philo. The big call comes to all of us at times, to most of us at thin-sown times. Some terrible possibility for us grows fact, the only fact. Some sorrow crashes into our placid life. The eerie words for us come true, "Behold, your house is left unto you desolate" (Matt. 23:38). And one must pull oneself together, and make shift to face it quietly, uncomplainingly, with honor, though the heart within one is so sore one wonders how it holds together. Or a war devastates the world. And a whole generation has to rise up, and leave all that they have, all that they are, all that they hope to be, paying that down to safeguard righteousness and liberty. Or to a woman, left behind, there comes one day the dreaded tidings. The home that was opening before her is gone. Her dream is out.

But, in the main, for most of us

> Of little threads our life is spun,
> And he spins ill, who misses one.[1]

Samuel Johnson remarks with truth in one of his wise essays that it is not sufficiently considered how much of human life passes in little

[7] Wordsworth, *The Excursion*, Bk. IX.

[8] See A. J. Gossip, "The Words from the Cross," *Expository Times*, XLI (1930), 198-202.

[9] *On the Ten Commandments* XXII.

[1] Matthew Arnold, "Horatian Echo."

28 ¶ After this, Jesus knowing that all things were now accomplished, that the Scripture might be fulfilled, saith, I thirst.

28 After this Jesus, knowing that all was now finished, said (to fulfill the scripture),

thirst; the third declares the consummation of the mission entrusted by the Father, in the word τετέλεσται, **It is finished.** Vs. 29 raises a question of interpretation and of textual conjecture: **So they put a sponge full of the vinegar on hyssop and held it to his mouth.** The word **hyssop** seems out of place here, since we are told in Mark 15:36 and in Matt. 27:48 that they put the sponge of vinegar on a reed to give it to Jesus. Hyssop is an herb, but it does not provide a long stalk such as a reed. Now *hyssos* (ὑσσός) is the Greek word for the Roman *pilum,* or javelin, and in one late MS of the eleventh century

incidents; and thinks it is a mistake that the moralists have endeavored to inculcate the awful virtues, without considering the lesser qualities which, though they produce no single acts of heroism nor astonish us by great events, do so much to make the draught of life bitter or sweet. That charge cannot be leveled against Jesus Christ. For even when saving a lost world, even when passing through waters so black and rushing that no one of us can picture them, he remembered his mother, and made provision for her future.

There are those who tell us confidently these days that the Christian morality is a quaintly obsolete affair, a garment so preposterously old-fashioned that up-to-date people would blush to be seen wearing it, that the recognized sanctities, like marriage and the family, have had their day and ought now to be left behind like the other barbarisms that we have outgrown, that our natural affections when dispassionately considered are seen to be only a subtler form of selfishness, a loving of our own simply because they are our own, and must be replaced by something wider and less personal and more catholic. So, long ago, D'Alembert declared, with a pompous complacency, that he preferred his family to himself, and his nation to his family, and humanity as a whole to his particular nation. Which surely is, one thinks, a silly and extremely doubtful saying. And Rousseau, for all his eloquent pratings about the rights of man, is a poor creature at whom one's gorge rises, as he sneaks through the dark to leave his babies on the door of the foundling hospital. Who can trust such a man whose fine tall talk about humanity in general is canceled out and derided by his pitiable failure toward his own flesh and blood? In every relationship of life the man proves himself, thereby, undependable and suspect.

But Christ, with all his huge ambitions for us in things spiritual, nonetheless put first the homely duties. These on occasion, he says, have to give way. Father and mother, wife and child, have to be left. But he himself worked on for years and years in the workshop in Nazareth putting through the ordinary duties of a village carpenter, although his heart was haunted by that dream of saving a whole world; and tarried there, ankle deep among the shavings, till some of the others could take his place, and he himself was free. And even upon Calvary the claims of family affection were conceded to the full. There is a fact that some of us are not remembering. It is natural for a young woman to seek to express herself, to find a satisfaction in an income of her own and in the wider life down in the office. But if her mother's life is dull and wearisome during her absence, how does Christ judge of that? For some churchiness is a kind of intoxication, little more. If, when John reached the heavenly places, he had explained to Christ that he had been so busy working for him and the cause, that he had not had time to think much about Mary, I do not think that Christ's "well done" would have been particularly hearty. In little things as well as those that catch the eye, we must learn Christ's unselfishness. And so to do our wisest plan is to live much beside him. Sometimes it seems as if a crisis lifts a man bodily above himself into a higher type of being. But, as a rule, it does not change, only reveals. All his days Jesus had been going about doing good, in sheer forgetfulness of himself. And so, even when they had nailed down his hands so that they could no longer leap out in generous kindliness and giving, the habit of his life still held. His heart, left free, ran out in its accustomed way to needy desperate sinful folk. "Sow a thought, and you reap an act. Sow an act, and you reap a habit. Sow a habit, and you reap a character. Sow a character, and you reap a destiny." [2] Normally, there is no other method.

28-29. ***I Thirst.***—It was characteristic of our Lord that only after he had arranged matters for his mother could a thought of his own desperate needs find entrance to his mind. That was his nature. Always he was thinking about

[2] Attributed to C. A. Hall.

29 Now there was set a vessel full of vinegar: and they filled a sponge with vinegar, and put *it* upon hyssop, and put *it* to his mouth.

"I thirst." 29 A bowl full of vinegar stood there; so they put a sponge full of the vinegar on hyssop and held it to his mouth.

---

(476) this word, shorter by two letters than the word for *hyssop* (ὑσσῷ for ὑσσώπῳ), is actually used in this passage. This might well seem to preserve the original reading, which has otherwise been lost in the entire MS tradition. (For a full treatment of this conjecture, first made by Joachim Camerarius in the sixteenth century, see Frederick Field, *Notes on the Translation of the New Testament* [Cambridge: University Press, 1899], pp. 106 ff.) On the other hand, many commentators (e.g., Bauer, Goguel, Loisy), remembering John's interpretation of the death of Christ by the symbolism of the

---

others. And always in his own life he came last. And since that is the essence of Christlikeness, if we are ever to attain to that, we also must acquire a like attitude of mind. Śānti Deva, the great Buddhist, says in his memorable book that people will have it that there is a something which they call the self; and that they make that something central in the planning of their lives and in the living out of it from day to day, so that everything else revolves around this self. They think of self, they work for self, they spend themselves for self. But if, said he, we could push this self out of the place of authority it has usurped in human minds, and would take other people, and not self at all, as the center around which our life turns, if we would think of them, work for them, spend ourselves for them, would not most of the problems that perplex the world solve themselves? So Śānti Deva centuries ago.[8] His prescription for our ailments is a sound one. But it is Jesus Christ who shows us how the thing is done, and who gives us the power, if we so choose, to do it.

At the same time, this saying of our Lord, **I thirst,** makes plain that the body has its rights. These, so Christ's teaching runs, must be restrained and subordinated and held firmly in check. Nonetheless, in their own place and in due measure they are legitimate. And the excesses of asceticism practiced by people who imagine that in this way they are being loyal to Christ have in reality no sanction from him whatsoever. **I thirst,** he said; and asked for some relief from this grievous addition to his many and intolerable sufferings. It is a moving cry to come from one who claimed that "he who believes in me shall never thirst" (6:35); but that the living water which he shall give him will be a perpetual ever-flowing fountain that can never run dry (4:14). That living water he does give. But to secure it for us he himself had to pass through "a dry and thirsty land, where no water is" (Ps. 63:1).

It was when our Lord said **I thirst** that there occurred one of the three incidents which alone redeem the shame of humanity on Calvary from absolute completeness. One of these was the presence of the little knot of loyal men and women who with what pain in their hearts stood near the Cross on to the very end—"afar off," so the Synoptists say. But apparently they had drawn closer. For this evangelist tells us that Christ spoke to them, and that, when his voice must have grown faint. We can be thankful for them. And a second incident is the noble conduct of two of the very Sanhedrin that had hounded Christ to his death, when they dared to care for the dishonored body. And the third is that someone, hearing Christ cry, **I thirst,** ran, "at once," so Matthew has it, and putting a sponge full of vinegar or sour wine upon a reed, held it to our Lord's parched and dying lips.

Apparently such wine was supplied for the use of the crucified—a surprising fact in those rough days. Luke indeed, with a harshness most unlike his generous nature, especially toward Gentiles, imputes the act to mockery and cruelty. But the other accounts have no suggestion of that kind. One hopes and thinks it was the kindly act of some soldier lad. "They shall look on him whom they have pierced" is quoted later in the narrative (vs. 37), in the first instance of these crucifiers of our Lord. But on the Day of Judgment, when one of them lifts up his eyes to him that sits upon the throne, with what amazement will he recognize one whom he once helped in his hour of utmost need!

John Duncan, that saint and acute mind of a century ago, once set it down that of all beings in the universe he would most like to have been the angel of the agony who was selected by God to strengthen Christ in the garden. And little wonder he so chose. And yet this soldier lad was kind to Jesus Christ,

[8] *The Path of Light,* from the Bodhi-Charyāvatāra of Śānti Deva, tr. L. D. Barnett (New York: E. P. Dutton & Co., 1909), pp. 88-89.

30 When Jesus therefore had received the vinegar, he said, It is finished: and he bowed his head, and gave up the ghost.

30 When Jesus had received the vinegar, he said, "It is finished"; and he bowed his head and gave up his spirit.

Passover, detect here an allusion to Exod. 12:22. In the ritual there prescribed the Israelites were to "take a bunch of hyssop, and dip it in the blood that is in the basin, and strike the lintel and the two side posts with the blood that is in the basin." The parallel is certainly not obvious, but the memory that hyssop is mentioned in the ritual of Passover may have led some unimaginative scribe to confuse ὑσσῷ περιθέντες with ὑσσώπῳ περιθέντες.

God's Son, when he was in the act of dying, and did something to help him through the waters of the river. And one covets his chance, and his prompt seizing of it. But after all, one need not envy him. For so really is Christ touched with the feeling of his people's needs and infirmities that he accounts anything done to aid the most insignificant of them as done to very him, and feels the self-same gratitude to those who so help them as he does, to all eternity, to this rough soldier. "Inasmuch as ye have done it unto one of the least of these my brethren, ye have done it unto me" (Matt. 25:40).

30. ***It Is Finished.***—And with that at long last, though one gathers sooner than usual to the crucified, death came to claim the Prince of life. Jesus was dead. The last chance for the world seemed gone. And hope was out, and black, and cold. So everyone, even those who had thought expectantly that this was he who should come, took sadly for granted. Yet Christ himself died with the shout of a conqueror; still undismayed, still valiant, still full of faith. As Matthew and Mark tell us, he had upon the Cross passed through dark, rushing, swollen waters, and a terrible midnight of the soul, when even God seemed to have deserted him. "My God, my God, why hast thou forsaken me?" But his heart rallied. And though everything for which he had toiled and sacrificed seemed down, and though nothing had come of all that he had taught and planned and done and suffered, nothing at all, except a little group of broken hearts that had loved him, and a knot of scattered men who had believed in him—and fled—he died still trusting God; himself by far the most audacious and intrepid of all believers, and so with the right to claim faith from the rest of us, sure that the work which had been given him to do was done. Gathering his last remnants of strength together, it was with a loud voice and exultantly that he cried, **It is finished;** and was gone.

Our Lord's assertion that what God had asked of him had been accomplished, that between his life as God had planned it and as it lay there now lived out there was no difference whatever, is a unique claim which no other of the sons of men could dream of making. John Ruskin says strikingly:

> Our best finishing is but coarse and blundering work after all. We may smooth, and soften, and sharpen till we are sick at heart; but take a good magnifying glass to our miracle of skill, and the invisible edge is a jagged saw, and the silky thread a rugged cable, and the soft surface a granite desert. . . . God alone can finish; and the more intelligent the human mind becomes, the more the infiniteness of interval is felt between human and divine work in this respect.[4]

He was speaking of course of art and craftsmanship; yet is it not still truer about life? What can the best of us take back to God except some broken purposes, and some attempts that came to little, and some dreams that went out, or that came true and proved most disappointing? We use all our brief span of life learning how to live; and having learned a little, get no chance to put it into practice. For our opportunity is over. We just begin, and then our work is done, poor fumbling blunderers that we are. But Christ knew that his work was finished and completely carried through. And is it not the simplest truth that that life of his has proved to be far the most momentous fact in human history? Has it not cleft time itself into two? And has not all that went before him, noble and impressive though much of it was, been wiped out as mere baby scribblings, and have we not started to count the years again as from a new beginning and as living in a new world, since Jesus lived and taught and died? Has he not enabled us to know God, and man, and life, as they were never known before? Has he not given us new powers and opened up new possibilities before us? Has he not proved himself in very deed to be that Savior who should come into the world, and a Savior sufficient even for the mighty task that God had set him?

[4] *Modern Painters* (Boston: Oldine Book Publishing Co., n.d.), III, 153.

31 The Jews therefore, because it was the preparation, that the bodies should not remain upon the cross on the sabbath day, (for that sabbath day was a high day,) besought Pilate that their legs might be broken, and *that* they might be taken away.

32 Then came the soldiers, and brake the legs of the first, and of the other which was crucified with him.

33 But when they came to Jesus, and saw that he was dead already, they brake not his legs:

34 But one of the soldiers with a spear pierced his side, and forthwith came there out blood and water.

31 Since it was the day of Preparation,
in order to prevent the bodies from re-
maining on the cross on the sabbath (for
that sabbath was a high day), the Jews
asked Pilate that their legs might be broken,
and that they might be taken away. 32 So
the soldiers came and broke the legs of the
first, and of the other who had been cru-
cified with him; 33 but when they came to
Jesus and saw that he was already dead,
they did not break his legs. 34 But one of
the soldiers pierced his side with a spear,
and at once there came out blood and

31-37. Foiled in their attempt to induce Pilate to change the inscription on the cross, the Jews petitioned Pilate that the death of the criminals might be hastened so that their bodies should not remain unburied. Deut. 21:23 forbade leaving a body all night upon the tree. Josephus (*Jewish War* IV. 5. 2) records Jewish precision in this matter: "They actually went so far in their impiety as to cast out the corpses without burial, although the Jews are so careful about funeral rites that even malefactors who have been sentenced to crucifixion are taken down and buried before sunset." Here it is suggested that the defilement would be even worse because this Friday was **Preparation,** not only for the sabbath, but for the first day of the paschal feast, and therefore especially holy (cf. Exod. 12:16). Soldiers were sent to perform the *crucifragium,* but found Jesus already dead (cf. vs. 30). To make sure, one of **the soldiers pierced his side with a spear,** and **blood and water** issued. However medical evidence may account for this phenomenon, the "witness" lays stress upon the validity of this tradition, which evidently represented some symbolic truth to the evangelist. It is doubtful whether I John 5:6 has the same

---

31-37. ***The Pierced Side.***—As a rule, crucifixion meant a pitilessly slow and lingering death. Not infrequently the unhappy sufferer might last on miserably for two or even three unending, crawling days. But the Jews had a notion that the exposed bodies of executed criminals polluted the sabbath. And as the next day was no ordinary sabbath but **a high day** (vs. 31), they asked the authorities that the three sufferers on Calvary should be despatched forthwith, and their bodies no doubt tossed into some rubbish heap or the like. Their request was granted; and a grim business, not uncommon, was ruthlessly carried through. The legs of the malefactors on Christ's right and left were broken with a heavy mallet—a hideous affair; yet probably accepted as a merciful release by those who had already borne more than a human being should be called upon to endure. But Jesus was already dead; to Pilate's surprise, as Mark tells us. Still, to make certain, for an error would have involved them in serious trouble, one of the soldiers thrust his spear (an ugly weapon, with a barbed iron head, that made a gaping wound) deep into Christ's side (20:27). **And,** we read, **at once there came out blood and water.**

It may be thought surprising that the evangelist who omits much that is central—e.g., the cry of dereliction—should have granted so much space and prominence to this incident. Yet be sure he had his reasons. He wants to save us from all fear of falling into Docetism (see Exeg.). And in view of what he is about to tell us in the last two chapters, he underlines the fact that there was no mistake, that the real Christ of God was really dead. As to the blood and water, certain medical explanations that have been ventured do not satisfy the mind and appear to be medically doubtful.

It would seem difficult to understand what happened. Nor do most of us feel much indebted to this particular scripture. Yet some turn to it and linger at it, as being very near the center. The pierced side of our Lord has a secure place among his stigmata, and a marked prominence in Christian thought and art and hymnody. Many, e.g., Augustus M. Toplady, have found here the perfect symbolism both of what they need in One who is to save them

35 And he that saw *it* bare record, and his record is true; and he knoweth that he saith true, that ye might believe.

36 For these things were done, that the Scripture should be fulfilled, A bone of him shall not be broken.

37 And again another Scripture saith, They shall look on him whom they pierced.

38 ¶ And after this Joseph of Arimathea, being a disciple of Jesus, but secretly for fear of the Jews, besought Pilate that he might take away the body of Jesus: and Pilate gave *him* leave. He came therefore, and took the body of Jesus.

water. 35 He who saw it has borne witness—
his testimony is true, and he knows that
he tells the truth—that you also may be-
lieve. 36 For these things took place that
the scripture might be fulfilled, "Not a
bone of him shall be broken." 37 And again
another scripture says, "They shall look on
him whom they have pierced."
38 After this Joseph of Ar-i-ma-the'a,
who was a disciple of Jesus, but secretly, for
fear of the Jews, asked Pilate that he might
take away the body of Jesus; and Pilate
gave him leave. So he came and took away

---

reference. There is no reason to suppose that this was regarded as a miracle. It is recorded for two reasons: It is an emphatic declaration that the death of Jesus was no mere semblance. The anti-Docetic motive is clear. But above and beyond the historic fact, a "fulfillment" of scripture was recognized and two citations are given. The first refers to the paschal lamb of Exod. 12:46, "Neither shall ye break a bone thereof," though the form of words is influenced by Ps. 34:20 (LXX 33:21). The second is from Zech. 12:10, correctly rendering the Hebrew where the LXX misreads the original. For the emphatic evidence in vs. 35, see on 21:24 and Intro., p. 446.

38-42. Joseph of Arimathea is named in all four Gospels. He was "a respected member of the council, who was also himself looking for the kingdom of God" (Mark 15:43), "rich" (Matt. 27:57), "a good and righteous man, who had not consented to their purpose and deed" (Luke 23:50-51). John adds that he **was a disciple of Jesus, but**

---

and of what they have found in Jesus Christ: forgiveness for the sin of the past, and power to resist it for the future.

> Let the water and the blood,
> From Thy riven side which flowed,
> Be of sin the double cure,
> Cleanse me from its guilt and power.[5]

So true is it that all Scripture is given by inspiration of God and is profitable.

38-42. ***The Burial of Christ.***—It is with relief that one comes upon the noble tale of Joseph of Arimathea and Nicodemus, of their unshaken loyalty to one who seemed fallen and utterly discredited, and of the kindliness and generosity and courage with which they acted. For it took courage to ask Pilate for a favor, and that concerning one whom he had that very day condemned to death. Besides, news of what they were about was certain to leak out and spread, and make them marked men in the city, awakening resentment against them in high quarters.

Of Joseph of Arimathea we know too little. "He was a member of the council," so Luke photographs him for us, "a good and righteous man, who had not consented to their purpose and deed, and he was looking for the kingdom of God" (Luke 23:50-51). This gracious personality it was who took the initiative. At the outset, it would seem, he dared alone. And that was noteworthy. For constitutionally the man was timid. He **was a disciple of Jesus,** says the evangelist, **but secretly, for fear of the Jews.** And so he would appear to come under that grave saying of the Master, "Whosoever shall be ashamed of me and of my words, of him shall the Son of Man be ashamed" (Luke 9:26). He was rich and comfortable and shrank from trouble and the upset and dangers of an open discipleship; yet he broke with his nature, defied and mastered it, boldly declared himself Christ's follower and friend, and proved that he was so, counting no cost, facing the consequences unafraid: and this when Peter had denied his Lord, and the rest had scattered; when the movement had been crushed and broken, and Christ proved to be a false prophet, so all men believed, and the last hope was out. A great deed greatly done! May God reward him for it! As be sure he has.

And Nicodemus joined him in his daring venture on behalf of Christ. It is a heartening study to keep one's eyes on Nicodemus, as on occasion he slips into the narrative and out of

[5] "Rock of Ages."

39 And there came also Nicodemus, which at the first came to Jesus by night, and brought a mixture of myrrh and aloes, about a hundred pound *weight*.

40 Then took they the body of Jesus, and wound it in linen clothes with the spices, as the manner of the Jews is to bury.

41 Now in the place where he was crucified there was a garden; and in the garden a new sepulchre, wherein was never man yet laid.

42 There laid they Jesus therefore because of the Jews' preparation *day;* for the sepulchre was nigh at hand.

his body. 39 Nic-o-de'mus also, who had at
first come to him by night, came bringing
a mixture of myrrh and aloes, about a hun-
dred pounds' weight. 40 They took the body
of Jesus, and bound it in linen cloths with
the spices, as is the burial custom of the
Jews. 41 Now in the place where he was
crucified there was a garden, and in the
garden a new tomb where no one had ever
been laid. 42 So because of the Jewish day
of Preparation, as the tomb was close at
hand, they laid Jesus there.

---

secretly, for fear of the Jews. Helped by **Nicodemus** (cf. 3:1; 7:50), who brought a **hundred pounds' weight** of spices, he lowered the body of Jesus from the Cross, wrapped it in linen with spices between the folds, and laid it in **a new tomb, in the garden,** near the place of execution, **where no one had ever been laid.** Matthew mentions that the tomb belonged to Joseph; Mark and Matthew say that a stone was rolled to close the door of the tomb.

---

it again. That first interview in Jerusalem that windy night, when he made his way through the darkness to judge of Jesus for himself and at first hand attracts one to the man. He too may have been timid, though there are worthier reasons that may be assigned for his caution. For he was a ruler, with responsibilities to the people; and before he declared for this young prophet, he must be sure of his ground lest he lead others astray. And so he sought out Christ, privately as yet, and put his difficulties directly to him, and talked them out with him, and listened to his answers. And all this while his colleagues for the most part had tossed the whole matter aside as either of no manner of importance or else as wicked heresy that must be put down.

It is so difficult to be old and yet open-minded and expectant of new truth; so easy to stop learning, imagining we have attained to the end of things, and that anything novel to us must be a declension and a sad falling away; so hard not to make up our little bundle of conclusions about things and to refuse to undo it in order to pack in something further or better that has come to light; to hold with comfortable assurance that we are the people and wisdom will die with us; and what does this young upstart know of matters we have studied all our days, and in which we are experts? Here was a man who, old though he was in years, had a young and adventurous mind; who kept his face turned to the light and sturdily made his way toward it. And for such there is always hope, as Nicodemus proves. For when we next see him, he has thrown off his timidity and in open council declares for Christ, at least so far as to protest with indignant vehemence against judging a man without any firsthand knowledge, swayed only by prejudice and nothing more. It was a bold speech that involved him in hot opposition; and an angry unpopularity that at once burst out around him. And it seems he made his stand quite alone. In the council that day Nicodemus was Christ's minority of one.

And now there is this last and crowning record—how Nicodemus stood by the dishonored Christ and brought his gracious offering; and better than that, gave his own personal and eager service. With their own hands, it seems, Joseph and he lowered our Lord from the Cross. With their own hands these two reverently prepared his body for seemly burial. With their own hands they managed to convey it to a nearby garden, apparently Joseph's garden, and to lay it in a tomb there, seemingly one that Joseph had made ready for his own funeral some day. They must have worked in haste. For the hour was growing late and the sabbath was approaching; and if Christ's body were not buried before it came, the Jewish authorities would no doubt ruthlessly take ugly action. And all this was carried out by two naturally cautious, even timid men!

The most heartening thing in Scripture is not even the amazing promises of Christ to ordinary people but the proof it gives time after time that they really work out, come true, in frail and stumbling men and women like

14 And when she had thus said, she
turned herself back, and saw Jesus stand-
ing, and knew not that it was Jesus.
15 Jesus saith unto her, Woman, why
weepest thou? whom seekest thou? She,
supposing him to be the gardener, saith
unto him, Sir, if thou have borne him
hence, tell me where thou hast laid him,
and I will take him away.
16 Jesus saith unto her, Mary. She turned
herself, and saith unto him, Rabboni; which
is to say, Master.

not know where they have laid him." 14 Say-
ing this, she turned round and saw Jesus
standing, but she did not know that it was
Jesus. 15 Jesus said to her, "Woman, why
are you weeping? Whom do you seek?"
Supposing him to be the gardener, she said
to him, "Sir, if you have carried him away,
tell me where you have laid him, and I
will take him away." 16 Jesus said to her,
"Mary." She turned and said to him in
Hebrew, "Rab-bo'ni!" (which means

---

name. She recognizes him with the exclamation **Rabboni,** an Aramaic title with the same meaning as rabbi, as the evangelist's translation into Greek shows. Dalman (*The Words of Jesus,* tr. D. M. Kay [Edinburgh: T. & T. Clark, 1902], p. 340) says that the context implies that by using this form of address, "Mary desires to resume the old attitude towards the 'Master' which is not permitted by Jesus." This title ceased to be used of the exalted Lord by the primitive community. Henceforth he is **Lord,** in Aramaic *Mārānā'* (cf. I Cor. 16:22, *Mārānā' thā'*, "Our Lord, come!" also John 20:28, *Mārî we'elāhî*).

In Matt. 28:9-10, Jesus is reported to have said to the women returning from the tomb with fear and great joy, "Hail," whereupon "they came up and took hold of his feet and worshiped him. Then Jesus said to them, 'Do not be afraid; go and tell my

---

again, search how we may, but even when we are alienated from him and do not miss him, when we are impudently and deliberately rebellious and set upon our unworthy ways. Even the wonderful story of the prodigal son is much less than the whole gospel. For after all, the wayward boy bethought himself, and repented, and came home hesitatingly, and by no means sure of his reception; still he turned home and reached it. After all, the sheep caught in the thicket bleated and let them know its whereabouts, though the shepherd did all the rest and effected its rescue. But the little piece of silver dropped and lost could do nothing for itself at all. Yet groping hands were seeking for it, drawing nearer and still nearer till they lit on it at last. If you have lost Christ, if your spiritual life has dimmed and become thin and drab and meager, you can be sure that he is searching for you—for he will not lightly let you go—has missed you, wants you back with him again. And, says the scripture confidently, he seeks "until he finds" (Luke 15:4, 8).

Third, although she was seeking him with her whole being, Mary did not recognize Christ when she saw him. That was not altogether her fault. For apparently the risen Christ was different in some ways from the Jesus she had known. Nor were the accounts of him given by those who had talked with him always meticulously consistent. He appeared to them "in another form," we read (Mark 16:12). Mary, face to face with Christ, her Christ to whom she owed so much, failed to recognize him, **Supposing him to be the gardener.** So it often is in life with all of us. Doggedly or sullenly or bravely we accept some untoward and wounding providence. For that is all we see in it. Yet God himself is in it and has come quite close to us; is calling us to some service for him; and with his own hands is fashioning us into the instrument he needs for some lofty end. But our eyes are holden and we do not see him. Thus Francis of Assisi was terrified of leprosy. And one day, full in the narrow path that he was traveling, he saw horribly white in the sunshine a leper! Instinctively his heart shrank back, recoiling shudderingly from the contamination of that loathsome disease. But then he rallied; and ashamed of himself, ran and cast his arms about the sufferer's neck and kissed him and passed on. A moment later he looked back, and there was no one there, only the empty road in the hot sunlight. All his days thereafter he was sure it was no leper but Christ himself whom he had met.[2] So, often all that we see is some needy and perhaps not attractive soul; someone who does not appeal to us, but who lacks friendship, claims assistance. "Did you not recognize me?" asks the Master. "That was I. And inasmuch as you do it to the least of these my brethren, you do it to very me." **Supposing him to be the gardener.** How blind we are!

[2] G. K. Chesteron, *St. Francis of Assisi* (London: Hodder & Stoughton, 1923), p. 57.

17 Jesus saith unto her, Touch me not; for I am not yet ascended to my Father: but go to my brethren, and say unto them, I ascend unto my Father, and your Father; and *to* my God, and your God.

Teacher). 17 Jesus said to her, "Do not hold me, for I have not yet ascended to the Father; but go to my brethren and say to them, I am ascending to my Father and your Father, to my God and your God."

---

brethren to go to Galilee, and there they will see me.' " Here (vs. 17) Jesus says to Mary, **Do not hold me, for I have not yet ascended to the Father; but go to my brethren and say to them, I am ascending to my Father and your Father, to my God and your God.** For "cease clinging to me" Bernard (*Gospel According to John,* II, 670) favors an earlier conjecture, "be not affrighted" (μὴ πτοοῦ for μή μου ἅπτου), which would agree with Matt. 28:10. But this has no MS support. According to the Johannine view (in this probably resembling the Epistle to the Hebrews), the Ascension took place on the day of the Resurrection. The thought appears to be that Mary must not hinder the Lord, who is on his way

---

17. *Touch Me Not.*—Why was Mary Magdalene forbidden to touch the risen Christ when certain others were permitted, and Thomas even commanded, so to do? The Exeg. properly rejects Archbishop Bernard's suggestion. For while the Synoptists represent the women as badly frightened, in this narrative Mary Magdalene has no fear at all. She is distracted and miserable, but markedly it is emphasized that she has not a trace of terror. The vision of angels in no way disturbs her. She seems not greatly interested in it. What she is seeking, what she must find, is the body of her Lord. And nothing else is of much consequence to her. If this report is accepted as authentic, then the suggestion falls. Christ does not throw words about for nothing. He does not say "Do not be frightened" to one who was not in the least bit afraid. Marcus Dods, who as usual sees further into the heart of things, says here:

> "For I have not yet ascended to my Father," implying that this was not His permanent return to visible fellowship with His disciples [cf. Exeg.]. Mary, by her eagerness to seize and hold Him, showed that she considered that the . . . "little time" of xvi.16 was past, and that now He had returned to be for ever with them. Jesus checks her with the assurance that much had yet to happen before that. His disciples must at once be disabused of that misapprehension.[3]

And so he sends her with a message to them. That may well be.

Is it permissible for us to find, not a parallel indeed, but at least an analogy in our experiences with our dead? In prayer we draw near to them and they to us, quite near. The veil that hides them from us does not break, but it grows thin and tenuous and diaphanous. We feel that they are there. And yet we cannot get through to them and reach and touch them—not yet. But one day when this mortal has put on immortality and we have gained the other world, please God, that may be possible. Meantime we cannot have the old intimate face-to-face communion with them as we used to do. Not yet.

17-18. *The Risen Christ's Message to His Friends.*—And that was Christ's message to his followers after their sorry flight and ugly failure! One sometimes wonders if the Day of Judgment will be as alarming as we think. Here there is no word of condemnation or reproach. But stepping across the wide gulf of their shame that had opened between him and them, our Lord begins again on the old friendly and trustful terms, even draws nearer to them than ever. In the upper room he had told them, "Henceforth I call you not servants, . . . I have called you friends" (15:15). But here he takes a further step, and speaks of them and to them as **my brethren.** That indeed was not altogether new. Once when a man interrupted him to tell him that his mother and brothers out on the edge of the crowd were asking to speak to him, he stretched out his hand to his disciples and said, "Here are my mother and my brothers! For whoever does the will of my Father in heaven is my brother, and sister, and mother" (Matt. 12:49-50). But these men of whom he was thinking now had not done the will of God, but had lamentably failed. Yet he will not lose faith in them, nor his affection for them. So true is it, as the writer to the Hebrews tells us, that he is not ashamed to call us brothers, as he well might be. For as John Tillotson put it long ago, "We have no cause to be ashamed of the gospel of Christ, but the gospel of Christ may justly be ashamed of us."[4] Nonetheless, Christ is not. Such is his loyalty even to the most undeserving of us as we limp back out of the sad mess we have made of things,

[3] "The Gospel According to John," *Expositor's Greek Testament, ad loc.*

[4] *The Golden Book of Tillotson,* ed. James Moffatt (London: Hodder & Stoughton, 1926), p. 215.

18 Mary Magdalene came and told the disciples that she had seen the Lord, and *that* he had spoken these things unto her.

19 ¶ Then the same day at evening, being the first *day* of the week, when the doors were shut where the disciples were assembled for fear of the Jews, came Jesus and stood in the midst, and saith unto them, Peace *be* unto you.

18 Mary Mag'da-lene went and said to the disciples, "I have seen the Lord"; and she told them that he had said these things to her.

19 On the evening of that day, the first day of the week, the doors being shut where the disciples were, for fear of the Jews, Jesus came and stood among them and said to them, "Peace be with you."

---

to the Father. She is to prepare the disciples for that meeting when they will receive from him the gift of the Spirit, which has so often been promised (cf. 7:39; 14:26; 16:7) after his return to the Father (cf. 7:33; 13:1, 3; 14:4, 23; 16:5, 17, 28; 17:13). It is characteristic of this Gospel that stress is laid on the unique relationship of Jesus to his God and Father. Jesus could not say "our Father" or "our God" when speaking to his disciples, least of all after the Resurrection. **My brethren** (cf. Matt. 28:10) reflects the usage of the early church (cf. I John 3:14, 16; Mark 3:34). The testimony of Mary Magdalene that she had actually **seen** and heard the risen **Lord,** and her report of his message to the disciples, lead up to the story of the insufflation.

19-22. The scene is Jerusalem, the date the evening of Easter day. **The disciples** is an inclusive term, and there is no indication that only the ten were present (cf. Luke 24:33, 36). **The doors were shut** suggests the nature of the resurrection body. While

---

unkempt and ragged creatures, with no case, and not a shadow of excuse. The Lord never disowns us, does not ostentatiously look the other way, but comes out eagerly to meet us, letting us see the difference our coming makes to him. It is all very wonderful and sounds impossible. And yet experience proves it true. For says Paul, "God never goes back upon his gifts and call" (Rom. 11:29 Moffatt).

The writer to the Hebrews accounts for it in part on the ground that he who sanctifies and they who are sanctified are all of one Father (Heb. 2:11 Weymouth). So Christ here. **Go to my brethren and say to them, I am ascending to my Father and your Father, to my God and your God.** What Christ tells us about God is true not only of God's attitude toward him, but of God's attitude toward us. It is not surprising that God should be loving and gracious to him who is lovable and pure and like God himself. But how can he be all that to us who are none of these things; who indeed must surely be repulsive to the clean eyes of the holy God? That was a real perplexity to Paul. He knew that it was so. He walked with gladness in the sunshine of it. But how it could be, God being what he is, we being what we are, was a moral enigma to him; and he could find an explanation of it only in the one direction where an explanation can be found. As the prophet told us long ago, God's ways are not as our ways, nor his thoughts as our thoughts; but rather as the heaven is high above the earth, so great is his mercy toward them that fear him—even if and when they make a sorry mess of their blundering endeavors.

All of which Mary Magdalene reported to the disciples, and was met, as was natural, so Luke tells us, with the blankest incredulity and open disbelief. "But these words seemed to them an idle tale, and they did not believe them" (Luke 24:11)—though some ancient authorities declare that Peter, and he apparently alone, thought or half thought there might just possibly be something in it, thought it at least worth testing, and ran to the tomb to see (see Luke 24:12 KJV). That moves one. For if Christ were alive, Peter must tell him how much he repented of his cowardice and treason. He ran.

19-20. ***Jesus Appears to the Disciples.***—However that may be, on the evening of that same day the disciples, a little band of threatened and badly frightened men, were huddled together, feeling far from secure. Shut that door! And keep it shut and bolted! For Calvary was so horridly near. And crucifixion was such a dreadful death. And to them too Christ appeared, so evidently and obviously and undeniably that their incredulity was gone, and their unbelieving minds convinced once and for all that this impossible thing was true. When Faithful in *Pilgrim's Progress* was being mercilessly mauled and battered by one too strong for him, whom he could not resist, "One came by, and bid him forbear. I did not know him at first; but as he went by, I perceived the

20 And when he had so said, he showed unto them *his* hands and his side. Then were the disciples glad, when they saw the Lord.

21 Then said Jesus to them again, Peace *be* unto you: as *my* Father hath sent me, even so send I you.

22 And when he had said this, he breathed on *them*, and saith unto them, Receive ye the Holy Ghost:

20 When he had said this, he showed them his hands and his side. Then the disciples were glad when they saw the Lord. 21 Jesus said to them again, "Peace be with you. As the Father has sent me, even so I send you." 22 And when he had said this, he breathed on them, and said to them, "Receive the

---

recognizable, and capable of communicating thought, the body of Jesus appeared and disappeared at will in spite of closed doors (cf. vs. 26). It is in keeping with this that Jesus **showed them his hands and his side.** But John does not—like Luke 24:39-43 and Ign. Smyr. 3—speak of the risen Lord as eating or being touched. The second greeting, **Peace be with you** (vs. 21), as well as the words which follow, may be intended to recall words spoken in the upper room (cf. 14:27; 17:18; 13:20). **He breathed on them** (vs. 22) suggests the symbolism of Gen. 2:7. This gift of the Spirit could be bestowed only after the glorification (i.e., the crucifixion) of Christ, according to the view of the evangelist.

---

holes in his hands and his side; then I concluded that he was our Lord." These were the marks and proofs of his identity on which our Lord himself relied. And they convinced his disciples.

What, one wonders, are the characteristics by which we betray our presence and convince others that it is really we. For we all have such characteristic marks. Good humor or temper, courage or a continual whine of grievance and complaint. Something makes people certain that it is very us beyond all question, and no possible other. Christ **showed them his hands and his side.** And by that they knew that it was he.

21-23. ***The Risen Christ's Gifts to His Friends.*** —Again as in the upper room, and undeterred by the miserable happenings since then, he offers them **peace.** That was of course the customary social greeting. But the fact that Christ repeats it shows that he had more in his mind by far than simply that; what he meant was peace in their own hearts and consciences. And indeed they had grievous need of it! No more dispirited and unhappy people could be found the whole world over than that discomfited and frightened little group of broken men. For on the one side, they had failed Christ, sadly and inexcusably. And their consciences must have been clamorous and sore, their self-respect wounded and raw. And on the other side, far worse even than that, was the incredible fact, yet fact it was, that Christ, their Christ, had failed them no less tragically; that his confident promises had proved to be only cheating words, with no body or substance in them; that the Master to whom they had pinned their faith, and for whom they had risked everything, had proved, if not an impostor, at least woefully and miserably self-deceived; that the wonderful dream he had awakened in them was out, had come to absolutely nothing, was only a mocking memory that would jeer at them down the years.

And suddenly their Lord broke in upon them in that darkness of disillusionment and despair. "I, on my side," he said, "am proving that your doubts of me are ungenerous and wrong. And I want you to know that whatever you have done and whatever you have been, I still trust you, and still believe in you; want you to take it in that God's love is big enough to cover your case, your need, your sin; and God's power strong enough to lift you up above all that; want you to accept and to walk in the sunshine of God's forgiving grace." As Paul put it to the Romans, if we really believe in the immeasurable, generous lovingkindness of God toward us in spite of our unworthinesses, let us have peace with God through our Lord Jesus Christ (Rom. 5:1; see Moffatt, Weymouth, ERV). Do not let your past get you down. But shake it off, rise up above it, humbly accepting God's unthinkable grace.

Christ startles the disciples out of their downheartedness and the belittling of themselves as proved failures by throwing himself frankly on their help and asking for it. Again he reminds them of the fundamental fact: "You have not chosen me. But I have chosen you. I did it deliberately, believing you the likeliest to be of service to God and to me in our vast plans for the saving of the world. And knowing all there is to know, the very worst, remembering how you have failed me in the last few hours, I stand

23 Whosesoever sins ye remit, they are remitted unto them; *and* whosesoever *sins* ye retain, they are retained.

Holy Spirit. 23 If you forgive the sins of any, they are forgiven; if you retain the sins of any, they are retained."

23. This highly controversial passage must be regarded as a variant of the tradition preserved in Matt. 16:19 and 18:18. In the former passage Peter is addressed in the singular; in the latter the verb is in the plural, and the reference must be as general as it is in the following words (i.e., Matt. 18:19), "If two of you agree on earth about anything they ask, it will be done for them by my Father in heaven." The words "binding" and "loosing" are used there (Matt. 18:18) in their technical meaning of a rabbi's responsibility for declaring in the light of tradition and experience that an action

to my choice. I look to you with confidence. I lean my cause against your loyalty. I leave my hopes unafraid in your hands. The dream has not faded away. The adventure has not broken down in a ridiculous fiasco. For with me you are going to make it all come true. **As the Father has sent me, even so I send you.** And greater works than mine shall you do."

So Christ to men who had abjectly failed him. In World War I a fine lad in the battalion with which I was serving failed through illness in face of the enemy and was court-martialed and punished. All that the colonel said to me was, "We must show him that we still trust him, or the lad will go to pieces." And not once did he allude to the unhappy incident, but not only treated the boy with the old friendliness, but a few weeks later in a particularly tight corner put him in command of the very company with whom he had been when he made his slip. In a few days' grim fighting the lad won honor after honor, and promotion for gallantry in the field. "What else could I do?" he said to me. "I failed him; and he trusted me." We too have failed Christ often and wretchedly and without excuse. Yet he too somehow still dares to trust us. Are we big enough to respond to that call on our gratitude and manhood?

But how? It is all very well for the old poet to tell us that

> Unless above himself he can
> Erect himself, how poor a thing is man![5]

But how does one erect himself above himself? Experience has proved disheartening, has shown us how unstable are our sturdiest and most vehement resolutions, how frail and undependable these fickle hearts of ours. How?

The answer is that by ourselves the thing just cannot be done at all. But then, Christ does not ask impossibilities from his people. He gives what makes it possible. So here. **He breathed on them, and said to them, "Receive the Holy Spirit."** He gave them something of his own ways and mind and nature, his own spirit, God's own Spirit. And with something of Christ within them, all things spiritual came within their reach. Alone you cannot do it. But Christ and you together can confront anything and see it through with honor.

It is no use to push all this aside impatiently as mere words which mean really nothing at all. For the facts are there, plain, obvious, undeniable; facts that prove that ordinary people, once Christ's Spirit has touched and inspired and quickened them, can live and do live, can serve God and the cause and do serve God and the cause, as they could not do before. Look at these very men. How abjectly they failed! And yet once this Spirit entered into them, how valiant, daring, unbreakable they became! These things are hard and solid facts that must be faced, and of which account must be taken.

As Robert Bridges put it:

> Not ev'n the Apostles, in the days
> They walked with Christ, lov'd him so well
> As we may now, who ken his praise
> Reading the story that they tell,
> Writ by them when their vision grew
> And he, who fled and thrice denied
> Christ to his face, was proven true
> And gladly for his memory died:
> So strong the Vision, there was none
> O'er whom the Fisher's net was cast,
> Ev'n of the fearfullest not one
> Who would have left him at the last.[6]

The fact that **he breathed** on them seems to imply that he felt that he could now communicate to them something of his own nature as hitherto he had not been able to do. Why? Perhaps because heretofore, in spite of all that he could say to them in warning, they had been too self-assured, too confident; but now, taught by their own tragic experiences, humbled and made aware of their shocking instability and

[5] Samuel Daniel, "To the Countess of Cumberland," st. xii.

[6] "Vision," from *The Poetical Works of Robert Bridges.* Used by permission of the Clarendon Press, Oxford.

24 ¶ But Thomas, one of the twelve, called Didymus, was not with them when Jesus came.

25 The other disciples therefore said unto him, We have seen the Lord. But he said unto them, Except I shall see in his hands the print of the nails, and put my finger into the print of the nails, and thrust my hand into his side, I will not believe.

24 Now Thomas, one of the twelve, called the Twin, was not with them when
Jesus came. 25 So the other disciples told
him, "We have seen the Lord." But he said to them, "Unless I see in his hands the print of the nails, and place my finger in the mark of the nails, and place my hand in his side, I will not believe."

---

was forbidden (i.e., "bound"), or permitted (i.e., "loosed"). But in the Johannine form of the saying the commission to the church goes rather further, **If you forgive the sins of any, they are forgiven; if you retain the sins of any, they are retained.** The force of the tenses in the two independent clauses must not be overlooked. The perfect is used each time (ἀφέωνται—the better-supported reading—and κεκράτηνται): "they have been forgiven"; "they have been retained." This implies insight into a granting or withholding of forgiveness already determined in the divine judgment. Probably we should take into account the thought behind I John 5:16-17.

24-29. Thomas has already been introduced to the readers of this Gospel (11:16) as a courageous pessimist, and again (14:5) as an honest skeptic. Absent on this first

---

insufficiency, they were at last willing and ready to receive what Christ could give them. So William Temple

> He imparts to them His own life-breath; the outward sign, helped by the play on words, suggests that henceforth His own spiritual energy will be within them. *Receive holy spirit.* The gift is freely offered, but it can be refused; there is a definite act of reception. The Lord now fulfils the promise of the Baptist concerning Him (i, 33); He baptises His disciples, not in water which washes away stains, but in holy spirit—the energy of a holy life in obedience to God.
>
> *Receive holy spirit*—not "the Holy Spirit." What is bestowed is not the Divine Person Himself but the power and energy of which He is the source. Earlier it had been said *not yet was there spirit, because Jesus was not yet glorified* (vii, 39). But now that glorification is complete, and it is possible for the new divine energy, which operates through man's response to the manifested love of God, to begin its activity.[7]

There is a lesson for all days, and not least for our day. Of ourselves we can do nothing. To attempt in our own strength the life we feel we ought to live is to be dogged by failure. Anatole France quotes Prévost, "How difficult it is to pick up a little strength when one has made a habit of one's weakness, and how much it costs us to fight for victory when for long past one has found it sweet to yield!"[8] We must live in Christ, and draw from him what in ourselves we have not got, if we are to be fit for what he asks of us. In particular, so Christ promises, it is a Spirit of discernment that they are receiving, enabling them to know what kind of life a man should live; to recognize what things are wrong and evil, and what are worthy and right; to determine when repentance is genuine, and when it is only an empty sham. **If you forgive the sins of any, they are forgiven; if you retain the sins of any, they are retained.** Confessedly the church has stumbled disastrously in these matters, mistaking prejudice for principle and mere human whims and preferences for the eternal will of God. All that often and scandalously. Yet is not Moehler justified when he declares that as they look back, subsequent ages watch with amazement and awe how the church has found its way through difficulties that seemed inescapable and problems that could not apparently be solved. In very truth a pillar of fire has led Christ's blundering people through the darkness of the night.

24-31. *Thomas.*—That night that Christ came Thomas had not been present. We do not know why. But is there not here a warning for us not to forsake the assembling of ourselves together? How much many must miss who make only an occasional, spasmodic, irregular appearance at the worship of God in his house! "For where two or three are gathered together in my name, there am I in the midst of them," so Christ promises (Matt. 18:20). And sometimes surely had they been there, to them too he would have appeared!

When the other disciples told him of what

[7] *Readings in St. John's Gospel,* 2nd ser. (London: Macmillan & Co.; New York: The Macmillan Co., 1940), pp. 386-87. Used by permission of Mrs. Temple.

[8] *The Latin Genius,* tr. Wilfrid S. Jackson (London: John Lane, 1924), p. 181.

26 ¶ And after eight days again his disciples were within, and Thomas with them: *then* came Jesus, the doors being shut, and stood in the midst, and said, Peace *be* unto you.

27 Then saith he to Thomas, Reach hither thy finger, and behold my hands; and reach hither thy hand, and thrust *it* into my side; and be not faithless, but believing.

28 And Thomas answered and said unto him, My Lord and my God.

29 Jesus saith unto him, Thomas, because thou hast seen me, thou hast believed: blessed *are* they that have not seen, and *yet* have believed.

26 Eight days later, his disciples were
again in the house, and Thomas was with
them. The doors were shut, but Jesus came
and stood among them, and said, "Peace be
with you." 27 Then he said to Thomas,
"Put your finger here, and see my hands;
and put out your hand, and place it in my
side; do not be faithless, but believing."
28 Thomas answered him, "My Lord and
my God!" 29 Jesus said to him, "Have you
believed because you have seen me? Blessed
are those who have not seen and yet believe."

---

appearance of the risen Lord to the assembled disciples, Thomas could not accept their evidence. He demanded a tangible test. A week later Thomas was present in the house with the rest when Jesus appeared and gave the greeting of peace. Jesus challenged the skeptic to carry out his test. He knew that Thomas would shrink from the crude and abhorrent literalism. The sight of the wounded hands and side in that transfigured body was enough to banish his doubts and melt his heart. There was a reproach in Jesus' challenge. **Do not be faithless, but believing.** Thomas' reply expresses the faith of the Christian church (cf. I John 5:4-5). The prologue to the Gospel begins with the assertion of the divinity of the Logos; ch. 1 closes with the confession of Nathanael (1:49), "Rabbi, you are the Son of God! You are the King of Israel!" The exclamation heard from the lips of Thomas is the mature creed of the worshiping church when this Gospel was written. Jesus responds with the last beatitude of the Gospels: **Have you believed because you have seen me? Blessed are those who have not seen and yet believe.**

---

had happened, Thomas was flatly and openly incredulous, pushing the whole thing aside as on the face of it ridiculously impossible. As to the first reports, it had been dark, or nearly so; the women were strained and overwrought by all they had been through; their eyes were full of tears and did not see clearly; they had imagined what was not there and could not have been there, for Christ was dead, and dead men do not rise. And as for this alleged appearance to the ten, self-evidently the thing could be nothing more than sheer hallucination born of frayed nerves or of longing for what could never be. It was wishful thinking that had seemed to come true.

Nearly everybody is severe with Thomas, a notable exception being a subtly discriminating study of the apostle's mind by A. B. Davidson.[9] Had we been there, we should likely have argued as he argued and said what he said. His tests sound crude, almost repulsively so. But were they? His was a doggedly honest mind, almost stolidly so. For he had not much poetry in him, one thinks; was a matter-of-fact person, with his feet planted firmly on the solid ground; not one to be rushed into believing what he wanted to believe, but sincere enough to face the facts and to accept them, however grim and dark. Essentially he was a valiant soul, loyal to Christ even when in his own mind the last hope was out. Certain that if the little band made for Jerusalem it meant the inevitable end, he yet leaped to his feet. "Let us also go," he said, "that we may die with him" (11:16). He did not stand to it, alas! But there spoke the real man. So here. With no such hope as the others had to encourage him, Thomas stood fast by the lost cause, for so it seemed to him; waited to go down with the sinking ship. For days on end nothing further happened, and with that, no doubt, the man grew more and more confirmed in his rejection of the wild rumors. Till suddenly Christ again appeared and accepted his disciple's challenge. **Put your finger here, and see my hands; and put out your hand, and place it in my side; do not be faithless, but believing.**

Often he acts so to people, blowing their truculent doubts into thin air; shutting them

[9] *Called of God,* pp. 319 ff.

30 ¶ And many other signs truly did Jesus in the presence of his disciples, which are not written in this book:

30 Now Jesus did many other signs in the presence of the disciples, which are not

B. The Purpose of the Gospel (20:30-31)

30-31. A selective interest has chosen a few typical "signs" out of the multitude retained in the tradition of the church (cf. 21:25). Those which have been recorded are told to fulfill the purpose of the Gospel—to create faith and to impart **life.** Belief in **Jesus** as **the Christ, the Son of God,** brings **life** in virtue of the **name** of Jesus. In the O.T. and in Judaism this title, **Son of God,** was messianic. In Hellenism it was applied to the Roman emperors. But for the evangelist the term is used in its highest and exclusive sense of him who, as the Logos, is the perfect revelation of God (cf. 1:34, 49; 3:8; 5:25; 10:36; 11:4, 27; 19:7). The prologue asserts that "in him was life" (1:4); throughout the Gospel the purpose of the mission of the Son is announced as "that they might have life" (cf. 5:40; 6:53; 10:10); now the first ending of the Gospel sums up its contents as a record of the works of Jesus to create faith leading to life.

The closing words of this evangelic story, as it was originally told before the appendix was added, form the beatitude declared to those who believe without seeing. This is the climax of the evangelist's teaching about the relative place of ocular demonstration and the response of faith. The fullest treatment which this aspect of the Fourth Gospel has received is in an essay by Oscar Cullmann entitled, Εἶδεν καὶ ἐπίστευσεν: *La vie de Jésus, objet de la "vue" et de la "foi" d'après le quatrième Evangile,* and contributed to *Aux Sources de la Tradition Chrétienne—Mélanges offerts à M. Maurice Goguel* (Neuchatel and Paris: Delachaux & Niestlé, 1950). This writer has shown that the connection between Jesus and the Christ is not that between a historical figure and a metaphysical entity, but that between a visible history compressed within a few years and a history continuously unfolded throughout the ages, which is known as "the history of salvation." The Johannine Gospel, in a degree only paralleled by the Epistle to the Hebrews, emphasizes both the real humanity of Jesus and the true divinity of the Christ and unites them in one Person. We are told that "the Word became flesh." Hence every incident recorded in the earthly life of Jesus has its own significance. This life in the "flesh" was and is a revelation of the divine nature. Hence the importance that attaches to the evidence received through the eyes and ears of the spectators. The authority of the first apostles was that they could say, "We have beheld his glory" (1:14). When

up into belief by the facts of their own experience; facts there, unanswerable and indisputable. In one real sense only thus does a man really believe at all. "What this parish needs," wrote Carlyle, "is what every parish needs, a man who knows God at more than second hand." Only when the gospel of Christ is for us no carried story, no rumor heard and passed on by us for what it may be worth; but first-hand evidence, what we have seen, what we have looked upon with our own eyes, what we have handled with our own hands, what we have proved in our own experience, not simply an unthinking acquiescence in what others say, which may be all very well as a beginning, but something that has happened to us—only then does our belief grow vital.

Yet Christ tells us here that there is a bigger faith even than that, a faith that can dispense with tangible proofs and visible evidence, that believes heroically even when there is no obvious and immediate confirmation, building unafraid and confident on God's naked word. This is true in many ways. The masters of devotion are unanimous in their assertion that no prayer is so real a prayer as that which seems to ourselves no prayer at all, so cold and dry and lifeless are our hearts, so dull and wingless our ineffectual words. And the saints are sure that the most heroic of believers is not he who is swept on happily and without effort by a gale of the Spirit in his sails, visibly making progress, but he who like Christ himself on the cross can believe on undauntedly in the utter darkness, and when all seems lost. It is easy to be faithful when set in a sphere where there is much to encourage one—crowded pews, and a buzzing of pleased excitement, and souls being saved. Easy for them who so see to believe. But his is a harder task which needs a deeper faith,

31 But these are written, that ye might believe that Jesus is the Christ, the Son of God; and that believing ye might have life through his name.

written in this book; 31 but these are written that you may believe that Jesus is the Christ, the Son of God, and that believing you may have life in his name.

Philip said, "Lord, show us the Father, and we shall be satisfied," Jesus replied, "He who has seen me has seen the Father" (14:8-9). So the apostolic testimony handed on to succeeding generations is: "That which was from the beginning, which we have heard, which we have seen with our eyes, . . . that which we have seen and heard we proclaim also to you, so that you may have fellowship with us" (I John 1:1-3).

Nevertheless, there are passages which show that merely seeing with the eyes of the body is not enough. The mighty acts of Jesus are always called "signs" in this Gospel; yet often those who saw them were not led to faith by what they saw. It was to the very crowd which had demanded, "What sign do you do, that we may see, and believe you?" (6:30) that Jesus said a little later, "You have seen me and yet do not believe" (6:36). The three synonyms used by John, ὁρᾶν, θεᾶσθαι, and θεωρεῖν, are all used of the physical organ of vision, but they are sometimes used in a double sense. Thus, "For judgment I came into this world, that those who do not see may see, and that those who see may become blind" (9:39), or again, "For this is the will of my Father, that every one who sees the Son and believes in him should have eternal life" (6:40). There is thus a spiritual vision which is needed to interpret the acts and words of Christ, and to see their abiding significance. Thus the two incidents in ch. 20 show the relation between seeing and believing. Peter had seen all that the other disciple saw in the empty sepulcher; but the disciple whom Jesus loved interpreted the situation in the light of all that he had already seen and heard of Jesus. "He saw and believed" (20:8). Thomas was not present on Easter evening when Jesus appeared to his disciples. But he had the testimony of those who had seen for themselves, and he should have grasped the significance of their testimony by his previous knowledge of Jesus.

The final beatitude is the charter of the church's faith. In the view of this evangelist a special privilege belongs to those who live under the dispensation of the Spirit. He tells us repeatedly that the relevance of some passage from the O.T., or the deeper meaning of some word or act of Jesus, was understood by the disciples only after the Resurrection, or when the Spirit had been given (cf. 2:19; 7:39; 14:26; 16:12). The apostolic testimony has preserved for the church of the future the record of what the first "eyewitnesses and ministers of the word" (Luke 1:2) saw and heard. Yet their record, if merely accepted as a statement of historic fact, would not suffice to produce belief. The happiness that is promised to those "who have not seen and yet believe" is the gift of the Spirit who will glorify Christ, "for he will take what is mine and declare it to you" (16:14-15).

who, set down in some cramped, dead, impervious congregation spends himself to the last ounce and has no flicker of encouragement; for all his labor seems a loss of time, and all his sacrifice a foolish waste with no results at all to justify it. Christ, the Christ who himself often lived through that experience, who died without one soul that really understood or who believed, worth calling believing, looks understandingly at such tried folk and smiles encouragement to them, **Blessed are those who have not seen and yet believe.**

Thomas may have been slow in starting. But at a bound he leaped ahead of all the rest and reached the full truth. **My Lord and my God!** —a saying which, as this Gospel was originally planned, was its apex and climax and culmination and end. Here was a man who had seen Jesus as he really was—the Christ, the Son of God. Through him he had learned to know God as he is, arguing from the Christ to him, sure that if Christ's life was one uninterrupted unselfishness, and his character a purity and grace which spent itself ungrudgingly for others, so must God live, so must God be. And seeing that, life grew another thing for Thomas. New standards for it thrust themselves upon him. New possibilities leaped into view and offered themselves to him. With such a Savior representing such a God, the old way of things would

21 After these things Jesus showed
himself again to the disciples at the
sea of Tiberias; and on this wise showed he
himself.

2 There were together Simon Peter, and
Thomas called Didymus, and Nathanael of
Cana in Galilee, and the *sons* of Zebedee,
and two other of his disciples.

3 Simon Peter saith unto them, I go a
fishing. They say unto him, We also go
with thee. They went forth, and entered
into a ship immediately; and that night
they caught nothing.

21 After this Jesus revealed himself
again to the disciples by the Sea of
Ti-be'ri-as; and he revealed himself in this
way. 2 Simon Peter, Thomas called the
Twin, Na-than'a-el of Cana in Galilee, the
sons of Zeb'e-dee, and two others of his dis-
ciples were together. 3 Simon Peter said
to them, "I am going fishing." They said
to him, "We will go with you." They went
out and got into the boat; but that night
they caught nothing.

Thus the faith which finds expression in the credo of Thomas is one with that which inspired Paul. "No one can say 'Jesus is Lord' except by the Holy Spirit" (I Cor. 12:3).

Charles Wesley, in his hymn "Spirit of faith, come down," has combined the Pauline and the Johannine testimony that appeals to the "Spirit of faith":

> No man can truly say
> That Jesus is the Lord,
> Unless thou take the veil away,
> And breathe the living word;
> Then, only then, we feel
> Our interest in his blood,
> And cry, with joy unspeakable,
> "Thou art my Lord, my God!"

C. Epilogue (21:1-25)

This chapter seems to be a later addition (see Intro., p. 446, on the suggestion that it was added by the evangelist himself). Mark's story breaks off abruptly with the women fleeing from the tomb in fear and trembling. Matthew, after telling of the appearance of the Lord to the women, records the revelation of Jesus to the disciples in Galilee. Luke's Easter appearances all take place in or near Jerusalem. In this last chapter John completes his Jerusalem Christophanies with the story of one by the lakeside in Galilee.

1. The Appearance Beside the Lake (21:1-14)

21:1-3. The lake is called **Tiberias,** as in 6:1, but nowhere else in the Gospels, though Josephus and Pausanias use the name. Six disciples join **Simon Peter** in a night's unsuccessful fishing. **Thomas and Nathanael** (here mentioned as **of Cana in Galilee**) are prominent in this Gospel. **The sons of Zebedee** are not mentioned elsewhere in John. The two unnamed disciples might well be Andrew and Philip who are named together in 1:43; 6:5, 7; 12:22.

---

no longer do. Thomas was being fashioned into a new type of being, was henceforth a new creature, living in a new world, endowed in Christ with quite new possibilities and powers.

"And that," says the evangelist as he lays down his pen, "is what I have written my book to prove that Christ can do for any one who will accept it from him" (vs. 31).

21:1-15. ***The Sanctity of Common Work.***—This chapter, whether or not by the hand of the original author, constitutes an appendix to the Gospel as it stands and as it has always stood, setting forth for the reader a dramatic tale vividly told. Seven of the disciples were back at the Sea of Galilee. Probably enough they had to face the ridicule of the village street. "The great adventurers are back again! I always said that their daft scheme would come to nothing, and it has." So, if not openly and to their faces, then behind their backs, people no doubt scoffed and jeered. But of that we hear nothing. Yet they themselves were puzzled.

4 But when the morning was now come, Jesus stood on the shore; but the disciples knew not that it was Jesus.

5 Then Jesus saith unto them, Children, have ye any meat? They answered him, No.

6 And he said unto them, Cast the net on the right side of the ship, and ye shall find. They cast therefore, and now they were not able to draw it for the multitude of fishes.

4 Just as day was breaking, Jesus stood
on the beach; yet the disciples did not know
that it was Jesus. 5 Jesus said to them,
"Children, have you any fish?" They an-
swered him, "No." 6 He said to them, "Cast
the net on the right side of the boat, and
you will find some." So they cast it, and
now they were not able to haul it in, for

4-8. Jesus, standing on the beach, was at first unrecognized. This might have been due to the morning haze (cf. 20:14). The story of the night's failure, the word of Jesus to lower the nets again, the astonishing haul, recall Luke 5:1-11, which may be a reminiscence of the same tradition, with Peter's sense of shame and his commission. There is no suggestion in the narrative that this is to be regarded as a "sign," and it is possible that Jesus was thought of as seeing a shoal of fish approaching the farther side of the boat. The question (μή τι προσφάγιον ἔχετε;), translated **Have ye any meat?** (KJV) or **Have you any fish?** (RSV), is shown by Wetstein—cited, with additional examples, by Field (*Notes on Translation of the N.T.*, p. 109)—to be an idiom for "Have you taken any fish?" Moulton and Milligan (*Vocabulary of Greek Testament,* pp. 551-52) show that the use of the word in the papyri, as well as some ancient textual authorities, supports the translation of the ERV, "Have ye aught to eat?"

They had seen the risen Lord; they had been given audacious promises by him; they had again been called to a high service for him and the world. Yet day crept after day and nothing happened. If they still held together, if they still waited, it was in a growing perplexity, and with minds tiring under the strain of this unexpected delay. Until at last Peter's patience snapped. Quite suddenly, it seems; perhaps while watching the other boats putting out for the fishing grounds, "I'm off to fish," he said; and the rest, at once falling in with the suggestion, they were with that making for the shore, hoisting the sails, and the accustomed feel of the ropes in their hands again, were back at the familiar, long-deserted tasks.

For themselves it was a wise move. But for Christ and his cause it was a crisis of the first importance. Wise for themselves. For idleness is a precarious condition, bringing many dangers. If grief comes, it is best not to sit solitary, moping and desolate, but to get back to one's daily work. It will be dazedly that one puts it through, moving about in an insubstantial world of shadows, and of things that have lost their momentousness. Yet it is wise. And in temptation it is common sense to fall back at once on some hobby or play or game or interest that will hold the attention, fill the mind, crowd out the evil thing. In light of this, our self-excusing plea that if we had been given a chance, some breathing space, some elbowroom, we could and would have served God loyally, whereas in the jostle and hubbub where we are set, with our minds of necessity clogged and cluttered up by daily duties urgently clamoring for our attention, the thing is out of the question—all that is a poor bleat. No doubt busyness has its perils. Since in the rush and noise and dust of life one can lose touch with God, get separated from him in the press. As Benjamin Jowett of Balliol put it, "God pity me! I cannot keep the thought of God in my mind." Yet idleness is far more dangerous. So Bishop Thomas Wilson, that busiest of men, that saintly soul, laid it down with confidence, he who had had experience of both ways of it: "To dispose our hearts to devotion, the active life is to be preferred to the contemplative."[1] That is a fact we are forgetting, with our insistence upon shorter working hours and more extensive leisure. For everything depends on how we use and fill the leisure. So long as a man is at decent work, his soul as a rule is fairly safe. It is when he is idling in his own time, lounging perhaps at the street corners, that he invites temptation. And it comes.

Yet while all that is so, it is with alarm that we watch that narrow ribbon of water widening between the shore and the departing boat. For if these men are caught into the old life again, will there be, can there be, a Christian church at all? Are they not going to turn their backs upon the great adventure; to settle down, disillusioned if not grown cynical, contemptuous of

[1] *Sacra Privata,* "Devotion."

7 Therefore that disciple whom Jesus loved saith unto Peter, It is the Lord. Now when Simon Peter heard that it was the Lord, he girt *his* fisher's coat *unto him,* (for he was naked,) and did cast himself into the sea.

8 And the other disciples came in a little ship, (for they were not far from land, but as it were two hundred cubits,) dragging the net with fishes.

9 As soon then as they were come to land, they saw a fire of coals there, and fish laid thereon, and bread.

the quantity of fish.
7 That disciple whom
Jesus loved said to Peter, "It is the Lord!"
When Simon Peter heard that it was the
Lord, he put on his clothes, for he was
stripped for work, and sprang into the sea.
8 But the other disciples came in the boat,
dragging the net full of fish, for they were
not far from the land, but about a hundred yards[k] off.

9 When they got out on land, they saw a charcoal fire there, with fish lying on it,

[k] Greek *two hundred cubits.*

On their confession of failure, Jesus told his disciples to cast the net on the side furthest from the shore. This would be indicated by a gesture. Strack and Billerbeck (*Kommentar zum N.T. aus Talmud und Midrasch,* I, 980) give evidence for the meaning "lucky" for **right side** (cf. also Luke 1:11; Matt. 25:33; Mark 16:5). The success of this attempt led the Beloved Disciple to recognize the Lord. Peter, with characteristic impetuosity, flung himself into the sea on the landward side, now clear of the net, hastily donning his outer garment and tucking it into his girdle the more easily to wade ashore. Because of the shallow water, the other six came ashore in the dinghy dragging after them the net with its great haul of fish.

9-14. This narrative recalls the Eucharistic meal of ch. 6. Some expositors credit Peter with the preparation of the charcoal fire, but the more obvious intention of the

---

all idealisms and suspicious of all generous enthusiasms? "For the deadliest of all wet blankets," said John Morley, out of his wide experience, "give me a middle-aged man who has been most of a visionary in his youth."[2] There is a pathetic passage in the life of Buddha. He, a young chieftain, had abandoned everything because he had recognized the evanescence of the things men covet, and for which they pay their lives, and had sought for something better and more permanent. For years he was zealous and wholehearted in his quest. He fasted all but unto death. He tried teacher after teacher. But nothing came of it. Till one day suddenly out of nowhere an intolerable craving for the old home life assailed him. He had tried hard. He had done all that man could do. And he had failed. Better surely be sensible and face the facts, and give it up, and go back to his wife and child and home. Buddha resisted that enticement and held on. Something perhaps not unlike that had come that day to these disciples. Was Christ's call to them to fade out after all? Were they to jolt back into the old familiar rut in which they used to travel?

Are not the two main lessons to be gathered from this passage these? First, our Lord's gracious sanctifying of common work. Not here for the first time of course. The long years spent at Nazareth in the carpenter's shed, his hand resting on ordinary manual daily toil, have glorified that. But here again he emphasized the fact that we can obey and help him by the willingness and thoroughness with which we put through our common tasks. In the Middle Ages that truth was largely challenged and forgotten, though indeed many a monk carved, and for that matter plowed, to the glory of God. Still common work fell in men's estimation to a very secondary place, till the Reformers broke in with their reminder that Christ can be served out in the fields as really as at the altar, as truly and as literally in the kitchen as in the holy place. Thus Karl Heim:

> "God dwells not in temples made with hands." It seemed that everything had become secular. But it was precisely this collapse of the temple-walls, this apparent secularization of all life, that was to lead to the most profound religious discovery. When the temple was overthrown, the whole world became the temple of God. The workshop became a church, a man's native land became a sanctuary; all who were engaged in maintaining human life became consecrated priests in this vast Church of God. [And again, quoting from Luther] A cobbler, a smith, a peasant, whatever he may be, a man has the labour and occupation of his craft, and yet all men alike are consecrated bishops and priests. A poor servant-girl may say: "I cook the meals, I make up the beds, I dust the rooms. Who has bidden me do it? My master and my mistress have

[2] *Aphorisms* (London: Macmillan & Co., 1887), p. 48.

10 Jesus saith unto them, Bring of the fish which ye have now caught.

11 Simon Peter went up, and drew the net to land full of great fishes, a hundred and fifty and three: and for all there were so many, yet was not the net broken.

12 Jesus saith unto them, Come *and* dine. And none of the disciples durst ask him, Who art thou? knowing that it was the Lord.

13 Jesus then cometh, and taketh bread, and giveth them, and fish likewise.

and bread. 10 Jesus said to them, "Bring
some of the fish that you have just caught."
11 So Simon Peter went aboard and hauled
the net ashore, full of large fish, a hundred
and fifty-three of them; and although there
were so many, the net was not torn. 12 Jesus
said to them, "Come and have breakfast."
Now none of the disciples dared ask him,
"Who are you?" They knew it was the
Lord. 13 Jesus came and took the bread
and gave it to them, and so with the fish.

---

evangelist is that Jesus had prepared a simple meal. On the arrival of the seven, Jesus invited them to bring some of the fish from their catch, and Peter drags the net to the beach. The strangeness of the event perplexed the disciples, yet they dared not put their wonder into words because they knew that this was the risen Lord. It is unnecessary to find here an allusion to the promise in 16:23 (see Exeg.). Any lingering doubts entertained at first were dispelled when Jesus, as in other days, **took the bread and gave it to them** (cf. Luke 24:30-31, 35; Mark 6:41; 8:6). This episode is regarded by many as allegorical. Farfetched meanings have been discovered. Jerome (see his commentary on Ezek. 47 in Migne's *Patrologia Latina,* XXV, 474) is responsible for the statement that according to Oppian, a Cilician poet of the second century, there are a **hundred and fifty-three** species of fish. There is no such statement in Oppian. If that was a common belief in the ancient world, it would be possible to infer that the evangelist is thinking of the universal mission of the apostles, and that by the unbroken net he was thinking of the power given to the church to hold together men of every race. The number is probably

---

bidden me. Who has given them the right to command me? God has given it them. So it is true that I am serving God in Heaven as well as them. How happy can I feel now! It is as if I were in Heaven, doing my work for God!" [8]

All of which has been again largely forgotten and is by many openly and angrily denied. For masses of people work has neither dignity nor interest, is a sheer nuisance, an intolerable necessity that has to be grudgingly put through. And not till it is safely over does life, to be called life, begin. Carlyle's eulogies of it come to us from a far-off land and awaken no echo whatsoever in the typical present-day mind.

> All true work is sacred; in all true work, were it but true hand labour, there is something of divineness. . . . Sweat of the brow; and up from that to sweat of the brain; sweat of the heart . . .—up to that "Agony of bloody sweat," which all men have called divine! O brother, if this is not "worship," then I say, the more piety for worship; for this is the noblest thing yet discovered under God's sky.[4]

There are few facts needing more urgently to be relearned than the sacredness and sanctity of common work. If men would only cease from these eternal ululations and self-commiseratings, and would grasp that in and through every proper task they can serve not man alone but the Lord Christ, putting their loyalty to him into the doing of it, they would again find that it is really true.

So the Jesuit priest, Gerard Manley Hopkins:

> It is not only prayer that gives God glory but work. Smiting on an anvil, sawing a beam, whitewashing a wall, driving horses, sweeping, scouring, everything gives God some glory if being in his grace you do it as your duty. To go to communion worthily gives God great glory, but to take food in thankfulness and temperance gives him glory too. To lift up the hands in prayer gives God glory, but a man with a dungfork in his hand, a woman with a sloppail, give him glory too. He is so great that all things give him glory if you mean they should. So then, my brethren, live.[5]

But while all that is indisputably so, this narrative goes on to show us that some are called to a more definite serving of the Master and his kingdom in more definitely spiritual ways, and in more definitely spiritual things. The disciples had not had a successful night. And

[8] *Spirit and Truth,* tr. E. P. Dickie (London: The Lutterworth Press, 1935), pp. 165-66, 171. Used by permission.

[4] *Past and Present,* Bk. III, ch. xii.

[5] Quoted in Rainer Maria Rilke, *Poems from the Book of Hours,* tr. Babette Deutsch (Norfolk, Conn.: New Directions Press, 1941), p. 7.

14 This is now the third time that Jesus showed himself to his disciples, after that he was risen from the dead.

15 ¶ So when they had dined, Jesus saith to Simon Peter, Simon, *son* of Jonas, lovest thou me more than these? He saith unto him, Yea, Lord; thou knowest that I love thee. He saith unto him, Feed my lambs.

14 This was now the third time that Jesus was revealed to the disciples after he was raised from the dead.

15 When they had finished breakfast, Jesus said to Simon Peter, "Simon, son of John, do you love me more than these?" He said to him, "Yes, Lord; you know that

---

the tradition of the fishermen's counted haul of fish. If the writer saw some symbolical meaning in the tradition, he has kept his secret. The main purpose is to record a third revelation of the risen Christ to his disciples (vs. 14). The appearance to Mary Magdalene is not included in the number.

2. Peter and the Beloved Disciple (21:15-23)

15-17. The restoration of Peter after his denial of Jesus takes the form of a threefold question and a triple commission, corresponding to the triple denial. The three questions are in substance one. The triple trust is that of a true pastor. There is no need to distinguish between the two words for **love** (as Goodspeed does) in these verses, since

---

when in the gray light of the dawn a voice hailed them across the waters from the shore, "Have you got anything, lads?" they had to answer, "No!" Whereat the stranger bade them cast on the right side of the ship. Thinking that from his slight vantage ground a little way up the beach he must have seen some evidence of a shoal or the like, they did as he said and found a catch indeed. **It is the Lord!** said John at once to Peter; and he with his usual impulsive impetuousness leaped overboard and swam and splashed ashore. A foolish action; and even a bit selfish! He would have done better taking his fair share at the oars and not leaving that to others. For it would seem that the water thereabouts was too shallow for the fishing boat, so shallow that they had to take to the dinghy and pull in, dragging the full net behind them.

There are many whose religion is like Peter's action. It is hectic, emotional, a thing largely of feeling. It takes the eye and seems impressive and makes others about them look formal and cold. But it does not set them to their tasks with a new faithfulness. And one wonders if it means much as Christ judges. Indeed, Peter himself seems to have felt this. For when Christ said, **Bring some of the fish that you have just caught,** it was he who sprang up and he who hauled the heavy net ashore; and he who brought what Christ had asked. And then there followed that strange, eerie, constrained breakfast beside the lake.

It would seem that Christ had prepared it for them with his own hands, knowing that they would be cold and wet and tired and disappointed; but that he allowed them to make their own contribution to it—both characteristically Christlike actions. Every child wants to be allowed to help; and a wise parent finds means of enabling him to do so. And there are few of the lovingkindnesses of the Lord greater or more moving than that he too allows us in our childish way to help him.

15-25. *The Questioning of Peter.*—With that we reach the scene which has made so deep an impression on the mind of Christendom—the searching threefold questioning of Peter.

(*a*) **Lovest thou me more than these?** Who or what are these? Most commentators hold, with the Exeg., that Christ meant the other disciples, referring back to Peter's confident boasting that even though all men should fail him, he for one certainly would not. That seems unlike Christ. It was not his way so to handle people, so to harass a fallen and repentant man, fretting his sore, or so to pit one of his followers against the others, and still less in these others' presence. And so some think that Christ's question meant—"Once on a day I called you, Peter; and then you responded, rose up at once, left all, and followed. But you are back at the old life again. And are you going to abandon me? Are you pulling out of the adventure? Having put your hand to the plow, are you now looking back? Do the old ties tug at your heart? And are they drawing you away from me? Or do you still love me more than these? You must decide between them and me; today, in this old familiar place. You are in danger of deserting. That is why I am here."

16 He saith to him again the second time, Simon, *son* of Jonas, lovest thou me? He saith unto him, Yea, Lord; thou knowest that I love thee. He saith unto him, Feed my sheep.

17 He saith unto him the third time, Simon, *son* of Jonas, lovest thou me? Peter was grieved because he said unto him the third time, Lovest thou me? And he said unto him, Lord, thou knowest all things; thou knowest that I love thee. Jesus saith unto him, Feed my sheep.

I love you." **16** He said to him, "Feed my lambs." A second time he said to him, "Simon, son of John, do you love me?" He said to him, "Yes, Lord; you know that I love you." He said to him, "Tend my sheep." **17** He said to him the third time, "Simon, son of John, do you love me?" Peter was grieved because he said to him the third time, "Do you love me?" And he said to him, "Lord, you know everything; you know that I love you." Jesus said to

---

ἀγαπάω and φιλέω are used interchangeably in this Gospel, even in the same context. The first question (vs. 15) takes the form **Do you love me more than these?** Of the two possible interpretations—"more than these do" or "more than you love these"—the former is preferable in view of Mark 14:29. The Johannine mannerism of ringing the changes on pairs of synonyms in the Greek makes it unwise to base any exegetical subtleties on the different words used for **feed** (βόσκειν) and **tend** (ποιμαίνειν) or even for **lambs** (ἀρνία) and **sheep** (προβάτια). The correct reading in vs. 17 is the diminutive προβάτια (A B C W), which is also read by B C 19 O.L. (*b*) in vs. 16. Some, however, would read ἀρνία (vs. 15), προβάτια (vs. 16), πρόβατα (vs. 17) on the strength of the Vulg.

Well, that is like him. For certainly he has often broken in on us in the very nick of time. We were in jeopardy. We were deciding, and deciding wrongly. And suddenly some word of his sprang into our mind. Some remembrance of him rose up and steadied us. And with that we rallied, and the crisis safely passed.

(*b*) **Do you love me?** Christ's questions to Peter show the test by which he judges that we stand or fall. Francis Bacon protests his amazement that Aristotle in his ethical writings never deals with the affections. For, thinks Bacon, these are fundamental, all-important, decisive.[6] It is by our likings that we are saved; and by our likings that we are lost. **Lovest thou me more than these?** So once. And then the twice-repeated, "Do you love me at all, to be called loving?" It is a drastic test. And Peter, faced by it, wisely does not protest or argue or asseverate. He knows that if he is challenged, he has small evidence of his affection to put forward. For he has failed Christ, denied Christ, deserted Christ with every aggravation of disloyalty. That he does not forget. And yet though it may not look like it, though he cannot prove it, though many things rise up to mock the claim, he knows that he does love Christ through and in spite of everything; and confidently calls Christ himself as his witness, challenging him to deny it; agreeing that he will stand or fall by the Master's decision in the matter. **You know,** he says; and again, **You know;** and then in a kind of desperation, "You who know all things must know this—that I do love you."

And in the end of the day what other plea has any one of us? We too have failed and faltered and deserted Christ too often. And yet we also can protest that in spite of much which we do not deny seems to make the claim ridiculous, we do love Christ, and he knows it. And with us as with Peter he accepts that plea. To the disciple he gave a wonderful promise: that though he had so sadly broken down, he would be faithful even unto death. And with that, the past blotted out, trustfully, hopefully, as sanguine about this man and what he could do for the cause as when he first chose him years ago, **Follow me,** Christ said.

And so it has been often and often with us too. What strange, dogged faith he has in us that will not break or die! O God, prayed Lancelot Andrewes, I thank Thee, "for my call, recall, yea, many calls besides."[7]

(*c*) It is impressive also to mark the criterion which our Lord gives us whereby we can gauge the value of what we claim to be our affection for him; and much more important, by which he himself judges of it. That criterion is service. Every affection worthy of the name is no mere sentiment, but is eager to do and give on behalf of the loved one. And so it is with a genuine Christian and the Master. Thus Paul: "For the love of Christ controls us, because we are convinced that one has died for all; therefore all have died. And he died for all, that those who

[6] *Advancement of Learning,* Bk. VII, ch. iii.

[7] *Private Devotions,* "Fifth Day: Praise."

18 Verily, verily, I say unto thee, When thou wast young, thou girdedst thyself, and walkedst whither thou wouldest: but when thou shalt be old, thou shalt stretch forth thy hands, and another shall gird thee, and carry *thee* whither thou wouldest not.

19 This spake he, signifying by what death he should glorify God. And when he had spoken this, he saith unto him, Follow me.

him, "Feed my sheep.
18 Truly, truly, I say to you, when you were young, you girded yourself and walked where you would; but when you are old, you will stretch out your hands, and another will gird you and carry you where you do not wish to go."
19 (This he said to show by what death he was to glorify God.) And after this he said to him, "Follow me."

(*agnos . . . agnos . . . oves*) and the Syriac versions. This charge to pastoral fidelity recalls the allegory of the good shepherd (10:1-18) and points forward to I Pet. 5:2-4.

18-19. Vs. 18 applies a proverbial expression to Peter: Youth is free to go its own way; old age means the loss of freedom. But in view of the many warnings uttered by Jesus of the fate that his followers must expect, it was natural to think of this as a prediction of martyrdom. The metaphor of stretching out the hands to be dressed, or to be led in helpless old age, was wrongly taken as a prophecy that Peter would be crucified. Field (*Notes on Translation of the N.T.*, p. 109) has certainly proved that Greek writers (Artemidorus, Arrian, Dionysius of Halicarnassus) used the term

---

live might live no longer for themselves but for him who for their sake died and was raised" (II Cor. 5:14-15). One is called of God not to privilege only but also to service. Which is true and yet quite a wrong way of putting it. For the opportunity of service is a major portion of the privilege, and is seized naturally, gladly, eagerly. So Karl Heim:

> The Heidelberg Catechism sums up the whole of Christian morality under one comprehensive topic: "Part Three: Concerning Thankfulness." "Since we are delivered from our suffering through grace alone, by Christ, and without any service of our own, why is it necessary to engage in good works? For this reason, that we must employ our whole life in expressing our gratitude to God for His goodness and in praising Him." When . . . a man experiences the miracle of forgiveness, it follows unavoidably that he must lay his whole life at the feet of Him who has blessed him so marvellously. Inevitably and naturally, without any striving, there comes to the man that which cannot be brought about by any laws or any asceticism, namely, the impulse to devote himself to God. . . . A man whose soul is filled to overflowing with gratitude does more, of his own free will, as Luther says, than is demanded from him. . . . He would like best if he could do the impossible . . . , and yet —this is true of all that a man does from this impulse of gratitude—he never reflects on what he does, he never dreams that he is doing anything out of the ordinary. His left hand knows not what his right hand does. His actions are free from all self-consciousness. "Faith does not ask whether it ought to do good works: it has done them already." [8]

[8] *Spirit and Truth*, tr. E. P. Dickie (London: The Lutterworth Press, 1935), pp. 155-56. Used by permission.

To Peter there was given a thrilling promise, but it was a twofold promise. The Moravians have as the symbol of their church an ox standing between an altar and a plow, with the inscription "Ready for either." Peter was guaranteed that in the end his life would flame itself out in a glorious act of crowning sacrifice; but also that before that he was to be given days and months and years of serving Christ by helping those dear to him. Not all Christians give the impression that they have entered any way at all into that side of their privileges in Christ. There are congregations which seem little more or better than religious clubs, run for the interest, or at most for the spiritual profiting of their members—just like any other club, a purely self-centered thing. But we are called of God not only for the saving of our own souls, but to help him in his saving of the world. And we should be his fellow laborers, with our hands touching his at the common task. Even some who are accounted saints look as if they were egregiously self-centered, and even unpleasantly selfish, absorbed in what happens to interest them, though in their case that is their own salvation; continually feeling their own spiritual pulse, and nervously examining yet again their own spiritual tongue, in a kind of fussy invalidism. Yet Christ summons us to health and manliness and efficiency. "Remember," so Bishop Thomas Wilson warned himself, "that the life of man is only to be valued for its usefulness," [9] a fact worth remembering even of the life in Christ.

Even when due weight is given to the warning

[9] *Maxims of Piety and Morality*, Maxim 1084.

20 Then Peter, turning about, seeth the
disciple whom Jesus loved following; which
also leaned on his breast at supper, and
said, Lord, which is he that betrayeth thee?
21 Peter seeing him saith to Jesus, Lord,
and what *shall* this man *do?*

20 Peter turned and saw following them
the disciple whom Jesus loved, who had
lain close to his breast at the supper and
had said, "Lord, who is it that is going to
betray you?" **21** When Peter saw him, he
said to Jesus, "Lord, what about this man?"

"stretching the hands" in connection with crucifixion, and Bernard (*The Gospel According to John,* II, 708-10) cites numerous passages from early fathers to prove that the phrase standing alone was sometimes used for crucifixion. But vs. 19 is a characteristic Johannine comment which probably indicates that Simon Peter had actually died, like his Master, on a cross. The command **Follow me** (vss. 19, 22) was the sign of restoration. It was spoken to Simon when he was first called to discipleship (Mark 1:17); it was spoken to him again at the crisis of faith and confession at Caesarea Philippi (Matt. 16:24). Peter would now understand the words spoken at 13:36. This conversation between the Lord and Peter may be the interview referred to by Paul in I Cor. 15:5.

20-23. Turning and seeing the Beloved Disciple following, Peter asked, **Lord, what about this man?** Jesus always rebuked curiosity about the future (cf. Luke 13:23-24; Mark 13:4, 32). Now he predicts nothing, but asks a hypothetical question. It is no concern of Peter's if the other disciple is called to a longer term of service on earth.

---

of the Exeg., it is possible to believe that in his commission to Peter, Christ thinks first of the little ones and their needs. **Feed my lambs.** About them the founders of the other religions are not impressive. It was Christ who brought to light the worth of a man, of any man, of the most ordinary individual. It was Christ who revealed the value of woman. And it was Christ who discovered the importance of the child. Goethe remarks loftily in an unbelievably silly finding that the scene when Christ called the children round about him is of no moment and importance, and that a picture of it would necessarily be pointless. As a matter of history, few things have been more formative or fruitful than Christ's interest in children and the passing on of something of his spirit in this matter to his church.

Feed my lambs, said Christ, putting that first, making it fundamental. Sometimes it may seem to have small results. Often enough youth seems to be greedy for the clubs and the gymnastics and the good times that the church organizes for them, yet while clutching at these to have no interest in its services and no time for its religion. Hence often enough Sunday-school teachers tend more or less to lose heart. For nothing seems to come of it. At the beginning they were thrilled. For they were going to work for Christ; and anything might happen any day. But now, it may be, it is less hopefully that they turn in week by week. For they know only too well what awaits them—the usual little row of swinging feet, of restless hands, of frankly bored faces! But more is happening than they realize. Are not modern psychologists almost frightening about that? Are we not told authoritatively by these psychologists that what happens to and in us during the first four or five years, or little more, is of such immense importance that it fixes, if not our fate, certainly our struggle throughout life? Our own eyes tell us that if one tugs at a grown branch it may give a little, but the moment one lets go, springs back into its set position; whereas a tendril can be permanently trained in the desired direction. Mothers, nurses, teachers—who can begin to reckon up the momentousness of the task committed to them! **Feed my lambs,** said Christ; that first.

And then twice over he commends the older people to Peter's care, urging on him to spend himself for them. For they too need continual help. C. G. Jung is of the opinion that at about forty or so many lives change their course and find a new channel; many folk tire and throw in their hand, and nearly everyone then has special need of new help and heartening and direction.[1] But indeed that need continues through life to its end. For every stage in it has its own problems to be faced, and its own difficulties to be met, while some run on almost from birth to death.

It is to be noted that in his commission to Peter, Christ bids him do not one thing, but two things for his sheep (but note Exeg.): first, he is told to tend and shepherd them, and then to feed them. Failure to give itself wholeheartedly to the fulfilling of these orders seems to be the reason of the church's ineffectiveness and comparative failure in our time. Organized

[1] *Modern Man in Search of a Soul,* pp. 124-25.

22 Jesus saith unto him, If I will that he tarry till I come, what *is that* to thee? follow thou me.

23 Then went this saying abroad among the brethren, that that disciple should not die: yet Jesus said not unto him, He shall not die; but, If I will that he tarry till I come, what *is that* to thee?

22 Jesus said to him, "If it is my will that he remain until I come, what is that to you? Follow me!"
23 The saying spread abroad among the brethren that this disciple was not to die; yet Jesus did not say to him that he was not to die, but, "If it is my will that he remain until I come, what is that to you?"

Until I come: The older eschatology retains its place in Johannine thought side by side with its "transmuted eschatology," and is clearly present in the first epistle. This was evidently preserved in early Christianity as a traditional saying and was misunderstood as an indication that this venerable disciple would survive till the Parousia. It is a reasonable inference that vs. 23 was written after his death to remove this misunderstanding, and the distress caused by the delayed return of the Lord.

Christianity is as a rule breathlessly busy about many things. It is hot and tired and panting. It is immensely energetic. But it is prone to lose its way among a multitude of lesser and secondary matters, forgetting that Christ lays the stress on shepherding the flock and feeding it, and bids us give ourselves to these. Yet in the many other things that we essay, which we declare must be done, these two are being pushed into a corner.

Dogged, tiring, persistent pastoral visitation is not spectacular. Yet to neglect it is disastrous. Canon Peter Green, with his immense influence in Manchester, declares bluntly that the Church of England is giving itself with zeal to everything except the one thing needful, the one thing that can alone meet the situation—faithful and devoted and affectionate pastoral visitation. The Edinburgh Presbytery of the Church of Scotland, disquieted by the constant leakage from the membership of the church, trickling out year by year, although the country-wide total is not falling, declared with assurance in a pamphlet that where elders and ministers were faithful in their visitation there was no lapsing. And young ministers who have returned to the old conception of their duties in this matter are reporting results with something of the amazed enthusiasm of the seventy on their return to Christ, and are no doubt being met, as those were, by the Master's eager approbation, and by an enthusiasm greater even than their own.

While as to the feeding of the flock, judged by the standards of our fathers, we are not taking preaching seriously these days, not as they did, not accounting it a lifework, claiming and getting a man's all. Read the outstanding preachers of the past, and we must see that though fashions in preaching change, these were great preachers of a great gospel, whereas we have been merely playing at it. And without the Word of God, which is our only hope, men cannot manage. **Tend my sheep;** and again, **Feed my sheep,** said Jesus Christ, our risen Lord, to Peter—and to us.

Yet to that climax there comes anticlimax. These hearts of ours are strange creations, unpredictable and unaccountable. One would have thought that Peter would have been awed and solemnized. And in a sense he was. And yet almost at once he was blundering once more. "Lord, you have been foretelling how it will be with me. But **what about this man?** he said, pointing to John, and met with a sharp reprimand.

There is an inquisitiveness that hangs idly about the environs of religion that Jesus will not satisfy; a meddling with many things that are no concern of ours. A hundred interesting problems are waiting to distract us and cajole us into wasting time. So Buddha felt in his day and kept insisting that to make real progress we must emancipate our minds from much that fascinates them but that is not fitted to help us in the task which will take all our time and energy—the task of cleansing our hearts and lives. It vexed him that so many paid no heed to this urgency of his but dallied on their way, discussing about this and that, all hugely interesting, yet in the old sense of the word impertinent matters. As he put it in a vivid metaphor: A man is wounded by a poisoned arrow still sticking deep in his flesh. And unconcernedly he keeps posing questions to himself. "Now of what wood is this arrow made, I wonder? And what bird gave these feathers? And what type of person shot it, dark or fair, short or tall?" Until those around him cry out in a fever of impatience, "What does all that matter? Pluck it out, man! For the thing is poisoned! Pluck it out! Or you must die." So our Lord here. Our road lies before us. It is for us to take it. Other things can wait. And

24 This is the disciple which testifieth of these things, and wrote these things: and we know that his testimony is true.

25 And there are also many other things which Jesus did, the which, if they should be written every one, I suppose that even the world itself could not contain the books that should be written. Amen.

24 This is the disciple who is bearing witness to these things, and who has written these things; and we know that his testimony is true.

25 But there are also many other things which Jesus did; were every one of them to be written, I suppose that the world itself could not contain the books that would be written.

---

3. Conclusion (21:24-25)

The reputation of the Beloved Disciple for veracity is well known in the church at large. His **testimony** lies behind this written Gospel. Such is the authentication offered by those who published it to the world. Whoever that disciple may have been, they believed that directly or mediately he was the author, and that this was a sufficient guarantee that it was worthy of acceptance. Vs. 25 repeats in heightened language the reminder given at the end of ch. 20, that only a selection is offered from the tradition of the life of Jesus to prove its inexhaustible wealth.

---

many of them are not our concern. A truth which has innumerable applications.

25. ***A Magnificent Hyperbole.***—And so with that this Gospel reaches its second and final end. Feeling that he has drawn only one little cupful out of an illimitable ocean, and shown us only a star here and there out of the endless constellations there are in Christ, its author closes with a magnificent hyperbole. **But there are also many other things which Jesus did; were every one of them to be written, I suppose that the world itself could not contain the books that would be written.**

And yet in sober fact is that really an exaggeration? For as T. R. Glover put it, "The Gospels are not four but 'ten thousand times ten thousand, and thousands of thousands,' and the last word of every one of them is, 'Lo, I am with you alway, even unto the end of the world.' "[2]

According to the Christian faith, the Lord Christ is not dead. Multitudes the world over have daily communion with him. But that apart, cannot we say of him with far more truth than Epictetus did about another, "And now Socrates being dead, no less useful to men, and even more useful, is the remembrance of that which he did and said when he was alive"?[3]

[2] *Conflict of Religions in Early Roman Empire,* p. 140.
[3] *Discourses* IV. 1. 170.